Introduction to
Mythology

About the Cover

On our cover are photographs representing a contemporary painting of Hera, the Greek goddess of motherhood, and an ancient statue of Athena the virgin warrior goddess, two illustrations of the power, the charm, and the timelessness of mythology. Painter Francis Picabia led or participated in a variety of styles of modern art, but in every one of these, he left us passionate images of women conveying his sense of their mystery and allure. From 1928 to the early 1930s, he painted what he called "transparencies." These dreamlike works, which included the Hera on the cover, were made up of multiple layers of transparent images based on Classical and Renaissance works. In 1930, Leonce Rosenberg, Picabia's principal dealer, wrote that the transparencies embody "the association of the visible and the invisible" and they represent "the notion of time added to that of space," moving beyond "instantaneity towards the infinite." Marcel Duchamp, the famous modern artist, said they created an impression of "the third dimension without the aid of perspective" (Calte 6). The large statue of Athena is from the Parthenon that preceded the one on the Acropolis of Athens today; it adorned the temple destroyed by the Persians in 480 B.C.E. Athena is brandishing a snake in her left hand, fighting with fierce grace on the side of the Olympian gods in their war against the Giants. Taken together, these two works of art illustrate the broad range of mythological imagery and its influence on religion, the state, and the individual.

Introduction to
Mythology

Contemporary Approaches to Classical and World Myths

Second Edition

Eva M. Thury
Drexel University

Margaret K. Devinney
Temple University

New York • Oxford
OXFORD UNIVERSITY PRESS
2009

Oxford University Press, Inc., publishes works that further Oxford University's
objective of excellence in research, scholarship, and education.

Oxford New York
Auckland Cape Town Dar es Salaam Hong Kong Karachi
Kuala Lumpur Madrid Melbourne Mexico City Nairobi
New Delhi Shanghai Taipei Toronto

With offices in
Argentina Austria Brazil Chile Czech Republic France Greece
Guatemala Hungary Italy Japan Poland Portugal Singapore
South Korea Switzerland Thailand Turkey Ukraine Vietnam

Published by Oxford University Press, Inc.
198 Madison Avenue, New York, New York 10016
http://www.oup.com

Oxford is a registered trademark of Oxford University Press

Library of Congress Cataloging-in-Publication Data

Thury, Eva M.
    Introduction to mythology: contemporary approaches to classical and world myths/Eva
M. Thury, Margaret K. Devinney.—2nd ed.
        p. cm.
    Includes biblographical references and index.
    ISBN 978-0-19-533294-0 (alk. paper)
    1. Mythology   I. Devinney, Margaret Klopfle, 1941–   II. Title.
    BL312.T48   2009
    2019.3—dc22

                                                        2008038439

Printing number: 9 8 7 6 5 4 3

Printed in the United States of America
on acid-free paper

Contents

Preface

This second edition of our text incorporates a new cover design which once again reflects our philosophy and intentions, while indicating some of the new material embodying our particular perspective on mythology. Two of the four new chapters present stories about goddesses (Tiamat and Nü-Kwa), while the chapter about Harry Potter contains a revision of Otto Rank's theory providing equal emphasis on the importance of Harry's mother and father to his development. Because the feminine dimension of mythology has received what we believe is a more balanced emphasis in this edition, we are pleased that this book features two goddesses on the cover. The statue of Athena from the Acropolis well represents the stories that make up the received mythological tradition, while the painting by Francis Picabia shows us the ways mythological figures acquire new, contemporary meanings. We delight in the multiple perspectives we have been able to provide in this book for traditional stories, suggesting that they are in some ways eternal and immutable, while showing how we see them differently because of the world we live in and highlighting the kinds of insights that have become available to us as a result.

As authors and editors, we felt we could not produce a work on mythology that did not recognize contemporary perspectives and beliefs as the cultural context for any study of mythological texts. In our view, this mitigates against the view that mythology is to be viewed as the ridiculous stories told by uneducated peoples as they struggled to make sense of their world—a perspective we often hear from our students at the start of a mythology course. Rather, we wanted our book to show the kinds of meanings that scholars, artists, and thinkers of all sorts find in mythological texts today. And that meant presenting the original texts of myths along with twentieth-century interpretations of them by scholars in a variety of academic fields.

It has been a challenge to shape and structure the material we wanted to include into a coherent and meaningful whole. In various forms, the text you see today has been through many levels of scholarly review. At every stage of this review process, there were readers who suggested trimming the contents, while at the same time proposing additions to what was already here. It took fortitude and patience to consider and reconsider the suggestions of competing claimants, and the revisions in this edition are a result of an ongoing process of dialogue and deliberation. We hope that our final choices will be useful to most students of mythology, though we understand that some will continue to note the absence of stories and traditions that fire their imagination and their enthusiasm. Later in this preface, we will attempt to trace a series of what we hope will be interesting paths of discovery through the ensuing variety of mythological material.

How to Read This Book

The organization of this book is based on the assumption that various readers like to read differently, so there is a variety of paths you may want to take as you read (see the section in this preface titled "Paths of Discovery Through This Book"). If you are reading the book as a text in a course, you may also want to pay attention to the course guidelines about which parts to give priority to.

New to this edition is an extensive illustrated time line which we would like to call to your attention. You may want to locate the material in the chapter you are reading on the time line at various points in your reading. This can help you ground your understanding of the stories in the chapter in a perspective that incorporates the other material in the book as well as major events in history.

What Everybody Should Read

We intend the first two chapters for all readers. Even if you already know what mythology is, you probably will want to read how *we* explain it to help guide your thinking about the rest of what we present in the book. In addition, if you are reading a chapter in any new part of the book, we suggest that you start with the introduction to that part, to provide a general orientation to why we grouped together the stories and mythological themes found there.

For the rest, we have tried to design the book so that individual chapters are self-contained and can be read as separate modules, so there is no need, after Part 1, to read the chapters in sequence. The "What to Expect" modules at the start of each chapter serve as advance organizers, designed to make suggestions about how to structure your exploration of the chapter. The "Paths of Discovery" section of the preface could be considered a kind of wide-ranging "What to Expect" segment spanning the book as a whole.

You will see that the book's text is divided into a main column and marginal notes. It contains two kinds of material in the main column: the texts of myths ("primary sources") and contemporary interpretations of them ("secondary sources")—as well as synthesized or interpretive material from us, the authors of this book ("secondary sources"). The primary and secondary texts from other authors are given in a font that looks like this, while the material from your authors comes in a font that looks like this. From time to time, the main column also contains tables, boxes, and illustrations to help you understand and appreciate the other material in the book.

Again, there is no right order in which to read the material in the main column, or even the chapters themselves. For example, we have chapters with primary sources like the *Epic of Gilgamesh* and secondary sources like J. S. Kirk's analysis of the *Epic of Gilgamesh* (Chapters 15 and 16, respectively). Many literature teachers will tell you that it's best to read the literary text first and have your own thoughts about it, before you even consult the marginalia and especially before you read a secondary source about it. We don't disagree with this view: we are, after all, literature teachers ourselves. However, we recognize that, for some readers, the secondary material makes the stories more meaningful, and such readers maintain their own views are not compromised by reading it first. So, if the choice is yours, try different approaches and select the one that results in the greatest enjoyment of the stories we include in the book.

The margins contain notes, definitions, cross references, headings, examples, and illustrations (or "marginalia") to guide and expand your appreciation of the main text.

Since the book contains many different kinds of texts, in some chapters, the marginalia is more full, or more varied, than in others. The purpose of these marginal comments is

- to highlight the structure of the discussion and thus make the argument easier to follow
- to explain and expand concepts and expressions in the main text and thus make the complex material of mythology more accessible
- to help you review the material by making skimming and navigating the text easier
- to show links between parts of the book to allow you to pinpoint connections that may have been lurking unspoken in your own thinking, or to notice relationships that may not have been obvious to you
- to spell out connections between the material of the book and other aspects of contemporary life, like television, the movies, and other pursuits and interests, including other academic disciplines
- to inspire further study by noting the sources of the ideas and perspectives in the text to give you access to concepts and ideas beyond the scope of the text.

Many readers will want to read the main column of text and jump to the margins only when they encounter material they have questions about. However, when you are looking at a chapter for the first time, you may want to skim through the marginalia to get an idea of the structure of what you are going to be reading. When you are studying for a test, you can use the marginalia as a guide as you skim the material you have read before. Sometimes the marginalia also contain definitions and concepts you may want to review or learn, depending on the guidance of your instructor.

Paths of Discovery Through This Book

The realm of "world myth" is vast, and the possibilities for exploration in it are many. As noted earlier, we suggest that, no matter where in the book your journey takes you, you start with the first two chapters to provide a useful overview of the kind of material you will be reading. In addition, any use of material in an as-yet-unfamiliar part of the book is, we believe, best preceded by reading the introduction to that part.

Here are some possible paths you may take in reading this book:

CLASSICAL MYTH

Chapter 2   Greek Creation Stories
Chapter 3   Ovid's Creation Story
Chapter 11   Ovid's Flood Story
Chapter 14   *The Hero with a Thousand Faces*: The book by Joseph Campbell, discussed by Dave Whomsley
Chapter 19   *Oedipus the King*—Sophocles
Chapter 20   The Structural Study of Myth—Claude Levi-Strauss
Chapter 24   Prometheus: The Greek Trickster
Chapter 25   Looking Back at Heroes: The Different Versions of a Myth
Chapter 27   Demeter and Persephone: The Homeric *Hymn to Demeter*
Chapter 28   Isis and Osiris (The second half of this chapter deals with Isis' role in the Roman Empire.)
Chapter 31   Heracles and Dionysus
Chapter 37   Cupid and Psyche—Apuleius

WORLD MYTH

In some sense, every chapter in this book is relevant to world myth; hence the title. However, it may be useful to point out the chapters in the book that deal with stories from parts of the world other than America, or ancient Greece or Rome. These are, grouped according to their cultures:

Chapter 5   Biblical Creation Stories
Chapter 6   *Enuma Elish*: A Mesopotamian Creation Story
Chapter 10   Nü Kwa: A Chinese Creator Goddess
Chapter 12   Biblical Flood Stories
Chapter 29   "Deciphering a Meal"—Mary Douglas

Chapter 6   The *Prose Edda*'s Creation Stories
Chapter 13   Ragnarok
Chapter 18   Heroes in the *Prose Edda*—Snorri Sturluson
Chapter 30   The Rituals of Northern Europe—H. R. Ellis Davidson

Chapter 15   The *Epic of Gilgamesh*
Chapter 16   A Levi-Straussian Analysis of the *Epic of Gilgamesh*—G. S. Kirk
Chapter 17   The *Ramayana*

Chapter 9   African Creation Stories
Chapter 23   African and African-American Trickster Stories
Chapter 28   Isis and Osiris

Chapter 14   *The Hero with a Thousand Faces*: The book by Joseph Campbell, discussed by David Whomsley

LITERATURE AND MYTH

Most of the stories in this book come from literary works, and this certainly includes most of the chapters listed as "Classical Myth" and "World Myth " (except Chapters 14, 16, 20, 25, 29 and 30). Thus, we do not relist these chapters here. Beyond this, what is included here depends on the definition each person will accord to literary works. Some will consider fairy tales as "literary works" while others will focus more on works of "high" culture. However, of particular interest in relation to this theme may be:

Chapter 17   The *Ramayana*
Chapter 19   *Oedipus the King*—Sophocles
Chapter 22   The Mwindo Epic
Chapter 25   Looking Back at Heroes: The Different Versions of a Myth
Chapter 42   Mythological Themes in Poetry
Chapter 43   Mythological Themes in Native American Literature
Chapter 44   Mythological Themes in Modern Narrative

ORAL STORYTELLING

Although the first two chapters listed treat literary stories, these stories derive from an oral tradition, and we try to elucidate that tradition in our account.

Chapter 3   Greek Creation Stories
Chapter 5   Biblical Creation Stories
Chapter 6   *Enuma Elish*: A Mesopotamian Creation Story
Chapter 8   Native American Creation Stories from the Southwestern United States
Chapter 9   African Creation Stories

MYTH AND RITUAL

THEORETICAL APPROACHES TO MYTH

The three chapters of Part 7, "Myth in a Contemporary Context." In some views, these chapters may be seen as theoretical: the former is a historical analysis with some application of Campbell's ideas about myth and the latter uses communications theory to study mythic concepts.

Myth from a Feminine Perspective

The Graeco-Roman culture is highly patriarchal, but the stories it tells often represent the strength and resilience of women. Of particular interest in this respect is the discussion of the Greek gender gap in Chapter 3, p. 28, and Chapter 27, p. 385. The Homeric *Hymn to Demeter* and the rituals involving it show the important role that the feminine force can have, even in a society where sexual equality is unheard of. "Cupid and Psyche" features the coming-of-age story of Psyche and her development as a significant force in Graeco-Roman society.

The Egyptian goddess Isis is a power in her own right, as is the Chinese goddess Nü Kwa. Chapter 10 also has methodological importance as it traces the ways scholars of mythology can identify feminine perspectives even in societies that have developed away from the espousal of these figures.

Modern psychological theories, including those of Jung (Chs. 32 and 33) and Rank (Ch. 41) have made significant contributions to our understanding of the importance of women in mythology.

In modern Western society, greater emphasis is placed on the contribution of women, and this is reflected in the stories that come from these cultures, including Harry Potter (Ch. 41), *Firefly* (Ch. 40), and "The Tiger's Bride" (Ch. 44). In addition, fairy tales often feature strong heroines, including Dorothy in *The Wizard of Oz* (Ch. 35) and the Goose Girl (Chs. 36 and 38). And finally, contemporary literature represents the importance of women's mythological insights, as shown by the work of Leslie Marmon Silko (Ch. 43), and Anne Sexton and Hilda Doolittle (Ch. 42).

Chapter 3   Greek Creation Stories
Chapter 4   Ovid's Creation Story
Chapter 6   *Enuma Elish*: A Mesopotamian Creation Story
Chapter 10   Nü Kwa: A Chinese Creator Goddess
Chapter 11   Ovid's Flood Story
Chapter 15   The *Epic of Gilgamesh*
Chapter 24   Prometheus: The Greek Trickster
Chapter 27   Demeter and Persephone: The Homeric *Hymn to Demeter*
Chapter 28   Isis and Osiris
Chapter 35   A Proppian Analysis of *The Wizard of Oz*
Chapter 36   Household Tales—Wilhelm and Jakob Grimm
Chapter 37   Cupid and Psyche—Apuleius
Chapter 38   Using Multiple Analyses to Highlight Different Aspects of the Same Tale
Chapter 40   *Stagecoach* and *Firefly*: Science Fiction and the Journey into the Unknown
Chapter 41   Harry Potter: A Rankian Take on the Hero of Hogwarts
Chapter 42   Mythological Themes in Poetry
Chapter 43   Mythological Themes in Native American Literature ("Yellow Woman")
Chapter 44   Mythological Themes in Modern Narrative ("The Tiger's Bride")

Companion Website and Instructor's Manual

Students and instructors may visit the **Companion Website** at www.oup.com/us/thury. Chapter objectives and summaries, study questions, suggested essay topics, self-correcting review quizzes, and glossary term flashcards are available here. There are also web links to sites relevant to chapter content. Finally, instructors may access several sample syllabuses and a PowerPoint-based Lecture Guide.

An **Instructor's Manual and Testbank** accompanies this book. Here instructors will find summaries, discussion questions, pedagogical suggestions, suggested essay questions, fill-ins, and multiple-choice tests for each chapter.

Acknowledgments

This work has been in progress for such a long time that particular mention of all those colleagues, friends, and family who helped us on the journey is very difficult.

We do wish to note our appreciation to our very generous colleagues who lent their professional expertise to commentary and suggestions on particular subjects: Amy Slaton on the relationship of science and myth, Seydev Kumar on the *Ramayana*, Daniel Biebuyck and Abioseh Porter on the Mwindo epic, G. Ronald Murphy on the Grimm Brothers tales, Michael O'Shea on Joyce's *Ulysses*, Paul Zolbrod on Native American literature, Keith Knapp on Chinese myth, and Éva Liptay and István Nagy on Egyptian myth.

A special note of thanks goes to Joseph Russo, who helped Eva Thury develop her first-ever syllabus on mythology when she was teaching at Wheaton College in 1976. Eva dates aspects of her approach to myth to Joe's insights and the bibliography he recommended. Also formative of Eva's appreciation for myth in that era were Jennifer T. Roberts, her colleague at Wheaton, and Dorothea Wender, whose translation of Hesiod appears in this book. We also would like to offer special thanks to Roger Abrahams, who generously shared his sources of inspiration on tricksters and ritual as well as suggesting primary and secondary material, and to Daniel Biebuyck whose unfailing generosity with respect to the Mwindo epic extended to careful textual editing and to supplying us with photographs from his collection of the performance of the Mwindo epic.

We also thank all who read the manuscript and offered helpful advice: M. Carl Drott, Jeff Drott, Marianne Henderson, Gertje Reichenbach, Will Mason, and Eileen Devinney. And we are indebted to the efforts of Charlotte Lenox, who handled the complex permissions research. We would like to thank those who read the manuscript for Oxford University Press, including those who were anonymous, as well as Fred Giacobazzi, Carol Stewart Grizzard, André P. M. H. Lardinois, William Magrath, Rick Phillips, Polly Stewart, and Michael Webster.

Saving the best for last, we thank our husbands, M. Carl Drott and Edward Devinney, for their astute reading, their technical assistance, and most important of all—for their encouragement and support during the long gestation period of this labor.

We particularly appreciate the artistic work of Mickey Drott who created the final illustrations we could get nowhere else; and we laud our editors at Oxford University Press, Robert Miller, Sarah Calabi, Christina Mancuso, Kristin Maffei, and Barbara Mathieu, for their valuable direction in helping us hone the focus of our project and prepare the manuscript for publication.

We dedicate this book to Martha B. Montgomery, who, in her time as the Head of what was then the Department of Humanities and Communications, hired each of us to work at Drexel University. Martha was an outstanding educator, a terrific boss, and an inspiring friend; we hope the work we do today carries on her vision of rigorous scholarship and dedicated teaching.

Eva Thury and Margaret Devinney

8000 BCE — **7500 BCE** Early Egyptians live in the desert areas, which are green at this time.

7000 BCE — **7000 BCE** Mesopotamians begin living in towns.

c. **7000 BCE** First farmers settle in Greece.

6000 BCE — c. **5400–4400 BCE** Farmers start to grow forms of wheat and barley and to keep animals nearer the Nile River in Egypt.

5000 BCE

4000 BCE — c. **3400 BCE** First use of hieroglyphics.

c. **3200 BCE** The Bronze Age: name given to the time when this metal first begins to be used.

c. **3200 BCE** Sumeria falls to the Akkadians.

3000 BCE — c. **3000 BCE** Writing system called cuneiform is invented in lower Mesopotamia.

2800 to 2500 BCE Gilgamesh is King of Uruk.

2375–2345 BCE Pyramid texts at Saqqara.

2350–2150 BCE Akkadian Empire

c. **2300 BCE** Sargon's birth, according to an inscription.

2125–2016 BCE Thebes becomes an important city. Rulers from the 11th dynasty become strong and start to control large parts of Egypt.

c. **2100 BCE** Earliest written versions of the *Epic of Gilgamesh*.

2000 BCE

1831–1786 BCE Egyptian art reaches a high point during the reign of Amenemhat III.

1792–1750 BCE Reign of Hammurabi, a Babylonian king who developed a code of laws.

c. 1700 BCE A form of writing known today as Linear A is developed on the island of Crete.

1550 BCE The Theban god Amun becomes one of the most important gods in Egypt.

c. 1530 BCE Volcanic explosion on the island of Thera. Today, some people believe this huge eruption may be the origin of the legend of Atlantis.

1500 BCE

1352–1336 BCE Reign of Amenhotep IV/Akhenaten, who closes the old temples and makes Aten the most important god in Egypt.

1336 BCE Tutankhamun becomes king and restores the cults of the old gods.

c. 1200 BCE The version of the *Epic of Gilgamesh* used in this book.

c. 1200 BCE Mycenean civilization.

1180 BCE Traditional date for the Trojan War. This legendary war was fought between an alliance of Greek cities and the Anatolian city of Troy.

1100–900 The Greek Dark Age: The skills of reading and writing are lost. Trade between Greece and other countries goes into decline. The population becomes much smaller.

1099 BCE Ramses XI becomes king—the last of the New Kingdom.

1069–715 BCE The south of Egypt is controlled by the High Priests of Amun.

1000 BCE

c. 950–550 BCE Versions of Genesis, the first book of the Hebrew Bible.

c. 950 BCE Jehovist version of Genesis.

900 BCE

c. 850 BCE Elohist version of Genesis.

800–480 BCE Greek settlements, known as colonies, are set up in Asia Minor, Italy, Sicily, North Africa, Egypt, and around the Black Sea.

800 BCE

776 BCE The first Olympic games are held in honor of the god Zeus.

c. 750 BCE Traditional date for the poet Homer, who composed the *Iliad* and the *Odyssey*.

c. 750 BCE Supposed earliest version of the Oedipus myth. (Homer referred to it in his *Odyssey*.)

750–700 BCE First temple of Pallas Athena is built in Athens.

c. 740 BCE The Greek alphabet, based on the Phoenician writing system, is created.

c. 721 BCE J-E version of Genesis.

700 BCE Shabaka Stone in Memphis.

700–480 BCE The Archaic Period in Greece: Greek cities increase trade with each other and with other cultures. Arts and crafts flourish. Great temples are built to honor the gods.

c. 700–650 BCE Hesiod the poet writes *Works and Days* and *Theogony*.

7th c. BCE *Hymn to Demeter*.

7th c. BCE Assurpanipal rules; creates a comprehensive library.

7th c. BCE Earliest versions of the Ramayana are surmised to have originated at this time.

700 BCE

671 BCE The Assyrians capture the city of Memphis.

663 BCE The Assyrians capture Thebes and control the whole country.

621–620 BCE Drako issues the first written law code in Athens.

620–580 BCE Poet Sappho of Lesbos writes nine books of poetry.

600 BCE

600–221 BCE Classical/Pre-Han era in China

590 BCE First Pythian Games held in Delphi in honor of the god Apollo.

c. 560–480 BCE Life of Pythagoras, Greek mathematician and philosopher.

c. 550 BCE Priestly version of Genesis.

550 BCE Persian king Cyrus the Great conquers Media.

534 BCE The first tragedy is performed in Athens at a festival dedicated to the god Dionysos.

525–456 BCE Life of the playwright Aeschylus.

500–428 BCE Life of Greek philosopher Anaxagoras.

500 BCE

495–405 BCE Life of the playwright Sophocles.

492–432 BCE Life of the philosopher Empedocles.

490 BCE The Battle of Marathon, at which the Athenian army defeats the invading Persian Empire.

487 BCE The first comedy play is performed in Athens at a festival dedicated to the god Dionysos.

c. 485–425 BCE Life of the historian Herodotus.

480–323 BCE The Greek Classical Period: artists began to portray humans and animals in a more natural and realistic way.

c. 480–407 BCE Life of the playwright Euripides.

c. 456 BCE Aeschylus's *Prometheus Bound*.

447 BCE The building of the Parthenon begins in Athens.

432–404 BCE Peloponnesian War between Athens and Sparta and their allies. Athens is defeated, and the city never fully recovers its miliary strength and power.

429–425 BCE Sophocles's *Oedipus the King*.

427–347 BCE Life of Greek philosopher Plato.

425 BCE Great plague in Athens.

400 BCE

399 BCE Socrates is sentenced to death.

387 BCE Plato, the Greek philosopher, founds his school at the Academy in Athens.

384–322 BCE Life of Aristotle.

341–270 BCE Life of Greek philosopher Epicurus.

335 BCE Aristotle founds his school at the Lyceum in Athens.

335–263 BCE Life of philosopher Zeno, who begins the Stoic movement.

332 BCE Alexander the Great becomes the new ruler of Egypt.

331 BCE New city of Alexandria is founded.

323 BCE Death of Alexander the Great. His generals divide his empire among them. For the next 40 years, these generals fight to expand their territory.

323–31 BCE The Hellenistic Period: Greek ideas and styles of art spread throughout Alexander's former empire.

c. 300 BCE Euclid founds a mathematical school in Athens.

300 BCE

290 BCE The library in Alexandria is founded. It holds half a million scrolls and conserves many of the great works of ancient Greek literature.

287–212 BCE Life of Archimedes, Greek mathematician and philosopher.

279 BCE Celtic tribes from the north invade Greece and reach as far as Delphi.

270 BCE Greek astronomer Aristarchus announces that the earth revolves around the sun each year and rotates on its own axis each day.

264–241 BCE Rome's First Punic War with the city of Carthage. Rome gains control of Sicily as its first overseas province.

254–184 BCE Life of the Roman playwright Olautus, who wrote over 130 comic plays.

221-220 BCE Han Dynasty rules China.

300 BCE
continued

218–202 BCE Rome's Second Punic War. Hannibal of Carthage crosses the Alps and invades Italy, but he is not able to take control of the city of Rome and eventually withdraws back to Africa.

200–100 BCE Songs of Ch-u, earliest Chinese sacred mythological texts.

200 BCE

c. 170 BCE Romans begin to interfere in the government of Egypt.

c. 150 BCE The Venus de Milo, one of the most famous sculptures in the world, is created.

c. 150 BCE Valmiki writes a version of the *Ramayana*. (It is used in this book.)

149–146 BCE Rome's Third Punic War. Rome destroys and takes control of Carthage, along with much of North Africa.

146 BCE The Romans conquer Corinth. The Greek mainland becomes a Roman province.

146 BCE Temple of Jupiter Stator is rebuilt. It is the first marble temple built in Rome and demonstrates the huge wealth pouring into the city.

100 BCE

59 BCE Julius Caesar becomes a consul in Rome and is appointed governor of two Gallic provinces.

58–50 BCE Gallic War. Julius Caesar greatly entends the territory that Rome controls in western Europe.

51 BCE Cleopatra VII becomes the queen of Egypt.

48 BCE Cleopatra VII's brother, Ptolemy XIII, tries to remove her from power, but the Roman leader, Julius Caesar, helps her to regain the throne.

44 BCE Julius Caesar proclaims himself permanent ruler of Rome. He is assassinated a month later on 15 March. Civil war follows, leading to the end of the Republic.

43 BCE–17 BCE Life of the Roman poet Ovid, who writes an epic poem called *Metamorphoses* about people who change into plants and animals.

100 BCE
continued

41 BCE Marc Antony comes to Egypt and forms an alliance with Cleopatra.

31 BCE Marc Antony is defeated at the Battle of Actium by Octavian, (who later changes his name to Augustus).

100 CE

31 CE–476 CE Roman Imperial Period: Rome is ruled by emperors.

31 BCE–14 CE Reign of Octavian, who is granted the title Augustus in 27 BCE.

43 BCE–17 CE Life of the Roman poet Ovid, who writes an epic poem called *Metamorphoses* about people who change into plants and animals.

30 CE Marc Antony and Cleopatra commit suicide, and the Roman emperor, Augustus, takes control of Egypt.

27 BCE–200 CE Many religious movements spread throughout the early Roman Empire.

40–120 CE Life of Plutarch.

41–54 CE Reign of the emperor Claudius. During this time Britain becomes part of the Roman Empire.

54–68 CE Reign of the Roman emperor Nero.

1st c. CE Seneca's *Oedipus.*

1st c. CE *Metamorphoses* by Apuleius.

79 CE Mt. Vesuvius erupts, destroying the towns of Pompeii and Herculaneum in Italy.

98–117 CE Reign of the Roman emperor Trajan. During his reign the empire is at its largest extent including territory in Europe, Africa, and Asia.

200 CE

122–123 CE Hadrian's Wall is built across north Britain.

146–170 CE Astronomer Ptolemy writes that the earth is the center of the universe, and all the planets and stars revolve around it.

180 CE Alexandria becomes a center of the Christian religion in Egypt.

220–280 CE China's Three Kingdom era. Hsu Cheng writes a version of the P'An Ku myth.

300 CE

303 CE The Roman emperor Diocletian tries to destroy Christianity.

306–337 CE Constantine I becomes emperor, and the Roman Empire, including Egypt, becomes Christian. Egyptian Christians are called Copts.

313 CE Christianity is tolerated throughout the Roman Empire

329 CE St. Peter's church in Rome is completed.

360 CE First church of St. Sophia is completed in Constantinople.

393 CE The Olympic Games are banned by the Roman emperor.

394 CE The last inscription in hieroglyphic script is inscribed on a wall at the temple of Isis at Philae.

395 CE Greece becomes part of the Byzantine Empire when the Roman Empire is divided in two. The capital of the Byzantine Empire is Constantinople, which was previously the Greek city Byzantium.

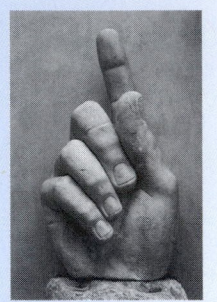

500–1100 CE **late 5th to 11th. CE** European Dark Ages.

1200 CE

c. 1200 Gottfried von Strassburg writes *Tristan and Isolde*.

1216–1223 Saxo Grammatikus writes Gesta Danorum.

1270–1280 The *Volsung Saga*.

1300 CE

13th c. CE Pueblo cultures thrive in the southwestern United States.

1400 CE

1455 Printing press invented by Johannes Gutenberg in Mainz, Germany.

1500 CE

1550–1750 Pastoral poetic form popular in England.

1600 CE to 1900 CE

1600 CE

1608–1674 Life of poet John Milton.

1611 and 1616 George Chapman publishes translations of Homer's *Iliad* and *Odyssey*.

1659 Pierre Corneille's *Oedipe.*

1679 John Dryden's *Oedipus.*

1697 Charles Perrault's *Tales of My Mother Goose.*

1700 CE

1718 Voltaire's *Oedipus.*

1734–1820 Life of Daniel Boone.

1784 Publication of John Filson's *Kentucke,* which incorporated a life of Daniel Boone

1795–1821 Life of poet John Keats.

1800 CE

1856–1936 Life of Sigmund Freud.

1865–1939 Life of poet William Butler Yeats.

1869–1948 Life of Mahatma Ghandi.

1870s U.S. government mandates education of Native American children in English-only boarding schools.

1875–1961 Life of Carl Gustav Jung.

1882–1941 Life of James Joyce.

1884–1939 Life of Otto Rank.

1889 Freud's *Interpretation of Dreams.*

1900 CE

1904 Swanton collects Raven myth versions at Wrangell and Sitka, Alaska.

1904–1987 Life of Joseph Campbell.

1922 First edition of James Joyce's *Ulysses.*

1932 American writer John Updike born.

1932 Jean Cocteau's *La Machine Infernale* (an Oedipus drama).

1900 CE
continued

1935 Anthropologist Ruth Benedict publishes *Zuni Mythology*.

1939 Release of John Ford's film *Stagecoach*

1939 *The Wizard of Oz*.

1947 India wins its freedom from the British Empire using nonviolent tactics, as taught by Mahatma Ghandi.

1948 Leslie Marmon Silko born; grows up in the Laguna Pueblo.

1963 Anthropologist Claude Levi-Strauss publishes *Structural Anthropology*.

1966–1969 The three seasons of the original version of the television show *Star Trek*.

1971 Anthropologist Mary Douglas publishes "Deciphering a Meal."

1987–1994 The seven seasons of *Star Trek: the Next Generation*.

1993–1999 The seven seasons of *Star Trek: Deep Space Nine*.

1993–2002 The seven seasons of the television show *The X-Files*.

1995–2001 The seven seasons of *Star Trek: Voyager*.

1997–2007 Publication of the seven Harry Potter books by J. K. Rowling.

2000 CE

2001–2005 The four seasons of *Enterprise*, the last television series set in the *Star Trek universe*.

2002 The single season of Joss Whedon's science fiction program *Firefly*.

2005 Release of the film *Serenity*, set in the *Firefly* universe.

Part 1

Introduction to Studying Myth

Mystical – Supernatural aspect of the world.
    – explores what is strictly beyond the surface of reality,
cosmological – Myths reflect the scientific thought of specific time period.

Sociological – validates and maintains the social order of specific society.

Pedagogical – guiding the individual through the inevitable crises of
    the stages of life.
    – Struggles character encounters directly reflect their
    particular society.

Paratactic Composition – contradicts itself
Syntactic composition – chronological

Folk Ideas   – variation in myths particular to cultures
Elementary Ideas – common themes that persist through all myths,

What Is Myth?

WHAT TO EXPECT . . . This chapter introduces you to the style of presentation used in this book. You can see that there is a main text on the right, with definitions, cross references, and other study aids in the left margin. In addition, wherever possible, the discussions are based not on retellings of myths, but on original versions. This allows you to enjoy and appreciate the literary style of the myths, and it makes your study of mythology more immediate—in many cases you are reading the same story heard by the original audience, not a watered-down version.

We start by defining mythology and explaining what a "contemporary" view of it is. Despite the widespread use of the word to mean fiction, mythology actually refers to stories that tell us about reality. One definition of myth that we introduce refers to it as "a traditional narrative that is used as a designation of reality."

In this chapter we show that the same story can provide a wide range of different kinds of insights into basic human questions, such as: What is it to be human? How do we fit into the scheme of things? How did our physical universe get to be the way it is? We illustrate these insights by examining the story of the Trojan War, as well as several other examples.

Mythology allows you to take a journey into an exciting and mysterious world. In your travels, you can expect to encounter gods, heroes, monsters, exotic countries, and amazing adventures. For pure story value, readings in mythology have no match. In addition, the experience of mythology will enrich your understanding of literary and artistic works created throughout the ages. You will see that you have entered a living tradition: we continue to incorporate mythological themes and messages in our culture today. Even our modern mass media reflect the motifs and characters which can be found in ancient stories from around the world. Myths are as close to us today as the adventures of Indiana Jones, the Starship Enterprise, or *Lost*.

The title of this book uses the word "contemporary" for two reasons. In the first place, we will be considering stories from a variety of societies and time periods, including those told in modern times by novelists, poets, dramatists, and filmmakers. Secondly, we will not be satisfied to tell these wonderful stories for their own sake. We will also consider what the stories mean, what message they convey about the people and cultures that originated them. In this effort, we will bring to bear insights from a variety of academic disciplines. As far as we can tell, human beings have always collected and analyzed the stories they came across in their society: some early instances are the accounts of Herodotus in the fifth century B.C.E. and those of Apollodorus in the first century B.C.E. Our investigations will include the work of some modern scholars who delve into the meaning and significance of mythological stories. More detail on the structure and philosophy of this book is found in the last section of this chapter, p. 14.

Andy Warhol, *Botticelli's Venus*, from details of Renaissance paintings, 1984 (left). Botticelli, *The Birth of Venus* (detail; right). We have juxtaposed detail from Botticelli's Venus with a modern version of the image. There is no need to prefer one rendering over the other: the meaning of each image is different. Each artist presents an artistic response to mythology. In this book, we are dedicated to remembering the effect of mythology on modern as well as traditional sensibilities.

Marginal comments are found throughout much of this text. For a description of the different kinds of marginal comments and suggestions on how they might be used, see the Preface.

What Mythology Is

In the first place, myths are stories. In every culture and every country, during every period of time from Ancient Egypt to the modern United States, people have told stories. Of these, perhaps the most captivating have been the sacred stories handed down as a part of religions, as well as the narratives that explain and define the great acts of nations and peoples: mythology in the strict sense refers to these. Usually these accounts are so old that their origins are shrouded in mystery. For us modern readers, part of their appeal is in their evocation of a long-gone era in which members of communities shared the same values and guided their lives by the stories they told. Rooted as we are in the ever-shifting, diverse, multifaceted world of the twenty-first century, we turn to mythology first for the entertainment value of a good story. Our impulse is sound: in the treasure house of mythological stories, we readily find the entertainment we are seeking.

And yet, the term "mythology" is usually applied to a body of stories whose purpose is not limited to entertainment. As Northrop Frye puts it, the stories of mythology are often "charged with a special seriousness and importance." Some stories are associated with a living religion still being **practiced at the time the myth is told;** others are more secular in nature, but still include values and perspectives that inform the society and culture of the storytellers.

Many people believe that myths are *false* stories that primitive people used to tell to explain the nature of the universe before a better, more "scientific" explanation for the world was available. This view is related to the popular use of "myth" to mean "false story." For instance, you may have heard people say that it is a myth that the sun travels around the earth, or that thunder is really the sound of two clouds colliding.

Marc Chagall, *The Creation of Man*, 1956–1958. Marc Chagall's 20th-c. painting captures a modern vision of the mystery and drama of creation. For more on creation stories, see Part 2, p. 23.

What Mythology Is Not

We will see that mythological stories often contain elements that do not accurately reflect the scientific understanding of the societies that tell them, but this literal falseness can also be a reflection of their importance. Because mythological narratives are important to a society, they are often handed down unchanged from generation to generation. As a result, the scientific details embedded in these stories are unchanged even as new scientific discoveries alter the people's understanding of their world.

In our study of mythological stories, it should become clear that any *false* or outdated science they contain is not intrinsic to the points they are making about the nature of human beings and their role in the world. Thus, even stories about the formation of the cosmos can convey important truths to subsequent generations, although the scientific views in them are outmoded. To a reader from outside the culture, however, the false science of a mythological tale may be much more obvious than its unchangingly *true* values and world view. As students of myth, we will see that mythological stories reveal true things about the culture that originated them, and may include values and perspectives that can be meaningful even for those of us outside that culture.

Alligators in the Sewers: an Urban Legend as an Oral Tale

In our print- and media-oriented culture, we do not have many examples of stories that are primarily oral. Among the few examples are the so-called urban legends which are found around the world. These are not myths in the strict sense, but they can help us see the nature of the oral tales that are still transmitted in our own time. You may have heard the story that giant alligators live in the sewers of New York City. This story is a myth in the popular sense of the word: it is a false story. Although **it is not a myth in the same sense** as most of the stories we will examine in this book, it bears examination here because it helps us see that oral storytelling, even in modern times, emphasizes the themes and issues that concern human beings at their core.

Thus, this urban legend allows us to think about the power of storytelling. It is familiar to people around the United States, not because people literally believe it—though some do!—but because it seems to express concerns that many people believe are worth thinking about. We will examine this story in detail here to suggest some of the insights that can be gained from looking at the stories people tell, whether they are true or false.

The story about alligators in the sewers is actually quite well developed, and there are many versions of it. Jan Harold Brunvand has compiled a discussion of all the different forms of the story. A common one has it that the animals were the survivors and descendants of pets given to children during the late fifties when pet baby alligators were a fad. When the pets got too big or

Genesis Frontispiece Depicting the Creation. This 16th-c. illustration shows the artist's vision of the world as it was being created. Compare with Chagall on p. 4.

"practiced at the time the myth is told"—Mircea Eliade believes that the power of myths is associated with their relationship to rituals, an aspect explored in Part 4.

"it is not a myth in the same sense"—This story is actually, as its name implies, a legend. Myths and legends are related: both are oral stories that are refined through repetition by one storyteller after another. A legend, however, is usually associated with a historical basis.

Alligator, the 1980 horror movie by John Sayles, represents one instance of the urban legend about alligators in the sewers.

This story comes from: Jan Harold Brunvand, *The Vanishing Hitchhiker: Urban Legends and Their Meanings.*

 Psychological Insights

psychology The study of the mental states and processes involved in the development of individuals.

Examples:
Otto Rank and Carl Jung study those workings of the human mind that occur without our notice. This "unconscious" is often represented by patients in their dreams as a maze or labyrinth. On Rank, see Introduction to Part 3, p. 155 and Ch. 25, p. 362.

 Anthropological Insights

anthropology The study of cultures: "culture" refers to the values and principles of a society, as well as to the artworks ("Culture" with a capital "C") that express those values.

Example:
Claude Levi-Strauss, see Ch. 20, p. 280). Levi-Strauss' theory, "structuralism," examines stories to study the mental structures or underlying concepts they represent. From these, he determines the values and principles of the culture that tells the stories.

 Social or Sociological Insights

sociology The study of the groups that people belong to or participate in. Groups of interest to sociologists can be as large as the American nation or as small as the family.

became too much trouble, they were flushed down the toilet and flourished in the sewer system. Some versions of the story say that the alligators are albino because they do not get any sun, or that they survive by eating rats. It turns out that all over the United States, people are familiar with this urban legend.

Brunvand traces the origins of the story to a February 10, 1935, *New York Times* account that says that an alligator was found in a New York City sewer. As far as we know, however, the other elements of the story are false, and thus the story is a "myth" in the colloquial sense of the word: a false story that people told to explain a rumor about an alligator whose path to a metropolitan sewer was unknown, and therefore mysterious.

The Meaning of the Urban Legend

Brunvand, who collected different versions of this urban legend about alligators, points out that the story is related to a whole family of other stories, like the one about the woman who found a rat in her fast-food fried chicken. You may be surprised to discover that we can gain a variety of different insights into our experiences from simple stories like this one. All of these stories suggest that there is something unclean and scary hidden underneath the pleasant surface of civilized life. We could add that the story about alligators in the sewers tells us a lot about the experience of living in cities. A city has a giant infrastructure which is unknown and mysterious to us. Under city streets are tunnels, subways, sewers, and conduits for water and steam, as well as abandoned buildings and structures of all sorts.

Psychologists tell us that an intricate maze like this represents our unconscious hopes and fears as we struggle to become mature human beings. By traversing the maze, we are working out problems that we may not even be aware of having. We will be studying more about these views in Chapter 32 on the mythological theories of Jung, who was a psychologist.

The story of alligators in the sewers can be taken more literally, as well. In a city, women and men do not walk on the ground. They are cut off from nature by the ground they walk on, which is not the ground at all, but a thin veneer that masks our nature, the unmentionable biological and physiological processes that lurk beneath civilized life. The alligators then, are an expression of the fears we have of all the unknown parts of living in a city, all the natural or instinctual parts of ourselves that, as civilized people, we are not completely comfortable or completely familiar with. The Sumerian *Epic of Gilgamesh* is a widely studied myth, which dates from about 2000 B.C.E., and expresses some of the same worries about how civilization distances human beings from their natural selves (for excerpts, see Ch. 15, p. 166). We will be studying more about these views in Chapter 20 on the theories of Levi-Strauss, who looks at all myth as a conflict between forces of nature and culture.

In addition to the other insights it provides, the story of alligators in the sewers expresses the fears we have of each other in a community. Working together in a community is a good way to get more done than could be accomplished by any single individual. Living in a community, however, also means being stuck with the ill effects of the actions of others. In a city, people live close together. If you flush away your pet alligator or other unwanted items, your neighbor may well have to deal with the aftereffects of your carelessness. The city involves you in the lives of people you do not know, some of whom lived in the distant past and left behind their triumphs and their failures to be dealt with by the next generation—which must build, literally, on their ruins. The story of the pet alligators points to the uneasiness most of us feel about other people's monsters.

Myths and Legends as True Stories

Looking back at the story of the alligators, we can see that the story was false in the literal sense: it is safe to say that alligators do not live in the sewers of New York City. And yet, **the story expresses**

some true concerns and conflicts of human beings who live in cities and participate in cultures, concerns that have been true of humans for many thousands of years, if the *Epic of Gilgamesh* can be believed.

Although it shares some characteristics with mythological accounts, an urban legend is not really a myth in the strict sense of the word. As you may already have known, myths are stories about gods and heroes performing fantastic and amazing adventures, rather than about alligators terrorizing nameless people in the streets of New York.

This book will introduce you to a great many gods and heroes, but thinking about the story of the alligators is appropriate to an introduction to mythology, because legends and myths are related to each other. Both are stories people tell, over and over, in different forms and versions. As you can see from the preceding explanation, the story about the alligators in the sewers is not just a false story. Rather, it tells us quite a lot about ourselves and our culture.

What about Gods and Heroes?

Some of you may be surprised that we have gotten this far without mentioning gods and heroes. Many people understand myths as stories of gods and heroes, and so they are. Like the cosmological accounts mentioned previously, these stories can provide us with an understanding of the nature of human life. The ancient Greek story of Heracles can serve as an example. Heracles, a human, is the illegitimate son of Zeus, the head of the Greek gods. Hera, Zeus' wife, is resentful of her husband's bastard by another woman and drives Heracles crazy, so he kills his own wife and children. Thus, his story also shows the limits of human freedom: a fundamentally good man must deal with the consequences of actions that seem beyond his control.

Heracles must perform a series of amazing deeds or labors to atone for his crimes. In addition, upon completing these labors, he achieves immortality. Although the story of Heracles' labors emphasizes the fact that, as a rule, human beings are subject to death, it also suggests that through great deeds, human beings can challenge and overcome this destiny by becoming immortal. For more about Heracles and his labors, see Chapter 31, p. 446.

Myth and Science

Many people think of myths as stories told to explain scientific facts, or to describe the origin of natural phenomena. This is called *aetiology* or *the aetiological function,* from the Greek word αἰτία, or "cause." For example, a Native American story from the Pacific Northwest explains that the raven is black because he once flew through the smoke hole or chimney of the house while trying to get away from Petrel after stealing fresh water from him. The story goes on to provide further aetiology, explaining that, in his flight, Raven dropped the water here and there as he went along, and that this is the origin of the great rivers of the world.

In the story, Petrel is hoarding fresh water until Raven distributes it freely. In thwarting Petrel, Raven's impulse is at the same time generous and mischievous, but his method of distributing his "gift" is not orderly or systematic. The story demonstrates the bounty available from nature, but suggests that **the world is not orderly or predictable,** and that survival in it requires cleverness, generosity, and the flexibility involved in changing your colors to suit the situation.

Heracles with Cerberus before Eurystheus.

"the story expresses some true concerns and conflicts . . . "— An episode of the television series *The X-Files* contains much the same theme. In it, the monster in the sewers is human and was created by genetic mutations arising from the atomic accident at Chernobyl in the Ukraine. The themes expressed remind us of Brunvand's version of the urban legend, except on a global scale. For more on the meaning of *The X-Files*, see Ch. 40, p. 589.

Metaphysical Insights

metaphysics This part of philosophy goes beyond ("meta" means "beyond") physics to study the nature and meaning of human life.

Aetiological Insights

aetiology Explaining the origin or cause of a custom or a fact of the physical universe. For the full story of Raven and Petrel, see Ch. 21, p. 295.

"the world is not orderly or predictable"—In contrast, the creation story told by Ovid (Ch. 4) emphasizes the orderly nature of the world. In it, the world is created by a god who lays out its boundaries like a surveyor. This image is especially appropriate coming from a Roman author, as Rome was especially proud of its technology, which included engineering and surveying.

Cosmological Insights

cosmology The study of the origin and structure of the universe.

"[Myth] incorporates what we might call the best scientific knowledge of its time."—Joseph Campbell calls this the "cosmological function" of myth.

 Historical Insights

history The study of past events, especially in relation to a particular person or culture.

Example:
Imagine composing a mythic story about Ronald Reagan or Bill Clinton. Some people would disagree with some of the events you included as facts and with the motivations that underlie them. It may well be the case that everyone did not agree about Gilgamesh or Daniel Boone. If one of the brides whom Gilgamesh raped was a member of your family or village, or if Daniel Boone owed you money, you might not see these figures as heroes.

This story comes from: Anthony DePalma, "Canadian Indians Win a Ruling Vindicating Their Oral History," *The New York Times*, February 9, 1998.

"an Indian woman is taken to the sky"—Leslie Marmon Silko, a contemporary writer in the Native American tradition, bases a story on this theme. (See Ch. 43, p. 642.)

It is clear that this story about Raven does not agree with modern theories about how rivers are formed or how animals obtain their coloration. It does, however, represent some important truths about the Native American view of the world.

On a more basic level, the story of Raven and Petrel provides its audience with an accurate mental representation of their physical environment. Thus, **it incorporates what we might call the best scientific knowledge of its time.** Mircea Eliade would say that archaic societies used myth to master the universe, whereas we use science. In this view, myth does not contain science, but represents an alternative way of viewing the universe. Our argument here, however, is that science and myth cover the same domain: the characterization of the natural world for the purpose of understanding and predicting the behavior of nature. In this sense, we can say that myth performs some of the same functions as what we might call science. For example, from the story of Raven and Petrel, Native Americans could formulate a mental map of their area, so they could plan how to find fresh water, which is abundant in the region, but not distributed according to any discernable pattern—like the flight of a bird being pursued.

More than any other aspect or quality, the scientific views a myth incorporates are likely to make it seem outdated, irrelevant, or "false." However, if these views are understood in the context of what is known at the time, they may well provide us with insights useful to the science of our times. For example, the myth of Raven and Petrel emphasizes the randomness found in nature. Mathematicians and computer scientists recently discovered that natural phenomena like clouds, trees, and bodies of water are not regular, and to study them, they have invented fractal geometry, which incorporates a random element in their description.

For some people, the most important question about myth is "Did it really happen?" However, this turns out to be a more complex issue than it first seems. Some myths deal with events in the lives of historical characters. These figures range from Gilgamesh, the ancient king of Uruk in 2600 B.C.E., to Cyrus who was the king of the Medes in the fifth century B.C.E., to Daniel Boone, the eighteenth-century American pioneer.

In many instances, historical details may have been modified, or their emphasis changed in mythical stories told about historical figures. In this sense, the myth may not be true. It is, however, difficult to determine the motivations or character of any historical figure, and all the people in a society do not agree on the facts surrounding a figure or on the motivations for her or his actions. At the same time, though, mythical stories flesh out a historical framework otherwise represented only in inscriptions and treaties, telling us how people of a particular era felt and thought. In addition, myths can often alert us to the existence of historical events that might be unknown except for their preservation in a story.

For example, the Supreme Court of Canada has recognized the claim of the Gitxsan tribe to 22,000 square miles of territory in British Columbia because a Gitxsan story shows that the tribe has inhabited the land for hundreds of years. In the story, **an Indian woman is taken to the sky** and brought back by a man who turns into a grizzly bear. Without realizing the bear is their sister's husband, the woman's brothers kill and skin it. The brothers take the skin to "where the river calls back the salmon every year," and the story states that "the Gitxsan people have been in Kispiox ever since."

Judgment of Paris, Cecchino da Verona (detail)

Greece and Troy

The Trojan War as an Example of Myth

The preceding discussion showed that legends and myths can provide us with a variety of insights into the minds and aspirations of the people who tell them. We have given a series of examples of these insights. However, the in-depth discussion of one story can show more clearly the range and depth of the insights provided by the study of mythology. The Greek story of the Trojan War provides a good example.

Greek mythology has it that Greek forces destroyed Troy after a long siege. **Eratosthenes** put the date of the war at 1184 B.C.E. The war arose over the kidnapping of the Greek **Helen,** wife of Menelaus, by the Trojan **Paris,** son of **Priam,** the king of Troy.

According to the myth, Paris at least believed that he was entitled to Helen. He received her from Aphrodite as a reward for granting the goddess of love first prize in a beauty contest he was judging. The story is as follows.

One day, **Hera,** the queen of the gods, **Athena,** the goddess of wisdom, and **Aphrodite,** the goddess of love, got into an argument about which of them was most beautiful. Zeus decided to put the matter before a judge, and selected Paris, son of Priam, the King of Troy. At the time, Paris was living outside his father's city and working as a shepherd, because there had been a prophecy that he would destroy his father's kingdom.

As it turned out, the prophecy was well founded. The three goddesses did not really want an impartial solution to the matter of who was most beautiful; each of them decided to win the contest by forming an alliance with the judge. The traditional way to do this was through the exchange of gifts, so each goddess offered Paris a gift. Hera offered him political power over Europe and Asia, Athena offered to make him the bravest and wisest warrior in the world, and Aphrodite offered him the most beautiful woman in the world, who was Helen, the wife of Menelaus. Paris rejected political power and honor as a warrior and chose success in love. Accounts differ about whether Paris kidnapped Helen or persuaded her to go with him.

 Introduction

Eratosthenes Head of the library in Alexandria, lived at the end of the 3rd c. B.C.E.

Helen Wife of Menelaus.
Priam King of Troy.
Paris His son.

 The Judgment of Paris

Hera Queen of the Greek gods.
Athena Greek goddess of wisdom.
Aphrodite Greek goddess of love.

This story comes from:
1. Euripides' fragmentary play, *Alexander,* ca. 415 B.C.E.
2. A lost poem called the *Cypri,* of which we have only second-hand accounts.

 Political Background of the Trojan War

Menelaus and Agamemnon Leaders of the Greek army at Troy.

This story comes from:
1. Euripides, *Iphigeneia in Aulis,* after 406 B.C.E.
2. Apollodorus, *Library,* ca. 2nd c. C.E.
3. Pausanias, *Guide to Greece,* 2nd c. C.E.

At the time of the Trojan War, Greece consisted of a group of city-states with separate governments. However, the leaders of these cities had made an alliance years earlier, when Helen was just a girl and all the men of Greece were competing with each other to be her husband. They agreed that they would all protect the rights of the man she chose. As a result, when Helen was kidnapped, the members of the alliance formed an expedition to get her back. This expedition accepted the common leadership of **Menelaus** and his brother **Agamemnon.** The Greeks sent a large force across the Aegean sea to Troy and besieged the city for ten years. It was on top of a great hill and thus very hard to capture.

The greatest warrior among the Greek leaders was **Achilles.** When the war first started, however, it looked as if he would not take part in it at all. His mother **Thetis** knew of a prophecy saying that if her son went to Troy, he would die there. He would either have a short and glorious life, or a long and ordinary one. Thetis hid her son on an island and disguised him as a girl. However, Odysseus, a very clever Greek leader, persuaded Achilles to join the expedition. Throughout the war, Thetis made a series of attempts to save Achilles' life, most notably by having **Hephaistos,** the blacksmith of the gods, make a suit of armor to protect him in battle. Her efforts were not able to prevent her son's death in the course of the war, but Achilles' participation was able to turn the tide in favor of the Greeks—he died, as the prophecy promised, gloriously.

In the tenth year of the war, on the advice of Odysseus, the Greeks built a large wooden horse, filled it with armed men, and pretended to sail away. The Trojans, thinking the horse was an offering to the gods that would bring them luck, took it into their citadel. At night, the Greek warriors climbed out of the horse, opened the gates to their fellow soldiers who had sneaked back, and together they captured the city. The Greeks burned Troy and took Helen back home again to her husband.

After the Trojan War was over, many Greek leaders had a difficult time getting home. The voyage across the Aegean Sea was treacherous, and many of the leaders had offended the gods in one way or another while capturing and pillaging Troy. They suffered for their sins on the homeward journey. Some died in trying to get home. Some, like Agamemnon, were killed by conspirators after they got home.

Odysseus was the Greek leader who had the most extensive adventures while trying to get home. It took him ten years to return to Ithaca: this meant he was away for twenty years altogether, since the war itself also took ten years.

Odysseus was a strong, brave fighter and a great leader who was especially known for his intelligence and quick wit. He came up with the idea of the Trojan horse. Ultimately, though, it was his wit that got him in trouble: he offended **Poseidon,** the Greek god of the sea, and the god interfered with his attempts to get back to Ithaca. Odysseus' adventures as he struggled to get home form the bulk of the work called the *Odyssey* by the poet Homer. Even when Odysseus got back home, his troubles were not over. He found that a group of rowdy young men had taken over his house and were trying to convince his wife **Penelope** to marry one of

 The Decision of Achilles

Achilles Noblest Greek warrior at Troy.
Thetis Achilles' mother.

Hephaistos Blacksmith of the Greek gods.

This story comes from: Homer's *Iliad*, ca. 750 B.C.E.

 The Capture of Troy

"After the Trojan War was over"— The traditional date set by Eratosthenes for the fall of Troy was 1184 B.C.E. Archeologists today believe that the settlement which may correspond to Troy fell ca. 1300–1200 B.C.E.

🌐 **The Story of Odysseus**

This story comes from: Homer's *Odyssey*, ca. 750 B.C.E.

Odysseus Greek leader from Ithaca.

Poseidon Greek god of the sea.

Penelope Odysseus' wife, who rejected the advances of the suitors. Greeks considered her the model of the faithful wife.

Telemachus Son of Odysseus.

NOSTALGIA

The Greeks told many different stories about the adventures of leaders in trying to get home after the Trojan War. The Greek word for homecoming is νόστος (*nostos*), and a story about a hero's homecoming was also called a νόστος. Our word "nostalgia" comes from the word νόστος or "homecoming" and -algia from ἄλγος (*algos*) meaning "pain." In its root sense, nostalgia is the pain you experience in trying to achieve a homecoming. In our language it tends to mean the sadness we feel about what we have lost in the past.

them, so they could take over his kingdom. With the help of his son **Telemachus** and of the goddess Athena, who was his special protector, Odysseus defeated the troublemakers.

Telemachus was only a baby when his father went off to war, but by the time Odysseus got home, he was able to help his father defeat his mother's suitors. In the *Odyssey,* Homer tells us the story of how Telemachus grew from being a helpless boy to asserting himself like a warrior.

The boy was raised mostly by his mother Penelope. He looked upon his family's swineherd, Eumaeus, as a father figure in the absence of Odysseus. At first Telemachus feels powerless to stop the boisterous suitors who insist on coming to his house every day to eat and drink and flirt with his mother. Eventually, with the help of Athena, Telemachus stands up to the suitors, organizes an expedition to look for his father, and returns to fight the intruders, alongside the swineherd Eumaeus and Odysseus himself.

Insights Provided by the Myth of the Trojan War

There is **archeological evidence** that suggests that the account of the Trojan War is not just a false story. The descriptions of Troy given by Homer have allowed archeologists to locate a city in a strategic position on a height overlooking the Dardanelles, the entrance to the Black Sea in modern Turkey. Many archeologists believe that this was the city Homer described in his poems. From the excavations of the site, we know that, over the centuries, people built different versions of this city, one on top of the other, in the same place. Archeologists numbered these cities. The one called Troy VIIa shows signs of having been burned and destroyed at around the time usually suggested for the Trojan War. Archeologist Carl Blegen believed that this confirmed Homer's account of the Trojan War. Other archeological evidence suggests the existence of commerce between the area widely identified as Troy and contemporary Greece, raising the possibility that a war occurred in relation to trade rivalries.

However, the kidnapping of Helen may have been part of the conflict at Troy. We know from our own experience that wars are not usually caused by just one event, but by a series of conflicts. You may remember from your modern European history that the cause of World War I was the assassination of Archduke Francis Ferdinand, but that Europe had been undergoing a series of conflicts and rivalries for quite some time. The assassination simply triggered hostilities.

How much of Homer's tale corresponds to historical facts? Modern archeologists have made a range of discoveries which complicate our understanding of what happened at the site. Manfred Korfmann says, "In its nucleus, the *Iliad* may reflect historical reality." He has recently found defensive structures on the site which match those described in detail by Homer. This is remarkable in itself because in Homer's time the walls of Troy were no longer standing: he lived some 400 years after the date traditionally given for its fall and must have learned about the events at Troy from a vigorous oral tradition. Yet we do not know the extent to which the myth of the Trojan War was a false story, as we know that oral tradition often distorts historical events, reshaping them to express the concerns of the poet's own era. Kurt Raaflaub argues that the gap between the historical events and the era of the poet Homer may well reduce the "historical core of the Trojan War tradition . . . to a minimum."

Of course, there is another sense in which the myth of the Trojan War told a true story for the people who originated it and for us as we study it. As we will show, the stories about Troy provide a variety of insights into the culture, thinking, and way of life of the people who originated them.

The story of the Trojan War provides insight into Greek culture, at least at the time of Homer. From the decision of Achilles to choose a short and glorious life over a long and uneventful one, we can see that the Greeks attached great value to victory in battle. The story of the Trojan War shows that, in their view, war represented a contest of wits as much as one of military prowess and strength. The war shows us that Greek society was based on the alliances a person made with others: this is why the Greeks so readily mounted an expedition that spent ten years trying to recover

 The Coming of Age of Telemachus

 "archeological evidence"—The site of Troy is thought to be at Hisarlik in modern Turkey. Frank Calvert, who started in 1863, was the first archeologist to excavate this site in search of Priam's city. The excavation of businessman Heinrich Schliemann, which began in 1870, was perhaps the most famous. Further excavations were carried out by Dörpfeld (1893–94) and Blegen (1932–38). In recent times, the area has been excavated by Manfred Korfmann.

 Historical Insights

Deal with: verifiable historical events reflected in mythical stories.

Anthropological Insights

Deal with: culture, the values and principles of a society.

one man's wife. The judgment of Paris also suggests the same aspect of Greek culture: victory in the beauty contest among the goddesses was not judged according to any objective standards, but according to which goddess could form the best alliance with Paris through gift giving.

From the story of the Trojan War, we can see how the Greeks saw human freedom and its limitations. It is easy to oversimplify the role of the gods and suggest that the Greeks believed they were enslaved by divine commands, or that they used the gods as an excuse for their actions, shirking responsibility for them by saying, in effect, "the devil made me do it." Neither view is accurate.

In Homer's story, the Greek gods represent higher forces in the universe which determine the fate of humans. For instance, the account of the Trojan War shows that human beings often feel powerless as they are swept away by forces like war that affect their destinies and change, or end, their lives. The actions of Aphrodite should be seen in this light: for the most part, **she represents the power of passion** to sway the decisions made by human beings, not an irresistible impetus that compels them to act in a certain way. Throughout the story, Helen and Paris take on themselves the responsibility for their actions and do not blame the goddess of love. For more on the Greek view of the gods in relation to events in human lives, see Chapter 31 on the role of Hera in causing Heracles' madness, p. 452.

In addition, the story of the Trojan War has other metaphysical implications. It emphasizes the limitations that mortality places on human beings' attempts to achieve eternal fame. The decision of Achilles shows a human being's quandary in deciding between living a long, uneventful life, and a short, glorious one. Achilles ultimately decides to extend his life beyond death by achieving fame and glory that will live on after him.

The story of the Trojan War also provides insight into Greek cosmology by incorporating contemporary scientific explanations of the nature of the universe. This is especially clear in the various accounts we have of heroes' adventures on the way home from the war. They encounter gods who control natural phenomena, like Aeolus, god of the winds, Proteus, a sea god who can change himself into any natural phenomenon, and Poseidon, the great god of the sea. Early Greek science portrayed the physical universe as made up of conflicting and complementary natural forces—wind, water, air, and fire. The myths of the time portrayed these forces as arising from differences of opinion among the gods.

The Aegean Sea is a treacherous body of water even today, when traversed by modern ships. Greek sailors traveled in small vessels that held fifty to a hundred men. Their ships were not self-contained entities that reached their destination after many uninterrupted days on the ocean. Rather, they navigated along the coastline and landed on shore each night for sleep and provisions. The *Odyssey* makes clear that the open sea, out of sight of land, is a dangerous place; humans lacked control and were buffeted by forces that could easily destroy them. This account was scientifically accurate, representing the nature of the Aegean and the state of Greek science and technology at the time.

In the story of the Trojan War, we can see the forces which the Greeks felt were operating on their families and their cities. As we know from recent events like the United States' involvement in Iraq or Vietnam, a war can have a significant effect on society.

Wars are especially hard on families. When soldiers go away to war, their property and family become vulnerable to other forces. We see this reflected in the story about the family of Odysseus, who was once the unchallenged leader of Ithaca. After he left, the suitors claimed his wife and property, and on his return, he had to fight for what was once his.

Because his father was away, Telemachus was raised by his mother, who was not able to instill in him a good sense of what it is to be a man. He enjoyed a warm relationship with Eumaeus, a slave, who functioned as a father substitute and role model for the boy. This turned the old relationships of society upside down.

There were economic effects of the war as well. Before the war, masters protected slaves like Eumaeus, providing them with a livelihood and protection from enemies. After the war,

---

 Metaphysical Insights

Deal with: what it means to be human, typical characteristics and limitations of humans, their relationship to a larger reality or principle.

"she represents the power of passion"—E. R. Dodds, in *The Greeks and the Irrational*, argues that the Greeks in Homer saw their gods as the source of what we would call unforeseen psychological powers that deprived them of their free will. Of course, as with us, different ancient authors portrayed the events of the war differently. In contrast with Homer, Euripides' play *Helen* represents Helen as never actually going to Troy with Paris, despite rumors to the contrary.

 Cosmological Insights

Deal with: the universe as understood by science.

For more about Greek science, see Ch. 3, p. 26.

Sociological Insights

Deal with: groups that people belong to or participate in—values about group behavior, standards for admission.

Insights Obtained from Myths

Insight	Deals with	Example
Historical	Verifiable historical events reflected in mythical stories	Homer's account allowed archeologists to determine an actual site which may have been Troy.
Anthropological	Culture—the values and principles of a society	Achilles was willing to die young because his culture valued glory in battle.
Metaphysical	What it means to be human—typical characteristics and limitations of humans; their relationship to a larger reality or principle	Aphrodite gave Helen to Paris: this represents the limitations passions impose on human freedom, and it shows that a complex event like war is determined by a variety of causes.
Cosmological	The universe as understood by the best science available at the time	Poseidon, the god of the sea, prevented Odysseus from going home. This story allowed its audience to understand the perils sailors encounter on the Aegean sea.
Aetiological	Explaining the origin or cause of a custom or a fact of the physical universe	Ravens are black because Raven escaped from Petrel through the smoke hole.
Sociological	Groups that people belong to or participate in—values about group behavior; standards for admission	The Trojan War changed the nature of the family because fathers were away fighting and sons were often raised by their mothers, or by servants.
Psychological	The struggles of individuals to become mature human beings and useful members of society	Telemachus comes of age by defending his home against the suitors. He serves as a role model for those seeking a mature role in Greek society; his actions show what the society requires of a grown man.

Odysseus, the master, needed the help of his swineherd. He came to Eumaeus' house and asked him for clothes and lodging. Eventually he asked the swineherd to fight alongside him to help him regain his wife and property.

The story of the Trojan War represents the Greeks' struggle to deal with stages in their personal development. Their stories show how war affects individuals in what we might call their personal lives. There is the story of Telemachus, who grows up without a father, but finds suitable role models to become a man and take a responsible part in his society. There is Achilles, who chooses glory over long life. And Thetis, Achilles' mother, expresses her fears as a mother for the well-being of her child as he struggles to live out the destiny he has chosen for himself.

Myth and Many Voices

This book will suggest a variety of insights into stories from different cultures and time periods. If we consider our own culture, however, we realize that not everyone in it shares the same beliefs. It is important to realize that the experiences of Odysseus do not sum up the experiences of all Greeks. In addition, for all the connections we can make between mythological stories and our own time period, it is important to note that there are differences as well. When you are looking at a culture from the outside, it is easy to think that you are seeing elements that resemble your own views and values.

We can look, for instance, at the story of the Trojan War and suggest that the effects of this war were like that of the Vietnam War in late-twentieth-century United States. Both wars caused a generation of young men to go off and fight in a foreign land for a cause they understood and valued only dimly and abstractly. Odysseus, who pretended to be insane to avoid going to Troy,

 Psychological Insights

Deal with: the struggles of individuals to become mature human beings and useful members of society.

Although reading myths can provide cross-cultural insights, it is important to remember the differences in cultures and historical periods while noticing the similarities in their stories.

"the Greeks practiced slavery"—Wendy Doniger points out that myths always express the political views of a particular segment of the population and must be studied with their historical and cultural context in mind. She gives the Old Norse myth of the Valkyries as an example. The stories about these worshippers of Odin (see Ch. 30, p. 436) took on a different meaning when included by Wagner in his operas. The Nazis then reinterpreted both the original stories and Wagner's version to express their vision of Germany and what they saw as its divine mission. C. B. Rose makes a similar point about stories of the Trojan War, which were used by the Romans to legitimize their empire by connecting its founding to Aeneas, a Trojan whose mother, Venus, is the goddess of love.

Contents of This Book:

- Part 1: Introduction

Mythic Themes:

- Part 2: Creation and Destruction
- Part 3: Heroes and Tricksters
- Part 4: Ritual

Related Topics:

- Part 5: Myths and Dreams
- Part 6: Folktales
- Part 7: Contemporary Myths
- Part 8: Myth and Literature

might be considered the first draft dodger in the tradition of the Vietnam war protesters in the 1960s.

At the same time, it is important to remember the differences between the two nations and eras as well as the similarities. For example, **the Greeks practiced slavery.** When the citizens of its city-states sailed off to war, they left their culture and civilization in the hands of people whom they viewed as their property. To get a good sense of what the Trojan War might have been like, we need to consider not just the experiences of Odysseus, but also those of his slave Eumaeus.

There are many other differences between the two societies as well. Homer's Greece was not actually a country; it was an uneasy international alliance forged for the purpose of the War among city states, many of whom were used to thinking of each other as enemies. And during the Trojan War, Greek families are portrayed as completely out of touch with their loved ones' experiences for ten to twenty years, whereas Americans saw the day's events on Vietnamese battlefields as they ate dinner every night.

It is only with caution that parallels can be drawn between the experiences of different cultures. This is not to say that we should not apply the experiences of gods and heroes to our own lives: such identification is at the heart of the pleasure of reading mythology. At the same time, however, it is important, while drawing parallels, to consider as much as possible the unique characteristics of each culture in the stories we read.

What We Mean by a Contemporary View of Myth

In this book, we present a great many stories for you to enjoy. In addition, we have included a variety of theoretical readings that describe some of the kinds of insights you can gain from looking at mythology from the standpoint of different disciplines, including history, sociology, anthropology, and psychology. This introduction has previewed some ideas on mythology from the work of theoreticians like Jung and Levi-Strauss. This book will include excerpts from works like theirs, so that you can acquire first-hand experience of thinking about myths in different ways.

The next chapter will provide you with some techniques for reading myths. After that, the next three sections of this book are organized thematically. Part 2 is about creation and destruction myths; Part 3 is about heroes and tricksters; Part 4 is about ritual and myth. The final part of the book describes phenomena that are related to myths: Part 5 is about symbols and dreams; Part 6 is about folktales and fairy tales; Part 7 is about American myths; and Part 8 is about mythic themes found in literature.

Further Reading

Brunvand, Jan Harold. *The Vanishing Hitchhiker: Urban Legends and Their Meanings*. New York: Norton, 1981.

Campbell, Joseph. "Mythological Themes in Creative Literature and Art." In *Myths, Dreams and Religion,* ed. Joseph Campbell, 138–75. New York: E. P. Dutton, 1970.

Wood, Michael. *In Search of the Trojan War*. Rev. ed. Berkeley: University of California Press, 1996.

Ways of Understanding Myth

WHAT TO EXPECT . . . People with widely varying fields of interest benefit from studying mythology. In this chapter, we explain why many professionals specializing in a wide range of areas study mythology. At the same time, readers of myths are enriched by keeping in mind that the original goals of their tellers were different from ours today. That is, because myths represent a window into the world of the mythmakers, you can expect to gain through them an understanding of cultures other than your own.

Because myths are old stories, reading them requires some techniques not called for in reading retellings. This chapter provides you with guidance on the characteristics. To help you become an effective reader of the myths in later chapters, this one includes a discussion of the characteristics of *oral* myth (repetition, an abundance of names and titles, and parataxis) and of *written* myth (a literary framework, the author's goals, and rationalization).

There are many paths to the enjoyment of mythology. Your first appreciation for it may have come from storybooks read to you when you were little, or even from popular television shows like *Duck Tales* or *Hercules*. Grown-ups also have a variety of choices in approaching the experience of mythology. Many books provide an introduction to the stories of gods and heroes: among the most popular are accounts like Edith Hamilton's *Mythology* and *Bulfinch's Mythology,* which is now available on the web. These are books by scholars who have read the original versions of mythological stories and retell them in their own style. The result is an exciting and pleasing story that can be enjoyed by a wide range of audiences.

This book is devoted to the understanding that a single mythological story may exist in a variety of different versions, each of which will have advantages for the audience and purpose for which it is designed. In writing this mythology book, however, we have decided whenever possible to present myths in translations that are as faithful as possible to the written texts that record the ancient versions of the stories. We have done this out of the belief that a college-level course can make these versions accessible to students and thus provide them with an understanding of certain aspects of the myth that are necessarily eliminated from such retellings as Hamilton's. We feel that some of the pleasure to be gained from the examination of mythological material comes from an appreciation of the literary style in which it is written. In many cases, mythological stories are very old, and they come from cultures that did not use writing, or did not use it for recording these stories, which may have been considered too important to store anywhere but within a living mind and an active memory. You know what a short story is, and if you are reading one that follows the rules for the genre, you know how to read and appreciate the text. However, when you are dealing with a prayer composed for inscription on the inside of an Egyptian coffin, or a poetic epic on the families of the gods composed for oral presentation in ancient Greece, you are less likely to be familiar with the characteristics that were considered appropriate.

The goal of this chapter is to acquaint you with the literary characteristics of such mythological stories and to suggest techniques to help you read them. Before we embark on this subject, we will briefly consider all the different categories of readers who are interested in mythology, and the kinds of evidence they typically derive from it. An additional point to be made here is that the original goals of mythological composition do not match the uses to which mythological texts are put these days. For those "in the know" about how to read mythology, this multiplicity of purposes can add to its appeal.

Who Studies Myth?

As Chapter 1 suggests, there is more to mythology than false stories. This is why a lot of serious attention is paid to myths by people in all sorts of different fields and professions. People have been studying mythology for almost as long as human beings have been telling stories. And mythological accounts have been studied from a lot of different points of view.

Why Scientists Study Myth

You may not have realized that mythology would be studied, for instance, by scientists. Scientists are always reexamining their understanding of the way the universe works. They may be looking for an answer to questions about the way the body heals, or where a star was in ancient times, or the best way to improve ecological systems. Often they can learn from stories about ancient healing rituals or dietary customs that are explained in mythical accounts. Or a myth might describe a journey taken by a hero in a way that gives insight into what the earth or the heavens were like at the time the story was told. Scientists study myths because they do not want to become so wrapped up in their own world view that they fail to notice a different perspective on the question at hand.

Why Historians Study Myth

Historians study past events, reconstructing what happened to a particular people, country, period, or individual. They base their findings on accounts written by the people they are studying, as well as on their laws and commercial documents. To complete the picture, they also use the evidence provided by archeologists, including samples of the houses the people lived in, the tools they used, how they dressed, what they ate, and so on.

Mythology also fits into this understanding. Historians get a better sense of the motivations and mindset of the people they are studying by considering the stories they told, the heroes they patterned themselves on, and the customs or ceremonies they participated in. All of these can be learned from a study of mythology.

How to Read Myth

Introduction: Characteristics of Old Stories

A myth does not have to be old: at this very moment, our own society is full of stories of gods and heroes, and these narratives tell us about ourselves in the same way that the story of the Trojan War characterizes the ancient Greeks.

However, many of the stories we will be studying in this book are very old, probably older than anything you have read before. If you have read Shakespeare or Beowulf in an English class, you know that texts from a different era require some getting used to. They may use language in ways we are unaccustomed to, or they may describe customs and habits we are unfamiliar with. The writers of such texts may have goals and values that are different from what we expect from a novel or play today.

Since many mythological stories are so old, many of them were composed at a time when writing had not been invented or was not widely used for literary purposes. Of course, these stories were later written down or we would not have them today. However, many mythological

Professions	What They Study[1]
Psychologists	The mind and mental processes
Sociologists	Origin, development, organization, and functioning of human social relations and human institutions
Anthropologists	Origins, physical and cultural development, social customs, and beliefs of humans
Folklorists	Traditional beliefs, legends, and customs of people
Historians	Past events
Archeologists	Culture of people as revealed by their artifacts, inscriptions, and monuments
Scientists	Physical and material world
Philosophers	Principles of being, knowledge, or conduct
Artists	Production of work according to aesthetic principles

[1] Adapted from *The Random House College Dictionary,* Revised Edition, 1982.

texts originated in oral form, and have the characteristics of oral composition, including the extensive repetition of words and phrases and an abundance of names and titles. To help you in your reading, we will illustrate these and other characteristics of orally composed works.

Oral stories often contain lines, or even whole incidents that are repeated, sometimes word for word, often with some variation. Ancient audiences liked such repetitions and looked forward to them, but to our ears they may sound confusing or boring.

Here is an example of the kind of repetition that is often found in oral myth:

Then Siduri said to him, "If you are that Gilgamesh who seized and killed the Bull of Heaven, who killed the watchman of the cedar forest, who overthrew Humbaba that lived in the forest, and killed the lions in the passes of the mountain, why are your cheeks so starved and why is your face so drawn? Why is despair in your heart and your face like the face of one who has made a long journey? Yes, why is your face burned from heat and cold, and why do you come here wandering over the pastures in search of the wind?"

Gilgamesh answered her, "And why should not my cheeks be so starved and my face drawn? Despair is in my heart and my face like the face of one who has made a long journey, it was burned with heat and with cold. Why should I not wander over the pastures in search of the wind? My friend, my younger brother, he who hunted the wild ass of the wilderness and the panther of the plains, . . . Enkidu my younger brother whom I loved, the end of mortality has overtaken him. I wept for him for seven days and nights till the worm fastened on him. Because of my brother I am afraid of death, because of my brother I stray through the wilderness and cannot rest."

Why does myth contain this kind of repetition?

The oral poet would be composing the poem on the spot, in front of his audience. He would not be creating the story from scratch, though. An oral poet would learn a large repertoire of fixed phrases or **formulas** to use as modular units from which to build his poems. This would mean that, as he was building his story, he would plug in a modular section and repeat it word for word. While he was doing this, he could think ahead and decide where his story would go next, what he would include or leave out.

The performance of an oral poet would be judged on a variety of factors. Of course his story would have to be interesting and his language polished and elegant. Because the oral poet

Bust of Homer, Capitoline Museum. Homer, the ancient Greek poet, lived so long ago that no one knows what he looked like. This bust from the 2nd c. B.C.E. shows him as old, but infuses him with a vitality attributable to the power of his compositions.

Examples:
The *Odyssey* (Homer). (See Ch. 1, pp. 9–14.)

The *Epic of Gilgamesh*. (See Ch. 15, p. 166.)

 Characteristics of Oral *Myth*: 1. Extensive Repetition

This example comes from: The *Epic of Gilgamesh*, 1200 B.C.E. For excerpts, see Ch. 15.

"formulas"—The name for modular units of rhythm and sound from which oral poets composed their works. For more on oral composition, see Alfred Lord, *The Singer of Tales*.

2. Abundance of Names and Titles

This example comes from: The Prologue of the *Prose Edda*. See Chapter 7, p. 78, for the complete text of the Prologue.

3. Paratactic Storytelling

Example of paratactic storytelling: A child might say, "I was in the park and I saw a bird and I chased it and it flew away."

Example of syntactic storytelling: "**When** I was in the park, I saw a bird. **Because** I chased it, it flew away."

"one after the other"—Walter Ong refers to this as the episodic construction of narrative.

Paratactic Storytelling in Biblical Myth

For the text of the creation story in Genesis, see Ch. 5, p. 51.

Paratactic Storytelling in Greek Myth

For the text of Hesiod's stories about the creation of the human race, see Ch. 3, p. 29.

usually could not read or write, his success would depend in great part on his memory. A good poet knew not just the rough outline of the story, but even its most minute details, so oral poets would provide long lists of names and places to show how well they had mastered the story. Listening to an oral poet give these details accurately would please an audience as any feat of artistic virtuosity pleases its audience. Just think how audiences are impressed with the number of notes a guitarist like Eric Clapton can play at once and not lose the tune. That is virtuosity, as is the ability to remember and elegantly describe all the generations of the hero's family.

Here is an example of the extensive use of names and titles in oral myth:

> Loridi, who resembled his father, was their son. Loridi's son was Einridi, his son Vingethór, his son Vingener, his son Módi, his son Magi, his son Seskef, his son Bedvig, his son Athra whom we call Annar, his son Itrmann, his son Heremód, his son Skjaldun whom we call Skjöld, his son Bíaf whom we call Bjár, his son Ját, his son Gudólf, his son Finn, his son Fríallaf whom we call Fridleif; he had a son named Vóden whom we call Odin.

There are two ways of telling a story, paratactic and syntactic.

The simplest example of paratactic storytelling is the speech of young children. They represent ideas, one after the other, without showing the temporal or logical connections between them. Syntactic storytelling, in contrast, does include logical connections and temporal (time-related) indicators.

In paratactic composition, the audience does not expect the author to provide logical connectives. The audience also is not bothered by logical inconsistencies. When a story is not written down, the listeners do not have written versions to put next to each other and compare word for word, the way we would. So the audience just does not think that way, and they are not interested in contradictions in the story. They are listening to the story for the main point, not checking for the consistency of incidental details.

The Genesis account of creation contains two creation stories, **one after the other,** within three pages or so of each other. In the first one, the earth is created in six days by God. Humans are created at the end of the process on the sixth day. Right after this is an account, in which God creates man first, before anything else is created. These stories were originally told separately to different audiences. Eventually, they were combined into one account in the version we have today. The audience of this combined work would not be bothered by these inconsistencies because they saw both stories as illustrating the same thing: human beings were important to God.

There are two ways to show something is important: by placing it first, or by placing it last, the climax of everything else. One of the versions of the creation story does the former, and one the latter.

Hesiod provides two stories about the origin of the human race. In the five ages of man, he explains that the first race of men were the Golden Age and that every age after them declined until the Iron Age, in which we are presently living. From the description it is clear that Hesiod is talking about the origin of men and women, as the races are described as reproducing themselves. This suggests that women always existed, in every race of human beings. In the immediately following story, however, Hesiod suggests that human beings consisted only of men until a fateful day when Zeus punished them by giving them a woman.

It is no use trying to fit the two stories together. We cannot tell which age of mankind Pandora belonged to; she is simply part of a different story. In the first story, Hesiod is trying to make the point that the world is worse now than it once was. In the other, he is talking about what a great evil women are, in his view. The two stories are not meant to fit together, and their audiences would not have thought to consider their inconsistency, not because they did not notice it or know about it, but because it did not matter to the main point of the story.

Paratactic storytelling, then, is storytelling whose author was not very interested in logical consistency or a sensible temporal order, because his audience was less interested in these elements that in the main point of the story being told.

The characteristics you have just been introduced to are well known to people studying mythology and to writers who want to compose narratives using mythological characters and places. It often happens, therefore, that authors who in other contexts would write quite differently, nevertheless use these characteristics to make their writing seem more like the stories of traditional mythology.

Of course, not all myths come from texts that were orally composed. Some of them come from written works, and very sophisticated ones at that. These texts also pose problems for students of mythology.

Unlike oral texts, these texts are usually not hard to understand, they are just hard to interpret correctly. To interpret these stories, the reader needs an understanding of the author's artistic perspective, style of writing, and goals in writing the text. Of course, all authors shape their texts to fit their artistic goals, but in written texts the revamping of the story tends to be more deliberate and free-spirited. An author may be writing a story with a particular theme in mind and may shape her or his characters and stories to make them fit this motif. The audience does not necessarily expect to hear a story that conforms to the versions they are familiar with. A good example is Ovid, whose *Metamorphoses* is often used as a source for mythological stories.

This literary work was constructed to have a very complex unity. Every story in it describes or refers to a shape change. The stories are chosen with this theme in mind, and stories which in other versions do not include a metamorphosis or shape change acquire one in this work of Ovid.

Ovid may well have had a specific reason in mind for the stories he was telling. He was not just telling them for our information, or even just to collect a lot of stories about myth. He was using the stories he told to show different aspects of the theme of change or metamorphosis. In

Later Texts Imitate the Oral Style

Examples:
The *Prose Edda* (Snorri Sturluson). (See Ch. 7, p. 78.)

Metamorphoses (Ovid). (See Ch. 4, p. 42.)

 Characteristics of Written Myth: 1. *The Literary Frame*

Ovid—A Roman writing poetic verse in Latin. He lived from 43 B.C.E. to 17 C.E.

Example:
The story of Medea as told by the Greek dramatist Euripides includes no shape changes, but as told by Ovid includes at least three.

 2. Goals of the Author

These quotes come from:
Charles Segal's *Landscape in Ovid's "Metamorphoses,"* pp. 92–93, and from K. Sara Myers' *Ovid's Causes*, pp. 26, 59, 142–43.

Flora's Realm, by Nicolas Poussin. This 17th-c. tableau shows some of the complexity of Ovid's world. To the left, Ajax, the hero of the Trojan war is committing suicide. In the middle is Hyacinth, who is killed by a discus thrown by Apollo. To the right, Venus is holding her wounded lover, Adonis. Overhead, Phaethon is driving the chariot of his father, the Sun, before his disastrous plunge from the heavens.

addition, Ovid describes the atmosphere of the times he lived in. Charles Segal explains that the world of the poem is one in which "the hard barriers of reality yield to the slightest touch of fancy and imagination" and one which "holds out the risk of moral chaos, of purposeless change, movement without meaning or end." He describes the theme of *Metamorphoses* as "abrupt, radical, irreversible change at the hands of strange, impetuous divinities." K. Sara Myers suggests that by representing ceaseless change, Ovid was making a statement about the contrasting permanence of poetry; she also notes that scholars have found in Ovid's representation of the nature of the gods a political message about the arbitrary rule of the Roman emperor.

The atmosphere Ovid created **reflected his own times.** When his *Metamorphoses* was written, Rome was ruled by the Emperor Augustus. To survive in this Empire, people had to accept and echo the emperor's views. Cases were not decided according to justice, but according to what the Emperor thought. You had to please the Emperor and to be especially careful not to offend any of his friends. This meant that as the Emperor was influenced by one person or the other, what was right and wrong changed. It was a highly unstable time.

Ovid created a literary world in which everything was highly subject to change. His characters acted in arbitrary and cruel ways to each other. As he set this world in mythological times, no one could say he was writing about the conditions in his own time. So we have to be careful in reading the myths written by Ovid. We have to remember that he wrote not to give us an accurate account of mythological stories as they were told in his time, but to reformulate them in such a way that they helped him represent the instability and unfairness of his own time.

In a sense, everyone who tells a story changes it, making it conform more or less to her or his world view: Homer and Hesiod reshaped the stories of their time to form them into unified works that reflected the world as they saw it. In particular, because oral tales can seem illogical, repetitious, and confusing, later authors who give us versions of myths often will "clean them up," making them seem more logical and less confusing. This often happens when two religious systems known in a country contradict each other. Often someone will come up with a story that will fit them together, or **rationalize** them.

There is reason to think that the worship of Thor was once independent of the worship of Odin. Some people worshipped Thor and some worshipped Odin; they were unrelated gods. But as their worshippers met, they wanted to know how Odin and Thor were related. Stories arose that Thor was Odin's son. In fact, these gods rarely appear in stories together because they are not deeply connected.

When Snorri Sturluson (1179–1241 C.E.) wrote the *Prose Edda* about the Icelandic gods, Christianity was already widely accepted in his country. So Snorri wrote a Prologue to his work, explaining why people came to worship the Icelandic gods, even though the Christian faith was the true religion. Snorri explained that people used to worship the god of the Bible, but through ignorance lost his name. Then, Snorri says, people began to worship men like Thor and Odin, who were great leaders, and they came to believe that Thor and Odin were gods.

In telling this story, Snorri was providing an explanation of how the two religions were connected. In addition, he was satisfying the Christian church that he did not believe the Icelandic myths were true, and he was not telling these stories to spread their worship. This was important at a time when the only means of publication of a literary work was by the copying of monks in monasteries.

Further Reading

Lord, Alfred. *The Singer of Tales*. New York: Atheneum, 1970.

Sidebar:

"reflected his own times"—Augustus exiled Ovid in 8 C.E., forcing him to leave the Rome he loved and live the rest of his life in Tomis, a dangerous and culturally isolated border town.

 3. The Rationalization of Myth

rationalize—Make something more logical or reasonable, usually by adding a made-up reason.

Rationalization in the *Prose Edda*

Example:
Snorri starts his Prologue as if he were quoting from the Bible: "In the beginning Almighty God created heaven and earth and everything that goes with them. . . ." He then quickly moves forward to the time when Priam ruled in Troy. He says that Thor was Priam's descendant. In this account, Snorri creates connections between the Biblical belief system, the ancient Greek myths, and finally the stories he wants to tell about the Icelandic gods. He does this by rationalization, adding a set of connections between these stories that were never made before. See Ch. 7, p. 79, for the text of the Prologue of the *Prose Edda*.

Part 2

Myths of Creation and Destruction

Creation myths address the most fundamental concerns of existence. Just as children ask, "Where did I come from?" adults continue to try to fathom the beginnings not only of their own existence, but also of all of their surroundings. At the same time, these stories represent a way of knowing and a way of structuring experience. That is, they focus our attention not just on the origin of aspects of our world, but on the priorities and categories that seem important to the tellers of creation myths. We learn a great deal about the daily lives of people and the hopes and fears that they experience, from the ways that they structure their stories of how the world came to be.

At first glance, it would appear that myths of destruction represent quite a different tradition than myths of creation. However, the destruction of the world is for the most part presented as an additional refinement of creation. Creation myths frequently represent the formation of the world in a series of stages. In some stories, the destruction of an earlier stage makes way for the development of a world more closely resembling our own. Creation may be accomplished by a god or may involve the descent or evolution of humans from an earlier divine state. Destruction can sweep away evils arising from the incomplete separation of humans from their divine origin, and help them reconcile their current mundane existence with a divine nature or destiny. In many stories, the destruction is represented as punishment sent to human beings by the gods. Humans may be guilty of a sin, or their transgressions may be sins of omission—like neglecting to worship the gods in Ovid's *Metamorphoses*. The work of a trickster may be involved in the sin which is punished and in the process of creation. In each case, however, the stories allow human beings to start anew in accordance with their relationship to the same divine forces that brought about their creation in the first place: the destruction can serve as a warning to the people to live their lives differently, or it can represent a harsh time visited upon them by capricious gods.

To highlight the thematic similarities between myths of creation from different cultures and traditions, as well as to show the connections between myths of destruction from all over the world, we group together the stories embodying each of these themes. Thus, Chapters 3 to 10 will present, in succession, the story of the creation of the world as found in Greek, Roman, Biblical, Mesopotamian, Icelandic, Native American, African, and Chinese stories. Then will follow, in Chapters 11 to 13, stories of destruction from most of these traditions. Looking at these stories in this order will highlight interesting similarities and differences among the traditions they come from. As a secondary emphasis, however, it may also be worthwhile to consider the common links between the myths of creation and destruction from the same tradition, and to skip between Parts 2A and 2B, looking at the story of creation and the story of destruction from an individual tradition. This way of reading can provide additional insight into the way the storytellers thought of themselves in relation to their gods and their world.

Another area of interest with respect to creation and destruction is the work of the tricksters Raven (Ch. 21, p. 295) and Prometheus (Ch. 24, p. 353), who create a world or a civilization by overturning the status quo.

Part 2A

Myths of Creation

In this section, we present a wide variety of creation stories: the Judaeo-Christian tradition of the Bible, Snorri Sturluson's *Prose Edda*, ancient Greek and Roman stories by Hesiod and Ovid, as well as Mesopotamian, Native American, African, and Chinese stories. These stories encompass a wide variety of perspectives on the human condition. Hesiod does not get around to the story of the creation of human beings except as an afterthought to his account of the birth of the gods. In contrast, human beings play a central role in the accounts in the Bible. Several creation stories, including one in the Bible, those from Mesopotamia and Africa, and those by Hesiod, Ovid, and Snorri, emphasize the loss of early perfection. In contrast, Native Americans see the present world, and their particular homelands, as an achievement, the culmination of their journey. Although these creation stories are diverse, they represent a coherent whole that allows us to consider the nature and function of myth, including particularly its role in "formulating and rendering an image of the universe . . . in keeping with the science of the time" and, to a lesser extent, its role in "validating and maintaining some specific social order" (discussed in Ch. 1, p. 4).

Creation from Nothing

Creation myths evolve over time and may be altered by recent scientific discoveries as well as religious and psychological influences. Sometimes this means that new concepts are added, or attributes of one character are melded with another, or linguistic aberrations are made to fit the perceived logical structure of the more current narrative. Because creation myths reflect the science of their time, they share the perspectives and limitations of that work. For example, modern readers may be surprised that many of the creation myths in this section represent the world as being made from the arrangement or rearrangement of already existing elements. They do not involve creation from nothing, which is a relatively modern scientific concept. Early Greek creation stories postulated fundamental substances or beings that always existed, like Hesiod's Earth (Gaia), and did not ask where these came from. The emphasis was on deriving the genealogy of the gods, not on proving their power by asserting that they made all things. This was in line with the science of the time, which traced the origins of the universe back to fundamental substances—like earth, air, fire, and water—and did not ask where these elements came from.

In the same vein, the Priestly creation story which begins the Bible originally seems to have said, "In the beginning, *when* God created the heavens and the earth, the earth was without form and void, and darkness was upon the face of the deep; and the Spirit of God was moving over the face of the waters." This sounds like the heavens and the earth were equal to God, since they came into existence when God did. And yet it was not the Priestly writer's intention to suggest that God had not made the heavens and the earth. He was more interested in discussing what God had done to make the earth especially suitable for human beings. Later, when philosophers were more interested in tracing all things back to a logical single source, this account was rendered, "In the beginning God created the heavens and the earth. The earth was without form and void, and darkness was upon the face of the deep; and the Spirit of God was moving over the face of the waters." This emphasized that God had made the world from nothing: a fact that the Priestly writer would probably have agreed with, but did not explicitly state.

Greek Creation Stories

WHAT TO EXPECT . . . In a way, this chapter represents the *real* beginning of the book, as it contains the first story you encounter from an oral source. With this excerpt, you can begin the process of appreciating the characteristics of the paratactic style, and especially of distinguishing the names of the main characters from the "background" of names and other details included by the oral poet to show his virtuosity.

Over several centuries, the ancient Greeks developed a range of versions of how the world was created. This chapter presents the views of one writer, Hesiod, but in it we can detect traces of the different kinds of explanations in his works, the *Theogony* and the *Works and Days*.

In the *Theogony,* Hesiod incorporates scientific and mythological explanations of the creation of the world. You can see the basics of his literary style, as well as the characteristics of the oral performance that preceded the written version. Two excerpts from the *Works and Days,* "Pandora" and "The Ages of Man," confront such universal themes as the presence of evil in the world and the belief that the present is only a distant, pale remnant of an original "golden age."

In this chapter you meet some amazingly fantastic characters, some physically grotesque and others psychologically depraved. You also make the acquaintance of Prometheus, who returns in the trickster section (Ch. 24). He is seen as a god or a hero, depending on which story you consider: here, the Greeks view him as the cause of the creation of woman, represented by Hesiod as a disruptive source in society. However, later on, it is his son who survives the flood (Ch. 12) to reshape mankind after the gods destroy it. Later, when you read about him as a trickster (Ch. 24), you will see that the disruption represented in myth can have a positive side, as Prometheus is also seen as the cause of civilization.

Hesiod, a Greek poet, lived in about 700 B.C.E. He composed two great poems, the *Theogony* and the *Works and Days,* both of which contain parts of the creation stories excerpted in this chapter. Gregory Nagy has argued that Hesiod and his predecessor, Homer, played an active role in the formulation of Greek traditions about the gods, synthesizing diverse local stories into a "unified pan-Hellenic model that suits most city-states but corresponds exactly to none." This would explain why the stories of these poets were acceptable to Greeks at a time when "[e]ach polis or 'city' was a state unto itself, with its own traditions in government, law, religion" (37).

Hesiod's stories sound like the adventures of gods and heroes, and in a way they are. However, Hesiod is included in Kirk and Raven's *Presocratic Philosophers* as a forerunner of the scientific explanations provided by later thinkers. You may not have realized that in ancient Greece, scientific speculation about the nature of the universe was the province, not of physicists and other scientists, but of philosophers. And Hesiod's poems, while containing some exciting stories that are pure mythology, are also a good source for some of the theories and scientific explanations developed by the Greeks in his time and before it.

The first excerpt from the *Theogony* describes how the world was made, and it incorporates both a scientific explanation and a mythological one. Hesiod begins by suggesting a scientific explanation when he describes impersonal figures which seem more like scientific elements than persons (Chaos, Earth, Tartarus, Love). He describes how these elements are derived from one another by asexual reproduction. This asexual reproduction is a representation of the way that atomic particles unite to form elements or that elements unite to form compounds. Hesiod did not know about particles and atoms, but he had observed chemical changes—the way that wood burns or iron rusts—and realized that such change could explain the formation of our present world.

In an extensive discussion of the opening of the *Theogony,* G. S. Kirk and J. E. Raven point out that Hesiod views Chaos (meaning "gap" or "space," not "disorder") as a fundamental constituent of his explanation. It is the first aspect of the universe, but to explain it, he needs to describe Earth, Tartarus, and Love. Tartarus, the underworld, is here described as a part of Earth, though he later becomes her consort in the generation of Typhon (*Theogony* 822). From Chaos, Hesiod derives Erebos and Night by asexual production, but they then become the parents of Day and Space, and there we have the entry into the story of Love. Like Tartarus, Erebos is a "place of nether darkness, . . . a passageway from Earth to Hades."[1] The majority of these early constituents (with the possible exception of Love) seem to be locations or divisions where things can happen; they are spaces rather than substances or objects, and at the same time, they are gods. Hesiod's conception of the world in this opening segment rather resembles that of Thales, the philosopher whose study of the heavens and whose calculations of celestial orbits allowed him to predict an eclipse of the sun which occurred on 28 May 585 B.C.E. Thales argued that water represents the underlying nature of all things, but he also said that all things are full of gods. This may have been his way of describing the physical forces operating within the substances he described.

Hesiod's account begins by saying, in effect, "Let me tell you how Chaos, the gap, came into being." He briefly mentions the spaces where life is lived by the men and gods: Earth, Olympus, Tartarus, Erebus. This scientific phase of the explanation, however, is over almost before you notice it. Led to the topic of Love, Hesiod soon combines and interlaces his scientific explanation with a mythological account in which families grow up by sexual reproduction. Then he shifts to an account of the adventures of the gods who arise. His main focus is the castration of Heaven by Ouranos' son Kronos. At the same time, as shown by the marginal notes to the accounts, this castration is part of Hesiod's explanation of the scientific development of the universe. He uses this story to explain how the gap, or Chaos, between heaven and earth arose. His shift from science to storytelling would not have seemed illogical to his audience, who in any case expected to be entertained, one way or the other, and who would not have been bothered by the paratactic nature of his account. See Chapter 2, p. 18, on this characteristic of myth.

HESIOD'S STYLE

Traditionally, scientific explanation was provided by philosophers in poetry. This was as standard in ancient Greece as scientists' writing lab reports is today. The poetic form Hesiod used was called dactylic hexameter; it was the same meter used by Homer for the *Odyssey* and the *Iliad,* epic poems describing the exploits of heroes and gods. In fact, Homer and Hesiod did not write their poems down; they composed them orally. They lived in a time when writing was

---

[1] Henry George Liddell and Robert Scott, *A Greek-English Lexicon*.

known, but it was used primarily for business matters and keeping records. The characteristics of oral myth were introduced in Chapter 2, p. 17. We repeat here the points relevant to the appreciation of Hesiod.

Oral composition did not mean that the poets memorized their poems and recited them. Actually, they composed them on the spot! Poets built up repertoires of phrases, some long and some short, and put them together for each performance. The phrases they used would fit into particular parts of a poetic meter; the better the poet, the more ways he (or she) would have mastered to say a particular thing. As we read Hesiod's poetry, we will see that he repeats certain phrases; they were the modular building blocks from which he built his poetic line.

At an oral performance, a poet was juggling many elements and varying the story to fit the reaction of the audience. As the story unfolded, the poet would display his virtuosity in performance, just as a modern jazz artist shows virtuosity by working elaborate improvisations into a piece of music and not losing the structure of the piece. One of the greatest displays of virtuosity was the insertion of numerous names. The poet would show that he remembered all the different titles that a god or goddess would have, and could work them, seemingly effortlessly, into the rhythm and plot he was constructing as he stood before his audience. Hesiod's poetry is especially full of elaborate lists of names and places which can be intimidating to the modern reader. It is a good idea to remember why these names are in the poem: they show the skill of the poet. The notes accompanying the readings point to names that are important to the understanding of Hesiod's main points; the other names he provides are best considered background.

Of course, like all successful performers, the oral poets of ancient Greece were always being asked by their audiences to repeat the works they were famous for. As time went on, these poems began to have standard forms. Eventually a different group of poets arose, called *rhapsodes,* who did not create new poems at each performance, but performed the classic poems word for word. In time, these versions were written down; they have come down to us. As a result of this process, Nagy notes that we have access in Hesiod's poems to the "culmination of what must have been countless successive generations of singers interacting with their audiences throughout the Greek speaking world" (79).

THE GREEK GENERATION GAP

After mentioning the origin of Chaos, Hesiod moves on to talk about the rivalries between generations of Greek gods. In the stories he tells, fathers see themselves in rivalry with their children, and mothers ally themselves with sons against the fathers. First Ouranos (Heaven; the origin of the name of the planet Uranus) turns against his children by Gaia (Earth) and hides them away. Gaia conspires with her son Kronos to punish Ouranos. Then Kronos, in turn, swallows the children he has by Rhea, afraid that they will displace him. Rhea, however, tricks her husband and saves Zeus, who as his father feared, takes over power.

Zeus seems to be haunted by the same fears as his father and grandfather but is more successful in managing them. He is told that his first wife, Metis, will bear a son who will be the king of gods and men. To prevent this, he swallows her and takes on a rapid succession of wives and lovers, settling at last upon Hera, whose children with him, Hebe, Ares, and Eileithyia, seem no threat to their father. Ares, the only male son of Hera and Zeus, is certainly warlike and troublesome, but he seems to channel his aggressive drives into making misery for men as the god of war, and not into challenging his father.

The *Theogony* is the story of the generations of the gods. Human beings are described only as peripheral players in the world of the gods. However, the rivalry between fathers and sons even among the gods sets the tone for the Greek mythical system. When we learn in Hesiod's

Works and Days (Ch. 3, p. 37.) that the gods withhold good things from human beings, we are not surprised. The fearfulness and selfishness of the gods to their own children makes it appropriate that they should treat even helpless humans as a threat.

Philip Slater points out that the attitude of Greek fathers to their sons is related to the marriage practices and family structure of the Greeks. Greek men tended to marry when they had already established themselves, at 30 or so. Women, on the other hand, were much younger when they married and tended not to be educated outside the house. Slater puts the age of marriage at 14; Hesiod recommends marrying a girl who is "in her fifth year" of maturity, which implies a marriage age of 16 to 18 (*Works and Days* 698). In any case, these women were closer in maturity and experience to their children than to their husbands, and not surprisingly, would take a child's side against his father. This situation was exacerbated by the lack of opportunity Greek men had to obtain their own station in life. If there happened to be no available war or adventure by which a young man could make his fortune, he had no choice but to wait for his inheritance from his father. The father's property passed to the son only on his father's death: ample reason for a father to feel his son's impatience to replace him.

This Roman statue shows the beauty and power that may have once belonged to the goddess Hera. It represents Juno, the Roman equivalent of Hera. The statue was damaged in ancient times; as with many classical statues, its head was destroyed. It has been repaired with a head of Venus, the goddess of beauty. The transformation allows us to see the kind of commanding queen of the gods postulated by Joan V. O'Brien before Hesiod and the author of the *Hymn to Apollo* redefined the nature of Hera's power.

THE GREEK GENDER GAP

It is fairly clear that the Greek generation gap also represented a gender gap. Sons were allied with their mothers in their efforts to defeat their fathers. It has been suggested that these stories may hark back to an era in which women were much more important in Greek society and myth. There is some reason to think that Hera may not always have been the wife of Zeus; she seems to have been an independent goddess with her own powers and worship. A large and majestic sanctuary of hers existed at Samos, going back as far as the tenth century B.C.E. Herodotus, the fifth-century B.C.E. Greek historian, called this temple the greatest he had ever seen (3.60.4).

Our main source of information about Hera comes from Homer and Hesiod, where she is secondary and subservient to her husband. But in the Homeric *Hymn to Apollo,* Hera is presented as the mother of Typhon, the monstrous creature who attacks Zeus in Hesiod. This battle may well have represented a more general conflict between the gods. Jenny Strauss Clay points out that there are suggestions in Homer's *Iliad* of an earlier stage in the history of the Olympian gods when Zeus' authority was not yet firmly established, and even indications of a challenge by an alliance of Hera and the Titans. Joan V. O'Brien has argued that Hesiod was familiar with an older, more powerful Hera, who was herself an earth goddess. In her view, Hesiod weakens the primeval female goddess by distributing her power to a variety of goddesses and attributing the birth of Typhon to Gaia, or Earth. Traces of the older story about Hera have been found also in Homer, who describes Zeus and Hera as husband and wife in an antagonistic relationship dominated for the most part by Zeus. Homer's Hera does not fight with her own powers but uses trickery and persuasion to overcome Zeus' plans. It may be that, as the structure of the Greek family changed, women were relegated to a more minor role in the human family, as well as in the family of the gods.

There are other indications of traditions that gave a greater role to women. The Hesiodic *Catalogue of Women,* a work we have only in fragmentary form, begins "Sweet-voiced Olympian Muses, daughters of aegis-bearing Zeus, now sing of the tribe of women who were the best of their time, and loosened their garments to have sex with the gods." Doherty suggests it "may have been at home in a women's tradition which may have differed from, while overlapping with the 'public' androcentric tradition" (310).

In fact, it is not just through his portrait of Hera that Hesiod emphasizes the male gods at the expense of the female. He presents us with a succession of three gods (Ouranos, Kronos,

Zeus), each of whom supplants his father. Male power is consolidated as each male god incorporates elements of his predecessors. Ouranos prevents the birth of his children, pushing them down into the Earth. Kronos improves on his father's stratagem by waiting until after they are born to swallow them, presumably out of their mother's control. And Zeus defeats his father by getting help from Ouranos and Gaia, and by solidifying his rule with the help of the Cyclopes, who were rejected by Ouranos but forge Zeus' thunderbolt—the basis of his power—for him. When his time comes to worry about being usurped, he exerts power over his wives directly. He swallows Metis so she never bears the son she is destined to have, who will be greater than his father. By contrast, the female forces in the universe are fragmented. Initially, Gaia's power over fertility is distributed, first to Aphrodite, goddess of animal fecundity, then to Demeter, goddess of vegetable fertility. Aphrodite, the source of procreation, herself has no divine children except, in later myth, the harmless Cupid. Demeter bears only a daughter, who is no threat to her father, in part because Zeus marries her off to his brother. For more on the Greek attitude toward women, see the introduction to the Homeric *Hymn to Demeter,* Chapter 27, p. 389.

The Creation

Hail, daughters of Zeus! Give me sweet song,
To celebrate the holy race of gods
Who live forever, sons of starry Heaven
And Earth, and gloomy Night, and salty Sea.
Tell how the gods and earth arose at first,   5
And rivers and the boundless swollen sea
And shining stars, and the broad heaven above,
And how the gods divided up their wealth
And how they shared their honours, how they first
Captured Olympus with its many folds.   10

Tell me these things, Olympian Muses, tell
From the beginning, which first came to be?
Chaos was first of all, but next appeared
Broad-bosomed **Earth,** sure standing-place for all
The gods who live on snowy Olympus' peak,   15
And misty Tartarus, in a recess
Of broad-pathed earth, and Love, most beautiful
Of all the deathless gods. He makes men weak,
He overpowers the clever mind, and tames
The spirit in the breasts of men and gods.   20
From Chaos came black Night and Erebos.
And Night in turn gave birth to Day and Space
Whom she conceived in love to Erebos.
And Earth bore starry **Heaven,** first, to be
All over, and to be a resting-place,   25
Always secure, for all the blessed gods.

This story comes from Hesiod, *Theogony.**

"Hail, daughters of Zeus!"—At the beginning of his poem, the poet asks for divine help. Here, he prays to the Muses, the goddesses of art, inspiration, and poetry. He asks them to help him tell the story well.

Chaos—Does not mean disorder but comes from the Greek word χάος and refers to a gap or void. As the story will show, Hesiod uses it to refer to the gap between heaven and earth. In the first nine lines, Earth resembles a place rather than a person, and the creation described is asexual. Here Hesiod relies on the accounts of ancient scientists who viewed the world as being formed from primeval elements. Mondi notes that χάω in Greek is neuter, and its lack of gender points to its "lack of definiteness and form"; gender arises later in the creation process (30–31).

Earth—Gaia.

Heaven—Ouranos.

* Hesiod. *Theogony, Works and Days: Theogonis, Elegies.* Trans. Dorothea Wender. Copyright © 1976. Used by permission of Penguin Books, Ltd.

Birth of the 12 Titans

"without pleasant love"—Hesiod shifts from asexual (scientific) reproduction to sexual (mythical) reproduction. Heaven lies on top of Earth. When his son Kronos emasculates Heaven, Chaos (the gap between Earth and Sky) will be formed. The process of sexual reproduction between Earth and Sky will end.

Birth of the Cyclopes

Birth of the Hundred Armed

The Revenge of Gaia

"And these most awful sons"—Hesiod shifts from the series of births comprising creation to the adventures of the families of the gods.

"Quickly she made grey adamant, and formed, a mighty sickle"—Earth (Gaia) makes the instrument of punishment (actually a useful tool) from ores found within her.

Then she brought forth long hills, the lovely homes
Of goddesses, the Nymphs who live among
The mountain clefts. Then, **without pleasant love,**
She bore the barren sea with its swollen waves,   30
Pontus. And then she lay with Heaven, and bore
Deep-whirling Oceanus and Koios; then
Kreius, Iapetos, Hyperion,
Theia, Rhea, Themis, Mnemosyne,
Lovely Tethys, and Phoebe, golden-crowned.   35
Last, after these, most terrible of sons,
The crooked-scheming Kronos came to birth
Who was his vigorous father's enemy.
Again, she bore the Cyclopes, whose hearts
Were insolent, Brontes and Steropes   40
And proud-souled Arges, those who found and gave
The thunder and the lightning-bolt to Zeus.
They were like other gods in all respects,
But that a single eye lay in the brow
Of each, and from this, they received the name,   45
Cyclopes, from the one round eye which lay
Set in the middle of each forehead. Strength
And energy and craft were in their works.

Then Ouranos and Gaia bore three sons
Mighty and violent, unspeakable   50
Kottos and Gyes and Briareus,
Insolent children, each with a hundred arms
On his shoulders, darting about, untouchable,
And each had fifty heads, standing upon
His shoulders, over the crowded mass of arms,   55
And terrible strength was in their mighty forms.

And these most awful sons of Earth and Heaven
Were hated by their father from the first.
As soon as each was born, Ouranos hid
The child in a secret hiding place in Earth   60
And would not let it come to see the light,
And he enjoyed this wickedness. But she,
Vast Earth, being strained and stretched inside her, groaned.
And then she thought of a clever, evil plan.
Quickly she made grey adamant, and formed   65
A mighty sickle, and addressed her sons,
Urging them on, with sorrow in her heart,
'My sons, whose father is a reckless fool,
If you will do as I ask, we shall repay
Your father's wicked crime. For it was he   70
Who first began devising shameful acts.'

She spoke, but fear seized all of them, and none
Replied. Then crooked Kronos, growing bold,

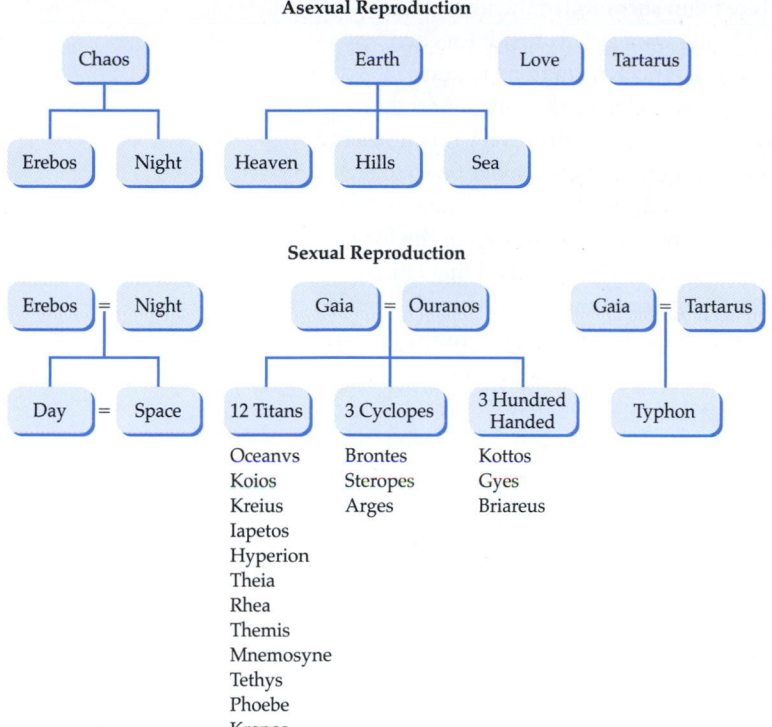

Asexual Reproduction

Chaos → Erebos, Night

Earth → Heaven, Hills, Sea

Love

Tartarus

Sexual Reproduction

Erebos = Night → Day = Space

Gaia = Ouranos → 12 Titans, 3 Cyclopes, 3 Hundred Handed

Gaia = Tartarus → Typhon

12 Titans	3 Cyclopes	3 Hundred Handed
Oceanvs	Brontes	Kottos
Koios	Steropes	Gyes
Kreius	Arges	Briareus
Iapetos		
Hyperion		
Theia		
Rhea		
Themis		
Mnemosyne		
Tethys		
Phoebe		
Kronos		

Creation According to Hesiod's *Theogony*

Answered his well-loved mother with these words:
'Mother, I undertake to do the deed;   75
I do not care for my unspeakable
Father, for he first thought of shameful acts.'
He spoke, and giant Earth was glad at heart.
She set him in a hiding-place, and put
Into his hands the saw-toothed scimitar,   80
And told him all the plot she had devised.

Great Heaven came, and with him brought the night.
Longing for love, he lay around the Earth,
Spreading out fully. But the hidden boy
Stretched forth his left hand; in his right he took   85
The great long jagged sickle; eagerly
He harvested his father's genitals
And threw them off behind. They did not fall
From his hands in vain, for all the bloody drops
That leaped out were received by Earth; and when   90
The year's time was accomplished, she gave birth
To the Furies, and the Giants, strong and huge,
Who fought in shining armour, with long spears,
And the nymphs called Meliae on the broad earth.
The genitals, cut off with adamant   95
And thrown from land into the stormy sea,
Were carried for a long time on the waves.

"He harvested his father's genitals"—Walcot explains that Chaos (the gap between Heaven and Earth) is created here: "The castration of Ouranos represents the separation of heaven and earth, and it repeats what Hesiod has already described when we read that first Chaos, a gap, came into being . . ." (6).

Aphrodite—Greek goddess of love. As Hesiod explains, she is also called Cytherea, Cyprogenes ("born on Cyprus"), and Philommedes ("genital- or smile-loving").

White foam surrounded the immortal flesh,
And in it grew a girl. At first it touched
On holy Cythera, from there it came   100
To Cyprus, circled by the waves. And there
The goddess came forth, lovely, much revered,
And grass grew up beneath her delicate feet.
Her name is **Aphrodite** among men
And gods, because she grew up in the foam,   105
And Cytherea, for she reached that land,
And Cyprogenes from the stormy place
Where she was born, and Philommedes from
The genitals, by which she was conceived.
Eros is her companion; fair Desire   110
Followed her from the first, both at her birth
And when she joined the company of the gods.
From the beginning, both among gods and men,
he had this honour and received this power:
Fond murmuring of girls, and smiles, and tricks,   115
And sweet delight, and friendliness, and charm.
But the great father Ouranos reproached
His sons, and called them **Titans,** for, he said
They strained in insolence, and did a deed
For which they would be punished afterwards.   120

Titans—"strainers." Hesiod derives their name (probably incorrectly) from the Greek verb τείνω, meaning to strain.

Kronos and Rhea

"And Rhea"—Here we skip a long series of stories about the generation of more of the gods. Eventually Hesiod turns to the story of Ouranos and Gaia's offspring, Kronos and Rhea, the parents of Zeus.

And Rhea, being forced by Kronos, bore
Most brilliant offspring to him: Hestia,
Demeter, golden-slippered Hera, strong
Hades, who has his home beneath the earth,
The god whose heart is pitiless, and him   125

Sandro Botticelli, *The Birth of Venus*. This 15th-c. painting represents the birth of Aphrodite (Roman Venus) as an independent event, not as in Hesiod's story, one linked to strife in the family of Ouranos and Gaia. The detail of her emergence from the sea, however, is retained.

Who crashes loudly and who shakes the earth,
And thoughtful Zeus, father of gods and men,
Whose thunder makes the wide earth tremble. Then,
As each child issued from the holy womb
And lay upon its mother's knees, each one   130
Was seized by mighty Kronos, and gulped down.
He had in mind that no proud son of Heaven
Should hold the royal rank among the gods
Except himself. For he had learned from Earth
And starry Heaven, that his destiny   135
Was to be overcome, great though he was,
By one of his own sons, and through the plans
Of mighty Zeus. Therefore he never dropped
His guard, but lay in wait, and swallowed down
His children. Rhea suffered endless grief;   140
But when she was about to bring forth Zeus,
Father of gods and men, **she begged the Earth**
And starry Heaven, her parents, to devise
A plan to hide the birth of her dear son
And bring the Fury down on Kronos, for   145
His treatment of his father and his sons
Whom mighty, crooked Kronos swallowed down.
They heard their daughter and agreed, and told
Her all that fate would bring upon the king
Kronos, and to his mighty-hearted son.   150
They sent her to the fertile land of Crete,
To Lyctus, when she was about to bear
Her youngest child, great Zeus. And in broad Crete
Vast Earth received the child from her, to raise
And cherish. And she carried him, with speed,   155
Through the black night, and came to Lyctus first.
She took him in her arms and hid him, deep
Under the holy earth, in a vast cave,
On thickly-wooded Mount Aegeum. Then,
To the great lord, the son of Heaven, the past   160
King of the gods, she handed, solemnly,
All wrapped in swaddling-clothes, a giant stone.
He seized it in his hands and thrust it down
Into his belly, fool! He did not know
His son, no stone, was left behind, unhurt   165
And undefeated, who would conquer him
With violence and force, and drive him out
From all his honours, and would rule the gods.
The strength and glorious limbs of the young lord
Grew quickly and the years went by, and **Earth**   170
Entrapped great clever Kronos with shrewd words
Advising him to bring his offspring back
(His son, by craft and power, conquered him.)
And first he vomited the stone, which he
Had swallowed last. At holy Pytho, Zeus   175

Francisco de Goya y Lucientes, *Saturn Devouring One of His Sons*. In Goya's imagination, Kronos (Roman Saturn) devours his children. In Hesiod's version, Kronos swallows his children to prevent them from taking over his position.

"she begged . . . her parents, to devise a plan"—Ouranos and Gaia play a complicated role in the events which follow. They warn Kronos that his destiny is to be replaced by Zeus. However, they provide Rhea with the same information, allowing her to bring it to pass.

"Earth entrapped great clever Kronos"—Gaia persuades her son Kronos to bring back his son Zeus. This seems incompatible with the explanation provided previously that Gaia helped fool Kronos into believing that he had swallowed Zeus, and not a stone.

"Advising him to bring his offspring back"—This does not fit with the version presented previously, in which Gaia helps keep Kronos from swallowing Zeus. See Ch. 2, p. 18, on the lack of logic in mythical accounts.

Set firm the stone in broad-pathed earth, beneath
Parnassus, in a cleft, to be a sign
In future days, for men to marvel at.
He freed **his uncles** from their dreadful bonds,
The sons of Heaven; his father, foolishly,   180
Had bound them. They remembered gratitude
And gave him thunder and the blazing bolt
And lightning, which, before, vast Earth had hid.
Trusting in them, he rules both men and gods.

"his uncles"—Kottos, Gyes, and Briareus, sons of Ouranos. Zeus frees Gaia's monstrous children, presumably pleasing his grandmother.

The Rule of Zeus

Now Zeus, king of the gods, **first took to wife**   185
Metis, wisest of all, of gods and men.
But when she was about to bear her child
Grey-eyed Athene, he deceived her mind
With clever words and guile, and thrust her down
Into his belly, as he was advised   190
By Earth and starry Heaven. In that way
They said, no other god than Zeus would get
The royal power over all the gods
Who live forever. For her fate would be
To bear outstanding children, greatly wise,   195
First, a girl, Tritogeneia, the grey-eyed,
Equal in spirit and intelligence
To Zeus her father; then she would bear a son
With haughty heart, a king of gods and men
But Zeus, forestalling danger, put her down   200
Into his belly, so that the goddess could
Counsel him in both good and evil plans.
And shining Themis was his second wife.
She bore the Horae: Order, blooming Peace,
And Justice, who attend the worlds of men,   205
And then the Fates, to whom wise Zeus has paid
The greatest honour: Clotho, Atropos
Lachesis, who give men all good and bad.
The daughter of Ocean, fair Eurynome,
Next bore to him three daughters, the fair-cheeked   210
Graces Aglaia and Euphrosyne,
And lovely Thalia. From their glancing eyes
Flowed love that melts the strength of a man's limbs,
Their gaze, beneath their brows, is beautiful.

Demeter, who feeds all, came to the bed   215
Of Zeus, and bore white-armed **Persephone,**
Whom Aidoneus stole away from her,
But Zeus the counselor approved the match.
Again, he loved fair-haired Mnemosyne,
Who bore the **Muses,** golden crowned, the Nine,   220

"Now Zeus"—Here we omit the story of Zeus' defeat of the monster Typhon.

"first took to wife"—Early in his career, Zeus marries several wives, in somewhat quick succession. The first one, Metis, is swallowed by him and becomes part of him. The second, Themis, simply fades from sight. His actions replace female generative power with male authority, even to his actions in giving "birth" to Athena, called by the mysterious term "Tritogeneia." See O'Brien's comments on the rivalry between Zeus and Hera, p. 28. Metis means "applied intelligence" and Themis, "law." Perhaps the function of these stories was to show the evolution of Zeus from a petty tyrant to a wise ruler who embodied wisdom and justice. After these wives, Zeus becomes involved with Eurynome (mother of the Graces), Demeter (mother of Persephone), Mnemosyne (mother of the Muses), and Leto (mother of Apollo and Artemis). Zeus' next wife was Hera, and he remained with her, although he continued to have an extensive love life, including a variety of human women, another way of showing independence from female divinities.

Persephone—Daughter of Demeter and Zeus. Her abduction by Aidoneus (Hades), god of the underworld, is described in detail in the Homeric *Hymn to Demeter*. (See Ch. 27, p. 385.)

Muses—The nine muses were goddesses who provided inspiration to artists and writers. Hesiod began his poems with a prayer to them for inspiration. For prayers to the Muses, see p. 29 and p. 36.

Whose pleasure is in feasting and sweet song.
And Leto joined in love with Zeus who holds
The aegis, and the offspring which she bore
Were lovelier than all the sons of Heaven:
Apollo and the huntress Artemis.   225
Last he took blooming Hera for his wife;
Uniting with the king of gods and men,
She gave him Hebe and Ares, and she bore
The goddess Eileithuia to her mate.
But Zeus himself produced, from his own head,   230
Grey-eyed **Athene,** fearsome queen who brings
The noise of war and, tireless, leads the host,
She who loves shouts and battling and fights.
Then Hera, angry, quarreled with her mate
And bore, without the act of love, a son   235
Hephaistos, famous for his workmanship
More skilled in crafts than all the sons of Heaven.
Amphitrite and **He who Shakes the Earth,**
The crashing god, produced a mighty son,
Wide-ruling Triton, he who holds the deep,   240
A fearsome god, who lives in a golden house
Beside his mother and the lord
His father. And to Ares, who pierces shields,
Cytherea bore Terror and Fear, dread gods
Who come with Ares, sacker of towns, and spread   245
Confusion in the close-packed ranks of men
In numbing war; then Cytherea bore
Harmonia, bold-hearted Cadmus' wife.
And Maia, daughter of Atlas, came to Zeus
And to his holy bed, and bore to him   250
Glorious **Hermes,** herald of the gods.
Semele, Cadmus' daughter, lay with Zeus
And bore to him a brilliant son, a god,
Glad **Dionysus,** mortal though she was,
And now they both have joined the ranks of gods.   255

Alcmene, lying in love with Zeus, who drives
The clouds, gave birth to **Heracles** the strong.
The famous limping god, Hephaistos, made
Aglaia, youngest Grace, his blooming wife.
And golden Dionysus took to wife   260
The fair-haired Ariadne, Minos' child:
The son of Kronos saved her from death and age.
And then strong Heracles, the glorious son
Of trim-ankled Alcmene, at the end
Of all his painful labours, made his bride   265
Hebe, the modest child of mighty Zeus
And golden-slippered Hera, on snow-clad
Olympus. Happy god! For he has done

Athene—Goddess of wisdom and war, child of Zeus.

Hephaistos—God of the forge, child of Hera "without the act of love." This again suggests a rivalry between Zeus and Hera. (See p. 29f.)

"He who Shakes the Earth"— Poseidon, god of the sea, and brother of Zeus.

Cytherea—Aphrodite, Greek goddess of love, who was born from the genitals of Ouranos. (See p. 32.)

Hermes—Messenger of the Greek gods; son of Zeus and Maia.

Dionysus—Greek god of wine; son of Zeus and Semele, a human being.

Heracles—Son of Zeus and a mortal woman, Alcmene. He became a god after a series of labors; see Ch. 31, p. 446. There is no explanation for why some offspring of gods and humans become gods and others remain human.

His great work and he lives among the gods
Forever young, forever free from pain.   270
And now, farewell, Olympians, and you
Islands and continents and salty sea.

The Creation of Pandora

The next excerpts come from Hesiod's *Works and Days*. This work devotes more attention to the affairs of humans than does the *Theogony. Works and Days* is a miscellaneous poem that contains, among other things, a series of precepts for how to live industriously (the works), and a description of the days of the month, and what activities are suitable for each (the days). Berkley Peabody maintains that the *Works and Days* was a celebration of Zeus and his power: certainly the following excerpt, about Pandora and the Ages of Man, shows the mastery of Zeus and his control of gods and humans. In addition, the poem may have been written to be performed at a poetic competition. This may explain Hesiod's early emphasis on strife in general, and the strife between poets in particular.

Strife, however, is also an appropriate concept to describe the spirit of Greek mythology. In the previous story of creation, we saw that Heaven tried to withhold power from his sons by hiding them in the earth. The spirit of Strife is also operative in relations between the gods and humans: the gods display this same mean-spiritedness to all those who are weaker than they are. At Mekone, Prometheus obtains meat for human beings by tricking Zeus into accepting a sacrifice of bones and fat rather than meat. Rather than gladly granting humans the nourishment they need, the gods respond by withholding fire from them. Then the first woman, Pandora, is created as another punishment for human beings, this time for stealing fire from the gods.

The story of Pandora is followed immediately by an account of the Ages of Man. This shows that the world has declined since its beginning; Hesiod describes himself as living in a time when it is difficult to eke out an existence. This fits with his vision of the gods in the other two excerpts as withholding good things from man. It may be noted, however, that strictly speaking, the two accounts are incompatible with each other. The story of Pandora suggests that there was no woman until Pandora; the story of the Ages of Man implies the existence of women at each of the points of human development. This kind of inconsistency would not have distressed Hesiod. He was not trying to produce a systematic account of the origin of the world, but rather a narrative which described what it was like to live in the world. Two aspects of this were his vision of women as a drain on productivity (Pandora) and his view that the world has gotten worse (Ages of Man). On the paratactic nature of myth, see Chapter 2, p. 18, and Chapter 25, p. 363.

Prometheus, the god who tries to help humans by getting fire for them, is one of the great figures in Greek mythology. We will learn more about him in Part 3 on heroes.

Jan Cossiers, *Prometheus carrying fire.* In stealing fire, the god helps human beings create civilization, as will be clear from the other stories about him. (See Ch. 24, p. 353.)

This story comes from: Hesiod, *Works and Days.**

"Pierian Muses . . . come tell of your father, Zeus"—The poet asks for divine help at the beginning of his poem. Here, he prays to the Muses, the goddesses of art, inspiration, and poetry. He asks them to help him tell the story well. The poem's emphasis on Zeus starts here and continues throughout.

**PIERIAN Muses, bringers of fame: come
Tell of your father, Zeus,** and sing his hymn,
Through whom each man is famous or unknown,
Talked-of or left obscure, through his great will
With ease he strengthens any man; with ease   5
He makes the strong man humble and with ease
He levels mountains and exalts the plain,

---

* Hesiod. *Theogony, Works and Days: Theogonis, Elegies.* Trans. Dorothea Wender. Copyright © 1976. Used by permission of Penguin Books, Ltd.

Withers the proud and makes the crooked straight.
With ease, the Thunderer whose home is high.
Hear, Zeus, and set our fallen laws upright   10
And may my song to **Perses** tell the truth.
Strife is no only child. Upon the earth
Two Strifes exist; the one is praised by those
Who come to know her, and the other blamed.
Their natures differ: for the cruel one   15
Makes battles thrive, and war; she wins no love
But men are forced, by the immortals' will,
To pay the grievous goddess due respect.
The other, first-born child of blackest Night,
Was set by Zeus, who lives in air, on high,   20
Set in the roots of earth, an aid to men.
She urges even lazy men to work:
A man grows eager, seeing another rich
From ploughing, planting, ordering his house;
So neighbour vies with neighbour in the rush   25
For wealth: this Strife is good for mortal men
Potter hates potter, carpenters compete,
And beggar strives with beggar, bard with bard.
O Perses, store this in your heart; do not
Let Wicked Strife persuade you, skipping work,   30
To gape at politicians and give ear
To all the quarrels of the market place.
He has no time for courts and public life
Who has not stored up one full year's supply
Of **corn, Demeter's gift,** got from the earth.   35
When you have grain piled high, you may dispute
And fight about the goods of other men.
But you will never get this chance again:
Come, let us settle our dispute at once,
And **let our judge be Zeus, whose laws are just.**   40
We split our property in half, but you
Grabbed at the larger part and praised to heaven
The lords who love to try a case like that,
Eaters of bribes. The fools! They do not know
That half may be worth more by far than whole,   45
Nor how much profit lies in poor man's bread.

The gods desire to keep the stuff of life
Hidden from us. If they did not, you could
Work for a day and earn a year's supplies;
You'd pack away your rudder, and retire   50
The oxen and the labouring mules. But Zeus
Concealed the secret, angry in his heart
At being hoodwinked by **Prometheus,**
And so he thought of painful cares for men.
First he hid fire. But the son of Iapetos   55
Stole it from Zeus the Wise, concealed the flame

Perses—Person to whom this poem is addressed; may be Hesiod's brother, or perhaps a rival in a poetry contest.

"Strife is no only child"—The goddess Strife plays a prominent role in Hesiod's understanding of the nature of the world. Notice that Hesiod ends his catalogue of the activities of Strife by saying "bard [strives with] bard." This may be a reference to the poetic contest at which the *Works and Days* was performed.

"corn, Demeter's gift"—Refers to all grain. Demeter is the Greek goddess of the harvest.

"let our judge be Zeus, whose laws are just"—Hesiod is referring to a dispute he had with Perses. He seems to be describing brothers settling a family inheritance, or contestants sharing a prize.

"The gods desire to keep the stuff of life hidden from us"—Another manifestation, this time in the human world, of the spirit of Strife which was first seen in the rivalry between father and son in Hesiod's *Theogony*. (See p. 30f.)

Prometheus—Son of Iapetos; a trickster who deceives Zeus to help human beings.

In a fennel stalk, and fooled the Thunderer.
Then, raging, spoke the Gatherer of Clouds:
"Prometheus, most crafty god of all,
You stole the fire and tricked me, happily,   60
You, plague on all mankind and on yourself.
They'll pay for fire: I'll give another gift
To men, an evil thing for their delight,
And all will love this ruin in their hearts."
So spoke the father of men and gods, and laughed.   65

Hephaistos—Lame blacksmith of the Greek gods.

He told **Hephaistos** quickly to mix earth
And water, and to put in it a voice
And human power to move, to make a face
Like an immortal goddess, and to shape
The lovely figure of a virgin girl.   70

Athene—Greek goddess of wisdom, war, weaving.

Aphrodite—Greek goddess of love.

Hermes—Greek messenger god; god of thieves.

Athene was to teach the girl to weave,
And golden **Aphrodite** to pour charm
Upon her head, and painful, strong desire,
And body-shattering cares. Zeus ordered, then,
The killer of Argos, **Hermes,** to put in   75
Sly manners, and the morals of a bitch.

"son of Kronos"—Zeus.

The **son of Kronos** spoke, and was obeyed.
The lame God moulded earth as Zeus decreed
Into the image of a modest girl,
Grey-eyed Athene made her robes and belt,   80
Divine Seduction and the Graces gave
Her golden necklaces, and for her head
The Seasons wove spring flowers into a crown.
Hermes the Messenger put in her breast
Lies and persuasive words and cunning ways;   85
The herald of the gods then named the girl

Pandora—First woman.

Pandora, for the gifts which all the gods
Had given her, this ruin of mankind.

The deep and total trap was now complete;
The Father sent the gods' fast messenger   90

Epimetheus—Brother of Prometheus ("forethought"); his name means "afterthought."

To bring the gift to **Epimetheus**
And Epimetheus forgot the words
His brother said, to take no gift from Zeus,
But send it back, lest it should injure men.
He took the gift, and understood too late.   95

"the woman opened up the cask, and scattered pains and evil among men"—Pandora actually opened a storage jar which was more usually a container for food like wine, olives, or grain. Hesiod uses the story to justify Greek misogyny (the dislike of women). For an alternative view, we have Odysseus' positive estimation of his wife Penelope's importance in Homer's *Odyssey*.

Before this time men lived upon the earth
Apart from sorrow and from painful work,
Free from disease, which brings the Death-gods in.
But now **the woman opened up the cask,**
And scattered pains and evils among men.   100
Inside the cask's hard walls remained one thing,
Hope, only, which did not fly through the door.
The lid stopped her, but all the others flew,
Thousands of troubles, wandering the earth.

The earth is full of evils, and the sea.   105
Diseases come to visit men by day
And, uninvited, come again at night
Bringing their pains in silence, for they were
Deprived of speech by Zeus the Wise.
And so there is no way to flee the mind of Zeus.   110

The Ages of Man

As noted in the previous introduction, the next excerpt also comes from Hesiod's *Works and Days,* following immediately upon the story of Pandora. Stories of the ages of man are found in a variety of different cultures. In some of these traditions, time is seen as periodically renewing itself in an infinite cycle that begins with a golden age from which creation declines but then recovers itself. Among these cyclic stories are the Vedic tradition from India and the Germanic tradition of Ragnarok, which we meet again when we discuss Destruction Myths. Mircea Eliade saw these stories as reflecting a characteristic universal to all primitive religions: reference to a great cosmic cycle of renewal and return to an era in which historical time itself is suspended in favor of eternal, mythical time (35–36). If Hesiod's story harks back to such an era, traces of a more optimistic perspective have well nigh disappeared, leaving only the grim reality of the present day and decline from a better age.

And now with art and skill I'll summarize
Another tale, which you should take to heart,
Of how both gods and men began the same.
The gods, who live on Mount Olympus, first
Fashioned a golden race of mortal men;   5
These lived in the reign of Kronos, king of heaven,
And like the gods they lived with happy hearts
Untouched by work or sorrow. Vile old age
Never appeared, but always lively-limbed,
Far from all ills, they feasted happily.   10
Death came to them as sleep, and all good things
Were theirs; ungrudgingly, the fertile land
Gave up her fruits unasked. Happy to be
At peace, they lived with every want supplied,
[Rich in their flocks, dear to the blessed gods.]   15

And then this race was hidden in the ground.
But still they live as spirits of the earth,
Holy and good, guardians who keep off harm,
Givers of wealth: this kingly right is theirs.
The gods, who live on Mount Olympus, next   20
Fashioned a lesser, silver race of men:
Unlike the gold in stature or in mind.
A child was raised at home a hundred years

This story comes from: Hesiod, Works and Days.*

 1. The Golden Race

2. The Silver Race

And played, huge baby, by his mother's side.
When they were grown and reached their prime, they lived   25
Brief, anguished lives, from foolishness, for they
Could not control themselves, but recklessly
Injured each other and forsook the gods;
They did not sacrifice, as all tribes must, but left
The holy altars bare. And, angry, Zeus   30
The son of Kronos, hid this race away,
For they dishonoured the Olympian gods.

The earth then hid this second race, and they
Are called the spirits of the underworld,
Inferior to the gold, but honoured, too.   35
And Zeus the father made a race of bronze,
Sprung from the ash tree, worse than the silver race,
But strange and full of power. And they loved
The groans and violence of war; they ate
No bread; their hearts were flinty-hard; they were Terrible men;
their strength was great, their arms   40
And shoulders and their limbs invincible.
Their weapons were of bronze, their houses bronze;
Their tools were bronze: black iron was not known.
They died by their own hands, and nameless, went   45
To **Hades'** chilly house. Although they were
Great soldiers, they were captured by black Death,
And left the shining brightness of the sun.

3. The Bronze Race

Hades—Greek god of the under-world; also called Aidoneus.

But when this race was covered by the earth,
The son of Kronos made another, fourth,   50
Upon the fruitful land, more just and good,
A godlike race of heroes, who are called
The demi-gods—the race before our own.
Foul wars and dreadful battles ruined some;
Some sought the flocks of Oedipus, and died   55
In Cadmus' land, at seven-gated Thebes;
And some, who crossed the open sea in ships,
For fair-haired Helen's sake, were killed at **Troy.**
These men were covered up in death, but Zeus
The son of Kronos gave the others life   60
And homes apart from mortals, at Earth's edge.
And there they live a carefree life, beside
The whirling Ocean, on **the Blessed Isles.**
Three times a year the blooming, fertile earth
Bears honeyed fruits for them, the happy ones.   65
[And Kronos is their king, far from the gods,
For Zeus released him from his bonds, and these,
The race of heroes, well deserve their fame.

4. The Race of Heroes or Demi-Gods

Troy—See Ch. 1, p. 9f., for the story of the Trojan War.

"the Blessed Isles"—The English poet, Alfred Lord Tennyson, picks up on this theme in his poem "Ulysses" in which the aged hero proposes a last journey in search of the carefree life Hesiod describes here. (See Ch. 42, p. 631.)

5. The Iron Race

"who live now"—Hesiod is describing his own times, as they seem to him.

Far-seeing Zeus then made another race,
The fifth, **who live now** on the fertile earth.]   70

I wish I were not of this race, that I
Had died before, or had not yet been born.
This is the race of iron. **Now, by day,**
Men work and grieve unceasingly; by night,
They waste away and die. The gods will give   75
Harsh burdens, but will mingle in some good;
Zeus will destroy this race of mortal men,
When babies shall be born with greying hair.
Father will have no common bond with son,
Neither will guest with host, nor friend with friend;   80
The brother-love of past days will be gone.
Men will dishonour parents, who grow old
Too quickly, and will blame and criticize
With cruel words. Wretched and godless, they
Refusing to repay their bringing up,   85
Will cheat their aged parents of their due.
Men will destroy the towns of other men.
The just, the good, the man who keeps his word
Will be despised, but men will praise the bad
And insolent. Might will be Right, and shame   90
Will cease to be. Men will do injury
To better men by speaking crooked words
And adding lying oaths; and everywhere
Harsh-voiced and sullen-faced and loving harm,
Envy will walk along with wretched men.   95
Last, to Olympus from the broad-pathed Earth,
Hiding their loveliness in robes of white,
To join the gods, abandoning mankind,
Will go the spirits Righteousness and Shame.
And only grievous troubles will be left   100
For men, and no defence against our wrongs.

> "Now, by day, men work and grieve unceasingly"—This is the reign of bad Strife, which, as Hesiod explained at the beginning of this poem, is already widespread.

Further Reading

O'Brien, Joan V. *The Transformation of Hera: A Study of Ritual, Hero, and the Goddess in the "Iliad."* Lanham, MD: Rowman & Littlefield, 1993.

Slater, Philip. *The Glory of Hera: Greek Mythology and the Greek Family.* Boston: Beacon Press, 1971.

4

Ovid's Creation Story

WHAT TO EXPECT . . . In this chapter, you encounter a story that at first sight seems quite similar to Hesiod's in Chapter 3. However, the reading is Ovid's Roman version of the creation of the universe, and when you get beyond your first impression, a careful reading will allow you to see that it is quite different from Hesiod's creation.

Look for the ways that Ovid's story reveals his own personality and perspectives, and shows the culture of his time as well as the expectations of the audience. For example, in comparing Ovid's Ages (Golden, Silver, and Iron) with those of Hesiod, you might think about how Ovid adapted a pessimistic story to express his own view of the world, that his was a great time to live in the Roman Empire.

To help you put Ovid's work into context, the marginal notes identify the prevalent scientific theories in Ovid's time and show how he used them to make his story sound scientific, even though he was primarily interested in telling a good story.

Ovid was cited in Chapter 2 (p. 19) as an example of a writer who told mythological stories in a literary frame. Ovid's *Metamorphoses* is a collective poem, a work that pulls together a variety of different legends to tell a story. As we noted in Chapter 2, Ovid's poem was not written to give us information about myths, but to illustrate the theme of metamorphosis or change.

It must be understood that Ovid wrote in a highly sophisticated time. The serious narratives of Homer and Hesiod were only a memory. The purpose of art was to be creative and to show the free play of the poet's fanciful imagination. Poets wrote with the assumption that their readers were educated, that they were familiar with the classics of their day. In our times, for instance, Tom Stoppard wrote *Rosencrantz and Gildenstern Are Dead* not to retell Shakespeare's story of Hamlet, but to provide a commentary and a perspective on it for our own times. The resulting play is not a homage to Shakespeare, but a statement of its own. It is at the same time very serious, and very funny. Similarly, in Ovid's time, it was not the poet's job to repeat the feats of previous writers, but to recast them for modern times. And as in modern times, people enjoyed poems that were frivolous, playful, iconoclastic, and funny.

Ovid produced a series of stories about metamorphosis, often adding this element to stories that in other versions did not include it. We should not think, however, that the poem emphasizes metamorphosis over all its other elements. Often the change is only a minor part of a story Ovid tells. Yet metamorphosis is much more than a theme of the poem. Rather, it describes the way Ovid handles his material: his approach is ever-changing. He juxtaposes straightforward elements and playful ones, serious themes and comic ones. He does not sustain a consistent mood or tone, preferring to move between scenes and motifs that are dramatic, high-minded, and emotional and those which are amusing, grotesque, or entertaining. Ovid keeps the

Metamorphosis of Narcissus. This painting by Salvador Dali captures the eclectic tone and mocking style of Ovid's narrative. The painting is a grimly humorous juxtaposition of several aspects of the myth. Narcissus was the boy who was so enthralled by his own reflection that he was turned into a flower. Dali represents the transformation of the human being into a stone-like hand. He shows the unnatural creation of the flower by having it spring forth from an egg, and he incorporates a statue of Narcissus who placed himself on a pedestal.

reader's attention by keeping his work moving as the narrative jumps from story to story, theme to theme, and mood to mood.

Hesiod's story of creation has a serious purpose, exploring the underlying principles that govern the universe and showing the moral implications of those principles for human beings, in their interactions with the gods and with each other. Ovid, on the other hand, refuses to involve himself in moral conflicts: the purpose of his story is to amuse and delight the reader. If deep reflection is to result from reading his narrative, it will be about the nature of art and the effect of different ways of telling a story.

For all its frivolity, however, Ovid's poem provides us with an account in accord with the best science of his time. Although Ovid's purpose is not consistently serious throughout, we see reflections throughout the poem of other works involving serious attempts to describe the nature of the universe. Although Ovid himself lived much later (43 B.C.E. to 17 C.E.), the science of his day incorporated ideas from a long line of Greek scholarship dating back to Thales (who lived before 585 B.C.E.), Pythagoras (born mid-6th-c. B.C.E.), Anaxagoras (500–428 B.C.E.), and Empedocles (492–432 B.C.E.). More recent thinkers in this vein included Plato (429–347 B.C.E.), Aristotle (384–322 B.C.E.), and Epicurus (341–270 B.C.E.) and Zeno (335–263 B.C.E.), the founders of Epicureanism and Stoicism, respectively. In this tradition, science was considered a part of philosophy. Today, we view science as "factual," and consider philosophy "subjective," but in ancient times, philosophy was considered "objective": it was philosophers who studied the nature of the universe or natural philosophy, and it was they who were known for the thoroughness and accuracy of their scientific and medical observations.

Ovid's explanations reflect the theories of the Epicureans, the Stoics, and other older natural philosophers who studied the nature of the universe. By including as many as possible of the views of these scientists, Ovid gives his poem what K. Sara Myers calls a pseudo-scientific tone (54). He does not subscribe to the views of any one scientist; rather, he uses technical language to provide an eclectic blend of the scientific views of his time. The picture he paints from the beginning of the flux of unstable elements ever separating and reuniting provides the perfect scientific backdrop for his mythological stories of metamorphosis. Today we can see a similar phenomenon in the television show, *The X-Files*. The stories told rely on a variety of scientific explanations and thus, to some extent, the series represents science accurately. The purpose of

Empress Livia Drusilla, wife of the Emperor Augustus, as Ceres, in 38 B.C.E. Here the Empress Livia is portrayed as Ceres (the Greek Demeter) as part of an effort by the Emperor Tiberius to recommend a more elevated code of conduct to the people of the Empire. In real life, however, Augustus and Livia were not above taking extraordinary powers upon themselves. Augustus respected the sensibilities of the Roman people and did not declare himself divine. However, from the beginning of his rule, he associated himself with a variety of deities, including his uncle Julius Caesar, who was declared a god, and "genuine" deities like Apollo, to whom he attributed his decisive victory in the sea battle at Actium.

the series, however, is to raise questions about the adequacy of scientific explanation. Similarly, Ovid's account represents the best science of his day, but his explanations raise questions about the adequacy of these explanations. For more about the science and the mythology of *The X-Files,* see Chapter 40, p. 589.

In addition, Ovid's *Metamorphoses* allows us to understand the spirit and mood of his times. Near the end of his poem, Ovid provides the praise of the emperor that was nearly obligatory in the poetry of the Empire, identifying Augustus, the first Emperor, with Jupiter, the Roman equivalent of Zeus. Yet the world Ovid creates in this poem reflects the arbitrariness and cruelty that were not atypical of his time. The Roman Empire under Augustus was a democracy in name only. Decisions were made by the emperor and his friends: they could seem arbitrary when looked at from other points of view. The account excerpted here traces human development from creation to an iron age in which "dread stepmothers ply their fatal poisons," a reflection of rumors about the bloody tactics used by Livia, the wife of Augustus in arranging succession to the throne. These stories suggest that it was difficult, in Ovid's time, to believe in a reign of order and reason. Myers explains Ovid's poetic mission as the desire to cast doubt "on the power of any poet to explain and perhaps even survive in a universe in which power is ultimately arbitrary and beyond the control of any poets or philosophers, since it rests in the hands of the powers in the heavens and on the Palatine" (25–26).

This story comes from: Ovid, *Metamorphoses,* I , 1–150.*

"breathe your breath"—Normally, poets start with a prayer to the Muse, the goddess of poetry. Ovid, however, starts with a prayer to the unnamed gods who cause metamorphoses, changes of form.

Creation

MY SOUL WOULD SING of metamorphoses.
But since, O gods, you were the source of these
bodies becoming other bodies, **breathe
your breath** into my book of changes: may
the song I sing be seamless as its way   5
weaves from the world's beginning to our day.

Before the sea and lands began to be,
before the sky had mantled every thing,
then all of nature's face was featureless—
what men call chaos: undigested mass   10
of crude, confused, and scumbled elements,

---

* Allen Mandelbaum. *The* Metamorphoses *of Ovid: A New Verse Translation* (New York: Harcourt, Inc.). Copyright © 1993 by Harcourt, Inc.

a heap of seeds that clashed, of things mismatched.
There was no Titan Sun to light the world,
no crescent Moon—no Phoebe—to renew
her slender horns; in the surrounding air,   15
earth's weight had yet to find its balanced state;
and **Amphitrite's** arms had not yet stretched
along the farthest margins of the land.
For though the sea and land and air were there,
the land could not be walked upon, the sea   20
could not be swum, the air was without splendor:
no thing maintained its shape; **all were at war;**
in one same body cold and hot would battle;
the damp contended with the dry, things hard
with soft, and weighty things with weightless parts.   25

A god—and nature, now become benign
ended this strife. He separated sky
and earth, and earth and waves, and he defined
pure air and thicker air. Unraveling
these things from their blind heap, assigning each   30
its place—distinct—he linked them all in peace.
Fire, the weightless force of heaven's dome,
shot up; it occupied the highest zone.
Just under fire, the light air found its home.
The earth, more dense, attracted elements   35
more gross; its own mass made it sink below.
And flowing water filled the final space;
it held the solid world in its embrace.
When he—whichever god it was—arrayed
that swarm, aligned, designed, allotted, **made**   40
each part into a portion of a whole,
then he, that earth might be symmetrical,
first shaped its sides into a giant ball.
He then commanded seas to stretch beneath
high winds, to swell, to coil, to reach and ring   45
shorelines and inlets. And he added springs
and lakes and endless marshes and confined
descending streams in banks that slope and twine:
these rivers flow across their own terrains;
their waters sink into the ground or gain   50
the sea and are received by that wide plain
of freer waters—there, they beat no more
against their banks, but pound the shoals and shores.

At his command, the fields enlarged their reach,
the valleys sank, the woods were clothed with leaves,   55
and rocky mountains rose. And as the sky
divides into two zones on its right side,
with just as many to the left, to which
the hottest zone is added as a fifth,

"what men call chaos"—Ovid explains chaos as a mess, or an "undigested mass of . . . scumbled elements." In contrast, Hesiod defined chaos as a void: see p. 29. Ovid's account incorporates the best currently influential scientific views of the origin of the world. An important view was that of Empedocles, who argued that the earth consists of four elements—earth, air, fire, and water—that combine to make up all things. This view is reflected in the text below. In Ovid's day, most people believed that the world was made of small elements called atoms. Lucretius, an earlier Epicurean poet, described the motions of these "elements" in extensive detail.

Amphitrite—Goddess of the sea, wife of Neptune, Roman god of the sea.

"all were at war"—Empedocles argued that the primal elements were originally unstable.

"A god—and nature . . . ended this strife"—Ovid was not a monotheist, although for much of the Middle Ages, he was viewed as holding such beliefs. The Stoics believed that the force of reason operated as a guiding principle of the universe and manifested itself as a divine force in nature. Earlier, Anaxagoras had held that Reason created the world by imposing order on chaos. Ovid here combines these two ideas, which were widely held by the natural philosophers (scientists) of his day. The act of creation here represents the first metamorphosis in the poem whose title is *Metamorphoses*.

"made each part into a portion of a whole"—When the elements are unscrambled, they become homogeneous substances (fire, earth, water, and air), and the universe is created from them. Note that fire is a characteristic element of the sky, above the air; we see it in the sun and the stars.

the god provided regions that divide   60
the mass the heavens wrap, and he impressed
as many **zones upon the earth.** Of these,
the middle zone, because of its fierce heat,
is uninhabitable; and thick snows
cover two outer zones; between them he   65
aligned two other regions, and to these
he gave a clement climate, mixing heat
and cold. Above, the air extends; and for
as much as earth is heavier than water,
so is the air more ponderous than fire.   70
He ordered fog and clouds to gather there—
in air—and thunder, which would terrify
the human mind; there, too, the god assigned
the winds that, from colliding clouds, breed lightning.

Yet he who was the world's artificer   75
did not allow the winds to rule the air
unchecked, set free to riot everywhere.
(But while each wind received a separate tract,
it still is difficult to curb their blasts,
to keep the world, which they would rend, intact: 80
though they are brothers, **they forever clash.**)
Eurus retreated toward Aurora's lands,
into the Nabataeans' kingdom and
to Persia, where the rays of morning meet
the mountain crests. And **Zephyrus** now went   85
to shorelines warm with sunset, in the west.
To Scythia, beneath the northern Wain,
swept horrid **Boreas.** Incessant rain
and mists that drench the southlands opposite—
this was the work of **Auster. The god placed**   90
above these winds the ether, without weight,
a fluid free of earth's impurity.

No sooner had he set all things within
defining limits than the stars, long hid
beneath the crushing darkness, could begin   95
to gleam throughout the heavens. That no region
be left without its share of living things,
stars and the **forms of gods then occupied**
the porch of heaven; and the waters shared
their dwelling with the gleaming fishes; earth   100
received the beasts, and restless air, the birds.
An animal with higher intellect,
more noble, able—one to rule the rest:
such was the living thing the earth still lacked.
Then man was born. Either the **Architect**   105
of All, the author of the universe,
in order to beget a better world,

Prometheus (left) is shown on this 3rd-c. c.e. sarcophagus as the creator of man, with the help of Athena (right). In the excerpted account, Ovid suggests this theory of the origin of man as one among many possible explanations. This allows him to tell a good story while still reserving his judgment in favor of the more scientific explanation of the origin of life which was prevalent among the scientists of his day, the Stoics and the Epicureans.

created man from seed divine—or else
Prometheus, son of Iapetus, made man
by mixing new-made earth with fresh rainwater   110
(for earth had only recently been set
apart from heaven, and the earth still kept
seeds of the sky—remains of their shared birth);
and when he fashioned man, **his mold recalled
the masters of all things, the gods.** And while   115
all other animals are bent, head down,
and fix their gaze upon the ground, to man
he gave a face that is held high;
he had man stand erect, his eyes upon the stars.
So was the earth, which until then had been   120
so rough and indistinct, transformed: it wore
a thing unknown before—the human form.

That first age was an age of gold: no law
and no compulsion then were needed; all
kept faith; the righteous way was freely willed.   125
There were no penalties that might instill
dark fears, no **menaces inscribed upon
bronze tablets;** trembling crowds did not implore
the clemency of judges; but, secure,
men lived without defenders. In those times,   130
upon its native mountain heights,

"seeds of the sky"—Atoms, according to Lucretius and the atomists, are the basis of all things. According to Empedocles, all things are made from four elements which are also present in this account ("new-made earth," "fresh rainwater," and "seeds of the sky," which would contain both air and fire).

"his mold recalled the masters of all things, the gods"—The Stoics believed that human beings were made in the image of the gods.

 The Golden Age

"menaces inscribed upon bronze tablets"—In Rome, laws were engraved and posted in public places.

"men lived without defenders"—Despite Rome's pride in the achievements of her army, Ovid envisions a better time when an army was not needed.

"no wood had yet been hauled down to the limpid waves"—The impiety of navigation was often discussed. Horace, another Roman poet, says that sea travel arose because of the limitless audacity of human beings determined to explore forbidden realms (*Odes*, Book 1, Poem 3).

the pine still stood unfelled;
**no wood had yet been hauled
down to the limpid waves,** that it might sail
to foreign countries; and the only coasts   135
that mortals knew in that age were their own.

The towns were not yet girded by steep moats;
there were no curving horns of brass, and no brass
trumpets—straight, unbent; there were no
swords, no helmets. No one needed warriors;   140
the nations lived at peace, in tranquil ease.
Earth of itself—and uncompelled—untouched
by hoes, not torn by ploughshares, offered all
that one might need: men did not have to seek:
they simply gathered mountain strawberries   145
and the arbutus' fruit and cornel cherries;
and thick upon their prickly stems, blackberries;
and acorns fallen from Jove's sacred tree.
There spring was never-ending. The soft breeze
of tender zephyrs wafted and caressed   150
the flowers that sprang unplanted, without seed.
The earth, untilled, brought forth abundant yields;
and though they never had lain fallow, fields
were yellow with the heavy stalks of wheat.
And streams of milk and streams of nectar flowed, 155
and golden honey dripped from the holm oak.

The Silver Age

After the golden age comes the rule of Jove (Jupiter). He is the Roman equivalent of Greek Zeus.

But after Saturn had been banished, sent
down to dark Tartarus, Jove's rule began;
the silver age is what the world knew then—
an age inferior to golden times,   160
but if compared to tawny bronze, more prized.
Jove curbed the span that spring had had before;
he made the year run through four seasons' course:
the winter, summer, varied fall, and short
springtime. The air was incandescent, parched   165
by blazing heat—or felt the freezing gusts,
congealing icicles: such heat and frost
as earth had never known before. **Men sought—
for the first time—the shelter of a house;**
until then, they had made their homes in caves,   170
dense thickets, and in branches they had heaped
and bound with bark. Now, too, they planted seeds
of wheat in lengthy furrows; and beneath
the heavy weight of yokes, the bullocks groaned.

"Men sought—for the first time—the shelter of a house"—The stated purpose is to show the degeneration of man, as did Hesiod. But Ovid held a belief in progress at the same time. Here he describes humans as progressing from caves to houses. Such a positive view of human development is well supported in antiquity: see the account of human civilization given by Aeschylus (525–456 B.C.E.) as part of his description of the role of Prometheus, Ch. 24, p. 356ff.

The Bronze Age

The third age saw the race of bronze: more prone   175
to cruelty, more quick to use fierce arms,
but not yet sacrilegious.
                   What bestowed

its name upon the last age was hard iron.
And this, the worst of ages, suddenly   180
gave way to every foul impiety;
earth saw the flight of faith and modesty
and truth—and in their place came snares and fraud,
deceit and force and sacrilegious love
of gain. Men spread their sails before the winds,   185
whose ways the mariner had scarcely learned:
the wooden keels, which once had stood as trunks
upon the mountain slopes, now danced upon
the unfamiliar waves. **And now the ground,**
which once—just like the sunlight and the air—   190
had been a common good, one all could share,
was marked and measured by the keen surveyor—
he drew the long confines, the boundaries.
Not only did men ask of earth its wealth,
its harvest crops and foods that nourish us,   195
they also delved into the bowels of earth:
there they began to dig for what was hid
deep underground beside the shades of Styx:
the treasures that spur men to sacrilege.
And so foul iron and still fouler gold   200
were brought to light—and war, which fights for both
and, in its bloodstained hands, holds clanging arms.
Men live on plunder; guests cannot trust hosts;
the son-in-law can now betray his own father-in-law;
and even brothers show   205
scant love and faith. The husband plots the death
of his own wife, and she plots his. And **dread**
stepmothers ply their fatal poisons; sons
now tally—early on—how many years
their fathers still may live. Now piety   210
lies vanquished; and the maid **Astraea,**
last of the immortals, leaves the blood-soaked earth.

 The Iron Age

Roman engineering produced elegant and enduring structures like this aqueduct built in 19 B.C.E. and still standing in Nimes, France.

"And now the ground . . . was marked and measured by the keen surveyor"—The Romans were justly proud of their engineering skills.

"the son-in-law can now betray his own father-in-law"—The most famous contemporary instance of this was that Pompey betrayed his wife's father, Julius Caesar.

"dread stepmothers ply their fatal poisons"—There were rumors that Livia, the emperor Augustus' wife, had poisoned her stepsons.

Astraea—Justice.

Further Reading

Myers, K. Sara. *Ovid's Causes: Cosmogony and Aetiology in the "Metamorphoses."* Ann Arbor: University of Michigan Press, 1994.

5 Biblical Creation Stories

WHAT TO EXPECT . . . In this chapter, you see parataxis (the idea that myths often weave together different stories without logical connection), an idea from Chapter 2, occurring in the stories found in the Bible. That is, Genesis incorporates two separate creation scenarios, and the story of creation found in it is actually a compilation of the work of three different authors, identified as Priestly, Jehovist (or Yahwist), and Elohist.

The sources of these stories come from different time periods, from approximately 950 to 550 B.C.E., and they impart different slants to their versions of creation. You can track which source you are reading from clues in the writing: differences in their name for God and, in the case of the Priestly writer, a reflection of the Babylonian creation stories. The different versions of the creation story reinforce and complement each other to give a richer picture of the Biblical God. You encounter these writers again in Chapter 12, "Biblical Flood Stories," and the introduction there gives more information on them.

The next excerpt comes from the Old Testament of the Bible and includes the creation stories believed by Christians and Jews. This text is revered and accepted as true by many members of our society. In presenting it here, we are acknowledging this important role. In Chapter 1, we said, "We would like to suggest that [mythological] stories are not just false stories, but that they are true if looked at differently from the logically drawn and empirically verifiable standards we are accustomed to using."

Traditionally, the authorship of Genesis is attributed to Moses. Biblical scholars have observed that this part of Genesis is actually a compilation of the work of three different authors. We do not know the names of these authors, but we can tell them apart by their writing style, the points they emphasize, and even the landscape in which they set their stories. Scholars refer to these authors by the letters J (or Y), E, and P, which stand for the Jehovist or Yahwist, Elohist, and Priestly sources. More detail about each of these authors is given in the table titled "Authors of Genesis" (p. 52).

The section of Genesis excerpted in this chapter consists of the work of the Priestly source and the J-E source (an early combination of the work of J and E). You can tell them apart because the J-E source always calls God "Lord God," while the Priestly writer calls him "God." There are other differences between them, as well. The excerpt starts "In the beginning, God created the heavens and the earth." Scholars have argued that the text here should be interpreted as, "In the beginning *when* God created the heavens and the earth, the earth was without form and void." That is, the earth existed, but was formless. As in the other accounts of creation given in this section, the Priestly source did not portray God as creating the world from nothing, but from previously existing elements. This does not diminish the authority of God, but puts the account in line with the science of the time.

Many people read the accounts of the Priestly writer and the J-E source without even noticing that there are disparities between them: they take the expanded creation story in the J-E source to be an expansion of the brief account in the Priestly writer. As we will see, however, a careful reading of the two stories shows that such a rationalization does not account for all the differences of detail. And yet, these two accounts are presented in the Bible one after the other, without intervening commentary. This suggests that they seemed coherent despite their disparities, and Biblical scholars have pointed out that it is in their vision of the relationship between God and the Israelites that the two versions of creation are most in agreement. The Israelites, or Jews, viewed themselves as the chosen People of God, and both creation stories show the special relationship between God and his People. For more on this issue, see the Introduction to Chapter 12, "Biblical Flood Stories."

Another issue that arises here is the way God is portrayed. In the previous chapters, we saw that the gods of the Greeks and Romans looked like human beings and behaved like them, as well. They are referred to as *anthropomorphic* gods, deities in the shape of human beings. The God of the Bible is not anthropomorphic. For the most part, God in Genesis does not have human form—even the use of the word "he" with respect to God is somewhat of a metaphor and has been the source of debate among scholars. There are some comments about God in Genesis that are worth considering in this respect. In the Priestly account, God says "Let us make man in our image ." (1:26), and then the author says, "So God created man in his own image, in the image of God he created him; male and female he created them" (1:27). Does this mean that God is male and female, or was the author speaking of other aspects of God's image? This is an issue for theologians and Biblical scholars, but we point it out here as a matter of interest to those who concern themselves with this text.

A less controversial aspect of the image of God is the degree to which he involves himself in human activities. A god who is very involved in human life is described as *immanent,* while a god who remains aloof from humans is known as *transcendent.* These terms are not absolutes; rather, they represent a scale of behavior. It is important to recognize that this scale does not necessarily represent the degree to which deities are sympathetic to human beings. Either term can characterize a caring deity. As a commonplace example, think of two parents. The first one says, "I want the garage cleaned on Saturday" and plainly intends the other members of the family to perform this task while she is involved in other tasks also important to the welfare of the family. This kind of parent is analogous to the transcendent god, while the immanent god corresponds to the parent who says, "Let's clean the garage on Saturday" and expects to roll up her shirtsleeves and participate in the task.

Clearly, the anthropomorphic Greek and Roman gods are very immanent, and, relative to them, the God of Genesis is rather transcendent. He is not described as having a human body, and his behavior for the most part transcends the human realm. For example, the Priestly writer describes him as saying "Let there be light" (1:3) without concern about how the order is to be carried out. And yet there are variations even within Genesis: the Priestly writer describes God as making the firmament and separating the light and the darkness (1:6–7); this description sounds as if God were doing the work himself in an immanent fashion. The portrait of God found in the J-E writer has even more immanent touches: he forms "man of dust from the ground" and breathes "into his nostrils the breath of life" (2:7), he walks "in the garden in the cool of the day" (3:8), and he makes "garments of skins" for Adam and his wife and clothes them (3:22).

1 1 In the beginning God created the heavens and the earth. 2 The earth was without form and void, and darkness was upon the face of the **deep;** and the Spirit of God was moving over the face of the waters.

This excerpt comes from: Genesis, 1–4.*

The Priestly Account of Creation

"deep"—Hebrew "tehom." This word is the equivalent of the Babylonian word "Tiamat." Tiamat was a Babylonian deity identified with salt water and killed by the head god Marduk. Here the Priestly writer is showing that Yahweh, not Marduk, prevailed over the deep.

"God called the dry land Earth"—The Babylonian religion held that there were separate gods in charge of the earth and its fertility. The Priestly writer here explains that the earth is not under the jurisdiction of a separate god: his one God is in charge of all of creation.

"'Let there be lights in the firmament'"—The Babylonians were renowned for their charting of the heavens. They were the first to calculate the circumference of the earth by triangulating from the heavens. They believed that each planet, star, and constellation had its own god. The Priestly writer writes to refute that view.

"God created the great sea monsters"—God is seen as ruling over the sea or defeating a sea monster in other parts of the Bible, as well. Often, this creature is called Leviathan. See Job 38:4–17; Psalm 74:13–14; Psalm 104:26; Isaiah 27:1. The presence of the sea monsters here is probably the result of the Priestly writer's response to Tiamat: as a dragon of watery chaos.

"Then God said, 'Let us make man in our image . . .'" —Human beings are made last, as the culmination of creation. They are made male and female.

3 And God said, "Let there be light"; and there was light. 4 And God saw that the light was good; and God separated the light from the darkness. 5 God called the light Day, and the darkness he called Night. And there was evening and there was morning, one day.

6 And God said, "Let there be a firmament in the midst of the waters, and let it separate the waters from the waters." 7 And God made the firmament and separated the waters which were under the firmament from the waters which were above the firmament. And it was so. 8 And God called the firmament Heaven. And there was evening and there was morning, a second day.

Authors of Genesis

950 B.C.E.	The **Jehovist** or **Yahwist** (often referred to as **J** or **Y**). This writer referred to God by the Hebrew word "Yahweh," which was sometimes rendered "Jahweh." To help in identifying this source, the translation used here always renders "Yahweh" as "Lord." **Origin:** Judaea, South Israel.
850 B.C.E.	The **Elohist** (often referred to as **E**). This writer referred to God by the Hebrew word "Elohim." To help in identifying this source, the translation used here always renders "Elohim" as "God." **Origin:** Ephraim, North Israel.
721 B.C.E.	**Jehovist-Elohist** version (often referred to as **J-E**). **Origin:** After the fall of the Northern Kingdom, Judaean editors combined parts of the J and E traditions. In parts of Genesis (including this excerpt), they were so effective in weaving these sources together that we can no longer separate them.
550 B.C.E.	The **Priestly** writer (often referred to as **P**). This writer also referred to God by the Hebrew word "Elohim," but his account can be distinguished from the Elohist by what he writes about. He demonstrates the concerns of a priest: he writes about how Jewish rituals and holy days began, and he keeps track of the generations—the so-called "begats." This is because a person's ancestry determines eligibility for religious functions. To help in identifying this source, the translation used here always renders "Elohim" as "God." **Origin:** In 587 B.C.E., the Jews were captured by Nebuchadnezzar and carried off to Babylon. This is known as the Babylonian Captivity. It ended in 538, when Cyrus allowed the Jews to return to their homeland, Israel. In his creation story, the Priestly writer is largely concerned with refuting the Babylonian religion, so we can tell he wrote after the Exile, expressing ideas that were current during it.

9 And God said, "Let the waters under the heavens be gathered together into one place, and let the dry land appear." And it was so. 10 **God called the dry land Earth,** and the waters that were gathered together he called Seas. And God saw that it was good. 11 And God said, "Let the earth put forth vegetation, plants yielding seed, and fruit trees bearing fruit in which is their seed, each according to its kind, upon the earth."

And it was so. 12 The earth brought forth vegetation, plants yielding seed according to their own kinds, and trees bearing fruit in which is their seed, each according to its kind. And God saw that it was good. 13 And there was evening and there was morning, a third day.

14 And God said, "**Let there be lights in the firmament** of the heavens to separate the day from the night; and let them be for signs and for seasons and for days and years, 15 and let there be lights in the firmament of the heavens to give light upon the earth." And it was so. 16 And God made the two great lights, the greater light to rule the day, and the

Differences between the J-E Writer and the Priestly Writer

	Priestly Genesis 1:1–2:4a	J-E Genesis 2:4b–3:24
Concerns	Explains the reason behind religious ceremonies like the Sabbath day. Refutes Babylonian polytheism by showing that all the parts of the universe were made by one God and are not ruled by separate deities, as the Babylonians believed.	Focuses on the covenant between God and Israel. A covenant is like a contract which binds both God and his people, Israel. Under the covenant, God functions as a kind master or patron and promises to take care of his people, who also promise to be loyal to him.
Landscape	Wet. Originates in Mesopotamia, a fertile land irrigated by the Tigris and Euphrates rivers. This account begins with the Spirit of God "moving over the face of the waters."	Dry. Originates in the deserts of Palestine. This account describes the planting of a garden, an important event in a desert. Man is made from dust.
Order of creation	Man is made last, showing his importance to God. The world is prepared for him before his creation.	Man is made on the first day, showing his importance to God. After man's creation, everything else is created for his use.
Nature of humans	Created male and female at the same time. Do not sin against God.	The man is created first. The woman is created later, after all other creatures. Sin against God.
View of God	Aloof from his creation. Seems to delegate his work: "Let there be light."	Involved with humans and with the act of creation: *forms* man of dust; *breathes* life into his nostrils; *walks* in garden (Genesis 3:8).

lesser light to rule the night; he made the stars also. 17 And God set them in the firmament of the heavens to give light upon the earth, 18 to rule over the day and over the night, and to separate the light from the darkness. And God saw that it was good. 19 And there was evening and there was morning, a fourth day.

20 And God said, "Let the waters bring forth swarms of living creatures, and let birds fly above the earth across the firmament of the heavens."

21 So **God created the great sea monsters** and every living creature that moves, with which the waters swarm, according to their kinds, and every winged bird according to its kind. And God saw that it was good. 22 And God blessed them, saying, "Be fruitful and multiply and fill the waters in the seas, and let birds multiply on the earth." 23 And there was evening and there was morning, a fifth day.

24 And God said, "Let the earth bring forth living creatures according to their kinds: cattle and creeping things and beasts of the earth according to their kinds." And it was so. 25 And God made the beasts of the earth according to their kinds and the cattle according to their kinds, and everything that creeps upon the ground according to its kind. And God saw that it was good.

26 **Then God said, "Let us make man in our image,** after our likeness; and let them have dominion over the fish of the sea, and over the birds of the air, and over the cattle, and over all the earth, and over every creeping thing that creeps upon the earth." 27 So God created man in his own image, in the image of God he created him; male and female he created them. 28 And God blessed them, and God said to them, "Be fruitful and multiply, and fill the earth and subdue it; and have dominion over the fish of the sea and over the birds of the air and over every living thing that moves upon the earth." 29 And God said, "Behold, I have given you every plant yielding seed which is upon the face of all the earth, and every tree with seed in its fruit; you shall have them for food. 30 And to every beast of the earth, and to every bird of the air, and to everything that creeps on the earth, everything that has the

"he rested on the seventh day from all his work . . . ."—The origin of the custom of dedicating the seventh day (the Sabbath) as a day of rest to God. One of the goals of this Priestly writer is to show the origin of this ritual.

 The J-E Account of Creation (p. 54)

"In the day that the LORD God made the earth"—The J-E account of creation starts here, beginning with the most important element of creation: man. Note that the terrain is dry before God makes it rain: the geography of this version is quite different from that of the Priestly version.

"the LORD God planted a garden"—A garden would not have been needed in the watery terrain of the Priestly version.

"tree of the knowledge of good and evil"—Many traditions have stories in which a tree has cosmic significance. See for instance, the world tree Yggdrasil in Icelandic myth, Ch. 7, p. 87.

Constancy of the Jews in Captivity. Psalm 137. It is from the culture of the Jews of the Babylonian Captivity that the Priestly source derives his story of creation.

breath of life, I have given every green plant for food." And it was so. 31 And God saw everything that he had made, and behold, it was very good. And there was evening and there was morning, a sixth day.

2 1 Thus the heavens and the earth were finished, and all the host of them. 2 And on the seventh day God finished his work which he had done, and **he rested on the seventh day from all his work** which he had done. 3 So God blessed the seventh day and hallowed it, because on it God rested from all his work which he had done in creation.

4 These are the generations of the heavens and the earth when they were created.

In the day that the LORD God made the earth and the heavens, 5 when no plant of the field was yet in the earth and no herb of the field had yet sprung up—for the LORD God had not caused it to rain upon the earth, and there was no man to till the ground; 6 but a mist went up from the earth and watered the whole face of the ground—7 then the LORD God formed man of dust from the ground, and breathed into his nostrils the breath of life; and man became a living being. 8 And **the LORD God planted a garden** in Eden, in the east; and there he put the man whom he had formed. 9 And out of the ground the LORD God made to grow every tree that is pleasant to the sight and good for food, the tree of life also in the midst of the garden, and the **tree of the knowledge of good and evil.**

"to till it and keep it"—The man is given a job to do. The terms set by God include forbidding the tree of the knowledge of good and evil.

Man Works in the Garden

"the Lord God caused a deep sleep to fall upon the man"—Woman is made from a part of man. In contrast, in Babylonian mythology, the male god Marduk makes the world out of the body of the female Tiamat.

"This at last is bone of my bones"—The Biblical account often incorporates older poetic sections like this.

"the man and his wife . . . were not ashamed"—Their nakedness does not disturb them until after they have sinned, Genesis 3:7.

15 The LORD God took the man and put him in the garden of Eden **to till it and keep it.** 16 And the LORD God commanded the man, saying, "You may freely eat of every tree of the garden; 17 but of the tree of the knowledge of good and evil you shall not eat, for in the day that you eat of it you shall die."

18 Then the LORD God said, "It is not good that the man should be alone; I will make him a helper fit for him." 19 So out of the ground the LORD God formed every beast of the field and every bird of the air, and brought them to the man to see what he would call them; and whatever the man called every living creature, that was its name. 20 The man gave names to all cattle, and to the birds of the air, and to every beast of the field; but for the man there was not found a helper fit for him. 21 **So the LORD God caused a deep sleep to fall upon the man,** and while he slept took one of his ribs and closed up its place with flesh; 22 and the rib which the LORD God had taken from the man he made into a woman and brought her to the man. 23 Then the man said,

> **This at last is bone of my bones** and flesh of my flesh;
> she shall be called Woman, because she was taken out of Man.

24 Therefore a man leaves his father and his mother and cleaves to his wife, and they become one flesh. 25 And **the man and his wife were both naked, and were not ashamed.**

Michelangelo, *Creation of Adam: Detail of the Sistine Chapel.* This famous picture represents God as creating man by the touch of a finger. In it, Michelangelo's focus is on the astonishing creative power of God. The J-E version, however, depicts God as more active and immanent in his creation: "the LORD God formed man of dust from the ground, and breathed into his nostrils the breath of life; and man became a living being"(2:7). This portrait of God's activity has been compared to the work of a potter.

3 1 Now the serpent was more subtle than any other wild creature that the LORD God had made. He said to the woman, "Did God say, 'You shall not eat of any tree of the garden'?" 2 And the woman said to the serpent, "We may eat of the fruit of the trees of the garden; 3 but God said, 'You shall not eat of the fruit of the tree which is in the midst of the garden, neither shall you touch it, lest You die.'" 4 But the serpent said to the woman, "You will not die. 5 For God knows that when you eat of it your eyes will be opened, and you will be like God, knowing good and evil." 6 So when the woman saw that the tree was good for food, and that it was a delight to the eyes, and that the tree was to be desired to make one wise, she took of its fruit and ate; and she also gave some to her husband, and he ate. 7 Then the eyes of both were opened and they knew that they were naked and **they sewed fig leaves together** and made themselves aprons.

8 And they heard the **sound of the LORD God walking in the garden** in the cool of the day, and the man and his wife hid themselves from the presence of the LORD God among the trees of the garden. 9 But the LORD God called to the man, and said to him, "Where are you?"

10 And he said, "I heard the sound of thee in the garden, and I was afraid, because I was naked; and I hid myself." 11 He said, "Who told you that you were naked? Have you eaten of the tree of which I commanded you not to eat?" 12 The man said, "The woman whom thou gavest to be with me, she gave me fruit of the tree, and I ate." 13 Then the LORD God said to the woman, "What is this that you have done?" The woman said, "The serpent beguiled me, and I ate."

> 14 The LORD God said to the serpent,
> Because you have done this
> cursed are you above all cattle,
> and above all wild animals;
> upon your belly you shall go,
> and dust you shall eat
> all the days of your life.
>
> 15 I will put enmity between you and the woman
> and between your seed and her seed;
> he shall bruise your head,
> and you shall bruise his heel.
>
> 16 To the woman he said,
> I will greatly multiply your pain in childbearing;

The Appearance of the Serpent

"they sewed fig leaves together"— After they sin, the man and the woman know they are naked.

"sound of the LORD God walking in the garden"—The anthropomorphic detail here can be taken as a sign of the immanent view the J-E writer has of the deity.

The Yahwist incorporates another poetic section into his account. The emphasis in this poem is on punishment. The Yahwist is more interested in the protection that God extends to the man and the woman after they have sinned; see verse 21.

"And to Adam he said"—This is the first mention of his name. Until now "Adam" has been referred to only as "the man." His name is the Hebrew word for "human being."

Eve—The first mention of her name. It means "mother of all living."

PUNS IN THE J-E CREATION STORY[2]

The writers of the Hebrew Bible made good use of the flexibility of their language to convey additional layers of meaning through the employment of word play. At 2:23, "woman" *ishshah* incorporates the rib of "man" *ish*, just as our word "woman" incorporates the word "man." The creation of the first "man" *'adham* is from "the ground" *'adhamah*. He is not explicitly named as Adam until 3:17, but the description of his origins prepares the reader for his name. Similarly, Eve's name is not mentioned until 3:20, where its meaning "mother of all living," emphasised by the pun on it: Eve, *hawwa* sounds like *hay* "life."

---

[2] These observations, based on Speiser's notes, and many other helpful but hard-to-credit contributions of emphasis and detail are included here as a result of the remarks of Michael Webster, one of the reviewers of this book in manuscript form.

Edgar Tolson, *Adam and Eve*. This modern version of the story of the garden of Eden uses sensuous curved lines to show the attractiveness of the temptation offered by the snake.

"garments of skins"—God clothes the man and the woman. He is satisfying their need for clothing, not his own concerns. The gesture shows his ongoing concern for them and expresses his protection of them under the covenant. The Yahwist is showing that God's concern endures even in the consequences of human sin.

in pain you shall bring forth children,
yet your desire shall be for your husband,
and he shall rule over you.

17 **And to Adam he said,**
Because you have listened to the voice of your wife,
and have eaten of the tree of which I commanded you,
'You shall not eat of it,'
cursed is the ground because of you;
in toil you shall eat of it all the days of your life;
18 thorns and thistles it shall bring forth to you;
and you shall eat the plants of the field.
19 In the sweat of your face you shall eat bread
till you return to the ground,
for out of it you were taken;
you are dust,
and to dust you shall return.

20 The man called his wife's name **Eve,** because she was the mother of all living. 21 And the LORD God made for Adam and for his wife **garments of skins,** and clothed them.

22 Then the LORD God said, "Behold, the man has become like one of us, knowing good and evil; and now, lest he put forth his hand and take also of the tree of life, and eat, and live for ever"— 23 therefore the LORD God sent him forth from the garden of Eden, to till the ground from which he was taken." 24 He drove out the man; and at the east of the garden of Eden he placed the cherubim, and a flaming sword which turned every way, to guard the way to the tree of life.

Further Reading

Speiser, E. A. *Genesis: Anchor Bible*. Garden City, NY: Doubleday Anchor, 1964.

Enuma Elish

A Mesopotamian Creation Story

WHAT TO EXPECT . . . *Enuma Elish*, also called *Epic of Creation*, contains many of the very early beliefs of the Mesopotamians concerning the origins of their world, their gods, and their ancestors. This sacred document was recited during the important New Year celebration, and as a political document extolling the primacy of Babylon, it is a key text for study of the Cradle of Civilization. Besides describing how Marduk created the world, it lays out a case for his preeminence among the gods and with that, the importance of Babylon, his special city where his temple is located.

As you read, notice the similarities between the creation by the Lord God in Genesis and the creation by Marduk: the separation of earth and sky, the ordering of the astronomical components, and the origin of human beings. Compare Marduk's ancestors and their actions with the anthropomorphic Greek pantheon and their problem-solving methods. Ask yourself what this combination of creation narrative and heroic epic tells us about the inhabitants of Mesopotamia. Can you see how the story was altered as it was handed down for millennia? Do you see ways it expresses the needs and beliefs of those who told it? Consider *Enuma Elish* in relation to the other stories of creation in Part 2, "Myths of Creation and Destruction."

Enuma Elish is one of the main sources for the stories told by the Mesopotamians to describe the origin of their world. This epic describes the struggle for control of the universe between the primeval goddess Tiamat and her descendant, the hero-god Marduk. After defeating Tiamat, Marduk creates the world from her body. Like many early creation stories, *Enuma Elish* does not describe creation from nothing ("ex nihilo"); rather, the universe begins with the gods already in place and representing the forces of nature. (For an explanation of this kind of creation, see the Introduction to "Myths of Creation and Destruction," p. 21.) The epic opens with the primeval cosmogony of the ancient Mesopotamians: the already-existing Apsu and Tiamat, water gods who personify chaos. In the forms of sweet and salt water, they mingle and produce five offspring: Mummu, the oldest, followed by two male/female pairs, Lahme and Lahame and then Anshar and Kishar. This last pair gives birth to Anu, father of Nudimmud (Ea), who with his consort Damkina, produces Marduk.

Enuma Elish features the activities of Marduk, the Babylonian pantheon's preeminent god. It describes the struggles of the primary gods in a way that enhances Marduk's stature and preeminence. Because this epic was fundamental to both the Babylonian and Assyrian peoples, it gives us a great deal of information about the theogony and cosmology of ancient Mesopotamia and contributes significantly to our understanding of ancient Near Eastern religious beliefs. However, scholars like Joan Oates caution that we should not assume we can reconstruct a systematic presentation of Mesopotamian religion and myth, since the available evidence reveals only a few aspects of it.

Principal Mesopotamian Deities in
Enuma Elish

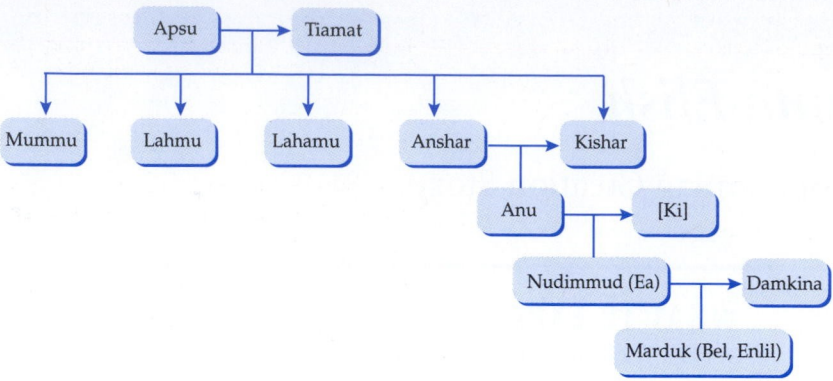

POLITICAL SIGNIFICANCE OF THE EPIC

The first fragments of *Enuma Elish* were discovered in1848 among the ruins of King Ashurbani-pal's library at Nineveh. This Akkadian version of the story was a Babylonian reworking of a Sumerian original. (For an explanation of the production of these tablets, and cuneiform, see the Introduction to Chapter 15, p. 166.) Further excavations turned up fragments of an Assyrian version, and even later ones yielded Neo-Babylonian versions at Kish and Uruk. Although the tablets found at Nineveh go back to the seventh century B.C.E., others have been dated much earlier, and an inscription from the fifteenth century B.C.E. leads scholars to surmise that the epic existed even then.

As noted above, many scholars believe *Enuma Elish* was intended as a literary monument to honor Marduk, the chief god who created and maintains the universe, and was not primarily composed as an account of creation. At the time, each city-state had its own patron and protector god. However, Babylon considered itself the most important of these realms, so the Babylonians wanted to emphasize that theirs was the ultimate deity. As a hymn of praise to Marduk's amazing deeds and a chronicle showing the acknowledgement of his supremacy by the other gods, the epic also serves the political purpose of claiming supremacy for the god's city, Babylon. Thus, it represents Marduk's ascension from chief god of Babylon to the highest position of all Babylonian deities. In addition, it explains the foundation of Babylon as an act of gratitude by the Anunnaki, the elder gods whom Marduk rewarded by establishing proper stations for them: three hundred in heaven and three hundred below.

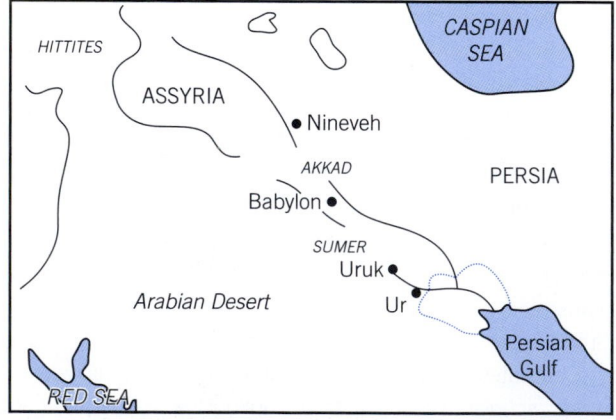

Ancient Babylon, the city of Marduk, and its surroundings. To the southeast of Babylon is the city of Uruk, where Gilgamesh was king. See Chapter 15 p. 166 for the epic which describes his exploits.

Timeline: Ancient Mesopotamia until 700 C.E.[1]

From Villages to Towns	6000–4000 B.C.E.	People settled in Mesopotamia and changed from dwelling in small villages to living in towns surrounded by smaller supporting communities.
The First Cities	4000–2900 B.C.E.	The Sumerians invented a writing system and quickly became the first literate urban civilization in the ancient world.
City-States	2900–2350 B.C.E.	Southern Sumerian city-states shared the same language and culture, but they often fought over land and water rights. Nomadic desert people, the Akkadians and Amorites, migrated into Mesopotamia.
The Akkadian Empire	2350–2150 B.C.E.	King Sargon of Akkad established control of southern Mesopotamia by 2330 B.C.E. The Akkadians controlled all of Mesopotamia and parts of Syria and Iran. They adopted many Sumerian customs including the cuneiform writing system, but they adapted it to their own language.
The Sumerian Revival	2100–2000 B.C.E.	After the collapse of the Akkadian Empire, King Ur-Nammu reunited Mesopotamia and revived Sumerian traditions for another century. Earliest written version of the *Epic of Gilgamesh*.
Rival Kingdoms	2000–1600 B.C.E.	Mesopotamia was divided into rival city-states. Hammurabi, King of Babylon, united most of Mesopotamia. The city of Babylon became an important economic center in southern Mesopotamia.
An International Age	1600–1000 B.C.E.	Assyria, in the north, emerged as the dominant military force in Mesopotamia. A period of political and economic crisis swept the region after 1200 B.C.E., causing severe upheavals in Assyria and Babylonia.
Late Empires	900–539 B.C.E.	By the seventh century B.C.E., the Assyrian Empire grew to become the largest the world had ever known, stretching from Egypt to Iran. Babylon reemerged as a world power after defeating the Assyrians in 612 B.C.E. The arts and sciences flourished during this period, and Babylon became the largest city in the ancient world. The most complete ancient version of *Enuma Elish* was in the Library of Assurbanipal in Nineveh in the seventh century B.C.E.
After the Fall of Babylon	539 B.C.E.–700 C.E.	Mesopotamian dominance ended with the fall of Babylon to the Persians in 539 B.C.E. Persian kings ruled the largest, most efficiently organized empire in the ancient world. Southern Mesopotamia flourished, and Babylon served as the winter residence of the Persian court. In 331 B.C.E., Alexander the Great conquered Babylon and ushered in an era of Greek control over much of the Middle East. Iranian dynasties controlled Mesopotamia until the Islamic conquest.

[1]From http://mesopotamia.lib.uchicago.edu/learningcollection/index.php?a=timeline.

RITUALS REFLECTED IN THE EPIC

Historians believe that *Enuma Elish* was meant to be presented orally at ceremonies dedicated to Marduk. It was recited by the high priest during the New Year ritual each Nisun (April) in Babylon, and parts may have been acted out. The recitation served as a kind of incantation against the flooding of the city caused by the spring rising of the Tigris and Euphrates rivers. The ritual represented this inundation as an annual battle between Marduk and watery chaos (Tiamat).

Water was a central component of religion and cosmology, as it represented survival for this ancient civilization. Moderate spring flooding irrigated the life-giving crops, but too much caused destruction. Thus, the religious ritual praises the gods for providing sustenance while pleading for protection. The cosmology also reflects the importance of water: the mingling of the fresh and salt water is the first act of creation. The homeland of the storytellers lay between the Tigris and Euphrates rivers and extended along the southern coast of the Arabian Gulf to present-day Bahrain (see map on p. 58). In this region, people could easily observe the confluence of fresh and salt water where these rivers meet the gulf. In addition, they would observe that the shifting shoreline of the sea (represented by Tiamat), when it was out of control, could undermine the groundwater, polluting wells and devastating agriculture in the affected region.

Enuma Elish also provides us with valuable information about particular Mesopotamian beliefs. For example, references to the Tablet of Destinies illustrate the way the deity in power (first Tiamat's vizier Qingu and then Marduk) has total control of the life of each individual. The Tablet contained the fates of all, though the keeper did not have power to determine that fate. The responsibility of the keeper was tremendous, however: to avoid the chaos that would ensue if the tablet fell to an unscrupulous deity who might destroy the social order. In turn, this recognition of the dependence of each person—and deity—on the keeper of the Tablet leads humans to seek a life totally conforming to the expectations of the gods, aiming to excel in their assigned roles rather than trying alternate paths to personal fulfillment.

For more on ancient Mesopotamian religion, see the Introduction to the *Epic of Gilgamesh*, Chapter 15, p. 166.

THE GENERATION GAP IN BABYLONIAN CULTURE

Besides its theological and political functions, *Enuma Elish* provides a window from which we can observe some Mesopotamian cultural norms. Most prominent among these are intergenerational conflict and the related representation of noise as aggression. As in most societies, the Babylonians extolled the wisdom of age and preached respect, obedience, and caring for the aged by the young. But researchers have noted that, in practice, the opposite occurred more often than not.

In *Enuma Elish*, we encounter a compromise between generations that is the foundation of a new social order as well as the justification for Babylon's supremacy over other Mesopotamian cities. From earlier Sumerian times, the patriarchal Mesopotamian society recognized the father as keeper of his family's land and primary decision maker. Land usually came to the son upon the father's death. But since life expectancy was low, and a man did not usually marry until his late twenties (though brides were usually in their teens), it was not unusual for a son to inherit upon marriage. In this epic, Marduk's military, creative, and administrative success prompts a generally enthusiastic acclamation, and his father Ea and grandfather Anu, who had failed to defeat Tiamat, give him special weapons in preparation for his battle. Afterward, along with Marduk's great grandfather Anshar, they rejoice and spread the good news of his success. In turn, Marduk honors Ea by seeking his counsel on the reorganization and supervision of their world. Thus, scholars have viewed Marduk's experiences in *Enuma Elish* as an endorsement for allowing the young the opportunity to achieve power. At the same time, the epic can be seen as presenting a solution to the problems of generational conflict by advocating that the younger generation should behave toward parents as tradition requires, while the older generation should recognize its limitations and value the young as providers and protectors.

At the same time, the epic and the ritual associated with it would help diffuse some of the negative feelings in the society. Scholar Nancy Foner observes that the myths allow the young to express hostility toward the old indirectly; Rikvah Harris explains that myths function as safety valves to deflate the pressures caused by generational inequalities; and Roy Wagner sums up the value of myths in this conflict: "Myths model and resolve certain recurrent interpersonal and kin tensions and relationships" (Harris, 629). These statements all apply to *Enuma Elish* as well as to many other myths, including *Oedipus, Cupid and Psyche*, and *Mwindo*. (See Introduction to Chapter 3 for a discussion of the Greek Generation Gap and Gender Gap.)

Intertwined with the theme of generational conflict in *Enuma Elish* is the motif of noise. The extreme reaction of Apsu to the young gods is represented as a series of complaints about their festive noises. The equation of noise and the rebellious behavior of the young is found throughout Babylonian culture. Peter Machinist explains the psychology of the society: "Activity is necessary for the universe to function. But too much activity brings on violence and potential chaos. Likewise, a certain inactivity, if understood as peace and calm, helps to insure a balanced and just order. But too much inactivity is the equivalent of paralysis and death, and invites violent activity to fill the void it has left" (225). Thus, the noisemaking of the young gods in *Enuma Elish* is a type of activity resulting in violence and subsequent punishment.

In *Enuma Elish*, Apsu's decision to "abolish [the] ways [of the younger gods] and disperse them" ignites the conflict driving all of the action in Tablets I–III. Although boisterous behavior is common to the young and a desire to live quietly and sleep is desired by the old, the response to the conflict in Tablet I is crucial to the epic: Marduk proves himself superior as a god, hero, and leader of his people, both young and old. In addition, the secondary resolution to the conflict, peace and prosperity for Babylon under Marduk's protection, reveals the principle that peace (quiet) and violence (noise and war) are both necessary for a balanced functioning of the universe.

THE CHARACTER AND EVOLUTION OF TIAMAT

As we read *Enuma Elish*, we see how the characterization of Tiamat evolves, giving us insights into the beliefs of ancient Mesopotamian society. In the first lines, Tiamat is described neutrally, if not positively, as the primordial salt water, a necessary component of creation of the world. In fact this identification was so strong that some versions of the manuscript actually use the word "sea" instead of "Tiamat" (Jacobsen, 105).

When Apsu explains his distress at the noise made by their offspring, Tiamat reacts maternally, defending the exuberance of their young. And later her plan to avenge Apsu's death at the hands of Ea can be seen as rooted in loyalty. However, as she prepares for this battle, we see her

giving birth to giant venomous snakes, contributing dragons, a rabid dog, demons, and other monstrous creatures, and making ferocious dragons look like gods, in order to deceive her opponents. And finally, in combat with Marduk, she is portrayed as totally monstrous, with the physical characteristics of lower creatures and the raging instincts of a wild animal.

This evolution of Tiamat from primordial mother to monstrous adversary who relies on magic spells and demons reveals a shift in viewpoint from a quasi-matriarchal to a patriarchal society (Knapp, 21). Her contribution to society remains, as Marduk creates the world from her body parts. She retains the role of ultimate mother, but the authoritative position of creator is firmly attributed to her male progeny.

COMPARISON TO OTHER CREATION STORIES

As a creation myth, *Enuma Elish* shares many characteristics with creation stories from other cultures. Of the traditions discussed in this book, the Greek (Chapter 3), the Hebrew Bible (Chapter 5), and the Northern European (Chapter 7) provide some interesting similarities. Such a comparison helps us to understand better the nature of mythology and the part that humans play in it, though none of the other myths completely parallels the Babylonian one.

The mythical figure of Tiamat was not herself a dragon, but a goddess who gives birth to dragons in her battle with Marduk. Later tradition represents her as a dragon and sea monster. In the modern role-playing game *Dungeons and Dragons*, Tiamat is a queen of evil dragons and a member of the game's pantheon. The picture shows this many-headed Tiamat in the background with her human form in the foreground.

Like *Enuma Elish*, the Greek poet Hesiod's description of creation in his *Theogony* (Chapter 3) begins with the primeval void (Chaos) and involves intergenerational conflict. Chaos is followed by Earth (Gaia), who gives birth to Heaven (Ouranos). Hesiod describes the interactions of the family of the gods, the offspring of Gaia and Ouranos (see chart, p. 31). The Greco-Roman creation story, as told by Hesiod and the Roman poet Ovid (Chapters 3 and 4), describes the strife between the generations of the gods as well as their conflicts with human beings and their ultimate destruction of this world. Also, in *Works and Days*, Hesiod details the creation of humans starting with "a golden race of mortal men" formed by the Olympian gods and ending with a decline to depravity in the present.

Creation in Genesis, the first book of the Hebrew Bible, is often compared to *Enuma Elish* in part because scholars have shown that one of the accounts incorporated in Genesis was influenced by the Jews' protracted stay in Mesopotamia during the Babylonian Captivity. The Genesis account, written by a source designated as P, also begins "without form and void" (1:1, p. 51). (For a more comprehensive discussion of the two narratives of creation in Genesis, see Chapter 5, p. 50f.) As in the other creation narratives discussed above, Genesis represents humans, the epitome of creation, as soon exhibiting negative characteristics and having to deal with evil, illness, and death. The Hebrew Bible also includes an account of the destruction of the world as a result of the moral decline of human beings (Chapter 12). The chart on page 63 compares the Mesopotamian and Hebrew sources with respect to their creation stories.

Enuma Elish

Tablet I

This story comes from: Stephanie Dalley, *Myths of Mesopotamia.* *

"When . . . above"—These words are the translation of *enuma elish,* the first on the original clay tablet.

Apsu, Tiamat The progenitors of all creation, including the deities. There is no explanation of how and when they came into existence.

Anshar Akkadian sky god, descendant of Apsu and Tiamat, great-grandfather of Marduk.

"Nudimmud, was superior to his forefathers"—This is an example of the generation gap discussed in the Introduction, p. 60.

When heaven **above** was not yet named	
Nor earth below pronounced by name,	
Apsu, the first one, their begetter	
And maker **Tiamat**, who bore them all,	
Had mixed their waters together,	5
But had not formed pastures, nor discovered reed-beds;	
When yet no gods were manifest,	
Nor names pronounced, nor destinies decreed,	
Then gods were born within them.	
Lahmu and Lahamu emerged, their names pronounced.	10
As soon as they matured, were fully formed,	
Anshar and Kishar were born, surpassing them.	
They passed the day at length, they added to the years.	
Anu their first-born son rivaled his forefathers:	
Anshar made his son Anu like himself,	15
And Anu begot Nudimmud in his likeness.	
He, **Nudimmud, was superior to his forefathers**:	
Profound of understanding, he was wise, was very strong at arms.	
Mightier by far than Anshar his father's begetter,	
He had no rival among the gods his peers.	20

---

* Stephanie Dalley, ed. and trans. "The Epic of Creation," in *Myths from Mesopotamia*. Oxford: Oxford University Press, pp. 228–77. ©1989. Used by permission.

Comparison of Creation in *Enuma Elish* and the Hebrew Bible

Subject	*Enuma Elish*	Genesis, Hebrew Bible
Creator(s)	Apsu and Tiamat	One God, creator of all
Origin of Matter	Matter is eternal.	God creates heaven and earth; their relationship to the preexisting deep and the waters is not specified.
Deities	Offspring of Apsu and Tiamat	The Lord God is creator of all.
Primeval Conditions	Watery chaos Day and night already exist before Anu's revolt against his children. (Marduk is a solar deity: luminous.)	Primeval water Lord separates light from darkness. Day and night exist, but light is a condition, not an attribute.
Extent	Creation covers less than 2 of 7 tablets. (Most of the work deals with the contest between Marduk and Tiamat.)	The struggle between God and primeval forces is only vestigial. God is seen as ruling over the great sea monsters (see note on p. 52).
Creation of the Firmament Both describe a parting of primeval waters.	Three types of water: Apsu—sweet water Tiamat—salt water Mummu—fog Ea kills Apsu and builds his home on sweet waters. Ea captures Mummu, and after defeating Tiamat, he divides the waters half earth, half sky.	"In the beginning, God created heaven and earth." (1:1) God creates the firmament, dividing earth and sky "to separate the waters from the waters." (1:6–8)
Creation of Earth	Marduk uses half of Tiamat's body, after establishing the other half as sky.	On the third day, earth becomes visible when God gathered together the waters. (1:1) He names the dry land "Earth" and the waters "Seas." (1:9–10)
Creation of Celestial Bodies In both: to provide light and a way of measuring time.	Babylonians describe it in astronomical terms. Marduk creates celestial bodies and the means of marking time (zodiac, designation of year, months, days, moon, sun).	Hebrews describe it in lay terms. The Lord created sun, moon, and stars to designate day, night, seasons, years.
Creation of Vegetation	Not in *Enuma Elish*, but in some sources; may be on one of the missing sections. Tablet VII refers to Marduk as "The creator of grains and legumes."	On the third day, God commands: "Let the earth put forth vegetation. . . ." (1:11–14)
Creation of Sea and Land Creatures	Not in the Babylonian sources.	On the fifth day, God creates "every living creature that moves" (1:20–21, 24–25) and "the great sea monsters." (1:21–22)
Creation of Humans	In this version of creation, Marduk creates humans to take over the care of sacred places, thus mollifying the gods. Creation of humans from dust is also described in *Atrahasis*, another Mesopotamian epic.	The Lord created man in His image from dust "and breathed life into him" (2:7), and gave him "dominion" over all the earth." (1:26–28)

"The gods of that generation"—
Apsu and Tiamat's great-
grandchildren.

"their clamor reverberated"—
Noise was generally viewed negatively in Babylonian mythology. In
the *Epic of Gilgamesh*, the great
flood occurs because the gods
can no longer tolerate the noise
made by humans. Enlil says to the
gods in council, "The uproar of
mankind is intolerable and sleep is
no longer possible by reason of
the babble" (p. 188).

vizier Counselor, minister, one
who carries out a lord's wishes.
In fact, he is the second in command, who acts in his lord's place
when assigned. In Tablet I, Tiamat appoints him her vizier.

"How could we allow . . ."
—Tiamat reacts maternally, in
contrast with her behavior toward
her great-grandson Marduk.

"put an end to their troublesome
ways"—Ovid describes the Roman
head god Jove as calling a council
of the gods to deal with human
beings whose moral turpitude
appalls him, Ch. 11, p. 131f.

"everything . . . was relayed"—
An explanation of how this was
done is not necessary in a myth.
See Ch. 2, p. 18.

"and put it on himself"—Ea, the
younger god, usurps Apsu's symbols of kingship, and thus his
power.

The gods of that generation would meet together
And disturb Tiamat, and **their clamour reverberated**.
They stirred up Tiamat's belly,
They were annoying her by playing inside Anduruna.
Apsu could not quell their noise   25
And Tiamat became mute before them;
However grievous their behaviour to her,
However bad their ways, she would indulge them.
Finally Apsu, begetter of the great gods,
Called out and addressed his vizier Mummu,   30
   'O Mummu, **vizier** who pleases me!
   'Come, let us go to Tiamat!'
They went and sat in front of Tiamat,
And discussed affairs concerning the gods their sons.
Apsu made his voice heard   35
And spoke to Tiamat in a loud voice,
   'Their ways have become very grievous to me,
   'By day I cannot rest, by night I cannot sleep.
   'I shall abolish their ways and disperse them!
   'Let peace prevail, so that we can sleep.'   40
When Tiamat heard this,
She was furious and shouted at her lover;
She shouted dreadfully and was beside herself with rage,
But then suppressed the evil in her belly.
   'How could we allow what we ourselves created to perish?'   45
   'Even though their ways are so grievous, we should bear it
      patiently.'
Vizier Mummu replied and counseled Apsu;
The vizier did not agree with the counsel of his earth mother.
   'O father, **put an end to their troublesome ways,**
   'So that we may be allowed to rest by day and sleep by night.'   50
Apsu was pleased with him, his face lit up
At the evil he was planning for the gods his sons.
Vizier Mummu hugged him,
Sat on his lap and kissed him rapturously.
But **everything they plotted between them**   55
Was relayed to the gods their sons.
The gods listened and wandered about restlessly;
They fell silent, they sat mute.
Superior in understanding, wise and capable,
Ea who knows everything found out their plot,   60
Made himself a design of everything, and laid it out correctly,
Made it cleverly, his pure spell was superb.
He recited it and it stilled the waters.
He poured sleep upon him so that he was sleeping soundly,
Put Apsu to sleep, drenched with sleep.   65
Vizier Mummu the counselor was in a sleepless daze.
Ea unfastened Apsu's belt, took off his crown,
Took away his mantle of radiance **and put it on himself**.

He held Apsu down and slew him;
Tied up Mummu and laid him across him. 70
He set up his dwelling **on top of Apsu**,
And grasped Mummu, held him by a nose-rope.
When he had overcome and slain his enemies,
Ea set up his triumphal cry over his foes.
Then he rested very quietly inside his private quarters 75
And named them Apsu and assigned chapels,
Founded his own residence there,
And Ea and Damkina his lover dwelt in splendour.
In the chamber of destinies, the hall of designs,
Bel, cleverest of the clever, sage of the gods, was begotten. 80
And **inside Apsu**, Marduk was created;
Inside pure Apsu, Marduk was born.
Ea his father created him,
Damkina his mother bore him.
He suckled the teats of goddesses; 85
The nurse who reared him filled him with awesomeness.
Proud was his form, piercing his stare,
Mature his emergence, he was powerful from the start.
Anu his father's begetter beheld him,
And rejoiced, beamed; his heart was filled with joy. 90
He made him so perfect that **his godhead was doubled**.
Elevated far above them, he was superior in every way.
His limbs were ingeniously made beyond comprehension,
Impossible to understand, too difficult to perceive.
Four were his eyes, four were his ears; 95
When his lips moved, fire blazed forth.
The four ears were enormous
And likewise the eyes; they perceived everything.
Highest among the gods, his form was outstanding.
His limbs were very long, his height outstanding. 100
　　　　(Anu cried out)
　　'**Mariutu**, Mariutu,
　　　Son, majesty, majesty of the gods!'
Clothed in the radiant mantle of ten gods, worn high above
　　his head
Five **fearsome rays** were clustered above him.
Anu created the four winds and gave them birth, 105
Put them in Marduk's hand, 'My son, let them play!'
He fashioned **dust** and made the whirlwind carry it;
He made **the flood-wave** and stirred up Tiamat.
Tiamat was stirred up, and heaved restlessly day and night.
The gods, unable to rest, had to suffer . . . 110
They plotted evil in their hearts, and
They addressed Tiamat their mother, saying,
　　'Because they slew Apsu your lover and
　　You did not go too his side but sat mute,
　　He has created the four, fearful winds 115

"on top of Apsu"—From this point, Apsu is the name of a place as well as the god.

Bel An Akkadian name meaning "master," earlier representing Enlil and then Marduk. The purpose of this epic is to celebrate Marduk as the replacement for Enlil. Here, after a single mention, Bel/Enlil is replaced by Marduk.

"inside Apsu"—Apsu in this statement refers predominantly to the place which arises when the god is killed, though both meanings seem to be implied.

"his godhead was doubled"—To signify Marduk's superiority, Anu has bestowed on him physical characteristics that are "impossible to understand" by the human adherents of these beliefs.

Mariutu This could be a play on the logogram for Marduk, AMAR.TU, or a diminutive of the word for son.

"fearsome rays"—In many traditions, brilliant rays of light denote majesty and blessedness. Compare Exodus 34:34 ("Moses' face shone)," and the Transfiguration of Christ in the New Testament (Matt. 17:1–5) and haloes in Western artworks representing saints.

"Anu created . . . winds . . . dust . . . the flood-wave . . . " —Thus, basic creation of the tangible world is a gift to Marduk from his grandfather.

To stir up your belly on purpose, and we simply cannot sleep!'
Was your lover Apsu not in your heart?
And vizier Mummu who was captured? No wonder you sit
    alone!
Are you not a mother? You heave restlessly
But what about us, who cannot rest? Don't you love us?   120
Our grip is slack, and our eyes are sunken.
Remove the yoke of us restless ones, and let us sleep!
Set up a battle cry and avenge them!
Conquer the enemy and reduce them to naught!'
Tiamat listened, and the speech pleased her.   125
    'Let us act now as you were advising!'
    The gods inside Apsu will be disturbed,

"Because they adopted evil for the gods who begot them"—Tiamat chooses to act out of a sense of righteousness.

Because they adopted evil for the gods who begot them.'
They crowded round and rallied beside Tiamat.
They were fierce, scheming restlessly night and day.   130
They were working up to war, growling and raging.
They convened a council and created conflict.

Mother Hubur Dalley suggests this might be a pun on the word "hubur" for "river" or hubura for "hubbub."

Mother Hubur, who fashions all things,
Contributed an unfaceable weapon: she bore giant snakes,
Sharp of tooth and unsparing of fang.   135
She filled their bodies with venom instead of blood.
She cloaked ferocious dragons with fearsome rays
And made them bear mantles of radiance, made them godlike,
                (chanting this imprecation)
    'Whoever looks upon them shall collapse in utter terror!
    Their bodies shall rear up continually and never turn away!'   140
She stationed a horned serpent, a *mushussu*-dragon, and a
    lahmu-hero,
An *ugallu*-demon, a rabid dog, and a scorpion-man,
Aggressive *umu*-demons, a fish-man, and a bull-man
Bearing merciless weapons, fearless in battle.

A Mushussu dragon as represented on the Gate of Ishtar at Babylon.

Her orders were so powerful, they could not be disobeyed.   145
In addition she created eleven more likewise.
Over the gods her offspring who had convened a council
    for her
She promoted Qingu and made him greatest among them,
Conferred upon him leadership of the army, command of the
    assembly,
Overall command of the whole battle force.   150
And she set him upon a throne.
    'I have cast the spell for you and made you greatest in the
        gods' assembly!
    I have put into your power rule over all the gods!
    You shall be the greatest, for you are my only lover!

Anukki variant of Anunnaki, referring to the group of older gods. See Introduction p. 58.

Tablet of Destinies The keeper of this controlled the fate of each individual. See Introduction p. 60.

    Your commands shall always prevail over all the **Anukki**!'   155
Then she gave him the **Tablet of Destinies** and made him clasp
    it to his breast.
    'Your utterance shall never be altered! Your word shall be law!'
When Qingu was promoted and had received the Anu-power

And had decreed destinies for the gods his sons, he said,
   'What issues forth from your mouths shall quench Fire!   160
   Your accumulated venom shall paralyse the powerful!'

Tablet II

Tiamat assembled her creatures
And collected battle-units against the gods her offspring.
Tiamat did even more evil for posterity than Apsu.
It was reported to Ea that she had prepared for war.   165
Ea listened to that report,
And was dumbfounded and sat in silence.
When he had pondered and his fury subsided,
He made his way to Anshar his father;
Came before Anshar, the father who begot him   170
And began to repeat to him everything that Tiamat had planned.

[Omitted section: Ea repeats to Anshar Tiamat's plan as detailed in
Tablet I. Anshar urges Ea and then Anu to defeat Tiamat. Both are
defeated.]

Anshar listened, and the report was very disturbing.
He twisted his fingers and bit his lip;
His liver was inflamed, his belly would not rest.
Then Ea from his secret dwelling called   175
The perfect one of Anshar, father of the great gods,
Whose heart is perfect like a fellow-citizen or countryman,
The mighty heir who was to be his father's champion,
Who rushes fearlessly into battle: Marduk the Hero!
Ea told him his innermost design, saying,   180
   'O Marduk, take my advice, listen to your father!
   You are the son who sets his heart at rest!
   Approach Anshar, drawing near to him,
   And make your voice heard, stand your ground:
   He will be calmed by the sight of you.'   185
The Lord rejoiced at the word of his father,
And he approached and stood before Anshar.
Anshar looked at him, and his heart was filled with joy.
He kissed him on the lips, put away his trepidation.
          (*Then Marduk addressed him, saying*)
'Father, don't stay so silent, open your lips,   190
Let me go, and let me fulfill your heart's desire.
Anshar, don't stay so silent, open your lips,
Let me go, and let me fulfill your heart's desire.'
          (*Anshar replied*)
   'What kind of man has ordered you out to his war?
   My son, don't you realize that it is **Tiamat, of womankind,**   195
      who will advance against you with arms?'
          (*Marduk answered*)
   'Father, my creator, rejoice and be glad!
   You shall soon set your foot upon the neck of Tiamat!

> "The perfect one of Anshar"—Ea extols his grandfather Anshar as progenitor, and himself as father of Marduk. This is a signal of generational awareness common in ancient Mesopotamian myths.

> "Tiamat, of womankind"—She is his great-great-great-great grandmother.

'Ansher, my creator, rejoice and be glad,
You shall soon set your foot upon the neck of Tiamat!   200

(Anshar replied)

'Then go, son, knowing all wisdom!
Quell Tiamat with your pure spell!
Set forth immediately in the storm chariot;
Let them be not driven out, but turn them back!'
The Lord rejoiced at the word of his father;   205
His heart was glad and he addressed his father,
   'Lord of the gods, fate of the great gods,
   If indeed I am to be your champion,
   If I am to defeat Tiamat and save your lives,
   Convene the council, name a special fate,   210
   Sit joyfully together in **Ubshu-ukkinakku**:
   My own utterance shall fix fate instead of you!
   Whatever I create shall never be altered!
   The decree of my lips shall never be revoked, never changed!'

Tablet III

Anshar made his voice heard   215
And addressed his speech to Kakka his vizier,
   'O Kakka, vizier who pleases me!
   I shall send you to Lahmu and Lahamu.
   You know how to probe, you are skilled in speaking.
   Have the gods my fathers brought before me;   220
   Let all the gods be brought to me.
   Let there be conversation, let them sit at a banquet,
   Let them eat grain, let them drink choice wine,
And then let them decree a destiny for Marduk their champion.
   Set off, Kakka, go and stand before them, and   225
   Everything that I am about to tell you, repeat to them.
      "Anshar your son has sent me,
      He has told me to report his heart's message,
      To say, **Tiamat who bore us is rejecting us**!
      She has convened a council, and is raging out of control."'   230

[Omitted section: Kakka delivers Anshar's message. He explains the difficulty of finding a god to confront Tiamat and repeats her vengeful plans as described in Tablet I and repeated by Ea in Tablet II. The text below continues with Kakka's recitation of Anshar's message to the Council of the Gods.]

'I sent Anu, but he was unable to face her.
Nudimmud panicked and turned back.
Then Marduk, sage of the gods, your son, came forward.
He wanted of his own free will to confront Tiamat.
He spoke his words to me,   235
   "If indeed I am to be your champion,
   To defeat Tiamat and save your lives,
   Convene the council, name a special fate,

"You shall . . . You shall . . ."—Such repetition usually indicates that a work had at least originally been recited.

Ubshu-ukkinakku Meeting place of the Council of the Gods.

"Anshar made his voice heard"—At the request of Marduk, the Council of the Gods is called together.

"Tiamat who bore us is rejecting us"—Kakka delivers to Lahmu and Lahamu the specific words that Anshar mandated in the omitted section.

Nudimmud Another name for Ea.

Sit joyfully together in Ubshu-ukkinakku:

And let me, my own utterance, fix fate instead of you.   240

Whatever I create shall never be altered!

Let a decree from my lips never be revoked, never changed!"

Hurry and decree your destinies for him quickly,

So that he may go and face your formidable enemy!'"

Lahmu and Lahamu listened and cried out aloud.   245

All the **Igigi** then groaned dreadfully,

'How terrible! Until Anshar decided to report to us,

We did not even know what Tiamat was doing.'

They milled around and then came,

All the great gods who fix the fates,   250

Entered into Anshar's presence and were filled with joy.

Each kissed the other: in the assembly

There was conversation, they sat at the banquet,

Ate grain, drank choice wine,

Let sweet beer trickle through their drinking straws.   255

Their bodies swelled as they drank the liquor;

They became very carefree, they were merry,

And they decreed destiny for Marduk their champion.

> **Igigi** Younger gods who did all of the work while the older gods rested. See chart, p. 63, for the relationship of these gods to the creation of humans.

Tablet IV

They founded a princely shrine for him,

And he took up residence as ruler before his fathers,   260

(who proclaimed)

'You are honoured among the great gods.

Your destiny is unequaled, your word has the power of Anu!

O Marduk, you are honoured among the great gods.

Your destiny is unequaled, your word has the power of Anu!

From this day onwards your command shall not be altered.   265

Yours is the power to exalt and abase.

May your utterance be law, your word never be falsified.

None of the gods shall transgress your limits.

May **endowment, required for the gods' shrines**

Wherever they have temples, be established for your place.   270

O Marduk, you are our champion!

We hereby give you sovereignty over all of the whole universe.

Sit in the assembly and your word shall be pre-eminent!

May your weapons never miss the mark, may they smash
   your enemies!

O lord, **spare the life** of him who trusts in you,   275

But **drain the life of the god who has espoused evil**!'

They set up in their midst one constellation,

And then they addressed Marduk their son,

'May your decree, O lord, impress the gods!

Command to destroy and to re-create, and let it be so!   280

Speak and let the constellation vanish!

Speak to it again and let the constellation reappear.'

He spoke, and at his word the constellation vanished.

> "endowment, required for the gods' shrines"—Upkeep of temple and service to the gods was a central obligation in Mesopotamian religion. To appease the younger gods who complain, Marduk creates humans to take over the tasks. (See Tablet VI, ll. 1–8.)

> "spare the life . . . drain the life of the god who has espoused evil"—Deities are not necessarily immortal. Humans will not be created until Tablet VI.

> "He spoke, and at his word . . ." —The control of nature proves the special power of a leader.

He spoke to it again and the constellation was re-created.
When the gods his fathers saw how effective his utterance was,   285
They rejoiced, they proclaimed: 'Marduk is King!'
They invested him with sceptre, throne, and staff-of-office.
They gave him an unfaceable weapon to crush the foe.
    "Go, and cut off the life of Tiamat!"
    Let the winds bear her blood to us as good news!'   290
The gods his fathers thus decreed the destiny of the lord
And set him on the path of peace and obedience.
He fashioned a bow, designated it as his weapon,
Feathered the arrow, set it in the string.
He lifted up a mace and carried it in his right hand,   295
Slung the bow and quiver at his side,
Put lightning in front of him,
His body was filled with an ever-blazing flame.
He made a net to encircle Tiamat within it,
Marshalled the four winds so that no part of her could escape: 300
South Wind, North Wind, East Wind, West Wind,
The **gift of his father Anu,** he kept them close to the net at
    his side.
He created the *imhullu*-wind, the tempest, the whirlwind,
The Four Winds, the Seven Winds, the tornado, the unfaceable
    facing wind.
He released the winds which he had created, seven of them.   305
They advanced behind him to make turmoil inside Tiamat.
The lord raised the flood-weapon, his great weapon,
And mounted the frightful, unfaceable storm-chariot.
He had yoked to it a team of four and had harnessed to its side
'Slayer', 'Pitiless', 'Racer', and 'Flyer';   310
Their lips were drawn back, their teeth carried poison.
They know not exhaustion, they can only devastate.
He stationed on his right Fearsome Fight and Conflict,
On the left Battle to knock down every contender.
Clothed in a cloak of awesome armour,   315
His head was crowned with a terrible radiance.
The Lord set out and took the road,
And set his face towards Tiamat who raged out of control.
In his lips he gripped **a spell,**
In his hand he grasped **an herb** to counter poison.   320
Then they thronged about him, the gods thronged about him;
The gods his fathers thronged about him, **the gods thronged
    about him**.
The Lord drew near and looked into the middle of Tiamat:
He was trying to find out the strategy of Qingu her lover.
As he looked, his mind became confused,   325
His will crumbled and his actions were muddled.
As for the gods his helpers, who marched at his side,
When they saw the warrior, the leader, their looks were strained.
Tiamat cast her spell. She did not even turn her neck.
In her lips she was holding falsehood, lies, wheedling,   330

'"Go, and cut off the life of Tia-mat!"—The gods send Marduk to overcome Tiamat only after they observe his special powers.

"Marshalled the four winds"—Preparation for attack includes calling on nature as a co-warrior.

"gift of his father Anu"—Anu was god of the winds.

"He created the *imhullu*-wind . . ." —Marduk shows his preeminence by outdoing his father: another sign of generational conflict, as explained in the Introduction, p. 60.

"His head was crowned with a ter-rible radiance"—As in Tablet I's description of Marduk's preemi-nence from birth, the inclusion here of radiance signifies his sta-tus as a hero.

"a spell . . . an herb"—Marduk relies on magic as well as on tradi-tional combat items and tech-niques.

"the gods thronged about him"—This type of emphasis through repetition is also used in the *Epic of Gilgamesh*, Ch.15, p. 166.

'How powerful is your attacking force, O lord of
   the gods!
The whole assembly of them has gathered to your place!'
      (*But he ignored her blandishments*)
The Lord lifted up the flood-weapon, his great weapon
And sent a message to Tiamat who feigned goodwill, saying:
   'Why are you so friendly on the surface   335
   When your depths conspire to muster a battle force?
   Just because the sons were noisy and disrespectful to
      their fathers,
   Should you, who gave them birth, reject compassion?
   You named Qingu as your lover,
   You appointed him to rites of Anu-power, wrongfully his.   340
   You sought out evil for Anshar, king of the gods,
   So **you have compounded your wickedness** against the
      gods my fathers!
   Let your host prepare! Let them gird themselves with
      your weapons!
   Stand forth, and you and I shall do single combat!'
When Tiamat heard this,   345
She went wild, she lost her temper.
Tiamat screamed aloud in a passion,
Her lower parts shook together from the depths.
She recited the incantation and kept casting her spell.
Meanwhile the gods of battle were sharpening their
   weapons.   350
Face to face they came, Tiamat and Marduk, sage of the gods.
They engaged in combat, they closed for battle.
The Lord spread his net and made it encircle her,
To her face he dispatched the ***imhullu*-wind**, which had
   been behind:
Tiamat opened her mouth to swallow it,   355
And he forced in the *imhullu*-wind, so that she could not
   close her lips.
Fierce winds distended her belly;
Her insides were constipated and she stretched her mouth wide.
He shot an arrow which pierced her belly,
Split her down the middle and split her heart,   360
Vanquished her and extinguished her life.
He threw down her corpse and stood on top of her.
When he had slain Tiamat, the leader,
He broke up her regiments; her assembly was scattered.
Then the gods her helpers, who had marched at her side,   365
Began to tremble, panicked, and turned tail.
Although he allowed them to come out and spared their lives,
They were surrounded, they could not flee.
Then he tied them up and smashed their weapons.
They were thrown into the net and sat there ensnared.   370
They cowered back, filled with woe.
They had to bear his punishment, confined to prison.

"Just because the sons were noisy"—Marduk confronts the elder Tiamat about her injustice to the young gods. (For more on the intergenerarional conflict in the epic, see the Introduction, p. 60f.)

"you have compounded your wickedness"—Marduk declares righteous revenge as his motivation.

"*imhullu*-wind"—The evil wind.

And as for the dozens of creatures, covered in fearsome rays,
The gang of demons who all marched on her right,
He fixed them with nose-ropes and tied their arms.   375
He trampled their battle-filth beneath him.
As for Qingu, who had once been the greatest among them,
He defeated him and counted him among the dead gods,
Wrested from him the Tablet of Destinies, wrongfully his,
Sealed it with his own seal and pressed it to his breast.   380
When he had defeated and killed his enemies
And had proclaimed the submissive foe his slave,
And had set up the triumphal cry of Anshar over all the enemy,
And had **achieved the desire of Nudimmud**, Marduk the
    warrior
Strengthened his hold over the captive gods,   385
And to Tiamat, whom he had ensnared, he turned back.
The Lord trampled the lower part of Tiamat,
With his unsparing mace smashed her skull,
Severed the arteries of her blood,
And **made the North Wind carry it off as good news**.   390
His fathers saw it and were jubilant: they rejoiced,
Arranged to greet him with presents, greetings gifts.
The Lord rested, and inspected her corpse.
He divided the monstrous shape and created marvels from it.
He sliced her in half like a fish for drying: 395
Half of her he put up to roof the sky,
Drew a bolt across and made a guard hold it.
Her waters he arranged so that they could not escape.
He crossed the heavens and sought out a shrine;
He leveled Apsu, dwelling of Nudimmud.   400
The Lord measured the dimensions of Apsu
And the large temple (Eshgalla), which he built in its image,
    was **Esharra**:
In the great shrine Esharra, which he had created as the sky,
He founded cult centers for Anu, Ellil, and Ea.

Tablet V

He fashioned stands for the great gods.   405
As for the stars, **he set up constellations** corresponding to them.
He designated the year and marked out its divisions,
Apportioned three stars each to the twelve months
When he had made plans of the days of the year,
He founded the stand of **Neberu** to mark out their courses,   410
So that none of them could go wrong or stray.
He fixed the stand of Ellil and Ea together with it,
Opened up gates in both ribs,
Made strong bolts to left and right,
With her liver he located the Zenith;   415
He made the crescent moon appear, entrusted night to it
And designated it the jewel of night to mark out the days.

"Wrested from him the Tablet of Destinies"—Marduk's rightful booty. Only the most important god should be in charge of the destinies of all.

"achieved the desire of Nudimmud"—Nudimmud (Ea) had sent his son Marduk to vanquish Tiamat.

"made the North Wind carry it off as good news"—Ancient Mesopotamians considered the North Wind the most favorable (Dalley, 275).

"His fathers"—This refers to Marduk's father Ea, his grandfather Anu, and great-grandfather Anshar.

"Half of her he put up to roof the sky . . . Her waters he arranged"—Marduk's separating Tiamat's body into earth and sky is echoed in Genesis 1:6–8 when the Lord separates the firmament and waters.

"He leveled Apsu"—Again Marduk surpasses his father Ea's accomplishments.

Esharra Sky, heaven.

"He founded cult centers"—In ancient Mesopotamia, worship of gods in their own temples was a central aspect of religion.

"he set up constellations"—The following description of the constellations, the moon, and measuring periods of time are accurate astronomical descriptions.

Neberu Here, this seems to be a bright star, most likely Sirius in the constellation Canus Major. In Tablet VII, it is also one of the names given Marduk to praise him by extolling all of his attributes.

'Go forth every month without fail in a corona,
At the beginning of the month, to glow over the land.
You shine with horns to mark out six days;   420
On the seventh day the crown is half.
The fifteenth day shall always be the mid-point, the half of
    each month.
When **Shamash** looks at you from the horizon,
Gradually shed your visibility and begin to wane.
Always **bring the day of disappearance close to the path of
    Shamash**,   425
And on the thirteenth day, the year is always equalized, for
    Shamash is responsible for the year.'
He made clouds scud.
Raising winds, making rain,
Making fog billow, by collecting her poison,   430
He assigned for himself and let his own hand control it.
He placed her head, heaped up mountains.
Opened up springs: water gushed out.
He opened the Euphrates and the Tigris **from her eyes**,
Closed her nostrils.   435
He piled up clear-cut mountains from her **udder**,
Bored waterholes to drain off the catchwater.
He laid her **tail** across, tied it fast as the cosmic bond,
He set her thigh to make fast the sky,
With half of her he made a roof; he fixed the earth.   440
He made the insides of Tiamat surge,
Spread his net, made it extend completely.
He touched heaven and earth.
Their bounds established.
When he had designed its cult, created its rites,   445
He threw down the reins and made Ea take them.
The Tablet of Destinies, which Qingu had appropriated,
    he fetched
And took it and presented it for a first reading to Anu.
The gods of battle whom he had ensnared were disentangled;
He led them as captives into the presence of his fathers.   450
And as for the eleven creatures that Tiamat had created, he
Smashed their weapons, tied them at his feet,
Made images of them and had them set up at the door of Apsu.
    'Let this be a sign that will never in future be forgotten!'
The gods looked, and their hearts were full of joy at him.   455
Lahmu and Lahamu and all his fathers
Embraced him, and Anshar the king proclaimed that there
    should be a reception for him.
Anu, Enlil, and Ea each presented him with gifts.
Damkina his mother exclaimed with joy at him;
She made him beam inside his fine house.   460
Marduk appointed **Usmu**, who had brought his greetings
    present as good news,
To be vizier of the Apsu, to take care of shrines.

"You shine with horns"—The shape of the crescent moon is often described as having horns.

Shamash Mesopotamian sun god. (Compare his role in the *Epic of Gilgamesh*, Ch. 15.)

"bring the day of disappearance close to the path of Shamash"—This is an accurate astronomical explanation of the relationship of the sun and moon. For example, the full moon sets at sunrise.

"from her eyes"—The word on the tablet, *inu*, means both "eyes" and "springs." Tiamat was the primeval water deity.

"udder . . . tail"—The coexistence of these parts creates the impression that Tiamat is monstrous, unlike the other deities—or the humans who are reciting the epic.

Neo-Assyrian cylinder seal representing Marduk defeating Tiamat.

Usmu Vizier of Ea in the Akkadian tradition. Thus, Marduk continues the influence of his father.

The Igigi assembled, and all of them did obeisance to him.

The Anunnaki, each and every one, kissed his feet.

The whole assembly collected together to prostrate themselves. 465

With cypress branches they sprinkled his body.

He put on a princely garment,

A royal aura, a splendid crown.

He took up a mace and grasped it in his right hand.

He set a *mushussu*-dragon at his feet. 470

Slung the staff of peace and obedience at his side.

When they gave kingship to Marduk,

They spoke an oration for him, for blessing and obedience.

    'Henceforth you shall be the **provider of shrines for us**.

    Whatever you command, we shall perform ourselves.' 475

Marduk made his voice heard and spoke,

Addressed his words to the gods his fathers,

    'Over the Apsu, the sea-green dwelling,

    In front of Esharra, which I created for you,

    Where I strengthened the ground beneath it for a shrine, 480

    I shall make my house to be a luxurious dwelling for myself

    And I shall establish my private quarters, and confirm

      my kingship.

    Whenever you come up from the Apsu for an assembly,

    Your night's resting place shall live in it, receiving you all.

    I hereby name it Babylon, home of the great gods. 485

    We shall make it the center of religion.

    Babylon, whose name you have just pronounced,

    Found there our night's resting place forever!'

They did obeisance to him and the gods spoke to him,

They addressed their lord **Lugal-dimmer-ankia**, 490

    'Previously the Lord was our beloved son.

    But now he is our king. We shall take heed of his command.'

Tablet VI

When Marduk heard the speech of the gods,

He made up his mind to perform miracles.

He spoke his utterance to Ea, 495

And communicated to him the plan that he was considering.

    'Let me put blood together, and make bones too.

    Let me set up primeval man: Man shall be his name.

    Let me create a primeval man.

    The work of the gods shall be imposed on him, and so 500

      they shall be at leisure.

    Let me change the ways of the gods miraculously,

    So they are **gathered as one, yet divided in two**.'

Ea answered him and spoke a word to him,

Told him his plan for the leisure of the gods.

    'Let **one who is hostile to them** be surrendered up, 505

    Let him be destroyed, and let people be created from him.

    Let the great gods assemble,

"He took up a mace"—In many traditions royalty carry a symbolic weapon as a sign of authority. Compare Kintu's conga scepter (Ch. 9), the light-saber in *Star Wars*, or Harry Potter's magic wand (Ch. 41).

"provider of shrines for us"—Like the gods in the Roman flood story (Ch. 11), the gods expect to be worshipped.

"I hereby name it Babylon"—Marduk established Babylon as the center of religious life. Since he has proven himself as a warrior and preeminent leader, it is also the center of power and authority. In this capacity, Marduk's role is not merely theological but also aetiological: this story about him explains the origins of Babylon as a city. For more on aetiology, see Chapter 1, p. 13.

"Lugal-dimmer-ankia"—Sumerian for "king of the gods of heaven and earth," an epithet of Marduk.

"He made up his mind to perform miracles"—Marduk's performing miracles is his own decision, not bestowed on him by a higher power. This signifies that he *is* that power.

"they [the gods] shall be at leisure"—Marduk shows his respect for the younger gods by creating human beings to relieve them of their ritual work in the temples.

"gathered as one, yet divided in two"—The council has gathered all the gods together, the older and the younger ones.

"one who is hostile to them"—Humans are created from the hostile god Qingu, who was Tiamat's vizier and lover.

Let the culprit be given up, and let them convict him.'
Marduk assembled the great gods,
Gave them instructions pleasantly, gave orders.   510
The gods paid attention to what he said.
The king addressed his words to the Anunnaki,
   'Your election of me shall be firm and foremost.
   I shall declare the laws, the edicts within my power.
   Whosoever started the war,   515
   And incited Tiamat, and gathered an army,
   Let the one who started the war be given up to me,
   And he shall bear the penalty for his crime, that you may
      dwell in peace.'
The Igigi, the great gods, answered him,
Their lord Lugal-dimmer-ankia, counselor of the gods,   520
   'It was Qingu who started the war,
   He who incited Tiamat and gathered an army!'
They bound him and held him in front of Ea,
Imposed the penalty on him and cut off his blood.
He created mankind from his blood,   525
Imposed the toil of the note and released the gods from it.
When Ea the wise had created mankind,
Had imposed the toil of the gods on them—
That deed is impossible to describe,
For Nudimmud performed it with the miracles of Marduk—   530
Then Marduk the king divided the gods,
The Anunnaki, all of them, above and below.
He assigned his decrees to Anu to guard,
Established three hundred as a guard in the sky;
Did the same again when he designed the conventions of earth,   535
And made the six hundred dwell in both heaven and earth.
When he had directed all the decrees,
Had divided lots for the Anunnaki, of heaven and of earth,
The Anunnaki made their voices heard,
And addressed Marduk their lord,   540
   'Now, O Lord, that you have set us free,
   What are our favours from you?
   We would like to make **a shrine with its own name**.
   We would like our night's resting place to be in your
      private quarters, and to rest there.
   Let us found a shrine, a sanctuary there.   545
   Whenever we arrive, let us rest within it.'
When Marduk heard this,
His face lit up greatly, like daylight.
   'Create Babylon, whose construction you requested!
   Let its mud bricks be moulded, and build high the shrine!'   550
When they had done the work on Esagila,
And the Anunnaki, all of them, had fashioned their individual
   shrines,
The three hundred Igigi of heaven and the Anunnaki of the
   Apsu assembled.

'It was Qingu"—The Igigi, not Marduk, indict Qingu.

"He created mankind from his blood"—This statement is ambiguous: is the creator Ea or Marduk? Dalley notes that the ambiguity may be a deliberate blurring of the two gods (276), because within three lines we read that "Ea the wise had created mankind." The creation of humans from Qingu's blood is a favor to the gods, who are relieved of their temple duties.

"a shrine with its own name"—Shrines dedicated to specific deities were the ultimate expression of respect, as well as a means for continued worship. Compare Demeter's shrine at Eleusis, Ch. 27, p. 386.

"Create Babylon, whose construction you requested!"—Marduk commissions the gods to build Babylon and thus, their own specific shrines.

Bab-ili Babylon, "Gateway of the Gods." This name, along with its founding by Marduk, gives Babylon exceptional status among Mesopotamian communities.

"*taqribtu*-offering"—A supplication offering, asking the gods for a blessing.

"He gave to the bow her names"—It was not uncommon, from earliest records, for heroes to name weapons. For an example in later Europe, see Thor's hammer Mjollnir (Ch. 30, p. 437.)

Bowstar Sirius. Dalley suggests that the bow refers to Ishtar, since the month of her great festival was called "Month of the heliacal rising of the bowstar."

"Thus they granted . . ."—Such a ritual signifying acceptance confirms the gods' acceptance of Marduk.

The Lord invited the gods his fathers to attend a banquet
In the great sanctuary which he had created as his dwelling.   555
　'Indeed, **Bab-ili** is your home too!
　　Sing for joy there, dwell in happiness!'
The great gods sat down there,
And set out the beer mugs; they attended the banquet.
When they had made merry within,   560
They themselves made a ***taqribtu*-offering** in splendid Esagila.
All the decrees and designs were fixed.
All the gods divided the stations of heaven and earth.
The fifty great gods were present, and
The gods fixed the seven destinies for the cult.   565
The Lord received the bow, and set his weapon down in front
　of them.
The gods his fathers looked at the net which he had made,
Looked at the bow, how miraculous her construction,
And his fathers praised the deeds that he had done.
Anu raised the bow and spoke in the assembly of gods,   570
He kissed the bow. 'May she go far!'
He gave to the bow her names, saying,
　'May Long and Far be the first, and Victorious the second;
　　Her third name shall be **Bowstar**, for she shall shine in
　　　the sky.'
He fixed her position among the gods her companions.   575
When Anu had decreed the destiny of the bow,
He set down her royal throne. You are highest of the gods!'
And Anu made her sit in the assembly of gods.
The great gods assembled
And made Marduk's destiny highest; they themselves did   580
　obeisance.
They swore an oath for themselves,
And swore on water and oil, touched their throats.
Thus they granted that he should exercise the kingship of the
　gods
And confirmed for him mastery of the gods of heaven and
　earth.

Tablet VII

The following is a condensation of the final tablet, which is a paean to Marduk via a compilation of 50 epithets. The final verses praise Marduk, describe his attributes, and direct the faithful:

"the Elil of the gods"—Elil (Enlil) was the Sumerian king of the gods—here, an example of syncretism. (For an explanation of syncretism, see Ch. 15, p. 166.)

With fifty epithets the great gods   585
Called his fifty names, making his way supreme.
May they always be cherished, and may the older explain to
　the younger.
Let the wise and learned consult together,
Let the father repeat them and teach them to the son.
Let the ear of shepherds and herdsman be open,   590
Let him not be negligent to Marduk, **the Elil of the gods**.

May his country be made fertile, and himself be safe and sound.
His word is firm, his command cannot alter;
No god can change his utterance.
When he is angry, he does not turn his neck aside;   595
In his rage and fury no god dare confront him.
His thoughts are deep, his emotions profound;
Criminals and wrongdoers pass before him.
The scribe wrote down the secret instruction which older
    men had recited in his presence,
And set it down for future men to read.   600
May the **people of Marduk whom the Igigi gods created**
Weave the tale and call upon his name
In remembrance of the song of Marduk
Who defeated Tiamat and took the kingship.

> "people of Marduk whom the Igigi gods created"—The high priest reciting *Enuma Elish* calls upon those present (the humans, created from Qingu) who have taken over service of the gods from the Igigi.

Further Reading

Dalley, Stephanie, ed. and trans. "The Epic of Creation." In *Myths from Mesopotamia*, 228–77. Oxford: Oxford University Press, 1989.

Knapp, Bettina L. "Enuma Elish: The Feminine Maligned." In *Women in Myth*. Albany, N.Y.: State University of New York Press, 1997, 21–43.

7

The *Prose Edda*'s Creation Stories

WHAT TO EXPECT . . . The *Prose Edda* is a literary work incorporating a great number of myths from the old Norse tradition, which included much of what is now northern Europe. Because Snorri, the writer, wanted to preserve this knowledge of a belief system that was disappearing, it contains both parataxis (the idea that myths often weave together different stories without logical connection) and rationalization (adding logic to an explanation after the fact). It also exhibits characteristics of both oral and written accounts, as explained in Chapter 2.

This chapter contains excerpts from the *Edda* describing the pantheon of the pagan gods and the creation of the world—actually, six different accounts based on varying sources. For more from the world of the *Edda*, see Chapter 13, which tells the story of Ragnarok, the end of the world, from the *Prose Edda*; Chapter 18, which has stories of Norse heroes from the *Prose Edda*; and Chapter 30, which has an excerpt from Davidson's *Gods and Myths of Northern Europe*.

With respect to Snorri's *Prose Edda,* contests are an important theme to notice. The main part of this work, called "The Deluding of Gylfi," is structured as a contest, and the stories Snorri tells often contain games and contests of various sorts, as well. Look for the old woman Gefjon's laughter at defeating Gylfi, for instance.

While reading the creation stories here, compare the different roles of human beings in the various creation stories you have been reading. The Norse stories in this chapter give more prominence to human beings than the Greek creation story in Chapter 3.

Snorri Sturluson lived in Iceland from 1179 to 1241 C.E. This was a time in which Christianity was already widespread in Celtic countries, so the knowledge of pre-Christian religion was being rapidly lost. Iceland was an especially good place to find information on the old religion, because it was the last of these countries to become Christianized. Snorri wrote the *Prose Edda* in about 1200 C.E. as a way of compiling as many as he could of the stories, legends, and poems about the old gods before they were lost completely. He did not record the information he gathered into an encyclopedia or dictionary, as we might today. Instead, he wove it into a lively and exciting story of a contest undertaken by the king of Sweden.

SNORRI'S STYLE

The resulting work, *Prose Edda*, has the characteristics of an oral account even though it is actually an instance of written myth. Often one version of a story follows directly upon another, without much logical connection. This is called *parataxis* and is one of the characteristics of oral myth. (See Ch. 2, p. 18, for a more extensive discussion of this style of composing myth.) For example, in this account of creation in "The Deluding of Gylfi," Snorri listed six different creation stories. He brought them together only by implying that each one happened after the other, but these seem to be independent stories that contradict each other. The first one says that the universe was created from nothing. This is a relatively modern and sophisticated view of creation. In the modern view, it was no longer sufficient to show how the components of the universe came to be as they are; it was felt that the creation should be traced back to the origin of all things. This account says that out of a collision of heat and cold in Ginnungagap, the body of Ymir was created. This is essentially a scientific explanation that bases creation on physical forces in an already existing universe. Several other accounts which follow attribute creation to the activities of powerful, godlike creatures—a very different kind of creation story.

SNORRI'S RATIONALIZATION OF MYTH

The production of the old stories Snorri uses was essentially unplanned. People had been telling them for so long that no one knew where they really came from. Before the stories were all brought together in one place, any contradictions in them were not as apparent. Snorri, in contrast, had a plan: he took these stories from some of the major pieces of literature of his day and combined them, making the discrepancies between them obvious to his reader. Snorri, however, was not troubled by these inconsistencies; he was quite willing to show the limitations of the stories. He was, after all, a Christian writing for a Christian audience. Since it was written before the invention of the printing press in 1455 C.E., his book would become known to people only by being hand-copied by Christian monks in Christian monasteries. Snorri did not need to make the stories believable; he was not trying to recruit believers for the old religion. Pagan religion still had followers in his time, but was no longer the official religion of Iceland. He only wanted to preserve these stories as part of his national heritage.

In fact, the problem Snorri had in telling his story was just the opposite. His audience believed in the Christian account of the origin of the universe. So he had to explain how the pagan religion that worshipped Odin and Thor could have become so widespread, when it was, in the view of his readers, plainly false. How could the much older Judaeo-Christian account, based on the Bible, have become neglected? Snorri answered this question by emphasizing the inconsistencies in his account: the people who told these stories, he suggests, had forgotten the truth, and thus made up the best explanation they could. Snorri thus rationalized myth, making it fit with current beliefs. Interestingly enough, rationalization did not make the myths more rational, but less. In this case, it meant making the inconsistencies and contradictions found in the stories he told apparent to his audience, so that they would understand that these are just stories. Snorri even introduced inconsistencies into his account. The main part of his account was a story called "The Deluding of Gylfi." He added to this a "Prologue" in which he speaks in his own person, as Snorri, to his audience. The two sections of the book are actually incompatible and contradict each other. In the "Prologue," Snorri explains how he really thinks the stories he is telling arose: this part of his account is not part of real Norse mythology. In "The Deluding of Gylfi," he just gives his readers the stories that make up the Norse mythological system. The notes accompaning the excerpt will point out inconsistencies between these two sections.

This excerpt comes from: Snorri Sturluson, *The Prose Edda*.*

Prologue

In the beginning Almighty God created heaven and earth and everything that goes with them and, last of all, two human beings, Adam and Eve, from whom have come families. Their progeny multiplied and spread over all the world. As time went on,

 The Biblical Story of Creation

"In the beginning Almighty God"—Snorri's account resembles the origin of the world as described in Genesis in the Bible. See Ch. 5, p. 50 for the text of the Biblical account.

---

* Snorri Sturluson. *The Prose Edda: Tales from Norse Mythology.* Trans. Jean I. Young, 23–37, Copyright © 1954. Used by permission of the University of California Press.

The People Lose Their Understanding of God

"In the end they lost the very name of God"—Snorri's account also differs from the story in the Bible: as time goes on, people lose all knowledge of the true God. This is why, later, they go on to invent the Icelandic gods for themselves.

The People Try to Learn about the Gods

"They observed"— Since people have lost true wisdom (the knowledge of God), they try to figure out the nature of the world by empirical observation.

"from their ancestors"—The accounts of other sources supplement the empirical investigation mentioned previously.

"there must be someone who ruled the stars"—The investigation imagined by Snorri comes to a preliminary conclusion.

however, inequalities sprang up amongst peoples—some were good and righteous but by far the greater number, disregarding God's commandments, turned to the lusts of the world. For this reason God drowned the world and all creatures living in it—with the exception of those who were with Noah in the ark. Eight persons survived Noah's flood and these peopled the world and founded families. As the population of the world increased, however, and a larger area became inhabited, the same thing happened again; the great majority of mankind, loving the pursuit of money and power, left off paying homage to God. This grew to such a pitch that they boycotted any reference to God, and then how could anyone tell their sons about the marvels connected with Him? **In the end they lost the very name of God** and there was not to be found in all the world anyone who knew his Maker. Notwithstanding, God granted them earthly gifts, worldly wealth and prosperity, and He also bestowed on them wisdom so that they understood all earthly things and all the ways in which earth and sky were different from each other.

They observed that in many respects the earth and birds and beasts have the same nature and yet exhibit different behaviour, and they wondered what this signified. For instance, one could dig down into the earth on a mountain peak no deeper than one would in a low-lying valley and yet strike water; in the same way, in both birds and beasts, the blood lies as near to the surface of the skin of the head as of the foot. Another characteristic of the earth is that every year grass and flowers grow on it and that same year wither and die; similarly fur and feathers grow and die every year on beasts and birds. There is a third thing about the earth: when its surface is broken into and dug up, grass grows on the topsoil. Mountains and boulders they associated with the teeth and bones of living creatures, and so they looked on earth as in some way a living being with a life of its own.

They knew it was inconceivably ancient as years go, and by nature, powerful; it gave birth to all things and owned all that died, and for that reason they gave it a name and reckoned their descent from it. They also learned **from their ancestors** that the same

Ptolemy, World Map. This 15th-c. C.E. map according to Ptolemy shows the divisions of the world Snorri is talking about. The superimposed numbers indicate 1–Europe, 2–Africa, 3–Asia, and 4–Troy near the center of the world.

earth and sun and stars had been in existence for many centuries, but that the procession of the stars was unequal; some had a long journey, others a short one. From things like this they guessed that **there must be someone who ruled the stars,** who, if he desired, could put an end to their procession, and that he must be very powerful and strong.

They reckoned too, that, if he controlled the primal bodies; and they realized that, if he guided these, he must rule over the shining of the sun and the dew-fall and the growth of plants resultant on these, and the winds of the air and storms of the sea as well. They did not know where his kingdom was, but they believed that he ruled everything on earth and in the sky, heaven and the stars, the ocean and all weathers. In order that this might be related and kept in mind, they gave their own names to everything, but with the migrations of peoples and multiplication of languages this belief has changed in many ways. They understood everything in a material sense, however, since they had not been given spiritual understanding, and so they thought that everything had been made from some substance.

The world was divided into three parts. From south to west up to the Mediterranean was the part known as Africa, and the southern portion of this is so hot that everything there is burned by the sun. The second part, running from west to north up to the ocean, is called Europe or Énéa, and the northern half of this is so cold that no grass grows there and it is uninhabited. From north to east and down to the south is Asia, and these regions of the world have great beauty and magnificence; the earth yields special products like gold and precious stones. The centre of the world is there also, and just as the earth there is more fertile and in every way superior to that found elsewhere, so the human beings living there were endowed beyond their fellows with all manner of gifts—wisdom, strength, beauty, and every kind of ability.

Near **the centre of the world** where what we call Turkey lies, was built the most famous of all palaces and halls—Troy by name. That town was built on a much larger scale than others then in existence and in many ways with greater skill, so lavishly was it equipped. There were twelve kingdoms with one overking, and each kingdom contained many peoples. In the citadel were twelve chieftains and these excelled other men then living in every human fashion. One of the kings was called **Múnón** or Mennón. He married a daughter of the chief king **Priam** who was called Tróán, and they had a son named Trór—we call him **Thór**. He was brought up in Thrace by a duke called **Loricus** and, when he was ten years old, he received his father's arms. When he took his place amongst other men he was as beautiful to look at as ivory inlaid in oak; his hair was lovelier than gold.

At twelve years old he had come to his full strength and then he lifted ten bear pelts from the ground at once and killed his foster father Loricus with his wife Lóri or Glóri, and took possession of the realm of Thrace—we call that Thrúdheim.

After that he travelled far and wide exploring all the regions of the world and by himself overcoming all the berserks and giants and an enormous dragon and many wild beasts. In the northern part of the world he met with and married a prophetess called Sibyl whom we call **Sif.** I do not know Sif's genealogy but she was a most beautiful woman with hair like gold. Loridi, who resembled his father, was their son. **Loridi's son was Einridi,** his son Vingethór, his son Vingener, his son Módi, his son Magi, his son Seskef, his son Bedvig, his son Athra, whom we call Annar, his son Itrmann, his son Heremód, his son Skjaldun, whom we call Skjöld, his son Bíaf whom we call Bjár, his son Ját, his son Gudólf, his son Finn, his son Fríallaf whom we call Fridleif; he had a son named Vóden whom we call Odin; he was a man famed for his wisdom and every kind of accomplishment. His wife was called Frígída, whom we call **Frigg.**

Odin, and also his wife, had the gift of prophecy, and by means of this magic art he discovered that his name would be famous in the northern part of the world and honoured above that of all kings. For this reason he decided to set out on **a journey from**

⬤ The Geography of the Time

⬤ **Adventures of the Heroes of Troy**

"the centre of the world"—When people tried to figure out what the gods were like, they looked at the exploits of a famous and powerful family from Troy, and decided that these people must be gods.

Múnón One of the twelve kings of Troy.

Priam Chief King of Troy.

Thór Son of Múnón and the daughter of Priam.

Loricus Foster father of Thor.

Sif Thor's wife.

"Loridi's son was Einridi"—Snorri presents these long lists of names to show his readers how well he knows the story. Most of them do not matter for an understanding of the main point he is making here. See also note on "he had twelve names," p. 84.

Frigg Odin's wife.

Odin Here Snorri says that Odin is one of Thor's descendents, but according to the rest of the *Prose Edda*, Thor is descended from Odin, not vice versa. Snorri does this to illustrate the fact that, as he has said, ancient men understood the world imperfectly.

"a journey from Turkey"—As Snorri says, Troy is in Turkey. See map, Ch. 1, p. 9.

Turkey. He was accompanied by a great host of old and young, men and women, and they had with them many valuables.

Through whatever lands they went such glorious exploits were related of them that they were looked on as gods rather than men. They did not halt on their journey until they came to the north of the country now called Germany. There Odin lived for a long time taking possession of much of the land and appointing three of his sons to defend it. One was called Vegdeg; he was a powerful king and ruled over east Germany; his son was Vitrgils; his sons were Vitta, father of Heingest and Sigar, father of Svebdag, whom we call Svipdag. Odin's second son was called Beldeg, whom we call **Baldr;** he had the country now called Westphalia; his son was Brand; his son, Frjódigar, whom we call Fródi; his son, Freóvin; his son, Wigg; his son, Gevis, whom we call Gave. Odin's third son was called Sigi; his son, Rerir; this pair ruled over what is now called France, and the family known as Volsungar come from there. Great and numerous kindreds have come from all of them. Then Odin set off on his journey north and coming to the land called Reidgotaland took possession of everything he wanted in that country. He appointed his son Skjöld to govern there; his son was Fridleif; from thence has come the family known as Skjöldungar; they are kings of Denmark and what was then called Reidgotaland is now named Jutland.

Thereafter Odin went north to what is now called Sweden. **There was a king there called Gylfi** and, when he heard of the expedition of the **men of Asia,** as the Æsir were called, he went to meet them and offered Odin as much authority over his kingdom as he himself desired. Their travels were attended by such prosperity that, wherever they stayed in a country, that region enjoyed good harvests and peace, and everyone believed that they caused this, since the native inhabitants had never seen any other people like them for good looks and intelligence. The plains and natural resources of life in Sweden struck Odin as being favourable and he chose there for himself a townsite now called Sigtuna. There he appointed chieftains after the pattern of Troy, establishing twelve rulers to administer the laws of the land, and he drew up a code of law like that which had held in Troy and to which the Trojans had been accustomed. After that, he travelled north until he reached the sea, which they thought encircled the whole world, and placed his son over the kingdom now called Norway. Their son was called Saeming and, as it says in the Háleygjatal together with the earls and other rulers the kings of Norway trace their genealogies back to him. Odin kept by him the son called Yngvi, who was king of Sweden after him, and from him have come the families known as Ynglingar.

The Æsir and some of their sons married with the women of the lands they settled, and their families became so numerous in Germany and thence over the north that their language, that of the men of Asia, became the language proper to all these countries. From the fact that their genealogies are written down, men suppose that these names came along with this language, and that it was brought here to the north of the world, to Norway, Sweden, Denmark and Germany, by the Æsir. In England, however, there are ancient district and place names which must be understood as deriving from a different language.

The Deluding of Gylfi

King Gylfi ruled the lands that are now called Sweden. It is told of him that he gave a ploughland in his kingdom, the size four oxen could plough in a day and a night, to a beggar-woman as a reward for the way she had entertained him. **This woman, however, was of the family of the Æsir;** her name was Gefjon. From the north of Giantland she took four oxen and yoked them to a plough, but those were her sons by a giant. The plough went in so hard and deep that it loosened the land and the oxen dragged it westwards into the sea, stopping in a certain sound. There Gefjon set the land for good and

---

Baldr A son of Odin.

⊛ **The Travels of Odin**

"There was a king there called Gylfi"—Snorri introduces Gylfi, who will be his protagonist. The trip taken by Gylfi, the central event of the work, is mentioned here.

"men of Asia"—Odin's family are called the Æsir (AY-seer). It is the Æsir whom Gylfi decides to visit and learn about in the next section, "The Deluding of Gylfi."

⊛ **Odin Settles in Sweden**

⊛ **The Conquests of the Æsir**

"This woman . . . was of the family of the Æsir"—The Prologue explains that the Æsir are the family descended from Odin. The story of "The Deluding of Gylfi" has some of the same characters as the Prologue, but many of the details and relationships are different.

gave it a name, calling it Zealand. But **the place where the land had been torn up was afterwards a lake.** It is now known in Sweden as "The Lake." And there are as many bays in "The Lake" as there are headlands in Zealand. **As the poet Bragi the Old says:**

> Gefjon dragged with laughter
> from *Gylfi* liberal prince what made Denmark larger,
> so that beasts of draught
> the oxen reeked with sweat;
> four heads they had, eight eyes to boot 5
> who went before broad island-pasture
> ripped away as loot.

King Gylfi was a wise man and skilled in magic. He marvelled that the Æsir were so knowledgeable that everything came to pass by their will, and he wondered if that was on account of their own strength or whether the divinities they worshipped brought that about. **He set out on a secret journey** to Asgard, changing himself into the likeness of an old man by way of disguise. But the Æsir were wiser than he, in that they had foreknowledge. They saw his journey before he came, and worked spells against him. When he came into the stronghold, he saw a hall so lofty that he could scarcely see over it; its roofing was covered with golden shields like a shingled roof. So Thjódolf of Hvin says that Valhalla was roofed with shields:

> Fighting men showed prudence
> when with stones being pelted;
> they let the War-God's roofing
> glitter on their backs.

Gylfi saw a man in the doorway who was juggling with knives, of which he had seven in the air at a time. This man at once asked him his name. He said he was called **Gangleri** and that he had come a long way, and he requested a lodging for himself for the night, asking who owned the hall. The other replied that it was their king. "I can take you to see him, but you must ask him his name yourself"; and he wheeled round into the hall. Gylfi went after him, and at once the door shut on his heels. There he saw many rooms and a great number of people, some playing, others drinking, some had weapons and were fighting. As he looked about him much of what he saw puzzled him, and he said:

> At every door
> before you enter
> look around with care;
> you never know
> what enemies 5
> aren't waiting for you there.

He saw three high-seats one above the other, and a man seated in each of them. Then **he asked what names those chieftains had.** The man who had taken him inside answered that the one sitting on the lowest seat was a king called High One, the next was Just-as-high, and the topmost one was called Third. Then High One asked the stranger if he had any more business, although he was as welcome to food and drink as anyone else in High-hall.

[Gylfi] replied that **first of all he wanted to know** if there was anyone within who was a well-informed man. High One said that he would not get out safe and sound unless he was still better informed:

> Whilst you ask, stand forward please,
> the answerer shall sit at ease.

"the place where the land had been torn up was afterwards a lake"—This illustrates the process called rationalization of myth. (See Ch. 2, p. 20.)

"As the poet Bragi the Old says"—To make his point more convincing, Snorri includes quotes from poets and poems famous in his day.

"He set out on a secret journey"—The Prologue explains Gylfi's journey differently: "When he heard of the expedition of the men of Asia, as the Æsir were called, he went to meet them and offered Odin as much authority over his kingdom as he himself desired," p. 82.

"Gylfi saw a man in the doorway"—The king arrives at the hall of the Æsir.

Gangleri "The weary walker," the false name taken by Gylfi, who is being cautious in his handling of the tricky Æsir.

"he asked what names those chieftains had"—The Æsir say their names are High One, Just-as-high, and Third.

"first of all he wanted to know"—Gylfi and the Æsir argue about which of them is well-informed. They spend the rest of the poem in a riddle contest. (See box.)

THE CONTEST IN THE *PROSE EDDA*

The Rules: Gylfi will keep asking the Æsir questions. The Æsir have to answer Gylfi's questions. **Conditions:**

- Gylfi wins if they cannot answer his questions, or they run out of answers before he runs out of questions.
- The Æsir win if they answer all of Gylfi's questions, and he runs out of questions before they run out of answers.

Meaning: The Christian king Gylfi has gone to the land of the pagan gods. The contest is between Christian religion and the pagan Æsir, the gods of the "old religion." Gylfi defeats the Æsir, so Christianity triumphs over paganism.

The Challenge: "[Gylfi] replied that first of all he wanted to know if there was anyone within who was a well-informed man. High One said that he would not get out safe and sound unless he was still better informed. . . . Gylfi began his questioning."

The Struggle: Gylfi says, about halfway through the *Prose Edda*: "It seems to me I've asked you something no one is prepared to tell me about. I'll stand here all ears for the answer to my question. On the other hand, if you can't tell me what I am asking, I maintain I've got the better of you."

The Resolution: Gylfi wins. At the end of the *Prose Edda*, the High One says to Gylfi, "And now, if you have anything more to ask, I can't think how you can manage it, for I've never heard anyone tell more of the story of the world. . . . The next thing was that Gangleri heard a tremendous noise on all sides and turned about; and when he had looked all round him [he found] that he was standing in the open air on a level plain. He saw neither hall nor stronghold. Then he went on his way and coming home to his kingdom related the tidings he had seen and heard, and after him these stories have been handed down from one man to another."

The consequences: When Gylfi wins, the stronghold of the Æsir is destroyed and vanishes.

All-father Another name for Odin.

"he had twelve names"—Snorri has the Æsir provide long lists of names to demonstrate how well they can answer Gylfi's questions. Most of them do not matter for an understanding of the main point he is making here. See also note on "Loridi's son . . . ," p. 81.

"His greatest achievement . . . is the making of man"—This sets the stage for the account of creation, which is the main point of this part of the *Prose Edda*.

Gylfi began his questioning: "Who is the foremost or oldest of all the gods?" High One replied: "He is called **All-father** in our tongue, but in ancient Asgard **he had twelve names:** one is All-father; the second, Herran or Herjan; the third, Nikar or Hnikar; the fourth, Nikuz or Hnikud; the fifth, Fjölnir; the sixth, Oski; the seventh, Omi; the eighth, Biflidi or Biflindi; the ninth, Svidar; the tenth, Svidrir; the eleventh, Vidrir; the twelfth, Jálg or Jálk."

Then Gangleri asked: "Where is that god? What power has he? What great deeds has he done?"

High One said: "He lives for ever and ever, and rules over the whole of his kingdom and governs an things great and small."

Then Just-as-high said: "He created heaven and earth and the sky and all that in them is."

Then Third said: "**His greatest achievement, however, is the making of man** and giving him a soul which will live and never die, although his body may decay to dust or burn to ashes. All righteous men shall live and be with him where it is called Gimlé or Vingólf, but wicked men will go to Hel and thence to Niflhel that is down in the ninth world."

Then Gangleri said: "**What was he doing before heaven and earth were made?**"

High One replied: "At that time he was with the frost ogres."

Gangleri said: "What was the origin of all things? How did they begin? What existed before?"

High One answered: "As it says in the *Sibyl's Vision*:

> In the beginning
> not anything existed,
> there was no sand nor sea
> nor cooling waves;
> earth was unknown   5
> and heaven above
> only Ginnungagap
> was—there was no grass."

Then Just-as-high said: "It was many aeons before the earth was created that Niflheim was made, and in the midst of it is a well called Hvergelmir, and thence flow the rivers with these names: Svöl, Gunnthrá, Fjörm, Fimbulthul, Slíd, Hríd, Sylg, Ylg, Leipt, and Gjöll which is next to Hel's gate."

Then Third said: "The **first world to exist,** however, was Muspell in the southern hemisphere; it is light and hot and that region flames and burns so that those who do not belong to it and whose native land it is not, cannot endure it. The one who sits there at land's end to guard it is called Surt, he has a flaming sword, and at the end of the world he will come and harry and will vanquish all the gods and burn the whole world with fire. As it says in the Sibyl's Vision:

> Surt from the south comes
> with spoiler of twigs
> blazing his sword
> [like] sun of the Mighty Ones:
> mountains will crash down,   5
> troll-women stumble,
> men tread the road to Hel,
> heaven's rent asunder."

Gangleri asked: "How were things arranged before families came into existence or mankind increased?"

High One said: "When those rivers which are called Elivagar came so far from their source that the yeasty venom accompanying them hardened like slag, it turned into ice. Then when that ice formed and was firm, a drizzling rain that arose from the venom poured over it and cooled into rime, and one layer of ice formed on top of the other throughout Ginnungagap."

Then Just-as-high said: "That part of Ginnungagap which turned northwards became full of the ice and the hoar frost's weight and heaviness, and within there was drizzling rain and gusts of wind. But the southern part of Ginnungagap became light by meeting the sparks and glowing embers which flew out of the world of Muspell."

Then Third said: "Just as cold and all harsh things emanated from Niflheim, so everything in the neighbourhood of Muspell was warm and bright. Ginnungagap was as mild as windless air, and where the soft air of the heat met the frost so that it thawed and dripped, then, by the might of that which sent the heat, life appeared in the drops of running fluid and **grew into the likeness of a man.** He was given the name Ymir, but the frost ogres call him Aurgelmir, and that is where the families of frost ogres come from, as is said in the Shorter Sibyl's Vision:

> All the sibyls
> are from Vidólf

Andreas Tille, *Geysir Strokkur*. This photograph of volcanic activity in the Icelandic landscape shows the meeting of hot and cold that Snorri describes as the beginning of the creation of Ymir.

"What was he doing before heaven and earth were made?"—Snorri begins an elaborate explanation of creation that includes six different creation stories. He can do this in part because he has structured his story as a contest, and so the Æsir want to be very thorough in answering Gylfi's questions.

 Account 1: Creation Begins from Ginnungagap, the Void

"the first world to exist"—The stories starting here could be viewed as stages in a single story, or as six separate stories stitched together by Snorri. Several explicitly say that a human being is created, though, strictly speaking, only the last story results in the creation of human beings.

 Account 2: Ymir Is Created as Hot and Cold Meet in Ginnungagap

"grew into the likeness of a man"—Ymir's progeny are frost ogres, not men, but the text could as well be reporting the origins of human beings.

all the wizards from Vilmeid,
but the sorcerers from Svarthöfdi,
all the giants have come   5
from Ymir.

"And here is what the giant Vafthrudnir said [in answer to Odin's question]:

Whence first from giant-kin
came Aurgelmir the well-informed?
From the Elivágar
oozed drops of venom
that grew till they fashioned a giant,   5
all our kindred came from thence,
because of this birth
they are aye far too barbarous."

Then Gangleri said: "How did families grow thence? How was it arranged that men became numerous? Do you believe it was a god you were speaking about just now?"

High One replied: "In no wise do we consider he was a god. He and all his family were evil; we call them frost ogres. But it is said that while he slept he fell into a sweat; then there grew under his left arm a man and woman, and one of his legs got a son with the other, and that is where the families of frost ogres come from. We call that old frost ogre Ymir."

Then Gangleri said: "Where was Ymir's home and what did he live on?"

High One replied: "As soon as the frost thawed, it became a cow called Audhumla, and four rivers of milk ran from her teats, and she fed Ymir."

Then Gangleri asked: "What did the cow live on?" High One answered: "She licked the ice-blocks which were salty, and by the evening of the first day of the block-licking appeared a man's hair, on the second day a man's head, and on the third day **the whole man was there.** He was called Buri. He was handsome and tall and strong. He had a son called Bor, who married a woman called Bestla, daughter of the giant Bölthorn. They had three sons; the first Odin; the second, Vili; the third, Vé; and it is my belief that that Odin, in association with his brothers, is the ruler of heaven and earth. We think that that is his title; it is the name given to the man we know to be greatest and most famous, and you can take it that that is his [Odin's] title."

Then Gangleri asked: "How did they get on together? Was one group more powerful than the other?"

Then High One answered: "Bor's sons killed the giant Ymir, and when he fell, so much blood poured from his wounds that they drowned the whole tribe of frost ogres with it—except for one who escaped with his household; this one is known to the giants as Bergelmir. He climbed up on to his **lur** and his wife with him, and there they were safe. From them spring the families of frost ogres, as it is said here:

Innumerable years ago,
before the earth was made,
was born the giant Bergelmir;
the first thing I remember
was when they laid   5
that wise one down on a 'lur.'"

Then Gangleri said: "What did the sons of Bor do next, since you believe they are gods?"

High One said: "There is a great deal to be told about this. They took Ymir and carried him into the middle of Ginnungagap, and made the world from him: from his **blood** the

---

Account 3: A Man, a Woman, and Children Grow from Ymir

Account 4: A Cow Licks a Man from the Ice

"the whole man was there"— Once again, Buri, the creature created here, is not a man, but is the ancestor of the Æsir family of gods. However, he is described as if he were human, and this account may well hark back to a story of the origins of human beings.

lur Boat hollowed out of a tree trunk. It could also serve as a coffin.

sea and lakes, from his **flesh** the earth, from his **bones** the mountains; rocks and pebbles they made from his teeth and jaws and those bones that were broken."

Just-as-high said: "From the blood which welled freely from his wounds they fashioned the ocean, when they put together the earth and girdled it, laying the ocean round about it. To cross it would strike most men as impossible."

Third added: "They also took his **skull** and made the sky from it and set it over the earth with its four sides, and under each corner they put a dwarf. These are called: East, West, North, and South. Then they took the sparks and burning embers that were flying about after they had been blown out of Muspell, and placed them in the midst of Ginnungagap to give light to heaven above and earth beneath. They gave their stations to all the stars, some fixed in the sky; others [planetary] that had wandered at will in the firmament were now given their appointed places and the paths in which they were to travel. So it is said in ancient poems that from that time sprang the reckoning of days and years, as it is said in the Sibyl's Vision:

> The sun did not know
> where she had her home,
> the moon did not know
> what might he had,
> stars did not know   5
> where their stations were.

Thus it was before this was done."

Then Gangleri said: "Great tidings I'm hearing now. That was a marvelous piece of craftsmanship, and skillfully contrived. How was the earth fashioned?"

Then High One answered: "It is round, and surrounding it lies the deep sea, and on the strand of that sea they gave lands to the families of giants to settle, but inland they [Bor's sons] built a stronghold round the world on account of the hostility of the giants; for this stronghold they used Ymir's eyebrows, and they called it **Midgard.** They took his brains too and flung them up into the air and made from them the clouds, as it is said here:

> From Ymir's flesh
> the earth was made
> and from his blood the seas,
> crags from his bones,
> trees from his **hair,**   5
> and from his skull the sky.

> From his eyebrows
> the blessed gods
> made Midgard for the sons of men,
> and from his **brains**   10
> were created
> all storm-threatening clouds."

Then Gangleri said: "It seems to me they made great progress when heaven and earth were created and the sun and the stars given their stations and arrangements made for day and night, but **whence came the men** who inhabit the world?"

Then High One answered: "When they were going along the sea-shore, the sons of Bor found two trees and they picked these up and created men from them. The first gave them spirit and life; the second, understanding and power of movement; the third, form, speech, hearing and sight. They gave them clothes and names. The man

This carving represents the world tree, Yggdrasil, whose branches spread all over the world and whose roots stretch to the court of the Æsir as well as to the land of the dead. (See p. 221.) In the previous story the sons of Bor make human beings out of trees, giving them a kinship with the framework that undergirds the universe.

 Account 5: Bor's Sons Make the World from Ymir's Body

Ymir's blood The sea.

Ymir's flesh The earth.

Ymir's bones The mountains.

Ymir's skull The sky.

Midgard A fortress around the world of humans to protect it from the giants. It was built from Ymir's eyebrows.

Ymir's hair Trees.

Ymir's brains Clouds.

 Account 6: Bor's Sons Make Men and Women from Trees

"whence came the men?"— Unlike the account of creation in Hesiod's *Theogony* (Ch. 3, p. 29ff.), the Icelandic creation story includes human beings. Unlike the Biblical creation story, however, it is not focused on the relationship between the deity and human beings (Ch. 5, p. 50).

Asgard A fortress for the gods, built in the middle of the world, near Troy.

was called Ask and the woman Embla; and from them have sprung the races of men who were given Midgard to live in. Next they built a stronghold for themselves in the middle of the world, which is called **Asgard**—we call it Troy. There the gods and their kindred lived, and from then on came to pass many events and memorable happenings both in heaven and earth. There is a place there called Hlidskjalf, and when Odin sat there on his high seat he saw over the whole world and what everyone was doing, and he understood everything he saw. His wife, the daughter of Fjörgvin, was named Frigg, and from that family has come the kindred that inhabited ancient Asgard and those kingdoms belonging to it; we call the members of that family the Æsir and they are all divinities. He [Odin] may well be called All-father for this reason—he is the father of all the gods and men and of everything that he and his power created. The earth was his daughter and his wife; by her he had his first son, Asa-Thor. Might and strength were Thor's characteristics, by these he dominates every living creature."

Further Reading

Davidson, H. R. Ellis. *Gods and Myths of Northern Europe*. London: Penguin Books Ltd., 1964.

Sturluson, Snorri. *The Prose Edda: Tales from Norse Mythology*. Trans. Jean I. Young. Berkeley: University of California Press, 1954.

Native American Creation Stories from the Southwestern United States

8

WHAT TO EXPECT . . . In this chapter, look for a new kind of mythological story, the working version. These myths from Native Americans of the Southwestern United States were collected by ethnographers, not literary texts like those in the Graeco-Roman and Norse traditions. They reflect an ongoing tradition of rituals practiced by a community, and thus can be connected with the discussion of ritual in Part 4.

You might compare the stories in this chapter to creation myths in the Judaeo-Christian tradition, in which deities create the universe, and then humans are placed in the world and given dominion over nature. Native American stories, like the stories in Genesis, place humans at the center: they actually help create their physical world. In reading these stories, you may want to consider your own cultural values and expectations and how they affect your response.

The cultural elements in this chapter will also be found in Chapter 21 on Raven, a Native-American trickster, and in Chapter 43, which includes a story from Leslie Marmon Silko that gives a contemporary perspective on Native-American mythology.

It is often amazing to American students reared in the Judaeo-Christian tradition, especially those living in the eastern United States, that the Native Americans of the Southwest celebrate a creation myth that is quite different in many ways from the events reported in Genesis.

In Genesis, humans are given dominion over the earth and its nonhuman creatures that are thus considered inferior to humans. Conversely, Native American peoples see themselves as participants rather than overseers. They see this world and their particular homelands as the culmination of their journeys, rather than as a result of losing paradise. We can compare this with various aspects of our Judaeo-Christian tradition. Hesiod's account of the Ages of Mankind represents the world as having fallen away from a perfect or golden race (Ch. 3, p. 39ff.). In the Yahwist-Elohist version of creation in Genesis (Ch. 5, p. 53), Adam and Eve were created by God, were given dominion over the earth, broke the commandment that had been given them regarding eating the fruit of the tree of the knowledge of good and evil, and were expelled from the Garden of Eden to a life of pain and toil. According to the view in Genesis, then, living on the earth as we know it is a punishment, compared with Eden. While on this earth, however, we can be satisfied that we are privileged over all other creatures. This has been interpreted by some as having the right to dispose of nature as we please.

In contrast, Native Americans view this world not as a punishment but as the place where their destinies will be fulfilled, not by domination but by maintaining a balance achieved by living in harmony with themselves and other humans, as well as with animals and the exterior world.

Paul Zolbrod, who provided the version of the Navajo Creation Story in this chapter, stresses the need for us to try to understand Native American culture and literature on its own terms, not according to Judaeo-Christian expectations. He is cautious against oversimplifying and encourages attention to the panoply of Native American groups. In the Introduction to *Diné Bahane'*, he also discusses a dilemma common to almost all research into myths: when the story remains in the oral tradition, it is constantly changing; when someone writes it down or transcribes what a storyteller is saying, it is no longer alive. Zolbrod's view of the value of his own work seems to apply to the dilemma. On the one hand, at least some of the belief group appreciate an apparently durable record of their beliefs; on the other, the text is "fossilized." He writes: "No text could ever represent the fluid, all-encompassing narrative cycle. . . . At best a printed work like this one would be to the whole dynamic tradition what a fossilized pawprint would be to some giant prehistoric creature typical of its species and total environment" (19–20).

The creation stories of the Zuni, Hopi, and Navajo excerpted in this chapter are by far not the only groups or stories in the Southwestern United States. Several other cultures live in the area covered by New Mexico, Arizona, Utah, and Colorado. These include a broad range of Puebloan peoples, such as the communities of the Acoma and Laguna; Apache communities that extend from northern New Mexico and the southern Rio Grande into the White Mountains of Arizona; Pimas, Papagos, and Yaquis of the Sonora Desert; and the Havasupi community in the area along the western Colorado River.

Generally, these creation myths hold that life began below ground and that the first creatures were prehuman, insect-like beings. They developed physically and socially into recognizable ancestors of the inhabitants of the contemporary community. And like most myths, they reveal the social and religious belief structures of the engendering communities.

The Zuni Emergence Myth

Ruth Fulton Benedict (1887–1948) was a cultural anthropologist who published studies on the relationships of folklore and religion and of culture and personality. She began her career as an English major at Vassar College and later went on to study anthropology with the great Franz Boas at Columbia University. Benedict's first major publication was called *Patterns of Culture.* It reflected what she termed *cultural relativism,* the theory that the study of any culture must take place within the context of that culture. For anthropologists, this meant trying to understand the whole life of a people, not just using them as a source of attractive or unusual artifacts. For students of mythology, cultural relativism means reading mythological texts as part of a developing understanding of the society, beliefs, and customs of a people. Benedict collected this version of the Zuni emergence tale during the summers of 1922 and 1923.

Any version of a myth represents some sort of editing and refining process. The myths we have considered in the preceding Greek, Roman, Biblical, Mesopotamian, and Icelandic sections are literary versions of myths. In contrast, the Native American myths presented in this section are working versions collected by ethnographers. This means that a scholar or student of a culture lived among the people and perhaps learned their language. He or she found people to recite the myths and stories of the people or tried to witness their ceremonies and rituals. The ethnographer then wrote down the myth, presenting it in translation to other scholars in her or his home country.

In selecting myths, versions of myths, and even translations for Native American words, the ethnographer makes choices which will affect our perception of the myth. The myths presented in this way reflect the stories told by the peoples they come from, but they also represent the writing style and personality of the person who collected them. An important difference that is apparent when we compare versions of collected myths and rituals is that they may vary widely in how explicit their language is. For example, the Zuni emergence myth collected by Benedict describes bodily functions more graphically than we are used to in the sacred stories of Western society. We cannot be sure if this is because the stories we are more familiar with were "cleaned up" before living memory by persons unknown, or because these Native American stories have a quality which our tradition does not possess. (Zolbrod also thought this was overinterpretation.)

The Zuni are Pueblo Indians who call their ancestors *Anasazi,* meaning "the Old Ones." We can still see remnants of the highly organized Anasazi society in the extensive multistory stone structures in places like Chaco Canyon, Arizona, and the cliff dwellings on Mesa Verde, Colorado.

The expertly engineered irrigation systems, the sophisticated highway networks between settlements, and the vibrant relationship between their society and their myths indicate that these people are intrinsically connected with the practical side of life as well as with the spiritual. Anasazi rituals performed today still include chanting their sacred narratives and performing dances that portray their union with nature and emphasis on maintaining balance and harmony in life.

Rituals are active, formal, dramatic presentations of sacred beliefs. The stories which belong to the myth are acted out so that young people and old can learn the myths and understand their timeless value to the group. In addition, acting out the myth provides a more intense sense of participation and ownership, even to those who are already quite familiar with the story. Paul Zolbrod speaks of the ceremonial life engendered by ritual, which involves ingathering found not only in ceremonial gatherings such as the Native American Church, but in seemingly more secular events such as powwows and festivals.

According to the Zuni creation story, the lowest world is populated by larval creatures with no discernible human qualities. Two small boys who are children of the Sun create access to this world using prayersticks, and they give the larval creatures the human physical traits of fingers, toes, a mouth, and an anus. The creatures travel vertically upward through four worlds before finding their ideal home on earth.

The excerpt of Benedict's version of the creation story begins with the fourth world.

Part of the Cliff Palace at Mesa Verde showing dwellings and kivas. The kivas may be distinguished by their circular shape. Basketmaker and Pueblo Indian, 12th c. C.E. Mesa Verde, Colorado, U.S.A.

The Zuni Emergence Myth

They were living in the fourth world. It was dark. They could not see one another. They stepped upon one another, they urinated upon one another, they spat upon one another. They could not breathe.

They lived there for four days. The Sun took pity on them.

He saw that the world was covered with hills and springs but **there were no people to give him prayersticks.** He thought, "My people shall come to the daylight world."

The earth was covered with mist. He threw his rays into the mist and there in the world his sons stood up. They were two boys. Their hair was tangled, they had long noses, long cheeks. Next day, they played together. The third day the younger brother said to the elder, "Let us go and look for beautiful places. I will go to **Corn Mountain** and you shall go to the south **Where the Cotton Hangs**."

The third day they went. The younger looked over the world and he saw that nobody lived there. He said to himself, "**Tomorrow we shall be old enough to work.**"

This excerpt comes from: Ruth Benedict, *Zuni Mythology*, Vol. I.*

"They lived there for four days"— These days are like those in Genesis: general designations for a period of time.

"there were no people to give him prayersticks"—Creators are often motivated by a desire to be worshipped.

"Corn Mountain" and "Where the Cotton Hangs"—These are actual places. Benedict tells us that they are local shrines today.

"Tomorrow we shall be old enough to work"—The children are simultaneously gods, because they are descended from the sun, and humans. This is an example of paratactic writing (Ch. 2, p. 18). Here the children already mention their own offspring.

* Ruth Benedict, *Zuni Mythology*, Vol. I, excerpts from pages 1–6. Copyright © 1935. Reprinted by permission of Columbia University Press.

When the next day came he called his brother. Elder Brother came and said, "What is it that you have to say that you have called me?" Younger Brother said, "We are four days old and we are old enough to work. This is a good world and nobody lives in it. Let us go to the southwest. There below the people are living in the fourth world. They are our fathers and mothers, our sons and daughters.

The two went to the southwest and they came to the entrance to the fourth world. They went in and came to the first world. There was just a little light there. They came to the second world. It was dark. They came to the third world. It was darker still. They came to the fourth world. It was black. The people could not see each other. They felt one another with their hands and recognized their faces. They said, "Some stranger has come. Where is it that you have come from? It is our fathers, the bow priests."

They ran to feel them and they said, "Our fathers, you have come. Teach us how to get out of this place. We have heard of our father Sun and we wish to see him." The two answered, "We have come to bring you to the other world where you can see him. Will you come with us?" The people answered, "Yes, we wish to go. It is nasty here. We wish to see our father Sun. We have been waiting for someone to show us the way, but our brothers must come too. As the priest of the north says, so let it be." **The two "needed" the priest of the north.** He came and said, "I have come. What is it that you wish to ask?" "We want you to come into the daylight world."

"Yes, we shall be glad to come. We want to see our father Sun, but my brothers must come too. As the priest of the east says, so let it be."

[Because repetition is a feature of oral tradition, this section, like the others in this myth-ritual, is repeated for the east, south, and west.]

They said to them, "Do you know how we can get to the daylight world?" Younger Brother went to the north. He took the seeds of the **pine** tree and planted them. He turned about and when he looked where he had planted, the pine had already grown. He turned again and when he looked at the tree, the branches were grown to full size. He tore off a branch and brought it back to the people. He went to the west and planted the seeds of the **spruce.** He turned about and when he looked where he had planted, the spruce had already grown. He turned again and when he looked at the tree, the branches were grown to full size. He tore off a branch and brought it back to the people. He went to the south and planted the seeds of the silver spruce. He turned about and when he looked where he had planted the seeds, the **silver spruce** had already grown.

He turned again and when he looked at the tree the branches were grown to full size. He tore off a branch and brought it back to the people. He went to the east and planted the seeds of the **aspen.** He turned about and when he looked where he had planted the seeds, the aspen had already grown. He turned again and when he looked, the branches had grown to full size. He tore off a branch and brought it back to the people. He said, "This is all. We are ready to go up to the upper world. My people, make yourselves ready. Take those things that you live by."

The bow priests took the long prayerstick they had made from the pine of the north. They set it in the earth. The people went up the prayerstick and came into the third world. There was rumbling like thunder. It was lighter in that world and the people were blinded. The bow priests said, "Have we all come out?" They answered,

"Yes. Is it here that we are going to live?" They answered, "Not yet. This is not the upper world." They lived there four days. The bow priests took the crook of the west that they had made from the spruce. They set it in the earth. There was rumbling like thunder and the people came up into the second world. It was twilight there and the people were blinded. The bow priests said, "Have we all come out?" "Yes. Is it here that we shall live?" "Not yet." They remained there four days and the two took the long

"The two 'needed' the priest of the north."—People want to go to the higher world, but must ask the priest.

"pine . . . spruce . . . silver spruce . . . aspen"—These trees correspond to the four directions. They are also kinds of trees indigenous to the region.

"The bow priests took the long prayerstick"—The twins here are functioning as bow priests. The bow priests preside at the ceremony associated with this myth. The Zuni pueblo still maintains a Bow Priest Society.

Petroglyphs at Newspaper Rock State Historic Monument, Utah, depict many kinds of images, both abstract and representative of animals and people.

prayerstick that they had made from the silver spruce of the south and set it in the earth. There was rumbling like thunder and the people came up into the first world. It was light like red dawn. They were dazzled and they said, "Is it here that we shall live?" They answered, "Not yet." The people were sad. They could see each other quite plain. Their bodies were covered with dirt and with ashes. They were stained with spit and urine and they had green slime on their heads. Their hands and feet were webbed and they had tails and no mouths or exits. They remained there four days. The bow priests took the long prayerstick they had made from the aspen of the east and they set it in the earth. There was rumbling like thunder and the people came up into the daylight world. The two bow priests came first and after them those who carried the medicine bundles, the ka'etone, tcu'etone, mu'etone and le'etone. When they came into the sunlight the tears ran down their cheeks.

Younger Brother said to them, "Turn to the sun and look full at our father Sun no matter how bright it is." They cried out for it hurt them and their tears ran to the ground. Everywhere they were standing the sun's flowers (sunflowers and buttercups) sprang up from the tears caused by the sun. The people said, "Is this the world where we shall live?" "Yes, this is the last world. Here you see our father Sun." They remained there four days and they went on.

They came to Slime Spring (Awico). They lived there four days and the bow priests said, "It is time our people learned to eat." They took the corn of the witch and they put it in the fields to **itsumawe.**

When it had grown they harvested it and the men took it home to their wives. They smelled it, but they had no way to eat. The bow priests were sad and Younger Brother said, "Elder Brother, the people have made itsumawe and I am sorry for them that they cannot eat. Let us cut them so that they can enjoy food." Elder Brother agreed and his brother said, "When everyone is asleep we shall go to each house and cut mouths in their faces." That night after the people were asleep **the bow priests took their (ceremonial) stone knives** and sharpened them with a red whetstone. They went to each house. They cut each face where the skin of the mouth was puffed up.

The knife made the lips red from the red of the whetstone. They went home. When the sun rose the people found that they had mouths. They said, "What makes our faces so flat?" They began to get hungry and the men brought in corn and water and they ate. That night they were uncomfortable because they had no exits. They could not defecate. Younger Brother thought, "We should cut the anus so that they can defecate." He went to his brother and he said, "These people should have the anus. Let us cut it tonight when they are asleep." Elder Brother agreed and they took the smaller stone knives and sharpened them on a soot whetstone. They cut the anus for all the people and the soot colored those parts black. Next morning the people were uncomfortable and they went outside. They thought they had broken open in their sleep.

They tried to break up the corn so that they could eat it better. They took whetstones in their webbed hands and rubbed the corn on the hearthstone. They mixed porridge and made corncakes. After they had made it, it was hard to clean their hands for they were webbed and Younger Brother said to Elder Brother, "I am sorry for my people that their hands are webbed. Let us cut their fingers apart." Elder Brother agreed and that night they took the larger stone knife and cut the webbed hands and feet of the people. In the morning the people were frightened but **when the sun had risen** they did not notice any more.

They worked better with fingers and toes. The next day Younger Brother said to the older, "Our people have been cut. They still have tails, and horns. Let us cut them away." Elder Brother agreed and they took the smaller stone knife. They went to each house and cut the tails and horns from their people. In the morning the people were frightened but when the sun rose they did not mind any more. They were glad that

itsumawe—To increase by magic. This shows us that the Zuni view the earth as sacred, the source of magical power.

"the bow priests took their . . . stone knives"—The young brothers are cocreators of their people. They use recognized ceremonial tools to adapt the creatures for life in this world.

"when the sun had risen"—Since the Sun is their father, the people are comforted by him.

"they were finished"—The metamorphosis into human shape is complete. Here again, the emphasis is on the twins as creators, a frequent motif in American Indian myths.

"It is better for us to separate"—Early recognition of the ability of the earth to support a limited number of people.

Migration story

"they started toward the east"—Most tribes have a migration story. The story typically names the clans and explains the location of their homeland.

"to find where the middle is"—Finding the middle is indicative of the Native American emphasis on harmony and balance in all aspects of life.

Water Spider The spider is most often a helper to the Anasazi. Here it is the Water Spider finding the center of the earth. In other parts of the Zuni Emergence Myth, Spider Grandmother is a nurturer and helper.

Information in this section is based on: Harold Courlander, *The Fourth World of the Hopi.*

"donor"—For a Proppian view of the role of this figure in folktales, see Ch. 34, p. 507.

"evil lives"—Because humans see failings in themselves and others, their myths must explain the presence of evil in their world. According to Hopi mythology, powakas, or evil ones, are shut out by society.

sipapuni The opening between worlds that allows passage from one world to another.

they were finished. They stayed there four days. They came to Watercress Spring. They stayed there four days.

They came to Prayerstick Place. The bow priest said, "Our people are too many. **It is better for us to separate.** Who will go to the south side and who will go to the middle?"

The next day **they started toward the east.** The people of Le'etone went to the north to Rope Hill and then to the east to the Nutria spring and turned back again toward the west. The people who were seeking the middle had come to Matsaka. They heard the Le'etone coming at Eastern Road and went out to meet them. They brought the Le'etone back with them into Matsaka and that is why salt weed always grows there. That is why Nutria is cold and the wind is from the east.

At Matsaka, each family built a house for themselves. The bow priests said, "It is time to try again **to find where the middle is.**" He called the Water Spider and he put his heart down at Matsaka. He touched the corners of the east and north, but he could not touch the corners of the west and the south. He said, "You are very near. I will go and find the place where my arms will touch the horizon in all four directions." The bow priests went with him.

Water Spider said, "I have to go back. Let us try Halona (ant place). My heart will be on an anthill." He stretched out his arms and legs and touched the horizon at the north, west, south and east. He was in the middle of the world. He said, "My people shall live here always. They will never be overthrown for their hearts will not be to one side (of the world)."

They returned to Matsaka and they said, "We have found the place. We shall go there. We have found the middle of the world." They left their houses standing in Matsaka and went to Halona to the middle of the world.

The Hopi Creation Story

Like the Zuni Emergence Myth, the Hopi Creation Story represents the first creatures as passing through four worlds before finding their ideal home. This myth, however, postulates the creation of the First World by Tawa, the Sun Spirit, who regretted the emptiness. This first world is again underground, the creatures are again insect-like, and a leader emerges to initiate the journey. This time, it is Spider Grandmother, a traditional helper and **donor** in the Proppian sense.

Daniel O. Stolpe, *Coyote Howling at the Moon*. It is easy to see from the vigorous motion captured by the artist why the Hopi see Coyote as fiercely flinging paint at the sky. Coyote is a creator and a trickster. For more on this combination, see Ch. 21, p. 295.

As they ascend to the second world, the insects evolve into higher-level creatures such as dogs, bears, and coyotes. And a similar evolution on the way to the third world replaces tails, fur, and webbed fingers with human physical characteristics.

But this second world has no light or warmth, and powakas have been causing people to lead **evil lives.** Spider Grandmother leads the group to the third world. Medicine men create a clay catbird and breathe life into it so that it can find the **sipapuni,** or entry hole, to the land beyond the sky. All help: Spider Woman's grandsons look for the sipapuni; chipmunk plants bamboo that will grow high enough to reach the hole; all sing in order to make the plants grow.

When they reach the fourth world, the boys' ball playing causes the earth to harden into mountains. But the earth is still cold and dark. Again all help to create their world: they build disks made of leather stretched over a wooden form and paint them with egg yolk and dyes so that they will shine; then they sing the disks up into the sky. So long as they sing, the disks rise, and the sun and the moon are soon in place. A coyote finds the paint bucket after they have finished; he swings it so fiercely that flecks reach the sky and become stars. Now that there are heavenly bodies to warm and light the plants, the corn will grow and feed and nourish the group.

Since the people cannot all cultivate the immediate area, they disperse as destined by the ritual of **selecting the corn.** Each clan chooses a hidden ear of various types of corn. The growing conditions required by that type determine where the group will settle.

"selecting the corn"—This represents why particular crops grow in particular regions. See Campbell's cosmological function of myth in Ch. 1, p. 8.

Diné Bahane': The Navajo Creation Story

The Navajo are descendants of the Athapaskans, not of the Anasazi like the Zuni, Hopi, and the other Pueblos. They are related to groups living much farther north and seem to have traveled south from Canada more than 500 years ago. Today we find Athapaskan communities in Alaska, the Yukon Territory in Canada, northern California, and in the United States Southwest; the Apaches and other neighbors of the Navajo are also Athapaskan. Paul Zolbrod, author of the following text, notes that the Navajo creation cycle bears a resemblance to the other Athapaskan stories, and most closely to the Myths of the Zia. In the Four Corners region, where Utah, Colorado, Arizona, and New Mexico meet, the Navajos are neighbors of the Pueblo groups. As an indication of the related belief systems of these communities, we might note that the Navajo creation myths are similar in interesting ways to the Zuni Emergence Tale, showing also that similar motifs are widespread among Native American groups. In the Navajo myth as in the other Native American stories we have been considering, the primary movement of creation is upward from beneath the earth. Each world has a sky that is represented as a hard shell. As in Hopi myth, those traveling upward through the successive worlds must find an opening—*sipapuni* or slit—that allows passage from one world to another. Rather than climbing, as in the Zuni story, the Navajo Air-Spirit People fly. In this story, the people receive much help in finding their earthly home. A swallow leads them to the second world, while the Wind and the Red Wind help guide them.

Students from the tradition of Western philosophy and religion might be tempted to compare the Fall of Adam and Eve and their expulsion from the Garden of Eden with the misdeeds of the Navajo Air-Spirit People and their expulsion from each world into the next. However, in the study of mythology and culture, it is important to consider the stories of a community from within their own belief system. The Navajo word *hozho,* which is difficult to translate with a single English word, is the essential principle necessary for living in society. It incorporates qualities inherent in the words "beauty," "balance," and "harmony." Just as Coyote and other tricksters risk disrupting the balance by insisting on their self-serving individualism, the insect people of the Navajo Creation Story are forced to move from world to world because they repeatedly defy the basic harmonious relationship that must exist between the male and female couple that unites in procreation. (For more on tricksters, see Chs. 21–24.)

The story begins by describing four streams, each flowing in a different direction, then naming a place located in each of the four directions. Then insects are introduced. This excerpt is from this first section, "The Emergence." It represents only a small part of the cycle, which covers the group's migrations, their encounters with threats and overcoming monsters, the creation of the Earth Surface People from an ear of corn, and the bringing together of the clans.

The Navajo Creation Story

These excerpts come from: Paul Zolbrod, *Diné Bahane'*: The Navajo Creation Story.*

"Many of the men were to blame, but so were many of the women"—The story suggests equal responsibility between the sexes for human transgression. Compare the presentation of Eve in the Bible and Pandora in Greek myth.

"They tried to stop, but they could not help themselves"—Social conflict, or the absence of solidarity, is the result of not being able to control what one should be able to. Control is a valued quality in Navajo society, and sexual excesses are often responsible for disharmony or social disorder.

"But the people still could not help it"—This account suggests a shrewd understanding of human psychology: just wanting to change behavior is not always enough to effect a change.

"a high, insurmountable wall of water"—A sudden wall of water comes from all directions at once. If the people were not able to fly, they would have perished.

We call them Air-Spirit People. For they are people unlike the five-fingered earth people who come into the world today, live on the ground for a while, die at a ripe old age, and then leave the world. They are people who travel in the air and fly swiftly like the wind and dwell nowhere else but here.

It is also said that the Air-Spirit People fought among themselves. And this is how it happened. They committed adultery, one with another. **Many of the men were to blame, but so were many of the women.**

They tried to stop, but they could not help themselves. The One That Grabs Things In the Water, who was chief in the east, complained, saying this: "They must not like it here," he said. And the Blue Heron, who was chief in the south, also complained: "What they do is wrong," he complained.

The Frog, who was chief in the west, also complained. But he took his complaint directly to the Air-Spirit people, having this to say to them: "You shall no longer be welcome here where I am chief," is what he said.

"That is what I think of you." And from his home in the north where he was chief, the Winter Thunder spoke to them also.

"Nor are you welcome here!" he, too, said to them.

"Go away from this land."

"Leave at once!"

But the people still could not help it: one with another they continued to commit adultery. And when they did it yet another time and then argued with each other again, The One That Grabs Things In the Water would no longer speak to them. The Blue Heron would no longer speak to them. Likewise the Frog would say nothing to them. And the Winter Thunder refused to say anything.

Four days and four nights passed. Then the same thing happened. Those who lived in the south repeated their sins. Finally they went to the north to speak with the Winter Thunder. He, too, drove them away, breaking his silence to say this to them:

"None of you shall enter here," he said to them.

"I do not wish to listen to you.

"Go away, and keep on going!"

[Each of the events in this narrative is reported four times, once for each of the places or characters involved. From here on, however, we will condense our retelling to only the first event in the series of four.]

But the people did not leave right away. For four nights the women talked and squabbled, each blaming the other for what had happened. And for four nights the men squabbled and talked. They, too, blamed one another.

At the end of the fourth night as they were at last about to end their meeting, they all noticed something white in the east. They also saw it in the south. It appeared in the west, too. And in the north it also appeared. It looked like an endless chain of white mountains. They saw it on all sides. It surrounded them and they noticed that it was closing in on them rapidly. It was **a high, insurmountable wall of water!** And it was flowing in on them from all directions, so that they could escape neither to the east nor to the west; neither to the south nor to the north could they escape. So, having nowhere else to go, they took flight. Into the air they went. Higher and higher they soared, it is said.

* Paul G. Zolbrod. *Diné Bahane'*, 36–42, 45–47, 49–52. Copyright © 1984. Used by permission of the University of New Mexico Press.

It is also said that they circled upward until they reached the smooth, hard shell of the sky overhead. When they could go no higher they looked down and saw that water now covered everything. They had nowhere to land either above or below.

Suddenly **someone with a blue head** appeared and called to them: "Here," he called to them. "Come this way. Here to the east there is a hole!" They found that hole and entered. One by one they filed through to the other side of the sky. And that is how they reached the surface of the second world.

The blue-headed creature was a member of the Swallow People. It was they who lived up there. While the first world had been red, this world was blue. The swallows lived in blue houses, which lay scattered across a broad, blue plain. Each blue house was cone-shaped; each tapered toward the top where there was a blue entry hole. At first the Swallow People watched them silently. Nobody from either group said anything to any member of the other. Finally, when darkness came and the exiled Air-Spirit People made camp for the night, the blue swallows left.

In the morning the insect people from the world below decided that someone should explore this new world. So they sent a plain locust and a white locust to the east, instructing them to look for people like themselves. Two days came and went before the locusts returned. They said that they had traveled for a full day. And as darkness fell they reached what must have been the end of the world. For they came upon the rim of a great cliff that rose out of an abyss whose bottom could not be seen. Both coming and going, they said, they found no people, no plants, no rivers, no mountains. They found nothing but bare, blue, level ground.

Next the two messengers were sent south to explore. Again, two days came and went while they were gone. And they again reported that after traveling for a full day they reached the end of the world. And they reported again that neither in going nor in coming back could they find people or plants, mountains or rivers.

[This account is repeated for west and north.]

After the scouts had returned from their fourth trip, the Swallow People visited the camp of the newcomers. And they asked why they had sent someone to the east to explore.

This is what the insect people from the lower world replied: "We sent them out to see what was in the land," they replied.

"We sent them out to see if there were people here like ourselves."

Then the swallows asked this:

"What did your scouts tell you?" they asked.

To which the newcomers replied this way:

"They told us that they reached the end of the world after traveling a full day," they replied.

"They told us that wherever they went in this world they could find neither people nor plants. Neither rivers nor mountains could they find."

To all of which the Swallow People then had this to say:

"Your couriers spoke the truth," they then said.

"But their trips were not necessary."

"Had you asked us what the land contained, **we would have told you.**

"Had you asked us where this world ended, we would have told you.

Hopi Jeddito black-on-yellow bowl. Pottery such as this often has a painted decoration representing what might be called migration maps of the various clans of Southwest U.S. Native Americans.

"someone with a blue head"—The stranger guides them to a *sipapuni*. The story of the head is repeated for each region. The color of the head is always that of its entire world: red, blue, white, yellow.

"we would have told you"—The Swallow People act as tutelaries for the Air-Spirit People.

"We could have saved you all that time and all that trouble.

"Until you arrived here, no one besides us has ever lived in this world. We are the only ones living here."

The newcomers then had this suggestion to make to the swallows:

"You are like us in many ways," they suggested.

"You understand our language.

"Like us you have legs; like us you have bodies, like us you have wings; like us you have heads.

"Why can't we become friends?"

To which the swallows replied:

"Let it be as you say," they replied.

"You are welcome here among us."

So it was that both sets of people began to treat each other as members of one tribe. **They mingled one among the other** and called each other by the familiar names. They called each other grandparent and grandchild, brother and sister; they called each other father and son, mother and daughter.

For twenty-three days they all lived together in harmony. But on the night of the twenty-fourth day, one of the strangers became too free with the wife of the swallow chief.

Next morning, when he found out what had happened the night before, the chief had this to say to the strangers:

"We welcomed you here among us," was what he had to say to them.

"We treated you as friends and as kin.

"And this is how you return our kindness!

"No doubt **you were driven from the world below** for just such disorderly acts.

"Well! you must leave this world, too; we will have you here no longer.

"Anyhow, this is a bad land. There is not enough food for all of us.

"People are dying here every day from hunger. Even if we allowed you to stay, you could not live here very long."

When they heard the swallow chief's words, the locusts took flight. And all the others followed. Having nowhere else to go, they flew skyward.

Into the air they went. Higher and higher they soared. They circled upward until they reached the smooth, hard shell of the sky overhead, it is said.

And like the sky of the world below this one seemed to have no opening. When the insect people reached it they flew around and around, having nowhere to land either above or below.

But as they circled, **they noticed a white face** peering at them. This was the face of *Nilch'i*. In the language of the White Man he would be called Wind. And they heard him cry to them:

"Here!" he cried.

"Here to the south you will find an opening.

"Come this way."

So off they flew to the south, and soon they found a slit in the sky slanting upward in a southerly direction. One by one they flew through it to the other side. And that is how they reached the surface of the third world.

[The incidents of the Swallow People are repeated for the Grasshopper People. Their story involves the appearance of the yellow head and the yellow world.]

It is also said that they again had to circle around for quite some time, looking in vain for some way to get through the sky overhead. Finally they heard a voice and they noticed a red head peering at them. The voice they heard and **the head they saw belonged to the Red Wind.**

Sidebar annotations:

"They mingled one among the other"—The Swallow People and the Air-Spirit People mingle, but the relationship proves disastrous because the visitors overstep their boundaries.

"you were driven from the world below"—The Air-Spirit People have not changed their ways and are not living in balance and harmony.

"they noticed a white face"—Once again, the Air-Spirit People are guided to a sipapuni.

"the head . . . belonged to the Red Wind"—The wind is again the primary tutelary.

Doing as they were told, they found a passage which twisted around through the sky's other surface like the tendril of a vine. It had been made this way by the wind.

They flew into it and wound their way to the other side. And that is how they reached the surface of the fourth world.

Four of the grasshoppers had come with them. One was white. One was blue. One was yellow. And one was black. To this very day, in fact, we have grasshoppers of those four colors among us.

The surface of **the fourth world** was unlike the surface of any of the lower worlds. For it was a mixture of black and white. The sky above was alternately white, blue, yellow, and black, just as it had been in the worlds below.

> "the fourth world . . . was a mixture"—It is a combination of the others, and superior to all of them.

But here the colors were of a different duration.

In the first world each color lasted for about the same length of time each day. In the second world the blue and the black lasted just a little longer than the white and the yellow. But here in the fourth world there was white and yellow for scarcely any time, so long did the blue and black remain in the sky. As yet **there was no sun and no moon;** as yet there were no stars.

> "there was no sun and no moon"—The fourth world of the Navajo is also dark, like that of the Hopi. (See p. 94.)

When they arrived on the surface of the fourth world, the exiles from the lower worlds saw no living thing. But they did observe **four great snow-covered peaks** along the horizon around them. One peak lay to the east. One peak lay to the south. One peak lay likewise to the west. And to the north there was one peak.

> "four great snow-covered peaks"—Mountains function as directional markers, indicating an emerging sense of balance and harmony.

[This is repeated for all four directions.]

The insect people sent two scouts to the east, who returned at the end of two days. Those two said that they had not been able to reach the eastern mountain after an entire day's flight. And although they had traveled far indeed they could see no living creature. Neither track nor trail could they see; not one sight of life were they able to detect.

Finally, two scouts were sent to explore the land that lay to the north. And when they returned they had a different story to tell. For they reported that **they had found a strange race** unlike any other. These were people who cut their hair square in front. They were people who lived in houses in the ground. They were people who cultivated the soil so that things grew therein. They were now harvesting what they had planted, and they gave the couriers food to eat.

> "they had found a strange race"—This new "strange race" is actually more advanced. They have developed from a hunter-gatherer society into an agricultural one. Some scholars have suggested that this section describes the first contact between the Navajo and the Pueblo people.

It was now evident to the newcomers that the fourth world was larger than any of the worlds below.

On the very next day, two members of the newly found race came to the camp of the exiles. They were called *Kiis'aanii*, they said, which means People Who Live in **Upright Houses.** And they wished to invite the exiles to visit their village.

> "Upright Houses"— May refer to the multistory pueblo communal construction. Thus, the travelers would be finding their proper home.

THE STAGES OF HUMAN CREATION IN NAVAJO MYTH

The creatures described in the story preceding this are called "people," and seem human, despite the constant mention of them as insects. For instance, they are described as committing adultery, an idea meaningful for humans but not for insects. We might look at the story that begins here as a new and final creation of human beings as we know them. Or it may be a different creation story, presented paratactically. We might also attribute this to the elasticity of oral tradition: presenting two versions of the same story, one after the other, without much of an attempt to make them fit together. (See Ch. 2, p. 18.)

The exiles were given corn and pumpkins to eat. And they were asked by their new friends to stay. For quite some time, in fact, they stayed in the village of the upright houses. There they lived well on the food that the *Kiis'aanii* gave them. Eventually they all lived together like the people of one tribe. Soon the two groups were using the names of family and kin between themselves. They called each other father and son, mother and daughter, grandparent and grandchild, brother and sister.

The land of the *Kiis'aanii* was a dry land. It had neither rain nor snow and there was little water to be found. But the people who had been dwelling there knew how to irrigate the soil to make things grow, and **they taught the newcomers** to do so.

"they taught the newcomers"—Practical information like this may be handed down in a myth and may be acted out in ritual songs and dances.

Twenty-three days came and went, and twenty-three nights passed and all was well. And on the twenty-fourth night the exiles held a council meeting. They talked quietly among themselves, and they resolved to mend their ways and to do nothing unintelligent that would create disorder. This was a good world, and the wandering insect people meant to stay here, it is said.

Creation of Humans

"[they] wanted the gods . . . to make humans"—The tellers of this story know their own physical characteristics, so the explanation of the creation of their ancestors demonstrates this. As they create the narrative, they explain their own existence.

Those creatures who had found the fourth world **wanted the gods of their new-found world, whom they called Holy People, to make humans.** One of the four leaders of the descendants of the Air-Spirit People said: "They want more people to be created in this world. But they want intelligent people, created in their likeness, not in yours. . . . The new creatures are to have hands like ours. They are to have feet like ours. They are to have mouths like ours and teeth like ours. They must learn to think ahead, as we do."

They prepared for the coming of the four Holy People by bathing carefully on the appointed day. The Holy People appeared among them, carrying a sacred buckskin and **two ears of corn.**

"two ears of corn"—Humans are created from corn, a major product of the earth for the Native Americans of the Southwest U.S.

"careful . . . just as careful . . . making sure"—The ritual achieves the spiritual balance by ascertaining the physical balance of the sacred objects.

One ear of corn was yellow. The other ear was white. Each ear was completely covered at the end with grains, just as sacred ears of corn are covered in our own world now.

Proceeding silently, the gods laid one buckskin on the ground, **careful** that its head faced the west. Upon this skin they placed the two ears of corn, being **just as careful** that the tips of each pointed east. Over the corn they spread the other buckskin, **making sure** its head faced east.

Under the white ear they put the feather of a white eagle.

And under the yellow ear they put the feather of a yellow eagle.

Then they told the onlooking people to stand at a distance. So that the wind would enter.

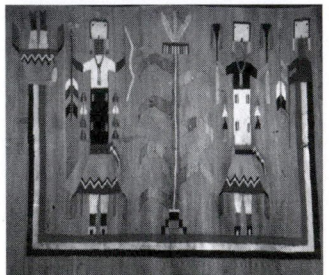

Blanket based on a sand painting design. Two supernatural "holy people" flank the sacred maize plant, which was their gift to mortals. They are enclosed by rainbow arc. Creation myth. Navajo, 19th c.

Then from the east the White Wind blew between the buckskins. And while the wind thus blew, each of the Holy People came and walked four times around the objects they had placed so carefully on the ground. As they walked, the eagle feathers, whose tips protruded slightly from between the two buckskins, moved slightly. Just slightly. So that only those who watched carefully were able to notice.

And when the Holy People had finished walking, they lifted the topmost buckskin.

And lo! The ears of corn had disappeared.

In their place there lay a man and there lay a woman.

The white ear of corn had been transformed into our most ancient male ancestor. And the yellow ear of corn had been transformed into our most ancient female ancestor.

It was the wind that had given them life: the very wind that gives us our breath as we go about our daily affairs here in the world we ourselves live in!

When this wind ceases to blow inside of us, we become speechless. Then we die.

In the skin at the tips of our fingers we can see **the trail of that life-giving wind.**

Look carefully at your own fingertips.

"the trail of that life-giving wind"—If you lived in the arid regions of the Southwest, you would be familiar with the way the wind blows sand into ridges and whorls. Here one natural phenomenon (sand dunes) is related to the similar form of another.

There you will see where the wind blew when it created your most ancient ancestors from two ears of corn, it is said.

The gods told the people to build a shelter for the couple, then directed them to "live here together as husband and wife." After four days, a set of hermaphroditic twins were born; these were followed by four sets of male-and-female twins, born at four day intervals. Only the first set chose not to marry after they had matured in four days.

The Holy People took First Man and First Woman, and each set of twins, in turn, to their home on the eastern mountain to educate them.

Soon after the First Man and the First Woman and all of their children had gone to the eastern mountain and returned, it was observed that **they occasionally wore masks** something like the masks worn by the Talking God and by the House God.

Whenever these masks were worn, those who wore them prayed for the good things and the necessary things. They prayed for such things as the steady rain, or for things like abundant crops.

But it also seems that during their visit to the eastern mountain the people learned terrible secrets, too. For witches also possess masks like these, and they too marry their close relatives.

"they occasionally wore masks"— Masks and symbolic costumes continue to be integral to Navajo dances and other religious ceremonies.

Further Reading

Benedict, Ruth Fulton. *Zuni Mythology,* Vol. I, 1–6. New York: Columbia University Press, 1935.

Courlander, Harold. *The Fourth World of the Hopi: The Epic Story of the Hopi Indians as Preserved in Their Legends and Traditions.* Albuquerque: University of New Mexico Press, 1987.

Zolbrod, Paul D. *Diné Bahane':* *The Navajo Creation Story.* Albuquerque: University of New Mexico Press, 1964.

CHAPTER

9

African Creation Stories

WHAT TO EXPECT . . . The readings in this chapter, from Uganda and Nigeria, provide examples of African creation stories. Look for characteristics they share with other creation accounts you have been studying: for example, recounting the deeds of the first human and explaining the existence of death. There are also differences: for example, the story from Uganda provides a justification for the Ugandan kingship; also, animals as well as humans are used as active characters to tell the story, communicating a closer kind of relationship between humans and their environment.

You can also note the fundamental connections between the stories told here and those in the Trickster section, especially those from Africa and the African-American tradition, Chapter 23, p. 339.

It is especially appropriate to be looking at creation stories from Africa. Paleontologists disagree about where human beings first appeared on the earth, but a likely theory places the first creatures we would recognize as human in East Africa, somewhere between 4 and 1.5 million years ago. However, it is important to remember that today Africa is a vast continent with several thousand different peoples, each with its own culture, language, traditions, and mythology. There is a wide range of creation stories found in Africa, including

- The complex tradition from the Dogon people of Mali in West Africa, about Amma, the egg-shaped creation god who gives birth to two sets of twins and struggles with Ogo, one of her creations, making the earth from a fragment of his placenta. Ogo is eventually turned into Yuguru, the Pale Fox who wanders the earth, eternally in revolt.

- The stories from the Bambara who live along the Niger River in Mali in West Africa. These are about the creative spirit Yo who gives birth to Faro, who creates seven heavens, Pemba, who creates the earth, and Teliko, who is the parent of aquatic twins whose descendents are fishermen, from whom come all human beings.

- The story from the Fon or Dahomey people from southern Benin in West Africa, which describes creation as arising from the androgynous Nana Boluku who begins the creation of the universe, but leaves its completion to her offspring, daughter Mawu and son Lisa.

- The lengthy mythological tradition arising from the ancient civilization of Egypt, represented by the story of creation arising from Atum, the Sun god, whose descendents are Geb (Earth) and Nut (Sky). (See Ch. 28, p. 403.)

The creation stories presented in this chapter are "how and why" tales. The events in these stories result in an *aetiological* explanation that shows us the origin of features of our world. Notably, these stories explain how the world got to be as it is and where death comes from.

Both stories reflect the widespread African belief in a sky god associated with thunder and lightning. Other African tales are presented in Chapters 22 (p. 305) and 23 (p. 339).

The first story, "The Creation," comes from the Ganda people of Uganda in East-Central Africa. The story describes the legendary ancestor of the kings of the ancient kingdom of Buganda, a man named Kintu, who, according to the version of the story given in this chapter, came from the north. Kintu is the name of the first king of Uganda, but accounts of the historical person have become interwoven with stories of the legendary figure involved in the creation of the world. "The Creation" describes Kintu's coming to Uganda and founding a family by intermarriage with the gods. It accounts for the fruits, vegetables, and animals found in the Uganda of its time, and explains why the chiefs of Uganda, though they are descended from the gods, are nonetheless mortal. At the same time, the story is about a man who must perform a series of tasks for a father in order to be allowed to marry his daughter.

The second story, "The Origin of Death," comes from the Bura people of Nigeria in West Africa. In this story, a worm is dispatched by the sky god to tell the people how to banish death. A self-important lizard comes along more quickly with a bogus answer, however, and the people believe the message he claimed to obtain from the sky god. As a result, the real message of the sky god is not observed, and death remains on earth. Hans Abrahamsson calls the theme of this story "the message that failed," and notes that it is the most common African myth about the origin of death. He finds many variants of this story all over Africa. The animals in the story vary: in some stories it is a chameleon who is overtaken by a lizard, a rabbit, or a snake. The point is always the same, though: the real message arrives too late, and as a result, human beings are subject to death.

Henry Louis Gates, Jr., has pointed out that many parts of West Africa have a tradition of a trickster figure like the one in "The Origin of Death." This trickster is a messenger interpreting the wishes of the gods to human beings. Gates calls him Esu-Elegbara and explains that he guards the barrier that separates the worlds of the humans and the gods. He is the originator of storytelling and the god of interpretation, in this respect resembling Hermes, the ancient Greek messenger god who links the Olympian gods to the world of the dead. "The Origin of Death" also has some similarities to the Biblical story of Adam and Eve in which a snake brings a false message whose result is the introduction of misery and death into the world. For more on trickster figures, see Part 3, especially Chapters 21 on Raven (p. 295), 23 on African and African-American tricksters (p. 339), and 24 on Prometheus (p. 353).

The Creation

Kintu was **the first man,** and when he came from **the unknown,** he found nothing in Uganda—no food, no water, no animals, nothing but a blank. He had a cow with him, and when he was hungry he drank her milk.

One day, as he roamed about searching for something, he saw two girls just dropped down from Heaven. He stopped. The girls also stopped a long way off. They were **Mugulu's** daughters, Nambi and her sister. The girls were surprised, and Nambi said, "Sister, look at the two things over there. What can they be?" The sister looked, but said nothing. Nambi continued: "We never saw anything like them before! Just go down and see what brings things like this to such a place as the earth." "How can I?" asked the sister. **"Look at those horns!"**

"I don't mean that one. Try the other."

The sister then advanced a little way, and when Kintu saw her coming, he also advanced to meet her. The then sister ran back to Nambi, and they both prepared to run away. Kintu, however, did not continue the pursuit, but returned to the cow.

This story comes from: Sir Harry Johnston, *The Uganda Protectorate.**

 The Arrival of Kintu

"the first man"—The other beings in the story are divine, not human.

"the unknown"—The north.

Mugulu Gulu, the sky, was an important deity.

"Look at those horns!"—Although the story is a serious one, the storyteller uses humor throughout to keep the attention of the audience. You have to listen carefully, because you do not know when the next joke will come.

---

* Sir Harry Johnston. *The Uganda Protectorate*, Vol. II, 700–705. (London: Hutchinson & Co., 1902.)

Map of Africa, showing Uganda

After some time, Nambi and her sister decided to come close to Kintu, and when only one hundred paces separated them, Nambi spoke to him: "Who are you?"

"I am Kintu."

"And what is that?" pointing to the cow.

"That is my cow."

Nambi and her sister withdrew to consider whether this could possibly be true. They returned directly, and asked: "We have never seen anything like you before; where did you come from?"

"I do not know."

Kintu at this point milked the cow, and put milk on the palm of his left hand, and drank it.

"What do you do that for?" asked Nambi.

"That's my food," said Kintu.

"We see no water here. What do you drink?"

"I drink milk."

The then girls retired for another conference, and Nambi confided to her sister that she believed that this was a man. Nothing else could do such extraordinary things. They returned to Kintu and submitted their decision, and Kintu said, "Yes, I am a man."

Nambi then told him all about themselves, and suggested that he should accompany them to heaven. Kintu agreed, on condition that they also took his cow.

This they declined to do, and they disappeared. As soon as they arrived in heaven, they told Mugulu that they had found a man and a cow.

"Where?" asked Mugulu.

"On the earth."

"Not a real man, surely?" Mugulu smiled as if he did not believe them, but they suspected that he knew all the time.

"Yes, a real man! **We know he is a real man because he wants food,** and when he is hungry he drags the udder of his cow, and squeezes out white juice, which he drinks."

"I shall make inquiries."

"He is very nice," said Nambi, "and I wanted to bring him up here. May I go and fetch him?"

"Leave the matter to me," said Mugulu, and the girls withdrew.

As soon as they had gone, Mugulu called his sons, and said, "Go to the earth and test this story about a real man being there. Nambi says that she saw a wild man and a cow, and that the man drank the cow's juice. Fetch the cow."

The boys prepared to start at once.

"Wait a bit," said Mugulu. "I don't want the man. **He will probably die** when he sees you; bring the cow only."

The boys arrived near Kintu's resting place, and he was asleep. **They took the cow,** and carried her off. When Kintu awoke, he did not see the cow, but just then he did not start in search of her, because he supposed that she had only wandered a short distance.

Presently, he got hungry, and tried to find the cow, but in vain. He ultimately decided that the girls must have returned and stolen her, and he was very angry and hungry. He used many words not of peace, and he sat down and pointed his nails and sharpened his

 "We know he is a real man because he wants food"—Later the girls' father will test Kintu's ability to eat, because it is characteristic of a man, as opposed to a god.

"He will probably die"—Mankind is portrayed as weak. Kintu must change this condition.

The First Test of Kintu

"They took the cow"—Mugulu's sons steal Kintu's cow. He must find alternate ways of feeding himself to survive.

Burnished pottery vessels resembling calabash bottles, 19th c. Pots of this type were made exclusively for the royal court of Uganda. These particular vessels were donated to the British Museum by Sir Harry Johnston, who collected the story of Kintu in this chapter. Compare them with the next illustration, a modern version crafted by Magdalene Odundo.

teeth, but there was no one with whom to fight. **He then peeled the bark off a tree and sucked it,** and thus he fed himself.

Next day, Nambi saw Kintu's cow as the boys arrived, and she exclaimed, "You have stolen Kintu's cow! That cow was his food and drink, and now what has he to eat? I like Kintu, if you do not. I shall go down tomorrow, and if he is not dead I shall bring him up here," and she went and found Kintu.

"So they have taken away your cow?"

"Yes."

"What have you been eating since?"

"I have been sucking the bark of a tree."

"Did you really do that?"

"What else was there to do?"

"Come with me to Mugulu, and your cow shall be given back to you."

They went, and Kintu, when he arrived, saw a vast multitude of people and plenty of bananas and fowls and goats and sheep—**in fact, everything was there in plenty.** And the boys, when they saw Nambi arrive with Kintu, said, "Let us tell our father, Mugulu." And they went and told him, and Mugulu said, "Go, and tell my chiefs to build a big house without a door for the stranger Kintu." The house was built, and Kintu went into it.

Mugulu then gave the following lavish order: "My people, go and cook ten thousand dishes of food, and roast ten thousand cows, and fill ten thousand vessels with beer, and give it to the stranger. If he is a real man, he will eat it, if not—the penalty is death."

The food was prepared and taken to Kintu's house. As there was no door, the members of the crowd put their shoulders to one side of the house and raised it off the ground, and put the food inside. They told Kintu that, if he did not finish it all at a meal, **the result would be death.** Then they dropped the side of the house down again, and waited outside.

Kintu surveyed the mass of food with dismay, and then started to walk round it, muttering his feelings to himself. As he went around the heap, his foot slipped into a hole, and on examination, he found that it was the opening of a cavern. "Ha! ha!" he said. "This cave has a good appetite; let me feed it," and **he took the ten thousand measures of beer and spilled them in,** laying the empty vessels on one side. Then the ten thousand carcasses of roast cows were pitched into the cavern, and lastly the food from the ten thousand baskets. Then, after he had closed the hole, he called to the people outside:

"Haven't you got a little more food out there?"

"No," they replied. "Did we not give you enough?"

"Well, I suppose I must do with it, if you have nothing more cooked."

"Have you finished it all?"

"Yes, yes. Come, and take away the empty dishes."

The crowd raised the side wall of the house, came inside, and asked Kintu whether he had really disposed of the food. He assured them that he had, and they, with one accord, then cried out, "Then it is a man indeed!" They went directly to Mugulu, and told him that the stranger had finished his meal, and asked for more.

Mugulu at first branded this statement as a falsehood, but on consideration he believed it. He pondered for a moment, then taking up a copper axe, he said to his chiefs, "Take this to Kintu. Tell him I want material to make a fire. Tell him that Mugulu is old and cold, and that Mugulu does not burn wood for a fire. Tell him I want stones, and tell him that he must cut up rocks with this copper axe and fetch the pieces and light me a fire. If he does so, then he may claim his cow. He may also have Nambi, and he can return to the earth."

"He then peeled bark off a tree and sucked it"—The world at this time contained no other forms of food for humans than the cow. By the end of the story, Kintu will have obtained a variety of edible plants and farm animals from his visit to heaven.

"in fact, everything was there in plenty"—Heaven is a sharp contrast to the empty void that is Uganda.

 The Second Test of Kintu

"the result would be death"—Mugulu's people cook an enormous meal for Kintu, and he must eat it or die. Kintu meets the test by using his wits.

"he took the ten thousand measures of beer and spilled them in"—We might imagine the storyteller acting out this part of the story.

The Third Test of Kintu

"a fire made of stones"—Kintu must light a fire for Mugulu. The fuel is to be stones, and they are to be cut with a soft copper axe.

"Just strike and see."—The axe gives special power to Kintu, just as tools give all people power over their environment.

 ### The Fourth Test of Kintu

"if he is a man he is to fetch it quickly"—In his fourth test, Kintu must bring back a bucket of dew for Mugulu. As with the previous test, accomplishing the task shows human control over nature.

"he suspected that there was something wrong"—The words echo Kintu's reaction when he is given the axe earlier. Such repetition is characteristic of oral storytelling.

"it only remains for you to get your cow"—The story returns to its beginning, and Kintu's final test involves picking out his cow from the herds of Mugulu.

Ceramic object, Magdalene Odundo, 2000. The artist was born in Kenya, but admires the vessels produced for the royal court of Uganda (see the previous illustration). To create this object, she employed a traditional technology to create a modern shape of her own imagining.

The chiefs went to Kintu, and told him that Mugulu wanted **a fire made of stones,** and that he must chop a rock with the copper axe.

Kintu suspected there was something wrong, but he spoke no words to that effect. He put the axe on his shoulder and went out before they allowed the wall to drop to the ground. He walked straight to a big rock, stood in front of it, placed the head of the axe on the rock, and rested his chin on the tip of the handle.

"It does not seem easy to cut," he said to the axe.

"It is easy enough to me," replied the axe. **"Just strike and see."**

Kintu struck the rock, and it splintered in all directions. He picked up the pieces of rock, and went straight to Mugulu, and said, "Here is your firewood, Mugulu. Do you want any more?"

Mugulu said, "This is marvelous! Go back to your home. It only remains now for you to find your cow."

And Kintu went away.

Next morning, the chiefs were called before Mugulu.

He said, "Take this bucket to Kintu, and tell him to fetch water. Tell him that Mugulu does not drink anything but dew, and **if he is a man he is to fetch it quickly.**"

Kintu received the bucket and the message, and again **he suspected that there was something wrong,** and he said words within himself, but he spoke nothing to that effect. He took the bucket and went out, and he set it down on the grass, and he said to the bucket, "This does not seem very easy." The bucket replied, "It is easy enough to me," and when Kintu looked down he saw that the bucket was full of dew. He took it to Mugulu, and said, "Here's your drinking water, Mugulu. Do you want any more?"

Mugulu said, "This is marvelous! Kintu, you are a prodigy. I am now satisfied that you are a man indeed, and **it only remains for you to get your cow.** Whoever took Kintu's cow, let him restore it."

"Your own sons stole my cow," said Kintu.

"If so," replied Mugulu, "drive all the cows here, and let Kintu pick out his cow if she is amongst them."

Ten thousand cows were brought in a herd.

Kintu stood near the herd in great perplexity, lost in thought. A hornet came and sat on Kintu's shoulder, and, as Kintu gave no heed, the hornet prepared his sting and drove it home.

Kintu struck at the hornet and missed him, and the hornet said, "Don't strike! I'm your friend."

"You have just bit me," replied Kintu.

"It wasn't a bite. Listen. You'll never be able to find your cow amongst all that herd. Just wait until I fly out and sit on the shoulder of a cow. That's yours. Mark her."

The herd of ten thousand cows was driven past, but the hornet did not move, and Kintu said aloud, "My cow is not amongst them."

Mugulu then ordered another herd to be brought, numbering twice as many cows as the last herd, but the hornet did not move, and Kintu said aloud, "My cow is not amongst them."

The herdsmen drove the cows away, and another herd was brought, and the hornet flew off and sat on the shoulder of a cow. Kintu went forward and marked her. "That's mine," he said to Mugulu. The hornet then flew to another, a young cow, and Kintu went forward and marked her, and said, "That also is mine."

The hornet flew to a third cow, and Kintu went forward and marked this one also, and said, "That cow is mine also."

Mugulu said, "Quite correct. Your cow had two calves since she arrived in heaven. You are a prodigy, Kintu. Take your cows, and **take Nambi also,** and go back to the earth. But first wait a bit." Mugulu called his servants and said to them, "Go to my store, and fetch one banana plant, one potato, one bean, one Indian corn, one ground-nut, and one hen." The things were brought, and Mugulu then addressed Kintu and Nambi: "Take these things with you; you may want them." Then, addressing Kintu, he said, "I must tell you that Nambi has a brother named Warumbe (meaning "disease" or "death"). He is mad and ruthless. At the moment, he is not here, so you had better start quickly, before he returns. If he sees you, he may want to go with you, but you are certain to quarrel." Mugulu then said to Nambi, "Here is some millet to feed the hen on the road down. **If you forget anything, don't come back to fetch it.** That is all. You may go."

Kintu and Nambi started, and when they were some distance on the journey, Nambi suddenly remembered that it was time to feed the hen. She asked Kintu for the millet, but it was nowhere to be found, and now it was clear that they had forgotten it in the hurry of departure.

"I shall return and fetch it," said Kintu.

"No, no, you must not! Warumbe will have returned, and he will probably wish to accompany us. I don't want him, and you had better not return."

"But the hen is hungry, and we must feed it."

"Yes, it is," said Nambi.

Nambi remained where she was, and Kintu returned to Mugulu, and explained that he had forgotten the millet.

Mugulu was angry that Kintu had returned, and Warumbe, who just then arrived, asked, "Where is Nambi?"

"She is gone to the earth with Kintu."

"Then I must come, too," said Warumbe.

After some hesitation, Kintu agreed to this, and they returned together to Nambi.

"How do you do," said Nambi.

"How do you do," replied Kintu.

"Hum."

"Ham."

"Hum."

"Ham."

"Hum."

"Ham."

Nambi then objected to Warumbe accompanying them, but he insisted, and finally it was agreed that he should come for a time and stay with Nambi and Kintu.

They all three proceeded, and reached the earth at a place called Magongo in Uganda, and they rested. Then the woman planted the banana and the Indian corn, the bean and the groundnut, and there was a plentiful crop.

In the course of time, three children were born, and **Warumbe claimed one of them.**

"Let me have this one," he said to Kintu. "You still have two children remaining."

"I cannot spare one of these," Kintu said, "but later on, perhaps, I may be able to spare one."

Years passed by, and many more children were born, and Warumbe again begged Kintu to give him one. Kintu went round to all the children with the object of selecting one for Warumbe, and he finally returned, and said, "Warumbe, I cannot spare you one just yet, but later on, perhaps, I may be able to do so."

"When you had three you said the same thing. Now you have many, and still you refuse to give me one. Mark you, I shall now kill them all. Not today, not tomorrow, not this year, not next year, but one by one I shall claim them all."

Kintu choosing his cow.

The Fifth Test of Kintu

"Ten thousand cows were brought in a herd"—When Nambi and her sister first saw Kintu's cow, they were astonished by it. Here, it turns out that they have a large herd of cows at home. This kind of inconsistency is typical of oral storytelling. (See Ch. 2, p. 18.)

"take Nambi also"—Mugulu sends Kintu back to earth with Nambi and a variety of provisions as a dowry. With these provisions, Kintu will turn the void which was Uganda into a prosperous place supporting many humans.

"If you forget anything, don't come back to fetch it."—Mugulu gives Nambi a command, but Kintu violates it. The result is that Warumbe, Nambi's brother, whose name means "disease" or "death" comes back to Uganda with Kintu. The story explains why human beings die, even though they are descended from the gods through Nambi.

"How do you do"—Elaborate greetings are traditional in Uganda. We can imagine Nambi eyeing Kintu, who now has her brother Warumbe at his side. A scene like this provides opportunity for the storyteller to employ disdainful tones and horrified looks to dramatize the calamity that has befallen. What follows is a traditional Ugandan exchange of grunts: all polite greeting would include these. Here they can be imagined to be full of negative feeling.

"Warumbe claimed one of them"—In traditional Ugandan society, the brother of the wife made her marriage arrangements and had a legitimate right to claim her children unless they were redeemed by a gift. Usually he relinquished his right to the eldest and youngest, but he was within his rights to take them all.

"I cannot spare one of these"— Kintu is able to defer death for a while, but in the end, it prevails.

Next day, one child died, and Kintu charged Warumbe with the deed. Next day again another died, and next day again another; and at last, Kintu proposed to return to Mugulu and tell him how Warumbe was killing all his children.

Kintu accordingly went to Mugulu, and explained matters. Mugulu replied that he had expected it. His original plan was that Kintu and Warumbe should not have met. He had told Kintu that Warumbe was a madman, and that trouble would come of it, yet Kintu had returned for the millet against the orders of Mugulu, and this was the consequence.

"However," continued Mugulu, "I shall see what can be done." And with that, he called his son Kaikuzi (literally, "the digger"), and said to him, "Go down and try to bring me back Warumbe."

Kintu and Kaikuzi started off together, and when they arrived were greeted by Nambi. She explained that in his absence Warumbe had killed several more of her sons. Kaikuzi called up Warumbe, and said, "Why are you killing all these children?"

"I wanted one child badly to help me cook my food. I begged Kintu to give me one. He refused. Now I shall kill them, every one."

"Mugulu is angry and he sent me down to recall you."

"I decline to leave here."

"You are only a small man in comparison to me. I shall fetch you by force."

With this they grappled, and a severe contest ensued. After a while, Warumbe slipped from Kaikuzi's grasp, and ran into a hole in the ground. Kaikuzi started to dig him out with his fingers, and succeeded in reaching him, but Warumbe dived still deeper into the earth. Kaikuzi tried to dig him out again, and had almost caught him when Warumbe sunk still further into the ground.

"I'm tired now." said Kaikuzi to Kintu. "I shall remain for a few days, and have another try to catch him."

"Kaikuzi then issued an order that there was to be two days' silence on the earth"—The test set by Kaikuzi is impossible for humans to fulfill. By making noise, they show their humanity. Many stories show that humans cannot overcome their limitations and become immortal. For example, in the Mesopotamian *Epic of Gilgamesh,* Utnapishtim asks Gilgamesh to stay awake for seven days, but he is not able to do so (Ch. 15, p. 190f).

Kaikuzi then issued an order that there was to be two days' silence on the earth, and that Warumbe would come out of the ground to see what it meant.

The people were ordered to lay in two days' provisions, and firewood and water, and not to go out of doors to feed goats or cattle. This having been done, Kaikuzi went into the ground to catch Warumbe, and pursued him for two days, and he forced Warumbe out at a place called Tanda. At this place there were some children feeding goats, and when they saw Warumbe they cried out, and the spell was broken, and Warumbe returned again into the earth. Directly afterwards, Kaikuzi appeared at the same place, and asked why the children had broken the silence. He was angry and disappointed, and he said to Kintu that the people had broken his order, and that he would concern himself no further with the recalling of Warumbe.

"I am tired now," said Kaikuzi.

"since you cannot expel him"— Once again, the story finds humor in serious events.

"Never mind him," said Kintu. "Let Warumbe remain, **since you cannot expel him.** You may go back to Mugulu now, and thank you."

Kaikuzi returned to Mugulu, and explained the circumstances.

"Very well," said Mugulu, "Let Warumbe stay there."

And Warumbe remained.

Map of Africa, showing Nigeria

The Origin of Death

Long ago, there was no such thing as death. There was no crying, there was no disease. Everybody was well and happy. They did not know anything by the name, death.

One day, everybody was amazed when a man sickened and died. No one knew what to do with him. They decided that they would ask the sky what to do with him.

They called a worm, and said, "Go and tell the sky that a man has died, and ask the sky what we should do with him."

The worm went to the sky, and said, "A man has died, and they have sent me to ask you what they should do with him."

The sky said to the worm, "Go and tell them to take the corpse, and hang it in the fork of a tree and throw mush at it until it comes back to life. When it comes back to life, no one else will ever die."

The worm started back.

A lizard named Agadzagadza ran ahead of the worm. He had heard everything that the sky had said. **He wanted to deceive the people on the earth.** Agadzagadza therefore ran very hard. When he reached the village, he said, "The worm does not travel fast enough, so the sky sent me. The sky said that I should tell you that you should dig a grave, wrap the corpse in cloth, and bury it in the grave."

The people did as Agadzagadza told them. They dug a grave, wrapped the corpse in cloth, and buried it.

Presently, the worm arrived.

They scolded him, and said, "Why did you not come back sooner? If the lizard had not come and told us what the sky said we should do, we would still be waiting for you." They told him what they had done to the corpse, as Agadzagadza had instructed them.

The worm said, "Who sent Agadzagadza? The sky did not send him. You have taken his word and you have done what he said, but it is not what the sky said you should do. **You accepted the wisdom of the lizard.** What the sky told me is different from what you have done. The sky told me that I should come back and tell you to take the corpse, hang it up in the fork of a tree, and it would come back to life. The sky also said that, when it came back to life, no one else would ever die. But now you have buried it. You had better take it out of the grave, and let us do what the sky said we should do."

The men were overcome by laziness, and they said to the worm, "It is because you did not come back more quickly that we have already buried the corpse. Who wants to work at this any more? We shall leave it, that is what we shall do."

Our ancestors refused to do what the sky asked them to do, they followed the lie of Agadzagadza. Because of this, people still die. It is the crime that Agadzagadza committed against us.

Further Reading

Gates, Henry Louis, Jr. *The Signifying Monkey: A Theory of African-American Literary Criticism.* New York: Oxford University Press, 1988.

Scheub, Harold. *A Dictionary of African Mythology: The Mythmaker as Storyteller.* Oxford: Oxford University Press, 2000.

---

* Albert D. Helser. *African Stories*, 192–93. Copyright © 1930, Fleming H. Revell Co. Used by permission of Baker Book House Company.

This story comes from Albert D. Helser, *African Stories**.

This bowl from the Yoruba people of Nigeria is decorated with lizards. It would typically hold kola nuts to welcome a guest.

"He wanted to deceive the people on the earth."—The lizard passes himself off as a representative of the sky god. However, ironically, by the role he plays, the lizard becomes a creator god, for he is the origin of death on earth. For more on the role of tricksters, who function in both creative and destructive ways, see Chapter 23, p. 339.

"You accepted the wisdom of the lizard"—This does not speak well for human intelligence.

"The men were overcome by laziness"—The lizard Agadzagadza tricks the people, but their fate is fair, because they contribute to it through their own laziness.

10

Nü Kwa

A Chinese Creator Goddess

WHAT TO EXPECT . . . Chinese myths, like most sacred stories, are expressions of religious belief and ritual; and, like them, change according to the evolving beliefs of the keepers (Ch. 2, p. 20). This chapter presents a selection of creation myths from ancient China to the present, focusing on goddesses and the pivotal role of the feminine in creation and culture.

The Introduction to this chapter contains a great deal of material that will give you background on Chinese culture and allow you to put the main reading in perspective. Look for the discussion of the principal philosophies underlying these myths. The philosophy can help you understand how the culture evolved over centuries. There is also a brief historical overview: you may want to make note of the different eras of Chinese history and the creation figures favored during each. In addition, the fragmentary nature of the myths in this chapter gives us the opportunity to illustrate additional methodologies used in studying mythology, beyond those outlined in Chapter 2.

Also important is the role of ritual in Chinese culture. Before you read this chapter, you may want to refer to the discussion of mythology and ritual in the introduction of Part 4, and if you want to delve deeper, read Victor Turner's observations about how belief systems (and therefore mythology) change as societies shift from an agricultural focus to an industrial one (pp. 378–82).

When you get to the main reading, look for the changes Knapp describes as occurring in the stories told about the creator goddess Nü Kwa. They illustrate many aspects of Chinese culture and religion, and offer us the opportunity to compare this culture with other traditions. As you read, compare the transformation of Nü Kwa's body into the cosmos with that of Ymir in Norse mythology (Ch. 7); note the similarities and differences between Nü Kwa and Demeter (Ch. 4) and Isis (Ch. 28).

The chart on page 118 will help with pronouncing the Chinese names, which might be unfamiliar to you.

INTRODUCTION TO CHINESE CREATION MYTHS

The creation myths of the Chinese differ from the Judaeo-Christian and other traditions as they do not involve a god who sets the universe in motion. Rather, a variety of different cosmological acts are involved with creation in the Chinese view (Birrell 1993, 24). This chapter features Nü Kwa (pronounced "Noo kwah"; the oo sound is made with lips rounded; see pronunciation guide, p. 118), the subject of one of the earliest creation stories told in China. We have also included a variety of stories in the marginalia which represent other aspects of creation, most of them having to do with the contribution of divine figures to human cultural development, like the invention of musical instruments or the bestowal of the methods of agriculture. In some other traditions, the culture hero who is credited with provision of such gifts is a trickster like Prometheus (ancient Greece) or Raven (northwestern North America and northeastern Asia);

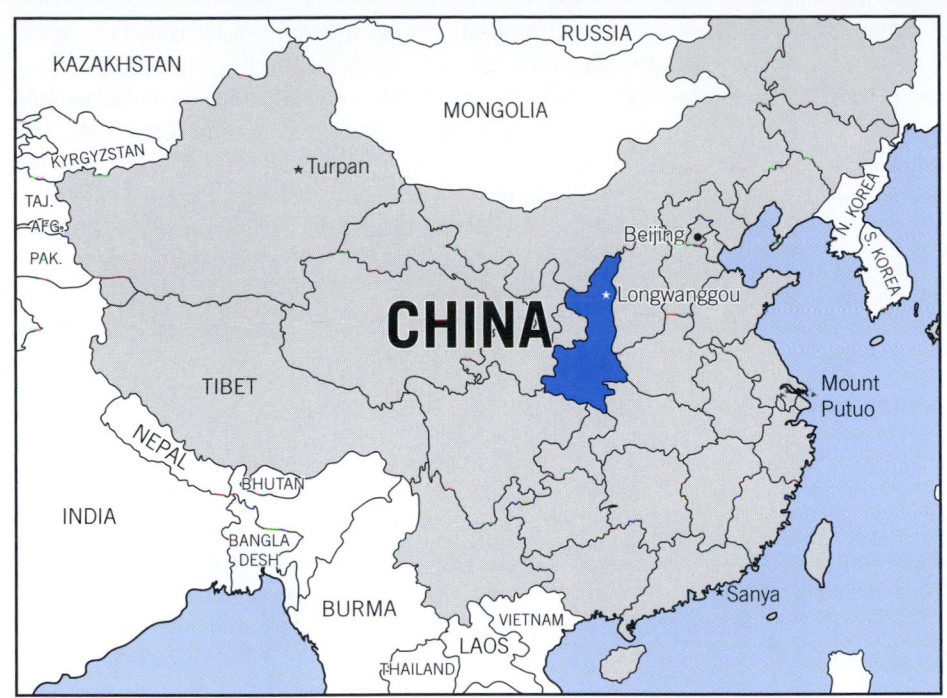

The stars on this map of China show the location of some of the main topics in this chapter: Turpan to the northwest is the site of the Astana tombs from which the painting of Nü Kwa on p. 122 comes; Long-wanggou in north-central China is the sight of the study by Adam Chau discussed extensively in the intro-duction, p. 110; giant statues of Kuan Yin (p. 121) are found at Mount Putuo in the east and Sanya in the south.

see Chapter 24 (p. 353) and Chapter 21 (p. 295); respectively. Though not a trickster, Nü Kwa herself is a participant in this tradition; in one of the stories about her told by Bettina Knapp, she is the inventor of metallurgy.

There are six separate Chinese creation stories (Birrell 2000, 16). According to the earliest, found in the most sacred mythological text (Chapter 3 of the third century B.C.E. *Songs of Ch'u*, which is titled "Questions of Heaven"), creation arises from a "primeval vapor" that embodies "cosmic energy governing matter, time and space." At the time of creation, the vapor "becomes differentiated into dual elements of male and female, Yin and Yang, hard and soft matter, and other binary elements" (Birrell 1993, 23).

The world that results from this creation consists of a square earth with a dome-shaped sky above it, which is held up by four pillars. Anne Birrell notes that this resembles the ancient Egyptian mythic cosmos from two and a half millennia earlier, and that the similarity might result from Egyptian influence on China by way of Central Asia (1993, 24).

P'AN KU, THE "COSMIC MAN"

The best known Chinese creation stories feature the universe we have just described, but graft onto it a human-like figure named P'An Ku: "Heaven and earth were in chaos like a chicken's egg, and P'An Ku was born in the middle of it." The story goes on to say that it took eighteen thousand years for heaven and earth to open and unfold, and "P'An Ku lived within them, and in one day he went through nine transformations, becoming more divine than Heaven and wiser than earth." Each day P'An Ku grew ten feet taller and developed in wisdom as the heavens rose ten feet higher and the earth grew ten feet thicker. "In eighteen thousand years the heavens reached their fullest height, earth reached its lowest depth, and P'An Ku became fully grown" (Birrell 1993, 32–33).

When P'An Ku had lived out his life, he died and was transformed, his body forming the world as we know it: "his breath became the wind and clouds; his voice became peals of thunder. His left eye became the sun; his right eye became the moon. His four limbs and extremities became the four cardinal points and the five peaks. His blood and semen became water and rivers. His muscles and veins became the earth's arteries; his flesh became fields and land. His hair and beard became the stars; his bodily hair became plants and trees. His teeth and bones became metal and rock; his vital marrow became pearls and jade. His sweat and bodily fluids became streaming rain. All the mites on his body were touched by the wind and were turned into the black-haired people" (Birrell 1993, 32–33)

STUDYING THE MYTH OF P'AN KU: THE METHODOLOGIES OF MYTHOLOGY

Let us consider these P'An Ku myths with respect to the various methodologies used in studying mythology. Every version of a myth is an important piece of evidence, but when we are trying to characterize a tradition, we would like to know which stories are most closely related to the ancient sacred traditions of a culture and people. This can be more difficult than it may seem at first sight because not all the texts we find have a known date. And in fact, as we mentioned in Chapter 2, writers are often so fond of the "mythic style" that they tell more recent stories using older diction to give their stories more "atmosphere." As a result, scholars have developed a series of techniques to determine the date and provenance of a literary text.

Both of the texts about P'An Ku quoted above come from Hsu Cheng, an author from the third century C.E., China's Three Kingdom era (220–280 C.E.). In the preceding Han period (221 B.C.E. to 220 C.E.), the feudal stages that comprised China were united into an empire, and this resulted in some changes in the nature of the stories told. Local traditions were, as Birrell says, "homogenized" into a national mythology (1993, 19). Her point involves introducing *political insight*s about the era in which a body of mythological texts originates.

In studying the myth of P'An Ku, Birrell uses *literary analysis* to explain that the first story differs from earlier texts about creation because it has a literary rather than a sacral or mythological character. She is referring to the simile comparing chaos to an egg: often this version of the story includes a description of an actual egg floating on the chaos, but that is not what the narrative says (1993, 29). She then uses *philosophical methods* to trace the viewpoint in this passage to early Han philosophers like Tung Chung-Shu, a second-century B.C.E. Confucian scholar. He divided the world into Heaven, earth, and the human domains to explain how the Han emperor mediated between them as the "archetypal human" (1993, 30). As noted above, in the Han period, many such changes were made to provide a mythology for the newly consolidated empire (1993, 19).

The second P'An Ku text is the transformation narrative. To characterize it, Birrell uses *a comparative approach*, citing the work of Bruce Lincoln, who studied Indo-European myths

The Three Main Eras of Chinese History with Respect to Mythology (Birrell 1993, 18–20)

Era	Dates	Dynastic Equivalent
Classical or pre-Han	600 B.C.E. to 221 B.C.E.	Middle to late Chou dynasty
Late classical and postclassical	221 B.C.E. to fifth century C.E.	Ch'in, Han and post-Han periods
Traditional	Sixth to seventeenth century C.E.	Sui-T'ang to Ming dynasty

Birrell's Methodologies in Comparing the Mythological Accounts P'An Ku and Nü Kwa

Methodology	Application
Political	Considers the unification of the Chinese empire in the Han period and notes that, as a result, Chinese mythology became more structured and less authentic
Literary	Identifies a literary device (simile) in the text of the P'An Ku story, noting this represents a divergence from the style of early mythological narratives
Philosophical	Traces the viewpoint in a passage in the story to points made by earlier Han philosophers
Comparative	Relates the transformation narrative in the story to European myths describing the cosmos as a human body
Comparative	Identifies aspects of the text as a borrowing by relating them to classical mythic texts
Historical	Applies the work of other scholars about the date of a particular mythological source, placing it in the time period of a particular government
Literary	Uses close reading to note details in the phrasing of the text and to consider their meaning

describing the cosmos as a human body. Lincoln identifies a series of "homologic alloforms" (natural forms in the world which correspond to body parts); the transformation narrative has sixteen such alloforms, marking it as a late borrowing from a non-Chinese source, probably one from central Asia. Birrell also adds other *comparative evidence* that the transformation narrative is a borrowing, noting that it does not appear in classical Chinese mythic texts and is not found until the third century C.E. (1993, 29–31).

In contrast, the first of the stories about Nü-Kwa (see p. 124) comes from the "Questions of Heaven," which is Chapter 3 of the *Songs of Ch'u*, a text dated to the third century B.C.E. Thus the account of creation by Nü-Kwa predates those about P'An Ku by six hundred years. In addition, Birrell cites another by the late Han author, Ying Shao: "People say that when Heaven and earth opened and unfolded, human kind did not yet exist. Nü Kwa kneaded yellow earth and fashioned human beings." The rest of the reading, which Knapp quotes below in another translation (p. 122), presents the aetiology of the current social order. As the reading opens with "people say that," Birrell concludes that in the late Han period, Nü Kwa was already well known as an ancient goddess (1993, 26–27, 33, 35). In these arguments, Birrell draws upon *historical evidence* and performs a close reading of the text, a literary technique. With these techniques of analysis, Birrell is able to determine the antiquity of the mythological figure of Nü Kwa, and to show her importance, even though the political and philosophical views of later generations led to her neglect. An older story is of course not necessarily better, but the techniques practiced by students of mythology allow them to see how mythology changes as culture changes. It is the cultural change that is the focus of Knapp's work in the reading, which makes up the main part of this chapter.

MYTHOLOGY AND RITUAL IN CHINA

Those of us in the West may wonder how the mythology outlined in this chapter is relevant to the everyday practices of people in China, either in the days these stories were told or in today's religious practices. A thorough answer is, of course, too large for a book of this scope, and yet even an indication of the answer may help us appreciate the meaning of the stories. As noted in other parts of this book, myth and ritual are closely related, though theories on their exact relationship vary (see p. 371). However, we can say that some of the stories told in this chapter are still important in the life of Chinese people, and that Chinese religion still continues to exert an influence on the world.

The first issue is that recent history has brought about a series of abrupt changes in Chinese religious practices. After a civil war that lasted from April 1947 to May 1950, the Chinese Communist Party defeated the Chinese Nationalist Party and established the People's Republic of China. In this Communist state, all religion was viewed as backward and was discouraged. Under the Cultural Revolution (1966–1976), a movement launched by the Chinese government under Mao Zedong, there was an even greater effort to eliminate the "bourgeois" aspects of the culture, including religion; houses of worship were destroyed and religious leaders were widely persecuted. Today, some of these conditions have been reversed, but the results of the Cultural Revolution persist. Today, most Chinese consider themselves nonreligious (*World Desk Reference* 188). However, ritual life persists as an important aspect of the culture.

There are many kinds of religious expression in China, but ancestor worship has been central to the culture for millennia: "family religion is basic, while individual and communal religion are secondary" (Thompson 34). In this context, marriage was "primarily a family matter," and the provision of children, especially male children, was "essential to the completion of the couple's filial responsibilities" (41). The three main components of the reverence for ancestors are the performance of elaborate funeral rites, the observance of extensive mourning, and ongoing sacrifices to the spirits of the ancestors (47). In pre-Communist China, the family maintained a small shrine commemorating each of its ancestors. Incense and candles were lit before this shrine twice a month in familial ceremonies and offerings were made (Maspero 122). In addition, the family had another shrine close by, a family tabernacle honoring "Heaven, the Emperor, and Ancient Masters" as well as other deities traditional to the locality and the family. Kuan Yin, the goddess of compassion, a deity discussed in this chapter (see p. 115 and p. 118), is featured in this shrine in some localities (123).

There were also other figures throughout the house, like a shrine to the Kitchen God, and pictures of the two gods of the Gate, the Lord and Lady of the Bed, and the God of Wealth (Maspero 112, 118, 120). The ritual role of these figures has reemerged, especially in rural areas in modern China (Gunde 51). This means that religion continues to be an important force, especially since Chinese religion has always been more a manifestation of culture than a matter of belief; and Thompson notes that it "was so woven into the fabric of family and social life that there was not even a special word for it until modern times, when one was coined to match the Western term" (1).

With respect to the community and the individual, Taoism, Confucianism, and Buddhism are the three major religious traditions discussed below by Knapp in introducing Chinese religious life (see p. 117ff). In addition, many people follow a "popular" or "folk religion" that mixes together gods and cults from a variety of sources. Such religion humanizes deities, filling in their mythology by giving them human lives, even though they were not in fact historical persons (Thompson 56). As a result, as Henri Maspero noted in observing China before Communism, "There is an extraordinary swarm of gods and spirits of every kind, a countless throng" (88). Adam Chau is an anthropologist who studied a temple in Longwanggou in Shaanbei in north-central China from 1995 to 1998, after the Communist government had eased some restrictions on religion. He notes, "Even though the popular religious landscape consists of a large number of deities, sacred sites, and religious specialists, each Shaanbei person's set of meaningful deities, sacred sites, and religious specialists is a limited one" (88).

Some scholars studying Chinese ritual have distinguished between the religion of the elite and that of peasant villages. Chau is more inclined to note the different modalities or ways of

Chau's Explanation of the Ways the Chinese "Do Religion"

Modality	Activity	Characteristics
discursive/scriptural	Reading and discussing religious texts	Requires strong reading skills
personal-cultivational	Meditation, chanting	Private or small group
liturgical/ritual	Religious services led by trained person	Large group, often related to special festivals
immediate-practical	Prayer, sacrifice, divination	Private or may involve a "gifted" intermediary

philosophy in China. The first of these is the "discursive/scriptural modality," which calls for a high level of literacy and thus is virtually inaccessible to the uneducated. However, Thompson notes that "the gulf between the peasant masses and the philosophers was not nearly so great as that between a laborer and an academic philosopher today." The concepts of philosophy were "not only comprehensible in their elementary form to the untutored peasant mind, but must actually have derived originally from the 'nature wisdom' of the peasant" (Thompson 17).

Chau calls the second modality "personal-cultivational": it involves practices like meditation and chanting. The "liturgical/ritual modality" involves practices aiming at "more immediate transformations of reality done in highly symbolic forms." This modality enlists the services of religious specialists like monks, priests, and Confucian ritual masters. The "immediate-practical modality" also aims at immediate, more direct, and simple results than the liturgical modality by using what Chau calls "minimal ritual elaborations" like "divination, getting divine medicine from a deity, charms, and consulting a spirit medium" (75).

Traditional temples range in size from simple shrines to elaborate multibuilding complexes. Some of the activities Chau outlines take place in temples; others do not. The conduct of weddings and funerals is centered in the home, as is mourning (Thompson 40–42, 47–55). Chau notes that the village temple is "usually located on a hill at a distance from the center of village life," and "it is generally deserted except during the temple festivals and when individual villagers come to consult the temple oracle or to burn incense" (38). We will see below in our examination of the goddess Kuan Yin that nowadays the Communist government is espousing a new, less traditional use of temples as tourist destinations.

Chau explains that some aspects of ritual life have reemerged in the People's Republic of China today: "Thousands of temples were destroyed during the Maoist era in Shaanbei, but today a significant proportion of them have been rebuilt (though not necessarily in the same locations). As tradition dictates, people stage temple festivals at least twice a year, one during the Lunar New Year and the other for the deity's birthday" (52). Which deity is so honored is largely a matter of "historical accident," Chau says. "Sometime in the past a deity might have appeared to a villager either in a dream or through a medium, asking the villagers to build a temple for him (or her), or a villager felt grateful for the help of a particular deity and decided to build the deity a temple in his own village, or a deity decided to make a villager his spirit medium by possessing the latter" (52).

KUAN YIN: HER INFLUENCE AND HER RITUALS

In the section of Knapp's work excerpted in this chapter, there is brief mention of Kuan Yin, the goddess of compassion, a deity of great repute both among Chinese Buddhists and in popular religion, though her characteristics are somewhat different in each case (Maspero 168). This figure is a Chinese transformation of Avalokiteśvara, an Indian Bodhisattva ("a person devoted to seeking enlightenment"), who is male and sometimes represented as having a thousand arms. This characteristic has caused her story to be linked with the story of Miao Shan, an actual person who is said to have blinded herself and cut off her arms to make medicine for her father's ailment. The process of linking a mythological story with a historical figure, or euhemerism, is typical of Chinese mythology. Servants misunderstood the grateful father's order to sculpt a statue of his daughter "with completely formed arms and eyes" and made one with a thousand eyes and a thousand arms. Knapp notes that this seems to be the basis of Miao Shan's association with Kuan Yin (197). The goddess' role was progressively expanded and elevated through the centuries and she "who exuded tenderness, compassion, love and eros, filled the void that had been created by the rigid and austere patriarchal consciousness that dominated the culture" (Knapp, 198). She is often represented as thousand-armed (see, p. 121) and thousand-eyed.

Though she was introduced to China in only the second century C.E. (Maspero 167), appearing much later than the creator goddess Nü Kwa, the main subject of the excerpt in this chapter, Kuan Yin has played a larger role in Chinese ritual life to this day. Thompson describes her as "no doubt the most popular deity in all of China" (59). In pre-Communist China, Maspero says, "in almost every house there are crudely colored statues or pictures of her. On her birthday festival, and for the most devout families also on her two other festivals, women give her skimpy plates of offerings, with sticks of incense. Aside from these regular festivals, they ask her especially that they be given children. But as no statue is to be found in most temples, it does not matter which of the Avalokiteśvara the women pray to. After having burned incense, they leave a little shoe as a votive offering, or sometimes people take away one of the shoes already left" (171). The importance of Kuan Yin may well be related to the importance of children to a society where they represent the fulfillment of the main religious principle driving the culture—the veneration of ancestors. Indeed, in a study of folk religion in rural southern China, Law has found an increased role for Kuan Yin in newly rebuilt village temples (94–95).

Kuan Yin's popularity has caused even the Communist government of the People's Republic to pay her homage, building a 108-meter statue of her in the seaside resort of Sanya, on Hainan island, facing the South China Sea (Tan). It is in the same complex as the Nanshan Buddhist Temple, which "comes across more as a theme park than a temple" (King). The statue was dedicated in 2005 as part of the Nanshan Cultural Tourism Zone and is, King says, part of "a temple made for tourists." Earlier, a 33-foot statue of Kuan Yin was erected at Mount Putuo, southeast of Shanghai, facing the East China Sea, and it too has become a major tourist destination. Each site has earlier, less imposing but more traditional statues and temples. The erection of such new temples and statues can be seen as the manipulation of mythological material to accommodate the economic and political goals of the current government. It also represents an adaptation of mythological traditions such as occurs in a society that is changing from a tribal agrarian form to a modern industrial or post-industrial one, as Victor Turner explains (pp. 378–81).

In contrast, as Knapp explains in the excerpt below, the importance of Nü Kwa faded over time, as other philosophical and political forces asserted themselves in the history of China. However, the need for a "feminine principle" remained and was filled in Chinese culture by Kuan Yin, the goddess of compassion. Interestingly, in the West there is a widespread belief in a substantial link between the two goddesses. This connection, which is found all over the Internet, seems to come from a popular book by Merlin Stone, who says:

> The Goddess Kuan Yin (Kwan Yin) is still revered in China today, but it may well be that Kuan Yin is a relatively recent reflection of the more ancient Nu Kwa. Both Nu and Yin mean woman, while the word Kuan means earth, and although the connection is not certain, both names may refer to a concept of the Goddess as Earth or Nature. Some of the accounts of Kuan Yin, still told today,

describe her as having originally been a male who had reached the state of Buddha being, but who then decided to return to earth as a Bodhisattva, a spiritual teacher—taking the form of Kuan Yin. This idea, that the Goddess was once a Buddhist devotee, can of course only have developed after the birth of the first Buddha, Gautama Siddhartha (about 560 B.C.E.), and may reflect the influence of one set of beliefs upon the other, the newer concepts of Buddhism superimposed upon beliefs about the ancient Goddess. Images of Kuan Yin, riding upon a dolphin, may be related to the fish tailed images of Nu Kwa (28–29).

In fact, Kuan means "to look or to gaze," and "Yin" means "sound," so "Kuan Yin" means "perceiver of sounds." Stone's discussion can be put in the category of popular goddess literature, which often makes connections between traditions and cultures that are unsupported by serious scholarly study like that described by Birrell earlier in this chapter. Philip Davies considers such work unacceptable and applies a "truth" standard to it, stating his dissatisfaction thus: "Factual information is used in the Goddess movement as raw material for constructing a narrative which will be personally and politically useful, not as a binding test of objective veracity." It might be better, until further substantiation is provided from ancient texts, to suggest that the story Merlin Stone tells is interesting, but it is about our own culture's need for feminist models. As students of mythology, we can then be aware of the nature of the support Stone provides for her views, which is presented in her own words above.

THE SCHOLARSHIP OF BETTINA KNAPP

A multifaceted scholar, Bettina Knapp has written 40 books on a wide range of subjects, including the arts in general and literature in particular. Her work on mythology is an especially important part of these studies, and within this area she explores the feminine aspects of mythology in several works. In *Women in Myth*, from which our excerpt is taken, Knapp builds her study around terms drawn from Jungian psychologist Karl Kerényi, who distinguishes between the archetypal, which refers to the "original and timeless" elements of mythology, and the ectypal, which refers to the elements of a myth corresponding to our temporal world, the world of sense (xviii).

Knapp's work in this volume can be construed as a feminist approach to mythology. As we saw above, Anne Birrell has highlighted the story of Nü Kwa that was hidden behind that of more recent deities in China's pantheon. In turn, in her chapter on "China's Fragmented Goddess Images," Knapp amplifies the changes Birrell has identified by providing us with historical and sociological insights into the story of Nü Kwa.

Knapp begins with an extensive introductory overview; our introduction to China's three great literary traditions comes from this section. She next provides an ectypal analysis of the myths discussed, and then an archetypal analysis. The former describes the historical situation represented by particular texts, as well as the condition and status of women at the time. The latter concerns the ritual and theological matters found in the myth. The description of Nü Kwa is taken from the latter section.

This excerpt comes from Bettina Knapp, "China's Fragmented Goddess Images," in *Women in Myth*.*

A Brief Introduction to China's Three Main Belief Systems

Whereas Western myths are wholly recorded by poets such as Homer, Aeschylus, Euripides, Sophocles, Ovid, and Virgil, **Chinese religious texts are fragmented,** episodic, contradictory, and obscure. Cosmogonic, creation, stellar, and flood myths,

"Chinese religious texts are fragmented"—These qualities also describe the Egyptian texts discussed in Chapter 28, p. 403.

Bettina Knapp. "China's Fragmented Goddess Images," in *Women in Myth* (Albany, NY: State University of New York Press, 1996).

Pronunciation Guide

In the table below, the word "aspirated" refers to pronouncing the word with a heavy puff of air following the sound, as with the p's in the English word 'pop,' and is indicated by an apostrophe.

ch'(aspirated)	ch
ch (unaspirated)	j (Thus, the name of Mao's widow is written "Chiang Ch'ing" and would be pronounced "Jiang Ching.")
k'(aspirated)	k
k (unaspirated)	g
p'(aspirated)	p
p (unaspirated)	b
t'(aspirated)	t
t (unaspirated)	d
ts'and tz'(aspirated)	ts
ts and tz (unaspirated)	s or ds (ds as in "woods")
hs	sh
j	French j plus r (no exact English equivalent)
a	a (as in star)
e	e (as in set)
i	e (as in he) or i (as in machine)
ou	o (as in over)
u	oo (as in too)
en	un (as in under)
ih	ir (as in bird; no exact English equivalent)
ü	German ü (oo sound made with lips rounded; no exact English equivalent)
ai	ie (as in lie) or i (as in I)
ei	ay (as in day)
ao	ow (as in now)
uo	oo (as in too) plus ou (as in ought)
ui, uei	oo (as in too) plus ay (as in day)
ung	oo (as in book) plus ng (as in thing)

"The Chinese Language." Columbia University, East Asian Curriculum Project, April 11, 2007. http://afe .easia.columbia.edu/china/language/teach.htm (accessed December 21, 2007).

Chinese goddesses:

- Nü Kwa creates women and men. She saves humankind from cosmic catastrophe when one of the pillars holding the sky collapses.

- Hsi Wang Mu represents the element "yin." She cultivates the peach tree of immortality and brews an elixir from its fruit.

- Ch'ang-O moon goddess, stole the elixir of immortality that had been provided her husband Yi the archer. She did not swallow enough to take her to heaven, but she reached the moon.

- Pi-hia yüan-kün protects women in childbirth and with her helpers assists with childhood diseases.

- Kuan Yin represents compassion. She forgave her father all the torments he inflicted on her for wanting to enter a convent instead of marrying. For more about her, see the Introduction, p. 115.

as well as tales of divine and/or virgin births, visitations, and apparitions overlap and reoccur, forever altering the emphases and philosophical impact of the particular passage involved. Allusions and brief statements about miraculous or monstrous deeds of divinities, as well as incredible feats of heroines and heroes, are generally diffused in bodies of ancient esoteric astrological, scientific, historical, and geographic works.

Because the Chinese have tended, since earliest times, "to reject supernatural explanations for the universe," they have chosen to humanize or take a euhemeristic approach to what "had originally been myth" and made it come "to be accepted as authentic history." This may offer partial explanation of why myths were not recorded "in their pristine mythological form" (Bodde 1981, 79).

The present approach to the study of Chinese myth will be to present sections of myths drawn from specific ancient sources. In that the feminine principle is to be highlighted, focus will be placed on the accomplishments of goddesses such as **Nü-Kwa** (or Nü Wa or Nü Gua), creatrix of women and men, and savior of humankind from cosmic catastrophe; **Hsi Wang Mu** (or the Queen Mother of the West), ruler of the Western Paradise and purveyor of the elixir of immortality; **Ch'ang-O** (or Heng-O), the beautiful goddess of the moon; **Pi-hia yüan-kün** (or the Holy Mother), the protectress of childbirth; and Kuan shih yin tzu tsai (or **Kuan Yin**), goddess of compassion.

It has been suggested that the honor accorded to such goddesses as Nü Kwa and Hsi Wang Mu indicates the prior existence of a less intransigent patriarchal society than the one that came into being with the rise of phallocentric Confucianism that repressed women (Kuo Mo-jo, quoted in Loewe 1979, 58).

The underlying philosophical and religious principles, as well as the climate that nurtured Chinese mythology, are contained in Taoism, Confucianism, and Buddhism, whose precepts provide obvious but also subtle insights into the manner in which mythical women—by extension earthly females—were perceived and treated in China. Unfortunately only a brief purview will be given of these religious concepts, but it will be sufficient, hopefully, to familiarize the reader with their broad concepts.

Intuitive, ambiguous, and mystical in essence, the Taoist approach to life is conceptually **bipolar.** Nature's cyclical processes (seasonal changes, growth and decline, night and day, etc.) indicate two factors at work in the universe: yang (viewed empirically as masculine) and yin (viewed empirically as feminine). Both life principles form a *whole*, each containing its opposite. Woman, as "the *mother* of all things" participated and participates fully in cosmic functioning; she, as yin, plays as significant a role as the male, albeit different, in maintaining a balance in the bipolar universe. We read in Lao Tzu's *Tao Te Ching* (*The Way and Its Power*, c. sixth century B.C.E.):

> The Tao [Way] that can be told of
> Is not the eternal Tao;
> The name that can be named
> Is not the eternal name.
> Nameless, it is the origin of Heaven and earth;　　　5
> Namable, it is the mother of all things.
>> (Quoted in de Bary 1960, 51)

The notion of the Great Mother, which suggests the existence of a limitless supply of energy or life force, is continuously feeding the limited if not weak capacities of the male. Interesting as well is the fact that Taoism praises inactivity rather than activity, holding weakness above strength.

Paradoxes, ambiguities, and symbols prevail in the mysterious timed/timeless worlds of the nonmanifest/manifest.

> Always nonexistent,
>   That we may apprehend its inner secret;
> Always existent,
>   That we may discern its outer manifestations.　　　10
> These two are the same;
> Only as they manifest themselves they receive different names.
>> (Ibid.)

Images and abstractions are gender-oriented.

> That they are the same is the mystery.
> Mystery of all mysteries!
> The door of all subtleties! . . .　　　15
>
> . . .
> The Tao is empty [like a bowl],
> It is used, though perhaps never full.
> It is fathomless, possibly the progenitor of all things. . . .
>> (Ibid.)

"bipolar"—This word is widely used to refer to manic-depressive illness, but Knapp uses it in its more traditional meaning of "characterized by two extremes."

"The Tao [Way]"—"Tao" is often translated as "Way." Thus these lines could read "The Way that can be told of is not the eternal Way."

The Taoist symbol, the *Taijitu* or *yin-yang* is a popular decoration in the West. It represents the universe as a dynamic swirl of yin (female) and yang (male) forces, each with a small circle of the other in it. Pictured at the right is an intricate handmade quilt by Barbara Gail Blate of Columbus, North Carolina, which represents the sky as lighter colored and the earth as darker, the opposite of the traditional symbolism.

In the above quotations, we note that words such as "door," "fathomless," and "progenitor" suggest the yin principle. The same applies to the following images:

> The spirit of the valley never dies.
> This is called the mysterious female.   20
> The gateway of the mysterious female
> Is called the root of heaven and earth.
> Dimly visible, it seems as if it were there,
> Yet use will never drain it.
>
> (*Tao Te Ching* 6.62)

Confucius—The name "Confucius" is a creation of western translators. His name has also been rendered as K'ung-fu-zi or Kong-fu-tzu.

Confucius (Master K'ung; c. 551–479 B.C.E.) preaches character building, learning, virtue, filial and ancestral piety, and a family-style morality based on the ethical wisdom of "cultivated" or "superior men." For Confucius, "filial duty and fraternal duty" were "fundamental to Manhood-at-its-best." In the *Canon of Filiality* (or the *Hsiao ching*, third century B.C.E.), a collection of pronouncements allegedly made by Confucius, we read: "Filiality is the root of virtue, and that from which civilization derives" (Thompson 1969, 39).

Because only the wisest and most honorable men were capable of governing society, moral integrity was stressed. No one but a "gentleman" was capable of ruling China, and it was incumbent upon him to elevate those he governed by serving as an example rather than by exercising autocratic control.

Women, virtually spurned, were barely mentioned in Confucius' writings; when they were, it was negatively. In the master's opinion, women were clearly inferior to men.

> The Master said, "In one's household, it is the women and the small men that are difficult to deal with. If you let them get too close, they become insolent. If you keep them at a distance, they complain." (*Analects* 17.25)

By separating the sexes male purity could be maintained; thus, women lived in the inner rooms of the house, while the men occupied outer ones. The existence and function of women as individuals were reduced to procreation and adherence to the prevailing societal regulations.

Buddhism, up to the time of the writing of the *Pure Land Sutra* (100 B.C.E. to 100 C.E.), one of the most popular of philosophical writings, considered woman to be an obstacle to man's spiritual evolution. Her sexual energy led to desire, bondage (*samsara*), pain, and suffering, culminating in cycles of rebirths (Paul 1985, 5). Because women represented a threat to the stability of the monastic communities and the discipline practiced therein, male chastity was emphasized. The following is an exchange between the Buddha and Ananda, his favorite disciple:

[ANANDA:]—"How are we to conduct ourselves, Lord, with regard to womankind?"

[THE BUDDHA:]—"As not seeing them, Ananda."

[ANANDA:]—"But if we should see them, what are we to do?"

[THE BUDDHA:]—"Not talking, Ananda."

[ANANDA:]—"But if they should speak to us, Lord, what are we to do?"

[THE BUDDHA]—"Keep wide awake, Ananda." (Quoted in ibid., 7)

According to the *Pure Land Sutra*, any and every worshipper who invokes Amida Buddha's name will be released from the pain of this world. Pictorially, Amida Buddha has been depicted seated on a lotus throne in his Western Paradise next to his attendant bodhisattva Avalokiteśvara, the androgynous Kuan Yin, "Goddess [God] of Compassion," savior/savioress. To men who come for solace, Kuan Yin appears as a male; to females who are anguished, she manifests herself most frequently as a beautiful and gracious woman with a child in her arms (*Kuan Yin* 1944, 4).

Whereas Confucianism and Buddhism considered the feminine as fearsome and destructive, although necessary in the procreating process, Taoism alone accepted women as a power implicit in nature's cyclical process and as part of the ordering principle of eternally interacting and continuously transforming elements making up Tao.

Turning back the centuries to China's uncertain beginnings, we find its origins, as in many a land, bathed in mystery. The latest archeological digs in China suggest that (as in India, Japan, and other nations) ancient China enjoyed, if not a matrilineal culture, at least a far less stringent form of a patriarchate. A mother or earth goddess was worshipped in Paleolithic, Neolithic, and early historical periods. Among some small statues unearthed by archeologists are the head of a female (c. 3000 B.C.E.), and a pregnant goddess figure encircled with birds, tortoises, and dragons of jade.

Nevertheless, China's legendary culture heroes are, as to be expected, male: **Fu Hsi** invented writing, music, and domestication of animals; **Shen Nüng** introduced agriculture, commerce, and pharmacopoeia to humankind; **Ch'ih Yu** brought metallurgy and metal weapons to the land; **the Yellow Emperor** taught the potter's art and shipbuilding, as well as the use of armor and wheeled vehicles; **Ti K'u** invented music; and **Hou Chi** taught how to sow grain. Three virtuous demigod rulers—Yao, Shun, and Yü—revealed the meaning of wisdom, courage, and integrity. **Yü the Great,** allegedly

"The Thousand Hand Guanyin" performed by the China Disabled People's Performing Art Troupe. This dance represents the attributes of Kuan Yin, who in some of her forms has a thousand arms and a thousand eyes. YouTube videos may be available showing this dance. See Introduction above, p. 116.

China's male culture heroes:

- Fu Hsi invented writing, music, and domestication of animals. He was a minor figure in ancient mythology whose role was much enhanced in the Han era.

- Shen Nüng introduced agriculture, commerce, and pharmacopoeia to humankind. He was a minor figure in early mythological texts but his role was enhanced by Han period mythographers.

- Ch'ih Yu invented metallurgy and metal weapons. He was also the god of war and accounts of him are early.

- the Yellow Emperor taught pottery and shipbuilding, the use of armor and wheeled vehicles. In the early tradition, his role was minor, but later he became a major Taoist deity.

- Ti K'u invented music. Birrell notes that much of the material about him comes from rationalizing Han sources (1993, 53).

- Hou Chi taught how to sow grain. Birrell suggests that like Ceres this figure may have originally been female and later transformed to fit into a hierarchy of male gods (301).

- Yü the Great allegedly born miraculously from a rock, "pacified" a terrible flood by digging channels for the excess water, thus saving humanity. These stories are, in Birrell's view, in the authentic narrative style of archaic myth (121) and not a Han reformulation, though Yu also is found in Han stories that add philosophical abstractions or literary flourishes to his story (157).

"Nü Kwa duly became his wife"— Many cultures have deities who are siblings but have married, including Zeus and Hera (Greek), Geb and Nut (Egyptian), Inti and Mama Quilla (Inca).

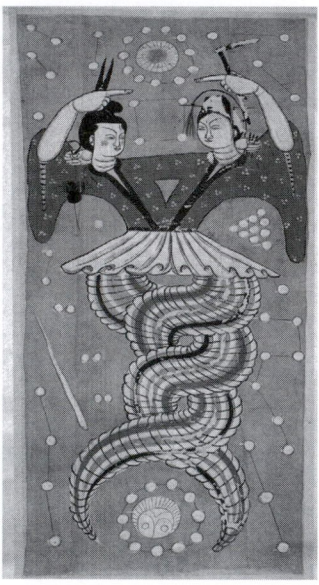

This Tang dynasty (618–907 C.E.) painting found in the Astana Tombs near Turpan represents Nü Kwa (left) and Fu Hsi with human upper bodies and snakelike entwined lower bodies. With her right hand, the goddess holds compasses representing the sky and has four small sticks in her other hand. The god has a carpenter's square symbolizing the earth in his left hand and an ink marker in his right. The wheel above the pair represents the sun, and the wheel below has the head of a toad and symbolizes the moon. Around the figures are small circles representing stars and a streak which is the tail of a comet.

born miraculously from a rock, "pacified" a terrible flood by digging channels into which the excess water flowed, thus saving humanity.

NÜ KWA: CREATOR AND SAVIOR

Nü Kwa (the prefix Nü means woman), the "Goddess of Go-betweens" or "Arranger of Marriages," was said to have existed originally as both an empress and a female spirit. Her sexual ambiguity persisted, however, until the first century C.E., when she was definitively identified as a female (Bodde 1981, 62).

Born three months after her brother, Fu Hsi, one of the ancient culture heroes, **Nü Kwa duly became his wife.** Thus did she come to be known as the inventor of the institution of marriage. In Han times, the brother and sister relationship symbolized feminine and masculine principles or the yin and yang system. The relationship was looked upon as a hierogamy, and each gender was endowed with some attributes of the other.

Nü Kwa and Fu Hsi were said to have been provided with human bodies and intertwining dragon tails. In other versions of the myth, Nü Kwa was described as having "a long head with two fleshy horns" and the body of a snake; or as formed with "the body of a serpent and [the] head of an ox." Elsewhere she is rendered as an icon with a human head (Liehtze 1990, 54).

According to the *Shan Hai Ching*, Nü Kwa not only was endowed with a woman's face and the body of a snake, but she had the power to alter her appearance seventy times a day (16.239).

> There are ten spirits here called Nü Kwa Chih Ch'ang (Nü Kwa's bowels [intestines]). They changed to spirits [from her intestines after her death] and dwell in Li Kuang (chestnut wide) wilderness where they block the roads. (*Shan Hai Ching* 16.233)

That Nü Kwa could transform herself at will was a fact of life for the Chinese. It was not unusual for foxes, tigers, dragons, and other animals to assume human shapes—a skill interpreted as manifestations of creative ability and capacity for self-renewal.

During Nü Kwa's early years, she considered earthly existence pleasurable, but in time her loneliness saddened her. To allay her melancholy, she grasped a handful of yellow earth and kneaded and fashioned it into human likenesses. In another version of the myth, we read:

> It is popularly said that when Heaven and Earth had opened forth, but before there were human beings, Nü Kwa created men by patting yellow earth together. But the work tasked her strength and left her no free time, so that she then dragged a **string** through mud, thus heaping it up so as to make it into men. Therefore the rich and the noble are those men of yellow earth, whereas the poor and the lowly—all ordinary people—are those **cord**-made men. (Ying Shao, Feng-su t'ung-yi, quoted in Bodde 1981, 64)

A T'ang dynasty version (ninth century B.C.E.) of the Nü Kwa legend presents her incestuous relationship with her brother, and the very notion of sexual intercourse in general, as a factor that introduces into the world the notion of "shame and guilt" (as in the case of Adam and Eve).

> Long ago, when the world first began, there were two people, Nü Kwa and her older brother. They lived on Mount K'un-lun. And there were not yet any ordinary people in the world. They talked about becoming husband and wife, but they felt ashamed. So the brother at once went with his sister up Mount K'un-lun and made this prayer:
>
> Oh Heaven, if Thou wouldst send us two forth as man and wife, then make all the misty vapor gather.
> If not, then make all the misty vapor disperse.

At this, the misty vapor immediately gathered. When the sister became intimate with her brother, they plaited some *grass* to make a fan to screen their faces. Even today, when a man takes a wife, they hold a fan, which is a symbol of what happened. *(Tu yi chih,* quoted in Birrell 1994, 35)

The Taoist *Huai-nan Tzu* (compiled by Liu An, c. 139 B.C.E.) introduced other elements into the Nü Kwa myth. A primeval god, Kung-kung (**euhemerized** as a human "rebel" in Chou writings, but depicted "as a horned monster with serpent's body" in the late Han period), functioned as the administrator of punishment. On one occasion, he battled against the monstrous god Chuan-hsü (an ancient legendary ruler) for the godheadship (Bodde 1981, 63). In so doing, Kung-kung knocked down **Pu-Chou Mountain, one of the four supporting pillars** on which Heaven rested (Birrell 1994, 97). In another section of the *Huai-nan Tzu,* it was said that not one but "four poles collapsed," after which the sky fell (69). The absence of sky subsequently caused the displacement of astral bodies, accounting to a great extent for the earth's disequilibrium and for the onset of terrestrial floods. Because the sun's rays were unable to reach the earth (due to the tear in the sky), the power of the flaming dragon who had meanwhile taken over the space increased in intensity, causing fires to rage on earth.

> In very ancient times, the four pillars [at the compass points] were broken down, the nine provinces [of the habitable world] were split apart, Heaven did not wholly cover [Earth], and Earth did not completely support [Heaven]. Fires flamed without being extinguished, waters inundated without being stopped, fierce beasts ate the people, and birds of prey seized the old and weak in their claws. Thereupon Nü Kwa fused together stones of the five colors with which she patched together azure Heaven. She cut off the feet of a turtle with which she set up the four pillars. She slaughtered the Black Dragon in order to save the province of Chi [the present Ho-pei and Shansi provinces in North China]. She collected the ashes of reeds with which to check the wild waters. (Bodde 1981, 62)

Thanks to Nü Kwa's knowledge of the science of metallurgy, she repaired the fault in the sky. Thus did she virtually single-handedly avert the deadly cosmic disaster. On a human level, the torn sky and the ensuing cataclysmic events that had given rise to a break in communication between heaven and earth had now been mended by Nü Kwa.

Nü Kwa's understanding of engineering, in this instance, dam building, saved the world from devastating floods. Following her great achievement, as detailed in the *Huai-nan Tzu,* not only was harmony between beasts and humans restored, but cosmic and seasonal order was ushered in.

> Ever since then, there have been no birds or beasts, no insects or reptiles, that do not sheathe their claws and fangs and conceal their poisonous venom, and they no longer have rapacious hearts. When one considers her achievement, it knows only the bounds of Ninth Heaven above and the limits of Yellow Clod below. She is acclaimed by later generations, and her brilliant glory sweetly suffuses the whole world. She rides in a thunder-carriage driving shaft-steeds of winged dragons and an outer pair of green hornless dragons. She bears the emblem of the Fortune of Life and Death. Her seat is the Visionary Chart. Her steeds' halter is of yellow cloud; in the front is a white calf-dragon, in the rear a rushing snake. Floating, drifting, free and easy, she guides ghostly spirits as she ascends to Ninth Heaven. She has audience with god inside the holy gates. Silently, solemnly, she comes to rest below the High Ancestor. Then, without displaying her achievements, without spreading her fame, she holds the secret of **the Way of the True Person** and follows the eternal nature of Heaven and earth. *(Huai-nan Tzu,* quoted in Birrell 1993, 71)

Nü Kwa's character traits, intellectual capabilities, and sense of responsibility, as distinguished from those of her brother, are depicted semiotically in the legend. Because Fu Hsi had been given a carpenter's square, an instrument designed to measure and trace quadrangular forms, he was identified with the earth. Nü Kwa, on the other hand, was provided with a compass, which served to trace circles, thus connecting her with heaven.

"string . . . cord"—The act of creation by Nü Kwa is seen as building or construction. A cord with knots at regular intervals can be used as a kind of ruler by a builder.

euhemerized Euhemerism refers to the practice of reinterpreting old myths as being about historical or legendary figures. See also Chapter 30, p. 431.

"Pu-Chou Mountain, one of the four supporting pillars"—Birrell notes that the *Huai-nan Tzu* is a collection of writings by various authors. In the one-pole variation of the story, there is no Nü-Kwa to restore order, and the point of this version is the aetiology of why Chinese rivers flow east, as a result of the damage done by Kung-kung (69).

"the Way of the True Person"—Birrell points out that this is Taoist philosophical terminology and that the narrative "results in a subversion of the myth of the goddess Nü Kwa, for she is transposed from the status of an independent primeval deity to that of a lesser goddess under the power of a supreme god, named High Ancestor (T'ai-tsu), in the Taoist pantheon." This, in Birrell's view, represents the beginning of the Han era in which the ancient gods and goddesses are "demythologized" and a new group of deities is put into place (Birrell 1993, 71).

An instrument associated with the precision of mathematics and exact sciences, the compass was believed to represent also rectitude and imagination. In that it was used by the Chinese as an important astrological symbol, it served as a link between heavenly and earthly spheres. Understandably, then, did Nü Kwa function, as we have seen, as the restorer of order and the maintainer of cosmic equilibrium (Christie 1985, 88).

Although Nü Kwa's power and achievements were great, the Chinese had problems rationalizing her creative abilities. For example, since she had been provided with a body prior to her own creation of humankind, questions as to who had endowed her with form were posed in the *Tian Wen* ("Questions of Heaven," from the *Ch'u-tz'u*, third century B.C.E.).

> **Nü Kwa had a serpent tail**.
> By what standard was her body formed?
>
> (Field 1986, 98)

No answer was put forward. Not only did the question remain unanswered; others arose. As the primordial creator of both women and men, from what prototype did she fashion them?

A **dichotomy** existed between the Nü Kwa worshipped in ancient times and the depotentiated deity of later centuries. Her early attributes identified her as creatrix of humankind and mender of the cataclysmic cosmic fault, and thus the savior of the universe. Moreover, her repairs had been accomplished with such expertise and such profound knowledge in a variety of disciplines, namely engineering and the sciences, that she succeeded in both balancing and steadying the earth's extremities. With an increase in patriarchal power in post-Han times, however, Nü Kwa was no longer considered a model of perfection. Divested to a great extent of her miraculous powers, she was no longer worshipped as humanity's redeemer and rescuer. With her demotion, there followed a concomitant diminution of feminine power in the new and evolving Chinese pantheon. Scholars have come to believe, therefore, that the ancient myth of Nü Kwa was what remained of China's early less intransigent phallocentric culture.

Further Reading

Birrell, Anne. *Chinese Myths*. London: British Museum Press, 2000.

Sidebar notes:

"Nü Kwa had a serpent tail" — This mention of the creator goddess predates the stories about P'An Ku by six centuries (Birrell, 1993, 33). See Introduction, p. 113.

dichotomy Birrell also compares the account from the "Questions of Heaven" to the one by Ying Shao in which Nü Kwa creates humans from yellow earth and the one from the T'ang Dynasty that sees the union of Nü Kwa and her brother as shameful (see above, p. 122). Her comment is that the various accounts of Nü Kwa "demonstrate the ways in which an arcane primal myth develops into a specific theme, from creative power to the act of creation, and then further evolves, or degenerates, into a myth that contradicts the original intent and meaning of the early mythic expression" (Birrell 1993, 34–35).

Part 2B

Myths of Destruction

As noted at the beginning of the part on creation, myths of destruction represent a refinement on creation rather than simply the annihilation of a world or a mythological system. As noted in the Introduction to Hesiod's story of the Ages of Man (p. 39), Mircea Eliade maintained that all ancient mythologies represent the world we live in as based on a timeless celestial model to which history returns in a kind of cosmic cycle of creation and destruction. We will see that each of the myths of destruction presented in this part contains a new message of rebirth and hope for the culture that originated it. By and large, these stories represent ways of emphasizing and celebrating the important aspects of a mythological system: we will see that it is the characteristic and the essential that survives the remaking of the world. This is perhaps most obvious in the Biblical story in Genesis, where the flood provides an opportunity for God to explicitly expound his ongoing relationship with his people in the form of a covenant—a formal, nearly contractual bond whose explicit outward signs are established in the rainbow—and in the newly found right to eat meat. As we will see, in other mythological systems where the links between gods and humans are less positive, a myth of destruction will nonetheless emphasize the positive aspects of human existence.

Among the mythical traditions of destruction studied in this book, the most predominant punishment by far is a flood; only in the *Prose Edda* is there destruction of the world by other means—fire and warfare. The account there also differs in another way from those of Genesis and Ovid's *Metamorphoses*. In the *Prose Edda,* Ragnarok comes about from what might be considered natural causes: a spark from Muspel causes the fire, and the anger of the Midgard Serpent sparks the final battles between the gods and their traditional enemies.

Destruction by Flood

The story of the flood in the Western tradition probably arose in Mesopotamia, "the land between rivers," where flooding was common. The story was told by different peoples to make different points. In Genesis the point of the story is that, after the flood, God establishes a covenant with his people (see Ch. 12, p. 141). In Ovid, the story provides another instance of the metamorphoses that represent the poet's theme: at the end, new human beings are created from the rocks thrown by Deucalion and Pyrrha, the survivors of the flood. In *Metamorphoses,* the gods tolerate humans only insofar as they are useful and not a nuisance (see Ch. 11, p. 131f).

In the *Epic of Gilgamesh,* the flood story provides an understanding of the mortal nature of human beings: they will all die, except Utnapishtim. It is the hero Gilgamesh who brings back this understanding to his people. Thus he is able to transform his personal suffering at the death of his friend Enkidu into a benefit to his people. Because it is so deeply embedded in the narrative itself, the flood story in Gilgamesh has been left in its original context in that text (see Ch. 15, p. 188).

It seems reasonable that a flood story would have different meanings according to when and where it was told. In Mesopotamia, the experience of a flood must have been much like the accounts from the eastern United States heard from time to time on the evening news. Heavy rains continue for several days, the ground becomes saturated, rivers rise and overflow their banks, and emergency workers in boats rescue survivors. In the desert southwest, the experience of a flood can be quite different. Much of the land is dry and rocky so that the rain runs off rapidly rather than soaking in. This gives rise to flash floods that can fill an arroyo with fast rushing water in only a few minutes. In fact, run-off from distant rainstorms can cause floods in areas where no rain has fallen, making the destruction seem to come from nowhere. The means of salvation too may need consideration: of course, it is not the ark which saves Noah and his family, but God, who provides detailed instructions on how to build it.

The following table points out the differences mentioned previously and many others. It compares events in the versions of the great flood story in *Gilgamesh,* the Bible, and Ovid's *Metamorphoses.*

Destruction by Fire

In the *Prose Edda,* Snorri Sturluson describes Ragnarok as the end of the old world order, a total annihilation of what had been. At Ragnarok, the earth will burn up. The gods and heroes will kill the monsters, and they themselves will be killed in the battle. The bridge Bifrost, which connects earth and heaven, will break. For a detailed account of this, see Chapter 13.

Snorri's account presents the end of the worship structure of the ancient gods. There is a link, however, between the old order and the new. As a "green and fair" earth rises out of the sea after the fire, bearing new human beings, worship is transferred to the sons of Thor and of Odin who are still alive. In this way Snorri allows continuity between the old order and the new.

Rebirth: New Creation after the Destruction

In each of the accounts presented here, the destruction of the world is followed by a renewal of the earth and a repopulation by righteous survivors or fresh, new beings. In Genesis, the Lord has chosen Noah and has instructed him very specifically

Comparison of Accounts of the Flood

	Gilgamesh	Bible (Genesis)	Metamorphoses
Causes	Enlil complains that the people of Shurrupak are too loud.	Mankind is increasingly sinful.	Humans had grown evil and scorned the gods.
Taking Action	"So the gods agreed to eliminate mankind."	"When the Lord saw how great was man's wickedness on earth, . . . he said: I will wipe out from the earth the men whom I have created . . . for I am very sorry that I made them." (6:7)	Jupiter (Zeus) observes from his throne on Olympus and calls together the council of the gods.
Exceptions	(The choosing of Utnapishtim is not explicitly described.)	"But Noah found favor with the Lord." (6:8) "You alone in this age have I found to be truly just." (7:1)	Jupiter announces that he must destroy the mortals "lest the uninfected part be contaminated." (Demigods, rustic deities, nymphs, fauns, satyrs should be able to stay on the lands given to them by the gods.)
Warning	Ea warns Utnapishtim to tear down his house and build a boat. He tells him: "despise worldly goods." Ea gives the measurements: "the ground space was one acre, each side of the deck measured 120 cubits, making a square."	The Lord tells Noah to build an ark. The Lord gives dimensions: 300 x 50 x 33 cubits.	Some of the gods at the council speak in agreement, some agree silently. "They all, however, felt grief over the sacrifice [elimination] of the human race." (They would miss sacrifices to themselves.)
Survivors	(Ea does not explicitly say that Utnapishtim is chosen, but it is clear from the warning that he is.)	The Lord tells Noah that he and his family will survive.	Righteous survivors are not chosen. Deucalion and Pyrrha seem to survive almost by accident. Jupiter promises a different, wonderful race.
Provisions	Utnapishtim brings all his gold and livestock and wild animals, his family and all his craftsmen.	Noah is to bring two of every creature (two of unclean, seven of clean).	No one is expected to survive, so no provision is made for life after the flood.
The Storm	Gods cause the storm. Nergel pulls out the dams of the nether waters. Ninurta throws down the dikes. The god of the storm turns daylight into darkness.	(The fury of the storm is not described in Genesis. The account emphasizes that it lasts 40 days and that it causes such a flood that the waters recede only after 150 days.)	Jupiter unleashes storm clouds without warning. Neptune calls on rivers to break loose and produces high winds. Crops are destroyed.
Gods' Fear of Destruction	Even the gods were terrified of the flood. They fled to the highest heaven. The great gods of heaven and hell wept.	(Such a reaction is not reported in Genesis.)	The gods decide that a flood is safer than fire, which may reach up to heaven.
Gods' Regret	Ishtar lamented her actions: "Why did I command this evil in the council of the gods?"	The Lord says: "Never again will I doom the earth because of man nor will I ever again strike down all living beings."	Jupiter sees the sole survivors as worthy and pious. Therefore he stops the storm and restores the world.
Landfall	The boat lands on a mountain.	The Ark comes to rest on Mt. Ararat.	Deucalion and Pyrrha's boat lands on Mt. Parnassus.
Thanksgiving	Utnapishtim offers sacrifice.	Noah builds an altar and offers a sacrifice.	Deucalion and Pyrrha pray and visit Themis at the oracle.
Rewards	Ishtar and the gods gather. Ishtar excludes Enlil for bringing about the flood. To atone, Enlil makes Utnapishtim and his wife immortal.	The Lord tells Noah: "Every creature that is above shall be yours to eat; I give them all to you as I did the green plants." (9:3)	They follow upon the oracle to "throw the bones of your great mother behind your backs." This creates more humans.

how to build an ark and how to stock it with the beginnings of the new civilization. In the Roman flood story, Pyrrha and Deucalion are spared because of their moral goodness, and from them the new human race is to be born.

In the *Prose Edda,* after Ragnarok, new life emerges from the warm, moist earth. The heirs of Odin and Thor have survived; and the sun, which had been eaten by Fenrir the wolf, has borne a daughter. Thus the personification of the sun allows the restoration of the world through her progeny, and life proceeds.

In Genesis and *Metamorphoses,* the destruction has taken place in the distant past, and we, as the propagators of the myth, are the descendants of the righteous survivors. For us, the story is a cautionary tale, reminding us that if we sin, we will be punished. This is a good, if simplified example of Levi-Strauss's view that myth teaches people how to behave properly as members of a community (see Ch. 20, p. 280f).

Like the other tales of destruction, Snorri's narrative also teaches. Its perspective is different, though, since both the teller and the listener are outside the ancient tradition described. Snorri constantly cites the old sagas and reports, so his account does provide information. His audience, however, is *between* traditions, so that the teaching it receives is not integrated into its function in any community or society. Thus, the pull to participate both morally and emotionally is very weak.

In fact, some students of myth would say that Snorri's audience was a lot like us: living as we do in a pluralistic society, many of us are between traditions as well. Although myths continue to speak to us regardless of our relationship to the tradition that they come from, our commitment to them may not be as strong as it was for the people who used them as guides to a way of life. Victor Turner points out that the lack of societal commitment to a myth or a ritual affects the nature and perhaps the quality of participation in it (see Ch. 26, p. 381). That is perhaps why *Star Trek* occupies a mythical status in our lives (see Ch. 40, p. 590), but it does not, for the most part, involve us in as high a level of belief and participation as the Zuni myths do for those living in the communities guided by them. In addition, our distance from the belief system of a myth may explain why we have a tendency to regard it as only a "false story" rather than a meaningful one (see p. 1).

Further Reading

Dundes, Alan. *The Flood Myth.* Berkeley: University of California Press, 1988.

Eliade, Mircea. *The Myth of the Eternal Return: Or Cosmos and History.* Trans. Willard R. Trask. Bollingen Series XLVI. Princeton, NJ: Princeton University Press, 1974.

Ovid's Flood Story

WHAT TO EXPECT . . . The Roman poet Ovid included a section on the great flood in his major work, *Metamorphoses*. There is an introduction to Ovid's writing style in Chapter 4 (pp. 42–44) and a discussion of some of his aims as a writer of mythology in Chapter 2 (pp. 19–21). The writing style of the selection in this chapter is sophisticated, and the content is presented with wit and humor: you might think about what the scene between Pyrrha and Deucalion would look like if it were acted out on stage. However, despite the light-hearted aspects of his story, as Ovid's audience expected, *Metamorphoses* presents insights for us into ideas that the Romans would have recognized as scientifically accurate about their world.

In this chapter, you will encounter a section on the Ages of Man, which you can compare with Hesiod's (Ch. 3, pp. 39–41); sections on Pyrrha and Deucalion, to compare with Noah and his family (Ch. 12, pp. 134–35) and with Utnapishtim and his wife, the survivors of the flood in the *Epic of Gilgamesh* (Ch. 15, p. 190–91).

Ovid, the Roman poet, is most famous for *Metamorphoses,* a long work that incorporates a great deal of mythic material. In focusing on these stories, it is important to understand that Ovid was a sophisticated and complex writer who did not write to give us information about myths, but to illustrate the theme of metamorphosis or change. Chapter 4, p. 42, includes Ovid's story of creation. The introduction to that chapter contains an extensive discussion of Ovid's writing style and his aims in writing about mythology.

Stories about the destruction of the world through floods are widespread in mythology. This text contains several, including the one from Ovid that follows, as well as those in Genesis and in the *Epic of Gilgamesh*. A comparison of these flood stories is found on page 127. Despite the widespread distribution of these stories, Ovid's turns out to be especially important because it is the only extensive flood story from the mythology developed by Greek and Roman culture. Other Roman writers like Lucretius mention the story of a flood, but only Ovid reports it in detail.

The flood story in Ovid seems to be related to Middle Eastern accounts through the character of Prometheus. Scholar Charles Penglase suggests that it represents a Mesopotamian tradition in which the god Enki rebels against the head god Enlil and protects humans from his wrath. In this view, the Greek figure of Prometheus represents the trickster figure Enki. It has been noted that the story of the flood does not fit the physical environment of Greece, while periodic flooding is related to fertility in the Mesopotamian region. The creation of Pandora in Hesiod is reminiscent of Mesopotamian stories in which Enki shapes mankind from clay, and Penglase suggests that her origin represents the creation of all mankind, not of women alone. In Hesiod, Pandora is led out and given to Epimetheus, Prometheus' brother. A variety of stories connect Pandora to Deucalion. In some she and Prometheus are his parents, while in others they are the parents of his wife, Pyrrha. After the flood, it is Pyrrha and Deucalion who create mankind. Ironically, despite their association with the rebel Prometheus, they are the most pious of mortals and most suited to repopulate the earth.

It is interesting to compare Ovid's flood story with his account of creation, which is also in *Metamorphoses*. Although the two accounts occur in rather quick succession in the long poem, the creation story is much more dry and abstract. Except for the occasional mention of "some god" who had a role in ordering and organizing the world, the story lacks a hero or agents and is presented mainly in scientific terms. In contrast, Ovid's story of the flood contains well-developed narrative elements, including a council meeting of the gods presided over by a blustering Jupiter, outraged at the behavior of human beings. The story follows the account of the four Ages of Man, and in the Iron Age, human beings have become, in Jupiter's view, totally depraved and must be eliminated. In another memorable scene, Pyrrha and Deucalion, the survivors of the flood, are at a loss for what to do next. Ovid imbues their dilemma with a comic touch as he has them debate the interpretation of the cryptic oracle they are to follow to renew life on earth.

Such lighthearted and frivolous treatment of divine matters raises the question of what a story like this one meant to its Roman audience. However, to answer this question, it is necessary to remember that the worship of the Greek gods was conceived quite differently from modern religions. The Homeric gods represented a time-honored tradition with extensive meaning to their worshippers, but were not, for the most part, the focus of personal dedication and piety. Homeric religion was a community activity, not a personal one: worship of the gods did not mean belief in them, so much as regular participation in their ceremonies. These rituals bound the community together in shared actions and values, as would a modern-day civic organization like the Lions Club. For all his light-hearted portrayal of the gods, Ovid represents them as holding the community-oriented values that would have seemed appropriate to his audience.

Although the stories told by Ovid would not have represented theological revelations to be incorporated into the personal belief systems of his audience, they nonetheless included ideas which the audience would recognize as truths about their world. The allegorical interpretation of Homeric stories was widespread and dated back to the sixth and fifth centuries B.C.E. That is, the gods and stories found in Hesiod and Homer were taken to represent "disguised philosophical truths" (Myers, 9) about the physical world. The Stoics, a fourth-century B.C.E. group of philosophers, were especially active in developing such interpretations.

Johannes Baur. Ovid represents Jupiter calling together the Council of the Gods as if it were Augustus convening a meeting of the Roman Senate. This 18th-c. C.E. engraving shows the distance between "the Emperor" and the Senators as Jupiter tells the story of Lycaeon. For more on the political dimension of Ovid's epic, see Ch. 2.

In examining Ovid's story of the flood, we cannot lose sight of his literary style and the expectations of his audience. As discussed in more detail in Chapter 4, Ovid was a sophisticated writer writing for an audience that was expecting a novel, witty story. As a result, Ovid often introduces elements that distance him and his audience from the stories he tells, including passages where he seems to break out of the story he is telling and addresses the audience in a wry aside.

> And now, within the marble council hall,
> the gods were seated. Throned above them all,
> and leaning on his ivory scepter, **Jove**—
> three times and then a fourth—shook his dread locks
> and so perturbed the earth and seas and stars.   5
> Then, opening his angry lips, he said:
>
> "Now, more than ever, I am plagued, beset
> by cares in governing the world; I faced
> **those horrid Giants,** with their snake-shaped feet,
> each monster, with the hundred hands he had,   10
> was ready to assail the sky, to seize
> these heavens—but that challenge was much less
> than what confronts us now. For, in the end,
> however fierce they were, those Giants all—
> when they attacked—formed part of one same pack.   15
> But now I must contend with scattered men;
> throughout the world, where Nereus' waves
> resound, I shall destroy the mortals' race.
> I **swear on the infernal streams** that glide
> **beneath the woods of Styx,** that I have tried   20
> all other means; and now I must excise
> that malady which can't be cured: mankind—
> lest the untainted beings on the earth
> become infected too. Can you, O gods,
> believe they are secure when I myself,   25
> who am the lord of lightning and your lord,
> met with the trap Lycaon set for me—
> Lycaon, famed for his ferocity?"
> **All shouted,** keen to hear who had been guilty
> of such sacrilege.   30
>
> But Jove, with word and gesture, curbed the uproar;
> when they had quieted, his words once more
> could break the silence in the hall: "Be sure—
> he has already paid the penalty.
> But I'll tell you his crime and punishment.   35
> I'd heard about this age of infamy;
> and hoping to disprove such tidings, I

This story comes from: Ovid's, Metamorphoses I, 177–437.*

Jove Also called Jupiter, the head of the gods in Roman myth, equivalent to Greek Zeus.

 The Angry Gods

"those horrid Giants"—As part of the violence and impiety of the Iron Age, the Giants, rebelling against the gods, pile up mountains to reach Jupiter's throne and unseat him. The Giants, creatures with great strength but not necessarily great size, represent an intermediate stage between the gods and humans, and have been identified with men of the Bronze Age in the four ages of man, who Hesiod says were "Terrible men; their strength was great" (Ch. 3, p. 40).

"swear on the infernal streams . . . beneath the woods of Styx"—The Styx was a river deep in the underworld. Oaths on it were considered unbreakable, even by the gods.

"All shouted"—Ovid has some fun in portraying the council of the gods as being like a rowdy meeting of the Roman Senate.

"I went from land to land, a god in human guise"—In the Greek and Roman tradition, a visitor should receive hospitality, even from strangers, since Zeus protected guests. In Homeric stories, the gods often disguised themselves as humans. It was not unreasonable to ask a stranger, "Are you a god?"

Lycaeon, already a wolf, fleeing from his own house. Illustration from Ovid's *Metamorphoses*.

Arcadia Maenala, Cyllene, and Lycaeus are three mountains in different parts of Arcadia in central Greece, indicating that Jove wandered far and wide.

Lycaeon founder of the town of Lycosura, whose claim to be the earth's oldest city is unsubstantiated. Like Prometheus at Mekone (see Ch. 24, p. 355), Lycaeon presented Zeus with a meal whose contents needed to be analyzed and in so doing he challenged the power of the god. Zeus recognized the nature of the meal and punished the preparer. The name Lycaeon comes from the Greek word for wolf, and is thought to be associated with one of Zeus' names, "Lycaeus." Stories were told in ancient times of rituals at Mount Lycaeon in Arcadia where worshippers ate human flesh and were changed into wolves.

"just as he was always keen on slaughter, now he turns against the sheep"—The transformation of Lycaeon provides a good illustration of Ovid's skill at representing metamorphosis. Computer graphics today have given us "morphing" to produce such a transformation before our eyes. Ovid's description does much the same, showing the change in stages that occur in a split second, and depicting the commonalities that link the resulting creature with his old self.

descended from Olympus' heights; **I went
from land to land, a god in human guise.**
Just now, it would be useless to describe   40
each sacrilege I found—upon all sides:
the truth was far, far worse than what I'd heard.
And I had crossed Mount Maenala's dread slopes,
home of wild beasts; I passed Cyllene's peak
and chill Lycaeus' pine grove. So I reached   45
the region and the uninviting home
of the **Arcadian** tyrant. Dusk had fallen,
and night was soon to follow. I'd made known
I was a god, and an Arcadian crowd
began to worship me. At first **Lycaeon**   50
just jeered at all their pious prayers, but then
he said: 'I mean to test him; let us see
if he, beyond all doubt—infallibly—
is god or man.' This was the test he'd planned:
by night—with me asleep—treacherously   55
to murder me. And not content with that,
he seized a hostage the Molossians
had sent to him; Lycaon cut his throat;
some of the still warm limbs he boiled in water,
and some he roasted on the fire. No sooner   60
had he set these before me as my meal than I,
with my avenging lightning bolt,
struck down his home, which caved in on itself—
walls worthy of their owner. He ran off
in panic, and when he had reached the fields,   65
within the stillness, he began to howl:
he tried to utter words—to no avail.
Wrath rises to his mouth; he foams; and **just
as he was always keen on slaughter, now
he turns against the sheep;** indeed he's pleased   70
to shed more blood. His clothes are changed to fur,
his arms to legs: he has become a wolf.
But he keeps traces of his former shape.
His hair is gray; he has the same fierce gaze;
his eyes still glitter, and he still presents   75
a savage image. Yes, one house collapsed;
but it was more than one I should have smashed.
Wherever earth extends, fierce fury reigns!
A vast cabal of crime—that's what I see.
Let them all pay the proper penalties   80
without delay. For such is my decree."

Some of the gods approve Jove's words with shouts,
inciting him still more; some indicate
assent with silent signs. In any case,
complete destruction of the human race   85
saddens them all. What aspect would earth take

once it was stripped of men. Who'd offer incense
upon the altars? Had Jove planned by chance
on wild beasts as earth's sole inhabitants
and overlords? Such were the things they asked.   90
Their king was quick to set their fears at rest:
he would take care of everything; he swore
a new race, one far different from the first,
emerging wondrously, would share the earth.

And now, as Jove was just about to hurl   95
his thunderbolts at the whole earth, **he stayed**
his hand: he was afraid that all those flames
might set the sacred sky ablaze, ignite
the world from pole to pole. He brought to mind
that, in the book of fates, this was inscribed: 100
a time would come when sea and land would burn,
a conflagration that would overturn
the palace of the sky—in fact destroy
the stunning fabric of the universe.

And so Jove set aside his lightening bolts   105
forged by the Cyclops; in their stead he chose
another punishment: he planned to drown
the race of men beneath the waves: he'd send
a deluge down from every part of heaven.
At once, within the caves of **Aeolus,**   110
Jove shuts up **Boreas** and other gusts
that might disperse the clouds. But he frees **Notus,**
who flies out on drenched wings: his awesome face
is veiled in pitch-black darkness, and his beard
is heavy with rainclouds, and water flows   115
down his white hairs; dark fog rests on his brow;
his wings and robes are dripping. Suddenly
his vast hands press against the hanging clouds;
and from the sky, rain pours as thunder roars.

Then Iris, **Juno's** messenger—her robes   120
are many-colored—fetches water, fuels
the clouds with still more rain. The crops are felled;
the wretched farmer weeps as he sees all
his hopes forlorn, in ruins on the ground—
the labor of long years—useless, gone.   125

But **angry Jove** is hardly satisfied
with just the waters of his realm on high:
he needs his azure brother's aid, his waves—
and **Neptune** offers help without delay.
That lord of waters summons all his rivers;   130
they hurry to his halls. This is his speech:

"complete destruction of the human race saddens them all"—The gods' love of humans is based on their fondness for the status quo and their attachment to the offerings they receive from humans. In this respect, the story resembles the Babylonian flood (see pp. 188–190). However, when God floods the earth in Genesis, it is his commitment to the Israelites that causes him to restrain the destruction he wreaks (see p. 144).

"he stayed his hand . . . [lest he] ignite the world from pole to pole"—Myers suggests that Jupiter seems to pause in his plans because he recalls the theory of the Stoic philosophers that the world will be destroyed by fire (43).

 The Flood

Aeolus God of wind.

Boreas, Notus Winds from the north and south.

"Notus . . . flies out on drenched wings . . . his beard is heavy with rainclouds"—In a universe where metamorphosis is the rule, Ovid introduces fleeting features even where a transformation does not take place. It is as if the world were everywhere imbued with changing, shifting forms.

Juno Married to Jove, the queen of the gods in Roman myth, equivalent to Greek Hera.

"angry Jove"—Ovid portrays the head of the gods as an out-of-control bully rather than an orderly leader delivering a well-chosen punishment.

Neptune Roman god of the sea, equivalent to Greek Poseidon.

"That lord of waters summons all his rivers; they hurry to his halls"—Divine power is portrayed as a highly centralized force like the Roman army. However, Neptune, like his brother, deploys his forces in raging fury rather than orderly conquest.

"The time is late. No long harangues. In brief:
Set all your forces free—that's what we need!
Open your gates and let your currents speed:
loosen the reins; don't slow or stay your streams!"   135
So he commands. His river-gods disband;
returning to their homes, they all unleash
their founts and springs; and these—rush toward the sea.
Neptune himself lifts high his trident, strikes
the earth: it shakes and, as it shudders, frees   140
a pathway for the waters. **As they leap
across their banks, they flood the open fields;
orchards and groves, and herds, and men and homes,
and shrines and all the sacred things they hold
are swept away.** And if some house remains   145
in place despite the fury it has faced,
the rising waters overtop the roof;
the towers can't be seen beneath the eddies.
Between the sea and land one cannot draw
distinctions: all is sea, but with no shore.   150

One man seeks refuge on a hill, another
rows in his curving boat where, just before,
he'd plowed; one sails across his fields of grain
or over the submerged roof of his villa;
sometimes an anchor snags in a green meadow;   155
sometimes a curving keel may graze the vines.

Where grateful **goats** had grazed along the grass,
the squat **sea-lions** sprawl and undersea,
the Nereids, amazed, stare hard at cities

"As they leap across their banks, they flood the open fields . . . men and homes, and shrines and all the sacred things they hold are swept away"—By Ovid's account, the devastation caused by the flood is extensive. It represents another "metamorphosis" as the institutions and structures associated with civilization are swept away and replaced by the wild surge that commingles incompatible forces as "the wolf now swims among the sheep." Humans are seen as victims struggling in vain to escape destruction by the violence of Jupiter who indiscriminately punishes innocent and guilty alike.

"goats . . . sea-lions . . . dolphins . . . wolf"—Ovid shifts from the destruction of humans to the plight of the animals caught in the flood. As a result, his younger contemporary, the Stoic philosopher Seneca, criticized him for insensitivity to human suffering. However, the picture Ovid paints represents the grotesque metamorphosis of the earth's neatly ordered farmland to a chaotic and disordered menagerie.

Peter Paul Rubens, *Deucalion and Pyrrha,* creators of humanity after the first flood. Museo del Prado, Madrid, Spain.

and homes and groves; through woodlands, **dolphins** roam;   160
they bump against tall branches, knock and shake
oak trees. The **wolf** now swims among the sheep;
the waves bear tawny lions, carry tigers;
the boar is swept along—his lightening force
is useless; and the stag's swift legs can't help;   165
the bird that searched so long for land where he
might rest, flight-weary, falls into the sea.

By now the heights are buried by sea swells;
the surge—a thing no one has seen before—
beats on the mountaintops. Most men are drowned   170
among the waves; and those who have escaped,
deprived of food, become starvation's prey.
The land that lies between Boeotia
and Oeta's fields is **Phocis**—fertile land

> **Phocis** Central Greece.

as long as it was land, but now a mass   175
the sudden surge had changed into a vast
sea-tract. There, Mount Parnassus lifts, star-high,
its two steep peaks that tower over clouds.

And here (the only place the flood had spared)

 The Survivors

Deucalion and his wife, in their small skiff,   180
had landed. First, they prayed unto the nymphs
of the Corycian cave, the mountain gods,
and Themis—she, the goddess who foretells
the future, in those early days, was still
the keeper of the Delphic oracle.   185

One could not point to any better man,
a man with deeper love for justice, than
Deucalion; and of all women, none

> **Deucalion** Ovid reports (line 232) that he is the son of Prometheus. In some versions it is his father who advises Deucalion to build a craft to escape from the flood. He and his wife, Pyrrha, represent a contrast to Lycaeon's impious ways.

matched Pyrrha in devotion to the gods.
And **when Jove saw the flooded world**—by now   190
a stagnant swamp—and saw that just one man
was left of those who had been myriads,
that but one woman had escaped the waves—
two beings who were pious, innocent—
he rent the clouds, then sent out Boreas   195
to scatter them; the sky could see again
the land, and land again could see the heavens.

> "when Jove saw the flooded world"—Pyrrha and Deucalion survive seemingly by accident, not because of a divine plan. Although Jove has said he would repopulate the earth, we have not heard of any provision to do so. It is Themis, the goddess of justice, who helps the survivors, not Jupiter.

The fury of the sea subsided, too.
And Neptune set aside his three-pronged weapon;
the god of waters pacified the waves   200
and summoned sea-green Triton, bidding him
to blow on his resounding conch—a sign
for seas and streams to end the flood, retreat.
The rivers fall back, and the hills emerge;

the sea has shores once more; the riverbeds,   205
however full their flow, now keep it channeled;
the land increases as the waters ebb;
the soil can now be seen; and then, at last,
after that long night, trees show their bare tops
with traces of the flood-slime on their boughs.   210
The world had been restored to what it was.
But when Deucalion saw earth so forlorn,
a wasteland where deep silence ruled, a bare
and desolate expanse, **he shed sad tears** and said to Pyrrha:

"O my wife, dear **sister,**   215
the only woman left on earth, the one
to whom I first was linked as a dear **cousin**
and then as husband, now we are together
in danger: all the lands both east and west
are empty now—and we alone are left: 220
the sea has taken all the rest. And we
may not survive: we have no certainties—
that vision of the clouds still haunts my mind.
How would you feel, sad heart, if you'd survived
the fatal flood, but I had lost my life?   225
How would you, all alone, have borne the fear?
With whom would you—alone—have shared your tears?
For if the sea had swallowed you, dear wife,
I too—believe me—would have followed you
and let the deluge drown me, too. **Would I**   230
were master of the arts my father plied;
then I, son of Prometheus, would mold
and so renew mankind—its many tribes.
But now the race of men has been reduced—
so did the gods decree—to me and you: 235
We are the last exemplars."

                                            So he said;
together they shed tears and then resolved
to plead with the celestial power, to pray
unto the sacred oracle for aid.   240
Then, side by side, they went without delay
to seek the waters of Cephisus' stream;
although its waters were not limpid yet,
the river flowed along its normal bed.
They took some water and, upon their heads   245
and clothing, sprinkled it, then turned their steps
to holy Themis' shrine. The roof was grimed
with pallid moss, the altars had no flame.
They reached the temple steps, and there they both
kneeled down, bent to the ground; in awe, they kissed   250
the cold stones, saying: "If the gods are pleased,
by righteous prayers, and their wrath can be

"he shed sad tears"—Although it was considered acceptable for heroes to cry, Ovid's representation makes Deucalion seem comic in the extent to which he gives voice to his despair, particularly as this speech continues.

"sister . . . cousin"—The Romans used *soror* (sister) also of a cousin. If Pyrrha was the daughter of Epimetheus, and Deucalion of Prometheus, this would make them cousins. Their actual relationship varies with the source.

"Would I were master of the arts my father plied"—The contrast between the wily Prometheus and his helpless son heightens the comic effect.

"They took some water and . . . sprinkled it"—Part of the ritual of approaching a god's shrine would involve purifying yourself.

appeased, then tell us, Themis, by what means
the ruin of our race can be redeemed;
and, kindest goddess, help this flooded world."   255
The goddess had been moved; her oracle
gave this response: "Now, as you leave the temple,
cover your heads and do not bind your clothes,
and **throw behind you, as you go, the bones
of the great mother."**   260

They are stunned, struck dumb;

and Pyrrha is the first to break their long
silence: she says she cannot do as told;
with trembling voice she begs the goddess' pardon,
but she cannot offend her mother's Shade   265
by scattering her bones. Again, again,
they ponder all the oracle had said;
those words obscure and dark—leave them perplexed.
At last, Prometheus' son speaks words that would
allay the fears of Epimetheus' daughter: 270
"I may be wrong, but I think Themis' answer
did not involve impiety or ask
for any sacrilege. By the great mother,
the earth is meant; and bones, I think, mean stones,
which lie inside earth's body. It is these   275
that we must throw behind us as we leave."

Her husband's explanation solaced Pyrrha;
yet hope was not yet firm—for, after all,
they both were doubtful of the oracle.
But what is wrong in trying? They set out;   280
they veil their heads, they both ungird their clothes;
and they throw stones behind them as they go.
And yes (**if those of old did not attest
the tale** I tell you now, who could accept
its truth), the stones began to lose their hardness;   285
they softened slowly and, in softening,
changed form. Their mass grew greater and their nature
more tender, one could see the dim beginning
of human forms, still rough and inexact,
the kind of likeness that a statue has   290
when one has just begun to block the marble.

Those parts that bore some moisture from the earth
became the flesh; whereas the solid parts—
whatever could not bend—became the bones.
What had been veins remained, with the same name.   295
And since the gods had willed it so, quite soon
the stones the man had thrown were changed to men,
and those the woman cast took women's forms.

"throw behind you . . . the bones of the great mother"—The oracle that Themis sends Deucalion and Pyrrha is confusing, in accordance with the nature of oracles. Their efforts to interpret it are comically obtuse, especially for two members of the family of Prometheus.

"if those of old did not attest the tale"—Ovid's aside comically undermines the belief in the metamorphosis he is describing.

 The Rebirth

"From this, our race is tough"—The story provides aetiological insight as Ovid explains that bones made of stones are the source of the human race's strength. On the aetiological aspect of myth, see Ch. 1, p. 7.

"the fertile seeds were nourished . . . as in a mother's womb"—Reference to a theory held by the natural scientist and philosopher Empedocles about how life on earth first began. In the science-studded account of the earth's creation, Ovid refers frequently to such contemporary scientific theories. In the flood story, references to them are much more rare.

"So, when the Nile . . . recedes"—The previous reference to Empedocles marked the beginning of Ovid's return to the perspective of philosophical inquiry. Although natural science is by no means his main concern, he returns to it again and again in his account, as a way of attaching verisimilitude to his fantastic transformations. A comparison can be made to the scientific explanations found in the fantastic events of the TV show *The X-Files*. Ovid's next topic in the current section, the origin of the flooding of the Nile, was an issue of much concern. To be adequate, any scientific explanation had to account for peculiar events like this one.

"she . . . fashioned shapes not seen before"—This explanation serves as the basis for upcoming stories about strangely shaped creatures.

From this, our race is tough, tenacious; we
work hard—proof of our stony ancestry.   300
The other animals—arrayed in forms
of such variety—were born of earth
spontaneously; the torrid sun began
to warm the moisture that the flood had left
within the ground. Beneath that blazing heat,   305
soft marshes swelled; **the fertile seeds**
were nourished by the soil that gave them life
as in a mother's womb; and so, in time,
as each seed grew, it took on its own form.
So, when the Nile, the stream with seven mouths,   310
recedes from the soaked fields and carries back
its waters to the bed they had before,
and slime, still fresh, dries underneath the sun,
the farmers, turning over clods, discover
some who are newly born, who've just begun   315
to take their forms, and others who are still
unfinished, incomplete—they've not achieved
proportion; and indeed, in one same body,
one part may be alive already, while
another is a lump of shapeless soil.   320
For, tempering each other, heat and moisture
engender life: the union of these two
produces everything. Though it is true
that fire is the enemy of water,
moist heat is the creator of all things: 325
discordant concord is the path life needs.
And when, still muddy from the flood, the earth
had dried beneath the sunlight's clement warmth,
she brought forth countless living forms: while some
were the old sorts that earth had now restored,   330
she also fashioned shapes not seen before.

Further Reading

Penglase, Charles. *Greek Myths and Mesopotamia: Parallels and Influence in the Homeric Hymns and Hesiod.* London: Routledge, 1994.

CHAPTER

12

Biblical Flood Stories

WHAT TO EXPECT . . . The account of the Biblical flood, like other stories of destruction, describes a new beginning. In this instance, a covenant is forged between human beings and God. This agreement spells out God's promise to accept humans in their imperfect state and to refrain from destruction in the future. As a result, God is seen as engaged in the lives of humans, rather than aloof. (For more on this, see Ch. 5, p. 51.) The covenant also reflects political relationships established in the ancient world between a king and his subordinates.

As you read, you may want to refresh your memory of Chapter 5's introduction to the various sources woven together to form the text you are reading (p. 50). That will enable you to note the different ways in which the Priestly, Yahwist, and Elohist writers handle details of the story. Another useful perspective may arise from comparing this flood story with those in Ovid's *Metamorphoses* (Ch. 11, p. 134) and *Gilgamesh* (Ch. 15, pp. 188–190). Look also for examples of the cosmological and aetiological aspects of myth.

The story recounted in the Old Testament of the Bible represents a significant variation on the theme of a world flood. The *Epic of Gilgamesh* comes from the same part of the world, and its flood story (see Ch. 15, pp. 188–190) shares a number of characteristics with the Biblical one, including the building of an ark which comes to rest on a high mountain. However, the emphases of the two stories are quite different. The story in *Gilgamesh* emphasizes the inferiority of humans to the gods. The hero Gilgamesh learns that only one man, Utnapishtim, was saved by the gods from the destruction of the flood, but Utnapishtim's salvation has no implications for other humans. In contrast, the flood story in Genesis represents a promise of protection or covenant that God makes not only with one survivor, but with all human beings. In fact, this story contains the first explicit mention in the Bible of the covenant, a special relationship between God and his chosen people, the Israelites. Even before this story, in Genesis 1–5, there are other indications that God has a covenant with human beings. He protects Adam and Eve after they are forced to leave the Garden (see Ch. 5, p. 155–156), and he guards Cain from retaliation for murdering his brother (Genesis 4:15). The covenant is discussed in more detail in a later section of this introduction.

THE TWO SOURCES OF THE BIBLICAL FLOOD STORY

For a more complete introduction to the stories in the Bible, see Chapter 5, p. 50. We note there that this part of Genesis is actually a compilation of the work of three different authors whose names are not known. Instead, they are referred to by the characteristics of their writing.

They are called the Yahwist, the Elohist, and the Priestly writer, or J, E, and P for short. The narratives of these authors can be distinguished in various ways. The J source always calls God "Yahweh," which the Revised Standard translation of the Bible (used herein) always translates "Lord." ("Yahweh" was originally written by German scholars as "Jahweh"; that is where "J" comes from.) In contrast, the Elohist and the Priestly writer call God "Elohim," which in this version is always translated "God." There are other differences between the various writers of Genesis, as well. The Priestly writer received his name because he pays more attention to the things a priest would care about: the proper way to conduct the worship of God; what ceremonies should be performed when, how, and by whom. The Priestly version is the one that gives the long lists of who is the father of whom, sometimes known as the "begats." Certain ceremonies in Judaism can only be performed by those who are the members of certain families, so a priest needs to be able to trace back the family lineage of the people in these sacred stories.

The story of the flood in Genesis weaves together the accounts of the Yahwist and the Priestly writer; in the translation provided in this chapter, it is easy to distinguish them by looking for changes from "Lord" to "God." After the prologue, which explains the reasons for the flood (6:5–8), the story begins with a brief account of the flood by the Priestly writer (6:9–22), who starts, predictably, with an account of the "generations of Noah," explaining who has a right to be considered a member of the family of Noah. The account of the Priestly writer is then interspersed throughout the lengthier narrative of the Yahwist. It can be found at 7:6, 11, 13–16a, 17a, 18–21, 24; 8:1–2a, 3b, 4–5, 7, 13a, and 15–19. Later, the Priestly writer describes God's covenant with Noah (9:1–17), emphasizing how to prepare meals in accordance with God's plan (9:3–4).

The Yahwist and the Priestly writer produce versions of the flood story that feel quite different from each other. The Priestly writer emphasizes the religious aspects of the agreement between God and humans, describing, as the later section on covenant explains, the progress human beings have made in understanding their relationship with God. In contrast, the Yahwist tells a story with characters who feel for and care about each other. He represents God in a quite anthropomorphic (human-like) way. In his version of the story, God is "grieved to his heart" at the wickedness of humans (Genesis 6:8), and when Noah enters the ark, it is God who shuts him in (Genesis 7:16).

To show the duration of the flood, the Yahwist describes the three birds that Noah sends out in a very simple way reminiscent of a fairy tale (Genesis 8:6b, 8–12). The first returns to the ark because it has no place to land. The second comes back with an olive leaf in its mouth, indicating that the vegetation has begun to recover from the flood, but it is not yet possible to roost on the earth. The third does not return at all to the ark, indicating that the earth has recovered and is suitable again for habitation. This story tells us about the receding of the waters, and about the longing and disappointment of the human beings waiting to return to their familiar haunts. When Noah leaves the ark, the Yahwist explains that his first act is to offer a sacrifice. God, who smells the pleasing odor of the offering, promises man that he will protect him forever (Genesis 8:21–22).

TWO VERSIONS OF THE COSMOLOGY OF THE BIBLICAL FLOOD STORY

The two sources represent the Biblical flood story as showing God's love for human beings through the covenant. However, the Yahwist and the Priestly writer differ in their representation of the nature and mechanics of the flood, even though both drew on the same tradition about its occurrence. The Israelites who came to Canaan encountered an independent tradition of a great flood. E. A. Speiser points out that the basis of the Biblical flood may be found in the geological background of Lower Mesopotamia, and that stories about it may be based on a geological era when the waters of the Persian Gulf rose and flooded a large area of its coastland (55–56). When

J and P made use of this tradition, each incorporated his current understanding of the geography of the world into the story.

The Priestly writer's story was influenced by the Mesopotamian society he inhabited and its beliefs about the nature of the universe or cosmology. In this view, the earth had been created out of a watery waste or chaos. In accordance with Mesopotamian cosmology, the Priestly writer explained, earlier in Genesis, that before God created the world, there existed only an expanse of waters (Genesis 1:1). In the course of creation, God fixed into place the firmament, a giant hemisphere which became a separating wall between the waters. After God installed the firmament, the area under it became dry land; this is the earth, a disk resting on and surrounded by water. Above the firmament were the waters which had been dislocated from around the earth. In the Mesopotamian view, this water was the domain of Tiamat, a god who ruled the watery chaos, while in the Biblical tradition it was inhabited by Leviathan, a sea monster that contended with, but was subordinate to, God (Job 38:8–11; Psalm 104:5–9).

In accordance with this cosmology, the Priestly writer describes the flood not as rain, but as the release of part of the world structure, the ocean above the firmament. His word for the flood is *mabbul,* a technical word for this part of the world. In contrast, the Yahwist calls the flood *gesem,* the word for abnormal rainfall. Thus, for the Priestly writer, the flood was a catastrophe on a worldwide scale. Its destruction, which lasted a year and ten days, in comparison with the Yahwist's 61 days, threatened to return the earth to primeval chaos. As a result, the state of affairs that arises after the Priestly writer's account of the flood very clearly represents God's new creation: the world has been brought to the brink of dissolution into its first principles, to be reshaped into a form that suits God better.

COVENANT

The story of the flood seems to describe the destruction of the world, but like many such stories, it portrays the elimination of the old world as an opportunity for the fashioning of a new one that more closely approximates our own. Because this is a story written by the Israelites for their own people, it takes no account of those who are not part of this group and views all humankind as Jewish. Thus the refashioning of the earth is seen as fully explained in God's covenant with the Israelites.

In destroying the earth with a flood, God prepares the way for a new stage of relations with his people, which can be seen as the completion of his creation. The Priestly writer represents this relationship as explicitly articulated in terms of a covenant, or formal agreement between God and his people. He includes it in the series of covenants described in the Old Testament of the Bible. In the Priestly writer's view, the covenant with Noah is the precursor of the agreements that God makes with Abraham (Genesis 17) and Moses (Exodus 31). According to his account, it is through the covenant related to the flood story that humans become as we know them today, with the characteristics and rights that are familiar to us.

The terms of each of the covenants represented in the Old Testament are different, but in some form, all of them represent the extension of protection by God, to be reciprocated by the incurring of certain obligations to God on the part of the humans who enter into the covenant with him. The first covenant represented by the Priestly writer is a promise that God makes to Noah as the representative of all human beings, not only of the Jews. The other two agreements—the one made with Abraham and the one at Sinai—are concluded by God in relation to the Israelites alone.

There are also implicit accounts of covenant relationships that occur when God makes clothes for Adam and Eve after they leave the garden (Genesis 3:21) and when he places a mark on Cain protecting him from retaliation for his crime (Genesis 4:15). The accounts of covenant formation in Genesis are modeled on political relationships established between a

Mihály Mészáros, Moses receiving the ten commandments on Sinai, described in Exodus 31. This is another sign of the covenant, the ongoing relationship between God and the Israelites in the Old Testament.

great king and his subordinates. By such an agreement (Hebrew *berît*), the vassal or subordinate obtains protection from the lord in exchange for the obligation to fulfill his commands. Although such an agreement does not infringe on the king's powers, it does require him to act on behalf of his vassal.

In both Biblical versions of the flood story, God makes an agreement with human beings after the waters recede. The Yahwist portrays God simply as declaring that he will never again destroy every living creature as he did in the flood (Genesis 8:21–22). In the Priestly version, God's promise is presented in a more elaborate and formal way. He concludes an agreement with Noah that he explicitly calls a covenant. This agreement completes the creation of human beings by protecting them from destruction and giving them new rights in relation to God. In the earlier part of his creation story, the Priestly writer had explained that when God created human beings, he prescribed for them a vegetarian diet, saying, "See, I give you every seed-bearing plant on earth and every tree that bears fruit; they shall be yours for food" (Genesis 1:29). Now, after the flood, God gives humans the right to eat meat, saying "Every moving thing that lives shall be food for you; as I gave you green plants, now I give you everything" (Genesis 9:3). Gerhard von Rad points out that this detail is intended to deal with issues that would be of concern to contemporary Israelites (127).

According to this theological perspective, human society is characterized by violence and killing, but God has accepted this degeneration of human beings from his original plan for them and is nonetheless willing to take them as they are. That is, human beings do not need to return to a previous state of ideal purity before God will accept them; his granting them the right to eat meat, in accordance with their usual violent practices, represents God's willingness to enter into a relationship with them nonetheless. As a sign of this covenant with human beings, God declares that he is placing his weapon of destruction, his bow, in the clouds, indicating that he will not use it again against humans. The rainbow, visible regularly to human beings, will serve as a sign of their new status with respect to God. The story provides the aetiological insight of explaining the origins of the rainbow, while providing it with a significance relating to the agreement or covenant with God.

6 1 When men began to multiply on the face of the ground, and daughters were born to them, the **sons of God** saw that the daughters of men were fair; and they took to wife such of them as they chose. 3 Then the LORD said, "My spirit shall not abide in man for ever, for he is flesh, but his days shall be a hundred and twenty years." 4 The **Nephilim** were on the earth in those days, and also afterward, when the sons of God came in to the daughters of men, and they bore children to them. These were the mighty men that were of old, the men of renown.

5 **The LORD** saw that the wickedness of man was great in the earth, and that every imagination of the thoughts of his heart was only evil continually.

6 And **the LORD was sorry that he had made man** on the earth, and it grieved him to his heart. 7 So the LORD said, "I will blot out man whom I have created from the face of the ground, man and beast and creeping things and birds of the air, for I am sorry that I have made them." 8 But Noah found favor in the eyes of the LORD.

9 These are the generations of Noah. Noah was a righteous man, blameless in his generation; **Noah walked with God.** 10 And Noah had three sons, Shem, Ham, and Japheth.

11 Now the earth was corrupt in God's sight, and the earth was filled with violence. 12 And God saw the earth, and behold, it was corrupt; for all flesh had corrupted their way

---

This excerpt comes from: Genesis 6–9.*

"sons of God"—Not physical descendants of God, but angelic beings who get involved with human women. As a result, human beings acquire divine power ("my spirit") beyond God's original plan.

"Nephilim"—Mighty ones, giants, or heroes. Their presence on earth shows that this was a time of violence and impiety. This motif is found in other traditions as well: see Ovid's flood story, Ch. 11, p. 129.

"The LORD"—The use of this name tells us that the writer of this part of the flood story is the Yahwist or J source. For a discussion of the three writers whose work is combined to make up our current version of Genesis, see p. 52.

"the LORD was sorry that he had made man"—It is important to note that the focus of this account is not the evil nature of humans, but the goodness of God. Here God regrets creating humans, but by the next verse, the emphasis is on Noah, whom God will save.

"Noah walked with God"—The use of the name "God" tells us that we are no longer reading the J source.

---

upon the earth. 13 And God said to Noah, "I have determined to make an end of all flesh; for the earth is filled with violence through them; behold, I will destroy them with the earth. 14 Make yourself an ark of **gopher wood;** make rooms in the ark, and cover it inside and out with pitch. 15 **This is how you are to make it:** the length of the ark three hundred cubits, its breadth fifty cubits, and its height thirty cubits. 16 Make a roof for the ark, and finish it to a cubit above; and set the door of the ark in its side; make it with lower, second, and third decks. 17 For behold, I will bring **a flood of waters** upon the earth, to destroy all flesh in which is the breath of life from under heaven; everything that is on the earth shall die. 18 But **I will establish my covenant with you**; and you shall come into the ark, you, your sons, your wife, and your sons' wives with you. 19 And of every living thing of all flesh, you shall bring two of every sort into the ark, to keep them alive with you; they shall be male and female. 20 Of the birds according to their kinds, and of the animals according to their kinds, of every creeping thing of the ground according to its kind, two of every sort shall come in to you, to keep them alive. 21 Also take with you every sort of food that is eaten, and store it up; and it shall serve as food for you and for them." 22 Noah did this; he did all that God commanded him.

7 1Then the LORD said to Noah, "Go into the ark, you and all your household, for I have seen that you are righteous before me in this generation. 2 Take with you **seven pairs of all clean animals,** the male and his mate; and **a pair of the animals that are not clean,** the male and his mate; 3 and seven pairs of the birds of the air also, male and female, to keep their kind alive upon the face of all the earth. 4 For in seven days I will send rain upon the earth forty days and forty nights; and every living thing that I have made I will blot out from the face of the ground." 5 And Noah did all that the LORD had commanded him.

6 **Noah was six hundred years old** when the flood of waters came upon the earth. 7 And Noah and his sons and his wife and his sons' wives with him went into the ark, to escape the waters of the flood. 8 Of clean animals, and of animals that are not clean, and of birds, and of everything that creeps on the ground, 9 two and two, male and female, went into the ark with Noah, as God had commanded Noah. 10 And after seven days the waters of the flood came upon the earth.

11 In the six hundredth year of Noah's life, in the second month, on the seventeenth day of the month, on that day all the fountains of the great deep burst forth, and the windows of the heavens were opened. 12 And rain fell upon the earth forty days and forty nights. 13 On the very same day Noah and his sons, Shem and Ham and Japheth, and Noah's wife and the three wives of his sons with them entered the ark, 14 they and every beast according to its kind, and all the cattle according to their kinds, and every creeping thing that creeps on the earth according to its kind, and every bird according to its kind, every bird of every sort. 15 They went into the ark with Noah, two and two of all flesh in which there was the breath of life. 16 And they that entered, male and female of all flesh, went in as God had commanded him; and **the LORD shut him in.**

17 The flood continued forty days upon the earth; and the waters increased, and bore up the ark, and it rose high above the earth. 18 The waters prevailed and increased greatly upon the earth; and the ark floated on the face of the waters. 19 And the waters prevailed so mightily upon the earth that all the high mountains under the whole heaven were covered; 20 the waters prevailed above the mountains, covering them fifteen cubits deep. 21 And **all flesh died that moved upon the earth,** birds, cattle, beasts, all swarming creatures that swarm upon the earth, and every man; 22 **everything on the dry land in whose nostrils was the breath of life died.** 23 He blotted out every living thing that was upon the face of the ground, man and animals and creeping things and birds of the air;

"gopher wood"—The exact kind of wood this represented is not known. Some scholars believe the ark must have been built of cypress.

"This is how you are to make it"—The ark was to be 440 feet long, 73 feet wide, 44 feet high; it was a vessel of 43,000 tons.

"a flood of waters"—Hebrew *mabbul* refers to the part of the heavenly sea which was believed to exist above the firmament. (See Introduction, p. 140.)

"I will establish my covenant with you"—The covenant was a formal agreement between God and his people. (See Introduction, pp. 141–142.)

"seven pairs of all clean animals . . . a pair of the animals that are not clean"—The Yahwist here ensures the preservation of all life on earth. The Priestly version (verse 6:20), more concerned about proper ritual observance, calls for the preservation only of those animals which are necessary according to Jewish law.

"Noah was six hundred years old"—Biblical scholars disagree about the actual number of years intended by the Priestly writer. However, the most noteworthy aspect of his account is the steady decline in human life span. From Adam to Noah, 700–1000 seems to be the normal life span. From Noah to Abraham it is 200–600 years; for the patriarchs it is 100–200 years. In the present it is 70–80 years.

"the LORD shut him in"—God is portrayed as immanent, acting directly and personally in human affairs. See Ch 5, p. 51, for a discussion of immanent and transcendent deities.

"all flesh died that moved upon the earth . . . everything on the dry land in whose nostrils was the breath of life died"—The Priestly writer is thought to be the author of verse 21, while verses 22–23, which are more vivid, are assumed to be written by the Yahwist.

they were blotted out from the earth. Only Noah was left, and those that were with him in the ark. 24And the waters prevailed upon the earth a hundred and fifty days.

8 1But God remembered Noah and all the beasts and all the cattle that were with him in the ark. And **God made a wind blow over the earth, and the waters subsided;** 2 **the fountains of the deep and the windows of the heavens were closed,** the rain from the heavens was restrained, 3 and the waters receded from the earth continually. At the end of a hundred and fifty days the waters had abated; 4 and in the seventh month, on the seventeenth day of the month, the ark came to rest upon the mountains of Ar'arat. 5 And the waters continued to abate until the tenth month; in the tenth month, on the first day of the month, the tops of the mountains were seen.

6 **At the end of forty days Noah** opened the window of the ark which he had made, 7 and **sent forth a raven;** and it went to and fro until the waters were dried up from the earth. 8 Then he sent forth a dove from him, to see if the waters had subsided from the face of the ground; 9 but the dove found no place to set her foot, and she returned to him to the ark, for the waters were still on the face of the whole earth. So he put forth his hand and took her and brought her into the ark with him. 10 He waited another seven days, and again he sent forth the dove—out of the ark; 11 and the dove came back to him in the evening, and lo, in her mouth a freshly plucked olive leaf; so Noah knew that the waters had subsided from the earth. 12 Then he waited another seven days, and sent forth the dove; and she did not return to him any more.

13 In the six hundred and first year, in the first month, the first day of the month, the waters were dried from off the earth; and Noah removed the covering of the ark, and looked, and behold, the face of the ground was dry. 14 In the second month, on the twenty-seventh day of the month, the earth was dry. 15 Then God said to Noah, 16 "Go forth from the ark, you and your wife, and your sons and your sons' wives with you. 17 Bring forth with you every living thing that is with you of all flesh—birds and animals and every creeping thing that creeps on the earth—that they may breed abundantly on the earth, and be fruitful and multiply upon the earth." 18 So Noah went forth, and his sons and his wife and his sons' wives with him. 19 And every beast, every creeping thing, and every bird, everything that moves upon the earth, went forth by families out of the ark.

20 Then Noah built an altar to the LORD, and took of every clean animal and of every clean bird, and offered burnt offerings on the altar. 21 And **when the LORD smelled the pleasing odor,** the LORD said in his heart, "I will never again curse the ground because of man, for the imagination of man's heart is evil from his youth; neither will I ever again destroy every living creature as I have done. 22 While the earth remains, seedtime and harvest, cold and heat, summer and winter, day and night, shall not cease."

9 1**And God blessed Noah** and his sons, and said to them, "Be fruitful and multiply, and fill the earth. 2 The fear of you and the dread of you shall be upon every beast of the earth, and upon every bird of the air, upon everything that creeps on the ground and all the fish of the sea; into your hand they are delivered. 3 Every moving thing that lives shall be

---

"God made a wind blow over the earth, and the waters subsided; the fountains of the deep and the windows of the heavens were closed"—The mention here of the deep marks this as the work of the Priestly writer, as does the reference to the 150-day duration of the flood.

"At the end of forty days Noah . . . sent forth a raven"—The several birds Noah sent out to determine if the flood was over provide a vehicle for the Yahwist to portray the human emotions in the story. They tangibly represent the process of waiting for the floodwaters to subside.

"when the LORD smelled the pleasing odor"—This detail appears also in the flood account in the *Epic of Gilgamesh* (see Ch. 15, p. 190), and so it must have been part of the Middle Eastern flood story which the Yahwist adapted for his own purposes. In *Gilgamesh* the detail suggests the greed and self-centeredness of the gods. The Yahwist here shows a new relationship between God and humans: God finds the sacrifice pleasing, since it shows Noah's piety.

"And God blessed Noah"—The text shifts here to the account of the Priestly writer. In his creation story (Genesis 1:29), he represents God as limiting humans to a vegetarian diet. (See Introduction, p. 142.)

This 13th-c. C.E. mosaic shows Noah releasing the dove.

food for you; and **as I gave you the green plants, I give you everything.** 4 Only you shall not eat flesh with its life, that is, its blood. 5 For your lifeblood I will surely require a reckoning; of every beast I will require it and of man; of every man's brother I will require the life of man. 6 Whoever sheds the blood of man, by man shall his blood be shed; for God made man in his own image. 7 And you, be fruitful and multiply, bring forth abundantly on the earth and multiply in it."

8 Then God said to Noah and to his sons with him, 9 "Behold, **I establish my covenant with you** and your descendants after you, 10 **and with every living creature that is with you,** the birds, the cattle, and every beast of the earth with you, as many as came out of the ark. 11 I establish my covenant with you, that never again shall all flesh be cut off by the waters of a flood, and never again shall there be a flood to destroy the earth." 12 And God said, "This is the sign of the covenant which I make between me and you and every living creature that is with you, for all future generations: 13 **I set my bow in the cloud,** and it shall be a sign of the covenant between me and the earth. 14 When I bring clouds over the earth and the bow is seen in the clouds, 15 I will remember my covenant which is between me and you and every living creature of all flesh; and the waters shall never again become a flood to destroy all flesh. 16 When the bow is in the clouds, I will look upon it and remember the everlasting covenant between God and every living creature of all flesh that is upon the earth." 17 God said to Noah, "This is the sign of the covenant which I have established between me and all flesh that is upon the earth."

18 The sons of Noah who went forth from the ark were Shem, Ham, and Japheth. Ham was the father of Canaan. 19 These three were the sons of Noah; and from these the whole earth was peopled.

20 **Noah was the first tiller of the soil.** He planted a vineyard; 21 and he drank of the wine, and became drunk, and lay uncovered in his tent. 22 And Ham, the father of Canaan, saw the nakedness of his father, and told his two brothers outside. 23 Then Shem and Japheth took a garment, laid it upon both their shoulders, and walked backward and

> "as I gave you the green plants, I give you everything"—Humans are given the right to eat meat, as long as they avoid the blood. The avoidance of blood represents one of the dietary laws that Jews respect as their duty because of their covenant with God. For an extensive discussion of the significance of these dietary restrictions, see Ch. 29.

> "I establish my covenant with you . . . and with every living creature that is with you"—On the covenant agreement, see Introduction.

> "I set my bow in the cloud"—The bow is God's bow of war, which he would use to punish evildoers. Here, however, he has set it aside, vowing to be merciful in the future. The rainbow, which is shaped like the archer's bow, will serve as a representation of this promise. This story provides an aetiology for the rainbow. See Ch. 1, on the aetiological aspect of myth.

> "Noah was the first tiller of the soil"—This refers to Cain, who is first described as a tiller of the ground (Genesis 4:2), but after his sin is cut off from the fertility of the earth (Genesis 4:12). Noah, who has demonstrated his righteousness through his sacrifice to God, represents the restoration of this link. Thus, von Rad points out that his drunkenness here is in no way blameworthy, but represents his discovery of the hitherto unknown gift of wine, and shows the restoration of human beings to a degree of harmony with the fertility of the earth (132).

Marc Chagall, *Noah and the Rainbow*. This modern painting represents the rainbow as a solid arc of light, rather than showing its multiple colors.

covered the nakedness of their father; their faces were turned away, and they did not see their father's nakedness. 24 When Noah awoke from his wine and knew what his youngest son had done to him, 25 he said, "Cursed be Canaan; a slave of slaves shall he be to his brothers." 26 He also said, "Blessed by the LORD my God be Shem; and let Canaan be his slave." 27 God enlarge Japheth, and let him dwell in the tents of Shem; and let Canaan be his slave." 28 After the flood Noah lived three hundred and fifty years. 29 All the days of Noah were nine hundred and fifty years; and he died.

Further Reading

Speiser, E. A. *Genesis: Anchor Bible.* Garden City, NY: Doubleday Anchor, 1964.

Ragnarok

WHAT TO EXPECT . . . In this chapter, Gylfi, the King of Sweden, disguised as Ganglieri, asks the High One about the history of his people. Using a question-and-answer format, Snorri Sturluson describes Ragnarok, the series of catastrophes that caused the end of the ancient, pagan world of the Norse tradition. As the world still burns, two humans who are hidden away in a woods are destined to repopulate the earth, and a new sun is born.

Bear in mind as you read this story, that it, like the other destruction stories in this section, involves a new creation. You may want to look back at the first creation in Norse legend, in Chapter 7, and see if the beginning and the end convey the same atmosphere or spirit. Compare this story—and the role of the gods in it—with those of the flood in Chapters 11 (p. 110), 12 (p. 139), and 15 (p. 166). For example, who is responsible? What actually causes the destruction? Why are the two humans in Hoddmimir's Wood spared? What might the answers tell you about Nordic culture in Snorri's time and before?

Myths of destruction describing the annihilation of a people, a place, or a culture are widespread. In these stories, people may be punished for doing something they had been commanded not to do, or for neglecting to do something that was expected by the ruling deity. However, in the Norse *Ragnarok* (doom of the gods), the destruction of the world and the gods is due not to actions of men, but to natural causes and warfare among the gods. Snorri's description in the *Prose Edda* is the most vivid and complete in the Norse literature.

The section excerpted in this chapter follows the section excerpted from the *Prose Edda* in Chapter 7. Gangleri is Gylfi, the king of Sweden in disguise, seeking information about a tricky race of gods called the Æsir. He is engaged here in a kind of contest with the Æsir, who are called High One, Just-as-high and Third. For more information, see the introduction to Chapter 18, p. 219.

During the battle of the gods, several pairs of enemies annihilate each other: Fenrir the wolf devours Odin, the king of the gods, and is then slain by Odin's son; Thor and the Midgard Serpent kill each other; Garm the monster-dog and Tyr kill each other; and Loki and Heimdall also kill each other. Life and authority as it has been known—in both its positive and negative aspects—are gone. In the older sagas, the story of Ragnarok ended there, with the destruction of the world and all it contained.

However, in Snorri's version of Ragnarok, as in many other such stories, destruction leads to a new order of life for human beings (see p. 153). From the almost total elimination of the old divine order comes a rejuvenation of nature and the birth of a new generation of people, promising hope for the future. The new creatures consist of humans as we know them, and there is

Thor fishing with the giant Hymir. During this adventure, Thor nearly defeats the Midgard Serpent, his adversary at Ragnarok, a child of Loki, and the giantess Angrboda. (See Ch. 18, p. 226.)

little mention of a regeneration of the old order: the new gods seem to be benign creatures whose role is to support human beings, not to conduct destructive wars with each other or with monsters. Perhaps in this version, Snorri, a learned man who traveled widely, wanted to reconcile what he studied in the great old sagas and his more recent Christian beliefs. A review of the events described by Snorri in the Ragnarok of the *Prose Edda* suggests the movement from the old, pagan past reported in the Norse sagas to the end of these ancient beliefs.

Because Ragnarok represents the destruction of the entire old order of gods, its events are highly complex and can be confusing. The events described are the finale of all previous actions of the ancient Norse deities, and thus many adventures and rivalries are intertwined to provide a suitable conclusion to all these different stories. The following outline is intended to help show the underlying structure beneath the complex events described in this story.

OUTLINE OF RAGNAROK—HOW THE WORLD ENDS AND IS REBORN

Signs and Portents

- Three harsh winters without summers
- Sun and moon are swallowed
- Earthquakes—the mountains fall
- War and strife—brothers kill brothers
- Rough seas caused by the writhing serpent

The Enemies of Good Assemble

- Fenrir the Wolf advances—his jaws stretch from earth to sky
- Midgard Serpent sprays poison into the sea and sky
- Surt and his army break the rainbow bridge
- Loki and Hyrm, the giant, arrive by ship
- The family of Hel and the frost giants arrive with Loki
- All gather on the vast plain of Vigrid

The Gods Prepare

- Heimdall blows his horn to wake the gods
- Odin rides to the spring of Mimir seeking prophesy
- Other gods join Odin
- Spirits of dead warriors, the Einherjar, follow Odin to Vigrid

The Battle—Death for Good and Evil

- Odin is killed fighting Fenrir, the wolf
- Frigg fights Surt
- Vidar, Odin's son, kills the wolf
- Thor kills the Midgard Serpent, but is felled by its poison
- Loki and Heimdall kill each other
- Surt sets fire to the world
- Heaven and earth burn and earth sinks into the sea

After the Battle—A Different Life

- The good and righteous live in golden halls with food and drink
- Perjurers and murderers live in a hall of poisonous serpents
- Corpses (of the bad) are eaten by Nidhogg the serpent

The Survivors

- Sons of Odin, Vidar and Vali, go to live at the site of Valhalla
- Sons of Thor, Modi and Magni, have Thor's magical hammer
- Baldr and Hod return from Hel

The New World

- Earth rises from the sea with crops and plants growing
- A new sun appears, the daughter of the old sun
- Two humans, Lif and Lifthrasir, survive the end of the earth
- Whole world is repopulated

Ragnarok

This excerpt comes from: Snorri Sturluson, the *Prose Edda*.*

 The Beginning of the End

Bifrost   Rainbow bridge connecting heaven and earth.

"the sons of Muspell"—The giant Surt rules Muspell to the south. He will bring an army to challenge the gods and will burn the earth with an ember from Muspell.

"there is nothing in this world that can be relied on when the sons of Muspell are on the warpath"—The gods did good work, but evil can ruin it.

"First will come the winter"—Before Ragnarok, there will be long, bad winters and bad humans.

"the wolf will swallow the sun"—Snorri maintained that the sun and moon are brother and sister. Sun drives the chariot of light made from a spark from Muspell. They are chased by two wolves, sons of a giantess, who will eventually catch and devour them.

"The wolf Fenrir"—Thought to be a child of Loki. He will get loose when the earth trembles at Ragnarok. See the story of Tyr and the binding of Fenrir, Ch. 18, p. 223.

Then Gangleri asked: "What is the way from earth to heaven?"

Then High One answered, laughing: "No one well informed would ask such a question. Have you never been told that the gods built a bridge from earth to heaven called **Bifrost?** You will have seen it, [but] maybe you call it the rainbow. It has three colors and is very strong, and made with more skill and cunning than other structures. But strong as it is, it will break when **the sons of Muspell** ride out over it to harry, and their horses [will] swim over great rivers; and in this fashion they will come on the scene."

Then Gangleri said: "It doesn't seem to me that the gods built a reliable bridge when it is going to break, and [yet] they can do what they will."

High One said: "The gods are not to blame for this structure. Bifrost is a good bridge, but **there is nothing in this world that can be relied on when the sons of Muspell are on the warpath.**"

Then Gangleri said: "What is there to relate about Ragnarok? I have never heard tell of this before."

High One said: "There are many and great tidings to tell about it. **First will come the winter** called Fimbulvetr. Snow will drive from all quarters, there will be hard frosts and biting winds; the sun will be no use. There will be three such winters on end with no summer between. Before that, however, three other winters will pass accompanied by great wars throughout the whole world. Brothers will kill each other for the sake of gain, and no one will spare father or son in manslaughter or in incest. As it says in the *Sibyl's Vision:*

> Brothers will fight
> and kill each other,
> siblings
> do incest;
> men will know misery,   5
> adulteries be multiplied,
> an axe-age, a sword-age,
> shields will be cloven,
> a wind-age, a wolf-age,
> before the world's ruin.   10

"Then will occur what will seem a great piece of news, **the wolf will swallow the sun** and that will seem a great disaster to men. Then another wolf will seize the moon and that one too will do great harm. The stars will disappear from heaven. Then this will come to pass, the whole surface of the earth and the mountains will tremble so [violently] that trees will be uprooted from the ground, mountains will crash down, and all fetters and bonds will be snapped and severed. **The wolf Fenrir** will get loose then. The sea will lash against the land because the Midgard Serpent is writhing in giant fury trying to come ashore. At that time, too, the ship known as Naglfar will become free. It is made of dead men's nails, so it is worth warning you that, if anyone dies with his nails uncut, he will greatly increase the material for that ship which both gods and men devoutly hope will take a long time building. The wolf Fenrir will advance with wide open mouth, his upper jaw against the sky, his lower on the earth (he would gape more widely still if there were room) and his eyes and nostrils will blaze with fire. The

* Snorri Sturluson. *The Prose Edda: Tales from Norse Mythology.* Trans. Jean I. Young, 39–40, 86–93. Copyright © 1954. Used by permission of the University of California Press.

Midgard Serpent will blow so much poison that the whole sky and sea will be spattered with it; he is most terrible and will be on the other side of the wolf.

"In this din the sky will be rent asunder and the sons of Muspell ride forth from it. Surt will ride first and with him fire blazing both before and behind. He has a very good sword and it shines more brightly than the sun. When they ride over Bifrost, however—as has been said before—that bridge will break. The sons of Muspell will push forward to the plain called Vigrid and the wolf Fenrir and the Midgard Serpent will go there too. **Loki and Hrym** with all the frost giants will also be there by then, and all the family of Hel will accompany Loki. The sons of Muspell, however, will form a host in themselves and that a very bright one. The plain **Vigrid** is a hundred and twenty leagues in every direction.

"When these things are happening, **Heimdall** will stand up and blow a great blast on the horn Gjoll and awaken all the gods and they will hold an assembly. Then Odin will ride to **Mimir's spring** and ask Mimir's advice for himself and his company. The ash Yggdrasil will tremble and nothing in heaven or earth will be free from fear. The **Æsir and all the Einherjar will arm themselves** and press forward on to the plain. Odin will ride first in a helmet of gold and a beautiful coat of mail and with his spear Gungnir, and he will make for the wolf Fenrir. Thor will advance at his side but will be unable to help help him, because he will have his hands full fighting the Midgard Serpent. Frey will fight against Surt and it will be a hard conflict before Frey falls; the loss of the good sword that he gave to Skirnir will bring about his death. Then the hound Garm, which was bound in front of Gnipahellir, will also get free; he is the worst sort of monster. He will battle with Tyr and each will kill the other. Thor will slay the Midgard Serpent but stagger back only nine paces before he falls down dead, on account of the poison blown on him by the serpent. The wolf will swallow Odin and that will be his death. Immediately afterwards, however, **Vidar** will stride forward and place one foot on the lower jaw of the wolf. On this foot he will be wearing the shoe which has been in the making since the beginning of time; it consists of the strips of leather men pare off at the toes and heels of their shoes, and for this reason people who want to help the Æsir must throw away these strips. Vidar will take the wolf's upper jaw in one hand and tear his throat asunder and that will be the wolf's death. Loki will battle with Heimdall and each will kill the other. Thereupon **Surt will fling fire over the earth and burn up the whole world.** As it says in the *Sibyl's Vision:*

> Heimdall blows loud
> his horn raised aloft,
> **Odin speaks with Mimir's head;**
> Yggdrasil trembles,
> old outspreading ash,   5
> and groans as the giant gets free.
>
> Hrym drives from the east
> holds high his shield before him,
> Jormungand writhes in giant rage;
> the serpent churns up waves;   10
> screaming for joy
> ghastly eagle will tear
> dead bodies with his beak.
>
> **From the east sails a ship,**
> from the sea will come   15
> **the people of Muspell**

This carving represents Odin, with his raven on his shoulder, being eaten by the wolf at Ragnarok.

"Loki and Hrym"—It was believed that Loki would arrive on the ship Naglfar, which Hrym, the giant, steered.

Vigrid The final battlefield.

Heimdall The god who guards Asgard.

The Great Battle

Mimir's spring It flows under Yggdrasil, the World Tree, and provides great wisdom. Mimir, the owner, drank from it and is very wise. In most accounts, he is dead, but his head continues to advise those who visit.

"Æsir and all the Einherjar will arm themselves"—The gods (Æsir) and the warriors (Einherjar) will take part in the battle.

Vidar Odin's son avenges him by slaying Fenrir.

"Surt will . . . burn up the whole world"—Surt is a giant from the land of fire. He causes complete destruction, far beyond the death of the Æsir.

with Loki as pilot;
all sons of fiends
are rowing with Fenrir,
with them on this voyage
is **Byleist's brother** 　　　　　20

Then occurs Hlin's second grief,
when Odin goes
to fight the wolf
and **Beli's bane** 　　　　　25
turns, fair, on Surt,
then will Frigg's beloved die.
To fight the wolf
goes Odin's son,
Vidar is on his way; 　　　　　30
sword in hand
he will pierce the heart
of Hvedrung's son.
Thus is his sire avenged.

The famous son 　　　　　35
of Earth falls back,
fainting from the serpent
fearing not attack.

All mankind must abandon home
when Midgard's Buckler 　　　　　40
strikes in wrath.

The sun will go black
earth sink in the sea
heaven be stripped
of its bright stars; 　　　　　45
smoke rage **and fire,**
leaping the flame
lick heaven itself.

Then Gangleri asked: "What will happen afterwards, when heaven and earth and the whole world has been burned and all the gods are dead and all the Einherjar and the whole race of man? Didn't you say before that **everyone will go on living for ever in some world or other?**"

Then Third answered: "**There will be many good dwelling places then and many bad.** The best place to be in at that time will be Gimle in heaven, and for those that like it there is plenty of good drink in the hall called Brimir that is on Okolnir. There is also **an excellent hall** on Nidafjoll called Sindri; it is made of red gold. Good and righteous men will live in these halls. On Nastrandir there is **a large and horrible hall** whose doors face north; it is made of the backs of serpents woven together like wattle-work, with all their heads turning in to the house and spewing poison so that rivers of it run through the hall. **Perjurers and murderers** wade these rivers as it says here:

I know a hall whose doors face north
on Nastrand far from the sun,
poison drips from lights in the roof;

Sidebar:

"Odin speaks with Mimir's head"—After Mimir was killed by the Vanir, Odin kept his head at the spring of wisdom and received from it knowledge of the future.

"From the east sails a ship"—Naglfar.

"the people of Muspell"—Surt's people.

"Byleist's brother"—Loki. He arrives with the giants from Muspell. Elsewhere, the giants cross the rainbow bridge and break it.

"to fight the wolf"—Each hero who overcomes a monster will also be killed by it:

- Odin and Fenrir (the wolf) who is shown to be an adversary of the gods in the story of Tyr (See Ch. 18).
- Thor and Midgard Serpent
- Frey and Surt (giant king of Muspel)
- Tyr and Garm (the hound)

"Beli's bane"—Epithet for Frigg. An epithet: a word or phrase used to describe a person or a thing. For example, Achilles is "swift-footed."

"The famous son of Earth"—Thor.

"and fire . . . lick heaven itself"—It had been prophesied that Surt would start the final destructive fire with a spark from Muspell.

"everyone will go on living for ever in some world or other"—Indicates a belief in a cyclical existence. This reminds us of Hindu belief that people are reborn according to their behavior in their previous life (Ch. 17, p. 206).

"There will be many good dwelling places then and many bad"—Good and evil will continue to exist in the next world.

"an excellent hall . . . a horrible hall"—The next life is envisioned as an extension of the present.

"Perjurers and murderers"—Naming only these two offenses might indicate what the Norse societies held as the highest moral values.

that building is woven
of backs of snakes.   5
There heavy streams must be waded through
by breakers of pledges and murderers.

"But it is worst [of all] in **Hvergelmir.**

There **Nidhogg** bedevils
the bodies of the dead."   10

Then Gangleri asked: "Will any of the gods be living then? Will there be any earth or heaven then?"

High One said: "At that time earth will rise out of the sea and be green and fair, and fields of corn will grow that were never sown. **Vidar and Vali** will be living, so neither the sea nor Surt's Fire will have done them injury, and they will inhabit Idavoll where Asgard used to be. And **the sons of Thor, Modi and Magni will come there and possess Mjollnir.** After that **Baldr and Hod will come from Hel.** They will all sit down together and converse, calling to mind their hidden lore and talking about things that happened in the past, about the Midgard Serpent and the wolf Fenrir. Then they will find there in the grass the golden chessmen the Æsir used to own. As it is said:

Vidar and Vali
when Surt's fire has died
will dwell in the temples,
Modi and Magni
Thor's Mjollnir will own   5
at the end of the battle.

"While the world is being burned by Surt, **in a place called Hoddmimir's Wood, will be concealed two human beings** called Lif and Lifthrasir. Their food will be the morning dews, and from these men will come so great a stock that the whole world will be peopled, as it says here:

Lif and Lifthrasir
in Hoddmimir's wood will be hidden;
the morning dews their food and drink
from thence will come men after men.

"And you will think this strange, but **the sun will have borne a daughter** no less lovely than herself, and she will follow the paths of her mother, as it says here:

Glory-of-elves to a girl
will give birth
before Fenrir overtakes her,
when the gods are dead
she will pursue the paths of her mother.   5

"And now, if you have anything more to ask, I can't think how you can manage it, for I've never heard anyone tell more of the story of the world. Make what use of it you can."

The next thing was that Gangleri heard a tremendous noise on all sides and turned about; and when he had looked all round him [he found] that he was standing in the open air on a level plain. **He saw neither hall nor stronghold.** Then he went on his way and coming home to his kingdom related the tidings he had seen and heard, and after him these stories have been handed down from one man to another.

Hvergelmir A well in Niflheim, under the third root of Yggdrasil.

Nidhogg—Serpent who gnaws at the root of Yggdrasil, and feeds on corpses.

 Rebirth after Ragnarok

Vidar and Vali Sons of Odin who survive Ragnarok.

"the sons of Thor . . . will possess Mjollnir"—Mjollnir is Thor's hammer. The text suggests that rightful inheritance will continue. However, it is paratactic, since it does not explain how this will be done.

"Baldr and Hod will come from Hel"—Rebirth of the earth includes an idyllic return of those who had died.

Modi and Magni Sons of Thor who survive Ragnarok.

"in . . . Hoddmimir's Wood . . . two human beings . . ." —The beginnings of a renewed human race are preserved in the remains of the old world, a tree (possibly Yggdrasil) of Germanic religion's cosmos.

"the sun will have borne a daughter"—In the new world, a new sun continues the job of her mother.

"Glory-of-elves"—epithet for the Sun. For other examples of epithets, see the *Epic of Gilgamesh*, Ch. 15, p. 173, and the *Hymn to Demeter*, Ch. 27, p. 391.

"He saw neither hall nor stronghold"—Here we see the outcome of the riddle contest between Gylfi and the Æsir (see Ch. 7, p. 84).

Further Reading

Davidson, H. R. Ellis. *Gods and Myths of Northern Europe*. London: Penguin Books Ltd., 1964.

Sturluson, Snorri. *The Prose Edda: Tales from Norse Mythology*. Trans. Jean I. Young. Berkeley: University of California Press, 1954.

Part 3

Heroes and Tricksters

The hero is the figure whose accomplishments and adventures can serve as models for the rest of us, inspiring us to feats in the realm of sociology, religion, or science. The deeds of heroes are as various as the values of the societies they come from. In this section, we will explore a variety of mythological heroes, considering the journeys they undertake and the great deeds they perform.

The idea of a hero has been carried through literature and storytelling into our own day and our own situation. We speak of the hero of a novel or a ballad; we have sports heroes, comic book heroes, "unsung" community heroes, to name just a few. Without being quite sure of what a hero is, most of us would agree that genuine hero figures transcend time and place because they embody virtues and traits that are universal.

Freud and Rank: Early Psychological Insights into the Hero

Sigmund Freud (1856–1939) was a therapist whose discoveries about the nature of hero stories remain influential to this day. He was greatly affected by the experiences and pathologies of his patients. One day, in reading Sophocles' play *Oedipus the King* (see p. 231), Freud was amazed to note that Jocasta says, "Many men have slept with their mothers in their dreams." He felt that this statement, which described Oedipus' fears in the play, represented the feelings he was seeing in his patients. For Freud's work had led him to believe that a son is strongly attracted to his mother and is capable of directing substantial anger at his father for also wanting her attention. He called this the Oedipus Complex. Like Freud, Otto Rank (1884–1939) emphasized the interaction of family members, which he described as the family romance, and the psychological development of the individual.

Rank, whose work first appeared in his native Germany early in the twentieth century, was a student of Freud's. Rank was instrumental in developing the modern definition of the role of the hero in mythology. His work is a good example of how scholars in other fields make connections with studies in mythology to answer questions of interest to their own work. In this case, the field that gains insights from mythology is psychology, and the questions that are illuminated involve relationships among family members. The myth of the hero is used to explain experiences that all humans undergo in their unconscious minds.

According to his best-known book, *The Myth of the Birth of the Hero*, a great number of stories from a variety of cultures fit the pattern of the family romance, including:

- Sargon the First, who founded Babylonia in the twenty-fourth century B.C.E. and destroyed the walls of Uruk, the city whose construction is celebrated in the *Epic of Gilgamesh*. Rank's analysis is based on an account of Sargon's birth found in an inscription dating to 2300 B.C.E.
- Moses, the Biblical leader who led the Israelites out of Egypt. Rank based his analysis on the birth history of Moses as told in the Bible in the second chapter of Exodus.
- Oedipus, the king of Thebes. Rank's analysis relies on the story of Oedipus as told by Sophocles (see Ch. 19, p. 231).
- Gilgamesh, the Babylonian hero (see Ch. 15, p. 166). Rank based his analysis on the "Animal Stories" of Claudius Aelian, who lived about 200 C.E., which includes an account of Gilgamesh as a boy who was saved by an eagle.
- Cyrus the Great, the king of Anshan in Persia who conquered Media in 550 B.C.E. His story is told in Herodotus' *Histories,* Book I.
- Tristan, the knight of King Arthur's court whose story is best known from the opera by Richard Wagner. Rank based his analysis on the epic composed by Gottfried von Strassburg in about 1200 C.E.
- Romulus, the mythical founder of Rome. Rank based his analysis on the story of Romulus in Fabius as reconstructed by Theodore Mommsen near the end of the nineteenth century from the accounts of Dionysius and Plutarch.
- Hercules, the Greek hero. Rank's analysis seems to be based on Apollodorus' version of the infancy of the hero (see Ch. 33, p. 453).
- Jesus of Nazareth, whose birth story is described in the Bible in the Gospel according to Luke.

In his book Rank uses the stories of these heroes to show that the pattern he identified was widespread enough to be considered universal. It is noteworthy that these heroes are for the most part not private individuals but the leaders of nations or peoples. Thus Rank's analysis not only considers the models of great deeds that might be emulated by private citizens, but has significance as well for the images that people hold of their heroism as represented by their country and their religion.

The so-called *Capitoline wolf* represents *Romulus and Remus* with the she-wolf. This statue is actually a composite, made up of a 5th-c. B.C.E. Etruscan bronze wolf and 15th-c. C.E. twins.

Joseph Campbell's Insights into Mythology

For most people today, the books of Joseph Campbell provide a more familiar introduction to the nature of the hero in mythology than the works of Sigmund Freud, Otto Rank, or Carl Jung (see Part 5, Ch. 432), whose psychological theories Campbell drew upon. According to Campbell's *The Hero with a Thousand Faces*, heroes from every culture typically undertake a journey to a far-off land. In their travels, they encounter villains, other heroes, and temptresses, and often have the opportunity to bring back magical elixirs.

Mythological Heroes from around the World

Heroes can be great kings or leaders like Gilgamesh, or Oedipus, or Mwindo, or Rama. They can be divine benefactors who provide human beings with their needs like Prometheus and Raven. Or they can be humble figures who live on the edges of society like the African tricksters.

There are many theories about the meaning of the hero's deeds. They show us how to conquer the wilderness (Gilgamesh), how to perform our duties in society (Rama), how to become a great leader (Mwindo), or how to honor the gods (Oedipus). While heroes represent the heights that human beings can achieve, they also allow us to investigate the limits of what humans can accomplish (Oedipus, Gilgamesh). The quests of heroes are not merely to be imitated. They not only have implications for extraordinary figures with great talents, but they also represent the inward path that must be taken by every human being. As we encounter heroes from mythologies spanning great distances and more than fifty centuries, we can see for ourselves that the characteristics that defined these heroes have endured and are still relevant today.

The Hero with a Thousand Faces

The book by Joseph Campbell, discussed by Dave Whomsley

WHAT TO EXPECT . . . Joseph Campbell, a well-known teacher of mythology, devoted his life to understanding various aspects of the stories we tell, both in traditional tales and in popular culture. He saw these stories as directly relevant to all of us. In his view, all humans are involved in a struggle to accomplish the adventure of the hero in their own lives. The reading in this chapter gives you an account of Campbell's ideas in his most widely influential book.

As you read this chapter, you may be surprised to find how many theories deal with the meaning of the hero's journey, especially in the field of psychology. Campbell outlines this journey with the expectation that it will help you organize and compare the various stories you study throughout this book and beyond. (Other organizational principles for use in comparison are discussed in Chapters 16, 20, 32, 33, 34, 35, and 38.)

Joseph Campbell (1904–1987) was a famous teacher of mythology. For four decades, his ideas excited and inspired students. He wrote numerous books about mythology, the most famous of which is probably *The Hero with a Thousand Faces,* which Dave Whomsley summarizes here.

In *The Hero with a Thousand Faces*, Campbell discusses many versions and variations of the hero myth. His purpose is to show the underlying structure of that myth and to help us understand why humans have kept telling versions of that myth, over and over, in culture after culture. He believes that the hero myth is really written about every human being: *each of us* is the hero struggling to accomplish his adventure. As human beings, we engage in a series of struggles to develop as individuals and to find our place in society. Beyond that, we long for wisdom: we want to understand the nature of the universe and the significance of our role in it. Campbell shows that the hero myth, in its many forms, tells versions of this struggle. Some heroes are successful and achieve glory, riches, and fame. Others are destroyed by forces that are more powerful than they. By studying both kinds of stories, we can learn about the stages of our own struggle to become the heroes of our own lives.

Campbell was a great synthesizer. Robert Segal shows that, in his effort to help us appreciate and identify with the hero, he brings together a variety of different psychological theories. In particular, Campbell helps show that the adventure of the hero involves coming to terms with many conflicting feelings. Otto Rank and Carl Jung were psychologists who strongly disagreed about what was important about being human. In very simple terms, Rank thought that psychologists needed to look at the male aspects of every human's nature, while Jung thought truth lay in studying the female aspects. Campbell did not resolve this disagreement, but he chose to disregard the differences between them. In doing so, he allows us to appreciate the insights of both men into the way mythology portrayed fundamental aspects of the human

Joseph Campbell

mind. (See Part 3 Introduction, pp. 155–157, for more on Rank, and Chapter 32, p. 468, for more on Jung.)

In addition, Campbell was a fine storyteller. *The Hero with a Thousand Faces* is full of stories, all brought together to show us the nature of the hero and ourselves. His analysis allows us to notice that despite their great variety, all hero stories follow the same pattern. The events he identifies can be found in many stories, some mentioned in his book and some not. To be analyzed according to *The Hero with a Thousand Faces*, a story does not need to have all of the elements Campbell mentions, nor do the elements have to be in the specific order he identifies as typical. What is essential to this analysis, then? Campbell's thinking suggests the importance of both male and female figures in the adventure of the hero. According to his analysis, a hero story should contain both father atonement and a meeting with a goddess or temptress.

By itself, Campbell's overview of the hero's journey provides a useful framework for many of the stories about heroes that occur later in this section. As an example, we have included in the introduction to the *Epic of Gilgamesh* (Ch. 15, pp. 170–171) the rudiments of an analysis according to *The Hero with a Thousand Faces*. It may also be interesting to read the excerpts from Jung that are found later in this book and to consider how Campbell's analysis combines elements from both of these psychologists.

Introduction to Joseph Campbell

In the PBS series, *The Power of Myth,* Bill Moyers described Joseph Campbell as the world's foremost authority on myth. During his lifetime, Campbell wrote extensively about many aspects of myth. In one of his earlier works, *The Hero with a Thousand Faces,* he argues that all heroes described in myth undergo a common development cycle. Despite the infinite variety of setting and incident, all the myths follow the same pattern. Campbell refers to this concept as the **monomyth:** no matter where you look, you'll see the pattern emerge.

Campbell bases his insights on the work of modern-day psychologists such as **Freud, Jung,** and their followers, who he says have "demonstrated irrefutably that the logic, the heroes, and the deeds of myth survive into modern times." Like Jung, Campbell suggests that myth itself is the result of a collective consciousness pouring down through the heavens and exiting from the mind of a human being. The symbols of myth are not manufactured by the author; they are created by a cosmic source and fed through the consciousness of the writer. Campbell writes, "they [the symbols] cannot be ordered, invented, or permanently suppressed. They are **spontaneous productions of the psyche,** and each bears with it, undamaged, the germ power of its source." Jung felt that a hero's quest was significantly shaped by his encounters with a female force called the anima. In contrast, Freud emphasizes the role of a child's father in the development of the child's sense of himself in the world. In *The Hero with a Thousand Faces,* Campbell integrated the Jungian view of the importance of the mother figure with the Freudian emphasis on the father.

Dave Whomsley wrote this summary and analysis of Joseph Campbell's *The Hero with a Thousand Faces* when he was a student at Drexel University.*

monomyth The narrative structure underlying all myths. Based on the view that all myths follow the same pattern.

"Freud, Jung"—Both Rank and Jung were students of Freud who developed ideas in different directions from their teacher. For more about their work, see the Part 3 Introduction and Ch. 32, p. 465 and p. 468, respectively.

The quotes in this overview come from: Joseph Campbell, *The Hero with a Thousand Faces.*

"spontaneous productions of the psyche"—Campbell believed myths from different countries and time periods arise from similar patterns in the human unconscious.

---

* David Whomsley. "*The Hero with a Thousand Faces.*" © 2002. Used by permission of author.

Campbell believes that the mythological adventure of the hero is related to **rites of passage.** These ceremonies celebrate the birth and naming of a child, a young person's growth into puberty, as well as milestones like marriage and burial. They mark the physical, mental and spiritual changes that young women and men undergo as they grow and develop to fill a variety of roles in society. "Apparently," says Campbell, "there is something in these initiatory images so necessary to the psyche that if they are not supplied from without, through myth and ritual, they will have to be announced again, through dream, from within."

"rites of passage"— These rituals are fundamental to Campbell's insights into the hero's journey. Examples include baptism, graduation, first haircut, driver's license, prom, etc. For more on ritual and its relation to myth, see Part 4, p. 367.

Overview of the Hero's Journey

In Campbell's view, the hero follows a well defined path. The first step, the separation or departure "consists in a radical transfer of emphasis from the external to the internal world." The hero must "**retreat from the world** to the realm of the unconscious. It is here that he will find the resolution of his conflicts and fears. This part of the hero's adventure contains the following five elements: "The Call to Adventure," the "Refusal of the Call," "Supernatural Aid," "Crossing the First Threshold," and "In the Belly of the Whale."

1. Separation or Departure

"retreat from the world"—The hero's adventures in fantastic lands relate, in Campbell's view, to internal psychic states.

The **second part** of the hero's path is called the trials and victories of initiation. Here the hero proves his merit, is tempted by evil, and learns the secrets of the gods. This stage contains the following six elements: "The Road of Trials," "The Meeting with the Goddess," "Woman as the Temptress," "Atonement with the Father," "Apotheosis," and "The Ultimate Boon."

2. Trials and Victories

"second part"—This is the main part of the story, the adventure itself.

The third part of the hero's journey is the return and reintegration with society. After his trials, **the hero returns,** "transfigured, [to] teach the lesson he has learned of life renewed" to make a difference in the everyday world. The six parts of this stage are "Refusal of the Return," "The Magic Flight," "Rescue from Without," "Crossing the Return Threshold," "Master of the Two Worlds," and "Freedom to Live."

3. Return

"the hero returns"—This part of the story can be minimal or even omitted.

Detailed View of the Hero's Journey

Destiny calls the hero, and transfers his "spiritual center of gravity" from his own world to an unknown zone, a world which fascinates and challenges him. The land of adventure is full of danger, and treasure.

 The Call to Adventure

"Destiny calls the hero"—The adventure may be voluntary or forced upon the hero. It may even be accidental or not noticed: the hero may suddenly find himself in the midst of an unexpected quest.

Campbell describes the transformation of Gautama Sakyamuni into the Buddha as an example of the call. The prince had been spoiled with wealth and lust by a father who wanted him to be a great emperor. But he was unfulfilled, ready to experience something more of life. "The time for the enlightenment of the Prince Siddhartha draweth nigh," thought the gods; "we must show him a sign," and they appeared to him in a variety of guises, as an old man, a diseased man, and a dead man, to show him the emptiness of his way of life.

The adventure can begin in an active or passive way. When Theseus arrived in Athens, he voluntarily started the adventure and chose his own course of action. Odysseus, on the other hand, wasn't looking for another adventure to begin; the gods made that choice for him. He also was passive about the course of the adventure, having to endure the winds of Poseidon blowing him across the seas like a piece on a chessboard.

Occasionally the hero of the myth refuses the call. He may do this because he thinks he's acting in his own interest—perhaps things should remain the way they are. The refusal shows that the psyche sees the change implied by the quest as a kind of death and resists it. Refusal can often result in a paralysis or enchantment. Campbell cites the story of Daphne running from Apollo as an example. Running in fear, she calls to her father to take away the beauty that caused Apollo to chase her. In response, she is turned into a tree.

 Refusal of the Call

Supernatural Aid

"protective figure"—Campbell views the initiation ceremony as the basis of the hero's journey. Because the adventure is internal in origin, representing the hero's readiness for a mature life, the characters encountered on the journey depend upon the hero's readiness for a particular adventure.

Crossing the First Threshold

"unknown zone"—In the first PBS TV series, *The Power of Myth,* Campbell uses the example of the bar at Mos Eisley in *Star Wars.* When Luke and Ben Kenobi enter, the place is full of creatures with unusual shapes and harsh habits. They meet Chewbacca and Han Solo, who become an essential part of Luke's adventure. While they are in the bar, Kenobi cuts off an attacker's arm to protect Luke. In it, Kenobi functions as his guardian.

Sticky-hair Campbell points out that the adventure of Prince Five-weapons provides the earliest example we have of the tar baby motif. For other examples, see Ch. 23, pp. 344 and 348.

In the Belly of the Whale

"The hero is swallowed up"—in the course of his adventure, the hero may disappear, be magically transported, or even die.

Osiris The powerful god whose rebirth represented the renewal of life conveyed by the flooding of the Nile. (See Ch. 28, p. 403.)

The Road of Trials

"a series of tasks"—Campbell characterizes this as "a favorite phase of the myth adventure." Indeed the trials of the hero may be extensive, occupying the majority of his adventures.

Cupid and Psyche For this story, see Ch. 37, p. 541.

Bernini's *Daphne and Apollo.* The story is from Ovid's *Metamorphoses* where rape is common and indicates the lack of control humans have over their destinies.

When the hero finally faces the challenge, he prepares himself with the provisions and weapons needed for his quest. In this stage, he often encounters a **protective figure** who will provide him with the means necessary to succeed.

An East African tribe tells of a hero who is met by an old woman who wraps her garment around the hero, transporting him to a brilliant chieftain who lives at the zenith of the sun. The chieftain blesses the hero and sends him home to live a prosperous life. The helper may not always be portrayed as a benign figure, however. He may appear as a tempter who lures innocent souls into trials from which they may not emerge unscathed, as Mephistopheles guides Faust to his damnation.

With the aid of a supernatural guide who represents his destiny, the hero sets out on his adventure. He reaches the gates of an **unknown zone,** where he encounters a threshold guardian who represents the limits of his current life. Sometimes this guardian assists the hero, while at others, he is deceitful and dangerous. The guardian represents the risky challenge of an adventure into the unknown.

As an example of crossing the first threshold, Campbell describes a caravan driver who encounters an ogre in the deserted wilderness. He has wisely included urns of water in his provisions, but believing the ogre's story about an abundance of water in the area, he decides to lighten the load to quicken travel. The whole caravan is weakened and is slaughtered by a group of ogres.

In another example, Prince Five-weapons is attacked by the fierce ogre Sticky-hair at the entrance of the forest. The prince uses each of his five weapons to slay the monster but each of them sticks to the ogre's body. Finally, he threatens and defeats the ogre with the thunderbolt he has in his belly, his knowledge or enlightenment.

Campbell offers a psychological/spiritual theory to explain the story of **Sticky-hair.** The ogre symbolizes the world to which we are stuck by the five senses. The prince (who is actually the Buddha in a different incarnation), having lost the protection of the five senses, transcends the need for them and resorts "to the unnamed, invisible sixth: the divine thunderbolt of the knowledge of the transcendent principle." In other words, the Buddha has a breakthrough and comes to understand the world on a much higher plane of consciousness. Sticky-hair recognizes his new status and honors him.

The hero is swallowed up because he does not successfully conciliate the guardian of the threshold; it appears that he has died. This stage of the journey reminds us that crossing the threshold is a form of death; the hero is swallowed up, and disappears, into another world, or into the inside of an animal. For example, Heracles rescues Hesione from a sea monster by diving into the monster's throat and cutting his way out through its belly. In some stories the hero is actually torn to pieces and is regenerated; this is true of the Egyptian story of **Osiris.**

One by one, the hero completes **a series of tasks.** The tasks function as tests or ordeals to show the hero's worthiness. Campbell describes the story of **Psyche,** who loses her husband **Cupid,** and must perform a series of tasks to win him back. These include sorting a great mixed pile of wheat, beans, millet, barley, lentils and peas. She must also get wool from dangerous poisonous sheep, bring back a bottle of water from a high dangerous stream, and even go to the land of the dead to bring back a box of Persephone's beauty.

Campbell describes the trials of the hero as **symbolic of psychological dangers** associated with overcoming the real problems of our lives. For instance, a stutterer dreamed of climbing a mountain and overcoming a series of obstacles that make him lose his breath. A young woman who lamented the loss of her virginity dreamed of traveling in a car through storm and rain.

Jung emphasized the **importance of the women** the hero encountered during his adventures: they represent the anima, or the female part of a man's psyche. This archetypical figure is essential to the development of a complete and mature personality. Campbell's analysis incorporates two aspects of Jung's anima: the hero with a thousand faces encounters the goddess, and the temptress. In addition, it is worth noting that Campbell's analysis, like those of Rank and Jung, applies primarily to the exploits of a male hero. This is because the psychological theories Campbell draws upon represent the experiences of men. When dealing with a story whose hero is a woman, we would need to look for "Mother Atonement," and meetings with a tempter and a god. Because stories of male heroes are so much more influential, we often find, even in stories with female heroes, that the villain is male and the apotheosis involves meeting with a **goddess,** not a god. This represents a distortion of the pattern Campbell described and is interesting as such.

The hero meets a goddess, who can be good or evil. To unite with her, the hero must ignore the temptations of human life, break the bonds of humanity to see beyond that which his human senses experience and win the boon of love "which is life itself enjoyed as the encasement of eternity." She may represent a creator goddess who nourishes and protects the world, as in the story of the Prince of the Lonesome Isle and the Lady of Tubber Tintye. The Prince's adventure is to find the healing water of the flaming well of Tubber Tintye. He enters the castle of Tubber Tintye and comes upon the most beautiful woman he has ever seen, lying asleep. He has nothing to say to her, and leaves the room. He finds twelve women, each more beautiful than the next, and leaves each. In the thirteenth room, his eyes are dazzled by a golden light. He finds the Queen of Tubber Tintye and stays with her for six days and six nights. The encounter eventually allows him to complete his quest almost effortlessly.

However, in giving life, the goddess starts humans on their road to death: "she is also the death of everything that dies." She can be destructive, representing an absent or unattainable mother. For example, in Greek myth Actæon encounters the virgin goddess Diana while she is bathing. He is turned into a stag and set upon by his own hunting dogs. Another example, in Hindu myth, is Kali, the goddess of the Totality of the universe, who represents Cosmic Power. The image of Kali at the temple where Ramakrishna was priest displayed both her positive and her terrible sides. Her four arms represent this tension: with them she waved a bloody saber, gripped a human head by the hair, made a gesture that said "fear not" and extended a hand to bestow favors.

Part of the hero's expression of his maturity is union with this "Queen Goddess of the World." However, insofar as the union with her represents sexual passion, **the hero may recoil from her** as hindering his quest for purity and enlightenment. Such entanglement may inhibit the hero's ability to perform his quest. Campbell refers to the revulsion Hamlet feels for the sexual aspect of his mother, as well as the revulsion of Oedipus from Jocasta, who he learns is his mother as well as his wife and the mother of his children. When the hero identifies the woman with his mother, he cannot entertain sexual feelings for her.

In some stories, the hero's revulsion causes the woman to be portrayed as an evil temptress, luring the hero into the sins of the flesh. The goal of the hero then becomes

Kali. Although this deity embodies female destructive power, she represents positive creativity as well.

"symbolic of psychological dangers"—As a result of his emphasis on rituals of initiation, Campbell sees the hero's adventures as representing internal challenges.

"importance of the women"—In its emphasis on the hero's interaction with a female figure, Campbell's analysis incorporates the thinking of Jung. (See Ch. 32, pp. 479–80.)

"goddess"—Campbell's view of women is, like Freud's, highly symbolic. A woman is not a complete entity in his analysis, but a projection, a part of a man's soul. This limitation is found also in the theories of Rank and Jung.

 The Meeting with the Goddess

 Woman as the Temptress

"the hero may recoil from her"—The hero's rejection of physical sexuality can be partial or absolute. The hero may reject a particular woman, or he may simply not have time for relationships with women.

St. George and the Dragon. The father figure does not have to be the hero's actual father, or even a human villain. Rather, Rank argues that "attenuation" (the process of making the story less harsh) may apply.

Atonement with the Father

atonement Making the father or father figure (any male villain) pay for his supposed mistreatment of the boy. Here Campbell's analysis incorporates the thinking of Freud and Rank. Rank explains that the mistreatment by the father is not real, but imagined by the little boy to justify his own anger in the family romance. See Part 3 Introduction, p. 156.

"rites of passage"—Times when we celebrate human milestones, also called initiation ceremonies. These rituals reflect the values of the community and may be linked with myths or stories. See Victor Turner, Ch. 26, p. 373.

resisting the call of the seductress. "The seeker of life must press beyond her, surpass the temptations of her call, and soar to the immaculate ether beyond."

The mythical father figure represents the initiatory priest who allows only the prepared hero to pass into the transformed world. His role is to test the hero to ascertain his worthiness. Like the guardian of the gate, he has both an evil and a benign aspect. He must be stern in testing the hero, but becomes loving once the hero has proven himself worthy.

Following Freud and Rank, Campbell's understanding of myth emphasizes the boy's interaction with his father. The little boy views his father as an ogre who interferes with his blissful union with his mother. Any ogre or monster in a story can, then, represent this aspect of the father. Campbell says, "As the original intruder into the paradise of the infant with its mother, the father is the archetypical enemy; hence throughout life all enemies are symbolical (to the unconscious) of the father."

The story of the hero on a quest is based on **rites of passage,** or initiation rituals, in which the hero represents the boy who is introduced to the practices of manhood. In this process, it is the father or father-figure who leads the boy into manhood, testing him and purging him of his childish ways. Campbell refers to the story of the Twin Warriors of the Navajo whose father is the bearer of the Sun. They go to his house to prove themselves worthy of being his sons. Their father hurls them first to the four points of the compass to test if they have any flaws that will appear there, but they bounce back to him unscathed. He tries to steam them to death and to poison them, but they outwit him in each case. Thus, he is forced to acknowledge them as his children. Testing by the father does not always result in acceptance, however. The Greek story of Phaethon also describes a sun god who tests his son. Phaethon is burnt up when he drives his father's chariot but does not heed his advice about the course he should take.

The hero's quest, if successful, incorporates the defeat of an ogre or villain who represents the fearsome aspect of the father. Like the mother, the father is seen as contradictory, both a creator and a destroyer, both a villain and a savior.

Through his adventure, the hero achieves **illumination** and understanding; he is raised to a godlike stature, often by communication with a higher figure which may be male, or female, or androgynous. Campbell suggests that the hero outgrows mere mortality, and is no longer blinded by his senses' misinterpretation of the true nature of things. In this stage, he meets a spiritual guide and becomes awakened, an enlightened one, able to see through the shell of his existence and the true reality beyond.

An example of apotheosis is the story of the Confucian scholar who went to the Buddhist patriarch Bodhidharma, asking for peace to be brought to his soul. "Bodhidharma retorted, 'Produce it and I will pacify it.' The Confucian replied, 'That is my trouble, I cannot find it.' Bodhidharma said, 'Your wish is granted.'" The scholar understood and left with the peace he had sought. Apotheosis often represents the achievement of such a new level of understanding by the hero.

At the end of the adventure, the hero gains possession of an object which symbolizes the Truth experienced in the apotheosis. The elixir is often food which can never be completely depleted (a bottomless cup, a few fish which fed thousands, the ambrosia of the Olympian gods) or an inextinguishable flame.

Campbell equates **these symbols** to the "perpetual life-giving, form-building powers of the universal source." Possession of this final blessed gift is often a simple task. At other times, the hero may have to steal the elixir from the magic castle, sneak past the guardian monsters, and battle through the elements to reach his homeland. In either case, the symbol of the ultimate boon remains to be possessed and returned to those who will benefit from its magical powers.

The hero's return may include a variety of elements. The hero may become so integrated with the land of adventure that he chooses to remain there, and does not return to his everyday life (Refusal of the Return). Or he may leave in haste, pursued by forces from the land of adventure (The Magic Flight). He may be brought back by other adventurers from his own world (Rescue from Without). In leaving an unknown and magical realm, the hero may encounter signs that he has returned to a more ordinary, everyday world (Crossing the Return Threshold). Some heroes achieve the ability to pass back and forth at will between the ordinary human world and the mythical land of adventure which is the source of enlightenment and transcendence (Master of the Two Worlds). Upon completion of his journey, the hero **does not, however, sequester himself** in elusive superiority. Rather, he is wise enough to lead an ordinary life, although one that is enlightened by his adventure (Freedom to Live).

The Spiritual Quest of the Hero

The journey of the hero is not, in Campbell's view, a mere story. Nor is it merely a psychological phenomenon. Rather it represents a **spiritual reality:** the hero is grappling with the place of all humans in the universe. In the world of human beings who are subject to death, the hero seeks, and finds that which is deathless. In thousands of stories, mythology chronicles the work of the hero to rediscover and show forth the undying essence of the universe.

Further Reading

Campbell, Joseph. *The Hero with a Thousand Faces*. Princeton, NJ: Princeton University Press, 1968.

Segal, Robert A. *Joseph Campbell: An Introduction,* Rev. ed. New York: Mentor-Penguin, 1990.

 Apotheosis

"illumination"—In many stories, the hero comes to understand that the spiritual side of human existence is as real as the physical part. This understanding may grow as the hero pursues his quest, or it may come as a sudden change in his view of the world.

 The Ultimate Boon: Elixir Quest

"these symbols"—Because the adventure of the hero is in fact internal, the ultimate boon obtained by the hero actually symbolizes the universal force or power found within him.

 Return, or Refusal of Return

"does not . . . sequester himself"—The return gives the hero an opportunity to apply his new understanding of the world. He may live an ordinary life with great wisdom or continue his magical adventures with a new inner power.

"spiritual reality"—The universality of the myth of the hero lies in the discovery of spiritual truths.

15

The *Epic of Gilgamesh*

WHAT TO EXPECT . . .   The *Epic of Gilgamesh,* one of the earliest myths to come down to us in written form—a nonalphabetic writing called cuneiform—is still being "completed," as contemporary archeologists continue to discover more ancient clay tablets that are inscribed with parts of the story of Gilgamesh.

In this chapter, you see a hero-king who at first behaves badly toward his subjects and his gods, but ultimately redeems himself. Although he fails to gain immortality, he achieves a type of eternal fame in the memory of his people for bringing back a story of the gods and building the great walls of his city, Uruk.

As you read, note how Gilgamesh's unsuccessful search for immortality, which is central to the epic, demonstrates the religious beliefs of this ancient culture. According to Mesopotamian religion, only the gods are immortal: Gilgamesh is two-thirds god and one-third human. Also, notice the marginal notes analyzing Gilgamesh's adventures by means of Joseph Campbell's view of the hero's journey. Consider Gilgamesh in relation to other fallible heroes: Hercules, who murders his own wife and children; Oedipus, who kills his father and marries his mother; and Mwindo, who hunts and kills Kirimu the Dragon. What role, if any, do the gods have in each hero's acts, and what can be learned about the values of a culture from the hero's eventual triumph?

The *Epic of Gilgamesh* is the story of the heroic deeds of a great leader. Ancient historic records show that there really was a Gilgamesh, and he was king of Uruk in the empire of Sumeria sometime between 2800 and 2500 B.C.E. In about 2300 B.C.E., Sumeria fell to the Akkadians, but even these conquerors regarded Gilgamesh as a great hero, and some subsequent peoples referred to him as a god.

The epic itself is more than 4,000 years old and may be the oldest written version of a heroic narrative in the world. Versions of it were written down as early as 2100 B.C.E. and underwent numerous changes in content and style in the following centuries. The text is a translation of a version which scholars estimate had been written about 1200 B.C.E. Although there are later versions, they do not essentially change or further develop ideas presented in this one.

We will notice as we read this text that, although the story is no longer an oral account, it still retains some of the characteristics of oral myth, like parataxis and epithets. As Chapter 2 makes clear, even written stories often include these because they are part of the genre, in effect creating for the new audience the experience of the earlier, more immediate style. We will also see another characteristic of oral myth: the mixture of Sumerian and Akkadian names for gods. This happens because the story developed over the many centuries during which the Akkadians—and subsequently others—conquered Sumeria. New people brought new deities, and through the process called *syncretism,* the characteristics of the old and new gods melded, and often both the old and new names were used.

The story comes from the early inhabitants of the land between the Tigris and Euphrates Rivers, modern-day Iraq. Gilgamesh survives because it was carved into soft clay tablets that were then hardened by baking. Generally, the tablets survived well, but all Gilgamesh-related tablets have damaged areas and missing sections. Archeologists hope that as more tablets are found, they will be able to fill in gaps to complete the stories. The writing system used is called cuneiform, which means "wedge-shaped," because its characters were made with the pointed or wedge-shaped end of a stick. This is one of the earliest forms of writing, invented around 3000 B.C.E. in the city-states of lower Mesopotamia.

This 15th-c. B.C.E. Babylonian fragment shows the *Epic of Gilgamesh* in cuneiform writing.

Archeologists have found versions of the story of Gilgamesh in the older Sumerian as well as in Akkadian and in other local languages. These versions were found throughout the Middle East, suggesting that the story of Gilgamesh was widely known in the second millennium B.C.E. and continued to draw learned audiences for centuries. Current scholars point out that the Akkadian version of the epic, the text translated in this chapter, may have been written by one or more poets, and that the style and composition is not merely a compilation of stories, but a well-organized narrative.

Among the several sets of Gilgamesh tablets, the most complete—and the one which scholars think represents the latest compilation and editing—comes from the library of Assurbanipal, the ruler of the Assyrian Empire in the seventh century B.C.E. In the history of his reign, Assurbanipal explains that he sent out emissaries to bring back old texts for his library in Nineveh, and that he had scholars copy and translate texts from Babylon, Uruk, and Nippur from their older Sumerian language into Akkadian. But shortly after Assurbanipal collected and collated the *Epic of Gilgamesh*, it was lost until the mid-nineteenth century when Austen Henry Layard made extensive archeological discoveries in Mesopotamia.

THEMES: UNIVERSAL AND PARTICULAR

The major themes, Gilgamesh's fear of death and his despair when he realizes that he cannot attain immortality, are important even for twenty-first-century readers because they speak to our basic concerns as human beings. In the introduction to his translation of *Gilgamesh,* Andrew George points out that besides these universal themes, we learn much that helps us understand the values of ancient Mesopotamian society. In particular, we find these beliefs in the epic:

- A hero develops through both successes and failures.
- Lasting achievements are the only way to attain a kind of immortality.
- The opposition between nature and culture, or wildness and civilization, is fundamental to Mesopotamian civilization.
- The king and the ruling class have very specific and serious responsibilities to the gods and society.
- A man has responsibilities to his family.

Ultimately, George says, "even for the ancients, the story of Gilgamesh was more about what it is to be a man than what it is to serve the gods" (xxxiii).

ANCIENT MESOPOTAMIAN RELIGION[1]

Many texts in this book are written versions of stories that were originally part of an oral tradition: for example, the Native American stories in Chapters 8 (p. 89) and 21 (p. 295). However, except for the earliest times in the third millennium B.C.E., the story of Gilgamesh was most likely read from a written text, and read aloud to an elite audience. That is, it did not grow out of a folk tradition, but from one that dealt with the role of kings in ancient Mesopotamian society. Studies of religion in Mesopotamia show that kings were viewed as earthly parallels of the gods and were responsible for setting an example as providers for the gods, thus inspiring their subjects to act piously in divine service. Kings of Mesopotamia were expected to achieve success in bringing their subjects—and their gods—peace and prosperity by making sure that the divine will was carried out. They were considered intermediaries for divine messages, and were responsible for making sure that these messages were acted on by their subjects.

Ultimately, the gods were in control of all aspects of social and economic life, and the ancient Mesopotamians believed that the divine was to be feared. The gods had created humans to be their servants. Temples resembled regal palaces, and the deities were considered to live in them, cared for by clergy-servants participating in various rituals. The staff—headed by both male and female priests—must have been huge, since many aspects of daily life were also administered from the temples.

Mesopotamian gods were anthropomorphic and were responsible for specific natural phenomena. Their behavior was a reflection of human behavior, both positive and negative. Their worshippers believed that these gods were actually present *in* their statues, and therefore *resided in* the temples in a very real way. They also believed that their primary duty in life was to serve the gods. Jean Bottero tells us that the duty of the temple servants was to maintain all aspects of daily life and building maintenance for the gods, while the duty of the rest of society was to serve the gods by accomplishing the work they believed they were put on earth to do: preparing, manufacturing, and delivering the associated goods and services.

A result of the Mesopotamians' view of religion was a belief that one should not try to change one's life, but to succeed in it. That is, one should not seek heroism, but look for happiness within the status quo of human existence. This lesson is learned by Gilgamesh, who struggles valiantly to escape death. However, he learns that the only type of immortality he can achieve is to behave like a king and accomplish great things. In that way, he will live on in the memory of future generations.

THE STRUGGLES OF THE HERO AND THE STRUCTURE OF THE EPIC

The story of Gilgamesh's adventures illustrates the difficulties and tensions that a hero must be ready to address on an ongoing basis. As the *Epic of Gilgamesh* opens, Gilgamesh is king of Uruk. However, his reign is not a happy one: he bullies and abuses his people. Through his friendship with Enkidu, Gilgamesh eventually becomes a worthy king of his people. In the course of the epic, Gilgamesh and Enkidu together conquer Humbaba, the king of the cedar forest. In this quest, Gilgamesh fulfills Joseph Campbell's definition of the hero: the figure who leaves home, performs a significant deed, returns, and is recognized for that deed. (See the chart on pp. 170–171 and Chapter 14, p. 159.)

Despite his heroic deeds, however, Gilgamesh, who has inherited divine attributes from his goddess mother Ninsun, faces continual problems because of the tension between his semi-divine nature and his daily human experiences. Although he is superior to the other inhabitants of Uruk in love and war, they resent him and complain to the gods about his behavior. And his periods of glory are always brief, followed by problems or disappointments. For example, after

---

[1] Most information in this section is taken from Jean Bottero, *Religion in Ancient Mesopotamia*.

winning the combat in the forest, Gilgamesh appears glorious, as it were, dressed finely and looking divinely beautiful. But immediately Ishtar confronts him, and his rejection of her sets in motion his next trial-success-disappointment cycle. Ishtar sends the Bull of Heaven as punishment, but Gilgamesh kills him. Gilgamesh then has to atone for this transgression.

Events follow a somewhat cyclical pattern throughout the work. In addition, there is a similar pattern at the beginning and end of the eleven-tablet version that is considered the standard: in the beginning, when Enkidu acquires culture to help Gilgamesh, and at the end, when he cannot transcend death, he has only culture to console him. We see this near the conclusion in the description of Gilgamesh as builder of the great wall that mirrors the description at the start.

In these first lines of the poem, Gilgamesh is already hailed as a hero for having built the great walls of Uruk, but it is not his role as founding father that ultimately gives him heroic stature. Rather, his significant mythic accomplishments are related to his development as a human being: his deep friendship with Enkidu, his overcoming sorrow and disappointment at the loss of his friend, and his search for eternal life for himself and others.

HEROISM AS A WAY OF DEALING WITH LIMITATIONS

The nature of heroic deeds may vary from culture to culture and from age to age, but in general, heroes are characterized by courage, wit, strength, physical beauty, virtue, and a willingness to take substantial risks to reach their goals. We can certainly see that Gilgamesh is a hero, but when we look closely at him, we also find difficulties and shortcomings. Gilgamesh journeys far from his home. His adventures with Enkidu against Humbaba lead to his losing his best friend. He goes off to seek the ancestral wisdom of Utnapishtim, and when he ultimately loses the Plant of Youth Regained, he learns that he is not only powerless to bring Enkidu back from the dead, but that he is equally unable to thwart his own mortality.

In the end, it is the way that Gilgamesh deals with these limitations which allows us to see him as a hero. He is the person who has seen all, who has experienced the most profound failures and disappointments, but who at the same time has tried to accomplish the most for humanity and has succeeded in understanding the cosmic order. His journey is as much psychological as it is geographical. After losing Enkidu, his friend and brother, he passes through a dark emotional period of sorrow and self-doubt, but emerges much more altruistic in nature. He has experienced the elusiveness of the secret of youth, and he has learned that there is no escape from death for humans.

Gilgamesh wants to escape human limitations, to get answers to questions not available to his contemporaries, and perhaps most importantly, he wants to overcome mortality both for himself and others. But ultimately his story shows us that, despite his extraordinary talents, in these matters he is not different from other humans. Thus, we see that it is precisely his human limitations that make him truly heroic.

GILGAMESH AND THE HERO'S JOURNEY

As mentioned before, one of the many ways to look at Gilgamesh is to relate his heroic deeds to the journey of the hero as defined by Joseph Campbell in *The Hero with a Thousand Faces*. Accordingly, we might compare the events of this epic to the elements of that journey as listed in the following chart. See Chapter 14, p. 159, for a more extensive discussion of these elements.

THE GENRE OF THE STORY OF GILGAMESH

We call the story of Gilgamesh an epic because it has the characteristics of that literary genre: that is, what has come down to us is a long poem that tells of the heroic deeds of an important historical figure. However, the version presented in this chapter is not written as a poem. N. K.

The Hero's Path	The Event in the *Epic*	The *Gilgamesh* Text
Refusal of the Quest (by Enkidu)	Gilgamesh is eager to establish himself as a hero by destroying Humbaba. But Enkidu knows of the giant's tremendous destructive powers.	"I tell you, weakness overpowers whoever goes near it: it is not an equal struggle when one fights with Humbaba; he is a great warrior, a battering-ram. Gilgamesh, the watchman of the forest never sleeps."
Supernatural Aid (by Shamash)	Gilgamesh has second thoughts about his ability to overpower Humbaba, so Shamash answers his plea and provides helpers.	"So Shamash accepted the sacrifice of his tears; like the compassionate man he showed him mercy. He appointed strong allies for Gilgamesh, sons of one mother, and stationed them in the mountain caves."
Meeting with the Goddess	Gilgamesh's mother, goddess Ninsun, asks Enkidu to go along to serve and protect Gilgamesh.	"Then Ninsun the mother of Gilgamesh extinguished the incense, and she called to Enkidu with this exhortation . . ."
Crossing the First Threshold	Enkidu warns Gilgamesh about the gate to Humbaba's forest. He will later remember crossing this threshold as the beginning of his death.	"When I opened the gate my hand lost its strength."
In the Belly of the Whale	Gilgamesh and Enkidu are stupefied by the grandeur of the forest. It represents another world.	"There [at the forest] they stood still; they were struck dumb. . . . They gazed at the mountain of cedars, the dwelling place of the gods and the throne of Ishtar."
Atonement with the Father	Humbaba is not, of course, Gilgamesh's father, but he is a father figure—strong, fierce, and threatening as a father would be to a boy undergoing an initiation ritual.	"By the life of Ninsun my mother and divine Lugulbanda my father . . . I have discovered your dwelling . . . and now I will enter your house."
Meeting with the Goddess	After killing Humbaba, Gilgamesh washes and puts on his royal robes and crown. Ishtar then approaches him.	"Ishtar lifted her eyes, seeing the beauty of Gilgamesh. She said, 'Come to me, Gilgamesh, and be my bride-groom . . .'"
Woman as the Temptress	Ishtar wants Gilgamesh to marry her, so she promises luxurious comforts and tremendous power.	"Kings, rulers, and princes will bow down before you . . ."
The Call to Adventure	Out of fear and grief, Gilgamesh plans to search for the secret of eternal life. This adventure occurs almost accidentally; it is not a planned quest like the search for Humbaba.	"Because I am afraid of death I will go as best I can to find Utnapishtim whom they call the Faraway, for he has entered the assembly of the gods."
Crossing the Threshold	On his quest for eternal life, Gilgamesh comes to the mountains which guard the rising and setting sun. The passage is guarded by monsters.	"At its gate the Scorpions stand guard, half man and half dragon; their glory is terrifying, their stare strikes death into men . . ."
In the Belly of the Whale	Gilgamesh disappears into the dark world beyond the mountain.	"When he had gone one league the darkness became thick around him, for there was no light, he could see nothing ahead and nothing behind him. After two leagues the darkness was thick and there was no light . . ."
Supernatural Aid	Shamash tells Gilgamesh the outcome of his journey, but Gilgamesh will not accept it until his experience confirms it.	"And to Gilgamesh he said, 'You will never find the life for which you are searching.'"
Meeting with the Goddess	Siduri is a goddess of brewing and wisdom, whom Gilgamesh meets on his travels and who gives him advice.	"Beside the sea she lives, the woman of the vine, the maker of wine; Siduri sits in the garden at the edge of the sea . . ."
Atonement with the Father	It is not clear why Gilgamesh regards Urshanabi as a villain to be defeated, but that is certainly how he treats him.	"Urshanabi saw the dagger flash and heard the axe, and he beat his head, for Gilgamesh had shattered the tackle of the boat in his rage."

The Hero's Path	The Event in the *Epic*	The *Gilgamesh* Text
Apotheosis	Gilgamesh learns a secret of the gods (the story of the flood) from Utnapishtim.	"[Gilgamesh] was wise, he saw mysteries and knew secret things, he brought us a tale of the days before the flood. "
The Road of Trials	Gilgamesh is given a task to show he deserves immortality.	"But if you wish, come and put it to the test: only prevail against sleep for six days and seven nights."
The Ultimate Boon: Elixir Quest	Gilgamesh gets, and loses, an elixir in the form of the flower of rejuvenation that restores youth.	"Come here, and see this marvellous plant. By its virtue a man may win back all his former strength . . ."
The Return	Gilgamesh goes back to Uruk the same way he came.	"So Gilgamesh returned by the gate through which he had come, Gilgamesh and Urshanabi went together."

Sandars, the translator, notes in her introduction that she aims to present a smooth and consistent story for the nonspecialist. The cuneiform tablets from which we get the story were often cracked and broken, leaving gaps in the text. For the most part, Sandars has not added anything to the text or altered the paratactic nature of the myth, but she has not indicated these gaps. Line-by-line translations, such as the editions by Stephanie Dalley and Benjamin Foster, provide an accurate and intriguing view of the challenge of ancient texts, but they can be more difficult to read and enjoy.

The *Epic of Gilgamesh*

I will proclaim to the world the deeds of Gilgamesh. This was the man to whom all things were known; this was the king who knew the countries of the world. He was wise, he saw mysteries and knew secret things, he brought us a tale of the days before the flood. He went on a long journey, was weary, worn-out with labour, returning he rested, he engraved on a stone **the whole story.**

When the gods created Gilgamesh they gave him a perfect body. **Shamash** the glorious sun endowed him with beauty, Adad the god of the storm endowed him with courage, the great gods made his beauty perfect, surpassing all others, terrifying like a great wild bull. Two thirds they made him god and one third man.

In Uruk he built walls, a great rampart, and the temple of blessed Eanna for the god of the firmament Anu, and for **Ishtar** the goddess of love. **Look at it** still today: the outer wall where the cornice runs, it shines with the brilliance of copper; and the inner wall, it has no equal. Touch the threshold, it is ancient. Approach Eanna the dwelling of Ishtar, our lady of love and war, the like of which no latter-day king, no man alive can equal. Climb upon the wall of Uruk; walk along it, I say; regard the foundation terrace and examine the masonry: **is it not burnt brick** and good? The seven sages laid the foundations.

The Coming of Enkidu

Gilgamesh went abroad in the world, but he met with none who could withstand his arms till he came to Uruk. But the men of Uruk muttered in their houses, "Gilgamesh sounds the tocsin for his amusement, his arrogance has no bounds by day or night. No son is left with his father, for Gilgamesh takes them all, even the children; yet **the king**

This excerpt comes from: The *Epic of Gilgamesh**

"the whole story"—Probably refers to Utnapishtim's story in Tablet XI.

Shamash God of the sun.

Ishtar Goddess of love and fertility, also of war.

"Look at it . . ."—The narrator speaks directly to the audience. The directions to touch the wall, to examine the foundation, and to approach the temple suggest that they were still intact when this version was written down.

"is it not burnt brick"—Baked bricks were used only for the most important construction; otherwise, sun-dried mud bricks were common.

"the king should be a shepherd to his people"—Although recognized as a hero, Gilgamesh is chastised for his arrogance.

Anu Father of the gods; god of the firmament. Zeus and Jupiter are also head gods who are "sky" gods.

"the gods cried to Aruru"—There is a hierarchy among the gods, and each has a specific responsibility. Aruru, the goddess of creation is called upon to create a companion for Gilgamesh.

"the goddess conceived an image"—First there is a mental creation, representing the sky god. This is followed by a creation from clay. Note that the creator here is female.

"he knew nothing of the cultivated land"—Agriculture was considered a more advanced occupation than hunting.

"the trapper was frozen with fear"—Enkidu has no fear of the trapper, suggesting that the primitive is more of a threat to the civilized, than vice versa.

"let her woman's power overpower this man"—In a land where the primary goddess, Ishtar, was the patroness of "free love," there was a positive connection between the practice of prostitution and religious values. Here, the harlot helps bring Enkidu from a wild existence into a civilized one.

"Trapper, go back"—Gilgamesh's advice to the trapper needlessly repeats the advice of the trapper's father. Here we note the paratactic nature of myth (see Ch. 2, p. 18).

"the harlot and the trapper . . . waited for the game"—They lie in wait for Enkidu, just as they would for wild prey.

should be a shepherd to his people. His lust leaves no virgin to her lover, neither the warrior's daughter nor the wife of the noble, yet this is the shepherd of the city, wise, comely, and resolute."

The gods heard their lament, the gods of heaven cried to the Lord of Uruk, to **Anu** the god of Uruk: "A goddess made him, strong as a savage bull, none can withstand his arms. No son is left with his father, for Gilgamesh takes them all; and is this the king, the shepherd of his people? His lust leaves no virgin to her lover, neither the warrior's daughter nor the wife of the noble." When Anu had heard their lamentation **the gods cried to Aruru,** the goddess of creation, "You made him, O Aruru, now create his equal; let it be as like him as his own reflection, his second self, stormy heart for stormy heart. Let them contend together and leave Uruk in quiet."

So **the goddess conceived an image** in her mind, and it was of the stuff of Anu of the firmament. She dipped her hands in water and pinched off clay, she let it fall in the wilderness, and noble Enkidu was created. There was virtue in him of the god of war, of Ninum himself. His body was rough, he had long hair like a woman's; it waved like the hair of Nisaba, the goddess of corn. His body was covered with matted hair like Samuqan's, the god of cattle. He was innocent of mankind; **he knew nothing of the cultivated land.**

Enkidu ate grass in the hills with the gazelle and lurked with wild beasts at the water-holes; he had joy of the water with the herds of wild game. But there was a trapper who met him one day face to face at the drinking-hole, for the wild game had entered his territory. On three days he met him face to face, and **the trapper was frozen with fear.** He went back to his house with the game that he had caught, and he was dumb, benumbed with terror. His face was altered like that of one who has made a long journey. With awe in his heart he spoke to his father: "Father, there is a man, unlike any other, who comes down from the hills. He is the strongest in the world, he is like an immortal from heaven. He ranges over the hills with wild beasts and eats grass; he ranges through your land and comes down to the wells. I am afraid and dare not go near him. He fills in the pits which I dig and tears up my traps set for the game; he helps the beasts to escape and now they slip through my fingers."

His father opened his mouth and said to the trapper, "My son, in Uruk lives Gilgamesh; no one has ever prevailed against him, he is strong as a star from heaven. Go to Uruk, find Gilgamesh, extol the strength of this wild man. Ask him to give you a harlot, a wanton from the temple of love; return with her, and **let her woman's power overpower this man.** When next he comes down to drink at the wells she will be there, stripped naked; and when he sees her beckoning he will embrace her, and then the wild beasts will reject him."

So the trapper set out on his journey to Uruk and addressed himself to Gilgamesh saying, "A man unlike any other is roaming now in the pastures; he is as strong as a star from heaven and I am afraid to approach him. He helps the wild game to escape; he fills in my pits and pulls up my traps." Gilgamesh said, "**Trapper, go back,** take with you a harlot, a child of pleasure. At the drinking-hole she will strip, and when he sees her beckoning he will embrace her and the game of the wilderness will surely reject him."

Now the trapper returned, taking the harlot with him. After a three days' journey they came to the drinking-hole, and there they sat down; **the harlot and the trapper sat facing one another and waited for the game** to come. For the first day and for the second day the two sat waiting, but on the third day the herds came; they came down to drink and Enkidu was with them. The trapper spoke to her: "There he is. Now, woman, make your breasts bare, have no shame, do not delay but welcome his love. Let him see you naked, let him possess your body. When he comes near uncover yourself and lie with him; teach him, the savage man, your woman's art, for when he murmurs love to you the wild beasts that shared his life in the hills will reject him."

She was not ashamed to take him, she made herself naked and welcomed his eagerness; as he lay on her murmuring love she taught him the woman's art. For six days and seven nights they lay together, for Enkidu had forgotten his home in the hills; but when he was satisfied he went back to the wild beasts. Then, when the gazelle saw him, they bolted away; when the wild creatures saw him they fled. Enkidu would have followed, but his body was bound as though with a cord, his knees gave way when he started to run, his swiftness was gone. And now the wild creatures had all fled away; **Enkidu was grown weak,** for wisdom was in him, and the thoughts of a man were in his heart. So he returned and sat down at the woman's feet, and listened intently to what she said. "You are wise, Enkidu, and now you have become like a god. Why do you want to run wild with the beasts in the hills? Come with me. I will take you to **strong-walled** Uruk, to the blessed temple of Ishtar and of Anu, of love and of heaven: there Gilgamesh lives, who is very strong, and like a wild bull he lords it over men."

When she had spoken Enkidu was pleased; he longed for a comrade, for one who would understand his heart. "Come, woman, and take me to that holy temple, to the house of Anu and of Ishtar, and to the place where Gilgamesh lords it over the people. **I will challenge him** boldly, I will cry out aloud in Uruk, 'I am the strongest here, I have come to change the old order, I am he who was born in the hills, I am he who is strongest of all.'"

"O Enkidu, you who love life, I will show you Gilgamesh, a man of many moods; you shall look at him well in his radiant manhood. His body is perfect in strength and maturity; he never rests by night or day. He is stronger than you, so leave your boasting. **Shamash** the glorious sun has given favours to Gilgamesh, and Anu of the heavens, and **Enlil,** and **Ea** the wise has given him deep understanding. I tell you, even before you have left the wilderness, Gilgamesh will know in his dreams that you are coming."

Now Gilgamesh got up to tell his dream to his mother, **Ninsun,** one of the wise gods. "Mother, last night **I had a dream.** I was full of joy, the young heroes were round me and I walked through the night under the stars of the firmament, and one, a meteor of the stuff of Anu, fell down from heaven. I tried to lift it but it proved too heavy. All the people of Uruk came round to see it, the common people jostled and the nobles thronged to kiss its feet; and to me its attraction was like the love of woman. They helped me, I braced my forehead and I raised it with thongs and brought it to you, and you yourself pronounced it my brother."

Then Ninsun, who is well-beloved and wise, said to Gilgamesh, "This star of heaven which descended like a meteor from the sky; which you tried to lift, but found too heavy, when you tried to move it, it would not budge, and so you brought it to my feet; I made it for you, a goad and a spur, and you were drawn as though to a woman. This is the strong comrade, the one who brings help to his friend in his need. He is the strongest of wild creatures, the stuff of Anu; born in the grasslands and the wild hills reared him; when you see him you will be glad; you will love him as a woman and he will never forsake you. This is the meaning of the dream."

Gilgamesh said, "Mother, I dreamed a second dream. In the streets of strong-walled Uruk there lay an axe; the shape of it was strange and the people thronged round. I saw it and was glad. I bent down, deeply drawn towards it; I loved it like a woman and wore it at my side." Ninsun answered, "That axe, which you saw, which drew you so powerfully like love of a woman, that is the comrade whom I give you, and he will come in his strength like one of the host of heaven. He is the brave companion who rescues his friend in necessity." Gilgamesh said to his mother, "A friend, a counsellor has come to me from Enlil, and now I shall befriend and counsel him." So Gilgamesh told his dreams; and the harlot retold them to Enkidu.

And now she said to Enkidu, "When I look at you, you have become like a god. Why do you yearn to run wild again with the beasts in the hills? **Get up from the**

"Enkidu was grown weak"—He becomes weaker physically as he becomes stronger intellectually.

"strong-walled"—Resembles a Homeric epithet: a two-word construction used to describe a person or a thing. For example, Achilles is "swift-footed."

"I will challenge him"—Even though Enkidu longs for a comrade, he aims to demonstrate his superiority to him.

Shamash God of the sun; lawgiver; husband and brother of Ishtar.

Enlil God of earth and wind; Sumerian for Ellil; father of Ninurta.

Ea God of wisdom and sweet waters; one of the creators of mankind. Ea = Sumerian Enki, god of fresh water, of wisdom; helper of mankind. Epithet: "far-sighted."

Ninsun Sumerian goddess noted for wisdom; wife of Lugulbanda.

"I had a dream"—In this story, dreams are a very important means of communication and of foretelling events.

Metaphor of the first dream: Enkidu is compared to a meteor— He is seen therefore as a descendant of Anu and as having heavenly power.

Metaphor of the second dream: Enkidu is compared to an axe— He is seen therefore as a physical protector.

"Get up from the ground, the bed of a shepherd."—The harlot continues to educate Enkidu, clothing him and teaching him to eat and drink as a human.

"Enkidu could only suck the milk of wild animals."—In this, he resembles Romulus and Remus, founders of Rome who were reared by a she-wolf. On other stories of this type, see the Introduction to Part 3, p. 156.

"He took arms to hunt the lion"— Enkidu uses his abilities as a wild animal to aid his new human companions. Compare this with his helping the animals to evade the hunter earlier.

"He does strange things in Uruk"— The unacceptable behavior of Gilgamesh in Uruk has been referred to earlier. But now, the complaint is made to Enkidu, who declares himself stronger than Gilgamesh and claims he will change his behavior.

"Then immediately his fury died."—Heroic companions often start off as adversaries. Examples include Arthur and Lancelot, Robin Hood and Little John.

Gilgamesh, as shown by an Assyrian relief from Palace of Sargon II, Khorsabad. 8th c. B.C.E.

"The meaning of the dream is this"—Enkidu interprets Gilgamesh's dream, a sign that he has been fully endowed with superior human wisdom.

ground, the bed of a shepherd." He listened to her words with care. It was good advice that she gave. She divided her clothing in two and with the one half she clothed him and with the other herself; and holding his hand she led him like a child to the sheepfolds, into the shepherds' tents. There all the shepherds crowded round to see him, they put down bread in front of him, but **Enkidu could only suck the milk of wild animals.** He fumbled and gaped, at a loss what to do or how he should eat the bread and drink the strong wine. Then the woman said, "Enkidu, eat bread, it is the staff of life; drink the wine, it is the custom of the land." So he ate till he was full and drank strong wine, seven goblets. He became merry, his heart exulted and his face shone. He rubbed down the matted hair of his body and anointed himself with oil. Enkidu had become a man; but when he had put on man's clothing he appeared like a bridegroom. **He took arms to hunt the lion** so that the shepherds could rest at night. He caught wolves and lions and the herdsmen lay down in peace; for Enkidu was their watchman, that strong man who had no rival.

He was merry living with the shepherds, till one day lifting his eyes he saw a man approaching. He said to the harlot, "Woman, fetch that man here. Why has he come? I wish to know his name." She went and called the man saying, "Sir, where are you going on this weary journey?" The man answered, saying to Enkidu, "Gilgamesh has gone into the marriage-house and shut out the people. **He does strange things in Uruk,** the city of great streets. At the roll of the drum work begins for the men, and work for the women. Gilgamesh the king is about to celebrate marriage with the Queen of Love, and he still demands to be first with the bride, the king to be first and the husband to follow, for that was ordained by the gods from his birth, from the time the umbilical cord was cut. But now the drums roll for the choice of the bride and the city groans." At these words Enkidu turned white in the face. "I will go to the place where Gilgamesh lords it over the people, I will challenge him boldly, and I will cry aloud in Uruk, 'I have come to change the old order, for I am the strongest here.'"

Now Enkidu strode in front and the woman followed behind. He entered Uruk, that great market, and all the folk thronged round him where he stood in the street in strong-walled Uruk. The people jostled; speaking of him they said, "He is the spit of Gilgamesh" "He is shorter." "He is bigger of bone." "This is the one who was reared on the milk of wild beasts. His is the greatest strength." The men rejoiced: "Now Gilgamesh has met his match. This great one, this hero whose beauty is like a god, he is a match even for Gilgamesh."

In Uruk the bridal bed was made, fit for the goddess of love. The bride waited for the bridegroom, but in the night Gilgamesh got up and came to the house. Then Enkidu stepped out, he stood in the street and blocked the way. Mighty Gilgamesh came on and Enkidu met him at the gate. He put out his foot and prevented Gilgamesh from entering the house, so they grappled, holding each other like bulls. They broke the doorposts and the walls shook, they snorted like bulls locked together. They shattered the doorposts and the walls shook. Gilgamesh bent his knee with his foot planted on the ground and with a turn Enkidu was thrown. **Then immediately his fury died.** When Enkidu was thrown he said to Gilgamesh, "There is not another like you in the world. Ninsun, who is as strong as a wild ox in the byre, she was the mother who bore you, and now you are raised above all men, and Enlil has given you the kingship, for your strength surpasses the strength of men." So Enkidu and Gilgamesh embraced and their friendship was sealed.

The Forest Journey

Enlil of the mountain, the father of the gods, had decreed the destiny of Gilgamesh. So Gilgamesh dreamed and Enkidu said, "**The meaning of the dream is this.** The father of the gods has given you kingship, such is your destiny, **everlasting life is not your destiny.** Because of this do not be sad at heart, do not be grieved or oppressed. He has given you power to bind and to loose, to be the darkness and the light of mankind. He has given you unexampled supremacy over the people, victory in battle from which no fugitive returns, in forays and assaults from which there is no going back. But do not abuse this power, deal justly with your servants in the palace, deal justly before Shamash."

The eyes of Enkidu were full of tears and his heart was sick. He sighed bitterly and Gilgamesh met his eye and said, "My friend, why do you sigh so bitterly?" But Enkidu opened his mouth and said, "I am weak, my arms have lost their strength, the cry of sorrow sticks in my throat, I am oppressed by idleness." It was then that the lord Gilgamesh turned his thoughts to the Country of the Living; on the Land of Cedars the lord Gilgamesh reflected. He said to his servant Enkidu, "I have not established my name stamped on bricks as my destiny decreed; therefore I will go to the country where the cedar is felled. I will set up my name in the place where the names of famous men are written, and where no man's name is written yet I will raise a monument to the gods. Because of the evil that is in the land, we will go to the forest and destroy the evil; for in the forest lives Humbaba **whose name is 'Hugeness,'** a ferocious giant." But Enkidu sighed bitterly and said, "When I went with the wild beasts ranging through the wilderness I discovered the forest; its length is **ten thousand leagues** in every direction. Enlil has appointed Humbaba to guard it and armed him in sevenfold terrors, terrible to all flesh is Humbaba. When he roars it is like the torrent of the storm, his breath is like fire, and his jaws are death itself. He guards the cedars so well that when the wild heifer stirs in the forest, though she is sixty leagues distant, he hears her. What man would willingly walk into that country and explore its depths? I tell you, weakness overpowers whoever goes near it: it is not an equal struggle when one fights with Humbaba; he is a great warrior, a battering-ram. Gilgamesh, the watchman of the forest never sleeps."

Gilgamesh replied: "Where is the man who can clamber to heaven? Only the gods live for ever with glorious Shamash, but as for us men, our days are numbered, our occupations are a breath of wind. How is this, already you are afraid! **I will go first** although I am your lord, and you may safely call out, 'Forward, there is nothing to fear!' Then if I fall I leave behind me a name that endures; men will say of me, 'Gilgamesh has fallen in fight with ferocious Humbaba.' Long after the child has been born in my house, they will say it, and remember." Enkidu spoke again to Gilgamesh, "O my lord, if you will enter that country, go first to the hero Shamash, tell the Sun God, for the land is his. The country where the cedar is cut belongs to Shamash."

Gilgamesh took up a kid, white without spot, and a brown one with it; he held them against his breast, and he carried them into the presence of the sun. He took in his hand his silver sceptre and he said to glorious Shamash, "I am going to that country, O **Shamash,** I am going; my hands supplicate, so **let it be well with my soul** and bring me back to the quay of Uruk. Grant, I beseech, your protection, and let the omen be good." Glorious Shamash answered, "Gilgamesh, you are strong, but what is the Country of the Living to you?"

"O Shamash, hear me, hear me, Shamash, let my voice be heard. **Here in the city man dies oppressed at heart,** man perishes with despair in his heart. I have looked over the wall and I see **the bodies floating on the river,** and that will be my lot also. Indeed I know it is so, for whoever is tallest among men cannot reach the heavens, and the greatest cannot encompass the earth. Therefore I would enter that country: because I have not established my name stamped on brick as my destiny decreed, I will go to the country where the cedar is cut. I will set up my name where the names of famous men are written; and where no man's name is written I will raise a monument to the gods." The tears ran down his face and he said, "Alas, it is a long journey that I must take to the Land of Humbaba. If this enterprise is not to be accomplished, why did you move me, Shamash, with the restless desire to perform it? How can I succeed if you will not succour me? If I die in that country I will die without rancour, but if I return I will make a glorious offering of gifts and of praise to Shamash."

So Shamash accepted the sacrifice of his tears; **like the compassionate man he showed him mercy.** He appointed strong allies for Gilgamesh, sons of one mother, and stationed them in the mountain caves. The great winds he appointed: the north wind, the whirlwind, the storm and the icy wind, the tempest and the scorching wind. Like vipers, like dragons, like a scorching fire, like a serpent that freezes the heart, a destroying flood and the lightning's fork, such were they and Gilgamesh rejoiced.

He went to the forge and said, "I will give orders to the armourers; they shall cast us our weapons while we watch them." So they gave orders to the armourers and the craftsmen sat down in conference. They cast for them axes of nine score pounds, and great swords they cast with blades of six score pounds each one, with pommels and hilts of thirty pounds. They cast for Gilgamesh the axe **"Might of Heroes"** and the bow of Anshan; and Gilgamesh was armed and Enkidu; and the weight of the arms they carried was thirty score pounds.

The people collected and the counsellors in the streets and in the market-place of Uruk; they came through the gate of seven bolts and Gilgamesh spoke to them in the market-place: "I, Gilgamesh, go to see that creature of whom such things are spoken, the rumour of whose name fills the world. I will conquer him in his cedar wood and show the strength of the sons of Uruk, all the world shall know of it. I am committed to this enterprise: to climb the mountain, to cut down the cedar, and leave behind me an enduring name." The counsellors of Uruk, the great market, answered him, "Gilgamesh, you are young, your courage carries you too far, you cannot know what this enterprise means which you plan. We have heard that Humbaba is not like men who die, his weapons are such that none can stand against them; when he roars it is like the torrent of the storm, his breath is like fire and his jaws are death itself. Why do you crave to do this thing, Gilgamesh? It is no equal struggle when one fights with Humbaba, that battering-ram."

When he heard these words of the counsellors Gilgamesh looked at his friend and laughed, "How shall I answer them; shall I say I am afraid of Humbaba, I will sit at home all the rest of my days?" Then Gilgamesh opened his mouth again and said to Enkidu, "My friend, let us goto the Great Palace, to Egalmah, and stand before Ninsun the queen. **Ninsun is wise** with deep knowledge, she will give us counsel for the road we must go." They took each other by the hand as they went to Egalmah, and they went to Ninsun the great queen. Gilgamesh approached, he entered the palace and spoke to Ninsun. "Ninsun, will you listen to me; I have a long journey to go, to the Land of Humbaba, I must travel an unknown road and fight a strange battle. From the day I go until I return, till I reach the cedar forest and destroy the evil which Shamash abhors, pray for me to Shamash."

Ninsun went into her room, she put on a dress becoming to her body, she put on jewels to make her breast beautiful, she placed a tiara on her head and her skirts swept the ground. Then she went up to the altar of the Sun, standing upon the roof of the palace; she burnt incense and lifted her arms to Shamash as the smoke ascended: "**O Shamash, why did you give this restless heart to Gilgamesh,** my son; why did you give it? You have moved him and now he sets out on a long journey to the Land of Humbaba, to travel an unknown road and fight a strange battle. Therefore from the day that he goes till the day he returns, until he reaches the cedar forest, until he kills Humbaba and destroys the evil thing which you, Shamash, abhor, do not forget him; but let the dawn, **Aya,** your dear bride, remind you always, and when day is done give him to the watchman of the night to keep him from harm." Then Ninsun the mother of Gilgamesh extinguished the incense, and she called to Enkidu with this exhortation: "Strong Enkidu, you are not the child of my body, but I will receive you as my adopted

---

"like the compassionate man he showed him mercy"—Shamash, the sun god, shows compassion here: this is an example of anthropomorphism, the gods acting like humans.

 Supernatural Aid (by Shamash)

"Might of Heroes"—The naming of weapons is prominent in many mythic traditions, for millennia. For example, see the Icelandic *Prose Edda*, p. 222.

 The Hero Must Leave Home

"Ninsun is wise"—Gilgamesh takes Enkidu to Ninsun, his wise mother.

 Meeting with the Goddess

"O Shamash, why did you give this restless heart to Gilgamesh"—Ninsun's prayer to Shamash is almost a rebuke in which she places the responsibility of protection on the god, because he has given Gilgamesh the drive to heroism.

Aya Dawn, bride of the sun gods.

son; you are my other child like the foundlings they bring to the temple. Serve Gilgamesh as a foundling serves the temple and the priestess who reared him. In the presence of my women, my votaries and hierophants, I declare it." Then she placed the amulet for a pledge round his neck, and she said to him, "I entrust my son to you; bring him back to me safely."

And now they brought to them the weapons, they put in their hands the great swords in their golden scabbards, and the bow and the quiver. Gilgamesh took the axe, he slung the quiver from his shoulder, and the bow of Anshan, and buckled the sword to his belt; and so they were armed and ready for the journey.

The counsellors blessed Gilgamesh and warned him, "Do not trust too much in your own strength, be watchful, restrain your blows at first. The one who goes in front protects his companion; the good guide who knows the way guards his friend. Let Enkidu lead the way, he knows the road to the forest, he has seen Humbaba and is experienced in battles; let him press first into the passes, let him be watchful and look to himself."

Again to Gilgamesh they said, "May Shamash give you your heart's desire, may he let you see with your eyes the thing accomplished which your lips have spoken; may he open a path for you where it is blocked, and a road for your feet to tread. May he open the mountains for your crossing, and may the nighttime bring you the blessings of night, and **Lugulbanda,** your guardian god, stand beside you for victory. Wash your feet in the river of Humbaba to which you are journeying; in the evening dig a well, and let there always be pure water in your waterskin. Offer cold water to Shamash and do not forget Lugulbanda."

Then Enkidu opened his mouth and said, "Forward, **there is nothing to fear.** Follow me, for I know the place where Humbaba lives and the paths where he walks."

After twenty leagues they broke their fast; after another thirty leagues they stopped for the night. Fifty leagues they walked in one day; in three days they had walked as much as a journey of a month and two weeks. They crossed seven mountains before they came to the gate of the forest. Then Enkidu called out to Gilgamesh, "Do not go down into the forest; **when I opened the gate my hand lost its strength.**" Gilgamesh answered him, "Dear friend, do not speak like a coward. Have we got the better of so many dangers and traveled so far, to turn back at last? You, who are tried in wars and battles, hold close to me now and you will feel no fear of death; keep beside me and your weakness will pass, the trembling will leave your hand. Would my friend rather stay behind? No, we will go down together into the heart of the forest. Let your courage be roused by the battle to come; forget death and follow me, a man resolute in action, but one who is not foolhardy. When two go together each will protect himself and shield his companion, and if they fall they leave an enduring name."

Together they went down into the forest and they came to the green mountain. There they stood still, they were struck dumb; they stood still and gazed at the forest. They saw the height of the cedar, they saw the way into the forest and the track where Humbaba was used to walk. The way was broad and the going was good. They gazed at the mountain of cedars, the dwelling-place of the gods and the throne of Ishtar. The hugeness of the cedar rose in front of the mountain, its shade was beautiful, full of comfort; mountain and glade were green with brushwood.

There **Gilgamesh dug a well** before the setting sun. He went up the mountain and poured out fine meal on the ground and said, "O mountain, dwelling of the gods, bring me a favourable dream." Then they took each other by the hand and lay down to sleep; and sleep that flows from the night lapped over them. Gilgamesh dreamed, and at midnight sleep left him, and he told his dream to his friend. "Enkidu, what was it that woke me if you did not? My friend, I have dreamed a dream. Get up, look at the mountain precipice. The sleep that the gods sent me is broken. Ah, my friend, **what a dream I**

"The counsellors blessed Gilgamesh and warned him"—The elders try to protect the youth with last-minute instructions. Although they make a very brief appearance, they might be considered representatives of Carl Jung's archetype of the Self. (See Ch. 32, p. 483.)

Lugulbanda A king of Uruk, god, and shepherd; protector of Gilgamesh.

"there is nothing to fear"—Enkidu has taken responsibility for protecting Gilgamesh.

 Crossing the First Threshold

"After twenty leagues . . . after another thirty"—Repetition is a narrative device that builds suspense about what will happen next. It is a characteristic of oral composition. See p. 180 and Ch. 1, p. 17.

"when I opened the gate my hand lost its strength"—The gate is the gate of the forest: Enkidu will later remember crossing this threshold as the beginning of his death.

In the Belly of the Whale

"Gilgamesh dug a well"—Digging a well and strewing flour was a ritual to pacify the demons and ghosts that haunted the open countryside. For a discussion of ritual and its relation to mythology, see Part 4.

"what a dream I have had! Terror and confusion"—Carl Jung would say that Gilgamesh's dream was of a Shadow figure: a frightening figure which represented all that Gilgamesh was not. The dream, of course, is also about Humbaba. The king of the cedar forest is the opposite of the king of Uruk (see Ch. 32, p. 476).

"this dream was altogether frightful"—The original clay tablets of the epic have a 23-line section which is too damaged to be readable. It seems that these lines must have contained the interpretation of this dream.

This neo-Assyrian relief from the 8th-c. B.C.E. palace of Sargon shows the transport of wood by sea. It was this important raw material that Gilgamesh and Enkidu's quest provided.

"I who know him, I am terrified."—Once again, Enkidu draws on the knowledge he acquired of Humbaba while he was still roaming among the animals. See his earlier declarations in the section labeled "Refusal of the Quest," p. 175.

"the boat of Magilum"—The meaning is uncertain, perhaps "boat of the dead."

have had! **Terror and confusion;** I seized hold of a wild bull in the wilderness. It bellowed and beat up the dust till the whole sky was dark, my arm was seized and my tongue bitten. I fell back on my knee; then someone refreshed me with water from his water-skin." Enkidu said, "Dear friend, the god to whom we are travelling is no wild bull, though his form is mysterious. That wild bull which you saw is Shamash the Protector; in our moment of peril he will take our hands. The one who gave water from his water-skin, that is your own god who cares for your good name, your Lugulbanda. United with him, together we will accomplish a work the fame of which will never die."

The next day after twenty leagues they broke their fast, and after another thirty they stopped for the night. They dug a well before the sun had set and Gilgamesh ascended the mountain. He poured out fine meal on the ground and said, "O mountain, dwelling of the gods, send a dream for Enkidu, make him a favourable dream."

The mountain fashioned a dream for Enkidu; it came, an ominous dream; a cold shower passed over him, it caused him to cower like the mountain barley under a storm of rain. But Gilgamesh sat with his chin on his knees till the sleep which flows over all mankind lapped over him. Then, at midnight, sleep left him; he got up and said to his friend, "Did you call me, or why did I wake? Did you touch me, or why am I terrified? Did not some god pass by, for my limbs are numb with fear? My friend, I saw a dream and **this dream was altogether frightful.** The heavens roared and the earth roared again, daylight failed and darkness fell, lightning flashed, fire blazed out, the clouds lowered, they rained down death. Then the brightness departed, the fire went out, and all was turned to ashes fallen about us. Let us go down from the mountain and talk this over, and consider what we should do."

When they had come down from the mountain Gilgamesh seized the axe in his hand: he felled the cedar. When Humbaba heard the noise far off he was enraged; he cried out, "Who is this that has violated my woods and cut down my cedar?" But glorious Shamash called to them out of heaven, "Go forward, do not be afraid."

Gilgamesh put on his breastplate, "The Voice of Heroes," of thirty shekels' weight; he put it on as though it had been a light garment that he carried, and it covered him altogether. He straddled the earth like a bull that snuffs the ground and his teeth were clenched. "By the life of Ninsun my mother who gave me birth, and by the life of my father, divine Lugulbanda, until we have fought this man, if man he is, this god, if god he is, the way that I took to the Country of the Living will not turn back to the city."

Then Enkidu, the faithful companion, pleaded, answering him, "O my lord, you do not know this monster and that is the reason you are not afraid.

"**I who know him, I am terrified.** His teeth are dragon's fangs, his countenance is like a lion, his charge is the rushing of the flood, with his look he crushes alike the trees of the forest and reeds in the swamp. O my Lord, you may go on if you choose into this land, but I will go back to the city. I will tell the lady your mother all your glorious deeds till she shouts for joy: and then I will tell the death that followed till she weeps for bitterness."

But Gilgamesh said, "Immolation and sacrifice are not yet for me, the boat of the dead shall not go down, nor the three-ply cloth be cut for my shrouding. Not yet will my people be desolate, nor the pyre be lit in my house and my dwelling burnt on the fire. Today, give me your aid and you shall have mine: what then can go amiss with us two? All living creatures born of the flesh shall sit at last in the boat of the West, and when it sinks, when the **boat of Magilum** sinks, they are gone; but we shall go forward and fix our eyes on this monster. If your heart is fearful throw away fear; if there is terror in it throw away terror. Take your axe in your hand and attack. He who leaves the fight unfinished is not at peace."

Humbaba came out from his strong house of cedar. Then Enkidu called out, "O Gilgamesh, remember now your boasts in Uruk. Forward, attack, son of Uruk, there is nothing to fear." When he heard these words his courage rallied; he answered, "Make haste, close in, if the watchman is there, do not let him escape to the woods where he will vanish. He has put on the first of his seven splendours but not yet the other six, let us trap him before he is armed." Like a raging wild bull he snuffed the ground; the watchman of the woods turned full of threatenings, he cried out. Humbaba came from his strong house of cedar. He nodded his head and shook it, menacing Gilgamesh; and on him he fastened his eye, the eye of death. Then Gilgamesh called to Shamash and his tears were flowing, "O glorious Shamash, I have followed the road you commanded but now if you send no succor how shall I escape?" Glorious Shamash heard his prayer and he summoned the great wind, the north wind, the whirlwind, the storm and the icy wind; they came like dragons, like a scorching fire, like a serpent that freezes the heart, a destroying flood and the lightning's fork. The eight winds rose up against Humbaba, they beat against his eyes; he was gripped, unable to go forward or back. Gilgamesh shouted: "By the life of Ninsun my mother and divine Lugulbanda my father, in the Country of the Living, in this Land I have discovered your dwelling; my weak arms and my small weapons I have brought to this Land against you, and now I will enter your house."

So he felled the first cedar and they cut the branches and laid them at the foot of the mountain. At the first stroke Humbaba blazed out, but still they advanced. They felled seven cedars and cut and bound the branches and laid them at the foot of the mountain, and seven times Humbaba loosed his glory on them. As the seventh blaze died out they reached his lair. He slapped his thigh in scorn. He approached like a noble wild bull roped on the mountain, a warrior whose elbows are bound together. The tears started to his eyes and he was pale, "Gilgamesh, let me speak. I have never known a mother, no, nor a father who reared me. I was born of the mountain, he reared me, and Enlil made me the keeper of this forest. Let me go free, Gilgamesh, and I will be your servant, you shall be my lord; all the trees of the forest that I tended on the mountain shall be yours. I will cut them down and build you a palace." He took him by the hand and led him to his house, so that the heart of Gilgamesh was moved with compassion. He swore by the heavenly life, by the earthly life, by the underworld itself: "O Enkidu, should not the snared bird return to its nest and the captive man return to his mother's arms?" Enkidu answered, "The strongest of men will fall to fate if he has no judgement. **Namtar,** the evil fate that knows no distinction between men, will devour him."

"**If the snared bird** returns to its nest, if the captive man returns to his mother's arms, then you my friend will never return to the city where the mother is waiting who gave you birth. He will bar the mountain road against you, and malice the pathways unpassable."

Humbaba said, "Enkidu, what you have spoken is evil: you, a hireling, dependent for your bread! In envy and for fear of a rival you have spoken evil words." Enkidu said, "Do not listen, Gilgamesh: this Humbaba must die. Kill Humbaba first and his servants after." But Gilgamesh said, "If we touch him the blaze and the glory of light will be put out in confusion, the glory and glamour will vanish, its rays will be quenched." Enkidu said to Gilgamesh, "Not so, my friend. First entrap the bird, and where shall the chicks run then? Afterwards we can search out the glory and the glamour, when the chicks run distracted through the grass."

Gilgamesh listened to the word of his companion, he took the axe in his hand, he drew the sword from his belt, and he struck Humbaba with a thrust of the sword to the neck, and Enkidu his comrade struck the second blow. At the third blow Humbaba fell. Then there followed confusion for this was the guardian of the forest whom they had felled to the ground. For as far as ten leagues the cedars shivered when Enkidu felled the watcher of the forest, he at whose voice Hermon and Lebanon used to tremble.

Now the mountains were moved and all the hills, for the guardian of the forest was killed. They attacked the cedars, the seven splendours of Humbaba were extinguished.

 Atonement with the Father

Humbaba is not, of course, Gilgamesh's father, but he is a father figure, strong, fierce, and threatening as a father would be to a boy undergoing an initiation ritual. For more on the nature of this element of the hero's journey, see Ch. 14, p. 140.

Namtar A demon of the underworld; the negative aspect of fate.

"If the snared bird"—Enkidu once again calls upon his experience in the wild to advise Gilgamesh about Humbaba.

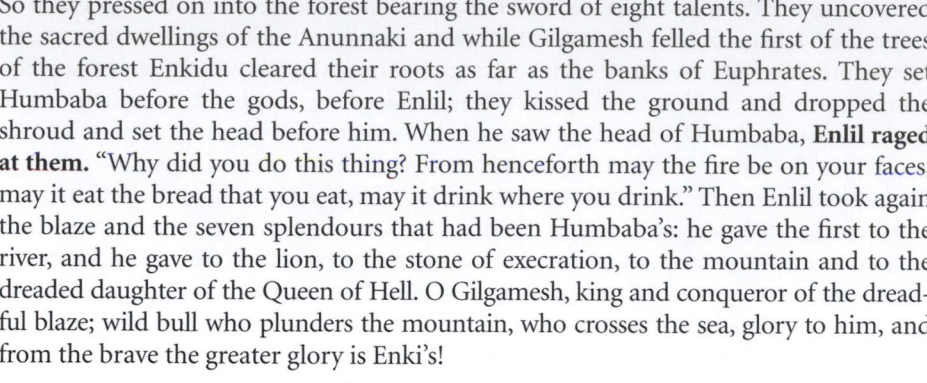

So they pressed on into the forest bearing the sword of eight talents. They uncovered the sacred dwellings of the Anunnaki and while Gilgamesh felled the first of the trees of the forest Enkidu cleared their roots as far as the banks of Euphrates. They set Humbaba before the gods, before Enlil; they kissed the ground and dropped the shroud and set the head before him. When he saw the head of Humbaba, **Enlil raged at them.** "Why did you do this thing? From henceforth may the fire be on your faces, may it eat the bread that you eat, may it drink where you drink." Then Enlil took again the blaze and the seven splendours that had been Humbaba's: he gave the first to the river, and he gave to the lion, to the stone of execration, to the mountain and to the dreaded daughter of the Queen of Hell. O Gilgamesh, king and conqueror of the dreadful blaze; wild bull who plunders the mountain, who crosses the sea, glory to him, and from the brave the greater glory is Enki's!

"Enlil raged at them."—Enlil, god of the earth, had made Humbaba the keeper of the forest, as Humbaba reminded Gilgamesh before he died.

Ishtar and Gilgamesh

 Meeting with the Goddess

Gilgamesh washed out his long locks and cleaned his weapons; he flung back his hair from his shoulders; he threw off his stained clothes and changed them for new. He put on his royal robes and made them fast. When Gilgamesh had put on the crown, glorious Ishtar lifted her eyes, **seeing the beauty of Gilgamesh.** She said, "Come to me Gilgamesh, and be my bride-groom; grant me seed of your body, let me be your bride and you shall be my husband. I will harness for you a chariot of lapis lazuli and of gold, with wheels of gold and **horns of copper;** and you shall have mighty demons of the storm for draft mules. When you enter our house in the fragrance of cedar-wood, threshold and throne will kiss your feet. Kings, rulers, and princes will bow down before you; they shall bring you tribute from the mountains and the plain. Your ewes shall drop twins and your goats triplets; your pack-ass shall outrun mules; your oxen shall have no rivals, and your chariot horses shall be famous far-off for their swiftness."

"seeing the beauty of Gilgamesh"—Ishtar is drawn to Gilgamesh because of his appearance, which denotes his high status. This kind of attraction is common in medieval European epics.

"horns of copper"—The "horns" of the chariot were most likely the yoke terminals.

Gilgamesh opened his mouth and answered glorious Ishtar, "If I take you in marriage, what gifts can I give in return? What ointments and clothing for your body? I would gladly give you bread and all sorts of food fit for a god. I would give you wine to drink fit for a queen. I would pour out barley to stuff your granary; but as for making you my wife—that I will not. How would it go with me? **Your lovers have found you like a brazier** which smoulders in the cold, a backdoor which keeps out neither squall of wind nor storm, a castle which crushes the garrison, pitch that blackens the bearer, a water-skin that chafes the carrier, a stone which falls from the parapet, a battering-ram turned back from the enemy, a sandal that trips the wearer. Which of your lovers did you ever love forever? What shepherd of yours has pleased you for all time? Listen to me while I tell the tale of your lovers.

Woman as the Temptress

"Your lovers have found you like a brazier"—Gilgamesh heaps up negative metaphors in rejecting Ishtar's proposal of marriage. Although she is the goddess of love, as the goddess of war she is often cruel and vindictive.

"There was **Tammuz,** the lover of your youth, for him you decreed wailing, year after year. You loved the many-coloured roller, but still you struck and broke his wing; now in the grove he sits and cries, 'kappi, kappi, my wing, my wing.' **You have loved** the lion tremendous in strength: seven pits you dug for him, and seven. **You have loved** the stallion magnificent in battle, and for him you decreed whip and spur and a thong, to gallop seven leagues by force and to muddy the water before he drinks; and for his mother Silili lamentations. You have loved the shepherd of the flock; he made meal-cake for you day after day, he killed kids for your sake. You struck and turned him into a wolf; now his own herd-boys chase him away, his own hounds worry his flanks. And did you not love Ishullanu, the gardener of your father's palm grove? He brought you baskets filled with dates without end; every day he loaded your table. Then you turned your eyes on him and said, 'Dearest Ishullanu, come here to me, let us enjoy your manhood, come forward and take me, I am yours.' Ishullanu answered, 'What are you asking from me? My mother has baked and I have eaten; why should I

Tammuz Sumerian god; name means "Faithful son."

"You have loved . . . You have loved"—The repetition is a rhetorical device used for emphasis. It is also a characteristic of oral composition. See Ch. 1, p. 17.

come to such as you for food that is tainted and rotten? For when was a screen of rushes sufficient protection from frosts?' But when you had heard his answer you struck him. He was changed to a blind mole deep in the earth, one whose desire is always beyond his reach. And if you and I should be lovers, should not I be served in the same fashion as all these others whom you loved once?"

When Ishtar heard this she fell into a bitter rage, she went up to high heaven. Her tears poured down in front of her father Anu, and Antum her mother. She said, "My father, Gilgamesh has heaped insults on me, he has told over all my abominable behaviour, my foul and hideous acts." Anu opened his mouth and said, "Are you a father of gods? Did not you quarrel with Gilgamesh the king, so now he has related your abominable behaviour, your foul and hideous acts."

Ishtar opened her mouth and said again, "My father, give me the **Bull of Heaven** to destroy Gilgamesh. Fill Gilgamesh, I say, with arrogance to his destruction; but if you refuse to give me the Bull of Heaven I will break in the doors of hell and smash the bolts; there will be confusion of people, those above with those from the lower depths. I shall bring up the dead to eat food like the living; and the hosts of dead will outnumber the living."

When Anu heard what Ishtar had said he gave her the Bull of Heaven to lead by the halter down to Uruk. When they reached the gates of Uruk the Bull went to the river; **with his first snort cracks opened in the earth** and a hundred young men fell down to death. With his second snort cracks opened and two hundred fell down to death. With his third snort cracks opened, Enkidu doubled over but instantly recovered, he dodged aside and leapt on the Bull and seized it by the horns. The Bull of Heaven foamed in his face, it brushed him with the thick of its tail. Enkidu cried to Gilgamesh, "My friend, **we boasted that we would leave enduring names** behind us. Now thrust in your sword between the nape and the horns." So Gilgamesh followed the Bull, he seized the thick of its tail, he thrust the sword between the nape and the horns and slew the Bull. When they had killed the Bull of Heaven they cut out its heart and gave it to Shamash, and the brothers rested.

But Ishtar rose up and mounted the great wall of Uruk; she sprang on to the tower and uttered a curse: "Woe to Gilgamesh, for he has scorned me in killing the Bull of Heaven." When Enkidu heard these words **he tore out the Bull's right thigh and tossed it in her face** saying, "If I could lay my hands on you, it is this I should do to you, and lash the entrails to your side." Then Ishtar called together her people, the dancing and singing girls, the prostitutes of the temple, the courtesans. Over the thigh of the Bull of Heaven she set up lamentation.

But Gilgamesh called the smiths and the armourers, all of them together. They admired the immensity of the horns. They were plated with **lapis lazuli** two fingers thick. They were thirty pounds each in weight, and their capacity in oil was six measures, which he gave to his guardian god, Lugulbanda. But he carried the horns into the palace and hung them on the wall. Then they washed their hands in Euphrates, they embraced each other and went away. They drove through the streets of Uruk and Gilgamesh called to the singing girls, "Who is most glorious of the heroes, who is most eminent among men?" "Gilgamesh is the most glorious of heroes, Gilgamesh is most eminent among men." And now there was feasting, and celebrations and joy in the palace, till the heroes lay down saying, "Now we will rest for the night."

The Death of Enkidu

When the daylight came Enkidu got up and cried to Gilgamesh, "O my brother, such a dream I had last night. Anu, Enlil, Ea and heavenly Shamash took counsel together, and Anu said to Enlil, "Because they have killed the Bull of Heaven, and because they

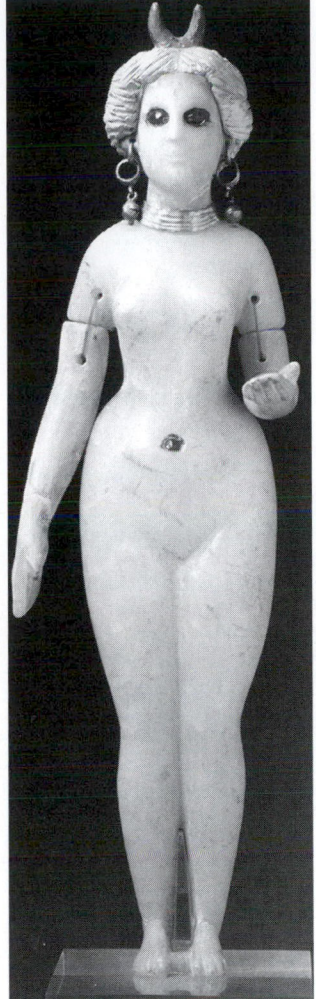

Ishtar, the powerful goddess of fertility, is shown in this statue from 4th-c. B.C.E. Babylon.

Bull of Heaven Anu is the sky-god, the owner of the Bull of Heaven.

"with his first snort cracks opened in the earth"—The Bull's first actions wreak havoc in Uruk.

"we boasted that we would leave enduring names"—Enkidu directs Gilgamesh to kill the Bull of Heaven, not to protect the heroes from destruction, but to achieve fame.

"he tore out the Bull's right thigh and tossed it in her face"—Enkidu's insult to Ishtar parallels that of Gilgamesh earlier. Both are shocking because Ishtar is a goddess and the insulters are humans.

This Assyrian relief representing a winged bull can give us an idea of how we might picture the Bull of Heaven.

lapis lazuli A deep blue stone, was one of the most important gemstones of ancient Mesopotamia. Its source was the mountainous area in present-day northeast Afghanistan.

"must Enkidu die although innocent?"—Human beings often find the idea of death unfair. This is a reflection of the metaphysical insights provided by myth: helping humans cope with their limited lives on earth (see Ch. 1, p. 7).

"he cursed the gate"—Enkidu, the child of nature, has been helping Gilgamesh to destroy natural forces like Humbaba and the Bull of Heaven. His love for Gilgamesh has made him destroy his own heritage. Now he curses his first steps in this direction, when he crossed the threshold into Humbaba's domain.

"that Trapper of nothing"—Enkidu curses the trapper who first told Gilgamesh about him.

"he turned on the harlot"—Enkidu's curse of the harlot is much stronger and more detailed than that of the trapper. It reaches "to all eternity."

"why are you cursing the woman"—The exchange with Shamash emphasizes the conflict over the role of woman. On the one hand, she is seen as the author of civilization with man. On the other hand, she weakens man and takes him away from his unity with nature. (See also p. 173.)

have killed Humbaba who guarded the Cedar Mountain one of the two must die." Then glorious Shamash answered the hero Enlil, "It was by your command they killed the Bull of Heaven, and killed Humbaba, and **must Enkidu die although innocent?**" Enlil flung round in rage at glorious Shamash, "You dare to say this, you who went about with them every day like one of themselves!"

So Enkidu lay stretched out before Gilgamesh; his tears ran down in streams and he said to Gilgamesh, "O my brother, so dear as you are to me, brother, yet they will take me from you." Again he said, "I must sit down on the threshold of the dead and never again will I see my dear brother with my eyes."

While Enkidu lay alone in his sickness **he cursed the gate** as though it was living flesh, "You there, wood of the gate, dull and insensible, witless, I searched for you over twenty leagues until I saw the towering cedar. There is no wood like you in our land. Seventy-two cubits high and twenty-four wide, the pivot and the ferrule and the jambs are perfect. A master craftsman from Nippur has made you; but O, if I had known the conclusion! If I had known that this was all the good that would come of it, I would have raised the axe and split you into little pieces and set up here a gate of wattle instead. Ah, if only some future king had brought you here, or some god had fashioned you. Let him obliterate my name and write his own, and the curse fall on him instead of on Enkidu."

With the first brightening of dawn Enkidu raised his head and wept before the Sun God, in the brilliance of the sunlight his tears streamed down. "Sun God, I beseech you, about that vile Trapper, **that Trapper of nothing** because of whom I was to catch less than my comrade; let him catch least, make his game scarce, make him feeble, taking the smaller of every share, let his quarry escape from his nets."

When he had cursed the Trapper to his heart's content **he turned on the harlot.** He was mused to curse her also. "As for you, woman, with a great curse I curse you! I will promise you a destiny to all eternity. My curse shall come on you soon and sudden. You shall be without a roof for your commerce, for you shall not keep house with other girls in the tavern, but do your business in places fouled by the vomit of the drunkard. Your hire will be potter's earth, your thievings will be flung into the hovel, you will sit at the crossroads in the dust of the potter's quarter, you will make your bed on the dunghill at night, and by day take your stand in the wall's shadow. Brambles and thorns will tear your feet, the drunk and the dry will strike your cheek and your mouth will ache. Let you be stripped of your purple dyes, for I too once in the wilderness with my wife had all the treasure I wished."

When Shamash heard the words of Enkidu he called to him from heaven: "Enkidu, **why are you cursing the woman,** the mistress who taught you to eat bread fit for gods and drink wine of kings? She who put upon you a magnificent garment, did she not give you glorious Gilgamesh for your companion, and has not Gilgamesh, your own brother, made you rest on a royal bed and recline on a couch at his left hand? He has made the princes of the earth kiss your feet, and now all the people of Uruk lament and wail over you. When you are dead he will let his hair grow long for your sake, he will wear a lion's pelt and wander through the desert."

When Enkidu heard glorious Shamash **his angry heart grew quiet,** he called back the curse and said, "Woman, I promise you another destiny. The mouth which cursed you shall bless you! Kings, princes and nobles shall adore you. On your account a man though twelve miles off will clap his hand to his thigh and his hair will twitch. For you he will undo his belt and open his treasure and you shall have your desire; lapis lazuli, gold and carnelian from the heap in the treasury. A ring for your hand and a robe shall be yours. The priest will lead you into the presence of the gods. On your account a wife, a mother of seven, was forsaken."

As Enkidu slept alone in his sickness, in bitterness of spirit he poured out his heart to his friend. "It was I who cut down the cedar, I who levelled the forest, I who slew Humbaba and now see what has become of me. Listen, my friend, this is the dream I dreamed last night. The heavens roared, and earth rumbled back an answer; between them **stood I before an awful being,** the sombre-faced man-bird; he had directed on me his purpose. His was a vampire face, his foot was a lion's foot, his hand was an eagle's talon. He fell on me and his claws were in my hair, he held me fast and I smothered; then he transformed me so that my arms became wings covered with feathers. He turned his stare towards me, and he led me away to the palace of **Irkalla,** the Queen of Darkness, to the house from which none who enters ever returns, down the road from which there is no coming back.

"There is the house whose people sit in darkness; dust is their food and clay their meat. They are clothed like birds with wings for covering, they see no light, they sit in darkness. I entered the house of dust and I saw the kings of the earth, their crowns put away for ever; rulers and princes, all those who once wore kingly crowns and ruled the world in the days of old. They who had stood in the place of the gods like Anu and Enlil, stood now like servants to fetch baked meats in the house of dust, to carry cooked meat and cold water from the water-skin.

"In the house of dust which I entered were high priests and acolytes, priests of the incantation and of ecstasy; there were servers of the temple, and there was **Etana,** that king of Kish whom the eagle carried to heaven in the days of old. I saw also Samuqan, god of cattle, and there was **Ereshkigal** the Queen of the Underworld; and **Belit-Sheri** squatted in front of her, she who is recorder of the gods and keeps the book of death. She held a tablet from which she read. She raised her head, she saw me and spoke: "Who has brought this one here?" Then I awoke like a man drained of blood who wanders alone in a waste of rushes; like one whom the bailiff has seized and his heart pounds with terror."

Gilgamesh had peeled off his clothes, he listened to his words and wept quick tears, Gilgamesh listened and his tears flowed. He opened his mouth and spoke to Enkidu: "Who is there in strong-walled Uruk who has wisdom like this? Strange things have been spoken, why does your heart speak strangely? The dream was marvellous but the terror was great; we must treasure the dream whatever the terror; for the dream has shown that misery comes at last to the healthy man, the end of life is sorrow." And Gilgamesh lamented, "Now I will pray to the great gods, for my friend had an ominous dream."

This day on which Enkidu dreamed came to an end and he lay stricken with sickness. One whole day he lay on his bed and his suffering increased. He said to Gilgamesh, the friend on whose account he had left the wilderness, "Once I ran for you, for the water of life, and I now have nothing." A second day he lay on his bed and Gilgamesh watched over him but the sickness increased. A third day he lay on his bed, he called out to Gilgamesh, rousing him up. Now he was weak and his eyes were blind with weeping. **Ten days he lay and his suffering increased, eleven and twelve days** he lay on his bed of pain. Then he called to Gilgamesh, "My friend, the great goddess cursed me and I must die in shame. I shall not die like a man fallen in battle; I feared to fall, but **happy is the man who falls in the battle,** for I must die in shame." And Gilgamesh wept over Enkidu. With the first light of dawn he raised his voice and said to the counsellors of Uruk:

> **Hear me, great ones of Uruk,**
> I weep for Enkidu, my friend,
> Bitterly moaning like a woman mourning
> I weep for my brother.
> O Enkidu, my brother,   5
> All the wild things of the plain and pastures;
> The paths that you loved in the forest of cedars
> Night and day murmur.
> Let the great ones of strong-walled Uruk
> **Weep for you.**   10

Sidebar notes:

"his angry heart grew quiet"—Shamash's words soften Enkidu's heart. He blesses the woman: she shall have wealth, love, and acceptance by the gods.

"[I stood] before an awful being" —Enkidu's terrifying dream predicts what will happen in the land of the dead.

Irkalla Another name for Ereshkigal, Queen of the Underworld.

Etana Twelfth king of Kish, a Sumerian and Akkadian city near Babylon, after the Flood.

Ereshkigal Another name for Irkalla, Sumerian goddess, Queen of the Underworld, sister of Ishtar, spouse of Nergal, mother of Ninazu.

Belit-Sheri "Mistress of open country," where the ghosts of those who had not been buried were thought to roam the wild countryside. Like many civilizations, the Mesopotamians also believed that phantoms of the dead who had not been provided a subsistence of food as offerings remained on earth and were responsible for many fearsome misdeeds.

"Ten days . . . eleven and twelve days"—This is an example of the counting by repetition which characterizes the poet's style. (See also p. 185.)

"happy is the man who falls in the battle"—Compare the *Prose Edda*, in which the Valkyries bring those who died in battle to a place of honor in Valhalla. (See Ch. 30, p. 436.)

"Hear me, great ones of Uruk"— Gilgamesh first calls upon the most important members of society. This indicates the status of Enkidu, as well as the gravity of the situation.

"Weep for you" and later "Mourn for you now" are repeated. This extensive repetition intensifies the emotional effect of the literary format, and harks back to an earlier oral tradition. See p. 169, on the genre of the *Epic of Gilgamesh*.

Enkidu, young brother. Hark,
There is an echo through all the country
Like a mother mourning.
Weep all the paths where
We walked together;   15
And the beasts we hunted, the bear and hyena,
Tiger and panther, leopard and lion,
The stag and the ibex, the bull and the doe.
The mountain we climbed where we slew the Watchman,
Weeps for you.   20
The warriors of strong-walled Uruk
Where the Bull of Heaven was killed,
Weep for you.
The harlot who anointed you with fragrant ointment
Laments for you now;   25
The women of the palace, who brought you a wife,
A chosen ring of good advice,
Lament for you now. **What is this sleep** which holds you now?
You are lost in the dark and cannot hear me.

He touched his heart but it did not beat, nor did he lift his eyes again. When Gilgamesh touched his heart it did not beat. So Gilgamesh laid a veil, as one veils the bride, over his friend. **He began to rage like a lion,** like a lioness robbed of her whelps. This way and that he paced round the bed, he tore out his hair and strewed it around. He dragged off his splendid robes and flung them down as though they were abominations.

In the first light of dawn Gilgamesh cried out, "I made you rest on a royal bed, you reclined on a couch at my left hand, the princes of the earth kissed your feet. I will cause all the people of Uruk to weep over you and raise the dirge of the dead. The joyful people will stoop with sorrow; and when you have gone to the earth I will let my hair grow long for your sake, **I will wander through the wilderness** in the skin of a lion." The next day also, in the first light, Gilgamesh lamented; seven days and seven nights he wept for Enkidu, until the worm fastened on him. Only then he gave him up to the earth, for the **Anunnaki,** the judges, had seized him.

Then Gilgamesh issued a proclamation through the land, he summoned them all, the coppersmiths, the goldsmiths, the stone-workers, and commanded them, "Make a statue of my friend." The statue was fashioned with a great weight of lapis lazuli for the breast and of gold for the body. A table of hard-wood was set out, and on it a bowl of carnelian filled with honey, and a bowl of lapis lazuli filled with butter. These he exposed and offered to the Sun; and weeping he went away.

The Search for Everlasting Life

Bitterly Gilgamesh wept for his friend Enkidu; he wandered over the wilderness as a hunter, he roamed over the plains; in his bitterness he cried, "How can I rest, how can I be at peace? Despair is in my heart. What my brother is now, that shall I be when I am dead. Because I am afraid of death I will go as best I can to find **Utnapishtim** whom they call the **Faraway,** for he has entered the assembly of the gods." So Gilgamesh traveled over the wilderness, he wandered over the grasslands, a long journey, in search of Utnapishtim, whom the gods took after the deluge; and they set him to live in the land of **Dilmun,** in the garden of the sun; and to him alone of men they gave everlasting life.

At night when he came to the mountain passes Gilgamesh prayed: "In these mountain passes long ago I saw lions, I was afraid and I lifted my eyes to the moon; I prayed and my prayers went up to the gods, so now, O moon god Sin, protect me." When he

"Weep all the paths where we walked together"—This lament has many of the characteristics of the English pastoral elegy. See John Milton's "Lycidas," Ch. 42, p. 639.

"What is this sleep"—These lines give us an idea of Sumerians' view of the afterlife in the Netherworld.

"He touched his heart"—Like Gilgamesh here, in *The Iliad* (XVIII, 317), Achilles, mourning Patroclus, puts his hands on his dead friend's heart.

"He began to rage like a lion"—In his grief, Gilgamesh rejects what civilization has given him, and behaves like a wild creature.

"I will wander through the wilderness"—Just as Enkidu has left the joys and protection of society, Gilgamesh will give up his "life" and wander, like the unsettled spirits. See p. 177, where Enkidu and Gilgamesh perform the ritual to ward off such restless souls.

Anunnaki The Sumerians grouped old gods of fertility and gods of the underworld together under Anu. They came to be known as judges of the underworld.

 The Call to Adventure

This adventure occurs almost accidentally; it is not a planned quest like the search for Humbaba.

Utnapishtim This name may mean "he found life." Like Noah, Utnapishtim was spared from the destruction of the flood.

Faraway An epithet for Utnapishtim.

Dilmun Sumerian paradise, sometimes described as the "land of the living." Scholars locate it in present-day Bahrain.

had prayed he lay down to sleep, until he was woken from out of a dream. He saw the lions round him glorying in life; then he took his axe in his hand, he drew his sword from his belt, and he fell upon them like an arrow from the string, and struck and destroyed and scattered them.

So at length Gilgamesh came to **Mashu,** the great mountains about which he had heard many things, which guard the rising and the setting sun. Its twin peaks are as high as the wall of heaven and its paps reach down to the underworld. At its gate Scorpions stand guard, **half man and half dragon;** their glory is terrifying, their stare strikes death into men, their shimmering halo sweeps the mountains that guard the rising sun. When Gilgamesh saw them he shielded his eyes for the length of a moment only; then he took courage and approached. When they saw him so undismayed the Man-Scorpion called to his mate, "This one who comes to us now is flesh of the gods." The mate of the Man-Scorpion answered, "Two thirds is god but one third is man."

Then he called to the man Gilgamesh, he called to the child of the gods: "Why have you come so great a journey; for what have you travelled so far, crossing the dangerous waters; tell me the reason for your coming?" Gilgamesh answered, "For Enkidu; I loved him dearly, together we endured all kinds of hardships; on his account I have come, for the common lot of man has taken him. I have wept for him day and night, I would not give up his body for burial, I thought my friend would come back because of my weeping. **Since he went, my life is nothing;** that is why I have travelled here in search of Utnapishtim my father; for men say he has entered the assembly of the gods, and has found everlasting life. I have a desire to question him concerning the living and the dead." The Man-Scorpion opened his mouth and said, speaking to Gilgamesh, "No man born of woman has done what you have asked, **no mortal man has gone into the mountain,** the length of it is twelve leagues of darkness; in it there is no light, but the heart is oppressed with darkness. From the rising of the sun to the setting of the sun there is no light." Gilgamesh said, "Although I should go in sorrow and in pain, with sighing and with weeping, still I must go. Open the gate of the mountain." And the Man-Scorpion said, "Go, Gilgamesh, I permit you to pass through the mountain of Mashu and through the high ranges; may your feet carry you safely home. The gate of the mountain is open."

When Gilgamesh heard this he did as the Man-Scorpion had said, he followed the sun's road to his rising, through the mountain. When he had gone one league the darkness became thick around him, for there was no light, he could see nothing ahead and nothing behind him. After two leagues the darkness was thick and there was no light, he could see nothing ahead and nothing behind him. **After three leagues** the darkness was thick, and there was no light, he could see nothing ahead and nothing behind him. After **four leagues** the darkness was thick and there was no light, he could see nothing ahead and nothing behind him. At the end of five leagues the darkness was thick and there was no light, he could see nothing ahead and nothing behind him. At the end of six leagues the darkness was thick and there was no light, he could see nothing ahead and nothing behind him. When he had gone seven leagues the darkness was thick and there was no light, he could see nothing ahead and nothing behind him. When he had gone eight leagues Gilgamesh gave a great cry, for the darkness was thick and he could see nothing ahead and nothing behind him. After nine leagues he felt the north wind on his face, but the darkness was thick and there was no light, he could see nothing ahead and nothing behind him. After ten leagues the end was near. After eleven leagues the dawn light appeared. At the end of twelve leagues the sun streamed out.

There was the garden of the gods; all round him stood **bushes bearing gems.** Seeing it he went down at once, for there was fruit of carnelian with the vine hanging from it, beautiful to look at; lapis lazuli leaves hung thick with fruit, sweet to see. For thorns and thistles there were hæmatite and rare stones, agate, and pearls from out of the sea. While Gilgamesh walked in the garden by the edge of the sea Shamash saw him, and he saw that he was dressed in the skins of animals and ate their flesh. He was

Mashu "Twin": mountains at the edge of the world where the sun rises. Gilgamesh has already gone beyond the point where humans should be.

 Crossing the Threshold

"half man and half dragon"— Scorpion men are often found in Mesopotamian myth as guardians of the boundary between earth and sky. See Levi-Strauss (Ch. 20, p. 285) on creatures resulting from the union of different species, such as humans and animals. Such aberrations are either extraordinary heroes or monsters. Gilgamesh is described at the beginning of this epic also as 2/3 god and 1/3 man.

"Since he went, my life is nothing"—It is ironic that Gilgamesh has the courage to pursue the questions about everlasting life precisely because he is so distraught about Enkidu's death and the inevitability of his own dying.

"no mortal man has gone into the mountain"—Gilgamesh has gone beyond the human sphere; he is traveling beyond the rising sun. The Greek hero Heracles also has adventures in this realm, see Ch. 31, p. 458.

 In the Belly of the Whale

"After three leagues . . . four leagues"—The repetition here is an effective technique to heighten suspense. It is also a characteristic of oral composition. See p. 169 on the genre of the *Epic of Gilgamesh.*

"bushes bearing gems"—In this world beyond nature and beyond human needs, the fruits are jewels, rather than food.

Supernatural Aid

Shamash tells Gilgamesh the outcome of his journey, but Gilgamesh will not accept it until his experience confirms it.

 Meeting with the Goddess

Siduri Goddess of brewing and wisdom. The origin of the name is unknown.

"Young woman, maker of wine"—Selling beer provided by a palace to travelers was a traditionally female profession. It is referred to in several laws of Hammurabi's Code, the earliest complete legal code, developed by the Babylonian king Hammurabi (1792–1750 B.C.E.).

"I will break in your door"—Gilgamesh threatens Siduri, as Ishtar threatened her father after being spurned by Gilgamesh. (See p. 181.)

"If you are that Gilgamesh who seized and killed the Bull of Heaven . . ."—This highly stylized, repetitive passage summarizes Gilgamesh's deeds for the audience.

"why should not my cheeks be starved . . ."—Like Siduri, Gilgamesh offers a stylized summary of events. He will repeat this explanation to Urshanabi and Utnapishtim. This kind of repetition is a hallmark of the poet's style. See Ch. 1, p. 17.

distressed, and he spoke and said, "No mortal man has gone this way before, nor will, as long as the winds drive over the sea." And to Gilgamesh he said, "You will never find the life for which you are searching." Gilgamesh said to glorious Shamash, "Now that I have toiled and strayed so far over the wilderness, am I to sleep, and let the earth cover my head for ever? Let my eyes see the sun until they are dazzled with looking. Although I am no better than a dead man, still let me see the light of the sun."

Beside the sea she lives, the woman of the vine, the maker of wine; **Siduri** sits in the garden at the edge of the sea, with the golden bowl and the golden vats that the gods gave her. She is covered with a veil; and where she sits she sees Gilgamesh coming towards her, wearing skins, the flesh of the gods in his body, but despair in his heart, and his face like the face of one who has made a long journey. She looked, and as she scanned the distance she said in her own heart, "Surely this is some felon; where is he going now?" And she barred her gate against him with the cross-bar and shot home the bolt. But Gilgamesh, hearing the sound of the bolt, threw up his head and lodged his foot in the gate; he called to her, "**Young woman, maker of wine,** why do you bolt your door; what did you see that made you bar your gate? **I will break in your door** and burst in your gate, for I am Gilgamesh who seized and killed the Bull of Heaven, I killed the watchman of the cedar forest, I overthrew Humbaba who lived in the forest, and I killed the lions in the passes of the mountain."

Then Siduri said to him, "**If you are that Gilgamesh who seized and killed the Bull of Heaven,** who killed the watchman of the cedar forest, who overthrew Humbaba that lived in the forest, and killed the lions in the passes of the mountain, why are your cheeks so starved and why is your face so drawn? Why is despair in your heart and your face like the face of one who has made a long journey? Yes, why is your face burned from heat and cold, and why do you come here wandering over the pastures in search of the wind?"

Gilgamesh answered her, "And **why should not my cheeks be starved** and my face drawn? Despair is in my heart and my face is the face of one who has made a long journey, it was burned with heat and with cold. Why should I not wander over the pastures in search of the wind? My friend, my younger brother, he who hunted the wild ass of the wilderness and the panther of the plains, my friend, my younger brother who seized and killed the Bull of Heaven and overthrew Humbaba in the cedar forest, my friend who was very dear to me and who endured dangers beside me, Enkidu my brother, whom I loved, the end of mortality has overtaken him. I wept for him seven days and nights till the worm fastened on him. Because of my brother I am afraid of death, because of my brother I stray through the wilderness and cannot rest. But now, young woman, maker of wine, since I have seen your face do not let me see the face of death which I dread so much."

She answered, "Gilgamesh, where are you hurrying to? You will never find that life for which you are looking. When the gods created man they allotted to him death, but life they retained in their own keeping. As for you, Gilgamesh, fill your belly with good things; day and night, night and day, dance and be merry, feast and rejoice. Let your clothes be fresh, bathe yourself in water, cherish the little child that holds your hand, and make your wife happy in your embrace; for this too is the lot of man."

But Gilgamesh said to Siduri, the young woman, "How can I be silent, how can I rest, when Enkidu whom I love is dust, and I too shall die and be laid in the earth. You live by the seashore and look into the heart of it; young woman, tell me now, which is the way to Utnapishtim, the son of Ubara-Tutu? What directions are there for the passage; give me, oh, give me directions. I will cross the Ocean if it is possible; if it is not I will wander still farther in the wilderness."

The wine-maker said to him, "Gilgamesh, there is no crossing the Ocean; whoever has come, since the days of old, has not been able to pass that sea. The Sun in his glory crosses the Ocean, but who beside Shamash has ever crossed it? The place and the passage are difficult, and the **waters of death** are deep which flow between. Gilgamesh, how will you cross the Ocean? When you come to the waters of death what will you do? But Gilgamesh, down in the woods you will find Urshanabi, the ferryman of Utnapishtim; with him are the holy things, the things of stone. He is fashioning the serpent prow of the boat. Look at him well, and if it is possible, perhaps you will cross the waters with him; but if it is not possible, then you must go back."

When Gilgamesh heard this he was seized with anger. He took his axe in his hand, and his dagger from his belt. Then he went into the forest and sat down. Urshanabi saw the dagger flash and heard the axe, and he beat his head, for Gilgamesh had shattered the tackle of the boat in his rage. Urshanabi said to him, "Tell me, what is your name? I am Urshanabi, the ferryman of Utnapishtim the Faraway." He replied to him, "Gilgamesh is my name, I am from Uruk, from the house of Anu." Then Urshanabi said to him, "**Why are your cheeks so starved** and your face drawn? Why is despair in your heart and your face like the face of one who has made a long journey; yes, why is your face burned with heat and with cold, and why do you come here wandering over the pastures in search of the wind?"

Gilgamesh said to him, "Why should not my cheeks be starved and my face drawn? Despair is in my heart, and my face is the face of one who has made a long journey. I was burned with heat and with cold. Why should I not wander over the pastures? My friend, my younger brother who seized and killed the Bull of Heaven, and overthrew Humbaba in the cedar forest, my friend who was very dear to me, and who endured dangers beside me, Enkidu my brother whom I loved, the end of mortality has overtaken him. I wept for him seven days and nights till the worm fastened on him. Because of my brother I am afraid of death, because of my brother I stray through the wilderness. His fate lies heavy upon me. How can I be silent, how can I rest? He is dust and I too shall die and be laid in the earth for ever. I am afraid of death, therefore, Urshanabi, tell me which is the road to Utnapishtim? If it is possible I will cross the waters of death; if not I will wander still farther through the wilderness."

Urshanabi said to him, "Gilgamesh, your own hands have prevented you from crossing the Ocean; when you destroyed the tackle of the boat you destroyed its safety." Then the two of them talked it over and Gilgamesh said, "Why are you so angry with me, Urshanabi, for you yourself cross the sea by day and night, at all seasons you cross it." "Gilgamesh, those things you destroyed, their property is to carry me over the water, to prevent the waters of death from touching me. It was for this reason that I preserved them, but you have destroyed them, and the **urnu snakes** with them. But now, go into the forest, Gilgamesh; with your axe cut poles, one hundred and twenty, cut them sixty cubits long, paint them with bitumen, set on them ferrules and bring them back."

When Gilgamesh heard this he went into the forest, he cut poles one hundred and twenty; he cut them sixty cubits long, he painted them with bitumen, he set on them ferrules, and he brought them to Urshanabi. Then they boarded the boat, Gilgamesh and Urshanabi together, launching it out on the waves of Ocean. For three days they ran on as it were a journey of a month and fifteen days, and at last Urshanabi brought the boat to the waters of death. Then Urshanabi said to Gilgamesh, "Press on, take a pole and thrust it in, but do not let your hands touch the waters. Gilgamesh, **take a second pole, take a third, take a fourth pole.** Now, Gilgamesh, take a fifth, take a sixth and seventh pole. Gilgamesh, take an eighth, and ninth, a tenth pole. Gilgamesh, take an eleventh, take a twelfth pole." After one hundred and twenty thrusts Gilgamesh had used the last pole. Then he stripped himself, he held up his arms for a mast and his covering for a sail. So Urshanabi the ferryman brought Gilgamesh to Utnapishtim, whom they call the Faraway, who lives in Dilmun at the place of the sun's transit, eastward of the mountain. To him alone of men the gods had given everlasting life.

Now Utnapishtim, where he lay at ease, looked into the distance and he said in his heart, musing to himself, "Why does the boat sail here without tackle and mast; why

"waters of death"—This might be a metaphor for achieving eternal life. But it is more likely literal, based on the widespread ancient belief that the underworld is surrounded by water. Also, in ancient Greek tradition, the dead cross the River Styx to enter Hades. (See Ch. 37, p. 557.)

 Atonement with the Father

Gilgamesh treats Urshanabi as a villain because he is frustrated that the ferryman has told him he might have to return from the land of Utnapishtim, and thus fail in his attempt to become immortal.

"Why are your cheeks so starved"—Rather than react to Gilgamesh's rage and the destruction of the boat, Urshanabi first questions Gilgamesh, just as Siduri had done.

"*urnu* snakes"—The definition of this is unclear. It might refer to ropes used to pull the boat along or to a cedar tree or pole used to support the ropes.

"take a second pole, take a third, take a fourth pole"—This is another example of counting by repetition which characterizes the poet's style; that is, instead of saying "take 120 poles," the phrase is repeated for each numbered item.

are the sacred stones destroyed, and why does the master not sail the boat? That man who comes is none of mine; where I look I see a man whose body is covered with skins of beasts. Who is this who walks up the shore behind Urshanabi, for surely he is no man of mine?" So Utnapishtim looked at him and said, "**What is your name,** you who come here wearing the skins of beasts, with your cheeks starved and your face drawn? Where are you hurrying to now? For what reason have you made this great journey, crossing the seas whose passage is difficult? Tell me the reason for your coming."

"What is your name"—Utnapishtim and Gilgamesh repeat the dialogue first spoken by Siduri and Gilgamesh.

He replied, "Gilgamesh is my name. I am from Uruk, from the house of Anu." Then Utnapishtim said to him, "If you are Gilgamesh, why are your cheeks so starved and your face drawn? Why is despair in your heart and your face like the face of one who has made a long journey? Yes, why is your face burned with heat and cold; and why do you come here, wandering over the wilderness in search of the wind?"

Gilgamesh said to him, "Why should not my cheeks be starved and my face drawn? Despair is in my heart and my face is the face of one who has made a long journey. It was burned with heat and with cold. Why should I not wander over the pastures? My friend, my younger brother who seized and killed the Bull of Heaven and overthrew Humbaba in the cedar forest, my friend who was very dear to me and endured dangers beside me, Enkidu, my brother whom I loved, the end of mortality has overtaken him. I wept for him seven days and nights till the worm fastened on him. Because of my brother I stray through the wilderness. His fate lies heavy upon me. How can I be silent, how can I rest? He is dust and I shall die also and be laid in the earth for ever." Again Gilgamesh said, speaking to Utnapishtim, "It is to see Utnapishtim whom we call the Faraway that I have come this journey. **For this I have wandered over the world,** I have crossed many difficult ranges, I have crossed the seas, I have wearied myself with travelling; my joints are aching, and I have lost acquaintance with sleep which is sweet. My clothes were worn out before I came to the house of Siduri. I have killed the bear and hyena, the lion and panther, the tiger, the stag and the ibex, all sorts of wild game and the small creatures of the pastures. I ate their flesh and I wore their skins; and that was how I came to the gate of the young woman, the maker of wine, who barred her gate of pitch and bitumen against me. But from her I had news of the journey; so then I came to Urshanabi the ferryman, and with him I crossed over the waters of death. Oh, father Utnapishtim, you who have entered the assembly of the gods, I wish to question you concerning the living and the dead, how shall I find the life for which I am searching?"

"For this I have wandered all over the world"—Gilgamesh here describes his transformation during his journey from a cultural figure, the king of an important city, to a more natural life as a nomadic hunter.

Utnapishtim said, "**There is no permanence.** Do we build a house to stand for ever, do we seal a contract to hold for all time? Do brothers divide an inheritance to keep for ever, does the flood-time of rivers endure? It is only the nymph of the dragonfly who sheds her larva and sees the sun in his glory. From the days of old there is no permanence. The sleeping and the dead, how alike they are, they are like a painted death. What is there between the master and the servant when both have fulfilled their doom? When the Anunnaki, the judges, come together, and Mammetun the mother of destinies, together **they decree the fates of men.** Life and death they allot but the day of death they do not disclose."

"There is no permanence."—Utnapishtim ignores the fact that Gilgamesh is two-thirds divine. However, the events of the epic, and Gilgamesh's ultimate resignation, suggest that Gilgamesh will die, too. Utnapishtim's explanation seems to be for the audience as well as for the hero.

"they decree the fates of men"—Like the Fates of the ancient Greeks, the Anunnaki and Mammetun decide when humans will die.

Then Gilgamesh said to Utnapishtim the Faraway, "I look at you now, Utnapishtim, and your appearance is no different from mine; there is nothing strange in your features. I thought I should find you like a hero prepared for battle, but you lie here taking your ease on your back. Tell me truly, how was it that you came to enter the company of the gods and to possess everlasting life?" Utnapishtim said to Gilgamesh, "I will reveal to you a mystery, I will tell you a secret of the gods."

The Story of the Flood

As a description of a devastating flood sent by the gods, this portion of the Gilgamesh epic could well belong in Part 2 with other Myths of Destruction. However, we include it here to complete the story of the hero Gilgamesh and his quest for eternal life. The episode seems to make the point that immortality can be achieved by only one man, Utnapishtim. For the rest of humans, death is inevitable. Read the Introduction to Destruction Myths in Part 2B, p. 125, for a comparison of this section of Gilgamesh with other flood stories.

Utnapishtim's Story

"You know the city Shurrupak, it stands on the banks of Euphrates? That city grew old and the gods that were in it were old. There was Anu, lord of the firmament, their father, and warrior Enlil their counsellor, **Ninurta** the helper, and Ennugi watcher over canals; and with them also was Ea. In those days the world teemed, the people multiplied, the world bellowed like a wild bull, and **the great god was aroused by the clamor.** Enlil heard the clamor and he said to the gods in council, 'The uproar of mankind is intolerable and sleep is no longer possible by reason of the babel.' So the gods agreed to exterminate mankind. Enlil did this, but **Ea because of his oath warned me in a dream.**

"**He whispered their words to my house** of reeds, 'Reed-house, reed-house! Wall, O wall, hearken reed-house, wall reflect; O man of Shurrupak, son of Ubara-Tutu; tear down your house and build a boat, abandon possessions and look for life, despise worldly goods and save your soul alive. Tear down your house, I say, and build a boat.

"'These are the measurements of the barque as you shall build her: let her beam equal her length, let her deck be roofed like the vault that covers the abyss; then take up into the boat the seed of all living creatures.'"

"When I had understood I said to my lord, 'Behold, what you have commanded I will honour and perform, but how shall I answer the people, the city, the elders?' Then Ea opened his mouth and said to me, his servant, 'Tell them this: I have learnt that Enlil is wrathful against me, I dare no longer walk in his land nor live in his city; I will go down to the Gulf to dwell with Ea my lord. But on you he will rain down in abundance rare fish and shy wild-fowl, a rich harvest-tide. In the evening the rider of the storm will bring you wheat in torrents.'

"In the first light of dawn all my household gathered round me, the children brought pitch and the men whatever was necessary. On the fifth day I laid the keel and the ribs, then I made fast the planking. The ground-space was one acre, each side of the deck measured one hundred and twenty cubits, making a square. I built six decks below, seven in all, I divided them into nine sections with bulk-heads between. I drove in wedges where needed, I saw to the punt-poles, and laid in supplies. The carriers brought oil in baskets, I poured pitch into the furnace and asphalt and oil; more oil was consumed in caulking, and more again the master of the boat took into his stores. I slaughtered bullocks for the people and every day I killed sheep. I gave the shipwrights wine to drink as though it were river water, raw wine and red wine and oil and white wine. There was feasting then as there is at the time of the New Year's festival; I myself anointed my head. **On the seventh day the boat was complete.**

"Then was the launching full of difficulty; there was shifting of ballast above and below till two-thirds was submerged. **I loaded into her all that I had** of gold and of living things, my family, my kin, the beast of the field both wild and tame, and all the craftsmen. I sent them on board, for the time that Shamash had ordained was already fulfilled when he said, 'In the evening, when the rider of the storm sends down the destroying rain, enter the boat and batten her down.' The time was fulfilled, the evening came, the rider of the storm sent down the rain. I looked out at the weather and it was terrible, so I too boarded the boat and battened her down. All was now complete, the battening and the caulking; so I handed the tiller to Puzur-Amurri the steersman, with the navigation and the care of the whole boat.

 Apotheosis

Gilgamesh learns a secret of the gods from Utnapishtim.

Ninurta The south wind; god of war, and also of wells and irrigation.

"the great god was aroused by the clamor"—As in Ovid's story of the flood, the gods are disturbed by humans.

"Ea . . . warned me in a dream"—Utnapishtim, like Noah, but unlike Deucalion, is warned of the flood.

"He whispered their words to my house"—Because he has sworn an oath of secrecy, Ea must speak to Utnapishtim's house, not to the person.

"On the seventh day the boat was complete."—In Genesis, the creation of the world takes seven days; here, Utnapishtim takes seven days to prepare for the destruction of the flood.

"I loaded into her all that I had"—Like Noah, Utnapishtim brings all necessities to begin a new life. For a chart comparing the Flood in Genesis, Ovid's *Metamorphoses*, and *Gilgamesh,* see the Introduction to Destruction Myths, Part 2B, p. 127.

"it thundered within where Adad, lord of the storm was riding"—Compare this help from the gods with that in Ovid's *Metamorphoses* (Ch. 11, p. 133), where Jupiter unleashes storm clouds and Neptune causes rising waters and winds.

"With the first light of dawn a black cloud came from the horizon; **it thundered within where Adad, lord of the storm was riding.** In front over hill and plain Shullat and Hanish, heralds of the storm, led on. Then the gods of the abyss rose up; Nergal pulled out the dams of the nether waters, Ninurta the warlord threw down the dykes, and the seven judges of hell, the Annunaki, raised their torches, lighting the land with their livid flame. A stupor of despair went up to heaven when the god of the storm turned daylight to darkness, when he smashed the land like a cup. One whole day the tempest raged, gathering fury as it went, it poured over the people like the tides of battle; a man could not see his brother nor the people be seen from heaven. Even the gods were terrified at the flood, they fled to the highest heaven, the firmament of Anu; they crouched against the walls, cowering like curs. Then Ishtar the sweet-voiced Queen of Heaven cried out like a woman in travail: 'Alas the days of old are turned to dust because I commanded evil; why did I command this evil in the council of all the gods? I commanded wars to destroy the people, but are they not my people, for I brought them forth? Now like the spawn of fish they float in the ocean.' The great gods of heaven and of hell wept, they covered their mouths.

"For six days and six nights the winds blew"—The storm lasts seven days. In Genesis, it lasts 40 days.

"**For six days and six nights the winds blew,** torrent and tempest and flood overwhelmed the world, tempest and flood raged together like warring hosts. When the seventh day dawned the storm from the south subsided, the sea grew calm, the flood was stilled; I looked at the face of the world and there was silence, all mankind was turned to clay. The surface of the sea stretched as flat as a roof-top; I opened a hatch and the light fell on my face. Then I bowed low, I sat down and I wept, the tears streamed down my face, for on every side was the waste of water. I looked for land in vain, but fourteen leagues distant there appeared a mountain, and there the boat grounded; on the mountain of Nisir the boat held fast, she held fast and did not budge. One day she held, and a second day on the mountain of Nisir she held fast and did not budge. A third day, and a fourth day **she held fast on the mountain** and did not budge; a fifth day and a sixth day she held fast on the mountain. When the seventh day dawned I loosed a dove and let her go. She flew away, but finding no resting-place she returned. Then I loosed a swallow, and she flew away but finding no resting-place she returned. I loosed a raven, she saw that the waters had retreated, she ate, she flew around, she cawed, and she did not come back. Then I threw everything open to the four winds, I made a sacrifice and poured out a libation on the mountain top. Seven and again seven cauldrons I set up on their stands, I heaped up wood and cane and cedar and myrtle. When the gods smelled the sweet savor, they gathered like flies over the sacrifice. Then, at last, Ishtar also came, she lifted her necklace with the jewels of heaven that once Anu had made to please her. 'O you gods here present, by the lapis lazuli round my neck I shall remember these days as I remember the jewels of my throat; these last days I shall not forget. Let all the gods gather round the sacrifice, except Enlil. He shall not approach this offering, for without reflection he brought the flood; he consigned my people to destruction.'

"she held fast on the mountain"—Noah's boat also comes to rest on a mountain; and he, too sends out birds who at first return because they find no resting place. Noah's dove signals the end of the flood by bringing back an olive branch; Utnapishtim's raven finds food and stays away.

"When Enlil had come, when he saw the boat, he was wrath and swelled with anger at the gods, the host of heaven, 'Has any of these mortals escaped? Not one was to have survived the destruction.' Then the god of the wells and canals **Ninurta** opened his mouth and said to the warrior Enlil, 'Who is there of the gods that can devise without **Ea?** It is Ea alone who knows all things.' Then Ea opened his mouth and spoke to warrior Enlil, 'Wisest of gods, hero Enlil, how could you so senselessly bring down the flood?'"

Ea   The god of wisdom chastises Enlil for bringing the flood "so senselessly."

"Do not drive him too hard"—Ea seems to argue for a more just treatment of humans by gods. In Genesis, God makes a covenant with his people, an arrangement to protect them (see Ch. 12, p. 141).

"'Lay upon the sinner his sin,
Lay upon the transgressor his transgression,
Punish him a little when he breaks loose,
Do not drive him too hard or he perishes;
Would that a lion had ravaged mankind

5

> Rather than the flood,
> Would that a wolf had ravaged mankind
> Rather than the flood,
> Would that famine had wasted the world
> Rather than the flood,   10
> Would that pestilence had wasted mankind
> Rather than the flood.'"

"'It was not I that revealed the secret of the gods; the wise man learned it in a dream. Now take your counsel what shall be done with him.'"

"Then Enlil went up into the boat, he took me by the hand and my wife and made us enter the boat and kneel down on either side, he standing between us. He touched our foreheads to bless us saying, 'In time past Utnapishtim was a mortal man; henceforth he and his wife shall live in the distance at the mouth of the rivers.' Thus it was that the gods took me and placed me here to live in the distance, at the mouth of the rivers."

The Return

Utnapishtim said, "As for you, Gilgamesh, who will assemble the gods for your sake, so that you may find that life for which you are searching? But if you wish, come and put it to the test: **only prevail against sleep for six days and seven nights.**" But while Gilgamesh sat there resting on his haunches, a mist of sleep like soft wool teased from the fleece drifted over him, and Utnapishtim said to his wife, "Look at him now, the strong man who would have everlasting life, even now the mists of sleep are drifting over him." His wife replied, "Touch the man to wake him, so that he may return to his own land in peace, going back through the gate by which he came." Utnapishtim said to his wife, "All men are deceivers, even you he will attempt to deceive; therefore bake loaves of bread, each day one loaf, and put it beside his head; and make a mark on the wall to number the days he has slept."

So she baked loaves of bread, each day one loaf, and put it beside his head, and she marked on the wall the days that he slept; and there came a day when the first loaf was hard, the second loaf was like leather, the third was soggy, the crust of the fourth had mould, the fifth was mildewed, the sixth was fresh, and the seventh was still on the embers. Then Utnapishtim touched him and he woke. Gilgamesh said to Utnapishtim the Faraway, "I hardly slept when you touched and roused me." But Utnapishtim said, "Count these loaves and learn how many days you slept, for your first is hard, your second like leather, your third is soggy, the crust of your fourth has mould, your fifth is mildewed, your sixth is fresh and your seventh was still over the glowing embers when I touched and woke you." Gilgamesh said, "What shall I do, O Utnapishtim, where shall I go? Already the thief in the night has hold of my limbs, death inhabits my room; wherever my foot rests, there I find death."

Then Utnapishtim spoke to Urshanabi the ferryman, "Woe to you Urshanabi, now and for ever more you have become hateful to this harborage; it is not for you, nor for you are the crossings of this sea. Go now, banished from the shore. But this man before whom you walked, bringing him here, whose body is covered with foulness and the grace of whose limbs has been spoiled by wild skins, take him to the washing-place. There he shall wash his long hair clean as snow in the water, he shall throw off his skins and let the sea carry them away, and the beauty of his body shall be shown, the fillet on his forehead shall be renewed, and he shall be given clothes to cover his nakedness. Till he reaches his own city and his journey is accomplished, these clothes will show no sign of age, they will wear like a new garment." So Urshanabi took Gilgamesh and led him to the washing-place, he washed his long hair as clean as snow in the water, he threw off his skins, which the sea carried away, and showed the beauty of his

The Road of Trials

Gilgamesh is given a task to show he deserves immortality.

"only prevail against sleep for six days and seven nights"—In overcoming sleep, Gilgamesh would overcome his nature as a mortal human. For Hesiod, too, the relationship of sleep to death is very close. In the *Theogony*, he describes them as brothers.

body. He renewed the fillet on his forehead and to cover his nakedness gave him clothes which would show no sign of age, but would wear like a new garment till he reached his own city and his journey was accomplished.

Then Gilgamesh and Urshanabi launched the boat on to the water and boarded it, and they made ready to sail away; but the wife of Utnapishtim the Faraway said to him, "Gilgamesh came here wearied out, he is worn out; **what will you give him** to carry him back to his own country?" So Utnapishtim spoke, and Gilgamesh took a pole and brought the boat in to the bank.

"Gilgamesh, you came here a man wearied out, you have worn yourself out; what shall I give you to carry you back to your own country? Gilgamesh, I shall reveal a secret thing, it is a mystery of the gods that I am telling you. There is a plant that grows under the water, it has a prickle like a thorn, like a rose; it will wound your hands, but if you succeed in taking it, then your hands will hold that which restores his lost youth to a man."

When Gilgamesh heard this he opened the sluices so that a sweetwater current might carry him out to the deepest channel; he tied heavy stones to his feet and they dragged him down to the waterbed. There he saw the plant growing; although it pricked him he took it in his hands; then he cut the heavy stones from his feet, and the sea carried him and threw him on to the shore. Gilgamesh said to Urshanabi the ferryman, "Come here, and see this marvellous plant. By its virtue a man may win back all his former strength. I will take it to Uruk of the strong walls; there I will give it to the old men to eat. Its name shall be 'The Old Men Are Young Again'; and at last I shall eat it myself and have back all my lost youth." So Gilgamesh returned by the gate through which he had come, Gilgamesh and Urshanabi went together. They travelled their twenty leagues and then they broke their fast; after thirty leagues they stopped for the night.

Gilgamesh saw a well of cool water and he went down and bathed; but deep in the pool there was lying a serpent, and **the serpent** sensed the sweetness of the flower. It rose out of the water and **snatched it away,** and immediately it sloughed its skin and returned to the well. Then Gilgamesh sat down and wept, the tears ran down his face, and he took the hand of Urshanabi; "O Urshanabi, was it for this that I toiled with my hands, is it for this I have wrung out my heart's blood? For myself I have gained nothing; not I, but the beast of the earth has joy of it now. Already the stream has carried it twenty leagues back to the channels where I found it. I found a sign and now I have lost it. Let us leave the boat on the bank and go."

After twenty leagues they broke their fast, after thirty leagues they stopped for the night; in three days they had walked as much as a journey of a month and fifteen days. When the journey was accomplished, they arrived at Uruk, the strong-walled city. Gilgamesh spoke to him, to Urshanabi the ferryman, "Urshanabi, climb up on to the wall of Uruk, inspect its foundation terrace, and examine well the brickwork; see if it is not of burnt bricks; and did not the seven wise men lay these foundations? One third of the whole city, one third is garden, and one third is field, with the precinct of the goddess Ishtar. These parts and the precinct are all Uruk."

This too was the work of **Gilgamesh, the king, who** knew the countries of the world. He **was wise,** he saw mysteries and knew secret things, he brought us a tale of the days before the flood. He went a long journey, was weary, worn out with labour, and returning engraved on a stone the whole story.

Further Reading

Bottero, Jean. *Religion in Ancient Mesopotamia*. Trans. Teresa Lavender Fagan. Chicago, IL: The University of Chicago Press, 2001.

Sandars, N. K. *The Epic of Gilgamesh: An English Version with an Introduction*. London: Penguin Books, 1972.

"what will you give him"—The plant is a token gift. For example, in the *Prose Edda,* when Hermod visits Baldr and Nanna, he receives gifts for Odin and Frigg; in the *Ramayana,* Sita gives Hanuman her jewel to pass on to Rama.

Some uses of gifts in myths:
- proof that the visitor has actually met the donor
- proof that the personages are actually who they say they are
- fulfillment of the convention of hospitality
- ways of transmitting magical objects from one realm to another.

 **The Ultimate Boon: Elixir Quest**

Gilgamesh gets, and loses, an elixir that restores youth.

The Return

Gilgamesh goes back the same way he came.

"the serpent . . . snatched it away"—As in Genesis, the serpent is a villain. This motif continues in western tradition through the Middle Ages: for example, St. George slays the dragon.

"Gilgamesh, the king, who . . . was wise"—The epithets of Gilgamesh here are identical to those in the first paragraph of the prologue.

A Levi-Straussian Analysis of the *Epic of Gilgamesh*

G. S. KIRK

WHAT TO EXPECT . . . Chapter 2 represented the different kinds of uses that scholars find for mythic material. In this chapter, you see the application of the theories of Claude Levi-Strauss, the French sociologist and linguistics scholar. Levi-Strauss, whose theories are elaborated in Chapter 20, finds that mythology helps show the nature of a culture: how it is organized, what its values are, what sorts of issues concern people in that society.

In this chapter, G. S. Kirk, a classics scholar, applies the ideas of Levi-Strauss to the *Epic of Gilgamesh*. You may want to read Chapter 15, the text of the story of Gilgamesh, before this one. Kirk's analysis shows aspects of the relationship between the two main characters, one of whom represents nature and the other culture. As you read, you may want to consider how the nature versus culture motif relates to the mortality theme in the *Epic of Gilgamesh*.

In addition to seeing Levi-Strauss' theory in action, you can get a better sense of his view of myth as a fundamental mode of human communication. As you read Kirk's analysis, compare it to the perspective on the myth provided by Campbell in the marginalia of Chapter 15.

The ideas of Claude Levi-Strauss have had wide influence in a variety of different fields. See Chapter 20 for excerpts from Levi-Strauss' "The Structural Study of Myth" and from Edmund Leach's *Claude Levi-Strauss*. Scholars have applied his methods in their study of the literature and anthropology of a variety of peoples. In the excerpt, G. S. Kirk, a scholar of Latin and ancient Greek, applies the theories of Levi-Strauss to the *Epic of Gilgamesh*. As Kirk begins with a general view of Levi-Strauss' theories, the resulting analysis provides additional insight into both the Sumerian epic and the theories of the French anthropologist.

In his analysis, Kirk suggests that in the *Epic of Gilgamesh,* the meaning has to do with the relationship between two characters, one of whom is identified with nature and the other with culture. This relationship is actually a complex one that is described in detail. Here we can say that Enkidu, Gilgamesh's friend and companion, starts off "close to nature" but ends up moving toward culture. He helps Gilgamesh destroy Huwawa (or Humbaba), the guardian of the cedar forest. As a result, Enkidu loses touch with what he is, a child of nature. In Kirk's view, it is this break with his real nature that causes Enkidu's death.

LEVI-STRAUSS' ANALYSIS OF LANGUAGE

Claude Levi-Strauss bases his analysis of myth on the model of the study of language, so it will be helpful to the understanding of his ideas to introduce some terminology from linguistics, the study of languages. Levi-Strauss notes that we determine the meaning of language not only by looking at the meanings of the individual elements or words, but also by noticing their relationship to each other in phrases, sentences, and paragraphs. This is called the syntagmatic relationship;

that is, the words in a sentence are related to each other syntagmatically. See "Deciphering a Meal," by Mary Douglas, Ch. 29, p. 423. We define syntagmatic as the relationship of the words in a sentence to each other. By contrast, the words that can be plugged into any specific point in the sentence have a paradigmatic relationship to each other.

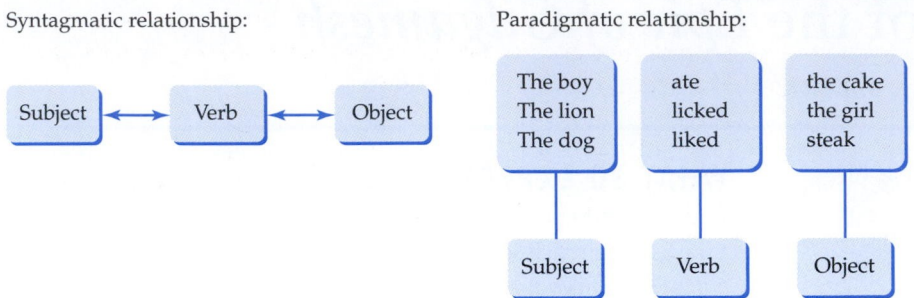

In this example, the syntagm or chain is the sentence; the paradigms consist of the words that can fulfill the same role, say that of verb, in the sentence. The words "ate," "licked," and "liked" are members of the same paradigm. These paradigms can produce a variety of syntagms, including "The boy licked the cake" and "The lion ate the girl." You need both syntagmatic and paradigmatic relationships to make up language. Levi-Strauss believes that myth is a kind of language, and its analysis works the same way: we examine not just the individual figures or characters in a myth, but how they are related to each other. These relationships tell us the meaning of a myth.

In this language, Enkidu and Huwawa (Humbaba) belong to the same paradigm. We can show that Levi-Strauss and Kirk's ideas are meaningful to our own times by coining the syntagm "Huwawa died for our sins." This saying would be based on the syntagm, "Jesus died for our sins." This referred to the Christian belief that Jesus Christ, who himself committed no sins, died to atone for the sins of others. Thus, he was innocent and he died for the guilt of others. In the 1960s for the environmental movement, this sentence became the basis for the saying: "King Kong died for our sins." Thus, "King Kong" was plugged into the original syntagm to make a point about the environment. In the new syntagm, environmentalists were suggesting that King Kong, the huge ape in the 1933 movie, was an innocent victim who died because he was taken from his jungle home to provide a profit for his captors. They felt that the greedy military-industrial complex was destroying nature for profit. This slogan was also used as a statement about the Vietnam war. War protesters argued that innocent Americans had to go to war because war was "good for the economy." Kirk's view of the *Epic of Gilgamesh* would allow us to add Huwawa and Enkidu to the paradigm for this syntagm. The resulting statements would be "Huwawa died for our sins" and "Enkidu died for our sins."

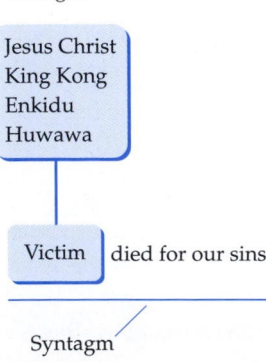

Being part of the same paradigm does not mean that these characters are the same, any more than the parts of the verb paradigm—"ate," "licked," and "liked"—were the same. In the case of the sentence " . . . died for our sins," each of the choices fits the paradigm because it is a subject. In this case, each of the characters fits the paradigm because in a sense he is an innocent victim. More particularly, the innocence stems from being a representation of a creature in a natural state who was killed by forces associated with civilization. In the same paradigm, Jesus Christ is sometimes called the "new Adam" as a reference to the belief that when the original Adam was created by God, he was without sin.

In the study of myth, we often want to compare the myths of different peoples. One way to do this is to identify an underlying syntagm and look for characters or events from different systems which fill the same paradigms in the syntagm. In the example above we can use the syntagm

| Victim | died for our sins. |

to compare the ancient story of Gilgamesh with the modern tale of King Kong. Of course, like any method of analysis, we then must use our own judgment to see if this comparison of paradigms helps us in our understanding of the stories.

Introduction

There have been three major developments in the modern study of myths. The first was the realization, associated especially with Tylor, Frazer, and Durkheim, that the myths of primitive societies are highly relevant to the subject as a whole. The second was Freud's discovery of the unconscious and its relation to myths and dreams. The third is the structural theory of myth propounded by the great French anthropologist Claude Levi-Strauss.

The essence of his belief is that myth is a **mode of human communication.** It is a product of language, which itself, together with music and rhythmical sound, forms a fourth or auditory mode. Just as the elements of language—sounds or phonemes—are meaningless in isolation, and only take on significance in combination with other phonemes, so the elements of myth—the individual narrative elements, the persons or objects—are meaningless in themselves, and only take on significance through their relation with each other. But it is not the formation of mere narrative as such that is significant; rather it is the underlying structure of relations that determines the real "meaning" of a myth, just as it is the underlying structure of a language that gives it significance as a means of communication. Variant versions of a myth may show changes in the surface meaning, but the structure and basic relationships will often remain constant—indeed may even be emphasized by the alteration of the overt symbols and by consequent inversions or other forms of transformation. Yet this significant structure is usually, in tribal societies at least, an unconscious one—which does not prevent it from reflecting popular preoccupations with social or seasonal contradictions, like those presented by sisters-in-law or by the growth and decay of vegetation and men.

Within a myth, according to Levi-Strauss, a structure can reveal itself at different levels, or by means of different codes. Among South American myths he distinguishes a sociological, a culinary (or techno-economic), an acoustic, a cosmological, and an astronomical **code.** Any one myth may contain all or most of these. If so, then its "message," and the significant relationships that compose it, will be reproduced more

*G. S. Kirk, *The Myth: Its Meaning and Functions in Ancient and Other Cultures*, excerpts from 41–48, 131–32, 141–51. Copyright © 1970 G. S. Kirk. Used by permission of the University of California Press.

This excerpt comes from: G. S. Kirk, *The Myth: Its Meaning and Functions in Ancient and Other Cultures.**

"mode of human communication"—According to Levi-Strauss, myth is a kind of language. See the preceding introduction and p. 282f.

 Ceci n'est pas une pipe.

René Magritte, *La trahison des images, 1929*. The words translate, "This is not a pipe." Kirk's and Levi-Strauss' point about myth is that it (like painting) is a language, and as such is not to be confused with what it represents.

Codes for the Analysis of Myth

"code"—a set of symbols, each of which has a meaning, like Morse code. The individual elements of a code can be combined to carry messages. Any one myth is likely to contain different codes, or levels of meaning. For Levi-Strauss' analysis of the Oedipus myth, see Ch. 20, p. 280.

or less analogously in each of the separate codes—assuming, that is, that the myth is complete. In his provisional interpretation of the Oedipus myth he uses the sociological code as a means of revealing something about the origins of men on the cosmological level. His interpretation of the myth's implication is summarized in these words: "Although experience contradicts theory, social life validates cosmology by its similarity of structure. Hence cosmology is true." Similarly his analysis, in the same article, of the Pueblo creation myth claims to reveal a message concerned with the **relation of life and death:** namely that some mediation is possible between the two, in this case through the concept of hunting as a way of getting food. Hunting is a mean between agriculture (which furthers life by producing food without killing) and warfare (a special kind of hunting which causes human death). This mediation is confirmed by a further one: for if grass-eating animals are on the side of life, and predatory animals on the side of death, there is a third kind, namely carrion-eaters, which mediate between the two because they do not kill, but eat raw animal food all the same. In other words, a kind of logic is being elicited from certain relationships in nature—one that makes death appear as an acceptable element of human experience.

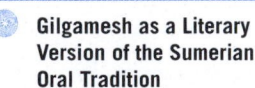

> "relation of life and death"—In the view of Levi-Strauss, myth represents an attempt to mediate between opposites like life and death.

Kirk Defines His Focus in Levi-Straussian Analysis

I propose to concentrate on Levi-Strauss's non-philosophical—one might almost say non-mystical—side; to assume that his theory of myth can be adequately summed up by his statement (in his preliminary article, "The Structural Study of Myth") that "the purpose of myth is to provide a logical model capable of overcoming a contradiction."

One such contradiction, the theme of mortality and immortality, is brought in the ***Epic of Gilgamesh*** into contact with the theme of nature in relation to the whole of culture. The epic brings the whole Mesopotamian tradition to its emotional and speculative, as well as its narrative, climax. The underlying implication of this poem seems to be associated with the valuation of the sometimes **opposing ideas of nature and culture**—an opposition given modern expression by Jean-Jacques **Rousseau,** but one that Levi-Strauss has shown to be of deep interest to the Indian tribes of central Brazil, and one that also impinged on ancient Greek culture. If so, then the nature-culture relationship is beginning to manifest itself as one of the central and most universal preoccupations of speculative myths, and the relation of different kinds of human, animal, and agrarian fertility. In fact, many myths are speculative above and beyond the straightforward allegory of trivial and concrete etiology.

In one sense this extraordinary poem is a compendium of some of the best-known and most successful stories of the Sumerian narrative tradition, including the myth of the flood, and the tale (which likewise looks like an originally independent poem) of Ishtar's passion for Gilgamesh and his violent rejection of her, followed by the successful disposal of the Bull of Heaven. Many other minor motifs, such as the journey through the mountain of Mashu, the jewelled garden, and the crossing of the waters of death, were possibly incorporated from other poems. Yet **the whole composition** has a life and unity of its own. The main underlying theme, as has long been recognized,

> **Introduction to the *Epic of Gilgamesh***

> *Epic of Gilgamesh*—A literary work composed in ancient Iraq. Gilgamesh was king of Uruk in Sumeria in about 2700 B.C.E. For the text, see Ch. 15, p. 166.

> "opposing ideas of nature and culture"—One of the fundamental pairs of relationships which Levi-Strauss finds underlying mythological stories.

> **Rousseau** 18th-century French philosopher who argued that human beings in the state of nature are superior to those in so-called civilized societies.

> **Gilgamesh as a Literary Version of the Sumerian Oral Tradition**

> "the whole composition"—For more on the development of literary versions of myths, see Ch. 25, p. 361.

Ben (1935–), *Mourir c'est facile*, 1979. The title of this painting, "Dying: that's easy" is a modern commentary on the complexity and difficulty of death.

is mortality; yet the problem presented is more complex than is suggested by phrases like "man in his search for understanding of death." To perceive the proper emphases of a work that is often allusive and obscure even where it is not fragmentary, it is essential to notice the changes introduced in relation to surviving Sumerian poems. In the Sumerian poem of "Gilgamesh and the Land of the Living" the hero "sets his mind" towards **Huwawa's** precinct in order to establish his own name and the names of the gods. He tells the sun-god Utu that men die in his city, that he has seen their bodies in the river and knows that he too will die; therefore he wants to set up his name, accomplish a deed that will be remembered long after his death.

Bill of sale of a field and one house paid in silver ca. 2550 B.C.E. This Sumerian terracotta tablet suggests that when it fell to the Akkadians, the Sumerian culture was well developed and prosperous.

The main motive, the establishment of a reputation, is the same in the **Sumerian and the Akkadian versions;** but it is made much clearer in the Sumerian that Gilgamesh accepts the full facts of death, that he has seen the corpses of ordinary men and is aware that he will suffer the same fate. This detail is suppressed in the Akkadian version, since Gilgamesh's grief and despair at Enkidu's death have to be fully motivated—and the motive offered is that now for the first time does Gilgamesh understand what death really means. And yet the change is not quite so straightforward. In the Sumerian poem on "The Death of Gilgamesh," Gilgamesh has a dream that portends his own imminent demise. The manner of its interpretation implies that he has not, after all, accepted the inevitability of death for himself as great king of Uruk: "Enlil, the great mountain, the father of the gods—O lord Gilgamesh, the meaning of the dream is—has destined thy fate, O Gilgamesh, for kingship, for eternal life he has not destined it." One of the purposes of this poem, or the original that lies behind it, was surely to emphasize that even the king, in spite of his divine associations, must die; and to assert that this was no anomaly reflecting on the king's authority on earth, but the result of a solemn divine decree. Echoes of such an emphasis descended into the Akkadian epic, although it is not there made explicit that it is Gilgamesh *as king* who cannot accept his fate as that of all other men.

In the Sumerian poem about the attack on Huwawa, Enkidu plays a lesser part, as it seems, than in the Akkadian version (although he similarly refers Gilgamesh to the sun-god for help, then tries to deter him from the actual encounter with the giant, and finally insists, as in the Akkadian version, on Gilgamesh killing the giant).

In all the Sumerian poems where he appears Enkidu is the servant of Gilgamesh and not his near-equal as in the Akkadian epic. The difference is significant. The whole theme of the creation of Enkidu by the gods as an equal and counterweight to Gilgamesh is unknown in the surviving fragments of Sumerian poetry. It may yet appear, or be present in tablets still undeciphered; it is more probable than not that some rudimentary predecessor of the theme was known before the Gilgamesh epic was composed. Even so, it is strange that none of our Sumerian Gilgamesh-poems foreshadows Enkidu as the wild man from the desert, the man who was gradually introduced to civilization and culture. In "Gilgamesh and the Land of the Living" it is made clear at one point that Enkidu has already seen Huwawa—but that is not explicitly related, as it is in the Gilgamesh epic, to his days as the companion of the wild animals, when he roamed at large through the desert places. It would be a reasonable conjecture that the author or authors of the Akkadian composition at the least emphasized

Huwawa Another form of the name Humbaba. Huwawa, guardian of the cedar forest, is killed by Gilgamesh.

The Akkadian Version Changes the Sumerian Version

"Sumerian and Akkadian versions"—Around 2300 B.C.E. the Sumerian empire, which told stories about the great leader Gilgamesh, was conquered by the Akkadians. The conquerors continued the tradition of Gilgamesh stories. The most complete version of the poem that we have is mostly in Akkadian. For a more general discussion of the nature of oral myth, see Ch. 2, p. 17.

Sumerian version Gilgamesh has seen the corpses of ordinary men and now comes to fear death. Even the king must die.

Akkadian version Gilgamesh understands death fully for the first time, since his friend Enkidu has died. The story deals with each individual's reluctance to believe that he must die.

Sumerian, ca. 2600 B.C.E. The impression of this cylinder seal shows a warrior usually held to be Gilgamesh on the left, fighting two bulls and a lion.

The Epic of Gilgamesh and the Acceptance of Death

Sumerian version Since Enkidu plays a lesser part, his gradual dying is less emphasized. Gilgamesh drops a drum and drum stick into the nether world, and Enkidu dies in attempting to retrieve them.

Akkadian version Enkidu's death is linked to what he has become, overly civilized. He dies because, by association with Gilgamesh, he has lost his essence as a person of nature.

Royal portrait head, "*Head of Sargon the Great.*" Akkadian, ca. 2300–2200 B.C.E. This portrait of a ruler shows that the Akkadian culture had also achieved a high degree of artistic skill in the period when it conquered the Sumerians.

"various attitudes to death"— Humans come to terms with the inevitability of their own deaths in a series of stages.

the motif of Enkidu's original wildness, gave it a prominence and a point that it does not seem to have had in earlier versions.

In the Sumerian poem about the death of Enkidu, of which Tablet XII, appended to the Akkadian epic, is a direct translation, the motive of Enkidu's gradual dying, and of his despair at what association with Gilgamesh has turned him into, simply does not exist. There Enkidu's death is caused by his own heedlessness in not following Gilgamesh's advice. He deliberately challenges the underworld, and as a consequence is finally detained. The poem is in any case rather mysterious: how did Gilgamesh drop his drum and drumstick into the nether world, why did Enkidu so readily volunteer to retrieve them and then act so imprudently? When not even the goddess Inanna could escape from the House of Dust without the fullest efforts of the great gods above, how could Enkidu, a mere mortal, hope to do so? Conceivably his function is precisely to emphasize that, for a mortal, death is absolutely irreversible. But what is the implication of the refrain "Namtar did not seize him, Fever did not seize him; the nether world seized him," and so on (e.g. XII, 51)? It is an odd story, part of the purpose of which was to provide another opportunity for a description of the conditions of the dead; but one that confirms the impression that Enkidu's complex role in the Akkadian epic is the result of much new speculation, and does not reproduce a standard Sumerian view.

Out of the incompletely homogeneous Sumerian background the Akkadian authors seem to have created a consistent picture of change and development in Gilgamesh's view of death. At the beginning of the epic he is carefree and extroverted, uncontrolled and autocratic. The provision of a companion and equal turns his mind elsewhere, to the making of a name. He knows that men must die, and determines to achieve a kind of immortality by a deed of prowess. Enkidu, who knows Huwawa, tries to deter him, but Gilgamesh presses forward in spite of an unfavorable dream. When the monster is slain they are both irrepressible, and insult Ishtar; this results in the gods decreeing Enkidu's death. The loss of a close companion, someone he loved, makes death very much more real to Gilgamesh; so do the lingering nature of Enkidu's death and his graphic predictions of what awaits him below. His statement that in the underworld even kings act as servants may have had some special effect, and reproduces a motif outlined in the Sumerian "Death of Gilgamesh." When at last Enkidu dies, Gilgamesh cannot understand it until the visible sign of corruption, the worm, appears. Then he behaves like a madman—carries grief to exceptional extremes, and allies it with new fears about his own death. He, too, he now perceives, will completely die; his body, too, will be corrupted. This causes him to set off on the lonely journey to Utnapishtim, to face every kind of danger, despite all warnings that Utnapishtim is a special case who cannot be copied. This message is repeated by Utnapishtim himself; the test of wakefulness, miserably failed, finally persuades Gilgamesh to depart. The unexpected information about the plant of rejuvenation (a folktale-type motif) and his consequent joy and sorrow, together with the sign glimpsed beneath the sea, complete his acceptance of failure in his quest, and he returns to Uruk. The myth exemplifies, through a single legendary figure, the **various attitudes to death** that humans tend to adopt: theoretical acceptance, utterly destroyed by one's first close acquaintance with it in someone loved; revulsion from the obscenity of physical corruption; the desire to surmount death in one's own private case, either by means of a lasting reputation or by the desperate fantasy that oneself could be immortal. Finally, a kind of resignation— but before that, perhaps, an attempt to delay death by emulating youth.

Nature and Culture in *The Epic of Gilgamesh*

The interpretation offered so far depends on neglecting several details of the tale that cannot be reconciled with the scheme of consequential action. Closer examination suggests that this kind of more or less literal interpretation is seriously incomplete—that some of the most fantastic and apparently arbitrary components are probably significant, and give the story a more fully mythical (because less directly allegorical and logical) status.

Leaving aside **fantastic elements of fairy-tale or folktale origin**—like the garden of jewels, the waters of death and the means found to cross them—which add greatly to the richness of the narrative but little to its central subject, we find that the main unexplained element is the insistence on Enkidu as a wild man from the desert. This at first sight arbitrary theme, inconspicuous in the Sumerian versions, is emphasized, not only in the earlier part of the poem, but also, by reminiscence, up to Enkidu's death. What is its point, does it serve any real purpose in the epic as a whole, and how did it become so prominent a motif in the Akkadian elaboration?

One of the main preoccupations of the Central Brazilian Indians was seen to be the relationship between nature and culture, the untamed and the tamed, the raw and the cooked, and the tensions, contradictions and paradoxes that operated between these extremes. I believe the Gilgamesh epic in its developed Akkadian form to be partly concerned with exploring, **consciously or not,** something of the same polarity. Men have always been preoccupied with status: with their relations as individuals to families, as families to clans, as clans to tribes—more generally still with their own society's relation to the whole world outside. That world extends from its broadest cosmological aspects (sky and heavenly bodies, for many the abode of gods or spirits) to the **immediate terrestrial environment.** It is here that the nature-culture contrast is seen at its most striking, in differences between the organization of the village and its surrounding fields or the whole cultivated area and the enfolding forest or desert; between the customs and rules of men and women and those applied between animals; between human cultural techniques and the natural processes they seem either to imitate, as Aristotle put it, or to counteract. At all events the investigation, in some sense, of the relationship between nature and culture is not improbable for the Mesopotamian peoples, especially since their myths certainly dwelt on the difference between the irrigated and the barren and on the gods who were responsible.

I want now to reconsider the poem, selecting for notice those phrases and actions which suggest that a contrast between nature and culture, primarily through Enkidu but also though his counterpart Gilgamesh, is implicit in the whole composite story; a meaningful contrast, in which positions are being opposed or reversed in order to explore and illuminate their full relationships. First, it is emphasized that Enkidu is created "on the steppe"; moreover he is shaggy all over, like an animal. And it is as an animal that he lives: he feeds and drinks like animals and in their company; he not only runs with the gazelles, but he also jostles with the wild beasts at the watering-place. But in some ways he behaves more craftily than they, since he tears up the traps set by the hunter. So Enkidu, although a man, is also the very antithesis of man and his works. Then comes the harlot, who introduces him not only to love—which the animals, too, can practice—but also, later, to shelter, company, clothes, cooked food, strong drink, and all the benefits of culture. But first, when he has grown tired of love for the time being, he tries returning to the animals, who reject him and with whose running he can no longer keep pace. The harlot consoles him by telling him that he is now "like a god"; it is no longer fitting that he should roam the steppe. She tells him, too, of Gilgamesh back in Uruk, who lords it "like a wild ox." Enkidu immediately feels the need for a friend, especially perhaps for one with some of his own latent wildness. Already there is an element of mutual reversal of roles: in the desert Enkidu has rejected the animals and become wise like a god, while in the city Gilgamesh, who is king and should be wise, behaves like a wild beast. Meanwhile Enkidu proves that he has indeed "forgotten where he was born" by taking a weapon and chasing off, or capturing, the

"fantastic elements of fairy-tale . . . origin"—Kirk believes that to find meaning in a myth, we must look beyond many of the details that simply make it an exciting story.

This idea comes from: Claude-Levi Strauss' *The Raw and the Cooked* (143).

"consciously or not"—People who create and tell myths may not be intentionally trying to include the "truths" that we discover as part of the myth.

"immediate terrestrial environment"—Culture is represented by the village and its cultivated fields. Nature is seen in the forest and in the desert.

Start of the poem:

Enkidu encounters the harlot:

Gilgamesh misbehaves in the city:

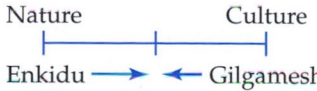

lions and wolves, so that the cattlemen and shepherds may rest in peace. He has become one of them, has turned utterly against the world of wild animals, just as they have rejected him.

He wrestles with Gilgamesh and they become fast friends. Now Gilgamesh conceives the Huwawa project; Enkidu (who seems uncomprehending of Gilgamesh's motive) is dismayed, since he had learned all about the cedar forest "in the hills, as I was roaming with the wild beasts." That implies that the cedar forest represents the steppe, the wild; and it certainly lies, as is proper for a monster's lair, beyond the civilized world. Admittedly there is probably more to it than that. Why is it called "the land of the living" in the Sumerian version? To be sure, it belongs to Enlil, who has set the giant there to guard the cedars; but Huwawa himself is hardly a vivifying force, and rather his forest, which lies in the mountains—the Kur, the name that also means the underworld—may represent death, and give a presage of its power by paralyzing Enkidu's hand (Akkadian version), or sending Gilgamesh into a death-like sleep (Sumerian version). At all events, in order to make a name, to overcome death in a modified way, Gilgamesh has to move from culture and the city into the mountain wilderness, to overcome the savage Huwawa, and to bring back the cedars to Uruk.

The details of the penetrating of the forest and the slaying of Huwawa are too uncertain to form the basis of further speculation. After the slaughter, Gilgamesh washes himself and puts on clean clothes. In rejecting Ishtar's love he adduces some remarkable reasons; for **what the goddess seems to have done to most of her previous lovers is to reverse their position as between nature and culture.** The lion, the embodiment of power and freedom, through having been loved by her is liable to be trapped and confined in the hunter's pit; the stallion has been subjected to the whip and spur. Conversely the herdsman has been turned into a wolf, and Ishullanu, Enlil's gardener (who had insultingly rejected Ishtar's love), has been turned into a mole, or some animal that is stuck, perhaps in a burrow, and can go neither up nor down. Being turned into one's opposite is a drastic punishment, and perhaps that is why these pairs seem to fit the nature-culture reversal so well—only Tammuz, changed into a wounded bird, somewhat obscurely, remains apart. Even so the grouping by pairs (nature-culture twice, and culture-nature twice) is remarkable.

Enkidu sickens and curses three instruments of his downfall: the gate, the hunter and the harlot. It is perhaps significant that two of these three are directly associated with his passage from nature to culture. Why does he mention both the hunter and the harlot, when just one of them would have adequately represented that whole stage in his history, and the third curse could then have been directed (for example) at the Bull of Heaven or his own rash hurling of its thigh at Ishtar? I believe it to be a legitimate conjecture that Enkidu takes the main reason for his lingering death to be his passage from the desert into the world of culture; and that is why he stresses the two similar incidents. At least two of these curses, against the hunter and harlot, are eventually reversed under the persuasion of Shamash, who points out the benefits of culture—especially the friendship of Gilgamesh and the lamentations to be received from the whole of Uruk and from Gilgamesh himself, who will let his hair grow, clothe himself in a lion-skin, and roam over the steppe (in other words, will simulate nature in a **typical *rite de passage* inversion**). At this thought Enkidu grows quiet and changes his curses into blessings. Once again, however, he claims that he is accursed, because he is dying not like someone who falls in battle but, presumably, slowly and from illness. Therefore it is death by disease, as much as dying itself, that Enkidu seems to resent; and disease may well be something he associates with culture and civilization. Is this, then, the reason for his cursing the hunter and the harlot—not so much because they had introduced him to Gilgamesh (the thought of whose friendship, after all, assuages his wrath against them), but because they enticed him into a world of disease and slow

---

Enkidu's friendship with Gilgamesh:

With respect to Huwawa, the extremes seem different, however:

"what the goddess seems to have done . . . is to reverse their position as between nature and culture"—As the story of Ishtar shows, there are other transformations in the story that reflect the nature-culture dichotomy.

The full movement of Enkidu:

"typical *rite de passage* inversion"—The story of the hero's adventure is often related to a society's rituals, especially to the initiation ceremony that marks the passage to manhood. On this link, see Part 4 on Ritual and Myth, and the analysis by Joseph Campbell of the hero myth, Chapter 14, p. 159.

death, away from the world of the steppe in which death tends to come suddenly and before the onset of old age and corruption?

Gilgamesh refuses to accept the reality of Enkidu's death—dresses him like a bride (a symbol of culture, or rather fertility: a *rite de passage,* but the wrong passage). Whether or not he hopes to preserve his friend by asserting his connection with culture, Gilgamesh himself finally responds to the situation by moving over to the world of nature and rejecting culture entirely. First he storms over the body like a lion deprived of its whelps, then he tears his hair and his garment (perhaps no more than regular signs of mourning), finally he does what Shamash had predicted to Enkidu, by roaming over the steppe clad in skins. It is true that any act of mourning is liable to involve an alteration of clothing and of the length of one's hair (either by cutting it off or by letting it grow). The motives are complex, although the rejection of the world of culture by the mourner, and on his own behalf, is probably not part of them. But by any standards **Gilgamesh's actions are extreme,** and they are heavily stressed in one aspect: he himself, the embodiment of culture, now rejects the cultured world and roams like an animal in the wild—not only like an animal, but also clad in a wild animal's skin.

It is not altogether easy to see why, either in his own mind or in the minds of those who created his mythical *persona,* Gilgamesh resorted to the desert. For at this point in the composite epic a drastic piece of rearrangement takes place. At one moment the hero is roaming the steppe, clothed in skins because of the death of Enkidu; at the next he is beginning his journey to Utnapishtim dressed in ordinary clothes—or so we may infer, since he specifically tells Utnapishtim on arrival that "I had not reached the alewife's house, When my clothing was used up"; and that only at that point did he slay "the wild beasts and creeping things of the steppe," eat their flesh and wrap their skins about him. There is an undeniable change of viewpoint here: clearly the whole episode of the journey to Utnapishtim has been joined on to the description of Enkidu's death and Gilgamesh's subsequent grief, and that accounts for the inconsistency. In its way the conversion of Gilgamesh's reason for being clothed in skins, from an act of mourning to an act of necessity, is very neat. Yet it tends to obscure the significance of his resort to the wilderness, and may be responsible for a further confusion about what Gilgamesh is wearing as he crosses the waters of death in Urshanabi's boat; for he takes off his cloth and uses it as a sail, whereas on any explanation he is dressed only in skins by this point.

In spite of this, those who thrust Gilgamesh upon Utnapishtim seem to have remained aware, for most of the time, that **his clothing was an important index** of his state of mind. So much is suggested by the emphasis placed by Utnapishtim, in his instructions to Urshanabi, on taking Gilgamesh to the washing-place as he leaves for his homeward journey, so that he may wash himself thoroughly and cast his soiled skins into the sea. Utnapishtim carefully specifies the dirt of Gilgamesh's limbs, the skins that have distorted them, the need for the sea to carry off the skins, the putting on of a completely new cloak. One might also ask why Utnapishtim and his wife tolerated Gilgamesh's foul condition for so long, including his seven days' sleep in their house. That sounds like an absurd piece of pedantry that pushes the evidence, and the obviously loose narrative techniques, too far. Yet there would be no conceivable reason for reintroducing the motif of Gilgamesh's being clothed in skins, after the natural assumption that on arrival in Utnapishtim's house he would be treated in the normal way of hospitality, were it not remembered that this was an important part of his characterization after the death of Enkidu. In short, the theme of Gilgamesh's becoming like an animal has been partly, but not completely, overlaid by the accretion of the popular Utnapishtim story.

Why does Gilgamesh withdraw from the world of culture into that of nature after his friend's death? Why is that idea so important that it runs even through the

"Gilgamesh's actions are extreme"—As Gilgamesh mourns Enkidu, he rejects culture in favor of nature.

"his clothing was an important index"—Kirk believes that some of the paratactic elements of this section come from the conflicting need to tell a "good story" and yet retain the important theme of the conflict of nature and culture. On parataxis, see Ch. 2, p. 18.

elaborated theme of his visit to Utnapishtim in search of personal immortality? It is not merely an exaggerated form of mourning; it is too emphatic for that, and the stress on the mode of clothing, and its relation to his return to Uruk, too pronounced. Does he hope to restore Enkidu to a kind of life? I doubt it; his concern seems to be more for himself, at this stage, than for Enkidu. It is his own preoccupation with death, as much as guilt for Enkidu, that he is expressing by these means. If so, then I suggest that **his rejection of the world and of the appurtenances of culture is a rejection of death itself.** Just as Enkidu blamed his acculturation for the manner, if not the inevitability, of his dying, so Gilgamesh rejects the actuality of Enkidu's death by seeking out the world of nature, of the animals who were Enkidu's companions and seemed to symbolize freedom, lack of restraint, lack of corruption—and yet some of them he slaughtered, much as Enkidu had attacked them after his initial assimilation to culture. Later, in returning to Uruk, washed and dressed in clean clothes, he not only signifies his resignation to death, but he also seems to imply that culture is not, after all, to blame for disease and the lingering aspects of mortality—or at least that man cannot avoid them, that there is no point in altering one's life because of them. Culture is in many ways questionable, and in the end it did Enkidu little good; although Enkidu had been comforted by Shamash's listing of its benefits (living like a king, being Gilgamesh's friend) in his own case. Wisdom, too, he had gained, as the harlot told him, like a god. And so this whole myth, revealing a persistent preoccupation that overrides the mechanical complexity of narrative accumulation, explores the relations of culture and nature, resignation and despair, disease and sudden death, mourning and madness. It balances one against the other, investigates ways out of the confrontation, and **achieves, as a myth perhaps should, a valuation that is complex,** ambiguous, emotional, and personal.

According to the interpretation here suggested, the *Epic of Gilgamesh* is something more, on the speculative plane, than an investigation of man's attitude to death; and the investigation of death is itself more subtle than had been supposed. Once again the question must be posed, Is the epic mythical in essence? Incorporated in an ancient setting and touching matters of universal concern, it possesses many of the characteristics of myth. Yet is the underlying speculation, such as it is, **"mythopoeic,"** conducted by developing intuitive associations and images arising out of the tale itself, or is it primarily the result of more rational processes? No final answer can be given, but I venture one conjecture: that the confrontation between nature and culture at least, with its effects on the assessment of death, is primarily intuitive. The more overt sides of Gilgamesh's obsession with mortality, on the other hand, may suggest a more deliberate elaboration of motifs and attitudes implicit in Sumerian predecessors like "The death of Enkidu" and "The death of Gilgamesh."

"his rejection of the world . . . is a rejection of death itself"—Gilgamesh's journey to Utnapishtim represents a rebellion against the very notion of death, just as he rejected civilization. It was civilization that brought about the death of Enkidu.

"achieves . . . a valuation that is complex"—The relationship between nature and culture is many sided. Kirk sees the Gilgamesh story as emphasizing this complexity rather than providing easy answers.

mythopoeic This term literally means "making myth," but it implies a particular view of the origin of myth. Here Kirk assumes that myth arises only out of subconscious processes. He wonders whether the *Epic of Gilgamesh* is a rational meditation on death or a myth that arose from the poet's intuitive mythmaking.

Further Reading

Kirk, G. S. *Myth: Its Meaning and Functions in Ancient and Other Cultures.* Berkeley, CA: University of California Press, 1970.

Levi-Strauss, Claude. *The Raw and the Cooked.* Trans. John and Doreen Weightman. New York, NY: Harper & Row, 1969.

The *Ramayana*

WHAT TO EXPECT . . . The *Ramayana,* one of the key myths of India, not only portrays events concerning its hero, Rama, it also illustrates *dharma,* the valued life-principle of Hindu society.

In this chapter, you learn that the Hindu gods took a personal and sympathetic interest in the lives of humans. The myth's characters—many of whom are deities—grapple with situations that parallel human dilemmas at a basic level. The grandeur and splendor of the story are enhanced beyond that of our everyday lives, as the frequent use of magic and illusion allows the characters to operate on a level far beyond human possibilities. Still, we can see the universal qualities that link their striving to ours.

As you read, notice how the principle of *dharma* affects the events of the story, providing valuable guidelines for ethical behavior.

The *Ramayana* is a very old and important myth from India. In fact, we might say that the importance of the *Ramayana* to the Indian tradition is as great as that of the *Iliad* and the *Odyssey* to the Greek. Like these, the *Ramayana* is a compilation and integration of stories from the core of tradition and culture, formed into a unified work of art. The old stories have been enriched with powerful and enduring descriptions, figures of speech, and, most important, verse forms which have served as the predominant style in India for centuries. Even today, the *Ramayana* is a core text in the Hindu tradition, and versions are adapted by storytellers and folk performers.

Over the centuries, Rama's story has maintained its relevance to philosophical and social values in India. Continuing into the present, the *Ramayana* has a very palpable modern presence; through the importance accorded to Rama's story, mythology is embedded in the body politic of a nation. We can, for instance see the place of the *Ramayana* by looking at the philosophy of Mahatma Gandhi (1869–1948), statesman and spiritual leader, who was instrumental in winning India's freedom from the British Empire through nonviolence in 1947. Gandhi talked of establishing Rama Rajya, "the kingdom of Rama," in India. For him and many others, this meant the kingdom of God on earth—a realm full of *dharma,* and thus just, merciful, and caring. More recently, because of sectarian violence and the destruction of the mosque in Auyodhaya in 1992, Rama's birthplace and other sites in Auyodhaya have assumed an importance for many Hindus that melds their traditional mythology with the events of present-day politics.

Like most ancient myths, the story of Rama was passed along by word of mouth long before it was written down. Because it remains such a meaningful story, there are many versions. The one most popular in India today is that by Tulsides. However, because of the availability of a concise translation, the version included here is the one said to have been composed by a poet named Valmiki around 150 B.C.E. Valmiki says that he was present at a sacrifice offered by Rama when he was asked to write down Rama's story. But the story was old even in Valmiki's time; it was a part of the folk tradition perhaps as early as the seventh century B.C.E. And so, the version that has come down to us is probably a mixture of several separate stories. For example, the episode dealing with the Rakshasas and Ravana and those dealing with the Vanara could have come from different traditions.

As a literary version of the myth (see Ch. 25, p. 361), Valmiki's *Ramayana* is a reworking of collected stories aimed at presenting a particular point of view. He has selected and combined elements that have found their way into the Rama myth as it passed through countless narrations. As he wrote, he integrated and synthesized elements of an oral storytelling tradition that spanned centuries. (For more on oral storytelling, see Ch. 2, p. 17, and Ch. 23, p. 341.) For example, the Vanara in Valmiki's story are monkey people and Lanka is an island in the southern sea, but these descriptions are not consistent in all *Ramayana* versions.

There are various possible explanations for Valmiki's portrayal of the Vanara as monkey people. Perhaps they represent the dark-skinned southern Aryan peoples. The light-skinned inhabitants of northern India (like Valmiki) did not have much contact with these southern peoples and saw them as "others," not people like themselves. Monkeys are common on the Indian subcontinent and are considered clever and helpful. Therefore, Valmiki's description is not necessarily negative, but naive and fanciful. His Vanara are noble, faithful, powerful warriors; their leader Hanuman is Rama's best friend and is given the job of rescuing Sita. And after the Rakshasas are defeated and Indra agrees to grant any wish Rama may have, the hero asks that all the dead Vanara warriors be brought back to life.

But maybe the Vanara became monkey people not because they were unfamiliar, but because of a misunderstanding. Nobin Chandra Das notes that the word "vanar" was originally the generic name for the many tribes who lived in southern India. But the word also meant "monkey," so it is possible that in an oral tradition, the more widely recognized word became the standard and descriptions were made to fit. In some legends, the vanara are semidivine creatures with special powers who sometimes live as humans in houses and sometimes as monkeys in the forest.

Conflicting information on the identification and location of Lanka might also be due to storytellers' modifications. Each person telling the story fitted what it was saying with his own experience, so the location of Lanka may well have shifted in the telling. According to events in the *Ramayana,* Lanka could be Sri Lanka, an island off the coast of southern India (see map). However, the Rama story originated in the northern areas of India populated by the Aryans. If this is the case, it is not likely that Rama's exile, Sita's abduction, and the related events would take place so far away as the southern tip of India. Rather, there would be a much shorter journey to a "Lanka" in west-central India.

THE *RAMAYANA* AS MORE THAN A HEROIC EPIC

Rama is a hero by standard definition: one who is chosen and who is recognized by his own people as well as his enemies as possessing extraordinary virtue, courage, and humanity. Like Campbell's hero (see Ch. 14, p. 161), he goes through a period of initiation, then leaves his home, performs extraordinary deeds, and returns to be acknowledged by his people. In the *Ramayana,* we see Rama as the pure and noble hero. Not only is he devoted, loyal, and courageous, he is very human in his emotions and in his failures and his striving. He is a much more credible hero because we react to his noble suffering and sympathize with his tragedy.

However, the *Ramayana* is more than a record of the heroism of Rama. It is a mirror of

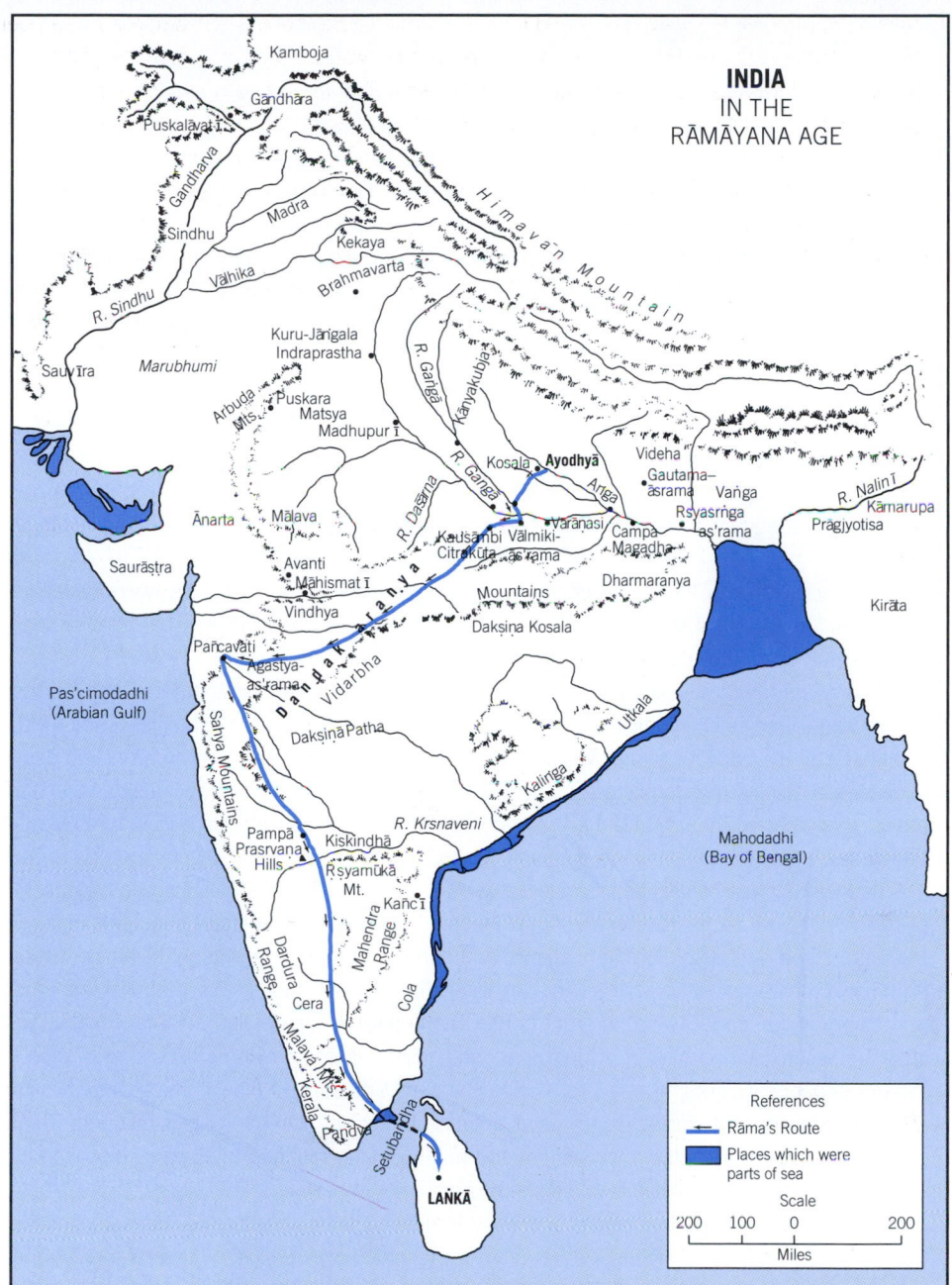

INDIA
IN THE
RĀMĀYANA AGE

Kamboja

Gandhāra

Puskalāvatī

Gāndharva

Sindhu

Madra

Vālhika

Kekaya

R. Sindhu

Brahmavarta

Sauvīra

Marubhumi

Kuru-Jāngala
Indraprastha

Arbuda Mts.

Puskara

Matsya

Madhupurī

Ānarta

Mālava

Avanti

Māhismatī

Vindhya

Saurāṣṭra

R. Daśārṇa

R. Gangā

R. Gangā

R. Kālakūpa

Kosala   **Ayodhyā**

Anga

Gautama–āsrama

Videha

Vanga

Rsyasrnga
as'rama

R. Nalinī

Kāmarupa

Prāgjyotisa

Kausāmbi Vālmiki-
Citrakūta as'rama

Vārānasi

Campa
Magadha

Dharmaranya

Kirāta

Mountains

Daksina Kosala

Pañcavati

Agastya-
as'rama

Dandaka ranya

Vidarbha

Pas'cimodadhi
(Arabian Gulf)

Sahya Mountains

Daksina Patha

Utkala

Kalinga

R. Krsnaveni

Pampā
Prasrvana
Hills

Kiskindhā

Rsyamūkā
Mt.

Kañcī

Mahodadhi
(Bay of Bengal)

Dardura
Range

Mahendra Range

Cera

Cola

Malaya Mts.

Kerala

Pandya

Setubandha

LANKĀ

References

Rāma's Route

Places which were
parts of sea

Scale

200   100   0   200

Miles

The subcontinent of India, showing a path that Rama and Sita might have taken to Lanka. Those who
advocate this route assume that Lanka in the *Ramayana* is present-day Sri Lanka. Others argue that
events could have only taken place in a limited area in the north-central region. The map also shows the
valley of the Indus River in the far northwest, where the Aryans settled.

Hindu society, with Rama and his family as models of how one should live. At the heart of the
Ramayana is the portrayal of the hero as one who always tries to act in accordance with
dharma. We can appreciate Rama's dilemma and his heroism even more if we understand that
it grows out of his conscientious adherence to the beliefs of his culture, rather than simply
reflecting his reactions to adversity. Sita and Bharata, like Rama, are heroes because they are
fulfilling the requirements of *dharma*.

DHARMA

Above all, the *Ramayana* portrays Rama as the human defender of ideals, rather than as one who can enjoy the powers of a god. The ideals he displays include *dharma* (righteousness and duty), *artha* (material prosperity), *karma* (legitimate sex and other pleasures), and *moksa* (liberation of the soul)—goals of moderation and dedication. These are the four principles or goals that should guide humans in all activities. Throughout the *Ramayana,* there is evidence of all of these, but the most prominent by far is *dharma*. *Dharma* is the moral principle governing social behavior, as well as moral and legal behavior. In the epic, Valmiki stresses ethical virtues such as truth, compassion, and kindness, and he shows that all must work toward keeping order in society, for the good of all.

In ancient times, Indian society was divided into four segments, or "varnas," according to social class. The result of this division was that by custom and by law, specific types of people did specific work. Vestiges of this division can still be found. For example, the highest level was devoted to learning and priesthood; the second, to ruling and winning battles. The third group consists of traders, artisans, and farmers; and the lowest group has to do the most unpopular jobs.

This social division has as its underlying principle that all social classes were necessary "limbs" of the "body" of society. All are necessary, and when all people follow the rules of operation, society is healthy and prosperous.

Dharma has both secular and religious connotations, and generally, it deals with correct behavior in all facets of life, including morality, duty, custom, law, virtue, and established order. It is based on the principle that each person has a specific role in life, related to his or her place in society, and this role requires a particular behavior in all aspects of daily existence. This includes all actions, thoughts, and speech in keeping with living a virtuous life. As a result, the people refer their activities throughout each day to the rules of *dharma*. This means, for example, that Rama must behave appropriately as a son, a brother, a military leader, and a protector of his beloved, as each situation demands. He is heroic because he finally succeeds in being the faithful and dutiful son, loving husband, and caring brother, while also being a stern leader and powerful warrior. It is *dharma* that explains Rama's behavior to his wife Sita after her abduction by the titan Ravana. In order to lure Rama away while he abducts Sita, Ravana has Maricha assume the form of a golden deer, which Sita wants and Rama chases and shoots. When the deer calls out in Rama's voice, Sita is tricked and sends Rama's brother, Lakshmana after him. Ravana then comes disguised as a hermit to abduct Sita. After Sita is rescued, Rama subjects her to a trial by fire to prove that she has not been touched by Ravana, because his *dharma* requires him to shun his wife if she has dishonored him.

Rama's motivation in this part of the story is difficult for any audience. In more detailed translations of the Rama stories, Sita is often represented by an illusory figure—a double or phantom figure—that she herself creates as a protection from genuine harm. In these versions of the *Ramayana,* it is the illusory Sita who sees the illusory deer. When Rama returns after his long exile, he forgets that the Sita in Ravana's power is illusory and orders her to undergo the ordeal of fire because he believes she has shamed him. The illusory Sita walks into the fire and disappears, leaving the genuine Sita to remain with Rama. Wendy Doniger O'Flaherty suggests that the story may feature this illusory Sita to justify Rama's subjecting her to the fire ordeal. In this view, he may have known it was not the real Sita, or the presence of Sita's double may help mollify Rama's (and the reader's) uneasiness that Sita has been with Ravana.

Sita, in fact, conducts herself as the dutiful Hindu wife who stands by her husband through all adversity. Her commitment to her *dharma* is so strong that when Rama does not want her to accompany him on his 14-year exile in the forest, she threatens suicide. It is to Rama's credit also that he allows her to come with him and fulfill her *dharma*. Secondary characters also represent ideal behavior: Dasaratha, as a caring and wise father to all of his sons; Sugreeva, as a faithful friend; Hanuman, as one devoted to his superior.

In contrast, some characters cause difficulty by ignoring *dharma*. For example, Kaikeyi, Dasaratha's wife and Bharata's mother, lets her desire for wealth and power (*artha*) blind her to righteous living. She is not virtuous because she ignores Rama's rightful claim to the throne and her duty to her husband.

The concept of *dharma* also makes the characters of the *Ramayana* act in ways that may seem surprising to a Western reader. After Rama has risked many lives rescuing Sita from Ravana and his people, he rejects her; this action is in accordance with his *dharma*. He must insist that his wife live according to the *dharma* of the good woman. Rama assumes that because she has lived among the Rakshasas for more than a year, she must have been defiled. It is only when the ordeal of fire proves her faithfulness to Rama that he can allow his emotions to surface. And just as the fire ordeal proves Sita's innocence, Dasaratha himself comes down from his home in heaven to ask Sita to forgive Rama, thus preserving *dharma*.

Bharata's *dharma* rules his actions as a younger brother to Rama and as a staunch defender of family tradition. He refuses to be crowned because kingship belongs to the eldest son. Even when Rama chooses to continue his exile, Bharata still refuses to act as king. Instead, he sets Rama's sandals on the throne as a representative of the man himself. This way, he satisfies his *dharma* as an adherent of tradition while preserving the role of younger brother.

VEDIC AND HINDU GODS

The *Ramayana* developed from the Aryans, who settled in the valley of the Indus River in the northwest of today's India around 1500 B.C.E. They originated in Brahmavarta, which lies between the Saravati and Darshadvati Rivers. These people, who had moved in from the north, had a more finely developed culture than the original tribes living throughout central and southern India. Therefore, their religion as well as their customs had a great influence. There were four books of sacred hymns, written in their Sanskrit language, called the Vedas. The religion of the Vedas, or Vedic religion, was based on offering sacrifice to the gods in the hope of obtaining earthly power and wealth rather than rewards in an afterlife. These hymns have been memorized and recited for countless generations and are today the basic scriptures of Hinduism. The last of them, the Rig Veda, derives from about 1000 B.C.E.

By the time of Valmiki, Vedic religion emphasized the importance of the Aryan priests who had become so powerful that they often claimed to have godlike qualities. At around this time, the influential preacher, Gautama Buddha, simplified the focus of religion by advocating mastery of oneself, virtuous conduct, a search for wisdom, and compassion for all as the means of achieving eternal satisfaction (nirvana). Humans could, therefore, become like gods through virtuous acts. Buddha's teachings were so popular that they caused the Vedic religion to be modified, incorporating an emphasis on the four principles that individuals need to guide their lives (*dharma, artha, karma,* and *moksa*). The result, Hinduism, is one of the world's major religions today.

In the *Ramayana,* the gods of both traditions take a personal and sympathetic interest in the affairs of mortals:

- **Agni,** the god of fire, and **Indra,** the chief god from Vedic times, save Sita from the fire and prove her virtue. Indra also appears in a chariot and rescues Rama from the belligerent shape-changing Rakshasas.
- **Shiva,** who emerged in Vedic times, but later became central in the Hindu tradition, is the god of destruction, as represented by his bow, he is also a god of sensuality and aestheticism. In these aspects, he has the power to purify the world by the fire of destruction, but

is easily moved to help humans. He is closely related to the Hindu belief in reincarnation, the return of humans to another body after death to partake in a higher, or lower, form of existence as a reward for a righteous, or unsatisfactory, life in the previous one. Although Shiva may not appear personally, his presence is noted by the importance of his bow— Rama reveals himself as a very special hero by stringing it. Thus, Shiva's bow represents the test of a worthy husband for Sita.

- **Vishnu** is the most important and supreme Hindu god. Like Shiva, he was worshipped in the earlier Vedic tradition, but his power became even stronger over time. He takes on various human and animal forms that are referred to as incarnations. All four of Dasaratha's sons in the *Ramayana* are incarnations of Vishnu.

SONS OF DASARATHA AS INCARNATIONS OF VISHNU

The four sons of Dasaratha are incarnations of the god Vishnu, who had chosen them to help in conquering the Rakshasas. Vishnu had promised that he would not harm the Rakshasas by anything that was in the heavens or on the earth. The sons of Dasaratha would conquer the Rakshasas for Vishnu by using the arrow of Brahma.

Vishnu descended to earth in the form of a tiger and brought sacred rice and milk from Brahma. He instructed Dasaratha to give the food to his wives so that they would bear him sons. All four are incarnations of Vishnu. However, this society bases its rules of inheritance on primogeniture (literally, first-birth). Thus Rama, the first-born, is most important of Dasaratha's sons. This is why Dasaratha acknowledges Rama as his heir, and Bharata agrees to act only as regent while Rama serves his 14-year banishment in the forest.

THE RAKSHASAS AS TITANS

Throughout the *Ramayana,* Vishnu and Rama work to defeat the Rakshasas, who are also referred to as titans. Just as the Titans in Greek mythology are very powerful creatures who threaten the Olympian gods, the titans in the *Ramayana* are negative forces which must be overcome. Led by Ravana, they are portrayed as devious creatures who have the power to transform themselves into various shapes and to conjure up magical deceptions. Although the Greek Titans, who are the children of Ouranos and Gaia, cannot change shape, many are portrayed with monstrous physical characteristics. For example, Titans Cottos, Briareus, and Gyges have a great advantage in battle because of their multiple heads and limbs (see Ch. 3, p. 31).

SAGES

Men and women who have chosen to live a rigorous religious life apart from the activity of the city provide crucial advice and protection to Rama and his family. These sages live in hermitages called ashrams, which are usually situated in the forest. They spend the day carrying out religious rituals and doing penance. Their rituals include chanting, offering gifts and flowers to the gods, and reciting the Vedas aloud.

The sages subsist only on what is to be found in the woods, but they are always hospitable to guests. In the *Ramayana,* sages are respected for their holiness and wisdom. Because they are not involved in everyday life or politics, they are a potent source for showing the way to harmony and integrity. As a result, they become custodians of the spiritual heritage and have a right to chastise kings as well as to offer advice.

The Story of the *Ramayana* according to Valmiki

Book I

King Dasaratha, of the Ikshwaku dynasty, ruled the kingdom of Kosala, with Ayodhya as the capital city. The people of Ayodhya were prosperous, happy, and righteous. Dasaratha had **three principal wives,** namely, Kausalya, Kaikeyi and Sumitra. In the midst of all happiness and prosperity around him, the King had but one worry, namely, he had no children. In order to beget sons, **Dasaratha celebrated the horse-sacrifice** and he was blessed with four sons. Rama, the eldest, was born of Queen Kausalya and Bharata was born of Kaikeyi. Lakshmana and Satrughna, the twins, were Sumitra's sons.

The four princes grew up splendidly. They were given all the education and training prescribed for princes. They were brave, virtuous and lovable, Rama being **the most accomplished and respected** among the four. While all the brothers were very much attached to one another, Rama and Lakshmana were especially close to each other; the same was true of Bharata and Satrughna.

When the princes were twelve years old, Dasaratha thought of celebrating their wedding. Just then, sage Vishwamitra came to Ayodhya to see Dasaratha. The King welcomed him with due homage and promised to do whatever the sage desired. Vishwamitra asked the King to send Rama with him for some days in connection with a holy sacrifice he was scheduled to celebrate; **Rama was required to deal with the titans Maricha,** Subahu, etc., who were bent upon disturbing and defiling the sacrifice. Dasaratha, who, it would appear, had the habit of promising in haste and repenting at leisure, balked, saying that Rama was too young to be able to fight the powerful titans. But, on the intervention of the royal priest and preceptor, sage Vasishta, Dasaratha agreed to send Rama.

Since Lakshmana was inseparable from Rama, he also went to Vishwamitra. The two young princes helped the great sage to complete the sacrifice successfully. Before bringing them back to Ayodhya, Vishwamitra took them to Mithila, the capital of the kingdom of Videha, which was ruled by a sagacious king, Janaka. The King had a daughter, **Sita, who was found in a field** which Janaka ploughed on the conclusion of a sacrifice. Janaka had offered Sita in marriage to anyone who could string the great bow of **Shiva.** No one had so far succeeded in doing it; in fact, none had been able even to lift it a bit. Vishwamitra was certain Rama could do it. So he asked Janaka to show the bow to the princes. Rama lifted the bow effortlessly, fixed the string and then drew it with such force that the bow snapped, with a terrific bang. **Janaka was overjoyed and immediately offered Sita's hand to Rama.** Naturally, King Dasaratha's consent had to be obtained. Messengers were dispatched immediately to Ayodhya, and Dasaratha, who too was happy at this alliance, hastened to Mithila. The marriage was celebrated in a fitting manner.

Indeed it was not a single marriage—all four princes were married. Lakshmana wedded Janaka's daughter Urmila; Janaka's brother's daughters, Mandavi and Srutakirti, were married to Bharata and Satrughna, respectively, on the initiative of sages Vishwamitra and Vasishtha. The princes lived happily in Ayodhya with their wives. After some time, Dasaratha mentioned to Bharata that his maternal uncle had been waiting in Ayodhya to take him to his place for a visit and that he should go with him. Accordingly, Bharata left Ayodhya, accompanied by Satrughna.

This story comes from: *Ramayana for the Modern World.**

"three principal wives"—In Valmiki's time, polygamy was common. Kings had harems, and even ascetics had more than one wife. Dasaratha had 350 wives besides these three.

"Dasaratha celebrated the horse-sacrifice"—This is probably related to a fertility ritual because Dasaratha needed sons to carry on tradition.

"the most accomplished and respected"—Rama is the first-born, and therefore especially blessed. But he is also special because he has more of Vishnu's divinity than the others.

"Rama was required to deal with the titans"—Being especially blessed means that the hero has additional tasks and challenges.

Maricha Rakshasa demon; Ravana's adviser.

"Since Lakshmana was inseparable from Rama"—*Dharma* requires family members to be faithful to one another. Lakshmana always acts as a brother should.

Sita Wife of Rama; daughter of Mother Earth and King Janaka; incarnation of Lakshmi, Vishnu's wife.

"who was found in a field"—Sita's birth is miraculous: she is the daughter of Mother Earth.

Shiva God of destruction.

"Janaka . . . offered Sita's hand to Rama"—Rama wins the bride, and is awarded her by her father. Compare the father "giving the bride away" at American weddings.

*S. L. N. Simha. *Ramayana for the Modern World*. Bharatiya Vidya Bhavan, Kulapati Munshi Marg, Mumbai India. Copyright © 1965. Used by permission of Bharatiya Vidya Bhavan.

Ravana, *Ramayana* dance performance, Siem Reap (Angkor Wat), Cambodia.

"Dasaratha felt . . . he should crown Rama as the heir apparent"—Dasaratha's *dharma* is to pass his power on to his eldest son, because primogeniture—the right of the firstborn son to inherit—was the custom in Valmiki's time. Dasaratha serves as a social model, showing how people should strive to fulfill their *dharma*. In keeping with *dharma* and tradition, Dasaratha secures the approval of counselors and nobles.

Book II

Rama spent twelve years with Sita in supreme happiness and was also a source of great joy to his father, whose favorite son he was. He was the embodiment of all good qualities and won the affection of one and all. One day, King **Dasaratha felt that in view of his advanced age, he should crown Rama as the heir apparent** and pass on to him the burden of administration. The King took counsel with his ministers, who warmly endorsed the proposal. The King then summoned the sages and wise men of the city, the subject princes as well as rulers from the different countries and placed before them his proposal to anoint Rama as the prince consort and sought their concurrence. This was given unanimously and most enthusiastically. The Assembly recounted all the great qualities of Rama, which made him a more than worthy successor to Dasaratha. Rama was sent for and informed of the decision regarding his coronation.

Dasaratha decided to celebrate the coronation the very next day. Preparations were begun for the purpose and the whole city wore a festive appearance. Queen **Kausalya** distributed gifts freely, hearing the glad tidings.

Kausalya Rama's mother.

However, it was not destined that things should move smoothly. Manthara, the favorite maid and companion of Queen **Kaikeyi,** on learning about the coronation of Rama on the next day, grew jealous and angry and went to Kaikeyi to poison her mind, saying that Rama's coronation would be a disaster to her and her son Bharata. Kaikeyi at first rejoiced at the news Manthara had given. But Manthara persisted in her evil counsel and Kaikeyi succumbed. Then Manthara outlined the strategy for getting Bharata anointed heir-apparent instead of Rama. Years ago, Manthara recalled, Kaikeyi had saved Dasaratha's life in one battle, in token of which the King had granted her two boons, which the Queen had said she would ask on a suitable occasion. Manthara said this was the occasion to ask two boons, namely, that Bharata should be anointed heir-apparent and Rama should be banished to the forest for fourteen years, so that Bharata may rule the kingdom without fear of hindrance from Rama.

Kaikeyi Bharata's mother.

Kaikeyi took up Manthara's suggestion enthusiastically and before the King came to her apartment in the night as usual, **she went into the chamber of wrath** and lay on the floor with disheveled hair. When the King arrived there in all anxiety, she placed before him her demands. **The King writhed in agony** at this and appealed to her, in vain, to give up her demands. The King was powerless, for the rulers of the Ikshwaku dynasty always honored their pledges. But it was too much for Dasaratha himself to convey the terrible news to Rama; Kaikeyi was only too ready to do this. She sent for Rama early in the morning and broke it to him, in Dasaratha's presence, the demands she had made on the King in fulfillment of the boons he had conferred on her earlier. Rama was not a bit perturbed and replied that he was only too happy to carry out his father's promise to her. Forthwith, he began to prepare to leave Ayodhya, disregarding the laments of his mother.

"she went into the chamber of wrath"—This probably refers to the room reserved for mourning loved ones. Kaikeyi is mourning as if Bharata had died.

"The King writhed in agony"—His dilemma: which is primary, following the accepted social custom for royalty or keeping a promise? Throughout the *Ramayana,* keeping one's word is the mark of a hero.

Sita and Lakshmana, after protracted arguments, obtained Rama's consent to accompany him to the forest. **Sita argued vigorously** that it was the duty of a wife to be with the husband wherever he went. Lakshmana was furious at the turn of events and wanted Rama to ignore what he considered a senile King's promise to a young wife. But when Rama could not be swerved from his resolve, **Lakshmana insisted on his accompanying** his brother. Without lingering a bit, Rama, Sita and Lakshmana left for the forest, with matted locks and clothes of bark. The whole of Ayodhya, cast in deep gloom, tried to follow the three to the forest but were soon eluded by the trio in the thick forest.

"Sita argued vigorously"—Sita insists on accompanying Rama in his exile. This is the *dharma* of the good wife.

"Lakshmana insisted on accompanying . . ."—Lakshmana behaves as his *dharma* as a brother demands, i.e., seek the best for your sibling. But when he realizes that Rama is determined to obey his father, Lakshmana, the good brother, accompanies Rama and Sita to the forest.

Within a few days of Rama's departure to the forest, King Dasaratha breathed his last, overpowered by grief at the turn of events. Immediately, sage Vasishtha dispatched messengers to bring Bharata to Ayodhya and Bharata hastened back, with deep anxiety, as he witnessed evil omens. He found the city enveloped in deep gloom. Very soon he learned from his mother the chain of events; Kaikeyi tried to break the news to Bharata in what she thought was a clever way. Bharata broke down at the news of his father's death and was wild beyond description with his mother for her vile design to get him installed as the heir-apparent. He rushed to Queen Kausalya to console her and seek her forgiveness for his mother's villainy. After he had performed the obsequies of his father, the elders like Vasishtha suggested to Bharata that he be anointed king, since it was not desirable that the kingdom should remain without a ruler for long. Not only did Bharata not agree to this, but he resolved to go to the forest and bring Rama back to be installed as king.

Preparations were made immediately for the whole family, accompanied by the army and a big retinue, to proceed to the forest. On the way, they rested for a night at the hermitage of **sage Bharadwaja,** who **directed them to the place of Rama's abode** in the Chitrakoota hill. Bharata met Rama and pleaded fervently for his return. But Rama did not relent. Bharata threatened to fast indefinitely but was prevailed upon by Rama to give up the idea. Rama promised to accept the kingdom *after* his return from the fourteen-year exile but not before. Finally, a happy solution was offered by sage Vasishtha, according to which Bharata was to carry on the administration as a regent until Rama's return from the exile. Bharata and Rama both consented to this arrangement. For this purpose Rama was asked to bless Bharata with his sandals; Bharata had specially brought a pair of golden sandals into which Rama stepped. The matter having thus been resolved fairly satisfactorily, Bharata and the whole contingent returned to Ayodhya. Bharata anointed Rama's sandals and carried on the administration with righteousness and efficiency. However, he decided not to live in Ayodhya until Rama's return but stay in the nearby village Nandigram, with matted locks and clothes of bark. He wanted to live the same ascetic life which Rama, with Sita and Lakshmana, was going to lead for fourteen years.

After Bharata's departure, **Rama decided to leave** Chitrakoota, partly because of the sad memories of his mother and brothers which the place had brought to him and partly because it had been defiled by the horses and elephants of Bharata's army. The three entered the Dandaka forest.

Book III

Rama was welcomed by the ascetics, who entreated him to deliver them from **the oppression of titans. He gave them the assurance** this would be done. The first misfortune which befell the trio in the forest was the attack on them by a demon, named Viradha. But Rama and Lakshmana vanquished the demon, who it appears was a celestial being, but had taken the form of a demon under curse.

Thereafter, the trio spent ten years in the Dandaka forest very happily, going from hermitage to hermitage. They also visited sage Agastya, who offered them excellent hospitality; Agastya also gave Rama a **celestial bow,** two inexhaustible quivers and a sword.

The sage advised them to take abode at Panchavati, on the banks of the Godavari. As they were proceeding to Panchavati, they came across a very old and huge eagle, named Jatayu. The celestial eagle told Rama that he was a friend of Dasaratha and promised to keep watch over Sita whenever the brothers went out hunting, etc. Lakshmana built a beautiful hut for their dwelling.

Life went on happily for some time, but adversity was lurking round the corner. Khara and his brother Dooshana, with their army of fourteen thousand, launched an attack on Rama, who, single-handedly, vanquished the entire force, including Khara and Dooshana.

One of the titans, Akampana, told **Ravana** that Rama could be vanquished not by battle but by abduction of his lovely wife, consequent to which he would not survive. Accordingly, Ravana set out to seek his relative **Maricha's** help on this ignoble mission, but Maricha dissuaded him from it.

Hardly had Ravana returned to Lanka when **Shurpanakha** came taunting Ravana over the destruction of his forces in Janasthana. By abducting Sita, Ravana would be avenging the defeat of his army.

This time Ravana was determined to abduct Sita and so he went to Maricha again and by threatening Maricha's own life forced him to agree to aid him in the sinister

---

"sage Bharadwaja . . . directed them to the place of Rama's abode"—This is an important role for Jung's Senex: protector and director. (See Ch. 32.) The sages were wise and holy men who lived alone in the forests. People sought them out for advice about religious as well as practical matters.

"Rama decided to leave"—The map in the introduction follows the route Rama probably took. Archeologists and historians have worked to identify the topographical features and ancient settlements that were most likely those named in the *Ramayana.*

"the oppression of titans"—These are the same "titans" referred to in Book I, the Rakshasas.

"He gave them assurance"—Since the mission of the ascetics is to pray and to help visitors live a more perfect religious and ethical life, negative forces would naturally aim to destroy them.

"celestial bow"—It belonged to Vishnu, and the quivers belonged to Indra. Heroes are often given miraculous aids or powers by sages. For example, in *Star Wars,* Ben Kenobi gives Luke Skywalker the light-saber and teaches him to use the Force.

Ravana With ten heads and twenty arms, he might have influenced the ancient Greek conception of Giants and Titans, such as Briareus.

Maricha One of the demons whom Rama subdued in Book I.

Shurpanakha Ravana's younger sister.

METONYMY

Metonymy is a way of representing an object or a person by using a word or an object closely identified with a person. For example, we sometimes refer to the American president and his advisers as "the White House" or to the British monarch as "the crown." In this event in the *Ramayana*, Rama's golden sandals will stand in for him as if he were actually present. Such a situation also occurs in Friedrich Schiller's play *William Tell*, where Governor Gessler puts his hat on a post in the market place for all to respect and greet, just as they would the governor. But, unlike Rama, Gessler was a tyrant and the people were so incensed at this indignity, they revolted and took back their rights as citizens. Rama is the acknowledged rightful ruler, so his sandals are accepted as the symbol of his presence.

mission. The plan which Ravana outlined was that **Maricha should, by assuming the form of a golden deer,** draw away Rama and Lakshmana from the hermitage, so that Ravana could carry away Sita. Things happened thus. When the captivating golden deer appeared near the hermitage, Sita at once desired to have the animal. Lakshmana warned that it was Maricha in the form of a deer; but **Sita was so enchanted by the deer that she insisted on getting it** alive or dead. Rama went after it and when at last he shot an arrow at it the deer raised false alarm, shouting in Rama's voice "O Sita, O Lakshmana." Lakshmana knew very well this was foul play by the demon. He was confident that Rama could take care of himself and did not wish to leave Sita alone.

But Sita was alarmed. By uttering harsh words and imputing unworthy motives to Lakshmana, she forced him to go in search of Rama. Sita was thus left alone in her hermitage. Ravana snatched this opportunity to abduct her. He approached her in the disguise of a hermit and then revealing his identity proposed that she become his wife. At

"Maricha . . . [will assume] the form of a golden deer"—He will change himself into a deer to lure Rama. Although Maricha does this because his life is threatened, he is still guilty of trickery. Trickery is often used to defeat heroes because it is very difficult to overcome their superior abilities.

"Sita . . . insisted on getting it"—She forces Rama to go after the deer. Like the Grimm Brothers' Snow White, Sita helps bring on her own downfall because she is taken in by the trickery of Ravana.

Rama and Sita.

"Ravana . . . assuming his monstrous form"—This is not just a change of clothes; Rakshasas can physically transform the shape of their bodies.

Ashoka A kind of tree; also the name of the very early Aryan leader.

"Shabari . . . who was a devotee of Rama"—This shows us again how respected Rama is, even in exile. It shows also that Shabari is acting according to the *dharma* of the hermitage in being ready to care for Rama.

Sugreeva Monkey king. Kabandha told Rama and Lakshmana that Sugreeva would help them find Sita.

Vali Sugreeva's elder brother, who had banished him.

Hanuman Noble monkey who leads the monkey army to fight for Rama.

"in the presence of fire"—It seems that fire is considered a very special element, and that it is part of a traditional ceremony here.

"the quarrel between Vali and [Sugreeva]"—This takes us away from the story of Rama. Valmiki based it on spoken stories. In oral storytelling, it is not unusual to go off on tangents like this. See the discussion of oral tradition and parataxis in Ch. 2, pp. 16–19.

"a demonstration of his might"—Heroes must always prove physical prowess. One of the most extensive examples is Hercules (Ch. 31, p. 446).

this preposterous proposal, Sita poured scorn and admonition on **Ravana.** He became furious, and **assuming his monstrous form,** lifted her by force into his chariot and began to move. Hearing Sita's cries for help, the eagle Jatayu, despite his age, gave a fierce battle, but Ravana clipped his wings and resumed the flight to Lanka, carrying Sita. On the way, Sita, with remarkable presence of mind, tied a few of her ornaments in her mantle and threw them towards a collection of monkeys she saw on the way so that the news of her abduction might reach Rama. Ravana soon reached Lanka and interned Sita in his harem under strict guard. He tried to win her affection alternately by frequent entreaties of all sorts, but Sita spurned Ravana's advances with utter contempt and wrath. Subsequently, she was removed to the **Ashoka** gardens where she lived underneath a Shimshapa tree, surrounded by titan women guards, who tried, in vain, all means to make Sita consent to become Ravana's consort.

Here, in Panchavati, Rama killed the illusory deer and returned to the hermitage, and on the way met Lakshmana, whom he blamed for leaving Sita alone in the hermitage. Then, not finding Sita in the hermitage, the two brothers started searching for her, and asking even the trees and the beasts about her whereabouts. They met Jatayu who was lying in a pool of blood. He had just a little energy to tell them how he was mortally injured by Ravana when he tried to combat with him; he then breathed his last.

Pursuing their search for Sita, Rama and Lakshmana then met **Shabari, an ascetic woman who was a devotee of Rama.** She had been collecting fresh fruits for Rama, each day for several years, in the hope that he would turn up some day. Rama enjoyed her hospitality and blessed her.

Book IV

When Rama and Lakshmana arrived at the Pampa lake, **Sugreeva** and his followers, seated on a mountain, saw them. Sugreeva thought that they were sent by **Vali** to slay them; but his chief counselor, **Hanuman,** spoke reassuringly, that there was no cause for apprehension. Then Sugreeva sent Hanuman to find out the intentions of the two lustrous young men, after inspiring them with confidence by pleasant and courteous words. Hanuman disguised himself as a bachelor brahmin, went to the two brothers and introducing himself as Sugreeva's minister, sought Rama's friendship with Sugreeva. Rama came to like Hanuman instantly and Hanuman in turn became his devotee. Lakshmana narrated to Hanuman their story and sought Sugreeva's help in the search for and recovery of Sita. Hanuman carried both the brothers on his shoulders to Sugreeva and introduced them to him, saying they deserved his help and friendship. Sugreeva most warmly and respectfully offered his friendship to Rama. An alliance was forged between the two **in the presence of fire.** Rama promised to kill Vali and in turn Sugreeva promised to help Rama in the search for Sita. Sugreeva's monkeys brought to Rama the ornaments which Sita had thrown from her garment. On seeing Sita's ornaments, Rama wailed for Sita all the more.

Sugreeva told Rama of **the quarrel between Vali and himself.** Once Vali went to kill the demon Mayavi, pursuing him inside a cave. Since he did not return for quite a long time, Sugreeva, who had been asked to wait outside, thought that he (Vali) was dead and allowed himself to be installed as king of Kishkindha on the counsel of his ministers. Vali, however, returned after slaying Mayavi and in spite of Sugreeva's entreaties, turned his wrath on him. He drove him away from the city, depriving him of his wife too. Sugreeva also told Rama of the might of Vali and his exploits. In **a demonstration of his might** to inspire confidence in Sugreeva, Rama, with the forefinger of his toe, threw the carcass of the demon Dundubhi twenty miles away. As Sugreeva was still not convinced of his prowess, Rama, with a single arrow, pierced through seven huge sala trees. This was enough to satisfy Sugreeva. Both these feats had been asked for by Sugreeva.

It was agreed between Rama and Sugreeva that the search for Sita would be launched as soon as the monsoon was over. Meanwhile, Sugreeva got engrossed in a life of pleasure, enjoying the fruits of victory after a long exile. During this period, **Rama became quite desolate and melancholy** and his yearning for Sita deepened. In this mood, as soon as the monsoon was over, Rama sent Lakshmana to Sugreeva to remind him of his part of the alliance, the search for Sita. Lakshmana reprimanded Sugreeva for the delay in instituting the search for Sita, though it turned out that Sugreeva had taken some preliminary steps in that regard. However, Sugreeva decided to intensify the efforts and thereupon collecting his army went to meet Rama to pacify him and told him that the search for Sita was being launched earnestly. The monkey army was split up and sent in all directions in search of Sita.

Hanuman, with Angada, the son of Vali, went to the South, with a big army. Rama, who had great confidence in Hanuman, gave him a ring to serve as a token which Sita could recognize. The monkey chiefs chanced to meet **a vulture,** Sampati, who was the elder brother of Jatayu. Sampati **told the monkeys of the whereabouts of Sita.** He said that Sita, surrounded by titan women guards, was in the city of Lanka in the kingdom of Ravana. Sampati urged the monkey chiefs to make the effort to go to Lanka with confidence and without delay. As Lanka was several hundred miles across the seas, the monkeys became despondent for a while, doubting the ability of any of them to cross the sea and get back. Finally the choice fell unanimously on Hanuman, the son of the God of the Wind, as the only one who could accomplish the mighty task of crossing the sea to Lanka and back. Hanuman undertook this assignment with great enthusiasm and confidence.

Book V

Before launching on the flight, Hanuman increased his size several-fold and prayed for the blessings of the Sun and the Wind. **The flight was in no sense uneventful** and devoid of obstacles, but Hanuman overcame them. Soon he reached the shores of Lanka city. He waited until dusk and then entered the city, reducing his size to that of an ordinary monkey. **Lanka was a magnificent city,** the multi-story buildings standing on golden pillars, opulent mansions, wide and beautiful lakes and gardens. He first entered Ravana's palace, by about midnight. Ravana was fast asleep; so were a number of women, but Hanuman could not locate anyone resembling Sita. He searched diligently for her everywhere but could not find her. He even wondered whether Sita was alive at all. He became despondent, and contemplated the disastrous consequences of his not finding Sita. However, with remarkable perseverance he continued the search, and came to the Ashoka garden.

Hanuman, King of the Monkeys, goes to Ceylon.

"It was agreed"—Sugreeva keeps his promise to Rama and begins searching for Sita.

"Rama became quite desolate and melancholy"—Even though he is a hero and is half divine, Rama still has very human emotions and human limitations. These qualities contribute to a hero's stature, because those telling the story can feel a special kinship with him.

"a vulture . . . told the monkeys the whereabouts of Sita"—Birds are often news reporters because they can travel where humans cannot. Compare the birds on Odin's shoulders in the *Prose Edda*. The popular expression "A little bird told me" may be a remnant of this belief.

"[Hanuman's] flight was in no sense uneventful"—Only very special people, either good or bad, could fly. Hanuman's flying here is good, because he is being helped by the Sun and the Wind. He is son of the Wind.

"Lanka was a magnificent city"—Lanka was a heavily fortified city on the Trikuta Hill. It is generally assumed to be present-day Sri Lanka. See map, p. 205, and Introduction, p. 204.

He did find a woman beneath a tree and it was not difficult for Hanuman to conclude that she was Sita. She was looking emaciated and terribly grief-stricken, dressed in soiled clothes and **without ornaments.** Titan women were keeping watch over her.

Hanuman perched himself on a nearby tree and reflected on the greatness of Sita and the sorrow which had befallen her. Soon Ravana came to the Ashoka garden to woo Sita, but she spurned him in harsh words. Ravana, becoming furious at this, said he was giving her two months to decide; if she refused his wish, she would be cut to pieces by his cooks! After Ravana left, Sita was overcome with extreme sorrow and even thought of committing suicide, but soon many auspicious signs appeared to her. At this moment, Hanuman skillfully opened conversation with Sita, by reciting in sweet tones Rama's praise. He said that he had been sent by Rama and wished to convey to her his well-being. **Sita first suspected that he could be Ravana himself in disguise** and asked him to go away. But **Hanuman** described to her the luster of Rama and his virtues and also **showed her the signet ring** which Rama had given to him for identification. Sita was convinced of Hanuman's bona fides.

Seeing Sita so grief stricken because of the pangs of separation from Rama, Hanuman offered to take her on his shoulders across the seas to Rama. At first, Sita doubted his ability to do so, but Hanuman demonstrated to her his prowess and said he could even lift the whole of Lanka. Sita, however, raised other objections; in particular **it was proper that her lord rescue her** and thus retrieve his honor and glory. So, Hanuman gave up the idea and promised to return swiftly to Kishkindha, to mobilize their ranks to launch the attack on Lanka. In token of his meeting with Sita, **Hanuman took from Sita a jewel** which she had carefully concealed in her sari; also, she narrated to Hanuman a couple of incidents relating to their personal life which only she and Rama knew.

The return flight was uneventful. Hanuman was welcomed by Angada and other colleagues, who were gladdened by the news that he had seen Sita. Soon they returned to Kishkinda and Hanuman narrated to Rama all that he had accomplished; he gave him the jewel Sita had given him in token of his having met her. **Hanuman told him** that Ravana would keep Sita alive only for a month before which she should be liberated. Seeing the token of recognition, Rama pined for Sita all the more.

Book VI

Rama was filled with joy at the discovery of Sita and expressed his warm appreciation of Hanuman's exploits. But soon he became despondent on account of the near impossibility of a whole army being able to cross the sea. But Sugreeva cheered him and the army of monkeys set out, with tremendous enthusiasm, towards the shores of the sea.

Meanwhile, in Lanka, Ravana held a council of his ministers, at which his brother Vibhishana advised him to give up Sita and spare destruction of Lanka. But Ravana did not heed this and in fact he rebuked Vibhishana severely for his advice. The virtuous Vibhishana left Lanka and sought asylum in Rama's camp, which was given. Vibhishana, whom Rama crowned king of Lanka in advance, was of great help to Rama in the war against Ravana. **Kumbhakarna,** another brother of Ravana, **also felt that Ravana had erred** seriously in having abducted Sita, but he said he would fight for Ravana.

Prayer having failed, Rama managed to get, by threat of force, from **the sea lord** a passage in the sea for a causeway to be built up. The whole army crossed the sea and reached the outskirts of Lanka. The battle between Rama's and Ravana's forces raged fiercely for several days. **Great valor was displayed on both sides.** The fortunes of the

---

"without ornaments"—This shows just how desolate and demeaned Sita is. Men, women, and animals wore ornaments.

"Sita first suspected that he could be Ravana himself in disguise"—As a Rakshasa, Ravana could transform himself into other shapes.

"Hanuman . . . showed her the signet ring"—The ring token proves that Hanuman is Rama's emissary.

"it was proper that her lord rescue her"—Sita wants Rama to rescue her, because a husband is dishonored if another man kidnaps her, as Ravana has done with Sita, but he is also dishonored if another man rescues her. It is the husband's *dharma* to take care of his wife, so Rama must retrieve his honor and rescue Sita himself.

"Hanuman took from Sita a jewel"—Now he has a token to prove he has spoken with Sita.

"Hanuman told [Rama]"—He is not reporting accurately. He heard Ravana threaten to have Sita cut to pieces if she did not decide in his favor within two months.

"Rama was filled with joy"—His first emotion is joy that his wife has been found. But soon he will consider the ethical problems associated with her having lived among the Rakshasas.

"Kumbhakarna . . . also felt that Ravana had erred"—Despite finding fault with his brother Ravana, he stays with him. This could be a fulfillment of *dharma* as a brother.

"the sea lord"—In the *Ramayana,* the sea lord is the personification of the ocean. As a favor to Rama, the sea lord keeps the waters still while a bridge is being built.

"Great valor was displayed on both sides."—The battle is nobler and more difficult when this happens. It enhances the glory of the hero in victory.

war moved up and down for both sides. There were occasions when Rama and Laksh-mana lay prostrate or were despondent. On such occasions, the monkey chiefs and Vibhishana offered solace and courage. But steadily the fortunes of Rama gained ascendancy, and one after another the titan warriors were killed.

The combat between Rama and Ravana was most fierce, but finally, by the use of **the Brahma arrow,** Rama vanquished Ravana, to the tumultuous joy of the vast army of monkeys and the world of celestial beings.

After the performance of Ravana's obsequies, Rama had Vibhishana crowned king of Lanka. Rama had instructed Hanuman to enter Lanka, with the permission of Vib-hishana, and convey to Sita the news of Ravana's destruction. This Hanuman did. Sita was overjoyed and said she wanted to see her lord, which message was conveyed to him. Rama became thoughtful for a while and then asked Vibhishana to bring Sita to his presence forthwith, after she had bedecked herself.

When Sita was brought to his presence, **Rama was overcome with many emo-tions—joy, grief and rage.** Everyone present anticipated trouble. Rama spoke to Sita in harsh words, as follows: "I have defeated the enemy and avenged the insult to me. This campaign was not undertaken wholly for your sake; it was to uphold the honor of my illustrious family. Your very sight is now painful to me. Go where you like, for no man of honor can take back a beautiful woman who lived for a year in the house of a titan. Stay with anybody you like."

Sita was thunderstruck at these words of Rama, but she answered him in dignified and strong terms. His suspicions were most unjust and unworthy. She came from a noble family. Since he suspected her character, the only course left to her was to undergo **the fire ordeal.** She asked Lakshmana to raise a pyre for her; on perceiving that Rama had no objection to this, Lakshmana did what Sita told him. No sooner had Sita entered the fire, than the fire god rose from it carrying Sita in his arms, with her clothes and jewels unscathed, and presented her to Rama. Rama accepted her, saying that he knew fully well that Sita was pure, but the fire ordeal was necessary to satisfy public opinion. Then **Dasaratha himself appeared** from his heavenly abode and asked Sita to forgive Rama for what he did, the object of which was to preserve *Dharma.* Rama begged of his father to give his blessings to Kaikeyi and Bharata, whom he had renounced earlier. Dasaratha said, "Be it so." On Rama's request, **Indra,** the celestial chief, restored to life all the monkeys which had been killed in the war.

Rama, accompanied by Sita, Lakshmana, Vibhishana and all the monkeys flew to Ayodhya in the celestial chariot Pushpaka. He sent word to Bharata in advance, through Hanuman, about his homecoming. Bharata's joy knew no bounds when he met Rama, Lakshmana and Sita. The whole of Ayodhya was bedecked to receive Rama. The joy that had been cut short fourteen years earlier had been restored in full meas-ure. Elaborate arrangements were swiftly made for Rama's coronation, which took place with due splendor. Rama gave Sita a beautiful pearl necklace, which she, with his approval, gave to Hanuman, that supreme devotee.

Rama offered to make Lakshmana the heir-apparent, but he declined; then Rama crowned Bharata as the heir-apparent. Rama ruled over the kingdom for over ten thousand years, enhancing the joy of his people, who were endowed with good qualities.

Further Reading

Simha, S. L. N. *Ramayana for the Modern World.* Bombay: Bharatiya Vidya Bhavan, 1965.

Vyas, Shantikumar N. *India in the Ramayana Age.* Delhi: Atma Ram & Sons, 1967.

"the Brahma arrow"—Vishnu gave Rama this powerful weapon to kill Ravana. Vishnu had promised the Rakshasas that he would not attack them with anything on the earth or in the sky. But Rama's using the arrow was an ethical solution to Vishnu's dilemma.

"Rama was overcome with . . . joy, grief and rage."—This mixture of emotions indicates not only Rama's love of Sita, but also his anger because he feels that she has betrayed him, and his sorrow that he may not take her back as his wife. His *dharma* is to over-power the person who dishonored his family by abducting his wife. At the same time, he fears also that she might have given in to the titan Ravana.

"the fire ordeal"—Trial by fire was used to prove a woman's charac-ter. If she survived, she was assumed to be protected by the gods, and therefore innocent. Sita's virtue is more evident because the fire god carries her from the flames to Rama.

"Dasaratha himself appeared"—Rama's father helps restore the balance of love and trust in the family.

Indra Chief of the Vedic gods who leads them in battle and cannot be beaten. For war, Indra, dressed in a warrior's suit, sits in a chariot that is pulled through the air by green horses.

"Rama offered to make Laksh-mana the heir-apparent"—This would preserve the faithful brother's *dharma.* But it is fitting for Lakshmana to refuse—also because of *dharma*—since Bharata is the second-born son and should be the immediate heir.

18

Heroes in the *Prose Edda*

SNORRI STURLUSON

WHAT TO EXPECT . . . Snorri Sturluson's accounts of the ancient Norse gods show deities who are not always godlike, heroic, or even effective. Their limitations may be caused by Snorri's reluctance to be associated with the deities he wrote about. As a Christian, he was writing to preserve the memory of an ancient belief system that was no longer relevant. Alternatively, the fallibility of these gods may reflect the ritual practices of the old Norse peoples or the world view of Snorri's contemporary Icelandic audience. This chapter's introduction and marginal notes provide you with evidence to consider these possibilities.

As you read, note specifically the differences between the *Prose Edda* and the other hero stories you have read. It may also be interesting to consider the discussion in Chapter 7 of the contest motif in Snorri's writing (p. 84) and how it applies to the stories told in this chapter.

As noted in the introduction to his creation story (Ch. 7, p. 78), Snorri Sturluson was a synthesizer who worked to preserve stories of a religion that was not his own. He was a widely traveled, sophisticated diplomat who collected stories of his people's past and united them into a dramatic narrative. One purpose of the *Prose Edda* was to teach poetry writing—the word "edda" means "poetic art"—in the style of the ancient Viking poets, who were called skalds.

The deeds recounted in the *Prose Edda* portray a golden past in which the gods had great powers of magic and strength, but it is not an era that we can tie to the active practice of a religion. In a sense, it is a recording of traditions by a man who wishes to preserve the memory of those traditions, but who is already beyond them.

SNORRI'S HERO-GODS HAVE LIMITATIONS

Although stories of heroes as a rule portray the hopes and aspirations of a people, it is difficult to determine the status of the characters of the *Prose Edda* as heroes. Most of them are gods, but they do not all represent the urge to transcendence characterized by Joseph Campbell in *The Hero with a Thousand Faces* (see Ch. 14, p. 159). Some are wicked, some are frail, and all seem flawed in a fundamental way. Loki, who is one of the gods, often works against their best interests, and his companions are unable to control him. Baldr, who is viewed as the "shining light" of the gods, is lost to them until the end of the world. Thor, the great hero of the gods, at times seems to pursue quests he cannot win without having the wit to notice his limitations. And the gods themselves are destined to be destroyed in Ragnarok, a great battle that will end the world as we know it (see Ch. 13, p. 147).

These weaknesses may be an indication that the stories Snorri includes are no longer able to bear the brunt of sustaining man through religious feeling. But this is not the only possible explanation: these stories of an imperfect world and its limited gods may, in fact, portray the Icelandic view of the universe. It may be that Icelandic myth represents life as a more cyclical phenomenon, an integration or alteration of good and evil, as Mircea Eliade would have it; see the Introduction to the Destruction section, p. 155. In this view, Loki and the destructive forces he embodies may indicate an acceptance of human fallibility that is lacking in the portrait of other, more powerful heroes.

THE *PROSE EDDA* IS A DIFFERENT KIND OF HERO EPIC

There are other differences between the *Prose Edda* and other hero tales such as the *Epic of Gilgamesh* and the *Ramayana* included in this book. In Snorri's account, there is no sustained action and no emphasis on ethical dilemmas. As a result, Snorri's heroes do not go through the development process described by Campbell in the way that Gilgamesh does. In addition, Snorri seems to assume that the reader is already acquainted with Odin and Thor and the gods in Valhalla. Therefore, his account seems more like a summary or overview than the fresh telling of an unknown story. He has Gylfi ask about various gods, and the Æsir answer with great authority. They often quote from the old songs and point out that they know what they say to be true because it is in the lay (the recorded saga). They often mock Gylfi because his knowledge is so limited, but they always provide the information requested.

THE *PROSE EDDA* AS A CONTEST

In fact, as noted in Chapter 7 (p. 84), the *Prose Edda* is organized as a kind of contest. Gylfi goes to visit the Æsir because he has been tricked by one of them. The object of his journey is not to sit at their feet and soak up their wisdom, but to test himself against them, to see whose learning is more powerful. Gylfi's battle with the Æsir mirrors the way the gods contend with each other in Snorri's stories. The main battle of the *Prose Edda* can be viewed as a struggle between Christianity and the pagan gods. The nature of the contest is that of a struggle between kinds of wisdom. Snorri asks the Æsir questions. Since he has more questions than they have answers, he wins. If the Æsir had had more answers than Gylfi had questions, then the pagan religion would have prevailed. At the end of Snorri's account, the Æsir are defeated. This may be an indication of a complex and subtle world view that accepts limitation as part of its nature, or it may be a representation by a nonbeliever of the failure of a religion which to him has more charm than authority.

In line with the overall structure of the *Prose Edda* as a contest we can see that several episodes within the larger work are also contests or challenges of a sort. For example, when Thor and his cohort visit the home of Utgard-Loki, they pit their strengths and talents against the host in order to assert their worthiness and authority. Although they lose, they are greatly admired: Utgard-Loki tells his adversary that he had feared Thor would succeed in the tasks, which had actually been tricks. If Thor had succeeded, the balance of nature itself would have been upset: old age would have been defeated, the oceans would have dried up, and the Midgard Serpent, who circles the earth, would have been moved from his crucial position.

The tricks presented in this episode—the Midgard Serpent as a cat, age as an old woman— are in fact a type of riddle. If Thor had figured out the identity of his adversary, he would have known that the contests in which he was engaged were not what they seemed. In this respect, Utgard-Loki's tricks are related to the type of word tricks children use. The person challenged must be clever enough to look past the obvious answer. Snorri includes riddles, perhaps to enhance the level of competition: one must not only perform the deed, but must also understand what makes the accomplishment so difficult.

THE *PROSE EDDA* AS A REFLECTION OF NORSE RITUAL PRACTICES

Although Snorri's story has highly literary characteristics, it nonetheless seems to be a reflection of the actual beliefs and practices of the Icelandic people. This is made clear by the abundance of archeological evidence which corresponds to the stories told in the *Prose Edda*. For example, in the story of Baldr's death excerpted in this chapter, we read that Baldr's body is burned on a funeral fire, or pyre, placed on a ship. His wife, who has died of grief, is also placed on the pyre, along with his horse. This event in the myth corresponds to rituals actually practiced by the Icelandic people in burying their dead, as H. R. Ellis Davidson shows in *Gods and Myths of Northern Europe*. For more of her discussion of Icelandic rituals and their correspondence to the stories found in the *Prose Edda,* see Chapter 30, p. 429.

LOKI AS A TRICKSTER HERO

In Norse mythology, Loki is an inconsistent character. He is a god, but he is also a thief and a deceiver who is often helpful to others, including the gods. As Snorri presents him in the *Prose Edda,* Loki is mischievous rather than evil. In a section of the *Prose Edda* not printed here, Loki turns himself into a mare to frustrate the aims of the giant who undertakes the building of a stronghold for the gods. Loki "romances" the builder's horse, thus preventing him from finishing the stronghold on time. This saves the Æsir from having to keep a bargain they had regretted making. Loki can also take on a completely positive role. In this excerpt, he helps the gods when he visits Utgard-Loki with Thor. In this adventure, Loki tries to uphold the honor of the

This 9th-c. C.E. Swedish burial site is one of many archeological sites with stones forming the shape of a ship.

Æsir by competing in the eating contest. Although he loses, he displays his solidarity with Thor and his men.

Georges Dumézil, the French comparative philologist and mythology scholar, also found redeeming characteristics in Loki, giving examples of him as very intelligent but impulsive, with an uncontrollable desire to act dramatically. Utilizing a comparative approach, Dumézil pointed out a significant resemblance between Loki and Syrdon, a figure from Caucasian legends who also has positive and negative characteristics, and traced the Loki-as-trickster motif to the *Maharabhata* of the Hindu tradition.

In some ways, Loki can be compared to the trickster heroes of Native American mythology, as described in Chapter 21, p. 295. He is a being with godlike powers who lives between worlds, rather than exclusively in the world of humans or that of special or magical beings. Like Raven and many other American Indian tricksters, Loki can change his shape, and like them, he often uses his powers to outwit figures of authority.

In this respect, Loki reflects the ambiguity we frequently see in Icelandic myth. His role emphasizes the fallibility and frailty of the gods. See p. 218 for a discussion of the significance of this aspect of the Icelandic gods as presented by Snorri Sturluson.

Then **Ganglieri** asked: "Where is the chief place or sanctuary of the gods?"

High One replied: "It is by the ash Yggdrasil. There every day the gods have to hold a court."

Then Ganglieri asked: "In what way is that place famous?"

Then Just-as-high said: "The ash is the best and greatest of all trees; its branches spread out over the whole world and reach up over heaven. The tree is held in position by three roots that spread far out; one is among the Æsir, the second among the frost ogres where once was Ginnungagap, and the third extends over Niflheim, and under that root is the well Hvergelmir; but Níðhögg gnaws at the root from below. Under the root that turns in the direction of the frost ogres lies the spring of Mímir, in which is hidden wisdom and understanding.

"The third root of the ash tree is in the sky, and under that root is the very sacred spring of Urð. There the gods hold their court of justice. The Æsir ride up to that place every day over the bridge Bifröst, which is also known as the Bridge of the Æsir."

The Major Gods

Then **Gangleri** asked: "Who are the gods men ought to believe in?"

High One replied: "The divine gods are twelve in number."

Just-as-high added: "The goddesses are no less sacred and no less powerful."

Then Third said: "Odin is the highest and the oldest of the gods. He rules all things and, no matter how mighty the other gods may be, they all serve him as children do their father. His wife is Frigg and she knows the fates of all men, although she does not prophesy.

"Odin is called All-father because he is the father of all the gods. He is also called Valfather because **all who fall in battle are his adopted sons.** He allots to them Valhalla and Vingolf, and then they are called Einherjar. He is also called Hangagud, Haptagud, Farmagud, and he named himself in many other ways when he came to King Geirrod."

Then Ganglieri said: "It would show great learning to know and cite in each instance the events that had given rise to the these names."

This excerpt comes from: Snorri Sturluson, *The Prose Edda.**

 Odin

Gangleri This is the name Gylfi assumes when he arrives at the Æsir stronghold. Not speaking his real name may be rooted in the ancient Germanic belief that if an evil one knows your name, he or she can cast a spell over you.

"all who fall in battle are his adopted sons"—To die in battle is the only honorable end for a warrior. Those who do are sent to Valhalla; the others go to Niflheim, where they are ruled by Hel, a daughter of the evil Loki.

*Snorri Sturluson. *The Prose Edda: Tales from Norse Mythology*. Trans. Jean I. Young, 48–64, 69–85. Copyright © 1954. Used by permission of the University of California Press.

"it will be impossible for you to be called a well-informed person"—This seems to point out the competitive nature of Snorri's work. See the Introduction for a discussion of the *Prose Edda* as a contest (p. 219).

 Thor

"As it says in the *Lay of Grimnir*"—Snorri often establishes authority for his story by citing other well-known stories. This is also a sign that he is writing a literary version of the myths.

 Baldr

Baldr   God who is wise, handsome, sweet, and pure.

Njord, Frey, and Freyja

Njord   God who controls the wind and sea, as the Greek Poseidon, and Roman Neptune.

Frey   Son of the wind and sea god Njord; controls the sun, rain, and harvest.

Njord, Frey, and Freyja   Belong to the Vanir; Odin's family are the Æsir. Both lived in Asgard, but the Vanir granted "peace and plenty," while the Æsir most often caused destruction.

"Then Gangleri said"—Snorri's dramatic technique is a kind of syntactic storytelling because it sets up links between parts of the narrative. For more on syntactic storytelling, see Ch. 1, p. 18.

 Tyr

"It is a proverbial saying"—Snorri often points out the connections between folk sayings and ancient beliefs.

Then High One said: "It would take a vast amount of knowledge to go over them all. It will, however, be quickest to tell you that most of these names have been given him because the many different nations in the world, all speaking different tongues, felt the need of translating his name into their several languages in order to worship and pray to him. Some incidents giving rise to these names, however, took place on his journeys, and these have been made into tales, and **it will be impossible for you to be called a well-informed person** if you cannot relate some of these great events."

Then Gangleri asked: "What are the names of the other gods? How do they occupy themselves? What have they done to distinguish themselves?"

High One said: "Thor, who is called Asa-Thor or Thor-the-charioteer, is the foremost of them. He is strongest of all gods and men. He rules over that kingdom called Thrudvangar, and his hall is called Bilskirnir; in that building are six hundred and forty floors—it is the largest house known to men. **As it says in the *Lay of Grimnir*:**

> Bilskirnir with its winding ways
> I know has more
> than six hundred and forty floors,
> of those buildings
> I know to be roofed   5
> I know my son's is the largest.

"Thor has two goats known as Tooth-gnasher and Gap-tooth, and the chariot he drives in. The goats pull the chariot, and for this reason he is called Thor-the-charioteer. He also owns three precious things. One is the hammer Mjollnir, which the frost ogres and cliff giants know when it is raised aloft, and that is not surprising since he has cracked the skulls of many of their kith and kin. His second great treasure is a belt of strength, and when he buckles that on his divine might is doubled. And he owns a third thing of great value in his iron gauntlets; he cannot do without these when he grips the handle of the hammer."

Then Gangleri said: "I would like to hear about more of the gods."

High One said: "Another son of Odin, is called **Baldr,** and there is [nothing but] good to be told of him. He is the best of them and everyone sings his praises. He is so fair of face and bright that a splendor radiates from him. From that you can tell how beautiful his body is, and how bright his hair.

"The third god is the one called **Njord.** He lives in heaven at a place called Noatun. He controls the path of the wind, stills sea and fire, and is to be invoked for seafaring and fishing.

"Njord of Noatun had two children after this, a son called **Frey** and a daughter **Freyja.** They were beautiful to look at, and powerful. Frey is an exceedingly famous god; he decides when the sun shall shine or the rain come down, and along with that the fruitfulness of the earth, and he is good to invoke for peace and plenty. But Freyja is the most renowned of the goddesses. She owns that homestead in heaven known as Folkvangar, and whenever she rides into battle she has half the slain and Odin half.

"Her hall Sessrumnir is large and beautiful. When she goes on a journey she sits in a chariot drawn by two cats. She enjoys love poetry, and it is good to call on her for help in love affairs.

Then Gangleri said: "The Æsir appear to me to be very powerful, and it is not surprising that you have great authority, since you possess such understanding of the gods and know how each should be prayed to. Are there more gods still?"

High One said: "There is a god called **Tyr.** He is the boldest and most courageous, and has power over victory in battle; it is good for brave men to invoke him. **It is a proverbial saying** that he who surpasses others and does not waver is 'Tyr-valiant.' He is also so well informed that a very knowledgeable man is said to be 'Tyr-wise.' Here is one proof of his daring. When the gods tried to persuade the wolf **Fenrir** to allow the fetter Gleipnir to be placed on him, he did not believe that they would free him until they put Tyr's hand in his mouth as a pledge. Then, when the Æsir would not loose him, he bit off the hand.

"One [god] is called **Bragi.** He is famous for wisdom and most of all for eloquence and skill with words; he knows most about poetry, and **from him poetry gets its name,** and from his name the man or woman who can use words better than others is called a poet. His wife is Dun. She keeps in her box the apples the gods have to eat, when they grow old, to become young again, and so it will continue up to Ragnarok.

"Also reckoned amongst the gods is one that some call the mischief monger of the Æsir and the father-of-lies and the disgrace-of-gods-and-men. He is **the son of the giant** Farbauti and his name is **Loki.** His mother's name is Laufey, and Byleist and Helblindi are his brothers. Loki is handsome and fair of face, but has an evil disposition and is very changeable of mood. He excelled all men in the art of cunning, and he always cheats. He was continually involving the Æsir in great difficulties and he often helped them out again by guile. His wife's name is Sigyn; their son [is] Nari.

"Loki had still more children. There was **a giantess in Giantland called Angrboda.** Loki had three children by her, the first was the wolf Fenrir, the second, Jormungand—that is the Midgard Serpent—and the third, Hel. Now when the gods knew that these three children were being brought up in Giantland and had gathered from prophecy that they would meet with great harm and misfortune on their account (and they all anticipated evil, first from the mother and still worse from the father), **All-father** sent some of the gods to capture the children and bring them to him. And when they came to him, he flung the serpent into the deep sea which surrounds the whole world, and it grew so large that it now lies in the middle of the ocean round the earth, biting its own tail. He threw Hel into Niflheim and gave her authority over nine worlds, on the condition that she shared all her provisions with those who were sent to her, namely men who die from disease or old age.

"The gods brought the wolf up at home, and only Tyr had the courage to go up to it and give it food. But when the gods saw how fast it was growing daily, and all prophecies foretold that it was doomed to do them injury, the Æsir adopted the plan of making a very strong fetter which they called **Loeding,** and they took it to the wolf and bade him try his strength against it. But the wolf thought that it would not be too difficult for him [to snap it] and allowed them to do as they would; and the first time the wolf strained against it the fetter broke, so he got free from Loeding.

"Then the Æsir made another fetter twice as strong, which they called Dromi, and bade the wolf test himself again against that fetter, saying that he would become very famous for strength if such a strong chain would not hold him. **The wolf, however, was thinking** that, although the fetter was very strong, he had grown in might since he had broken Loeding; it also occurred to him that he would have to expose himself to danger in order to become famous, so he let the fetter be put on him. When the Æsir said they were ready, he shook himself, knocking the fetter against the ground, and struggled against it, digging his feet in so hard that the fetter broke into pieces which flew far and wide; so he got himself out of Dromi.

"After that the Æsir feared that they would never be able to get the wolf bound. Then All-father sent one called Skirnir, Frey's messenger, down to the **World-of-dark-elves** to some dwarfs, and had made the fetter called Gleipnir. This was made from six things: the noise a cat makes when it moves, the beard of a woman, the roots of a mountain, the sinews of a bear, the breath of a fish, and the spittle of a bird. Now, although you may not have known this before, you can easily prove that you are not being told a falsehood, since you will have observed that a woman has no beard, a cat makes no noise when running, a mountain has no roots and, upon my word, everything I have told you is just as true, although there are some things that you can't put to the test."

"Tyr . . . Fenrir"—For the story of Fenrir and Tyr, see p. 435.

Bragi

"from [Bragi] poetry gets its name"—Old Icelandic for poetry is *bragi*. Snorri says the Vanir and Æsir sealed a truce by spitting into a crock; the gods made the spittle into a man. Dwarfs killed him and mixed his blood with honey—the mead of poets: whoever drank it became a poet or scholar.

Loki

"the son of the giant"—Levi-Strauss notes the special nature of creatures not born from two like parents. Such an offspring is often a monster or evil person. (See p. 284.)

"a giantess . . . called Angrboda"—Loki's children are feared because they are his and also because their mother is a giant. Two of Loki's children are monstrous: Fenrir the wolf and the Midgard Serpent.

All-father Odin. Snorri varies the name to create poetic interest, and because such virtuosity enhanced the storyteller's reputation.

The Binding of Fenrir

Loeding The Norse named weapons and special animals and objects. Note that Thor's hammer is called Mjollnir and Odin's horse is Sleipnir.

"The wolf . . . was thinking"—Fenrir seems like a person in many ways: the Æsir bargain with him, he reasons, and he plans for the future. Although he is an animal, he is the son of Loki, a major god.

"World-of-dark-elves"—Dwarfs are often pictured as miners or underground workers, as in the tale "Sleeping Beauty." The more derogatory connotation of this underground activity is that they cannot be normal human beings, whose place is *on* the earth, not under it or above it. (Note that witches *fly*.)

"I can easily tell you that"—There are small suggestions throughout Snorri's account that his story is about a contest. (See p. 219.)

"we will set you free again"—The gods lie to Fenrir.

"Tyr put out his right hand and laid it in the wolf's mouth"—Tyr is the only brave god. This scene portrays the gods as fallible and weak beings, although their reputations are great. Davidson points out that Tyr may well be related to a great ancient Norse war god (see Ch. 30, p. 449).

6th-c. C.E. bronze of *Tyr* and a chained animal, probably *Fenrir*.

"There he will lie until Ragnarok"—The gods finally bind and subdue Fenrir, but this portrayal suggests that the threat of the wolf is ever-present.

Then Gangleri said: "I can certainly understand it's true. I can see [that from] these things you have taken as examples, but how was the fetter made?"

High One replied: "**I can easily tell you that.** The fetter was as smooth and soft as a ribbon of silk, but as trusty and strong as you are now going to hear. When the fetter was brought to the Æsir they thanked the messenger very much for carrying out his mission.

"Then the Æsir, calling to the wolf to go with them, went out on to an island called Lyngvi in a lake called Amsvartnir. They showed him the silken band and bade him break it. They said it was a bit stronger than it appeared to be from its thickness and passed it from one to the other, testing its strength with their hands, and it did not break.

"They said, however, that the wolf would be able to snap it. The wolf's answer was: 'This ribbon looks to me as if I could gain no renown from breaking it—it is so slight a cord; but if it has been made by guile and cunning, slender though it looks, it is not going to come on my legs.' Then the gods said that he would soon snap so slight a ribbon of silk, when he had broken great fetters of iron before, 'and if you don't succeed in snapping this cord you need not be afraid of the gods; **we will set you free again.**' The wolf said: 'If you bind me so that I can't get free, then you will sneak away so that it will be a long time before I get any help from you. I don't want to have that ribbon put on me. But rather than be accused of cowardice by you, let one of you place his hand in my mouth as a pledge that this is done in good faith.' Each of the gods looked at the other then and thought that they were in a fix, and not one of them would stretch forth his hand, until **Tyr put out his right hand and laid it in the wolf's mouth.** Now when the wolf began to struggle against it, the band tightened, and the more fiercely he struggled the firmer it got.

"They all laughed except Tyr; he lost his hand. When the gods saw that the wolf was well and truly bound, they took the chain that was fast to this fetter and which was called Gelgja, and drawing it through a great boulder called Gjoll drove the boulder deep down into the earth. Then they took a huge stone called Thviti and sank it still deeper in the earth, and used this stone as a fastening peg.

"The wolf opened his mouth to a frightful width and struggled violently, wanting to bite them. Then they shoved a sword into his mouth so that the hilt was in its lower jaw and the point in the upper; that is his gag. He howls horribly, and the slaver running from his mouth forms the river called Von. **There he will lie until Ragnarok.**"

Then Gangleri said: "Loki had very evil children, but all these brothers and sisters have great power. Why didn't the gods kill the wolf, since they anticipated evil from him?"

High One replied: "The gods set such store by their sanctuary and temple that they would not pollute them with the wolf's blood, [even] although prophecies foretold that he would be the death of Odin."

Goddesses

Then Gangleri asked: "What goddesses are there?"

High One replied: "The foremost is Frigg. She owns that dwelling known as Fensalir, and it is most magnificent.

"Saga is another: she lives at Sokkvabekk, and that is a large estate.

"The third is Eir: she is the best of physicians.

"The fourth is Gefjoné: she is a virgin, and women who die unmarried serve her.

"The fifth is Fulla: she too, is a virgin and **wears her hair loose** and a golden band round her head. She carries Frigg's little box and looks after her shoes and knows her secrets.

"Frejya is as distinguished as Frigg. She is married to a man named Od; their daughter is Hnoss; she is so lovely that whatever is beautiful and valuable is called 'treasure' from her name.

"wears her hair loose"—This was the sign in many European cultures that a woman was unmarried.

High One lists ten more goddesses; none of them has a wide sphere of influence. Sif, Thor's wife, is not influential enough to be worthy of notice here.

"There are, moreover, others whose duty it is to serve in Valhalla, carry the drink round and look after the table service and ale-cups.

"These are called **Valkyries.** Odin sends them to every battle, and they choose death for the men destined to die, and award victory. Gud and Rota and the youngest norn Skuld always ride to choose the slain and decide [the issue of] battles."

Then Gangleri said: "You say that all the men who have fallen in battle since the beginning of the world have now come to Odin in Valhalla—what has he got to feed them with? I imagine that there must be a huge crowd of them there."

Then High One replied: "What you say is true. There is a huge crowd there, and there will be many more still, and yet they will seem too few when the wolf comes. But there is never so big a crowd in Valhalla that they don't get enough pork from **the boar called Saehrinmner. He is boiled every day, and comes alive every evening.** But as for the question you are putting now, it seems to me that not many people would know enough to give you the correct answer."

Then Gangleri asked: "Does Odin have the same food as the Einherjar?"

High One said: "He gives what food is on his table to two wolves called Geri and Freki; but **he himself needs nothing to eat.** Wine is for him both food and drink.

"Two ravens sit on his shoulders and bring to his ears all the news that they see or hear; they are called Hugin [Thought] and Munin [Memory]. He sends them out at daybreak to fly over the whole world, and they come back at breakfast-time; by this means he comes to know a great deal about what is going on, and on account of this men call him the god-of-ravens."

[Then Gangleri asked:] "Now has **Thor** never had an experience in which he **encountered something so strong in might and powerful in magic that it was too much for him?**"

Then High One said: "He has found many things hard to master but I doubt if anyone could tell you the stories and, even if something did overcome Thor on account of its magical power and strength, there is no need to tell the tale, since this happened more than once and yet everyone has to believe that Thor is exceedingly mighty."

Then Gangleri said: "It seems to me that I've asked you something no one is prepared to tell me about."

Then Just-as-high said: "Certain happenings have been reported to us that strike us as being incredible, but there is a man sitting nearby who will know the truth about them, and you may be sure, since he has never told a lie before, that he won't tell one for the first time now."

Then Gangleri said: "I'll stand here all ears for the answer to my question. On the other hand, if you can't tell me what I am asking, I maintain I've got the better of you."

Then Third said: "It is obvious that he wants to know this tale, although we don't think it a fine one to tell. You keep quiet.

"The beginning of the story is that Thor-the-charioteer was on a journey with his goats and in his chariot and with him the god Loki, when they came one evening to a farmer's where they got lodgings for the night. During the evening Thor took the goats and slaughtered them, then had them skinned and put into a cauldron. When they were cooked, Thor and his companion sat down to supper and Thor invited the farmer and his wife and children to the meal. The farmer's son was called Thjalfi and his daughter, Roskva. Thor spread the skins out away from the fire, and told the farmer and his household to throw the bones on to the skins. Thjalfi, the farmer's son, took firm hold of a thigh-bone of one of the goats and split it with his knife, breaking it for the marrow. Thor stayed there that night, and just before daybreak got up and dressed, took the hammer Mjollnir, raised it and consecrated the goatskins. Then the goats

 The Valkyries

Valkyries For more on these goddesses sacred to Odin, see Ch. 30, p. 435.

 Life in Valhalla

"the boar . . . comes alive every evening"—This magical renewal of a food source is common to myths in many cultures. Just below, Thor's goats are cooked and eaten, but the next day are alive and well.

"he himself needs nothing to eat"—As a god, Odin is beyond the physical needs of humans. But Thor seems to drink in his encounter with Utgard-Loki (p. 227). This may be a difference between the natures of the two gods. Odin is more removed from human life, or transcendent, whereas Thor gets involved with human life. He is an immanent god. (See Genesis creation story, Ch. 5, p. 50.)

"Thor . . . encountered something that . . . was too much for him"—The Norse gods sometimes show defects in ability and judgment. But the story also shows the power of Loki. For more on Snorri's portrayal of divine weakness, see the Introduction, p. 218.

 The Story of Thor and Utgard Loki

This 18th-c. statue shows the Saxon God *Thunor* (*Thor*) on his throne.

"when Thor saw their terror"—Thor is merciful to the family. Note that he takes the children as his servants "in reconciliation," not as a punishment. He becomes their patron, giving them opportunities for travel and adventure they would have never had if they had remained at home.

Loki's Contest: Eating

"Logi should . . . pit himself against Loki"—Here, Loki is no trickster; he is trying to help Thor retain his honor among arrogant challengers.

Thjalfi's Contest: Running

"Thjalfi said he would run a race"—Utgard-Loki has insulted him by calling him "the youngster." This gives Thjalfi the chance to participate as fully as the others.

stood up. One of them was lame of a hind leg; Thor noticed that and declared that the farmer and his household had done something silly with the bones; he knew that a thigh-bone was broken. There is no need to make a long story about it; everyone can guess how terrified the farmer would be when he saw Thor letting his eyebrows sink down over his eyes—but when he saw what he did of the eyes he thought he would drop down dead for the look in them alone. Thor gripped the handle of his hammer so that his knuckles went white. Then the farmer and his whole household did what you might expect, screamed out and begged for mercy for themselves, offering in compensation everything they possessed. But **when Thor saw their terror,** his anger left him and he calmed down and took from them in reconciliation their children Thjalfi and Roskva. They became his bondservants and accompanied him ever afterwards.

"He left his goats behind him there and set off on an expedition eastwards to Giantland, traveling all the way to the sea and then away over the deep ocean. When he came to land he went ashore and with him Loki and Thjalfi and Roskva. They had not walked very long before they came upon a big wood, and they walked the whole day till dark. Thjalfi, who could run faster than anyone else, was carrying Thor's knapsack, but they were not very well off for food.

"Thor and his companions continued their way and walked on till midday. Then they saw a stronghold on a plain. They had to bend their necks right back before they could see over the top of it. They went up to the stronghold and there was a gate in the entrance and it was shut. Thor went up to the gate but could not get it opened. Then they tried their hardest to get inside the stronghold and [finally] did so by squeezing between the bars of the gate. After that they saw a huge hall and went up to it.

"The door was open and, entering, they saw a large number of men and most of them pretty big, sitting on two benches. Next they came before the king, Utgard-Loki, and greeted him, but it was some time before he took any notice of them. He smiled contemptuously at them and remarked: 'News travels slowly from distant parts, or am I mistaken in thinking that this urchin is Thor-the-charioteer? You must be stronger than you look to me. At what arts do you and your companions think you excel? We don't allow anyone to stay with us who is not a past master of some craft or accomplishment.'

"Then the one who brought up the rear, Loki, said: 'I have an accomplishment which I am ready to try; there's no one here will eat faster than I can.' Utgard-Loki replied: 'That's a feat if you can perform it and we'll put it to the test.' He called over to the very end of the bench that the man called **Logi should** take the floor in front of the company and **pit himself against Loki.** Then a trencher was fetched and brought into the hall and filled with chopped-up meat. Loki sat down at one end and Logi at the other, and each of them ate as fast as he could. They met in the middle of the trencher and by then Loki had left only the bones of his meat, but Logi had eaten all his meat, bones, and trencher into the bargain, so everyone thought that Loki had lost the contest.

"Then Utgard-Loki asked what the youngster there could do. **Thjalfi said he would run a race** against anyone Utgard-Loki produced. Utgard-Loki said that that was a good accomplishment; he reckoned he must be very good at running to perform this feat, yet he agreed it should be tried forthwith. Utgard-Loki got up and went outside then, and there along a level bit of ground was a good running-track. Utgard-Loki called to him a lad whose name was Hugi and told him to run a race with Thjalfi. They ran the first race and Hugi was so far ahead that he turned back to meet Thjalfi at the end of it.

"Then Utgard-Loki said: 'You will have to exert yourself a bit more, Thjalfi, if you are to win this contest and yet it's true that no men have [ever] come here who have struck me as being quicker on their feet than this.' Then they ran the second race and this time when Hugi came to the end and turned round Thjalfi was a long cross-bow shot behind. Utgard-Loki said: 'I think Thjalfi is a good runner, but I don't believe he will win the contest now; we'll prove it, however, when they run the third race.' Then they ran yet another race. Hugi had reached the end and turned back, however, before Thjalfi had come halfway and everyone said that this sport had been put to the test.

"Then Utgard-Loki asked Thor what accomplishment it would be he was going to display to them—after telling such great tales of his mighty deeds. Thor answered that he would like best to pit himself against someone in drinking. Utgard-Loki said that that might well be and went into the hall and calling his cup-bearer bade him fetch the sconce-horn the retainers were accustomed to drink from. The cup-bearer at once came forward with the horn and placed it in Thor's hands.

"Utgard-Loki remarked: 'We consider it good drinking if this horn is drained at one drink, some men take two to empty it, but no one is such a wretched drinker that he can't finish it in three.' Thor looked at the horn. It did not strike him as being very big, although it was a bit on the long side, and he was very thirsty. He began drinking in great gulps and thought he would not need to bend to the horn more than once. When, however, his breath failed and he raised his head from it to see what progress had been made in the drinking, it seemed to him that it was only a little lower in the horn than before.

"Then Utgard-Loki said: 'You drank well but not too much; I would never have believed it if I had been told that Asa-Thor couldn't take a bigger drink. However, I know you will empty it at the second draught.' Thor made no reply, put the horn to his mouth intending to take a bigger drink and strove at the drinking until he was out of breath; yet he saw that the end of the horn would not tilt up as much as he would have liked. When he took the horn from his mouth and looked into it, it seemed to him that he had made still less impression than before, although there was now enough space between the rim and the liquor to carry the horn without spilling.

"Then Utgard-Loki said: 'What about it, Thor? Aren't you leaving more for the one drink left over than will be quite convenient for you? It seems to me, if you are going to empty the horn at the third draught, that this will have to be the biggest. You won't be considered so great a man here amongst us as you are with the Æsir, you know, unless you can give a better account of yourself in other contests than it seems to me you will in this.' At that Thor grew angry, put the horn to his mouth and took a tremendously long drink as hard as he could; and when he looked at the horn, he had at any rate made a slight difference. He then gave up the horn and would drink no more.

"Utgard-Loki remarked: 'It is evident that your strength is not as great as we had imagined. But do you want to make trial of any other feats? It is clear that you don't show to advantage in this one.' Thor answered: 'I can make trial of some feats yet; when I was at home with the Æsir, however, I'd have thought it strange for drinks like these to be called little—what sport are you proposing for me now?"

"Then Utgard-Loki said: 'Youngsters here perform the feat—it's not thought much of—of lifting my cat up from the ground; I would never have suggested such a thing to Asa-Thor if I'd not seen that you aren't nearly as strong as I thought you were.' Thereupon a gray cat jumped forward on to the hall floor. It was rather a big one, but Thor went up to it, put his arm round under the middle of its belly, and lifted up. The cat arched its back as Thor raised his arm, and when he was stretching up as high as he could, the cat had to lift one of its paws [from the floor]; that was all Thor could do in that trial of skill.

"Then Utgard-Loki said: 'This contest has gone as I expected; it's rather a big cat and Thor is a short little fellow compared with such big men as we have here.' At that Thor said: 'Call me little if you like, but **let someone come and wrestle with me now;** now I am angry!' Utgard-Loki looked along the bench and said: 'I don't see anyone here who wouldn't feel it beneath him to wrestle with you.' He added, however, 'Wait a bit, call my foster-mother, the old woman Elli, here, and let Thor wrestle with her if he wants to. She has brought down men who have struck me as being stronger looking than Thor.'

Thor's Contest 1: Drinking

Challenge: To empty the horn in one drink.

This is only one of the many contests in the *Prose Edda*. For a discussion of the role of contests—and that of the *Prose Edda* itself as a contest—see the Introduction, p. 219.

Thor's Contest 2: Physical Strength

Challenge: Lifting Utgard-Loki's cat.

Thor's Contest 3: Wrestling

Challenge: To bring down the opponent

"let someone come and wrestle with me now"—Thor offers to wrestle any opponent.

"I have deceived you with spells"—Utgard-Loki confesses that he had used magic and deceit. In fact, the contests set up for Thor challenged the very nature of the universe.

Trick in Loki's Contest: Loki was competing with fire, one of the elements.

Trick in Thjalfi's Contest: Thjalfi was contending with thought, the limits of what it means to be human.

Trick in Thor's Contest 1: The drinking horn was attached to the sea.

Trick in Thor's Contest 2: The cat was the Midgard Serpent. In trying to lift it, Thor was trying to alter the boundaries of the universe.

Trick in Thor's Contest 3: The opponent was old age. In wrestling her, Thor was trying to overcome the limitation of mortality that is attached to the Icelandic gods, who will perish at Ragnarok. (See Ch. 13, p. 147.)

"with some such magic or other"—Magic wins out over heroic physical deeds. This message is spoken to Thor, but is ominous to the listener, Gylfi.

Utgard-Loki's final trick: The stronghold disappears. This event is mirrored later in the scenes where Gylfi's "contest" is complete and the Æsir stronghold itself disappears. (See p. 153.)

The Death of Baldr

"Baldr the Good"—He represents the sort of absolute that cannot survive in the world. Thus, Loki eliminates Baldr and makes the world a more "normal" place. For more on Baldr, see Introduction, p. 220.

"Thereupon an aged crone came into the hall and Utgard-Loki said she was to come to grips with Asa-Thor. There is no need to make a long story of it. The wrestling went so that the harder Thor exerted himself the firmer she stood her ground. Then the old woman began trying holds and Thor lost his balance; there was a tremendous tussle, but it was not long before Thor fell on to one knee. Utgard-Loki went up to them then and told them to stop wrestling, saying there was no need for Thor to offer to wrestle with any more of his retainers. By that time it was late in the evening. Utgard-Loki showed **Thor and his companions** where to sit down and they stayed there the night and **were shown great hospitality.**

"As soon as dawn broke the next day Thor and his companions got up, dressed, and were ready to go away. Then Utgard-Loki came to where they were and had a table set up for them. There was no lack of good cheer in the way of food and drink. When they had finished the meal, they set out on their journey and Utgard-Loki accompanied them, going out of the stronghold with them. At their parting he addressed Thor, asking him how he thought his journey had turned out and whether he had ever met a man mightier than he [Utgard-Loki] was. Thor replied that he would not deny that he had been put to shame in their dealings with each other, 'I know besides that you'll dub me a nobody and I don't like that.'

"Then Utgard-Loki said: 'I'm going to tell you the truth now that you've come out of the stronghold—if I live and have any say in the matter, you are never going to come inside it again; upon my word you'd never have got in if I'd known you had so much strength; you nearly landed us in disaster. But **I have deceived you with spells** [in] the contests in which you strove against my retainers. The first was what Loki did. He was very hungry and ate fast, but the man called Logi was 'wildfire' and he burned the trencher as quickly as he did the chopped meat. And when Thjalfi was running against the one called Hugi, that was my thought, and Thjalfi couldn't be expected to compete in speed with that. And when you were drinking from the horn and thought you were being slow, upon my word, I never would have believed such a miracle possible; the other end of the horn was in the sea but you didn't perceive that, and now when you come to the ocean you'll see how much you have made it shrink.' That is called the ebb-tide now. He continued: 'I thought it no less wonderful when you lifted up the cat and, to tell you the truth, everyone who saw it was terrified when you lifted one of its paws from the ground. That cat was not what it appeared to be; it was the Midgard Serpent that lies curled round the world and is scarcely long enough head to tail to encircle the earth. You stretched up so high that it wasn't far to the sky. It was a marvelous thing, too, that you held out so long in the wrestling match and only fell down on to one knee when you were struggling with Elli, because there never has been, nor ever will be anyone (if he grows old enough to become aged), who is not tripped up by old age. And now, as a matter of fact, we are going to part and it will be better for us both for you not to come to see me again. I shall go on defending my stronghold **with some such magic or other** so that you will not win any power over me.'

"When Thor heard this speech he gripped his hammer and swung it aloft but, when he was going to strike, he saw no Utgard-Loki. Then he turned round to the stronghold with the idea of destroying it. He saw no stronghold there—[only] spacious and beautiful plains. He turned away and went on his journey until he came back to Thrudvangar. To tell you the truth, however, it was then he resolved to see if he could contrive an encounter with the Midgard Serpent, as he afterwards did. Now I don't think that anyone could tell you a better tale about this expedition of Thor's."

Then Gangleri asked: "Are there any more remarkable stories about the Æsir?"

High One replied: "I will tell you about something that seemed far more important to the Æsir. The beginning of this story is that **Baldr the Good** had some terrible dreams that threatened his life. When he told the Æsir these dreams, they took counsel together and it was decided to seek protection for Baldr from every kind of peril. Frigg exacted an oath from fire and water, iron and all kinds of metals, stones, earth, trees, ailments, beasts, birds, poison and serpents, that they would not harm Baldr. And when this had been done and put to the test, Baldr and **the Æsir used to amuse themselves** by making him stand up at their assemblies for some of them to throw darts at, others to strike and the rest to throw stones at. No matter what was done he was never hurt, and everyone thought that a fine thing. When **Loki,** Laufey's son, saw that, however, he was annoyed that Baldr was not hurt and he **went disguised as a woman** to Fensalir to visit Frigg. Frigg asked this woman if she knew what the Æsir were doing at the assembly. She answered that they were all throwing things at Baldr, moreover that he was not being hurt. Frigg remarked: 'Neither weapons nor trees will injure Baldr; I have taken an oath from them all.' The woman asked: 'Has everything sworn you an oath to spare Baldr?' Frigg replied: 'West of Valhalla grows a little bush called mistletoe, I did not exact an oath from it; I thought it too young.' Thereupon the woman disappeared.

"Loki took hold of the mistletoe, pulled it up and went to the assembly. Now Hod was standing on the outer edge of the circle of men because he was blind. Loki asked him: 'Why aren't you throwing darts at Baldr?' He replied: 'Because I can't see where Baldr is, and, another thing, I have no weapon.' Then Loki said: 'You go and do as the others are doing and show Baldr honor like other men. I will show you where he is standing: throw this twig at him.' Hod took the mistletoe and aimed at Baldr as directed by Loki. The dart went right through him and he fell dead to the ground. This was the greatest misfortune ever to befall gods and men.

"When Baldr had fallen, the Æsir were struck dumb and not one of them could move a finger to lift him up; each looked at the other, and all were of one mind about the perpetrator of that deed, but **no one could take vengeance;** the sanctuary there was so holy. When the Æsir did try to speak, weeping came first, so that no one could tell the other his grief in words. Odin, however, was the most affected by this disaster, since he understood best what a loss and bereavement the death of Baldr was for the Æsir. When the gods had recovered from the first shock **Frigg** spoke. She **asked which of the Æsir wished to win her whole affection and favor.** Would he ride the road to Hel to try if he could find Baldr, and offer Hel a ransom if she would allow Baldr to come home to Asgard? The one who undertook this journey was a son of Odin called Hermod the Bold. Then they caught Odin's horse, Sleipnir, and led him forward, and Hermod mounted that steed and galloped away.

"The Æsir, however, took Baldr's body and carried it down to the sea. Baldr's ship was called Ringhorn, it was a very large ship. **The gods wanted to launch it and to build Baldr's funeral pyre on it,** but they could not move it at all. They sent to Giantland then for the ogress called Hyrrokkin. And when she came—she was riding a wolf with vipers for reins—she jumped off her steed and Odin called to four berserks to guard it, but they were unable to hold it fast till they struck it down. Then Hyrrokkin went to the prow of the vessel and at the first shove launched it in such a way that the rollers burst into flame and the whole world trembled. Thor became angry then and seizing his hammer would have cracked her skull had not all the gods begged protection for her.

"Concerning Hermod, however, there is this to tell. **For nine nights he rode dales so deep and dark that he saw nothing,** till he came to the gates of Hel. Then he alighted and tightened his stirrups, remounted, and dug in his spurs, and the horse jumped over the gate with such vigor that it came nowhere near it. Then Hermod rode right up to the hall and dismounted. He went inside and saw his brother Baldr sitting on the high seat there. Hermod stayed there that night. In the morning he asked Hel if Baldr might ride home with him, telling her how much the gods were weeping. Hel said, however, that this test should be made as to whether Baldr was loved as much as people said. 'If everything in the world, both dead or alive, weeps for

"the Æsir used to amuse themselves"—Once again, the Icelandic gods display their fondness for games and contests.

"Loki . . . went disguised as a woman"—This is interesting in light of the reduced role that goddesses seem to play in these stories. It is also interesting in light of Loki's role as a liminal figure. For more on tricksters as liminal figures, see Ch. 24, p. 354.

"no one could take vengeance"—Despite their rage and grief, the Æsir respect the sanctity of the place.

"Frigg . . . asked which . . . wished to win her . . . favor"—The request, to find Baldr, and pay a ransom to bring him back, reveals a belief that the soul leaves the body after death.

"The gods wanted to launch it and to build Baldr's funeral pyre on it"—This type of sea funeral was customary. Remnants of ship graves have been found in several locations across northern Europe; archeologists estimate that these burials took place from the Iron Age through the 9th c. C.E.

"For nine nights he rode dales so deep and dark that he saw nothing"—Hel is far removed from the places of the living.

"*Bound Devil*." Loki is shown fettered after contriving Baldr's death.

The Punishment of Loki

him, then he shall go back to the Æsir, but he shall remain with Hel if anyone objects or will not weep.'

"Thereupon the Æsir sent messengers throughout the whole world to ask for Baldr to be wept out of Hel; and everything did that—men and beasts, and the earth, and the stones and trees and all metals—**just as you will have seen these things weeping when they come out of frost and into the warmth.** When the messengers were coming home, having made a good job of their errand, they met with a giantess sitting in a cave; she gave her name as Thökk. They asked her to weep Baldr out of Hel. She answered:

> Thökk will weep
> dry tears
> at Baldr's embarkation;
> the old fellow's son
> was no use to me   5
> alive or dead,
> let Hel hold what she has.

It is thought that the giantess there was Loki, Laufey's son—who has done most harm amongst the Æsir."

Then Gangleri said: "Loki has a great deal to answer for, since first he caused Baldr to be killed, and then prevented him from being freed from Hel. Was any vengeance taken on him for this?"

High One said: "This was requited him in a manner he will long remember. When the gods had become as wrathful with him as might be expected, he ran away and hid himself on a mountain. There he built himself a house with four doors so that he could see out of it in all directions. Often during the day, however, he changed himself into the shape of a salmon and hid in the place called the waterfall of Franang.

"The gods saw where he had gone; they went back again to the waterfall and dividing their forces into two groups, while Thor waded in mid-stream, they made for the [open] sea. Then Loki saw that he had only two means of escape, either to risk his life by jumping out to sea or to try once more to leap over the net. He chose the latter, jumping as quickly as possible over its edge-rope. Thor clutched at him and caught him, but he slipped through his hand until he had him fast by the tail, and **it is for this reason that the salmon tapers towards the tail.**

"After that Loki was taken unconditionally and put into a cave. Taking three flat stones, the gods set them up on end and bored a hole through each. Then Loki's sons were captured, Vali and Nari or Narfi. The Æsir changed Vali into a wolf and he tore asunder his brother Narfi. The Æsir took his entrails and with them bound Loki over the edges of the three stones—one under his shoulder, the second under his loins, the third under his kneejoints—and these bonds became iron. Then Skadi took a poisonous snake and fastened it up over him so that the venom from it should drop on to his face. His wife Sigyn, however, sits by him holding a basin under the poison drops.

"When the basin becomes full she goes away to empty it, but in the meantime the venom drips on to his face and then he shudders so violently that **the whole earth shakes—you call that an earthquake.** There he will lie in bonds until Ragnarok."

Further Reading

Davidson, H. R. Ellis. *Gods and Myths of Northern Europe.* London: Penguin Books Ltd., 1964.

Fee, Christopher R., with David A. Leeming. *Gods, Heroes and Kings: The Battle for Mythic Britain.* Oxford: Oxford University Press, 2001.

Sturluson, Snorri. *The Prose Edda: Tales from Norse Mythology.* Trans. Jean I. Young. Berkeley, CA: University of California Press, 1954.

Oedipus the King

SOPHOCLES

WHAT TO EXPECT . . . *Oedipus the King*, by the Greek dramatist Sophocles, is an ancient play based on an even older myth. Because the story was very well known even when this play was written, in the 420s B.C.E., the original Greek audience already knew the outcome and even the particulars of the myth. Therefore, as you read, look out for places where the audience could derive additional enjoyment from an ironic view of what was being said in the performance.

Unless you have read Greek plays before, some aspects of Greek drama may seem strange to you at first. This chapter provides you with an orientation to this classical art form, describing the structure of the Greek theater, the style of performance and its purpose. The role of the chorus in performance in particular may be new to you. Try to imagine as you read a group of Theban men who care deeply about Oedipus, but who are also worried about the fate of their city.

You may also consider the relationship between this play and the other Greek myths found in this book about Prometheus (Ch. 24, p. 353), Demeter (Ch. 27, p. 385), and Heracles (Ch. 31, p. 462), as well as the Greek creation stories in Ch. 3, p. 25. Sophocles' play reappears for consideration in Ch. 25 (p. 361) as a literary myth, in comparison with other kinds of mythic stories. And this play of Sophocles exercised a significant influence on the work of the founder of psychotherapy, Sigmund Freud, and his student Otto Rank, as discussed in the Introduction to Part 3, p. 155.

This play has been compared to a detective story because it describes the efforts of Oedipus, who is the current king of Thebes, to find the murderer of Laios, the previous king. Even though the murder happened many years before, Oedipus takes on the role of the investigator. Through his persistent questioning, even when other characters try to dissuade him, he assembles the evidence which inescapably proves that he himself is the murderer.

A modern mystery story is exciting because the reader is in suspense until the last minute, wondering who committed the crime. On the other hand, the ancient Greeks appreciated and enjoyed this story, even though they knew how it turned out. They came to the theater knowing the story of Oedipus, and this did not spoil the play for them.

The myth of Oedipus had been around at least since about 750 B.C.E., when Homer included it in the *Odyssey* (11.271–80). Versions of the story are included in many ancient works, including Euripides' lost play *Oedipus* and his *Phoenician Women* and Sophocles' *Phoenician Women* (written after 413 B.C.E.). The details of the story vary from version to version. We are not sure of the exact date of Sophocles' version, but scholars think it was written between 429 and 425 B.C.E. In the Sophoclean version, Jocasta hangs herself before Oedipus finds out the truth about his origin. He then blinds himself and leaves Thebes. However, in Euripides' *Phoenician Women,* Jocasta does not hang herself but dies much later, after her sons' death in civil war. In Homer, Oedipus does not blind himself or stop being king of Thebes, as he does in Sophocles (Ahl, 7). For Sophocles' audience, the excitement was contained not in the outcome of the story, but in how Sophocles told it and how he developed his characters.

Greek myths were a part of everyone's education. These stories of the gods and heroes were told and retold to children as well as adults. The major characters of myths were represented on all kinds of household objects, including dishes, vases, and jewelry. As a result, the Greeks knew, even before the play started, that Oedipus himself was the murderer of Laios, even though he himself did not realize it for most of the play. They also knew that Laios was Oedipus' father, so that, without realizing it, Oedipus had killed his own father. Oedipus was really a native Theban who had been taken from his home when he was a baby, and so he did not recognize any of his relatives. And, even worse, after Oedipus killed his father, he came to Thebes and married Jocasta, Laios' widow. Oedipus did not know that Jocasta was his mother, and that the children he had with her were his brothers and sisters, as well as his sons and daughters.

Knowing the solution to the "mystery" in the play certainly took away the suspense for the Greek audience. However, this amusement was replaced with another, equally satisfying activity: the appreciation of irony. Irony is a literary technique that refers to conveying the opposite of what is actually being said. That is, the characters say something, but the audience knows that the opposite is true, either because they have information that the characters do not, or because they know their real personality. Since the audience knew a great deal that Oedipus, the main character, did not, they appreciated the irony of his situation. Oedipus is a great hero and can perform all kinds of great deeds that ordinary people cannot. It is ironic that such a great man is more ignorant than the audience about the most important details of his own private life. The marginal notes will point out some instances where the audience would have understood the irony of Oedipus' situation.

The play provided its audience with some other kinds of irony as well. Even though this play is about Thebes, it was actually written by Sophocles for an audience in Athens. At the time, Athens and Thebes were, for all practical purposes, separate countries. Many scholars believe that Sophocles wrote *Oedipus the King* in 425 B.C.E., when a plague was raging in Athens. The inclusion of the plague in the myth of Oedipus was Sophocles' innovation (Ahl, 35). The audience would have been interested in the horrible disease that is at the core of this play, since they were experiencing an outbreak of it themselves. In the play, Oedipus himself is the cause of the disease in his city. The Athenians may even have looked at each other and wondered if one of them was the cause of the sickness and misery in their own midst.

THE GREEK THEATER

Greek playwrights followed certain conventions that might be unfamiliar to modern audiences. The theater itself did not have a high proscenium stage like most of our theaters. Rather, as shown in the diagram, there was a raised stage surrounded by a large circular area for the chorus. Beyond this, there was arena seating for the audience; as a result, as Peter Arnott notes, there was a significant sense of continuity between the chorus and the audience. The chorus is perhaps the most unfamiliar aspect of a Greek play. We think of choruses today as singers, but the Greek verb *chorizein* means "to dance." The chorus consisted of fifteen characters, all of whom came onstage performing a kind of dance. Their movements were not lyrical and emotive like those of ballet dancers; their dances included a variety of movement, some of which was more like the maneuvers of a marching band. The chorus performed to the music of a flute, singing as they danced.

The chorus actually performed two very different functions in different parts of the play. The play included episodes in which characters talked to each other as they would in a modern play: during these, the leader of the chorus behaved like a character who talked with the other characters. Between episodes, there were choral odes when the chorus moved as a group and sang an elaborate song together while they danced. In the choral odes, the chorus often reflected on the action that had taken place in the previous episode.

The chorus had a special relationship with the main character of the play. They were typically the same gender as that character, and expressed support for him or her. The chorus of *Oedipus the King* represent older men of Thebes who begin as loyal followers of Oedipus and continue to be very sympathetic to him as his misfortunes unfold.

Greek plays were performed with very simple scenery. They were mostly set in front of the doors of a house. Characters appeared in front of the house and often described what went on inside. The audience learned about most of the action through the words of the characters, rather than seeing it directly. In *Oedipus the King,* for instance, we do not see Oedipus kill his father; we hear about the incident from Oedipus himself and from the messenger who was present at the scene. We do not see Jocasta hang herself, rather we hear about it from a servant who reports on what happened inside the house.

In fact, most of the events we learn about have actually happened before the play starts. The drama of the play is the discovery of the events that have already occurred in the life of Oedipus. Greek audiences believed that action of a play should take place within one day. Sophocles describes one day in the life of Oedipus: a very critical day, on which he looks back on the events of his life and sees them in a new way.

This drawing shows the theater of Dionysus in Athens in the 5th c. B.C.E. The audience sat around the circular orchestra, where the chorus danced and from which they interacted with the other characters on the stage. There was a wooden building at the back of the orchestra which often, as in the Oedipus, represented a house. The actors stepped from the house and interacted in front of it, at times reporting the events within.

DOES OEDIPUS HAVE A TRAGIC FLAW?

Aristotle was a famous ancient Greek philosopher who made significant contributions to thought on a wide variety of topics from biology to physics and the nature of art. Even though he wrote in the late fourth century B.C.E., more than a hundred years after Sophocles' play, Aristotle's views have been very influential in coloring the appreciation of the play, and his ideas remain important today. Aristotle thought that the *Oedipus* in many ways represented the best of Greek drama, and he used it as an example at several points in his *Poetics.*

Aristotle had strong ideas about how drama should work, but his views have often been misinterpreted. He is often cited as arguing that the *Oedipus* was a play about a hero with a tragic flaw. This has been taken to mean that in some sense Oedipus did not have free will, but was destroyed by conditions over which he had no control. Of course, Aristotle lived and wrote some hundred years after Sophocles' play was written, so his opinion of it may not reflect either what Sophocles intended or his audience perceived. However, there are even greater problems with using his authority to support the idea of a tragic flaw in a hero. John Jones points out that Aristotle did not believe that plays were about heroes at all: he never used the word "hero" in his discussion of the play. "Tragedy," he says, "is an imitation not of human beings but of action and life, of happiness and misery" (*Poetics* 50a16).

And, in addition, as Jones makes clear, it is a misinterpretation of Aristotle to use him as an authority in the matter of a tragic flaw. He did use the word *hamartia,* which is usually translated "flaw" or even "tragic flaw," but such a translation does not accurately reflect what he was describing. Aristotle believed that, to provide a successful imitation of an action, a play should involve some kind of change of fortune. He described this as follows:

> The well-constructed plot must, therefore, have a single issue, and not (as some maintain) a double. The change of fortune must not be from bad to good but the other way around, from good to bad; and it must be caused, not by wickedness, but by some great error [*hamartia*] on the part of a man such as we have described, or of one better, not worse than that.
>
> (*Poetics* 53a13–17)

In this passage, Aristotle's focus is the plot of the play, not its characters, and he believed that the conditions about plot which he set out in the *Poetics* were achieved by Sophocles in his *Oedipus*.

Each reader will have her or his own view of Sophocles' play and its main character, but Aristotle's ideas should not be taken as meaning that the playwright was writing to show us a man defeated by fate. Classics scholar Bernard M. W. Knox provides an extensive literary analysis of the play, which shows that, in several instances, the play suggests that Oedipus himself chose his actions: they were the result of the kind of person he was and the kinds of choices he freely made. His fate was not forced upon him. For more on the literary themes associated with this play and how they complement its place in the spectrum of Greek mythology, see Chapter 25, p. 361.

Oedipus the King

This text comes from: Sophocles' *Oedipus the King.**

Cast of Characters

Major characters (speaking roles)

Minor characters (nonspeaking roles)

OEDIPUS, king of Thebes
PRIEST of Zeus
KREON, Oedipus' brother-in-law
CHORUS of Theban elders
LEADER of the chorus
TEIRESIAS, prophet, servant to Apollo
JOCASTA, wife of Oedipus
MESSENGER from Corinth
SHEPHERD, member of Laios' household
SERVANT, household slave of Oedipus;
Delegation of Thebans; servants to lead Teiresias and Oedipus; attendants to Oedipus, Kreon, Jocasta; and Antigone and Ismene, the daughters of Oedipus.

Setting the Scene for the Play

"suppliant boughs"—Someone who came asking for help from the gods was a suppliant. To identify themselves, suppliants carried green branches tied with pieces of wool.

"limping"—Oedipus limps because, as a child, he was put out on a mountainside to die with his feet tied together.

> *Dawn. Silence. The royal palace of Thebes. The altar of Apollo to the left of the central palace. A delegation of Thebans—old men, boys, young children—enters the orchestra by the steps below the altar, assembles, and waits. They carry* **suppliant boughs**—*olive branches tied with strips of wool. Some climb the steps between the orchestra and the altar, place their branches on the altar, and return to the orchestra. A PRIEST stands apart from the suppliants at the foot of one of the two stairs. Silence. Waiting. The central doors open. From inside the palace,* **limping,** *OEDIPUS comes through the palace doors and stands at the top of the steps*

---

*From *Oedipus the King* by Sophocles, translated by Stephen Berg and Diskin Clay. Copyright © 1988 by Stephen Berg and Diskin Clay. Used by permission of Oxford University Press, Inc.

leading down into the orchestra. He is dressed in gold and wears a golden crown.

OEDIPUS: **Why, children**,
why are you here, why
are you holding those branches tied with wool,
begging me for help? Children,
the whole city smolders with incense.   5
Wherever I go I hear sobbing, praying. Groans fill the air.
Rumors, news from messengers, they are not enough for me.
Others cannot tell me what you need.
I am king, I had to come. As king,
I had to know. Know for myself, know for me.   10
Everybody everywhere knows who I am: Oedipus. King.
Priest of Zeus, we respect your age, your high office.
Speak.
Why are you kneeling? Are you afraid, old man?
What can I give you?   15
How can I help? Ask.
Ask me anything. Anything at all.
My heart would be a stone
if I felt no pity for these poor shattered people of mine
kneeling here, at my feet.   20
PRIEST: Oedipus, lord of Thebes, you see us, the people of Thebes,
        your people,
crowding in prayer around your altar,
these small children here, old men bent with age, priests, and I, the
        priest of Zeus,
and our noblest young men, the pride and strength of Thebes.
And there are more of us, lord Oedipus, more—gathered in the city,   25
        stunned,
kneeling, offering their branches, praying before the two great
        temples of Athena
or staring into the ashes of burnt offerings, staring,
waiting, waiting for the god to speak.
Look,
look at it,   30
lord Oedipus—right there,
in front of your eyes—this city—
it reels under **a wild storm of blood,** wave after wave battering Thebes.
We cannot breathe or stand.
We hunger, our world shivers with hunger. A disease hungers,   35
nothing grows, wheat, fruit, nothing grows bigger than a seed.
Our women bear
dead things,
all they can do is grieve,
our cattle wither, stumble, drop to the ground,   40
flies simmer on their bloated tongues,
the plague spreads everywhere, a stain seeping through our streets,
        our fields, our houses,

Prologue—The parts of an ancient Greek play were set by tradition and included the Prologue, Parodos, Choral Odes, and Episodes. The start of each of these elements is indicated in the marginalia.

"Why, children"—Oedipus is the king, but he behaves with great tenderness to his subjects. He tries to help the Thebans with their problems, as would a parent taking care of his children.

"Everybody everywhere knows who I am"—The irony here is that everyone *does* know who he is, except for Oedipus. The audience knows that he has killed his father and married his mother. Oedipus himself knows only that he is the king, not the most important fact about himself. However, it is important to recognize that the Theban people, unlike the audience, do not know Oedipus' personal history. This makes possible the abundance of irony in the play. Sophocles uses a variety of puns on the name of Oedipus (which means "swollen foot") to remind the audience of the complex of ideas surrounding the main character. This includes references to a theme of knowledge/ ignorance evoked by puns on the verb οἶδα (oida) which means "I know," and sounds like the word οἰδέω or "to swell, become swollen," as well as a variety of uses of the word πούς (pous), or "foot."

"a wild storm of blood"—The priest describes very vividly the plague which is afflicting Thebes. The Athenian audience would have recognized its characteristics.

look—god's fire eating everyone, everything,
stroke after stroke of lightning, the god stabbing it alive—
it can't be put out, it can't be stopped,   45
its heat thickens the air, it glows like smoking metal,
this god of plague guts our city and fills the black world
          under us where the dead go
with the shrieks of women,
living women, wailing.
You are a man, not a god—I know.   50
We all know this, the young kneeling here before you know it, too,
but **we know how great you are,** Oedipus, greater than any man.
When crisis struck, you saved us here in Thebes,
you faced the mysterious, strange disasters hammered against us by
          the gods.
This is our history—   55
we paid our own flesh to the **Sphinx** until you set us free.
You knew no more than anyone, but you knew.
There was a god in it, a god in you. (*The* PRIEST *kneels.*)
Help us. Oedipus, we beg you, we all turn to you, kneeling to your
          greatness.
Advice from the gods or advice from human beings—you   60
          will know which is needed.
But help us. Power and experience are yours, all yours.
Between thought and action, between
our plans and their results a distance opens.
Only a man like you, Oedipus, tested by experience,
can make them one. That much I know.   65
Oedipus, **more like a god than any man alive,**
deliver us, raise us to our feet. Remember who you are.
Remember your love for Thebes. Your skill was our salvation once
          before.
For this Thebes calls you savior.
Don't let us remember you as the king—godlike in power—   70
who gave us back our life, then let us die.
Steady us forever. You broke **the riddle** for us then.
It was a sign. A god was in it. Be the man you were—
rule now as you ruled before.
Oh Oedipus,   75
how much better to rule a city of men than be king of
          empty earth.
A city is nothing, a ship is nothing
where no men live together, where no men work together.
OEDIPUS: Children, poor helpless children,
I know what brings you here, I know.   80
You suffer, this plague is agony for each of you,
but none of you, **not one suffers as I do.**
Each of you suffers for himself, only himself.
My whole being wails and breaks
for this city, for myself, for all of you,   85
old man, all of you.

"we know how great you are"—Although Oedipus is a man, he seems like a god. This is often a characteristic of heroes.

Sphinx Creature with the head of a woman, the body of a bird, and the hindquarters of a lion. When Oedipus first came to Thebes, she was terrorizing the countryside. He correctly answered the riddle she asked everyone and defeated her.

"more like a god than any man alive"—Once again, the priest compares Oedipus to a god.

"the riddle"—The Sphinx asked what were the creatures that walked on four legs, two legs, and three legs. Oedipus answered that they were humans, who crawled when they were young, walked on two feet in their prime, and used a cane when they were old.

"not one suffers as I do"—Oedipus shares the sufferings of his people. In addition, he is a man of action: he has already recognized the problem and has already taken action to help Thebes.

Everything ends here, with me. I am the man.
You have not wakened me from some kind of sleep.
I have wept, struggled, wandered in this maze of thought,
tried every road, searched hard—   90
finally I found one cure, only one:
I sent my wife's brother, **Kreon,** to great **Apollo**'s shrine at Delphi;
I sent him to learn what I must say or do to save Thebes.
But his long absence troubles me. Why isn't he here?
        Where is he?
When he returns, what kind of man would I be   95
if I failed to do everything the god reveals?

Kreon Oedipus introduces his brother-in-law, who will be appearing on stage in a minute.

Apollo God of the sun, poetry, and medicine. He also had a dark side and could send plague as well as healing.

> *Some of the suppliants by the steps to the orchestra stand to announce* KREON'S *arrival to the* PRIEST. KREON *comes in by the entrance to the audience's left with a garland on his head.*

PRIEST: You speak of Kreon, and Kreon is here.
OEDIPUS *(turning to the altar of Apollo, then to* KREON*):*
Lord Apollo, look at him—his head is crowned with laurel, his eyes
        glitter.
Let his words blaze, blaze like his eyes, and save us.   100
PRIEST: He looks calm, radiant, like a god. If he brought bad news,
would he be wearing that crown of sparkling leaves?
OEDIPUS: At last we will know.
Lord Kreon, what did the god Apollo say?
KREON: His words are hopeful.   105
Once everything is clear, exposed to the light,
we will see our suffering is blessing. All we need is luck.
OEDIPUS: What do you mean? What did Apollo say? What should
        we do?
Speak.
KREON: Here? Now? In front of all these people?   110
Or inside, privately?
KREON *moves toward the palace.*
OEDIPUS: Stop. **Say it.** Say it to the whole city.
I grieve for them, for their sorrow and loss, far more than I grieve
        for myself.

"Say it"—Oedipus does not want to have secret meetings. He is open with his people.

KREON: This is what I heard—there was no mistaking the   115
        god's meaning—
Apollo commands us:
Cleanse the city of Thebes, cleanse the plague from that city,
destroy the black stain spreading everywhere, spreading,
poisoning the earth, touching each house, each citizen,
sickening the hearts of the people of Thebes!   120
Cure this disease that wastes all of you, spreading, spreading,
before it grows so vast nothing can cure it
OEDIPUS: What is this plague?
How can we purify the city?
KREON: **A man must be banished.** Banished or killed.   125
Blood for blood. The plague is blood,
blood, breaking over Thebes.
OEDIPUS: *Who* is the man? *Who* is Apollo's victim?

"A man must be banished"—As the play goes on, we learn that the man is Oedipus.

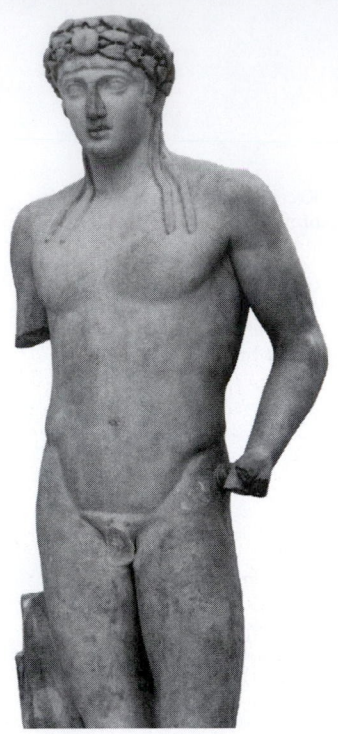

Apollo, Roman after a Greek 5th-c. B.C.E. original. Budapest Museum of Fine Art. The god is a commanding presence in this play. It is his oracle that prophesies Oedipus' fate, and the play represents him as one of the chief divinities of Thebes.

"not one man"—If more than one man had been involved, then Oedipus, who was alone, could not have done the killing.

"How could a single bandit"—The first suggestion that Oedipus suspects there was a plot to kill Laios.

"I will reveal the truth"—The audience knows Oedipus will accomplish this, but he himself does not recognize the price he will pay.

"the dead man"—The dead man is Laios, Oedipus' father.

KREON: My lord, before you came to Thebes, before you came
        to power,
Laios was our king   130
OEDIPUS: I know. But I never saw Laios.
KREON: Laios was murdered. Apollo's command was very clear:
Avenge the murderers of Laios. Whoever they are.
OEDIPUS: But where *are* his murderers?
The crime is old. How will we find their tracks?   135
The killers could be anywhere.
KREON: Apollo said the killers are still here, here in Thebes.
Pursue a thing, and you may catch it;
ignored, it slips away.
OEDIPUS: And Laios—where was he murdered?   140
At home? Or was he away from Thebes?
KREON: He told us before he left—he was on a mission to Delphi,
his last trip away from Thebes. He never returned.
OEDIPUS: Wasn't there a witness, someone with Laios who saw what
        happened?
KREON: They were all killed, except for one man. He escaped.   145
But he was so terrified he remembered only one thing.
OEDIPUS: What was it? One small clue might lead to others.
KREON: This is what he said: bandits ambushed Laios, **not one man.**
They attacked him like hail crushing a stalk of wheat.
OEDIPUS: **How could a single bandit** dare attack a king   150
unless he had supporters, people with money, here,
here in Thebes?
KREON: There were suspicions. But after Laios died we had no
        leader, no king.
Our life was turmoil, uncertainty.
OEDIPUS: But once the throne was empty,   155
what threw you off the track, what kept you from searching
until you uncovered everything, knew every detail?
KREON: The intricate, hard song of the Sphinx
persuaded us the crime was not important, not then.
It seemed to say we should focus on what lay at our feet, in front of us, 160
ignore what we could not see.
OEDIPUS: Now *I* am here.
I will begin the search again. **I
will reveal the truth,** expose everything, let it all be seen.
Apollo and you were right to make us wonder about **the dead man.**   165
Like Apollo, I am your ally.
Justice and vengeance are what I want,
for Thebes, for the god.
Family, friends—I won't rid myself of this stain, this disease,
        for them—
they're far from here. I'll do it for myself, for me.   170
The man who killed Laios might take revenge on me
just as violently.
So by avenging Laios' death, I protect myself.
(turning to the suppliants) Rise, children,

pick up your branches, 175
let someone announce my decision to the whole city of Thebes.
(*to the* PRIEST) I will do everything. Everything.
And, with the god's help, we will be saved.
Bright Apollo, let your light help us see.
Our happiness is yours to give, our failure and ruin yours. 180
PRIEST: Rise. We have the help we came for, children.
The king himself has promised.
May Apollo, who gave these oracles, come as our savior now.
Apollo, heal us, save us from this plague!

> OEDIPUS *enters the palace. Its doors close.* KREON *leaves by a door to the right on the wing of the stage. The* PRIEST *and suppliants go down into the orchestra and leave by the entrance to the left as a chorus of fifteen Theban elders files into the orchestra by the entrance on the right, preceded by a flute player.*

CHORUS: **Voice**   voice   voice 185
voice who knows everything o god
glorious voice of **Zeus**
how have you come from Delphi bathed in gold
what are you telling our bright city Thebes
what are you bringing me 190
health death fear
I know nothing
so frightened rooted here
awed by you
healer what have you sent 195
is it the sudden doom of grief
or the old curse the darkness
looming in the turning season
o holy immortal voice
hope golden seed of the future 200
listen be with me speak
these cries of mine rise
tell me
I call to you reach out to you first
holy **Athena** god's daughter who lives forever 205
and your sister Artemis
who cradles the earth our earth
who sits on her great throne at the hub of the market place
and I call to **Apollo** who hurls light
from deep in the sky 210
o gods be with us now
shine on us your three shields
blazing against the darkness
come in our suffering as you came once before
to Thebes o bright divinities 215
and threw your saving light against the god of grief
o gods
be with us now
pain pain my sorrows have no sound

Parados—The chorus enters, moving together in formation, in three rows of five. Their dance is a bit like the movement of a marching band. As they dance, they sing together as one body.

"Voice voice voice"—The language of the chorus is different from that of the rest of the characters. They do not speak in complete sentences. Rather, their emotional phrases are meant to express how upset they are. Their language makes a kind of emotional sense, but is not always understandable on the rational level.

Zeus Greek head god.

Athena Goddess of wisdom, and patron of the city of Athens. She, Artemis, and Apollo are viewed here as the patron gods of Thebes.

Apollo God of the sun, poetry, and medicine. He is the god of healing, but also of destruction.

"pain pain"—In the opening of the play, the priest described the effects of the plague almost clinically. Here the chorus shows what it feels like.

no name no word no pain like this   220
plague sears my people everywhere
everyone army citizens no one escapes
no spear of strong anxious thought protects us
great Thebes grows nothing
seeds rot in the ground   225
our women when they labor
cry Apollo Apollo but their children die
and lives one after another split the air
birds taking off
wingrush hungrier than fire   230
souls leaping away they fly
to the shore
of the **cold god of evening**

> "cold god of evening"—Hades, god of the underworld.

west
he death stain spreads   235
so many corpses lie in the streets everywhere
nobody grieves for them
the city dies and young wives
and mothers gray-haired mothers wail
sob on the altar steps   240
they come from the city everywhere mourning their bitter days
prayers blaze to the Healer
grief cries a flute mingling
daughter of Zeus o shining daughter show us
the warm bright face of peace of help   245
of our salvation

       The doors of the palace open. OEDIPUS *enters.*

and **turn back the huge raging jaws of the death god Ares**

> "turn back . . . the death god Ares"—It is not clear why the chorus prays to Ares here. The first time the plague hit Athens, the city was at war with Sparta. The chorus seems to see the plague as caused by the war, and thus by the war god.

drive him back drive him away
his flames lash at me
this is his war these are his shields   250
shouts pierce us on all sides

> **Ares**   God of war.

turn him back lift him on a strong wind
rush him away
to the two seas at the world's edge
the sea where the waters boil   255
the sea where no traveler can land
because if night leaves anything alive
day destroys it
o Zeus
god beyond all other gods   260
handler of the fire

> "handler of the fire"—Zeus' special weapon was the lightning bolt.

father
make the god of our sickness
ashes

> "great bowman of light"—This expression combines Apollo's role as god of the sun and his special weapon, the bow.

Apollo   265
great bowman of light draw back your bow
fire arrow after arrow

make them a wall circling us
shoot into our enemy's eyes
draw the string twined with gold   270
come **goddess**
who dances on the mountains
sowing light where your feet brush the ground
blind our enemy come
god of golden hair   275
piled under your golden cap **Bacchus**
your face blazing like the sea when the sun falls on it
like sunlight on wine
god whose name is our name Bacchus
god of joy god of terror   280
be with us now your bright face
like a pine torch roaring
thrust into the face of the slaughtering war god
blind him
drive him down from Olympus   285
drive him away from Thebes
forever
OEDIPUS: Every word of your prayers has touched me.
Listen. Follow me. Join me in fighting this sickness, this plague,
and all your sufferings may end, like a dark sky,   290
clear suddenly, blue, after a week of storms,
soothing the torn face of the sea,
soothing our fears.
Your fate looms in my words—
I heard nothing about Laios' death,   295
I know nothing about the murder,
I was alone, how could I have tracked the killer, without a clue,
I came to Thebes after the crime was done,
I was made a Theban after Laios' death. Listen carefully—
these words come from an innocent man.   300
(*Addressing the* CHORUS.) One of you knows who killed Laios.
Where is that man?
Speak.
I command it. Fear is no excuse.
He must clear himself of the dangerous charge.   305
Who did this thing?
Was it a stranger?
Speak.
I will not harm him. The worst he will suffer is exile.
I will pay him well. He will have a king's thanks.   310
But if he will not speak because he fears me,
if he fears what I will do to him or to those he loves,
if he will not obey me,
I say to him:
My power is absolute in Thebes, my rule reaches everywhere,   315
my words will drive the guilty man, the man who knows,
out of this city, away from Thebes, forever.

"goddess who dances on the mountains"—Artemis, goddess of the hunt.

Bacchus (or Dionysus) God of wine. He usually appears as a young man with long blond hair, holding a torch made of a stick with a pinecone stuck onto it. He is especially Theban because his mother, Semele, was a daughter of Cadmus, the founder of Thebes.

"I know nothing about the murder"—Oedipus knows more than he supposes about Laios' death: this is ironic. Here Oedipus' ignorance is once again put in terms of the verb "to know."

 Episode 1

Artemis of Ephesos, Capitoline Museum. The statue shows the virgin goddess, sister of Apollo, covered in bulls' testicles, presumably to emphasize the power derived from her virgin state.

"Let him be nothing"—Here Oedipus creates his own fate. There
are those who see him as trapped
by the fate Apollo has given him—
to kill his father and marry his
mother. He makes his own fate
even worse, however, by decreeing
exile for the man who killed Laios.
Exile does not just mean moving
from one city to another. It means
leaving your home, where you can
vote and own a business, and
going to a place where you can do
neither. By the end of the play,
Oedipus, by his own decree, will
be "nothing."

Nothing.
My word for him is nothing.
Let him be nothing.   320
Give him nothing
Let him touch nothing of yours, he is nothing to you.
Lock your doors when he approaches.
Say nothing to him, do not speak.
No prayers with him, no offerings with him.   325
No purifying water.
Nothing.
Drive him from your homes. Let him have no home, nothing.
No words, no food, shelter, warmth of hand, shared worship.
Let him have nothing. Drive him out, let him die.   330
He is our disease.
                 I know.
                         Apollo has made it clear.
Nothing can stop me, nothing can change my words.
I fight for Apollo, I fight for the dead man.   335
You see me, you hear me, moving against the killer.
My words are his doom.
Whether he did it alone, and escaped unseen,
whether others helped him kill, it makes no difference—
let my hatred burn out his life, hatred, always.   340
Make him an ember of suffering.
Make all his happiness
ashes.

"If he eats at my side"—These
ironic lines help remind the audience that Oedipus, without knowing it, is cursing himself.

If he eats at my side, sits at my sacred hearth, and I know these things,
let every curse I spit out against him find me,   345
come home to me.
Carry out my orders. You must,
for me, for Apollo, and for Thebes, Thebes,
this poor wasted city,
deserted by its gods.   350
I know—the gods have given us this disease.
That makes no difference. You should have acted,
you should have done something long ago to purge our guilt.
The victim was noble, a king—
you should have done everything to track his murderer down.   355
And so,
because I rule now where he ruled;

"because I share his bed"—Here
the audience is reminded that
Oedipus is sleeping with his own
mother.

because I share his bed, his wife;
because the same woman who mothered my children might have mothered his;
because fate swooped out of nowhere and cut him down;   360
because of all these things

"as I would fight for my own murdered father"—This is ironic: Laios
was Oedipus' father, but he does
not realize this yet.

I will fight for him **as I would fight for my own murdered father.**
Nothing will stop me.
No man, no place, nothing will escape my gaze. I will not stop
until I know it all, all, until everything is clear.   365
For every king, every king's son and his sons,
for every royal generation of Thebes, *my* Thebes,

I will expose the killer, I will reveal him
to the light.
Oh gods, gods, 370
destroy all those who will not listen, will not obey.
Freeze the ground until they starve.
Make their wives barren as stone.
Let this disease that shakes Thebes to its roots—
or any worse disease, if there is any worse than this—waste them, 375
crush everything they have, everything they are.
But you men of Thebes—
you, who know my words are right, who obey me—
may justice and the gods defend you, bless you,
graciously, forever. 380

LEADER: Your curse forces me to speak, Master.
I cannot escape it.
I did not murder the king, I cannot show you the man who did.
Apollo told us to search for the killer.
Apollo must name him. 385

OEDIPUS: No man can force the gods to speak.

LEADER: Then I will say the next best thing.

OEDIPUS: If there's a third best thing, say that too.

LEADER: **Teiresias** sees what the god Apollo sees.
Truth, truth. 390
If you heard the god speaking, heard his voice,
you might see more, more, and more.

OEDIPUS: Teiresias? **I have seen to that already.**
Kreon spoke of Teiresias, and I sent for him. **Twice.**
I find it strange he still hasn't come. 395

LEADER: And there's an old story, almost forgotten,
a dark, faded rumor.

OEDIPUS: What rumor? **I must sift each story,**
see it, understand it.

LEADER: Laios was killed by bandits. 400

OEDIPUS: I have heard that story: but who can show me the man who saw the
        murderer?
Has anyone seen him?

LEADER: If he knows the meaning of fear,
if he heard those curses you spoke against him,
those words still scorching the air, 405
you won't find him now, not in Thebes.

OEDIPUS: The man *murdered*. Why would words frighten him?
    TEIRESIAS has appeared from the stage entrance to the right of the audience. He
    walks with a staff and is helped by a slave boy and attendants. He stops at some dis-
    tance from center stage.

LEADER: **Here is the man who can catch the criminal.**
They're bringing him now—
the godlike prophet who speaks with the voice of god. 410
He, only he, knows truth.
The truth is rooted in his soul.

OEDIPUS: Teiresias, you understand all things,

LEADER The leader of the chorus interacts with the other characters, representing the viewpoint of the chorus.

Teiresias This prophet was struck blind by Hera when he issued an opinion unfavorable to her.

"I have seen to that already"—Sending for Teiresias was not Kreon's idea, but Oedipus'.

"Twice"—Teiresias has been reluctant to come: Oedipus has been sending for him without avail.

"I must sift each story"—Here we see Oedipus' drive to be the detective.

"Here is the man who can catch the criminal."—Ironically, the chorus leader is right: Teiresias does know the truth. That is why he has been so reluctant to come.

Earle Hyman as Teiresias in a production by The Shakespeare Theater in Washington, D.C.

"Study the cries of birds"—Oedipus recommends that Teiresias use the standard techniques of prophets to learn the will of the gods: study how birds are acting and study the remains of sacrifices burned to the gods.

"What have *you* said that helps Thebes?"—The prophet begins to challenge the king.

"my grief"—His knowledge makes Teiresias sad. In addition, he knows that Oedipus will not believe him.

"Stubborn old fool"—Since Oedipus is ignorant, his anger is, from his point of view, reasonable.

what can be taught, what is locked in silence,
the distant things of heaven, and things that crawl the earth.   415
You cannot see, yet you know the nature of this plague infesting our city.
Only you, my lord, can save us, only you can defend us.
Apollo told our messenger—did you hear?—
that we could be saved only by tracking down Laios' killers,
only by killing them, or sending them into exile.   420
Help us, Teiresias.
Study the cries of birds, study their wild paths,
ponder the signs of fire, use all your skills of prophecy.
Rescue us, preserve us.
Rescue yourself, rescue Thebes, rescue me.   425
Cleanse every trace of the growing stain left by the dead man's blood.
We are in your hands, Teiresias.
No work is more nobly human than helping others,
helping with all the strength and skill we possess.
TEIRESIAS: Wisdom is a curse   430
when wisdom does nothing for the man who has it.
Once I knew this well, but I forgot.
I never should have come.
OEDIPUS: Never should have come? Why this reluctance, prophet?
TEIRESIAS: Let me go home.   435
That way is best, for you, for me.
Let me live my life, and you live yours.
OEDIPUS: Strange words, Teiresias, cruel to the city that gave you life.
Your holy knowledge could save Thebes. How can you keep silent?
TEIRESIAS: **What have *you* said that helps Thebes?** Your words   440
          are wasted.
I would rather be silent than waste my words.
OEDIPUS Look at us, *(stands, the CHORUS kneel)*:
kneeling to you, Teiresias, imploring you.
In the name of the gods, if you know—
help us, tell us what you know.   445
TEIRESIAS: You kneel because you do not understand.
But I will never let you see **my grief.** Never.
My grief is yours.
OEDIPUS: What? You know and won't speak?
You'd betray us all, you'd destroy the city of Thebes?   450
TEIRESIAS: I will do nothing to hurt myself, or you. Why insist?
I will not speak.
OEDIPUS: **Stubborn old fool,** you'd make a rock angry!
Tell me what you know! Say it!
Where are your feelings? Won't you ever speak?   455
TEIRESIAS: You call me cold, stubborn, unfeeling, you insult
          me. But you,
Oedipus, what do you know about yourself,
about your real feelings?
You don't see how much alike we are.
OEDIPUS: How can *I* restrain my anger when I see how little you   460
          care for Thebes.

TEIRESIAS: The truth will come, by itself,
the truth will come
no matter how I shroud it in silence.
OEDIPUS: All the more reason why you should speak.
TEIRESIAS: Not another word.   465
Rage away. You will never make me speak.
OEDIPUS: I'll rage, prophet, I'll give you all my anger.
I'll say it all—
Listen: I think you were involved in the murder of Laios,
you helped plan it, I think you   470
did everything in your power to kill Laios,
everything but strike him with your own hands,
and if you weren't blind, if you still had eyes to see with,
I'd say you, and you alone, did it all.
TEIRESIAS: Do you think so? Then obey your own words, obey   475
the curse everyone heard break from your own lips:
Never speak again to these men of Thebes,
never speak again to me.
                                You, it's
you.   480
What plagues the city is you.
The plague is you.
OEDIPUS: Do you know what you're saying?
Do you think I'll let you get away with these vile accusations?
TEIRESIAS: I am safe.   485
Truth lives in me, and the truth is strong.
OEDIPUS: **Who taught you this truth of yours?** Not your
        prophet's craft.
TEIRESIAS: *You* taught me. You forced me to speak.
OEDIPUS: Speak what? Explain. Teach me.
TEIRESIAS: Didn't you understand?   490
Are you trying to make me say the word?
OEDIPUS: What word? Say it. Spit it out.
TEIRESIAS: Murderer.
I say *you,*
you are the killer you're searching for.   495
OEDIPUS: You won't say *that* again to me and get away with it.
TEIRESIAS: Do you want more? Shall I make you really angry?
OEDIPUS: Say anything you like. Your words are wasted.
TEIRESIAS: I say you live in shame, and you do not know it,
do not know that you   500
and those you love most
wallow in shame,
you do not know
in what shame you live.
OEDIPUS: You'll pay for these insults, I swear it.   505
TEIRESIAS: Not if the truth is strong.
OEDIPUS: The truth is strong, but not your truth.
You have no truth. **You're blind.**
Blind in your eyes. Blind in your ears. Blind in your mind.

"I'll say it all"—Oedipus expands on his earlier suspicion that there was a plot to kill Laios, now believing that Teiresias was involved with it.

"Who taught you this truth of yours?"—Oedipus is really saying, "who told you to tell this lie?" At the same time, he questions the value of prophecy, but it is he himself who is ignorant.

"You're blind."—Ironic: it is Oedipus who will be blind by the end of the play.

TEIRESIAS: And I pity you for mocking my blindness.   510
Soon everyone in Thebes will mock you, Oedipus. They'll
> mock you
as you have mocked me.
OEDIPUS: One endless night swaddles you in its unbroken black
> sky.
You can't hurt me, you can't hurt anyone who sees the light of
> day.
TEIRESIAS: True. Nothing I do will harm you. You, you   515
and your fate belong to Apollo.
Apollo will see to you.
OEDIPUS: Are these your own lies, prophet—or Kreon's?
TEIRESIAS: Kreon? Your plague is you, not Kreon.
OEDIPUS: Money, power, one great skill surpassing another,   520
if a man has these things, other men's envy grows and grows,
their greed and hunger are insatiable.
Most men would lust for a life like mine—but I did not demand
> my life,
Thebes gave me my life, and from the beginning, **my good friend
> Kreon,**
loyal, trusted Kreon,   525
was reaching for my power, wanted to ambush me, get rid of
> me by hiring this cheap wizard,
this crass, conniving priest, who sees nothing but profit,
whose prophecy is simple profit. You,
what did you ever do that proves you a real seer? What did you
> ever see, prophet?
And when the Sphinx who sang mysteriously   530
imprisoned us
why didn't you speak and set us free?
No ordinary man could have solved her riddle,
it took prophecy, prophecy and skill you clearly never had.
Even the paths of birds, even the gods' voices were useless.   535
But I showed up, I, Oedipus,
stupid, untutored Oedipus,
I silenced her, I destroyed her, **I used my wits, not omens,**
to sift the meaning of her song.
And this is the man you want to kill so you can get close to   540
> King Kreon,
weigh his affairs for him, advise him, influence him.
No, I think you and your master, Kreon, who contrived this plot,
will be whipped out of Thebes.
Look at you.
If you weren't so old, and weak, oh   545
I'd make you pay
for this conspiracy of yours.
LEADER: Oedipus, both of you spoke in anger.
Anger is not what we need.
We need all our wits, all our energy to interpret Apollo's words.   550
Then we will know what to do.

"my good friend Kreon"—Oedipus now believes that Kreon has betrayed him, so *he* is being ironic. The basis of Oedipus' suspicions is that it was Kreon who recommended Teiresias.

"this crass, conniving priest"— Oedipus shows that, although he summoned the prophet as Kreon suggested, he himself does not think well of prophets.

"I used my wits, not omens"— Oedipus is used to relying on his quick wit, but here it leads him astray. He jumps to the conclusion that there was a plot to kill Laios, and that Teiresias and Kreon were involved with it. Oedipus has decided that Kreon told him to send for Teiresias as part of a plot to discredit him and take over the throne.

TEIRESIAS: Oedipus, **you are king, but you must hear my reply.**
My right to speak is just as valid as yours.
I am not your slave. Kreon is not my patron.
My master is Apollo. I can say what I please.   555
You insulted me. You mocked me. You called me blind.
Now hear me speak, Oedipus.
You have eyes to see with,
but you do not see yourself, you do not see
the horror shadowing every step of your life,   560
the blind shame in which you live,
you do not see where you live and who lives with you,
lives always at your side.
Tell me, Oedipus, **who are your parents?**
Do you know?   565
You do not even know
the shame and grief you have brought your family,
those still alive, those buried beneath the earth.
But the curse of your mother, the curse of your father
will whip you, whip you again and again, wherever you turn,   570
it will whip you out of Thebes forever,
our clear eyes flooded with darkness.
That day will come.
And then what scoured, homeless plain, what leafless tree,
what place on **Kithairon,**   575
where no other humans are or ever will be,
where the wind is the only thing that moves,
what raw track of thorns and stones, what rock, gulley,
or blind hill won't echo your screams, your howls of anguish
when you find out that the marriage song,   580
sung when you came to Thebes, heard in your house,
guided you to *this* shore, this wilderness
you thought was home, *your* home?
And you do not see
all the other awful things   585
that will show you who you really are, show you
to your children, face to face.
Go ahead! Call me quack, abuse Kreon, insult Apollo, the god
who speaks through me, whose words move on my lips.
No man will ever know worse suffering than you,   590
your life, your flesh, your happiness an ember of pain. Ashes.
OEDIPUS (*to the* CHORUS): Must I stand here and listen to these
       attacks?
TEIRESIAS (*beginning to move away*): I am here, Oedipus, because
       you sent for me.

OEDIPUS: You old fool,
I'd have thought twice before asking you to come   595
if I had known you'd spew out such idiocy.
TEIRESIAS: Call me fool, if you like, but your parents,
who gave you life, they respected my judgment.

"you are king, but you must hear my reply"—Teiresias emphasizes the irony of the taunt Oedipus made earlier. It is Oedipus who will be blind by the end of the play. He will stab out his own eyes, when he learns that he has killed his father and married his mother.

"who are your parents?"—Angry, Teiresias strikes back at Oedipus, raising an issue that concerns his adversary. Oedipus left Corinth, where he was raised, because he was worried about who his real parents were. A drunk at a feast had called him a bastard, so Oedipus left Corinth to ask the Delphic oracle about his origins. He never returned to Corinth.

"Do you know?"—Teiresias here focuses on the theme of knowledge; in Greek this is another pun on Oedipus' name.

Kithairon High desolate mountain to the south of Thebes.

In this 19th-c. painting, Ingres represents Oedipus as engaged in a philosophical exchange, rather than a deadly struggle, with the Sphinx.

OEDIPUS: Parents?
     What do you mean?   600
       Who are my mother and father?
TEIRESIAS: This day is your mother and father—this day
will give you **your birth,**
it will destroy you, too.

"your birth"—The birth the prophet refers to is a birth of self-understanding.

OEDIPUS: How you love mysterious, twisted words.
TEIRESIAS: Aren't you the great solver of riddles?   605
Aren't you Oedipus?
OEDIPUS: Taunt me for the gift of my brilliant mind.
That gift is what makes me great.
TEIRESIAS: That gift is your destiny. It made you everything you are,
and it has ruined you.   610
OEDIPUS: But if this gift of mine saved Thebes, who cares what
   happens to me?
TEIRESIAS: I'm leaving. Boy, take me home.
OEDIPUS: Good. Take him home. Here
I keep stumbling over you, here you're in my way.
Scuttle home, and leave us in peace!   615

"I keep stumbling over you"—Irony: it is blind men who stumble over things.

TEIRESIAS: I'm going. I said what I came to say,
and that scowl, darkening your face, doesn't frighten me. How can
   you hurt me?

I tell you again:
the man you've been trying to expose—
with all your threats, with your inquest into Laios' murder   620
that man is here, in Thebes.
Now people think he comes from Corinth, but later
they will see he was born in Thebes.
When they know, he'll have no pleasure in that news.
Now he has eyes to see with, but they will be slashed out;   625
rich and powerful now, he will be a beggar,
poking his way with a stick, feeling his way to a strange country.
And his children—the children he lives with—
will see him at last, see what he is, see who he really is:
their brother and their father; his wife's son, his mother's husband;   630
the lover who slept with his father's wife; the man who murdered
        his father—
the man whose hands still drip with his father's blood.
These truths will be revealed.
Go inside and ponder that riddle, and if you find I've lied,
then call me a prophet who cannot see.   635

> OEDIPUS *turns and enters the palace.* TEIRESIAS *is led out*
> *through the stage entrance on the right.*

CHORUS: Who did crimes unnameable things
things words cringe at
which man did the rock of prophecy at Delphi say
did these things
his hands dripping with blood   640
he should run now flee
his strong feet swallowing the air
stronger than the horses of storm winds
their hooves slicing the air
now in his armor   645
Apollo lunges at him
his infinite branching fire reaches out
and the steady dread death-hungry **Fates** follow and never stop
their quick scissors seeking the cloth of his life
just now   650
from high snowy **Parnassus**
the god's voice exploded its blazing message
follow his track find the man
no one knows
a bull loose under wild bushes and trees   655
among caves and gray rocks
cut from the herd he runs and runs but runs nowhere
zigzagging desperate to get away
birds of prophecy birds of death circling his head
forever   660
voices forged at the white stone core of the earth
they go where he goes always
terror's in me flooding me
how can I judge

⟡ **Choral Ode 1**

"which man"—The chorus refers
to an earlier issue in the previous
scene: who could be the murderer of Laios?

Fates Goddesses who spin the
thread which represents the life
of a human (Clotho), measure
it out (Lachesis), and cut it off,
causing her or his death
(Atropos).

Parnassus Delphi, the shrine of
Apollo, is located in the southern
slopes of Mount Parnassus.

"a feud wounding the families of Laios or Oedipus"—In a trilogy dated 467 B.C.E., Aeschylus, another Greek dramatist, told a different version of the story of Oedipus and his family. Charles Segal explains that the *Laios,* a lost play of that trilogy, probably told the story of how Oedipus' father fell in love with Chrysippus' son, Pelops, and kidnapped him. Chrysippus killed himself in shame, and Pelops cursed Laios and his family (46). Sophocles, in his version of the story, minimizes the issue of a family curse, but there is a hint of it here. See the remarks of Claude Levi-Strauss for a different view of the significance of the history of Oedipus' family, Ch. 20, p. 284.

Episode 2

what the god Apollo says   665
trapped hoping confused
I do not see what is here now
when I look to the past I see nothing
I know nothing about **a feud**
wounding the families of Laios or Oedipus   670
no clue to the truth then or now
nothing to blacken his golden fame in Thebes
and help Laios' family
solve the mystery of his death
Zeus and Apollo know   675
they understand
only they see
the dark threads crossing beneath our life
but no man can say a prophet sees more than I
one man surpasses another   680
wisdom against wisdom skill against skill
but I will not blame Oedipus
whatever anyone says
until words are as real as things
one thing is clear   685
years back the Sphinx tested him
his answer was true
he was wise and sweet to the city
so he can never be evil
not to me   690
        KREON enters through the stage entrance at right, and
        addresses the CHORUS.
KREON: Men of Thebes, I hear Oedipus, our king and master,
has brought terrible charges against me.
I have come to face those charges. I resent them bitterly.
If he imagines I have hurt him, spoken or acted against him
while our city dies, believe me—I have nothing left to live for. 695
His accusations pierce me, wound me mortally—
nothing they touch is trivial, private—
if you, my family and friends,
think I'm a traitor, if all Thebes believes it, says it.
LEADER: Perhaps he spoke in anger, without thinking,   700
perhaps his anger made him accuse you.
KREON: Did he really say I persuaded Teiresias to lie?
LEADER: I heard him say these things,
but I don't know what they mean.
KREON: Did he look you in the eyes when he accused me?   705
Was he in his right mind?
LEADER I do not know or see what great men do. *(turning to*
        OEDIPUS, *who has emerged from the palace):*
But here he is—Oedipus.
OEDIPUS: What? You here? Murderer!
You dare come here, to my palace, when it's clear   710
you've been plotting to murder me and seize the throne of Thebes?

You're the bandit, you're the killer.

Answer me—

Did you think I was cowardly or stupid?
Is that why you betrayed me?   715
Did you really think I wouldn't see what you were plotting,
how you crept up on me like a cloud inching across the sun?
Did you think I wouldn't defend myself against you?
You thought I was a fool, but the fool was you, Kreon.
Thrones are won with money and men, you fool!   720
KREON: You have said enough, Oedipus. Now let me reply.
Weigh my words against your charges, then judge for yourself.
OEDIPUS: Eloquent, Kreon. But you won't convince me now.
Now that I know your hatred, your malice.
KREON: Let me explain.   725
OEDIPUS: Explain?
What could explain your treachery?
KREON: If you think this stubborn anger of yours, this perversity,
is something to be proud of, you're mad.
OEDIPUS: And if you think you can injure your sister's husband,   730
    and not pay for it, you're mad.
KREON: I would be mad to hurt you. How have I hurt you?
OEDIPUS: Was it you who advised me to send for that great holy
    prophet?
KREON: Yes, and I'd do it again.
OEDIPUS: How long has it been since Laios disappeared?
KREON: Disappeared?   735
OEDIPUS: Died. Was murdered. . . .
KREON: Many, many years.
OEDIPUS: And this prophet of yours—was he practicing his trade
    at the time?
KREON: With as much skill, wisdom and honor as ever.
OEDIPUS: Did he ever mention my name?   740
KREON: Not in my presence.
OEDIPUS: Was there an inquest? A formal inquiry?
KREON: Of course. Nothing was ever discovered.
OEDIPUS: Then why didn't our wonderful prophet, our Theban
    wizard, denounce me as the murderer then?
KREON: I don't know. And when I don't know, I don't speak.   745
OEDIPUS: But you know this. You know it with perfect certainty.
KREON: What do you mean?
OEDIPUS: This: if you and Teiresias were not conspiring against me,
Teiresias would never have charged me with Laios' murder.
KREON: If he said that, you should know.   750
But now, Oedipus, it's my right, my turn to question you.
OEDIPUS: Ask anything. You'll never prove I killed Laios.
KREON: Did you marry my sister, Jocasta?
OEDIPUS: I married Jocasta.
KREON: And you gave her an equal share of the power in Thebes?   755
OEDIPUS: Whatever she wants is hers.
KREON: And I share that power equally with you and her?

Domenico Fetti, *Socrates instructing two pupils.* In the dialogue with Oedipus, Kreon employs the method usually known as "Socratic questioning" to allow Oedipus to see that it would not be to his advantage to try to take over the throne of Thebes. The Greeks associated this technique with the philosophers known as the Sophists, who were seen as modern, successful thinkers. Sophocles wants his audience to make that connection, to show the great range of abilities achieved by human beings in his time. For more on the philosophical dimensions of the play, see Knox, (135–36).

OEDIPUS: Equally.
And that's precisely why it's clear you're false, treacherous.
KREON: No, Oedipus.   760
Consider it rationally, as I have. Reflect:
What man, what sane man, would prefer a king's power
with all its dangers and anxieties,
when he could enjoy that same power, without its cares,
and sleep in peace each night? Power?   765
I have no instinct for power, no hunger for it either.
It isn't royal power I want, but its advantages.
And any sensible man would want the same.
Look at the life I lead. Whatever I want, I get from you,
with your goodwill and blessing. I have nothing to fear.   770
If I were king, my life would be constant duty and constraint.
Why would I want your power or the throne of Thebes
more than what I enjoy now—the privilege of power
without its dangers? I would be a fool to want more
than what I have—the substance, not the show, of power.   775
As matters stand, no man envies me, I am courted
and admired by all. **Men wear no smiling masks for Kreon.**
And those who want something from you come to me
because the way to royal favor lies through me.
Tell me, Oedipus, why should I give these blessings up   780
to seize your throne and all the dangers it confers?
A man like me, who knows his mortal limits and accepts them,
cannot be vicious or treacherous by nature.
The love of power is not my nature, nor is treason
or the thoughts of treason that go with love of power.   785
I would never dare conspire against your life.
Do you want to test the truth of what I say?

"Men wear no smiling masks for Kreon"—Is Kreon suggesting that Thebans flatter Oedipus, and are afraid to bring their problems to him directly? He may be speaking in general here, or as Ahl suggests, his remarks may be a pointed attack on his adversary in this debate (115).

As a result of many earthquakes, the *great temple of Apollo at Delphi* is in ruins today, but it is still possible to imagine the grandeur of this site on the slope of Mount Parnassus.

Go to Delphi, put the question to the oracle,
ask if I have told you exactly what Apollo said.
Then if you find that Teiresias and I have plotted against you,   790
seize me and put me to death. Convict me
not by one vote alone, but two—yours and mine, Oedipus.
But don't convict me on the strength of your suspicions,
don't confuse friends with traitors, traitors with friends.
There's no justice in that.   795
To throw away a good and loyal friend
is to destroy what you love most—
your own life, and what makes life worth living.
Someday you will know the truth:
time, only time reveals the good man;   800
one day's light reveals the evil man.
LEADER: Good words
for someone careful, afraid he'll fall.
But a mind like lightning
stumbles.   805
OEDIPUS: When a clever man plots against me and moves swiftly
I must move just as swiftly, I must plan.
But if I wait, if I do nothing, he will win, win everything,
and I will lose.
KREON: What do you want? My exile?   810
OEDIPUS: No. Your death.
KREON: You won't change your mind? You won't believe me?
OEDIPUS: I'll believe you when you teach me the meaning of envy.
KREON: Envy? You talk about envy. You don't even know what
        sense is.
Can't you listen to me?   815
OEDIPUS: I am listening. To my own good sense.
KREON: Listen to *me*. I have sense on my side too.
OEDIPUS: You? You were born devious.
KREON: And if you're wrong?
OEDIPUS: I still must govern.   820
KREON: Not if you govern badly.
OEDIPUS: Oh Thebes, Thebes . . .
KREON: Thebes is mine too.
LEADER (*turning to* **JOCASTA,** *who has entered from the palace,*
        accompanied by a woman attendant):
Stop. I see   825
Jocasta coming from the palace
just in time, my lords, to help you
settle this deep, bitter feud raging between you.
Listen to what she says.
JOCASTA: Oedipus! Kreon! Why this insane quarreling?   830
You should be ashamed, both of you. Forget yourselves.
This is no time for petty personal bickering.
Thebes is sick, dying.
        —Come inside, Oedipus
—And you, Kreon, leave us.   835

JOCASTA Oedipus' wife appears and breaks up the quarrel, like a mother separating fighting boys.

Must you create all this misery over nothing, nothing?

KREON: Jocasta,

Oedipus has given me two impossible choices:

Either I must be banished from Thebes, my city, my home,

or be arrested and put to death.   840

OEDIPUS: That's right.

I caught him plotting against me, Jocasta.

Viciously, cunningly plotting against the king of Thebes.

KREON: Take every pleasure I have in life, curse me, let me die,

if I've done what you accuse me of, **let the gods**   845

destroy everything I have, let them do anything to me.

I stand here, exposed to their infinite power.

JOCASTA: Oedipus, in the name of the gods, believe him.

His prayer has made him holy, naked to the mysterious

whims of the gods, has taken him beyond what is human.   850

Respect his words, respect me, respect these men standing at your side.

CHORUS (*beginning a dirge-like appeal to* OEDIPUS):

listen to her

think yield

we implore you   855

OEDIPUS: What do you want?

CHORUS: be generous to Kreon give him respect

he was never foolish before

now his prayer to the gods has made him great

great and frightening   860

OEDIPUS: Do you know what you're asking?

CHORUS: I know

OEDIPUS: Then say it.

CHORUS: don't ever cut him off

without rights or honor   865

blood binds you both

his prayer has made him sacred

don't accuse him

because some blind suspicion hounds you

OEDIPUS: Understand me: 870

when you ask for these things

you ask for my death or exile.

CHORUS: no

by the sun

the god who bathes us in his light   875

who sees all

I will die godless no family no friends

if what I ask means that

it is Thebes

Thebes dying wasting away life by life   880

this is the misery

that breaks my heart

and now this quarrel raging between you and Kreon

is more more than I can bear

OEDIPUS: Then let him go, **even if it means I must die**   885

"let the gods destroy everything I have"—By calling on the gods to judge him, Kreon strengthens his case in the eyes of Jocasta and the chorus.

"even if it means I must die"—Oedipus believes that if Kreon remains alive, he will plot against him and destroy him.

or be forced out of Thebes forever, stripped of all my rights,
    all my honors.
Your grief, your words touch me. Not his.
I pity you. But him,
my hatred will reach him wherever he goes.
KREON: It's clear **you hate to yield,** clear   890
you yield only under pressure, only
when you've worn out the fierceness of your anger.
Then all you can do is sit, and brood.
Natures like yours are a torment to themselves.
OEDIPUS: Leave. Go!   895

> "you hate to yield"—Kreon is correctly describing Oedipus' personality. In some circumstances, his unyielding nature makes him an effective ruler, but it is a liability here.

KREON: I'm going. Now I know
you do not know me.
But these men know I am the man I seem to be, a just man,
not devious, not a traitor.
      KREON *leaves.*
CHORUS: woman why are you waiting   900
lead him inside comfort him
JOCASTA: Not before I know what has happened here.
CHORUS: blind ignorant words suspicion without proof
the injustice of it
gnaws at us   905
JOCASTA: From both men?
CHORUS: yes
JOCASTA: What caused it?
CHORUS: enough enough
no more words   910
Thebes is so tormented now
let it rest where it ended
OEDIPUS: Look where cooling my rage,
where all your decent, practical thoughts have led you.
CHORUS: Oedipus I have said this many times   915
I would be mad helpless to give advice
if I turned against you now
once
you took our city in her storm of pain
straightened her course found fair weather   920
o lead her to safety now
if you can

> "straightened her course"—The chorus describes Oedipus as a captain who led his ship (the city of Thebes) to safety in a storm (the assault of the Sphinx).

JOCASTA: If you love the gods, tell me, too, Oedipus—
      I implore you—
why are you still so angry, why can't you let it go?
OEDIPUS: I will tell you, Jocasta.   925
You mean more, far more to me than these men here.
Jocasta, it is Kreon—Kreon and his plots against me.
JOCASTA: What started your quarrel?
OEDIPUS: He said I murdered Laios.
JOCASTA: Does he know something? Or is it pure hearsay?   930
OEDIPUS: He sent me a vicious, trouble-making prophet
to avoid implicating himself. He did not say it to my face.

"no mortal can practice the art of prophecy"—Like her husband, Jocasta does not believe in the effectiveness of prophecy. Here she describes very personal reasons for her lack of faith.

"cut down at a crossroads"—It is this a reference that Oedipus reacts strongly to below: Laios was killed at a crossroads.

"abandon our child on a mountain"—Putting a child out to be destroyed by the elements was a common, if cruel, form of ancient Greek population control. Exposure, as it was called, was often practiced on girls, deformed children, and, as here, on children who were not wanted for other reasons. Oedipus' parents thought he would bring them bad luck. There are many stories from around the world about children cast out by their parents, as Oedipus was. All of the figures in these stories grew up to be great heroes.

"it flashed through my mind"—Oedipus is beginning to remember killing someone at a crossroads. If it turns out to be Laios, he has cursed himself by cursing the murderer.

JOCASTA: Oedipus, forget all this. Listen to me:
no mortal can practise the art of prophecy, no man can see the
    future.
One experience of mine will show you why.   935
Long ago an oracle came to Laios.
It came not from Apollo himself but from his priests.
It said Laios was doomed to be murdered by a son, his son and mine.
But Laios, from what we heard, was murdered by bandits from a
    foreign country,
cut down at a crossroads. My poor baby   940
was only three days old when Laios had his feet pierced together
    behind the ankles
and gave orders to **abandon our child on a mountain,** leave him
    alone to die
in a wilderness of rocks and bare gray trees
where there were no roads, no people.
So you see—Apollo didn't make that child his father's killer,   945
Laios wasn't murdered by his son. That dreadful act which so terrified
    Laios—
it never happened.
All those oracular voices meant was nothing, nothing.
Ignore them.
Apollo creates. Apollo reveals. He needs no help from men.   950
OEDIPUS (*who has been very still*):
While you were speaking, Jocasta; **it flashed through my mind**
like wind suddenly ruffling a stretch of calm sea.
It stuns me. I can almost see it—some memory, some image.
My heart races and swells—   955
JOCASTA: Why are you so strangely excited, Oedipus?
OEDIPUS: You said Laios was cut down *near* a crossroads?
JOCASTA: That was the story. It hasn't changed.
OEDIPUS: Where did it happen? Tell me. Where?
JOCASTA: In Phokis. Where the roads from Delphi and Daulis meet.   960
OEDIPUS: When?
JOCASTA: Just before you came to Thebes and assumed power.
Just before you were proclaimed King.
OEDIPUS: O Zeus, Zeus,
what are you doing with my life?   965
JOCASTA: Why are you so disturbed, Oedipus?
OEDIPUS: Don't ask me. Not yet.
                    Tell me about Laios.
How old was he? What did he look like?
JOCASTA: Streaks of gray were beginning to show in his black hair.   970
He was tall, strong—built something like you.
OEDIPUS: No! O gods, o
it seems each hard, arrogant curse
I spit out
was meant for me, and I   975
didn't
know it!

JOCASTA: Oedipus, what do you mean? Your face is so strange.
You frighten me.
OEDIPUS: It is frightening—can the blind prophet see, can he
    really see?   980
I would know if you told me . . .
JOCASTA: I'm afraid to ask, Oedipus.
Told you what?
OEDIPUS: Was Laios traveling with a small escort
or with many armed men, like a king?   985
JOCASTA: There were five, including a herald.
Laios was riding in his chariot.
OEDIPUS: Light, o light, light
now everything, everything is clear. All of it.
Who told you this? Who was it?   990
JOCASTA: A household slave. The only survivor.
OEDIPUS: Is he here, in Thebes?
JOCASTA: No. When he returned and saw that you were king
and learned Laios was dead, he came to me and clutched my hand,
begged me to send him to the mountains   995
where shepherds graze their flocks, far from the city,
so he could never see Thebes again.
I sent him, of course. He deserved that much, for a slave, and more.
OEDIPUS: Can he be called back? Now?
JOCASTA: Easily. But why?   1000
OEDIPUS: I am afraid I may have said too much—
I must see him.
Now.
JOCASTA: Then he will come.
But surely I have a right to know what disturbs you, Oedipus.   1005
OEDIPUS: Now that I've come this far, Jocasta,
hope torturing me, each step of mine heavy with fear,
I won't keep anything from you.
Wandering through the mazes of a fate like this,
how could I confide in anyone but you?   1010
My father was Polybos, of Corinth.
My mother, Merope, was Dorian.
Everyone in Corinth saw me as its first citizen
but one day something happened,
something strange, puzzling. Puzzling, but nothing more.   1015
Still, it worried me.
One night, I was at a banquet,
and a man—he was very drunk—said I wasn't my father's son,
called me "bastard." That stung me, I was shocked.
I could barely control my anger, I lay awake all night.   1020
The next day I went to my father and mother,
I questioned them about the man and what he said.
They were furious with him, outraged by his insult,
and I was reassured. But I kept hearing the word "bastard" "bastard"—
I couldn't get it out of my head.   1025
Without my parents' knowledge, I went to Delphi: I wanted the truth,

Marble relief, 3rd C. C.E., from a sarcophagus showing *Oedipus sacrificing to the Delphic Oracle* in front of
a statue of Apollo.

but Apollo refused to answer me.
And yet he did reveal other things, he did show me
a future dark with torment, evil, horror,
he made me *see*—   1030
see myself, doomed to sleep with my own mother, doomed
to bring children into this world where the sun pours down,
children no one could bear to see, doomed
to murder the man who gave me life, whose blood is *my* blood.
        My father.
And after I heard all this, I fled Corinth,   1035
measuring my progress by the stars, searching for a place
where I would never see those words, those dreadful predictions
come true. And on my way
I came to the place where you say King Laios was murdered.
Jocasta, the story I'm about to tell you is the truth: 1040
I was on the road, near the crossroads you mentioned,
when I met a herald, with an old man, just as you described him.
The man was riding in a chariot
and his driver tried to push me off the road
and when he shoved me I hit him. I hit him.   1045
The old man stood quiet in the chariot until I passed under him,
then he leaned out and caught me on the head with an ugly goad—
its two teeth wounded me—and with this hand of mine,
this hand clenched around my staff,
I struck him back even harder—so hard, so quick he couldn't dodge it,   1050
and he toppled out of the chariot and hit the ground, face up.
I killed them. Every one of them. I still see them.
(*to the* CHORUS)

If this stranger and Laios
are somehow linked by blood,   1055
tell me what man's torment equals mine?
Citizens, hear my curse again—
Give this man nothing. Let him touch nothing of yours.
Lock your doors when he approaches.
Say nothing to him when he approaches.   1060
                                    And these, these curses,
with my own mouth I
spoke these monstrous curses against myself.
(OEDIPUS *turns back to* JOCASTA)
These hands, these bloodstained hands made love to you in your
        dead husband's bed,   1065
these hands murdered him.
If I must be exiled, never to see my family,
never to walk the soil of my country
so I will not sleep with my mother
and will kill Polybos, my father, who raised me—his son!—   1070
wasn't I born evil—answer me!—**Isn't every part of me**
unclean? Oh
some unknown god, some savage venomous demon must have done
        this, raging, swollen with hatred. Hatred

"If this stranger and Laios are somehow linked"—This is ironic: Oedipus has already committed the acts he is worried about here.

"Isn't every part of me unclean?"—Oedipus has gone from being a self-confident ruler to dreading and raging at unknown demons.

for me.   1075
Holiness, pure, radiant powers, o gods
don't let me see that day,
don't let it come, take me away
from men, men with their eyes, hide me
before I see   1080
the filthy black stain reaching down over me, into me.
   (The CHORUS have moved away from the stage)
LEADER: Your words make us shudder, Oedipus,
but hope, hope
until you hear more from the man who witnessed the murder.   1085
OEDIPUS: That is the only hope I have. Waiting.
Waiting for that man to come from the pastures.
JOCASTA: And when he finally comes, what do you hope to learn?
OEDIPUS: If his story matches yours, I am saved.
JOCASTA: What makes you say that?   1090
OEDIPUS: Bandits—you said he told you bandits killed Laios.
So if he still talks about bandits,
more than one, I couldn't have killed Laios.
One man is not the same as many men.
But if he speaks of one man, traveling alone,   1095
then all the evidence points to me.
JOCASTA: Believe me, Oedipus, those were his words.
And he can't take them back: the whole city heard him, not only me.
And if he changes only the smallest detail of his story,
that still won't prove Laios was murdered as the oracle foretold.   1100
Apollo was clear—it was Laios' fate to be killed by my son,
but my poor child died before his father died.
The future has no shape. **The shapes of prophecy lie.**
I see nothing in them, they are all illusions.
OEDIPUS: Even so, I want that shepherd summoned here.   1105
Now. Do it now.
JOCASTA: I'll send for him immediately. But come inside.
My only wish is to please you.
      JOCASTA dispatches a servant.

CHORUS: fate
be here let what I say be pure   1110
let all my acts be pure
laws forged in the huge clear fields of heaven
rove the sky
shaping my words limiting what I do
Olympus made those laws not men who live and die   1115
nothing lulls those laws to sleep
they cannot die
and the infinite god in them never ages
arrogance insatiable pride
breed the tyrant   1120
feed him on thing after thing blindly
at the wrong time uselessly
and he grows reaches so high

"The shapes of prophecy lie"—
Jocasta again finds the issue that
concerned her earlier, the falseness
of oracles in general and of the one
about her child in particular.

 Choral Ode 2

"Olympus made those laws not
men who live and die"—At times,
the Greeks saw their gods as *tran-*
scendent, or distant from the
world of human beings, as here.
(See Ch. 5, p. 51.)

"arrogance insatiable pride breed
the tyrant"—Some scholars have
seen these comments as referring
directly to the tyrannical way Oedipus has behaved, especially to
Kreon. Charles Segal points out
that the chorus has been consistently on Oedipus' side, though
(120). He believes that here it is
contrasting the horrible fate the
oracles seem to have in store for
Oedipus with the uprightness of
his life. Choruses in Greek plays
often speak in mysterious ways.

nothing can stop his fall
his feet thrashing the air standing on nothing 1125
and nowhere to stand he plunges down
o god shatter the tyrant
but let men compete let self-perfection grow
let men sharpen their skills
soldiers citizens building the good city 1130
Apollo
protect me always
always the god I will honor
if a man walks through his life arrogant
strutting proud 1135
says anything does anything
does not fear justice
fear the gods bow to their shining presences
let fate make him stumble in his tracks
for all his lecheries and headlong greed 1140
if he takes whatever he wants right or wrong
if he touches forbidden things
what man who acts like this would boast
he can escape the anger of the gods
why should I join these sacred public dances 1145
if such acts are honored
no
I will never go to the holy untouchable stone
navel of the earth at Delphi
never again 1150
go to the temples at Olympia at Abai
if all these things are not joined
if past present future are not made one
made clear to mortal eyes
o Zeus if that is your name 1155
power above all immortal king
see these things look
those great prophecies are fading
men say they're nothing
nobody prays to the god of light no one believes 1160
nothing of the gods stays.

> JOCASTA *enters from the palace, carrying a branch tied with*
> *strands of wool and a jar of incense (the symbols of a suppliant).*
> *She is accompanied by a servant woman. She addresses the*
> CHORUS.

Lords of Thebes, I come to the temples of the god
with offerings—this incense and this branch.
So many thoughts torture Oedipus. He never rests.
He acts without reason. He is like a man 1165
who has lost everything he knows—the past
is useless to him; strange, new things baffle him.
And if someone talks disaster, it stuns him: he listens, he is afraid.
I have tried to reassure him, but nothing helps.

"if he takes whatever he wants"—This could be about Oedipus or about evil men in general.

"I will never go to the holy untouchable stone"—The beliefs of the chorus involve faith in oracles. The current situation threatens them in a complex way. Either they must reject Oedipus, their highly esteemed ruler, or they must question the tenets of their religion.

 Episode 3

So I have come to you—   1170
Apollo, close to my life, close to this house,
listen to my prayers: *(she kneels)*
                    help us purify ourselves of this disease,
help us survive the long night of our suffering,
protect us. We are afraid when we see Oedipus confused   1175
and frightened—Oedipus, the only man who can pilot Thebes
to safety.

> *A* MESSENGER *from Corinth has arrived by the entrance to the*
> *orchestra on the audience's left. He sees* JOCASTA *praying, then*
> *turns to address the* CHORUS.

MESSENGER: Friends,
can you tell me **where King Oedipus lives**
or better still, where I can find him?   1180
LEADER: Here, in this house.
This lady is his **wife and mother**
of his children.
MESSENGER: May you and your family prosper.
May you be happy always under this great roof.   1185
JOCASTA: Happiness and prosperity to you, too, for your kind words.
But why are you here? Do you bring news?
MESSENGER: Good news for your house, good news for King Oedipus.
JOCASTA: What is your news? Who sent you?
MESSENGER: I come from Corinth, and what I have to say I know   1190
    will bring you joy.
And pain perhaps. . . . I do not know.
JOCASTA: Both joy and pain? What news could do that?
MESSENGER: The people of Corinth want Oedipus as their king.
That's what they're saying.
JOCASTA: But isn't old Polybos still king of Corinth?   1195
MESSENGER: His kingdom is his grave.
JOCASTA: Polybos is *dead?*
MESSENGER: If I'm lying, my lady, let me die for it.
JOCASTA: You. *(To a servant)* Go in and tell Oedipus.
O oracles of the gods, where are you now!   1200
This man, the man Oedipus was afraid he would murder,
the man he feared, the man he fled from has died a natural death.
Oedipus didn't kill him, it was **luck,** luck.
She turns to greet OEDIPUS *as he comes out of the palace.*
OEDIPUS: Jocasta, why did you send for me? *(taking her gently by*   1205
    the arm)
JOCASTA: Oedipus,
listen to this man, see what those ominous, holy predictions of Apollo
    mean now.
OEDIPUS: Who is this man? What does he say?
JOCASTA: He comes from Corinth.
Your father is dead. Polybos is dead!   1210
OEDIPUS: What?
Let me hear those words from your own mouth, stranger.
Tell me yourself, in your own words.

"Apollo, close to my life"—Jocasta expresses a reverence for Apollo here that is unexpected in the light of her earlier skepticism about oracles. The Oedipus she describes is no longer a commanding and capable leader.

"where King Oedipus lives"—In Greek, the messenger's question is formulated in what Knox calls a "fantastic" series of variations on the expression "to know where" (184). This group of puns is intended to remind the audience that Oedipus, who claims to know so much, is ignorant of the fundamental facts about where he came from.

"wife and mother"—This unintentionally describes Jocasta's relationship to Oedipus.

Luck, Fortune Greek goddess Tyche or chance. Her worship replaces other gods. If chance rules our lives, there is no need to behave morally, or to seek the favor of other deities

MESSENGER: If that's what you want to hear first, then I'll say it:
Polybos is dead.   1215
OEDIPUS: How did he die? Assassination? Illness? How?
MESSENGER: An old man's life hangs by a fragile thread. Anything
    can snap it.
OEDIPUS: That poor old man. It was illness then?
MESSENGER: Illness and old age.
OEDIPUS: Why, Jocasta,   1220
why should men look to the great hearth at Delphi
or listen to birds shrieking and wheeling overhead—
cries meaning I was doomed to kill my father?
He is dead, gone, covered by the earth.
And here I am—my hands never even touched a spear—   1225
I did not kill him,
unless he died from wanting me to come home.
No. Polybos has bundled up all these oracles
and taken them with him to the world below.
They are only words now, lost in the air.   1230
JOCASTA: Isn't that what I predicted?
OEDIPUS: You were right. My fears confused me.
JOCASTA: You have nothing to fear. Not now. Not ever.
OEDIPUS: But the oracle said I am doomed to sleep with my mother.
How can I live with that and not be afraid?   1235
JOCASTA: Why should men be afraid of anything? Fortune rules
    our lives.
Luck is everything. Things happen. The future is darkness.
No human mind can know it.
It's best to live in the moment, live for today, Oedipus.
Why should the thought of marrying your mother make you so afraid?   1240
Many men have slept with their mothers in their dreams.
Why worry? See your dreams for what they are—nothing, nothing
    at all.
Be happy, Oedipus.
OEDIPUS: All that you say is right, Jocasta. I know it.
I should be happy,   1245
but my mother is still living. As long as she's alive,
I live in fear. This fear is necessary.
I have no choice.
JOCASTA: But Oedipus, your father's death is a sign, a great sign—
the sky has cleared, the sun's gaze holds us in its warm, hopeful light.   1250
OEDIPUS: A great sign, I agree. But so long as my mother is alive,
my fear lives too.
MESSENGER: Who is this woman you fear so much?
OEDIPUS: Merope, King Polybos wife.
MESSENGER: Why does Merope frighten you so much?   1255
OEDIPUS: A harrowing oracle hurled down upon us by some
    great god.
MESSENGER: Can you tell me? Or did the god seal your lips?
OEDIPUS: I can.
Long ago, Apollo told me I was doomed to sleep with my mother

"Many men have slept with their mothers in their dreams"—Freud drew on this observation of Jocasta's in formulating his "Oedipus principle." See Part 3 Introduction, p. 155.

"but my mother is still living"—Ironic, as Jocasta is standing there.

and spill my father's blood, murder him   1260
with these two hands of mine.
That's why I never returned to Corinth. Luckily, it would seem.
Still, nothing on earth is sweeter to a man's eyes
than the sight of his father and mother.
MESSENGER: And you left Corinth because of this prophecy?   1265
OEDIPUS: Yes. And because of my father. To avoid killing my father.
MESSENGER: But didn't my news prove you have nothing to fear?
I brought good news.
OEDIPUS: And I will reward you for your kindness.
MESSENGER: That's why I came, my lord. I knew you'd remember me   1270
when you returned to Corinth.
OEDIPUS: I will never return, never live with my parents again.
MESSENGER: Son, it's clear you don't know what you're doing.
OEDIPUS: What do you mean? In the name of the gods, speak.
MESSENGER: If you're afraid to go home because of your parents.   1275
OEDIPUS: I *am* afraid, afraid
Apollo's prediction will come true, all of it,
as god's sunlight grows brighter on a man's face at dawn
when he's in bed, still sleeping,
and reaches into his eyes and wakes him.   1280
MESSENGER: Afraid of murdering your father, of having his blood
on your hands?
OEDIPUS: Yes. His blood. The stain of his blood. That terror never
     leaves me.
MESSENGER: But Oedipus, then you have no reason to be afraid.
OEDIPUS: I'm their son, they're my parents, aren't they?   1285
MESSENGER: Polybos is nothing to you.
OEDIPUS: Polybos is not my father?
MESSENGER: No more than I am.
OEDIPUS: But you are nothing to me. Nothing.
MESSENGER: And Polybos is nothing to you either.   1290
OEDIPUS: Then why did he call me his son?
MESSENGER: Because I gave you to him. With these hands
I gave you to him.
OEDIPUS: How could he have loved me like a father if I am not
     his son?
MESSENGER: He had no children. That opened his heart.   1295
OEDIPUS: And what about you?
Did you buy me from someone? Or did you find me?
MESSENGER: I found you squawling, left alone to die in the thickets
     of Kithairon.
OEDIPUS: Kithairon? What were you doing on Kithairon?
MESSENGER: Herding sheep in the high summer pastures.   1300
OEDIPUS: You were a shepherd, a drifter looking for work?
MESSENGER: A drifter, yes, but it was I who saved you.
OEDIPUS: Saved me? Was I hurt when you picked me up?
MESSENGER: Ask your feet.
OEDIPUS: Why,   1305
why did you bring up that childhood pain?

MESSENGER: I cut you free. Your feet were pierced, tied together at
    the ankles
with leather thongs strung between the tendons and the bone.

OEDIPUS: That mark of my shame—I've worn it from the cradle.

MESSENGER: That mark is the meaning of your name: 1310
Oedipus, **Swollenfoot**, Oedipus.

OEDIPUS: Oh gods
who did this to me?
My mother?
My father?   1315

MESSENGER: I don't know. The man I took you from—he would
    know.

OEDIPUS: So you didn't find me? Somebody else gave me to you?

MESSENGER: I got you from another shepherd.

OEDIPUS: What shepherd? Who was he? Do you know?

MESSENGER: As I recall, he worked for Laios.   1320

OEDIPUS: The same Laios who was king of Thebes?

MESSENGER: The same Laios. The man was one of Laios' shepherds.

OEDIPUS: Is he still alive? I want to see this man.

MESSENGER *(pointing to the CHORUS)*: These people would know
    that better than I do.

OEDIPUS: Do any of you know this shepherd he's talking about?   1325
Have you ever noticed him in the fields or in the city?
Answer, if you have.
It is time everything came out, time everything was made clear.
Everything.

LEADER: I think he's the shepherd you sent for.   1330
But Jocasta, she would know.

OEDIPUS *(to JOCASTA):* Jocasta, do you know this man?
Is he the man this shepherd here says worked for Laios?

JOCASTA: **What man?** Forget about him. Forget what was said.
It's not worth talking about.   1335

OEDIPUS: How can I forget
with clues like these in my hands?
With the secret of my birth staring me in the face?

JOCASTA: No, Oedipus!
No more questions.   1340
For god's sake, for the sake of your own life!
Isn't my anguish enough—more than enough?

OEDIPUS: You have nothing to fear, Jocasta.
Even if my mother
and her mother before her were both slaves,   1345
that doesn't make you **the daughter of slaves.**

JOCASTA: Oedipus, you must stop.
                        I beg you—stop!

OEDIPUS: Nothing can stop me now. I must know everything.
Everything!   1350

JOCASTA: I implore you, Oedipus. For your own good.

OEDIPUS: Damn my own good!

JOCASTA: Oh, Oedipus, Oedipus

Swollenfoot Oedipus means "swollen foot."

"What man?"—Jocasta recognizes the man as the shepherd to whom she gave her baby, long ago.

"with clues like these"—Oedipus, like a detective, wants to follow the available clues.

"Isn't my anguish enough"—Jocasta has figured out that Oedipus is the child she gave to the shepherd.

"the daughter of slaves"—Oedipus thinks that Jocasta is worried that his mother was a slave.

I pray to god you never see who you are!
OEDIPUS *(to one of the attendants, who hurries off through the exit*   1355
     stage left):
You there, go find that shepherd, bring him here.
Let that woman bask in the glory of her noble birth.
JOCASTA: God help you, Oedipus—
you were born to suffer, born
to misery and grief.   1360
These are the last last words I will ever speak, ever
Oedipus.
(JOCASTA *rushes offstage into the palace. Long silence.)*
LEADER: Why did Jocasta rush away,
Oedipus, fleeing in such pain?   1365
I fear disaster, or worse,
will break from this silence of hers.
OEDIPUS: Let it break! Let everything break!
I must discover who I am, know the secret of my birth,
no matter how humble, how vile.   1370
Perhaps Jocasta is ashamed of my low birth, ashamed to be my wife.
Like all women she's proud.
But Luck, Goddess who gives men all that is good, made me,
and I won't be cheated of what is mine, nothing can dishonor me, ever.
I am like the months, my brothers the months—they shaped me   1375
when I was a baby in the cold hills of Kithairon,
they guided me, carved out my times of greatness,
and they still move their hands over my life.
I am the man I am. I will not stop
until I discover who my parents are.   1380
CHORUS: If I know if I see
if the dark force of prophecy is mine
Kithairon
when the full moon
rides over us tomorrow   1385
listen listen to us sing to you
dance worship praise you
mountain where Oedipus was found
know Oedipus will praise you
praise his nurse country and mother   1390
who blessed our king
I call on you Apollo
let these visions please you
god Apollo
healer   1395
Oedipus son
who was your mother
which of the deathless mountain nymphs who lay
with the great god Pan
on the high peaks he runs across   1400
or with Apollo
who loves the high green pastures above

Fortuna Nemesis, Aquincum
Museum, Budapest. The cult of the
goddess Fortune or Luck was
becoming more popular in Athens at
the time Sophocles wrote this play.
One of his reasons for writing was to
show that new cults like hers should
not replace the worship of the traditional gods. (On other changes in
Greek religion, see Ch. 27, p. 387.)

Choral Ode 3

"But Luck . . . made me"—
Oedipus sees himself as a child of
Fortune or Luck, a nobody who
made good on his own. The irony
of his fate is that he will soon see
that he is not a nobody: he is the
legitimate son of the king.

"who was your mother"—The chorus here represents the gods as
immanent, or highly involved in
the actions of human beings. This
is in direct contrast with the views
in the previous choral ode. This
violent swing of attitude indicates
how upset the chorus is.

"which one bore you"—The chorus imagines that Apollo, Hermes, or Dionysus had an affair with one of the female nature spirits called nymphs, and that Oedipus was their son.

 Episode 4

"the shepherd we are looking for"—This is the man who ran away from Laios' murder. Oedipus has summoned him to question him about the details of that incident. By coincidence, he turns out to be the man the messenger was just describing, who gave him the infant Oedipus.

which one bore you
did the god of the bare windy peaks Hermes
or the wild, dervish Dionysus   1405
living in the cool air of the hills
take you
a foundling
from one of the nymphs he plays with
joyously lift you hold you in his arms   1410
OEDIPUS: Old men, I think the man coming toward us now
must be **the shepherd we are looking for.**
I have never seen him, but the years, chalking his face and hair, tell me
he's the man. And my men are with him. But you probably know him.
LEADER: I do know him. If Laios ever had a man he trusted,   1415
this was the man.
OEDIPUS *(to the* MESSENGER*):* You—is this the man you told me
     about?
MESSENGER: That's him. You're looking at the man.
OEDIPUS *(to the* SHEPHERD *who has been waiting, hanging back):*
You there, come closer   1420
Answer me, old man.
Did you work for Laios?
SHEPHERD: I was born his slave, and grew up in his household.
OEDIPUS: What was your work?
SHEPHERD: Herding sheep, all my life.   1425
OEDIPUS: Where?
SHEPHERD: Kithairon, mostly. And the country around Kithairon.
OEDIPUS: Do you remember ever seeing this man?
SHEPHERD: Which man?
OEDIPUS *(pointing to the* MESSENGER*):*   1430
This man standing here. Have you ever seen him before?
SHEPHERD: Not that I remember.
MESSENGER: No wonder, master. But I'll make him remember.
He knows who I am. We used to graze our flocks together
in the pastures around Kithairon.   1435
Every year, for six whole months, three years running.
From March until September, when the Dipper rose, signaling
     the harvest.
I had one flock, he had two.
And when the frost came, I drove my sheep back to their winter pens
and he drove his back to Laios' fold.   1440
Remember, old man? Isn't that how it was?
SHEPHERD: Yes. But it was all so long ago.
MESSENGER: And do you remember giving me a baby boy at
     the time—
to raise as my own son?
SHEPHERD: What if I do? Why all these questions?   1445
MESSENGER: That boy became King Oedipus, friend.
SHEPHERD: Damn you, can't you keep quiet.
OEDIPUS: Don't scold him, old man.
It's you who deserve to be punished, not him.

SHEPHERD: What did I say, good master?   1450
OEDIPUS: You haven't answered his question about the boy.
SHEPHERD: He's making trouble, master. He doesn't know a thing.
(OEDIPUS takes the SHEPHERD by the cloak)
OEDIPUS: Tell me or you'll be sorry.
SHEPHERD: For god's sake, don't hurt me, I'm an old man.   1455
OEDIPUS *(to one of his men):* You there, hold him. We'll make
    him talk.
      (The attendant pins the SHEPHERD'S arms behind his back.)
SHEPHERD: Oedipus, Oedipus,
god knows I pity you.
What more do you want to know?   1460
OEDIPUS: Did you give the child to this man?
                            Speak. Yes or no?
SHEPHERD: Yes.
And I wish to god I'd died that day.
OEDIPUS: You *will* be dead unless you tell me the whole truth.   1465
SHEPHERD: And worse than dead, if I do.
OEDIPUS: It seems our man won't answer.
SHEPHERD: No. I told you already. I gave him the boy.
OEDIPUS: Where did you get him? From Laios' household?
    Or where?
SHEPHERD: He wasn't my child. He was given to me.   1470
OEDIPUS *(turning to the CHORUS and the audience):*
By whom? Someone here in Thebes?
SHEPHERD: Master, please, in god's name, no more questions.
OEDIPUS: You're a dead man if I have to ask you once more.
SHEPHERD: **He was one**   1475
of the children
from Laios'
household.
OEDIPUS: A slave child? Or Laios' own?
SHEPHERD: I can't say it . . . it's   1480
awful, the words
are awful . . . awful.
OEDIPUS: And I,
I am afraid to hear them . . .
but I must.   1485
SHEPHERD: He was Laios' own child.
Your wife, inside the palace, she can explain it all.
OEDIPUS: *She* gave you the child?
SHEPHERD: My lord . . . yes.
OEDIPUS: Why?   1490
SHEPHERD: **She wanted me to abandon the child** on a mountain.
OEDIPUS: His own mother?
SHEPHERD: Yes. There were prophecies, horrible oracles. She
    was afraid.
OEDIPUS: What oracles?
SHEPHERD: Oracles predicting he would murder his own father.   1495
OEDIPUS: But why did you give the boy to this old man?

> "He was one . . ."—The line breaks here emphasize the reluctance of the shepherd to state the origin of the child.

> "She wanted me to abandon the child"—Jocasta (p. 256) has said that Laios had her child's feet pierced and gave orders for his abandonment. She may have meant, however, that Laios ordered her to have it done.

SHEPHERD: Because I pitied him, master, because I
thought the man would take the child away, take him to another country.
Instead he saved him. Saved him for—oh gods,
a fate so horrible, so awful, words can't describe it.   1500
If you were the baby that man took from me, Oedipus,
what misery, what grief is yours!
OEDIPUS (*looking up at the sun*):
LIGHT   LIGHT   LIGHT
never again flood these eyes with your white radiance, oh gods, my eyes.   1505
All, all
the oracles have proven true. I, Oedipus, I
am the child
of parents who should never have been mine—doomed, doomed!
Now everything is clear—I   1510
lived with a woman, she was my mother, I slept in my mother's bed, and I
murdered, murdered my father,
the man whose blood flows in these veins of mine,
whose blood stains these two hands red.

> OEDIPUS *raises his hands to the sun, then turns and walks into the palace.*

CHORUS: man after man after man   1515
o mortal generations
here once
almost not here
what are we
dust ghosts images a rustling of air   1520
nothing nothing
we breathe on the abyss
we are the abyss
our happiness no more than traces of a dream
the high noon sun sinking into the sea   1525
the red spume of its wake raining behind it
we are you
we are you Oedipus
dragging your maimed foot
in agony   1530
and now that I see your life finally revealed
your life fused with the god
blazing out of the black nothingness of all we know
I say
no happiness lasts nothing human lasts   1535
wherever you aimed you hit
no archer had your skill
you grew rich powerful great
everything came falling to your feet
o Zeus   1540
after he killed the Sphinx
whose claws curled under
whose weird song of the future baffled and destroyed
he stood like a tower high above our country
warding off death   1545

"LIGHT LIGHT LIGHT"—Now that Oedipus has seen the light with his mind, he wants never to see the light again with his eyes.

Choral Ode 4

Oedipus abandoned on Mount Kithairon by the shepherd. Marble relief from a sarcophagus, 3rd C. C.E.

"we are you Oedipus"—For all its horror at what Oedipus has done, the chorus does not reject him. Rather, they identify with him. It is not unusual for a hero to engender this kind of empathy.

and from then on Oedipus we called you
king our king
draped you in gold
our highest honors were yours
and you ruled this shining city   1550
Thebes   Thebes
now
your story is pain pity no story is worse
than yours Oedipus
ruined savage blind   1555
as you struggle with your life
as your life changes
and breaks and shows you who you are
Oedipus   Oedipus
son father you harbored in the selfsame place   1560
the same place sheltered you both
bridegroom
how could the furrow your father plowed
not have cried out all this time
while you lay there unknowing   1565
and saw the truth too late
time like the sun sees all things
and it sees you
you cannot hide from that light
your own life opening itself to you   1570
to all
married unmarried father son
for so long
justice comes like the dawn
always   1575
and it shows the world your marriage now
I wish
o child of Laios
I wish I had never seen you
I grieve for you   1580
wail after wail fills me and pours out
because of you my breath came flowing back
but now
the darkness of your life
floods my eyes   1585

> The palace doors open. A SERVANT *enters and approaches the*
> CHORUS *and audience.*

SERVANT: Noble citizens, honored above all others in Thebes,
if you still care for the house of Laios,
if you still can feel the spirit of those who ruled before, now
the horrors you will hear, the horrors you will see, will shake
>   your hearts and shatter you with grief beyond enduring.
Not even the waters of those great rivers Ister and Phasis   1590
could wash away the blood
that now darkens every stone of this shining house,

> "the darkness of your life floods my eyes"—The chorus predicts Oedipus' blinding himself: the blindness of his life will flood his eyes.

 Episode 5

> "the horrors you will hear"—Violence was usually not presented on stage in Greek tragedies. Here Sophocles provides us with a narrative of the death of Jocasta and the blinding of Oedipus, rather than allowing us to witness them directly.

this house that will reveal, soon, soon
the misery and evil two mortals,
both masters of this house, have brought upon themselves.   1595
The griefs we cause ourselves cut deepest of all.
LEADER: What we already know
has hurt us enough,
has made us cry out in pain.
What more can you say?   1600
SERVANT: This:
Jocasta is dead. The queen is dead.
LEADER: Ah, poor
unhappy Jocasta,
how did she die?   1605
SERVANT: She killed herself. She did it.
But you did not see what happened there,
you were not there, in the palace. You did not see it.
I did.
I will tell you how Queen Jocasta died,   1610
the whole story, all of it. All I can remember.
After her last words to Oedipus
she rushed past us through the entrance hall, screaming,
raking her hair with both hands, and flew into the bedroom, their bedroom,
and slammed the doors shut as she lunged at her bridal bed,   1615
crying "Laios" "Laios"—dead all these years—
remembering Laios—how his own son years ago
grew up and then killed him, leaving her to
sleep with her own son, to have his children, their children,
children—**not sons, not daughters,** something else, monsters. . . .   1620
Then she collapsed, sobbing, cursing the bed where she held
        both men in her arms,
got husband from husband, children from her child.
We heard it all, but suddenly, I couldn't tell what was happening.
Oedipus came crashing in, he was howling,
stalking up and down—we couldn't take our eyes off him—   1625
and we stopped listening to her pitiful cries.
We stood there, watching him move like a bull, lurching, charging,
shouting at each of us to give him a sword, demanding we tell him
where his wife was, that woman whose womb carried him,
him and his children, that wife who gave him birth.   1630
Some god, some demon, led him to her, and he knew—
none of us showed him—
suddenly a mad, inhuman cry burst from his mouth
as if the wind rushed through his tortured body,
and he heaved against those bedroom doors so the hinges whined   1635
and bent from their sockets and the bolts snapped,
and he stood in the room.
There she was—
we could see her—his wife
dangling by her neck from a noose of braided, silken cords   1640
tied to a rafter, still swaying.

"not sons, not daughters"—The servant's language here illustrates what anthropologists say is the problem with incest: it makes it hard for members of society to identify the resultant offspring, and thus, to relate to them. See also p. 276.

"shouting at each of us to give him a sword"—It is not clear why Oedipus wants a sword at this point. He does not yet know that Jocasta has hanged herself, so he cannot be wanting to cut her down. Does he want to do her violence? Or to harm himself?

And when he saw her he bellowed and stretched up and loosened
    the rope,
cradling her in one arm,
and slowly laid her body on the ground.
That's when it happened—he   1645
ripped off the gold
brooches she was wearing—one on each shoulder of her gown—
and raised them over his head—you could see them flashing—
and tilted his face up and
brought them right down into his eyes   1650
and the long pins sank deep, all the way back into the sockets,
and he shouted at his eyes:
**"Now you won't see me, you won't see
my agonies or my crimes,
but in endless darkness,** always, there you'll see   1655
those I never should have seen.
And those I should have known were my parents, father
    and mother—
these eyes will never see their faces in the light.
These eyes will never see the light again, never."
Cursing his two blind eyes over and over, he   1660
lifted the brooches again and drove their pins through his eyeballs up
to the hilts until they were pulp, until the blood streamed out
soaking his beard and cheeks,
a black storm splashing its hail across his face.
Two mortals acted. Now grief tears their lives apart   1665
as if that pain sprang from a single, sorrowing root
to curse each one, man and wife. For all those years
their happiness was truly happiness, but now, now
wailing, madness, shame and death,
every evil men have given a name,   1670
**everything criminal and vile
that mankind suffers** they suffer. Not one evil is missing.
LEADER: But now
does this torn, anguished man
have any rest from his pain?   1675
SERVANT: No, no—
then he shouted at us to open the doors and show everyone in
    Thebes
his father's killer, his mother's—I cannot say it.
Once we have seen him as he is
he will leave Thebes, lift the curse from his city—   1680
banish himself, cursed by his own curses.
But his strength is gone, his whole life is pain,
more pain than any man can bear.
He needs help, someone to guide him.
He is alone, and blind. Look,   1685
look—the palace doors are opening—now
a thing
so horrible will stand before you

"Now you won't see me…but in endless darkness."—This poetic paradox makes a kind of psychological sense. Oedipus' blindness will proclaim his shame. No one will be able to say that he committed his crimes unscathed. See also p. 273.

"everything criminal and vile that mankind suffers"—The pain of Oedipus and Jocasta is compared to all human suffering.

you will shudder with disgust and try to turn away
while your hearts will swell with pity for what you see.   1690

> *The central doors open.* OEDIPUS *enters, led by his household*
> *servants. His mask is covered with blood. The* CHORUS *begin a*
> *dirge to which* OEDIPUS *responds antiphonally.*

CHORUS: **horror horror** o what suffering
men see
but none is worse than this
Oedipus o
how could you have slashed out your eyes   1695
what god leaped on you
from beyond the last border of space
what madness entered you
clawing even more misery into you
I cannot look at you   1700
but there are questions
so much I would know
so much that I would see
no   no
the shape of your life makes me shudder   1705
OEDIPUS: **I   I**

this voice of agony
I am   what place am I
where? Not here, nowhere I know!
What force, what tide breaks over my life?   1710
Pain, demon stabbing into me
leaving nothing, nothing, no man I know, not human,
fate howling out of nowhere   what am I
fire   a voice   where   where
is it being taken?   1715
LEADER: Beyond everything to a place
so terrible nothing is seen there, nothing is heard.
OEDIPUS *(reaching out, groping)*:
Thing   thing   darkness
spilling into me, my   1720
black cloud smothering me forever,
nothing can stop you, nothing can escape,
I cannot push you away.
I am
nothing but my own cries breaking   1725
again and again
the agony of those gold pins
the memory of what I did
stab me
again   1730
again.
LEADER: What can you feel but pain.
It all comes back, pain in remorse,
remorse in pain, to tear you apart with grief.
OEDIPUS: Dear, loyal friend   1735

"horror horror . . ."—The chorus sings a dirge, a song of sorrow in reaction to what has happened to Oedipus. It suggests that he may not have been responsible for his actions. However, Oedipus will reject this suggestion.

"I I this voice of agony"—Oedipus sings in sorrow, in response to the dirge of the chorus.

you, only you, are still here with me, still care
for this blind, tortured man.
Oh,
I know you are there, I know you friend
even in this darkness, friend, touched by your voice.   1740
LEADER: What you did was horrible,
but how could you quench the fire of your eyes,
what demon lifted your hands?
OEDIPUS: Apollo   Apollo
it was Apollo, always Apollo,   1745
who brought each of my agonies to birth,

but I,

nobody else, *I*,

I raised these two hands of mine, held them above my head,
and plunged them down,   1750
I stabbed out these eyes.
Why should I have eyes? Why,
when nothing I saw was worth seeing?
Nothing.
LEADER: Nothing. Nothing.   1755
OEDIPUS: Oh friends. Nothing.
No one to see, no one to love,
no one to speak to, no one to hear!
        Friends, friends, lead me away now.
Lead me away from Thebes—Oedipus,   1760
destroyer and destroyed,
the man whose life is hell
for others and for himself, the man
more hated by the gods than any other man, ever.
LEADER: Oh I pity you,   1765
I weep for your fate
and for your mind,
for what it is to be you, Oedipus.
I wish you had never seen the man you are.
OEDIPUS: I hate   1770
the man who found me, cut the thongs from my feet,
snatched me from death, cared for me—
I wish he were dead!
I should have died up there on those wild, desolate slopes of
        Kithairon.
Then my pain and the pain   1775
those I love suffer now
never would have been.
LEADER: These are my wishes too.
OEDIPUS: Then I never would have murdered my father,
never heard men call me my mother's husband.   1780
Now
I am
Oedipus!
Oedipus, who lay in that loathsome bed, made love there in that bed,

> "but I, nobody else, *I* "—Oedipus recognizes two forces that produced his current condition: the god Apollo and his own actions. The relationship between these two forces is mysterious, but the god cannot be said to have destroyed Oedipus.

> "I should have died"—Oedipus' lament over his life, which begins here, makes clear that humans produce their fate through their own decisions.

his father's and mother's bed, the bed   1785
where he was born.
No gods anywhere now, not for me, now,
unholy, broken man.
What man ever suffered grief like this?
LEADER: How can I say that what you did was right?   1790
Better to be dead than live blind.
OEDIPUS: **I did what I had to do.** No more advice.
How could *my* eyes,
when I went down into that black, sightless place beneath the earth,
the place where the dead go down, how,   1795
how could I have looked at anything,
with what human eyes could I have gazed
on my father, on my mother—
oh gods, my mother!
What I did against those two   1800
not even strangling could punish.
And my children, how would the sight of them, born as they
        were born,
be sweet? Not to these eyes of mine, never to these eyes.
Nothing, nothing is left me now—no city with its high walls,
no shining statues of the gods. **I stripped all these things from**   1805
        myself—
I, Oedipus, fallen lower than any man now, born nobler than the best,
born the king of Thebes! Cursed with my own curses, I
commanded Thebes to drive out the killer.
I banished the royal son of Laios, the man the gods revealed
is stained with the awful stain. The secret stain   1810
that I myself revealed is my stain. And now, revealed at last,
how could I ever look men in the eyes?
Never. Never
If I could, I would have walled my ears so they heard nothing,
I would have made this body of mine a wall.   1815
I would have heard nothing, tasted nothing, smelled nothing, seen
nothing.
        No thought. No feeling. Nothing. Nothing.
So pain would never reach me any more.
O Kithairon,   1820
why did you shelter me and take me in?
Why did you let me live? Better to have died on that bare slope
        of yours
where no man would ever have seen me or known the secret of
        my birth!
Polybos, Corinth, that house I thought was my father's home,
how beautiful I was when you sheltered me as a child   1825
and oh what disease festered beneath that beauty.
Now everyone knows the secret of my birth, knows
how vile I am.
O roads, secret valley, cluster of oaks,
O narrow place where two roads join a third,   1830

"I did what I had to do."—On the rational level, Oedipus is fulfilling the terms of his own curse by wanting to cut himself off from human contact by blinding himself and exiling himself. However, his actions make sense on the emotional plane as well. Psychologists would point out that his reaction is not an unusual one for someone who has suffered a series of traumatic events.

"I stripped all these things from myself"—Oedipus recognizes the effects of the curse he himself placed on the murderer of Laios.

roads that drank my blood as it streamed from my hands,
flowing from my dead father's body,
do you remember me now?
Do you remember what I did with my own two hands, there
        in your presence,
and what I did after that, when I came here to Thebes?   1835
O marriage, marriage, you gave me my life, and then
from the same seed, my seed, spewed out
fathers, brothers, sisters, children, brides, wives—
nothing, no words can express the shame.
No more words. Men should not name what men should never do.   1840
        (To the CHORUS*)*
Gods, oh gods, gods,
hide me, hide me
now
far away from Thebes,   1845
kill me,
cast me into the sea,
drive me where you will never see me—never again.
(Reaching out to the CHORUS, *who back away.)*
Touch this poor man, touch me,   1850
don't be afraid to touch me. Believe me, nobody,
nobody but me can bear
this fire of anguish.
It is mine. Mine.
LEADER: Kreon has come.   1855
Now he, not you, is the sole guardian of Thebes,
and only he can grant you what you ask.
OEDIPUS *(turning toward the palace):*
What can I say to him, how can anything I say
make him listen now?   1860
I wronged him. I accused him, and now everything I said
proves I am vile.
KREON *(enters from the entrance to the right. He is accompanied
        by men who gather around OEDIPUS):*
I have not come to mock you, Oedipus; I have not come to blame
        you for the past.
(To attendants) You men, standing there, if you have no respect for   1865
        human dignity,
at least revere the master of life,
the all-seeing sun whose light nourishes
every living thing on earth.
Come, cover this cursed, naked, **holy thing,** hide him
from the earth and the sacred rain and the light,   1870
you powers who cringe from his touch.
Take him. Do it now. Be reverent.
Only his family should see and hear his grief.
Their grief.
OEDIPUS: I beg you, Kreon, if you love the gods,   1875
grant me what I ask.

> "holy thing"—Oedipus was venerated as a hero at Colonus, just north of Athens, and perhaps in Athens itself.

I have been vile to you, worse than vile.
I have hurt you, terribly, and yet
you have treated me with kindness, with nobility.
You have calmed my fear, you did not turn away from me.   1880
Do what I ask. Do it for yourself, not for me.
KREON: What do you want from me, Oedipus?
OEDIPUS: Drive me out of Thebes, do it now, now—
drive me someplace where no man can speak to me,
where no man can see me anymore.   1885
KREON: Believe me, Oedipus, I would have done it long ago.
But I refuse to act until I know precisely what the god desires.
OEDIPUS: Apollo has revealed what he desires. Everything is clear.
I killed my father, I am polluted and unclean.
I must die.   1890
KREON: That is what the god commanded, Oedipus.
But there are no precedents for what has happened.
We need to know before we act.
OEDIPUS: Do you care so much for me, enough to ask Apollo?
For me, Oedipus?   1895
KREON: Now even you will trust the god, I think.
OEDIPUS: I will. And I turn to you, **I implore you, Kreon**—
the woman lying dead inside, your sister,
give her whatever burial you think best.

        As for me,   1900
never let this city of my fathers see me here in Thebes.
Let me go and live on the mountain, on Kithairon—the mountain
my parents intended for my grave.
Let me die the way they wanted me to die: slowly, alone—
die *their* way.   1905
And yet this much I know—
           no sickness,
no ordinary, natural death is mine.
I have been saved, preserved, kept alive
for some strange fate, for something far more awful still.   1910
When that thing comes let it take me
where it will.
    (OEDIPUS *turns, looking for something, waiting*):
As for **my sons**, Kreon,
they are grown men, they can look out for themselves.   1915
But **my daughters,** those two poor girls of mine,
who have never left their home before, never left their father's side,
who ate at my side every day, who shared whatever was mine,
I beg you, Kreon,
care for them, love them.   1920
But more than anything, Kreon,
I want to touch them,
    (he begins to lift his hands)
let me touch them with these hands of mine,   1925
let them come to me so we can grieve together.
My noble lord, if only I could touch them with my hands,

"I implore you, Kreon"—Although Oedipus has been reduced to a blind man and, by his own decree, an outcast, he has not changed his fundamental nature or lost his heroic stature. Even from his reduced circumstances, he is still giving orders here. Despite his blindness, he has a clear vision of how he wants his affairs to be handled, and he issues a series of commands to Kreon: "give her whatever burial you think best," "let me die the way they wanted me to die," "let me touch [my daughters]," "let them come to me," etc.

"my sons"—Oedipus' sons are Eteocles and Polyneices, who later kill each other in a civil war described in Aeschylus' play *Seven Against Thebes*.

"my daughters"—Oedipus' daughters are Antigone and Ismene, whose story is told in Sophocles' play *Antigone*.

Charles Francois Jalabert, *Oedipus and Antigone, or the Plague of Thebes, 1843.* In the vision of the artist, Oedipus' daughter is no longer small, as suggested by the stage direction in our text. However, the scene reflects the commanding majesty of Oedipus, even given his sufferings.

they would still be mine just as they were
when I had eyes that could still see.
     (Oedipus' two small daughters are brought out of the palace)
O gods, gods, is it possible? Do I hear   1930
my two daughters crying? Has Kreon pitied me and brought me
what I love more than my life—
my daughters?
KREON: I brought them to you, knowing how much you love them,
    Oedipus,
knowing the joy you would feel if they were here.   1935
OEDIPUS: May the gods who watch over the path of your life, Kreon,
prove kinder to you than they were to me.
Where are you, children?
Come, come to your brother's hands—
     (taking his daughters into his arms)   1940
his mother was your mother, too,
come to these hands which made these eyes, bright clear eyes once,
sockets seeing nothing, the eyes

of the man who fathered you. Look . . . your father's eyes,
your father—   1945
who knew nothing until now, saw nothing until now, and became
the husband of the woman who gave him birth.

                                               I weep for you
when I think how men will treat you, how bitter your lives will be.
What festivals will you attend, whose homes will you visit   1950
and not be assailed by whispers, and people's stares?
Where will you go and not leave in tears?
And when the time comes for you to marry,
what men will take you as their brides, and risk **the shame of**
    marrying
the daughters of Oedipus?   1955
What sorrow will not be yours?
Your father killed his father, made love
to the woman who gave birth to him. And he fathered you
in the same place where he was fathered.
That is what you will hear; that is what they will say.   1960
Who will marry you then? You will never marry,
but grow hard and dry like wheat so far beyond harvest
that the wind blows its white flakes into the winter sky.
Oh Kreon,
now you are the only father my daughters have.   1965
Jocasta and I, their parents, are lost to them forever.
These poor girls are yours. Your blood.
Don't let them wander all their lives.
begging, alone, unmarried, helpless.
Don't let them suffer as their father has. Pity them, Kreon,   1970
pity these girls, so young and helpless except for you.
Promise me this. Noble Kreon,
touch me with your hand, give me a sign.
                      (KREON *takes his hands.)* Daughters,
daughters, if you were older, if you could understand,   1975
there is so much more I would say to you.
But for now, I give you this prayer—
                                        Live,
live your lives, live each day as best you can,
may your lives be happier than your father's was.   1980
KREON: No more grief. Come in.
OEDIPUS: I must. But obedience comes hard.
KREON: Everything has its time.
OEDIPUS: First, promise me this.
KREON: Name it.   1985
OEDIPUS: Banish me from Thebes.
KREON: I cannot.   Ask the gods for that.
OEDIPUS: The gods hate me.
KREON: Then you will have your wish.
OEDIPUS: You promise?   1990
KREON: I say only what I mean.
OEDIPUS: Then lead me in.

"the shame of marrying the daughters of Oedipus"—The incest taboo is found in many societies, but the relationships it prohibits vary from society to society, depending on the rules for kinship and marriage in that society. Anthropologists explain the function of the idea of incest in different ways, but they would agree that a practical basis of the taboo is to prevent the kind of confusion Oedipus outlines here, the confusion over how people in a society are related to each other.

(OEDIPUS reaches out and touches his daughters, trying to take them with him.)

KREON: Oedipus, come with me. Let your daughters go. Come.

OEDIPUS: No. You will not take my daughters. I forbid it.

KREON: You *forbid* me?   1995

You have no power any more.

All the great power you once had is gone,

gone forever.

> *The* CHORUS *turn to face the audience.* KREON *leads* OEDI-
> PUS *toward the palace. His daughters follow. He moves slowly,*
> *and disappears into the palace as the* CHORUS *ends.*

CHORUS: O citizens of Thebes, this is Oedipus,

who solved the famous riddle, who held more power than any mortal.   2000

See what he is: all men gazed on his fortunate life,

all men envied him, but look at him, look.

All he had, all this man was,

pulled down and swallowed by the storm of his own life

and by the god.   2005

Keep your eyes on that last day, on your dying.

Happiness and peace, they were not yours

unless at death you can look back on your life and say

I lived, I did not suffer.

● **Epilogue**

"Keep your eyes on that last day"—The chorus' summary of Oedipus' experiences does not do justice to the complex issues and perspectives presented by the play.

Further Reading

Knox, Bernard M. W. *Oedipus at Thebes*. New Haven, CN: Yale University Press, 1957.

Sophocles, *Oedipus the King*. Trans. Stephen Berg and Diskin Clay. New York, NY: Oxford University Press, 1978.

20

The Structural Study of Myth

CLAUDE LEVI-STRAUSS

WHAT TO EXPECT . . .   While history tells us about specific events that happen in a society, myth provides an additional perspective: it describes the most fundamental ideas and ideals shared by a group. For Claude Levi-Strauss, it is the passing on of this message that forms the basis for each culture's storytelling. In his view, getting to the most complete message requires studying all possible versions of the myth (called a cycle), since each version contains at least some elements of the ideals people believe in.

This chapter describes Levi-Strauss' principles of structural analysis and illustrates his method for comparing stories to identify the cultural values of a group. Also in this chapter, Edmund Leach explains Levi-Strauss' theories, especially that of weighing apparent contradictions in various versions of a myth and coming to the point of finding an all-encompassing belief characteristic of the culture, e.g., oppositions such as Nature versus Culture and Life versus Death. Levi-Strauss' interest is not so much in the oppositions themselves, but in how the society, or the story, achieves a balance between them. Using the Oedipus story, Leach shows the interconnectedness of the versions and how they convey basic beliefs of the ancient Greeks.

Because Levi-Strauss focuses on achieving a balance between the fundamental oppositions found in myth, the trickster is very important to his structural study of myth. This chapter contains the first description of this figure found in a variety of cultures, including Native American (Ch. 21, p. 295), Greek (Ch. 24, p. 353), and African and African-American (Ch. 23, p. 339). And finally, if you have not already done so, you may want to go back, after reading this chapter, to G. S. Kirk's application of Levi-Strauss' ideas to the *Epic of Gilgamesh* in Ch. 16, p. 193.

Claude Levi-Strauss was a French anthropologist who studied the religious beliefs and practices of peoples in places as varied as North America, Brazil, Australia, and the South Pacific islands. However, Levi-Strauss' contribution to mythology ranged beyond the study of particular cultures. He was a great theoretician who was interested not just in the stories, customs, and ceremonies of people, but in the understanding of human nature and society that can be developed by studying these aspects of culture.

As he collected and analyzed the stories that people in a community pass on from family to family and from generation to generation, Levi-Strauss observed the patterns of significance which emerge. He noted that, because these stories are deeply influential in the creation and development of human societies, myth can often function as the "formulation of a sacred mystery" (Leach, 58). As explained in Chapter 1, it seems that people have always told stories to explain the world and their place in it. Communities have defined themselves by telling tales of epic heroes and clever tricksters, and they have handed down stories explaining their own origins and describing where they expected to spend eternity. It is this transmission of vitally important cultural and spiritual information that was, for Levi-Strauss, the most important function of myth.

THE FUNCTION OF MYTH

What, then, makes a people unique or special? Some would say it is their history. As a cultural anthropologist, Levi-Strauss found that a people defines itself by its myths. Like history, myth tells us about what happened to the people who shared a culture. But myth does much more than record a series of events: this differentiates it from history. Rather than merely reporting specific events in the political or cultural development of a society, myth tells us about the most fundamental ideas and ideals of a group. It perpetuates a tradition by carrying a message from one generation to the next, and even to those following many generations later.

However, it is hard to be sure what the message of a myth is. A myth is a story told by different storytellers. With each telling, the focus, the details, even the meaning of a story change. Which is the true meaning? Levi-Strauss explained that the message is not complete in any single version of a myth, and that we must include all possible forms of a myth in an interpretation. Each version of the story contains at least some elements of the ideas people believe in. As we study different versions of the same myth, we formulate a more complete picture of the "message" being transmitted. Edmund Leach compares this process to trying to understand a message sent from far away (63). One person is trying to relay a message to another who is almost out of earshot and in an area where there is interference (from wind, traffic). The first person shouts the message several times, and each time the listener comprehends some part of what is being said and writes it down as heard. Eventually, the listener puts together all of the elements and deciphers the entire message.

For Levi-Strauss, our understanding of myths develops in the same way: a version is told, then another, then another. Over time, a story takes on new characteristics important to the current keepers of the myth and leaves out other details no longer important to them. Levi-Strauss proposes that the transmission of myths over time and geographical area operates in a similar manner, and that in order to get the message, we need as many variants of a myth as possible. This collection of versions is also called a cycle. For the cultural group which "owns" the myth, this constant reshaping transmits to junior members the basic messages of their belief system. In other words, it teaches.

LEVI-STRAUSS' METHOD OF ANALYSIS

To unravel the layers of meaning in a myth, Levi-Strauss has developed a method of dissecting them into their various elements. This allows the methodical analysis of the elements and ideas of the myth cycle. The stages of this technique are:

- Write each individual element of the myth on a card.
- Arrange these cards in columns and rows, according to the topics or issues they contain.

Categories of Interpretation of Myth

"collective dreams"	Carl Jung (see Part 5 of this book, on myths and dreams)	Myths tell us about the inner psychology of people—how they think and feel.
"aesthetic play"	Johan Huizinga	The early myth tellers expressed abstract ideas by personifying them, for example, as humans or animals. He called personification "a playing of the mind" (*Homo Ludens*, 64)
"the basis of ritual"	Many writers (see Part 4 of this book, on ritual)	Myths are stories told to explain religious ceremonies.

The cards then resemble a grid of elements. If they are read *across* the rows from upper left to lower right, they follow the story line. However, when we scan the cards vertically, going *down* the columns, the elements of the myth are organized according to idea groupings. These idea groupings are most important for Levi-Strauss' analysis. He sees in them relationships and oppositions which can tell us much about the ideas inherent in the message of the myth. This, in turn, can identify the cultural values of the group. The excerpt in this chapter from his article "The Structural Study of Myth" contains a detailed explanation of this method and applies the method to the Oedipus myth. Levi-Strauss begins by considering various types of interpretations of myths.

These excerpts come from: Levi-Strauss, *Structural Anthropology,* Ch. XI, "The Structural Study of Myth."*

"collective dreams . . . esthetic play . . . ritual"—For examples, see the chart on categories of interpretation.

"phenomena which they cannot otherwise understand"—Levi-Strauss discounts what Joseph Campbell describes as the cosmological aspect of myth. (See Ch. 1, p. 8.)

Of all the chapters of religious anthropology probably none has tarried to the same extent as studies in the field of mythology. From a theoretical point of view the situation remains very much the same as it was fifty years ago, namely, chaotic. Myths are still widely interpreted in conflicting ways: as **collective dreams, as the outcome of a kind of esthetic play, or as the basis of ritual.** Mythological figures are considered as personified abstractions, divinized heroes, or fallen gods. Whatever the hypothesis, the choice amounts to reducing mythology either to idle play or to a crude kind of philosophic speculation.

Some claim that human societies try to provide some kind of explanations for **phenomena which they cannot otherwise understand:** astronomical, meteorological, and the like. But why should these societies do it in such elaborate and devious ways, when all of them are also acquainted with empirical explanations? On the other hand, psychoanalysts and many anthropologists have shifted the problems away from the natural or cosmological toward the sociological and psychological fields. But then the interpretation becomes too easy: If a given mythology confers prominence on a certain figure, let us say an evil grandmother, it will be claimed that in such a society grandmothers are actually evil and that mythology reflects the social structure and the social relations; but should the actual data be conflicting, it would be as readily claimed that the purpose of mythology is to provide an outlet for repressed feelings. Whatever the situation, a clever dialectic will always find a way to pretend that a meaning has been found.

Mythology confronts the student with a situation which at first sight appears contradictory. On the one hand it would seem that in the course of a myth anything is likely to happen. There is no logic, no continuity. Any characteristic can be attributed to any subject; every conceivable relation can be found. With myth, everything becomes possible. But on the other hand, this apparent arbitrariness is belied by the astounding similarity between myths collected in widely different regions. Therefore the problem: **If the content of a myth is contingent,** how are we going to explain the fact that myths throughout the world are so similar?

"If the content of a myth is contingent"—People put what is around them ("contingent") into their stories.

"long ago"—Myths are not rooted in a specific period, as historical events are.

On the one hand, a myth always refers to events alleged to have taken place **long ago.** But what gives the myth an operational value is that the specific pattern described is timeless; it explains the present and the past as well as the future.

Myth as a Kind of Language

We have so far made the following claims: (1) If there is a meaning to be found in mythology, it cannot reside in the isolated elements which enter into the composition of a myth, but only in the way those elements are combined. (2) Although **myth**

---

*Claude Levi-Strauss, "The Structural Study of Myth." *Structural Anthropology,* Ch. XI, 207–30. Copyright © 1963 by Basic Books, Inc. Reprinted by permission of Basic Books, a member of Perseus Books, L.L.C.

belongs to the same category as language, being, as a matter of fact, only part of it, language in myth exhibits specific properties. (3) Those properties are only to be found *above* the ordinary linguistic level, that is, they exhibit more complex features than those which are to be found in any other kind of linguistic expression.

If the above three points are granted, at least as a working hypothesis, two consequences will follow: (1) Myth, like the rest of language, is made up of constituent units. (2) These constituent units presuppose the constituent units present in language when analyzed on other levels but they belong to a higher and more complex order. For this reason, we shall call them **gross constituent units.**

How shall we proceed in order to identify and isolate these gross constituent units? We should look for them on the sentence level. The only method we can suggest at this stage is to proceed tentatively, by trial and error, using as a check the principles which serve as a basis for any kind of structural analysis: economy of explanation; unity of solution; and ability to reconstruct the whole from a fragment, as well as later stages from previous ones.

The technique which has been applied so far by this writer consists in analyzing each myth individually, breaking down its story into the shortest possible sentences, and writing each sentence on an index card bearing a number corresponding to the unfolding of the story.

Practically each card will thus show that **a certain function** is, at a given time, linked to a given subject. Or, to put it otherwise, **each gross constituent unit will consist of a relation. . . .**

The true constituent units of a myth are not the isolated relations but *bundles of such relations,* and it is only as bundles that these relations can be put to use and combined so as to produce a meaning. Relations pertaining to the same bundle may appear **diachronically** at remote intervals, but when we have succeeded in grouping them together we have reorganized our myth according to a time referent of a new nature, corresponding to the prerequisite of the initial hypothesis, namely **a two-dimensional time referent** which is simultaneously diachronic and synchronic. Two comparisons may help to explain what we have in mind.

Let us first suppose that archaeologists of the future coming from another planet would one day, when all human life had disappeared from the earth, excavate one of our libraries. Even if they were at first ignorant of our writing, they might succeed in deciphering it—an undertaking which would require the discovery that the alphabet, as we are in the habit of printing it, should be read from left to right and from top to bottom. However, they would soon discover that a whole category of books did not fit the usual pattern—**these would be the orchestra scores** on the shelves of the music division. But after trying, without success, to decipher staffs one after the other, from the upper down to the lower, they would probably notice that the same patterns of notes recurred at intervals, either in full or in part, or that some patterns were strongly reminiscent of earlier ones. Hence the hypothesis: What if patterns showing affinity, instead of being considered in succession, were to be treated as one complex pattern and read as a whole? By getting at what we call *harmony,* they would then see that an orchestra score, to be meaningful, must be read diachronically along one axis—that is, page after page, and from left to right—and synchronically along the other axis, all the notes written vertically making up one gross constituent unit, that is, one bundle of relations.

The Oedipus Myth as an Example of Levi-Strauss' Method

Now for a concrete example of the method we propose. We shall use the Oedipus myth. I am well aware that the Oedipus myth has only reached us under late forms and through literary transmutations concerned more with esthetic and moral preoccupations than

---

"myth belongs to the same category as language"—For discussion of the way Levi-Strauss treats myth as a language, see the Introduction, p. 281.

"*gross constituent units*"—The individual elements of the story.

"a certain function"—Levi-Strauss uses the example "Oedipus marries his mother, Jocasta."

"each gross constituent unit will consist of a *relation*"—The most important part of studying mythology for Levi Strauss is this classification and grouping of the fundamental units of myth.

"diachronically"—The same story may be told in different time periods. Levi Strauss will argue that every such version must be considered as the myth is studied.

"a two-dimensional time referent"—The string of events is diachronic, covering more than one time period; the bundles are synchronic, occurring at the same time.

"Let us first suppose"—Levi-Strauss' method of proof often consists of hypothetical examples. Here he is asking his reader to consider what someone who had never heard of musical notation would make of an orchestra score. The idea is to decode the message even if the details of the code are unknown.

"these would be the orchestra scores"—An orchestra score is an example of synchronic *and* diachronic organization of information: the progression of notes that form the melody is diachronic; the simultaneous playing of several notes for harmony is synchronic.

"we shall not . . . offer an explanation acceptable to the specialist"—This analysis relies on a literary version of the story, not a "working version" (see Ch. 25, p. 361), which would be more useful to an anthropologist.

with religious or ritual ones, whatever these may have been. But **we shall not** interpret the Oedipus myth in material terms, much less **offer an explanation acceptable to the specialist.** We simply wish to illustrate—and without reaching any conclusions with respect to it—a certain technique, whose use is probably not legitimate in this particular instance, owing to the problematic elements indicated above.

The myth will be treated as an orchestra score would be if it were unwittingly considered as a unilinear series; our task is to reestablish the correct arrangement. Say, for instance, we were confronted with a sequence of the type: l, 2, 4, 7, 8, 2, 3, 4, 6, 8, 1, 4, 5, 7, 8, 1, 2, 5, 7, 3, 4, 5, 6, 8, . . . , the assignment being to put all the l's together, all the 2's, the 3's, etc.; the result is a chart:

1	2		4			7	8
	2	3	4		6		8
1			4	5		7	8
1	2			5		7	
		3	4	5	6		8

We shall attempt to perform the same kind of operation on the Oedipus myth, trying out several arrangements of the constituent parts until we find one which is in harmony with the principles enumerated above. Let us suppose, for the sake of argument, that the best arrangement is the following (although it might certainly be improved with the help of a specialist in Greek mythology).

We thus find ourselves confronted with four vertical columns, each of which includes several relations belonging to the same bundle. Were we to *tell* the myth, we would disregard the columns and read the rows from left to right and from top to bottom. But if we want to *understand* the myth then we will have to disregard one half of the diachronic dimension (top to bottom) and read from left to right, column after column, each one being considered as a unit. (See the chart on p. 285.)

In the Oedipus Story Levi-Strauss Finds These Relationships:

1. Overrating of blood relationships
2. Underrating of blood relationships
3. Monsters being slain
4. Difficulty in walking straight and standing upright.

"one common feature"—After arranging the story in a table, Levi-Strauss looks for relationships among the bundles in each column.

All the relations belonging to the same column exhibit **one common feature** which it is our task to discover. For instance, all the events grouped in the first column on the left have something to do with blood relations which are overemphasized, that is, are more intimate than they should be. Let us say, then, that the first column has as its common feature the *overrating of blood relations.* It is obvious that the second column expresses the same thing, but inverted: *underrating of blood relations.* The third column refers to monsters being slain. As to the fourth, a few words of clarification are needed. The **remarkable connotation of the surnames** in Oedipus' father-line has often been noticed. However, linguists usually disregard it, since to them the only way to define the meaning of a term is to investigate all the contexts in which it appears, and personal names, precisely because they are used as such, are not accompanied by any context. With the method we propose to follow the objection disappears, since the myth itself provides its own context. The significance is no longer to be sought in the eventual meaning of each name, but in the fact that all the

"remarkable connotation of the surnames"—Oedipus' name means "swollen foot"; his grandfather's name, Labdacus, means "lame"; and his father's name means "left-sided."

Il Riccio (1470–1523), *Europa on the Bull.* In the view of Levi-Strauss, this represents the first episode of the story of Oedipus (see the chart).

1	2	3	4
Cadmus seeks his sister Europa who was ravished by Zeus.			
		Cadmus kills the dragon.	
	The Spartoi kill one another.		
			Labdacus (Laius' father) = lame.
	Oedipus kills his father.		
			Laius (Oedipus' father) = left-sided.
		Oedipus kills the Sphinx.	
			Oedipus = swollen-foot.
Oedipus marries his mother, Jocasta.			
	Eteocles kills his brother, Polyneices.		
Antigone buries her brother, Polyneices, despite prohibition.			

This chart illustrates Levi-Strauss' use of the terms *synchronic* and *diachronic*.

diachronic Read top to bottom, moving left to right. The story of the myth emerges from this method of reading.

synchronic Consider each column as a separate unit. Read top to bottom only. The meaning of the myth emerges from this method of reading.

names have a common feature: All the hypothetical meanings (which may well remain hypothetical) refer to *difficulties in walking straight and standing upright.*

What then is the relationship between the two columns on the right? Column three refers to monsters. The dragon is **a chthonian being** which has to be killed in order that mankind be born from the Earth; the sphinx is a monster unwilling to permit men to live. The last unit reproduces the first one, which has to do with the *autochthonous origin* of mankind. Since the monsters are overcome by men, we may thus say that the common feature of the third column is *denial of the autochthonous origin of man.*

This immediately helps us to understand the meaning of the fourth column. In mythology it is a universal characteristic of **men born from the Earth** that at the moment they emerge from the depth they either cannot walk or they walk clumsily. This is the case of the chthonian beings in the mythology of the Pueblo: Muyingwu, who leads the emergence, and the chthonian Shumaikoli are lame ("bleeding-foot," "sore-foot"). The same happens to the Koskimo of the Kwakiutl after they have been swallowed by the chthonian monster, Tsiakish: When they returned to the surface of the earth "they limped forward or tripped side-ways." Thus the common feature of the fourth column is *the persistence of the autochthonous origin of man.* It follows that **column four is to column three** as column one is to column two. The inability to connect two kinds of relationships is overcome (or rather replaced) by the assertions that contradictory relationships are identical inasmuch as they are both self-contradictory in a similar way.

Although this is still a provisional formulation of the structure of mythical thought, it is sufficient at this stage.

Turning back to the Oedipus myth, **we may now see what it means.** The myth has

"a chthonian being"—χϑῶν (chthōn) is the Greek word for "earth." Cadmus buried the dragon's teeth in the earth, and the "crop" that grew was the army of Spartoi. Thus they are not born of the union of two creatures, but they sprang from the earth. The English word for this is "autochthonous."

"men born from the Earth"—The Greeks believed that humans were the product of the union of a man and a woman, who are viewed as like creatures. In their stories, creatures not born of two like creatures (like those that spring from the earth) are abnormal and usually monsters.

"column four is to column three"— Here Levi-Strauss takes his analysis even further, finding relationships *between* the columns or bundles he has already identified. Columns 1 and 2 show opposite views of the value of kinship; columns 3 and 4 show opposing views of man's origin from the earth.

"we may now see what it means"—Levi-Strauss identifies the meaning of the myth. The Oedipus myth provides a way of grappling with a problem which is basic to the beliefs of the people who told it. It wonders where human beings come from, and therefore, what the point of their life is. In telling the story, people were able to think about issues that bothered them, but in a way that minimized their anxiety.

"some basic elements are lacking"—Events and details may vary from one version of a myth to another, but this variation adds value to a Levi-Straussian interpretation. Although some elements may be omitted or new ones added, the substance of the myth remains.

"the quest for the *true* version, or the *earlier* one"—Myth is always changing. We may look for an earlier version, but this is not intrinsically more valuable, since the problems are forever current. For example, the Oedipus story is so popular today because we find in it human values which appeal to us. Our beliefs and experiences are certainly different from those of the original ancient Greek audience, but we interpret the myth according to our knowledge and values.

"Freud . . . should [also] be included"—For a discussion of Freud's view of family relationships, see the Introduction to Part 3, p. 155.

"Labdacus' collateral line"—Cousins: those from the same grandparents, but not his brothers and sisters.

Agave, Pentheus Pentheus was the king of Thebes when the worship of Dionysus was being introduced there. When he opposed the new cult, Dionysus arranged his death at the hands of his own mother, Agave.

to do with the inability, for a culture which holds the belief that mankind is autochthonous, to find a satisfactory transition between this theory and the knowledge that human beings are actually born from the union of man and woman. Although the problem obviously cannot be solved, the Oedipus myth provides a kind of logical tool which relates the original problem—born from one or born from two?—to the derivative problem: born from different or born from same? By a correlation of this type, the overrating of blood relations is to the underrating of blood relations as the attempt to escape autochthony is to the impossibility to succeed in it. Although experience contradicts theory, social life validates cosmology by its similarity of structure. Hence cosmology is true.

Two remarks should be made at this stage.

In order to interpret the myth, we left aside a point which has worried the specialists until now, namely, that in the earlier (Homeric) versions of the Oedipus myth, **some basic elements are lacking,** such as Jocasta killing herself and Oedipus piercing his own eyes. These events do not alter the substance of the myth although they can easily be integrated, the first one as a new case of autodestruction (column three) and the second as another case of crippledness (column four). At the same time there is something significant in these additions, since the shift from foot to head is to be correlated with the shift from autochthonous origin to self-destruction.

Our method thus eliminates a problem which has, so far, been one of the main obstacles to the progress of mythological studies, namely, **the quest for the *true* version, or the *earlier* one.** On the contrary, we define the myth as consisting of all its versions; or to put it otherwise a myth remains the same as long as it is felt as such. A striking example is offered by the fact that our interpretation may take into account the Freudian use of the Oedipus myth and is certainly applicable to it. Although the Freudian problem has ceased to be that of autochthony *versus* bisexual reproduction, it is still the problem of understanding how *one* can be born from *two:* How is it that we do not have only one procreator, but a mother plus a father? Therefore, not only Sophocles, but **Freud himself, should be included** among the recorded versions of the Oedipus myth on a par with earlier or seemingly more "authentic" versions.

An important consequence follows. If a myth is made up of all its variants, structural analysis should take all of them into account. After analyzing all the known variants of the Theban version, we should thus treat the others in the same way: first, the tales about **Labdacus' collateral line** including **Agave, Pentheus,** and Jocasta herself; the Theban variant about Lycos with Amphion and Zetos as the city founders; more remote variants concerning Dionysus (Oedipus' matrilateral cousin); and Athenian legends where Cecrops takes the place of Cadmus, etc. For each of them a similar chart should be

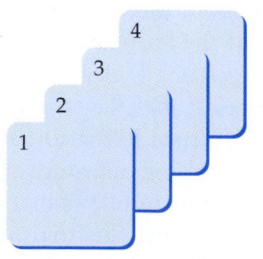

To analyze a myth comprehensively, all known variants should be considered. Each variant is represented on a two-dimensional chart; these are then organized in three-dimensional order, making different readings possible.

drawn and then compared and reorganized according to the findings: Cecrops killing the serpent with the parallel episode of Cadmus; abandonment of Dionysus with abandonment of Oedipus; "Swollen Foot" with Dionysus' loxias, that is, walking obliquely; Europa's quest with Antiope's; the founding of Thebes by the Spartoi or by the brothers Amphion and Zetos; Zeus kidnapping Europa and Antiope and the same with Semele; the Theban Oedipus and the Argian Perseus, etc. We shall then have several two-dimensional charts, each dealing with a variant, to be organized in a three-dimensional order, as shown in the figure [to the left], so that three different readings become possible: left to right, top to bottom, front to back (or vice versa). All of these charts cannot be expected to be identical; but experience shows that **any difference to be observed** may be correlated with other differences, so that a logical treatment of the whole will allow simplifications, the final outcome being the structural law of the myth.

At this point the objection may be raised that the task is impossible to perform, since we can only work with known versions. Is it not possible that **a new version might alter the picture?** This is true enough if only one or two versions are available, but the objection becomes theoretical as soon as a reasonably large number have been recorded. Let us make this point clear by a comparison. If the furniture of a room and its arrangement were known to us only through its reflection in the **two mirrors placed on opposite walls,** we should theoretically dispose of an almost infinite number of mirror images which would provide us with a complete knowledge. However, should the **two mirrors be obliquely set,** the number of mirror images would become very small; nevertheless, four or five such images would very likely give us, if not complete information, at least a sufficient coverage so that we would feel sure that no large piece of furniture is missing in our description.

On the other hand, it cannot be too strongly emphasized that all available variants should be taken into account. There is no single true version of which all the others are but copies or distortions. **Every version belongs to the myth.**

The reason for discouraging results in works on general mythology can finally be understood. They stem from two causes. First, comparative mythologists have selected preferred versions instead of using them all. Second, we have seen that the structural analysis of *one* variant of one myth belonging to one tribe (in some cases, even one village) already requires two dimensions. When we use several variants of the same myth for the same tribe or village, the frame of reference becomes three-dimensional, and as soon as we try to enlarge the comparison, the number of dimensions required increases until it appears quite impossible to handle them intuitively. The confusions and platitudes which are the outcome of comparative mythology can be explained by the fact that multi-dimensional frames of reference are often ignored or are naively replaced by two- or three-dimensional ones. Indeed, progress in comparative mythology depends largely on the cooperation of mathematicians who would undertake to express in symbols multi-dimensional relations which cannot be handled otherwise.

To check this theory, **an attempt was made from 1952 to 1954 toward an exhaustive analysis** of all the known versions of the Zuni origin and emergence myth: Cushing, 1883 and 1896; Stevenson, 1904; Parsons, 1923; Bunzel, 1932; Benedict, 1934. Furthermore, a preliminary attempt was made at a comparison of the results with similar myths in other Pueblo tribes, Western and Eastern.

As the chart indicates, the problem is the discovery of a life-death mediation. For the Pueblo, this is especially difficult; they understand the origin of human life in terms of the model of plant life (emergence from the earth). **They share that belief with the ancient Greeks,** and it is not without reason that we chose the Oedipus myth as our first example. But in the American Indian case, the highest form of plant life is to be found in agriculture which is periodical in nature, that is, which consists in an alternation between life and death. . . .

By systematically using this kind of structural analysis it becomes possible to organize all the known variants of a myth into a set forming a kind of permutation group, the two variants placed at the far ends being in a symmetrical, though inverted, relationship to each other.

Our method not only has the advantage of bringing some kind of order to what was previously chaos; it also enables us to perceive some basic logical processes which are at the root of mythical thought. Three main processes should be distinguished.

"any difference to be observed"—Levi-Strauss encourages collecting and analyzing the greatest possible number of variants, which, when charted according to his method, provide the most comprehensive meaning of the myth—what he here calls "the structural law of the myth."

"a new version might alter the picture"—If we have several versions already, a new one cannot affect the picture much.

"two mirrors placed on opposite walls"—The mirrors would reflect each other's content back and forth infinitely. However, the infinite copies of them would still only be referring to one subset—that is, we would see the same furniture in both mirrors (although from different directions) and would have no way of guessing what other furniture there was.

"two mirrors . . . obliquely set"—Here each mirror would reflect a different part of the room, giving us a better guess as to what furniture was in it.

"Every version belongs to the myth."—All available versions should be included in the structural analysis of a myth.

"an attempt . . . toward an exhaustive analysis"—For a selection from the work of Ruth Benedict, see Ch. 8.

"They share that belief with the ancient Greeks"—Like the Oedipus myth, the Zuni cycle of stories also deals with basic human questions concerning life and death.

"Our method . . . has the advantage"—Levi-Strauss emphasizes the basic logical processes of his structural method.

A Simplified Chart of the Zuni Emergence Myth

Change			Death
Mechanical value of plants (used as ladders to emerge from lower world)	Emergence led by Beloved Twins	Sibling incest (origin of water)	Gods kill children of men (by drowning)
Food value of wild plants	Migration led by the teo Newekwe (ceremonial clowns)		Magical contest with People of the Dew (collecting wild food *versus* cultivation)
		Brother and sister sacrificed (to gain victory)	
Food value of cultivated plants			
		Brother and sister adopted (in exchange of corn)	
Periodical character of agricultural work			
			War against the Kyanakwe (gardeners *versus* hunters)
Food value of game (hunting)			
	War led by the two War-Gods		
Inevitability of warfare			Salvation of the tribe (center of the World found)
		Brother and sister sacrificed (to avoid the Flood)	
DEATH			PERMANENCE

Tricksters

The trickster of American mythology has remained so far a problematic figure. Why is it that throughout North America his role is assigned practically everywhere to either coyote or raven? If we keep in mind that mythical thought always progresses from the awareness of oppositions toward their resolution, the reason for these choices becomes clearer. We need only assume that two opposite terms with no intermediary always tend to be replaced by two equivalent terms which admit of a third one as a mediator; then one of the polar terms and the mediator become replaced by a new triad, and so on. Thus we have a mediating structure of the following type:

This carved spoon comes from the Haida or Tlingit culture on the Northwest Coast of North America. The handle represents a raven and a doubled-up human. Raven and Coyote are trickster figures throughout North America.

Initial pair	First triad	Second triad
Life	Agriculture	
		Herbivorous animals
		Carrion-eating animals (raven, coyote)
		Beasts of prey
	Hunting	
	Warfare	
Death		

The unformulated argument is as follows: carrion-eating animals are like beasts of prey (they eat animal food), but they are also like food-plant producers (they do not kill what they eat). Or to put it otherwise, Pueblo style (for Pueblo agriculture is more "meaningful" than hunting): ravens are to gardens as beasts of prey are to herbivorous animals. But it is also clear that herbivorous animals may be called first to act as **mediators** on the assumption that they are like collectors and gatherers (plant-food eaters), while they can be used as animal food though they are not themselves hunters. Thus we may have mediators of the first order, of the second order, and so on, where each term generates the next by a double process of opposition and correlation.

This kind of process can be followed in the mythology of the Plains, where we may order the data according to the set:

> Unsuccessful mediator between Earth and Sky
> (Star-Husband's Wife)
>
> Heterogeneous pair of mediators
> (grandmother and grandchild)
>
> Semi-homogeneous pair of mediators
> (Lodge-Boy and Thrown-away)

While among the Pueblo (Zuni) we have the corresponding set:

> Successful mediator between Earth and Sky
> (Poshaiyanki)
>
> Semi-homogeneous pair of mediators
> Uyuyewi and Matsailema)
>
> Homogeneous pair of mediators
> (the two Ahaiyuta)

> **mediators** Myth-makers gradually rationalize opposites by incorporating intermediate processes or characters.

Ash Boy and Cinderella

On the other hand, correlations may appear on a horizontal axis: (this is true even on the linguistic level; see the manifold connotation of the root *pose* in Tewa according to Parsons: coyote, mist, scalp, etc.). Coyote (a carrion-eater) is intermediary between herbivorous and carnivorous just as mist between Sky and Earth; as scalp between war and agriculture (scalp is a war crop); corn smut between wild and cultivated plants; as garments **between "nature" and "culture"**; as refuse between village and outside; and as ashes (or soot) between roof (sky vault) and hearth (in the ground). This **chain of mediators,** if one may call them so, not only throws light on entire parts of North American mythology—why the Dew-God may be at the same time the Game-Master and the giver of raiments and be personified as an "Ash-Boy"; or why scalps are mist-producing; or why the Game-Mother is associated with corn smut; etc.—but it also probably corresponds to a universal way of organizing daily experience. See, for instance, the French for plant smut (*nielle,* from Latin *nebula); the luck-bringing power attributed in Europe to refuse (old shoe) and ashes (kissing chimney sweeps); and compare the American Ash-Boy cycle with the Indo-European Cinderella: Both are phallic figures (mediators between male and female); masters of the dew and the game; owners of fine raiments; and social mediators (low class marrying into high class); but they are impossible to interpret through recent diffusion, as has been contended, since Ash-Boy and Cinderella are symmetrical but inverted in

> "between 'nature' and 'culture'"— This opposition is at the root of Levi-Strauss' anthropological study of myth. For an application of this methodology to the story of Gilgamesh, see Ch. 16, p. 198ff.

> "chain of mediators"—The relations between nature and culture found in the stories of a society are also reflected in the language and values.

every detail (while the borrowed Cinderella tale in America—Zuni Turkey-Girl—is parallel to the prototype). Hence the chart:

	Europe	America
Sex	female	male
Family Status	double family (remarried father)	no family (orphan)
Appearance	pretty girl	ugly boy
Sentimental status	nobody likes her	unrequited love for girl
Transformation	luxuriously clothed with supernatural help	stripped of ugliness with supernatural help

"like Ash-Boy . . . the trickster is a mediator"—For more on tricksters, see Chs. 21 (p. 296f), 23 (p. 339), and 24 (p. 353).

Thus **like Ash-Boy and Cinderella, the trickster is a mediator.** Since his mediating function occupies a position halfway between two polar terms, he must retain something of that duality—namely an ambiguous and equivocal character. But the trickster figure is not the only conceivable form of mediation; some myths seem to be entirely devoted to the task of exhausting all the possible solutions to the problem of bridging the gap between *two* and *one*.

The Structure of Myths

"quadruplication"—See the Native American creation myths in Ch. 8, p. 89.

The question has often been raised why myths, and more generally oral literature, are so much addicted to duplication, triplication, or **quadruplication** of the same sequence. If our hypotheses are accepted, the answer is obvious: The function of repetition is to render the structure of the myth apparent. For we have seen that the synchronic-diachronic structure of the myth permits us to organize it into diachronic sequences (the rows in our tables) which should be read synchronically (the columns). Thus, a myth exhibits a "slated" structure, which comes to the surface, so to speak, through the process of repetition.

 **The Proliferation of Myths**

The Logic of Myths

However, the slates are not absolutely identical. And since the purpose of myth is to provide a logical model capable of overcoming a contradiction (an impossible achievement if, as it happens, the contradiction is real), a theoretically infinite number of slates will be generated, each one slightly different from the others. Thus, myth grows spiral-wise until the intellectual impulse which has produced it is exhausted. Its *growth* is a continuous process, whereas its *structure* remains **discontinuous.**

discontinuous The structure of myths exhibits this quality because new tellings produce versions which are somewhat different from existing ones.

Prevalent attempts to explain alleged differences between the so-called primitive mind and scientific thought have resorted to qualitative differences between the working processes of the mind in both cases, while assuming that the entities which they were studying remained very much the same. If our interpretation is correct, we are led toward a completely different view—namely, that the kind of logic in mythical thought is as rigorous as that of modern science, and that the difference lies, not in the quality of the intellectual process, but in the nature of the things to which it is applied. This is well in agreement with the situation known to prevail in the field of technology: What makes a steel ax superior to a stone ax is not that the first one is better made than the second. They are equally well made, but steel is quite different from stone. In the same way we may be able to show that the same logical processes operate in myth as in science, and that man has always been thinking equally well; the improvement lies, not in an alleged progress of man's mind, but in the discovery of new areas to which it may apply its unchanged and unchanging powers.

Edmund Leach on Levi-Strauss

Edmund Leach explains the theories of Levi-Strauss for the nonspecialist in his book called *Claude Levi-Strauss*. He makes it clear that the point of view is his, and that he is restating and interpreting the original. However, the book is an excellent introduction to a difficult body of work, and for that reason, it is excerpted in this chapter. For Leach and Levi-Strauss, the primary role of myth is the weighing of apparent contradictions in the various versions of the myths and achieving a mediation between them. That is, myths present opposing ideas because we often see our lives in terms of opposites that present choices. For example, in choosing a college, we might weigh the question of whether to live at home and attend a nearby school, or to move far away and live more independently. Our decision might be affected by emotional factors (closeness to family and friends versus making new friends and developing as an individual) or economic ones (living at home is probably cheaper). At any rate, we look at the pros and cons and decide which is best for us. Levi-Strauss and Leach emphasize that on a deeper level, we make the same kinds of decisions about our cultural values; and our acceptance of a particular set of values is often the result of our weighing the positive and negative factors. We may not carry out the process as consciously, but we do come to a conclusion that makes the unwelcome contradiction acceptable to us. For example, in the previous example, we might finally choose to strike a balance by living on campus, but going home for weekends.

Myths, then, help us deal with the contradictions in our lives. Another instance of such a contradiction occurs when new scientific evidence contradicts old beliefs. Levi-Strauss shows the way the Oedipus cycle of stories resolves this contradiction in the preceding excerpt from "The Structure of Myth."

THE STRUCTURAL METHOD

Levi-Strauss' structural analysis of myth cycles (p. 284ff.) is scientific and systematic. He gathers the largest possible sample, dissects it into constituent units, and observes and analyzes these units in relationship to the whole, noting logical patterns in their use. By examining these relationships, we start to see the logical connections that might help explain the underlying— maybe even subconscious—message.

Leach uses the Oedipus story to illustrate Levi-Strauss' analytical principles. As we saw, Levi-Strauss finds that the Oedipus myth tries to achieve a balance between these extremes:

Extreme	**Example**
1. Overrating of blood relationships	incest
2. Underrating of blood relationships	killing your father
3. Monsters being slain	the death of the Sphinx
4. Difficulty in walking straight and standing upright	Oedipus' damaged feet

The first two of the extreme elements listed above are in fact the poles of a scale useful for studying Greek mythology as well as a wide range of stories. This scale represents the tension between the extremes of incest (element 1) and exogamy (element 2, marrying outside of your tribe or group). The scale can be represented as follows:

Incest   Exogamy

Nature   Culture

This scale allows us to consider individual actions of characters in a story and to track the tensions they struggle with in the course of a story. (See Ch. 14, pp. 159–165.) The best outcome to

Cadmus killing the dragon of Thebes. Laconian cup, ca. 550 B.C.E. From the teeth of the dragon sprang autochthonous "earth-born" men (the Spartoi) who had trouble walking. See the discussion by Leach (292).

the struggle, in the view of Levi-Strauss, would be to achieve a balance between the extremes of the scale, but in the case of tragic tales, this outcome is not realized in many cases. Because incest here refers to the overrating of blood relations, it does not necessarily imply the actions usually associated with the everyday use of the word. Rather, it can refer to any set of actions that suggest an extreme respect for one's blood relations, like Antigone's burial of her brother (in Sophocles' play *Antigone*), even though this action is illegal according to the laws established by Creon.

In describing Levi-Strauss' work, Leach shows that the story of Oedipus and other Greek myths are so interrelated that it is possible to view the whole of Greek mythology as a single system. That is, the collection of Greek myth cycles provides a single mega-message that contains all the values and beliefs of the ancient Greek world. Leach finds that Greek myth is full of examples of the differences among humans, animals, and gods, and that these contrasts point out contradictions that we (and the Greeks) encounter in life.

The most important and most basic of these oppositions is that of nature versus culture. As humans move from being at home in nature toward a dependence on a world of more complicated structure and laws, they lose their relationship with the gods and the ideal of paradise. The theme of a contrast between nature and culture is only one of the oppositions Leach finds in Greek mythology; others are the opposition between life and death, between sky and underworld, and between this world and the other world beyond it. Leach's analysis illustrates Levi-Strauss' theory that "collectively the sum of what all myths say is not expressly said by any of them, and that what they thus say (collectively) is a necessary poetic truth which is an unwelcome contradiction" (Leach, 77).

To elucidate this theory, Leach retells all the incidents involved in the Oedipus myth, highlighting the fundamental patterns of opposition that Levi-Strauss identified. In the excerpt below, we include four of the eight stories Leach recounts in his comprehensive analysis of the Oedipus myth. Even with this subject, we will be able to show that the stories about Oedipus are interrelated, and that this myth is effective at teaching the wide range of values of the early Greeks.

This section comes from: Edmund Leach, *Claude Levi-Strauss.**

"a bull . . . carries off . . . Europa . . . a cow [leads] Cadmus"—Demonstrates the oppositions—divine: human and wild: tame.

"to follow a particular cow"—See the Oedipus story chart, column 1: Overvaluation of kinship, p. 285.

"Having killed the dragon"—column 3: Men kill monsters.

"Cadmus sows the dragon's teeth"—domestic: wild.

"[Spartoi] kill one another"—Undervaluation of kinship. Spartoi means "(men) sowed from the dragon's teeth."

"Nature : Culture :: Gods : Men"—Should be read, "Nature is to culture as gods are to men."

"unstable alliance"—See Introduction, p. 281.

Cadmus, Europa, and the Dragon's Teeth

Story: Zeus (God) in the form of **a tame wild bull** (mediator between wild and tame) **seduces and carries off a human girl, Europa.**

Europa's brother, Cadmus, and mother, Telephassa, search for her. The mother dies and is buried by Cadmus. Cadmus is then told **to follow a particular cow** (domestic animal: replacement of sister and mother). Where the cow stops, Cadmus must found Thebes, having first sacrificed the cow to Athena. (Cow forms link between man and gods just as bull formed link between the gods and man.) In seeking to provide water for the sacrifice Cadmus encounters a dragon (monster) guarding a sacred pool. The dragon is a son of Ares, god of war. Cadmus and the dragon engage in battle. **Having killed the dragon, Cadmus sows the dragon's teeth** (a domestic action applied to wild material). The crop is men (the Spartoi) without mothers.

They kill one another, but the survivors cooperate with Cadmus to found Thebes. Cadmus makes peace with Ares and marries his daughter Harmonia. The gods give Harmonia a magical necklace as dowry, which later brings disaster to everyone who possesses it. At the end of the story Cadmus and Harmonia change into dragons.

Comment: The story specifies the polarity **Nature : Culture : : Gods : Men** and affirms that the relationship between gods and men is one of ambiguous and **unstable**

---

*Leach, Edmund, *Claude Levi-Strauss* (New York: Viking Press, 1970), 78–89.

alliance—exemplified by marriage followed by feud followed by marriage accompanied by poisoned marriage gifts. There is also the ambiguity of autochthony/nonautochthony. Cadmus, who slays the dragon from whom are born the Spartoi, is himself the dragon and ancestor of the Spartoi.

Laius, Chrysippus, and Jocasta

Story: During the reigns of Lycus, Amphion, and Zethus, Laius goes into banishment and is befriended by Pelops. **He falls in love with Pelops' son,** Chrysippus, whom he teaches to drive a chariot. After returning to the throne of Thebes he marries Jocasta but avoids sleeping with her because of the prophecy that her son will kill him. The conception which results in the birth of Oedipus follows a bout of lust when Laius has got drunk at a religious feast. On the occasion when he encountered Oedipus "at the crossroads," Oedipus was a "young man driving a chariot."

"He falls in love with Pelops' son"—The homosexual aspect of this story creates a way for parallel actions of Laius with a young boy who is or should be like a son.

Comment: The myth establishes an equivalence between Chrysippus and Oedipus, and the incest between Oedipus and his mother is matched by **homosexual incest between Laius and his son.**

"homosexual incest between Laius and his son"—Actually Pelops' son Chrysippus.

Oedipus

Story: The King (Laius) and the Queen (Jocasta) rule in Thebes. The son (Oedipus) is exposed on a mountain with his ankles staked and thought to be dead. He survives. The son meets the King-father "at a crossroads" and kills him. The Queen's brother (Creon) acts as regent. Thebes is beset by a monster (Sphinx, female). The Queen's hand in marriage is offered to anyone who will get rid of the monster by answering its riddle. Oedipus does so. The monster commits suicide. The son assumes all aspects of the deceased father's role. On discovery, the Queen commits suicide; son-King (Oedipus) blinds himself and becomes a seer (acquires supernatural sight).

This story comes from: Sophocles' *Oedipus the King*. However, the scenes with the Sphinx are not included in the play. See Ch. 19, p. 231, for the full text of Sophocles' play, and Ch. 25, p. 360, for B. M. W. Knox's discussion of *Oedipus*.

Antigone, Eteocles, and Polyneices

Story: Oedipus has two sons, Eteocles and Polyneices, who are also his half-brothers, since they are sons of Jocasta. Oedipus having abdicated, Eteocles and Polyneices are supposed to hold the throne alternately. Eteocles takes the throne first and refuses to give it up; Polyneices is banished and leads an army of heroes from Argos against Thebes. The expedition fails. Eteocles and Polyneices kill each other. Antigone, in defiance of Creon, performs funeral rites over Polyneices. In punishment she is walled up alive in a tomb, where she commits suicide. Later the sons of the dead heroes lead another expedition against Thebes and are triumphant.

This story comes from: Sophocles' *Antigone*.

Wedding of Iocaste and Oedipus, by Giovanni Boccaccio. 15th-c. illustration for *Des Cleres et Nobles Femmes.* In the background their sons, Polyneices and Eteocles, prepare for battle, throwing Thebes into civil war, the backdrop for Sophocles' *Antigone.*

Comment: Levi-Strauss' own treatment of [the stories relating to Oedipus and his family is handled in "The Structure of Myth" section].

It will be seen that if we proceed in this way there never comes a point at which we can say that we have considered "all the variants," for **almost any story** drawn from the general complex of classical Greek mythology **turns out to be a variant** in one way or another. If, for example, we take as our central theme the Oedipus complex as understood by Freud—the story of a son who kills his father and then becomes the paramour of his mother—we shall find that **the following well-known stories are all "variants."** Thus:

Oedipus: son kills father and becomes paramour.
Agamemnon: paramour [Clytemnestra] kills father, inviting vengeance from the son.
Odysseus: father merges with son and destroys the would-be paramours. Odysseus has no descendants.
Menelaus: paramour (Paris) is destroyed by a third party and there is no heir (son).
Hippolytus: innocent son, falsely accused of being paramour, is killed by father.

What emerges from such a comparison is that each story is seen to be **a combination of relational themes,** that each theme is one of a set of variations, and that what is significant about these relational themes is the contrast between the variations.

The message contained in the whole set of stories cannot readily be put into words; otherwise there would be no need for such circumlocution. But roughly, what it amounts to is simple enough: if society is to go on, daughters must be disloyal to their parents and sons must destroy (replace) their fathers.

Here then is the **irresolvable unwelcome contradiction,** the necessary fact that we hide from consciousness because its implications run directly counter to the fundamentals of human morality.

There are no heroes in these stories; they are simply epics of unavoidable human disaster. The disaster always originates in the circumstances that a human being fails to fulfill his or her proper obligations toward a deity or a kinsman, and this, in part at least, is what Levi-Strauss is getting at when he insists that the fundamental moral implication of mythology is that "Hell is ourselves," which I take to mean "self-interest is the source of all evil."

But I must again remind the reader that this whole example is **Leach imitating Levi-Strauss** and not a summary of a Levi-Strauss original. It has been necessary to go to this length in order to display the "theme and variations" aspects of a typical Levi-Straussian analysis, but in all other respects the material is thin and atypical. There is a paucity of magical happenings and a monotonous concentration on the bedrock issues of homicide and sexual misdemeanor. In Levi-Strauss' own examples these ultimate conflicts are usually transformed into a language code of some other kind.

Further Reading

Leach, Edmund. *Claude Levi-Strauss.* New York: Viking Press, 1970.

"almost any story . . . turns out to be a variant"—Structural analysis of a myth cycle requires consideration of all variants. The cycle involves enough redundancy that the meaning comes across nonetheless.

"the following well-known stories are all 'variants'"—The range of relations experienced between father and son: in some cases, the relationship is too close and interferes with the survival of the family. In others, the relationship is too distant, with the same result. Charting and analyzing relationships such as these is at the root of Levi-Straussian structural analysis.

"a combination of relational themes"—For an explanation of relationships, see Levi-Strauss, p. 273f.

"The message"—Greek myth, like myth in general, transmits a cultural message: that is, it tells members of a society how to behave if the society is to continue.

"irresolvable unwelcome contradiction"—According to Levi-Strauss, the complexity of mythological stories serves to blunt their painful message. The variations in the story show the pain human beings cause when they overreach themselves. The message is, we are only human beings, not gods.

"There are no heroes in these stories"—Greek myth teaches that disaster results because of human error.

"Leach imitating Levi-Strauss"—Leach reminds us that he is interpreting the ideas of Levi-Strauss. He emphasizes that the original is deeper and more complex.

Raven

A Native American Trickster

WHAT TO EXPECT . . . The discussion of tricksters was begun as part of Claude Levi-Strauss' theory in Chapter 20 (p. 288) and continues in this chapter. The trickster is typically a figure between two worlds who gains inspiration and power from the realms he bridges. Because he is not completely invested in these societies, the trickster is freer to disregard the morals and standards held dear by them, and to behave in ways that their members would find improper or unacceptable. From his unique position, the trickster can also be a valuable asset to humans by creating and providing what they need. This chapter introduces Raven, a complex figure from the Northwestern coast of North America. In the context of trickster figures, Raven's bringing light to the world has similarities to the Greek figure Prometheus' bringing fire, or to other characteristics of Greek Hermes and Norse Loki.

Like African and African-American tricksters (Ch. 23, p. 339), Raven lives on the fringes of society. Although he may have some godlike attributes, he is different from the trickster-gods in the Greek and Norse traditions. In Native American mythology, there is a symbiotic relationship that extols the idea that all of nature participates in creation as keepers of the earth.

As you read, you may want to consider the role of the storyteller in producing different versions and styles of the same myth. Also, it may be useful to compare these stories and the Zuni, Hopi, and Navajo creation stories in Chapter 8, p. 89. Finally, Chapter 25, p. 364, contains discussion of the meaning and significance of working versions of a myth like the ones found in this chapter.

The Native American culture hero Raven is a raucous trickster who pulls outrageous pranks to get what he wants. At the same time, he is also a creator and provider who gives humans what they need and teaches them both practical and moral lessons. As a benefactor of humans, he reinforces the notion that humans are responsible for what happens to their world. (For more on this view of the world, see the discussion under Native American creation myths, Ch. 8, p. 94.) The broad spectrum of American Indian myths and rituals shows us the value of a close relationship with extraordinary beings like Raven, because they emphasize the importance of a symbiotic relationship of humans and nature. In this interaction, all beings are appreciated according to their individual capabilities. Thus, Native Americans do not believe in a single supreme deity or a group of chosen gods with extraordinary powers, although some beings in their world are more important than others.

Raven tales are prominent throughout a broad area of northwestern North America and northeastern Asia. They are the myths of the people whose ancestors crossed the Bering Strait tens of thousands of years ago when a land-bridge between Siberia in Asia and Alaska in North America existed. The groups who remained in what is now Alaska and the Northwest Coast of Canada, along the coast of British Columbia, include the Haida, Tlingit, Tsimshian, and Kwaki-utl peoples.

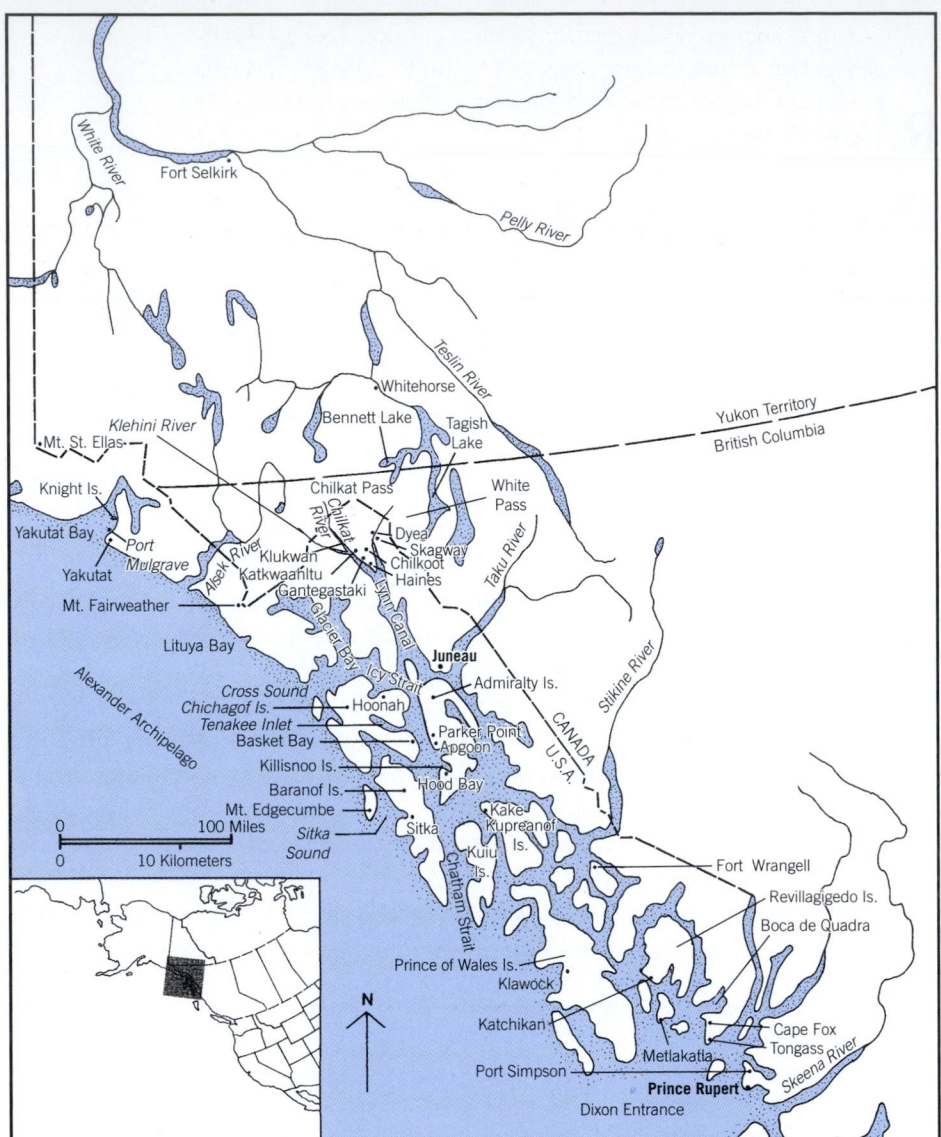

Map of Southeastern Alaska, showing the Native American communities.

RAVEN AND THE TRICKSTER TRADITION

In some ways, the story of Raven parallels the characteristics of trickster gods and demigods in other mythic traditions, such as the Greek and the Norse. However, the differences among these trickster figures reveal specific beliefs of their cultural groups. For example, Hermes in the Greek tradition and Loki in the Norse belong to the families of gods who are in charge of the world. As noted, Raven, strictly speaking, is not a god. Nonetheless, we might think that Raven resembles other godlike beings, because he has some of the characteristics we associate with divinity. For instance, the circumstances of his birth are unusual and fantastic. Raven always existed, but he was born of a virgin whom he tricked into eating a seed. He also shares the god-like attribute of creator. Raven created land by dropping grains of sand into the sea, and he caused different types of animals to be created.

The Raven trickster tales also have characteristics in common with some of the other trickster traditions presented in this book, including Kweku Anansi from Africa (Ch. 23, p. 345), Anancy from African-American stories (Ch. 23, p. 346), Loki from Icelandic myth (Ch. 18, p. 220), and the Greek trickster-god, Prometheus (Ch. 24, p. 353).

Like African and African-American tricksters, Raven also lives outside the community. That is, even though he is well-known to the community and sometimes provides good things for the people, he is not really accepted by society because he does not care to be a part of the standard social structure. In this respect, he is like the liminal trickster figures in African myth who exist on the fringes of human society (see Ch. 23, p. 339). He does not take part in the activities of the group, but instead, often prevents those activities to get what he wants. For example, Raven behaves as a child might to get his grandfather to give him the boxes containing the sun and the moon: he cries. In another story, he lies to Petrel to get him to leave his house so that Raven can drink all of his water.

Raven is, like Anancy, often motivated by his appetites and desires. His ability to reason is used primarily to devise ways to get what he wants. However, the results of his actions very often have the effect that they benefit others, enhancing his stature in the eyes of humans. For example, in the tales recounted in this chapter, Raven brings light and fire to the world for all humans.

19th-c. c.e. *Haida chest* made of argillite. On the lid is raven with both human and birdlike attributes.

Although Raven has brought good things to earth, his actions are the result of his wanting to get something for himself, not for mankind. The Norse trickster-god Loki also behaves in this way; his actions are directed toward fulfilling his own wishes. He often makes trouble, but he is not really evil. Often, though, his amusement is gotten by "puncturing the bubble" of the right and normal way of doing things. Loki, who is neither entirely good nor entirely bad, is a trickster who brings both comedy and tragedy to the Norse myths. He is an ambivalent character: he is respected among the company of the highest gods, but is also described as "mischief monger," "father of lies," and "disgrace of gods and men." He is praised for his good looks and superior abilities, but is also known to be a cheat and a troublemaker. Like Raven, Loki is a mischievous character who is often admired for his resourcefulness and for the beneficial results of his selfish deeds.

Unlike other Native American tricksters, Raven never becomes a savior or benefactor to human beings; however, his activities, though undertaken for his own reasons, often benefit human beings. Raven's trickery on behalf of humans can be contrasted with the Greek trickster Prometheus, who also helped human beings. Prometheus saw that the gods had fire, but kept it to themselves, so he stole it and brought it to earth. (See Chapter 24, p. 353, for more on Prometheus.) Zeus was so angry that he punished Prometheus unmercifully, chaining this

Insights Obtained from Myths

	Raven	Prometheus
Origin	Unknown. May be a self-made creature.	Son of the gods Iapetus and Clymene.
Motivation	His own reasons, perhaps just the fun of the trick.	Wants to help mankind.
Method	Complex plan. Uses social conventions (e.g., grandfather-grandson relationship) to achieve his end.	Steals by stealth like an ordinary thief.
Effect	Some creatures are happy and some are afraid. Raven doesn't seem to care.	People have an easier life than Zeus intended. This pleases Prometheus.
Result	Raven's act is accepted as part of his nature.	Prometheus is severely punished by the gods.
Moral	We admire a strong spirit.	Do not break the rules of the gods.

benefactor of mankind to a rock in the Caucasus Mountains where each day an eagle pecked out his liver.

Like Prometheus, Raven got things for humans through trickery. For example, he tricked his grandfather into letting the sun, moon, stars, and daylight take their places in the sky, and he tricked Petrel and stole the spring of water for his world. And, like Prometheus, Raven gave human beings fire: he taught the people how to bring fire from its origin and keep it for their use. But in spite of the similarities of their stories, Prometheus and Raven are quite different kinds of tricksters.

There is at least one viewpoint, however, from which Prometheus and Raven resemble each other. Both seem to have dual aspects: as a greedy manipulator and as a culture hero. As the section on Prometheus shows, the Greek hero is in some instances a cunning figure out to capture food to satisfy his appetite. However, in other stories he is a benefactor who provides human beings with the basis of their civilization. In *The Trickster,* Paul Radin argues that there is good evidence that Native American trickster-heroes were always divine culture-heroes as well as being divine buffoons. He also shows that, in the stories of many Native American tricksters, there is a development or evolution of the character of the trickster himself. Trickster figures often start their careers as simple figures who perform tricks to satisfy their own appetites. However, the trickster becomes a figure whose tricks are directed toward the needs of others. He is a savior who undergoes difficulty and suffering to provide the necessities of life to others. This change or evolution may occur in a subsequent part of the same story, or in other later versions of the adventures of the trickster.

RAVEN AS A SHAPE-CHANGER

Like trickster figures in many traditions, Raven is a shape-changer. He uses his shape-changing ability to shift back and forth from bird to child to accomplish his heroic deeds. We should keep in mind, however, that no matter what his physical form, Raven has the same mindset and the same way of behaving. His shape changes, but his spirit does not.

In one story, Raven changes himself into a tiny speck of dirt so that the rich man's daughter will swallow it as she drinks and thus conceive a child—a child who is actually Raven! Therefore, he has changed his shape twice here to trick the rich man who keeps the world's light hidden in a box.

Among the Northwest Coast tribes there are many stories of both people and animals changing their shape. In the Wrangell Raven myth, for example, people are so shocked when daylight is let out of the box that some run into the water and some into the woods. They have been wearing animal-skin clothing, and now they actually become the animals whose skin they were wearing.

RAVEN AS A TRANSFORMER

Raven's ability to change his shape does not, however, exhaust his magical properties of transformation. He is a creature who transforms the world. His transformational ability is in the first place an instance of his nature as a trickster, as he provides human beings with light by trickery. However, he transforms in other ways also: creating one thing out of another. For example, he forms the major rivers by flying along and spitting out the water he stole from Petrel. And in a related myth, Raven creates by transforming single grains of sand into large masses of land. In that story he has asked Mermaid to marry him, and she is willing, so long as he is able to provide her a place to sit down and rest. Raven makes a deal with Frog who gives him a bag of sand. Then Raven flies over the sea, dribbling the sand as he goes; each grain of sand becomes an island.

MYTH IS INTERWOVEN WITH LIFE

Northwestern Native American myths are very closely interconnected with the daily life of the people who live by them; what is narrated in the myth is lived through ritual. (See Part 4 for more detailed discussion of ritual, p. 373.) On a most basic level, ritual is a word we can use to describe actions regularly performed in a set manner. We carry out many rituals in our everyday actions; for example, we shake hands in greeting. For the native peoples of the Northwest Coast, ritual can include everyday tasks like the making of clothes from the skins of animals, or it can refer to special ceremonies in which the hunter releases the spirit of the dead animal so that it will return next year in a new body, ready for a new hunt. Groups of people who share the same values may act them out in actions or in words. For example, they may have special dances or songs, or stories that belong to specific holidays or family occasions.

Raven is one of the most important figures in the belief system of the native peoples of the Northwest Coast. They give him prestigious names such as "He-Whose-Voice-Is-Obeyed" in Haida and "Great Inventor" and "Chief" in Kwakiutl. Raven is also one of the most frequently used motifs in Northwest Coast native artwork. His form and his personality represent a bird prominent throughout the region. Thus, like most of the mystical beings of these peoples, he is a member of the animal kingdom. By contrast, Western peoples have more of a tendency to envision their gods as anthropomorphic, that is, having human forms and characteristics. The Native American tradition focuses on the interlocking spiritual nature of all things. The Raven myth *encourages* appreciation of creatures who benefit humans. Like other Native American myths, it extols the idea that all of nature participates as keepers of the earth, and it reveals the importance of animals to the people, both ritually and practically.

HOW THESE RAVEN STORIES WERE COLLECTED

John R. Swanton was an anthropologist who lived with the Tlingit during the first decade of the twentieth century, learning their beliefs and documenting their way of life through notes and photographs. Careful to use the most reliable sources he could find, Swanton sought out Katishan, chief of the Kasq!aque'dé of Wrangell in the southeastern part of Alaska, which shares a border with Canada. (See map, p. 296.) Katishan, whose mother was a very famous storyteller, was a chief who had the reputation for the best knowledge of myths in his area. Swanton did not always identify his source by name, so his acknowledgement of Katishan suggests he regarded the chief as a very important source. Swanton also recorded another, unnamed storyteller presenting the Raven myth at Sitka. (See map, p. 296.) Since the invention of the tape recorder was decades in the future, Swanton had to copy by hand all that was said as the storytellers spoke. Given in this chapter are two versions of essentially the same Raven myth which he collected at Wrangell and Sitka between January and April 1904. These communities are located on islands separated by a hundred-mile sea voyage.

As you read, you can compare the styles and contents of these different versions of the same myth to determine which one satisfies you better, and to figure out *why*. This also gives you the chance to observe the method used by researchers like Swanton. When they are comparing versions of a myth, they look for stories that follow ancient patterns, because they consider them to be more accurate. But in reading these versions, we can see that the two storytellers made different assumptions about the background of their audience.

For instance, the story from Sitka is probably being told for the benefit of listeners more familiar both with the Raven myth and with other stories which explain the origins of bodies of water, various animals, and the reputation of Petrel. Katishan, the storyteller at Wrangell, was assuming less familiarity on the part of his audience. His version seems to explain everything from the very first sentence and gives the story a historical perspective whenever possible. For example, it describes Raven-at-the-Head-of-the-Nass as "the principal deity to whom the Tlingit formerly prayed." An insider would not have to be told this. In addition, Katishan adds several summaries of myths unrelated to his story as background information, presumably for listeners who are unfamiliar with his native tradition.

The two stories represent differences of style and presentation. This may result from the different styles of the storytellers or it may reflect their perceptions of their individual audience. The Sitka storyteller's version is more lively and engaging. This may be because he is the more experienced storyteller: his version is directed more to the listener's participation. He expertly eases the listener into the story: "No one knows just how the story of Raven really begins, so each starts from the point where he does know it. Here it was always begun in this way." In contrast, Katishan, the storyteller at Wrangell, is more formal and distant. His opening is that of a lecture: "In olden times, only high-caste people knew the story of Raven properly because only they had time to learn it."

The differences between the two versions may also have something to do with the storytellers' perception of Swanton. Perhaps the Sitka storyteller viewed him as an "insider" with whom his tradition could be shared, while Katishan, the Wrangell storyteller, considered him an "outsider" who needed instruction in the lore of his people. However, we must be careful not to oversimplify the process of understanding the differences among the stories. For example, it may be that the Wrangell version was a particular attempt on the part of Katishan to educate the visitor he knows is in his audience. Or he may be giving more detail because he feels comfortable with his audience and knows they will enjoy the elements he adds. The Sitka storyteller may have found that his audience liked their stories told in a more traditional manner. We would have to study many more versions of the same story and many more stories by the same tellers before we could come to solid conclusions about the meaning and significance of the differences we find between these versions.

This text comes from: John Swanton, *Tlingit Myths and Texts.**

Raven Myth Recorded in English at Sitka

No one knows just how the story of Raven really begins, so each starts from the point where he does know it. Here it was always begun in this way. Raven was first called Kit-ka'ositiyi-qa-yit (Son of Kit-ka'ositiyi-qa). When his son was born, Kit-ka'ositiyi-qa tried to instruct him and train him in every way and, after he grew up, told him he would give him strength to make a world. **After trying in all sorts of ways** Raven finally succeeded. Then there was no light in this world but it was told him that far up the Nass was a large house in which someone kept light just for himself. Raven thought over all kinds of plans for getting this light into the world and finally he hit on a good one. The rich man living there had a daughter, and he thought, "I will make myself very small and drop into the water in the form of a small piece of dirt." **The girl swallowed this dirt** and became pregnant. When her time was completed, they made a hole for her, as was customary, in which she was to bring forth, and lined it with rich furs of all sorts. But **the child did not wish to be born** on those fine things. Then its grandfather felt sad and said, "What do you think it would be best to put into that hole? Shall we put in moss?" So they put moss inside and the baby was born on it. Its eyes were very bright and moved around rapidly.

The Thefts of Raven

Round bundles of varying shapes and sizes hung about on the walls of the house. When the child became a little larger it crawled around back of the people weeping continually,

"No one knows"—Telling the listeners that the origin of the story is not known is a common storyteller's technique.

"After trying in all sorts of ways"—Raven creates a world, but only after trial and error. This is not creation from nothing: some sort of world already exists, with dwellings and light, although the light is *within* the house.

"The girl swallowed this dirt"—Conception is not the result of a union between male and female of the same species. This is typical of hero myths.

"the child did not wish to be born"—Mwindo also asserted himself at a very young age. (See Ch. 22, p. 210.)

*John R. Swanton, *Tlingit Myths and Texts.* Smithsonian Institution Ethnology, Bureau of Bulletins, Vol. 39. (Washington DC: U.S. Government Printing Office, 1909, 1–5.)

and as it cried it pointed to the bundles. This lasted many days. Then its grandfather said, "Give my grandchild what he is crying for. Give him that one hanging on the end. That is the bag of stars." So the child played with this, rolling it about on the floor back of the people, until suddenly he let it go **up through the smoke hole.** It went straight up into the sky and **the stars scattered out of it** arranging themselves as you now see them. That was what he went there for.

Raven Hat. Members of the Raven moiety claimed the raven as their crest. Many crest objects including hats, dance batons, and carved wooden post and screens, refer to particular myths in the raven story.

Some time after this **he began crying again, and he cried so much** that it was thought he would die. Then his grandfather said, "Untie the next one and give it to him."

He played and played with it around behind his mother. After a while he let that go up through the smoke hole also, and there was the big moon.

Now just one thing more remained, the box that held the daylight, and he cried for that. His eyes turned around and showed different colors, and the people began thinking that he must be something other than an ordinary baby. But it always happens that a grandfather loves his grandchild just as he does his own daughter, so the grandfather said, "Untie the last thing and give it to him." His grandfather felt very sad when he gave this to him. When the child had this in his hands, **he uttered the raven cry,** "Ga," and flew out with it through the smoke hole. Then the person from whom he had stolen it said, "That old manuring raven has gotten all of my things."

Journeying on, Raven was told of another place, where a man had an everlasting spring of water. This man was named Petrel (Ganu'k). Raven wanted this water because there was none to drink in this world, but Petrel always slept by his spring, and he had a cover over it so as to keep it all to himself. Then Raven came in and said to him, "My brother-in-law, I have just come to see you.

How are you?" He told Petrel of all kinds of things that were happening outside, trying to induce him to go out to look at them, but Petrel was too smart for him and refused.

When night came, Raven said, "I am going to sleep with you, brother-in-law." So they went to bed, and toward morning Raven heard Petrel sleeping very soundly. Then he went outside, took some dog manure and put it around Petrel's buttocks. When it was beginning to grow light, he said, "Wake up, wake up, wake up, brother-in-law, you have defecated all over your clothes." Petrel got up, looked at himself, and thought it was true, so he took his blankets and went outside. Then **Raven went over to Petrel's spring,** took off the cover and began drinking. After he had drunk up almost all of the water, Petrel came in and saw him. Then Raven flew straight up, crying "Ga."

Before Raven got through the smoke hole, however, Petrel said, "My spirits up the smoke hole, catch him." So Raven stuck there, and Petrel put pitchwood on the fire under him so as to make a quantity of smoke. **Raven was white before that** time, but the smoke made him of the color you find him today. Still he did not drop the water. When the smoke-hole spirits let him go, he flew around the nearest point and rubbed himself all over so as to clear off as much of the soot as possible.

This happened somewhere about the Nass, and afterwards he started up this way. First **he let some water fall from his mouth** and made the Nass. By and by he spit more out and made the Stikine. Next, he spit out Taku river, then Chilkat, then Alsek,

"up through the smoke hole"— The traditional house has a fireplace in the center floor and a chimney, or smoke hole, directly above it in the roof.

"the stars scattered out of it"—An illustration of Joseph Campbell's cosmological aspect of myth. (See Ch. 1, p. 8.)

"he began *crying* again, and he *cried* so much"—Such repetition is common in an oral story.

"he uttered the raven cry"—Raven is revealed, but only after he succeeds and escapes.

"Raven went over to Petrel's spring"—Compare Raven's drinking here to Thor's drinking the sea in the *Prose Edda* (Ch. 18, p. 227f). But Raven is the trickster, and Thor is the dupe who has been tricked by Utgard-Loki.

"Raven was white before that"— Many myths focus on how animals got certain physical traits. This is another instance of the aetiological aspect of myth (Ch. 1, p. 7).

"he let some water fall from his mouth"—Raven spits out water as he flies to create bodies of water. This is an example of transformation. Objects are changed into other things and become geographical features of the world being created. A variation of this is the creation of the world from the body of Ymir in the *Prose Edda* (Ch. 7, p. 86).

and all the other large rivers. The small drops that came out of his mouth made the small salmon creeks.

After this Raven went on again and came to a large town where there were people who had never seen daylight. They were out catching **eulachon** in the darkness when he came to the bank opposite, and he asked them to take him across but they would not. Then he said to them, "If you don't come over **I will have daylight break** on you." But they answered, "Where are you from? Do you come from far up the Nass where lives the man who has daylight?" At this Raven opened his box just a little and shed so great a light on them that they were nearly thrown down. He shut it quickly, but they quarreled with him so much across the creek that he became angry and opened the box completely, when the sun flew up into the sky. Then those people who had sea-otter or fur-seal skins, or the skins of any other sea animals, went into the ocean, while those who had land-otter, bear, or marten skins, or the skins of any other land animals, went into the woods [**becoming the animals** whose skins they wore].

Raven Myth Recorded in English at Wrangell

In olden times **only high-caste people knew** the story of Raven properly because only they had time to learn it.

At the beginning of things there was no daylight and the world lay in blackness. Then there lived in a house at the head of Nass river a being called Raven-at-the-Head-of-the-Nass (Nas-ca'ki-yel), **the principal deity to whom the Tlingit formerly prayed** but whom no one had seen; and in his house were all kinds of things including sun, moon, stars, and daylight. He was addressed in prayers as Axcagu'n, or Axkinaye'gi, My Creator, and Wayigena'lxe, Invisible-Rich-Man. With him were two old men called Old-Man-Who-Foresees-All-Troubles-in-the-World and He-Who-Knows-Everything-that-Happens. Next to Nas-ca'ki-yel, they prayed to the latter of these. Under the earth was a third old person, Old-Woman-Underneath, placed under the world by Nas-ca'ki-yel. Nas-ca'ki-yel was unmarried and lived alone with these two old men, and yet he had a daughter, **a thing no one is able to explain.** Nor do people know what this daughter was. The two old persons took care of her like servants, and especially **they always looked into the water** before she drank to see that it was perfectly clean.

First of all beings **Nas-ca'ki-yel** created the Heron as a very tall and very wise man and after him the Raven, who was also a very good and very wise man at that time.

The Story of Raven's Birth

Raven came into being in this wise. His first mother had many children, but they all died young, and she cried over them continually. According to some, this woman was Nas-ca'ki-yel's sister and it was Nas-ca'ki-yel who was doing this because he did not wish her to have any male children. By and by Heron came to her and said, "What is it that you are crying about all the time?" She answered, "I am always losing my children. I cannot bring them up." Then he said, "Go down on the beach when the tide is lowest, get a small, smooth stone, and put it into the fire. When it is red hot, swallow it. Do not be afraid." She said, "All right." Then she followed Heron's directions and gave birth to Raven. Therefore Raven's name was really Itca'k!, the name of a very hard rock, and he was hence called Ta'qlik!-ie (Hammer-Father). This is why Raven was so tough and could not easily be killed.

Heron and Raven both became servants to **Nas-ca'ki-yel, but he thought more of Raven and made him head man over the world.** Then Nas-ca'ki-yel made some people.

eulachon A fish that is a major food source on the Northwest Coast.

"I will have daylight break"—Raven threatens the fishermen with daylight. This may seem strange, but they had to catch this night-feeding species in darkness.

"becoming the animals"—In many rituals, dancers wear animal skins to embody the spirit of the animal. An example is the buffalo dance of the Navaho.

"only high-caste people knew"—The storyteller begins with a sociological commentary.

"the principal deity to whom the Tlingit formerly prayed"—Such a description is a sign that the storyteller or his audience is outside the old belief system which generated the myth. It assumes that an explanation is necessary and provides one, which an insider would not need.

"a thing no one is able to explain"—The storyteller is self-conscious and anticipates his listener's questions.

"they always looked into the water"—This story builds on the Sitka version and assumes that the audience knows it.

Nas-ca'ki-yel—Means "Raven at the head of the Nass." However, this god creates Heron and then Raven. This is an example of parataxis. (See Ch. 2, p. 18.)

"Raven came into being in this wise"—This is a partial explanation of the origin, but is basically syntactic because the storyteller takes pains to provide a logical, well-developed story. (For an explanation of syntactic and paratactic storytelling, see Ch. 2, p. 18.)

"Nas-ca'ki-yel . . . made [Raven] head man over the world"—At this point, Nass-Raven is primary creator, who designates Raven as "head man."

All of the beings Nas-ca'ki-yel had created, however, existed in darkness, and this existence lasted for a long time, **how long is unknown.** But Raven felt very sorry for the few people in darkness and, at last, he said to himself, "If I were only the son of Nas-ca'ki-yel I could do almost anything." So he studied what he should do and decided upon a plan. **He made himself very small, turned himself into a hemlock needle,** and floated upon the water Nas-ca'ki-yel's daughter was about to drink. Then she swallowed it and soon after became pregnant.

Although all this was by the will of Nas-ca'ki-yel and although he knew what was the matter with his daughter, yet he asked her how she had gotten into that condition. She said, I drank water, and I felt that I had swallowed something in it. Then Nas-ca'ki-yel instructed them to get moss for his daughter to lie upon, and on that the child was born. **They named him Nas-ca'ki-yel also.** Then Nas-ca'ki-yel cut a basket in two and used half of it for a cradle, and he said that people would do the same thing in future times, so they have since referred its use to him.

Nas-ca'ki-yel tried to make human beings out of a rock and out of a leaf at the same time, but the rock was slow while the leaf was very quick. Therefore **human beings came from the leaf.** Then he showed a leaf to the human beings and said, "You see this leaf. You are to be like it. When it falls off the branch and rots there is nothing left of it." That is why there is death in the world. If men had come from the rock there would be no death. Years ago people used to say when they were getting old, "We are unfortunate in not having been made from a rock. Being made from a leaf, we must die."

Nas-ca'ki-yel also said, **"After people die, if they are not witches, and do not lie or steal, there is a good place for them to go to." Wicked people are to be dogs and such low animals hereafter.** The place for good people is above, and, when one comes up there, he is asked, "What were you killed for?" or "What was your life in the world?" The place he went to was governed by his reply. So people used to say to their children, "Do not lie. Do not steal. For the Maker (Nas-ca'ki-yel) will see you."

Because Nas-ca'ki-yel got it into his mind to wish for daylight in the world, he had wished for a grandchild through whom it might come. Now, therefore, although he knew what answer he would receive, he sent for Liu'wat-uwadji'gi-can and questioned him to see whether he would answer right: "Where did this child come from? Who is it? Can you tell?" And the other said, "His eyes look like the eyes of Raven." That's how he came to get the name Raven.

After a while the baby began to crawl about. His grandfather thought a great deal of him and let him play with everything in the house. Everything in the house was his. The Raven began crying for the moon, until finally they handed it to him and quick as a wink he let it go up into the sky. After he had obtained everything else, he began to cry for the box in which daylight was stored. He cried, cried, cried for a very long time, until he looked as though he were getting very sick, and finally his grandfather said, "Bring my child here." So they handed Raven to his grandfather. Then his grandfather said to him, **"My grandchild, I am giving you the last thing I have in the world."** So he gave it to him.

Then Raven, who was already quite large, walked down along the bank of Nass river until he heard the noise people were making as they fished along the shore for eulachon in the darkness. All the people in the world then lived at one place at the mouth of the Nass. They had already heard that Nas-ca'ki-yel had something

"how long is unknown"—The storyteller again anticipates the audience's question.

"He . . . turned himself into a hemlock needle"—Raven plans his own second birth, using trickery.

"They named him Nas-ca'ki-yel also."—The father and son bear the same name and become a single character in the story.

"human beings came from the leaf"—Because humans are made from the leaf instead of the rock, they die and disintegrate. See African stories on the origin of death in Ch. 9.

"After people die . . . there is a good place for them to go to"—In the *Prose Edda*, warriors who die in battle go to Valhalla, while those who do not are taken to the kingdom of Hel. (See Ch. 18, p. 221.)

"Wicked people are to be dogs and such low animals hereafter"—This reminds one of the Hindu concept of reincarnation: a person who has behaved badly is reincarnated as a lower form of life.

"My grandchild, I am giving you the last thing I have in the world."—As in the Sitka version, the grandfather gives the child everything out of love.

This *raven rattle*, collected by Louis Shotridge in Sitka, Alaska was used in ceremonies celebrating Raven's activities described in our stories in this chapter.

"They were afraid"—These people fear daylight, but those in the American Southwest sought the light or created it in order to grow corn for survival. See the Hopi myth, Ch. 8, p. 94.

"Then Raven opened the box"—He lets the light out to punish the fishermen. In the Sitka version, Raven also releases light as a punishment; but there it was because the people would not bring him to the opposite shore.

"Those that had hair-seal or fur-seal skin"—The fishermen's clothing determines what kind of animals they become. Believing that animals descended from people leads to an increased respect for their prey by hunters. We might also see this as fulfilling the psychological aspect of myth, because identifying with his prey becomes part of the hunter's sense of self. (Ch. 1, p. 6.)

"This is the origin of the great rivers of the world, the Nass, Skeena, Stikine, Chilkat, and others"—Giving the actual current names of the rivers is an indication of the syntactic nature of this version.

"Raven saw a fire far out at sea"—Raven causes fire to be brought to the people. In Hesiod's account of creation, Prometheus is punished for stealing fire from the gods and giving it to humans. This suggests a different relationship between gods and humans in ancient Greece than among the Tlingit.

"and so"—This condensed summary paragraph summarizes and judges rather than narrates, and thus seems to be informing a listener who is outside the belief system.

called "daylight," which would some day come into the world, and they used to talk about it a great deal. **They were afraid** of it.

Then Raven shouted to the fishermen, "Why do you make so much noise? If you make so much noise I will break daylight on you." Eight canoe loads of people were fishing there. But they answered, "You are not Nas-ca'ki-yel. How can you have the daylight?" and the noise continued. **Then Raven opened the box** a little and light shot over the world like lightning. At that they made still more noise. So he opened the box completely and there was daylight everywhere.

When this daylight burst upon the people they were very much frightened, and some ran into the water, some into the woods. **Those that had hair-seal or fur-seal skins** for clothing ran into the water and became hair seals and fur seals. Hair seal and fur seal were formerly only the names of the clothing they had. Those who had skins called marten skins, black-bear skins, grizzly-bear skins, etc., ran into the woods and turned into such animals. Petrel (Ganu'k) was one of the first persons created by Nas-ca'ki-yel. He was keeper of the fresh water, and would let none else touch it. The spring he owned was on a rocky island outside of Kuiu, called Deki'-nu (Fort-far-out), where the well may still be seen. Raven stole a great mouthful of this water and dropped it here and there as he went along. **This is the origin of the great rivers of the world, the Nass, Skeena, Stikine, Chilkat, and others.** He said, "This thing that I drop here and there will whirl all the time. It will not overflow the world, yet there will be plenty of water." Before this time Raven is said to have been pure white, but, as he was flying up through the smoke hole with Petrel's water, the latter said, "Spirits, hold down my smoke hole." So they held him until he was turned black by the smoke.

After this **Raven saw a fire far out at sea.** Tying a piece of pitchwood to a chicken hawk's bill, he told him to go out to this fire, touch it with the pitchwood, and bring it back. When he had brought it to him Raven put it into the rock and the red cedar saying, "This is how you are to get your fire, from this rock and this red cedar," and that is the way they formerly did. Thus Raven (Yel) went about among the natives of Alaska telling them what to do, but Nas-ca'ki-yel they never saw. Raven showed all the Tlingit what to do for a living, but he did not get to be such a high person as Nas-ca'ki-yel, and he taught the people much foolishness. At that time the world was full of dangerous animals and fish. Raven also tied up some witches, **and so** it was through him that the people believed in witchcraft. Then he told the people that some wild animals were to be their friends (i.e., their crest animals) to which they were to talk.

Further Reading

Radin, Paul. *The Trickster: A Study in American Indian Mythology*, 2nd ed. New York, NY: Schocken Books, 1972.

Swanton, John R. *Tlingit Myths and Texts*. Smithsonian Institution Ethnology, Bureau of Bulletins, Vol. 39. Washington, DC: U.S. Government Printing Office, 1909.

CHAPTER

22

The Mwindo Epic

WHAT TO EXPECT . . . This chapter deals with the story of the hero Mwindo from the Democratic Republic of Congo in Africa. In the course of the epic, Mwindo develops from a powerful but boastful young man to a moderate and responsible leader who has become an acceptable chief to the Nyanga people. The story was collected during an actual storytelling performance and can therefore provide a valuable view of the communal practice and its actual relationship to the story itself. Daniel Biebuyck, who transcribed and translated the epic, reports that the audience was made uncomfortable with Mwindo's boasting, but through all the trials and tribulations he undergoes heroically, Mwindo finally becomes moderate in thought and deed.

As you read the epic and the marginal notes, you see that such a story reflects the social and moral values, as well as the everyday activities, of the people involved in the storytelling ritual. You also see how the audience participates in this communal activity, as the storyteller frequently interrupts the narrative with songs and the reasons for including them. You may want to compare this experience with other accounts of this kind of storytelling as a way of transmitting myths. See Ch. 3, p. 27, and Ch. 27, p. 389, for accounts of this tradition in Greece, and Ch. 23, p. 341, for a narrative of an oral storytelling session in St. Vincent.

You may want to compare Mwindo as a hero to the Greek Heracles (Ch. 31, p. 446): both achieve greatness only after struggle and maturity. Heracles is opposed by stepmother Hera, and Mwindo must defeat, and come to terms with, his father. As you read, note that the story provides clues about the everyday activities of the society telling it. Do you see any similarities between the story of Mwindo and the other African stories in this book, the creation stories in Ch. 9, p. 102, and the trickster tales in Ch. 23, p. 339?

This story about the hero Mwindo is told by the Nyanga people from the Democratic Republic of the Congo, in central Africa. The Nyanga live simply, trapping, gathering, or growing their food. They also hunt and fish. In contrast they have very intensive social lives and a rich and varied oral literature. Every day after work, the men of the village gather in the men's meeting place to eat, drink, and talk. Women gather separately in groups. The groups discuss their work and their lives and they share stories, proverbs, and riddles. Stories come not just from professional storytellers; everyone knows some.

MWINDO AS A HERO

Mwindo is the son of a chief, but his father does not want a son and tries to have him killed. Like many heroes, however, Mwindo is an amazing prodigy from the time he is in his mother's womb. His birth is attended by miraculous circumstances, and he overcomes his father's attempts to harm him. His father runs away, and Mwindo pursues him even to the underworld, where he must perform the tasks set for him. Mwindo's story is not complete until he undergoes another journey, however. He kills the Dragon Kirimu, a friend of the lightning god Nkuba. Afterward, he must undergo a journey of suffering to atone for his offense.

In the course of the epic, Mwindo develops from a powerful but boastful young man to a moderate and responsible leader who deserves to be the next chief. Biebuyck reports that throughout the epic, the audience was made uncomfortable with Mwindo's boasting, but excused it because his father had treated him unjustly. Through all the trials and tribulations he undergoes heroically, Mwindo finally becomes moderate in thought and deed. Only then does he become an acceptable chief to the Nyanga, who make a clear distinction between heroism and leadership.

THE MWINDO EPIC AS AN ORAL TALE

The text of the Mwindo epic is an especially important one for students of mythology because it represents a live performance. It allows us to study an oral epic which is still being told, retold, and modified by members of the society that originated it. Many of the other myths we read here have already been written down and thus have stopped changing and developing. This version of the Mwindo epic was performed by Candi Rureke and recorded by Daniel Biebuyck, who translated it from the Nyanga in collaboration with Kahombo C. Mateene, a former Nyanga student of Biebuyck's who is now a linguist. Biebuyck has also collected other versions of the story.

In each version, the story is somewhat different. For example, version 1 (found in this chapter) gives a great deal of detail about Mwindo's relationships with his father Shemwindo and with his aunt Iyangura. Version 2 gives prominence to the hero's interactions with the Pygmies; the only family relation of any importance is that of Mwindo and his sister. In versions 3 and 4, Mwindo has a brother called Kabutwakenda (which means "Little One Just Born He Walked"; in version 1 this is one of Mwindo's names). In version 3, Kabutwakenda is born first, but soon flies away and disappears, leaving Mwindo to hunt with his Pygmies and visit Nyamurairi, as in version 1. In version 4, Kabutwakenda is the hero, and his half-brother Mwindo is the villain.

However, the different versions also agree in many ways: each version centers on a hero who has an unusual birth and performs mighty deeds; Mwindo's greatness is achieved primarily through wit, trickery, singing, dancing, and dice-playing rather than the physical prowess of a fighter. In most of the stories, the Pygmies and the hero's paternal aunt are his supporters and advisors. In versions 1 and 2, he is born against his father's will, and in versions 1–3, the gods themselves are unable to conquer him. Although each version of the epic is a different story by a different bard, many individual details and plot elements are repeated from version to version.

The bard Candi Rureke performing (around 1956, in his home village of Kisimba). He holds a conga scepter in his left hand and a calabash rattle in his right with which he always accompanied himself. The only other instrument used during the performance of *the Mwindo epic* was a Nkwangatiro percussion stick. The latter was rhythmically sounded by four young men accompanists.

THE EPIC SHOWS US THE LIVES OF THE PEOPLE

The version we present in this chapter paints a vivid picture of the lives of the Nyanga people, and gives us a feel for what it must be like to attend a live performance of such a myth. The story is full of songs, sections in which the storyteller shows off his abilities by describing in poetic form the boasts of Mwindo against his enemies, or by cataloguing the household goods to be found in the village of Tubondo. In the course of telling the story of Mwindo, Rureke talks to his audience, and adds details from his own life and region.

Imagine yourself at a performance of the Mwindo epic. You sit with a large crowd around the men's hut in the middle of a Nyanga village. While singing and telling the story, the storyteller dances, mimes, and acts out the main parts. Four young men accompany the performance on a percussion stick, which is beaten with drumsticks. The narrator shakes a calabash rattle containing seeds or pebbles and wears ankle-bells. The percussionist and the audience sing refrains of the songs or repeat phrases during pauses by the narrator. As the story goes on, the audience also encourages the storyteller with handclapping and whooping and with gifts of food, beer, money, beads, and jewelry.

Mwindo

The Courtship of Mukiti and Iyangura

Long ago there was a chief called Shemwindo. That chief built a village called Tubondo, in the state of Ihimbi. Shemwindo was born with a sister called Iyangura.

And in Shemwindo's village there were seven meeting places of his people. When he became chief, **Shemwindo married seven women.** After Shemwindo had married, he summoned his many people: the juniors and the seniors, the advisers, the counselors and the nobles. All people, young and old, male and female, officeholder and commoner, were called to meet with him in council.

Shemwindo sat down in the middle of them. He made a decree, saying: "You, my seven wives, the one who will bear a male child among you, I will kill; all of **you must give birth to girls only.**" Having made this interdiction, he threw himself hurriedly into the houses of the wives, and then launched the sperm where his wives were.

Among his wives there was one who was beloved and another who was despised. The despised one had her house built next to the garbage heap and his other wives lived in the clearing in the middle of the village. After a certain number of days, those seven wives became with child, and all at the same time.

Close to the village of Shemwindo there was a river in which there was a pool, and in this pool there was a water serpent, master of the unfathomable. The serpent **Mukiti** heard that **downstream from him there was a chief who had a sister called Iyangura.** She glistened like dew reflecting the rays of the sun, she was so beautiful. Mukiti heard the news of her beauty, and he went to court her.

Mukiti reached Tubondo; Shemwindo accommodated him in a guest house. After having eaten dinner and food, Mukiti said to Shemwindo, "You, **my uncle,** my mother's brother, I have come here where you are because of your sister Iyangura." Shemwindo gave Mukiti a black goat as a token of hospitality and, moreover, said to Mukiti that he would answer him tomorrow. Mukiti said: "Yes, my dear father, I am satisfied."

When night turned day, Mukiti dressed himself up like the anus of a snail, the very cleanest of the clean. He was clothed with bunches of raphia fronds on the arms and on the legs, and with a belt of bongo antelope, and he also wore the isia crest of elephant tail and whiskers of leopard fixed in a brass disk on his head. In their homestead,

This excerpt comes from: Daniel Biebuyck, *The Mwindo Epic: From the Banyanga* (Congo Republic).*

"Shemwindo married seven women"—Polygamy, the marrying of more than one wife, is an accepted practice among the Nyanga.

"you must give birth to girls only"—We learn later that Shemwindo wants daughters because they bring a dowry. When a daughter marries, her husband pays a price to her family; for a son, the family must provide a bride-price.

Mukiti   The water serpent is usually represented as a mild creature; in some stories, as here, he marries a human wife.

"downstream from him there was a chief who had a sister called Iyangura"—Here begins a long section dealing with the marriage of Iyangura, Mwindo's aunt, to Mukiti. This section may seem like an interruption of the main hero story, but it is actually strictly necessary to it. Among the Nyanga, a child has a special relationship to his father's sister. She is like a mother to him. If Iyangura had been around when Mwindo's father was trying to harm him, she would have protected the child. However, she had moved away to marry Mukiti. Mwindo's running away to reach her protection will be the first phase of his heroic deeds.

* Daniel Biebuyck; Kahombo Mateene. *The Mwindo Epic: From the Banyanga (Congo Republic).* Berkeley: University of California Press, pp. 41–145. © 1969. Used by permission granted by the Regents of the University of California.

"my uncle"—Mukiti and Iyangura are cousins, but Shemwindo is only the half brother of Mukiti's sister. The Nyanga accept such marriages but not the marriage of full cousins.

"I have never met with my sister"—Mukiti uses the title sister for his cousin Iyangura.

"irresistibly darted against each other's chest in salutation"—This was a normal Nyanga family greeting, but the attraction between Iyangura and Mukiti is an essential part of the story. It seals the marriage, and explains why Iyangura was not present to protect Mwindo.

"he had been asked for a great number of valuables"—Mukiti describes the negotiation of a bride price for a daughter: the reason Shemwindo wanted no sons.

Baniyana   The kinship group of the bats. The bats are Mwindo's maternal uncles who will make the hero's armor. They are represented as blacksmiths; the Nyanga connected bats and blacksmiths because of the sounds made by a bat.

Wooden Nyanga stool.

"they would bring his wife to him"—In a Nyanga marriage, the bride goes to live with the family of her husband. This practice is called by anthropologists exogamy, or marrying outside of your family unit. Of course, since Mukiti and Iyangura are half cousins, the distance is actually greater geographically than in terms of kinship.

Shemwindo and his sister Iyangura also outdid themselves in dressing up. The moment Mukiti and Shemwindo saw each other, Mukiti said to his uncle: "I am astonished. Since I arrived, **I have never met with my sister.**" Hearing that, Shemwindo assembled all his people; he went with them into secret council. Shemwindo said to his people: "Our sister's son has come to this village looking for my sister; and you then must answer him." The counselors and nobles, hearing that, agreed. saying: "It is befitting that you first present Iyangura to Mukiti." They passed with Iyangura before Mukiti. Mukiti, seeing the way in which Iyangura was bursting with mature beauty, said to himself in his heart: "Now, she is not the one I expected to see; she is like a ntsembe tree in her beauty and blood." Iyangura, indeed, was dressed in two pieces of bark cloth imbued with red powder and mbea oil. Seeing each other, Mukiti and Iyangura **irresistibly darted against each other's chest in salutation.** Iyangura said to Mukiti: "Do you really love me, Mukiti?" Mukiti told her: "Don't raise your voice anymore, my wife; see how I am dancing, my back shivering like the raphia-tree larvae, and my cheeks holding in my laughing."

After Mukiti and Iyangura looked on each other like this, the counselors and nobles of Shemwindo answered Mukiti, saying: "We are satisfied, Mukiti, because of your word. Now go forth to gain treasures and trophies for us." After Mukiti had been spoken to in such a manner, he returned home with soothed heart. During his absence, the villagers fixed him a seven-day feast in celebration of the valuables he would bring for his part of the marriage.

After Mukiti was home, he assembled his people and told them that he was just back from courting that **he had been asked for a great number of valuables,** nine thousand, and a white goat, and a reddish one, and a black one, and one for sacrifice, and one for the sacred calabash, and one for the mother, and one for the young men. The counselors and the nobles clapped their hands, saying to their lord that they were satisfied, that they could not fail to find that payment of goods reasonable, because this maiden was not to be lost. After the seven days were up, Mukiti took the marriage payments with him while his people remained behind.

On leaving his village the next morning, he went to spend the night in the village of the **Baniyana.** They gave him a ram as a token of hospitality. Mukiti and his people slept in their village. When Mukiti woke up, he propelled himself into the village of the Banamitandi, those kin of the spiders, those helpers of heroes. They gave Mukiti a goat as a token of hospitality. And so he spent the night there. In the morning, he and his people took a pathway out of the village, and at long last they came to the village of his wife's family, in Tubondo, at Shemwindo's.

When they arrived in Tubondo, Shemwindo showed them a guest-house to sleep in, and also gave them a ram-goat. In the evening, Iyangura heated water for her husband and they went together to wash themselves (for it is the custom for a wife to wash her husband's feet before bed). They anointed themselves with red powder and climbed into bed. Iyangura put a leg across her husband.

In the morning, there was a holiday. Shemwindo assembled all his people and they sat together in a group. Then, Mukiti came out with the marriage payments and placed them before the elders of the village, who were very satisfied. They told him: "Well, you are a man who cannot be stopped by anything, one who is able to overcome fear and doubt." After they had laid hold of the marriage payments, the people of Shemwindo told Mukiti to return to his village and **they would bring his wife to him** for the marriage. Hearing this, Mukiti said: "Absolutely all is well. What would be bad would be to be deceived." He returned to his village and had his people prepare much food to entertain the guests to come.

Shemwindo waited until Mukiti had been gone a day. In the morning, he set out to follow him, taking Iyangura with him. The attendants carried Iyangura, without allowing her foot to touch the ground, as they went through mud or water. When the attendants and the bride arrived at Mukiti's, he showed them to a guesthouse. A rooster was caught and cooked "to clean the teeth." In this guesthouse **the elders had Iyangura sit on a stool** to indicate how significant this wedding would be.

When she was seated, she took out the remainder of the banana paste from which she had had breakfast in her mother's house in their village. She and her husband, Mukiti, ate it. While they were eating, still more banana paste, with taro leaves, was being prepared for them.

When the paste and the leaves were ready, the elders told Mukiti also to sit down on a stool, and **they placed the paste between both of them.** They told Iyangura to grasp a piece of paste **in her right hand** and have her husband eat it along with a portion of meat. She took a piece of paste, and fed it to her husband; and her husband took a piece of paste, and he, too, fed it to his wife. After both husband and wife had finished the ceremonial eating of the paste, the counselors of Mukiti gave Shemwindo and his people a strong young steer.

After they had finished eating the steer, **they spoke to Mukiti,** saying: "Don't turn our child here, whom you have just married, into a woman in ragged, soiled clothing. Don't transform her into a servant who does nothing but work for you."

After they had said this, right after awakening, they went, having been given money as a going-away gift by Mukiti. When the bridal attendants arrived in Tubondo, they were very happy, along with their chief, Shemwindo. By the river, where Mukiti and his people and his wife, Iyangura, remained, he made a proclamation saying: "All my people, **if one day you see a man walking downstream** against the flow, then you will tear out his spinal column. For it is forbidden to walk this way, you all the people of Maka, of Birurumba, of Ankomo, and Mpongo. This other path here, the one that follows the flow of the river, this is the great path on which all people must pass." Now in this village there lived his headman called Kasiyembe.

After Mukiti had voiced this interdiction regarding the two paths, he told Kasiyembe: "Henceforth you must dwell with my wife, Iyangura, at the borders of the pool; and **I, Mukiti, shall reside here where all the dry leaves collect,** where all the fallen tree trunks are obstructed in the middle of the pool."

Mwindo's Unusual Birth and His Brief Early Years

Because of his power and virtues, Shemwindo, his wives and people, became very famous not only in Tubondo, but throughout the country. When many days had passed, his wives came into labor! They gave birth to female children only. One wife among them, the seventh and the Preferred One, lagged behind in her pregnancy. When she saw that her companions had already given birth, she continually complained: "How terrible this is! What then shall I do? I alone remain with this burden. What will come out of this pregnancy?"

Just after she had finished these sad reflections, she found a bunch of firewood at her door. She did not know from where it had come. **It was her child, the one that was inside her womb, who had just brought it.**

After some time, while looking around the house the Preferred One discovered a jar of water standing there. She did not know from whence it had come. It was as if it had brought itself into the house. And again, after some more time had passed, she found raw vegetables sitting in the house. Now, she was even more astonished. It was the child in her womb who was carrying out all these miraculous tasks for her.

When the inhabitants of the village saw that the Preferred One continued to drag on with her pregnancy, they started sneering at her: "When is this one going to give birth?" they would mock. The child, dwelling in the womb of its mother, meditated to

---

"the elders had Iyangura sit on a stool"—Normally, women sit on a piece of wood or an animal skin.

"they placed the paste between both of them"—We get a detailed description here of the final part of the Nyanga wedding ceremony, in which the husband and wife feed each other. In the United States, it is customary for the husband and wife to feed each other cake at their wedding reception.

"in her right hand"—The Nyanga attach great importance to the right in general, and to the right hand in particular.

"they spoke to Mukiti"—Such advice is a customary part of a Nyanga wedding ceremony.

"if one day you see a man walking downstream"—This seems to be part of Mukiti's establishing his household. Later, when Mwindo tries to reach his aunt Iyangura, this set of prohibitions will mean that he has to fight his way to her side.

"I, Mukiti, shall reside here where all the dry leaves collect"—Mukiti, following Nyanga custom, will not live with his wife.

"It was her child . . . who had just brought it"—Mwindo begins to perform amazing feats even while he is within his mother's womb.

itself, saying that it could not come out from the underpart of the body of its mother, because people might make fun saying that he was the child of a woman. He did not want to emerge from the mouth of his mother, for then they might make fun, saying that he had been vomited up like a bat.

The pregnancy had gone so far beyond its term that the old midwives came. They arrived when the Preferred One was already being troubled with labor pains. The child in the womb climbed to her belly, wandered through her limbs and torso, and went on and came out through her middle. The old midwives were astonished when they saw him wailing on the ground. They pointed at him, asking: "What kind of child is that?"

Some saw that it was a male child, and were worried and wanted to shout about the village that a male child had been born. Others refused, saying that no one should say, because when Shemwindo heard, he would kill him. The counselors sitting with Shemwindo shouted: "What sort of child is born there?" But the old midwives kept their silence. Afterwards, they gave him the name Mwindo—first-born male—for there had only been female children born in that family.

"Some . . . wanted to shout about the village"—The midwives usually announce the birth of the child and reveal its sex in the men's gathering place, but they do not want Shemwindo to harm the child.

In the house where the birth took place, a cricket appeared carrying omens of great and dreadful things. After Shemwindo had asked what child was born and the midwives refused to answer, the cricket had left the birthhouse and had carried the news to him: "Chief, a male child has been born to you. They call him Mwindo, and that is why they have not answered you." When Shemwindo heard that his Preferred One had given birth to a boy, he took up his spear. The moment he prepared to throw it into the birth hut, the child shouted from inside, saying: "Each time this spear is thrown, may it hit the bottom of the house pole, where the household spirits reside. May it never end up where these old midwives are seated. Neither may it arrive at the place where my mother is." Shemwindo threw the spear into the house six times, and each time it hit nothing but the pole. When the midwives saw those extraordinary happenings they swarmed out of the house. They fled, saying that they did not want to die in that place.

When Shemwindo became exhausted in his anger, he spoke to his counselors, saying that they should dig a grave to throw Mwindo into, for he did not want to see a male child. When the counselors had heard the order of the lord of their village, they did not argue with him. When the grave was finished, they went to fetch the child. They carried him gently and went to bury him. Mwindo howled from within the grave, saying: "Oh, my father, this is the death that you will die, but first you will suffer many sorrows." When Shemwindo heard the remarkable curse, he scolded his people telling them to cover the grave right away. They went to fetch the plantain and banana trees to lay on the grave, as is the custom. They placed them on top of him, but at that very moment, it became evident that **Mwindo had been born with a conga scepter,** the royal fly swatter made of the buffalo tail, which he held in his right hand. He also carried an adze, in his left hand. A little bag of the spirit of Kahombo, the carrier of good fortune, was slung across his back on the left side, and in that bag there was a long magic rope. Most wondrously, Mwindo was born laughing and also speaking, already a man among men.

"Mwindo had been born with a conga scepter"—The conga scepter will help him fly through the air, and to kill, to destroy, and to advise. It is the material symbol of the hero's force. See the picture of Candi Rureke holding a conga scepter, p. 306.

When the day was ending, those sitting outdoors looked to where Mwindo had been discarded, and saw light coming forth, as though the sun were shining from within. They ran to tell the others in the village. They saw the emanation, but they could not stand still because the great heat, which was like fire, burned them.

When everyone had fallen asleep for the night, Mwindo emerged from the grave and sneaked into his mother's house. There he began to wail. In his home, Shemwindo heard the child's wailing. He was totally astonished, saying: "Has my wife given birth to another child?" He was wracked with indecision, unsure whether or not he could even stand up because of his fear. But in his manliness, he did stand up, going to the house of his wife, slithering like a snake, without making a sound. He peeked through the open door, and cast his eye on the child sleeping on the floor. He entered the hut and questioned his wife, saying: "Where does this child come from? Did you leave another one in the womb to whom you have given another birth?" His wife replied to him:

"This is Mwindo here." Mwindo kept silent. Shemwindo left the house without being able to speak another word.

He went to wake his counselors. He told them: "I was not deceived. He has returned. It is astounding." He told them also: "Tomorrow, you will go to cut a piece from the trunk of a tree, carve in it a husk for a drum, and then put the hide of an antelope in the river to soften."

When the sky had become day, all the people assembled. Then, together they went to see Mwindo in his mother's house. After they had looked at him, the counselors went to the forest to cut a piece of wood for the husk of the drum; then they carved the wood, they hollowed it out so that it became a husk.

When the husk was finished, they went again to fetch Mwindo. **They carried him gently** and put him in the husk of the drum. Mwindo said: "This time, my father has no mercy. What! A small baby is being mistreated!" The people of Shemwindo went to get the hide for the drum. They covered the drum with it. When Shemwindo had seen his son placed in the drum, he declared to all his people that he wanted two expert swimmers, divers, to go the next day to throw the drum into the pool where nothing moves. After the swimmers were found, they picked up the drum. Then, all the people left the village to throw Mwindo into the water.

When they arrived at the pool, the divers dove into it with the drum. When they arrived in the middle of the pool, they asked in a loud voice: "Shall we drop him here?" Those sitting on the edge of the river answered: "Yes. Drop it there, so that you can't be accused of his return." They released the drum and it sank into the depths. The waves made rings above the place where it had entered.

The swimmers returned to the shore. Shemwindo was very pleased with them. **He awarded each swimmer a maiden.** That day when Mwindo was thrown away, earth and heaven joined together because of the heavy rain. It rained for seven days and that rain brought much famine in Tubondo.

After they had thrown Mwindo away, they returned to the village. When they arrived in Tubondo, Shemwindo threatened his wife **Nyamwindo,** the Preferred One, saying: "Don't shed tears weeping for your son. If you weep, I shall send you to the same place your son has been thrown." That very day, Nyamwindo, Mwindo's mother, turned into the Despised One. Unable to weep, Nyamwindo went on merely sobbing—but not one little tear did she shed.

Mwindo moaned within the drum. He listened closely to its sound, and said: "I must not wash downstream in the river. I cannot leave without warning my father and all his people who have cast me away of the consequences of throwing me here. They must be able to hear the sound of my voice. If I wash away, then I am not Mwindo."

The drum rose all alone to the surface of the pool. It did not go down the river, neither did it go up the river.

From Tubondo a row of maidens went to draw water from the river, at the wading place. As soon as they cast their eyes toward the middle of the pool, they saw the drum on the surface of the water, turning around and around. They inquired of each other: "Lo, the drum that was thrown with Mwindo in it—there it is!" Mwindo inside that drum said, "If I don't sing while these maidens are still here, then I shall not have anyone who will bring the news to where my father is in Tubondo."

While the maidens were drawing water and still had their attention fixed toward the drum, Mwindo threw sweet words into his mouth. **He sang:**

> I am saying farewell to Shemwindo!
> I shall die, O **Bira!**

"They carried him gently"— Shemwindo's counselors don't want to mistreat the child, but they follow the orders of their chief.

"He awarded each swimmer a maiden."—There are many occasions on which chiefs give women as "presents" to offficeholders, followers, or those who do special services for them.

Nyamwindo Mwindo's mother. Her name is taken from her son's and means "mother of Mwindo."

Performers playing the drums of different sizes, tensions and thus timbres that are used by the Nyanga in all of their dance performances. It is in such a drum that the infant Mwindo hid himself from his father.

"He sang"—The songs included in the epic do not advance the action of the story; rather, they allow the storyteller to elaborate parts of the story, to rest and to improvise comments on his own story, his performance, or his audience. In this song, Mwindo predicts that he will find his father's sister, his paternal aunt, and that he will defeat his father and his father's counselors.

Bira A Nyanga word for those not of their culture, especially their neighbors the Hunde. Mwindo is here saying, "Do you weaklings believe I will die now?"

My little father threw me into the drum!
I shall die, Mwindo!
The counselors abandoned Shemwindo;   5
The counselors will become dried leaves.
The counselors of Shemwindo,
The counselors have failed in their counseling!
My little father threw me into the drum! I shall not die,
while that little one survives!   10
The little one is joining Iyangura,
Iyangura, the sister of Shemwindo.

When the girls heard Mwindo singing, they climbed up to the village, leaving the water jars behind them in disarray. The men, seeing them appear, running and rushing, at the outskirts of the living area, took their spears and went out, believing that they were being chased by a wild beast. Seeing the spears, the maidens beseeched their fathers: "Hold it! We are going to bring the news to you of how the drum that you threw into the pool has remained there. In fact it is singing: 'The counselors of Shemwindo, the counselors have failed in their counseling.'" When he heard that, Shemwindo accused the girls of lying: "What? The drum has come to the surface again!" The maidens averred this was true: "Mwindo is still alive." When Shemwindo heard that, he assembled his people. Everybody went down to the river carrying spears, arrows, and torches.

From where Mwindo was floating, he was able to see that the maidens had run toward the village. So he stopped singing for a while, saying to himself that he would sing again when the people arrived. All the people of the village, seeing the drum, joined together in staring at it. When Mwindo saw them standing in a group on the shore, he threw sweet words into his mouth. He sang:

I am saying farewell to Shemwindo;
I shall die, O Bira!
The counselors abandoned Shemwindo.
The counselors will turn into dried leaves.
What will die and what will be safe   5
Are going to encounter Iyangura.

When Mwindo finished singing, bidding farewell to his father and to all the people of Shemwindo, the drum sank into the pool. The waves made rings at the surface. Shemwindo and his people were very perplexed. They shook their heads, saying: "How terrible it is! Will some day there be born what has never been born?" After they had witnessed this extraordinary event, they returned to Tubondo.

Mwindo headed upstream. He went to the river's source, at Kinkunduri's, to begin his journey. When he arrived at Kinkunduri's, he lodged there. He said he was going to join Iyangura, his paternal aunt, where Kahungu had told him she had gone. He met up with his aunt Iyangura downstream, and he sang:

"Mungai fish . . . kabusa fish . . . canta fish"—Mwindo addresses each of the allies of Mukiti the water serpent. After his wedding to Iyangura, Mukiti charged each of them to guard the passage downriver.

"Little One Just Born He Walked"—This name of Mwindo emphasizes the hero's ability to perform adult actions from the moment of his birth.

Mungai fish, get out of my way!
For Ikukuhi, should I go out of my way for you?
You are impotent against Mwindo,
Mwindo is the **Little One Just Born He Walked.**
I am going to meet Iyangura.   5
For **kabusa fish,** should I go out of my way for you?
You are helpless against Mwindo,
For Mwindo is the Little One Just Born He Walked.
Canta fish, get out of my way!

Canta, you are impotent against Mwindo.   10
I am going to encounter Iyangura, my aunt.
For mutaka fish, should I go out of my way for you?
You are helpless against Mwindo!
I am going to meet Iyangura, my aunt.
For kitoru fish, should I go out of my way for you?   15
You see, I am going to encounter Iyangura, my aunt.
For crabs, should I go out of my way for you?
You are impotent against Mwindo!
See, I am going to encounter Iyangura, my aunt, sister of Shemwindo.
For nyarui fish, should I go out of my way for you?   20
Whereas Mwindo is the Little One Just Born He Walked.
I am going to encounter Iyangura, my aunt, Sister of Shemwindo.
For nyarui fish, should I go out of my way for you?
Whereas Mwindo is the Little One Just Born He Walked.
I am going to encounter Iyangura, my aunt,   25
Sister of Shemwindo.
For cayo fish, should I go out of my way for you?
You see, I am going to encounter Iyangura, my aunt,
Sister of Shemwindo.
Look! You are impotent against Mwindo.   30
Mwindo, the Little One Just Born He Walked.
He who will go up against me, it is he who will die on the way.

> "You are helpless against Mwindo!"—Several species of fish and crabs, like mungai, ikukuhi, kabusa, canta, mutaka, kitoru, mushenge, nyarui, and cayo are mentioned in this song. They are all personifications of ugliness and hatred and considered allies of Mukiti.

Each time Mwindo arrived where there was a swimming animal, he said that it should get out of the way for him, that they were powerless against him, that he was going to his aunt, Iyangura. When Mwindo arrived at Cayo's, he spent the night; in the morning he traveled on right after awakening. Again he sang:

For ntsuka fish, should I go out of my way for you?
You see that I am going to encounter Iyangura.
You see that you are powerless against Mwindo.
Mwindo is the Little One Just Born He Walked.
For kirurumba fish, should I get out of the way?   5
You see that I am going to encounter Aunt Iyangura.
You see that you are powerless against Mwindo,
For Mwindo is the Little One Just Born He Walked.
For mushomwa fish, should I go out of the way?
You see I am going to encounter Aunt Iyangura.   10
You see that you are powerless against Mwindo.
For Mwindo is the Little One Just Born He Walked.

The Encounter with the Dreaded Mukiti

Musoka, the junior sister of the evil Mukiti, had gone to live upstream from hated Mukiti:

For **Musoka,** should I go out of my way for you?
You are powerless against Mwindo,
Mwindo is the Little One Just Born He Walked.

> **Musoka** A female water spirit for whom the Nyanga have a special cult.

When Musoka saw Mwindo arriving at her place, she sent an envoy to Mukiti to say that there was a person, who was about to join Iyangura. The envoy ran quickly to

Mukiti. Mukiti replied that the envoy should tell Musoka that the man must not pass beyond her place. That envoy arrived at Musoka's. He told how he had been spoken to by Mukiti. Then Musoka blocked Mwindo's passage, although she did not know that he was a child of Mukiti's wife, Iyangura. Musoka spoke to Mwindo, saying: "Mukiti refuses to let you by. So it is only by proving your manhood that you will be able to pass. I, Musoka, I am placing barriers here. You will not find a trail." Mwindo answered her, softening his voice: "I am Mwindo. **Never will I be forbidden to pass on any trail.** I will break through exactly at the place where you would prevent me." Mwindo left the water above him, dug inside the sand, and burrowed to a place somewhere between Musoka and Mukiti.

After Mwindo had passed Musoka in this way, he boasted: "Here I am, the Little One Just Born He Walked. No one ever points a finger at me." When Musoka saw him downstream, **she touched her chin,** saying: "How then has this tough one here gotten through? If he had passed above me, I would have seen his shadow; if he had passed below me, I would have heard the sound of his feet." Musoka railed at his escape, saying that she would be scolded by Mukiti.

After Mwindo had passed Musoka, he began to journey to Mukiti's. He sang:

> In Mukiti's, in **Mariba's** dwelling place!
> For Mukiti, should I go out of the way for you?
> You see I am going to encounter Iyangura,
> Iyangura, sister of Shemwindo.
> Mukiti, you are powerless against Mwindo.   5
> Mwindo is the Little One Just Born He Walked.

When Mukiti heard this, he asked who was talking about his wife. He shook heaven and earth. The whole pool moved. Mukiti said: "This time we shall really get to know each other, for I never fear a boasting and pampered child. I won't be worried about such a one until I have measured myself against him."

Mwindo, organizing himself, went to appear at the spot where the monster Mukiti was coiled up. When Mukiti saw him, he said: "This time it is not the one whom I expected to see. He surpasses all expectation! Who are you?" Mwindo responded that he was Mwindo, the Little One Just Born He Walked, **child of Iyangura.** Mukiti said: "What do you want?" Mwindo answered that he was going to be with Iyangura. Hearing that, Mukiti said to Mwindo: "You are lying. No one ever passes over these logs and dried leaves."

While Mukiti and Mwindo were still boasting and arguing, maidens went from Iyangura's place to draw water at Mukiti's place, because there is where the water hole was. As soon as the maidens heard the way in which Mwindo always referred to Iyangura as his aunt, they ran to tell her. "Over there, where your husband Mukiti is, a little man says that Mukiti should let him pass, for he is Mwindo, that he is going to meet with Iyangura, his paternal aunt." When Iyangura heard that, she said: "**Lo! That is my child.** I will go to where he is." Iyangura climbed up the slope. She looked to the river that she might see the man who was calling her his aunt. As soon as Mwindo saw Iyangura coming to him, he sang:

> I am suffering much, Mwindo.
> I will die, Mwindo.

While Iyangura was descending the slope, he went on singing.

> Aunt Iyangura,
> Mukiti has blocked the road to me.
> I am going to meet Aunt Iyangura,
> I am going to encounter Iyangura,
> Sister of Shemwindo.   5

Margin notes:

"Never will I be forbidden to pass on any trail."—Later in the story, Mukei the hedgehog will burrow tunnels for Mwindo. Here he seems to have the ability to perform this feat by himself.

"she touched her chin"—To express astonishment.

Mariba Mukiti is referred to by the word for "pool," his dwelling place.

"child of Iyangura"—The relationship between a child and his paternal aunt is a close one; she is like a mother to him, and he refers to himself as her child.

"Lo! That is my child"—Iyangura reflects the closeness of the tie to her nephew.

For Mukiti, shall I go out of the way?
I am joining Iyangura,
Sister of Shemwindo.
For **Mukiti, my father,** shall I go out of my way for him?
You are powerless against Mwindo.   10

Iyangura said: "**If my sister's son, the nephew of the people of Mitandi, is in this drum,** let him come here so that I can see him." But though his aunt cited the people of Mitandi in this way, Mwindo refused to move. From inside the drum, Mwindo complained that his aunt had missed the mark. She spoke again: "If you are the nephew of the One Who Hears Secrets, come here." Though his aunt mentioned the One Who Hears Secrets, the drum still refused to draw near. His aunt said anew: "If you really are **the nephew of the people of the Yana,** come before me." When Mwindo heard this, he went forth from the pool singing:

I am going to my Aunt Iyangura,
Iyangura, sister of Shemwindo.
Kabarebare and Ntabare mountain,
Where the husband of my senior sister sets fish traps.
And a girl who is nice is a lady,   5
And a nice young man is a house pole.
We are telling the story
That the Babuya have told long ago.
We are telling the story.

Kasengeri is dancing, wagging his tail;   10
And you see his tail of nderema fibers.
Nkurongo bird had gone to court mususu bird;
Muhasha bird has contracted asthma, is gasping for breath.
If I am at a loss for words in the great song,
If it dies out, may it not die out for me there.   15
They are accustomed to speak to Mukiti with bells.
The tunes that we are singing.
The uninitiated ones cannot know them.
I would like to be as perfect in body as the
Mburu monkey and still eat a lot,   20
I would remain satisfied with my flat belly.
I have seen a rooster cock-adoodle-dooing;
I also saw a muntori-bird pointing him out.
The little guardian of the rice field
Is never confused about   25
When sky has become day.
I see that meditations kill;
They killed the couple, otter and his mother.
If little pot travels too much,
It means little pot looks for crack.   30
He who one day ate ntsuka-fish does not sojourn long.
It is as though he had eaten the heart of the plunger.
If Nyabunge coils like the whirlpools,
Then she loses her way home.
I learned that a catastrophe happened: 35
One suffering from frambesia and a leper on a bed

"Mukiti, my father"—Mwindo calls Mukiti, his aunt Iyangura's husband, his father, reflecting the closeness of the tie between aunt and nephew.

"If my sister's son . . . is in this drum"—Here we are reminded that Mwindo is still imprisoned in the drum. This was not emphasized in his previous adventures on his way down the river.

"the nephew of the people of the Yana"—Only when his aunt calls him this, does he move. The Yana-Baniyana is the kinship group of the bats, Mwindo's maternal uncles who will make his armor.

"We are telling the story that the Babuya have told long ago"—The narrator, Mr. Rureke, steps out of the story and speaks in his own person. He explains that he is telling a story told by the Babuya descent group, a group represented in his village.

Kasengeri An animal often compared to a good dancer. The narrator dances while singing; here he is praising his own dancing and calling attention to the movement of his arms, which are decorated with fiber armlets.

"If I am at a loss for words"—The narrator loses the thread of the story he is telling and improvises until he recovers himself.

"He who one day ate ntsuka-fish"—The words here suggest that the narrator is hungry and that he is enjoying himself. He digresses by brief reference to several stories and proverbs and by making some personal reflections. Nyanga songs are often loosely pieced together unrelated verses. What matters here is the singing, dancing, rhythm, and music, much as in the lyrics of some rock and roll songs.

This statue is used in Nyanga mumbira initiation rituals. It represents an imaginary animal; its stylized carved head is topped by a real hornbill beak. The curved top and bottom represent limbs.

Kasiyembe Mukiti's head man, charged with guarding Iyanqura.

"Kasiyembe's foolish mop of hair"—A great mop of hair seems foolish or suggestive of evil to the Nyanga. As the description of Kasiyembe suggests, it is not hygienic or attractive.

"Widen your heart"—Iyangura speaks up for her husband and his household.

"Look, I am playing with my conga scepter"—The narrator dances with a conga scepter like that of Mwindo and here he calls attention to it.

> If you hear the uproar of an argument,
> It means that the old woman has gotten more than the young mother.
> I always sit down thinking about myself,
> As in the game "throat and top."   40
> I have cultivated bananas for the dragon
> So heavy that a cluster had no one to carry it.
> The muhangu-animal that tries to make the first banana fruits drop.
> If the mother of the girl dies because of the young man,
> It means an atumbu insect falls from the ntongi-tree.   45

Mwindo was still flowing with the river, and as he floated by his aunt, she seized the drum and she slashed it open. Removing the hide, she saw the multiple rays of the rising sun and the moon—such was the beauty of the child. Mwindo rose out of the drum, still holding his conga scepter and his adze, together with his little bag that contained the magical rope. When Hawk saw Mwindo meeting his aunt, he went to bring the news to the elder who had been sent to Iyangura to keep watch over her continually. He told him: "You who are here, it is not merely a little man who appears over there; he carries stories of his many attributes and feats. He is going to kill you." Hearing this **Kasiyembe** said: "Go! When you have arrived at Mwindo's, tell him he must not attempt to pass by this side, for if he tries, I will tear out his backbone. I am setting up traps here, pits and pointed sticks and razors in the ground, so that whenever he tries, I will catch him."

Then, by his great powers, Mwindo made **Kasiyembe's foolish mop of hair** catch on fire. Indeed, the tongues of flame rose into the air in such a way that all the lice and all the vermin that were nestled on his head were entirely consumed.

When they saw that Kasiyembe's mop of hair was burning, the people of Kasiyembe went to fetch water to put out the fire. But by the time they arrived with the jars, all the water had dried up in them. They went straight to the water-carrying plantain stalks, but these, too, were already dried up. They said: "I guess we will have to spit on his head!" But even that was impossible, for their mouths, too, were so dry that no one had any spit left.

As they were going through all of this, they said: "Kasiyembe is about to die. Go to Mukiti's place, and see if there is any help there, for there is a pool." But when they arrived, they found the whole pool had dried up. When his aunt saw what was happening, she went to beg before the boy: "**Widen your heart,** you my son 'of the body,' my nephew who is such a unique creature. Did you come here just to attack us? Widen your heart for us, and take the spell off my husband. Stretch your heart that you may heal the afflicted without harboring further resentment against them." After the aunt had finished humbly imploring, Mwindo cooled the anger of his heart. He awoke Kasiyembe, waving his conga scepter above him, and singing:

> He who went to sleep wakes up.
> You have no power against Mwindo,
> Mwindo is the Little One Just Born He Walked.
> He who went to sleep wakes up.
> **Look, I am playing with my conga scepter.**   5

Suddenly, Kasiyembe was saved. And in the storage jars water again appeared. And the green stalks of the plantains, again there was water in them. And where Mukiti was staying, there, too, the water came back. When the people saw this feat, they were astonished, saying: "Mwindo must be a great man." Kasiyembe saluted Mwindo, saying "Hail! Hail! Mwindo."

After he had accomplished that deed, Mwindo informed his aunt that he would be going to Tubondo the next day to fight his father, for twice his father had thrown him away, and so he would go to stand up against him. The aunt said to him: "O powerful one, you won't be able to overpower your father. For you are only yesterday's child. Will you be worthy of ruling Tubondo, village of seven meeting places? I, who had you taken from the drum, must strongly say no. No one should even try to go alone, for the lonely path is never a pleasant one to travel."

Mwindo refused to listen; he blocked out his aunt's words by humming to himself. She told him: "Do not go to fight your father. But if you do go, then I shall go with you to watch as your father cuts you into pieces."

She instructed the maidens to pack up her household objects so she could accompany Mwindo, for the lonely path is never pleasant, something comes along with the power to kill. When the sky had become daylight, they breakfasted before the journey. And Mwindo sang of deeds of glory to give him strength and attractiveness:

> I am going over there to Tubondo;
> I am going over there to Tubondo,
> Even though Tubondo has seven entries.
> We are saying, oh Bira!
> Aunt, give me advice   5
> To fight with the people downstream;
> They carry spears and shields.
> **In Ihimbi where dwelt Birori,**
> I shall die today, Mushumo.
> Sky became day, I was still speaking   10
> Like the sound of Mukuki.
> The sky in this village takes a long time to become day:
> **It is the single man** who is cooking hard-to-cook food.
> **Mikere-river is together with Tua-river,** his kinsman.
> May the people of Ntande not regret the lack of meat,   15
> For they have had a woman who fishes with a net.
> May the Batembo not regret the lack of meat.
> They hold Mutumba and Kunju.
> And Birere-hill of Rukobakoba;
> I cannot fish with the Baroba.   20
> From Europe there come all kinds of things!
> The sun is setting downstream
> From the Batika-Rukari.
> Maere, little girl of Rukunja,
> Maere, what did you eat when you came?   25
> I have not eaten anything extraordinary;
> I have eaten a goat for sharing purposes;
> And I also ate mususa-vegetables picked in the village.
> **They were full of sand and slime.**
> To a trap that is not well set   30
> Katiti-pigeon only leaves its tail.
> The nkurongo-birds of this village are mean;
> The nkurongo-birds, as soon as they have seen people,
> Flutter their tails.

Mwindo sang:

> I am going with the aunt.
> The Little One has slept, all prepared for the journey.

"In Ihimbi where dwelt Birori"—The storyteller inserts personal recollections into Mwindo's song. He speaks about Ihimbi, the region he is from.

"It is the single man . . ."—A proverb.

"Mikere-river . . . Tua-river . . ."—Here the narrator refers to rivers that are the limits of estates controlled by the descent groups to which he is personally linked.

"They were full of sand and slime"—The storyteller expresses frustration at the lack of consideration with which he is being treated by the village.

O my father, the Little One set out right after awakening,
I warn you, we are already underway.

The evening of this journey found him at his maternal uncles, among **the people of Yana.** They had killed a goat of hospitality for him. After they all had eaten, Mwindo said to his maternal uncles: "I am going to fight Shemwindo in Tubondo. You who are the blacksmiths of large light spears, my uncles, make me strong and resistant." The people of Yana said that they would remake him by the forge. They dressed him in shoes made entirely of iron and pants all of iron too, they also made him an iron shirt and hat. They told him: "As you are going to fight your father, may the spears that they will unceasingly hurl at you strike only this iron on your body." After his uncles had finished forging, they said they would go with him so that they might see the battle. In the morning, Mwindo set out with his uncles, and his aunt Iyangura, accompanied by all of her servants. Mwindo sang out angrily, boasting:

> I shall fight over there at Shemwindo's
> The cattle that Shemwindo possesses,
> May they join Mwindo.

When they had the village in sight, Mwindo's aunt said: "O our leader, let's get out of here. Just looking up at your father's village makes us dizzy with fear. Tubondo is a village of seven gates. There are too many people there. They will destroy us." Mwindo answered: "I am never afraid of anyone with whom I have not yet fought, much less that overgrown child. I want to try this Shemwindo. He is too much spoiled by pride."

When they arrived, he said: "Let us spend tonight in this village." His aunt howled, she said: "Where will we sleep, here there is no house, and Kiruka-nuambura has arrived, bearer of rain that never ceases." The aunt shouted: "Oh! my father, where shall we sleep? The rain has just rumbled, the young woman is destitute." Mwindo looked around, and said he wanted to have houses—and **houses assembled themselves** in two rows!

Mwindo indicated that his uncles should take one row of houses, and his aunt the other row. And Mwindo's house arose by itself in the middle of them all. His aunt shouted: "Our leader Mwindo, hail for these our houses. Shemwindo has fathered a hero. Kahombo, my father, I shall give you some children, my father's grandchildren. Let us go with our prestigious man. May he escape thunder and lightning! In spite of himself, Shemwindo brought forth a son who is never afraid. And Mwindo is making himself a hero already." Mwindo's aunt said to him: "O Mwindo, my leader, let us escape, for you are powerless in the face of this mass of people who are in Tubondo." Mwindo said that he must first test himself. Iyangura, said: "O Mwindo, what shall we eat then? Look, the great number of your uncles here, and I, too, have an entourage with me, and you, Mwindo, have drummers and singers with you. What will this whole group eat?" Mwindo saw that his aunt was telling him something important, and had to agree. He said to himself that he must begin with the food that was there in Tubondo, the village of his enemies, that this must be magically captured—and so great were his powers that it happened. The food came to him, so that he might go to fight. Mwindo sang while carrying back the food from his father's camp. His aunt was shouting out in hunger, "O my leader, what shall we eat today?" Mwindo howled back, singing:

> **The foods that are in Tubondo,**
> May the foods come to Mwindo,
> Mwindo, the Little One Just Born He Walked.
> The animals that are in Tubondo,
> May the animals come to Mwindo

"the people of Yana"—The Baniyana, Mwindo's maternal uncles, make an armor for him.

"houses assembled themselves"—Mwindo causes houses to build themselves.

"The foods that are in Tubondo"— This song gives us a clear idea of the furnishings and provisions of a Nyanga household. From the picture it paints of their diet and technology, we can imagine how the people of the society from which this story arose live.

5

The meats that Shemwindo stores,
May the meats come to Mwindo Mboru,
Mwindo, the Little One Just Born He Walked.
The wood that Shemwindo keeps,
O leader, may it come to Mwindo Mboru!   10
For Mwindo is the Little One Just Born He Walked.
And the fire that Shemwindo possesses,
May the fire also come to Mwindo.
And the water that Shemwindo possesses,
May the water also come to Mwindo Mboru.   15
The jars that are at Shemwindo's,
May the jars come to Mwindo,
Mwindo, the Little One Just Born He Walked
The clothes that are at Shemwindo's,
May the clothes come to Mwindo,   20
Mwindo is going to fight!
The wooden dishes that are in Tubondo
May the wooden dishes also come to Mwindo
O father, Little One Just Born He Walked.
Hopes to be victorious.   25
The beds that Shemwindo possesses,
May the beds come to Mwindo.
And the wicker plates that Shemwindo possesses,
May the wicker plates also come to Mwindo.
And the salt that Shemwindo possesses,   30
May the salt also come to Mwindo,
The Little One Just Born He Walked.

It was in this way that Mwindo was speaking!

And the chickens that Shemwindo possesses,
May the chickens also come to Mwindo.
The praise-singers of cheer sing together;
They began their praising together long ago,
The singers of praise sing as one voice;   5
They have achieved harmony in the middle of the village.
That which-will-die and that which-will-be-saved,
May it come to Iyangura here,
Iyangura, sister of Shemwindo.
The goats that are at Shemwindo's,   10
May the goats come to Mwindo.
The cattle bellowed, saying,
"O father, let us go to Mwindo!"
The dogs that are in Tubondo,
May the dogs come to Mwindo.   15
The dogs barked, saying,"
"O father, let us go to Mwindo!"
We are seated, stretching out our voices
Like the diggers of traps.
The banana groves that are in Tubondo,   20
May the banana groves come to Mwindo.

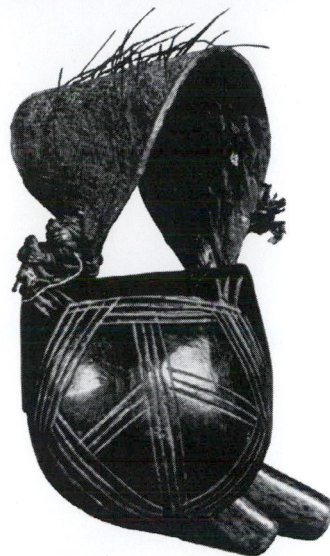

Wooden dog bell, with elephant bone clappers and elephant hide collar. Dogs' bells have a wide range of uses in the rituals of the Nyanga.

"The praise-singers of cheer"— The narrator interrupts the inventory of Nyanga culture to praise the singers and percussionists who accompany him.

And the tobacco that Shemwindo possesses,
May the tobacco also come to Mwindo.
The mukusa asp swallowed froth;
Anger is in the heart.   25
And the pipes that Shemwindo possesses,
May the pipes also come to Mwindo.
The spears that are at Shemwindo's,
May the spears come to Mwindo.
The adzes that are at Shemwindo's,   30
May the adzes come to Mwindo.
The billhooks that are at Shemwindo's,
O father, may the billhooks join Mwindo!
May there be none left to go gardening.
The pruning knives that are at Shemwindo's,   35
May the pruning knives come to Mwindo.
Little pruning knife, little scraper of mbubi lianas.
May the little pruning knife come to Mwindo.
The little dog bells that Shemwindo possesses,
May the little dog bells come to Mwindo.   40
May there be nobody left to go hunting.
The bags that Shemwindo possesses,
May the bags also come to Mwindo.
The razors that Shemwindo possesses,
May the razors also come to Mwindo;   45
May there be nobody left who is shaved.
The butea rings that Shemwindo possesses,
O father, the butea rings,
May they be ready to come to Mwindo;
May there be nobody left who wears them.   50
The necklaces that Shemwindo possesses,
May the necklaces also come to Mwindo;
May there be nobody left who wears these.
The needles that Shemwindo possesses,
May the needles also come to Mwindo;   55
May there be nobody left to do hook work.
The fire drill that Shemwindo possesses,
May the fire drill also come to Mwindo;
May there be nobody left who makes fire.
The hoes that Shemwindo possesses,   60
O father, the hoes,
May they come to Mwindo;
May there be nobody left who hoes.
The pots that Shemwindo possesses,
May the pots also come to Mwindo;   65
May there be nobody left who cooks.
The baskets that Shemwindo possesses,
May the baskets also come to Mwindo.
May there be nobody left who goes to work.
The mumanga piercer that Shemwindo possesses,   70
May the mumanga piercer come to Mwindo;

May there be nobody who bores shafts.
Let us recite from the story
That the Babuya are used to reciting.
The bisara billhooks that Shemwindo possesses,   75
May the bisara billhooks come to Mwindo;
May there be nobody who prunes banana trees.
And the bellows that Shemwindo possesses,
May the bellows also come to Mwindo;
May there be nobody left who smiths.   80
And the hammers that are at Shemwindo's,
May the hammers also come to Mwindo;
May there be nobody who smiths.
And the blacksmiths at Shemwindo's,
May the blacksmiths also come to Mwindo;   85
May there be nobody who smiths.
The nkendo knives that are in Tubondo,
The nkendo knives that Shemwindo possesses,
May the nkendo knives come to Mwindo.
May there be nobody who plaits.   90
The raphia palm trees that are at Shemwindo's,
May the raphia palm trees come to Mwindo;
May there be nobody who plaits
Or who traps. And the drums that are in Tubondo,
O father the drums!   95
May they join Mwindo;
May there be nobody who dances.

Thus did Mwindo invoke magically all of his father's possessions.

Mwindo and his uncles and his aunt and the servants, the singers and the drum-mers, when the latter opened their eyes—all the things that were in Tubondo and at Shemwindo's had come to them. When Mwindo's aunt saw all these things, she said to her son Mwindo: "You will suffer because of those things belonging to other people that you brought together here." And it was true, for all **those with Mwindo got sick,** gorging themselves with food. They said: "Lo! Mwindo is a man who does not lie when he says that he is the Little One Just Born He Walked. He always has something to rely upon. He is not a man to provoke."

> "those with Mwindo got sick"—Even though Mwindo has great power, he does not yet know how to use it wisely for his people.

When Mwindo saw that all the important things of his father had come to him, he said that now his father remained there, drunk and abandoned. He said to his aunt that he wanted his uncles to start the fight, and that he would remain there with her for a while so that he might see how his uncles handled themselves in battle. His uncles fought on the land and in the air, but the people of Tubondo said: "You will not win out today."

After a time, Mwindo's uncles were completely wiped out. They died. One of Mwindo's uncles escaped from the midst of the battle, but he was seriously injured. He ran to Mwindo to tell him: "The people of Tubondo have overcome us. All the people, all your uncles, are lying there in their own congealed blood."

Mwindo said: "First, I'm going to find out why my uncles were all defeated. And if Shemwindo does not meet me face to face, then I am not Mwindo."

Mwindo went climbing up to Tubondo. As soon as the people saw Mwindo arriv-ing, they pointed to him, saying to Shemwindo: "See the little man who just appeared at the village entrance alone." Shemwindo answered his people: "What can one little man do all by himself? We shall cut his throat and he will die." His people answered him:

"There, from where bisibisi insects emerge, one day red ants will come out. **This little man** will be able to make us run away and we won't be able to do anything against him." Shemwindo answered: "Let this little fool go swaggering into the garbage heap." Mwindo came through the village entrance singing and swinging his scepter around. He talked to the people. He demanded to dance to the rhythm of their drums.

While he was dancing he declaimed: "May whoever dies and whoever is saved join Iyangura." He raised his voice to the sky, singing:

> What will never die but will be saved,
> May it, O father, join Iyangura,
> Iyangura, sister of Shemwindo,
> The most exalted **mother of my cradling string.**
> O father, whoever will die and whoever will be saved,   5
> May they join their aunt,
> Sister of Shemwindo!

Mwindo shouted, saying:

> Hatred is in the heart,
> My friend **Nkuba,** god of lightning, may you be on my side
> And make me victorious.
> I shall fight here in Tubondo,
> Even if Tubondo has seven entrances.   5
> Here, in Tubondo, send seven lightning flashes to close them off.
> I shall fight here in Tubondo.
> May Tubondo turn into dried leaves, merely.
> The counselors ran away leaving Shemwindo;
> The counselors were not worthy of that office.   10
> May the counselors turn into dried leaves
> My friend Nkuba, may you strike in victory.
> Hatred is in the heart.
> I implored Aunt Iyangura,
> Whoever will die or be saved,   15
> May they join Iyangura,
> Aunt, sister of Shemwindo
> My little fiery father.
> My insignificant father threw me into the grave.
> My insignificant father believed that I would die.   20

Mwindo raised his eyes into heaven and said:

> My friend Nkuba,
> Here in Tubondo send seven lightning flashes!

While Mwindo was looking up, he pointed his scepter there as well. From the sky where Nkuba dwells, seven lightning flashes came, descending on Tubondo. It turned into dust, and all who lived there turned into mere dust. Where Shemwindo was sitting in his compound, he exclaimed: "There is no time for lingering here." He went down behind the house without looking back. He arrived at a place in which **there was a kikoka plant.** Tearing it out, he went into the ground at the base of its root.

"This little man"—Mwindo's size may link him to the Pygmies who are found throughout Nyanga country. They have strong political and religious ties to Nyanga chiefs. They hunt for the chief of the village, who is not allowed to hunt for himself, they participate in the ritual of the chief's enthronement, they provide the chief with one of his wives, and they are experts at narrating and singing the longer epic tales. The Nyanga believe that great epic texts like this one originated among those of their people who were most closely associated with the Pygmies.

"mother of my cradling string"— The most exalted title a person can give his mother or aunt. Nyanga women carry their babies tied on their backs in a network of finely woven raphia bands. These bands have a great emotional and religious significance and are said to represent the person.

Nkuba   God of lightning, who earlier tried to prevent Mwindo from reaching his aunt, has here become his ally.

"there was a kikoka plant"—This plant is used for brewing beer and for magical ceremonies. In tales, heroes and other characters are said to hide in this plant, or to go underground by entering it.

Mwindo said he could not chase his father so long as he had not resuscitated his uncles. Then he brought them back to life, smiting them with his scepter, and singing:

> He who went to sleep, awake!
> **My uncles, brothers of my mother, wake up.**
> I have been testing the people of Yana.
> My uncles, brothers of my mother, forge me!
> You who are powerful blacksmiths and followers of Nkuba, forge me.   5
> Shemwindo, you are powerless against Mwindo,
> Mwindo is the Little One Just Born He Walked.
> My uncles, brothers of my mother, forge me,
> You who are blacksmiths of light spears.

The Visit to the Underground

Mwindo finished waking up all of his maternal uncles. Where Shemwindo had fled, he went bumping into everything, and hurting himself. Finally, he got to the place of the god Muisa, who lives where no one ever clusters around the fire, for fire is unknown there in that dark place. In Tubondo, where Mwindo settled with his aunt, his uncles, and his servants, singers, and drummers, he told them: "Let's search out Shemwindo where he headed to Muisa's." His aunt gave him his bag in which there was the rope. She also handed him his axe; he still clasped his scepter in his hand, he the owner of its great powers. Mwindo said: "My aunt, stay here in the village of your birth. Here is the rope. **Stay here holding one end of it.** I'll follow my father to Muisa's dark and desolate realms. If you feel that this rope has stopped moving, then wait for me no longer, for lo, the fire will have dwindled and I will be dead then."

After he had spoken, Master Sparrow alit where Mwindo was sitting, and told him: "Come here, for I will show you the path your father took, and where he entered at the base of the root of the kikoka plant.

Indeed, when your father fled, I was on the roof of the world and saw him fleeing and stumbling." After Sparrow had given him this news, Mwindo said farewell to his aunt. Holding one end of the rope, he rushed toward the village gate. When he arrived at the kikoka plant, where his father had entered, he too pulled it up. Then **he went into the earth.** He went to the well at Muisa's place, and met Kahindo, the spirit of good fortune and daughter of Muisa. **Kahindo** embraced him, saying: "This is my welcome, Mwindo. First stop here where I am. In Muisa's village one can never get through. Will you succeed in getting by, when all others have not? If you are going to Muisa's, when you enter the meeting place, you will see a very big man curled up in the ashes near the hearth. He is Muisa. If he greets you, if he says: 'Blessing be with you, my leader,' you, too, will answer, 'Yes my leader.' When he offers you a stool, you will refuse it. You will tell him: 'No, my leader. Will the head of a man's father become a stool?' When he hands you a little gourd of banana beer to drink, you will refuse, answering: 'No, my father, **even though a person is one's child,** is that any reason why he should drink the urine of his father?' After Muisa has recognized you that way, he will say to you: 'Blessing, blessing, Mwindo.' And you will answer him: 'And to you blessing, blessing also, leader.' When he gives you paste to eat, you will answer him: 'Even though a person is one's child, is that a reason why he should eat the excrement of his father?'"

Now Mwindo went on ahead of Kahindo and climbed up to Muisa's. He headed for the meeting place. Muisa greeted him with "Blessing." Mwindo answered, "Yes, my father." Muisa recollected: "Bring a chair for Mwindo to sit on." Mwindo answered: "Not at all, don't bother, for **even though a man is a guest,** is that a reason for him to sit on the head of his father?" Muisa also said that he had a gourd of beer left there: "Let me pour

---

"My uncles . . . wake up"—In bringing his uncles back to life, Mwindo asks them once again to make him strong and resistant with armor, that is, to "forge" him.

"Stay here holding one end of it"—Mwindo and his aunt will communicate by way of the rope. A rope like this can be used to send a signal from one person to another over a fixed and limited space. Here one end stays with Mwindo, the other end with his aunt, and the rope expands magically as Mwindo travels.

"he went into the earth"—Mwindo enters the underworld in pursuit of his father. He will have to prevail over Muisa, prominent divinity of this world, before he can capture his father.

Kahindo Muisa's daughter. She provides Mwindo with the information he will need to pass the tests set by her father.

"even though a person is one's child"—Mwindo is so small that he looks like a child. He must still prove his ability to recognize the true nature of things.

"even though a man is a guest"— The repetition here of the words used by Kahindo in her instructions is characteristic of oral myth. In his answers, Mwindo changes the word "child" used by Kahindo to "guest." The connotations of the words are not far apart, as Mwindo uses the word for a guest who is related.

you a bit." Mwindo said: "No, I would not do that. For even though a man is a guest, is that a reason for him to drink the urine of his father?" Muisa said: "Let them prepare some paste for you, O Mwindo!" Mwindo answered him: "No, for even though a man father?" Hearing that, Muisa said to him: "Twice blessings, Mwindo."

Seeing Mwindo pass those tests, Muisa said: "Go and take a rest in Kahindo's house." Mwindo went inside and saw Kahindo cleansing herself, dressing up and rubbing herself with red powder and castor oil. Mwindo was stunned for she appeared as a sunbeam. Kahindo noticed, and greeted him: "Come in, O Mwindo!"

Mwindo said: "May the one who remains behind hurt himself, **O my sister!**" When she saw that Mwindo had come into the house, she said to herself: "Lo, Mwindo is hungry." She got up, she went to make some paste of ashes, the mythical food of Muisa. After she stirred it, she brought it there to Mwindo in her **sacred hut.** When Muisa saw Kahindo bringing the paste to Mwindo, he dashed quickly toward the house of his daughter where he might see where Mwindo was sitting. He said to Mwindo: "Oh, Mwindo, I see you are eating this food. Tomorrow, as soon as you are up and about, you must begin cultivating a new banana grove for me. **You must first cut leaves,** then plant the banana trees, then fell the trees. You must then cut the newly grown weeds, then prune the banana trees, then prop them up, then bring the ripe bananas to me. After you have performed all those works I shall know to return your father to you." After Muisa had spoken like that to Mwindo, he also said to him: "When you leave for the fields, I will send a man with you to make sure you are doing the farming correctly." After he had thus spoken, he left the doorway. Mwindo, sitting in the house, started eating the paste.

In the morning **Mwindo took up his billhook and went to cultivate the bananas** as he had been instructed. Muisa picked out a man to go with him to the fields. As they traveled, the man showed Mwindo a mountain with mango trees all over it. Mwindo, seeing that mountain, placed the billhooks on the ground, so that they might, by themselves, lay out fresh trails for them to get through the bush. When they finished cutting the trails, the billhooks mowed the grasses. Having cut the grasses, the banana trees planted themselves. Mwindo placed a number of axes there along with the billhooks. The axes felled the trees.

Having finished there, the billhooks went across the banana grove, cutting the newly grown weeds. Mwindo's companion returned to Muisa and brought the news: "This time he is not just a cultivator. He is a cultivator of marvelous things. He has not touched one iron tool. They themselves are hoeing and sawing and felling trees, and cutting weeds."

Having given the news, he returned again to where Mwindo was in the field of fresh bananas. The billhooks had finished cutting the weeds there, and now cut poles. The poles, by themselves, were propping up the banana trees. The poles completed the propping of the trees, and the banana stems were ripened. The observer ran back with this news to Muisa. "I have observed more than a man in the fields cultivating today. The banana trees already have stems and the bananas already are ripe." And Mwindo, he also exclaimed, was already on his way carrying a stem of bananas. Hearing this, Muisa said: "Lo, this boy is going to manage to pass all of these tests there in the forest. I slept having set traps for him last evening, but he freed himself by his wits and escaped those dangers. Today I have again tested him, but here he is about to escape again." Having thus been astonished because of Mwindo, Muisa sent his powerful belt of **cowries** over to where Mwindo was, saying to it: "My belt, you are going to Mwindo. You must break him in two and smash his mouth against the ground." The belt, obeying the instructions of its master, went to the banana grove.

When it saw Mwindo in the banana grove, it fell upon him and lashed at him, making him scream. It crushed him, smacking his mouth against the ground until froth came out.

Mwindo's First Task: Cultivating Bananas

"my sister"—They are not related, but they are of the same age.

"sacred hut"—A place to receive guests.

"You must first cut leaves"— Muisa lists the basic steps of banana growing.

"Mwindo . . . went to cultivate the bananas"—The prominence of this task represents the significance of banana growing to the Nyanga. It is their main form of agriculture, while banana paste is the main element of the Nyanga diet.

A wooden pot used for the eating of banana paste. This elaborately carved pot belonged to one of the divine kings of the Nyanga.

cowries A type of seashells.

He couldn't breathe. Urine and excrement flowed out of him, so little could he control himself. Seeing its master unable to find means to escape, Mwindo's scepter recalled its duty. It drew itself up above the head of Mwindo. He opened his eyes and gazed about.

During the time Mwindo had been pinned down by Muisa's belt, the rope that he was attached to did not move any more. His aunt, back in Tubondo, had held on to the other end of the rope. When it was still, she threw herself down, saying that her son was dead. She uttered a cry, low and high, imploring the gods, and she said: "However he returns, I will take care of him." Back where Mwindo was, he lifted up his eyes, and sang:

> Though Muisa slay Mwindo
> And I shall die,
> Muisa, you are really helpless against Mwindo,
> Against Mwindo, the Little One Just Born He Walked.

Mwindo, while singing, remembered his aunt: "You there in Tubondo, I felt that my rope did not move because Muisa had pinned me to the ground. He wrapped me up like a bunch of bananas. But don't worry any more, because I am saved. It is my scepter that brought me back to life."

Mwindo now sent his scepter to Muisa, saying: "You, my scepter, when you have arrived where Muisa is, you must smash him powerfully. You must force his mouth to the ground so that his tongue will cut the earth like a hoe. For as long as I stay away from the village, you must not let him loose again." The scepter went whirling around. When it arrived at Muisa's meeting place, it smashed him. It shoved his mouth to the ground. His tongue dug into the earth. He could not control his bowels and he messed himself badly. He couldn't breathe. Mwindo stayed in the banana grove preparing a load of bananas. When he returned to the village, he glanced over at the meeting place and he saw Muisa. Foam spewed out of his mouth and nose, he was so enraged. Kahindo, seeing Mwindo, hurried to him. She told him: "You are just coming here, while my father's body has already cooled in death." Mwindo answered her that he had come looking for his father. "Now bring my father here, so that I may go home with him." Kahindo answered: "First you must heal my father. Then I will show you your father, and deliver him to you." Mwindo sang while awakening Muisa:

> He who sleeps shall wake up.
> Muisa, you are powerless against Mwindo
> Because Mwindo is the Little One Just Born He Walked.
> Kahombo, whom Muisa brought forth,
> He-who-is-accustomed-to-mocking-himself.   5
> Muisa, you are helpless against Mwindo.
> **A bit of food, thanks, puts an end to a song.**

Mwindo went on singing like that while beating Muisa's head with his scepter to bring him back to life. When Muisa awakened and saw that he was safe, he said: "You, Mwindo, lo, you are a powerful man."

Muisa again tested Mwindo. "You, child, must go as soon as it is light and **gather for me the honey** that is in that tree there." Sky became night. Kahindo stirred paste for Mwindo. Having eaten the paste, they went to sleep.

When the sky had turned to day, Mwindo took up his axe and went to gather the honey. He took coals with him to start a fire. When he arrived at the base of the tree, he climbed up into it, arriving at the hive where the honey was. He made the fire, and used it to smoke out the bees. When it was ready, he struck his axe against the trunk, singing:

> I am extracting honey in Muisa's country.
> My friend Nkuba, may you be victorious.

Sidebar notes:

"Mwindo . . . remembered his aunt"—Even beyond the use of the rope for signaling, Mwindo communicates with his aunt by a kind of telepathy.

"A bit of food, thanks, puts an end to a song."—The storyteller is invited to eat and thanks his host.

 Mwindo's Second Task: Gathering Honey

"gather for me the honey"—Honey is regarded as a great delicacy among the Nyanga.

> Hatred is in the heart.
> My little father threw me into the drum into the river;
> My father believed that I would drift away.   5

Muisa, back in the village, said: "I think this man will finally gather this honey!" Muisa sent his magical belt. It flew and smashed Mwindo against the tree trunk. Again he couldn't breathe and he couldn't control his bowels. Urine and excrement ran down his legs.

Iyangura saw that the rope was still, and again she feared that he was dead. Where Mwindo had left it, his scepter realized that its master was dying. It climbed up to where he was, pressed against the tree trunk, and it beat and beat on the head of Mwindo. He sneezed, lifted his eyes and gasped. He said: "Lo, while I was perched here, I was on the verge of death." When he had opened his eyes, he implored his friend Nkuba, singing:

Nkuba The god of lightning, helps Mwindo to cut open the honey tree.

> My friend **Nkuba,** be victorious.
> Hatred is in the heart.

In climbing down, he gazed into the sky, saying: "My friend Nkuba, I am suffering." When Nkuba heard the cry of his friend Mwindo, he descended to the tree and cleaved it into pieces. On the ground, his friend Mwindo did not have a single wound.

Mwindo had come down with the basket of honey. He carried it to Muisa's and laid it at his feet. Then Muisa sent a boy to look for the place where he had hidden Shemwindo, but Shemwindo was gone. Having seen no one there, the boy returned to Muisa and Mwindo. He told them: "While you were waiting here Shemwindo has fled. He is not where he has been." Just then **Kahungu** came in and told Mwindo: "Your companion Muisa lies, for he has warned your father to flee to Ntumba's, the sacred aardvark, saying that you are too powerful." After Kahungu had told Mwindo the news in that manner, he flew away into the sky.

Kahungu Hawk.

Mwindo then told Muisa the truth bluntly. "Bring me my father right now! Have him emerge from where you have hidden him so that I may take him with me. You scoundrel, you said that when I plowed a field for you, and when I gathered honey for you, you would then give me my father. I want you to produce him right now." Muisa said: "This time, this boy is really getting annoying, and right here in my own village."

"He tossed his hooves up into the air"—This expression means that Muisa is really dead.

Mwindo began to beat Muisa on the head with his scepter. Muisa then couldn't control himself and excrement stuck to his buttocks. He fainted away. His urine ran all over the ground, and froth came out of his nose and eyes and covered his face. **He tossed his hooves up into the air** and he stiffened like a viper. Mwindo said, "Stay like that, you dog." He would not heal him until he came back. Mwindo was going in pursuit of his father, where he had gone to the aardvark, Ntumba's. Mwindo went on singing:

Ntumba The aardvark, lives in a huge lair in the underground world. Aardvarks are anteaters and are powerful diggers.

> I am searching for Shemwindo
> In the place where Shemwindo went.
> Shemwindo fled into Ntumba's dwelling.
> l am searching for Ntumba's dwelling
> **Ntumba,** open for me.   5
> Shemwindo is in flight inside Ntumba's dwelling.
> I am searching for my father Shemwindo
> In Ntumba's dwelling.
> The sun begins to set.
> I am searching for Shemwindo.   10
> Shemwindo is in flight inside Ntumba's dwelling.
> My little father threw me into the drum.

Mwindo implored lightning-bringing Nkuba, saying:

> My friend Nkuba, may you be victorious.
> Hatred is in the heart.
> My little father, the dearest one,
> I am searching for my father in Ntumba's dwelling,
> My friend Nkuba, may you be victorious,   5
> Hatred is in the heart.
> I am looking for my little father.
> My little father threw me into the drum,
> My little father, eternal malefactor among people.
> My little father shot me into the river.   10
> Ntumba, open for me.

Mwindo paced around Ntumba's cave where his father was, but Ntumba paid no attention to him. Then the aardvark, Ntumba, made a sign to Shemwindo, saying: "You be ready to go. The little man at the door is strong, and you see the way he is threatening." When Shemwindo heard how his son was toughening himself (like a hide drying in the sun), he said: "The little boy comes to us looking severe." Then he told his friend Ntumba that he was going to continue to run away. Shemwindo then escaped to **Sheburungu's**—the god of creation, known too as Onfo.

When he heard the voice of Mwindo, Nkuba said: "My friend is already tired of praying to me." He sent down seven bolts of lightning. They struck inside the cave, cleaving it into a million pieces. The cave turned into dust. Realizing that his friend Nkuba had struck the cave, Mwindo walked inside. He searched for his father but did not find him. Then he met Ntumba and told him: "Ntumba, where did you let my father go, where have you hidden him?" The aardvark kept silent as though he had not heard. Mwindo spat at him, saying: "Get out, you scoundrel! May you die of scrotal elephantiasis!"

When Ntumba saw how Mwindo proceeded to blame him, he said: "You see how my house was just destroyed and all my crop. What am I going to do now?" Where Kahungu dwelt in the sky, he came down. He went to bring the news to Mwindo, saying: "You know, Mwindo, that Ntumba has allowed your father to escape. Your father ran away to Sheburungu's." Kahungu again flew away. Mwindo remained at Ntumba's. Because of anger and weariness, he cursed the aardvark: "Ntumba, this is how you will die—may you never again find food in this country of yours." In Tubondo, Iyangura went on pondering sadly: "My heart will return to normal only when Mwindo is safely back." She looked at the rope that she was holding. She said: "Lo, Mwindo is still searching for the place to which his father has escaped."

Mwindo followed his father, all wrapped up in hatred. He arrived at the entrance of the creation god, Sheburungu's, village. He encountered a group of little children, who greeted him, saying: "Mwindo, don't run ahead of us. We are hungry and we need you to give us food." Mwindo implored Iyangura to send him food, telling her that the children of Sheburungu were hungry. While asking for food from his aunt, Mwindo sang:

> Oh, you there, where Iyangura has stayed,
> Sister of Shemwindo,
> **I must have seven portions of food.**
> You see where Mwindo passed,
> I am suffering from hunger.   5
> Aunt Iyangura,
> I am claiming meat.

Sheburungu A name given to Ongo, the creator god.

"I must have seven portions of food"—The connection between Mwindo and his aunt is magical, and allows him to ask for and receive this assistance from her.

Having said to his aunt that he needed seven portions of meat and paste to come to him, Mwindo looked up, and the pastes had already arrived. Mwindo gave them to the youngsters, and they began eating the paste. When they finished eating, **Mwindo returned the wicker plates to Iyangura,** telling her to line them up so that they might be used as steps to climb up to Sheburungu's. Mwindo sent back the wicker plates, singing:

> I send back the wicker and wooden plates.
> O Aunt Iyangura, (I pay you honor),
> I send back the wicker and wooden plates.

After he had sent back the wicker and wooden plates, he climbed up to Sheburungu's, and the youngsters followed him (as they always do when a visitor arrives). He went up to Sheburungu's, singing:

> Sheburungu, you,
> I am looking for Shemwindo.
> Shemwindo gave birth to a hero
> In giving birth to the Little One Just Born He Walked.
> Sheburungu,   5
> I am looking for Shemwindo.

Sheburungu shouted and said:

> O Mwindo, **let us gamble together!**

And Mwindo shouted and said:

> O my father Sheburungu,
> I am looking for Shemwindo.

And he—

> O Mwindo, let us gamble together!

And Mwindo shouted, he said:

> O my father, give me Shemwindo!
> My little father threw me into the drum,
> My little father threw me into the river.
> The youngsters asked me to gamble with them,
> The youngsters—I do not gamble with them.   5

After Mwindo had entreated him to return his father, Sheburungu said to him: "I cannot just give your father to you. First we must gamble. Then I will deliver your father, and then you may go home with him." Mwindo answered him: "Go ahead and spread the seed shells out on the ground that I may guess how many there are (for that was how they gambled). I will not run away from you for you know the dangers that I have already escaped from." After Sheburungu heard Mwindo's response, he brought a mat and the very old seed shells of the isea tree. Sheburungu wagered: "Mwindo, if you beat me, you will carry your father off with you. Here are three sums of money. If you beat me, you will carry them off, too." **Mwindo wagered three sums of money.** Sheburungu was the first to take a handful of seeds. With the first take-up, he won all of Mwindo's money. **Mwindo wagered the goats** that remained in Tubondo. Sheburungu took the seeds and he won all the goats from Mwindo. **Mwindo wagered everything, even his aunt. Sheburungu won all his goods and his followers and his aunt.** Mwindo simply sat there all alone with his scepter. And then Mwindo wagered his scepter. When Sheburungu tried to take the seeds, he failed. Mwindo took the seeds. He won back from She-

---

"Mwindo returned the wicker plates to Iyangura"—Nyanga men eat together in the men's hut, sharing the dishes prepared by their wives. When the meal is over, they return all the empty plates to their places immediately, so that an evil sorcerer may not use the remaining food particles against them. A housewife is always uneasy until the plates are returned.

Mwindo's Third Task: Gambling with the Creator God

"let us gamble together"—Sheburungu wants to play wiki with Mwindo. This game involves taking handfuls of black seed and guessing the number of seeds held in each hand. This game is played only by men and involves substantial wagering.

"Mwindo wagered . . . money . . . goats . . . all his goods and followers and his aunt."—In this wiki game, the participants can wager all their possessions, including their wives and daughters.

burungu all the money that he had wagered. Sheburungu wagered again and Mwindo again took the seeds. All that Sheburungu had bet, Mwindo won it back. Sheburungu wagered all his objects, together with his cattle. Mwindo took the seeds up again, and again he won. Finally he won all the things of Sheburungu— people, goats, cattle. Mwindo piled up everything and Sheburungu was left all alone.

Kantori and Kahungu ran to where Mwindo was, warning him: "You, Mwindo, come quickly, your father is trying to run away again." After he heard that, Mwindo abandoned the game and sped away to encounter his father in the banana grove of Sheburungu. Seeing his father, Mwindo inquired: "**O my father,** are you here?" (Now he was able to pay the respect due to a father, for he had defeated him properly.) Shemwindo answered: "Here I am."

After Mwindo had seized his father, he returned with him to Sheburungu's. Mwindo said: "Sheburungu, you have been hiding my father. This is my father, is he not?" Mwindo said to Sheburungu: "Sheburungu, I don't want any of your things that I have won. Just keep all, for I am leaving here with my father." Mwindo gave his respectful farewell to Sheburungu and his people: "O father Sheburungu, farewell!" Sheburungu answered: "Yes, you, too, Mwindo, go and be strong, along with your father Shemwindo." After Mwindo had said farewell to Sheburungu, he returned singing:

> Listen, Ntumba,
> He who went away comes back.

Mwindo shook the rope, reminding his aunt, and telling her of his return. And she had bells attached to the rope, Mwindo sang:

> He who went away comes back,
> You see **I am carrying Shemwindo.**

Mwindo rushed headlong to the cave, which Ntumba had already finished rebuilding. Mwindo said to him: "Why did you hide my father away?" Mwindo sang:

> Ntumba, even you are powerless against Mwindo,
> For Mwindo is the Little One Just Born He Walked.
> I am on my way home from this point on in Ntumba's house.
> Look, I am carrying Shemwindo,
> My father, the dearest one,   5
> Shemwindo, senior brother of Iyangura.
> It is Shemwindo,
> the one who gave birth to a hero.
> Aunt Iyangura, I am on my way back.
> Mwindo is the Little One Just Born He Walked.   10
> I am carrying my father, Shemwindo.

When Mwindo arrived at Ntumba's, he told him the whole story: "Ntumba, you were wrong to offend me." But he gave back all of Ntumba's things, his land and the banana groves, and his followers, everything. And Mwindo and his father Shemwindo spent the night there. The next day, Ntumba said to Mwindo: "Go, I will never utter slander against you. I have no dispute with you." When Mwindo left Ntumba's with his father, he went singing, reminding his aunt in Tubondo:

> Since Mwindo is the Little One Just Born He Walked,
> It is you who are wrong for offending me in vain.
> Look! I am carrying Shemwindo.
> Muisa, you are helpless against Mwindo,
> Since Mwindo is the Little One Just Born He Walked   5

Kantori Sparrow.

"Oh, my father"—Now that he has defeated his father properly, Mwindo pays him the respect due to a father. From this moment, the hero displays his true greatness and does not manifest excessive emotions.

"I am carrying Shemwindo"—This may mean that Mwindo literally carries his father or simply that they travel together.

Look! I am carrying Shemwindo.
I am returning to Tubondo,
Where remained my aunt Iyangura,
Iyangura, sister of Shemwindo,
Aunt, birth-giver, Iyangura.   10
I shall eat on the wicker and wooden plates
Only when I shall arrive in Tubondo.

"I shall eat . . . only when" —
Once again, the text suggests that
Mwindo does not eat while under-
going his adventures.

When Mwindo left Ntumba's village with his father, he went straight to Muisa's.
There, Kahindo came to Mwindo, saying:

"You see my father here, his bones fill a basket. What shall I do then? **It is fitting**
that you should heal my father. Don't leave him like that. May my father wake up,
because he is the chief of all the people." Mwindo woke up Muisa, singing:

"It is fitting that you should heal
my father"—Mwindo killed Muisa
before going on his trip to
Ntumba's.

He who went to sleep wakes up,
My Father Muisa,
He who went to sleep wakes up.
Look! You, it is you who have offended me in vain.
Look! I am carrying my father Shemwindo.   5
Muisa, he who went to sleep wakes up.
Muisa, you are helpless against Mwindo,
Mwindo is the Little One Just Born He Walked.
Shemwindo brought forth a hero.
I am going to Aunt Iyangura's village,   10
Iyangura, sister of Shemwindo.

"Mwindo is the Little One Just
Born He Walked"—Mwindo
reminds Muisa that his birth and
childhood were miraculous. The
narrative here is not needless
boasting: Mwindo's background is
necessary to explain his powers to
Muisa.

Mwindo was awakening Muisa, he kept striking him with his scepter, saying: "You
have offended me. You have tried to be equal to Mwindo, whereas **Mwindo is the Lit-**
tle One Just Born He Walked, the little one who does not eat earthly foods. The day he
was born, he did not drink at the breasts of his mother." When Mwindo had finished
awakening Muisa, Muisa was brought back to life.

Mwindo revealed to him his great secret, that he had been forged by his uncles, the
people of Yana. "My body is covered with iron, and you, don't you see me?" He told
him: "Muisa, have you never heard that I came out of the middle of my mother? I was
not born in the same way that other children are born, but I was born speaking and
even walking! Have you never heard that I was thrown into a grave, one that they had
even put banana stems on, but I came back to life. My father threw me into the drum,
which he threw into the river, but I emerged from the water once more. Have you not
heard all these marvelous things, Muisa? That is why you dared to make a fool of me."

When Mwindo was at Muisa's, he shook the rope to remind his aunt that he would
return. Iyangura said to Mwindo's uncles, the people of Yana, that Mwindo had captured his father, and that he was now on his way home with him. While returning to
Tubondo, Mwindo said farewell to Muisa:

You, Muisa,
You see me already leaving,
You Muisa, taker of others' things.
Where Aunt Iyangura remains
In Tubondo,   5
He who went away is back.

"it's befitting that you marry my
Kahindo"—Mwindo stayed with
Kahindo, Muisa's daughter, when
he first arrived at Muisa's.

When Muisa saw Mwindo going, he said to him: "Oh, Mwindo, my son, **it's befit-**
ting that you marry my Kahindo here." Mwindo answered him: "I cannot marry here,
I shall marry later in Tubondo.

Mwindo set forth. He and his father went home, emerging where they had entered, at the root of the kikoka fern. When they arrived at Tubondo, those who were in the village, Iyangura and the uncles of Mwindo, went to greet Mwindo and his father. Seeing him, Iyangura and the uncles of Mwindo lifted him up into the air carrying him on their fingertips. When they had walked around the village, Mwindo told them to let him down. They gathered many spear heads and put him on top of them. His maternal uncles put him to the test so they might know if their nephew had remained as he was when they had forged him. After Mwindo was seated in the middle of the village, he told his aunt the story of where he had been and how he had fought while searching for his father.

Iyangura gave her son this order: "Since you have arrived with your father, bring him first into **the shrine of good fortune** to let him rest there." In giving due hospitality to his father, Mwindo killed **the goat that never defecates and never urinates.** They cooked it, along with the rarest of **rice,** for his father. He said to his father: "Here are your goats! It is you who were wrong. You set yourself against Mwindo, the Little One Just Born He Walked, when you said that you did not want any boys. You did a deliberate wrong in the way you wished things to be. You did not know the strength of the blessing of Mwindo."

After Mwindo had given food to his father as a hospitality gift, Iyangura said to him: "My son, shall we go on living always in **this desolate village?** I want you to save all the people who lived here in this village. When you have brought them back to life it is then only that I shall be able to know how great you are in beating Shemwindo. Only then can I tell others the story of the ways in which he acted, and the evil that he did against you." Mwindo listened to the order to heal those who had died. His uncles, the people of Yana, beat the drum for him while he was dancing with the joy of seeing his father. They sang. His aunt shouted:

> My father, eternal savior of people.

Mwindo said:

> Oh, father, they tell me to save the people.
> I say: "He who went to sleep wakes up."
> Little Mwindo is the Little One Just Born He Walked.
> My little father threw me into the drum.
>
> Shemwindo, you do not know how to lead people.   5
> The habits of people are difficult.
> My little father, eternal malefactor among people,
> **Made bees fall down on me,**
> Bees of day and sun.
> I lacked all means of protection against them.   10

Mwindo was healing those who died in Tubondo in the following way: when he arrived at the bone of a man, he beat it with his scepter so that the man would then wake up. The resuscitation was as follows:

> Each one who died in pregnancy came back to life in her pregnancy.
> Each one who died in labor revived while still in labor.
> Each one who was preparing paste resuscitated stirring paste.
> Each one who died defecating was reborn defecating.
> Each one who died setting traps came to life trapping.   5
> Each one who died copulating came alive copulating.
> Each one who died forging was brought to life forging.

The Return of the Hero

"the shrine of good fortune"—A shrine for the spirit of good fortune, where guests are accommodated. Shemwindo is no longer treated as the chief, the possessor of the village, but only as an important guest.

"the goat that never defecates and never urinates"—A very fat goat.

"rice"—More trouble to cultivate than bananas. A very elegant meal is prepared for Mwindo to host his father.

"this desolate village"—All the inhabitants of the village were killed by Nkuba, lightning, in the attempt to capture Shemwindo. Mwindo immediately brought his uncles back to life, but not the other people of the village.

"Made bees fall down on me"—This stereotyped expression means that his father unexpectedly exposed him to all kinds of dangers. The dangers came suddenly, like a swarm of bees.

Each one who died cultivating came to life cultivating.
Each one who died making pots and jars was reborn shaping.
Each one who died carving dishes came to life carving.   10
Each one who died quarreling with a partner was brought back
    still quarreling.

Mwindo stayed in the village for three days bringing people back to life. He was bone weary. Each person he revived arose straight up like a tree. Tubondo was lively once again with the people and **the goats, the dogs, the cattle,** the poultry, the male rams, and the female ewes, the teenage boys and girls, the children and the youngsters, the old males and females. In the middle of all those people were the nobles and counselors and the Pygmies and all the royal initiators. All those also were planted back in their own places. All the groups that formerly dwelt in Tubondo came back to life. Each person who died having things of a certain quantity, came back to life still having his things. Tubondo again became the big village with seven entrances.

When the people were revived, Iyangura spoke in the middle of the crowd:

"You, Shemwindo, my brother, have your followers prepare quantities of beer and kill cows and goats for a feast. Let all the people meet here in Tubondo. Then we shall be able to examine in detail our deep concerns and to resolve them in our assembly." After Shemwindo had heard the voice of his sister, he uttered a cry, high and low, to all his people, saying that they should have beer together so they might meet together, discuss important things together.

The Royal Presentation

After the people had grouped themselves in the assembly, servants stretched mats out on the ground in the place where Mwindo and his father and his aunt would pass. Everyone kept silent, a sacred total silence. Those three radiant stars, Mwindo and his father and his aunt, appeared from inside the house, marching solemnly.

The people gathered themselves in an orderly manner, each group in its own cluster: Mwindo also ordered that all his father's wives, his seven mothers, be seated in one group but that Nyamwindo, the mother who gave birth to him, should separate herself somewhat from his other mothers, called "the little mothers." The little mothers moved to form their own cluster. His mother moved a short distance away, all the while remaining near her co-spouses so they might not spite her. Mwindo now ordered Shemwindo to speak: "My father, it is your turn. Explain to the chiefs why you have a grudge against me." Shemwindo was flabbergasted. Quivering, he spoke, choking a bit as he did so: all this brought about by the great evil that caused him to destroy Mwindo. He said: "All you chiefs, I don't deny the harm that I have committed against my son. Indeed, I had passed a law that I would kill any among my wives who would give birth to a son. My preferred wife became my despised one. In the middle of all this anger, I armed myself with a spear. I wanted to kill the child with its mother. When we woke up in the morning, upon awakening, we saw the child already wailing again in its mother's house. When I heard that, I asked myself in my heart: 'If I continue to fail to kill this child, then it will usurp my royal chair.' Where this child went, I believed that I was doing away with him, but I was only making him stronger. It is from these acts that the child's anger stems."

"From that point on I began to flee, all my people having been wiped out. My son set out in search of me. He went to deliver me from the abyss of evil in which I was involved. I was at that time withered like dried bananas.

"And it is like that, that I arrive here in the village of Tubondo. So may the male offspring be spared, for he has shown me the way in which the sky becomes daylight and

"the goats, the dogs, the cattle"—Listed are all the domestic animals traditionally known by the Nyanga, as well as cattle. Cattle are not widespread among the Nyanga; they are mentioned here either because the narrator was familiar with them from travels in neighboring areas, or because this reference preserves an ancient tradition known by the ancestors of the Nyanga before they migrated to their present home from the eastern grasslands.

has given me the joy of witnessing again the warmth of the people and of all the things here in Tubondo."

Then Iyangura spoke to the men who were sitting in the assembly, reproaching Shemwindo openly. "Here I am, aunt of Mwindo, you chiefs. Our young man here, Shemwindo, has married me to Mukiti. **I got accustomed to it** thanks to the confidence of my husband. Suddenly, this child appeared where I was living. Mukiti was then on the verge of killing him because he did not know of our relationship. But his intelligence and his anger saved him. From then on I followed him to show him the way to Shemwindo's. It's there that Mwindo's fights with his father began, because of the anger caused by all the evils that his father perpetrated against him. When he found him, he seized him. Then Mwindo made his father return again to this village, Tubondo. So it is that we are in this meeting of the assembly of the chiefs.

"You, Shemwindo, acted badly when you discriminated against the children, saying that some were bad and others good, whereas you did not know what was in the womb of your wife. What you were given by the creator god, you saw it to be bad. If the people had been exterminated here, it is Shemwindo who would have been guilty of exterminating them. I, Iyangura, I am finished." After Iyangura had spoken, Mwindo also stood up: he praised the assembly, he said: "As for me, I, Mwindo, man of many feats, the Little One Just Born He Walked, I will not hold a grudge against my father. May my father here not be frightened, believing that I am still angry with him. No, I am not angry with my father. What my father did against me and what I did against my father, **all that is already over.** Now let us examine what is to come, the evil and the good. Now, let us live in harmony in our country, let us care for our people well."

Shemwindo declared that as far as he was concerned, it was Mwindo who would succeed him, and if anyone insulted Mwindo, the seniors would denounce him. When Mwindo heard his father's voice, he answered him: "Father, sit down on your royal chair. I cannot be chief as long as you are alive, otherwise I would die suddenly." The counselors and nobles agreed with Mwindo. Shemwindo said: "Since you, my counselors and my nobles, come to give me this advice, so I am ready to divide the country into two parts—for Mwindo a part and for myself, a part, because of the fear you inspire."

After Shemwindo had spoken thus, he conferred the kingship upon his son. He stripped himself of all the things of kingship that he bore. **He gave Mwindo a dress dyed red and two red belts, he also gave him the expensive bracelets** made of raphia string to wear on his arms; he gave him a boar skin belt and gave him a raphia and hair belt as well; he gave him a powerful fur hat; he also gave him the hide of a white goat. Shemwindo dressed Mwindo in all those things while Mwindo was standing up, because a chief is always dressed in such things while he is standing. The counselors went to fetch the chair imbued with powerful powder and oil. They gave it to Shemwindo.

Shemwindo made Mwindo sit on it, and handed over to Mwindo the scepter of copper on which there were incisions imbued with the powerful powder and oil. When he stood up, his father also handed over to him the wrist protector and the bow, and the quiver in which there were arrows, with royal emblems on all of them.

After Shemwindo had thus enthroned his son, Mwindo shouted that **he now had become famous,** but he would not act as his father had, causing his own name only to be perpetuated by having only one group remain on earth, named after him and honoring his deeds. "May all the various families and groups be celebrated here. May many boys and girls be born and our people increase. May there be born also deaf and cripples, because a country is never without some handicapped."

After Shemwindo had dressed his son in the chiefly paraphernalia, **he distributed beer and meat** for the chiefs who were there. Each group took a goat and a cow. They also gave Iyangura one cow to bring back to her husband Mukiti. Then the chiefs and the counselors who were there, said: "Let Mwindo remain here in Tubondo and let Shemwindo go

"I got accustomed to it"—The Nyanga think that it is a good thing for a woman to become accustomed to her husband's family and not always seek excuses for frequently visiting her own family.

"all that is already over"—Mwindo displays the magnanimity that is appropriate for a chief.

"He gave Mwindo a dress . . . belts . . . bracelets"— Shemwindo gives his son all the traditional paraphernalia of a chief.

"he now had become famous"— Mwindo is referring to the fame he has achieved through his initiation as chief. He then shows his generosity by indicating that he will accept diversity among his followers.

"he distributed beer and meat"— As suggested here, it is customary during a chief's enthronement for the chief to feed the people and to provide them with other gifts. The people in turn provide him, without matrimonial payments, four wives.

to dwell on another mountain." Hearing this, Shemwindo clapped his hands—he was very satisfied. During Mwindo's enthronement, his uncles, the people of Yana, gave him a maiden. Mwindo's father, too, gave him a maiden called Katobororo and the Pygmies gave him one as well. During Mwindo's enthronement, he was given four women. After Mwindo had been enthroned, the assembly dispersed. All those who came from somewhere, returned there. Shemwindo also took possession of his mountain. He left Tubondo to his son.

When Iyangura, aunt of Mwindo, returned to her husband, **she anointed Mwindo** in the middle of the group, saying:

O, Mwindo, hail!
Blessing, here, hail!
If your father throws you into the grave, hail!
Don't harbor resentment, hail!
May you stand up and make your first step, hail!   5
May you be safe, may you be blessed, hail!
And your father and your mother, hail!
May you bring forth tall children, boys and girls.
Be strong, my father. As for me, there is nothing ominous left, hail!

When Mwindo took leave of his father, his father also gave him a blessing.

Confronting the Dragon, and Being Punished for His Deeds

After a fixed number of days had elapsed since he had been enthroned, Mwindo said that he had a terrible craving to eat some wild pig meat. **He sent his Pygmies forth,** for they were his hunters, out into the forest. Where the Pygmies went in the forest, when they had already been hither and yon, they felt tired, they slept halfway. In the morning they found the trail of wild pigs, followed them, met them. They sent the dogs after them, seeing that they were fleeing. Crossing two plateaus, they met a red-haired pig who was old and fat. They hurled a sharp spear at it. They cut it into pieces on the spot.

In the very dense forest, when they were cutting the pig to pieces, **Dragon** heard their mumbling. He said: "What now, people here again? I thought that I was the only one living here." He went after them, snakelike. When he came close to them, he threw himself onto them. He took away three Pygmies—he swallowed them. One among the Pygmies, called Nkurongo, wrestled himself loose. He fled and the dogs followed him. Dragon said to himself: "Let this wild pork remain here, for I will trap the dogs and the Pygmy who fled." Dragon nestled down beside the corpse of the pig. Nkurongo fled. When he arrived, he looked back, saying: "Lo, my companions have been overtaken by night. They are already dead." At the time when he fixed his eyes on the Dragon, he saw that he had seven heads and seven horns and seven eyes. When that little Pygmy there was already on the crest, he shouted: "I flee, eh!" He fled and the dogs followed him.

He appeared in Tubondo. at Mwindo's house. After he had rested awhile, Mwindo asked him: "Is there peace there, from where you are coming?" He answered him: "There is no peace there, chief! We went to the forest, four of us, and Dragon has swallowed three of us, and I, Nkurongo, escaped, together with the dogs. This Dragon, he is as large as the sky." Hearing that, Mwindo said: "Well, now, this time it's tough." He looked up to the sky, lowered his eyes to the ground, and said: "O, my scepter, be victorious tomorrow."

Very early in the morning, Mwindo took up his scepter and the Pygmy went before him. Thus they proceeded. At the place where they had cut the pig into pieces, the Pygmy pointed at Dragon, saying: "There he is."

Mwindo said to the Pygmy: "You stay here. When Dragon swallows me, it is you who will announce the news in the village." Mwindo took in hand his scepter. He went

The masked circumcisor is a composite being like the kirimu dragon and includes several bird components: honey bird, hawk, and hornbill. In his right hand, he carries an adze of the sort used for honey harvesting, he moves like a hawk, and his mask incorporates the beak of a hornbill.

snakelike after Dragon. When he was eye-to-eye with him, Mwindo said: "You will not be my measure today." Dragon was overcome with surprise. He stood up. When he was about to fly against Mwindo, Mwindo put sweet words into his mouth. He sang:

> Dragon, you are helpless against Mwindo,
> For Mwindo is the Little One Just Born He Walked.
> Dragon, you have challenged Mwindo.
> Dragon, you are powerless against Mwindo,
> For Mwindo is the Little One Just Born He Walked.   5
> Shemwindo gave birth to a hero.
> Comrade, you are powerless against Mwindo

When Dragon attempted to swallow him, Mwindo beat him with his scepter. Dragon fell upside down and died. Mwindo called, shouting to his Pygmy to come to cut up Dragon. When he was about to touch Dragon with his great knife Mwindo forbade him: "First, leave him like that. Let us call people in the village to carry him back so that Shemwindo may see the wonders I perform." He sent his scepter to fetch the people so that they could bring back this god of a dragon. He sang:

> O, my scepter, go for me.
> Those who have remained in Tubondo over there,
> At Shemwindo's, May Shemwindo send people to me.

The scepter arrived in front of Shemwindo. It wagged itself in front of him, and all the people of the village went to see. He said that the scepter was bearing the news: " If Mwindo is not dead, it is Dragon who is dead." Shemwindo sent a group of people there:

> Be ready to leave the village!
> Go and join Mwindo!
> In the dense forest there are many things—
> There are snakes that bite.
> Go and join Mwindo,   5
> Where Mwindo has gone.
> Shemwindo has given birth to a hero.

The scepter flew away together with the people whom Shemwindo had provided and came into Mwindo's hands. He told the men to lift up Dragon. They made a stretcher. It broke because of Dragon's weight. They made another and carried it to the village. They let Dragon down in the middle of the village. When the people saw him, they were astonished. They whooped: "Now, things will be coming out of the forest!" But some of them were worried, saying, **"Whoever has killed the Dragon cannot fail to kill one of us,** perhaps even all of us." Mwindo said to his people to cut up Dragon, and he, Mwindo, sang:

> Dragon is being skinned and cut up on the
> little raphia palms.

Mwindo howled, saying:

> Dragon is being skinned and cut up on the
> little raphia palms.
> Dragon always devours people;
> Dragon has exterminated people.
> Shemwindo, my father, be afraid of me.   5

When they opened the belly, there came out a man who leaped up, being alive, and another, and yet another. After Dragon had been cut up and the three Pygmies had

"Whoever has killed the Dragon cannot fail to kill one of us"—As will be clear from what follows, it is contrary to Nyanga custom for the chief to hunt and kill animals. This small scene suggests the dissension that can be sown by such activity of a chief.

come out alive, Mwindo gave an order: "When you begin to eat this Dragon, you will eat him with bones and all. Don't throw any of them away.

Mwindo distributed to his people all the meat with the mass of bones. He told them also that if he saw even a little bone behind somebody's house, he would make him pay for it for Dragon must be roasted in public.

When Dragon had been divided into many parts, they seized his eyes and roasted them hot on a piece of potsherd. Each time that there appeared a splatter and the eye burst open, there came out a man. When all the eyes of Dragon had been roasted, there had appeared one thousand people. Mwindo said: "These are my people." And **he gave them a mountain.**

It so happened that Nkuba had made a blood pact with Dragon. When he inhaled the odor of his friend Dragon, which was passing with the wind, froth dropped from his nose; tears came from his eyes; he said, "What shall I do with **this friend here, Mwindo?**" He said that he first wanted to make him suffer in order that he would not begin again. He also said, "If Mwindo had known that I had exchanged blood with Dragon, then he would not have killed my friend the Dragon. But he is safe because he did not know that he was my friend."

Mwindo sang:

> Nkuba has just come to take Mwindo;
> Nkuba came to carry Mwindo away
> From the heights of Tubondo,
> When he inhaled the smell of roasting.

Mwindo howled, he said:

> Eh! Nkuba, you are helpless against Mwindo;
> Shemwindo brought forth a hero.
> Eh! Nkuba, you are powerless against Mwindo Mboru.

Then Mwindo said farewell to the people one by one.

> My mother who carried me,
> You are seeing that I am already going.
> Nyamwindo howled, complaining:
> "What shall I do with my child?"
> Nyamwindo howled, saying: 5
> "I die, I die, along with my child."
> Shemwindo howled, saying:
> "I die, I die, along with my child."

After Nkuba had **inhaled the smell** of his friend Dragon which came from his friend Mwindo in Tubondo, he descended on the spot to take Mwindo. He said to Mwindo: "I come to take you, you my friend. I want to teach you because I am very vexed with you, you my friend, since you dared to kill Dragon, for Dragon, too, was my friend. So know that you are doing wrong."

Hearing this, Mwindo was not afraid of going away with Nkuba, but his people were stricken with anxiety, thinking that their chief was going forever. Mwindo sang:

> **Let us go up to Bisherya** over there,
> For Nkuba has come to take Mwindo.
> I am about to climb up to Bisherya over there,
> For Nkuba has come to take Mwindo.
> O, Nkuba, you are powerless against Mwindo,   5
> For Mwindo is the Little One Just Born He Walked.

"he gave them a mountain"—It is the custom for a Nyanga chief to provide his followers the use of parts of his domain.

"this friend here, Mwindo"—Nkuba, lightning, has been a friend to Mwindo, helping him in his adventures.

"inhaled the smell"—This section repeats some of the information found in the description of Nkuba's discovery that Dragon is dead. Such redundancy is typical of oral composition. The storyteller does not work with a written text, so he does not compare the two sections as we might and notice the inconsistencies. For a discussion of the characteristics of oral composition, see Introduction, p. 306.

"Let us go up to Bisherya"—Nkuba takes Mwindo on a journey by which he will make up for his wrongdoing in hunting and killing Dragon.

Shemwindo gave birth to a hero.
My friend, you are powerless against Mwindo.

Mwindo went on singing like that while Nkuba was climbing with him slowly into the air, and the people of Mwindo had their attention diverted by the spectacle. Nkuba disappeared into the clouds, together with Mwindo.

They arrived at Nkuba's. He asked: "My friend Mwindo, you acted wrongly when you dared to kill my friend Dragon, when you roasted his eyes so that the odor drifted up to me, so that I smelled it in the air. If only you had made the odor descend to earth, then I would not have been angry." Nkuba still said to Mwindo: "I have rescued you many times from many dangers, so now you show that you are equal to me."

Mwindo felt there much cold, and the icy wind there was strong. No house! They lived there in wandering, not settling in one spot. **Nkuba seized Mwindo** and climbed up with him to Rain. When Rain saw Mwindo, he told him: "You, Mwindo, never accept being criticized. Word of your toughness, your heroism, we surely have heard those stories. But here there is no room for your heroism." Rain fell upon Mwindo seven and seven times more. He made hail fall upon him, and he soaked him thoroughly. Nkuba lifted Mwindo up again. He had him ramble across Moon's territory. When Moon saw Mwindo, he pointed at him: "We heard you were tough, but here in the sky there is no room for your pride." Moon burned Mwindo's hair. Nkuba lifted Mwindo up again. He went and climbed up with him to the domain of **Sun.** When Sun saw Mwindo, he **harassed him with heat.** Mwindo lacked all means of defense against Sun—his throat became dry, **his thirst strangulated him.** He asked for water. They said to him: "No, there is never any water. Now we advise you to grit your teeth and take it." After Sun had made Mwindo sustain these pains, Nkuba lifted Mwindo up. He went and made him arrive in the domain of Star: "We have heard that surely you are very tough, but here there is no room for your heroism." Kubikubi-star ordered Rain and Sun to come.

All—Nkuba, Rain, Sun, Star—all those gave Mwindo but one message: "We have respect for you. Otherwise, you would vanish right here. **Never should you kill an animal** or even an insect like a centipede. If one day we learn the news that you begin to kill anything of these forbidden things, then you will die." They pulled his ears seven times and seven more, saying: "Do you understand?" And he: "Yes, I have understood." They also said to Mwindo: "It is Nkuba here who is your guardian. If you have done wrong, it is Nkuba who will give us the news, and that day he will seize you, without any chance to say goodbye to your people."

After Nkuba made Mwindo ramble everywhere through the sky, they let him return home. Mwindo had by then spent one year in the sky, seeing all the good and all the bad things that are there. Nkuba raised Mwindo up. He returned with him home to Tubondo. Mwindo sang:

> Mwindo was already arriving
> Where Shemwindo had remained.
> Where Shemwindo had remained
> Mwindo was already arriving.
> He who went away returns. 5
> Shemwindo brought forth a hero.
> What will die and what will be safe,
> O my senior sister, may it join Mwindo!
> My friend Nkuba, be victorious.
> Let me go to Tubondo, 10
> To Tubondo, village of my mothers.
> May I see my mother, descend here in Tubondo,
> In father's village, my dearest one.

"Nkuba seized Mwindo"—This passage relates Mwindo's sufferings in the realm of Lightning, Rain, Moon, Sun, and Star.

"Sun . . . harassed him with heat"—The Nyanga for this is, literally, "Sun stretched him out (like an animal hide set out for drying) on hot things."

"his thirst strangulated him"—The Nyanga verb means, "kneaded him like bananas for beer brewing."

"Never should you kill an animal"—Nyanga chiefs are prohibited from hunting and trapping.

The will says: "Mwindo, if you kill an animal, you die."

> O Mwindo, never try again!
> From now on may you refuse meat.

Nkuba said:

> "Never try again."

When Shemwindo saw his son being brought back by Nkuba, he rewarded Nkuba with a maiden dressed with a bracelet of copper, Nkuba's metal. They also gave him the prescribed white fowl. It is there that the custom of celebrating the cult of Nkuba originated. **From then on they always dedicated to him** a maiden wearing a copper bracelet. After Nkuba had received his gift, he returned to his domain in the sky.

Mwindo assembled all his people. He told them: "When I arrived in the sky, I met with Rain and Moon and Sun and Kubikubi Star and Lightning. These forbade me to kill the animals of the forest, the rivers, and the village." He also told them: "I have seen in the sky things unseen which I cannot divulge." Shemwindo's and Nyamwindo's many hairs had gone "high as that," as the long hairs of the ghost of the forest, and in Tubondo, the drums had not sounded anymore, the rooster had not crowed anymore. On the day that Mwindo appeared, his father's and his mother's long hairs were shaved, and the roosters crowed, and that day all the drums were beaten all around, throughout the earth and in the sky.

When Mwindo's fame grew and traveled widely, he passed laws for all his people, saying:

> May you grow many foods and many crops.
> May you live in good houses,
> May you moreover live in a beautiful village.
> Don't quarrel with one another.
> Don't pursue another's spouse.   5
> Don't mock the invalid passing in the village.
> And he who seduces another's wife will be killed!
> Accept the chief. Fear him. May he also fear you.
> May you agree with one another, all together,
> No enmity in the land nor too much hate.   10
> May you bring forth tall and short children—
> in so doing you will bring them forth for the chief.

After Mwindo had spoken, he remained always in his village. He had much fame, and his father and his mother, and his wives and his people! His great fame spread to other countries, and other people from other countries came to pay allegiance to him.

"From then on, they always dedicated to him"—The epic here explains the origin of a Nyanga custom. The Nyanga dedicate a large number of women to the deities of lightning, good fortune, etc. These women are considered married to a spirit and cannot marry normally. They do, however, have the right to enter into long-term relationships with men, married or unmarried. Any children they have, however, belong to the mother's family and not the father's, as they would in an ordinary Nyanga marriage. Mwindo, like most heroes, brings back wisdom and a new understanding of reality from his journey.

Further Reading

Biebuyck, Daniel. *The Mwindo Epic: From the Banyanga (Congo Republic).* Berkeley, CA: University of California Press, 1969.

African and African-American Trickster Stories

23

WHAT TO EXPECT . . . The introduction to this chapter explains that African and African-American trickster tales flourished as a response to scarcity and hardship. Although the underlying causes for this were different, the tradition moved with the enslaved Africans to the American South because such storytelling allows the audience to deal with ethical and social dilemmas in a specific way. See for yourself what differences there are between tales from the old world and the new. What would be the effect if the behavior described in these tales became the norm for everyone?

This chapter includes stories performed in Africa, the West Indies, and the American South. In your reading, consider the similarities of oral technique and trickster behavior, as well as differences. For example, the trickster in these stories often causes disharmony, but this is a part of the audience's enjoyment—vicarious participation in re-orienting their world. Also compare the account of storytelling found in this chapter with the account in Chapter 22, p. 306, of the performance of the Mwindo epic.

As you read, think about why many stories in this tradition feature animals, rather than humans, as characters. Consider the relationship between these animals and those appearing in the Nigerian creation story in Chapter 9, p. 108. In what ways is the behavior of the Native American Raven, Ch. 21, p. 295, and the Greek Prometheus, Ch. 24, p. 353, comparable?

The trickster is a kind of hero, but he often does not seem very heroic. The trickster may have various names or various forms, but his predominant characteristic is guile in human relations. Typically, the trickster forges a contract with a dupe and then betrays him. He is a power broker who achieves his strength by violating the boundaries set by society. Or he tries to play a trick and is caught and disgraced. In this case, the trickster is also the dupe, and other characters in the story are seen as power brokers who punish him. Some stories represent a contest of two tricksters. Unlike European folktales, which usually have a happy ending, trickster stories typically end in disharmony.

African-American folktales are based on the storytelling heritage of the enslaved Africans transplanted to the New World. However, some kinds of African traditional tales did not survive in America. Epic stories that required elaborate performance could not be hidden from slave owners. In addition, owners discouraged blacks' attempts to maintain their religious practices, so there was little opportunity to transmit the stories associated with religious rituals. Many of the tales that did survive depict the adventures of a trickster whose behavior can be laughed at, yet learned from.

African-American folktales represent a wide variety of topics and themes, but their plot lines tend to reflect the experiences of the storytellers. There is a significant group of tales in which animals speak and act like humans. There are also many tales dealing explicitly with the relationships of masters and slaves. Many of these are about a trickster who is a slave named John and someone called Old Master, Master, Massa, or Massa King. These include the story of the slave who finds a talking skull and reports it to his master. The slave swears to the truth of his unusual discovery, and backs it up by telling the master he can beat him if the skull does not talk. When the slave shows the skull to the master it is silent, and he is beaten. Later he sees the skull again, and it says to him, "I told you not to talk to the white man." This is actually an adaptation of an African folktale to a plantation setting. Some of these stories involve trickery on the part of the master, or the encouragement of the slaves' own cunning. However, the slave is not always the butt of these stories; in some of them, he outwits the master, who is lazy or deceitful. Nonetheless, the stories represent a grim world in which masters and slaves are pitted against each other, and the slave survives only by a combination of cunning and luck.

Different scholars focus on various aspects of the meaning or significance of trickster tales. John W. Roberts emphasizes the social dimension of the tales. He points out that, although trickster stories from Africa and the American South resemble each other greatly, the significance of these tales is quite different. In both cultures people had to contend with the shortage of everyday necessities, and the stories reflect this. In Africa, the greatest threat to the values of the community came from the practice of magic, the attempt to manipulate the forces of nature at the expense of other members of the community. Rather than magic, the African trickster used his wits to obtain the supplies he needed while respecting and even affirming the community's values and identity by his negative example. Thus the trickster's behavior was viewed as acceptable adaptive behavior to conditions of extreme physical hardship.

In America as well, trickster tales flourished as a response to scarcity and hardship. However, the nature of this privation reflected the injustice of the slaveholding system. In Africa, the shortages were due to natural disasters or war. In America, shortage of food and material goods was the rule for enslaved Africans, a rule artificially imposed by their white masters in the midst of the abundance produced by the slaves themselves. In this context, challenging the masters' power would have been too dangerous; thus, under the conditions of slavery, trickster behaviors became valued ways to subvert the system. However, the social context of the stories allowed African Americans to distance their own identity from the moral values represented by the trickster.

Jay Edwards believes that the importance of the trickster tale is that it captures important ethical dilemmas for both the individual and society. He focuses on the dual role played by the trickster in African-American stories: he gets the dupe to trust him, and then betrays the trust. The story is as much about the change in the trickster's behavior as it is about the relationship between the trickster and the dupe. The stories favor neither trickery nor trust, but allow the audience to reflect on certain moral dilemmas imposed by slavery, the dilemmas that account for the change in the trickster's role. These dilemmas deal with various opposites that the stories set out as possibilities: life and death, male and female, harmony and disharmony. Because of the nature of the social conditions imposed by slavery, the resolution of these dilemmas is always the same: trickster tales inevitably end in disharmony, and the trickster's strategy is to maximize short-term economic gain at the cost of long-term goals like social cohesion.

The moral distance provided by trickster tales operates on individuals as well as on the society as a whole. Roger Abrahams points to the trickster himself in these stories. He is a part of society, but functions at its limits. He lives between nature and culture, and because of his dual identity, is able to unmask or disorder the world of those with a more solid stake in the established norms of society. As an insignificant and almost invisible creature, the trickster is able to learn the secrets of others, and to unmask and undermine their doings.

One example he uses is "Crawling into the Elephant's Belly." In this story, Anansi, the trickster, learns he can get food by climbing into the belly of an elephant in the King's corral and feeding on the innards he finds there. He is warned not to eat too much; if he does the elephant will die and he will be trapped inside. However, he is unable to resist gorging himself and so is caught by the King's guard. Abrahams views the trickster's activities as "protorevolutionary" or amoral.

The trickster does not act to make right or wrong triumph; he operates for the sheer joy of disruption and boundary-breaking. It is this delight that accounts for the repetition and variation of actions that is characteristic of these stories. The trickster moves for the joy of movement, repeating and varying his tricks until he is free and his dupes must pay the price. Thus, trickster tales provide their audience with the delight of seeing how the world can be taken apart and put together, destroyed and rebuilt, without predictable logic.

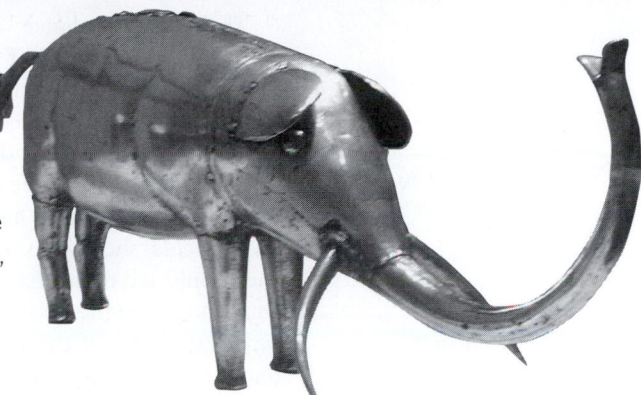

Elephant, 19th c. Republic of Benin, Fon peoples.

IMPORTANCE OF THE AUDIENCE

Trickster tales derive from a tradition based on oral performance. In Africa, as well as in America, these tales were meant to be told at gatherings, rather than written down. In the African village, people gathered after work or on special occasions to tell stories. The storyteller was not necessarily a professional, and storytelling contests were not uncommon. (See the performance of the Mwindo epic, Ch. 22, for more detail.) In America as well, enslaved Africans gathered in the evening to exchange stories and to vie with each other in storytelling. To fully appreciate these stories, it is important to imagine them as they were performed. The best storytellers would be those who could bring the stories to life by imitating a range of human and animal voices, by accompanying the story with a variety of sounds, squawks, screams, and by providing suitable singing, dancing, and gestures. Abrahams notes, "To an observer from another culture, the storytelling might seem to be as much a singing, dancing, and joking occasion as a recounting of a tale" (*Afro-American Folktales,* 26). To provide the flavor of such a gathering, we have enclosed Abrahams' account of a storytelling session he witnessed in St. Vincent in the West Indies.

Performance at a Wake in St. Vincent

A number of stories had been performed at a wake that I was attending in Richland Park, St. Vincent, when an old lady, Nora Bristol, broke into the already tumultuous proceedings, yelling out, **"See-ah."** A number of people looked her way but gave no vocal response. Again she shouted in her ancient growl, "See-ah." This time, two or three people responded, "See-ah," almost intoning the words. She then growl-sang, "See-ah, **Nanny**" to which everyone in the room responded, now singing:

> See-ah, Nanny, see-ah.

She took the audience one step further, singing in ringing tones:

> See-ah, Nanny, see-ah.

Knowing by now that others would repeat what she had sung, at this point she got up and began to do a little shuffle-dance, knees slightly bent and body turning slightly to the left as the singing began in earnest:

> See-ah, Nanny, see-ah.
> See-ah, Nanny, see-ah.
> **Me Mammy Nanny** coming (for to)
> See-ah, Nanny, see-ah.

This excerpt comes from: Roger D. Abrahams, Afro-American Folktales: Stories from Black Traditions in the New World.*

"See-ah"—means "look here" or "look there," or even "watch out."

Nanny The main character of a story which people in the room are familiar with. This is the first clue about the story Nora wants to tell.

"Me Mammy Nanny"—This song contains more clues about the story. It will be a story about Nanny and her Mammy.

*Roger D. Abrahams. *Afro-American Folktales: Stories from Black Traditions in the New World*, 26–30. Copyright © 1985. Pantheon Books.

This song and dance lasted at least five minutes and managed to involve, in some way or the other, most of the people in the room and many of those right outside the windows, in the yard of the recently deceased man. Then she suddenly yelled out, "Oh no, that is not my mother's voice up in the cotton on the mountain." Again the insistently repetitive song and dance started up, and lasted for another few minutes. At some point in the middle of a line, someone else called out, **"Crick!"** "Well then," Nora now said, "this woman had this only daughter, and whenever she left the house to go to the fields, she always told her daughter, if anyone came and called out to her, that she should tell them that she [her mother] had gone to the mountain [and therefore could not open the door]."

"Crick!"—The common West Indian way of calling attention to the story.

But the force of the singing and dancing was still coursing through the group, and they broke into the story, singing over and over:

> See-ah, Nanny, see-ah.
> See-ah, Nanny, see-ah.
> Me Mammy Nanny coming (for to)
> See-ah, Nanny, see-ah.

 Nora's Story: Part One

 Nora's Story: Part Two

Again, after a minute or so, she yelled, "Crick-crack!" now getting the traditional response from the others: "Rockland come." And she went on: "Then Nanny [the little girl's name] was surprised [by the witch-woman who had successfully imitated her mother's voice]. She went into the first bedroom, Nanny wasn't there. She went past the stairs and into the second bedroom, she couldn't find Nanny. She went downstairs, no Nanny. [Clearly Nanny had seen her mistake and run away.]"

> See-ah, Nanny, see-ah.
> See-ah, Nanny, see-ah.

Naturally, the song was again picked up by the entire group and carried on in three repetitions. This time, the singing came to a halt of its own, for the group was waiting for an indication of where the story was being taken. "No Nanny," she called to the mountain and she called to the cotton-field:

> See-ah, Nanny, see-ah.
> See-ah, Nanny, see-ah.

"deus-ex-machina trick"—The plot of some ancient Greek plays was so complicated that you couldn't figure out how it would ever be resolved. At the end, the author would have a god (deus) appear on stage and sort out all the problems. The god would appear with the help of a system of ropes and pulleys (ex machina).

Clearly, Nora and her audience were more interested in singing and dancing than in telling the story. Though I knew the language fairly well, I could not understand how the plot was being developed, for she had provided none of the clues to which I was accustomed. She proceeded to give a bit more dialogue, and to act out some more of the chase. But the tale was brought to a close, not through a profound ending to the action, but almost without warning, by a **deus-ex-machina trick:** "Her husband came down with his cutlass and ax and all and cut down all the trees, and gave that old lady a *whoppu!* and I came right here to tell all of you this story!"

Throughout the story, this immensely animated lady leaped about as if she were wound up like a spring, pointing her crooked finger in the face of all the little girls listening, chuckling to herself about these ridiculous doings even while she sang at the top of her lungs, danced around, and brought other people on the floor with her. Her performance was roundly enjoyed, not least because of her age and reputation, and because she was **breaking the rules of decorum** and obviously enjoying doing so. To be sure, such singing and dancing and other animating acts are the norm in West Indian performances at wakes, but few women—and especially, few older women— are willing to so perform. Far from being judged harshly for garbling the plot, she was applauded for her abundant energies and her ability to bring everyone into the performance.

 Nora's Story: Part Three (the conclusion)

"breaking the rules of decorum"—The narrator's function goes beyond telling the plot of the story.

Many storytellers attempt to gain everyone's attention by starting a song with which everyone will begin to sing; or by shouting out the conventional opening, "Crick-crack!" Often, of course, this ploy will not work, as more than one person will attempt to grab the audience's attention. There may also be too many other things going on at that moment for even the best of the storytellers to gain center stage.

A number of other features of storytelling in such communities underscore how narration is open to interruption and digression, preventing tales from being told from beginning to end. **Scenes are not necessarily recalled in chronological sequence;** I have recorded a great many stories that seem to begin in the middle or even the end, only to go back to some scene that occurs earlier in the string of actions that make up the "plot," as we think of it conventionally. The tales, after all, are made up of commonplace episodes and characters, recognizable to the audience, and can therefore be played around with. **The story may be stopped at any time, and on occasion, may be started again** some time later, even after another story or two has been told, or after other songs have been launched. In some cases, the sequence of episodes is fixed, and the effect of the story relies on a building of drama in a specific way. Naturally enough, these are the stories that have tended to be written down and put into folktale collections. But, equally often, stories are picked up and put down almost serendipitously, and the narrator may string together conventional episodes in any of a number of combinations, a practise that has led one observer to regard them as "pointless, disjointed, mutilated fragments . . . [which often] break off just when the interest has reached its highest point."

Nothing demonstrates the string-of-beads effect more than those stories, reported from a number of places in Afro-America, that begin or end with a song that seems to have little to connect it to the plot. For instance, the story "Assaulting All the Senses," from Surinam, concerns killing a tiger by getting him to drink monkey urine, yet ends with a song that apparently bears no relation to the story's action.

The use of such non-sequiturs has been reported from one end of the sphere of Afro-American culture to the other. Daniel Crowley, for instance, in his many intimate descriptions of tellings, tales, and tellers, includes interruptions to the narrative flow caused by audience questions and comments, parenthetical remarks (including jokes and elaborate "I was there"-type exaggerations by the narrator), and the inevitable breaking out in song.

In an even more radically punctuated tale tradition, described and summarized by Richard and Sally Price, among the Saramaka of Surinam, speakers introduce whole stories, little comic testimonial speeches about the truth of the story and the veracity of its teller, and songs that are by convention attached to another story, in addition to the usual running commentary on the effectiveness of the tale or the truths implied in its message.

To the uninstructed ear or eye the usual tale from this tradition often seems **formless and directionless,** wittily or eerily animated but without the strong sense of whole-plottedness to which we are accustomed. I am sure that if we were able to go back to the original oral versions of many of our most common literary folktales, we would be surprised at their rambling character, their repetitiveness and the number of parenthetical remarks introduced that sometimes develop into large-scale digressions. Storytelling, especially when it occurs at a wake (or some other celebration of life-transition), provides a context within which a number of other types of performance are encouraged, including riddles, games, and singing and dancing.

"Many storytellers attempt to gain everyone's attention—Storytelling sessions involve competition.

"Scenes are not necessarily recalled in chronological sequence"—Since the stories contain commonplace episodes and characters (like tricksters and dupes), people recognize them, even if the plot is not told in order.

"The story may be stopped . . . and . . . started again"—Interruption and digression are also a part of other oral traditions. Bernard Fenik has shown that Homer, who told stories about Odysseus' travels and the Trojan War, also inserted such interruptions into his story (61–104).

This quote comes from: Charles Rampini, *Letters from Jamaica* (London, 1877), 116.

"The use of such nonsequiturs"—The audience is very much a part of the telling of an African-American story and can interrupt with questions, comments, remarks, and songs.

These ideas come from: Daniel Crowley, *I Could Talk Old Story Good* (Berkeley, 1966). Richard and Sally Price, *Afro-American Arts of the Suriname Rain Forest* (Los Angeles, 1980).

"formless and directionless"—The oral versions of well-known literary folktales must have been rambling, repetitive, and full of digressions and parenthetical remarks.

African Trickster Tales

The first two African animal stories presented here are "How and Why" tales. The events in these stories result in an aetiological explanation of a feature of our world. Not all "How and Why" tales involve a trickster; see, for instance, the story of "The Creation" in Chapter 9, p. 103.

However, the typically disruptive actions of a trickster prove a useful way to explain some of the ways in which the world does not seem ordered or organized, or fair. The first story, "Why the Hare Runs Away," comes from the Ewe people of Togo and Benin in West Africa. In this story, the trickster himself is the dupe who is captured by the other animals. As expected in such a story, there is a contract, to build a well cooperatively, and the hare violates it and is punished for the infraction. The story contains the tar-baby motif also found in "Tricking All the Kings." The second story, "The Ant's Burden," comes from the Hausa people of Nigeria and Niger in West Africa. In this story, Kweku Anansi, the spider, attempts to trick the dwarf and his own son, Kweku Tsin, but is tricked in turn. Anansi's third attempt to find a dupe in the ant is more successful. Characteristically, he forges a contract and breaks it.

Why the Hare Runs Away

This is the story of the hare and the other animals.

The dry weather was drying up the earth into hardness. There was no dew. Even the creatures of the water suffered from thirst. **Famine soon followed,** and the animals, having nothing to eat, assembled in council.

"What shall we do," said they, "to keep ourselves from dying of hunger and thirst?" And they deliberated a long time.

At last **it was decided** that each animal should cut off the tips of its ears, and extract the fat from them. Then all the fat would be collected and sold, and with the money they would get for it, they would buy a hoe and dig a well, so as to get some water. And all cried, "It is well. Let us cut off the tips of our ears."

They did so, but when it came to the turn of the hare to cut off the tips of his ears, **he refused.**

The other animals were astonished, but they said nothing. They took up the ears, extracted the fat, went and sold all, and bought a hoe with the money.

They brought back the hoe and began to dig a well in the dry bed of a lagoon. "Ha! **Here is water at last.** At last we can slake our thirst a little."

The hare was not there, but when the sun was in the middle of the sky, he took a calabash and went towards the well.

As he walked along, the calabash dragged on the ground and made a great noise. It said, *"Chan-gan-**gan-gan**, Chan-gan-gan-gan."*

The animals, who were watching by the lagoon, heard this terrible noise. They were frightened. They asked each other, "What is it?" Then, as the noise kept coming nearer, they ran away. Reaching home, they said something terrible at the lagoon had put to flight the watchers by the lagoon.

Then all the animals by the lagoon were gone. The hare drew up water without interference. Then he went down into the well and bathed, so that the water was muddied.

When the next day came, all the animals ran to get water, and they found it muddied.

"Oh," they cried, "who has spoiled our well?"

Saying this, **they went and took an image.** They made birdlime and spread it over the image.

Then, when the sun was again in the middle of the sky, all the animals went and hid in the bush near the well.

This story comes from: Alfred Burden Ellis, *The Ewe-Speaking Peoples of the Slave Coast of West Africa.* *

"Famine soon followed"—The trickster tale is typically set in a context of scarcity.

"it was decided"—The animals make a contract.

"he refused"—The trickster acts against the contract.

"Here is water at last."—The story highlights the importance of a steady source of clean water for survival.

Gan-gan   A drum.

"Then all the animals were . . . gone"—The hare seems to succeed in his tricks.

"they went and took an image"— The tar-baby motif begins here.

*Alfred Burden Ellis. "Why the Hare Runs Away," in *The Ewe-Speaking Peoples of the Slave Coast of West Africa.* (London: Chapman and Hall, 1890), 275–77.

The hare came. His calabash cried, *"Chan-gan-gan-gan. Changan-gan-gan."* He approached the image. He never suspected that all the animals were hidden in the bush.

The hare saluted the image. The image said nothing. He saluted again, and still the image said nothing.

"Take care," said the hare, "or I will give you a slap."

He gave it a slap, and **his right hand was stuck fast** in the bird-lime. He slapped with his left hand, and that remained fixed also.

"Oh! oh!" cried he, "let us kick with our feet."

He kicked with his feet. The feet remained fixed, and the hare could not get away. Then the animals ran out of the bush and came to see the hare and his calabash.

"Shame, shame, oh, hare!" they cried together. "Did you not agree with us to cut off the tips of your ears, and, when it came to your turn, **did you not refuse?** What! You refused, and yet you come to muddy our water?"

They took whips, they fell upon the hare, and they beat him. They beat him so that they nearly killed him.

"We ought to kill you, accursed hare," they said. "But no—run."

They let him go, and the hare fled. **Since then, he does not leave the grass.**

The Ant's Burden

Kweku **Anansi** and Kweku Tsin, his son, were both very clever farmers. Generally, they had fine harvests from each of their farms. One year, however, they were very unfortunate. They had sown their seeds as usual, but no rain had fallen for more than a month after and it looked as if the seeds would never sprout.

Kweku Tsin was walking sadly through his fields one day, **looking at the bare, dry ground,** and wondering what he and his family would do for food, if nothing ever came up. To his surprise, there was a tiny dwarf seated by the roadside. The little hunchback asked why he was so sad, and Kweku Tsin told him. **The dwarf promised to help** him to bring rain to the farm. He had Tsin fetch two small sticks and tap him lightly on the hump, while singing

> **O water, go up,**
> O water, go up,
> And let rain fall, and let rain fall.

To Tsin's great joy it immediately began to rain, and it kept up until the ground was good and soaked. Then the seeds sprouted and the crops began to look very promising.

Anansi soon heard how well Tsin's crops were growing—while his were still languishing in the earth. He went straightaway to his son and demanded to know the cause. Kweku Tsin, being an honest fellow, at once told him what had happened.

Anansi quickly decided to get his farm watered in the same way, and immediately set out for the place where Tsin had met the little dwarf. As he went, he cut two big, strong sticks, thinking, "My son made him work with little sticks. I will make him do **twice as much** with my big ones." He carefully hid the big sticks, however, when he saw the dwarf coming toward him. Again the hunchback asked what the trouble was, and Anansi told him. "Take two small sticks, and tap me lightly on the hump," said the dwarf. "I will get rain for you."

"Take care"—Ironically, the hare, who does not respect social standards, expects others to honor them.

"his right hand was stuck fast"—The trickster is tricked: he is the dupe.

"did you not refuse?"—The power of the social group forged by the other animals is affirmed.

"Since then, he does not leave the grass"—The story is used to explain a natural phenomenon: the behavior of rabbits as observed in our world.

This story comes from: Roger D. Abrahams, *African Folktales.**

Anansi The spider, a West-African trickster. The name has many other forms, including Nancy, Anancy, Ananzi. He is widely known in the West Indies and coastal Central and South America, as well as in the American South.

"looking at the bare, dry ground"—Once again, the trickster tale is set in a context of scarcity.

"The dwarf promised to help"—The dwarf makes a contract with Kweku Tsin.

"O water, go up"—Songs like this one provide an opportunity for storytellers to display their virtuosity.

"twice as much"—The trickster's greed makes him disregard the details of the contract that the dwarf offers.

Linguist's staff from Ghana, 19th-20th
c. This golden staff associates the spider with verbal talent. The representation of Anansi as a spider seems to
come from the same impulse.

But Anansi took his big sticks and beat so hard that the dwarf fell down dead. The greedy fellow was now thoroughly frightened, for he knew that the dwarf was jester to the king of the country, and a big favorite of his. He wondered how he could **fix the blame on someone else.** He picked up the dwarf's body and carried it to a kola tree, climbed up, and laid it on one of the top branches. Then, he sat down under the tree to watch.

By and by, Kweku Tsin came along to see if his father had succeeded in getting rain for his crops. "Did you not see the dwarf, father?" he asked, as he saw the old man sitting alone. "Oh, yes!" replied Anansi, "but he climbed this tree to pick kola. I am now waiting for him." "I will go up and fetch him," said the young man—and immediately began to climb. As soon as his head touched the body, the dwarf, of course, fell to the ground. "Oh! what have you done, you wicked fellow?" cried his father. "You have killed the king's jester!" "That is all right," quietly replied the son (who saw that this was one of Anansi's tricks). "The king is very angry with him, and has promised a bag of money to anyone who would kill him. **Now I can go and get the reward.**" "No! No! No!" shouted Anansi. "The reward is mine. I killed him with two big sticks. I will take him to the king." "Very well!" was the son's reply. "You killed him, you may take him."

Off set Anansi, quite pleased with the prospect of getting a reward. But when he reached the king's court, it was only to find the king very angry at the death of his favorite. The body of the jester was shut up in a great box and **Anansi was condemned**—as a punishment—to carry it on his head forever. The king enchanted the box so that it could never be set down on the ground. The only way in which Anansi would ever be able to get rid of it was by getting some other man to put it on his head. This, of course, no one was willing to do.

At last, one day, when Anansi was almost worn out with his heavy burden, **he met Ant.** "Will you hold this box for me while I go to market and buy some things I need badly?" said Anansi to Mr. Ant. "I know your tricks, Anansi," replied Ant. "You want to be rid of it." "Oh no, indeed, Mr. Ant," protested Anansi. "Indeed, I will come back for it, I promise."

Mr. Ant, who was an honest fellow, and always kept his own promises, believed him. He took the box on his head, and Anansi hurried off. Needless to say, **the sly fellow** had not the least intention of keeping his word. **Mr. Ant waited in vain for his return, and was obliged to wander all the rest of his life with the box on his head.** That is the reason we so often see ants carrying great bundles as they hurry along.

African-American Trickster Tales

"The Ant's Burden" described the adventures of Anansi, the West-African trickster. The first story of this section makes it clear that the spider as trickster safely made the trip from Africa to America. On both continents, the spider seems to have a special role in the magic of storytelling and entertainment.

Why They Name the Stories for Anansi

"Why They Name the Stories for Anansi," a story from Tobago in the West Indies, represents a broad African-American tradition that all stories were called Anansi stories. The spider weaving webs makes a good symbol for the storyteller weaving stories. There are, also, versions of the story which come from Africa. In these, the trickster performs an impossible task, such as capturing the snake.

*Roger D. Abrahams. "Why They Name the Stories for Anansi," in *Afro-American Folktales: Stories from
Black Traditions in the New World*, 182–83. Copyright © 1985 by Pantheon Books.

Once upon a time, **Anansi** decided that children should call all their stories after him. So he went to **Master King** and told him this, and Master King said, "Well, as you know, Blacksnake is a very wise and clever creature. If you can trick him and bring him back to me full-length on a pole, then I will have all those stories named for you."

Well, **Nansi** really wanted his name to be known this way, but it is very hard even to catch a snake. Nansi knew that Blacksnake really loved to eat pigs, so he went and set a trap for Blacksnake with a pig as bait. Mr. Blacksnake, though, was very clever and saw immediately that it was a trap, so when he got to it he just raised up his tail and slithered right over it, catching the pig in his mouth as he went by. He took it home and had a good dinner for himself.

Well, Nansi then *really* had to think hard about how he was going to catch Blacksnake. So he tried again. He set another trap with a pig, this time in a place that he knew Mr. Snake passed each day of the week to go for water. Again, Mr. Blacksnake saw the trap, so he walked around it, took the pig, and went on his own way. He met Nansi then, and he said to him, "Nansi, you have been setting these traps for me all around. Why are you doing this when you know I am as wise and clever as you and any other creature?"

So Nansi said, "Well, Mr. Blacksnake, I must tell you the truth. They were talking up there in Master King's yard, and everyone was saying that of all the snakes, the longest is Mr. Yellowtail Snake. I tried to tell them you were *much* longer, but they just shouted, and so I bet money that you were the longest. So will you come with me and prove to Master King that you are longer than Mr. Yellowtail Snake? Now, Blacksnake was very proud of his length. So he said, "As a matter of fact. Mr. Nansi, I am much longer than Yellowtail Snake, and I'm glad you told the king because he should know such things."

So Nansi said, "Well, how can we prove it to Master King? **Why don't you lay down as long as you can make yourself,** and I'll take you to Master King that way and we'll just prove it together." So Blacksnake thought for a while and he couldn't see anything wrong with doing it that way, so he just lay down full-length, and stretched and stretched himself until he was stretched as full as he could get. And Nansi quickly tied him to a pole as tightly as he could.

Nansi just **threw that pole across his shoulder and carried him right up to the king:** "Well, Master King, you see I brought Mr. Blacksnake to you tied up on a pole." So the king said, "Well, after today, I'm going to call all those stories 'Nansi Stories,' and I'll order everybody else to do the same, because you were able to trick the wisest and cleverest of the creatures."

So that's how we get it that we call all these stories after Mr. Nansi.

Tricking All the Kings

This story begins with a king who is addressed as "Massa King," and it involves outwitting the master on the plantation. But this is a complicated story with several parts. The opening takes place on the plantation; from there the story shifts to the sea, and then to the jungle. The rambling story is held together by its emphasis on kings: Massa King of the first segment corresponds to the shark, the king of the water, in the second, and to the lion, the king of the jungle, in the final part of the story. The initial situation of the story resembles "Why the Hare Runs Away," p. 344. In that story, the rabbit fouls the animals' water hole and is caught. In "Tricking All the Kings," the trickster is not the rabbit, but "Buh (Brother) Nansi," the spider.

*Elsie Clews Parsons. "Tricking All the Kings," in "Folklore of the Antilles, French and English," in *Memoirs of the American Folklore Society*, Vol. 26, no. III (1943), 97–100. Used by permission of the American Folklore Society.

Master King Also called "the king," suggests the plantation owner, but also seems to have some of the characteristics of an African king or even the god who is in charge of the names of things.

Nansi Another name for Anansi.

Serpent headdress, from Guinea, 19th-20th c. Such masks can be as long as 260 cm and are used in initiation ceremonies. They seem to represent the characteristic which Mr. Snake in this story is most proud of.

"Why don't you lay down as long as you can make yourself"—The trickster makes a contract with his dupe.

"threw that pole across his shoulder and carried him right up to the king"—The trickster breaks the contract.

This story comes from: Elsie Clews Parsons, *Folklore of the Antilles, French and English.**

Illustration from Joel Chandler Harris' *Uncle Remus, His Songs and Sayings.* In *Uncle Remus,* it is Mr. Fox who makes the tar baby to catch Mr. Rabbit. In the Ewe version of the story, the reasons for the creation of the tar baby are more complex.

Buh [Brother] Nansi The spider. His name has many forms, including Nancy, Anancy, Ananzi. He is widely known in the West Indies and coastal Central and South America, as well as in the American South.

"you mean to pitch me in that blue, blue sea"—In this segment of the story, the king becomes the trickster's first dupe. A more familiar version of this tale may be "The Wonderful Tar Baby Story," the Uncle Remus story in which Brer Rabbit begs the Fox not to throw him into the briar patch.

"I'll have you drowned"—In effect, the trickster makes a contract with his dupe.

"It's my home."—The trickster triumphs over the dupe because he is comfortable in the wild parts of nature.

"let's go on and catch some"—Buh Nansi makes a contract with Buh Shark, who is the second dupe.

There was once a king who had a deep well that gave him lots of fresh water. One day, he began to notice that some of his water was gone, and the rest all muddied up, and he couldn't tell who had done this to him. He knew he had to catch the thief because the weather was so dry that no one could get any water except from the king's well.

So **the king made a man** out of tar and set it right by the mouth of the well. He put bread in one of the hands of the tar-man, and in the other, a fish. When the thief comes, the king figured, he will have to have a chat with him, and when he finds the tar-man won't talk, he'll hit him. And so he said, and so it happened. Up came the thief about eleven o 'clock that night, and when he came near the well, he was startled. He said, "Good evening to you, sir." But the tar-man didn't respond. He said, "I'm just taking a walk around tonight and I got thirsty, so I wanted to ask you for some water." The tar-man wouldn't speak. The thief said, "I will have to find out who you are." He went right up to the face of the image and he peered at it for a long time because it was so dark.

"Oh, I see now, you are a watchman Massa King put here to frighten me away. But you are no good here." And he slapped him in the jaw and his hand stuck.

He said, "Oh hell! You look gummy. Let me go, will you?" The tar-man said nothing. He said, "I'll give you another slap if you won't let me go." And he slapped him, and now his two hands were stuck. He said, "What do you mean by this? You won't let me go? I'll throw you into the well if you won't let me go." He said, "Massa King sent you here to hold me, and you are holding me, but I 'm going to toss you into the well and then both of us will be down there, I'll tell you." And he tried to toss him, in his struggle to get away, and he just stuck more and more until he was fastened on from head to toe. And who was the thief? **Buh Nansi.**

Now, the next morning, the king came and said, "Ah, I've caught the thief and his meat and bones will make my bread today!" And he took him by the shoulder and he pulled him off the tar-man, and he dragged him by the hair to the palace. He called his servant and said, "I caught the thief who has been stealing my water for many weeks, but he won't steal from me anymore." Then he sad, "Take him and hold him, and we'll chain him until we can think of the way we can kill him best." The servant asked what his sentence would be, so Massa King said, "Maybe we'll have to burn him." Buh Nansi never said a word. The servant said, "I think the best death for him is to shoot him." Still Buh Nansi kept quiet.

Then the king said, "The best way to take his life is to drown him." Then Buh Nansi said, "Oh, Massa King, **you mean to pitch me in that blue, blue sea?** Massa King, better to shoot me than pitch me in that blue sea water." But the king said, "No, I wouldn't. **I'll have you drowned.**" And he took a bit of rope and put it around Buh Nansi's neck and tied a piece of iron to it and took him to the beach. Massa King and his servant took him out in a boat about three miles out to sea, and flung him overboard.

And he went right to the bottom, sat down, loosened the iron from around his neck, and floated to the top, just like he knew he would. He was bobbing along even before the boat moved half a mile, and called out, "Ah, Massa King, you couldn't have done me a better favor than to fling me into this sea water. **It's my home.**"

He dove down again, feeling kind of happy, and he met up with a shark. "Oh, Buh Shark, you're the very man I've been looking for, for three nights and three days now."

Buh Shark asked why. And he said, "I want to get together to catch some small fish and go ashore and cook them up for a big feast this afternoon." Buh Shark said, "You would invite me to a big feast?" "Yes, I would. Come on, **let's go on and catch some** and I'll show you."

Well, they caught plenty, and they went ashore, and Buh Shark said to Buh Nansi, "You must go ashore alone, and leave me in the water, because I can't live out of the water for more than two minutes. You cook them up and just bring me my share." Buh

Nansi said, "Well, I'll have them all cooked up then, and I'll bring you your share. You stay in the water and sing some sweet songs thinking about this feast, while I get some kindling and get this fire going."

After the fire was going, he put a big copper pot on it, one that holds two hundred gallons of water. And he filled it with the small fish, and when they were all boiled up and the water was steaming hot, he said, "Buh Shark, come here in the sun for a while, and show me how you can stand on the tip of your tail, and tell some jokes. " Buh Shark said, "I'll come, but only for half a minute, you know, because otherwise I'll die." And as Buh Shark came up and stood on the tip of his tail, **Buh Nansi took out a bucket of the steaming water and he killed him.**

Buh Shark had nothing more to say ever again. Buh Nansi cut him in three pieces and put them in the copper pot with the little fishes and boiled it properly with peppers. And after it was cooked, he took it off the fire. He knew he couldn't eat it all alone, but being so selfish, he was going to throw away what was left over.

But just as he was beginning, **up came Buh Lion.** Buh Nansi said, "Ah, you are the man I wanted to see. I want you to help me eat some of my fish here. I have caught plenty and can't eat them all." He was afraid of Lion, but just smiled and said, "You just came in time."

And they both sat down to eat. When Buh Nansi ate about six pieces of fish, Lion had eaten just about all the rest. Buh Nansi, who didn't *really* want to share, grumbled to himself. "I have been here all the time, lighting the fire and straining to put that big copper pot on the fire and here you come just in time to eat." Lion said, "What are you saying? If you grumble any more, I'm going to kill you and eat you too. You just look at what I'm doing and keep quiet." Buh Nansi got really scared now, and didn't say anything until they had finished eating.

Then Buh Nansi said to Lion, **"Let's play the little game** we used to play when we were at school." And Lion said he didn't remember any games. Buh Nansi said, "Sure you do. We take a little piece of string, and you put your two hands behind your back, and we tie you to a tree, and take a little switch and touch your back with it, and when you make a rush you break the string and get away, and the other person has to do the same thing." Lion said to Buh Nansi, "If you let me tie you first, I'll play." Buh Nansi said that was all right, and they got a string and a switch, and Buh Lion tied him. And then when Buh Lion hit him with the switch he made a plunge and got away. Buh Nansi said, "Now let me tie you," and he pulled a cord-rope out of his pocket and tied Buh Lion's hands behind his back. And **he took out a whip from his pocket and really started to lick him hard.** Lion made a plunge at Buh Nansi with his paw to kill him, but he couldn't touch him, Buh Nansi was that quick.

And he shouted out, "My wife, my wife, you and all the children come out and get your licks on Buh Lion. A little while ago he ate all my fish, which I was going to bring home." So all his children started to beat Buh Lion too, until he was half dead. And they just left him there tied to the tree, Buh Lion lying on the ground half beat to death, and they went on home.

Buh Lion saw a woman coming his way on her way home. So he said, "My good lady, please let me loose or else I shall surely die." The lady said, "Who put you there, my good lion?" "Buh Nansi, ma'am." "Why did he tie you?" "He tied me here because we had a little game we played in school and he got me to remember it and play it with him. I tied him first, and he broke the string like we always used to, and he got away. Then he tied me, but not with the same string, but a much stronger cord-rope, and then he licked me, and his wife and children came and licked me and had me completely beaten." "But if I let you loose, my good lion, you will spring on me and eat me." He cried, "Oh now, my good lady, if I tried to do that all the trees and stones around here would cry 'shame.'" She said, "All right, then, I will." And she let him

M. Drott. *Lion Mask.*

"Buh Nansi . . . killed him"— The trickster betrays the dupe.

"up came Buh Lion"—The lion is Buh Nansi's third dupe.

"Let's play the little game"—Buh Nansi makes a contract with his third dupe.

"he . . . started to lick him hard" —Buh Nansi breaks his contract with Buh Lion.

"Shame, Lion, shame"—In his own way, Buh Lion is as dishonest as Buh Nansi; but unlike the trickster, he is subject to shame.

loose, and he immediately tried to spring on her and eat her. And all the trees and all the stones sang out: **"Shame, Lion, shame."** So he stopped.

So he went home and told his wife what Buh Nansi had done to him. And she said, "I always told you to stay away from Buh Nansi's reach. You are much stronger than he is, but you haven't got the tricks that he has. But we'll think of a way to get back at him."

So she thought and thought, and finally she said to Lion, "We'll have a dance tonight. You know how much Buh Nansi likes to dance. We'll figure out a way to fix him because he will come to the dance—he couldn't stand to stay away. I know, we'll get a revolver and shoot him."

"she should just throw him out of the window"—This section of the story is notable for the comic scene of the mother dancing with a child who eventually jumps out the window.

Well, Buh Nansi heard about how everybody else had been invited to the dance, and he wanted to go. So he told his wife to wrap him up in a white sheet and he would go as a little baby, and she could carry him into the dance. And if anyone notices that it is him, **she should just throw him out of the window** in the sheet. So said, so done. And the music struck up and they got right into the dancing. And Lion noticed a mother with this baby. And he said, "I don't think a baby has bones that big. It must be Buh Nansi pulling a trick."

So he found out by pulling on the sheet, and Buh Nansi told his wife to throw him out of the window. But his wife was so taken up in the dancing that she didn't hear him.

"he grabbed some peppers"—The hot pepper and limes mentioned in this section are typical of much West Indian cooking.

So Nansi gave a little jig and started to run, Lion behind him. He ran until he saw a crab hole just beside a pepper tree. So **he grabbed some peppers** and jumped down in the hole. He put the peppers in his mouth and crushed them up. Lion came to the hole and started to dig. He dug until he could just about see Buh Nansi, and then Buh Nansi spat out the mouthful of peppers into Buh Lion's eyes and made him blind. He rubbed both eyes out of his head with his paws, it hurt so much. And he died from the pain, and out came Buh Nansi and chopped him up and flung him on his shoulder and carried him home, piece by piece, to his wife. He said, "My wife, we can walk out proudly forever, day or night, because I have killed this great king of the woods, and we have Lion to eat tonight for dinner." So he got the pot on the fire and got some limes and made a lion soup.

"I went to this feast"—The story-teller appears as a witness to the tale, but reveals immediately that none of it is true.

"You must . . . never do evil"—The moral of the story is explicitly stated.

I went to this feast and enjoyed some of it, and I came directly here to tell you this big lie. That's why you see that today you must never do evil. **You must always do good to your friends, and never do evil.** You must always do good to your friends even if they do you bad.

This story comes from: Roger D. Abrahams, *The Man-of-Words in the West Indies.* *

A Boarhog for a Husband

We have seen that not all tricksters are animals like Brer Rabbit or Anancy. John the Slave represents another type of trickster, marginalized by his enslaved status, struggling with the Master for survival, as in the story of the talking skull. This story presents still another, almost invisible kind of trickster. He also operates on the edges of society. He plays a part in it, but his role is on the edge. From this vantage point, he can unmask the more successful members of society. Like all tricksters, he is a creature with strange powers who brings disorder to society. Roger Abrahams points out that he allows us, his audience, to delight in seeing society dismantled and built up again. He contrasts this story with European "Animal Bridegroom" stories like "The Frog Prince." The frog is revealed to be a human, and the result is a happy ending, just the opposite of what happens in this story.

*Roger D. Abrahams. "A Boarhog for a Husband," in *The Man-of-Words in the West Indies.* (Baltimore, MD: Johns Hopkins University Press, 1983), 171–72. Used by permission of author.

This version of the story comes from St. Vincent in the West Indies, but the story is known throughout the Antilles, and it resembles a number of African stories. Different versions vary what the husband turns into, including a reptile, a beast, and a cannibal.

Scalambay, scalambay
Scoops, scops, scalambay
See my lover coming there
Scoops, scops, scalambay.

Once upon a time—it was a very good time—Massa King had an only daughter. And all the young fellows were constantly talking with each other about who was going to be able to marry her. They all came by to call on her, but none of them suited her. Each time one would come, her father would say "Now this is the one!" But she kept saying, "No, Daddy, this fellow here, I just don't like him," or "No, Mommy, this one really doesn't please me." But the last one to come along was a handsome young fellow, and she fell in love with him right away. And of course, when she fell in love, it was deep and wide—she just lost her head altogether. What she didn't know was that she'd actually chosen a boarhog who had changed himself into a human to go courting.

Now the Massa King had another child, a **little Old Witch Boy** who lived there and did all the nasty stuff around the palace. He was always dirty and smelly, you know, and no one liked to be around him, especially the King's beautiful daughter. One day after work the young fellow came in to visit his bride, and the Old Witch Boy whispered, "Daddy, Daddy, did you know that the fellow my sister is going to marry is a boarhog?" "What? You better shut your mouth and **get back under the bed** where you belong." (That's where they made the Old Witch Boy stay, you see, because he was so dirty.)

Now when they got married, they moved way up on the mountain, up where they plant all those good things to put in the pot, roots like dasheen, tania, and **all those provisions that hogs like to eat,** too. One day, Massa King came up there and showed him a big piece of land he wanted his daughter and her husband to have for farming. The husband really liked that because he could raise lots of tanias—which is what boarhogs like to eat most.

So one day he went up to work, early early in the morning. Now there was this little house up by the land where he could go and change his clothes before he went to work. He went into one side of the little house, and he started singing:

Scalambay, scalambay
Scoops, scops, scalambay
See my lover coming there
Scoops, scops, scalambay.

And with each refrain he would take off one piece of clothing. And with every piece he took off he became more of a boarhog—first the head, then the feet, then the rest of the body.

Scalambay, scalambay
Scoops, scops, scalambay
See my lover coming there
Scoops, scops, scalambay.

Well, about noon, when he thought the time was coming for lunch to arrive in the field, he went back into the house and put back on his clothes, took off the boarhog suit and put back on the ordinary suit he came in. And as he got dressed he sang the same little song to change himself back into a handsome man.

"Scalambay, scalambay"—The song opening a story piques public interest and provides a focus for the performer and audience to interact. See Abrahams' narrative of oral performance on p. 341.

"little Old Witch Boy"—the trickster, who is actually the king's true son.

"get back under the bed"—Staying under the bed implies a kind of contract that the trickster makes. He stays out of the way, and allows himself to be forgotten, while having access to the secrets of those in the society around him.

"all those provisions that hogs like to eat"—The animal bridegroom indicates his true nature by his dietary preferences.

"Scalambay, scalambay"—Now we understand the role of the song: it is the "charm" that the husband uses for transformation. As the story goes on, the song will again change meaning.

Scalambay, scalambay
Scoops, scops, scalambay
See my lover coming there
Scoops, scops, scalambay.

After a while, the **Old Witch Boy as usual came with the food,** but this day he came early and saw what was going on, **heard the singing,** and saw the man changing. So he rushed home and told his father again, "Daddy, this fellow who married my sister up there is really a boarhog. It's true!" Massa King said, "Boy, shut your mouth," and his sister said, "Get back underneath the bed, you scamp you."

The next day, the Old Witch Boy got up very early and went up the mountain and heard the song again:

Scalambay, scalambay
Scoops, scops, scalambay
See my lover coming there
Scoops, scops, scalambay.

All right, he thought, and he went down again and he told his father what he had seen and heard. **He even sang the song.** Now Massa King didn't know what to think. But he knew he was missing a lot of tanias from his other fields, so he loaded up his gun and went to see what was going on up there in his fields. Mr. Boarhog was up there changing and didn't know he was being watched, but he thought he heard something so he kind of stopped. The Old Witch Boy started to sing, and Mr. Boarhog couldn't do anything but join in with him. And so there they both were, singing:

Scalambay, scalambay
Scoops, scops, scalambay
See my lover coming there
Scoops, scops, scalambay.

And the man **slowly changed into a boarhog.** When the King saw this he couldn't believe his eyes. He took his gun and he let go, pow! And he killed Mr. Boarhog, and carried him down the mountain. **The King's beautiful daughter couldn't believe what she saw and began to scream and cry,** but Massa King told her what he had seen and what he had done, and then she had to believe it.

They cleaned Mr. Boarhog's body and had him quartered. And **I was right there** on the spot, and took one of the testicles and it gave me food for nearly a week!

"Old Witch Boy . . . came with the food"—His position as servant echoes his role under the bed: he is at the margin of society. Since he is ignored, he can observe what he will.

"heard the singing"—The song changes function again. Now it becomes the sign by which the husband is recognized.

"He even sang the song."—Now the song unmasks the husband's deception and reveals that his role in society is even more tenuous than that of the little Old Witch Boy.

"slowly changed into a boarhog. . . . The king's beautiful daughter . . . began to scream and cry"—The dupes, the daughter and her husband, are destroyed by the implied contract they made with the little Old Witch Boy.

"I was right there"—Oral narrative often includes claims by storytellers to have witnessed the events they describe.

Further Reading

Abrahams, Roger D. "Eating in the Belly of the Elephant." *Folklife Annual* (1987): 10–23.

Roberts, John W. *From Trickster to Badman: The Black Folk Hero in Slavery and Freedom.* Philadelphia, PA: University of Pennsylvania Press, 1989.

Prometheus

The Greek Trickster

WHAT TO EXPECT . . . To the ancient Greeks, Prometheus was considered a transformer of culture because he stole fire from the gods and gave it to humans. Such activity, along with his tricking Zeus into giving up power, marks him as a supreme benefactor, but one who lives on the edge of society, functioning at its outer limits. Consider the relevance to his behavior of Victor Turner's concept of "liminality" (Ch. 26, p. 375). Levi-Strauss (Ch. 20, p. 280) argues that Greek myths represent a tension between overvaluing kin and undervaluing them: is there any sign of this strain in the story of Prometheus?

In his *Theogony,* Hesiod recounts how Prometheus tricks the head of the gods, and in *Prometheus Bound,* Aeschylus dramatizes his sufferings for his rebellion against Zeus, including Prometheus' description of his assistance to humans. Both of these works provide insights into the audiences' estimation of the gods and their view of the world. Consider the other stories Hesiod tells (Ch. 3, p. 25) and how they fit with the story of Prometheus. Do you get the same sense of Hesiod as a poet in these stories, or is your perspective on him changed? You may also want to relate Prometheus to other Greek figures you have read about in this book, and consider whether they have similar relationships to Zeus; Demeter (Ch. 27, p. 385) and Hercules (Ch. 31, p. 446) may be especially interesting in this regard. In Aeschylus, Prometheus becomes a tragic hero: to what extent does he resemble Sophocles' famous tragic hero, Oedipus (Ch. 19, p. 231)?

As you read, compare trickster elements in Hesiod and Aeschylus to those in other trickster stories, including African, African-American (Ch. 23, p. 339), Native American (Ch. 21, p. 295), and Norse (Ch. 18, p. 218) versions.

The Greek figure Prometheus is perhaps the best-known example of a trickster as a builder of culture. According to the story told by Hesiod in the *Works and Days* (see Part 2A, Myths of Creation and Destruction), he stole fire from the gods and gave it to human beings. Now fire, of course, is not just a good way to warm up hot dogs at a cookout. Rather, it is necessary to work metal and thus underlies all technology. It is also an essential element in the production of energy and represents the basis of ancient as well as modern industry. Thus, the story told by Hesiod implies that Prometheus is a great culture hero. In recognition of his contribution, there was a torch race at Athens in honor of Prometheus, as part of a ceremony celebrating the kindling of the year's new fire.

Ancient Greece was not the only culture which saw the trickster as a transformer of culture, or a culture hero. Even though tricksters from other mythological systems are in many ways quite different, they often share this characteristic. In Native American stories, the trickster is a figure who is often obsessed with his appetites for food and sex. However, as time passes, other stories of the trickster arise, representing him as a savior, a creator, and a benefactor of the people (see Ch. 21, p. 295).

In African tales, the trickster forges a contract with a dupe and then betrays him. Why does this make him a culture hero? In times of extreme physical hardship, this figure uses his wits to obtain the supplies he needs. However, his behavior is not viewed as a model to be followed by others. He does not represent the proper way to behave in this culture; rather, he is the exception that proves the rule. His negative example affirms the community's values and identity: his behavior is wrong, but necessary.

John W. Roberts explains that for African-Americans, the meaning of the trickster changed. In Africa, food shortages were due to natural disasters or war. In America, shortage of food and material goods was artificially imposed by white masters in the midst of the abundance produced by the slaves themselves. Thus, African-American trickster stories represent a grim world in which masters and slaves are pitted against each other, and the slave survives only by a combination of cunning and luck. The role of the trickster is based not on building culture, but on resisting and surviving a culture that is out to use him up. The trickster is a culture hero only in the sense of preventing the complete elimination of his culture by forces out to destroy it.

In all of these instantiations, the trickster is a "liminal" creature. That is, he is on the threshold (Latin *limen, liminis*) between two worlds. He is a part of society, but functions at its outer limits. He lives between nature and culture, and because of his dual identity, is able to unmask or disorder the world of those with a more solid stake in the established norms of society. He is a revolutionary who is likely to destroy the world as we know it, and forge a new reality from its ruins. (For more on liminal figures, see the work of Victor Turner, Ch. 26, p. 373.)

Prometheus too is a liminal figure. He is a god, but he takes the side of humans. His role is not to bolster the power of Zeus, but to question it. He is not just a builder of civilization who gave humans fire, he is the revolutionary who rebels against the despot and stirs up the existing order. Another story told by Hesiod about this great hero makes this clear. It is Prometheus who makes Zeus angry by tricking him into accepting the less desirable of two offerings. On the one hand, this makes Prometheus behave as tricksters always do: he is the clever figure who outwits a dupe and takes his food away. On the other hand, this represents Prometheus as a rebel against a certain divine order, the cosmic system in which human beings are not cherished, valued, and protected.

HESIOD ON PROMETHEUS

Hesiod, a Greek poet, lived in about 700 B.C.E. and composed two poems, the *Theogony* and the *Works and Days*. The Creation section of this book contains his story of Prometheus' theft of fire, as well as an extensive introduction to his style of writing and the social significance of his work (see Ch. 3, p. 26f). The excerpt in this chapter comes from Hesiod's *Theogony,* a poem describing the nature and generations of the gods, and it is in this context that the poet tells the story of Prometheus.

In this poem, Hesiod wants to show how Zeus became the supreme head of the gods. In recounting the struggle of Prometheus against Zeus, he is not very favorable to the rebel. Rather, he portrays Prometheus as playing an essentially pointless trick against the head god merely to win the better share of food for humans. As a paratactic poet, Hesiod does not tell the story in chronological order, but the sequence of events in his story is as follows:

Atlas and the Punishment of Prometheus,
Arkesilas Painter (6th C. B.C.E.).

Event	Source
1. Prometheus cheats Zeus of the better sacrifice.	Described in detail by Hesiod in the *Theogony* (see excerpt).
2. Zeus withholds fire from humans.	Mentioned in both *Theogony* and the *Works and Days*.
3. Prometheus steals fire for humans.	Mentioned in both *Theogony* and the *Works and Days*.
4. Zeus punishes him by inflicting Pandora, the first woman, on humans.	Described in detail by Hesiod in the *Works and Days* (found in Part 2A, on creation stories).
5. Zeus binds Prometheus to a rock in chains.	Mentioned in both *Theogony* and the *Works and Days*.
6. Zeus allows his son Heracles to free Prometheus to increase his son's fame.	Mentioned in the first part of the story that Hesiod describes, in the *Theogony*.

Prometheus at Mekone

This story comes from: Hesiod, *Theogony.**

Zeus Head of the gods in Greek mythology. For a genealogical chart of the early Greek gods, see Ch. 3, p. 31.

Clever Prometheus was bound by **Zeus**
In cruel chains, unbreakable, chained round
A pillar, and Zeus roused and set on him
An eagle with long wings, which came and ate
His deathless liver. But the liver grew   5
Each night, until it made up the amount
The long-winged bird had eaten in the day.
Lovely Alcmene's son, **strong Heracles,**
Killing the eagle, freed Prometheus
From his affliction and his misery,   10
And Zeus, Olympian, who rules on high,
Approved, so that the fame of Heracles
The Theban might be greater than before
Upon the fruitful earth; he showed respect,
And gave the honour to his famous son.   15
And angry though he was, he checked the rage
He felt against Prometheus, who dared
To match his wits against almighty Zeus.
For at Mekone, once, there was a test
When gods and mortal men divided up   20
An ox; Prometheus audaciously
Set out the portions, **trying to deceive**
The mind of Zeus. Before the rest, he put
Pieces of meat and marbled inner parts
And fat upon the hide, and hid them in   25
The stomach of the ox; but before Zeus
The white bones of the ox, arranged with skill,
Hidden in shining fat. And then he spoke,
The father of gods and men, and said to him,
"Milord, most famous son of Iapetos,   30

"strong Heracles, killing the eagle, freed Prometheus"—Hesiod tells us the outcome of the story at the beginning. He is not interested in building suspense, but in describing the plan of Zeus.

"trying to deceive the mind of Zeus"—Prometheus hides the meat in the stomach, making it look small and undesirable, and arranges the bones to stretch out the fat, making it look bigger and more appealing.

The shares you've made, my friend, are most unfair!"
Thus Zeus, whose plans are everlasting, spoke
And criticized. But sly Prometheus
Did not forget his trick, and softly smiled
And said, "Most glorious Zeus, greatest of all   35
The gods who live forever, choose your share,
Whichever one your heart leads you to pick"
He spoke deceitfully, but **Zeus who knows**
Undying plans, was not deceived, but saw
The trick, and in his heart made plans   40
To punish mortal men in future days.
He took the fatted portion in his hands
And raged within, and anger seized his heart
To see the trick, the white bones of the ox.
(**And from this time** the tribes of men on earth   45
Burn, on the smoking altars, white ox-bones.)
But Zeus, the gatherer of clouds, enraged,
Said, "Son of Iapetos, cleverest god
Of all: so, friend, you do not yet forget
Your crafty tricks!" So spoke the angry Zeus   50
Whose craft is everlasting. From that time
He bore the trick in mind and would not give,
To wretched men who live on earth, the power
Of fire, which never wearies. The brave son
Of Iapetos deceived him, and **he stole**   55
The ray, far-seeing, of unwearied fire,
Hid in the hollow fennel stalk, and Zeus
Who thunders in the heavens ate his heart,
And raged within to see the ray of fire
Far-seeing, among men. Immediately   60
He found a price for men to pay for fire.

[The story of Pandora is included with the creation stories in Chapter 3, p. 25.]

It is impossible to hoodwink Zeus
Or to surpass him, for Prometheus
The son of Iapetos, kind though he was
And wise, could not escape his heavy rage   65
But he was bound by force, with heavy chains.

Sidenotes:

"Zeus who knows undying plans, was not deceived"—Hesiod seems to have added this comment to rationalize his praise of Zeus. And yet the logic of the story suggests that the head god was deceived. On the rationalization of myth, see Ch. 2, p. 20.

"And from this time"—Hesiod's story provides an aetiology, or explanation, of why humans sacrifice bones to the gods. For more on this aspect of myth, see Ch. 1, p. 7.

"he stole the ray . . . of unwearied fire"—Prometheus steals fire from the gods for humans. Raven, the Native American trickster, also brings the light to human beings by stealing the sun. (See Ch. 21, p. 303.)

Aeschylus on Prometheus

Aeschylus was a Greek playwright who wrote the *Prometheus Bound* in about 456 b.c.e. The play is a tragedy that details the sufferings of Prometheus for his rebellion against Zeus and foreshadows his eventual release at the hands of Heracles, Zeus' son. Aeschylus' purpose in describing Prometheus is different from that of Hesiod. He is showing the nobility of Prometheus, his main character, at the expense of Zeus. Thus, he paints a picture of Zeus as a young god, a tyrant who had no special right to hold sovereignty over the other gods. In this play, Prometheus is portrayed as a rebel who fought against the heartless god to win.

For an introduction to Greek drama, see Ch. 19, p. 232. The following excerpt is an exchange between the chorus of the play and its main character, Prometheus. Choruses were groups who sang and danced in the play and helped to advance the story line. Typically, as here, they strongly supported the main character. The excerpt occurs near the opening of the play. Prometheus has been brought out and fastened to a rock. The chorus, who are daughters of Ocean, see him there and, filled with pity, ask the cause of his punishment. In response he describes the history of his assistance to human beings.

It is clear that by the time of Aeschylus, Prometheus was seen not just as a trickster stealing food because he was ruled by his appetites. Rather, he was considered a full-fledged savior of humankind, the source of every advance, from agriculture to literature. In celebrating his gifts, human beings were expressing pride in the technology they had developed and the civilization they had built by using it.

It is in Aeschylus that we see the full importance of the gift of fire. Prometheus describes early human beings as quite primitive, and elaborates in detail how they came to their present state. In fact, all of the accomplishments he lists are due to the introduction of fire. Fire allowed the fashioning of metal tools for building, navigation, and science. Language and reason itself are seen as deriving from toolmaking. Thus early human beings are described as "groping through their lives in a dreamlike stupor" because without language, they did not have names for things and thus had no intellectual tools for manipulating their world.

CHORUS:
I weep for you, weep for your bitter fate, Prometheus,
And the tears gleam on my cheek soft as the dewfall
In a shower of warm compassion.
The oppressor's hand is heavy
On the gods of old. **The Lord Zeus**   5
Is a self-willed, lawless despot.

And all the earth raises her voice in lamentation
For the glory and the greatness of the old world
And the immemorial splendors
That are gone. The whole of Asia   10
Is astir with sounds of weeping
From the stricken race of mankind.
A fate more cruel eyes have never seen.
I know of but one to compare,
The Titan, **Atlas,** who in the western isles   15
Is groaning day and night beneath
The whole sky's weight on giant shoulders.
The waves are sighing as they break,
Answered from the ocean bed,
And Hades stirs and mutters underground.   20
Streams are clamoring down from the hills
In flood with lamentation.

PROMETHEUS:
It is not pride or obstinacy that has prompted
My silence, but the bitter consciousness

This story comes from: Aeschylus, *Prometheus Bound.**

"The Lord Zeus is a self-willed, lawless despot"—After resisting the invasion of the kingdom of Persia in 490 and 480 B.C.E., the Greeks had strong negative feelings against tyrants of all sorts. Although this part of the play may seem irreverent in criticizing Zeus, the play as a whole demonstrated his power.

Atlas Prometheus' brother, who fought against Zeus and the Olympian gods. He was punished by having to hold the earth and heavens on his back.

*Aeschylus, *The Oresteia Trilogy, Prometheus Bound.* Ed. Robert W. Corrigan. Trans. George Thomson, 140–43. (New York: Dell Publishing Company, 1965).

Of what I have done to merit such maltreatment.   25
Who was it after all that first appointed
Their several powers for these new divinities?
You have heard that story and I will say no more,
But now listen to the sufferings of mankind,
In whom, once speechless, senseless, like an infant,   30
I have implanted the faculty of reason.
I speak of man not to reproach him, only
To proclaim the record of my services.
At first, with eyes to see, they saw in vain,
With ears to hear, heard nothing, groping through   35
Their lives in a dreamlike stupor, with no skill
In carpentry or brickmaking, like ants
Burrowing in holes, unpractised in the signs
Of blossom, fruit, and frost, from hand to mouth
Struggling improvidently, until I   40
Charted the intricate orbits of the stars;
Invented number, that most exquisite
Instrument; formed the alphabet, the tool
Of history and chronicle of their progress;
Tamed the wild beasts to toil in pack and harness,   45
And yoked the prancing mounts of opulence,
Obedient to the rein, in chariots;
Constructed **wheelless vehicles with linen**
Wings to carry them over the trackless waters;
Yet, having bestowed all these discoveries   50
On man, I have none for myself to win
Deliverance from what I suffer for them.

CHORUS:
It is a bitter irony that *you*
Should find yourself so helpless—a physician
Who taken sick despairs of his own skill.   55

PROMETHEUS:
There is more matter yet for you to admire
In the resource of my imagination,
And this above all—when sickness struck them down,
Having no herbal therapy to dispense
In salves and potions, their strength neglected ran   60
To waste in moping ignorance, till I
Compounded for them gentle medicines
To arm them in the war against disease.
And I set in order the forms of **prophecy,**
Interpreting the significance of dreams,   65
Voices, wayside meetings; trained them to observe
The flight of eagles, distinguishing the good
And evil auguries, describing for them
Their habits, matings, feuds, affinities;

Sidenotes:

"Who . . . first appointed their several powers for these . . . divinities?"—It was Prometheus' idea to assign different spheres to different gods. Zeus took charge of the heavens, his brother Poseidon of the sea, and Hades of the underworld.

"I speak of man not to reproach him"—Prometheus is not trying to make human beings sound weaker than they really were.

"At first, with eyes to see, they saw in vain"—Early humans did not have language, and so saw things but did not know their names.

"Burrowing in holes"—Prometheus' suggestion that early human beings lived in caves is well supported today.

"wheelless vehicles with linen wings"—Ships.

"Having no herbal therapy"—The distillation of medicinal potions called for fire.

prophecy Greek religion relied extensively on priests to foretell the will of the gods. This was done by examining the flight of birds, and by cutting open animals to examine their innards. Once again, the knives used would be tools made in the fire, and the sacrificed animals would be burned in homage to the gods.

This 20th-c. c.e. mural by David Alfaro Siqueiros shows the suffering Prometheus with the punishing eagle at the right. By virtue of the contributions to society Aeschylus ascribes to Prometheus, Siqueiros associates the god with industry and workers, represented at the lower right.

Taught them to inspect the entrails, of what hue 70
And texture they must be for heaven's favor,
So leading them in to the difficult art
Of divination by burnt sacrifice.
And last, who else can boast to have unlocked
The **earth's rich subterranean treasure-houses** 75
Of iron, copper, bronze, silver, and gold?
That is my record. You have it in a word:
Prometheus founded all the arts of man.

"earth's rich subterranean treasure-houses"—It was a common belief that humans' first access to precious metals occurred as rocks around their campfires oozed ore.

Further Reading

Conacher, D. J. *Aeschylus' "Prometheus Bound": A Literary Commentary.* Toronto: University of Toronto Press, 1980.

25

Looking Back at Heroes
The Different Versions of a Myth

WHAT TO EXPECT . . . The different versions of a myth represent adaptation to the needs of a group or individual. In this chapter, you once again encounter Sophocles' *Oedipus the King*, the main reading of Chapter 19, p. 231. Now you are encouraged to think of Sophocles' version of the story as one among many. His is a literary version of the myth that he made relevant to the Athens audience of his day (see Ch. 19 for a full discussion). In our own day, the story of Oedipus has continued to change its meaning and significance, since the tellers or writers change aspects of the story to express their ideas. This chapter introduces you to versions of the story from first-century C.E. Rome through twentieth-century Europe.

Rationalized versions of a myth are different from individual literary ones; they are syntheses of all known versions, designed to highlight a particular characteristic or theme. Examples related to the Oedipus myth come from Sigmund Freud, Otto Rank, and Claude Levi-Strauss.

Working versions, those myths that are still being told and modified by the society that originated them, also reflect the storytellers'—and audiences'—beliefs, although details may vary rather widely.

As you read, you may want to classify the myths and stories you know, or those you have read in this book, according to the categories found in this chapter, and explain the reasons for your decisions.

Thus far, we have described some of the characteristics of myth. In the first chapter, we said that myths are not just false stories, and suggested that they have a variety of kinds of importance to the society and the individuals who originated them. And we noted that mythological accounts have been studied from a variety of different points of view, including those of literature, philosophy, and social science.

In addition, myths are more likely to be about some topics than others. In Chapters 1 and 2, we suggested that many myths are about the origins of the world and about heroes. Other chapters of this book explore myths about destruction, as well as fairy tales and literary myths.

From looking at the examples of myth presented thus far, we can see that there are many versions of myth. Some myths, like the Genesis creation story, have a variety of different authors who can be identified by their writing styles and interests, but who are personally not known to us. Other myths, like *Oedipus the King,* were written by one person we can identify. Some myths, like the Mwindo epic, have been written down only recently and are still being told by the descendants of the society whose members originated them.

Different versions of a myth represent adaptation to the needs of a group or individual. As stories grow and develop, they pass through the activities of different storytellers. They come to have different meanings for individuals and groups in the society.

The stories may:

- be reworked by individuals who use them to express their personal perspectives and experiences—literary version of a myth
- be studied by scholars under whose influence they are used to draw inferences about people and societies—rationalized version of a myth
- become associated with a particular ritual or ceremony in the society—working version of a myth.

All of these different perspectives on a story shed light on the human process of mythmaking. The following discussion will consider each.

Literary Versions of Myth

In general, it can be said that critics and scholars hold a wide range of views about what is of primary importance in studying a literary work. The life story of the author, the historical times, the imagery and themes the author discussed, and the experience which the reader brings to the text are among the aspects of a work that receive study and emphasis.

Usually a literary work is written by one person whose techniques of artistic creation can be discovered and agreed upon, even if the value and meaning attached to them are more controversial. For example, Sophocles wrote *Oedipus the King* in Athens, probably in 425 B.C.E. At the time he wrote, however, **there were other versions** of the story by other people. Sophocles used some existing elements of the myth, and he himself changed and revised the myth to accomplish the ends that he wanted to achieve in his artistic creation. Thus, the myth was different when Sophocles was done with the play, which represented his unique artistic work. To some extent, though, it means that Sophocles' version is only one of the stages in the life of the myth. Every storyteller changes a story by telling it, some more, some less.

As noted in the introduction to the play (Ch. 19, p. 231), Sophocles probably wrote his drama when a plague was raging in Athens. Thus, he added to the "received version" of the myth a story of a plague: until that point the story of Oedipus had not included a plague (Ahl, 35). By including it, Sophocles made the old story relevant to the lives of his fellow citizens. The audience would have been interested in the horrible disease that is at the core of this play, since they were experiencing an outbreak of it themselves. Although he uses mythical material, we can see that Sophocles is talking about a unique Oedipus; Oedipus is not like other people in the play. And Sophocles makes a point of saying he's a king and a hero who stands up against the gods. He seems more unusual than ordinary, as befits a hero.

Bernard Knox, a noted literary critic, explains that, in some sense, the play is about intellectual blindness; it expresses irony through the actions and speeches of the characters. Irony is a literary technique that refers to conveying the opposite of what is actually being said; that is, the characters may say something, but the members of the audience know that the opposite is true, either because they have information that the characters do not, or because they know the real personality of the characters. Since the audience knew a great deal that Oedipus, the main character, did not know, they noticed the irony of his situation. Oedipus is a great hero and can perform all kinds of great deeds

Example of a Literary Version of a Myth:

Oedipus the King by Sophocles

For the text of Sophocles' play, see Ch. 19.

"there were other versions"—The child's game Telephone illustrates the changeability of oral tradition. Participants sit in a circle; one whispers a message to the next, who whispers it to the next, until the last one reports what he has heard. Invariably, through mishearings and misinterpretations, the message becomes altered substantially and often humorously.

The Triumph of Death, by the 16th-c. C.E. painter Pieter Brueghel the Elder, shows the devastation caused by the plague.

Knox's Analysis of Sophocles' Play

This view comes from: Bernard M. W. Knox, *Oedipus at Thebes.*

"[Oedipus] still has the same personality he always had"—Oedipus is a man of action. He likes to be the first person to understand and solve a problem. At the beginning of the play when the people of Thebes come to him for help, he says, "I know what brings you here," and he has already figured out a way of dealing with the problem. (See Ch. 19, p. 236.)

"at the end of the play . . . Oedipus remains who he always was"—Although Oedipus is reduced to a blind man and, by his own decree, an outcast, he has not changed his fundamental nature or lost his heroic stature. Despite his blindness, he has a clear vision of how he wants his affairs to be handled, and he issues a series of commands to Kreon: **give** her whatever burial you think best, **let me die** the way they wanted me to die, **let me touch** [my daughters], **let them come** to me, etc. (See Ch. 19, p. 276f.)

"if you believe in chance, you do not believe in any kind of order"—Oedipus tries to defy the gods and declares that he is a child of chance.

 Other Literary Versions of the Myth of Oedipus

"the writers adapt the story"—Each literary version is suited to its audience, and to the message the author wishes to convey.

that ordinary people cannot. It is ironic that such a great man is more ignorant than the audience about the most important details of his own private life.

Knox points out that Oedipus' name in Greek means "swollen foot," but the first part of it sounds like οἶδα (oida), a Greek verb meaning "I know." Thus, there is some sense in the play that there is a dichotomy between two aspects of the hero. On the one hand, he has the swollen feet of the son exposed by Laius, and on the other, he knows some things. He embodies the ongoing juxtaposition of the ugly and ill-shapen and possessing great wisdom, or at least attempts at great wisdom.

According to Knox, Oedipus begins by believing that he himself is godlike and does not need the gods: he is self-sufficient. This explains why he tries to defy the oracle of Apollo, and why he joins with Jocasta in her rejection of the gods' power.

Of course, Oedipus does not succeed at his attempts to solve his problems by himself. However, Knox goes on to point out that the play does not end with the defeat of Oedipus. At the end of the play, Oedipus has learned something. **He still has the same personality he always had,** but now he uses it differently. In fact, Knox notes that, **at the end of the play, despite the horrible facts he faces, Oedipus remains who he always was** and becomes even greater. He achieves a "terrible success" in "his search for the truth," and shows us his "greatness, not this time in defiance of the powers which shape human life but in harmony with those powers" (195). That is, Oedipus tries to defy the power of the gods, but he winds up accepting it.

The gods' power was an important issue in the time of Sophocles. Knox says, "the pessimistic mood of the end of the fifth century deepened in the fourth as Greece, torn apart by incessant warfare, succumbed to the perseverance, intrigue, and raw aggressiveness of a half-savage Macedonian king. . . . The goddess Chance . . . symbolized the century's 'sense of drift'" (167). Everything they had was slipping away from them, so they became followers of chance.

What does the worship of chance mean? Knox quotes Polybius as saying, "Chance, which makes no contracts with this life of ours, makes everything new contrary to our calculations and displays her power in the unexpected" (167).

If life is no longer subject to our calculations, this means believing in fortunetellers, it means believing in astrology, it means believing in the roll of the dice, believing that there is no point to putting forth effort. Here is an example: if class standing were assigned by chance, there'd be no point in studying for the exam, because the teacher would just roll the dice to assign the grades. So **if you believe in chance, you do not believe in any kind of order** which can be influenced by your efforts. And Greece was at a time in her history when all the greatness that she was seeing was slipping away from her so it was easy for people to say life has no meaning, there is no point to any of it, we should believe in chance.

"The goddess Tyche [which is Greek for "chance"] superseded the Olympians"—that is to say, if you worshipped her, you did not need to worship anybody else—"in the mind of the common man; she was the only appropriate icon of a world which persistently mocked all human calculation and the logic on which it was based" (167).

Each version is different; **the writers adapt the story** to suit the tastes of their audience and the message they want to convey. Seneca, the Roman dramatist, wrote one in Latin in the first century C.E. His Oedipus was the innocent victim of an evil fate, who endures his suffering to save his city. He mediates between helpless humans and an incomprehensible supernatural world. Pierre Corneille's *Oedipe* was produced in 1659 in Paris; this author felt that Sophocles' plot was too disturbing, and so blunted it by adding a romantic subplot. John Dryden's English version (1679) also included this romantic subplot, as well as the idea that Oedipus and Jocasta were deeply attracted to one another. Voltaire's 1718 version tries to make Oedipus' discovery more believable by making their marriage more recent. His hero is a king who focuses on the needs of his people and does his duty by them.

Modern versions include Andre Gide's *Oedipe* written in 1930. His Oedipus is a kind of existential hero, an independent spirit who seeks the truth, and his play is at the same time a parody of the play and a serious reinterpretation of it as dealing with issues of human freedom and the law. Jean Cocteau's *La Machine Infernale,* written in 1932, is also irreverent while at the same time suggesting the universal power of myth. The drama, influenced by surrealism, abounds in supernatural elements that inspire terror: dreams, miracles, monsters, and ghosts. Oedipus is given the answer to the riddle by the Sphinx, and believes he is a hero, but finds himself caught in the trap of fate.

Rationalized Versions of Myth

However, it is not just literary versions that contribute to the significance of the story of Oedipus. Freud, the founder of psychoanalysis, saw in Oedipus a malady that he believed all men are subject to, which he named the Oedipus complex. He said, "It may be that we are all destined to direct our first sexual impulses towards our mothers, and our first impulses of hatred and violence toward our fathers; our dreams convince us that we were [so destined]." In this sense, then, Oedipus is not a hero because he is unlike other men, but in fact because he is typical of them. He represents us all; he is an ordinary person. Freud's view of the myth then became part of the explanation or **rationalization** for why the story had retained its significance throughout the centuries.

Social scientists like Freud are interested not just in one single plot or version of the Oedipus myth, but they gather together all the known versions, listing them and incorporating them in a continuous narrative, a "life of Oedipus" or a "history of Oedipus." In their views, we find a very different sense of what a myth is: it is not a single literary text or version, but a synthesis of all known versions. This synthesis is designed to highlight a particular characteristic or feature of the myth that seems important to the thinker who is assessing it.

To Otto Rank, Freud's follower, Sophocles' story of Oedipus is not the most important or most interesting version of the myth. Rank saw the story as an expression of the family romance, the story a child tells to express and rationalize his own feelings about his father.

Rank did not think that the saga of the hero could be found only in Sophocles' play. He finds this same pattern in the stories of at least fifteen heroes—Sargon, Moses, Karna, Oedipus, Paris, Telephus, Perseus, Gilgamesh, Cyrus, Tristan, Romulus, Hercules, Jesus, Siegfried, and Lohengrin—from many different geographic locations and cultures, as early as 2800 B.C.E. The pattern occurs in a variety of disparate stories. For instance, Rank shows that the story of Judas Iscariot, which is much less familiar to people, fits the same pattern as the story of Oedipus.

Rank believes that the need to tell this story is intrinsically connected to how human beings are organized into families. The story, in his view, is very widespread because children are expressing their feelings as powerless beings in the family. To make themselves feel better, they identify with the long succession of heroes in the stories we have just listed. These heroes overcome their powerlessness by eventually defeating their powerful parents. The heroes of all these different stories do many of the same things, in Rank's view, because the feelings of children in families all over the world, in many time periods, are alike. Thus, for Rank, the Oedipus story is one among many that show that human beings all come from similar families, and they share certain characteristics as a result.

Claude Levi-Strauss is another social scientist who considered the myth of Oedipus. He believed that myth is a kind of language, and the constituent units of myth are the events that take place in a story. If myth is like a language, we understand it by figuring out the relationships between these constituent units. As a result, Levi-Strauss, like Freud and Rank, synthesized all the versions he could find of the myth of Oedipus. For him, however, they had an entirely different meaning and importance. He believed that the purpose of myth is to help us

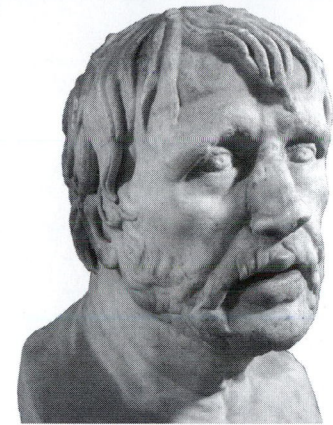

This 1st-c. C.E. bust represents *Seneca*, the philosopher and playwright, who adapted the story of Oedipus to represent the virtues and concerns of the Romans of his day.

 The Views of Sigmund Freud and Otto Rank

This view comes from: Sigmund Freud, *The General Introduction to Psychoanalysis*, trans. Joan Riviere (184–85).

rationalization—The term applies to myths told in a particular way for a particular reason. Thus, Snorri rationalized the ancient Icelandic myths by saying they were stories men came up with after they had lost the true religion of Christianity. (See Ch. 7, p. 79.)

The Saga of the Hero, According to Rank, Includes

- descent from noble, powerful parents
- exposure in a river, in a box
- raising by lowly parents
- return to his first parents
- punishment of the first parents.

FREUD, Andy Warhol. *Ten Portraits of Jews of the Twentieth Century:* Sigmund Freud, 1980.

understand and overcome the contradictions we find in our lives. Thus he identified a series of contradictions found in the Oedipus myth and showed a mediation or balance in each.

In the view of Levi-Strauss, the myth expresses the conflicts that a culture experiences when it tries to reconcile different views of how human beings came into existence. Some cultures believe that only one sex is necessary for reproduction, while others think that human beings are born of the union of a man and a woman.

The story of Oedipus dramatizes the problems with accepting our origins: the hero comes from a family that springs from the earth, but creatures who spring from the earth have jerky movements and seem crippled. They are monsters. The story includes elements about the destruction of monsters: for instance, Cadmus, Oedipus' ancestor, slays a dragon and sows its teeth into the ground. But creation also results. Men spring up from the teeth and found the city of Thebes. These earth-born men walk with a lurching gait, as, of course, does our hero Oedipus. On the one hand, we accept and admire our ancestors because they are the origin of our line. On the other hand, they were primitive, lurching, uncultured: for this we are inclined to reject them.

Levi-Strauss, like Rank, believed that the myth of Oedipus shows us something general about the nature of human beings, namely that human beings struggle to achieve a balance between nature and culture. They are driven to build cultural objects and institutions, but then to find that these frustrate and restrict their natural instincts and drives.

Working Versions of Myth

Now the story of Oedipus, if it holds any meaning for us, does so as a literary work or as a story expressing something essential that all human beings share, as Rank or Levi-Strauss suggest. There is no longer a society whose values and concerns it expresses. However, the Greeks venerated Oedipus as a hero or even a demigod. Pausanias tells us that his bones were brought to Athens from Thebes and buried in a hero-shrine there (*Description of Greece*, 3.50). In addition, he was worshipped at sanctuaries throughout Greece. So the myth was once alive, in that it explained the meaning or importance of a ritual or set of ceremonies performed as part of a religion. Also, looked at even more broadly, it expressed certain values and conflicts that were important to a society, probably different ones at different times.

In contrast with the story of Oedipus, some myths are still being told, retold, and modified by members of the society that originated them.

For example, Daniel Biebuyck has sought out storytellers and collected different **versions of the Mwindo epic.** Each storyteller's version differs from all others by emphasizing different aspects of the story and by including or omitting different details.

In fact, the people telling the tale may well not notice the differences at all. Albert Lord, in his studies of Yugoslav oral poetry that survived into modern times, has shown that even when there are substantial differences between two versions of an oral tale, differences in length and in details of the plot, the audience considers them the same story. This is not because the people telling these stories are primitive or unsophisticated. Rather, the aspects of the story that concern them are not different enough to be worth their attention. They would accuse us of quibbling if we insisted on pointing them out. Some contemporary African scholars have labeled concerns with exact detail a "pen and paper" mentality. They believe that such critics are missing the essential character of the myth. They might respond, as did Heraclitus (a philosopher whose career began in the late sixth century B.C.E.) that "all things are in process and nothing stands still." He also compares all existing things to the stream of a river, noting that "you would not step twice into the same river" (197). That is, even if we read exactly the same words on two different occasions, they are not exactly the same because we are reading them on different occasions. This idea is explored and legitimized by modern scholars as

The Views of Claude Levi-Strauss

For the text of Levi-Strauss' discussion of the Oedipus myth, see Ch. 20.

Contradictions Found in the Oedipus Myth

- *Overrating* of blood relations (Oedipus has sex with his mother) versus *underrating* of blood relations (he murders his father).
- *Autochthony* (Oedipus' ancestors sprang from the earth) versus *destroying monsters* (Oedipus overcomes the Sphinx).

The Young Poet: Portrait of Jean Cocteau, Romaine Brooks. The playwright adapted the Oedipus myth to fit the tastes and concerns of France in the early part of the 20th C. C.E.

"versions of the Mwindo epic"— For the text of the Mwindo epic, see Ch. 22, p. 305.

This view comes from: Albert Lord, *The Singer of Tales.*

This idea comes from: Plato, Cratylus 402 B.C.E.: tr. Kirk and Raven, *The Presocratic Philosophers.*

reader-response criticism, which suggests that, to some extent, each text is different for every reader on every occasion. "Different readings arise in part because each reader brings to a text a different general repertoire—a set of culturally conditioned experiences, beliefs, knowledge, and expectations. And, of course, you can change your readings of texts very drastically if your life experiences change" (22–23).

The tellers of the Mwindo epic would argue that its different versions agree in many ways: each version contains a hero who has an unusual birth and performs mighty deeds. Although each version of the epic is a different story by a different bard, many individual details and plot elements are repeated from version to version. And the meaning of the story is about the same for the society that tells it. It contains models of how a marriage should be performed, how a father should behave, what a good chief is like, and what it means to grow up.

In a sense, any version of a myth like the Mwindo epic that still expresses the values of the people who tell it is a working version, but there are stories whose function in a society is particularly evident because they are connected with a religious ritual or ceremony.

Thus, for instance, the Judaeo-Christian **scriptures found in the Bible are associated with various religious ceremonies and have a variety of significances** for the people involved in them. Parts of the Old Testament are associated with the ceremony of circumcision, for instance, and the ceremony itself has significance for defining and expressing membership in the Jewish religion. Parts of the New Testament are associated with Christian rituals of Eucharist and Communion. These rituals express the ideals and values Christians derive from their religion. These stories in the Bible are alive in the sense of giving meaning to the society. Throughout history, however, members of each society have been accustomed to regard their own stories as sacred texts and those of others as mere stories.

In a sense, the distinctions between versions of myths are not as hard and fast as the classification here makes them seem. For instance, the Bible, which contains working versions of myths, is also a literary work and worthy of study as such. However, the categorization presented here may help to explain why **myths are of interest to so many different kinds of professions.** Literary critics have a tendency to work with literary versions of myths; scientists and philosophers focus on working versions of myths; psychologists often work with rationalized versions of myths.

> **This idea comes from:** Kathleen McCormick, Gary Waller, and Linda Flower, *Reading Texts: Reading, Responding, Writing.*

> "scriptures found in the Bible . . . have a variety of significances"— For a discussion of the close link between the rituals of the Jewish dietary laws and the story of creation in the Bible, see Mary Douglas' "Deciphering a Meal," Ch. 29, p. 417.

> "myths are of interest to so many different kinds of professions"— See Ch. 2, p. 17, for a chart listing some of the different fields concerned with myth.

Further Reading

Knox, Bernard M. W. *Oedipus at Thebes.* New Haven, CN: Yale University Press, 1957.

Rank, Otto. *The Myth of the Birth of the Hero.* Ed. Philip Freund. New York, NY: Vintage Books, 1959.

Part 4

Ritual and Myth

What Does Ritual Have to Do With Mythology?

You may wonder why we have included a section on rituals in a book on mythology. In the context of religion, the connection is clear: myths are the stories told by those who participate in the group, while rituals are the actions performed by members of the group. However, we often study myths outside of their religious context, as literary works, as cultural objects, or just as entertaining stories. Nonetheless, there is a great deal to be learned about myths by considering them in the context of rituals. Take, for example, the story of the kidnapping of Persephone (see Ch. 27). In it, Demeter's daughter Persephone is seized by Hades and taken as his bride to live in the underworld. Demeter, who is the goddess of grain, wanders the earth and refuses to let the crops grow until Zeus arranges a compromise which returns Persephone to her mother for part of each year.

We can appreciate this by itself as an example of a good story that represents the relationship between mother and daughter. We can ponder the themes it emphasizes: sexuality and death, perseverance and regeneration. However, our view of the myth is expanded and enriched by recognizing that it was told as part of the ceremonies conducted at the temple of Demeter in Eleusis. In this context, the story is no longer about the efforts of individuals, it is also a public communication recounting the traditions and struggles of a society. We can then see the myth as a representation of marriage customs in a society where a daughter's consent was not required before she was given in marriage, and we can notice that it emphasizes the personal longing to survive death and return from the land of the dead, as Persephone did.

Because ritual deals with human activities rather than stories, its study brings us into some areas that may seem unexpected. Religious ceremonies, parades, festivals, even sporting events like the Balinese cockfight or American football, and children's activities like trick or treating all come into consideration when we look for activities related to beliefs and values expressed in mythological stories.

The Participant in Ritual: Passive or Active?

There are different ways to think about rituals. Mircea Eliade describes their origin in archaic times, saying that rituals arose because they "deliberately repeat . . . the acts posited [by] gods, heroes and ancestors." By this he means that through ritual, primitive human beings tried to recapture the primordial act of creation, the center, which is "pre-eminently the zone of the sacred, the zone of absolute reality." Thus, through rituals even today, the religious man is able to return to "mythical time" *in illo tempore:* Eliade uses this phrase, literally "in that time," to refer to the golden age posited by primitive men as existing before the start of historical time. Thus, in his view, rituals return the participants to the time-before-time found in their stories. This is a time when "the individual is truly himself": when the original revelation was made or when the creation occurred.[1] For more on Eliade's views, see the Introduction to Hesiod's "The Ages of Man," Chapter 3, p. 39.

Some scholars have studied ritual for the effects it has on the individual and on society, emphasizing how rituals help members of the society cope with their difficulties, channel negative emotions, learn about the stories and values of their society, and so forth. This approach makes the ritual seem like a force through which society affects its participants. The participants, on the other hand, seem like the passive recipients of the ritual's effects. This approach can seem very satisfactory because it focuses on an element we relate to easily: the psychology of the individual undergoing the ritual. However, when we consider only the individual, we are looking at a static model that cannot account for societal change. In contrast, Victor Turner has emphasized the active nature of ritual, which involves a more in-depth understanding of the community and the culture in which the ceremony is performed. According to Turner, the ritual is something the participants do: it is a drama in which they are the actors. As a result of their actions in the ritual, they are transformed, and through their experiences, they have the power to change the society itself. Rituals develop and maintain importance in a society because the society finds real meaning in them (see Ch. 26, p. 373).

Many rituals occur at particularly sensitive points in our lives: birth, coming of age, graduating from college, marriage, death. These rituals are called "rites of passage." It is through performing these ceremonies that individuals make the transition to a new role or condition in relation to society. In this view, the ritual is a living thing, and the participants are the actors in it. This perspective on ritual is powerful, because it takes into account the growing, changing nature of society.

The Characteristics of Rituals

Often we talk about personal rituals—the small, repetitive and regularly repeated patterns of behavior that we practice: the bedtime "rituals" of children, the competitive "rituals" of athletes, or the "rituals" we perform as we study for a test or write a paper. However, when we speak of rituals in a more technical sense, we mean more than just patterns of behavior that exhibit regularity and repetition. Usually a ritual in this sense refers to a public event that belongs to a community. A ritual

[1]This explanation of Eliade's view of ritual draws on ideas and phrases from pp. 5, 20, 35, and 86.

can, however, be private, as Erika Brady shows in discussing private rituals of grief that arise in cases of deep trauma.

Another characteristic of a ritual is that it expresses meaning. This meaning can be in terms of a myth or story associated with the ritual, as noted previously, or it may be that the ritual highlights values or conflicts found in the society. For example, in his analysis of the Balinese cockfight, Clifford Geertz describes a contest between fighting cocks that is of great importance on an island in the Indian Ocean that was once colonized by the Dutch. In this study, he shows that Balinese men identify with their cocks, much as American

Keith Haring (1958–1990), *Cockfight*. Haring represents the relationship between men and their cocks in our society, which is similar to that in Bali.

men identify with their football teams. In attending cockfights, the Balinese man does not necessarily bet on the best cock or the one he thinks is most likely to win. Rather, without particularly noticing it, he bets on the cock owned by someone from his village or from his occupational group or family. As a result, betting on cockfights reflects the organization and structure of Balinese society.

Because the meaning of ritual is typically of great importance to the participants, they become emotionally engaged in the actions they are performing. In discussing the Balinese cockfight, Geertz notes that some percentage of the fights he witnessed were what he calls "deep cockfights" in which the participants bet more than they can afford to lose. Rituals hit us "where we live" emotionally. Clyde Kluckhohn studied the Navajo, and in reporting on their rituals, he compares the emotional impact to that of literature among people whose culture is organized around the reading of books. He notes that the Navajo "have a keen expectation of the long recitals of myths (or portions of them) around the fire on long winter nights." He adds, quoting another scholar on ritual, A. M. Hocart, "Emotion is assisted by the repetition of words that have acquired a strong emotional coloring, and this coloring is again intensified by repetition."[2]

In addition to their strong emotional content, rituals usually exhibit a symbolic or vicarious nature. The meaning of the word "vicarious" derives from the story of King Vikar in Icelandic myth. The story describes the nature of the head god Odin. It was customary to offer Odin human sacrifice, and one day the members of King Vikar's army drew lots to decide who should die to propitiate the god. When the lot

---

[2] A. M. Hocart. "Ritual and Emotion," *Character and Personality* 7 (1939) 208, 210–11.

fell to the king himself, his ministers were appalled and suggested a symbolic sacrifice. The customary ritual of Odin involved hanging and stabbing the victim with a spear; instead, the king put on a noose of animal entrails, and his followers threw a pine bough at him. However, Odin was not to be cheated, and turned the entrails into a rope, and the bough became a spear, so the king was hanged and stabbed, dying as the ritual originally demanded. The story illustrates that Odin would not accept a substitute sacrifice, and ironically, the name of Vikar has ever since stood for "substitute" or "symbol." Unlike the sacrifice of King Vikar, most rituals are vicarious: they are symbolic actions which represent the effect desired by the participants, but do not cause it. For example, a festival of Dionysus at Athens (as described in Ch. 31) included a ritual that involved offering the wife of a city official to the god as a bride and acting out in lewd detail the particulars of the "marriage" that followed.

The Ritual as a Drama Acted on the Stage of Society

When we discuss the relationship of ritual to meaning, we need to consider the ways in which particular societies express meaning. In a traditional society, the members of the community all share the same complex of beliefs and values. Typically, their occupations and status in the society are related to these beliefs, as well. Thus, in such a society, it is possible to connect the meaning of a ritual to the dominant (and often only) belief system. In a modern pluralistic society, however, the community is not structured around a single system of beliefs and values. Rather, the emphasis is on the individual, and because the society includes a variety of belief systems, the power of any one is diminished, at least in terms of the community. As a result, it is much more difficult to determine the meaning of a ritual.

Take, for instance, the introduction of Halloween into France. In 1997 the holiday, previously unknown, became fashionable there. In the United States, the holiday is explained as relating to the Christian tradition. It is explained that on the night before All Saints' Day, known as All Hallows' Eve, the souls of the dead roam the earth. Child revelers dressed in fantastic costumes go house to house requesting treats and threatening tricks if they are not forthcoming. The French, whose tradition includes a Christian element, have always celebrated All Saints' Day, November 1st, as an occasion to bring flowers to the graves of their relatives, but had no celebration related to the eve. The *New York Times* attributed the French introduction of Halloween to marketing strategists, who wanted to create sales opportunities tantamount to those in the United States, where the holiday ranks second only to Christmas in retail sales. Some French, however, attributed their interest in Halloween to the desire for fun, while others pointed out that the festival was European before it was American. A pagan festival was celebrated in Britain and Ireland on October 31, the eve of the new year. On this date, the dead were believed to rise from the grave and walk the earth again.

It is clear that in a pluralistic society, the adoption of a new festival or a new ritual is not related to the beliefs of the community, or even the deeply felt needs of the individual. This is not to say that the festival does not and will not have meaning. Victor Turner has pointed out that the role reversal involved in Halloween accords children the power they do not ordinarily have in society, allowing them to consider the values of their society "from a new perspective." However, as the example of French Halloween shows, Turner makes clear that in modern society, participation in ritual is more a matter of individual choice than in traditional society, where rituals are interwoven with all aspects of daily life (see Ch. 26, p. 378ff).

The Relationship between Myth and Ritual

Theories about the relationship between myths and rituals have varied. Some scholars believe that myths are the more basic form, that is, that rituals have been developed as things to do to express the importance of the events and personages found in myths, in the lives of the people who tell them. Other scholars believe that rituals came first, and that myths are explanations or stories after the fact to make sense of the ceremonies people perform.

Anthropologists have sometimes postulated that every myth has an associated ritual, and that every ritual is related to a myth. However, as they have studied different cultures, they found abundant instances of myths without rituals and rituals without myths. In some cases, they suggested that a myth or ritual had once existed in conjunction with its counterpart, but had fallen into disuse and been forgotten. Especially in Greek culture, we often find instances of myths that do not seem to have associated rituals. On the other hand, the Ndembu, the African tribe studied by Victor Turner (see Ch. 26, p. 373), have rituals for which there is no myth. However, for our purposes here, the exceptions to the rule do not matter. As students of mythology, we can learn a great deal from thinking about the rituals associated with myths. Kluckhohn summarizes the situation well: "To a considerable degree, the question of the primacy of ceremonial or mythology is as meaningless as all questions of 'the hen or the egg' form. What is really important is the intricate interdependence of myth with ritual" (54).

Further Reading

Brady, Erika. "The 'Beau Geste': Shaping Private Rituals of Grief." *Folklife Annual* (1987): 24–33.

Cohen, Roger. "AH-lo-een: An American Holiday Moves to France." *The New York Times,* October 31, 1997, A1, A4.

Eliade, Mircea. *The Myth of the Eternal Return: Or Cosmos and History.* Trans. Willard R. Trask. Bollingen Series XLVI. Princeton, NJ: Princeton University Press, 1974.

Geertz, Clifford, ed. *Myth, Symbol and Culture.* New York, NY: Norton, 1971.

Kluckhohn, Clyde. "Myths and Rituals: A General Theory." *Harvard Theological Review* 35.1 (1942): 45–79.

Ritual

VICTOR TURNER

What to Expect . . . Victor Turner, an anthropologist whose writing is based on the study of traditional and modern societies, explains that ritual is a kind of symbolic language for participants that helps define any event in terms of the broader range of symbols found in that society. It is the mythology, the stories told in the society, that as a rule provide the script for the rituals in which the members participate. Consider which stories you have read thus far in this book are related to rituals, from the Greek torch race in honor of Prometheus to any rituals you may know of in relation to the stories of the Judaeo-Christian Bible.

While analyzing a broad range of rituals in different types of societies, Turner focuses especially on rites of passage, rituals that mark changes in status in a person's life. Such events are well characterized in mythology by the trickster, a creature possessing liminality, the state of being between two cultures or two statuses. In considering modern post-industrialist culture, which embraces a complex system of various belief systems, Turner identifies a characteristic he calls the liminoid, which accounts for the choice we have of belief systems in our pluralistic society.

As you read, think about how Turner's ideas about liminality and the crossing of thresholds play a role in a variety of the stories you have read thus far. For example, one of the elements Joseph Campbell (Ch. 14, p. 159) identifies as part of the hero's journey is the crossing of the threshold into the land where the adventures will take place.

Victor Turner was an anthropologist whose thinking has greatly influenced our ideas about ritual. In an article he wrote for the journal *Science,* Turner provides a definition of a ritual as "a stereotyped sequence of activities involving gestures, words, and objects, performed in a sequestered place, and designed to influence preternatural entities or forces on behalf of the actors' goals and interests."

For Turner, ritual is a symbolic language through which the participants communicate "many ideas, relations between things, actions, interactions, and transactions found in the society." Thus any action performed in a ritual is likely to have a variety of interrelated meanings. However, ritual is not just a symbolic language. It is a series of actions performed by participants who are affected by their role in the drama.

Turner describes what he calls the different dimensions of a ritual, a concept useful to those of us interested in rituals as a part of the study of mythology. These represent the different perspectives involved in the study of rituals. A ritual is different for those who participate in it than it is for the anthropologist who comes from outside the society to study it. The dimensions Turner speaks of are

- exegetic: the way an insider explains the ritual to someone outside the society. This reflects both the insider's personal understanding of the ritual, as well as his or her assumptions about what outsiders can understand and what they want to know.

- operational: the way an anthropologist, who is outside the society, records what is done in the ritual, and how the participants behave and appear to feel. The anthropologist must look for understanding in what is done, how it is done, and who does (or doesn't) do it. In other words, the members of the society can never tell outsiders everything they need to know (and might not want to).

- positional: the way an anthropologist, who is outside the society, describes the connections between the symbols found in a ritual and other symbols found in the society and the culture. When anthropologists try to understand ritual, they try to fit it to categories they can use to compare the rituals of different cultures.

As students of mythology, we are examining stories that can play an important part in the religion practiced by a community of worshippers. It is important for us to understand that these stories should not be viewed in isolation from the other important perspectives that provide meaning to the life of the community. In addition, we cannot assume that the community of the storytellers will look upon the story in the same way as we do, as we are taking on the role of honorary anthropologists who look at the stories from outside.

Turner classifies rituals as seasonal or cyclic and contingent. *Cyclic rituals* are those "hallowing a culturally defined moment of change in the climatic cycle or the inauguration of an activity such as planting, harvesting, or moving from winter to summer pasture." A Thanksgiving Day parade, for instance, celebrates the harvest at the end of the northern growing season and would be considered a cyclic ritual.

In contrast, *contingent rituals* are those "held in response to an individual or collective crisis." These include life crisis ceremonies "performed at birth, puberty, marriage, death, and so on, to demarcate the passage from one phase to another in the individual's life cycle" and rituals of affliction "performed to placate or exorcise preternatural beings or forces believed to have afflicted villagers with illness, bad luck, gynecological troubles, severe physical injuries, and the like." Turner shows that any ritual will incorporate a variety of symbols meaningful to the members of the society performing it.

Turner's definition of ritual is based on the anthropological field work he did among the Ndembu people of central Africa. In the course of this work, he formulated an understanding of ritual that can be applied beyond the culture and society that inspired it. In fact, the concepts he developed are applicable both to traditional societies like those in rural Africa and to pluralistic societies like that found in the United States. This is because Turner's ideas take into account that a society's culture, beliefs and rituals change over time.

The first reading is taken from Turner's book *The Forest of Symbols: Aspects of Ndembu Ritual*. It focuses on the rite of passage, a particular kind of ritual. Rites of passage are ceremonies that celebrate the movement of a member of society from one state or condition to another, like graduations or weddings. A graduation, for example, represents a passage of members of a school's student body out of the school and into another stage of education or experience. Rites of passage comprise a large and important category of rituals, but not all rituals are rites of passage.

This mural from 1923–24 by Diego Rivera represents the offerings at the Mexican *Day of the Dead*. This seasonal ritual takes place on November 1–2 and involves setting up altars in the home to welcome back the spirits of the dead with offerings of their favorite foods.

The second reading comes from Turner's book *On the Edge of the Bush: Anthropology as Experience*. In it he explains that the rite of passage has a characteristic called liminality, which is introduced in the first reading and discussed further in the second reading. Liminality allows those taking part in the ritual to see and understand their society in a new way. It allows the participants to support and in some cases to remake their society, adapting it to the understanding they have achieved through the ritual.

The third reading, excerpted from an article, applies to modern pluralistic societies the concepts developed from the study of traditional societies. This reading is interesting because in it Turner refers to ideas in the first reading, and explains how his thinking has grown and developed since he wrote the earlier passages.

Introduction to Rites of Passage

Rites de passage are found in all societies but tend to reach their maximal expression in small-scale, relatively stable and cyclical societies, where change is bound up with biological and meteorological rhythms and recurrences rather than with technological innovations. Such rites indicate and constitute transitions between states. By "state" I mean "a relatively fixed or stable condition" and would include in its meaning such social constancies as legal status, profession, office or calling, rank or degree. I hold it to designate also the condition of a person as determined by his culturally recognized degree of maturation as when one speaks of "the married or single state" or the "state of infancy."

Van Gennep has shown that all rites of transition are marked by three **phases:** separation, margin (or *limen*), and aggregation. The first phase of separation comprises symbolic behavior signifying the detachment of the individual or group either from an earlier fixed state in the social structure or a set of cultural conditions (a "state"); during the intervening liminal period, the state of the ritual subject (the "passenger") is ambiguous; he passes through a realm that has few or none of the attributes of the past or coming state; in the third phase the passage is consummated. The ritual subject, individual or corporate, is in a stable state once more and, by virtue of this, has rights and obligations of a clearly defined and "structural" type, and is expected to behave in accordance with certain customary norms and ethical standards.

As van Gennep, Henri Junod, and others have shown, *rites de passage* are not confined to culturally defined life-crises but may accompany any change from one state to the other, as when a whole tribe goes to war, or when it attests to the passage from scarcity to plenty by performing a first-fruits or harvest festival. *Rites de passage,* too, are not restricted, sociologically speaking, to movements between ascribed statuses. They can also concern entry in to a new, achieved status, whether this be a political office or membership of an exclusive club or secret society. They may admit persons into membership of a religious group where such a group does not include the whole society, or qualify them for official duties of the cult, sometimes in a graded series of rites.

The subject of a passage ritual is, in the liminal period, structurally, if not physically, "invisible." The structural "invisibility" of liminal *personae* has a twofold character. They are at once no longer classified and not yet classified. In so far as they are no longer classified, the symbols that represent them are, in many societies, drawn from the biology of death, decomposition, catabolism, and other physical processes that have a negative tinge such as menstruation (frequently regarded as the absence or loss of status). Thus in some boys' initiations, newly circumcised boys are likened to

---

Pablo Picasso, *The First Communion,* 1896. This coming-of-age ritual includes a shared meal representing the community, bread representing spiritual as well as physical nourishment, and white clothing associated with purity.

This reading comes from: Victor Turner, *The Forest of Symbols**

"Rites de passage"—In our society, an example would be initiation into a fraternity or sorority. This might include a "hazing" or test period in which the pledge must follow the orders of someone who is already a member of the organization. In effect, the pledge gives up any right to independence and ceases to be a person for the duration of the initiation.

phases The stages of a rite of passage are

- separation
- marginal or liminal period
- aggregation

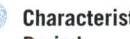 **Characteristics of the Liminal Period**

limen The Latin word for "threshold." From this word comes the idea of liminality. When you are on the threshold between two rooms, you are, in a sense, in both of them or in neither one; you are "in between." The idea of "liminality" refers to the state of being in between two stages of life, two communities, or two social statuses.

---

*Victor Turner. *The Forest of Symbols: Aspects of Ndembu Ritual* (Ithaca, NY: Cornell University Press, 1967), 93–111. First published in *The Proceedings of the American Ethnological Society,* 1964.

Villa of the Mysteries. This 1st-c. C.E. fresco shows an initiation into the worship of Bacchus at Pompeii. The initiates, young women on the threshold of adulthood, are whipped as part of the ceremony, as part of a temporary loss of status associated with the ceremony.

 Communitas

"set of relations"—Communitas is the recognition of a social bond and sense of interrelatedness achieved by initiates going through the liminal period. It transcends distinctions of rank, age, kinship position, and sometimes even sex.

Gabriele Bella, *Festival of the last Thursday of Carnival* (fl. 1700–1750). The exuberance of the crowd in carnival costumes represents communitas in the celebration, which lifted the bonds of proper social behavior.

Ndembu Turner did extensive anthropologic research among this people. (See p. 374 and p. 381.)

"special ties"—Turner's name for this was *communitas,* from the Latin word for community. He defined it as the recognition of a social bond and sense of interrelatedness achieved by initiates going through the liminal period.

This reading comes from: Victor Turner, *On the Edge of the Bush: Anthropology as Experience.**

menstruating women. In so far as a neophyte is structurally "dead," he or she may be treated, for a long time or a short time, as a corpse is customarily treated in his or her society. The neophyte may be buried, forced to lie motionless in the posture and direction of customary burial, may be stained black, or may be forced to live for a while in the company of masked and monstrous mummers representing *inter alia,* the dead, or worse still, the un-dead.

Since neophytes are not only structurally "invisible" (though physically visible) and ritually polluting, they are very commonly secluded, partially or completely, from the realm of culturally defined and ordered states and statuses. In liminal situations (in kinship-dominated societies), neophytes are sometimes treated or symbolically represented as being neither male or female. A further structural characteristic of transitional beings is that they have nothing. They have no status, property, insignia, secular clothing, rank, kinship position, nothing to demarcate them structurally from their fellows. Their condition is indeed the very prototype of sacred poverty. Rights over property, goods and services inhere in positions in the politico-jural structure. Since they do not occupy such positions, neophytes exercise no such rights. In the words of King Lear, they represent "Naked unaccommodated man."

I have spoken of the interstructural character of the liminal. However, between neophytes and their instructors (where these exist), and in connecting neophytes with one other, there exists a **set of relations** that compose a "social structure" of a highly specific type. It is a structure of a very simple kind: between instructors and neophytes there is often complete authority and complete submission; among neophytes there is often complete equality. Between incumbents of positions in secular politico-jural systems there exist intricate and situationally shifting networks of rights and duties proportioned to their rank, status, and corporate affiliation. There are many different kinds of privileges and obligations, many degrees of superordination and subordination. In the liminal period such distinctions and gradations tend to be eliminated. If complete obedience characterizes the relationship of neophyte to elder, complete equality usually characterizes the relationship of neophyte to neophyte, where the rites are collective. This comradeship must be distinguished from brotherhood or sibling relationship, since in the latter there is always the inequality of older and younger, which often achieves linguistic representation and may be maintained by legal sanctions. The liminal group is a community or comity of comrades and not a structure of hierarchically arrayed positions. This comradeship transcends distinctions of rank, age, kinship position, and, in some aspects of cultic group, even sex. Much of the behavior recorded by ethnographers in seclusion situations falls under the principle, "Each for all, and all for each." Among the **Ndembu** of Zambia, for example, all food brought for novices in circumcision seclusion by their mothers is shared out equally among them. No special favors are bestowed on the sons of chiefs or headmen. Any food acquired by novices in the bush is taken by the elders and apportioned among the group. Deep friendships between novices are encouraged, and they sleep around lodge fires in clusters of four or five particular comrades. However, all are supposed to be linked by **special ties** which persist after the rites are over, even into old age.

Play as a Characteristic of Liminality

For me the essence of liminality is to be found in its release from normal constraints, making possible the deconstruction of the "uninteresting" constructions of common sense, the "meaningfulness of ordinary life," discussed by phenomenological sociolo-

*Victor Turner. Excerpt from *On the Edge of the Bush: Anthropology as Experience,* 160–61, 235–36. © 1985 The Arizona Board of Regents. Reprinted by permission of the University of Arizona Press.

gists, into cultural units which may then be reconstructed in novel ways. Liminality is the domain of the "interesting," or of "uncommon sense." This is not to say that it is totally unconstrained, for in so far as it represents a definite stage in the passage of an initiand from status A to status B in a ritual belonging to a traditional system or sequence of rituals, liminality must bear some traces of its antecedent and subsequent stages. To use **Robert Merton's** terms, some symbols must accord with the "manifest" purposes of the ritual (to transform a boy into a man, a girl into a woman, a dead person into an ancestral spirit, etc.). But others have the "latent" capacity to elicit creative and innovative responses from the neophytes and their instructors.

The study of masks and costumes in African and Melanesian initiation rituals, whether of puberty or into secret societies, demonstrates the imaginative potential unlocked by liminality, for maskers (representing deities, arch-ancestors, territorial guardian spirits, or other supernaturals) typically appear in liminal sites sequestered from mundane life. Among the Ndembu of Zambia, for example, the makishi, masked figures, said to be ancient ancestors, of awesome shape and power, are believed by boy novices secluded in the bush camps during the Mukanda rites to spring from the blood-soaked site in the deep bush where they had recently been circumcised. The woodcarvers who create the masks, though they portray a limited range of types (the Foolish Young Woman, the Crazy One, the Wise Old Chief, the Fertility Binder, etc.), display a wide range of personal aesthetic initiative in generating variant forms.

In other words, there is an aspect of play in liminality. **Huizinga's** *Homo Ludens* (1955 [1938]) has sensitized anthropological thought to the play element in the construction and negotiation of meaning in culture, by his scrutiny of all kinds of playing from children's games to the dialectic of philosophy and the judicial process. After him, play is a serious business! Not all play, of course, is reserved, in any society, for liminal occasions in the strict van Gennepian sense of ritual stages. In tribal societies children and adults play games in nonritual, leisure contexts. But the serious games which involve the play of ideas and the manufacture of religiously important symbolic forms and designs (icons, figurines, masks, sand-paintings, murals in sacred caves, statues, effigies, pottery emblems, and the like) are often, in traditional societies, reserved for authentically liminal times and places.

Van Gennep distinguishes between those rites of passage which mark the nodes of individual development in any human life from beginning to end, varying chronologically from culture to culture, but marking changes of state and status, from womb to tomb, and those rites, which often involve popular festival with dramatized status, gender, and age reversals, and Rabelaisian emphases on catabolism and fecundity, which mark **nodes in the agricultural cycle** or calendar such as sowing, first fruits, and main harvest of the staple crop, or in the solstices, or the intersection of solar, lunar, and/or Venusian cycles. The former rites, referring to human development, are centered on individuals, who are initiated by adepts or elders and taught the meanings of symbols materialized as rock-paintings, masks, medicine-bundles, riddling utterances, gestures, dance-movements, figurines, sand paintings, and many other modes of sacral communication—or at least as much as the elders desire novices to know in the innocency of their initiation.

Some of these figurations are what Grathoff and Handelman call "symbolic types," akin to **Jung's "archetypes"** but derived from that portion of significant social experience transmitted and learned as culture rather than from the emergence into subjective awareness of genetically transmitted discrete numinous structures, unknowable in themselves, but clothed like caddis-fly larvae in forms derived from personal experience. As Aphrodite was born from sea-foam, such **symbolic types are generated from liminality;** they are its markers rather than its symbols, so to speak. They do not "stand for" liminality; they constitute it.

Robert Merton An influential late 20th-c. sociologist who studied the perspectives of "insiders" versus "outsiders" in society.

This mask was carved for an initiation ritual in the Democratic Republic of Congo, where such masks are typically destroyed after the ritual is concluded.

Johan Huizinga His study has shown the importance of play to passing on the values of a society.

"nodes in the agricultural cycle"— Rituals reflecting mileposts in the calendar may also involve status reversal, but of a temporary sort that does not involve liminality and communitas. For example, we have trick or treating every year on October 31st.

"Jung's 'archetypes'"—See Ch. 32, p. 468.

"symbolic types . . . generated from liminality"—In *The Ritual Process,* Turner argues that society supports certain liminal creatures who live in it, but are strictly speaking, not part of it. Depending on the society, they can include priests, clowns, court jesters, and other creatures who are tolerated despite, or perhaps because of, their ongoing challenge to the hierarchical structures and values which represent the essence of the society. Their experience represents a different sort of liminality, a permanent or long-term low status on the edges of society, not a stage in a journey or a rite of passage.

Helen Levitt, *Children*, 1940. For the children in the picture, the wearing of masks achieves a temporary status reversal that ends when the masks are put away. Such masking is part of the cyclic ritual of Halloween.

But liminality is also, even in tribal ritual, a time outside time in which it is often permitted to play with the factors of sociocultural experience, to disengage what is mundanely connected, what, outside liminality, people may even believe to be naturally and intrinsically connected, and to join the disarticulated parts in novel, even improbable ways. Even in solemn rites of passage and far more in calendrical festivals and carnivals it is considered licit to fool around with the factors of cultural construction, liberating the signifiers from the signified, filling the liminal scene with dragons, monsters, caricatures, fantasies made up of elements of everyday experience torn out of context and improbably combined with other disrupted elements. Alternatively, the ordinary, the expectable, is distorted. Human heads, limbs, genitalia are monstrously enlarged or unnaturally diminished, leaving the rest of the body of normal size. Such devices are used for mocking, critiquing, detaching the group from sober, normal, indicative orderings, and subverting the grammars of their arrangements.

Velazquez, *Portrait of the Jester Sebastian de Morra*, 1644. Court jesters lived on the edge between two worlds. They were "usually men of low class" who were able to interact with the nobility and express the people's outrage (Gluckman, 102–103).

This reading comes from: Victor Turner, "Liminal to liminoid in play, flow, and ritual: An essay in comparative symbology." In *The Anthropological Study of Human Play* (53–92).

"different explanatory stress"— Turner shows a traditional society does not separate work and play. Play is just an aspect of work in such societies.

THE LIMINOID: CHANGES TO LIMINALITY IN MODERN SOCIETY

In the next section, Turner explains the concept of the "liminoid," which he developed as an adaptation of the idea of liminality to modern, pluralistic society. Based as they are on the study of traditional societies, the concepts of communitas and liminality cannot be directly transferred to the rituals we experience in our modern pluralistic society. This is because we do not all share the same belief system, and we do not assign social status or roles within the community according to our beliefs.

Rather, our culture is a complex combination of various belief systems and values. As a result, we are to some extent distanced from our rituals: they do not have the same hold on us as the rituals of a traditional culture have on their participants. We can "take it or leave it": if one set of beliefs or values does not work out for us, we can select another. We may consider ourselves members of no social group, or we may consider ourselves casual participants in a variety of different communities, which can be non-overlapping and hold unrelated or even conflicting values. Despite these differences, Turner's insights can still serve to enlighten our experience in modern society.

In this selection, Turner makes a careful distinction between traditional and modern societies' attitudes toward work, play, and leisure. This discussion serves as the underpinning of his explanation of why liminality does not work in the same way for a modern pluralistic society as it does for traditional societies.

Work and Play in Traditional Society

Despite immense diversities within each camp, there still remains a fundamental distinction at the level of expressive culture between all societies before and all societies subsequent to the Industrial Revolution, including the industrializing Third World societies, which, though dominantly agrarian, nevertheless represent the granaries or playgrounds of metropolitan industrial societies.

Key concepts here are work, play, and leisure. Placing a **different explanatory stress** on each or any combination of these can influence how we think about symbolic manipulation sets, symbolic genres, in the types of societies we will consider.

It is, furthermore, a universe of work in which whole communities participate, as of obligation, not optation. The whole community goes through the entire ritual round, whether in terms of total or representative participation. Thus, some rites, such as those of sowing, first fruits, or harvest, may involve everyone, man, woman, and child, others may be focused on specific groups, categories, associations, etc., such as men or women, old or young, one **dan** or another, one association or secret society or another. Yet the whole ritual round adds up to the total participation of the whole community.

Sooner or later, no one is exempt from ritual duty, just as no one is exempt from economic, legal, or political duty. Communal participation, obligation, the passage of the whole society through crises, collective and individual, directly or by proxy, are the hallmarks of "the work of the gods" and sacred human work. Without it profane human work would be, for the community, impossible to conceive, though, no doubt, as history has cruelly demonstrated to those conquered by industrial societies, possible to live, or, at least, exist through.

Yet it can be argued that this "work" is not work, as we in industrial societies know it, but has in both its dimensions, sacred and profane, an element of "play." Insofar as the community and its individual members regard themselves as the masters or "owners" of ritual and liturgy or as representatives of the ancestors or gods who ultimately "own" them, they have authority to introduce, under certain culturally determined conditions, elements of novelty from time to time into the socially inherited deposit of ritual customs.

Liminality, the seclusion period, is a phase peculiarly conducive to such **"ludic"** invention. Perhaps it would be better to regard the distinction between "work" and "play," or better between "work" and "leisure" (which includes but exceeds play *sui generis*), as itself an artifact of the Industrial Revolution, and to see such symbolic-expressive genres as ritual and myth as being at once "work" and "play" or at least as cultural activities in which work and play are intricately interrelated.

Yet it often happens that the historically later can throw light on the earlier, especially when there is a demonstrable sociogenetic connection between them. For **there are undoubtedly "ludic" aspects in "tribal," etc., culture,** especially in the liminal periods of protracted initiation or calendrically based rituals. Such would include joking relationships, sacred games, such as the ball games of the ancient Maya and modern Cherokee, riddles, mock-ordeals, holy fooling and clowning, Trickster tales told in liminal times and places (in or out of ritual contexts), and a host of other types.

The point is, though, that these "play" or "ludic" aspects of tribal and agrarian ritual and myth are, intrinsically, connected with the "work" of the collectivity in performing symbolic actions and manipulating symbolic objects so as to promote and increase fertility of men, crops, and animals, domestic and wild, to cure illness, to avert plague, to obtain success in raiding, to turn boys into men and girls into women, to make chiefs out of commoners, to transform ordinary people into shamans and shamanins, to "cool" those "hot" from the warpath, to ensure the proper succession of seasons and the hunting and agricultural responses of human beings to them, and so forth. Thus the play is in earnest, and has to be within bounds. In the liminal phases and states of tribal and agrarian cultures—in ritual, myth, and legal processes—work and play are hardly distinguishable in many cases.

Work and Play in Contemporary Society

[In contrast,] technical innovations are the products of ideas, the products of what I will call the "liminoid" (the **"-oid"** here, as in asteroid, starlike, ovoid, egg-shaped, etc., derives from Greek *-eidos,* a form, shape, and means "like, resembling"; "liminoid" resembles without being identical with "liminal").

dan Rank.

"Sooner or later, no one is exempt from ritual duty"—There is not much freedom of choice about rituals in traditional society. On the other hand, Turner will show that participation in rituals tends to be optional in modern societies.

Liminality Having laid the groundwork with an account of how work is viewed in traditional societies, Turner now reintroduces liminality, explaining it is part of the playfulness of such a society, but this ludic aspect is part of a larger context which views all of life as a part of the work of the community.

ludic—This term refers to play and to play-like or playful activities that may be a part of work.

"there are undoubtedly 'ludic' aspects in 'tribal,' etc., culture"— Because members of tribal societies relate all of their activities to work, this does not mean that their members never have fun. It is just that "fun" occurs in the context of work-related activities and is seen as part of them.

 The Liminoid

-oid means "resembling." Thus, a "humanoid" is a creature that is not, for one reason or other, human, but resembles humans.

This 15th-c. fresco of a rural scene shows work and play as part of the routine of the community during the harvest.

"the Protestant ethic"—Americans once valued work in some of the same ways as tribal society. However, this code of values is no longer the dominant one in our society.

"symbolic genres, both of the entertainment and instructive sorts"—Drama in particular, and all the forms of entertainment which contain a dramatic element.

"is liminality an adequate label"—Turner's answer will be "no." He will revise what he said in his earlier work about the role of dramatic performance in modern society.

"Leisure is etymologically derived from Old French *leisir*"—In considering what a concept means to society, Turner often discusses the language and word it comes from. By itself, etymology can't explain a concept, but it can contribute to an understanding of it. Here this method suggests that the connotation of "leisure" includes the idea of choice, because it is related to the idea of buying things and selecting the item to purchase.

"But they do this in a much more complicated way"—In our society, creating the liminoid may be a full-time occupation. The creators (artists etc.) have much more individual freedom to create liminoid scenes and do so in very complex ways—in part because they perform these activities only. These artists may criticize the status quo as well as support it. When such creative activities support the values of the culture, they are closer to tribal myths and rituals, and therefore, more genuinely "liminal" than "liminoid."

America's forefathers believed strongly in the set of values known as **the Protestant ethic.** Devotion to work was a Christian virtue; and play, the enemy of work, was reluctantly and charily permitted only to children. Even now, these values are far from extinct in our nation, and the old admonition that play is the devil's handiwork continues to live in secular thought. Although play has now become almost respectable, it is still something in which we "indulge" (as in sexual acts), a form of moral laxness.

Nevertheless, modern industrial or post-industrial societies have shed many of these anti-leisure attitudes. Technological development, political and industrial organization by workers, action by liberal employers, revolutions in many parts of the world, have had the cumulative effect of bringing more leisure into the "free-time" of industrial cultures. In this leisure **symbolic genres, both of the entertainment and instructive sorts,** have proliferated. In my book *The Ritual Process,* I have spoken of some of these as "liminal" phenomena. In view of what I have just said, **is liminality an adequate label** for this set of symbolic activities and forms?

Leisure can be conceived of as a betwixt-and-between, a neither-this-nor-that domain between two spells of work or between occupational and familial and civic activity. **Leisure is etymologically derived from Old French *leisir,*** which itself derives from Latin *licere,* "to be permitted." Interestingly enough, it ultimately comes from the Indo-European base *leik-,* "to offer for sale, bargain," referring to the "liminal" sphere of the market, with its implications of choice, variation, contract—a sphere that has connections, in archaic and tribal religions, with Trickster deities such as Elegba, Eshu, and Hermes. Exchange is more "liminal" than production. Just as when tribesmen make masks, disguise themselves as monsters, heap up disparate ritual symbols, invert or parody profane reality in myths and folk-tales, so do the genres of industrial leisure, the theater, poetry, novel, ballet, film, sport, rock music, classical music, art, pop art, and so on, play with the factors of culture, sometimes assembling them in random, grotesque, improbable, surprising, shocking, usually experimental combinations.

But they do this in a much more complicated way than in the liminality of tribal initiations. They multiply specialized genres of artistic and popular entertainments, mass culture, pop culture, folk culture, high culture, counter-culture, underground culture, etc., as against the relatively limited symbolic genres of "tribal" society, and within each they allow lavish scope to authors, poets, dramatists, painters, sculptors, composers, musicians, actors, comedians, folksingers, rock musicians, "makers" generally, to generate not only weird forms, but also, and not infrequently, models, direct and parabolic or aesopian, that are highly critical of the status quo as a whole or in part. Of course, given diversity as a principle, many artists, in many genres, also buttress, reinforce, and justify the prevailing social and cultural mores and political orders. Those that do so, do so in ways that tend more closely than the critical productions to parallel tribal myths and rituals—they are "liminal" or **"pseudo-" or "post-" "liminal,"** rather than "liminoid."

Satire is a conservative genre because it is pseudo-liminal. Satire exposes, attacks, or derides what it considers to be vices, follies, stupidities, or abuses, but its criteria of judgment are usually the normative structural frame of values. Hence satirical works, like those of Swift, Castlereagh, or Evelyn Waugh, often have **a "ritual of reversal"** form, indicating that disorder is no permanent substitution for order.

A mirror inverts but also reflects an object. It does not break it down into constituents in order to remold it, far less does it annihilate and replace that object. But art and literature often do. **The liminal phases of tribal society invert but do not usually subvert the status quo,** the structural form, of society; reversal underlines that chaos is the alternative to cosmos, so they had better stick to cosmos, that is, the traditional order of culture—though they can for a brief while have a heck of a good time being chaotic, in some saturnalian or lupercalian revelry, some charivari, or institutionalized orgy. But supposedly "entertainment" genres of industrial society are often subversive, lampooning, burlesquing, or subtly putting down the central values of the basic, work-sphere society, or at least of selected sectors of that society. Some of these genres, such as the "legitimate" or "classical" theater, are historically continuous with ritual, and possess something of the sacred seriousness, even the "rites de passage" structure of their antecedents. Nevertheless, crucial differences separate the structure, function, style, scope, and symbology of the liminal in "tribal and agrarian ritual and myth" from what we may perhaps call the "liminoid," or leisure genres, of symbolic forms and action in complex, industrial societies.

This is but one of the **distinctive ways in which the liminal is marked off from the liminoid.** In the 1972 American Anthropological Association Meetings in Toronto, several examples were cited—from modern societies on the fringe of industrial civilizations which bore some resemblance to liminal inversions in tribal societies. But what was striking to me was how even in these "outback" regions optionality dominated the whole process. For example, when the masked mummers of La Have, usually older boys and young married men, known as "belsnicklers," emerge on Christmas Eve to entertain, tease, and fool adults, and to frighten children, they knock at house doors and windows, asking to be "allowed" entrance. Some householders actually refuse to let them in. Now I cannot imagine a situation in which Ndembu, Luvale, Chokwe, or Luchazi masked dancers (peoples I have known and observed), who emerge after the performance of a certain ritual, marking the end of one half of the seclusion period and the beginning of another, to dance in villages and threaten women and children, would be refused entry. Nor do they ask permission to enter; they storm in! Belsnicklers have to "ask for" treats from householders. Makishi (maskers) among Ndembu, Chokwe, etc., demand food and gifts as of right. Optation pervades the liminoid phenomenon, obligation the liminal. One is all play and choice, an entertainment, the other is a matter of deep seriousness, even dread; it is demanding, compulsory (though, indeed, fear provokes nervous laughter from the women, who, if they are touched by the makishi, are believed to contract leprosy, become sterile, or go mad!).

To the contrary, in tribal ritual, even the normally orderly, meek, and "law- abiding" people would be obliged to be disorderly in key rituals, regardless of their temperament and character. The sphere of the optional is in such societies much reduced. Even in liminality, where the bizarre behavior so often remarked upon by anthropologists occurs, the sacra, masks, etc., emerge to view under the guise at least of "collective

"'pseudo-' or 'post-' 'liminal'"— Almost liminal, closer to liminality than to the liminoid.

"a 'ritual of reversal'"—Such rituals are not really liminal, because they do not change the status of their participants or the nature of society. A modern example would be Halloween. (See p. 370.)

"The liminal phases of tribal society invert but do not usually subvert the status quo"—In a rite of passage, the participants glimpse a vision of their society without social barriers, an experience Turner calls *communitas*. However, while changes in society do occur as a result of this experience, they tend to be gradual ones that occur without sweeping it away completely. (See Ch. 31, p. 461f.)

 Choice as a Characteristic of Liminoid Activities

"distinctive ways in which the liminal is marked off from the liminoid"—In this section, Turner contrasts rituals in tribal societies with rituals and ritual-like activities in modern societies. Drawing on examples from his own field work and that of other anthropologists, he shows that the members of these two kinds of societies tend to participate in liminal and liminoid activities, respectively.

The Liminoid as the Domain of the Individual

Liminal versus Liminoid: A Comparison of Characteristics

Bases of Comparison:

1. Kind of Society
2. Frequency of Occurrence
3. Integration into the Social Process
4. Common Meaning for a Group
5. Nature of Criticism

ergic-ludic With play related to work.

representations." If there ever were individual creators and artists, they have been subdued by the general "liminal" emphasis on anonymity and normative communitas, just as the novices and their novice-masters have been. But in the liminoid genres of industrial art, literature, and even science (more truly homologous with tribal liminal thinking than modern art is), great public stress is laid on the individual innovator, the unique person who dares and opts to create. In this lack of stress on individuality, tribal liminality may be seen not as the inverse of tribal normativeness, but as its projection into ritual situations. However, this has to be modified when one looks at actual initiation rituals "on the ground."

I found that, among the Ndembu, despite the novices' being stripped of names, profane rank, and clothes, each emerged as a distinct individual; and there was an element of competitive personal distinctiveness in the fact that the best four novices in the terms of performance during seclusion (in hunting, endurance of ordeal, smartness in answering riddles, cooperativeness, etc.) were given titles in the rites marking their re-aggregation to profane society. For me, this indicated that **in liminality is secreted the seed of the liminoid,** waiting only for major changes in the sociocultural context to set it growing into the branched "candelabra" of manifold liminoid cultural genres.

If one has to, like Jack Horner, pull out a dialectical plum from each and every type of social formation, I would counsel that those who propose to study one of the world's fast disappearing "tribal" societies should **look at the liminal phases of their rituals** in order most precisely to locate the incipient contradiction between communal-anonymous and private-distinctive modes of conceiving principles of sociocultural growth.

In *The Ritual Process,* I noted that

> Liminality, marginality, and structural inferiority are conditions in which are frequently generated myths, symbols, rituals, philosophical systems, and works of art. These cultural forms provide men with a set of templates, models, or paradigms which are, at one level, periodical reclassifications of reality (or, at least, of social experience) and man's relationship to society, nature, and culture. But they are more than (mere cognitive) classifications, since they incite men to action as well as thought. (1969, 128–129)

When I wrote this, I had not yet made the distinction between **ergic-ludic** ritual liminality and anergic-ludic liminoid genres of action and literature. In tribal societies, liminality is often functional, in the sense of being a special duty or performance required in the course of work or activity; its very reversals and inversions tend to compensate for rigidities or unfair-nesses of normative structure. But in industrial society, the *rite de passage* form, built into the calendar and/or modeled on organic processes of maturation and decay, no longer suffices for total societies. Leisure provides the opportunity for a multiplicity of optional, liminoid genres of literature, drama, and sport, which are not conceived of as "antistructure" to normative structure where "antistructure is an auxiliary function of the larger structure" (Sutton-Smith 1972:17).

In the so-called "high culture" of complex societies, the liminoid is not only removed from a *rite de passage* context, it is also "individualized." The solitary artist creates the liminoid phenomena, the collectivity experiences collective liminal symbols. This does not mean that the maker of liminoid symbols, ideas, images, and so on, does so *ex nihilo;* it only means that he is privileged to make free with his social heritage in a way impossible to members of cultures in which the liminal is to a large extent the sacrosanct.

When we compare liminal with liminoid processes and phenomena, then we find crucial differences as well as similarities. Let me try to set some of these out.

1. Liminal phenomena tend to predominate in tribal and early agrarian societies.
2. Liminal phenomena tend to be collective, concerned with calendrical, biological,

social-structural rhythms or with crises in social processes, whether these result from internal adjustments or external adaptations or remedial measures. Thus they appear at what may be called "natural breaks," natural disjunctions in the flow of natural and social processes. They are thus enforced by sociocultural "necessity," but they contain *in nuce* "freedom" and the potentiality for the formation of new ideas, symbols, models, beliefs. Liminoid phenomena may be collective (and when they are so are often directly derived from liminal antecedents), but are more characteristically individual products, though they often have collective or "mass" effects. They are not cyclical, but continuously generated, though in the times and places apart from work settings assigned to "leisure" activities.

3. Liminal phenomena are centrally integrated into the total social process, forming with all its other aspects a complete whole, and representing its necessary negativity and subjunctivity. Liminoid phenomena develop apart from the central economic and political processes, along the margins, in the interfaces and interstices of central and servicing institutions—they are plural, fragmentary, and experimental in character.

Andrea Robbins and Max Becher, *German Indian*. Modern values of work and leisure give individuals more choices for how they will spend their time. Germans, influenced by the novels of Karl May, are fascinated by American Indians and stage events in which they act out select aspects of what they term "Indian life."

4. Liminal phenomena tend to confront investigators rather after the manner of Durkheim's "collective representations," symbols having **a common intellectual and emotional meaning** for all the members of a given group. They reflect, on probing, the history of the group, i.e., its collective experience, over time. They differ from preliminal or postliminal collective representations in that they are often reversals, inversions, disguises, negations, antitheses of quotidian, "positive," or "profane" collective representations. But they share their mass, collective character.

Liminoid phenomena tend to be more idiosyncratic or quirky, to be generated by specific named individuals and in particular groups—"schools," circles, and coteries. They have to compete with one another for general recognition and are thought of at first as ludic offerings placed for sale on the "free" market—this is at least true of liminoid phenomena in nascent capitalistic and democratic-liberal societies. Their symbols are closer to the personal-psychological than to the "objective-social" typological pole.

5. Liminal phenomena tend to be ultimately **eufunctional** even when seemingly "inversive" for the working of the social structure, ways of making it work without too much friction.

Liminoid phenomena, on the other hand, are often parts of social critiques or even revolutionary manifestoes—books, plays, paintings, films, etc., exposing the injustices, inefficiencies, and immoralities of the mainstream economic and political structures and organizations.

In complex modern societies **both types coexist** in a sort of cultural pluralism. But the liminal—found in the activities of churches, sects, and movements, in the initiation rites of clubs, fraternities, masonic orders and other secret societies, etc.—is no longer society-wide. Nor are liminoid phenomena, which tend to be the **leisure genres** of art, sport, pastimes, games, etc., practiced by and for particular groups, categories, segments, and sectors of large-scale industrial societies of all types. But for most people the liminoid is still felt to be freer than the liminal, a matter of choice, not obligation. The liminoid is more like a commodity—indeed, often is a commodity, which one selects and pays for—than the liminal, which elicits loyalty and is bound up with one's membership or desired membership in some highly corporate group. **One works at the liminal, one plays with the liminoid.**

There may be much moral pressure to go to church or synagogue, whereas one queues up at the box office to see a play by Beckett, a performance by Mort Sahl, a Superbowl Game, a symphony concert, or an art exhibition. And if one plays golf, goes yachting, or climbs mountains, one often needs to buy expensive equipment or pay for club membership. Of course, there are also all kinds of "free" liminoid performances and entertainments—Mardi Gras, charivari, home entertainments of various kinds— but these already have something of the stamp of the liminal upon them, and quite often they are the cultural debris of some unforgotten liminal ritual. There are permanent "liminoid" settings and spaces, too—bars, pubs, some cafes, social clubs, etc. But when clubs become exclusivist they tend to generate rites of passage, with the liminal a condition of entrance into the "liminoid" realm.

Further Reading

Gluckman, Max. *Politics, Law and Ritual in Tribal Society.* Chicago, IL: Aldine Publishing Company, 1965.

Turner, Victor. *The Forest of Symbols: Aspects of Ndembu Ritual.* Ithaca, NY: Cornell University Press, 1967.

Sidebar notes:

"a common intellectual and emotional meaning"—In modern society, each person chooses from a wide variety of entertainments. Thus, at any given time, the members of the society are engaged in a diverse range of activities. In traditional society, there is a limited number of genres, so people are more likely to be engaged in the same activity at any given time. An analogy can be made to television before cable. On any given night, Americans were likely to be watching the same shows. As a result, people with very different tastes and interests felt unified in their shared experiences of, say, Lucy Ricardo's baby, or what happened on the Ponderosa.

eufunctional Helping a society to run smoothly.

 Liminal and Liminoid in Modern Complex Societies

"both types coexist"—Modern liminality, like that in traditional societies, is bound up with a group.

"leisure genres"—The liminoid is likely to be connected with leisure, and may be associated with, or may itself be, a commodity.

"One works at the liminal, one plays with the liminoid"—In this explanation, Turner returns to the distinction between the views of work in traditional and modern society.

Demeter and Persephone

The Homeric Hymn to Demeter

27

WHAT TO EXPECT . . . Demeter, the Greek goddess of grain and agriculture, was an important figure in Greek religion, and the *Hymn* in this chapter tells the story of the struggle that was said to lie behind the founding of her temple at Eleusis, near Athens. According to this myth, Demeter contended with Zeus, the father of the gods, to have a say in the terms under which her daughter Persephone was to marry. As you read, compare Demeter to the other Greek figure who struggled against the power of Zeus, Prometheus. Consider the story according to the stages represented by Joseph Campbell as occurring in the journey of the hero: what difficulties arise in such an analysis because the hero you are considering is a woman?

The worship of Demeter was supposed to confer special blessings in the afterlife, and thus it reflects Greek beliefs with respect to death and a person's fate after it. In addition, this story about Demeter reflects cultural values related to marriage and the role of women. Consider the story of Demeter and Persephone in the light of what you have read in this book about the Greek gender gap (Ch. 3, p. 29).

Claude Levi-Strauss has argued that one of the main motifs running through all of Greek myth is a tension between undervaluing kinship and overvaluing it (Ch. 20, p. 284ff). Relate the story of Demeter and Persephone to these themes.

The *Hymn to Demeter* was a working version of a myth: a poem believed to have been used at ceremonies in honor of the goddess, at her shrine in Eleusis, a town near Athens in Greece. (For more on working myths, see Ch. 25, p. 360.) It was composed before the end of the seventh century B.C.E. In fact, the story told in the hymn explains the significance of Eleusis: it was the place Demeter came to when she went to earth to look for her daughter, Persephone. The Eleusinians built a temple for Demeter, and thus her visit led to the origin of her worship there. The main celebration took place in early autumn, when the drought of summer was ending and the fields were becoming green. This was the time of plowing and of sowing grain. As Helene Foley notes in her commentary on the *Hymn,* "In Greece the grain continues to grow after being sown in the fall, if slowly, throughout the winter season; growth then quickens in the spring" (59).

The time of year corresponds to the *Hymn*'s description of the end of the earth's infertility after Persephone returns from the underworld. The temple at Eleusis dates back to about 1300 B.C.E., and may have belonged to an even earlier fertility goddess than Demeter. There were also other rituals and celebrations of Demeter at Athens in the spring.

The worship of Demeter began as a local cult at Eleusis; that is, it was closed to anyone who was not Athenian or Eleusinian. But in 760 B.C.E., there was a famine in all of Greece. The oracle at Delphi told the Athenians to make a sacrificial offering to Demeter at Eleusis, not just for themselves, but for all the Greeks. This brought an end to the famine. As a result, all Greeks began to send the first fruits of their harvest to Demeter at Eleusis. The local cult of Demeter became one which was open to, and respected by, all Greeks.

THE POLITICAL SIGNIFICANCE OF THE MYTH AND CULT OF DEMETER

Eleusis was originally an independent state that was conquered by Athens because it was a rich source of grain. As the urban population of Athens grew in the seventh and sixth centuries B.C.E., it could no longer provide enough food for all its citizens, so it conquered Eleusis and exploited her agricultural bounty. The *Hymn to Demeter* represents the Eleusinian point of view, considering agricultural life and rural values superior to urban civilization. In the peace treaty in which Eleusis accepted Athenian domination, it maintained control of the mysteries of Demeter. The annual ceremony gave Eleusinians an opportunity to assert the value of their way of life. The *Hymn*, thought to be an integral part of the mysteries, represented agriculture as the source of civilization and asserted the autonomy and independence of Eleusis despite Athenian rule.

Despite its clear reference to a Homeric social world and its ties to Eleusis and the rituals practiced there, the *Hymn* is difficult to date. It concentrates on Eleusis and doesn't mention the parts of the ritual of Demeter which were performed at Athens, probably as part of an effort to recapture the mythical period of the foundation of the Mysteries, as Foley suggests.

THE CULT OF DEMETER AND ITS MYSTERIES

We don't know as much as we wish about the ceremony in which the *Hymn* was used because much of it was secret. The parts we know about involved a procession and a reenactment of the myth of Demeter and Persephone. Foley summarizes the details of the ritual:

- The Festival lasted a week or more in Boedromion (September, October).
- On the 13th of the month, the young men of military age left Athens and went to Eleusis to escort certain sacred objects (we don't know what they were) back to Athens.
- On the 15th, the Mysteries began with a proclamation at the Agora in Athens.
- On the 16th, those to be initiated purified themselves by bathing in the bay of Phaleron.
- On the 19th, the initiands processed on the Sacred Way from Athens to Eleusis, carrying the sacred objects and fasting on their journey. Ceremonies were performed at the bridge over the river at the boundary between Eleusis and Athens, including winding yellow woolen thread around the right hand and left leg of each initiand, and ritual bathing in the Kephisos River. When the procession arrived at Eleusis, there was a ritual meal and an all-night celebration that involved songs with obscene lyrics and dance. This was open only to women.
- The actual Mysteries themselves were conducted in the Telesterion at Eleusis, a hall that held several thousand people. We know they included drinking a concoction of barley, water, and herbs, and activities involving the Anaktoron, a small rectangular stone structure within the Telesterion with a fire burning at its top. The ceremony took place in darkness until the Anaktoron opened, and the chief priest appeared. At this point, the abduction of Persephone and the wanderings of Demeter are thought to have been reenacted, perhaps in a way that involved the Homeric *Hymn* included in this chapter (66–69).

Only those who had been initiated into the cult knew its secret practices, and they were not allowed to tell. Cults like this are known as mystery religions; only those who have been initiated into the mysteries reap their benefits.

The accounts gathered about the cult of Demeter suggest that it promised a privileged fate after death to its followers, and only to them. Through the cult, the worshippers of Demeter achieved a feeling of closeness to the gods. As a result, they felt that they would obtain blessings in the afterlife.

MYTHS AFFECT AND REFLECT OUR VIEW OF REALITY

Myths show how people think. In particular, myths can express how people feel about their bodies, their world, and each other. At the heart of these differences is how myths portray human beings. Some represent them as good; others show them as fundamentally wicked. Many mythological systems represent humans as having a body and a soul, but for some, these two aspects of human beings are closer in nature than for others.

Greeks of Homer's time tended to be monists who believed that a soul and body are really one inseparable substance, the soul being the way the body moves or acts. Thus, for a monist, when the body dies, the soul also is destroyed or recycled, like the other elements of the self. All that remains is a shade or pale ghost of the individual, and it lives a pale reflection of its former life, powerless and cut off from all its capabilities and achievements. The Greeks believed that the afterlife was such a grim place. We get a glimpse of it in the *Odyssey*, when Odysseus visits Hades and talks to the great Greek hero Achilles. That hero describes his fate as follows: "Better, I say, to break sod as a farm hand for some poor country man, on iron rations, than lord it over the exhausted dead."[1] Certainly Achilles deserved praise and glory, not punishment. And in fact, the fate of the dead in Hades is not, for the most part, a punishment, but a kind of shadow-life. They do not suffer; they are "exhausted."

Dualists, on the other hand, believe that the soul and body are separate. There are different degrees of dualism: some dualists believe that the soul and body are completely different, and only the soul survives after death. Others think that the body too survives, but in a different way, in a more spiritual form.

The myth of Demeter represents a change in perspective in Greek myth, toward a kind of dualism, because it suggests that the soul is saved not through the activities of the body, but through the knowledge obtained through the experience of the mysteries. In this respect, the worship of Demeter can be characterized as gnostic, from the Greek word $\gamma\nu\tilde{\omega}\sigma\iota\varsigma$ (*gnosis*) or "knowledge." Gnostic religions are based on a secret teaching or gnosis that is revealed only to initiates. Those who share the gnosis can achieve salvation, but the "ignorant" are excluded from it. Gnostics also believe that the soul is divine in origin, and that it has fallen from a higher world. The only way for the soul to return to its previous elevated state is through being initiated into the gnosis.

The followers of Demeter shared some, but not all aspects of this dualistic belief: like most fertility cults, her worship emphasized a cycle of birth, growth, and death related to the development of the seed in the ground. This seems different from the gnostic view that the soul moves in a straight line out of the lower state of this world back to its divine origins. However, followers of Demeter did seem to believe that they could achieve personal salvation of a sort not available to others through knowledge that was an otherworldly secret. This implies a kind of disregard for obtaining salvation through, say, performing good works in this world or having a more generalized faith in a god. The effect, then, of such a belief is to decrease the value of what cult members do on earth, and to emphasize what they know.

Gnosticism is interesting because it does not always produce its own mythology. Sometimes, gnostics just reinterpret existing stories to suggest a "secret" teaching behind a public form of

---

[1]Fitzgerald translation, book 11.544–6.

worship. As time went on, there arose more extreme forms of gnostic dualism. Docetism is a form of gnosticism that maintains that our earthly life is only an apparition or a shadow of real, divine life. According to docetism (from the Greek verb $\delta o\varkappa \varepsilon \tilde{\iota} \nu$, *dokein,* "to seem"), this world only seems real; the only reality is divine, and the best approach to living in this earthly world is to escape from its illusions, either by living a very simple life, *asceticism,* or by getting as much pleasure as possible, hedonism, until the time when the illusion passes and the initiate can enter true reality of the gnosis.

Myths show people how to behave by giving them heroes to look up to and imitate. If myths show heroes abstaining from food or sexual involvements to achieve success, then they reflect a set of values that are dualistic, suggesting opposition between body and soul, and superiority of the soul. Dualism, if it is very radical, can suggest that people don't need to care about what happens in the world of the body at all: all that matters is the world of the soul.

Gnosticism and docetism were at their height from the second century B.C.E. to the second century C.E. However, there were also earlier appearances of gnostic and docetist beliefs. A line in Homer's *Odyssey* tells us that the real Heracles lives among the gods, but his image can be found in Hades.[2] Stesichorus wrote a poem about Helen of Troy in which he claims that the real Helen never went to Troy with Paris, rather the Trojan War was caused by an image or a shadow of Helen.[3] Gnosticism is not in itself a single religion, but it is a way of looking at the world that attaches itself to different mythologies or belief systems. Thus there were pagan gnostics, Jewish gnostics, and Christian gnostics. Christian gnostics believed that Jesus Christ was purely God and did not die on the cross, but only seemed to participate in this world. Gnosticism and docetism are alive and well today and can be found in branches of all the major religions, as well as in unrelated cults, philosophies, and churches. Since gnosticism is a secret worship, followers of these cults will often deny any such characterization.

THE BACKGROUND OF THE STORY OF DEMETER

Demeter was the Greek goddess of grain and agriculture. She is worshipped with her daughter Persephone, or $K \acute{o} \rho \eta$ (*Kore*) meaning "girl," who represents the life force of the grain and disappears from the earth when the seed is put into the ground to die (as seed) and be born again (as grain).

The seed is planted in the ground when it is dormant; humans are buried in the ground when they are dead. In 1890, Sir James Frazer wrote a thirteen-volume study of myth and ritual connected with vegetation gods, *The Golden Bough.* In it, he suggested that since Demeter revitalizes the seed, she became associated with giving new life to the dead. This would explain her association with Aidoneus (Hades), the god of the dead, in this story, which makes her the death-god's mother-in-law.

GREEK MARRIAGE CUSTOMS

The *Hymn to Demeter* describes what in some ways was a typical Greek marriage, at least from the point of view of the wife. Greek women and men entered marriage at very different ages. Men tended to marry when they had already established themselves, at 30 or so. Women, on the other hand, married a few years after menarche, the start of their menstrual period, at the age of 16 to 18; Philip Slater puts the age of marriage even younger, at 14. It was thought, wrongly, that a woman would produce better, healthier children if she were very young. We now

---

[2](*Odyssey* 11.602): The *Odyssey* dates from about 750 B.C.E., but this line may have been added later.
[3]Stesichorus lived from about 630 to 550 B.C.E.

know that adolescent women's bodies have not yet stopped growing, and their underdevelopment is likely to harm both the mothers and their children. This meant that a husband and wife were intrinsically incompatible because of their levels of maturity and experience. They lived very separate lives, staying in different parts of the house. Wives lived in the women's quarters, and had more in common with their children than their husbands.

Although the story in the *Hymn to Demeter* has often been called a rape, the *Hymn* makes it clear that it was also a marriage. Persephone is betrothed by her father, Zeus, to his brother, Aidoneus. She is not consulted; her intended husband is old enough to be her father. However, these conditions were quite typical of marriages in Greece at this time. In fact, vase paintings and statues from the time period of the *Hymn* often portray Aidoneus and Persephone as a loving couple, the king and queen of Hades; Demeter is also portrayed as blessing their marriage. The *Hymn* gives us much the same perspective. Near the beginning of the story, Helios tells Demeter, who is distraught at the loss of her daughter, "Not an unseemly bridegroom among immortals is Aidoneus, Lord of Many" (p. 393). Near the end, Aidoneus tells Persephone, "I shall not be an unfitting husband among the immortals, as I am father Zeus' own brother. When you are here you shall be mistress of everything which lives and moves; your honors among the immortals shall be the greatest, and those who wrong you shall always be punished, if they do not propitiate your spirit with sacrifices, performing sacred rites and making due offerings" (p. 399). He sounds much more like a wooer pleading his case with his intended bride than a rapist imposing his will. In fact, if there is blame for Persephone's fate, the *Hymn* attaches it only to Zeus, the originator of the betrothal. Rhea, Demeter's mother tells her, "Come and do not nurse unrelenting anger against Kronion (Zeus), lord of dark clouds; Soon make the life-giving seed grow for men" (p. 401).

THE STYLE OF THE POEM

The *Hymn to Demeter* was composed in the style of Homer. Homer was an oral poet, who would perform his works from memory, creating them on the spot for his audience. He used modular units called *formulas* for building his poems. Each time a poem was performed, it was slightly different, because the poet would build it according to his moods and the response of his audience. You will see the formulas Homer's followers used in the poem. In the first few lines, these include "lovely-haired," which is used of Demeter, "slender-ankled" of Persephone, and "far-seeing and loud-thundering" of Zeus. The story also repeats longer sections, like "the many-named son of Kronos carried her away against her will." Such repetitions were very pleasing to their original audience, which enjoyed noticing repetitions as they listened. They are less pleasing to us who read the story in written form, so the translator of this *Hymn* has given us enough repetition to give us the flavor of the *Hymn*'s style, but not as much as is in the original.

In addition, like many works that are orally composed, the *Hymn to Demeter* is full of names. The oral poet showed his virtuosity by weaving into the poem all the names he could think of, even those of minor characters. In addition, to make the names fit the rhythm of the poem, he often used different forms or versions of names. For instance, he calls Demeter by her own name as well as Deo and Dos. The names were a delight to the poet's original audience, who knew them from having heard many such stories, but they often cause difficulties for modern readers.

THE GREEK GENDER GAP AND THE *HYMN TO DEMETER*

In the Introduction to Chapter 3 (p. 28), we discussed the attitude toward women as represented in Greek religion, notably in Hesiod's *Works and Days* and its version of the story of Pandora. We argued that there was a gender gap in Greek society that was reflected in the struggles between

Zeus and Hera in Greek mythology. Helene Foley states that "[t]he Hymn [to Demeter] repeats the pattern of sexual tensions among male and female deities found in Hesiod and prefigures the similar tensions that pervade Aeschylus' *Oresteia*" (116). The *Hymn* portrays the struggle of the mother, Demeter, to hold on to her child against the wishes of the father. Ultimately, Demeter has to give in to Zeus' "patriarchal agenda" (Foley 169), but the *Hymn,* and the ritual at Eleusis, give elaborate testimony to the power of her resistance, and, as a result, to her limited autonomy. Clay notes that the *Hymn* ultimately portrays the limitation of the power of Demeter. She suggests that this is because, as a local cult, the worship of Demeter at Eleusis represented a threat to the worship of the Panhellenic Olympian gods. "As a whole," she says, "the Hymn to Demeter may be understood as an attempt to integrate, and hence to absorb, the cult of Demeter and the message of Eleusis into the Olympian cosmos" (265), represented by the poetry of Homer and Hesiod. Thus constituted, the Eleusinian Mysteries were like other rituals: they provided a space, as Victor Turner would say, "to fool around with the factors of cultural construction." This permitted the symbolic expression of attitudes and emotions that went against the established structure of society, but after they were over, the society was able to function again, with renewed purpose and vigor. What remains are the "special ties [among participants] which persist after the rites are over, even into old age." For Turner's discussion of ritual, see Chapter 26, p. 373.

FEMINIST MEANINGS OF THE *HYMN*

For some time, the *Hymn to Demeter* has provided an image of women's values and perspectives for society. In 1861, Johann Jakob Bachofen suggested that in the remote past, Greece was a matriarchy, a society organized to protect the union of women and their children. He believed that the *Hymn* was not written during this time period, but later, when the matriarchy had been replaced by patriarchy, the rule of men. Bachofen felt the *Hymn* expressed longing for the now-vanished era of feminine authority and sharing, a period of closeness to nature and reliance on natural instincts and emotions. Unfortunately, he based his views on stories like the *Hymn to Demeter*, so his theories had a certain circularity. His ideas remain, however, as an indication of an important element in the Demeter story: the myth does express an alternative set of values that focuses on the importance of the mother-daughter bond and of women's emotions and priorities. Today, commentators doubt that this reflects a particular phase of Greek history; some are more inclined to think that the emotions expressed in the *Hymn* probably represent a part of human longing that may well be present in most eras of human history: the longing for the anima or feminine aspect of the soul, as described by Jung (see Ch. 32, p. 479).

For some women, the myth of Demeter and Persephone has been a source of strength

Demeter and Core, "Exaltation of the Flower." Greek relief from Pharsale, 470–460 B.C.E. For some modern readers, the story of Demeter represents the depth and strength of the relationship between mother and daughter.

because of the value it attaches to women and their emotions. To others, the *Hymn* is an account of rape which represents the intrusion of men into the peaceful lives and loves of women, the triumph of patriarchy, and the limitation of religion based on the feminine principle. Feminist thinkers do not necessarily believe that the myth describes a historical period, but rather they use it to reimagine society and their own role in it. This involves not allowing themselves to be defined only by their relationships to men, but attaching more importance to interactions between women. For example, the poet Alma Luz Villaneuva represents a mother as finding a stronger sense of herself through loving her daughter: ". . . your body slid out of mine; daughter. Loving you, I loved myself—badly, exquisitely."[4] Through reimaginings like this, the myth of Demeter and Persephone is very much alive today, because it provides us with an image which at the same time represents and transforms roles in our society.

Hymn to Demeter

The Abduction in the Meadow

I begin to sing of lovely-haired **Demeter,** the goddess august,
of her and her **slender-ankled daughter** whom **Zeus,**
far-seeing and loud-thundering, gave to Aidoneus to abduct.
Away from her mother of the golden sword and the splendid fruit
she played with the full-bosomed daughters of Okeanos, 5
gathering flowers, roses, crocuses, and beautiful violets
all over a soft meadow; irises, too, and hyacinths she picked,
and narcissus, which **Gaia,** pleasing the All-receiver,
made blossom there, by the will of Zeus, for a girl with a flower's
    beauty.
A lure it was, wondrous and radiant, and a marvel to be seen 10
by immortal gods and mortal men.
A hundred stems of sweet-smelling blossoms
grew from its roots. The wide sky above
and the whole earth and the briny swell of the sea laughed.
She was dazzled and reached out with both hands at once. 15
to take the pretty bauble; Earth with its wide roads gaped
and then over the Nysian field the lord and All-receiver,
the many-named son of Kronos, sprang out upon her with
    his immortal horses.
Against her will he seized her and on his golden chariot
carried her away as she wailed; and she raised a shrill cry, 20
calling upon father **Kronides,** the highest and the best.
None of the immortals or of mortal men heard
her voice, not even the olive-trees bearing splendid fruit.
Only the gentle-tempered daughter of Persaios,
Hekate of the shining headband, heard from her cave, 25
and lord **Helios,** the splendid son of Hyperion, heard
the maiden calling father Kronides; he sat
apart from the gods away in the temple of prayers,
accepting beautiful sacrifices from mortal men.
By Zeus' counsels, his brother, the All-receiver 30
and Ruler of Many, Kronos' son of many names,

This text comes from: *The Homeric Hymns.**

Demeter Also called Dos and Deo in what follows; goddess of grain.

slender-ankled daughter—Persephone, daughter of Demeter and Zeus.

"Zeus. . . gave to Aidoneus to abduct"—Aidoneus abducted her, but Zeus, her father, gave her to him.

Aidoneus Another form of the name Hades, god of the underworld. Aidoneus was Zeus' brother, and thus Persephone's uncle.

Gaia The Earth.

"the many-named son of Kronos—Aidoneus (Hades).

"Against her will he seized her"—This story is sometimes called the rape of Persephone; it reflects how the arranged marriage felt to Persephone.

Kronides Son of Kronos; another name for Zeus.

Hekate A goddess of the moon.

Helios God of the sun.

[4]Alma Luz Villaneuva, "The Crux," in Christine Downing, ed., *The Long Journey Home* (Boston: Shambhala, 1994), 119.
* *The Homeric Hymns,* Trans., Apostolos N. Athanassakis, pp. 1–15. © 1976. Reprinted with permission of The Johns Hopkins University Press.

was carrying her away with his immortal horses, against her will.
So while the goddess looked upon the earth and the starry sky
and the swift-flowing sea teeming with fish
and the rays of the sun and still hoped to see
her loving mother and the races of gods immortal,   35
hope charmed her great mind, despite her grief.

Demeter Seeks Her Daughter

The peaks of the mountains and the depths of the sea resounded
with her immortal voice, and her mighty mother heard her.
A sharp pain gripped her heart, and **she tore**   40
the headband round her divine hair with her own hands.
From both of her shoulders she cast down her dark veil
and rushed like a bird over the nourishing land and the sea,
searching; but **none of the gods or mortal men
wanted to tell her the truth** and none   45
of the birds of omen came to her as truthful messenger.
For **nine days** then all over the earth mighty **Deo**
roamed about with **bright torches** in her hands,
and in her sorrow never tasted ambrosia
or nectar sweet to drink, and never bathed her skin.   50
But when the tenth light-bringing Dawn came to her,
Hekate carrying a light in her hands, met her,
and with loud voice spoke to her and told her the news:
"Mighty Demeter, bringer of seasons and splendid gifts,
which of the heavenly gods or of mortal men   55
seized Persephone and pierced with sorrow your dear heart?
For I heard a voice but did not see with my eyes
who it was; I am quickly telling you the whole truth."
Thus spoke Hekate. And to her the **daughter of lovely-haired Rhea**
answered not a word, but **with her** she sped away   60
swiftly, holding the bright torches in her hands.
They came to Helios, watcher of gods and men,
and stood near his horses, and the illustrious goddess made a plea:
"Helios, do have respect for me as a goddess, if I ever
cheered your heart and soul by word or deed.   65
Through the barren ether I heard the shrieking voice
of my daughter famous for her beauty, a sweet flower at birth,
as if she were being overcome by force, but I saw nothing.
And since you do gaze down upon the whole earth
and sea and cast your rays through the bright ether,   70
tell me truly if you have seen anywhere
what god or even mortal man in my absence
seized by force my dear child and went away."
Thus she spoke and **Hyperionides** gave her an answer:
"Lady Demeter, daughter of lovely-haired Rhea,   75
you shall know; for I greatly reverence and pity you
in your grief for your slender-ankled child; no other immortal
is to be blamed save cloud-gathering Zeus

"So while the goddess looked upon the earth"—Persephone is looking in vain for her mother.

"she tore the headband"—A sign of mourning, as are the rejection of eating and bathing.

"none of the gods or mortal men wanted to tell her the truth"—The silence of gods and humans suggests that Zeus was within his rights in giving his daughter to Aidoneus.

"nine days"—A traditional period of mourning.

Deo Another name for Demeter, a diminutive.

"bright torches"—A torchlight procession was celebrated at Athens in honor of Demeter.

"Hekate carrying a light"—The torch symbolizes the moon goddess' reflected light.

"daughter of . . . Rhea"—Demeter. To the original Greek audience these names would have all been familiar.

"with her"—Demeter and Hekate together visit Helios, whose role here is the wise old man. He has seen what happened to Persephone and prophecies her future. See Jung, Ch. 32, p. 469, for an account of the importance of the Senex or wise old man in myth.

Hyperionides Another name for Helios, the sun. It means he was the son of Hyperion.

who gave her to Hades, his own brother, to become
his buxom bride. He seized her and with his horses   80
carried her crying loud down to misty darkness.
But, Goddess, stop your great wailing; you mustn't give
yourself to grief so great and fruitless. **Not an unseemly**
bridegroom among immortals is Aidoneus, Lord of Many,
your own brother from the same seed; to his share fell   85
honor when in the beginning a triple division was made,
and he dwells among those over whom his lot made him lord."
With these words, he called upon his horses, and at his command
speedily, like long-winged birds, they drew the swift chariot,
as a pain more awful and savage reached Demeter's soul.   90

From Olympus to Eleusis

Afterwards, angered with Kronion, lord of black clouds,
she withdrew from the assembly of the gods and from lofty
   Olympus
and went through the cities of men and the wealth of their labors,
tearing at her fair form for a long time; no man
or deep-girded woman looking at her knew who she was   95
before she reached the house of prudent Keleos,
who then was lord of **Eleusis,** a town rich in sacrifices.
Grieving in her dear heart, she sat near the road,
at Parthenion, the well from which the citizens drew water,
in the shade of a bushy olive-tree which grew above it.   100
She looked like an old woman born a long time ago
and barred from childbearing and the gifts of wreath-loving
   Aphrodite,
even as are nurses for the children of law-tending
kings and keepers of the storerooms in their bustling mansions.
The daughters of **Keleos Eleusinides** saw her   105
as they were coming to fetch easily-drawn water
in copper vessels to their father's dear halls,
four of them in their maidenly bloom, like goddesses,
Kallidike, Kleisidike and Demo the lovely,
and Kallithoe, who was the eldest of them all.   110
They did not know who she was; it is hard for mortals to see divinity.
Standing near they addressed her with winged words:
"Old woman, whence and from what older generation do you come?
Why have you wandered away from the city and not approached
a house; there in the shadowy halls live   115
women of your age and even younger ones
who will treat you kindly in both word and deed."
After these words, the mighty goddess answered:
"Dear children, whoever of ladylike women you are,
I greet you and will explain; indeed it is fitting   120
to tell you the truth, since you are asking.
Dos is the name which my mighty mother gave me.
And now from **Crete** on the broad back of the sea

"Not an unseemly bridegroom"—Hades will echo these words in pleading his case to Demeter at the end of the poem.

"your own brother"—Zeus, Demeter, and Aidoneus were siblings. Thus the relationship between Demeter and Zeus was between a brother and sister. The Greeks no longer permitted such liaisons, but they had been accepted at one time.

Gian Lorenzo Bernini (1598–1680), *Rape of Persephone*.

"she withdrew from the assembly of the gods"—Stories of withdrawal have the same pattern. The hero (Demeter, Achilles) withdraws, causing devastation, ambassadors are sent and rejected, reconciliation eventually takes place, but a substitute loses his/her life in the process (Persephone, Patroclus).

Eleusis   Demeter's chief temple was there, in commemoration of the hospitality of the Eleusinians, as is about to be described.

"She looked like an old woman"—Demeter disguises her appearance during her visit to earth. Her new form reflects her emotional condition, that of a woman whose ability to mother has passed away.

Keleos Eleusinides   Keleos from Eleusis.

"They did not know who she was"—The daughters of Keleos do not recognize Demeter as a goddess. There are many stories of Greek gods appearing to humans in disguise.

"who will treat you kindly in both word and deed"—It was Greek custom to treat a stranger with hospitality, even before she revealed her name.

Crete This island seems to figure strongly in the imaginations of Greeks at this time. In Homer's *Odyssey*, when Odysseus wants to disguise himself, he also tells stories in which he comes from Crete.

"carried me off against my will"— Stories of pirates' kidnapping people for ransom were not uncommon at this time. Although Demeter's story about herself is a lie, it accurately conveys the emotions she has endured. However, it is not for her own abduction that she is mourning, but her daughter's.

"in such tasks as befit a woman past her prime"—The main accomplishment of Greek women was the bearing of children. After Demeter loses her daughter Persephone, she immediately seeks out another child to take care of.

Triptolemos According to tradition, the son of Keleos who receives the gift of agriculture from Demeter and conveys it to all humankind. He appears on a votive relief found in the temple at Eleusis (see p. 401), but his role is not described in the *Hymn*. Foley suggests that this may be to lessen emphasis on the local aspects of Demeter's story and render it more meaningful to a Panhellenic audience (a broad audience all over Greece).

"each will receive you, for indeed you look like a goddess"—Despite all Demeter has been through, her divine nature shines through her earthly disguise.

I came unwillingly; marauding men by brute force
carried me off against my will, and later   125
they landed their swift ship at Thorikos, where the women
came out in a body and the men themselves
prepared a meal by the stern-cables of the ship.
But my heart had no desire for the evening's sweet meal;
I eluded them and, rushing through the black land,   130
I fled my reckless masters, so that they might not enjoy
the benefit of my price, since, like thieves, they carried me across
    the sea.
So I have wandered to this place and know not at all
what land this is and what men live in it.
But may all who dwell in the Olympian halls   135
grant you men to wed and children to bear
as your parents wish; and now have mercy on me, maidens
and, dear children, kindly let me go to someone's house,
a man's and a woman's, to work for them
in such tasks as befit a woman past her prime.   140
I shall be a good nurse to a new-born child,
holding him in my arms; I shall take care of the house,
and make the master's bed in the innermost part
of the well-built chamber and mind his wife's work."
So said the goddess, and forthwith Kallidike, still a pure virgin   145
and the most beautiful of Keleos' daughters, replied:
"Good mother, men must take the gifts of the gods
even when they bring them pain, since gods are truly much
    stronger.
I shall advise you clearly and give you the names
of the men who have great power and honor in this place;   150
these are leaders of the people who defend the towers
of the city by their counsels and straight judgments.
They are **Triptolemos,** shrewd in counsel, and Dioklos,
Polyxeinos and Eumolpos, untainted by blame,
Dolichos and our manly father,   155
and everyone has a wife managing his mansion.
No woman there, when she first looks upon you,
will dishonor your appearance and remove you from the mansion,
but **each will receive you, for indeed you look like a goddess.**
If you wish, wait here for us to go to the mansion   160
of our father and tell our deep-girded mother, Metaneira,
all these things from beginning to end, hoping that
she will bid you come to our mansion and not search for
    another's.
A growing son is being reared in the well-built mansion,
born late in her life, much wished for and welcome.   165
If you should bring him up to reach puberty,
some tender woman seeing you could easily
be envious; such rewards for rearing him she'll give you."
So she spoke, and the goddess nodded her head in assent,
and they proudly carried their shining vessels filled with water.   170

In the House of Keleos and Metaneira

Swiftly they reached their father's great mansion and quickly told
their mother what they had seen and heard. And she commanded
    them
to go forthwith and invite her to come for copious wages.
And they, **as deer or heifers** in the season of spring,
sated in their hearts with pasture **frisk over a meadow,**   175
held up the folds of their lovely robes
and **darted** along the hollow wagon-road, as their flowing hair
tossed about their shoulders, like the flowers of the crocus.
They met the glorious goddess near the road where
they had left her before; and then they led her to their father's   180
house. And the goddess walked behind them, brooding
in her dear heart, with her head covered, while a dark
cloak swirled about her tender feet.
Soon they reached the house of Zeus-cherished Keleos
and through the portico they went where **their lady mother**   185
sat by a pillar, which supported the close-fitted roof,
holding a child, a young blossom, on her lap; they ran
near her, and the goddess stepped on the threshold and touched
the roof with her head and filled the doorway with divine radiance.
Awe, reverence and pale fear seized the mother;   190
and she yielded her seat to the goddess and asked her to sit.
But Demeter, the bringer of seasons and splendid gifts,
did not want to sit on the lustrous seat;
she kept silent and cast down her beautiful eyes
until Iambe, knowing her duties, placed in front of her   195
a wellfitted seat and over it she threw a white fleece.
Demeter sat on it and with her hands she held in front of her a veil,
remaining on the seat for long, speechless and brooding,
doing nothing and speaking to nobody.
And without laughing or tasting food and drink   200
she sat pining with longing for her deep-girded daughter
until **Iambe,** knowing her duties, with her jokes
and many jests induced the pure and mighty one
to smile and laugh and have a gracious temper.
At later times, too, Iambe was able to please her moods.   205
Metaneira now filled a cup with wine and gave it
to her, but she refused it; it was not right for her, she said,
to drink red wine. She asked them to give her a drink
of barley-meal and water mixed with tender **pennyroyal.**
She mixed the drink and gave it to the goddess, as she had asked,   210
and mighty Deo accepted it, complying with holy custom.
Then among them fair-girded Metaneira started speaking.
"I salute you, lady, because I think you were born to noble
and not to lowly parents. Modesty and grace show
in your eyes, as if you were the child of law-giving kings.   215
But **man must take the gifts of gods** even when they are
grieved by them, for on their necks there is a yoke.

"as deer or heifers . . . frisk, [the daughters of Keleos] . . . darted"—This is called an extended simile. The style of Homer is characterized by these elaborate comparisons.

"in her dear heart"—In Greek the word for "dear" is φίλος (*philos*), which means "dear" or "own" heart, and refers to private, inward thoughts.

"their lady mother"—Metaneira is holding her young son Demophoön.

"Awe, reverence and pale fear seized the mother"—Metaneira's response here is dictated by the poet's reverence for Demeter, not the requirements of the narrative. Accordingly, the story continues as if there had been no epiphany; the members of the household treat the goddess like an ordinary woman. This disruption of the story's narrative thread is in keeping with the paratactic style of composition (see Ch. 2, p. 18).

Iambe An old woman tries to cheer up Demeter with what were probably obscene jokes and gestures. The procession of the initiands to Eleusis included such jokes and gestures, which are quite appropriate to a fertility goddess.

"Metaneira now filled a cup"—The sharing of a potion was part of initiation into the Eleusinian mysteries.

pennyroyal Mint.

"man must take the gifts of gods"—This is ironic, because in the story that follows it will be Metaneira who refuses the divine gift of Demeter.

"unhoped for and late-born"—In Greek, Metaneira's words are nearly identical with her daughter's earlier ones. The oral poet accomplished this by introducing slight variations to the same repeated phrases, or formulas. For more on oral composition, see the Introduction to Ch. 3. The effect is to emphasize the like-mindedness of mother and daughters, a theme of the poem, and the Mysteries themselves.

"the Undercutter . . . tree-felling creature"—Reference to a belief that toothaches are caused by a worm.

"she received him to her fragrant bosom"—According to Rank, the hero, the son of royal parents, is often raised by a lowly stepmother. (See Introduction to Part 3, p. 155.) This story fits Rank's pattern, since Demeter is disguised as a lowly woman, but adds an element of irony to it, as Demeter is in fact of higher status than his real mother.

"Demeter anointed [Demophoön] with ambrosia . . . At night she hid him like a firebrand in the blazing fire"—Achilles' mother Thetis tried to make him immortal by similar means. There are stories in Greek myth of heroes who do become divine, but they are rare. One was Heracles, who becomes a god after completing his labors. In the *Hymn*, Demeter's failure to make Demophoön immortal means that she will need to find another way of conveying benefits to humans, through her Mysteries. Unlike his brother Triptolemos, Demophoön does not figure in Eleusinian art or inscriptions.

"The shafts of terrible anger shot through Demeter"—We can imagine Metaneira's shock as her nursemaid reveals an unexpectedly terrifying rage.

Styx A river thought to flow through the underworld. In Homer, the gods swear unbreakable oaths on it.

And now since you have come here, what is mine will be yours.
Nurture this child of mine, whom **unhoped for and late-born**
the gods have granted me, in answer to my many prayers.   220
If you should bring him up to reach the age of puberty,
some tender woman seeing you could easily
be envious; such rewards for rearing him I will give you."
Fair-wreathed Demeter addressed her in turn:
''I salute you too, lady; may the gods grant you good   225
things. I will gladly accept the child as you ask me.
I will nurture him and I don't think that for his nurse's foolishness
either a spell or **the Undercutter** will harm him.
I know a remedy by far mightier than the **tree-felling creature,**
and for harmful bewitching I know a noble antidote."   230
With these words **she received him to her fragrant bosom**
and immortal arms, and the mother rejoiced in her heart.
Thus the fine son of prudent Keleos,
Demophoön, to whom fair-girded Metaneira gave birth,
was nurtured by her in the palace; and he grew up like a god,   235
not eating food or nursing at his mother's breast.
As if he were the child of a god, **Demeter anointed him with**
   ambrosia,
holding him to her bosom and breathing on him sweetly.
At night she hid him like a firebrand in the blazing fire,
secretly from his dear parents. To them it was a miracle   240
How he blossomed forth and looked like the gods.
And she would have made him ageless and immortal,
if fair-girded Metaneira, thinking foolish thoughts
and keeping watch by night from her fragrant chamber,
had not seen her; she raised a cry, striking her thighs   245
in fear for her child, and blindness entered her mind,
and weeping she spoke winged words:
"Demophoön, my child, this stranger hides you
in a great fire, bringing me grief and painful care."
Thus she spoke wailing, and the splendid goddess heard her.   250
The shafts of terrible anger shot through Demeter,
the fair-wreathed, who then with her immortal hands
took from the blazing fire and placed on the ground
the dear child born in the queen's mansion,
and at the same time addressed fair-girded Metaneira: 255
"Men are too foolish to know ahead of time
the measure of good and evil which is yet to come.
You too were greatly blinded by your foolishness.
The relentless water of the **Styx** by which gods swear
be my witness: immortal and ageless forever   260
would I have made your dear son and granted him everlasting honor;
but now it is not possible for him to escape the fate of death.
Yet honor everlasting shall be his because
he climbed on my knees and slept in my arms.
But in due time and as the years revolve for him,   265
the sons of the Eleusinians will join in war

and dreadful battle against each other forever.
I am Demeter the honored, the greatest
benefit and joy to undying gods and to mortals.
But come now, let all the people **build me**   270
a great temple and beneath it an altar under the steep walls
of the city, above Kallichoron, on the rising hill.
I myself shall introduce rites so that later
you may propitiate my mind by their right performance."
With these words **the goddess changed her size and form**   275
and sloughed off old age, as beauty was wafted about her.
From her fragrant veils a lovely smell
emanated, and from the immortal skin of the goddess a light
shone afar, as her blond hair streamed down over her shoulders,
and the sturdy mansion was filled with radiance as if from lightning.   280
Out she went through the mansion. The queen staggered,
and she remained speechless for a long time, forgetting
to pick her growing child up from the floor.
His sisters heard his pitiful voice,
and they ran from their well-spread beds; and then one   285
took up the child in her arms and held him to her bosom.
Another revived the fire and yet a third rushed
with her tender feet to rouse her mother from her fragrant chamber.
They gathered round the squirming child, bathed him
and fondled him, but his heart was not soothed,   290
for surely lesser nurses and governesses held him now.
All night long they propitiated the glorious goddess,
quaking with fear, and as soon as dawn appeared
they told the truth to Keleos, whose power reached far,
as the fair-wreathed goddess Demeter had ordered them.   295
He then called to assembly the people of every district
and bade them build an opulent temple to lovely-haired Demeter
and make an altar on the rising hill.
And they listened to his speech, and obeying forthwith
they built it as he ordered; and the temple took shape according to   300
    divine decree.

Demeter Withdraws Her Favors

Now when they finished the temple and refrained from labor,
each man went to his home, but blond Demeter,
sitting there apart from all the blessed ones,
kept on wasting with longing for her **deep-girded daughter.**
Onto the much-nourishing earth she brought a year   305
most dreadful and harsh for men; no seed
in the earth sprouted, for fair-wreathed Demeter concealed it.
In vain the oxen drew many curved plows over the fields,
and in vain did much white barley fall into the ground.
And **she would have destroyed the whole race of mortal men**   310
with painful famine and would have deprived
the Olympians of the glorious honor of gifts and sacrifices,

This 4th-c. B.C.E. votive relief shows the procession of believers' sacrifices to Demeter.

"build me a great temple. . . . I myself shall introduce rites"—Here we see the origins of the worship of Demeter at Eleusis.

"the goddess changed her size and form"—Demeter now proves the truth of her words by appearing as a goddess. The *epiphany* ("showing forth") of a god was an important element in the founding of rites. It is her appearance at a site that makes that site sacred to her, and suitable for her temple.

"All night long they propitiated the goddess"—This probably explains the origin of the παννυχίς (*pannychis*), a nightlong vigil kept by women at the shrine of Demeter as part of her worship at Athens.

"deep-girded daughter"—This phrase is often used of women in Homer and the Homeric hymns. It means "wearing a broad belt." The belt was worn across the lower hips and is often associated with brides (who loosen it to admit their husbands) and mature women, perhaps suggesting fertility or lasciviousness.

"she would have destroyed the whole race of mortal men"—The Graeco-Roman gods easily sacrifice human beings to their needs. See also Ovid's story of the flood, Ch. 11, in which the gods send a flood because of humans' sins.

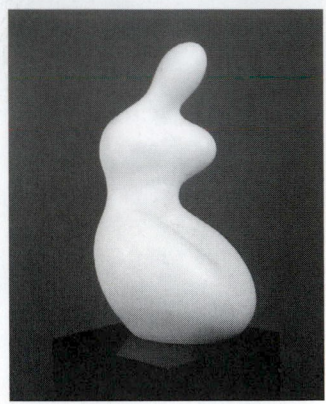

Jean Arp, *Demeter*, 1960. This modern representation of the goddess emphasizes her beauty. She was the wife of Zeus before Hera, and her attractiveness is reflected in the beauty of the earth in its crop-laden richness.

"the angry goddess"—Demeter did not approach Zeus when she originally learned from Helios that he had given Persephone to Aidoneus. Presumably she knew that it would do no good. Now that she has something to bargain with—the fate of mankind—she makes her demand. This suggests the authority of the father, and the irrevocable nature of arranged marriage.

Hermes The messenger of the gods is often represented as an intermediary who can communicate with the land of the dead. Turner would call him a liminal figure (see Ch. 26, p. 373).

Argeiphontes—A name for Hermes, probably meaning "slayer of [the monster] Argos."

"with smiling brows"—Foley suggests this may mean he is not able to express his feelings in a civilized way.

"prudent-minded"—This adjective may refer to Persephone's new status as a grown woman.

if Zeus had not perceived this and pondered in his mind.
First he sent golden-winged Iris to invite
the lovely-haired Demeter of the fair form.   315
He spoke to her and she obeyed Zeus, the son of Kronos and lord
of dark clouds, and ran swiftly mid-way between earth and heaven.
She reached the town of Eleusis rich in sacrifices,
found the dark-veiled Demeter in the temple
and spoke, uttering winged words to her: 320
"Demeter, Zeus the father, whose wisdom never wanes,
invites you to come among the tribes of the immortal gods.
But come and let not the word of Zeus be unaccomplished."
Thus she spoke begging her, but her mind was not persuaded.
So then again the father sent forth all the blessed   325
immortal gods. They ran to her, and each in his turn
summoned her and gave her many beautiful gifts
and whatever honors she might want to choose among the immortals.
But no one could persuade the mind and thought
of **the angry goddess** who stubbornly spurned their offers.   330
She said she would never set foot on fragrant Olympus
and never allow the grain in the earth to sprout forth
before seeing with her eyes her fair-faced daughter.
So when loud-thundering, far-seeing Zeus heard this,
he sent Argeiphontes of the golden wand to Erebos.   335
His mission was to win Hades over with gentle words,
and bring Persephone out of misty darkness
to light and among the gods, so that her mother
might see her with her eyes and desist from anger.
Hermes did not disobey and, leaving his Olympian seat,   340
with eager speed plunged into the depths of the earth.
He found the lord inside his dwelling,
sitting on his bed with his revered spouse; she was
in many ways reluctant and missed her mother, who far
from the works of the blessed gods was devising a plan.   345
Mighty **Argeiphontes** stood near and addressed him:
"Hades, dark-haired lord of those who have perished,
Zeus the father bids you bring noble Persephone
out of Erebos and among the gods, so that her mother,
seeing her with her eyes, may desist from anger   350
and dreadful wrath against the gods; because she is contemplating
a great scheme to destroy the feeble races of earth-born men,
hiding the seed under the earth and abolishing the honors
of the immortals. Her anger is dreadful, and she does not mingle
with the gods, but apart from them in a fragrant temple   355
she sits, dwelling in the rocky town of Eleusis."
Thus he spoke and Aidoneus, lord of the nether world,
with smiling brows obeyed the behests of Zeus the king
and speedily gave his command to **prudent-minded** Persephone:
"Persephone, go to your dark-robed mother,   360
with a gentle spirit and temper in your breast,
and in no way be more dispirited than the other gods.

I shall not be an unfitting husband among the immortals,
as I am father Zeus' own brother. When you are here
you shall be mistress of everything which lives and moves;   365
your honors among the immortals shall be the greatest,
and those who wrong you shall always be punished,
if they do not propitiate your spirit with sacrifices,
performing sacred rites and making due offerings."
Thus he spoke and wise Persephone rejoiced   370
and swiftly sprang up for joy, but he himself
gave her to eat a honey-sweet pomegranate seed,
contriving secretly about her, so that she might not spend
all her days again with dark-robed, revered Demeter.
Aidoneus, Ruler of Many, harnessed nearby   375
the immortal horses up to the golden chariot.
She mounted the chariot, and next to her mighty Argeiphontes
took the reins and the whip in his own hands
and sped out of the halls, as the horses flew readily.
Soon they reached the end of the long path, and neither   380
the sea nor the water of rivers nor the grassy glens
and mountain-peaks checked the onrush of the immortal horses,
but they went over all these, traversing the lofty air.

The Reunion of Mother and Daughter

He drove them and then halted near the fragrant temple
where fair-wreathed Demeter stayed. When she saw them,   385
she rushed as a **maenad** does, along a shady woodland on the
    mountains.
Persephone on her part, when she saw the beautiful eyes
of her mother, leaving chariot and horses, leaped down
to run and, throwing her arms around her mother's neck,
    embraced her.
And as Demeter still held her dear child in her arms,   390
her mind suspected trickery, and in awful fear she withdrew
from fondling her and forthwith asked her a question:
"Child, when you were below, did you perchance partake
of food? Speak out, that we both may know.
If your answer is no, coming up from loathsome Hades,   395
you shall dwell both with me and with father Kronion,
lord of dark clouds, honored by all the immortals.
Otherwise, you shall fly and go to the depths of the earth
to dwell there a third of the seasons in the year,
spending two seasons with me and the other immortals.   400
Whenever the earth blooms with every kind of sweet-smelling
springflower, you shall come up again from misty darkness,
a great wonder for gods and mortal men.
With what trick did the mighty All-receiver deceive you?"
Facing her now, beautiful Persephone replied: 405
"Surely, Mother, I shall tell you the whole truth.
When Hermes, the helpful swift messenger, came

"I shall not be an unfitting husband"—The story here is as much
about a husband trying to win
acceptance from his mother-in-law
as it is of the rectification of a kidnapping.

"gave her to eat a . . . pomegranate seed"—In Greece and the
Middle East, pomegranates were
often offered to fertility deities. The
apple-like shape of this fruit and
its many seeds connect it with
procreation and fertility. The seed
thus represents the consummation of the marriage between
Hades and Persephone. It was a
custom to give brides pomegranates. It also symbolizes Persephone's connection to her new
husband Aidoneus. Although originally she felt alienated from him,
over time she has formed an emotional link with him. This phenomenon has been observed among
captives and their captors and has
been called "Patti Hearst Syndrome," after the kidnapped
heiress who joined her counter-
culture captors in a series of
crimes.

maenad A follower of Dionysus,
who rushes freely through the
woods liberated from her household tasks, given over to wine,
performing the ceremonies of the
god. (See Ch. 31, p. 460.)

This 5th-c. B.C.E. votive relief represents *Persephone and Pluto*
enthroned, making them seem like
a harmonious and well-matched
couple.

from father Zeus and the other heavenly dwellers
to fetch me from Erebos, so that seeing me with your eyes
you might desist from your anger and dreadful wrath against the   410
   immortals,
I myself sprang up for joy, but **Aidoneus slyly placed
in my hands a pomegranate seed,** sweet as honey to eat.
Against my will and by force he made me taste of it.
How he abducted me through the shrewd scheming of Kronides,
my father, and rode away carrying me to the depths of the earth   415
I shall explain and rehearse every point as you are asking.
All of us maidens in a delightful meadow,
Leukippe, Phaino, Electra, Ianthe,
Melite, Iache, Rhodeia, Kallirhoe,
Melobosis, Tyche, Okyrhoe with a face like a flower,   420
Chryseis, Ianeira, Akaste, Admete,
Rhodope, Plouto, lovely Kalypso,
Styx, Ourania, charming Galaxaura,
battle-stirring Pallas, and arrow-pouring Artemis,
were playing and picking lovely flowers with our hands,   425
mingling soft crocuses and irises with hyacinths
and the flowers of the rose and lilies, a wonder to the eye,
and the narcissus which the wide earth grows crocus-colored.
So I myself was picking them with joy, but the earth beneath
gave way and from it the mighty lord and All-receiver   430
leaped out. He carried me under the earth in his golden chariot,
though I resisted and shouted with shrill voice.
I am telling you the whole truth, even though it grieves me."
So then all day long, being one in spirit,
they warmed each other's hearts and minds in many ways   435
with loving embraces, and an end to sorrow came for their hearts,
as they took joys from each other and gave in return.
Hekate of the shining headband came near them
and many times lovingly touched the daughter of pure Demeter.
From then on this lady became her attendant and follower.   440

The Compromise of Zeus

Far-seeing, loud-thundering Zeus sent them a messenger,
lovely-haired Rhea, to bring her dark-veiled mother
among the races of the gods, promising to give her
whatever honors she might choose among the immortal gods.
With a nod of his head he promised that, as the year revolved,   445
her daughter could spend one portion of it in the misty darkness
and the other two with her mother and the other immortals.
He spoke and the goddess did not disobey the behests of Zeus.
Speedily she rushed down from the peaks of Olympus
and came to **Rharion, life-giving udder of the earth**   450
in the past, and then no longer life-giving but lying idle
without a leaf. It was now hiding the white barley
according to the plan of fair-ankled Demeter, but later

"Aidoneus slyly placed in my hands a pomegranate seed"—Persephone places the blame for her divided loyalties on her new husband.

"Leukippe, Phaino . . ."—The oral poet shows his virtuosity by listing the names of all of Persephone's companions while maintaining the meter or rhythm of the poem.

"With a nod of his head he promised"—Zeus' words to Demeter are echoed below by Rhea. The repetition is typical of oral poetry.

"Rharion, life-giving udder of the earth"—It is here that Triptolemos was supposed to have first plowed and planted grain. Thus there is a hint here of the origins of agriculture which are otherwise omitted from the poem. (See previous note, p. 394.)

the fields would be plumed with long ears of grain,
as the spring waxed, and the rich furrows on the ground   455
would teem with ears to be bound into sheaves by withies.
There she first landed from the unharvested ether.
Joyfully they beheld each other and rejoiced in their hearts;
and Rhea of the shining headband addressed her thus:
"Come, child! Far-seeing, loud-thundering Zeus invites you   460
to come among the races of the gods and promises to give you
whatever honors you wish among the immortal gods.
With a nod of his head he promised you that, as the year revolves,
your daughter could spend one portion of it in the misty darkness
and the other two with you and the other immortals.   465
With a nod of his head he said it would thus be brought to pass.
But obey me, my child! Come and do not nurse
unrelenting anger against Kronion, lord of dark clouds;
Soon make the life-giving seed grow for men."
Thus she spoke and fair-wreathed Demeter did not disobey,   470
but swiftly made the seed sprout out of the fertile fields.
The whole broad earth teemed with leaves and flowers;
and she went to the kings who administer the laws,
Triptolemos and Diokles, smiter of horses, and mighty Eumolpos
and Keleos, leader of the people, and showed them the   475
celebration of holy rites, and **explained to all,**
to Triptolemos, to Polyxeinos and also to Diokles,
the awful mysteries not to be transgressed, violated
or divulged, because the tongue is restrained by reverence for the gods.
Whoever on this earth has seen these is blessed,   480
but **he who has no part in the holy rites has
another lot as he wastes away in dank darkness.**
After the splendid Demeter had counseled the kings in everything,
she and her daughter went to Olympus for the company of the
    other gods.
There they dwell beside Zeus who delights in thunder,   485
commanding awe and reverence; thrice blessed is he
of men on this earth whom they gladly love.
Soon to his great house they send as guest
Ploutos, who brings wealth to mortal men.
But come now, you who dwell in the fragrant town of Eleusis,   490
sea-girt Paros and rocky Antron,
mighty mistress Deo, bringer of seasons and splendid gifts,
both you and your daughter, beauteous Persephone,
for my song kindly grant me possessions pleasing the heart,
and I shall remember you and another song, too.   495

Demeter, Triptolemus, and Perse-phone. Votive relief from Eleusis, ca. 440–430 B.C.E. This relief comes from the site of the temple of Demeter at Eleusis and represents the giving of wheat to humankind in the person of Triptolemos.

"explained to all"—Demeter tells her followers in Eleusis exactly what she wants done in her ritual.

"he who has no part in the holy rites . . . wastes away in dank darkness"—The cult of Demeter was believed to provide her followers with life after death.

The Story of Demeter and the Insights Gained from Myth

In Chapter 1, p. 3, we describe what Joseph Campbell calls the four functions of myth, and which we have included, with other perspectives, in what we call the "insights" gained from myth, showing that mythology is important to human beings in a wide variety of ways. Campbell's list of the functions of myth includes mystical or metaphysical, cosmological, sociological and psychological. To these we have added the historical, anthropological, and aetiological insights we can gain from reading and studying myth. The story of Demeter well illustrates some of these insights.

Kind of Insight	Explanation	Manifestation in the *Hymn to Demeter*
Aetiological	Myth explains the origin or cause of a custom or a fact of the physical universe.	The myth explains the origin of worship at Eleusis, and the basis for building a temple there.
Historical	Myth reminds us of verifiable historical events reflected in historical stories.	We see the importance of Eleusis as an agricultural state, the basis of its ability to resist being completely swallowed up in the Athenian empire.
Mystical or Metaphysical	Myth reconciles us to losing "our animal innocence" and coming to understand that we are not immortal like the gods.	Persephone goes down into the underworld and comes back, thus conquering death. Her triumph over death suggests that human beings can also, to some extent, overcome death.
Cosmological	Myth helps us in "formulating and rendering an image of the universe, a cosmological image in keeping with the science of the time."	The myth explains the origin, and the significance, of the seasons. The science of the time understood, as we do today, that certain meteorological conditions are necessary for the seed to grow.
Sociological	Myth provides us the means of "validating and maintaining some specific social order."	Although the marriage to Aidoneus causes grief to Persephone and Demeter, the story shows that the girl and her family adjust to it.
Psychological	Myth has a role in "shaping individuals to the aims and ideals of their various social groups."	The myth shows us the grief of Persephone, and of Demeter, but it also shows us that the girl eventually comes to accept her husband, at least in a limited way.
Anthropological	Myth shows us the values and principles of a society.	We see both the subservience of women to men in Athenian society, and the basis of what can be their terrifying strength in resisting and defying the decisions of men.

Further Reading

Athanassakis, Apostolos N., trans. *The Homeric Hymns*. Baltimore, MD: The Johns Hopkins University Press, 1976.

Foley, Helene P. *The Homeric Hymn to Demeter: Translation, Commentary, and Interpretive Essays*. Princeton, NJ: Princeton University Press, 1994.

O'Brien, Joan V. *The Transformation of Hera: A Study of Ritual, Hero and the Goddess in the Iliad*. Lanham, MD: Rowman and Littlefield, 1993.

Isis and Osiris

28

WHAT TO EXPECT . . . Worship of the Egyptian goddess Isis, queen of heaven and premier mother goddess, healer, and sorceress, continued throughout every period of ancient Egypt's 3,000-year history. As religious/cultural centers shifted, religious belief and practices changed to reflect the values of the worshippers. With the rise of the Roman Empire, Isis, like Demeter (Ch. 27, p. 385), became the subject of a widespread cult, and her worship became a mystery religion.

As background, this chapter contains a summary of the characteristics of the best-known Egyptian deities. The creation story from Heliopolis includes the birth of Isis and Osiris and provides the background for the cycle of stories related to the death of Osiris and his resurrection through the devotion of Isis. The text by Plutarch presents a complete account of the story of Isis, but sometimes shows a bias in favor of Greek philosophy over Egyptian cult.

As you read, compare the content, style, and tone of the stories about Isis, and note how the ritual described by Apuleius differs from—as well as corresponds to—the early Isis stories. Consider the story of Isis according to the stages represented by Joseph Campbell as occurring in the journey of the hero, comparing her journey to that of Demeter or Gilgamesh (Ch. 15, p. 166). Compare the worship of Isis to that of Demeter. What was the basis of each?

The myth of Isis and Osiris originates in Egypt and is influential throughout the history of that great culture. Egypt was a great trading power, and some aspects of her culture became known in the Mediterranean area. Although Egyptian businessmen in some cases carried their religion with them, up to classical times (5th c. B.C.E.), there was not much attempt to make converts in the rest of the world. The greatest source of Egyptian influence on religion in the Graeco-Roman world came from the establishment of the Serapeum (temple of Serapis) in Alexandria in the fourth century B.C.E. With the rise of Rome, some stories about Isis became well known throughout the empire, and her cult became an important one in an area much wider than her original sphere of influence.

The worship of Isis became the basis of an important personal religion that, like the cult of Demeter (see Ch. 27, p. 385), involved an elaborate initiation ceremony into secret mysteries. It persisted in the Roman Empire at least until 394 C.E. Its allure was such that, at times, emperors erected temples in honor of the goddess in the center of Rome, while at other times her worship was persecuted by the Romans and eventually by the Christians.

In this chapter, we will examine some of the Egyptian stories associated with this goddess, as well as one of the rituals associated with her in the Roman Empire. Interestingly enough, Isis has continued to find devotees in modern times. The goddess is often included or featured in

Isis nursing Harpocrates, Late Period, Budapest Museum of Fine Art. After her search for the body of Osiris, she bore him this child, conceived after her husband's death.

religions aiming to recapture the roots of African spirituality. She was also the subject of the 1877 book by the theosophist leader Madame Blavatsky, *Isis Unveiled,* that embraces the myth of Isis and Osiris and attributes a new meaning to it by linking it to a secret doctrine of mystical spirituality.

Such modern efforts are often based on the teachings of spiritual leaders who combine an understanding of ancient beliefs with personal mystical experiences. Often these teachings involve a secret revelation that is presented only to initiates, and as such fits within the definition of gnosticism—a group offering salvation through belief in a secret doctrine, often one that represents the world of everyday experience as illusory or incomplete in some important way, which only the secret teaching can correct. Study of such modern-day gnostic groups is beyond the scope of this book, but understanding their teachings entails attention to both the ancient stories that are refocused in this way and to the philosophy or values to whose service they are applied. (For more on gnosticism, see Ch. 27, p. 388.)

HISTORY AND GEOGRAPHY OF EGYPT

Egyptian culture spans some 3,000 years and, not surprisingly, encompasses a great variety of historical periods, as well as mythological beliefs and rituals. The worship of Isis can be found at nearly every period.

In brief, the history of Egypt is usually organized as follows:

- Early Dynastic period, 3100–2686 B.C.E.
- Old Kingdom, 2686–2181 B.C.E. The great pyramids were built in this era.
- First Intermediate period, 2181–2040 B.C.E.
- Middle Kingdom, 2040–1650 B.C.E.
- Second Intermediate period, 1750–1550 B.C.E.
- New Kingdom, 1550–ca. 1069 B.C.E.
- Third Intermediate period, ca. 1069–656 B.C.E.
- Late Period, ca. 664–343 B.C.E.
- Graeco-Roman period, 332 B.C.E.–642 C.E.

Geographically, Egypt is a vast land stretched out along the Nile river. The country was originally centered along the upper (south) Nile and eventually came to include the lower (north) Nile.

In addition, the culture of Egypt was based at different historical eras in different cities, whose ascendancy affected the nature of religious beliefs and practice. The main religious/cultural centers were

- **Memphis:** At the beginning of Egypt's history, Menes, the king of Upper Egypt (the southern part) unified the country by conquering Lower Egypt (the northern part) and establishing a capital at Memphis, near modern-day Cairo, where he founded a temple to the creator god Ptah. The creator god was worshipped at Memphis along with his consort, the lion-headed goddess Sekhmet, and their child Nefertem.
- **Heliopolis,** near Memphis, was the dominant city of the Old Kingdom. According to the creation story originating here, Atum was the chief god, and his children, produced by a solitary act of ejaculation, were Shu and Tefnut. Shu and Tefnut give birth to Geb and Nut, who were the parents of two sons and two daughters: Osiris, Seth, Nephthys, and Isis, as well as of Horus in some versions. George Hart notes that the priests of Heliopolis formulated the version of the creation story that incorporated a previously existing cycle of myths about Osiris into the creation story featuring Atum, the sun god.

- **Hermopolis,** located in Middle Egypt, was an administrative center of the Middle Kingdom. According to the creation story based there, there were eight gods (an Ogdoad) consisting of four male-female pairs that represented the primeval forces of nature in what may have been a scientific account. The story is thought to have explained the original burst of energy that caused the creation of the sun from churned-up primal matter. Hermopolis was the city of Thoth, the scribe of the gods and the god of wisdom, and of the moon, whom the Greeks equated with Hermes, hence the city's name.

- **Thebes,** in the South, became the capital after Memphis. At the end of the First Intermediate period, Theban prince Mentuhotep reunited Egypt and initiated the Middle Kingdom, though subsequent kings returned the capital to the north. Amun was the predominant god of Thebes, and his ascendancy coincided with its role as a major religious center; it reached its height in the New Kingdom. Theologians there maintained that all significant gods are simply projections of Amun.

Ptah, Late period, Budapest Museum of Fine Art.

GODS AND GODDESSES: THE RELIGION OF EGYPT

The religion of Egypt included a variety of deities whose roles, functions, and stories were not standardized throughout the kingdom or throughout history. The Egyptian approach to religion allowed for the attributes of one god to be transposed or melded with those of another, so understanding some of the main figures can be quite useful to the appreciation of any one in particular. As a result, a variety of conflicting and contradictory stories existed about the gods of Egypt. The best-known Egyptian deities are

- **Atum,** a sun god of Heliopolis in Lower Egypt. For the most part, Atum refers to the setting sun; Re refers to the midday sun.

- **Re,** also a sun god whose cult was centered in Heliopolis. Later Re became merged with Amun into a deity known as Amun Re. Re could be combined with a variety of different gods; for example, he joined with Horus to form Re-Horakhty, or "Horus in the Horizon," a form of the morning sun.

- **Amun** ("the hidden one"), a god whose worship originated in Thebes. He was also worshipped in Hermopolis. According to an inscription found in a temple at Esna (south of Thebes), Amun causes the ram-headed Khnum to create human beings as a potter who molds clay on a potter's wheel.

- **Hathor** ("the mansion of Horus"), perhaps the first great mother goddess and represented with the attributes of a cow. She was a goddess of love and joy. In some early stories, she is the mother of Horus. At Edfu (south of Thebes), she was the consort of Horus who took on a warrior-aspect there.

- **Horus** ("the one who is above"), a sky god with a falcon shape. He represented the living, reigning, king of Egypt, and his name was used for the king. There was both an elder and a younger Horus. As the elder, he was a powerful warrior who defeated Seth, as shown on the temple walls at Edfu. As the younger, he was the child of Isis and Osiris, and was also known as Harpocrates, a child nursing at the breast of Isis.

- **Osiris** ("the Seat of the Eye": the place where the sun goes), a deity associated with earth. He was thought by some scholars to represent a predynastic king of Egypt. He is killed and

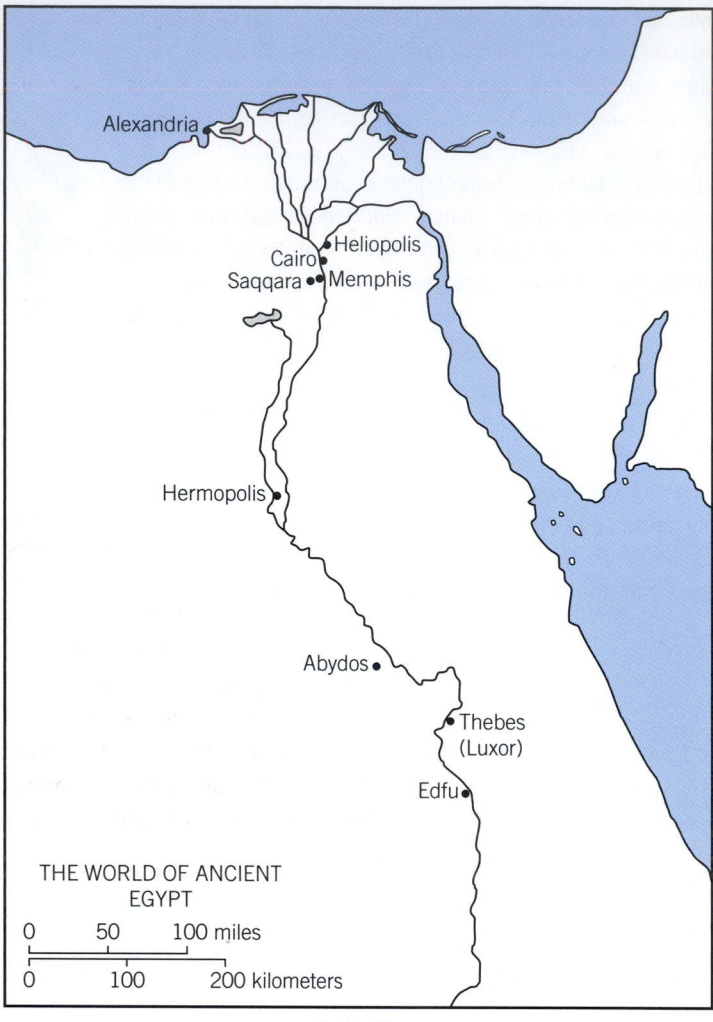

Map of Egypt

dismembered by his brother Seth, and reassembled by his sister and wife Isis to bear Horus, his son and avenger. Osiris was associated with the dead king. In addition to his role as the leading funerary deity, Osiris also had associations with the growth of agricultural crops, which were thought to undergo the same type of rebirth that Osiris experienced.

- **Anubis,** a deity represented as a jackal or a jackal-headed human. He conducts the final judgment before Osiris. The *Book of the Dead* provided guidance for this ritual, which was believed to take place after death. In it, the heart of the deceased was weighed against the feather of Maat, the symbol of truth. If the heart was not heavier than the feather, the deceased could enter the afterlife. If it was heavier, the heart was eaten by a monster.

The role of Anubis and Isis in the resurrection of Osiris becomes more important in the Middle Kingdom and the New Kingdom. Initially, Anubis' role is that of a *psychopompus,* the conductor of the dead to the underworld, but eventually he is seen as Re's representative in ensuring the treatment of Osiris' body that is necessary for his resurrection. As such, Anubis becomes the key god associated with the preparation of the mummy and even with the journey of the deceased in the underworld. Plutarch represents him as Isis' nephew; in some stories he is her son. He comes to take on increasingly more importance in assuring life after death and eventually is represented as teaching Isis what needs to be done to accomplish the resurrection of Osiris.

The return from the dead of Osiris provides the rationale for perhaps the best-known aspect of ancient Egyptian culture, the mummification practices that were believed to allow the survival of the body, and thereby to accord eternal life to the deceased. Originally in the Old Kingdom this opportunity was available only to a predominant group of pharaonic individuals, and later in the Middle Kingdom members of the privileged classes, including scribes and courtiers, could aspire to it as well.

Egyptian deities were represented in a variety of forms, often as animals or as creatures combining human and animal characteristics. These forms were viewed not as representing the actual appearance of the god, but as a manifestation of some aspect of his or her powers. In fact, the animal identified with the god often engaged in human activity or was a hybrid being with some human characteristics. For example, Hathor, perhaps the earliest mother goddess, is often represented as a cow or as a woman with some features of a cow. The connection of cows with fertility provides a straightforward rationale for this identification. A similar rationale exists for the frequent appearance of Horus, the sky god, as a falcon. However, the same god might be represented as different animals, and with no clear association: an example is Thoth, the god of writing and knowledge, who might be represented as an ibis (a water bird) or a baboon. Deities might share an animal: many gods were represented with the head of a lion, which was associated with the forces of destruction, or that of a falcon, which meant aggression. Sometimes this meant a connection between the deities, and sometimes not. For example, in later Egyptian history, Isis was identified with Bastet, the goddess who often had the features of a cat, and as a result she too was represented with a cat form.

CREATION OF THE WORLD

As may be evident from the account given about the religious/cultural centers of Egypt, each era and location had its version of a creation story. We will focus on the creation story from Heliopolis, which resulted in the development of the Ennead or group of nine gods. This story includes the birth of Isis and Osiris and provides the background for the cycle of stories related to the death of Osiris and his resurrection through the efforts of Isis. George Hart has derived this story from a variety of ancient texts, including the ancient *Pyramid Texts* and the Shabaka Stone, which dates to 700 B.C.E. but is thought to be the copy of a papyrus from circa the thirteenth century B.C.E. Hart notes that the priests at Heliopolis produced what in all likelihood was a novel synthesis of an older story of creation from Atum and the story of Osiris, which he notes was not attested before the Fifth Dynasty (ca. 2465–2323 B.C.E.).

This cycle of myths portrays life as a cyclical struggle based on the actions of Osiris, Isis, Seth, and Nephthys, a newer generation of gods representing opposing forces in the cosmic order. This newer portion of the creation story was formulated by the priests at Heliopolis to incorporate into the original creation story: the struggle of Seth against his first-born brother Osiris for the kingship, Seth's murder of Osiris, Isis' search for Osiris and her revitalizing her consort long enough for the conception of Horus, who was to avenge the death of Osiris. The story which arose at Heliopolis was remarkable also because it brought the god Horus, an important deity in his own right, into the family of Osiris. It provided a genealogy that showed the descent of the Pharaoh, the current occupant of the throne of Egypt, represented by Horus, from the primeval god of the sun, represented by Atum.

The creation story which results from this process can be represented as follows:

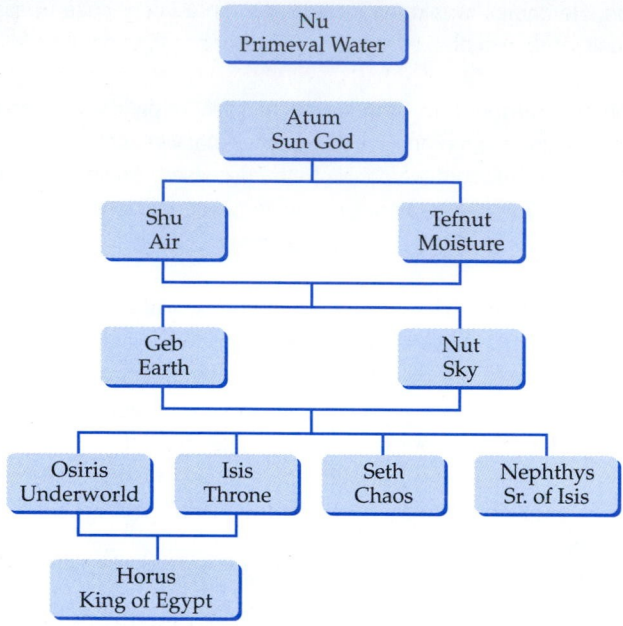

Adapted from G. Hart, *Egyptian Myths,* p. 15.

However, the texts on which this story is based do not provide us with a narrative of the sort we often see in the study of mythology. Rather, Hart and other Egyptologists have synthesized this story from a variety of disparate texts, including the *Pyramid Texts* (written during the Old Kingdom), the *Coffin Texts* (compiled near the end of the Old Kingdom), and various instantiations of the group of spells and incantations which are collectively known as the *Book of the Dead* (compiled in the New Kingdom).

The oldest texts available as sources for Egyptian mythology are the *Pyramid Texts,* which were inscribed by Pharaohs starting with those of Unas (2375–2345 B.C.E.) on the Pyramid at Saqqara. The *Coffin Texts* are for the most part later than the *Pyramid Texts* and were written on the insides of the coffins of private persons, not kings. They contain material that was also found in the *Pyramid Texts,* but with a different perspective, to suit the needs of the dignitaries whose coffins they adorn. Both *Pyramid* and *Coffin Texts* are for the most part working texts— stories everyone was familiar with, used to achieve a ritual result.

In the brief excerpts, we show the kinds of ancient texts from which the story of creation can be inferred. We start with a text that was one of the *Shu Texts* designed to show the multiplicity and timelessness of the god Shu. The excerpt starts with Shu, who has already been created by Atum, the sun god. It begins with the separation of Sky (Nut) from Shu and Tefnut (or Tefenet), the combination of Air and Moisture which was the first stage of Creation. After raising up the sky, Shu sets Geb (Earth) under his feet. The excerpt portrays the act of creation as tantamount to the act of unifying Egypt from "the Two Lands," the Upper and Lower Kingdoms.

Creation: Excerpt from the *Coffin Texts*

I lifted up my daughter Nut from upon myself, so that I might give her to my father Atum in his realm, and I have set Geb under my feet. This god knits up the Two Lands

This text comes from: The *Ancient Egyptian Coffin Texts,* Spell 76, trans. by R. O. Faulkner.* Notes are also based on Rundle Clark, *Myth and Symbol in Ancient Egypt.*

Re Visible form of the Sun god.

*The Ancient Egyptian Coffin Texts, Spells 74 and 76. Trans. R. O. Faulkner. Warminster, UK: Aris & Phillips, 1993.

for my father Atum, he gathers together for himself the celestial kine; I have set myself among them. I indeed am Shu whom Atum created, whereby **Re** came into being; I was not built up in the womb, I was not knit together in the egg, I was not conceived, but **Atum spat me out** in the spittle of his mouth together with my sister Tefenet. She went up after me, and I was covered with the breath of the throat. The phoenix of Re was that whereby Atum came into being in chaos, in the Abyss, in darkness and in gloom. I am Shu, father of the gods, and Atum once sent his **Sole Eye** seeking me and my sister Tefenet. I made light of the darkness for it, and it found me as an immortal.

Creation: Excerpt from the *Pyramid Texts*

The *Pyramid Text* excerpted also refers to the story of creation. It is written as a prayer, spoken first to Osiris and then to Nut, calling upon them to take the deceased king into their protection and assure him everlasting life. The sarcophagus of the king represents the earth (Geb) and the lid stands for the sky (Nut). The priest speaks the initial prayers to Osiris, while Geb speaks the rest of the passage to his sister-consort Nut (Rundle Clark, 48–51).

O **Osiris** the King, may you be protected! I give to you all the gods, their heritages, their provisions, and all their possessions, for you have not died.

O Osiris the King, appear as King of Upper and Lower Egypt, because you have power over the gods and their spirits.

"O Nut, **spread yourself** over your son Osiris the King that you may conceal him from **Seth**; protect him, O Nut. Have you come that you may conceal your son?

I have indeed come that I may protect this great one.

O Nut, fall over your son Osiris the King, protect him, O Great Protectress, this great one who is among your children.

Thus says Geb: O Nut, it is well with you; power was yours in the womb of mother Tefenet before you were born, that you might protect this King, for he has not died.

You are violent, moving about in your mother's womb **in your name of Nut.**

You are the daughter, mighty in her mother, who appeared as a bee; make the King a spirit within yourself, for he has not died.

O Great One, who came into being in the sky, you have achieved power, you have achieved strength, and have filled every place with your beauty; the entire land is yours. Take possession of it, for you have enclosed the earth and all things within your embrace, and you have set this King as an Imperishable Star who is in you.

As Geb I will make you fruitful, in your name of 'Sky,' for I will join the entire land to you everywhere.

The Egyptian Creation Myth, Third Intermediate Period, Budapest Museum of Fine Art. Illustration found on coffin fragment. The overarching figure of Nut is shown covering the earth. In the ritual in which the hymn to Osiris is used, the coffin lid, symbolizing Nut, is lowered on the base, symbolizing Geb.

"Atum spat me out"—Pyramid Utt. 527 says, "he put his penis in his hand that he might obtain pleasure of emission thereby and there were born brother and sister—that is Shu and Tefnut" (trans. Rundle Clark, 42).

Sole Eye An aspect of the sun, which looks much like a single eye. It is seen as blinding light, a destructive and terrible aspect of the Sun god, the means for him to burn his enemies with a terrible fury.

This text comes from: *The Ancient Egyptian Pyramid Texts.* Utterances, 425–34.* The notes are largely based upon, and the translation enhanced by turns of phrase from, Rundle Clark, *Myth and Symbol in Ancient Egypt* (48–51).

Osiris The hymn speaks to the dead king under the name of Osiris.

"spread yourself"—Nut is the mother of Osiris, in her role as Sky, she covers all the Earth.

Seth Osiris' brother, is the cause of his death, as will be seen in the excerpt from Plutarch given.

"You are violent"—This refers to an unknown story in which Nut rebelled against her mother while still in the womb.

"in your name of Nut"—Egyptian cosmology had it that there was one underlying divine reality, and the specific gods were manifestations of it.

"Be far from the earth"—Shu, Nut's father, as air, held her up in his arms, separating her from Geb. As a result, she gave birth to the stars, which moved upward into the sky.

Be far from the earth, for to you belongs the head of your father Shu; be powerful by means of it, for he has loved you and has set himself under you and (under) all things. You have taken to yourself every god who possesses his bark, that you may install them in the starry sky, lest they depart from you as stars. Do not let this King be far from you in your name of 'Sky.'

Calling Forth Osiris: Excerpt from the *Coffin Texts*

This text comes from: *The Ancient Egyptian Coffin Texts,* Spell 74, trans. by R. O. Faulkner.* The notes are largely based upon, and the translation has been enhanced by turns of phrase from: Rundle Clark, *Myth and Symbol in Ancient Egypt,* (125–29).

The *Coffin Text* represents a scene originally thought to be from a ritual called "the passion of Osiris," an eight-day ritual performed in the Middle Kingdom at the temple of Osiris in Abydos. This ritual was performed to call forth the rising waters of the Nile to flood the dead land, represented as Osiris. According to its story, it is Isis who gives him new life. With her sister Nephthys, she ministers to the unconscious god and gets him to rise on one side: the flood waters were believed to pour from the thigh of Osiris to revitalize the land.

"O sleeper"—Osiris.

"pools . . . streams"—Refers to parts of the great irrigation system which was maintained throughout Egypt to control and direct the flooding of the Nile so its waters could be harnessed for agriculture.

"the Nine Gods"—Groups of nine gods were popular in Egyptian religion, though the actual nine names varied. The reference seems to be to nine of the ten or eleven gods of creation, as shown in the diagram on p. 408: Nu, Atum, Shu, Tefnut, Geb, Nut, Isis, Osiris, Nephthys, Seth, Horus.

Turn about, turn about, **O sleeper,** turn about in this place which you do not know, but I know it. See now, I have found you (lying) on your side, O Great Listless One.

"My sister," says Isis to Nephthys, "this is our brother. Come, that we may raise his head. Come, that we may reassemble his bones. Come, that we may rearrange his members. Come, that we may make a dam in his side. Let not this one be limp in our hands; there drips the efflux which has issued from this spirit. The **pools** are filled for you, the names of the **streams** are made for you."

"O Osiris, live, O Osiris! The Great Listless One stands up from upon his side. I am Isis, I am Nephthys; Horus has addressed you, Thoth has protected you, and your two sons are Lords of the Great White Crown; what you have done shall be what you shall do. Geb has seen and **the Nine Gods** have heard that your power shall be visible in the sky and the dread of you among the [hostile] gods. Your son Horus has taken possession of the Great White Crown, which has been taken from the one who would harm you. Then will your father Atum call 'Come!' Osiris, live! Osiris, let the Listless One arise!"

Isis in the Early Roman Empire

The cult of Isis was one of many religious movements (Christianity was another) that was spreading throughout the early Roman empire (27 B.C.E.–200 C.E.). She became well established in the Greek centers of Eleusis and Delphi, formerly strongholds of the gods Demeter and Apollo. Her worship grew in northern Greece and Athens. There were harbors dedicated to her in the Arabian Gulf and the Black Sea. In the course of the spread of her cult, the role of Isis became broadened and universalized. She became the queen of heaven and the mother goddess par excellence, the healer and the sorceress above all others. She was worshipped by men and women, free and slave, and all her followers found something special in her message for themselves. Her worship became a mystery religion like that of Demeter, the Greek goddess of grain, and she had initiates and priests of her own. To those whose religion was imbued with philosophy, she became an abstract principle that ruled over Fate and overcame the dread determinism connected with astrology and the fixed destiny it preached.

As the cult of Isis spread, she became identified with a variety of Greek gods and goddesses: foremost among these were Demeter; Aesclepias, the god of medicine and healing; Aphrodite, the goddess of love; Tyche, the goddess of fortune; and Artemis, goddess of the hunt; as well as a variety of Middle-Eastern goddesses like Cybele, the Great Mother, and Astarte. In this atmos-

---

The Ancient Egyptian Coffin Texts, Spells 74 and 76. Trans. R. O. Faulkner. Warminster, UK: Aris & Phillips, 1993.

phere of borrowing and syncretism, the mixing together of elements from different religions, it is hard to sort out which aspects of Isis were properly hers and which ones were borrowed characteristics gained from her association with other deities.

PLUTARCH AS A TRANSMITTER OF EGYPTIAN MYTH

Plutarch was a Greek who lived from 40 to 120 C.E. and in all probability wrote his work on Isis and Osiris toward the end of his life. We are indebted to the story he tells, since we have no other complete account of the story of Isis, and none from an Egyptian source. However, the fairness and accuracy of Plutarch's view must be brought into question. Daniel S. Richter has shown that Plutarch's primary concerns were to show the superiority of Greek philosophy to Egyptian cult, which he regarded as atheistic and barbaric.

Perhaps even more problematic is Plutarch's assimilation of Egyptian deities into what he regards as their Greek equivalents. In the opening of his story, he presents the birth of Isis and Osiris, but the actual gods he names are Greek ones—Cronus, Rhea, Hermes, and Apollo. As a result, Plutarch alters the Egyptian story from the Pyramid texts and turns it into a hodge-podge whose components make sense neither as psychology nor as cosmology.

Plutarch's account begins with Cronus and Rhea, who must in his view be the equivalents of Nut and Geb, gods of heaven and earth. Yet the story as Plutarch tells it is confused in relation to Egyptian myth. His Rhea (= Nut) is represented as bearing children from Helius (= Re), Geb and Hermes (= Thoth). There is no indication in Egyptian sources that Nut had consorts other than Geb or fathered children with anyone else. Continuing with the story, Plutarch has Hermes (Thoth) playing draughts with the Moon. This opponent seems to represent darkness and so is likely to have been the Egyptian god Seth, whom Plutarch represents as Typhon.

In the next generation, Plutarch distorts the Ennead of Heliopolis by inserting into it the elder Horus as a sibling of Isis and Osiris. The order of the children of Geb and Nut is: Osiris, Aroueris or Apollo (elder Horus), Typhon (Seth), Isis, Nephthys. Gwyn Griffith points out that Plutarch was not an innovator: he must have been following sources which represented the stories as he does. However, since very few sources remain for the Egyptian stories, and none of them provides us with an extensive narrative, Plutarch's version is both valuable and frustrating for scholars and students of Egyptian mythology.

For all its limitations, Plutarch's version of mythology seems to be based on authentic material. Several ancient Egyptian sources corroborate his story of a battle between Typhon (Seth) and Horus (Apollo) for the kingship of Egypt. The Shabaka Stone, dated to 700 B.C.E. in Memphis, represents Geb as assigning Upper Egypt to Seth and Lower Egypt to Horus, but then deciding that Horus should wear the crown of both kingdoms. The *Pyramid Texts* contain references to Osiris' suffering fatal wounds from an attack by Seth. Plutarch's version accords well with the version Hart describes as having been developed by the priests of Heliopolis to integrate the original story of creation by Amun with the rise of Horus as representing the Pharaoh. In this version, Osiris is avenged by his son Horus, who eventually becomes the king. Plutarch, or his source, has matched these events in Egyptian mythology with counterparts in the stories of the Greek gods he views as equivalent deities. In Greek myth, Apollo (Horus) overcame Typhon (Seth); the defeat allowed him to take charge of Delphi and assume control of Greece through the proclamations of the oracle there.

Plutarch's *Isis and Osiris*

The story is related as follows in as brief a way as possible, omitting the utterly useless and superfluous features. They say that when **Rhea** secretly had intercourse with

The *Shabaka Stone*, which bears an ancient inscription, was later reused as a millstone; the grooves cut into it for this purpose damaged some parts of an earlier creation story inscribed on the stone. This closeup shows the original hieroglyphics as well as the later grooves.

The Birth of Osiris and Isis

This text, and much of the notes, comes from: Plutarch's *De Iside et Osiride.**

Rhea, Cronus Greek gods used by Plutarch for the Egyptian deities Nut and Geb.

Hermes Greek messenger god, stands for the Egyptian god Thoth, who is thought to have invented draughts.

draughts A game whose board had 30 squares. The squares may have been light and dark in a reference to the darkness and the light of the moon. The five days won by Thoth must have been days intercalated to adjust a calendar based on 12 lunar months of 30 days to the solar year.

Pamylia An Egyptian festival thought to have been established by Isis, in which women carry phallic images.

Phallephoria Processions in honor of Dionysus at which phalluses were carried. There seems not to be an equivalent Egyptian ritual associated with Osiris, but Plutarch regards Osiris as equivalent to the Greek Dionysus.

Typhon Greek monster, opponent of Zeus in Hesiod (see Ch. 3, p. 34). Here, Typhon is equated with the Egyptian god Seth.

"Osiris, when he was king"—The connection of Osiris with crop fertility is a Greek view, most likely derived from assimilating Isis in to Demeter.

The Rivalry of Seth and Horus for the Kingship

"Typhon secretly measured the body of Osiris"—This episode between Typhon (Seth) and Horus (Apollo) is corroborated by an inscription found on the Shabaka stone. (See p. 410.)

Pans and Satyrs Greek woodland demigods associated here with Dionysus.

"the city is called Coptos to this day"—Plutarch explains a variety of disparate elements in the course of his story: the causes of place names, the meaning of words, and the origin of customs. Collectively, these points are called *aitiai* or "causes," and providing aetiology is a traditional role of mythological accounts. (See Ch. 1, p. 7.)

 The Wanderings of Isis

Cronus, Helius came to know about it and set on her a curse that she should not give birth in any month or year. Then **Hermes,** falling in love with the goddess, became intimate with her, and then played **draughts** against the Moon. He won the seventieth part of each of her illuminations, and having put together five days out of the whole of his gains, he added them to the three hundred and sixty; these five the Egyptians now call the epagomenal days and on them they celebrate the gods' birthdays.

They say that on the first day Osiris was born, as he was delivered, a voice cried out that the Lord of All was coming to the light of day. Some say that a certain Pamyle, who was fetching water at Thebes, heard a voice from the temple of Zeus instructing her to cry out loudly that the great king and benefactor, Osiris, had been born; and that because of this she became Osiris' nurse, Cronus having entrusted him to her. The festival of the **Pamylia,** which is like the **Phallephoria,** is celebrated in her honor. On the second day, it is said, Aroueris was born, whom some call Apollo and the elder Horus; and on the third **Typhon** was born, not in the right time or place, but bursting through with a blow, he leapt from his mother's side. On the fourth day Isis was born, near very moist places, and on the fifth Nephthys, whom some call Teleutê (End) and Aphrodite, and some call Nikê (Victory). They say that Osiris and Aroueris were the offspring of Helius, Isis of Hermes, and Typhon and Nephthys of Cronus. For this reason kings used to regard the third of the epagomenal days as unlucky and on it they did no public business nor did they attend to their own persons until night. They say that Nephthys married Typhon, and that Isis and Osiris, being in love with each other even before they were born, were united in the darkness of the womb. Some aver that Aroueris was the fruit of this union and add that he is called the elder Horus by the Egyptians, and Apollo by the Greeks.

It is said that **Osiris, when he was king,** at once freed the Egyptians from their primitive and brutish manner of life; he showed them how to grow crops, established laws for them, and taught them to worship gods. Later he civilized the whole world as he traversed through it, having very little need of arms, but winning over most of the peoples by beguiling them with persuasive speech together with all manner of song and poetry. That is why the Greeks thought he was the same as Dionysus.

When he was away, Typhon conspired in no way against him since Isis was well on guard and kept careful watch, but on his return he devised a plot against him, making seventy-two men his fellow-conspirators and having as helper a queen who had come from Ethiopia, whom they name Asô. **Typhon secretly measured the body of Osiris** and got made to the corresponding size a beautiful chest which was exquisitely decorated. This he brought to the banqueting-hall, and when the guests showed pleasure and admiration at the sight of it, Typhon promised playfully that whoever would lie down in it and show that he fitted it, should have the chest as a gift. They all tried one by one, and since no one fitted into it, Osiris went in and lay down. Then the conspirators ran and slammed the lid on, and after securing it with bolts from the outside and also with molten lead poured on, they took it out to the river and let it go to the sea by way of the Tanitic mouth, which the Egyptians still call, because of this, hateful and abominable. They say that all these events occurred on the seventeenth day of the month of Athyr, when the sun passes through the scorpion, in the twenty-eighth year of the reign of Osiris. But some state that this was the period of his life rather than of his reign.

The first to hear of the misfortune and to spread the news of its occurrence were the **Pans and Satyrs** who live near Khemmis, and because of this, the sudden disturbance and excitement of a crowd is still referred to as "panic." When Isis heard of it she went there and then cut off one of her locks and put on a mourning garment. Accordingly **the city is called Coptos to this day.** Others think that the name indicates deprivation; for they use *koptein* to mean "to deprive," and they suggest that **Isis, when she**

was wandering everywhere in a state of distress, passed by no one without accosting him, and even when she met children, she asked them about the chest. Some of these had happened to see it and they named the river-mouth through which **Typhon's friends had pushed the box to the sea.** For this reason the Egyptians believe that children have the power of divination, and they take omens especially from children's shouts as they play near the temples and say whatever occurs to them.

When Isis found that Osiris had loved and been intimate with her sister while mistaking her for herself, and saw a proof of this in the garland of **melilot** which he had left with Nephthys, she searched for the child (for Nephthys had exposed it instantly upon giving birth to it, in fear of Typhon); and when Isis found it with the help of dogs which had led her on with difficulty and pain, it was reared and became her guard and attendant, being called **Anubis.** He is said to keep watch over the gods as dogs do over men.

They say that she learned as a result of this that the chest had been cast up by the sea in the land of **Byblos** and that the surf had brought it gently to rest in a heath-tree. Having shot up in a short time into a most lovely and tall young tree, the heath enfolded the chest and grew around it, hiding it within itself. Admiring the size of the tree, the king cut off the part of the trunk which encompassed the coffin, which was not visible, and used it as a pillar to support the roof. They say that Isis heard of this through the divine breath of rumor and came to Byblos, where she sat down near a fountain, dejected and tearful. She spoke to no one except the queen's maids, whom she greeted and welcomed, plaiting their hair and breathing upon their skin a wonderful fragrance which emanated from herself. When the queen saw her maids she was struck with longing for the stranger's hair and for her skin, which breathed ambrosia; and so Isis was sent for and became friendly with the queen and was made nurse of her child. The king's name, they say, was **Malcathros;** some say that the queen's name was **Astarte,** others Saôsis, and others Nemanous, whom the Greeks would call Athenais.

They say that Isis nursed the child, putting her finger in its mouth instead of her breast, but that in the night she **burned the mortal parts of its body,** while she herself became a **swallow,** flying around the pillar and making lament until the queen, who had been watching her, gave a shriek when she saw her child on fire, and so deprived it of immortality. The goddess then revealed herself and demanded the pillar under the roof. She took it from beneath with the utmost ease and proceeded to cut away the heath-tree. This she then covered with linen and poured sweet oil on it, after which she gave it into the keeping of the king and queen; to this day the people of Byblos venerate the wood, which is in the temple of Isis. The goddess then fell upon the coffin and gave such a loud wail that the younger of the king's sons died—the elder son she took with her, and placing the coffin in a boat, she set sail. When the river Phaedrus produced a somewhat rough wind towards dawn, in a fit of anger she dried up the stream.

As soon as she happened on a deserted spot, there in solitude she opened the chest and pressing her face to that of Osiris, she embraced him and began to cry. She then noticed that the boy had approached silently from behind and had observed her, whereupon she turned round and full of anger gave him a terrible look. The boy was unable to bear the fright, and dropped dead.

Osiris, Late Period, Budapest Museum of Fine Art. He wears elaborate headgear, the so-called atef crown. His body is wrapped up as if he were a mummy.

"Isis . . . wandering everywhere in . . . distress"—This image of Isis is well known in every phase of Egyptian mythology.

"Typhon's friends had pushed the box to the sea"—Seth has defeated Osiris and made away with his body.

melilot Sweet clover.

Anubis Egyptian god of the dead and of embalming, often represented with a dog's head. Some stories consider him the child of Isis. Apuleius includes a figure of Anubis in the procession of Isis carrying the herald's wand of Hermes and a green palm branch (see p. 416).

Isis Finds the Coffin of Osiris

Byblos A major port of Phoenicia, now Lebanon. This episode is thought to have been influenced by the experiences of Demeter when she goes to Eleusis to seek Persephone. (See Ch. 27, pp. 393ff.)

"Melcathros . . . Astarte"—The names of the king and queen are reminiscent of the Phoenician gods Melcarth, associated with Heracles, and Astarte, the Phoenician goddess of love who was associated with the Egyptian Hathor.

"burned the mortal parts of its body"—Demeter behaves similarly with her charge Demophoön. (See Ch. 27, p. 396.)

swallow The walls of the temple at Abydos describe Isis in the form of a sparrow hawk receiving the seed of Osiris. For the Greeks, the swallow represented mourning.

Maneros Herodotus identifies Maneros as the only son of the first king of Egypt, who died before his time and was the subject of songs of mourning. Herodotus also links him to Linus, who engages in a musical contest with Apollo. This story links Isis with Venus, the Roman goddess of love, who grieves over the death of her human lover Adonis. Plutarch may be thinking here of a ceremony in honor of Adonis which was performed at Byblos in the temple of Astarte.

"image of a dead man which is carried around in a chest"—We would describe such an image as a *memento mori*, Latin words meaning "be mindful of your death," or in a more familiar Latin warning, *carpe diem*, "seize the day," for whatever activity the speaker regards as worthy.

"Having journeyed to her son Horus"—The first mention of Isis' son Horus (as opposed to her brother Horus). Here the story returns to Egypt. Herodotus represents Leto (the mother of Apollo = Horus) as hiding her son in this area. In Egyptian myth, Wedjoyet and her son Nefertem are the main gods in this area. Egyptians linked Wedjoyet with Hathor, who may have been the first goddess represented as the mother of Horus. Nearby Khemmis is said to be the birthplace of Horus, son of Isis.

papyrus boat   In the procession of Isis, the high priest carries a lamp shaped like a boat, presumably in honor of Isis' voyage. (See p. 412.)

"distributed them to each city"—Besides the element of aetiology or explanation for the many tombs of Osiris, one in each district of Egypt, the story seems to suggest a ceremony in which a meal was divided into a precise number of parts to be shared by clan leaders.

"his male member"—In the Greek creation story, Cronus cuts off the penis of Uranus (see Ch. 3, p. 31). This motif may be an intrusion from the Greek tale, as Osiris will still procreate after this, or it may underline the miraculous nature of the generation of Horus.

"Horus won"—The battle was for control over Egypt. The victory indicates the Pharaoh's link with Horus.

"he ripped the crown from her head"—In the Egyptian version, which Plutarch found "useless," Horus rips off his mother's head. The process of rationalization makes the story seem more reasonable, but it destroys its original purpose—the explanation of why Isis had a cow's head in some of her appearances, a characteristic she takes from Hathor, the mother goddess of the previous generation. On the rationalization of myth, see Ch. 2, p. 20.

Some say that it did not happen so, but, as we said before, that he fell into the sea and is honored because of the goddess, being the same person as the **Maneros** of whom the Egyptians sing in their banquets. Some say the boy was called [Palaestinus or] Pelousius and that the city founded by the goddess (Pelusium) was named after him; also that the Maneros of whom they sing was the discoverer of music and poetry. Others again say that it is not the name of a man at all, but an expression such as comes naturally to men as they drink and make merry: "The best of luck to this and that!" For this sentiment, signified by the word Maneros, is expressed by the Egyptians on all festive occasions. For instance, there is the **image of a dead man which is carried round in a chest** and shown them: this is not, as some assume, a memorial of the suffering of Osiris, but they say that thus they exhort their inebriated companions to use the present and enjoy it, since every one will very soon be like the image seen; this is why they bring it into the feast.

Having journeyed to her son Horus who was being brought up in Buto, Isis put the box aside, and Typhon, when he was hunting by night in the moonlight, came upon it. He recognized the body, and having cut it into fourteen parts, he scattered them. When she heard of this, Isis searched for them in a **papyrus boat,** sailing through the marshes. That is why people who sail in papyrus skiffs are not harmed by crocodiles, which show either fear or veneration because of the goddess. From this circumstance arises the fact that many tombs of Osiris are said to exist in Egypt, for the goddess, as she came upon each part, held a burial ceremony. Some deny this, saying that she fashioned images and **distributed them to each city** as though she was giving the whole body, so that he (Osiris) might be honored by more people and that Typhon, if he overcame Horus, when he sought for the true tomb, might be baffled in his search because many tombs would be mentioned and shown.

The only part of Osiris which Isis did not find was **his male member;** for no sooner was it thrown into the river than the lepidotus, phagrus and oxyrhynchus ate of it, fish which they most of all abhor. In its place Isis fashioned a likeness of it and consecrated the phallus, in honor of which the Egyptians even today hold festival.

Afterwards Osiris came to Horus, it is said, from the underworld, and equipped and trained him for battle. Then he questioned him as to what he considered to be the finest action, and Horus said, "To succor one's father and mother when they have suffered wrong." Osiris asked him again what he considered to be the most useful animal for those going out to battle. When Horus replied, "The horse," he was surprised and he queried why he did not name the lion rather than the horse. Horus answered that the lion was helpful to someone in need of aid, but that the horse routed the fugitive and so destroyed completely the force of the enemy. Osiris was pleased on hearing this, thinking that Horus had adequately prepared himself. When many were coming over, as they say, to the side of Horus, there came also Thoueris, Typhon's concubine; and a snake which pursued her was cut in pieces by Horus, for which reason they now throw out a piece of rope in public and cut it up. The battle then lasted for many days and **Horus won.** When Isis came across Typhon tied in bonds, she did not kill him, but freed him and let him go. Horus did not take this at all calmly, but laying hands on his mother **he ripped off the crown from her head.** Hermes however put on her instead a cow-headed helmet. When Typhon brought a charge of illegitimacy against Horus, Hermes helped Horus, and the latter was judged by the gods to be legitimate. Typhon was defeated in two other battles, and Isis, having had sexual union with Osiris after his death, bore Harpocrates, prematurely delivered and weak in his lower limbs.

A Ritual of Isis

Although Egyptian civilization is usually considered to end with Roman occupation in 30 B.C.E., some Egyptian deities like Isis and Serapis survived and were incorporated into the complicated mixture of rituals, cults, and religions that made up the belief structure of the Roman Empire, at least until its Christianization in 337 C.E., and to some degree even after that. As explained in the introduction of this chapter (p. 410), the worship of Isis persisted in the Roman Empire at least until 394 C.E. As we have already seen in the preceding excerpt from Plutarch, Isis came to be identified with a variety of other goddesses from throughout the Roman Empire.

The following text comes from *The Golden Ass,* a Roman novel by Apuleius, who lived from 125 to ca. 170 C.E. The protagonist of the story, Lucius, is accidentally turned into an ass by dabbling in ill-understood magic, and has a wide range of adventures while in that form. He learns that only by eating roses can he return to his human form, but the flowers are scarce. At the end of the novel, he sees a vision of Isis, who calls upon him to become her follower, and the next day Lucius regains his human form upon seeing a procession of Isis, is described in detail, and munching on a garland of roses, which were sacred to the goddess.

The ritual which Lucius happens upon is the one called the *Ploiaphesia,* a springtime blessing of ships which celebrated the opening of the year's navigation after the dangers of winter storms were past. This festival is thought to be the origin of modern-day Carnival celebrations which often occur in relation to Easter or Christmas. Though not included in the account excerpted here, the floats of carnivals in Italy and the Rhineland are thought to derive from the ship-shaped floats used in the celebration of this ritual of Isis. However, many aspects of the ritual described by Apuleius are familiar to us from contemporary Carnival celebrations: the strewing of flower petals, the grotesque costumes, cross-dressing, elaborate regalia with sparkling headdresses, and the procession gleaming with lights and shimmering mirrors. Other elements, like carrying the figure of the goddess in procession, bear a resemblance to processions in honor of saints and of Mary, the mother of God, carried out in many Christian contexts to this day.

By this time the forerunners of the main procession were gradually appearing, every man richly decked **as his votive fancy suggested.** One fellow was girded about the middle like a soldier; another was scarfed like a huntsman with hunting-knife and shoes; another, wearing gilt sandals, silken gown, and costly ornaments, walked with a woman's mincing gait; another with his leg-harness, targe, helm, and sword, looked as if he had come straight from gladiatorial games. Then, sure enough, there passed by a man assuming the magistrate with fasces and purple robe; and a man playing the philosopher with cloak, staff, wooden clogs, and goat's beard; a fowler with bird-lime elbowing a fisherman with hooks. I also saw **a tame she-bear dressed as a matron** and carried in a sedan-chair; an ape with bonnet of plaited straw and saffron-hued garment, holding in his hand a golden cup and representing Phrygian **Ganymede** the shepherd; and lastly, an ass with wings glued on his back ambling after an old man—so that you could at once have exclaimed that one was Pegasus and the other **Bellerophon,** and would have laughed at the pair in the same breath.

Into this playful masquerade of the overflowing populace the procession proper now marched its way. Women glowing in their white vestments moved with symbolic gestures of delight. Blossomy with the chaplets of the Spring, they scattered flowerets out of the aprons of their dresses all along the course of the holy pageant. Others, who bore polished mirrors on their backs, walked before the Goddess and reflected all the people coming after as if they were advancing towards the Image. Others, again, carrying combs of ivory, went through the various caressive motions of combing and **dressing the queenly tresses of their Lady;** or they sprinkled the street with drops of unguent and genial balm.

There was a further host of men and women who followed with lanterns, torches, wax tapers, and every other kind of illumination in honor of Her who was **begotten of the Stars of Heaven.** Next came the musicians, interweaving in sweetest measures the notes of pipe and flute; and then a supple choir of chosen youths, clad in snow-white

Harpocrates, Late Period, Budapest Museum of Fine Art. The god is depicted sucking his finger, and wears the hair lock characterizing him as a child.

This text comes from: Apuleius, *The Golden Ass.* *

"as his votive fancy suggested"— The comic figures at the beginning of the procession poked fun at persons of authority and even the gods themselves. This would not have seemed strange to the Romans, who did not feel that seriousness was part of the honor due to a god. In fact, clowning and obscenity were often incorporated into the worship of the gods. An example from classical Greece includes the performance of comedies in honor of Dionysus in which actors wear oversized leather phalluses.

"a tame she-bear dressed as a matron"—One of Isis' most important associations was with Artemis, whose cult animal was the bear.

Ganymede The handsome boy carried off by Zeus to be his lover.

Bellerophon Accomplishes a series of difficult tasks with the help of Pegasus, a winged horse provided to him by Athena, the goddess of wisdom.

"dressing the queenly tresses of their Lady"—R. E. Witt notes that such "mistresses of the wardrobe" (183) are found to this day in the procession in honor of St. Agatha in Catania, Sicily.

* Apuleius, *The Golden Ass,* Trans. Jack Lindsay, 239–42. Copyright © 1932. Used by permission of University of Indiana Press.

"begotten of the Stars of Heaven"—Isis was born from the union of Geb (Earth) and Nut (Sky).

Serapis A deity of Egyptian origin who becomes a replacement for Osiris as Isis' consort in non-Egyptian versions of her cult, most notably at Alexandria.

"linen garments of the purest white"—Traditionally worn by initiates. This, and the shaven heads of the men (see below) mark their passage through the liminal period of initiation: see Turner, Chapter 26, p. 382.

"bore the relics of the mighty gods"—The items they carry are symbols of the powers of Isis and the deities associated with her. They may also figure in the ceremonies in her honor.

"a blazing lamp . . . its long bowl was gold"—The lamp may have been boat-shaped, in honor of Isis' own travels by boat to recover the body of Osiris. The goddess was also called "the Giver of Good Sailing." Her protection of sailors was also based on her connection with the moon.

"the wand of Mercury"—In Rome, the god was called "Hermanubis," a blending of Hermes, the Greek god who led the dead to the underworld, and Anubis, the Egyptian lord of the underworld.

"he let milk trickle to the ground"—See "Cow," below.

Cow Isis was associated with Hathor, the goddess who often bore the shape of a cow.

"Secret Things"—The contents of the chest are a mystery. According to some accounts, it contained the head of Osiris, or his penis.
"a small urn"—It was reminiscent of the canopic jars used in Egypt to hold the entrails of the mummified dead. It may have contained water from the Nile. The handle may recall the battle of Osiris with Seth, who could take on the form of a snake.

holiday tunics, came singing a delightful song which an expert poet (by grace of the Muses) had composed for music, and which explained the antique origins of this day of worship. Pipers also, consecrated to mighty **Serapis,** played the tunes annexed to the god's cult on pipes with transverse-mouthpieces and reeds held sidelong towards the right ear; and a number of officials kept calling out, "Make way for the Goddess!"

Then there came walking a great band of men and women of all classes and ages, who had been initiated into the Mysteries of the Goddess and who were all clad in **linen garments of the purest white.** The women had their hair anointed and hooded in limpid silk; but the men had shaven shining polls. Terrene stars of mighty deity were these men and women; and they kept up a shrill continuous tingle upon sistra of brass and silver and even gold. The chief ministers of the ceremony, dressed in surplices of white linen tightly drawn across the breast and hanging loose to the feet, **bore the relics of the mighty gods** exposed to view. The first priest held on high **a blazing lamp**—not at all like the lamps that illumine our evening suppers; for **its long bowl was gold,** and it thrust up from an aperture in the middle a fat flame. The second priest was similarly vestured, but he carried in both hands model altars to which the auxiliary love of the supreme Goddess has given the fitting title of Auxilia. The third priest grasped a palm tree with all its leaves subtly wrought in gold, and **the wand of Mercury.**

The fourth priest displayed the Symbol of Equity; a left hand molded with open palm (since the left hand seemed to be more adapted to administer equity than the busier, craftier right hand). The same man also bore a vessel of gold rounded into the shape of a woman's breast, from which **he let milk trickle to the ground.** The fifth priest had a winnowing-fan constructed with thickset sprigs of gold; and the sixth priest had an amphora.

After these came the Gods themselves (deigning to walk before our eyes on the feet of men). First we saw the dreadful messenger of the gods of heaven and hell, Anubis, with his face blackened on one side and painted gold on the other, lifting on high his dog's head and bearing his rod in his left hand. Close upon his heels followed a **Cow** (emblem of the Goddess that is fruitful mother of all) sitting upright upon the proud shoulders of her blessed worshipper. Another man carried the chest that contained the **Secret Things** of her unutterable mystery. Another bore in his beatified bosom a venerable effigy of Supreme Deity, which showed no likeness to any bird or beast (wild or tame) or even to man, but which was worthy of reverence because of its exquisite invention and originality: a symbol inexpressible of the true religion that should be veiled in Deep Silence. This effigy was of burnished gold, made as follows: **a small urn** was delicately hollowed out with a round bottom: the strange hieroglyphs of the Egyptians covered its outside; the spout was shaped rather low but jutting out like a funnel; the handle on the other side projected with a wide sweep; and on this stood an asp, stretching up his scaly, wrinkled, swollen throat and twining round the whole length.

Further Reading

Apuleius. *The Golden Ass.* Trans. Jack Lindsay. Bloomington, IN: University of Indiana Press, 1932.

Hart, George. *The Legendary Past: Egyptian Myths.* Avon: British Museum Publications, 1990.

Rundle Clark, R. T. *Myth and Symbol in Ancient Egypt.* London: Thames and Hudson, 1959.

Traunecker, Claude. *The Gods of Egypt.* Ithaca, NY: Cornell University Press, 2001.

Witt, R. E. *Isis in the Graeco-Roman World.* Ithaca, NY: Cornell University Press, 1971.

Deciphering a Meal

MARY DOUGLAS

WHAT TO EXPECT . . . In this chapter, you learn more about the close relationship of ritual and myth—that is, ritual is at least as strong a means of cultural communication as language. Anthropologist Mary Douglas shows that everyday practices, such as eating and drinking, can reflect the broader beliefs of a culture. Using the structuralist principles of Claude Levi-Strauss, she analyzes the components and relationships expressed by the simple rituals of mealtime. Douglas starts with a discussion of the meals in her own home, suggesting that the food served must meet certain criteria to be considered a meal. By degrees, she broadens her analysis to a study of the Jewish dietary laws to consider the ways in which they reflect components found in the mythology that attends them.

As you read, recall what you know about the covenant between God and the Israelites from the Biblical creation story (Ch. 5, p. 50) and the story of the flood (Ch. 12, p. 139). Consider mealtimes in your own family and community, and compare the weekly and yearly cycle of meals you experience to those described by Douglas.

A ritual can be something as ornate and public as a royal coronation, or as simple and private as praying at certain times of the day. Mary Douglas, an anthropologist, uses a structuralist approach in thinking about myth and ritual. This means that she is searching for the underlying "structure" or organization of ideas expressed in myths and rituals. For more discussion of this approach, which originates from the work of Claude Levi-Strauss, see Chapter 20, p. 280.

In "Deciphering a Meal," Douglas first examines a fundamental human activity—eating—and describes the ritualistic activities she has observed among her family and compatriots in England. Using these observations to formulate specific principles for considering meals as rituals, she then moves on to investigate the meaning and function of the Jewish dietary laws as rituals related to the belief system found in the myths of the Bible.

Like Levi-Strauss, Douglas advocates "decoding" meals to discover their meaning. She discovers in the usual structure of a western European meal the social expectations of the society. That is, she identifies the "codes" or rules that apply to mealtimes in her household and society, and eventually in other societies as well. For example, she explains that drinks are more inclusive than meals, since we might have a casual drink with an acquaintance or business associate whom we would not invite home for dinner. Meals, however, are "exclusive," since they are reserved for family and friends. And they become even more exclusive when they are more festive and laden with ritual.

MEALS AS RITUALS

The study of meals as rituals can take different forms. Nutritionists and philosophers tell us "You are what you eat." In the article excerpted in this chapter, Douglas shows the close, even interdependent, relationships between eating and broad cultural norms. People sharing a specific culture come to expect meals consisting of certain foods prepared in particular ways. Of course, the "normal" meal varies from group to group and occasion to occasion, and it is individualized or revised according to personal tastes and experiences. For example, Americans expect roasted turkey on Thanksgiving and a cookout with grilled hamburgers and hot dogs on Independence Day. Some families, however, do not like turkey, so they substitute ham or roast beef, or they may personalize the normal meal by incorporating elements from their ethnic tradition.

However, Douglas' observations about meal-related rituals go much deeper than this. She examines the Jewish dietary laws, viewing them as more than sensible health-related prescriptions. She finds rather that the codes that describe which foods are prescribed or rejected by ancient Mosaic Law are related to the stories told by the Jews about their relationship with God. Foods fit for the table are closely related to those acceptable as religious sacrifice. And those outside the permitted boundaries for sacrificial ritual are also excluded from permissible food for humans. Douglas shows that the dietary laws represent a unified system linking sacrificial, religious rituals and practical, daily eating rituals. Thus, the codes applying to meals are deeply embedded in the Israelite society's determination to maintain its exclusive status as the Chosen People. Douglas provides examples from other aspects of the dietary laws as well. She shows that food rules mandating against mixtures (such as that of meat and milk or meat and blood) carry over into other rules against mixing, such as that forbidding Jews to marry outside their society. Dietary laws thus mirror other cultural codes.

SYNTAGMATIC AND PARADIGMATIC RELATIONS

In her analysis, Douglas makes extended use of a concept developed by Levi-Strauss, so we will briefly discuss it here. He models his study of myth on the study of language, or linguistics (see Ch. 20, p. 272). Linguists have shown that we determine the meaning of language not only by looking at the meanings of the individual words, but by noticing how they are related to one another, in phrases, sentences, and paragraphs. Levi-Strauss carries this idea over into the study of myth.

Linguists identify two relationships in a language:

1. The sentence is a chain of related elements such as a subject, verb, and object. The relationship between these elements is called syntagmatic.
2. For any single element in a sentence, there is a group of words that can be placed into it. The relationship between these elements is called paradigmatic.

This is what these two relationships would look like:

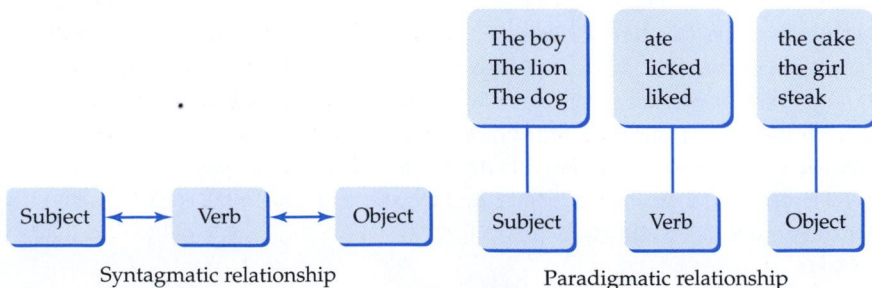

Syntagmatic relationship   Paradigmatic relationship

Douglas applies this method of analysis to her subject, meals. *Syntagmatic* is her name for the relationship of the individual servings (example: meat loaf + green beans + rice) that form courses, and courses that form meals (example: soup + main course + dessert). On the level of servings, items that have a syntagmatic relationship form a chain of items representing "normal" or "typical" meals. She describes such a typical dinner as consisting of a meat, a starch, and a vegetable; this chain could be described as a stressed element and two unstressed ones: *a + 2b*. Foods that might fit into one of the servings have a *paradigmatic* relationship to one another, such as beef, chicken, and pork in the meat (stressed: *a*) category. For example, you can't have a normal meal of potatoes, rice, and noodles because these are paradigmatically related. That doesn't mean you can't eat those items together, but they are not considered a meal in our society. The syntagmatic relationship then continues to include the meals of each day, week, and so on, until we are considering all the meals eaten in a year as a chain. If we describe our system of meals in this fashion, we are looking at it as a ritual, and we are then in a good position to think about whether this chain has anything to do with our belief system, as expressed in our myths.

Douglas answers this question for the Jewish dietary laws, but we can consider it briefly as applying to our own society. We could ask what the most complex meal of this chain was, and then see if that was related to our beliefs. For many of us, this would be the Thanksgiving dinner, the meal at which there are many courses, each with an elaborate structure. Each element of the meal would be elaborated. We would find in this abundant meal, however, some of the same structure that Douglas has identified in the smaller-scale members of the chain. That is, there would not be one meat item, but there could be several, and not one starch but several, and so on. And there would be turkey with dressing and gravy (*a + 2b*) and sweet potatoes with brown sugar and butter (*a + 2b*), and green beans with butter and almonds, and potatoes with cheese and butter, and so on.

Thanksgiving is a ritual that can easily be related to various kinds of meaning found in our society: the idea of being grateful to God for the harvest, the warm ties we feel to the members of our families, the story of the first Thanksgiving when the Pilgrims and Indians sat down together, the importance to our society of the sporting events held on Thanksgiving, excitement about the beginning of the Christmas season, a time for either personal piety or extended shopping and spending. All of these different dimensions of American beliefs and values find their culmination in Thanksgiving Day and its rituals.

Douglas would argue that Thanksgiving epitomizes the meaning of our chain of meals—a meaning that is reflected, in a lesser way, in the simpler elements of the chain: the Sunday or Saturday dinner we share with family and friends, and even the more informal and more hurried meals we make for just one or two people. The lowest link of the chain may be the TV dinner with a meat, a starch and a vegetable, or the hamburger with coleslaw and fries; but all the meals when taken together express something about our beliefs and values.

RITUAL AS MYTH-IN-ACTION

Douglas shows that ritual is at least as strong a means of cultural communication as language. In so doing, she shows an aspect of Levi-Straussian analysis: the perpetuation of myths and the transmission of cultural values from one generation to the next or from one participant to another. Societies build links to their sacred beliefs into the everyday activities of their members, and through these links, everyday life becomes as powerful a way of passing on beliefs and values as the teachings of the priest or the storyteller.

Ritual can be considered as myth-in-action, and in "Deciphering a Meal," Mary Douglas shows how ritual and myth work together to organize and give meaning to the basic activities of everyday life.

Deciphering a Meal

This text comes from: Mary Douglas, "Deciphering a Meal" in *Myth, Symbol, and Culture.**

"if food is a code"—In Ch. 20, Levi-Strauss explains how language—and myth, which he sees as a kind of language—is a code by which messages and teachings are passed among humans. Social events, like other rituals, contain sets of values important to those who observe them.

Malcah Zeldis (b. 1931), *Thanksgiving.* Douglas speaks of the ordered pattern of meals in a day or a week. In American society, the highest point of the yearly pattern is Thanksgiving Day dinner, which is analogous to Sunday in the week.

If language is a code, where is the precoded message? The question is phrased to expect the answer: nowhere. In these words a linguist is questioning a popular analogy. But try it this way: **if food is a code,** where is the precoded message? Here, on the anthropologist's home ground, we are able to improve the posing of the question. A code affords a general set of possibilities for sending particular messages. If food is treated as a code, the messages it encodes will be found in the pattern of social relations being expressed. The message is about different degrees of hierarchy, inclusion and exclusion, boundaries and transactions across the boundaries. The taking of food has a social component as well as a biological one. Food categories therefore encode social events. The next step is to take up a particular series of social events and see how they are coded.

---

*Mary Douglas, "Deciphering a Meal," in *Myth, Symbol, Culture,* edited by Clifford Geertz, 61–81. Copyright © 1971. Used by permission of Daedalus Press.

This will involve a close understanding of a microscale social system. **I shall therefore start** the exercise **by analyzing the main food categories used** at a particular point in time in a particular social system, **our home.** The humble and trivial case will open the discussion of more exalted examples.

Sometimes at home, I ask, "Would you like to have just soup for supper tonight? I mean a good thick soup—instead of supper. It's late and you must be hungry. It won't take a minute to serve." Then an argument starts: "Let's have soup now, and supper when you are ready." "No, to serve two meals would be more work. But if you like, why not start with the soup and fill up with pudding?" "Good heavens! What sort of a meal is that? A beginning and an end and no middle." "Oh, all right then, have the soup as it's there, and I'll do a Welsh rarebit as well." When they have eaten soup, Welsh rarebit, pudding, and cheese: "What a lot of plates. Why do you make such elaborate suppers?" They proceed to argue that by taking thought I could satisfy the full requirements of a meal with a single, copious dish. Several rounds of this conversation have given me a practical interest in the categories and meanings of food. I needed to know what defines the category of a meal in our home.

For analyzing the food categories used in a particular family the analysis must start with why those particular categories and not others are employed. **We will discover the social boundaries which the food meanings encode** by an approach which values binary pairs according to their position in a series. Between breakfast and the last nightcap, the food of the day comes in an ordered pattern.

Between Monday and Sunday, the food of the week is patterned again. Then there is the sequence of holidays and fast days through the year, to say nothing of life cycle feasts, birthdays, and weddings. In other words, the binary or other contrasts must be seen in their **syntagmatic relations.** The chain which links them together gives each element some of its meaning.

Eating, like talking, is patterned activity, and the daily menu may be made to yield **an analogy with linguistic form.** Being an analogy, it is limited in relevance; its purpose is to throw light on, and suggest problems of, the categories of grammar by relating these to an activity which is familiar and for much of which a terminology is ready to hand.

The two major contrasted food categories are **meals versus drinks.** Both are social events. Outside these categories, of course, food can be taken for private nourishment. Then we speak only of the item itself: "Have an apple. Get a glass of milk." If likely to interfere with the next meal, such eating is disapproved. But no negative attitude condemns eating before drinks. This and other indices suggest that meals rank higher.

Meals contrast with drinks in the relation between solids and liquids. Meals are a mixture of solid foods accompanied by liquids. With drinks the reverse holds. A complex series of syntagmatic associations governs the elements in a meal, and connects the meals through the day. One can say: "It can't be lunchtime. I haven't had breakfast yet," and at breakfast itself cereals come before bacon and eggs. Meals in their sequence tend to be named. Drinks sometimes have named categories:

"Come for cocktails, come for coffee, come for tea," but many are not named events: "What about a drink? What shall we have?" There is no structuring of drinks into early, main, light. They are not invested with any necessity in their ordering. Nor is the event called drinks internally structured into first, second, main, sweet. On the contrary, it is approved to stick with the same kind of drink. The same lack of structure is found in the solid foods accompanying drinks. They are usually cold, served in discrete units which can be eaten tidily with fingers. No order governs the choice of solids.

Meals properly require the use of at least one mouth-entering utensil per head, whereas drinks are limited to mouth-touching ones. A spoon on a saucer is for stirring, not sucking. Meals require a table, a seating order, restriction on movement and on alternative occupations.

"I shall therefore start . . . by analyzing the main food categories used . . . in our home"—Douglas sets up the rules for her scientific method, moving from an individual case to more universal conclusions.

"We will discover the social boundaries which the food meanings encode"—Putting the family's food preferences in order allows us to see the codes that underlie that order.

"syntagmatic relations"—This phrase refers to the relationship that the members of a chain have to each other. For a fuller discussion, see Introduction, p. 418.

"an analogy with linguistic form"—Eating and meals are considered as a kind of language. As with a sentence, we can ask of a meal, "What does it mean?" Douglas answers this question, first for her own household, then for the Jewish dietary laws.

"meals versus drinks"—In the author's social world, meals rank higher than drinks as signs that a person is included in a social group.

Drinks versus Meals:

- Structuring is much less stringent than with meals.
- Foods served with drinks are usually individual, "finger food" items requiring no utensils and no specific sequential order.
- Drinks are often consumed standing up or sitting in casual situations.

Meals versus Drinks:

- Meals require utensils that enter the mouth; drinks do not.
- Meals usually require sitting at a table.
- Meals require a contrast of tastes and textures.

Jean Dubuffet, (1901–1985), *Snack for Two*. Douglas notes that a snack is not a meal.

Even at Sunday breakfast, reaching for the newspapers is a signal that the meal is over. The meal puts its frame on the gathering. The rules which hedge off and order one kind of social interaction are reflected in the rules which control the internal ordering of the meal itself. Drinks and their solids may all be sweet. But a meal is not a meal if it is all in the bland-sweet-sour dimensions. A meal incorporates a number of contrasts, hot and cold, bland and spiced, liquid and semiliquid, and various textures. It also incorporates cereals, vegetables, and animal proteins.

Criticism easily fastens on the ordering of these elements in a given case.

Obviously **the meanings in our food system** should be elucidated by much closer observation. I cut it short by drawing conclusions intuitively from the social categories which emerge. Drinks are for strangers, acquaintances, workmen, and family. Meals are for family, close friends, honored guests. The grand operator of the system is the line between intimacy and distance. Those we know at meals we also know at drinks. The meal expresses close friendship. Those we only know at drinks we know less intimately. So long as this boundary matters to us the boundary between drinks and meals has meaning. There are smaller thresholds and halfway points. The entirely cold meal (since it omits a major contrast within a meal) would seem to be such a modifier. So those friends who have never had a hot meal in our home have presumably another threshold of intimacy to cross. The recent popularity of the barbecue and of more elaborately structured cocktail events which act as bridges between intimacy and distance suggests that our model of feeding categories is a common one. It can be drawn as in Figure 1.

Evidently the external boundaries are only a small part of the meaning of the meal. Somewhere else in the family system some other cognitive activity is generating the internal structuring.

We can go much further toward **discovering the intensity of meanings and their anchorage in social life** by attending to the sequence of meals. For the week's menu has its climax at Sunday lunch. By contrasting the structure of Sunday lunch with weekday lunches a new principle emerges. Weekday lunches tend to have a tripartite structure, one element stressed accompanied by two or more unstressed elements, for example a main course and cold supporting dishes. But **Sunday lunch has two main**

> "meanings in our food system"—By analyzing our food system, we determine the codes for showing inclusivity and exclusivity: who we feel close to and who we feel distant from. These social categories show that meals express more intimate relationships than do drinks.

> "discovering the intensity of meanings and their anchorage in social life"—Douglas is interested in studying meals as a way to understand the values expressed in the life of the people who take part in them.

> "Sunday lunch has two main courses"—This may not be true of American meals. Douglas is basing her argument on British customs, but this does not limit the value of her conclusions. Customs of other social groups can be charted in a similar way and would produce analogous results.

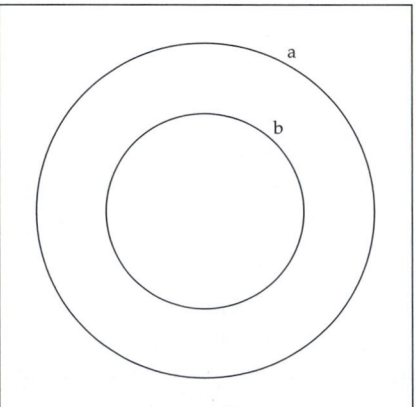

Figure 1. Social universe (a) share drinks; (b) share meals too.

courses, each of which is patterned like the weekday lunch—say, first course, fish or meat (stressed) and two vegetables (unstressed), second course, pudding (stressed), cream and biscuits (unstressed). Christmas lunch has three courses, each on the same tripartite model. Here we stop and realize that the analogy may be read in the reverse sense. **Meals are ordered in scale of importance** and grandeur through the week and the year. The smallest, meanest meal metonymically figures the structure of the grandest, and each unit of the grand meal figures again the whole meal—or the meanest meal. The perspective created by these repetitive analogies invests the individual meal with additional meaning. Here we have the principle we were seeking, the intensifier of meaning, the selection principle. A meal stays in the category of meal only insofar as it carries this structure which allows the part to recall the whole. Hence the outcry against allowing the sequence of soup and pudding to be called a meal.

As to the social dimension, admission to even the simplest meal incorporates our guest unwittingly into the pattern of solid Sunday dinners, Christmases, and the gamut of celebrations. Whereas the sharing of drinks (note the fluidity of the central item, the lack of structuring, the small, unsticky accompanying solids) expresses by contrast only too clearly the detachment and impermanence of simpler and less intimate social bonds.

Summing up, **syntagmatic relations** between meals reveal a restrictive patterning by which the meal is identified as such, graded as a minor or major event of its class, and then judged as a good or bad specimen of its kind. A system of repeated analogies upholds the process of recognition and grading. Thus we can broach the questions of interpretation which binary analysis by itself leaves untouched.

If I wish to serve **anything worthy of the name of supper** in one dish it must preserve the minimum structure of a meal. Vegetable soup so long as it had noodles and grated cheese would do, or poached eggs on toast with parsley. Now I know the formula. A proper meal is A (when A is the stressed main course) plus $2B$ (when B is an unstressed course). Both A and B contain each the same structure, in small, $a + 2b$, when a is the stressed item and b the unstressed item in a course. A weekday lunch is A; Sunday lunch is $2A$; Christmas, Easter, and birthdays are $A + 2B$. Drinks by contrast are unstructured.

To understand the categories we have placed ourselves at the hub of a small world, a home and its neighborhood. **The precoded message of the food categories** is the boundary system of a series of social events.

To sum up, the meaning of a meal is found in a system of repeated analogies. Each meal carries something of the meaning of the other meals; each meal is a structured social event which structures others in its own image. The upper limit of its meaning is set by the range incorporated in the most important member of its series. The recognition which allows each member to be classed and graded with the others depends upon the structure common to them all. **The cognitive energy** which demands that a meal look like a meal and not like a drink **is performing in the culinary medium the same exercise that it performs in language.** First, it distinguishes order, bounds it, and separates it from disorder. Second, it uses economy in the means of expression by allowing only a limited number of structures. Third, it imposes a rank scale upon the repetition of structures. Fourth, the repeated formal analogies multiply the meanings that are carried down any one of them by the power of the most weighty. By these four methods the meanings are enriched. There is no single point in the rank scale, high or low, which provides the basic meaning or real meaning. Each exemplar has the meaning of its structure realized in the examples at other levels.

From coding we are led to a more appropriate comparison for the interpretation of a meal, that is, **versification.** To treat the meal as a poem requires a more serious example than I have used hitherto. I turn to the Jewish meal, governed by the Mosaic dietary rules. For Lu Chi, a third century Chinese poet, poetry traffics in some way

---

"Meals are ordered in scale of importance"—This is true of American meals as well. We give meaning and importance to ordinary activities such as eating by expanding them for more meaningful occasions. The basic structure of the activity remains, but the more elaborate meal expresses more intense meaning.

"syntagmatic relations"—The relationship between members of a chain. For example, the parts of an individual serving (green beans-potatos-meat loaf) are syntagmatically related. (See Introduction, p. 419.)

"anything worthy of the name of supper"—For people to feel they have eaten a meal, even a one-dish supper must have all of the recognized elements of what is considered a "normal" meal in their culture.

"The precoded message of food categories"—For Douglas, rituals involving food reflect a society's expected and observed social boundaries.

"The cognitive energy . . . is performing . . . the same exercise that it performs in language"—Ritual is as effective a means of communication as language. See Ch. 20 for Levi-Strauss' theories on myth as a language that serves as society's basic means for communicating values.

"From coding we are led to . . . versification"—Douglas expands her anthropological argument by using less tangible, poetic analogies. Here she compares a meal to a poem: it is a condensed form of language that expresses a great deal of meaning. This transition allows her to talk about the meaning of the Mosaic dietary laws.

between the world and mankind. The poet is one who "traps Heaven and Earth in a cage of form." On these terms the common meal of the Israelites was a kind of classical poem. Of the Israelite table, too, it could be said that it enclosed boundless space.

At this point I turn to the rules governing **the common meal as prescribed in the Jewish religion.** It is particularly interesting that these rules have remained the same over centuries. Therefore, if these categories express a relevance to social concerns we must expect those concerns to have remained in some form alive. The three rules about meat are: 1) the rejection of certain animal kinds as unfit for the table (Leviticus 11), 2) of those admitted as edible, the separation of the meat from blood before cooking (Lev. 17:10), 3) the total separation of milk from meat, which involves the minute specialization of utensils (Exodus 23:19; 34:26; Deuteronomy 14:21).

I start with the classification of animals whose rationality I claim to have discerned. Diagrams will help to summarize the argument. First animals are classified according to degrees of holiness (see Figure 2).

At the bottom end of the scale some animals are abominable, not to be touched or eaten. Others are fit for the table, but not for the altar. None that are fit for the altar are not edible and vice versa, none that are not edible are sacrificeable. The criteria for this grading are coordinated for the three spheres of land, air, and water. Starting with the simplest, we find the sets as in Figure 3.

Water creatures, to be fit for the table, must have fins and scales (Lev. 13:9–12; Deut. 14:19). Creeping swarming worms and snakes, if they go in the water or on the land, are not fit for the table (Deut. 14:19; Lev. 11:41–43). "The term swarming creatures (*sherec*) denotes living things which appear in swarms and is applied both to those which teem in the waters (Genesis 1:20; Lev. 11:10) and to those which swarm on the ground, including the smaller land animals, reptiles and creeping insects." Nothing from this sphere is fit for the altar. The Hebrews only sanctified domesticated animals and these did not include fish. "When any one of you brings an offering to Jehovah, it shall be a domestic animal, taken either from the herd or from the flock" (Lev. 1:2). But, Assyrians and others sacrificed wild beasts, as S. R. Driver and H. A. White point out.

Air creatures (see Figure 4) are divided into more complex sets: (a), those which fly and hop on the earth (Lev. 11:12), having wings and two legs, contains two subsets,

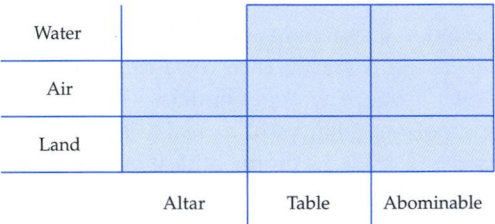

Figure 2.   Degrees of holiness.

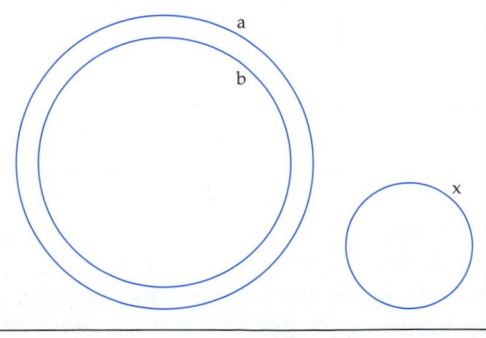

Figure 3.   Denizens of the water (a) insufficient criteria for (b); (b) fit for table; (x) abominable: swarming.

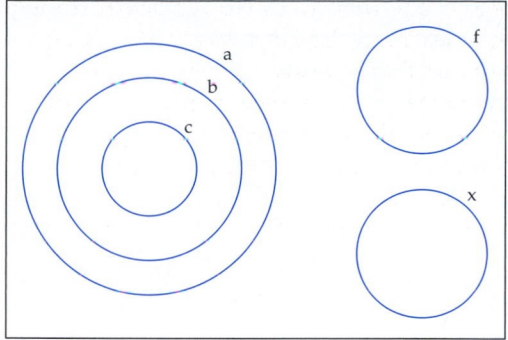

Figure 4. Denizens of the air (a) fly and hop: wings and two legs; (b) fit for table; (c) fit for altar; (f) abominable: insufficient criteria for (a); (x) abominable: swarming.

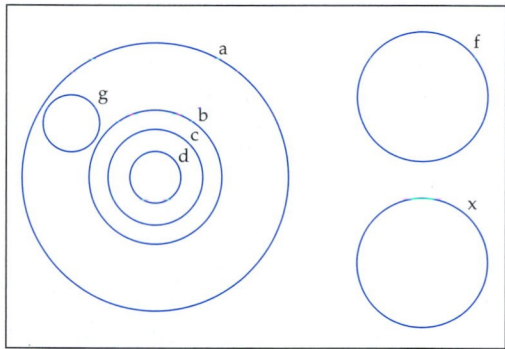

Figure 5. Denizens of the land (a) walk or hop with four legs; (b) fit for table; (c) domestic herds and flocks; (d) fit for altar; (f) abominable: insufficient criteria for (a); (g) abominable: insufficient criteria for (b); (x) abominable: swarming.

one of which contains the named birds, **abominable** and not fit for the table, and the rest of the birds (b) fit for the table. From this latter subset a sub-subset (c) is drawn, which is suitable for the altar—turtledove and pigeon (Lev. 14; 5:7–8) and the sparrow (Lev. 14:4g-53). Two separate sets of denizens of the air are abominable, untouchable creatures (f), which have the wrong number of limbs for their habitat, four legs instead of two (Lev. 9:20), and (x), the swarming insects we have already noted in the water (Deut. 14:19).

> "abominable"—Animals in each non-abominable category must have all of the characteristics for the category. If not, they are completely excluded.

The largest class of land creatures (a) (see Figure 5) walk or hop on the land with four legs. From this set of quadrupeds, those with parted hoofs and which chew the cud (b) are distinguished as fit for the table (Lev. 11:3; Deut. 14:4–6) and of this set a subset consists of the domesticated herds and flocks (c). Of these the first born (d) are to be offered to the priests (Deut. 24:33). Outside the set (b) which part the hoof and chew the cud are three sets of abominable beasts: (g) those which have either the one or the other but not both of the required physical features; (f) those with the wrong number of limbs, two hands instead of four legs (Lev. 11:27 and 29:31); (x) those which crawl upon their bellies (Lev. 11:41–44).

> 3. Land Creatures

The **isomorphism** which thus appears between the different categories of animal classed as abominable helps us to interpret the meaning of abomination. Those creatures which inhabit a given range, water, air, or land, but do not show all the criteria for (a) or (b) in that range are abominable. The creeping, crawling, teeming creatures do not show criteria for allocation to any class, but cut across them all.

> **isomorphism** This word is used in science to describe graphs and means "the same shape." Such graphs are thought to represent similar relationships. Here Douglas is saying that the diagrams for the laws about water, air, and land creatures have the same shape.

Here we have **a very rigid classification.** It assigns living creatures to one of three spheres, on a behavioral basis, and selects certain morphological criteria that are found most commonly in the animals inhabiting each sphere. It rejects creatures which are anomalous, whether in living between two spheres, or having defining features of members of another sphere, or lacking defining features. Any living being which falls outside this classification is not to be touched or eaten. To touch it is to be

> "a very rigid classification"—The Mosaic dietary laws require an animal classification based on the morphology or structural and behavioral characteristics of animals, and reject anomalies, forms which fall outside of the approved criteria.

	Under the Covenant	
Human	Israelites	others
Nonhuman	their livestock	others

Figure 6.   Analogy between humans and nonhumans

defiled and defilement forbids entry to the temple. Thus it can be summed up fairly by saying that anomalous creatures are unfit for altar and table. This is a peculiarity of the Mosaic code. In other societies anomaly is not always so treated. Indeed, in some, the anomalous creature is treated as the source of blessing and is specially fit for the altar, or as a noble beast, to be treated as an honorable adversary.

Since in the Mosaic code every degree of holiness in animals has implications one way or the other for edibility, we must follow further the other rules classifying humans and animals. Again I summarize a long argument with diagrams. First, note that **a category which divides some humans from others,** also divides their animals from others. Israelites descended from Abraham and bound to God by the Covenant between God and Abraham are distinguished from all other peoples and similarly the rules which Israelites obey as part of the Covenant apply to their animals (see Figure 6). The rule that the womb opener or first born is consecrated to divine service applies to firstlings of the flocks and herds (Exod. 22:29–30; Deut. 24:23) and the rule of Sabbath observance is extended to work animals (Exod. 20:10). The analogy by which Israelites are to other humans as their livestock are to other quadrupeds develops by indefinite stages, the **analogy between altar and table.**

Since Levites who are consecrated to the temple service represent the first born of all Israel (Numbers 3:12 and 40) there is an analogy between the animal and human firstlings. Among the Israelites, all of whom prosper through the Covenant and observance of the Law, some are necessarily unclean at any given time. No man or woman with issue of seed or blood, or with forbidden contact with an animal classed as unclean, or who has shed blood or been involved in the unsacralized killing of an animal (Lev. 18), or who has sinned morally (Lev. 20) can enter the temple. Nor can one with a blemish (Deut. 23) enter the temple or eat the flesh of sacrifice or peace offerings (Lev. 8:20). The Levites are selected by pure descent from all the Israelites. They represent the first born of Israel. They judge the cleanness and purify the uncleanness of Israelites (Lev. 13, 14). Only Levites who are without bodily blemish (Lev. 21:17–23) and without contact with death can enter the Holy of Holies. Thus we can present these rules as sets in Figures 7 and 8.

"a category which divides some humans from others"—For the Israelites, the classification of animals follows the pattern of their classification of humans.

"analogy between altar and table"—The classification in the dietary laws reflects the understanding of the world revealed by the Covenant or agreement which God made with the Israelites in the book of Genesis. See Ch. 12, pp. 141–42, for a fuller discussion of this important Biblical principle.

Analogy 1: Between humans and animals—Shows that rules concerning access to the temple apply to the Israelites as dietary rules apply to their livestock.

Meichel Pressman (1863–1953), *The Seder*. In the Jewish tradition, the home is the location of a great part of worship. The Passover seder represents the high point of the yearly cycle of Friday-night meals in celebration of the Sabbath.

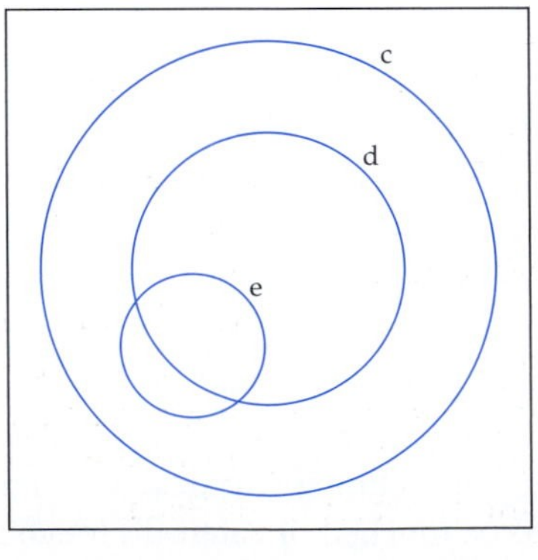

Figure 7.   The Israelites (c) under the Covenant; (d) fit for temple sacrifice: no blemish; (e) consecrated to temple service, first born.

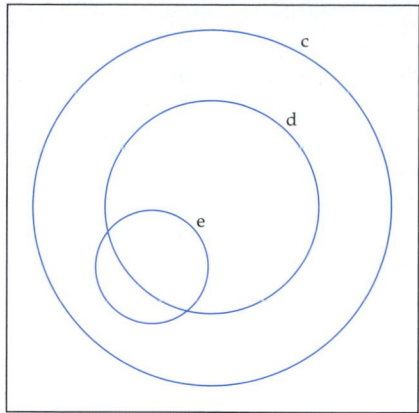

Figure 8.   Their livestock (c) under the covenant; (d) fit for temple sacrifice: no blemish; (e) consecrated to temple service, first born.

The analogy between humans and animals is very clear. So is the analogy created by these rules between the temple and the living body. Further analogies appear between the classification of animals according to holiness (Figure 2) and the rules which set up the analogy of the holy temple with its holier and holier inner sanctuaries, and on the other hand between the temple's holiness and the body's purity and the capacity of each to be defiled by the self-same forms of impurity. This analogy is **a living part of the Judeo-Christian tradition** which has been unfaltering in its interpretation of New Testament allusions. The words of the Last Supper have their meaning from looking backward over the centuries in which the analogy had held good and forward to the future celebrations of that meal. "This is my body . . . this is my blood" (Luke 22:19–20; Mark 14:22–24; Matthew 26:26–28). Here the meal and the sacrificial victim, the table and the altar are made explicitly to stand for one another.

Relating the Patterns to the Laws

Lay these rules and their patternings in a straight perspective, each one looking forward and backward to all the others, and we get the same **repetition of metonyms** that we found to be the key to the full meaning of the categories of food in the home. By itself the body and its rules can carry the whole load of meanings that the temple can carry by itself with its rules. The overlap and repetitions are entirely consistent.

What then are these meanings? Between the temple and the body we are in a maze of religious thought. What is its **social counterpart?** Turning back to my original analysis of the forbidden meats we are in a much better position to assess intensity and social relevance. For the metonymical patternings are too obvious to ignore. At every moment they are in chorus with a message about the value of purity and the rejection of impurity. At the level of a general **taxonomy of living beings** the purity in question is the purity of the categories. Creeping, swarming, teeming creatures abominably destroy the taxonomic boundaries. At the level of the individual living being impurity is the imperfect, broken, bleeding specimen. The sanctity of cognitive boundaries is made known by valuing the integrity of the physical forms. The **perfect physical specimens point to** the perfectly bounded temple, altar, and sanctuary. And these in their turn point to the hard-won and hard-to-defend **territorial boundaries of the Promised Land.** This is not reductionism. We are not here reducing the dietary rules to any political concern. But we are showing how they are consistently celebrating a theme that has been celebrated in the temple cult and in the whole history of Israel since the first Covenant with Abraham and the first sacrifice of Noah.

Analogy 2: Between the temple and the living body—Shows that only pure Levites representing the first born of Israel can enter the Holy of Holies.

"a living part of the Judeo-Christian tradition"—Christians believe that the analogies Douglas has identified in Jewish culture are continued in the New Testament's Last Supper.

"repetition of metonyms"—Just as food categories showed the beliefs of people in the home, so the Jewish dietary law's categories reveal what the Jews believe about their relationship with God.

"social counterpart"—The principles established to define the "fit for altar" category can carry over to analysis of how people behaved and why.

"taxonomy of living beings"—As Douglas has shown through the diagrams she has described, the dietary laws organize and explain the world according to Jewish faith.

"perfect physical specimens point to . . . territorial boundaries of the Promised Land"—The meals that the Jews eat remind them of the Covenant. Each meal is a celebration of their relationship with God. The importance of the Promised Land is not, in this view, political: it expresses what God has done for his people.

Conclusion

We are left the question of why, when so much else had been forgotten about the rules of purification and their meaning, **the rules governing the Jewish meal** have persisted. What meanings do they still encode, unmoored as they partly are from their original social context? It would seem that whenever a people are aware of encroachment and danger, dietary rules controlling what goes into the body would serve as a vivid analogy of the corpus of their cultural categories at risk. But here I am, contrary to my own strictures, suggesting a universal meaning, free of particular social context, one which is likely to make sense whenever the same situation is perceived. **We have come full-circle** to Figure 1, with its two concentric circles. The outside boundary is weak, the inner one strong. Right through the diagrams summarizing the Mosaic dietary rules the focus was upon the integrity of the boundary at (b). Abominations of the water are those finless and scaleless creatures which lie outside that boundary.

Abominations of the air appear less clearly in this light because the unidentified forbidden birds had to be shown as the widest circle from which the edible selection is drawn. If it be granted that they are predators, then they can be shown as a small subset in the unlisted set, that is as denizens of the air not fit for table because they eat blood. They would then be seen to threaten the boundary at (b) in the same explicit way as among the denizens of the land the circle (g) threatens it. We should therefore not conclude this essay without **saying something more positive** about what this boundary encloses. In the one case it divides edible from inedible. But it is more than a negative barrier of exclusion. In all the cases we have seen, it bounds the area of structured relations. Within that area rules apply. Outside it, anything goes. Following the argument we have established by which each level of meaning realizes the others which share a common structure, we can fairly say that the **ordered system** which is a meal represents all the ordered systems associated with it. Hence the strong arousal power of a threat to weaken or confuse that category. To take our analysis of the culinary medium further we should study **what the poets say** about the disciplines that they adopt. A passage from Roy Fuller's lectures helps to explain the flash of recognition and confidence which welcomes an ordered pattern. He is quoting Allen Tate, who said: "Formal versification is the primary structure of poetic order, the assurance to the reader and to the poet himself that the poet is in control of the disorder both outside him and within his own mind." The rules of the menu are not in themselves more or less trivial than the rules of verse to which a poet submits.

Further Reading

Douglas, Mary. "Deciphering a Meal." In *Myth, Symbol, Culture,* ed. Clifford Geertz, 61–81. New York, NY: Norton, 1971.

———. *Purity and Danger: An Analysis of Concepts of Pollution and Taboo.* London and New York: Routledge, 2002.

The Rituals of Northern Europe

H. R. ELLIS DAVIDSON

WHAT TO EXPECT . . . Scholar H. R. Ellis Davidson uses a variety of literary sources as well as archeological discoveries and historical accounts to reconstruct the world of the ancient Northern Europeans. The archeological component is important because the older societies she deals with did not have a written literary tradition. As a result, it is necessary to infer from material traces of the cultures the beliefs and values of the people who used them. However, Davidson warns, contemporary students must be ready to accept them on their own terms, as they are quite different from current beliefs and practices.

To help you formulate a more comprehensive view of the world than Snorri Sturluson presents in his *Prose Edda*, this chapter describes the integral role of the Norse gods in everyday life, and in doing so, helps you think about how myths and their attendant rituals evolve, depending on shifts in political boundaries and religious belief.

As you read, remember to compare the view of Northern European civilization in this chapter with the sense of it you obtained from reading the sections of the *Prose Edda* describing the Norse view of creation (Ch. 7, p. 78), the end of the world at Ragnarok (Ch. 13, p. 147), and the adventures of the gods (Ch. 18, p. 218). Also, note the terms "syncretism", "rationalization", and "euhemerism", and cite examples from the text.

We have seen that for many people and cultures, myths and rituals are closely intertwined. However, when we look for rituals associated with the stories found in Snorri Sturluson's *Prose Edda,* we find few, if any, remnants of such practices in the worship of Odin, Thor, and their companions. A valuable resource here is provided by Hilda R. Ellis Davidson, the author of *Gods and Myths of Northern Europe,* who studied archeology and English literature in England. In this book, she provides a good example of how both literature and material artifacts can help us understand the beliefs and rituals of peoples and cultures who disappeared long ago. The people of northern Europe gave up some of their ethnic characteristics as they lost their ethnic unity via emigration and intermarriage with other peoples.

The myths and beliefs of Northern Europeans are difficult to learn about because they did not have a written literary tradition, and it seems that they did not keep written records for government and trade. However, we can piece together a picture of their beliefs and customs by looking at the artifacts and buildings unearthed by archeologists and by studying the remnants of the old oral tradition which later poets wrote down in their work.

READING THE PAST: THE CONTRIBUTIONS OF ARCHEOLOGY

Many of the objects we might see in an archeological museum can tell us volumes about the people who used them. And if we take the time to learn about how and why people used these things—from everyday eating and grooming utensils to precious jewelry and ritual paraphernalia—we can "read" their values in the artifacts. Davidson tries to learn about people from the things they have left behind. For the Northern Europeans, these include artifacts such as stone and wood carvings, runes, amulets, engraved swords, helmets, and drums; sites such as ship burials and bogs in which bodies are preserved; names of places and sacred groves, trees, hills, and rivers which have inspired local lore.

Davidson reminds us that we can learn much from the mythologies of earlier peoples and, by doing so, enrich ourselves in viewing our own beliefs more clearly. She warns us, however, that we must be ready to accept them on their own terms, which are most likely very different from our beliefs and practices today. The early tribes of northern Europe may seem uncaring and even brutal in their rituals involving burning, stabbing, and sacrificing young people, wives, and beloved servants. But for them, these practices represented a very powerful belief, as they determined the sharing of the expected afterlife with those dearest to them on earth.

Through archeological evidence related to the rituals and beliefs of the early Northern European tribes, Davidson shows that some deities were immanent, while others were transcendent. As we learned in Chapter 5, gods are called transcendent when they remain more or less aloof and immortal in their own sphere and do not take part in the mortal activities of their worshippers (see p. 51). In contrast, gods are seen as immanent when they live and interact—or even interfere—with the world of worshippers. Odin is aristocratic and usually distant from the hurly-burly of everyday human activity, that is, roughly transcendent, whereas Thor is much more approachable, but crude and rough in his manners and activities, therefore immanent. For example, he even intervenes in battles to assure that his warrior-worshippers are victorious (see p. 438), and he is seen as intimately involved in the rituals of his worship. For Germanic believers, it must have been very reassuring to have the direct support of these more immanent gods and to be able to see that they displayed the same ideals, interests, and flaws as humans.

HISTORIES AND SAGAS: THE LITERARY RECORD

Davidson gathered her information from the early sagas and poetry collections of the northern European peoples, many of which were written down between the ninth and thirteenth centuries C.E. Because the writers spoke and wrote earlier versions of present-day Icelandic, Swedish, Danish, German, and English, and because the scholarly language of the time was Latin, these texts are more accessible to Westerners today than ancient writings of Mesopotamia (such as the cuneiform of *Gilgamesh*) or the pictorial narratives such as the Popol Vuh of the Mayans of Central America.

The later works, written after the Dark Ages of the late fifth through eleventh centuries C.E., had a different purpose and therefore provide a different type of information. Some, such as the *Gesta Danorum* (Deeds of the Danes), written by the Danish historian Saxo Grammaticus between 1216 and 1223, were intended as histories, providing tribute to the great warriors of the writer's ethnic group, and continued into "recent" history, up to 1187. But others, such as the *Volsung Saga* and the works bound together in the *Codex Regius* between 1270 and 1280 C.E., focused on ancient tales of gods and heroes that had been handed down in the oral tradition.

This book represents the stories told by northern European peoples through extensive excerpts from the *Prose Edda* (see Ch. 7, p. 78; Ch. 13, p. 147; and Ch. 18, p. 218). However, this literary work is just one of many fascinating sources recounting the exploits of these gods and heroes. Many characters, events, and ideas appear in several of these poems and sagas, and Snorri is known to have borrowed heavily from a variety of sources. Davidson also makes good use of them to substantiate her explanations of the rituals and beliefs of the Norse and Scandinavian tribes.

Because these works are composed by poets attempting to create an artistic piece as well as one reflecting the beliefs of the people, they fall into the category of rationalized versions of a myth, as described in Chapter 7, p. 79. The authenticity of these myths is also affected by changes in religion and ritual throughout the centuries that produced them. As the late sagas were being written down, Christianity was increasingly spreading through the descendants of the old Germanic tribes. Thus, these stories combine heathen and Christian traditions as their writers try to reconcile both worlds. For example, the *Voluspa,* a poem of the late thirteenth century which describes Ragnarok and the downfall of the Æsir, presents Baldr as a Christ-figure. The mixture of the traditions should probably be expected, especially since they had been in contact with each other for a very long time.

Through the years, scholars have come up with various ways to understand the mythology of the ancient Northern Europeans. One of the most influential has been Georges Dumézil, the French comparative philologist and mythologist, who argued that all Indo-European peoples developed a trilevel hierarchical system of organization in their society and, by extension, for their gods. The system, which Dumézil applied to societies from western Europe to areas in the Middle East and India, describes three classes of society—kings, warriors, and farmers. In addition, he argued that these classes correspond to a hierarchy of gods: the highest are those who represent wisdom, holiness, and nobility; the second, might and success in war; and the third, fertility and fruitfulness. As applied to the Norse deities, this system suggests the characteristics of Odin, Thor, and Freyr, respectively. However, Davidson's analysis should make clear that the actual functions undertaken by these gods were more complicated than Dumézil's schema allows.

CHANGING BELIEFS: RATIONALIZATION, SYNCRETISM, AND EUHEMERISM

Davidson's account helps us to track the developments in people's beliefs and practices by noticing changes in physical objects and artifacts they used. For example, she describes an object which represented an arrangement of the hammer of Thor laid out in the shape of a cross. This object was used at a time when the same person might find himself participating in some elements of the "old" religion along with practices that came from Christianity. Another example of what may represent a change in beliefs is found in Snorri Sturluson's account in the *Ynglinga Saga* of the war between the main Icelandic families of gods. The Vanir were fertility gods who may have represented a form of Norse worship preceding the Æsir who challenged them. Their hostilities seem to have ended in a draw with a truce and an exchange of hostages; by Snorri's time, the worship of the two families coexisted. The process of combining and blending separate religious traditions is called syncretism and involves rationalization, in which reasons are assigned after the fact to account for the linking of what were originally separate beliefs. For a more extensive discussion of rationalization in the context of Snorri's work, see Chapter 7.

As we study the works from this changing Northern European cultural and religious tradition, it might also help to bear in mind a theory employed by some scholars of ancient cultures. Euhemerism theorizes that people "invent" the old gods by looking backward and deifying their old historical and legendary heroes. As Christianity became more widespread in northern Europe, its adherents incorporated euhemeristic elements in their stories to downgrade the importance of ancient deities, arguing that they were not "real" gods but only rationalizations for ancient beliefs and practices. This made it easier to emphasize the importance of the new monotheistic religion and to represent recalcitrant believers in the old religions as mistaken or deluded (see Ch. 7, p. 80). In addition to Nordic textual sources, Davidson also uses a much earlier one—*Germania,* written by the Roman historian Tacitus in the first century C.E. *Germania* is different from the sagas in two major ways: it is written in classical Latin, and its purpose was a kind of propaganda. Tacitus went out from Rome to northern parts of the Empire inhabited by tribal groups who had migrated over many centuries from northern India and west-central Asia. He wanted to show the Romans that these new additions to the Empire were honorable, hospitable, resourceful, law-abiding people who would be assets to Roman civilization, although their culture and beliefs were quite different from those in the Mediterranean area. Although Tacitus selected his subjects extremely carefully, and sometimes altered details in order to fulfill his assignment, he did provide valuable information on what Davidson calls the heathen period of the Northern Europeans.

During that long period, there were times when missionaries more actively made contact with the tribes. At other times, some of the Norse and Germanic peoples were more interested in raiding monasteries and settlements of the descendants of the Roman Empire. Davidson is careful to remind us that we should not think that all of these people were engaged in similar activities at the same time or that they were affected by outside influences at the same time. She points out that tribes in the areas of present-day England, France, and Germany gave up or mediated their old beliefs long before the Scandinavians (i.e., Swedes, Danes, and Icelanders); for this reason, we get our best information on the ancient religious practices and beliefs by going back to the Nordic sources. The following excerpt from *Gods and Myths of Northern Europe* shows us how these writings, along with archeological evidence, can teach us much about the rituals and beliefs of those peoples.

This text comes from: H. R. Ellis Davidson, *Gods and Myths of Northern Europe.**

Gods and Myths of Northern Europe

Odin, Lord of Hosts

Odin as a God of Violence and Cunning

"late heathen period"—The 9th and 10th centuries.

"Odin appears . . . as . . . giver of victory"—If a warrior fell in battle, he enjoyed the best kind of afterlife.

"Snorri's account"—For sections of Snorri Sturluson's *Prose Edda*, see Ch. 7, 13, and 18.

"Valhalla . . . was peopled by the chosen ones"—Valhalla was not a paradise for all. Only warriors dedicated to Odin could be chosen.

Odin's Followers

"Like any earthly ruler"—Odin and his warriors had a mutually dependent relationship, much like earthly rulers and their vassals.

"Sigmund the Volsung"—The Volsungs were a line of kings whose ancestors included Odin himself and the daughter of a giant.

Violence and battle were always close at hand in the lives of men of the heathen period in northwestern Europe. It seems fitting then to begin our survey of the beliefs of the north by concentrating on the gods to whom they turned for help in the hazards and chances of warfare.

In the **late heathen period** there is no doubt as to the main figure who represented the God of Battle, for **Odin appears continually as the lord of hosts and giver of victory.** In **Snorri's account** and in many poems he is shown welcoming to his abode courageous men who fell in battle. His creatures were the raven and the wolf who feast upon the slain, while his dwelling was the hall of the slain, Valhalla. In Norwegian court poetry of the tenth century, he is pictured choosing champions to fall in battle, so that after death they can be enrolled in his warrior band and help him to go out to the last battle of the gods with a magnificent following.

This impressive conception has caught the imagination of later writers, and it is sometimes assumed that all men hoped to go to Valhalla after death. The literature however gives us no real reason to assume that **Valhalla** was ever regarded as a paradise for all; it **was peopled by the chosen ones,** the aristocratic warriors who had worshipped the god on earth. Those who joined Odin in Valhalla were princely warriors, kings, and distinguished leaders and heroes who followed the god in life and pledged him their loyal service in return for his help.

Like any earthly ruler, Odin handed out weapons to his chosen followers, and once they had received them, they were bound to give him loyal service till death and beyond it. Thus **Sigmund the Volsung** received a splendid sword, which the god himself brought into the hall and thrust into the great tree supporting the roof. The sword was regarded both as a family heirloom and a gift from Odin, and when Sigmund's time came to die, Odin appeared on the battlefield and shattered the blade with his spear. The pieces of the broken sword were reforged for Sigmund's son, Sigurd, who also found favor with Odin, and was given a wonderful horse bred from Odin's own steed, **Sleipnir.**

Not only treasures but valuable counsel might be given to chosen warriors. Odin taught Sigmund **spells of battle,** and he instructed Hadding, another of his heroes, how to draw up his forces in wedge formation. When Hadding profited by this advice, and led out his army, **Odin himself** in the form of an old man **stood behind them,** and shot so swiftly with his bow that ten arrows sped as one, while he drove away the storm clouds which the enemy had raised by magic. Similarly he gave advice to Harald Wartooth, king of the Danes, to whom he appeared as "an old man of great height, lacking one eye and clad in a hairy mantle." **He promised Harald** immunity from wounds, and in return Harald vowed to give him "all the souls which his sword cast out of their bodies!" **Saxo** has also preserved in the eighth book of his history the story of what happened to Harald **when the god's favour was withdrawn.** First Odin roused up enmity between him and his great friend King Ring, and then he gave to Ring the cherished secret of wedge formation. As Harald drove out to meet Ring in battle, he suddenly recognized the god in the place of his own charioteer. He begged him for one more victory, swearing to dedicate to Odin all who fell in battle. But the driver was relentless, and even as Harald pleaded he flung him down from the chariot, and slew him with his own sword as he fell.

In Old Norse literature the rites said to belong to Odin are dedication by a spear, hanging, and burning. Snorri tells us in *Ynglinga Saga* that marking with a spear at the time of death and burning of the dead were practices followed by the Swedish worshippers of Odin, and that they claimed to be following their god's own example. According to the poem *Havamal* (Utterance of the High One), Odin himself recounts how he was pierced with a spear and hanged on a tree, a sacrifice for the attainment of wisdom. We have independent evidence for the sacrifice of men and beasts by hanging as late as the eleventh century in Sweden.

An account of a sacrifice to Odin by hanging is given in one of the late sagas, *Gautreks Saga.* This has so convincing a ring that in spite of its late date it may be based on memories of the traditional sacrificial cult of the god. A Viking leader King **Vikar** prayed to Odin for a favourable wind, and when lots were drawn to decide who should be given to Odin in return for this, it fell upon the king himself. In this embarrassing situation his men decided to stage a mock sacrifice. Vikar was to stand on a tree-stump with a calf's intestines looped round his neck and fastened to the tree above. Starkad, a hero and follower of Odin, was to stand beside him with a long rod in his hand. He thrust this rod at the king, uttering the words, "Now I give thee to Odin." At this moment a deadly substitution took place and the ritual became reality.

> He let the fir bough go. The rod became spear, and pierced the king through. The stump fell from under his feet, and the calf's intestines became a strong rope, while the branch shot up and lifted the king among the boughs, and there he died.
>
> Gautreks Saga, 7

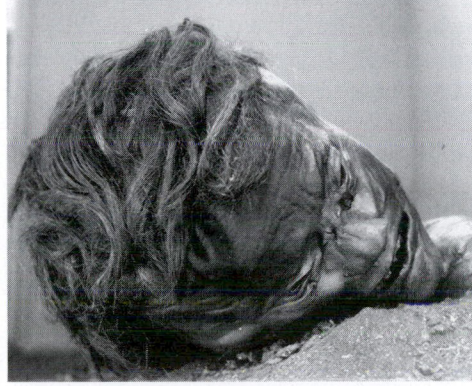

Woman victim of human sacrifice. Viking, Migration Period, from Jutland. There are grounds for believing that women also had the right of entry into Odin's Realm if they suffered a sacrificial death.

Sleipnir Snorri tells us that he had eight legs. (See p. 445.)

"spells of battle"—Supernatural help is added to practical instruction such as the wedge-shaped battle formation.

"Odin himself . . . stood behind them"—The god helps the warriors to take his advice and win.

"[Odin] promised Harald"—Odin strikes a deal: he will protect the warrior and will receive in return the souls of Harald's victims.

Saxo Saxo Grammaticus, who wrote a 16–volume history of the Danes covering events from before the birth of Christ to 1187 C.E.

"when the god's favour was withdrawn"—Odin orchestrates Harald's death.

 Odin's Ritual

Vikar Ironically, the name is the root of our word "vicarious" meaning "indirectly, through a representative."

Odin and Other Gods of Justice

Here noose and spear are used together in a ritual killing. Among the many titles of Odin, it is noticeable that we find Spear-Brandisher, and God of Hanged Men.

Snorri also emphasized the importance attributed to **the burning of the dead** among the followers of Odin. All objects burned on the pyre with their owners were deemed to pass with them to Valhalla, he tells us. The double ritual of hanging and stabbing is accompanied by burning in a tenth-century account of a sacrifice held on the **Volga,** among the Swedish settlers there. It was witnessed by **Ibn Fadlan,** an Arab traveller, who left a detailed account of what he saw, and he tells how a slave-girl was sacrificed at the funeral of her master.

Odin possessed the **great spear Gungnir,** and this was evidently used to stir up warfare in the world. In *Voluspa,* the cause of the first war among the gods is said to be brought about by Odin flinging his spear into the host. Thus up to the end of the heathen period the picture of the god as fierce provoker of war and giver of victory persisted in the north.

We have good reason to believe that Odin as god of war has developed out of earlier conceptions among the Germanic peoples on the Continent of the god who ruled over the battlefield. The god Wodan, or Wotan, had the same type of sacrifice associated with his name. The **Heruli,** for instance, worshippers of Wodan, practiced a double ritual of stabbing and burning. Among them the victims were not necessarily captives taken in war, but those also who were on the point of death from illness or old age.

Tacitus tells us that the Hermundari and the Chatti sacrificed to Mars and Mercury in return for victory. There is little doubt that Mercury represented the Germanic god Wodan at the time when Tacitus wrote. In England the same god, Woden, gave his name to the fourth day of the week, Wednesday, the day which in France is called *Mercredi* after the Roman god. Just as Odin was looked on as the divine ancestor of the Swedes, so Woden was believed to be the founder of many royal dynasties. Most of the Anglo-Saxon kings looked back to him as their divine ancestor.

At the time of Tacitus however there is reason to believe that the Roman god of war, Mars, was identified not with Wodan, but with another Germanic god, **Tiwaz.** Odin in fact appears to be the successor of both Wodan and Tiwaz, retaining some of the qualities and attributes of both these gods. In Snorri's account Tiwaz appears as Tyr. He is only a shadowy figure, but Snorri mentions that men prayed to him for victory, and also that he was renowned for his wisdom as well as for his valor. Tiwaz in his day must have been a very great power among the heathen Germans. The third day of the week, sacred in Rome to Mars, was called after him throughout the Teutonic world, so that against *Mardi* in France we have Tuesday in England. In Old Norse his name was used as a synonym for "god," and Odin bore among his titles that of *Sigtyr,* the *Tyr,* or god, of victory. The name Tiwaz is related to the Greek Zeus, and to the Roman Jupiter (who was originally *Dyaus pitar,* father Dyaus). All three are thought to be derived from *dicus,* the Indo-Germanic word for god, which stands also for the shining heaven and the light of day. It is probable that Tiwaz was the supreme sky god of the Germans as well as their god of battle.

Although Odin had in the main taken the place of Tiwaz at the close of the heathen period, memories of the earlier battle god still lingered. In one of the *Edda* poems dealing with spells to use in battle (*Sigrdr'fumál,* 5), men are told to carve runes of victory, giving the name of Tyr. We have what may be instances of this name on weapons. **A helmet from Negau** in Austria bears an inscription in North Italic letters of the second century B.C.E., which has been thought by some scholars to give the name *Teiwa,* an archaic form of the god's name. A spear from Kowel bears the rune which is the initial of the god's name. These may be a sign of the ancient Germanic war god, cut by one who wished to claim his help and protection in battle.

It is probably significant that the one myth about Tyr which has survived in the pages of Snorri concerns the **binding of the wolf Fenrir,** the adversary of the gods. Only Tyr was brave enough to feed him, and willing to sacrifice his hand in order that the monster should be bound. Later on, the wolf is the special adversary of Odin at Ragnarok. It seems likely that in earlier Germanic myths it was Tiwaz who was matched against him. Snorri tells us that Tyr was killed by **Garm, a hound of the underworld, who may well be Fenrir under another name.**

In Tiwaz we have an early Germanic war god, an ancestor of Odin. He had great powers, and extensive sacrifices were made to him. He was a one-handed god, and since a one-handed figure wielding a weapon is seen among Bronze Age rock-engravings in Scandinavia it has been suggested that his worship may go back to very early times in the north, and that the myth of the god binding the wolf is of great antiquity. Certainly Tiwaz differs in one respect from Wodan, who seems to have taken over his position as god of battle later in the heathen period. Tiwaz was associated with law and justice, whereas Wodan and Odin are reproached on many occasions for fickleness and treachery.

While Odin is renowned for wisdom and cunning, he is not represented as in any way concerned with justice among men. To find a reason for this change in the character of the war god, it will be necessary to return to the Scandinavian Odin and to consider some of his companions and followers in Asgard and on earth.

In **Snorri's description** of the after-life for warriors, there are certain beings who form a link between Odin and the slain, and between the worlds of the living and the dead. These are the female spirits called Valkyries, who wait on the warriors in Valhalla, and no description of the gods of battle can be complete without them. In the descriptions of the poets they appear as women who wear armor and ride on horseback, passing swiftly over sea and land. They carry out Odin's commands while the battle rages, giving victory according to his will, and at the close they lead the slaughtered warriors to Valhalla. Sometimes, on the other hand, they are pictured as the wives of living heroes. Human princesses are said to become Valkyries, as though they were the priestesses of some cult.

The conception of a company of women associated with battle among the heathen Germans is further implied by two spells which have survived into Christian times.

Franz Stassen, *Wotan*, 1914. For a series of illustrations for Wagner's "Das Rheingold."

"A helmet from Negau"—Here Davidson brings together evidence from archeology and literary texts, providing a well-rounded perspective of the lives and beliefs of the ancient Nordic peoples.

"binding of the wolf Fenrir"—For Snorri's account of this, see Ch. 18, p. 223.

"Garm . . . Fenrir under another name"—Snorri first tells the story of Tyr's losing his hand to the wolf Fenrir. But at Ragnarok Tyr kills—and is killed by—Garm. This may be Snorri's conscious attempt to create a parallel between Odin and Tyr, and Garm and Fenrir.

Odin's Companions Include:

- Valkyries, women who are "Choosers of the slain" (see Ch. 18, p. 225).
- Berserks, fierce, fearless warriors.

 The Valkyries of Odin

"Snorri's description"—He describes valkyries in similar language as heroes. Individual names are recorded in the *Grimnismal* and other manuscripts.

Valkyrie Activities Associated with Odin:

- binding and unbinding of fetters
- hurling of spears
- power to fly through the air.

"a different, cruder picture"—Earlier evidence of Valkyries ties them to a more primeval, grotesque world incorporating blood, human entrails, and the accompanying supernatural powers.

"the Irish sagas"—There is much historical and archeological evidence of Norse raids on Ireland, Scotland, and Britain, so it is not surprising that stories and beliefs eventually intermingle.

The raven In Ch. 18, p. 225, we read that Odin gets his information from ravens.

"as a result of the work of the poets"—Oral traditions change to fit the expectations of the audience. As the ancient tribes were Christianized, poets chose to "adjust" the old myths.

The Berserks of Odin

"In the later saga-literature"—As the culture develops and the stories are written down, they become more conventional, perhaps rationalized. For more on rationalized versions of a myth, see Ch. 25, pp. 363–364.

One comes from Merseburg in south Germany, and is a charm for the unloosing of fetters. It describes how certain women called the Idisi (like the Old Norse *disir* for goddess) sat together, some fastening bonds, some holding back the host, some tugging at fetters. It concludes with the words, "Leap forth from the bonds, escape from the enemy."

Old Norse literature has left us with a picture of dignified Valkyries riding on horses and armed with spears, but **a different, cruder picture** of supernatural women connected with blood and slaughter has also survived. Female creatures, sometimes of gigantic size, pour blood over a district where a battle is to take place; they are sometimes described as carrying troughs of blood or riding on wolves, or are seen rowing a boat through a rain of blood falling from the sky. Such figures are usually omens of fighting and death; they sometimes appear to men in dreams, and they are described more than once in skaldic verse of the tenth and eleventh centuries. The most famous example of this kind of dream vision is that said in *Njals Saga* to have been seen before the Battle of Clontarf, fought at Dublin in 1014. A group of women were seen weaving on a grisly loom formed from men's entrails and weighted with severed heads. They were filling in a background of grey spears with a weft of crimson. They were called by names of Valkyries. A poem is quoted in the *Saga* which is said to have been spoken by them, and in the course of this they declare that it is they who decide who is to die in the coming battle.

Other figures showing a close resemblance to Valkyries of this kind are found in stories of the Celtic peoples. Two "goddesses," Morrigu and Bobd, are mentioned in **the Irish sagas.** They were wont to appear on the battlefield, or were sometimes visible before a battle. They could take on the form of birds of prey, and they were accustomed to utter prophecies of war and slaughter. **The raven,** together with the wolf, is mentioned in practically all the descriptions of a battle in Old English poetry, and both were regarded as the creatures of the war god, Odin.

Such striking resemblances between the figures of supernatural battle-women in the literature of the Scandinavians and heathen Germans on the one hand, and the Celtic peoples on the other, are significant. There is little doubt that the figure of the Valkyrie has developed in Norse literature into something more dignified and less blood-thirsty **as a result of the work of the poets** over a considerable period. The alarming and terrible creatures who have survived in the literature in spite of this seem likely however to be closer in character to the choosers of the slain as they were visualized in heathen times.

The power which Odin was believed to possess over the minds of men at war was not limited to the sapping of their energy and will-power, the imposing of "fetters" on them in the heat of battle. He could give more positive help, as we see from the phenomenon of the berserks. These were warriors so full of the ecstasy of battle as to be impervious to wounds and to danger, and according to Snorri they derived this power from Odin:

> . . . his men went without mailcoats, and were frantic as dogs or wolves; they bit their shields and were as strong as bears or boars; they slew men, but neither fire nor iron could hurt them. This is known as running berserk.

> Ynglinga Saga, 6

In the later saga-literature the berserk has turned into something which resembles a fairy-tale monster, with whom the hero does battle against overwhelming odds and whom he of course defeats. The main characteristics of the berserk nevertheless are worthy of note. First, he fights in a state of wild frenzy; secondly, he is marked out as a member of a special class free from the laws which govern ordinary members of society. These characteristics have been recorded among the Germanic peoples long before Viking times.

Another aspect of the berserks is found among the warriors of the Harii, also described by Tacitus. Like the Chatti these were famed for their strength, and they cultivated the art of terrifying their enemies:

> They black their shields and dye their bodies black, and choose pitch dark nights for their battles. The terrifying shadow of such a fiendish army inspires a mortal panic, for no enemy can stand so strange and devilish a sight.

Germania, 43

At the time of Harald Fairhair, king of Norway in the ninth century, there were berserks in the king's bodyguard. In the *Hrafnsmal* they are called wolf-coats, and are said to be men of tried valour who never flinched at battle. We are told in *Heimskringla* that they had a place on the king's warship. The berserks who roamed through Scandinavia were apparently viewed as sacred to the god. They are frequently said to be **shapechangers,** and sometimes to take on animal form.

Thor, the Thunder God

In the myths as presented to us by Snorri, Thor is undoubtedly one of the gods who stands out most clearly. The champion of the Æsir and the defender of Asgard appears as a massive, red-bearded figure, armed with his hammer, his iron gloves, and his girdle of strength. The cult of Thor had a long life in western Europe. In the eleventh century **he was still worshipped** with enthusiasm by the Vikings of Dublin, and at the close of the heathen period it was he who was thought of as the principal adversary of Christ.

Of all the gods, it is Thor who seems the characteristic hero of the stormy world of the Vikings. Bearded, outspoken, filled with vigor and gusto, he puts his reliance on his strong right arm and simple weapons. He strides through the northern realm of the gods, a fitting symbol for the man of action. Like the Indian god Indra, who resembles him in some respects, Thor was a **tremendous trencher-man,** impressing even the giants by his capacity for eating and drinking. In the hall of Utgard-Loki he took part in an epic drinking contest, striving to empty a great horn whose tip went down into the sea, and though he was bemused by the cunning of the giant, he lowered the level of the ocean perceptibly by his efforts. There is not much doubt that tales like that of **Thor's humiliations** in the hall of Utgard-Loki were primarily for entertainment, acceptable at a time when the worship of Thor was no longer of serious concern among men. Nevertheless the very characteristics of the god seized upon to provide mirth must be in themselves significant, and much may be learned from them.

Thor's delight in eating and drinking was in accordance with his great vitality and physical strength. His progress through the realms of gods and giants was marked by the continual overthrowing of adversaries and overcoming of obstacles. His usual method of killing his enemies was simple and direct: without recourse to the tortuous wiles of Odin or Loki, he

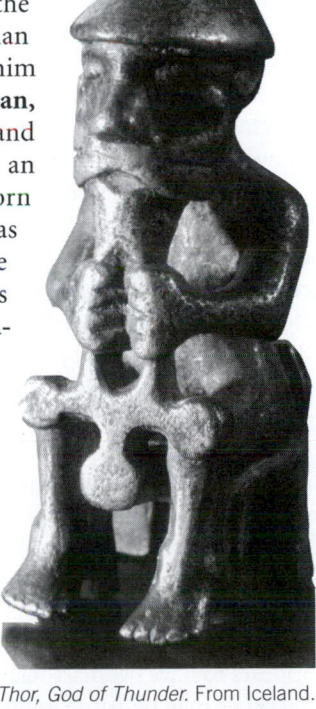

Thor, God of Thunder. From Iceland. Viking, ca. 100 C.E. Thor, seated on a throne with his hammer Mjollnir on his knees.

Characteristics of Berserks in Earlier Sources:

- fight in a wild frenzy
- exempted from some laws
- terrify enemies by appearing dreadful, sometimes bear-like or wolf-like, or by changing shape.

shapechangers For a discussion of this, see Ch. 21, p. 298.

 Thor in the Myths

"he was still worshipped"—During the transition period from paganism to Christianity in Northern Europe, the ancient worship structure overlaps the new. This can mean that people in adjacent areas might worship according to each of the traditions and that religious traditions overlap, with gods from one crossing over into the other.

"tremendous trencher-man"— Thor is a down-to earth god, and stories about him confirm his human-like strengths and weaknesses. See the discussion of him as immanent, p. 430.

"Thor's humiliations"—These are part of the *Prose Edda* (see Ch. 18, p. 225ff.), and are discussed later in this excerpt on p. 445.

Thor's Major Deeds:

- slays Midgard serpent at Ragnarok
- kills numerous giants with his hammer
- exhibits great strength and energy

A smith's mold for casting both Christian crosses and Thor's hammer. Viking, 10th c. C.E. This artifact shows that the transition from one religion to another can be accomplished gradually by a society.

 The Hammer of Thor

"The image of Thor in the temple"—The *Flateyjarbok*, written in the late 14th c., describes a very ornate statue of Thor in a temple in Thrandheim, and Saxo Grammaticus says that when a Swedish temple of Thor was pillaged in 1125, the raiders took huge bronze hammers.

Uses of Mjollnir:

- to bless a newborn child
- to bless a funeral ship
- to restore life
- for sacrifices
- as a protection against harm

"Donar . . . was considered to resemble Hercules"—In ancient times, a god who did "double duty" in this way could serve as a link between cultures.

swastika A cosmic symbol of good luck and well-being. Its ancient spiritual significance has been overshadowed since Adolf Hitler adopted it as the Nazi logo in 1935. He perverted many aspects of Germanic mythology for propaganda purposes. The Nazi swastika faced in the opposite direction than the traditional one.

"the sun-wheel"—The swastika representing the turning of the cosmos around the pole star.

simply struck at them with his hammer or hurled it through the air to shatter their skulls.

He slew giantesses with boulders, or broke their backs by forcing a weight down upon them. In such stories we are seeing Thor the Thunder God at work, felling trees and destroying men with his deadly bolts. Thor's realm is very different from that of Odin. His cult was not an aristocratic one, and indeed a taunt made against him in one of the *Edda* poems was that while Odin received kings who fell in battle, Thor got the thralls. But we shall see that his power extended far, and that he was the god supreme not only over the stormy sky, but also over the life of the community in all its aspects. If part of the mantle of the old sky god, Tiwaz, fell upon Odin, a great part of it undoubtedly covered the broad shoulders of Thor.

The image of Thor in the temple usually carried a hammer, and we hear much in the myths concerning this weapon of the god. Snorri tells us that the Æsir proclaimed that the hammer Mjollnir was the greatest treasure which they possessed, since it enabled them to hold Asgard secure against the giants. Clearly this hammer was something more than a weapon. We know that the hammer was raised to hallow the new-born child who was to be accepted into the community, and it seems also to have been used at funerals, since at Balder's death it was fetched to hallow the funeral ship before this was set alight. When Thor had feasted on his goats, he made the sign of the hammer over the bones and skin in order to restore them to life. In this new life given by the god, we can see a possible significance in the use of the hammer at sacrifices and funerals.

Like that of the Christian cross, the sign of the hammer was at once a protection and a blessing to those who used it. An early king of Norway, Hakon the Good, who became a Christian, was bullied into attending autumn sacrifices, and he strove to protect himself from the heathen rites by making the sign of the cross over the cup passed round in honour of the gods. When the company objected, one of his friends defended Hakon, saying: "The King acts like all those who trust in their strength and might. He made the mark of the hammer over it before he drank."

Men were accustomed in the tenth century to wear the symbol of Thor in the form of a hammer-shaped amulet on a chain or cord round their necks. The hammer amulet was also used at an earlier period, though in a slightly different form. Small amulets which resemble long-handled hammers and which may be Thor's hammers were found by Fausset in graves of an Anglo-Saxon cemetery at Gilton, Kent.

The hammer-shaped weapon is similar to the double axe of antiquity, which also represented the thunderbolt, and which was shown in various forms in temples of the ancient world. Among the early Germanic peoples the god **Donar, Thor's predecessor, was considered to resemble Hercules,** the mighty male figure armed with a club who battled against monsters, and part of the resemblance was evidently due to the weapon which the god carried. Tacitus tells us that the praises of Hercules used to be chanted by the Germans as they went into battle, and that they believed he had visited them.

The hammer could of course be used as a throwing weapon, and one of the characteristics of Mjollnir was that it would always return to the owner's hand. In this way it was a fitting symbol of the thunderbolt hurled by the angry god.

Sometimes on the drums a male figure with a hammer-like object in either hand is shown, and sometimes this is a kind of cross with hooked ends, resembling a swastika. The **swastika,** or hooked cross, is a sign found in many regions of the world and known from remote antiquity. It was very popular among the heathen Germans, and appears to have been associated with the symbol of fire.

There may be some connection between it and **the sun-wheel,** well known in the Bronze Age, or it may have arisen from the use of the hammer or axe to represent thunder, which was accompanied by fire from heaven.

Thor was the sender of lightning and the god who dealt out both sunshine and rain to men, and it seems likely that the swastika as well as the hammer sign was connected with him.

The swastika is also found on weapons and sword scabbards. It would seem indeed as though the power of the thunder god, symbolized by his hammer, extended over all that had to do with the well-being of the community. It covered birth, marriage, and death, burial, and cremation ceremonies, weapons and feasting, travelling, land-taking, and the making of oaths between men.

The famous weapon of Thor was not only the symbol of the destructive power of the storm, and of fire from heaven, but also a protection against the forces of evil and violence. Without it Asgard could no longer be guarded against the giants, and men relied on it also to give security and to support the rule of law.

The mother of Thor was said to be Earth herself, and in the earliest skaldic verse he is described in phrases meaning **"son of Earth."** Of his wife, Sif, we know little, except that she had wonderful golden hair; it has been suggested that this was the sign of an ancient fertility goddess, her abundant, **shining hair typifying the golden wheat.** There was an undoubted link between Thor as the thunder god and the fertility of the earth, on which the lightning strikes and the rain falls, causing increase.

It is in keeping with this link between Thor and the earth, that we find many of the first Icelandic settlers taking with them from Norway not only the high-seat pillars from Thor's temple, but also earth from between the pillars. Moreover they were careful to hallow the land which they took for themselves in the name of the god before they built their dwellings upon it and sowed their crops.

In his association with the natural world, Thor was thus both destroyer and protector. He was regarded in Viking times as a sure guide for those who traveled over the sea, because of his power over storms and wind. He was the god to be invoked for journeying, and even **Helgi the Lean,** one of the early Icelandic settlers who had been converted to Christianity, was said to continue **to call on Thor** whenever he had a sea voyage to make. Thor could call down storms against his adversaries. Thor's power over the sea might of course be used more positively to benefit his worshippers, as when he is said to have stranded a whale on the shores of Vineland in response to the prayers of Thorhall, one of the explorers.

Fertility Gods

Those gods who determined the course of war and sent thunder from heaven were essentially powers of destruction, although they might also give protection from chaos and disorder. Other powers were said to dwell in Asgard with Odin and Thor whose province was of a different kind, since their sphere of influence was over the peace and fertility of the inhabited earth.

These were called the **Vanir,** and Snorri tells us that the chief figures among them were the twin deities Freyr and Freyja, the children of Njord. We are not told much about them in the myths which he includes in the *Prose Edda*, but it is clear that he regarded them as powerful beings whose worship continued until late in the heathen period. Freyr he calls *Veraldar* god, god of the world.

The written sources represent Freyr as the sovereign deity of increase and prosperity. According to Adam of Bremen, **his image in the temple at Uppsala was a phallic one,** and he was the god who dispensed peace and plenty to mortals and was invoked at marriages. Saxo also tells us that there was worship of Freyr at **Uppsala.** He mentions a great sacrifice called *Froblod* which took place there at regular intervals, which included human victims. He also refers to the worship of Freyr accompanied by "effeminate gestures" and "clapping of mimes upon the stage," together with the

 The God of the Sky

"son of Earth"—This phrase, called an epithet, is common in ancient myths from the Mediterranean. See "The Trojan War" (Ch. 1, p. 9ff) and *Gilgamesh* (Ch. 15, p. 173) for more examples.

"shining hair typifying the golden wheat"—The golden tassels of wheat in the field are imagined as the hair of a beautiful woman. Based on this, some modern writers have compared Sif to Demeter, as a goddess of agriculture, but Sif does not have the powerful ritual status of the Greek goddess. (For more on Demeter, see Ch. 27, p. 385.)

"Helgi the Lean . . . to call on Thor"—During the transition from heathen to Christian times people combine aspects of worship from both traditions. Consider the Christmas tree, a pagan symbol incorporated into Christian celebrations.

Vanir In the *Ynglinga Saga*, Snorri describes the war of the Æsir against the Vanir, "the first in the world," which seems to have ended in a draw. The story may represent the bringing together of different belief systems. See Introduction, p. 431.

 Freyr, God of Plenty

"[Freyr's] image . . . was a phallic one"—See also use of phallus in the worship of Dionysus, Ch. 31, p. 462.

Uppsala The first great settlement in Sweden and the site of its oldest university, where many manuscripts important to Northern mythology are kept.

"This implies some kind of performance"—Researchers use written sources to learn about accompanying customs. Davidson links activities both synchronically and diachronically. (See also Levi-Strauss, Ch. 20, p. 280.)

"men dressed as women"—Role-playing by cross-dressing is a way of defining boundaries, a significant component of many rituals. (See Turner, Ch. 26, p. 373.)

Balder as a Fertility God

death [and] fertility The idea that new life springs from death is both old and widespread.

Frazer—Although Balder is not usually considered one of the Vanir, James G. Frazer believed that he resembled them in function.

"Balder represents Christ"—This is an example of the frequent mingling of heathen or heroic and Christian traditions in later writings about the Norse gods. Writers who know both traditions make connections they deem appropriate. See Introduction, p. 431.

"[Freyr's] descendants . . . are the later kings of the land"—This is an example of euhemerism, where a writer makes a genealogical connection between the later heroic period and the time of the gods. (See Introduction, p. 431.)

 Frigg, the Mother Goddess

"Mother Earth appears as the wife of the supreme sky god"—In the ancient Greek tradition, Gaia is embraced by Uranus, producing descendants Zeus, Hera, and their offspring (see Ch. 3, p. 29f.). Such a union of earth mother and sky father is also part of South-west American Indian mythology (see Ch. 8, p. 89)

"is little more than a name"—In general, Icelandic mythology seems not to invest female deities with wide-ranging influence on human life. Freyja, discussed in the next section, represents an exception to this rule.

"unmanly clatter of bells.'" **This implies some kind of performance,** possibly ritual drama, which to Saxo and the Danish heroes whom he describes appeared unmanly and debased. It may be noted that **men dressed as women** and the use of clapping and bells have survived into our own time in the annual mumming plays and the dances which go with them. Possibly some kind of symbolic drama to ensure the divine blessing on the fruitfulness of the season was once performed at Uppsala in Freyr's honor.

The sagas have preserved memories of **a fertility cult** associated with Freyr which is strongly at variance with the battle cult of Odin. The ban against weapons in Freyr's temples, his anger when blood is shed on his sacred land, the taboo against outlaws in his holy place, are all in accordance with his character as a bringer of peace. Freyr is linked also with the sun and the fruitful earth; a fertile field stands near his temple, and no frost is allowed to come between him and his faithful worshipper, while we are told also that he was connected with marriage and the birth of children. Like Nerthus, who was known as Mother Earth, and intervened in human affairs, Freyr was the deity who brought fertility to men. Freyr, again like Nerthus, inspired joy and devotion. Men rejoiced to share their possessions with him.

The idea of **death** in connection with the male deity brings in a new problem. In the Near East and the Mediterranean regions, we know that the dying gods of vegetation, Osiris, Tammuz, Adonis, and the rest, played a most important part in the religion of **fertility.** The god's death typified the coming of winter to the world, and all lamented him; then he emerged again from the darkness of death to give new life and bring rejoicing in the spring. In *The Golden Bough* **Frazer** fitted Balder, the dying god of Asgard, into this death and resurrection pattern.

Balder, son of Odin, was remembered by Snorri for his beauty and his tragic death. Already in the Viking age the resemblance to Christ had been noticed, and in *Voluspa* the ending of the poem seems to imply that **Balder represents Christ,** coming to reign over a new heaven and earth. Balder in his death was mourned by all the world of nature, and in the same way in the most moving of Old English Christian poems, the *Dream of the Rood,* all creation is said to weep at the death of Christ, as he hung upon the cross. But while Balder's death is deeply lamented, there is no indication in either Snorri's or Saxo's accounts that he was brought back to life to save the world.

It seems probable, however, that Snorri's impressive description of Balder's death and the grief it caused owes something to the memory of a god slain for men's preservation and for the fruitfulness of the earth. It is hard to doubt that the story owes something to the cult of the Vanir, even if Balder himself were not a true member of that family. The male god of fertility is bound to die, and his death must be universally lamented, as was that of Balder. In lamenting it, we mourn for our own fate, for "the blight that man is born for."

But the story of Balder does not fit wholly into the pattern. It may also be noted that Freyr leaves no son to avenge him; **his descendants,** like those of Frodi and Scyld, **are the later kings of the land** who follow him one by one into the land of the dead, some possibly by way of a sacrificial death. It remains to attempt to discover what was the part played by the goddesses of the north in the pattern of fertility.

The usual pattern in early religions is that in which the goddess **Mother Earth appears as the wife of the supreme sky god,** since the earth is embraced and made fruitful by the god of the heavens. The image of the Earth Mother, from whom we spring, by whom we are nourished, and into which we return when we die, has remained a fundamental one.

Indeed any clear proof of the worship of the Earth Mother in heathen Scandinavia is hard to find. The mother of Thor, Fjorgynn, **is little more than a name** for us, although her name is used by poets as a synonym for earth. The only maternal figure surviving in Snorri's Asgard however is the goddess Frigg, the wife of Odin and mother of Balder. Loki and Saxo accuse her of unfaithfulness to her husband Odin, but her essential function seems to be that of revered wife and mother, the consort of the high god, and queen of heaven. In her earlier Germanic form *Frija,* she gave her name to **Friday,** the day of Venus, throughout the Germanic world.

Frigg plays a consistent part in the poetry, and lack of detail about her in the myths and the failure to find places named after her may be due to the fact that she was remembered under other titles. She has become overshadowed in Snorri's pages by the more evocative figure of Freyja, and we must now consider why this is so.

When Snorri first introduced Freyja into his account of Asgard, he declared that she was the most renowned of the goddesses, and that she alone of the gods yet lived. This implies that he knew something of her worship continuing into his own day in Scandinavia, and it is well known that fertility cults die hard, particularly in remote country districts. The impressive list of **places called after Freyja,** especially in south Sweden and southwest Norway, shows that Snorri's estimate was no idle one. Freyja is not concerned only with human love. She seems to have had some authority in the world of death. Her name is specifically linked by Snorri with a special kind of witch-craft known as *seidr,* for he states that she was a priestess of the Vanir who first taught this knowledge to the Æsir. We know a good deal about *seidr* from prose sources, and it forms an interesting clue to the nature of her cult. The essentials of performing it were the erection of a platform or lofty seat on which the leading practitioner sat, the singing of spells, and the falling into a state of ecstasy by this leader, who is generally a woman, and is called a **volva.**

This is relevant to a study of the cult of Freyja. As we have seen, she is said to have been an expert on *seidr,* and to have introduced it. **She could take on bird-form,** which meant that she could journey far in some shape other than human. As goddess of the Vanir, the prosperity of the community and marriages of young people were within her province, and these were precisely the subjects on which the *volva* used to be consulted. The *volva* too was accustomed to journey round the countryside and be present at feasts just as Freyja's brother, Freyr, was said to do. Like Freyr, such women were asked to foretell the coming season.

Frigg, as we saw, has been left almost wholly free from such aspersions, and yet there is little doubt that Frigg and Freyja are closely connected. As the weeping mother, the goddess associated with childbirth and linked with the benevolent Mothers, Frigg appears to have her roots in the Vanir cult.

Snorri saw the Æsir and the Vanir as two powerful companies of gods, able to wage war against one another; yet the only names of male deities of the Vanir which are given in his account are **Njord** and **Freyr,** who were given as hostages to the Æsir when the war was over. Who were the rest of the company of the fighting Vanir? The most likely answer seems to be the vast assembly of gods of fertility from many different localities, of which a few names like Ing, Scyld, and Frodi have come down to us, while many more are utterly forgotten.

In orgies, ecstasies, and sacrificial rites, and in the turning to the earth and the dead, whose blessing would help to bring the harvest, it can be seen that the Vanir were the rivals of Odin, god of ecstasy and of the dead. It is hardly surprising that the idea of rivalry between the two cults is sometimes implied in the myths, and is symbolized by the tradition of a **war between the Æsir and the Vanir.** The Vanir also protected men in battle, and they were the gods of royal houses, worshipped for a long period by the Swedish kings who wore the boar image, and who were believed to be informed for a while by the spirit of the Vanir who possessed them. There seem to have been many who worshipped them with favour and devotion, finding their cult more rewarding and comforting than that of the sky god or the willful god of war. The friendship of

Friday Named for Frigg, wife of Odin and mother of Balder.

  The Goddess Freyja

"places called after Freyja"—Davidson also uses clues such as place names to judge the importance of a person or deity.

"seidr"—This means "sorcery" or "magic"; we get most of our information about it from Snorri.

"volva"—In some sources the volva is a wise woman who can foretell people's lives, but in others she is depicted as a sorceress, capable of evil.

"[Freyja] could take on bird-form"—Not only is Freyja exceptional because she is a shape-changer like berserks or were-wolves; being a bird signifies that she can go where humans cannot. See Ch. 18, p. 225, for Odin's ravens Hugin and Munin, Thought and Memory, who also represent this kind of power.

  The Power of the Vanir

Njord A fertility god himself, he is the father of Freyr and Freyja.

Freyr—We know from written accounts that he was the fertility god of the Swedes in the 11th c. and the chief deity after Thor. His name means "lord," and Freyja means "lady."

"war between the Æsir and the Vanir"—Both families of gods were involved with ecstatic rituals and fertility.

"treacherous, sliding quality of Odin's favours"—See the previous discussion of Odin as a transcendent, aristocratic god who does not deign to involve himself in commonplace human pursuits, p. 430.

Wodan Wodan was worshipped as the head god before Odin. As societal values change, deities may gain or lose characteristics, or may be forgotten as their worshippers turn to other gods.

Mercury To unify their empire, the Romans accepted the gods in a conquered country and recommended an equivalent Roman god to the newly annexed people to the Roman religion.

"Wodan . . . supplanted his rival [Tiwaz]"—Before Wodan's worhip, people paid homage to Tiwaz. Thus the complete succession was Tiwaz → Wodan → Odin.

"Snorri . . . made Thor the first of the gods"—He may have done this as part of his rationalization of pagan myth. On rationalization, see Ch. 7, p. 79.

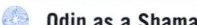 **Odin as a Shaman**

"to offer himself as a link"—Because he has undergone a ritual death and rebirth, the shaman is a liminal figure who is a part of both worlds and can pass between them to help his community. On liminality as element of ritual, see Ch. 26, p. 375–76.

World Tree We see the significance of the tree Yggdrasil in Ch. 7, p. 87. See also Ch. 13, p. 153, where humans survive Ragnarok by hiding in the woods.

"he has to undergo a ritual death"—Ordinary humans have no direct access to supernatural knowledge and must be changed to be made worthy. Ritual death is very real; the person involved has left his previous existence and takes on a genuine new one.

the Vanir had none of the **treacherous, sliding quality of Odin's favours,** and it extended, like his, beyond the grave.

The Many Faces of Odin

In Snorri's account Tiwaz appears as Tyr. He is only a shadowy figure, but Snorri mentions that men prayed to him for victory, and also that he was renowned for his wisdom as well as for his valor. Tiwaz in his day must have been a very great power among the heathen Germans.

Although Odin had in the main taken the place of Tiwaz at the close of the heathen period, memories of the earlier battle god still lingered. In one of the *Edda* poems dealing with spells to use in battle, men are told to carve runes of victory, giving the name of Tyr. We have what may be instances of this name on weapons. A helmet from Negau in Austria bears an inscription in North Italic letters of the second century B.C.E., which has been thought by some scholars to give Teiwa, an archaic name of the god. [This as well as runes carved into weapons found in England and the Ukraine] may be signs of the ancient Germanic war god, cut by those who wished to claim his help and protection in battle.

We know that in the early days the Germanic peoples made costly sacrifices both to Tiwaz and to Wodan, dedicating to them those who fell in battle or who came into their hands as captives. Gradually **Wodan,** whom the Romans called **Mercury, supplanted his rival.** He was regarded as the ancestor of kings, and he welcomed them to his halls after death; he was the deity to whom human sacrifices were offered by burning, strangling, and stabbing with a spear. In the myths known to Snorri he had grown greatly in stature, and become Odin, father of the gods and ruler of Asgard. Even the powerful Thunder God was now viewed as his son, although **Snorri** had doubts about this, and in his preface **made Thor the first of the gods** of the north. Odin, as we have seen, was the god of battle, whose symbols were the spear and the raven, but in the poems and sagas known to Snorri he is shown in other aspects. He was also the ancient one-eyed god, crafty and skilled in magic lore, a great shapechanger, and an expert in the consultation of the dead. He was the rider on the eight-legged steed, the wanderer up and down the earth, the god knowing the secrets of travel between the worlds.

The shaman's main function is to act as a kind of priest or witch-doctor—though neither term is wholly satisfactory—and **to offer himself as a link** between the human community to which he belongs and the Other World. While in a state of trance, he is believed to journey in spirit to the furthest heaven or to the land of the dead, so that he may visit the gods to obtain knowledge, or rescue some soul which disease or madness has expelled from its body. He acts as a seer, sometimes foretelling the future, finding the reason for calamities and disease, and answering questions concerning the destinies of those who consult him. We have seen that the *volva*, whose links appear to be with the Vanir, possessed certain of the characteristics of the shaman. The figure of Odin in his aspect as god of the dead undoubtedly fits into the same pattern, and this is an important side of his cult to set beside his character as a war god.

The **World Tree** is indeed the center of the shaman's cosmology, as it is in the world of the northern myths. The essential feature of the initiation ceremony, whether among the Eskimos, the American Indians, or the Siberian peoples, is the death and rebirth of the young shaman, and the torments and terrors which he has to undergo if he is to gain possession of the esoteric knowledge necessary to him in his new calling. Before he can attain ability to heal and to pass to the realms of gods and spirits, **he has to undergo a ritual death.** This may be experienced in dreams or visions, and the experience may be induced by means of meditation, fasting, or the use of drugs; in any case it causes the initiate terrible suffering. The World Tree plays a considerable part in these dreams and visions of the young shaman.

The hanging of Odin on the World Tree seems indeed to have two main conceptions behind it. First, Odin is made into a sacrifice according to the accepted rites of the god of death, who is Odin himself. We know that victims were hung from trees before the Viking age, and the custom continued at Uppsala until the tenth century. Secondly, Odin is undergoing a ceremony of initiation, gaining his special knowledge of magic by means of a symbolic death. In his *Prose Edda* Snorri has not shown much of this side of Odin's character, for he has concentrated on showing the god as the Allfather and ruler of Asgard.

Like the shamans also, Odin seeks knowledge by communication with the dead. He declares in *Havamal* that he knows spells which will make a hanged man walk and talk with him. He is represented as gaining knowledge of the future by consultation of **the severed head of Mimir,** the hostage said to have been killed by the Vanir. Another version of the story of his relations with Mimir is that he sacrificed one of his eyes so that Mimir, the giant guardian of the spring in the underworld, would permit him to drink from it, and so gain wisdom.

In later folk-beliefs Odin was associated with the "wild hunt," the terrifying concourse of lost souls riding through the air led by a demonic leader on his great horse, which could be heard passing in the storm. Later still, the leader became the Christian Devil.

The Gods of the Dead

There are several links between Odin and the Vanir which at first sight seem puzzling, since **the two cults were apparently opposed** to one another. The goddess Skadi, wife of **Njord,** is said to have borne children to Odin. Odin and Freyja are often mentioned together, and we have the strange double of Odin, the god Od who is said to have been Freyja's husband, for whom she wept after he left her. We may partly account for such links when we remember that Odin and Freyr were worshipped side by side, and both honored by the Swedish kings in the great temple at Uppsala. It is thus scarcely surprising if one cult influenced the other, especially in the last period of heathenism, when the powers of the old gods were waning, and distinctions between them became blurred. There is however another reason for a link between the two cults, and that is that the Vanir as well as Odin had undoubtedly power over the realm of the dead.

The Vanir are represented as having close connections with life in the **burial mound,** with the symbol of the funeral ship, and with the conception of a journey to the land of the dead across the sea. We know that Freyr himself was said to have been laid in a mound, and to have rested there while offerings were made to him. There is mention of a door in the mound, so that men could enter it, and of wooden figures kept inside. The idea that the dead men rested inside his grave mound as in a dwelling is one found repeatedly in the Icelandic sagas.

So far no mention has been made of the god Thor in connection with the dead. Yet we know the extent of his worship in the north, and **the mark of the swastika or hammer on cremation urns and memorial stones suggests** that he afforded his protection to his worshippers in the realm of death as in life. It seems as if both cremation and inhumation were associated with Thor. He

Thor's Hammer Amulet. Viking artifact from Iceland, 10th c. This is a small, ornate version worn to ward off danger.

"The hanging of Odin on the World Tree"—Because Odin is himself the god of death (see p. 225), he participates in the death-rebirth ritual to achieve the special knowledge necessary to the shaman.

"the severed head of Mimir"—In the *Prose Edda,* Snorri also tells us how Odin learns from the head of Mimir in a spring under a root of the World Tree. Even as a disembodied head, Mimir is extremely powerful because of his knowledge. In fact, wisdom is so important that Odin sacrificed his eye for it.

 The Burial Mound

"the two cults were apparently opposed"—As leader of the Æsir, Odin is the god of battle and death, while the Vanir are gods of peace and fertility.

Njord Vanir fertility god, father of Frey and Freyja.

"burial mound"—This is a tomb built above ground and covered with earth. Earlier funeral rites described in Norse literature include cremation with a memorial stone set on the site or casting the ashes in the sea, and burning the dead and his entourage in a ship as it was pushed out to sea. One excavated burial mound even contained a burial ship.

Thor and the Dead

"the mark of the swastika or hammer . . . suggests"—Sometimes found objects, such as cremation urns or memorial stones, provide as much information about the beliefs and rituals of people as literary and historical accounts.

had special links with fire, on account of his command over lightning, but in the later Viking age, when his worship still flourished, most of his worshippers were buried in the earth. Cremation lingered on for the most part in Sweden as the rite of the followers of Odin.

Evidently those who dwelled on the Ness and who were under Thor's protection were to pass into a holy hill after death. **Such a conception is closely linked** with the importance of the family. Like the idea of the dwelling within the burial mound or the departure over the sea, it emphasizes the significance of man's link with his ancestors, of the continuance of the family rather than the individual, and the importance of one particular sacred locality. The worship of Thor and Freyr is suited to life in a settled community, and in this differs from the cult of Odin, whose cremation pyres might be raised on battlefields far from home.

When we have mentioned the great gods, we realize that these do not by any means exhaust the inhabitants of Asgard, as Snorri presented them. Many so-called gods play a prominent part in the myths, and others are mentioned briefly by name, but we search in vain for any established cult connected with them in heathen times, while if we try to resolve the difficulty by defining them as literary creations they remain puzzling and contradictory. A number appear to be associated with the cult of the Vanir. Some may originally have been heroes who in the course of time were promoted by antiquaries into heaven. Some may have begun as abstractions used by the poets, and have gradually developed a literary personality of their own. Some may have been imported into the north from foreign sources, and ultimately gained a place in Asgard through the poets and storytellers. Some of the more interesting claimants to a place in Asgard include Loki, Balder [see also p. 228ff.] and Heimdall.

Loki: Hero, God, and Trickrster

The place which Loki occupies in the circle at Asgard is puzzling, although he is a prominent figure, and plays an important part in most of the well known myths. He is evidently an ambivalent character, neither wholly good nor wholly bad, although in Snorri's tales the bad side predominates. By the late Viking age the wicked and dangerous side of his character seems to have been strengthened by comparison with the Christian Devil. Loki appears in Snorri to have been directly **responsible for the death of Balder,** but outside Snorri the evidence is slender, and many have thought that the picture of him as Balder's murderer is a late development due to the gradual blackening of his reputation. This is perhaps the most difficult of the many problems connected with Loki.

A characteristic of Loki, shared by no other gods except Odin and Thor, is his sociability. He has adventures in company with nearly all the important inhabitants of Asgard, Freyr being the exception. He is the companion of Odin and Thor; he fights Heimdall and kills Balder; he plays a part in both the creation and destruction of the world; he helps in the building of Asgard; he is at home among the giants and the monsters as well as the gods. There is no doubt as to his importance in the mythology of the north.

It may be noted that even the **Loki of Snorri's tales is a mischievous rather than a wicked being.** Sometimes his actions cause inconvenience and suffering to the gods, as when he helps a giant to steal the apples of immortality, or, in his desire to steal a salmon, kills an otter who has powerful relations to avenge him. Yet on other occasions it is Loki who rescues the gods from serious predicaments, as when he helps to regain Thor's hammer by dressing him up as a bride. Sometimes Loki acts under compulsion, either because the giants get him into their power or the angry gods insist on his righting some wrong he has done them. There is no doubt however that many of his

---

"Such a conception is closely linked"—Belief and ritual are most often interdependent. For example, where the continuance of a family and the significance of a sacred place are most important, placement of the recognizable body (as opposed to ashes) in a mound seems more conducive to the belief that the deceased will live on in a parallel existence.

"responsible for the death of Balder"—For this story, see Ch. 18, p. 228f.

"Loki of Snorri's tales is a mischievous rather than a wicked being"—Loki shares many characteristics with tricksters in other traditions, especially in his being alternately helpful and bothersome. (For more on tricksters, see Chs. 21 and 23, and the Introduction, Ch. 18, p. 220.)

acts, like the cutting off of Sif's hair, are the doings of a naughty boy rather than crimes against the righteous gods. While he is both cunning and ingenious, it may be noted that his plans do not by any means always succeed.

Loki has certain magic powers, and the most outstanding is the **ability to change his shape.** When the giant was building the walls of Asgard, Loki turned himself into a mare and lured away the giant's horse which served him so faithfully. It was while he was in mare's form, according to Snorri, that Loki gave birth to Sleipnir, Odin's eight-legged steed. When he was concerned in the theft of the apples, Loki was in bird form. When he went to look for Thor's hammer, he was said to borrow the "feather form" of Freyja, which meant flying in the shape of a bird. To prevent the clever dwarfs from winning their wager, he turned himself into a fly and stung the smith at a critical moment. He is said to have taken the form of a flea when he wanted to steal Freyja's necklace.

The binding of Loki may also be an early tradition, although here again it is difficult to be sure how far there has been influence from learned works. This may have been because the idea of a bound giant was already familiar in heathen times. In northern England there are carved stones from the Viking age showing monstrous bound figures, which could be identified with either Satan or Loki.

Loki also seems to have become the hero of many folk-tales, told for entertainment purposes only, and many of them late in date; in these he usually plays a comic role. Loki as the ambivalent mischief-maker might similarly be seen as a kind of Odin-figure in reverse. It is certainly easier to understand some of the puzzling elements in him if we regard him as a parody of the great creator-gods rather than as consistently in opposition to them. Certain elements in the myths and poems suggest that at one time he was a chthonic figure, connected primarily with the world of the dead, and this would be comprehensible if we see him as a kind of shadow of Odin. Besides his links with Hel, the serpent, and the wolf, and with the horse that carries Odin to the realm of the dead, he appears alongside the giants at Ragnarok, steering the ship that brings them over the sea.

It is important to remember that there was also a Loki of the outer-regions, **Utgard-Loki,** who dwelt somewhere to the east of the land of the gods, and was visited on one famous occasion by Thor. This Loki is a giant of tremendous size and power, but his power is not really greater than that of Thor: it depends largely on his cunning and his capacity to perform sight-deceiving magic which makes things appear other than they are. The straightforward **Thor** is taken in and humiliated, whereas Odin, we feel, would have been perfectly at home in this bewildering world of sleight and fantasy. Comic fabrication though this story may be, it perhaps contains an element of truth in the way in which the Loki giant is set up against Thor.

No estimate of Loki can be complete which does not take into account **the grim and terrifying background of death to which Loki seems at times to belong.** If he were originally a giant of the underworld, with skill in deceiving and disguise, it is conceivable that he would gradually develop in later literature into the figure of the agile trickster, stirring up mischief and parodying the more dignified gods, and so have won a place of this kind in Snorri's Asgard. Continually following Odin and Thor, yet mocking at them and the goddesses, he has turned into the hero of a series of diverting, sometimes unseemly stories. Only at Ragnarok is it clear where Loki's real allegiance lies, when he seems to relapse again into the figure of a bound and monstrous giant, breaking loose to destroy the world. Then the nimble-witted **Thersites** of the court of the gods is replaced by a remote and terrible power.

"ability to change his shape"—A frequent motif among trickster figures. For an example from American Indian mythology, see the Raven story, Ch. 21, p. 298.

An 8th-c C.E. carved funerary stone from Gotland, Sweden, shows *Sleipnir.* ATA, Stockholm.

Utgard-Loki Utgard is the land outside Asgard and Midgard, the areas where the Æsir live. Utgard was said to be inhabited by giants and trolls, and was therefore quite forbidding. This suggests that Utgard-Loki is a more threatening form of the trickster.

Thor [and Utgard-Loki] For Snorri's telling of these adventures, see Ch. 18.

"the grim . . . background of death to which Loki seems at times to belong"—Loki as Trickster versus Loki as Destroyer of the World are two aspects of him that play prominent roles in Snorri's *Prose Edda:* the entertaining but humiliating trickster who brings down Thor with a series of impossible tasks, and the monstrous prime mover in the destruction of the old world.

Thersites In Greek mythology, he was known as a cruel trickster.

Further Reading

Davidson, H. R. Ellis. *Gods and Myths of Northern Europe.* London: Penguin Books Ltd., 1990.

31

Heracles and Dionysus

WHAT TO EXPECT . . . In this chapter, you encounter Heracles and Dionysus, and learn their stories as the first step toward becoming familiar with the rituals associated with each. Both were sons of Zeus and mortal women. Each was later considered divine, although they took different paths toward that status. Heracles was a hero figure of great power, but one who could also be dangerous to himself and others, murdering his wife and children, for example. Yet he served as a guardian of community life, a role model for Greek youth, and he became a participant in the Eleusinian mysteries (see Ch. 27, p. 385). Although Dionysus was certainly the god of wine, in classical times he was experienced more as a god of inspiration in whose honor dramatic festivals were held. The rituals of Dionysus contained subversive elements like cross-dressing, drunkenness, exchanges of insults, obscene songs, the acting out of sexual acts.

As you read the stories of these two sons of Zeus, consider the similarities and differences between them. With respect to Dionysus, reflect on what you have learned about the Greek gender gap in Chapter 3, p. 28f., and Chapter 27, p. 397, in light of what you are learning with respect to his relationship to women. Consider these two deities in light of the motif Claude Levi-Strauss found in Greek myth of a tension between overvaluing kinship and undervaluing kinship (Ch. 20, p. 281ff.).

Although Heracles[1] could have been included in the section on heroes, we discuss him under rituals, because he is associated with a variety of Greek customs and ceremonies. Dionysus is discussed in this section for the same reason. Both Heracles and Dionysus were the sons of Zeus and mortal women, and both were eventually considered gods. Their paths to acceptance as divinities were quite different, however. Heracles was considered quintessentially Greek, while the worship of Dionysus was associated with influences that came to Greece from the Orient. Unlike Dionysus, Heracles was originally human. However, he was a powerful and amazing human being, a true hero, and after he performed a series of labors, he became divine. Dionysus, on the other hand, seems to have wielded the power of a god from birth. Nonetheless, he had to overcome the resistance and slander of human leaders before his divinity was accepted and the rituals that he called for were widely practiced. Because their stories and rituals are different, we will consider these two sons of Zeus in separate sections.

---

[1] This is the Greek version of his name. The Romans called him Hercules, the form of the name which is more common in English.

Heracles

HERACLES AS A HERO

In addition to offering sacrifices to the gods, the Greeks were unusual among ancient peoples in paying reverence to a group of human beings called heroes. Originally, Heracles seems to have been one of these heroes, but over time, he came to be regarded as one of the gods. He was the illegitimate son of Zeus, the king of the gods, and Alcmene, a human woman. Having one divine parent did not guarantee divine status. While the offspring of such unions were as a rule blessed with special talents, they were also burdened with special problems. The name "Heracles," meaning "Glory of Hera," seems to have been intended to ward off the anger of Hera, Zeus' wife, as the result of her husband's adulterous union with Alcmene. As a protection against wrath, the name was singularly ineffectual: Hera was responsible for a variety of misfortunes Heracles endured throughout his time on earth, including several fits of murderous rage in which he caused the death of his tutor, his children, and one of his friends.

Because Heracles began life as a human being, he especially fired the imagination of the Greeks. His worship provided the opportunity to celebrate both the noble and the vulgar aspects of what it means to be human. As a hero, Heracles accomplished some amazing feats, but he was also guilty of horrendous crimes. Because he endured great suffering while carrying out his twelve labors, the Greeks viewed Heracles as a figure to emulate and a personal patron. Thus he figured in Greek personal piety, an aspect of Greek ritual that we have not yet considered in this book.

RITUALS ASSOCIATED WITH HERACLES

Heracles was the protecting deity of numerous towns and was worshipped at a variety of shrines and altars throughout Greece. Typically, his shrine would include a temple, dining facilities, and athletic facilities. By syncretism, a variety of local cults over time became transformed into the worship of Heracles. Syncretism means that the names and attributes of various gods are mingled, and the rituals and beliefs of different regions become intertwined. For example, at Thasos, he was considered a protector of the city, and his worship was blended with that of the Phoenician god Melqart of Tyre. The god Melqart actually had characteristics quite different from Heracles: he was a god of navigation, fertility, and prosperity, the founder of the city of Tyre, and the guardian of its orderly ongoing functioning. Despite the differences between the two deities, worshippers at Melqart's shrine in Tyre referred to the god they were honoring as both "Heracles" and "Melqart," as if these were names for the same being. In his study of Greek cults, L. R. Farnell suggests that the connection between the two gods arose because both were associated with rituals that burned their effigies on a pyre. For Heracles, the ritual probably commemorated his burning on a funeral pyre on Mount Oeta after being inadvertently poisoned by his wife Deianeira; we do not know the reason for the ceremony associated with Melqart.

In addition to his role as a guardian of community life, Heracles also served Greek youth as a role model. In many Greek cities, boys of eighteen, known as *ephebes,* underwent a two-year period of military training that was as much a rite of passage as a serious regimen for becoming a soldier. At Athens, Heracles served as a patron and military ideal to the *ephebes,* who made him a special offering at the ceremony where they cut their hair as a preparation for military service.

Heracles was also honored at some important ceremonies that involved people from more than one city, including some of the ceremonies at Eleusis, which drew worshippers from across Greece. The Eleusinian Mysteries were a yearly religious ritual performed in honor of the goddess Demeter (see Ch. 27, p. 393).

People who underwent this ritual were initiated and learned the secrets that gave them special powers in the afterlife. Therefore, when Heracles was ordered to bring Cerberus back from the underworld, he sought initiation at Eleusis. However, he first had to be cleansed for his part in the deaths of the Centaurs during his fourth labor. After being purified at Eleusis through special ceremonies, which came to be called the Lesser Mysteries, Heracles was initiated into the Eleusinian Mysteries.

According to a story told by the Greek poet Pindar, Heracles founded the Olympic Games using the payment he received from King Augeas for cleaning his stables in his fifth labor. Eurystheus did not accept this labor as one of the ten which he required because it was done for pay. However, Heracles put the payment he received to good use for the well-being of all Greece. In his eleventh labor, the hero brought back shade trees from the land of the Hyperboreans to make the site of the Olympic games more pleasant.

THE TWELVE LABORS

Perhaps the most famous stories involving Heracles are those about his Twelve Labors. Like most mythical stories, those about Heracles are told in different versions. According to some, he was driven mad by Hera and performed his labors in expiation of his guilt. According to other versions of his life, including one followed by the famous Greek dramatist Euripides in his play *Heracles,* the hero went mad *after* performing his labors.

The labors themselves had meaning to Greeks beyond their obvious quality as great deeds. To perform them, Heracles traveled far and wide: his adventures spanned all of Greece and the

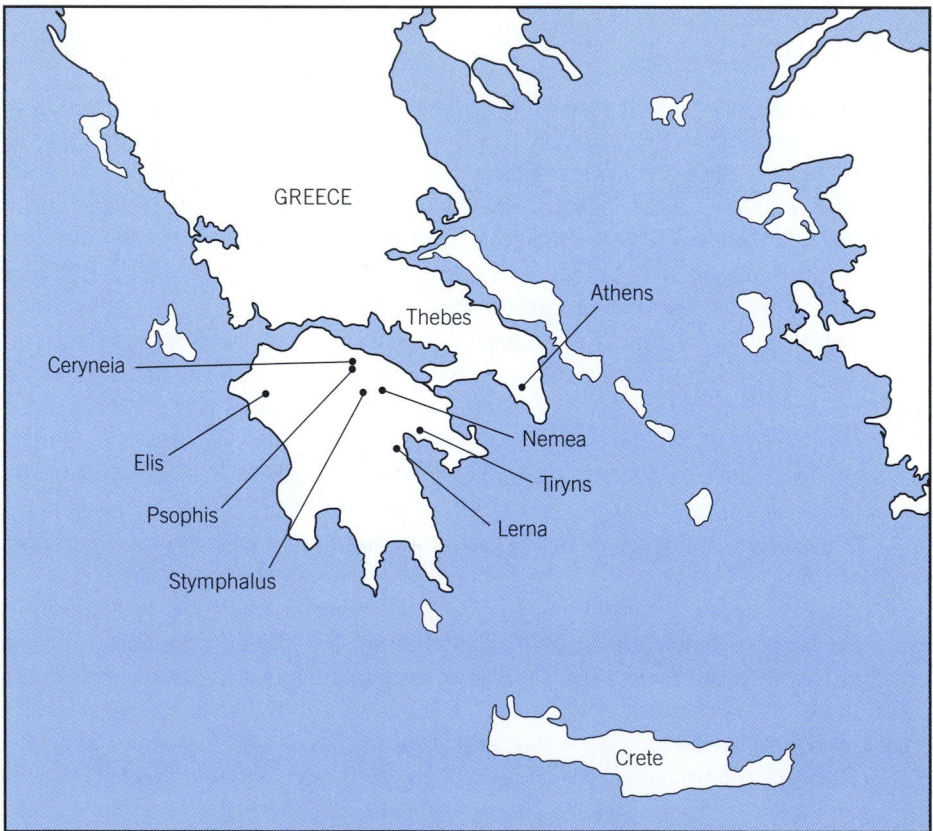

The locations of Heracles' first six labors. He started from Tiryns and went to Nemea (1), Lerna (2), Cerneia (3), Psophis (4), Elis (5), and Stymphalus (6).

known world. The first six were performed within the peninsula in the lower part of Greece called the Peloponnese. In the second group, Heracles traveled more widely, even going to parts of the world associated with the realm of death. He went to Crete to bring back the Cretan bull; to Thrace in northeastern Greece for the mares of Diomedes; to the land of the Amazons, which was thought to be in Asia, for the belt of Hippolyte; to Erythia, an island off the coast of southern Spain, for the cattle of Geryon; on a path through Italy, Libya, Egypt, Asia, Arabia, and Gibraltar for the apples of the Hesperides; and back to Laconia in the Peloponnese for the descent to Hades to bring back Cerberus.

These stories gave the Greeks insight into their cosmology, providing them with an understanding of the geographical boundaries and physical features of their world, while allowing them to feel that, through Heracles, they had achieved supremacy over all the dangers it offered. In addition, Heracles' adventures provided aetiological insights into some natural phenomena. (On the aetiological and cosmological insights provided by myths, see Ch. 1, pp. 7, 8, 12.) For example, in bringing back the cattle of Geryon, Heracles returned to Tiryns by way of Liguria in southern France. In his travels, he found himself in battle with brigands as well as with the natives. When he ran out of other missiles, he called upon Zeus, who sent a shower of stones against his opponents. This story was said to explain the rock-covered *Plaine de la Crau* in Liguria.

HERACLES' MANY-SIDED PERSONALITY

Heracles' character as a god was a complex and contradictory one. His nature included the following aspects:

- Heracles was a benefactor of human beings. As such, it was his task to free Prometheus, the great champion of humans, who had been chained to a rock for giving fire to them (on Prometheus, see Ch. 24, p. 353).

- He was a culture hero who founded the Olympic games with the payment obtained from King Augeas for cleaning his stables in his fifth labor. He was also associated with the founding of the Lesser Mysteries at Eleusis when he went there in preparation for a trip to the underworld.

- Heracles had a reputation for medical power and healing, perhaps because of his association with athletic contests and the physical well-being they required. During the plague at Athens in 428 B.C.E., Athenians dedicated a new statue at the shrine of Heracles Alexikakos at Melite in Attica, and his shrine in Boeotia at Huettos was regularly visited by patients seeking cures. Farnell reports that Heracles was frequently associated with natural springs and hot baths, which were ancient centers for healing. This association itself is complicated, because hot springs, which are often the source of sulfurous emanations, are thought to be entrances to the underworld, as well. (On Heracles' connection to the underworld, see pp. 451, 458.)

- A powerful and savage warrior, Heracles cut off the ears, noses, and hands of the Minyan heralds who came to Thebes to collect extortion money. He wandered through Greece and around the world wielding a large club and wearing the skin of the lion he killed at Nemea, with the lion's head covering his own.

- He was, by some accounts, a short man, and excessively hairy. According to one story, he defeated two Thessalian brothers who made a habit of attacking travelers. He slung them upside down from a pole he carried between his shoulders. From this vantage point, they had a good view of Heracles' hairy rump, and made so many jokes about it that he burst out laughing and let them go. The hero was called Melampygus, or "black bottom," because of this feature.

- He was a burlesque figure devoted to excessive eating and drinking, as well as other kinds of excess. The Greek comic writer Aristophanes portrays him as obsessed with food. According to some stories, he slept with the fifty daughters of Thespios in one night.

- Despite his role as a drunken buffoon, Heracles was not stupid. In some of his adventures, he was very canny and functioned as a trickster (see p. 339f. for more discussion of this kind of hero), persuading Atlas, the giant who held up the sky, to go and get the apples of the Hesperides. Heracles agreed to take over Atlas' burden while he was in the land of the Hesperides, and then persuaded Atlas to take up the sky again once he had gotten the apples for Heracles.

- Heracles was given to violence, but many of his violent deeds were directed at villains and miscreants, or those who deserved to die. This was, however, not always the case. When, as a youth, he killed his music teacher Linus, Heracles pleaded self-defense, as Linus had struck him in the course of a lesson. He was acquitted, but his father Amphitryon saw his violent nature and sent him away from home to tend his herds, thinking that this would keep him out of harm's way. Some of Heracles' violent deeds were viewed by the Greeks

Alexander Calder, *Hercules and Lion,* 1929. This modern mobile construction shows Heracles strangling the Nemean lion. Calder's use of basic lines emphasizes the similarity between the hero and the monster he is strangling, as well as the raw energy both contenders bring to the struggle. The lion's hand-like paw on Heracles' chest evinces pathos and sympathy for the victim whose smaller scale and compressed stance indicate his inferiority to the erect hero.

as especially horrific and he had to be purified from the resulting pollution. He was driven insane by Hera and killed his wife Megara and their children. Stories about him suggest that he had to perform his Twelve Labors to expiate these crimes. In another crime abhorrent to the Greeks, who thought it a sacrilege to mistreat guests, Heracles murdered Iphitus while this hero was visiting him at his house. Heracles had to agree to be sold as a slave to atone for this murder. There are so many different stories about the contamination that Heracles suffers that contamination, rather than the story line, seems to be the main point of the stories.

- Several stories connect Heracles to the Centaurs, half-civilized creatures who were half-man and half-horse. These creatures combined savage passions and civilized learning in much the same way as Heracles himself, and his struggles with them may well represent the conflicts within his own complex and contradictory nature. One story found in the excerpt that follows illustrates the civilized nature of these creatures. The Centaur Pholus himself ate his meat raw, but he served roasted meat to Heracles when he was on his way to capture the Erymanthian boar. Pholus, who knew how to welcome and entertain guests, embodied the virtues most valued by the Greeks. He represented the civilized aspect of the centaurs, as did Cheiron, the Centaur who educated Jason and Achilles and taught natural medicine to Asclepius, the god of medicine.

- Heracles' excessive and violent nature is illustrated in other interactions with Centaurs, most of whom were wild and savage creatures with unbridled passions and an uncontrollable

Hercules, Nessus, and Deianeira. Roman mosaic, 2nd–3rd c. C.E. Aquincum Museum (Budapest). Although this episode suggests an opposition between Heracles and the centaurs, the hero's life history indicates an ongoing relationship based on similarities of appetite and temperament.

longing for alcohol. Heracles persuaded Pholus to open a jar of wine that was the common property of all the Centaurs living on the mountain; the others smelled the wine and came armed to Pholus' cave. In the fight that ensued, Cheiron was shot by one of Heracles' arrows, and Pholus died accidentally from touching another. Another story (not included here) is about Heracles and the Centaur Nessus, who seemed to combine the civilized and savage aspects of the Centaurs. Nessus was the ferryman at the River Evenus and claimed to have been appointed to this post by the gods for his honesty. Yet in carrying her across the river, Nessus tried to rape Heracles' wife Deianeira, and Heracles killed him for it. As he lay dying, Nessus tricked Deianeira, instructing her to prepare what he claimed was a love potion. Later, when Heracles fell in love with Iole, Deianeira tried to recover his love with the potion, which turned out to be a poison that caused the hero a horribly painful death.

- One of Heracles' functions seems to have been to battle death. Cora Angier Sowa calls this the theme of "Wrestling with Death," and finds it associated with Heracles in Homer's story of the Trojan War, the *Iliad* (5. 395– 404), where he battles with Hades and wounds him with an arrow (130). In the adventures we excerpt, three of Heracles' labors involve raids on the west, thought to be the location of the underworld, to retrieve native treasures. G. S. Kirk points out that Geryon is associated in a variety of ways with Hades, the god of the dead: his cattle were pastured near the cattle of Hades, and before Geryon's home was shifted westward, he was originally associated with the hot springs of Thermopylae, reputed to be an entrance to the underworld. In his next labor, Heracles goes to the underworld to retrieve Cerberus, robbing the kingdom of death of the guardian of its gates. In his final labor, Heracles travels west to bring back the golden apples of the Hesperides, which are a symbol or a source of immortality or renewed youth, and thus involve defeating death.

- Stories about Heracles may suggest a complex sexuality. He was, on the one hand, a ladies' man who showed his sexual prowess by sleeping with great numbers of women. On the other hand, two stories about Heracles involve cross-dressing and passing himself off as a woman. After sacking Troy, Heracles was thrown off course by a storm sent by Hera and took refuge on Cos. According to some stories, to flee Hera, he disguised himself by dressing in women's clothes, and in fact eventually married Chalciope while thus attired, thus inaugurating a Coan marriage ritual. After killing Iphitus, Heracles was required to undergo a period of servitude to Queen Omphale of Lydia, who fell in love with him. According to some stories, Heracles and Omphale traded clothes: she put on his lion pelt, he wore her dresses. Although Heracles never married Omphale, the couple may have been celebrating their new-found relationship. Philip Slater suggests that Heracles' cross-dressing may have been occasioned by hidden feelings of inadequacy as a man, which he finds typical of men in Greek society, but Kirk points out that transvestism occurred regularly if not frequently in Greek myth, and mentions Achilles' disguise as a girl in Skyros, and Pentheus' disguise as a woman to spy on Dionysus. We could add Dionysus' effeminacy and his disguising himself as a woman to escape from Hera. Kirk suggests that cross-dressing might have had ritual significance, allowing men to shed a treasured social role to celebrate the transition from one social state to another in ceremonies like marriage. For the shift of status involved in such "rites of passage," see Turner, Chapter 26, p. 375f.

WHAT DOES IT MEAN TO SAY THAT HERA DROVE HERACLES MAD?

From some Greek myths, like the story of Hera's vengeance against Heracles, it is easy to believe that the gods are all-powerful beings who have humans at their mercy. However, Shakespeare's saying "As flies to wanton boys are we to the gods; they kill us for their sport"[2] does not accurately describe the Greeks' attitudes toward their gods. Neither do the scenes in the movie *The Clash of the Titans* where we see Zeus picking up giant chess pieces representing the other gods and humans in the story and positioning them on a board which represents the human world. The Greeks did not see their gods in this way; *The Clash of the Titans* is more accurate in describing the Roman attitude toward the gods than that of the Greeks. Even then, the Romans did not consider the gods to be malicious masters. Rather, they saw them as representatives of what could at times be a cruel and unbending Fate.

The Greeks, however, did not view the gods as taking away their freedom or responsibility. When they said that a god caused someone to do something, they were not implying that the human had not acted freely or was not responsible for his acts. For example, in the stories about Heracles killing his guest Iphitos, there is no suggestion that Heracles was not responsible because Hera "made him do it." The stories about Heracles make it clear that we are dealing with someone who had a rash and violent temper. There are people like this in our world, people who fall into a murderous rage over what seem to others to be trifles. How do *we* explain the actions of such a person? Depending on the circumstances and our own views of human nature and society, we speak of heredity, temperament, mental illness, or drug addiction, of neglect by society, or abuse by parents. To some extent, all of these are external forces affecting people's actions: although they are useful as explanations, they fail to represent what the experience seemed like to the person undergoing it.

Saying "He was driven mad by Hera" emphasizes the way such actions can feel to the individual: they appear as immensely powerful, irresistible forces that overpower a person and impel him toward an action. Was resistance possible? Yes. Was it likely? No, because such force

---

[2] Shakespeare, *King Lear* IV. i.

seems to have "a power of its own." It is in this light that we should consider Heracles' fate: he was a man of great power, but also a man who could be dangerous to himself and others.

The Birth and Early Life of Heracles

Before **Amphitryon** arrived back in **Thebes, Zeus** came to the city by night, and tripling the length of that single night, he assumed the likeness of Amphitryon and went to bed with **Alcmene,** telling her all that had happened in the war with the **Teleboans.** When Amphitryon arrived and saw that his wife was welcoming him with no great ardour, he asked her the reason; and when she replied that he had come the previous night and slept with her, he found out from Teiresias about her intercourse with Zeus.

Alcmene gave birth to two sons, Heracles, who was the son of Zeus and the elder by a night, and Iphicles, whom she bore to Amphitryon. When Heracles was eight months old **Hera, wanting to destroy the child,** sent two huge serpents to his bed. Alcmene cried out for Amphitryon, but Heracles leapt up and killed the serpents by strangling them, one in each hand. According to Pherecydes, however, it was Amphitryon who placed the serpents in the bed, because he wanted to find out which of the children was his own; and seeing that Iphicles fled while Heracles stood his ground, he realized that Iphicles was his child.

Heracles was taught chariot-driving by Amphitryon, wrestling by Autolycos, archery by Eurytos, fencing by Castor, and lyre-playing by Linos. This Linos was a brother of Orpheus, who had arrived in Thebes and become a Theban citizen, but was killed by Heracles with a blow from his lyre (for Linos had struck him, and Heracles lost his temper and killed him). When a charge of murder was brought against Heracles, he cited a law of Rhadamanthys saying that if a person defends himself against another who has initiated the violence, he should suffer no penalty. So Heracles was acquitted. And Amphitryon, fearing that he

Hercules strangling the snakes sent by Hera. This 2nd–3rd-c. c.e. statue is unusual in ancient sculpture as the hero seems to have been modelled on an actual baby. Some scholars believe the model was the young Caracalla (Roman Emperor from 211 to 217 c.e.).

might do something similar again, sent him to his herds; and there he grew up, surpassing all others in size and strength. The mere sight of him was enough to show that he was a son of Zeus: for his body measured four cubits, a fiery gleam shone from his eyes, and he never missed his mark with his arrows or javelins.

While he was still with the herds, and was now eighteen, he killed **the lion of Cithairon,** a beast that used to make incursions from Cithairon to destroy the cattle of Amphitryon and Thespios. This last was king of Thespiae, and Heracles visited him when he wanted to kill the lion. **He was entertained by him for fifty days,** and each night after Heracles went out to the hunt, Thespios arranged that one of his daughters should go to bed with him. For he had fifty of them, borne to him by Megamede, daughter of Arneos, and he was eager that they should all conceive children by Heracles. And Heracles, in the belief that he was always sleeping with the same woman, had intercourse with all of them. When he had overcome the lion, he dressed in its skin, and used its gaping mouth as a helmet.

This text comes from: *Apollodorus: The Library of Greek Mythology.**

Amphitryon Heracles' father.

Thebes See map on p. 448.

Zeus King of the Greek gods, a notorious womanizer.

Alcmene Heracles' mother.

Teleboans Admetus was away fighting these people.

Hera Queen of the Greek gods, notorious for taking vengeance on women Zeus became involved with.

"Hera, wanting to destroy the child"—Otto Rank includes Heracles among the heroes he studies in *The Myth of the Birth of the Hero.* However, Rank finds Heracles unusual in being persecuted by Hera and not, like other heroes, by a father figure. See Introduction to Part 3, p. 155.

"the lion of Cithairon"—This early adversary's skin provides Heracles with the distinctive costume he habitually wore.

"He was entertained by him for fifty days"—According to other versions of the story, Heracles slept with all the daughters of Thespios in one night.

Heracles with a many-breasted Hydra. 17th-c. restoration by Alessandro Algardi of a 2nd-c. C.E. Roman work.

Heracles' First Marriage, and Madness

As he was returning from the hunt, he was met by some heralds who had been sent by Erginos to collect tribute from the Thebans. Heracles, who had received arms from Athene, took command of the Thebans, killed Erginos, and put the Minyans to flight; and he forced them to pay tribute to the Thebans at twice the aforementioned rate. It happened that during the battle, **Amphitryon, fighting with courage, met his death.** As a prize of valour, Heracles received from Creon his eldest daughter, Megara, who bore him three sons, Therimachos, Creontiades, and Deicoon.

After his battle with the Minyans, it came about that Heracles was **struck by madness through the jealousy of Hera,** and threw his own children, who had been borne to him by Megara, into the fire, together with two of Iphicles' children. Condemning himself to exile on this account, he was purified by Thespios and went to Delphi to ask the god where he should settle. It was on this occasion that the Pythia called him Heracles for the first time (for until then he had been called Alceides). She told him to settle in Tiryns while he served Eurystheus for twelve years, and to accomplish the [ten] labours that would be imposed on him; and then, she said, **after the labours had been accomplished, he would come to be immortal.**

Labors of Hercules

On hearing this, Heracles went to Tiryns and fulfilled what Eurystheus demanded of him. **Eurystheus** began by ordering him to fetch the skin of the **Nemean lion;** this was **an invulnerable beast fathered by Typhon.** On reaching Nemea, he sought out the lion, and began by shooting arrows at it, but when he discovered that the beast was invulnerable, he raised his club and chased after it. When the lion took refuge in a cave which had two entrances, Heracles walled up one of them and went in through the other to attack the beast; and throwing his arm round its neck, he held it in a stranglehold until he had throttled it. And hoisting it on to his shoulders, he proceeded to Mycenae. Astounded by his bravery, Eurystheus refused him entry to the city from that day forth, and told him to exhibit his trophies in front of the gates. They say, furthermore, that in his alarm he had a bronze jar made for himself to hide in beneath the ground, and that he conveyed his commands for the labours through a herald, Copreus, a son of Pelops the Elean.

As a second labour, Eurystheus ordered Heracles to kill the **Lernaean hydra;** this creature had grown up in the swamp of Lerna, and used to make incursions into the plain and destroy the cattle and the countryside. The hydra had a body of enormous size, and nine heads, of which eight were mortal, but the one in the center immortal. So climbing on to a chariot driven by **Iolaos,** Heracles made his way to Lerna, and

"Amphitryon . . . met his death"— Heracles does not, like some of the heroes Rank considers, kill his father but, as leader of the expedition, he is in a sense responsible for his death.

"struck by madnesss through the jealousy of Hera"—On the role of Hera, and on the gods as "causing" human behavior," see p. 452.

"after the labours had been accomplished, he would come to be immortal"—In Euripides' play *Heracles,* the labors are accomplished before Heracles' fit of madness, his motivation for them is to restore honor to his father Amphitryon.

First Labor: the Nemean Lion

Eurystheus Hera hastened his birth before that of Heracles, because Zeus had declared that the child about to be born would be the next king of Mycenae.

"Nemean lion"—Nemea is near Tiryns in the Peloponnese (see map). Heracles' labors begin close to home, but later encompass all of the known world.

"an invulnerable beast fathered by Typhon"—Invulnerability meant the lion could not be pierced by a spear; Heracles therefore strangled him.

Second Labor: the Lernaean Hydra

Lernaean hydra A hydra is a water serpent. This one was, according to Hesiod, raised by Hera to be an adversary to Heracles.

Iolaos Son of Iphicles, Heracles' half-brother, accompanied Heracles on several of his adventures.

halting his horses there, he discovered the hydra on a hill by the springs of Amymone, where it had its lair. By hurling flaming brands at it, he forced it to emerge, and as it came out, he seized it and grasped it firmly. But it twined itself round one of his legs, and clung to him. By striking the hydra's heads off with his club Heracles achieved nothing, for as soon as one was struck off, two grew up in its place; and a huge crab came to its assistance by biting Heracles on the foot. So he killed the crab, and summoned assistance on his own account by calling Iolaos, who set fire to part of the neighboring forest, and using brands from it, burned out the roots of the hydra's heads to prevent them from regrowing. And when, by this means, he had prevailed over the regenerating heads, he cut off the immortal head, buried it, and placed a heavy rock over it by the road that leads through Lerna to Elaious. As for the body of the hydra, he slit it open and **dipped his arrows into its gall.** Eurystheus declared, however, that this labour should not be counted among the ten, because Heracles had not overcome the hydra on his own, but only with the help of Iolaos.

As a third labour, Eurystheus ordered him to bring the Cerynitian hind alive to Mycenae. This hind, which had golden horns, lived at Oinoe, and was sacred to **Artemis;** so Heracles, wanting neither to kill it nor wound it, pursued it for a full year. When the hind, worn out by the chase, fled for refuge to the mountain known as Artemision, and from there towards the River Ladon, Heracles struck it with an arrow as it was about to cross over the stream, and was thus able to catch it; and then, setting it on his shoulder, he hurried through Arcadia. But he came across Artemis in the company of Apollo, and she wanted to take the hind away from him, accusing him of trying to kill an animal that was sacred to her. By pleading necessity, however, and saying that the person responsible was Eurystheus, he allayed the anger of the goddess and brought the animal alive to Mycenae.

As a fourth labour, Eurystheus ordered him to bring the Erymanthian boar alive. This beast was causing havoc in Psophis, sallying forth from the mountain known as Erymanthos. While Heracles was passing through Pholoe, he was entertained as a guest by the **Centaur Pholos,** son of Seilenos and a Melian nymph. The Centaur served roasted meat to Heracles, but he himself ate it raw. When Heracles asked for wine, he said that he was afraid to open the jar that was the common property of the Centaurs; but Heracles urged him to take courage, and opened it up. Not long afterwards, the Centaurs became aware of the smell, and appeared at Pholos' cave armed with rocks and fir trees. A fight ensued and Cheiron was wounded by Heracles' arrows. He wanted to die, but was incapable of doing so because he was immortal. Only when **Prometheus offered himself to Zeus to become immortal** in his place was Cheiron able to die. Pholos pulled an arrow from a corpse, marvelling that so small a thing could kill creatures of such a size; but the arrow slipped from his hand and landed on his foot, killing him instantly. When Heracles returned to Pholoe and saw that Pholos was dead, he buried him and went out to hunt the boar. He chased the beast from the thicket with loud cries; and thrusting it exhausted into deep snow, he trapped it in a noose, and took it to Mycenae.

As a fifth labour, Eurystheus ordered Heracles to remove the dung of the cattle of Augeias without assistance in a single day. Augeias was the king of Elis, and, according to some, he was a son of the Sun, or according to others, of Poseidon, or again, of Phorbas; and he owned many herds of cattle. Heracles went up to him, and without disclosing Eurystheus' order, said that he would remove the dung in a single day if Augeias would give him a tenth of his cattle. Augeias gave his word, not believing that he could do it. After he had engaged Phyleus, the son of Augeias, as a witness, Heracles made a breach in the foundations of [the wall surrounding] the cattle yard, and then, diverting the courses of the Alpheios and the Peneios which flowed nearby, he channeled their water into the yard, after first making an outlet through another breach.

"dipped his arrows into its gall"— The Greeks regarded the use of poison as questionable. In Homer's *Odyssey,* Mentes explains his father gave Odysseus poison for his arrows where others had refused. Heracle's poisoned arrows caused the accidental death of Pholus and poison eventually led to his own death after the Centaur Nessus gave Deianeira, his wife, what she thought was a love potion to use on her husband (see p. 451).

 Third Labor: the Cerynitian Hind

Artemis Virgin goddess of hunting. As Lady of the Animals, she is often associated with deer. If harm came to her creatures, her reaction could be deadly. When the Greek leaders killed a pregnant hare at the start of the Trojan War, Artemis demanded that Agamemnon sacrifice his daughter Iphigeneia before the Greeks could proceed.

 Fourth Labor: the Erymanthian Boar

Centaur Pholos Centaurs were half-man and half-horse, and were subject to wild passions, but a few of them, like Pholos and Cheiron in this story, were dignified and cultured. Compare John Updike's rendering of the Cheiron/Cladwell character in the excerpt from his novel, *The Centaur,* in Ch. 44, p. 664.

"Prometheus offered . . . to become immortal"—Prometheus was undergoing a living death through a punishment from Zeus for having given fire to humans. He was chained to a rock, where an eagle each day pecked out his liver, which regrew each night. (See Ch. 24, p. 355.)

 Fifth Labor: the Cattle of Augeias

This Labor Shares Some Characteristics with Two Others:

• In the tenth labor, Heracles must bring back the cattle of Geryon. Here he winds up being entitled to (but not receiving) one tenth of Augeias' cattle.

- In the eleventh labor, Heracles travels to the land of the sun and brings back, golden apples. The repetition of these characteristics suggests the importance of Heracles' rivalry with the sun and his role as cattle drover.

"When the judges had taken their seats"—Heracles defends himself against Augeias. In representing his eloquence in pleading his case, Apollodorus emphasizes Heracles' intelligence, one of his aspects as a god (see p. 450).

⬤ Sixth Labor: the Stymphalian Birds

- "sixth labour"—The last of the labors Heracles performs locally in the Peloponnese (see map, p. 448). In the rest he roams the earth and visits the underworld.

⬤ Seventh Labor: the Cretan Bull

- "bull that had carried Europa"— This version is incompatible with the current story. If the bull had been Zeus, it would not still be there. On the lack of logic in mythical stories, or parataxis, see Ch. 2, p. 18f.

Europa Daughter of the king of Phoenicia, in the Middle East. When Zeus fell in love with Europa, he changed into a bull, and carried her to Crete (see map, p. 448), where she had Minos.

⬤ Eighth Labor: the Mares of Diomedes

Thrace Northernmost part of Greece. Greeks considered Thracians warlike and primitive people.

Ares Greek god of war.

⬤ Ninth Labor: the Belt of Hippolyte

River Thermodon In northeastern Asia Minor.

"pressed down their right breasts"—To keep them from developing.

When Augeias discovered that the task had been accomplished on the order of Eurystheus, he refused to pay the reward, and went so far as to deny that he had ever promised to pay a reward, saying that he was ready to submit to arbitration on the matter. **When the judges had taken their seats,** Phyleus was called by Heracles and testified against his father, saying that he had agreed to pay a reward to Heracles. Augeias flew into a rage, and before the vote had been cast, ordered both Phyleus and Heracles to depart from Elis. Eurystheus would not accept this labour either as one of the ten, saying that it had been accomplished for pay.

As a **sixth labour,** Eurystheus ordered him to drive away the Stymphalian birds. At the city of Stymphalos in Arcadia there was a lake called Stymphalis, in the depths of a thick forest; and innumerable birds had sought refuge there, fearing to become the prey of wolves. So when Heracles was at a loss as to how he could drive the birds from the wood, Athene gave him some bronze castanets which she had received from Hephaistos. By rattling these from a certain mountain that lay beside the lake, he frightened the birds. Unable to endure the noise, they flew up in alarm, and in that way Heracles was able to shoot them down with his arrows.

As a seventh labour, Eurystheus ordered him to fetch the Cretan bull. According to Acousilaos, this was the **bull that had carried Europa** across the sea for Zeus, but it is said by some that it was the bull that was sent up from the sea by Poseidon when Minos had promised to sacrifice to him whatever appeared from the sea. And they say that when Minos saw the beauty of the bull, he sent it to join his herds and sacrificed another to Poseidon; and the god in his anger turned the bull wild. Heracles arrived in Crete to confront this bull, and when Minos replied to his request for assistance by telling him to fight and capture it on his own, he captured it and took it to Eurystheus; and after he had shown it to him, he set it free. It wandered to Sparta and throughout Arcadia, and crossing the Isthmus, it arrived at Marathon in Attica and harassed the inhabitants.

As an eighth labour, Eurystheus ordered him to bring the mares of Diomedes the **Thracian** to Mycenae. This Diomedes, a son of **Ares** and Cyrene, was king of the Bistones, a highly belligerent people in Thrace, and owned man-eating mares. So Heracles sailed there with a company of volunteers, overpowered the men who were in charge of the mangers, and led the mares towards the sea. When the Bistones came fully armed to the rescue, he passed the mares over to Abderos to guard. (This Abderos, a Locrian from Opous who was a son of Hermes and a beloved of Heracles, was torn apart by the horses and killed.) So Heracles fought against the Bistones, killed Diomedes, and put the rest to flight. After founding the city of Abdera by the grave of Abderos, who had met his death in the meantime, he took the horses to Eurystheus and handed them over to him. But Eurystheus released them, and they went to the mountain called Olympus, where they were killed by the wild beasts.

As a ninth labour, Eurystheus ordered him to fetch the belt of Hippolyte. She was queen of the Amazons, who lived by the **River Thermodon** and were a people who excelled in war; for they cultivated manly qualities, and if they ever had intercourse with men and gave birth to children, they raised the girls. They **pressed down their right breasts** to ensure that they would not be hindered from throwing their javelins, but retained their left breasts to allow them to suckle their children. Hippolyte had the belt of Ares in her possession as a symbol of her supremacy over the others, and Heracles was sent to fetch the belt because Admete, the daughter of Eurystheus, wanted it for herself.

When he put in at the harbour of Themiscyra, Hippolyte came to see him, and she asked him why he had come and promised to give him the belt. But Hera assumed the likeness of an Amazon and wandered around in the crowd saying that the strangers who had just arrived were abducting the queen. Seizing their arms, the Amazons hastened to the ships on horseback; and when Heracles saw them there fully armed, he thought that this must be the result of a plot, and he killed Hippolyte and robbed her of the belt. And then, after fighting the rest of the Amazons, **he sailed away, and called in at Troy.**

It happened that the city was in a desperate plight at that time, through the wrath of Apollo and Poseidon; for wanting to put Laomedon's arrogance to the test, **they had taken on human form and undertaken to fortify Pergamon in return for pay.** But when they had constructed the wall, he refused to pay them their fee. In response, Apollo sent a plague, and Poseidon a sea-monster which was carried along on a flood and used to snatch away the inhabitants of the plain. When oracles declared that they would be delivered from these misfortunes if Laomedon offered his daughter, Hesione, as prey to the monster, Laomedon offered her up, binding her to some rocks by the sea. When Heracles saw her exposed there, he promised to rescue her if he received in return the mares that Zeus had presented [to Troy] in compensation for the abduction of

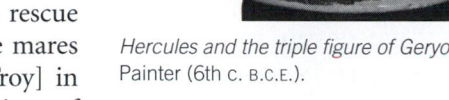

Hercules and the triple figure of Geryon. Group E Painter (6th C. B.C.E.).

Ganymede. Laomedon said that he would hand them over, and Heracles killed the monster and rescued Hesione. But **Laomedon refused to pay** the agreed reward, and Heracles put to sea threatening to make war on Troy at some future time. And taking the belt to Mycenae, he gave it to Eurystheus.

As a **tenth labour,** he was ordered to fetch the cattle of Geryon from Erytheia. **Erytheia** was an island that lay near the Ocean and is now called Gadeira; it was inhabited by Geryon, son of Chrysaor and Callirrhoe, daughter of Oceanos. He had the body of three men joined into one; these were united at the waist, but divided into three again from the hips and thighs downwards. He owned red cattle, which were herded by Eurytion and guarded by Orthos, a two-headed dog that Echidna had borne to Typhon. So travelling through Europe to fetch the cattle of Geryon, Heracles killed many savage beasts, and then arrived in Libya. He made his way to Tartessos, where he erected two pillars standing opposite one another at the boundaries of Europe and Libya, as memorials of his journey. In the course of his journey, he was overheated by the Sun, and aimed his bow against the god; and the Sun was so impressed by his bravery that he offered him a **golden cup** which he used when crossing the Ocean. Arriving at Erytheia, Heracles set up camp on Mount Abas. His presence was detected by the dog Orthos, which rushed to attack him; but he struck it with his club and when the herdsman Eurytion came to the dog's assistance, he killed Eurytion too. Menoites, who was pasturing the cattle of Hades in the area, informed Geryon of what had happened; and Geryon caught Heracles driving the cattle away near the river Anthemous, and engaged him in battle, but was killed by an arrow. Heracles put the cattle into the cup, and after he had made the crossing to Tartessos, he returned it to the Sun.

When he reached the top of **the gulf,** Hera sent a gadfly against the cattle and they dispersed among the foothills of the Thracian mountains. Heracles set out in pursuit, and recovering some of them, he drove them towards the Hellespont, but those that he

---

"he . . . called in at Troy"—Troy in Western Asia Minor would have been on Heracles' route home to Tiryns.

"they had . . . undertaken to fortify Pergamon [Troy] in return for pay"—The citadel of Troy was reputed to have been built by the gods because it resisted attack for ten years, until the Greeks conquered it with the Trojan horse.

"Laomedon refused to pay"— Having already cheated Apollo and Poseidon, Laomedon proceeded to cheat Heracles. This proves his undoing, as Heracles returns with an army and kills him. The story represents Heracles as a more formidable enemy than Apollo or Poseidon.

 Tenth Labor: the Cattle of Geryon

"tenth labour"—In his last three labors, Heracles leaves the physical world and travels to realms associated with death and the afterlife (see p. 449).

Erytheia Comes from the Greek word for "red," and with the red cattle, links Geryon and the setting sun, which colors the world red. There is also a link to the underworld, as Geryon's cattle are pastured near the cattle of Hades, the god of the underworld.

"golden cup"—the Greeks believed that the sun traveled each day from east to west across the sky, and returned to the east again each night by sailing on the river Ocean, which encircled the earth. Here, the Sun offers Heracles his sailing vessel.

"the gulf"—The Adriatic sea. Heracles is returning to Greece from the west.

Eleventh Labor: the Apples of the Hesperides

"the land of the Hyperboreans" — The Hyperboreans, a mythical people, lived in the far north. Heracles does not know their location, and must first defeat the sea god Nereus to learn it.

"he transformed himself into many different shapes"—In Homer's *Odyssey*, Menelaos describes a similar encounter with the sea god Proteus. To prevail, he must hold on to the god, who changes into a lion, and a rushing river.

"taking the fetters of olive for himself"—Hard suggests that Heracles put on a crown made of olive branches as a symbolic substitute for the chains which had bound Prometheus.

"followed the advice of Prometheus"—Heracles' liberation of this god emphasizes his role as a bringer of culture; in addition, he shows intelligence in listening to Prometheus' wise advice.

"It is said by some, however"—In an effort to be thorough, Apollodorus often presents alternate versions of his stories. In the 1st c. B.C.E., when he was working, written accounts were the norm. However, because myths originally derive from oral stories, he realized that there are often different versions told in different places. (See p. 448.)

Twelfth Labor: the Capture of Cerberos

Eleusis This town in Attica was the site of a very significant temple to Demeter, the goddess of agriculture. Many Greeks came from afar to participate in the ceremonies or mysteries performed in her honor. (See Ch. 27, p. 385.)

"she was an empty phantom"—In the Greek view, the afterlife, even for the virtuous, is a "shadow existence." In the *Odyssey*, Achilles describes it to a visiting Odysseus as worse than the life of a slave.

left behind were wild from that time forth. Having had difficulty collecting his cattle together, he blamed the River Strymon, and although it had been navigable previously, he made it unnavigable by filling it with rocks. He took the cattle to Eurystheus, and handed them over; and Eurystheus offered them in sacrifice to Hera.

When these labours had been accomplished in eight years and a month, Eurystheus, who would not acknowledge the labour of the cattle of Augeias or that of the hydra, ordered Heracles, as an eleventh labour, to fetch some golden apples from the Hesperides.

These apples were to be found, not in Libya, as some have claimed, but on Mount Atlas in **the land of the Hyperboreans.** They had been presented to Zeus [by Ge] at the time of his marriage to Hera, and were guarded by an immortal dragon, the offspring of Typhon and Echidna, which had a hundred heads and could speak with all manner of different voices. And with this dragon, the Hesperides—Aigie, Erytheia, Hesperia, and Arethousa by name—also kept guard. So Heracles proceeded on his way, until he arrived at the River Echedoros, where Cycnos, the son of Ares and Pyrene, challenged him to single combat [...] to avenge him, Ares too engaged him in single combat, but a thunderbolt was hurled between the two combatants, bringing the fight to an end. Travelling through the land of the Illyrians, Heracles hurried to the River Eridanos, where he visited the nymphs who were daughters of Zeus and Themis; and they told him where he could find Nereus. Heracles seized hold of him while he was asleep, and although **he transformed himself into many different shapes,** Heracles tied him up and refused to let him go until he had learned from him where the apples and the Hesperides were located.

On the Caucasos he shot the eagle, born to Echidna and Typhon, that fed on the liver of Prometheus. He then set Prometheus free, **taking the fetters of olive for himself,** and presented Cheiron to Zeus as an immortal being who was willing to die in Prometheus' place.

When he reached Atlas in the land of the Hyperboreans, Heracles **followed the advice of Prometheus,** who had told him not to go for the apples himself but to take over the sky from Atlas and send him instead. So Atlas took three apples from the Hesperides and returned to Heracles; and not wishing to hold up the heavens again, [he said that he himself would carry the apples to Eurystheus, and asked Heracles to support the sky in his place. Heracles promised that he would, but passed it back to Atlas by means of a ruse. For Prometheus, when offering his advice, had told him that he should ask Atlas to take the sky back until] he had prepared a pad for his head. And when Atlas heard his request, he placed the apples on the ground and took the sky back. In this way, Heracles was able to pick up the apples and depart. (**It is said by some, however,** that he did not get the apples from Atlas, but plucked them himself after killing the guardian snake.) He brought the apples back, and gave them to Eurystheus; but as soon as he received them, he returned them to Heracles. Then Athene took them from Heracles, and carried them back again; for it was unholy for them to be deposited anywhere else.

As a twelfth labour, he was ordered to fetch Cerberos from Hades. Cerberos had three dogs' heads, the tail of a dragon, and on his back, the heads of all kinds of snakes. When Heracles was about to depart for Cerberos, he went to Eumolpos in **Eleusis** with a view to being initiated, but since it was impossible for him to behold the Mysteries unless he had been purified from the murder of the Centaurs, he was purified by Eumolpos and initiated thereafter. He made his way to Tainaron in Laconia, where the mouth of the descent to Hades is located, and descended through it. When the souls caught sight of him, they fled, except for Meleager and the Gorgon Medusa. He drew his sword against the Gorgon as if she were still alive, but learned from Hermes that **she was an empty phantom.** As he drew close to the gates of Hades, he discovered

Theseus there, and Peirithoos, who had tried to gain Persephone as his bride, and had been imprisoned there for that reason.

When they saw Heracles, they stretched their arms towards him, hoping that his strength would enable them to be raised from the dead. He took Theseus by the hand and raised him up, but when he wanted to raise Peirithoos, the earth shook and he let him go. He also rolled aside the stone of Ascalaphos.

Wanting **to procure blood for the souls,** he slaughtered one of the cattle of Hades, but their herdsman, Menoites, son of Ceuthonymos, challenged him to a wrestling match. Heracles seized him round the middle and broke his ribs, but let him go when Persephone interceded. When he asked Pluto for Cerberos, Pluto told him to take the beast if he could overpower it without using any of the weapons that he was carrying. Discovering Cerberos by the gates of Acheron, Heracles, sheathed in his breastplate and fully covered by his lion's skin, grasped its head between his arms and never relaxed his grip and stranglehold on the beast until he had broken its will, although he was bitten by the dragon in its tail. Then he carried it off and made his way back, ascending through Troezen. As for Ascalaphos, Demeter turned him into an owl. **After Heracles had shown Cerberos to Eurystheus,** he returned the beast to Hades.

Further Reading

Slater, Philip. *The Glory of Hera: Greek Mythology and the Greek Family*. Boston, MA: Beacon Press, 1968.

Dionysus

Like Heracles, Dionysus was the illegitimate son of Zeus and a mortal woman. And, as with Heracles, there are stories that Hera persecuted Dionysus and his mother because of her jealousy of her husband. In fact, it was Hera who caused him to have an unusual birth. Zeus swore an oath to give Semele, his mother, anything she asked for. Hera persuaded her to ask to see Zeus in all his glory. When Zeus granted her wish, Semele was burned to a cinder, but he was able to snatch up his son's fetus before it was destroyed. He brought it to term by sewing it into his thigh. After Dionysus was born, Hera drove him mad, as she had Heracles.

However, these stories are much less important as an aspect of Dionysus' personality as a god. Most of the stories we have about him suggest that he was in control of his fate and his powers. Indeed, in many stories, including two presented in the excerpt, Dionysus is engaged in making other people uncomfortable because they chose to deny his power or criticize the virtue of his mother.

The stories we have about Dionysus portray him as a newcomer and an outsider who had trouble being accepted into Greek worship. As a result, scholars for a long time believed that his worship was a foreign cult that had been imported into Greece from Thrace. However, this turns out not to be the case.

Archeologists have discovered evidence that the worship of Dionysus in Greece goes back to the days of Mycenaean civilization, about 1200 B.C.E. This means that the difficulty of accepting Dionysus must have been psychological and not cultural; that is, the conflict was not between a foreign culture and a Greek one, but between the established values of Greek society and the values that the worship of Dionysus represented. In perpetuating stories about the "foreign" nature of Dionysus, the Greeks were unconsciously expressing their discomfort with the emotions and attitudes he stood for. Thus, the resistance to Dionysus arose from the mixed feelings occasioned by what we may call the subversive power of his myth. This is discussed in detail in the next section.

"to procure blood for the souls"— The shadowy souls could only communicate if visitors provided them with animal blood to drink. Odysseus on his visit is prepared for this by Circe and brings an animal with him to slaughter.

"After Heracles had shown Cerberos to Eurystheus"— In Apollodorus' version, Heracles does not become a god after completing his labors. Rather, he goes on to other adventures, including the murder of Iphitos and the sack of Troy. He does not become a god until his death on funeral pyre Mount Oeta, after his wife Deianeira unintentionally poisons him with a substance that the Centaur Nessus has told her is a love potion.

THE NATURE OF DIONYSUS

E. R. Dodds describes Dionysus most aptly, saying "To the Greeks of the classical age, Dionysus was not solely, or even mainly, the god of wine," and adding that the god's domain is "not only the liquid fire in the grape, but the sap thrusting in a young tree, the blood pounding in the veins of a young animal, all the mysterious and uncontrollable tides that ebb and flow in the life of nature" (Dodds, xi–xii). The Greeks experienced the inspiration of Dionysus not as drunkenness, but as a kind of fervent inspiration, a religious experience in which the worshippers' instincts were liberated from the bondage of reason and social custom and they "became conscious of a strange new vitality [attributable] to the god's presence [within]." The ceremonies associated with the god were designed to induce or celebrate this fervent inspiration, as the participants performed ritual dances and experienced day-long sessions of dramatic performances which moved them to bouts of what Aristotle called "pity and fear" (*Poetics* 1449b).

As can be seen from Dodds' description of Dionysus' nature, his worship involved feelings and attitudes that were in opposition to the values of a stable society as Greeks understood it. Perhaps the most famous story about Dionysus is that of his encounter with Pentheus, king of Thebes. This story is included in the excerpt from Apollodorus and is told at length in *The Bac-*

Dionysus and his followers, ca. 380–360 B.C.E., Budapest Museum of Fine Art. In Euripides' *Bacchae*, the followers of Dionysus are Theban women who roam the countryside in a frenzy. Much of the worship of the god had a calm, enlightened feel to it, as in the representation on this amphora.

chae, a play by Euripides. According to this story, Dionysus comes to Thebes, a new god demanding worship. However, Pentheus, the king, is scandalized by the ritual and, denying that Dionysus is a god, outlaws his worship. The rituals of Dionysus are performed by women called maenads or Bacchants[3] who leave their homes and roam the countryside, drinking wine, dancing, and hunting wild animals and tearing them to pieces as sacrifices to the god. Despite Pentheus' prohibition, increasing numbers of Thebans, young and old, male and female, are leaving the city to worship the god.

When Dionysus himself appears in Thebes, Pentheus imprisons him. However, the god is set free under mysterious circumstances when an earthquake destroys his prison. Pentheus, who is as fascinated by Dionysus as he is scandalized by him, goes off to the country in disguise to spy on the worshippers. However, Dionysus casts a spell over the worshippers, and they believe that the king is a wild animal, and led by Pentheus' mother Agave, they tear him to pieces. Seaford notes, "It is virtually certain that in the lost part of Dionysos' speech at the end of the play he announced the establishment of his cult at Thebes. *Bacchae* dramatises the aetiological myth of the Theban cult of Dionysos, i. e., the myth that explains and narrates its founding" (54), in the same way as the *Homeric Hymn to Demeter* represents the founding of the temple at Eleusis (see p. 385).

However, the ritual of Dionysus, as described in Euripides' *Bacchae,* would have seemed especially scandalous to the Greeks, as Greek women led very sheltered and circumscribed lives. They lived in a separate part of the house, apart from men, and hardly left the house. The term "white-armed" in Homer was a compliment routinely paid to noble women. Given the strength of the sun in Greece, a Greek woman would have to avoid going out almost completely to keep her skin white. In addition, Greek women had almost no rights and little power in their society. Thus, having them, on their own initiative, leave their homes and their endless round of household duties to establish and officiate at new rituals would seem quite outrageous. Giving women such power would seem to subvert the order of society.

In fact, these mythical accounts do not accurately reflect what was done in classical Greece to worship Dionysus. It is true that there was a society of women called *maenads* at Thebes, but these were not an impromptu gathering of women overcome with the madness of

---

[3] They were called bacchants or bacchae after Bacchus, another name for Dionysus.

Dionysus. Rather, they were office holders of high prestige who themselves represented not liberation from the rules made by society, but the orderly conduct of religious rites and rituals. The society of Thyiades at Delphi participated in ritual dances and torchlight processions that may have evoked those of the original *maenads,* but once again these rituals were more symbolic reminiscences than literal reenactments of the Bacchic revels found in mythology. In Miletus, there was a ritual of Dionysus that involved a piece of raw meat for divine or human consumption. We are unsure of the details, but there was no widespread rending or eating of sacrificed animals.

The myths of Dionysus may provide us with evidence of what it was like to be initiated into the mystery-cult of Dionysus. (On such cults, see p. 395.) Seaford argues that this may have been a "secret cult within a public festival of the whole community" (71). Some elements of the initiation may be found in the *Bacchae,* Seaford notes. The play suggests that initiates were subjected to a series of riddling questions and imprisoned in the dark. They were masked and dressed as satyrs. They experienced a miraculous light and were subjected to a symbolic death, identifying with a sacrificial animal. According to Seaford's reconstruction, the initiates underwent a frightening ritual experience, perhaps a trance, that represented a "radical transformation of identity" involving the "**dissolution of boundaries** between male and female, human and animal, and—above all—between life and death"(95). There is also reason to think that initiates into this secret community may have believed that their membership in the *thiasos* or following of Dionysus won for them a new life after death. Seaford describes small inscribed strips of gold buried with the dead throughout the Greek world. The inscriptions vary, but the strips seem to contain instructions for how to behave in the underworld. One from fourth century B.C.E. Thessaly says in part, "Now you died and now you come into being, thrice blessed one, on this day. Tell Persephone [the goddess of the underworld] that Bakhios [Dionysus] himself freed you" (Seaford 55).

In addition, the myths of Dionysus serve as an indication of one characteristic of the rituals in his honor. Because of the traditional importance of women to the worship of Dionysus, L. R. Farnell reports in his study of Greek cults that their involvement in the god's rituals was "strikingly frequent," a characteristic which placed these ceremonies at variance with the rest of Greek society. Yet, for the most part, the rituals of Dionysus were run by officials of the city government and by men and women who were prominent members of well-established religious groups, not by roaming bands of unknown or marginal social status. In some cases, these officiants were bound by oaths of purity, and all were expected to lead exemplary lives. Nonetheless, as will be clear from the detailed descriptions in the next section, the rituals of Dionysus did contain subversive elements like cross-dressing, drunkenness, exchanges of insults, obscene songs, the acting out of sexual acts. As such, they allowed the expression of some of what Dodds calls the "strange vitality" which is habitually repressed by social constraints (xx).

At the same time, festivals of Dionysus were also the time for Greeks to indulge in day-long bouts of watching dramatic performances, thus steeping themselves in the powerful emotions which these literary works typically expressed. Aristotle suggested that the viewers of Greek tragedy became better for having shared these feelings with the characters in the plays, and that by doing so, spectators experienced a cleansing or catharsis of their own negative feelings. Thus, the festivals of Dionysus would seem to have allowed Greeks to share in the trickster role of the god. He was considered an outsider, although he was one of the oldest of the Greek gods. His worship allowed Greeks to participate in what Victor Turner would call "liminal experiences" that allowed them in turn both to rebel against the strictures of their society and to become reconciled to it anew. Goldhill notes that Dionysus' "sphere would encompass [a] sense of paradox and reversal," and that his worship represented "the interplay between norm and transgression."

"dissolution of boundaries"— Turner refers to this as the "interstructural character of the liminal." By this he means that in the liminal stage of initiation rituals, the initiates (or "neophytes") are secluded and treated as if they did not belong to any of the "culturally defined and ordered states or statuses" in the society. When they reenter society, the initiates return to accepting its structure, but their liminal experience connects them to each other for the rest of their liminal lives. See Chapter 26, pp. 375–376.

RITUALS ASSOCIATED WITH DIONYSUS

The Greeks celebrated a variety of rituals honoring Dionysus. Here is a description of the main festivals in his honor, as they were practiced at Athens. Other Greek cities had similar or analogous ceremonies.

- The **Lenaia,** in late January or early February, included religious rituals as well as a procession and dramatic contests. The main ceremony was a torchlight ritual performed by the officials of the Eleusinian mysteries. It involved awakening the young god Dionysus, who was imagined to have slept through the winter. The procession was not a sedate event. It involved wild and boisterous behavior: marchers wore masks representing drunken men and sang obscene songs. The marchers included professional revelers in wagons who heckled and cursed the audience. In the processions, marchers carried about phalloi, large images of the penis, which represented fertility and regeneration.

- The **Anthestheria,** a festival of the new wine celebrated in late February. The first day of this three-day celebration was called Pithoigia ("opening the wine jars"), and on it, the new wine was opened, offered to the god, and sampled. The next day was called Choes, after the Greek name for a nine-pint measure, and was devoted to drinking parties. As at the Lenaia, the procession included hecklers in wagons mocking and reviling passers-by. On the final day, called Chytroi ("pots"), pots of seed and vegetable bran were offered to the dead. In the ceremony, the wife of one of the city officials was offered as a bride to Dionysus in a ceremony that involved acting out the physical consummation of the union.

- The **City Dionysia** was celebrated at the end of March and included processions, animal sacrifices, and dramatic performances. By contrast with the other festivals of Dionysus, it was a more dignified and formal event, although, like the other festivals, the processions included phalloi. The festival commemorated the arrival of a particular statue of Dionysus from the Boeotian town of Eleutherai to Athens. The arrival of the statue is thought to have represented a political alliance between the two regions. At the beginning of the festival, a procession escorted the wooden statue of Dionysus from its temple on the Acropolis near the theater to a small shrine on the road leading from Eleutherai to Athens. At the end of the festival, a torchlight procession returned the statue to its customary location. The festival made up in magnificent display what it lost in wanton high spirits: spectators were awed by elaborate and lavishly presented offerings of loaves, bowls, and animals, and entertained by elaborate performances both during the processions and at dramatic competitions that went on for five days. Poets and actors rehearsed throughout the year in preparation for the dramatic competitions at the City Dionysia, that included the presentation of tragedies, comedies, and the dithyramb, a kind of elaborate song performed with accompanying dancing.

- The **Rural Dionysia** were celebrated in December, on different days in different districts. These tended to be local versions of some of the elements found in the City Dionysia, and also involved processions and dramatic performances. These festivals were far less formal than the City Dionysia and incorporated more of the bawdy elements described in the account of the Lenaia.

- The **Oschophoria** was an autumn festival involving a procession from the temple of Dionysus at Athens to the temple of Athena Skiras at Phaleron. Its character was quite different from the other festivals of Dionysus, and Farnell suggests that it may have been an older festival of Athena that was refocused to include Dionysus. The procession was led by two men dressed as women and carrying bunches of grapes on the branch (*oschoi*). There followed races between *ephebes* (young men performing military service) who also carried bunches of grapes, and a banquet. At the banquet, female servers told stories from the life of Theseus, the legendary Athenian hero who killed the Minotaur. The festivities were punctuated by wild cries that combined grief and joy; we are not sure why.

The Birth of Dionysus

Cadmos had four daughters, Autonoe, Ino, **Semele,** and Agave, and a son, Polydoros. Ino became the wife of Athamas, Autonoe the wife of Aristaios, and Agave the wife of Echion. As for Semele, **Zeus** fell in love with her, and slept with her in secret from **Hera.**

Now Zeus had engaged to do whatever Semele asked, and as the result of a deception by Hera, she asked him to come to her just as he had come when he was courting Hera. Unable to refuse, Zeus came to her bedchamber in a chariot to the accompaniment of lightning and thunder, and hurled a thunderbolt. Semele died of fright, but Zeus snatched her aborted sixthmonth child from the fire, and sewed it into his thigh. (After Semele's death, the other daughters of Cadmos **spread the tale that Semele had slept with a mortal** but falsely laid the blame on Zeus, and that she had been struck down with a thunderbolt because of that.)

When the appropriate time arrived, Zeus brought Dionysos to birth by untying the stitches, and handed him over to Hermes, who took him to Ino and Athamas, and persuaded them to bring him up as a girl. But Hera in her fury drove them mad, and Athamas hunted his eldest son Learchos in the belief he was a deer and killed him, while Ino threw Melicertes into a cauldron of boiling water, and **carrying it with her dead child inside,** leaped into the sea. She is known as **Leucothea** and her son is known as Palaimon—these were the names given to them by mariners, who receive help from them when they are caught in storms. The **Isthmian Games** were founded in honour of Melicertes on the orders of Sisyphos.

As for Dionysus, Zeus rescued him from the anger of Hera by turning him into a kid; and Hermes gathered him up and took him to some nymphs who lived at Nysa in Asia, those whom Zeus later turned into a constellation, naming them the **Hyades.**

Struggles for Recognition

After his discovery of the vine, Dionysos was driven mad by Hera and roamed around Egypt and Syria. He was welcomed first by Proteus, king of the Egyptians, but then

Praxiteles, Hermes, and Dionysus, ca. 350–330 B.C.E. The myth of Dionysus' birth from Zeus' thigh raises questions about the fate of the child after it was born. According to one story, Zeus had him reared by nymphs in Nysia. In the version of his life told by Apollodorus, Dionysus was taken by Hermes to Ino, his mother's sister, who brought him up as a girl; presumably this story explains Dionysus' effeminate characteristics.

This story comes from *Apollodorus, The Library of Greek Mythology.**

Cadmos The founder of the Greek city of Thebes.

Semele The mother of Dionysus.

Zeus King of the Greek gods, a notorious womanizer.

Hera Queen of the Greek gods, who took vengeance on women Zeus became involved with.

"spread the tale that Semele had slept with a mortal"—Hard suggests that Dionysus later drove Theban women mad in retribution for this slander.

"carrying it with her dead child inside"—In several stories about Dionysus, parents harm their children. These stories may be the basis for some rituals of Dionysus in which an animal sacrifice representing a divine child was killed and eaten.

Leucothea A goddess who protected sailors. In the *Odyssey,* she saved Odysseus after Poseidon had capsized his vessel.

Isthmian Games Held on the isthmus of Corinth, near where a dolphin was said to have brought Melicertes' body to shore. It included horse and chariot races.

Hyades These seven stars make up the face of the bull in the constellation Taurus.

* *Apollodorus. The Library of Greek Mythology,* translated by Robin Hard, 101–103. Copyright © 1997. Reprinted by permission of Oxford University Press.

Rhea By syncretism (see p. 447), the worship of the Phrygian mother Cybele became identified with the Greek goddess Rhea. Dionysus was usually linked with Cybele, a fertility goddess whose worshippers also wandered through the mountains and participated in wild revels.

Thetis A sea goddess, mother of the Greek hero Achilles.

Bacchai Followers of Dionysus, usually women, who participated in orgiastic rites and wild dancing through the mountains.

Satyrs Wild creatures who had some animal features, and were preoccupied with drinking and lovemaking.

"India, where he set up pillars" — These marked the Eastern limits of the known world as did the pillars of Heracles on the West.

"forced the women to desert their houses and abandon themselves to Bacchic frenzy"— Apollodorus explains the spread of Dionysian worship as caused by revenge and force. In contrast, Euripides, in his play *The Bacchae,* makes it seem more attractive and desirable.

"chartered a pirate ship"—In another version of this story in the Homeric *Hymn to Dionysus,* the god turns himself into a lion to frighten the sailors. It is usually pirates who surprise their passengers when they reveal their identity, but here it is the god who provides the surprise to his captors.

"brought his mother up from Hades"—Some rituals of Dionysus reenacted the resurrection of Semele from the dead.

arrived at Cybela in Phrygia, and after he had been purified by **Rhea** and learned the rites of initiation, and had received the [initiate's] robe from her, he hurried through Thrace to attack the Indians. Lycourgos, son of Dryas, the ruler of the Edonians, who live by the River Strymon, was the first to insult and expel him. Dionysos sought refuge in the sea with **Thetis,** daughter of Nereus, while the **Bacchai** were taken prisoner along with the crowd of **Satyrs** who followed in his train. But later the Bacchai were suddenly set free, and Lycourgos was driven mad by Dionysos. During his madness, Lycourgos, believing that he was pruning a vine branch, killed his son Dryas with blows from his axe and had cut off his limbs by the time he recovered his senses. When the land remained barren, the god declared in an oracle that it would become fruitful again if Lycourgos were put to death. On hearing this, the Edonians took him to Mount Pangaion and tied him up, and there he died through the will of Dionysos, killed by horses.

After travelling through Thrace and the whole of **India, where he set up pillars,** he arrived in Thebes, where he **forced the women to desert their houses and abandon themselves to Bacchic frenzy** on Mount Cithairon. But Pentheus, a son of Echion by Agave, who had inherited the throne from Cadmos, tried to put an end to these practices, and when he went to Mount Cithairon to spy on the Bacchai, he was torn to pieces by his mother Agave, who, in her frenzy, took him for a wild beast. Having shown the Thebans that he was a god, he went to Argos, and there again, when they failed to honour him, he drove the women mad, and they carried their unweaned children into the mountains and feasted on their flesh. Wanting to make the sea-passage from Icarios to Naxos, he **chartered a pirate ship** with a crew of Tyrrhenians. When they had him on board however, they sailed past Naxos and pressed on towards Asia hoping to sell him. But he changed the mast and oars into snakes and filled the craft with ivy and the sound of flutes; and the pirates went mad, and jumped into the sea, where they turned into dolphins.

In this way, men came to know that he was a god and paid due honour to him; and after he had **brought his mother up from Hades** and named her Thyone, he ascended to heaven in her company.

Further Reading

Goldhill, Simon. "The Great Dionysia and Civic Ideology." In *Nothing to Do with Dionysos?* eds. John J. Winkler and Froma I. Zeitlin, 97–129. Princeton, NJ: Princeton University Press, 1990.

Seaford, Richard. *Dionysos.* London: Routledge, 2006.

Part 5

Myths and Dreams

Why Do We Talk about Dreams in a Mythology Book?

For a long time, students of mythology have noticed that myths share common elements, even though they originate in places that are geographically remote from each other, or come from time periods that are many centuries apart. There are many possible explanations for such similarities. Ancient writers like Herodotus tried to establish patterns of influence between the civilizations that originated the similar stories, looking for contact, known and unknown, between their cultures. In modern times, Otto Rank provides one of the more thoroughgoing discussions of the meaning behind the common elements of disparate myths in the first chapter of *The Myth of the Birth of the Hero* (3–7). He considers the possible explanations for the widespread similarities among myths, cataloguing them as follows:

1. The idea that "the unanimity of the myths is a necessary [result] of the uniform disposition of the human mind and the manner of its manifestation" (4).
2. The idea that the myths that are similar can be traced back to an "original community" of Indo-European peoples who told the same stories because they had a shared culture. The stories then diverged as the people dispersed throughout the world.
3. The idea that the similar stories were borrowed as peoples migrated and influenced each other's culture.

In the course of his discussion, Rank speaks in detail about studies undertaken by his contemporaries and dismisses the second and third possibilities. He argues for the first or "psychological explanation," maintaining that myths arise out of the human unconscious and that they reflect shared experiences we all have by virtue of being human beings. In this view, which Rank notes is based on pioneering work by Sigmund Freud, dreams are the everyday indications of the reality of a mechanism common to all human beings.

In this section, we consider the views of Carl Gustav Jung (1875–1961) who, like Rank, was a student of Freud, but whose explanation for the nature of myth is different from that of Rank. Both Jung and Rank drew upon Freud's influential description of the relationship between the wakeful experiences of his patients and the dreams they had while they were asleep. However, each psychologist developed a different theory about how myths, dreams, and the unconscious are structured and related. Jung's work developed a complete and far-reaching discussion of dreams as perhaps the most important component of a theory of human experience, and thus of mythology.

The Unconscious

Modern psychology was founded on the idea that, besides their conscious stream of life, human beings also experience another set of subconscious experiences whose role in their development is just as important to their fulfillment as human beings, if not more so. This insight was first articulated in 1889 by Sigmund Freud in *The Interpretation of Dreams*. Freud believed that his patients were expressing neurotic behavior based on feelings they experienced in infancy. He argued that these emotions survived in an area of their mind that stored memories, ideas, feelings, fears, and wishes that were "repressed," that is, preserved without conscious awareness. Freud felt that, in order to help his patients deal with neurotic behavior, he must enable them to deal with their unconscious processes, and that their dreams, which originated from the same source, could offer signs indicating the content of the unconscious.

Anonymous, *Portrait of Carl Gustav Jung*. This portrait of Jung represents the open and beneficent gaze of the psychologist. Glasses raised, he seems to be in pleasant speculation about the nature of the human psyche.

Jung, who was a student of Freud, also believed in the existence and importance of the unconscious, but explained its function differently from his teacher. Jung felt that the unconscious contained not only the feelings of the individual, but also the results of the collective experience of humankind. He reasoned by analogy with the other capacities he saw in human beings. That is, a human baby is born with a range of physical potentialities that she will develop in the course of maturation: the ability to walk upright, the power to reason logically, and the capacity to express herself through a language. Jung would say that in addition to these "innate" (inborn) abilities, a human being also is born with the potential to form archetypal images and express them in dreams and myths. These capacities are explored in the writings of Jung and his student M. L. von Frantz, excerpts from which are presented in Chapters 32 (p. 468) and 33 (p. 485).

The Scientific View of the Meaning of Dreams

You may wonder how the ideas of Jung compare with modern-day scientific accounts of the functioning and meaning of dreams. The short answer is that modern science has neither confirmed nor refuted Jung's observations. Scientists are by no means agreed on the meaning of dreams. Some view dreams as the result of nerve cell activity that is part of the physiological process of "clearing the decks" or "taking out the garbage" from the experiences of the wakeful part of the day. In a 1977 study, J. Allan Hobson and Robert McCarley suggested that the forebrain (the neocortex and associated structures) tries to fit a plot to meaningless associations and memories arising in response to random signals from the brain stem. The phenomenon known as the dream results and is developed in accordance with the individual's own emotional vocabulary. In this view, dreams have no meaning at all, but are simply constituted of meaningless debris that we are best rid of if we are to get on with our lives. However, there are two arguments against this view:

1. Dreams seem to have a significant relationship to myths, treating as they do motifs and figures that are also found in the sacred stories of most civilizations. This suggests that dreams, which are related to such important material, must have meanings of their own, whatever the nature of their physiological generation, in relation to the mythical material they are related to.
2. Human beings have seemingly always felt that dreams are significant. The emotional power of dreams has always suggested that they must have some meaning, because otherwise, we would look upon them more dispassionately.

Other scientists point to the generation of dreams. Dreams arise during what is called rapid-eye-movement (or REM) sleep, and numerous studies show that if human beings are deprived of this kind of sleep by organic or chemical failure or intervention, their health and well-being tends to deteriorate, and they may even die. In fact, all mammals experience REM sleep, and this physiological process is thought to be an important aspect of their development. Thus, some scientists reason that, since REM sleep is this important, and dreams occur primarily during this phase of the sleep cycle, dreaming too must also have importance for our well-being. Neurobiologists have formulated a range of theories about the importance of dreaming, postulating that it may help us to sort and process our memories, or that it may produce a synthesis of the attitudes and strategies we use to cope with the events of daily life.

Of course, the sense that dreams are important is not necessarily attended by unanimity about what, in fact, they mean. A great variety of theories have been used to explain the meaning of dreams. Freud and his students Rank and Jung have each developed extensive explanations of how therapists and their patients can use dream material to achieve a stable and mature psychic life.

The theories of Jung have been extensively based on the analysis of patients' dreams, and his understanding of dreams has been most influential in how turn of the twenty-first century theorists have understood the relationship between our dreams and the mythic material which most closely resembles them. For a more complete understanding of the workings of the unconscious, Jung's ideas can also be examined in relation with those of Freud and Rank. It has been suggested that Joseph Campbell, in *The Hero with a Thousand Faces,* tried to produce a synthesis of the ideas of Jung and Rank about mythology, aiming to maximize our understanding of the ways in which unconscious processes are manifested in mythology (see Ch. 14, p. 159).

Further Reading

Anon. "Unconscious." *Microsoft Encarta Reference Library* 2002. Redmond, WA: Microsoft Corporation, 2002.

Hobson, J. A. "Dreaming, Neural Basis of." In *International Encyclopedia of the Social & Behavioral Sciences.* Kidlington, Oxford, UK: Elsevier Science Ltd., 2001.

Rank, Otto. *The Myth of the Birth of the Hero.* New York, NY: Alfred A. Knopf, 1959.

Winson, Jonathan. "The Meaning of Dreams." *Scientific American* 263.5 (November 1990): 86–95.

Man and His Symbols

C. G. JUNG

WHAT TO EXPECT . . . For Carl Jung, myths and dreams are the primary pathway to self-realization because they allow human beings to understand and relate to parts of their psyches that would otherwise be inaccessible to them. Through what Jung called the process of individuation, the therapy he developed tries to deepen a person's experiences psychologically. Responding to dreams requires interplay of many aspects of the personality, which Jung called archetypes: the shadow, animus or anima, and Self. As you read, consider how the archetypes described by Jung can be identified in the stories you have read, and how their interplay results in a resolution that represents the growth of the individual. In particular, think in these terms about the interactions of Gilgamesh, Enkidu, and Ishtar (Ch. 15, p. 166); Rama, Sita, Ravana, and Hanuman (Ch. 17, p. 203); Mwindo, Shemwindo, and Iyangura (Ch. 22, p. 305); and Demeter, Persephone, and Aidoneus (Ch. 27, p. 385).

Carl Gustav Jung (1875–1961) was a Swiss psychoanalyst and psychiatrist. Like Sigmund Freud, who was his teacher, he had a significant clinical psychiatric practice, which led to his formulating theories about the human condition based on the symptoms presented by his patients. In developing these theories, Jung's aim was to help his patients by guiding them through a process of gaining an understanding of themselves. That is, he was seeking to find ways for individuals to discover themselves so they could participate more meaningfully in life. To do this, he believed that human beings need to connect with something higher, something transcendent. Jung sought this aspect of human life in a part of the human personality that Freud and other psychotherapists called the unconscious. His interest in mythology derived from the belief that both myths and dreams, which for him were the primary pathways into the unconscious, derived from the processes that were always underway in the unconscious of every human being. Thus the study of mythology could enhance the personal exploration that Jung felt each person needed to undertake into her or his unconscious processes.

Jung believed that the unconscious make-up of humans, the foundation of our personality, consists of several discrete perspectives or archetypes that come into play more or less forcefully, depending on the particular circumstance at hand. The archetype was defined as a tendency to form mythological patterns or motifs. These archetypes were characterized by typical figures common to psychic activity in every culture through history. Jung suggested that these motifs manifest themselves in a particular pattern in each person's unconscious: he calls this pattern the process of individuation. Since archetypes are typical of all human beings and endure in every phase of human culture, they help us to understand the human personality and to connect to a much broader, transcendent realm.

Jungian therapy seeks to identify and understand the process of individuation, and thus tries to deepen a person's experiences psychologically. The dreams of a person can often provide insight into the unconscious or archetypical forces operating in his psyche. That is, in Jung's view, the overt content of the dreams a person has is not their most important aspect: *the dreams of a person are not about what they seem to be about.* Rather, the figures and events of these dreams must be understood as manifestations of unconscious aspects of the person's personality. As people respond to these events, they draw on the aspects of personality that allow them to act in a way that reflects their individual values. And this requires a kind of dialectical interplay of many viewpoints or aspects of the personality, some of which rule their ideas and feelings about themselves and the world at one time, some at another.

The primary archetype is the *Self,* which is the fullest extension of the individual, because it comprises both the personal and the transcendental, and provides value to all aspects of human nature. The Self is part of the process of individuation whose other main archetypes (Shadow, Animus, Anima) are described in the selections in this chapter. Other archetypes are represented by names that reflect their functions. Some of those described by Jung or his associates include:

Archetype	Function
Senex	Wise old man. Coming from the Latin word for "old," this figure passes along wisdom that will help us cope with present situations. (For example, Obi Wan Kenobi in *Star Wars.*)
Great Mother	As a primary nurturer, she protects and consoles. Prehistoric fertility goddess figurines are proof that this archetype has been influential at least since very early human development. (For example, Demeter.)
Significant Animal	The creature usually has extraordinary powers, such as speech, and helps the human negotiate danger, solve problems, etc. (For example, Falada in "The Goose Girl.")

Jung's method has been useful to students of mythology because it gives us a way of explaining mythic phenomena in terms of the dichotomy or struggle among archetypes. It is hardly surprising that these archetypes represent a broad range of mythical figures, including those in this book and beyond. According to Jung, humans are born with an ability to create and combine archetypes into a "language" that reflects their experiences, much as they are born with an ability to develop language itself. A child is not born speaking English or Japanese, but with an ability to develop the language she is surrounded by. Similarly, a person is not born with stories, but with the ability to develop them. Jung calls this ability the *collective unconscious* and explains that it is collective because it is something we all have in common, something that makes us human beings. It relates us with the past via fantasy, dreams, and archetypal imagery.

As we participate in this through various personas, we are able to participate in a universal, enduring community, which is both reassuring and necessary for a fulfilled psychic life. And because myths incorporate and describe the activities and value of the archetypes, they move the personality to experience beyond itself and therefore provide a panorama of the psychological possibilities. Thus, myths teach us and help us to better understand ourselves.

The following selections introduce us to Carl Jung through his theory of the significance of dreams. This relates fundamentally to the study of myth, because both are dramatic presentations of human dilemmas. The ego interacts with the other personalities, and all of these aspects of the psyche struggle to resolve the situation. This drama results in a unity made up of the diverse parts.

These excerpts come from: C. G. Jung, "Approaching the Unconscious" in *Man and His Symbols.**

The Archetype in Dream Symbolism

The dream is a normal psychic phenomenon that transmits unconscious reactions or spontaneous impulses to consciousness. Many dreams can be interpreted with the help of the dreamer, who provides both the associations to and the context of the dream image, by means of which one can look at all its aspects.

Just as the human body represents a whole museum of organs, each with a long evolutionary history behind it, so we should expect to find that the mind is organized in a similar way. It can no more be a product without history than is the body in which it exists. By "history" I do not mean the fact that the mind builds itself up by conscious reference to the past through language and other cultural traditions. I am referring to the biological, prehistoric, and **unconscious development of the mind in archaic man,** whose psyche was still close to that of the animal.

"unconscious development of the mind in archaic man"—Jung's term for this is *collective unconscious.* For an explanation, see Introduction, p. 466.

This immensely old psyche forms the basis of our mind, just as much as the structure of our body is based on the general anatomical pattern of the mammal. The trained eye of the anatomist or the biologist finds many traces of this original pattern in our bodies. The experienced investigator of the mind can similarly see the analogies between the dream pictures of modern man and the **products of the primitive mind,** its "collective images," and its mythological motifs.

"products of the primitive mind"—"Primitive" does not mean "lacking culture" here. In the social sciences, it is a technical term for societies that don't use writing. Jung's point is that humans have always expressed their deepest beliefs through myths and mythical images.

Just as the biologist needs the science of comparative anatomy, however, the psychologist cannot do without a "comparative anatomy of the psyche." In practice, to put it differently, the psychologist must not only have a sufficient experience of dreams and other products of unconscious activity, but also of mythology in its widest sense.

The Archetype Defined

My views about the "archaic remnants," which I call "archetypes" or "primordial images," have been constantly criticized by people who lack sufficient knowledge of the psychology of dreams and of mythology. The term "archetype" is often misunderstood as meaning certain definite mythological images or motifs. But these are nothing more than conscious representations; it would be absurd to assume that such variable representations could be inherited.

The archetype is a tendency to form such representations of a motif—representations that can vary a great deal in detail without losing their basic pattern. There are, for instance, many representations of the hostile brethren, but the motif itself remains the same. They are, indeed, an **instinctive trend,** as marked as the impulse of birds to build nests, or ants to form organized colonies.

"instinctive trend"—In this respect, archetypes are similar to human language-learning ability. Babies are not born knowing a specific language (or archetype), but have the ability to learn a language (or to develop archetypes) in conjunction with their culture.

Here I must clarify the relation between instincts and archetypes: What we properly call **instincts** [emphasis added] are physiological urges, and are perceived by the senses. But at the same time, they also manifest themselves in fantasies and often reveal their presence only by symbolic images. These manifestations are what I call **archetypes** [emphasis added]. They are without known origin; and they reproduce themselves in any time or in any part of the world—even where transmission by direct descent or "cross fertilization" through migration must be ruled out.

Characteristics of the Archetype

1. Archetypal Images Develop in People from Different Cultures
   • Cross cultural
   • Strikingly similar

I vividly recall the case of a professor who had had a sudden vision and thought he was insane. He came to see me in a state of complete panic. I simply took a 400–year-old book from the shelf and showed him an old woodcut depicting his very vision. "There's no reason for you to believe that you're insane," I said to him. "They knew about your vision 400 years ago." Whereupon he sat down entirely deflated, but once more normal.

A very important case came to me from a man who was himself a psychiatrist. One day he brought me a handwritten booklet he had received as a Christmas present from

"A very important case"—As a clinician, Jung illustrates his theories with actual material from his psychoanalytical practice.

*Jung, C. G. *Man and His Symbols,* 56–66, 78. Trans. M. L von Franz, Joseph L. Henderson, Jolande Jacobi, Anita Jaffe. Copyright © 1968. Used by permission of Standard Educational Corporation.

his 10–year-old daughter. It contained a whole series of dreams she had had when she was eight. They made up the weirdest series of dreams that I have ever seen, and I could well understand why her father was more than just puzzled by them. Though childlike, they were uncanny, and they contained images whose origin was wholly incomprehensible to the father. Here are the relevant motifs from the dreams:

1. "The evil animal," a snakelike monster with many horns, kills and devours all other animals. But God comes from the four corners, being in fact four separate gods, and gives rebirth to all the dead animals.

2. An ascent into heaven, where pagan dances are being celebrated; and a descent into hell, where angels are doing good deeds.

3. A horde of small animals frightens the dreamer. The animals increase to a tremendous size, and one of them devours the little girl.

4. A small mouse is penetrated by worms, snakes, fishes, and human beings. Thus the mouse becomes human. This portrays the four stages of the origin of mankind.

5. A drop of water is seen, as it appears when looked at through a microscope. The girl sees that the drop is full of tree branches. This portrays the origin of the world.

6. A bad boy has a clod of earth and throws bits of it at everyone who passes. In this way all the passers-by become bad.

7. A drunken woman falls into the water and comes out renewed and sober.

8. The scene is in America, where many people are rolling on an ant heap, attacked by ants. The dreamer, in a panic, falls into a river.

9. There is a desert on the moon where the dreamer sinks so deeply into the ground that she reaches hell.

10. In this dream the girl has a vision of a luminous ball. She touches it. Vapors emanate from it. A man comes and kills her.

11. The girl dreams she is dangerously ill. Suddenly birds come out of her skin and cover her completely.

12. Swarms of gnats obscure the sun, the moon, and all the stars, except one. That one star falls upon the dreamer.

In the unabridged German original, each dream begins with the words of the old fairy tale: "Once upon a time. . . ." By these words the dreamer suggests that she feels as if each dream were **a sort of fairy tale,** which she wants to tell her father as a Christmas present. The father tried to explain the dreams in terms of their context. But he could not do so, so there seemed to be no personal associations to them.

Her dreams have a decidedly peculiar character. Their leading thoughts are markedly philosophic in concept. The first one, for instance, speaks of an evil monster killing their animals, but God gives rebirth to them all through a divine *Apokatastasis,* or restitution. In the Western world this idea is known through the Christian tradition. It can be found in the Acts of the Apostles III: 21: "[Christ] whom the heaven must receive until the time of restitution of all things." The early Greek Fathers of the Church (for instance, Origen) particularly insisted upon the idea that, at the end of time, everything will be restored by the Redeemer to its original and perfect state.

But according to St. Matthew XVII: 11, there was already an old Jewish tradition that Elias "truly shall first come, and restore all things." I Corinthians XV: 22 refers to the same idea in the following words: "For as in Adam all die, even so in Christ shall all be made alive."

One might guess that the child had encountered this thought in her religious education. But she had very little religious background. Her parents were Protestants in

"a sort of fairy tale"—Tales transmit the values of the tellers and thus inform the society (see Levi-Strauss, Ch. 20, p. 280). Without fully realizing her participation in the collective unconscious, the girl presents her father with the "gift" of her deepest feelings.

"Her dreams have a decidedly peculiar character"—Jung's methodology is to examine the various motifs in the little girl's dream and show that each of them appears in a variety of stories in a wide range of cultures. He carefully notes that the dreamer has no apparent knowledge of the situation.

name; but in fact they knew the Bible only from hearsay. It is particularly unlikely that the recondite image of *Apokatastasis* had been explained to the girl. Certainly her father had never heard of this mythical idea.

Nine of the 12 dreams are influenced by the theme of **destruction and restoration.** And none of these dreams shows traces of specific Christian education or influence. On the contrary, they are more closely related to primitive myths. This relation is corroborated by the other motif—the "cosmogonic myth" (the creation of the world and of man) that appears in the fourth and fifth dreams. The same connection is found in I Corinthians XV: 22, which I have just quoted. In this passage, too, Adam and Christ (death and resurrection) are linked together.

The general idea of Christ the Redeemer belongs to the world-wide pre-Christ theme of the hero and rescuer who, although he has been devoured by a monster, appears again in a miraculous way, having overcome whatever monster it was that swallowed him. When and where such a motif originated nobody knows. We do not even know how to go about investigating the problem. The one apparent certainty is that every generation seems to have known it as a tradition handed down from some preceding period when man did not yet know that he possessed a hero myth; in an age, that is to say, when he did not yet consciously reflect on what he was saying. **The hero figure is an archetype,** which has existed since time immemorial.

The production of archetypes by children is especially significant, because one can sometimes be quite certain that a child has had no direct access to the tradition concerned. In this case, the girl's family had no more than a superficial acquaintance with the Christian tradition. Christian themes may, of course, be represented by such ideas as God, angels, heaven, hell, and evil. But the way in which they are treated by this child points to a totally non-Christian origin.

Let us take **the first dream** of the God who really consists of four gods coming from the **"four corners."** The corners of what? There is no room mentioned in the dream. A room would not even fit in with the picture of what is obviously a cosmic event, in which the Universal Being himself intervenes. The quaternity (or element of "fourness") itself is a strange idea, but one that plays a great role in many religions and philosophies. In the Christian religion, it has been superseded by the Trinity, a notion that we must assume was known to the child. But who in an ordinary middle-class family of today would be likely to know of a divine quaternity? It is an idea that was once fairly familiar among students of the Hermetic philosophy of the Middle Ages, but it petered out with the beginning of the 18th century, and it has been entirely obsolete for at least 200 years. Where, then, did the little girl pick it up? From Ezekiel's vision? But there is no Christian teaching that identifies the seraphim with God.

In the second dream, a motif appears that is definitely non-Christian and that contains a reversal of accepted values—for instance, pagan dances by men in heaven and good deeds by angels in hell. This symbol suggests a relativity of moral values. Where did the child find such a revolutionary notion, worthy of Nietzsche's genius?

These questions lead us to another: What is the compensatory meaning of these dreams, to which the little girl obviously attributed so much importance that she presented them to her father as a Christmas present?

If the dreamer had been a primitive medicine man, one could reasonably assume that they represent variations of the philosophical themes of death, of resurrection or restitution, of the origin of the world, the creation of man, and the relativity of values. But one might give up such dreams as hopelessly difficult if one tried to interpret them from a personal level. They undoubtedly contain **"collective images"** and they are in a way analogous to the doctrines taught to young people in primitive tribes when they are about to be initiated as men. At such times they learn about what God, or the gods, or the "founding" animals have done, how the world and man were created, how the end of the world

---

John Armstrong, *Dreaming Head,* 1938. Art © John Armstrong/CARCC, Ottawa/VAGA, New York, NY. The girl in the picture is dreaming, and the flowers can be seen as the results of her dream, the images of completeness and fulfillment that Jung refers to as the Self (see p. 482). The flowers spring up of their own accord and not through the intellectual efforts of the dreamer. This insight accords well with the artist's motivation in a surrealist picture, whose inspiration relies not on the intellect but on instincts.

will come and the meaning of death. Is there any occasion when we, the Christian civilization, hand out similar instructions? There is: in adolescence. But many people begin to think again of things like this in old age, at the approach of death.

The little girl, as it happened, was in both these situations. She was approaching puberty and, at the same time, the end of her life. Little or nothing in the symbolism of her dreams points to the beginning of a normal adult life, but there are many allusions to destruction and restoration. When I first read her dreams, indeed, I had the uncanny feeling that they suggested impending disaster. The reason I felt like that was the peculiar nature of the compensation that I deduced from the symbolism. It was the opposite of what one would expect to find in the consciousness of a girl of that age.

These dreams open up a new and rather terrifying aspect of life and death. One would expect to find such images in an aging person who looks back on life, rather than to be given them by a child who would normally be looking forward. Experience shows that the unknown approach of death casts an *adumbratio* (an anticipatory shadow) over the life and dreams of the victim. Even the altar in Christian churches represents, on the one hand, a tomb and, on the other, a place of resurrection—the transformation of death into eternal life.

Such are the ideas that the dreams brought home to the child. They were a preparation for death, expressed through short stories, like the tales told at primitive initiations or the *Koans* of Zen Buddhism. This message is unlike the orthodox Christian doctrine and **more like ancient primitive thought.** It seems to have originated outside historical tradition in the long-forgotten psychic sources that, since prehistoric times, have nourished philosophical and religious speculations about life and death.

It was as if future events were casting their shadow back by arousing in the child certain thought forms that, though normally dormant, describe or accompany the approach of a fatal issue. Although the specific shape in which they express themselves is more or less personal, their general pattern is collective. They are found everywhere and at all times, just as animal instincts vary a good deal in the different species and yet serve the same general purposes.

We do not assume that each new-born animal creates its own instincts as an individual acquisition, and we must not suppose that human individuals invent their specific human ways with every new birth. Like the instincts, the collective thought patterns of the human mind arises, in more or less the same way in all of us.

"more like ancient primitive thought"—The dream motifs do not depend on learned or actual experience. They come from the girl's collective unconscious.

 Characteristics of the Archetype

2. The Unconscious

"even in animals"—Jung speaks of animals because he is introducing the concept of the unconscious, the instinctive aspect of the psyche that he believes explains many human impulses and moods that we can't account for by reflection.

Such emotional manifestations, to which such thought patterns belong, are recognizably the same all over the earth. We can identify them **even in animals,** and the animals themselves understand one another in this respect, even though they may belong to different species. And what about insects, with their complicated symbiotic functions? Most of them do not even know their parents and have nobody to teach them. Why should one assume, then, that man is the only living being deprived of specific instincts, or that his psyche is devoid of all traces of its evolution?

Naturally, if you identify the psyche with consciousness, you can easily fall into the erroneous idea that man comes into the world with a psyche that is empty, and that in later years it contains nothing more than what it has learned by individual experience. But **the psyche is more than consciousness.** Animals have little consciousness, but many impulses and reactions that denote the existence of a psyche; and primitives do a lot of things whose meaning is unknown to them.

"the psyche is more than consciousness"—Jung here lays the foundation for his view of the importance of unconscious thought.

You may ask many civilized people in vain for the real meaning of the Christmas tree or of the Easter egg. The fact is, they do things without knowing why they do them. I am inclined to the view that things were generally done first and that it was only a long time afterward that somebody asked why they were done.

Thought forms, universally understandable gestures, and many attitudes follow a pattern that was established long before man developed a reflective consciousness.

 Characteristics of the Archetype

3. Dynamic Aspects

It is even conceivable that the early origins of man's capacity to reflect come from the painful consequences of violent emotional clashes. Let me take, purely as an illustration of this point, the bushman who, in a moment of anger and disappointment at his failure to catch any fish, strangles his much beloved only son, and is then seized with immense regret as he holds the little dead body in his arms. Such a man might remember this moment of pain forever.

We cannot know whether this kind of experience was actually the initial cause of the development of human consciousness. But there is no doubt that the shock of a similar emotional experience is often needed to make people wake up and pay attention to what they are doing.

"archetypal forms are not just static patterns"—As explained below, Jung sees archetypes as participating in a process of individuation. Since a process implies change, the archetypes are seen as evolving and developing.

Such experiences seem to show that **archetypal forms are not just static patterns.** They are dynamic factors that manifest themselves in impulses, just as spontaneously as the instincts. Certain dreams, visions, or thoughts can suddenly appear; and however carefully one investigates, one cannot find out what causes them. This does not mean that they have no cause; they certainly have. But it is so remote or obscure that one cannot see what it is. In such a case, one must wait either until the dream and its meaning are sufficiently understood, or until some external event occurs that will explain the dream.

A Brief History of Dream Interpretations

Myths go back to the primitive storyteller and his dreams, to men moved by the stirring of their fantasies. These people were not very different from those whom later generations have called poets or philosophers. Primitive storytellers did not concern themselves with the origin of their fantasies; it was very much later that people began to wonder where a story originated. Yet, centuries ago, in what we now call "ancient" Greece, men's minds were advanced enough to surmise that the tales of the gods were nothing but archaic and exaggerated traditions of long-buried kings or chieftains. Men already took the view that the myth was all too improbable to mean what it said. **They therefore tried to reduce it to a generally understandable form.**

"They . . . tried to reduce it to a generally understandable form"—See the discussion of rationalization in myth, Ch. 25, p. 363.

In more recent times, we have seen the same thing happen with dream symbolism. We became aware, in the years when psychology was in its infancy, that dreams had some importance. But just as the Greeks persuaded themselves that their myths were merely elaborations of rational or "normal" history, so some of the pioneers of psychology came to the conclusion that dreams did not mean what they appeared to mean. The images or symbols that they presented were dismissed as bizarre forms in which repressed contents of the psyche appeared to the conscious mind. It thus came to be taken for granted that a dream meant something other than its obvious statement.

Imagination and intuition are vital to our understanding. And though the usual popular opinion is that they are chiefly valuable to poets and artists (that in "sensible" matters one should mistrust them), they are in fact equally vital in all the higher grades of science. Here they play an increasingly important role, which supplements that of the "rational" intellect and its application to a specific problem. Even physics, the strictest of all applied sciences, depends to an astonishing degree upon intuition, which works by way of the unconscious (although it is possible to demonstrate afterward the logical procedures that could have led one to the same result as intuition). Intuition is almost indispensable in the interpretation of symbols, and it can often ensure that they are immediately understood by the dreamer. But while such a lucky hunch may be subjectively convincing, it can also be rather dangerous. It can so easily lead to a false feeling of security. It may, for instance, seduce both the interpreter and the dreamer into continuing a cozy and relatively easy relation, which may end in a sort of mutual dream. The safe basis of real intellectual knowledge and moral understanding gets lost if one is content with the vague satisfaction of having understood by "hunch." One can explain and know only if one has reduced intuitions to **an exact knowledge of facts and their logical connections.**

The Process of Individuation

In the psychic life of the individual, the archetypes interact in a pattern that both reflects and fosters the development of the personality. This pattern is known as the process of individuation. The organization of this pattern, like that of any process, is linear and temporal. That is, the parts are related in a necessary way to each other. For example, baking a cake is a process, and its parts cannot be interchanged or substituted. You can't separate the eggs after you put the cake in the oven. Similarly, the stages of the process of individuation—encounters with the Shadow, Animus or Anima figures, and the Self—must be experienced more or less in order.

However, one individual may at different stages or points in life experience the process anew in a different context. In particular, the Animus and Anima figures can be experienced on a variety of different planes, from the purely physical to the abstract philosophical. After the individual has dealt with a Shadow on this level, and an Anima, he may encounter a very different sort of Shadow and Anima, and a new vision or sense of the Self. In this way, the fundamental process of individuation can be experienced several times to give the person a more intricate and meaningful understanding of his or her role and function in the world.

The Realization of the Shadow

When a child reaches school age, the phase of building up the ego and of adapting to the outer world begins. This phase generally brings a number of painful shocks. At the same time, some children begin to feel very different from others, and this feeling of being unique brings a certain sadness that is part of the loneliness of many youngsters.

"Imagination and intuition are vital to our understanding."—For some philosophers like Plato, our rational capacity has been viewed as the highest aspect of human thinking. Jung, however, argues that our humanity is at least as much dependent on those functions that do not depend on logic. They are also essential to learning and knowing.

"an exact knowledge of facts and their logical connections"—Jung believes that he has found a pattern of symbols that can be applied in a systematic and logical manner. However, the analyst must still possess good intuition to analyze dreams successfully.

The Process of Individuation
Stage 1   Shadow
Stage 2   Animus-Anima
Stage 3   Self

This text comes from: M. L. von Franz, "The Process of Individuation" in Jung, *Man and His Symbols.* * M. L. von Franz was a student of Jung who continued to develop and interpret Jung's ideas after his death.

The imperfections of the world, and the evil within oneself as well as outside, become conscious problems; the child must try to cope with urgent (but not yet understood) inner impulses as well as the demands of the outer world.

The actual processes of individuation—the conscious coming-to-terms with one's own inner center (psychic nucleus) or Self—generally begins with a wounding of the personality and the suffering that accompanies it. This initial shock amounts to a sort of "call," although **it is not often recognized as such.** On the contrary, the ego feels hampered in its will or its desire and usually projects the obstruction onto something external. That is, the ego accuses God or the economic situation or the boss or the marriage partner of being responsible for whatever is obstructing it.

Or perhaps everything seems outwardly all right, but beneath the surface a person is suffering from a deadly boredom that makes everything seem meaningless and empty. **Many myths and fairy tales symbolically describe** this initial stage in the process of individuation by telling of a king who has fallen ill or grown old. Other familiar story patterns are that a royal couple is barren; or that a monster steals all the women, children, horses, and wealth of the kingdom; or that a demon keeps the king's army or his ship from proceeding on its course; or that darkness hangs over the lands, wells dry up, and flood, drought, and frost afflict the country. Thus it seems as if the initial encounter with the Self casts a dark shadow ahead of time, or as if the "inner friend" comes at first like a trapper to catch the helplessly struggling ego in his snare.

Through dreams one becomes acquainted with aspects of one's own personality that for various reasons one has preferred not to look at too closely. This is what Jung called "the realization of the shadow." (He used the term "shadow" for this unconscious part of the personality because it actually often appears in dreams in a personified form.)

The shadow is not the whole of the unconscious personality. It represents unknown or little-known attributes and qualities of the ego—aspects that mostly belong to the personal sphere and that could just as well be conscious. In some aspects, the shadow can also consist of collective factors that stem from a source outside the individual's personal life.

When an individual makes an attempt to see his shadow, he becomes aware of (and often ashamed of) those qualities and impulses he denies in himself but can plainly see in other people—such things as egotism, mental laziness, and sloppiness; unreal fantasies, schemes, and plots; carelessness and cowardice; inordinate love of money and possessions—in short, all the little sins about which he might previously have told himself: "That doesn't matter; nobody will notice it, and in any case other people do it too."

If you feel an overwhelming rage coming up in you when a friend reproaches you about a fault, you can be fairly sure that at this point you will find a part of your shadow, of which you are unconscious. It is, of course, natural to become annoyed when others who are "no better" criticize you because of shadow faults. But what can you say **if your own dreams—an inner judge in your own being—reproach you?** That is the moment when the ego gets caught, and the result is usually embarrassed silence. Afterward the painful and lengthy work of self-education begins—a work, we might say, that is the psychological equivalent of the labors of Hercules. This unfortunate hero's first task, you will remember, was to clean up in one day the Augean Stables, in which hundreds of cattle had dropped their dung for many decades—a task so enormous that the ordinary mortal would be overcome by discouragement at the mere thought of it.

The shadow does not consist only of omissions. It shows up just as often in an impulsive or inadvertent act. Before one has time to think, the evil remark pops out, the plot is hatched, the wrong decision is made, and one is confronted with results that were never intended or consciously wanted. It is particularly in contacts with people of

Sidebar notes:

"it is not often recognized as such"—The projection of feelings is the basis for what Jung and von Franz view as the symbolic nature of dreaming. That is, your dreams are not about what they seem to be about. Rather, they symbolize other processes buried in your unconscious.

"Many myths and fairy tales symbolically describe"—Just as events in dreams should not be taken literally, other manifestations of our unconscious are also expressed in metaphoric and symbolic ways.

Definition of the Shadow

"if your own dreams . . . reproach you"—Von Franz is showing how the archetypes in our dreams enable us to know ourselves better. Since dreams come from our own unconscious, representation of faults and negatives brings us into direct contact with our shadow personality.

the same sex that one stumbles over both one's shadow and those of other people. Although we do see the shadow in a person of the opposite sex, we are usually much less annoyed by it and can more easily pardon it.

In dreams and myths, therefore, the shadow appears as a person of the same sex as that of the dreamer. The following dream may serve as an example. The dreamer was a man of 48 who tried to live very much for and by himself, working hard and disciplining himself, repressing pleasure and spontaneity to a far greater extent than suited his real nature.

I owned and inhabited a very big house in town, and I didn't yet know all its different parts. So I took a walk through it and discovered, mainly in the cellar, several rooms about which I knew nothing and even exits leading into other cellars or into subterranean streets. I felt uneasy when I found that several of these exits were not locked and some had no locks at all. Moreover, there were some laborers at work in the neighborhood who could have sneaked in.

When I came up again to the ground floor, I passed a back yard where again I discovered different exits into the street or into other houses. When I tried to investigate them more closely, a man came up to me laughing loudly and calling out that we were old pals from the elementary school. I remembered him too, and while he was telling me about his life, I walked along with him toward the exit and strolled with him through the streets. There was a strange chiaroscuro in the air as we walked through an enormous circular street and arrived at a green lawn where three galloping horses suddenly passed us. They were beautiful, strong animals, wild but well-groomed, and they had no rider with them. (Had they run away from military service?)

The maze of strange passages, chambers, and unlocked exits in the cellar recalls the old Egyptian representation of the underworld, which is a well-known symbol of the unconscious with its unknown possibilities. It also shows how one is "open" to other influences in one's unconscious shadow side, and how uncanny and alien elements can break in. The cellar, one can say, is the basement of the dreamer's psyche. In the back yard of the strange building (which represents the still unperceived psychic scope of the dreamer's personality) an old school friend suddenly turns up. This person obviously personifies another aspect of the dreamer himself—an aspect that had been part of his life as a child but that he had forgotten and lost. It often happens that a person's childhood qualities (for instance, gaiety, irrascibility, or perhaps trustfulness) suddenly disappear, and one does not know where or how they have gone. It is such a lost characteristic of the dreamer that now returns (from the back yard) and tries to make friends again. This figure probably stands for the dreamer's neglected capacity for enjoying life and for his extroverted shadow side.

But we soon learn why the dreamer feels "uneasy" just before meeting this seemingly harmless old friend. When he strolls with him in the street, the horses break loose. The dreamer thinks they may have escaped from military service (that is to say, from the conscious discipline that has hitherto characterized his life). The fact that the horses have no rider shows that instinctive drives can get away from conscious control. In this old friend, and in the horses, all the positive force reappears that was lacking before and that was badly needed by the dreamer.

This is a problem that often comes up when one meets one's "other side." The shadow usually contains values that are needed by consciousness, but that exist in a form that makes it difficult to integrate them into one's life. The passages and the large house in this dream also show that the dreamer does not yet know his own psychic dimensions and is not yet able to fill them out.

The shadow in this dream is typical for an introvert (a man who tends to retire too much from outer life). In the case of an extrovert, who is turned more toward outer objects and outer life, **the shadow would look quite different.**

"I owned and inhabited a very big house"—The house often appears as a symbol of the dreamer's personality.

"The maze of strange passages"—If the house represents the dreamer's whole personality, then the cellar (or attic) can symbolize the unknown or shadow as aspects of this whole.

Rene Magritte, *The Happy Donor*, 1966. The artist's vision here represents the house as within a man. In von Franz's explanation of Jung's theory, the house is seen from within, completing the picture and showing us the many stages and chambers contained in the personality. The unconscious serves as the support of the whole structure.

"the shadow would look quite different"—The classification of introvert or extrovert is quite important to Jung's theories, although it is not developed further in the excerpts given here. In these two dreams von Franz illustrates how the shadow can be significantly different, depending on the nature of the personality of the dreamer.

Louis Janmot (1814–1892), *Nightmare*. In this dream, the young girl on the right seems to be fleeing the older woman, who has already captured another girl. To the young woman, the old one represents all she is not, in age and power, and so she flees this shadow figure, whom she perceives as threatening her.

A young man who had a very lively temperament embarked again and again on successful enterprises, while at the same time his dreams insisted that he should finish off a piece of private creative work he had begun. The following was one of those dreams:

A man is lying on a couch and has pulled the cover over his face. He is a Frenchman, a desperado who would take on any criminal job. An official is accompanying me downstairs, and I know that a plot has been made against me: namely, that the Frenchman should kill me as if by chance. (That is how it would look from the outside.) He actually sneaks up behind me when we approach the exit, but I am on my guard. A tall portly man (rather rich and influential) suddenly leans against the wall beside me, feeling ill. I quickly grab the opportunity to kill the official by stabbing his heart. "One only notices a bit of moisture"—this is said like a comment. Now I am safe, for the Frenchman won't attack me since the man who gave him his orders is dead. (Probably the official and the successful portly man are the same person, the latter somehow replacing the former.)

The desperado represents the other side of the dreamer—his introversion—which has reached a completely destitute state. He lies on a couch (i.e., he is passive) and pulls the cover over his face because he wants to be left alone. The official, on the other hand, and the prosperous portly man (who are secretly the same person) personify the dreamer's successful outer responsibilities and activities. The sudden illness of the portly man is connected with the fact that this dreamer had in fact become ill several times when he had allowed his dynamic energy to explode too forcibly in his external life. But this successful man has no blood in his veins—only a sort of moisture—which means that these external ambitious activities of the dreamer contain no genuine life and no passion, but are bloodless mechanisms. Thus it would be no real loss if the portly man were killed. At the end of the dream, the Frenchman is satisfied—he obviously represents a positive shadow figure who had turned negative and dangerous only because the conscious attitude of the dreamer did not agree with him.

This dream shows us that the shadow can consist of many different elements—for instance, of unconscious ambition (the successful portly man) and of introversion (the Frenchman). This particular dreamer's association to the French, moreover, was that they know how to handle love affairs very well. Therefore the two shadow figures also represent two well-known drives: power and sex. The power drive appears momentarily in a double form, both as an official and as a successful man. The official, or civil servant, personifies collective adaptation, whereas the successful man denotes ambition; but naturally both serve the power drive. When the dreamer succeeds in stopping this dangerous inner force, **the Frenchman is suddenly no longer hostile.** In other words, the equally dangerous aspect of the sex drive has also surrendered.

Whether the shadow becomes our friend or enemy depends largely upon ourselves. As the dreams of the unexplored house and the French desperado both show, **the shadow is not necessarily always an opponent.** In fact, he is exactly like any human being with whom one has to get along, sometimes by giving in, sometimes by resisting, sometimes by giving love—whatever the situation requires. The shadow becomes hostile only when he is ignored or misunderstood.

"the Frenchman is suddenly no longer hostile"—When the shadow is accepted, it ceases to be a threat, and is integrated into the dreamer's personality.

"the shadow is not . . . always an opponent"—Jung's theory places a priority on helping people integrate their partial personalities into a whole that is satisfactory to them. Therefore, each archetype has both positive and negative aspects, to be dealt with as the individual sees fit.

Sometimes, though not often, an individual feels impelled to live out the worse side of his nature and to repress his better side. In such cases the shadow appears as a positive figure in his dreams. But to a person who lives out his natural emotions and feelings, the shadow may appear as a cold and negative intellectual; it then personifies poisonous judgments and negative thoughts that have been held back. So, whatever form it takes, the function of the shadow is to represent the opposite side of the ego and to embody just those qualities that one dislikes most in other people.

When dark figures turn up in our dreams and seem to want something, we cannot be sure whether they personify merely a shadowy part of ourselves, or the Self, or both at the same time. Divining in advance whether our dark partner symbolizes a shortcoming that we should overcome or a meaningful bit of life that we should accept—this is one of the most difficult problems that we encounter on the way to individuation.

Moreover, the dream symbols are often so subtle and complicated that **one cannot be sure of their interpretation.** In such a situation all one can do is accept the discomfort of ethical doubt—making no final decisions or commitments and continuing to watch the dreams. This resembles the situation of Cinderella when her stepmother threw a heap of good and bad peas in front of her and asked her to sort them out. Although it seemed quite hopeless, Cinderella began patiently to sort the peas, and suddenly doves (or ants, in some versions) came to help her. These creatures symbolize helpful, deeply unconscious impulses that can only be felt in one's body, as it were, and that point to a way out.

> "one cannot be sure of their interpretation"—Because individual psyches are so varied and dreams are so personal, the archetypes take on a personal aspect despite their universal nature. The need of one dreamer may be the opposite of another.

The Anima: The Woman Within

Difficult and subtle ethical problems are not invariably brought up by the appearance of the shadow itself. Often another "inner figure" emerges. If the dreamer is a man, he will discover a female personification of his unconscious; and it will be a male figure in the case of a woman. Often this second symbolic figure turns up behind the shadow, bringing up new and different problems. Jung called its male and female forms "animus" and "anima."

The anima is a personification of all feminine psychological tendencies in a man's psyche, such as vague feelings and moods, prophetic hunches, receptiveness to the irrational, capacity for personal love, feeling for nature, and—last but not least—his relation to the unconscious. It is no mere chance that in olden times priestesses (like the Greek Sibyl) were used to fathom the divine will and to make connection with the gods.

A particularly good example of how the anima is experienced as an inner figure in a man's psyche is found in the medicine men and prophets (shamans) among the Eskimo and other arctic tribes. Some of these even **wear women's clothes** or have breasts depicted on their garments, in order to manifest their inner feminine side—the side that enables them to connect with the "ghost land" (i.e., what we call the unconscious).

One reported case tells of a young man who was being initiated by an older shaman and who was buried by him in a snow hole. He fell into a state of dreaminess and exhaustion. In this coma he suddenly saw a woman who emitted light. She instructed him in all he needed to know and later, as his protective spirit, helped him to practice his difficult profession by relating him to the powers of the beyond. Such an experience shows the anima as the personification of a man's unconscious.

In its individual manifestation the character of a man's anima is as a rule **shaped by his mother.** If he feels that his mother had a negative influence on him, his anima will often express itself in irritable, depressed moods, uncertainty, insecurity, and touchiness. These "anima moods" cause a sort of dullness, a fear of disease, of impotence, or of accidents. The whole of life takes on a sad and oppressive aspect. Such dark moods can even lure a man to suicide, in which case the anima becomes a death demon. She appears in this role in Cocteau's film *Orphée*.

 Definition of the Anima

> "wear women's clothes"—Here we have an explanation for ritual cross-dressing that is quite different from, but not incompatible with that provided by Turner (Ch. 26).

 The Negative Anima

> "shaped by his mother"—Jung shares Freud's ideas about the influence of the mother's personality on her son.

"effeminate"—In his discomfort with behavior associated with homosexuality, Jung (and von Franz) reflect the prejudices of their time period.

"a negative anima appears in some fairy tales"—For example, looking at the Grimms' fairy tale "Rapunzel" from the point of view of the Prince, the witch who imprisons Rapunzel in the tower is a negative anima.

 The Positive Anima

"a creature who is fascinatingly vague"—Negative anima figures of this kind frequently appear in James Bond movies, for example, Elektra King, the daughter of the oil tycoon in *The World Is Not Enough.*

"the goddess Isis"—For a discussion of the appearance of Isis in Apuleius' novel, *The Golden Ass,* see Ch. 37, p. 542.

 Four Stages of the Anima:

1. Purely instinctual and biological—Eve
2. Romantic and aesthetic—Faust's Helen
3. Spiritual—Virgin Mary
4. Pure wisdom—Sapientia

If, on the other hand, a man's experience of his mother has been positive, this can also affect his anima in typical but different ways, with the result that he either becomes **effeminate** or is preyed upon by women and thus is unable to cope with the hardships of life. A still more subtle manifestation of **a negative anima appears in some fairy tales** in the form of a princess who asks her suitors to answer a series of riddles or, perhaps, to hide themselves under her nose. If they cannot give the answers, or if she can find them, they must die—and she invariably wins. The anima in this guise involves men in a destructive intellectual game. We can notice the effect of this anima trick in all those neurotic pseudo-intellectual dialogues that inhibit a man from getting into direct touch with life and its real decisions. He reflects about life so much that he cannot live it and loses all his spontaneity and outgoing feeling.

The most frequent manifestations of the anima take the form of erotic fantasy. Men may be driven to nurse their fantasies by looking at films and striptease shows, or by daydreaming over pornographic material. This is a crude, primitive aspect of the anima, which becomes compulsive only when a man does not sufficiently cultivate his feeling relationships—when his feeling attitude toward life has remained infantile.

All these aspects of the anima have the same tendency that we have observed in the shadow: That is, they can be projected so that they appear to the man to be the qualities of some particular woman. It is the presence of the anima that causes a man to fall suddenly in love when he sees a woman for the first time and knows at once that this is "she." In this situation, the man feels as if he has known this woman intimately for all time; he falls for her so helplessly that it looks to outsiders like complete madness. Women who are of "fairy-like" character especially attract such anima projections, because men can attribute almost anything to **a creature who is so fascinatingly vague,** and can thus proceed to weave fantasies around her.

The projection of the anima in such a sudden and passionate form as a love affair can greatly disturb a man's marriage and can lead to the so-called "human triangle," with its accompanying difficulties.

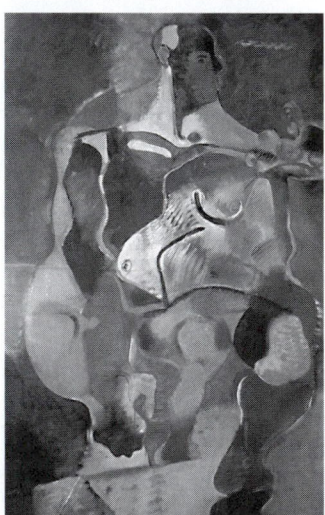

Gábor Tari, *Szibilla.* The rounded curves of the figure evoke the flowing power of the ancient Sibyl, the priestess of the goddess who prophesied the future at Delphi. She represents the anima of a man whose pronouncements come, as von Franz says, "from the depths" of the unconscious and whose guidance can set him on the path toward his Self.

But I have said enough about the negative side of the anima. There are just as many important positive aspects. The anima is, for instance, responsible for the fact that a man is able to find the right marriage partner. Another function is at least equally important: Whenever a man's logical mind is incapable of discerning facts that are hidden in his unconscious, the anima helps him to dig them out. Even more vital is the role that the anima plays in putting a man's mind in tune with the right inner values and thereby opening the way into more profound inner depths. It is as if an inner "radio" becomes tuned to a certain wavelength that excludes irrelevancies but allows the voice of the Great Man to be heard. In establishing this inner "radio" reception, the anima takes on the role of guide, or mediator, to the world within and to the Self. That is how she appears in the example of the initiations of shamans that I described earlier; this is the role of Beatrice in Dante's *Paradiso,* and also of **the goddess Isis** when she appeared in a dream to Apuleius, the famous author of *The Golden Ass,* in order to initiate him into a higher, more spiritual form of life.

As Jung has demonstrated, the nucleus of the psyche (the Self) normally expresses itself in some kind of fourfold structure. The number four is also connected with the anima because, as Jung noted there are four stages in its development. The first stage is best symbolized by the figure of Eve, which represents purely instinctual and biological relations. The second can be seen in Faust's Helen: She personifies a romantic and aesthetic level that is, however, still characterized by sexual elements. The third is represented, for instance, by the Virgin Mary—a figure who raises love (eros) to the heights of spiritual devotion. The fourth type is symbolized by Sapientia, wisdom transcending even the most holy and the most pure. Of this another symbol is the Shulamite in the Song of Solomon. (In the psychic development of modern man this stage is rarely reached. The Mona Lisa comes nearest to such a wisdom anima.) At this stage I am only pointing out that the concept of fourfoldness frequently occurs in certain types of symbolic material.

During the Middle Ages, the knightly cult of the lady signified an attempt to differentiate the feminine side of man's nature in regard to the outer woman as well as in relation to the inner world. The lady to whose service the knight pledged himself, and for whom he performed his heroic deeds, was naturally **a personification of the anima.** The name of the carrier of the Grail, in Wolfram von Eschenbach's version of the legend, is especially significant: Conduir-amour ("guide in love matters"). She taught the hero to differentiate both his feelings and his behavior toward women. Later, however, this individual and personal effort of developing the relationship with the anima was abandoned when her sublime aspect fused with the figure of the Virgin, who then became the object of boundless devotion and praise. When the anima, as Virgin, was conceived as being all-positive, her negative aspects found expression in the belief in witches.

> "a personification of the anima"— In fairy tales, the fairy godmother usually fulfills this function. See Ch. 35, p. 523, for a discussion of the Witch of the East in *The Wizard of Oz*. The opposite—the negative anima—is personified in characters like the stepmother in "Snow White."

The Animus: The Man Within

The male personification of the unconscious in woman, the animus exhibits both good and bad aspects, as does the anima in man. But the animus does not so often appear in the form of an erotic fantasy or mood; it is more apt to take the form of a hidden "sacred" conviction. When such a conviction is preached with a loud, insistent, masculine voice or imposed on others by means of brutal emotional scenes, the underlying masculinity in a woman is easily recognized. However, even in a woman who is outwardly very feminine, the animus can be an equally hard, inexorable power. One may suddenly find oneself up against something in a woman that is obstinate, cold, and completely inaccessible.

Just as the character of a man's anima is shaped by his mother, so the animus is basically influenced by a woman's father. The father endows his daughter's animus with the special coloring of unarguable, incontestably "true" convictions—convictions that never include the personal reality of the woman herself as she actually is.

This is why the animus is sometimes, like the anima, a demon of death. For example, in a gypsy fairy tale a handsome stranger is received by a lonely woman in spite of the fact that she has had a dream warning her that he is the king of the dead. After he has been with her for a time, she presses him to tell her who he really is. At first he refuses, saying that she will die if he tells her. She insists, however, and suddenly he reveals to her that he is death himself. The woman immediately dies of fright.

The negative animus does not appear only as a death-demon. In myths and fairy tales he plays **the role of robber and murderer.** One example is Bluebeard, who secretly kills all his wives in a hidden chamber. In this form the animus personifies all those semiconscious, cold, destructive reflections that invade a woman in the small hours, especially when she has failed to realize some obligation of feeling. It is then that she begins to think about the family heritage and matters of that kind—a sort of web of calculating thoughts, filled with malice and intrigue, which get her into a state where she even wishes death to others.

> ### Definition of the Animus

Mario Baert, *Blauwbaard*, 1983.

> ### The Negative Animus
>
> "the role of robber and murderer" —Examples of this in the Grimms' tales include the character Rumpelstiltskin.

The Positive Animus

 Four Stages of the Animus:

1. Wholly physical man—Tarzan
2. Romantic man or "man of action"—Indiana Jones
3. Orator or bearer of the "word"—Ronald Reagan or John F. Kennedy
4. Wise guide to spiritual truth—Gandhi

Like the anima, the animus does not merely consist of negative qualities such as brutality, recklessness, empty talk, and silent, obstinate, evil ideas. He too has a very positive and valuable side; he too can build a bridge to the Self through his creative activity.

The animus, just like the anima, exhibits four stages of development. He first appears as a personification of mere physical power—for instance, as an athletic champion or "muscle man." In the next stage he possesses initiative and the capacity for planned action. In the third phase, the animus becomes the "word," often appearing as a professor or clergyman. Finally, in his fourth manifestation, the animus is the incarnation of meaning. On this highest level he becomes (like the anima) a mediator of the religious experience whereby life acquires new meaning. He gives the woman spiritual firmness, an invisible inner support that compensates for her outer softness. The animus in his most developed form sometimes connects the woman's mind with the spiritual evolution of her age, and can thereby make her even more receptive than a man to new creative ideas. It is for this reason that in earlier times women were used by many nations as diviners and seers. The creative boldness of their positive animus at times expresses thoughts and ideas that stimulate men to new enterprises.

The Self: Symbols of Totality

If an individual has wrestled seriously enough and long enough with the anima (or animus) problem so that he or she is no longer partially identified with it, the unconscious again changes its dominant character and appears in a new symbolic form, representing the Self, the innermost nucleus of the psyche. In the dreams of a woman this center is usually personified as a superior female figure—a priestess, sorceress, earth mother, or goddess of nature or love. In the case of a man, it manifests itself as a masculine initiator and guardian (an Indian guru), **a wise old man,** a spirit of nature, and so forth. An Austrian folk tale illustrates the role that such a figure can play:

> A king has ordered soldiers to keep the night watch beside the corpse of a black princess, who has been bewitched. Every midnight she rises and kills the guard. At last one soldier, whose turn it is to stand guard, despairs and runs away into the woods. There he meets an "old guitarist who is our Lord Himself." This old musician tells him where to hide in the church and instructs him on how to behave so that the black princess cannot get him. With this divine help the soldier actually manages to redeem the princess and marry her.

"a wise old man"—This figure, also known as a *senex*, often appears in stories as the one who teaches the young hero essential skills or provides crucial information about himself, his family, or even his enemy. Examples include Obi Wan Kenobi or Yoda in *Star Wars* and Faithful John in the Grimms' tale (p. 534).

Clearly, "the old guitarist who is our Lord Himself" is, in psychological terms, a symbolic personification of the Self. With his help the ego avoids destruction and is able to overcome—and even redeem—a highly dangerous aspect of his anima.

The Self, however, does not always take the form of a wise old man or wise old woman. These paradoxical personifications are attempts to express something that is not entirely contained in time—something simultaneously young and old. The dream of a middle-aged man shows the Self appearing as a young man:

> Coming from the street, a youth rode down into our garden. (There were no bushes and no fence as there are in real life and the garden lay open.) I did not quite know if he came on purpose, or if the horse carried him here against his will.
>
> I stood on the path that leads to my studio and watched the arrival with great pleasure. The sight of the boy on his beautiful horse impressed me deeply.
>
> The horse was **a small, wild, powerful animal,** a symbol of energy (it resembled a boar), and it had a thick, bristly, silvery-gray coat. The boy rode past me between the studio and house, jumped off his horse, and led him carefully away so that he would not trample on the flowerbed with its beautiful red and orange tulips. The flowerbed had been newly made and planted by my wife (a dream occurrence).

"a small, wild, powerful animal"—As the individual matures and accepts his shadow, a figure which might have once been frightening is now seen as inspiring.

This youth signifies the Self, and with it renewal of life, a creative *elan vital,* and a new spiritual orientation by means of which everything becomes full of life and enterprise.

It is no wonder that this figure of the **Cosmic Man** appears in many myths and religious teachings. Generally he is described as something helpful and positive. He

Cosmic Man A figure who embodies the wisdom of the universe. Examples include Utnapishtim in *Gilgamesh* (see Ch. 15, p. 203).

appears as Adam, as the Persian Gayomart, or as the Hindu Purusha. This figure may even be described as the basic principle of the whole world.

We have already seen that symbolic structures that seem to refer to the process of individuation tend to be based on the motif of the number four—such as the four functions of consciousness, or the four stages of the anima or animus. It reappears here in the cosmic shape of **P'an Ku.** Only under specific circumstances do other combinations of numbers appear in the psychic material.

In our Western civilization, similar ideas of a Cosmic Man have attached themselves to the symbol of Adam, the First Man. There is a Jewish legend that when God created Adam, he first gathered red, black, white, and yellow dust from the four corners of the world, and thus Adam "reached from one end of the world to the other." When he bent down, his head was in the East and his feet in the West.

According to the testimony of many myths, the Cosmic Man is not only the beginning but also the final goal of all life—of the whole of creation. The whole inner psychic reality of each individual is ultimately oriented toward this archetypal symbol of the Self.

Because this symbol represents that which is whole and complete, it is often conceived of as a bisexual being. In this form the symbol reconciles one of the most important pairs of psychological opposites—male and female. This union also appears frequently in dreams as a divine, royal, or otherwise distinguished couple.

In medieval symbolism, **the "philosopher's stone"** (a pre-eminent symbol of man's wholeness) is represented as a pair of lions or as a human couple riding on lions. Symbolically, this points to the fact that often the urge toward individuation appears in a veiled form, hidden in the overwhelming passion one may feel for another person. (In fact, passion that goes beyond the natural measure of love ultimately aims at the mystery of becoming whole, and this is why one feels, when one has fallen passionately in love, that becoming one with the other person is the only worthwhile goal of one's life.)

In ways that are still completely beyond our comprehension, our unconscious is similarly attuned to our surroundings—to our group, to society in general, and, beyond these, to the space-time continuum and the whole of nature. Thus the Great Man of the Naskapi Indians does not merely reveal inner truths; he also gives hints about where and when to hunt. And so from dreams the Naskapi hunter evolves the words and melodies of the magical songs with which he attracts the animals.

But this specific help from the unconscious is not given to primitive man alone. Jung discovered that dreams can also give civilized man the guidance he needs in finding his way through the problems of both his inner and his outer life. Indeed, many of our dreams are concerned with details of our outer life and our surroundings. Such things as the tree in front of the window, one's bicycle or car, or a stone picked up during a walk may be raised to the level of symbolism through our dream life and become meaningful. If we pay attention to our dreams, instead of living in a cold, impersonal world of meaningless chance, we may begin to emerge into a world of our own, full of important and secretly ordered events.

I have already mentioned the fact that the Self is symbolized with special frequency in the form of a stone, precious or otherwise. In many dreams the nuclear center, the Self, also appears as a crystal. The mathematically precise arrangement of a crystal evokes in us the intuitive feeling that even in so-called "dead" matter, there is a spiritual ordering principle at work. Thus the crystal often symbolically stands for the union of extreme opposites—of matter and spirit.

The urge that we find in practically all civilizations to erect stone monuments to famous men or on the site of important events probably also stems from this symbolic meaning of the stone. The stone that Jacob placed on the spot where he had his famous dream, or certain stones left by simple people on the tombs of local saints or heroes, show the original nature of the human urge to express an otherwise inexpressible experience by the stone-symbol. It is no wonder that many religious cults use a

P'an Ku   According to Taoist thought, the first living being, who developed inside a cosmic egg. P'an Ku separated the world into *yin* and *yang* and created the sun, the moon, and the stars with the help of four creatures: a dragon, a unicorn, a tortoise, and a phoenix. When he died, the universe was made from his body. For more on P'an Ku as a creator, see chapter 10, pp. 111–113.

"the 'philosopher's stone'"—This was an instrument of the magician for turning base metals into gold. The search for a philosopher's stone is the main quest in the first of the Harry Potter books by J. K. Rowling.

Constantin Brancusi (1876–1957), *The Kiss.* The couple, royal or otherwise, evokes the totality of the Self through their complementarity, which represents completeness.

Master of the Campana Cassone (flourished ca. 1510), *Detail of Theseus and the Minotaur: The Labyrinth.* As the painting makes clear, the labyrinth, like the mandala, expresses the complex totality of the Self.

The Relation to the Self

"Navajo Indians . . . bring a sick person back into harmony"—For more on the concept of harmony in the Navajo belief system, see Ch. 8, p. 95.

stone to signify God or to mark a place of worship. The holiest sanctuary of the Islamic world is the Ka'aba, the black stone in Mecca to which all pious Moslems hope to make their pilgrimage.

Among the mythological representations of the Self one finds much emphasis on the four corners of the world, and in many pictures the Great Man is represented in the center of a circle divided into four. Jung used the Hindu word mandala (magic circle) to designate a structure of this order, which is a symbolic representation of the "nuclear atom" of the human psyche—whose essence we do not know. In this connection it is interesting that a Naskapi hunter pictorially represented his Great Man not as a human being but as a mandala.

Whereas the Naskapi experience the inner center directly and naively, without the help of religious rites or doctrines, other communities use the mandala motif in order to restore a lost inner balance. For instance, the **Navaho Indians** try, by means of mandala-structured sand paintings, to **bring a sick person back into harmony** with himself and with the cosmos—and thereby to restore his health.

An example of a spontaneously produced mandala occurs in the following dream of a 62–year-old woman. It emerged as a prelude to a new phase of life in which she became very creative:

> I see a landscape in a dim light. In the background I see the rising and then evenly continuing crest of a hill. Along the line where it rises moves a quadrangular disk that shines like gold. In the foreground I see dark plowed earth that is beginning to sprout. Now I suddenly perceive a round table with a gray stone slab as its top, and at the same moment the quadrangular disk suddenly stands upon the table. It has left the hill, but how and why it has changed its place I do not know.

Landscapes in dreams (as well as in art) frequently symbolize an inexpressible mood. In this dream, the dim light of the landscape indicates that the clarity of daytime consciousness is dimmed. "Inner nature" may now begin to reveal itself in its own light, so we are told that the quadrangular disk becomes visible on the horizon.

Hitherto the symbol of the Self, the disk, had been largely an intuitive idea on the dreamer's mental horizon, but now in the dream it shifts its position and becomes the center of the landscape of her soul. A seed, sown long ago, begins to sprout: for a long time previously the dreamer had paid careful attention to her dreams, and now this work bears fruit.

Now the golden disk suddenly moves to the "right" side—the side where things become conscious. Among other things "right" often means, psychologically, the side of consciousness, of adaptation, of being "right," while "left" signifies the sphere of unadapted, unconscious reactions or sometimes even of something "sinister." Then, finally, the golden disk stops its movement and comes to rest on—significantly—a round stone table. It has found a permanent base.

Further Reading

Jung, C. G. *Man and His Symbols.* Trans. M.L von Franz, Joseph L. Henderson, Jolande Jacobi, Anita Jaffe. New York, NY: Dell Publishing, 1968.

How to Perform a Jungian Analysis of a Myth or Fairy Tale

WHAT TO EXPECT . . . Carl Jung believed that dreams have symbolic meaning, rather than merely reflecting daily events in the life of the dreamer. As a practicing therapist, he helped patients live a more meaningful life by demonstrating that dreams, as well as stories, are symbolic representations of aspects of the *process of individuation*—understanding who we are psychically. He showed that in dreams and fairy tales we encounter archetypes from the collective unconscious.

In this chapter, you are shown how to carry out a Jungian analysis of a fairy tale by identifying and tracking the major archetypes: the shadow, anima, animus, and Self. The chapter talks about stories that resemble traditional tales as easier to interpret in this way, then it discusses the more ironic and "dark" stories that pose some problems for a Jungian analysis. Consider the films you have seen and the stories you have read, come up with your own examples of each kind, and consider what makes them easy or hard to interpret according to the Jungian model.

Carl Gustav Jung was a psychologist whose views have continued to enjoy a great deal of prominence up to the present. Today Jungian therapists still use the ideas he formulated to counsel their patients and lead them to richer, fuller lives. Jungian institutes provide detailed courses of study dealing extensively with the writings of Jung and of his students, who are called Jungians. These institutions serve students with a wide range of backgrounds, from doctors with medical school training and advanced degrees in psychiatry, to ordinary citizens who have no special training but are motivated by an interest in understanding themselves better.

This chapter is not intended to substitute for such in-depth study of Jungian ideas. However, in *Man and His Symbols,* Jung described his ideas about psychic development in an easily accessible form that can be read and applied without additional training (see Ch. 32, p. 468). Such an analysis can be useful to understanding the dynamics of a fairy tale and the effect it has on its audience. Marie-Louise von Frantz, who studied with Jung, points out that he "hated it when his pupils were too literal-minded" and applied his concepts mechanically, "[making] a system out of them," while forgetting that they had to adapt them to the experience of the particular person who was their patient (*Shadow and Evil,* 3). James Hillman, Jung's successor at the C. G. Jung Institute, warns that in our response to dream material, we should not lose sight of the depth and complexity of the images we find in our dreams.

This chapter incorporates a step-by-step series of directions for applying the ideas in *Man and His Symbols* to the study of folktales and myths, and illustrates the process of adapting Jung's methods of analysis to gain insight into these stories. For an examination of how other analytic perspectives can be combined with Jungian interpretation, see Chapter 38, p. 524f.

Introduction: Stories Resemble Dreams

Jungian analysis is based on the idea that myths and dreams are related. According to Jungian theory, storytellers create their narratives out of the elements they encounter in their own psychic development, fashioning them out of **archetypal images** to represent the individual's progress in this process of individuation. Just as human beings are born with the ability to learn a language and express themselves uniquely and creatively through it, Jung believed that each individual is born with the ability to develop a rich language of symbols called archetypes to express her or his development as a human being. A Jungian analysis of a fairy tale or other story locates these images and considers their patterns of interaction in the story, treating it as if it were a dream experienced by an individual.

Different Theories About the Meaning of Dreams

There are many theories about the significance of dreams. Some studies suggest that they are meaningless elements that are left over after the brain has processed the important things it has to deal with. In this view, dreams are like "taking out the garbage" and have no significance at all. However, many people believe that in their dreams, they are continuing to work out the problems that they were dealing with during the day, and thus they look upon dreams as a useful treatment of the everyday issues they deal with. They believe that in our dreams we see the people from our everyday lives, and that dreams may give us ideas, suggestions, or warnings about how to deal with these people and the issues involved with them.

A completely different view was held by Jung, who believed that dreams have symbolic meaning rather than reflecting directly on the people and forces operating in our everyday lives. That is, simply put, **Jung would say that the people and objects in your dreams do not represent the people and objects they seem to be.** Rather, they are symbolic figures that represent the struggle each of us undergoes throughout our lives to become a mature and complete person. Thus, in performing a Jungian analysis, we treat myths and fairy tales like dreams, and in our analysis we identify the archetypes found in these stories, keeping in mind, as J. Hillman warns, that the images in dreams are complex and may have more than one meaning. However, before we can do this, we must complete the analogy by deciding who is having the dream: from whose point of view will we look at the story? A mythical story or a fairy tale is told by many different people, and it cannot be the dream of just one person. However, typically, people who read or hear fairy tales imagine themselves as one of the characters and identify with the problems and successes of that character.

Bruno Bettelheim, an influential psychologist, suggested that this kind of identification can help a child cope with the difficulties of growing up. The child may, at different stages in his or her development, relate to different characters and problems in the same story. Naturally enough, this happens more with some stories than others. For example, in the Grimm Brothers' story "The Frog Prince," it is possible for a child to relate at one point to the little girl who loses her golden ball. The ball, symbolizing perfection, can represent childish innocence when the child begins to feel that life has become too "ugly and complicated" for her current understanding of the world. Although the frog in the story functions as an adversary to the princess, the tale is not so unilateral that the frog is a villain with whom the child can't empathize. It too represents a point of view that the child may relate to, recognizing some of his feelings about himself in the character who has to move from a lower animal form to a higher state of being.

In analyzing a fairy tale, we would like to capture the basic components of the meaning of the tale for its audience. To accomplish this, we can **treat it as a dream experienced by one of the characters.** We may even want to perform different analyses of the same story, looking at it from different perspectives, and noticing what the story can reveal to people at different stages

---

"archetypal images"—Jung saw these symbolic images as the basis of our dreams and stories. He said they "form a bridge between the ways in which we consciously express ourselves and a more primitive, colorful, and pictorial form of expression." (See Ch. 32.)

 Dreams Can Be Understood As:

1. Meaningless psychic debris
2. The continuation of our daily struggles
3. Symbolic stories

"Jung would say that the people . . . in your dreams do not represent the people . . . they seem to be"—That is, if you have a dream about your mother, the meaning of the dream probably has nothing to do with your mother. Rather, your mother is symbolic of something in your process of individuation.

This idea comes from: Hillman, *The Dream and the Underworld.*

Step 1: Determine Whose Dream It Is

This idea comes from: Bettelheim, *The Uses of Enchantment.*

"treat it as a dream experienced by one of the characters"—In a Jungian analysis, all the characters in a story are seen as representing different aspects of the unconscious of a single person. As Anthony Stevens says, "The multiplicity of symbols in dreams reflects [the] plurality of symbols within the psyche" (205). Jung saw fairy tales and myths as revealing hidden feelings and conflicts. This means that different characters in the stories can represent different points of view in the internal conflicts of the person.

of development. Thus, a single fairy tale can have as many different analyses as there are characters in it. Some of these analyses may be very difficult or impossible to perform, however, because fairy tales as a genre are not very rich in character development. That is, they often don't tell us much about their characters.

As we saw in our discussion of this genre, even the main character of a fairy tale is often not well developed, but may only have a "generic" name like "the prince" or "Jack" (which can be a particular name but can also be used to speak of an unknown person or a stranger). (For more on the characteristics of fairy tales, see Introduction to Part 6, p. 495.)

Although many different treatments of a story are possible, it is usual to start such a series of analyses with the main character, and that is how we will proceed here. For example, in studying the story of Cinderella, it would be reasonable to start by treating Cinderella, the main character, as the dreamer. We could go on also to look at the story from the point of view of the prince, and we will perform such an analysis later on. You could even do an analysis from the perspective of the stepmother or the wicked stepsisters, but this would be more difficult because so much material must be added to the fairy tale. The results, though, can often be highly imaginative and fun. For example, Donald Barthelme wrote a novel telling about the story of Snow White from the point of view of the seven dwarves. To create the kind of characters normally found in a novel, he had to add detail to the fairy tale about the dwarves' relationship to Snow White and their feelings about her. For example, at one point in the story, the dwarves are puzzled by Snow White's behavior and watch her closely because they fear she has fallen out of love with them and become interested in the Prince.

> "What are you doing there," we asked, "writing something?" Snow White looked up. "Yes" she said. And looked down again, not a pinch of emotion coloring the jet black of her jet-black eyes. "A letter?" We asked, wondering if a letter, then to whom and about what. "No," she said. "A list?" we asked, inspecting her white face for hint of tendresse. *But there was no tendresse. "No," she said. We noticed then that she had switched the tulips from the green bowl to the blue bowl.*

In this passage, Barthelme fills in the "generic" characters of the dwarves, giving them the kind of human reaction that would seem normal if someone you loved took up with someone else.

Briefly put, Jung believes that dreams and stories are symbolic representations of aspects of the process of **individuation**. Jungian writer M.-L. von Frantz describes this as the "slow, imperceptible process of psychic growth" by which "a wider and more mature personality emerges" (*Man and His Symbols,* 159–61).

In the course of individuation, Jung showed that a person deals with various unconscious forces that appear in dreams and can be identified with the characters of fairy tales. Thus, these characters can be treated as if they represented "the psychic potencies and personal tendencies" of the dreamer him- or herself. The psychic forces or archetypes that we can look for in fairy tales are called the shadow, anima or animus, and Self. The next sections of this chapter will introduce these archetypal forms and provide a rudimentary list of their characteristics. For a more complete discussion of these archetypes, see Chapter 32, p. 468.

In using the lists that follow, remember that the assignment of the archetypes always takes place **in relation to a point of view or perspective of one particular character** in the story, usually the hero. This person is represented as the dreamer whose dream the fairy tale becomes. It is in relation to this dreamer that other characters can then be considered as the shadow, the animus or anima, and the Self.

Once the basic identification and classification of archetypes have been completed, it will be possible to retell the story in symbolic form; that is, elements of the story represent aspects of the process of individuation for the person who identifies with the main character or hero whose perspective was undertaken in the analysis. But before we can interpret the dream in this fashion, we need to explore the nature and varieties of the archetypes to be found in it.

Joseph Edward Southall, *Cinderella,* 1893–1895. Determining the point of view or "the dreamer" is the first step in the Jungian analysis of a story or fairy tale. Here Cinderella, shown with the pear tree that grows from her mother's grave, is the natural choice. But other analyses, from the point of view of other characters, can be worthwhile as well.

This excerpt comes from: Barthelme, *Snow White* (10).

 Step 2: Assign the Archetypes

individuation Jung's term for growing up and becoming a fully developed individual.

This idea comes from: Jacoby, Kast, and Riedel, *Witches, Ogres and the Devil's Daughter* (12).

"in relation to a point of view or perspective of one particular character"—Jung's archetypes represent parts of an individual's personality. We need to identify the dreamer so we can understand how these different parts are interacting.

The Archetypes

The shadow is not the whole of the unconscious personality. It represents the unknown or little-known attributes and qualities of the ego. . . . When an individual makes an attempt to see his shadow, he becomes aware of . . . those qualities and impulses he denies in himself but can plainly see in other people. . . . The shadow usually contains values that are needed by consciousness, but that exist in a form that makes it difficult to integrate them into one's life.

The shadow is the same sex as the person, but has the opposite personality and self-image. Before it is accepted or dealt with (integrated into the psyche), the shadow can appear as a frightening animal, an enemy, a thief; the wicked stepmother is a classic shadow figure for a main character like Cinderella or Snow White. Or the shadow can appear simply as a neutral person who is different from the main character: a prince or a king, or a princess or a queen, a servant, a helper.

The anima is the personification of all feminine psychological tendencies in a man's psyche. . . . Often this second symbolic figure turns up behind the shadow, bringing up new and different problems. . . . In its individual manifestation, the man's anima is as a rule shaped by his mother. [The anima plays a role in] putting a man's mind in tune with the right inner values and thereby opening the way into more profound inner depths. [The anima] takes on the role of guide, or mediator, to the world within and to the Self.

A dreamer who is a boy or a grown man has an opposite-sex figure called the anima. If she is a positive anima, she can lead him to the next stage of growth and development, but if she is destructive, a "femme fatale," she can lead him to destroy himself. A common negative anima figure for a boy or man includes the witch in the Grimm brothers' tale, "The Raven."

The animus [is the] "male personification of the unconscious in woman . . . ." Just as the character of a man's anima is shaped by his mother, so the animus is basically influenced by a woman's father. [The animus can] build a bridge to the Self through his creative activity. Through him a woman can experience the underlying processes of her cultural and personal objective situation and can find her way to an intensified spiritual attitude toward life.

A dreamer who is a girl or woman has an opposite-sex figure called the animus. He leads her "to the next level," which can mean fulfillment and satisfaction if it is a positive animus figure, or death and destruction if it is a negative animus figure. He can appear as a prince, a king, a friend, a helper, or a robber. In **"The Goose Girl,"** Conrad, who tries to get the heroine into trouble, can be seen as an animus figure, as can the King who ultimately helps her defeat the wicked serving girl who has stolen her birthright. Bluebeard, who married seven wives and murdered each one, represents an animus figure for each of these wives. Different kinds of animus figures may be appropriate at different stages of a heroine's psychic development. An animus figure can be a muscle-studded strong man, a romantic hero, a wise leader, or a saint.

The Self can be defined as an inner guiding factor that is different from the conscious personality. . . . One could call it the inventor, organizer and source of dream images, [which creates] a slow, imperceptible process of psychic growth. . . . It is a regulating center that brings about the constant extension and maturing of the personality. . . . [It is] the innermost nucleus of the psyche.

The Self is a same-sex figure representing the totality or inner part of the person. It appears as a helpful animal, a wise old man or woman, or a royal couple and it can be represented by a rock, a crystal, a jewel, or a mirror. In *The Empire Strikes Back,* Yoda is a wise old man who knows how to use the Force, a transcendent power found throughout the Universe. In the part of the story involving Luke Skywalker, Yoda functions as a Self figure who trains Luke, helping him to master the Force rather than be consumed by it. The Self can be represented by a Cosmic Man who incorporates aspects of the whole world in his point of view or perspective, or by a group or collective who represents diverse perspectives of what it means to be human. Any circular object can embody the Self, including a small one like a ring, or a large one like a circular building or the wheel of a mill.

For each of the psychic forces identified, it is important to consider the kind or stage of the archetype embodied by the character. For example, in "The Goose Girl," we start by noting that Conrad is an animus figure for the main character, the princess who becomes a goose girl. Then we continue by adding that he is a negative animus figure who is bent on causing trouble for her, as he would like to get some of her golden hair, but she prevents him by making the wind carry off his hat.

However, it is not long before the Goose Girl encounters a positive animus figure in the old King to whom Conrad reports her activities. The King sees immediately that there is more to the Goose Girl than can be explained by Conrad's complaints, and sets to work to enable her to declare her real mission and purpose in his land. Thus, he develops a plan to free her from the vow of silence imposed on her by the servant girl. In this way, the King, like Conrad, functions as an animus figure, but of the positive kind, as he leads the Goose Girl to fulfill her real destiny, not to satisfy his own selfish needs.

Because Jung believed that the fairy tale or story represents the growth process of an individual, it is not sufficient to assign the characters in the story to particular archetypes. It is necessary in addition to chart the stages or steps in the process, which are played out in the story. That is, the fairy tale must be retold as a symbolic narrative, with its events corresponding to developments in the process of individuation attributed to the figure or character who is seen as the dreamer.

For a symbolic understanding of the events in the story, it is useful to focus on the points in the story at which the characters who have archetypal significance interact with each other. Often, these events can be localized as happening at the same physical location. For example, we **can divide the Grimm Brothers' fairy tale, "The Raven," into the following events,** at which there is interaction between

1. hero and witch (anima) at the witch's house
2. hero and giant (shadow) on the way to the glass mountain
3. hero and robbers (shadow) on the way to the glass mountain
4. hero at glass mountain (Self).

In some cases where the interaction is especially complex, it may be necessary to break a series of interactions in a single location into several events or stages. This division can be performed according to the passage of time, or according to the entrance or departure of other characters, or according to some other meaningful occurrence in the story. For example, consider the movie version of **The Wizard of Oz.** (For more discussion of this film, see Ch. 35, p. 514.)

Although a film is not, in the strict sense, a fairy tale, *The Wizard of Oz* can be treated as such because it was created communally by many writers, producers, directors, and actors, all of whom shaped the original story written by L. Frank Baum. Baum's version has little in common with a traditionally structured fairy tale. In fact, Baum himself was opposed to traditional fairy tales as misleading and tried to structure his story as a "rational" one that would communicate what he saw as truths about the nature of the world. However, the many people who worked on the film eventually shaped its plot into that of a classic fairy tale. In the same way, it is possible to consider any modern film as a fairy tale and analyze it according to Jung's theories. Of course, depending on the characteristics of the work being analyzed, the analysis may be unsuccessful. More on this in the final section of this chapter, "Puzzles and Problems," p. 492.

 Step 3: Break the Story into Parts, Stages, or Episodes

"divide [the story] into . . . events"—Look for points at which the character changes, especially when the change occurs through interaction with another archetype.

"The Raven"—See Ch. 36, p. 531, for the text and discussion of this fairy tale.

The Wizard of Oz—The 1939 film based on the book written by L. Frank Baum in 1900.

In *The Wizard of Oz,* there is a scene that occurs in Oz just after Dorothy's house arrives in Munchkinland. We may divide **this complex scene** into events in the following way:

1. Dorothy arrives and meets Glinda (shadow)
2. Dorothy meets the Wicked Witch of the West (shadow)
3. Dorothy is greeted by the Munchkins (Self)
4. Dorothy receives the ruby slippers (Self)

Note that the analysis of a story is not an objective process: there may be variations in what is considered an event or an episode. This classification is not the ultimate goal in analysis, but merely a step in finding patterns in the events. Thus, whether a pattern consists of several events with one main focus, or of one main event with many parts that have the same focus, will in all likelihood make no difference to the ultimate significance of the pattern of interaction shown in the analysis.

The main reason for dividing the story into events or episodes is to determine the pattern of interactions in the story among archetypal figures, with a view to retelling the story in symbolic terms. Thus we can notice that in *The Wizard of Oz,* Dorothy, upon her arrival in Oz, first encounters two shadow figures and, in between them, a Self figure. First, Dorothy's house falls on and kills the Wicked Witch of the East. Then Dorothy meets Glinda, who steps out of a kind of shining bubble to provide her with some useful advice for her journey, but cannot really solve her problems. Finally, Dorothy is briefly threatened by the Wicked Witch of the West. None of these encounters is decisive: Dorothy does not change, or grow, or accomplish anything while dealing with these Shadow figures. Glinda represents an interesting figure here: she clearly embodies characteristics Dorothy lacks, but she will reappear later in the story offering Dorothy the key to the mystery of the ruby slippers. She represents a less threatening form of the Shadow, one which will eventually manifest itself as an aspect of Dorothy's Self.

Jung suggests that the archetypes of **shadow and Self are closely linked** with each other. Although the shadow initially seems threatening, when we come to accept it and integrate its characteristics into our understanding of ourselves, it becomes clear that the shadow has been part of us all along. This also explains in Jungian terms why Glinda (who is, as she reveals to Dorothy, a "good witch") and the (bad) witches are not really all that different from each other. They all have characteristics that Dorothy lacks at this point, embodying the power and assertiveness that she will have to learn to wield as the story continues.

The next two events are equally tantalizing, but inconclusive. In them, Dorothy receives some other fleeting glances of what must surely be representatives of her innermost Self. Glinda gives her the ruby slippers, and she is entertained by the Munchkins, who celebrate their new freedom and consider her as their liberator. For Dorothy, these encounters with the Self are not lasting and productive: **she does not yet know how to use the ruby slippers,** and freeing the Munchkins was not a deliberate act on her part, but a fortuitous event she discovers with surprise.

After these brief interactions with Self figures, Dorothy prepares for what will turn out to be another, more meaningful encounter with the inner wisdom of the Self. She sets out on the Yellow Brick Road toward the home of the Wizard of Oz in Emerald City. Along the

---

Sidebar notes:

"this complex scene"—Several interactions between characters occur at the same time, and the archetypes they symbolize are affected.

"shadow and Self are closely linked"—The shadow shows us values that our consciousness needs, but does not recognize, while the Self already represents the fully integrated version of these characteristics.

 Step 4: Characterize the Events or Episodes in the Story

Example:
Pattern of interactions between archetypal figures in *The Wizard of Oz:*
- Wicked Witch of the East: shadow
- Glinda the Good Witch: shadow
- Wicked Witch of the West: shadow
- Ruby Slippers: Self
- Munchkins: Self
- Scarecrow: animus
- Tin Woodsman: animus
- Cowardly Lion: animus

"she does not yet know how to use the ruby slippers"—The Self, which facilitates the process of psychic maturity, shows itself briefly here, revealing aspects of the girl's personality that will become available to her later in the story.

Salvador Dali, *Swans Reflecting Elephants,* 1937. Here the elephants are the reflections of the swans. Both animals are beautiful, showing that the shadow, which expresses hidden aspects of the dreamer, need not be evil or harmful, but once accepted as accepted, is seen as part of the Self.

way, she collects a significant group of animus figures who will help her to achieve the goals set for her by her inner regulatory mechanisms: the Scarecrow, Tin Woodsman, and Cowardly Lion.

The Process of Individuation

The interaction of archetypes is described by Jung as the process of individuation, and like any process, it contains elements in certain order. For example, if we consider the process of baking a cake, we must proceed in a fixed order: separate the eggs, mix the dry ingredients, and so forth. We couldn't perform these steps in a random order: there must be growth and development, along with increasing complexity. It would not make sense to, say:

1. cream the butter and egg yolks
2. separate the eggs
3. put the batter in the oven
4. mix the wet and dry ingredients.

Thus, if we consider *The Wizard of Oz* from the point of view of Dorothy, we can see a process of growth that occurs in the main character as she moves through the story. Jung showed that it is important for the hero first to come to terms with her or his shadow, so the usual order of archetypes is

Shadow → Animus or Anima → Self

However, the way that the archetypes interact must be meaningful and will be different in every story. Thus, even though Dorothy defeats a shadow figure, the Wicked Witch of the East, early in the story, this hardly contributes to her process of individuation, as it is done accidentally and without any understanding on her part.

Later, we see a more meaningful event being prepared for as the animus figures in the story help Dorothy to prepare for dealing with the Wicked Witch of the West. The animus figures provide Dorothy with opportunities to be a grown-up who helps others, rather than a child who is always looking for someone to help her. They reassure her that she does in fact have grown-up qualities like determination and the power to protect her friends. The Wicked Witch of the West is a shadow figure with whom Dorothy deals much more deliberately and consciously than she had with the Wicked Witch of the East earlier. And, although Dorothy meets some Self figures, she is not interacting with them successfully until she defeats the Wicked Witch of the West. After this, she will be ready to have Glinda appear to her and tell her that she has always had the power to use the ruby slippers to get home.

Once the main archetypes are identified and the main patterns of interaction between them traced, it is time to retell the story in terms of the archetypes. In this process, it is important to remember that **the resulting story** must make sense in terms of the character identified as the dreamer in the first part of the analysis. Thus, the analysis provided of *The Wizard of Oz* would not be complete until we discussed the sort of person Dorothy appeared to be at the beginning of the story, and in what way the Witches were her shadow: What characteristics did they have that Dorothy seemed to lack? Then it would be necessary to consider the companions Dorothy acquires on the Yellow Brick Road, and to explain what they offered her as animus figures: Which kind of animus were they? What aspects of her Self were they guiding her toward? And how was her Self embodied in Glinda, and in the Munchkins, and in the ruby slippers? It is only after these explanations had been incorporated into the narration of the events of the story that the analysis could be represented as showing Dorothy's process of individuation.

Advanced Topics

We began by pointing out that the same story could be looked at from the perspective of any of the characters. Thus, it would be possible to look at the story of *The Wizard of Oz* from the

Example:
Archetypal patterns showing a process of individuation: Early interactions with self and shadow show Dorothy's early and passive stage of development. Later interactions with animus figures help her learn to become more active and self-directing.

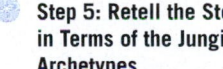

Step 5: Retell the Story in Terms of the Jungian Archetypes

"the resulting story"—Focusing on the archetypes changes the point of the story from Dorothy's external adventures to her internal growth and development. This brings out the universal characteristics of the story.

Retelling the Story from the Perspective of Another Character

perspective of, say, the Scarecrow. Then we would consider the Wizard as the shadow figure, and there would be a variety of anima figures, including Dorothy, as well as Glinda, and the Wicked Witch. Since several of these anima figures are at odds with each other, it would be necessary to explain how they represented various directions into which the Scarecrow could have developed, and which would have led him toward various, mutually exclusive hypothetical Self figures. However, the Self figures present in the story are the Tin Woodsman who is made of metal and the Cowardly Lion who proves to be a helpful animal: two forms which Jung notes are often taken by the Self.

Looking at *The Wizard of Oz* from this second perspective allows us to understand more about how the story works: we now see the importance of the mutual relationship between Dorothy and her friends. And we perceive more clearly the qualities of the Wizard as a failed ruler: for the Scarecrow, he is not a Self figure, but a shadow. As the deceitful ruler of Oz, the Wizard is the opposite of what the Scarecrow becomes with his friends: they emerge as the well-chosen and wise guardians of the city who will replace the government of the Wizard.

 Puzzles and Problems

Although it is possible to make Jungian analysis seem very simple in the abstract, in fact the interpretation of a story according to the psychic symbols Jung identified can be quite complex and may not be completely satisfying. A traditional fairy tale may have undergone many changes as it was shaped by a variety of storytellers. In the course of such a process, various aspects of the story may have been left out or changed according to the tastes and values of the time, rendering the story incomplete or unsatisfying to analyze. For example, in the Grimm Brothers' story "Robber Bridegroom," a young girl sees her unscrupulous bridegroom-to-be kill another young woman and succeeds in proving this to her friends and neighbors, with the result that he is executed. The tale provides us with an incomplete account of the heroine's process of individuation, though it does serve as a striking warning to young women about the dangers of following the demands of a destructive animus figure.

The difficulty of applying Jungian analysis to the interpretation of movies, plays, and television shows can be even greater than that encountered in using it for traditional stories. **It may well be that the artistic norms of a particular period or genre are in conflict with the sincere search for personal meaning** and value assumed by the Jungian model. There may be the feeling that life is hopeless, or that what is worth chronicling is the absurdity of seeking personal values or trusting anyone. This can be represented in grueling works of art like *Who's Afraid of Virginia Woolf,* a classic movie about the deterioration of a marriage as the main characters berate, belittle, and abuse each other. Or it may be embodied in lighthearted parodies like *The Water Boy* or *There's Something About Mary.* The plots of such films are deliberately quite childlike and simple, and thus can be analyzed easily by assigning archetypal figures to the characters and noting their interaction. However, such analysis does not begin to do justice to the additional perspectives introduced by the parodying within the film of the drama's own characters and dilemmas.

"It may well be that the artistic norms . . . are in conflict with the sincere search for personal meaning"—Writers of novels and movies may intentionally create characters who do not grow as people in the Jungian sense. This may be done to illustrate unfortunate aspects of society, or simply to create one-sided characters for comic effect.

"In many episodes, Mulder disagrees with or disapproves of Scully's approach . . . and her view . . . by no means triumphs"—Examples abound. In "731" (Episode 310), Scully debunks Mulder's notion that alien beings exist and have launched a conspiracy against human beings. The series eventually validates Mulder's view in "Two Fathers"/ "One Son" (Episodes 611 and 612). Thus, in the terms represented by the series, Scully is a negative anima figure who interferes with Mulder's understanding of the truth. For a more thorough discussion of *The X-Files,* see Ch. 40, p. 590.

To analyze such movies adequately, it is necessary to discuss the ironic aspects of the characters as well as their more straightforward qualities. For example, in considering a Jungian analysis of the popular television show *The X-Files,* it is not sufficient to point out that, from the point of view of the main character Fox Mulder, his partner Dana Scully represents a positive anima figure. If this were all we said, we would be neglecting the main part of a show whose motto is "Trust No One." It is necessary to take into account the underlying antagonism between Mulder and Scully that is as much a part of the show, as are the hints of the romantic relationship that many fans hope will take place between them. **In many episodes, Mulder disagrees with or disapproves of Scully's approach to the case at hand, and her view of the investigation by no means triumphs in many cases.**

However, this does not mean that a Jungian analysis is meaningless. It only shows that the series portrays Mulder as a man who is not always in touch with himself. We are not given the answer to the question of what represents Mulder's true self, and therefore we cannot be sure if Scully is a positive anima or a negative one. As an agent of the FBI, and one who is often more straightforwardly loyal to the organization than her partner, Scully represents an anima figure who is leading Mulder to a Self best represented by the agency itself. However, the show casts doubt upon the integrity and trustworthiness of the FBI and indeed of all large social organizations, often espousing the view that each person must function as an individual and "trust no one."

Failure to incorporate these complications into a Jungian analysis of episodes of a show like *The X-Files* can result in an interpretation as glib and empty as it is meaningless. However, taking into account the uncertainties of the main characters and the ambiguity for the viewer produced by the multiple levels of understanding such a story, the resulting Jungian analysis can provide an enlightening perspective on the individual's struggle to achieve psychic growth in a complex and in many ways disheartening era.

The X-Files' Mulder and Scully hunt for a killer who uses the Internet to attract his victims in "2Shy" (Episode 306). Care must be taken in the Jungian analysis of complex modern stories in which the characters are developed using multiple levels of irony.

Further Reading

Bettelheim, Bruno. *The Uses of Enchantment: The Meaning and Importance of Fairy Tales.* New York, NY: Knopf, 1976.

Part 6

Folktale and Myth

You may wonder why there is a section on fairy tales (or folktales; we use the terms interchangeably) in a book about mythology. It turns out that fairy tales and myths are related in a few ways. It has been suggested that myths reveal the fundamental nature of the human mind. Psychologists like Freud and Jung, who are interested in dreams, find that similar elements occur in their patients' dreams and in myths and fairy tales. If fairy tales are related to dreams, these stories may, like myths, represent something that is essential to what it is to be human.

Fairy tales share other characteristics with myths, as well. Like myths, they are often related orally as stories, rather than being written down as literary works. This means that they change and evolve in the telling the way that myths do; folklorists have often been able to track versions of a story and note how it is told differently in various regions. Even in one location, one person's telling of a fairy tale will be somewhat different from another's, although people hearing the two different versions will for the most part agree that they are the same story. In addition, because fairy tales are handed down (or transmitted) orally, they can be paratactic in the same way as myths. See Chapter 2, p. 18, for a discussion of this phenomenon.

It has been suggested that fairy tales, like myths, are related to rituals, and that they are stories that give meaning to patterns of action practiced in the society that tells them. Think of a child going to sleep at night, listening to different fairy tales, commenting on them and discussing them with a parent. The stories become an informal means of education for the child, giving meaning to the practices described in them. The stories also become part of role-playing games that allow children to deal with the conflicts and tensions inherent in their society.

Fairy tales also foster psychological growth and development. In our society, many of the stories from the Brothers Grimm are cleaned up to eliminate some of the violent parts of the story. For example, according to the Grimm version, Cinderella's stepsisters are punished by being blinded. In versions you may be familiar with, the sisters are not punished at all, or their punishment is simply that they continue to be their own unlovely selves. However, psychologist Bruno Bettelheim has argued that the stories should not be "toned down" in this fashion, since they give children an outlet for dealing with their negative and cruel feelings. His study of the tales by the Brothers Grimm suggests that fairy tales serve an important function, and that children will, at different points in their lives, have favorite tales that deal with unconscious problems and conflicts they are dealing with at the time.

Although myths and fairy tales are similar in some ways, they are different in others. Some of the main differences are

1. In myths, the heroes tend to be specific figures with specific talents. In fairy tales, the hero is often unnamed, or else his name is generic. "Heracles" as a hero is a particular individual with specific talents, strengths, and weaknesses, whereas "Jack" or "the prince" could be anybody.
2. In myths, the required feats of strength or the power of intellect are directly accomplished by the hero, while in fairy tales, the tasks to be done are usually performed through magic.

In rare instances, elements found in fairy tales can be combined with those in myths. For example, we include in this book the story of Cupid and Psyche (Ch. 37), which shares the characteristics of both a myth and a fairy tale. In structure, it resembles fairy tales, and can be analyzed by the Proppian method outlined in Chapter 34. However, the characters are not generic figures, but gods and goddesses, including Venus, goddess of love, and her son Cupid (the Roman versions of Aphrodite and Eros). This story represents an interesting blend of traditions, as its introduction shows (p. 541).

Now that we have established that fairy tales represent a reasonable part of a book about mythology, let us think about how to study them most effectively. It turns out that the characteristics we listed—generic heroes, use of magic—are not the most interesting qualities of fairy tales. Rather, scholars have been interested in why fairy tales have appealed to so many people, both children and grown-ups, for so long. It is true that people will sometimes say that fairy tales all seem the same to them. For some, this is viewed as a drawback, and they think of fairy tales as monotonous and childish. Other people find the simplicity of fairy tales delightful; they enjoy encountering the same elements over and over in stories that nonetheless manage to surprise and delight with their ingenuity. For a long time scholars noticed the similarities among fairy tales and wanted to understand more about how they worked.

Classifying Tales

As part of understanding the nature and meaning of fairy tales, scholars have developed systems of classification for them, in some cases relying on similarities of themes found in the stories. For example, is "Hansel and Gretel" similar to or different from "Aladdin"? Are the stories similar because each of them has a supernatural creature (witch, genie)? Are they different because one of them involves seeking treasure, while the other one involves trying to escape an evil captor? If we retold "Hansel and Gretel" and made the witch an evil genie who captured the children, would it be a different story or just modified slightly?

To answer questions like this, you would need to think about what makes stories similar. Folklorists have often classified fairy tales according to the plot elements they contain. These elements are often called themes or motifs. Stith Thompson's system of classification is a very broadly used system that works in this way.

Thompson's *Motif-Index of Folk Literature* categorizes these motifs under 26 major headings, such as Cleverness, Fools, or Transformation (gods turn into animals, devils turn into animals, men turn into animals, men turn into other men), identified by a capital letter for the major category and a number for the minor. In *The Folktale,* Thompson describes his work as supplementing the earlier classification system developed by A. A. Aarne (426). His system of classification is extremely detailed. For example, if magic as a motif is listed under "D," a heading such as "Magic Objects" covers subheadings D800–D1699, and a particular magical object such as "inexhaustible food" is D1652.1. Such detailed organization of material allows those who are comparing and analyzing tales to be very clear about what they mean when they describe two fairy tales as similar.

The motifs identified by Thompson are related to key elements of Propp's morphology of the folktale. Thompson explains that a motif is the smallest element in a tale that is important enough to survive many storytellings in the particular tradition (*Folktale,* 415). These include characters in the tale, certain items that play a role in the action, and single incidents or persons. Propp extended the value of motifs by using them to analyze the *structure* of the tale. The emphasis on structure allowed Propp to group folk- or fairy tales in ways that showed similarities between them.

Propp's study of structure also allowed him to identify types of tales. Thompson had studied types of tales, using them to describe the essential parts of a story. For example, to what extent are stories with the same motifs related to each other? "The Goose Girl" (p. 527) and "Tricking All the Kings" (p. 347) both have the motif "Imposture," and "The Raven" (p. 531) and "Faithful John" (p. 534) both involve transfer to a magical place. But are they alike? In what ways are they different? To consider this issue, Thompson set up a system of identifying types of tales. A type is a traditional tale that can stand alone and be told independently of any other story. It may consist of a single motif or several.

Propp, however, had a different idea. He was familiar with systems of classifying tales according to motifs (like that of Thompson), but wanted to resolve the question of which element takes priority in forming a family, and thus, which parts of a tale were necessary to its essence. This would allow him to determine the hierarchical relationship of the elements of a tale and to establish what elements of the tale were essential to it. In his studies, Propp determined that what was essential to a story was something he called a function, and he identified 31 of them. Functions are elements of the story that are linked to certain actions performed by characters, like hero or villain. Thus, Propp developed a system of classification that was based not on the subject or content of the fairy tale, but on its underlying actions or structure. This allowed him to show the similarities between stories with widely differing subject matters. After Propp, other theorists have adapted his system to their own ends. Perhaps the most influential of these is the system of analysis developed by A. J. Greimas, which generalizes Propp's system of classification so that it can apply to all kinds of narratives, not just folktales. To accomplish this,

Greimas reduces Propp's 31 functions to a pattern he calls "the Quest," which consists of a qualifying test, a main test, a glorifying test, and the consequence of each (237–39).

The Proppian morphology has provided a powerful and flexible tool for talking about fairy tales. You can see this method of analysis in action in the next chapter, which explores the extensive changes made in transforming the children's book by L. Frank Baum into a film version called *The Wizard of Oz*.

Further Reading

Aarne, Antti. *The Types of the Folk-Tale; a Classification and Bibliography*. Trans. and enl. by Stith Thompson. Helsinki: Suomalainen Tiedeakatemia, Academia Scientarum Fennica, 1928.

Greimas, A.-J. *Structural Semantics: An Attempt at a Method*. Trans. Daniele McDowell, Ronald Schleifer, and Alan Velie. Lincoln, NE: University of Nebraska Press, 1983.

Propp, Vladimir. *The Morphology of the Folktale*. Ed. Louis A. Wagner, trans. Laurence Scott. Austin, TX: University of Texas Press, 1968.

Thompson, Stith. *The Folktale*. Berkeley, CA: University of California Press, 1977.

———. *Motif-Index of Folk-Literature, a Classification of Narrative Elements in Folktales, Ballads, Myths, Fables, Mediaeval Romances, Exempla, Fabliaux, Jest-Books, and Local Legends* (6 volumes). Bloomington, IN: Indiana University Press, 1955–1958.

The Morphology of the Folktale

VLADIMIR PROPP

 **WHAT TO EXPECT . . .** Folktales belong to the world of mythology because they share many characteristics of myth, and in the view of many who study mythology, both emerge from the unconscious processes always underlying our everyday lives. In addition, both serve the same function for society: passing on cultural norms and values. Vladimir Propp provides a useful framework for comparing stories, and although he concentrates on Russian tales, you can apply his techniques to those in other traditions as well. Basically, he classifies the characters according to their actions, and he analyzes each tale into a series of plot elements called *functions* to determine the structure of the story.

As you read, note that Propp uses letters of the alphabet to designate plot elements, like departure and trickery. When considering his examples from Russian folktales, consider whether you know stories with similar elements from your reading or from movies you have seen.

Vladimir Propp's work, called *The Morphology of the Folktale,* uses the structure or form of the tale as the basis of classifying and comparing stories. The root of "morphology," *morph,* comes from the Greek word for "form," and is used widely in biology and anatomy. For example, it occurs in terms describing basic human body types such as *ectomorph* (a tall, slender shape), *endomorph* (a short, broad shape), and *mesomorph* (the body shape that is medium height and breadth). Anatomists determined these classifications by creating standards and measuring bone structures. Propp's method is similar, but he relies on the presence of particular characters and actions in a sequence to determine the form of a story. The examples in his system of classification are drawn from Russian folktales, which were part of his own native tradition, but it also works well for tales from other cultures.

PROPP'S SYSTEM OF ANALYSIS

The system of classification developed by Propp is very simple and easy to learn, since it is based, with some modification, on the sequence of letters in the alphabet. According to Propp, every fairy tale is made up of a series of plot elements, which he calls functions. The main part of a tale will start with one or more lacks or harms, the solving of which directs the action. The lack or harm is designated by the letters "a" (lack) or "A" (harm). Thus, the plot of a fairy tale will go from the lack or harm to its resolution, "K." Other elements can be encountered along the way, including meetings with donors, villains, and false heroes, and solving difficult tasks. Often the story will end in a wedding, "W." A story will not always contain all of these functions, but for the most part, the functions it does contain will be in order. That is, the basic structure of a story will go from "A" to "W," with omissions. Each of the functions or plot elements is designated by a letter or group of letters. For the most part, these letters are designed to help you remember

499

This excerpt comes from: *The Morphology of the Folktale**

"we shall separate . . . we shall make a comparison"—Is "Snow White" similar to "Hansel and Gretel"? Propp indicates that his classification scheme will give us the basis for answering this question through the comparison of the fairy tales.

morphology In science, this term indicates a systematic study to determine the structure and component parts of an organism.

dramatis personae This Latin phrase refers to the characters in a play or story as a group. (See "Functions characterize roles in the story," p. 501ff.)

"characters . . . often perform the same actions"—The genie in "Aladdin," and the fairy godmother in "Cinderella," for all their differences, are both donors, who give the heroes what they need to accomplish their tasks.

"The sequence of functions is always identical"—A great variety of fairy tales can be described by the same small group of letters, from A to W. Similarly, in chemistry we are able to describe the world, for all its diversity, as the patterns made by a small number of elements.

"by no means do all tales give evidence of all functions"—The key to Proppian analysis is not the presence of all the elements the analysis contains, but their *sequence*. Not every story fits Proppian analysis, because not every story is a fairy tale. A tale that fits can be considered a proper fairy tale because it has the *proper order* of functions. A story which is not a fairy tale will result in an alphabet soup of functions in an order very different from the one Propp has identified. However, small variations (some of which will be described below) do not affect the status of a story as a fairy tale.

what they stand for: for example, "D" is for Donor, and "L" (which can remind you of "lies") stands for the actions of the false hero.

The plot elements in Propp's method of analysis are even easier to learn because they often come in clusters or groups. For example, the functions D-E-F usually come together and make up what is called a "donor cycle. In this cycle, the donor tests the hero (D), the hero responds (E), and the hero obtains a magical agent from the donor (F). Other groupings include the combat cycle, which includes combat with the villain, being branded or marked, and defeating the villain (H-J-I); being assigned a task and completing it, (M-N); pursuit and rescue (Pr-Rs); lies of the false hero; and exposure of the false hero (L-Ex).

This work is dedicated to the study of *fairy* tales. We are undertaking a comparison of the themes of these tales. For the sake of comparison, **we shall separate** the component parts of fairy tales by special methods; and then, **we shall make a comparison** of tales according to their components. The result will be a **morphology** (i.e., a description of the tale according to its component parts and the relationship of these components to each other and to the whole).

In a tale, the names of the *dramatis personae* change, but neither their actions nor functions change. From this we can draw the inference that a tale often attributes identical attributes to various personages. This makes possible the study of the tale *according to the functions of its dramatis personae.*

Investigation will reveal that the recurrence of functions is astounding. Going further, it is possible to establish that **characters** of a tale, however varied they may be, **often perform the same actions.** The actual means of the realization of functions is a variable. But the function, as such, is a constant.

Thus the functions of the dramatis personae are basic components of the tale, and we must define and extract them. Definition must proceed from two points of view. First of all, definition should in no case depend on the personage who carries out the function. Secondly, an action cannot be defined apart from its place in the course of narration. The meaning which a given function has in the course of the action must be considered.

Function is understood as an act of a character, defined from the point of view of its significance for the course of the action.

1. Functions of characters serve as stable, constant elements in a tale, independent of how and by whom they are fulfilled. They constitute the fundamental components of a tale.
2. The number of functions known to the fairy tale is limited.
3. **The sequence of functions is always identical.**

As for groupings, it is necessary to say first of all that **by no means do all tales give evidence of all functions.** But this in no way changes the law of sequence. The absence of certain functions does not change the order of the rest. For the present we shall deal with groupings in the proper sense of the word. The presentation of the question itself evokes the following assumption: if functions are singled out, then it will be possible to trace those tales which present identical functions. Tales with identical functions can be considered as belonging to one type. On this foundation, an index of types can then be created, based not on theme features, which are somewhat vague and diffuse, but upon exact structural features.

4. All fairy tales are of one type in regard to their structure.

Morphology of the Folktale, Second Edition, by Vladimir Propp, translated by Laurence Scott, 19–65, 80–83, 91–94. Revised and edited with a Preface by Louis A. Wagner. Copyright (c) 1968. By permission of the University of Texas Press.

We shall now set about the task of proving, developing, and elaborating these theses in detail. Here it should be recalled that the study of the tale must be carried on strictly deductively, i.e., proceeding from the material at hand to the consequences.

Functions Characterize Roles in the Story

Propp calls the characters in a tale *dramatis personae*. This Latin phrase refers to the actors in a theatrical production, and it fits well with a system of classification based on the actions of the characters in a tale. Each of the various functions we just described is associated with, and is said to be in the sphere of, a particular *dramatis persona*. For example, the definition of the hero is as follows: ". . . that character who either directly suffers from the action of the villain in the complication (the one who senses some kind of lack [or harm; functions a or A), or who agrees to liquidate the misfortune or lack of another person [function K]. In the course of the action the hero is the person who is supplied with a magical agent [donor], and who makes use of it or is served by it [functions D-E-F]" (50). Propp sees the tales as a series of functions, or actions, carried out by the characters (or *dramatis personae*) as actors. The functions of the *dramatis personae* comprise the tale as a whole. Identifying these roles and functions, and their relationships to one another, allows you to analyze and compare tales from within a particular culture or even from different cultures.

How to Assign Functions to the Characters

Although functions, as such, are the subjects of the present study (and not their performers nor the objects dependent upon them), we nevertheless should examine the question of how functions are distributed among the *dramatis personae*. Before answering this question in detail, one might note that many functions logically join together into certain **spheres.** These spheres correspond to their respective performers. They are spheres of action. The following spheres of action are present in the tale:

1. The sphere of action of the *villain.* Constituents: villainy (A); a fight or other forms of struggle with the hero (H); pursuit (Pr).
2. The sphere of action of the *donor* (provider). Constituents: the preparation for the transmission of a magical agent (D); provision of the hero with a magical agent (F).
3. The sphere of action of the *helper.* Constituents: the spatial transference of the hero (G); liquidation of misfortune or lack (K); rescue from pursuit (Rs); the solution of difficult tasks (N); transfiguration of the hero (T).
4. The sphere of action of a *princess* (a sought-for person) and of her father. Constituents: the assignment of difficult tasks (M); branding (J); exposure (Ex); recognition (Q); punishment of a second villain (U); marriage (W). The princess and her father cannot be exactly delineated from each other according to functions. Most often it is the father who assigns difficult tasks due to hostile feeling toward the suitor. He also frequently punishes (or orders punished) the false hero.
5. The sphere of action of the *dispatcher.* Constituent: dispatch (connective incident, B).
6. The sphere of action of the *hero.* Constituents: departure on a search (Counteraction, Departure: C↑); reaction to the demands of the donor (E); wedding (W). The first function (C) is characteristic of the seeker-hero; the victim-hero performs only the remaining functions.
7. The sphere of action of the *false hero* also includes C↑, followed by reaction to a donor (E) and, as a specific function, unfounded claims (L).

"spheres"—Groups of functions that correspond to the particular performer. Here, the emphasis is on the character, whereas with pairs and sequences, the emphasis is on the action itself.

Some Spheres of Action:

- villain
- donor
- helper
- hero
- false hero

 Is It a Task or a Test?

In some cases, actions are hard to assign to a specific dramatis persona. Propp explains (elsewhere) that testing by a donor (D) can be distinguished from a difficult task (M) according to the consequences of the action, by what happens after it is completed. If the hero receives a magical agent which *later* helps him perform a task, then the action constitutes testing by a donor. If receipt of a bride and marriage follow, then it was a difficult task.

Distribution of Spheres of Actions among Characters:

1. The Sphere of Action Exactly Corresponds to the Character.
2. One Character Is Involved in Several Spheres of Action.

"intentions cannot be considered as an essential motif"—Characters must be evaluated in light of what they do for the hero and for the course of action of the tale. Sometimes, they do not intend the result achieved.

3. A Single Sphere of Action Is Distributed among Several Characters.

G. P. Jacomb Hood, Illustration for *"Little Red Riding Hood,"* 1919. The sphere of the villain includes functions in the preparatory part, where the harm or lack is precipitated. Here the wolf performs trickery: having eaten the grandmother, he lies in wait for the unsuspecting Little Red Riding Hood.

How are the above-mentioned spheres of action distributed among individual tale characters? There are three possibilities here:

1. The sphere of action exactly corresponds to the character. The witch who tests and rewards the hero, or the horse which brings the hero to the princess, helps in abducting her, rescues the hero from pursuit, etc., is a pure helper.

2. One character is involved in several spheres of action. For example, the little iron peasant who asks to be let out of a tower, thereupon rewarding the hero with strength and a magic tablecloth, but who eventually also aids in killing the dragon, is simultaneously both a donor and a helper. The category of grateful animals demands special scrutiny. They begin as donors (begging for help or mercy), then they place themselves at the disposal of the hero and become his helpers. Sometimes it happens that an animal which has been freed or spared by the hero simply disappears without even informing the hero of the formula to summon it, but in a critical moment it appears in the role of a helper. It rewards the hero with direct action. It may, for example, help the hero get to another kingdom, or it obtains for him the object of his search, and so on.

Several other cases of combination can be cited. The father who dispatches his son, giving him a cudgel, is at the same time both a dispatcher and a donor. The witch who kidnaps a boy, places him in her oven, and is then robbed by the boy combines the functions of villain and (unintentional, hostile) donor. We come upon the phenomenon that the will of personages, their **intentions, cannot be considered as an essential motif** for their definition. The important thing is not what they want to do, nor how they feel, but their deeds as such, evaluated and defined from the viewpoint of their meaning for the hero and for the course of the action.

3. The reverse case: a single sphere of action is distributed among several characters. For example, if a dragon is killed in a battle, it is incapable of pursuit. Elements D, E, and F are sometimes similarly distributed. One character does the testing while another one accidentally gives the reward.

Living things, objects, and qualities must be examined as equivalent quantities. However, it is more convenient to term living things "magical helpers" and objects and qualities as "magical agents," even though they both function in exactly the same manner. Hence it is apparent that the magical agent is actually nothing more than a particular form of magical helper.

One should also make mention of the fact that the hero often gets along without any helpers. He is his own helper, as it were. Conversely, a helper at times may perform those functions which are specific for the hero. Besides C, the only thing which is specific for him is his reaction to the activity of the donor. Yet here the helper often acts instead of the hero.

The Parts of a Fairy Tale

In Propp's method of analysis, a fairy tale can be described as a sequence of functions. The main part of the story consists of the functions a (lack) or A (harm) to W. The tale can begin with a Preparatory Part, which explains the causes of the harm or lack and incorporates a separate set of functions designated by Greek letters from α to θ (alpha to theta).

The Functions of *Dramatis Personae*

In this chapter we shall enumerate the functions of the *dramatis personae* in the order dictated by the tale itself.

For each function there is given: (1) a brief summary of its essence, (2) an abbreviated definition in one word, and (3) its conventional sign. (The introduction of signs will later permit a schematic comparison of the structure of various tales.)

All functions fit into one consecutive story. The **series of functions** given below represents the morphological foundation of fairy tales in general.

A tale usually begins with some sort of initial situation. The members of a family are enumerated, or the future hero is simply introduced by mention of his name or indication of his status.

Although this situation is not a function, it nevertheless is an important morphological element. The species of tale beginnings can be examined only at the end of the present work. We shall designate this element as the *initial situation*, giving it the sign α.

After the initial situation there follow functions:

Quick Greek Primer for Use with Propp's Functions

α	alpha	ε	epsilon
β	beta	ζ	zeta ("ZAY-ta")
γ	gamma	η	eta ("AY-ta")
δ	delta	θ	theta

I. ONE OF THE MEMBERS OF A FAMILY ABSENTS HIMSELF FROM HOME. (Definition: *absentation*. Designation: β.)

Usual forms of absentation: going to work, to the forest, to trade, to war, "on business." An intensified form of absentation is represented by the death of parents. Sometimes members of the younger generation absent themselves. They go visiting, fishing, for a walk, out to gather berries.

II. AN INTERDICTION IS ADDRESSED TO THE HERO. (Definition: *interdiction*. Designation: γ.)

"**You dare not look** into this closet." "Take care of your little brother, do not venture forth from the courtyard." Interdiction not to go out is sometimes strengthened or replaced by putting children in a stronghold. Sometimes an interdiction is evidenced in a weakened form, as a request or bit of advice: a mother tries to persuade her son not to go out fishing: "you're still little," etc. An inverted form of interdiction is represented by an order or a suggestion. "Bring breakfast out into the field." "Take your brother with you to the woods."

III. THE INTERDICTION IS VIOLATED. (Definition: *violation*. Designation: δ.)

The **forms of violation** correspond to the forms of interdiction. Functions II and III form a *paired* element. The second half can sometimes exist without the first. A fulfilled order corresponds to a violated interdiction.

At this point **a new personage,** who can be termed the *villain,* enters the tale. His role is to disturb the peace of a happy family, to cause some form of misfortune, damage, or harm. The villain may be a dragon, a devil, bandits, a witch, or a stepmother, etc.

IV. THE VILLAIN MAKES AN ATTEMPT AT RECONNAISSANCE. (Definition: *reconnaissance*. Designation: ε.)

The **reconnaissance** has the aim of finding out the location of children, or sometimes of precious objects, etc. A bear says: "Who will tell me what has become of the tsar's children? Where did they disappear to?"; a clerk: "Where do you get these precious stones?" In an inverted form of reconnaissance, the intended victim questions the villain.

V. THE VILLAIN RECEIVES INFORMATION ABOUT HIS VICTIM. (Definition: *delivery*. Designation: ζ.)

 Preparatory Part

"series of functions"—The first group of functions is designated by the Greek letters α to θ and sets up the lack or harm which drives the story. Stories don't necessarily have all of the preparatory functions; some have none at all. They simply start with the lack or harm, saying, "One morning Jack woke up and decided to seek his fortune." The preparatory part can also include a "donor cycle," which strictly speaking, is out of sequence with the order of a Proppian analysis.

 Absentation

Examples of Absentation:

- Parents leave for work
- Man goes off to war
- Parent dies
- Children go on an errand

 Interdiction

"You dare not look"—To interdict is to forbid. Another form of this function is a command. Sometimes the interdiction is understood, rather than expressed.

Examples of Interdiction:

- Command
- Request
- Order
- Suggestion
- Advice

 Violation of the Interdiction

"forms of violation"—Actions of the main characters inevitably go against the command, request, or suggestion.

"a new personage"—The violation of the interdiction is in the domain of the villain.

 Reconnaissance by the Villain

reconnaissance We use the word to mean gathering information secretly. Typically, the villain tries to find out the location of precious objects or children.

Delivery

"receives an answer"—This function refers to the success of reconnaissance in the previous one.

Examples of delivery:
The mirror tells Snow White's stepmother she is still alive.

Trickery

Examples of trickery:
At the opening of Disney's *Aladdin,* Jafar, the villain, tricks Aladdin into agreeing to go and get the lamp. First he has Aladdin followed and imprisoned for petty theft. This is the reconnaissance, and the trickery follows.

Complicity

"the victim"—One of the *dramatis personae.* In some cases, the hero is the victim; in others, a separate character.

Examples of complicity:
Aladdin goes to get the lamp.

"The hero takes the ring"—As interdictions are always broken, deceitful proposals are always accepted and fulfilled.

Villainy or Harm

"absentation . . . all prepare the way for [villainy]"—This is usually true, but a variation is also possible at this point.

Sometimes a story does not start with a lack or harm, but with a donor (p. 507).

"exceedingly varied"—Propp lists all the categories and subcategories of villainy found in a sample of 100 tales. He assigns a numerical superscript to each. We have condensed this section and do not include all the types of villainy listed by Propp.

"substitution"—May involve replacing one person with another, or changing a person *into* another creature.

"other beginnings"—Some tales don't start with a harm, but only its result, a lack.

The villain directly **receives an answer** to his question. The chisel answers the bear: "Take me out into the courtyard and throw me to the ground; where I stick, there's the hive." To the clerk's question about the precious stones, the merchant's wife replies: "Oh, the hen lays them for us," etc.

VI. THE VILLAIN ATTEMPTS TO DECEIVE HIS VICTIM IN ORDER TO TAKE POSSESSION OF HIM OR OF HIS BELONGINGS. (Definition: *trickery.* Designation: η.)

The villain, first of all, assumes a disguise. A dragon turns into a golden goat, or a handsome youth; a witch pretends to be a "sweet old lady" and imitates a mother's voice; a thief pretends to be a beggarwoman.

Other types of trickery: A witch tries to have a ring accepted; a godmother suggests the taking of a steam bath; a beggar seeks alms. The stepmother gives a sleeping potion to her stepson.

VII. **THE VICTIM** SUBMITS TO DECEPTION AND THEREBY UNWITTINGLY HELPS HIS ENEMY. (Definition: *complicity. Designation: θ.*)

The hero takes the ring, goes to steam bath, to swim, etc. A special form of deceitful proposal and its corresponding acceptance is represented by the deceitful agreement. ("Give away that which you do not know you have in your house.") Assent in these instances is compelled, the villain taking advantage of some difficult situation in which his victim is caught: a scattered flock, extreme poverty, etc.

VIII. THE VILLAIN CAUSES HARM OR INJURY TO A MEMBER OF A FAMILY. (Definition: *villainy.* Designation: A.)

This function is exceptionally important, since by means of it the actual movement of the tale is created. **Absentation, the violation of an interdiction, delivery, the success of a deceit all prepare the way for this function,** create its possibility of occurrence, or simply facilitate its happening. The forms of villainy are **exceedingly varied.** [For example:]

The villain abducts a person or takes away a magical agent or helper (A^1). A princess seizes a magic shirt; a finger-sized peasant makes off with a magic steed.

The villain plunders in other forms (A^5). The object of seizure fluctuates to an enormous degree. The object of plunder does not influence the course of action.

The villain causes bodily injury (A^6) or a sudden disappearance (A^7). Usually this disappearance is the result of bewitching or deceitful means. A stepmother puts her stepson into a sleep—his bride disappears forever; a wife flies away from her husband upon a magic carpet.

The villain demands or entices his victim (A^8). Usually this form is the result of a deceitful agreement. The king of the sea demands the tsar's son, and he leaves home.

The villain expels someone (A^9): a stepmother drives her stepdaughter out; parents launch a small boat, carrying their sleeping son, into the sea.

The villain casts a spell upon someone or something (A^{11}). A wife turns her husband into a dog and then drives him out; a stepmother turns her stepdaughter into a lynx and drives her out.

The villain effects a **substitution** (A^{12}). A nursemaid changes a bride into a duckling and substitutes her own daughter in the bride's place.

The villain orders a murder to be committed (A^{13}). A princess orders her servants to take her husband away into the forest and kill him. Usually in such instances a presentation of the heart and liver of the victim is demanded.

The villain imprisons or detains someone (A^{15}), or makes a threat of cannibalism (A^{17}). He or she torments a victim at night (A^{18}), or declares war (A^{19}).

However, far from all tales begin with the affliction of misfortune. There are also **other beginnings** which often present the same development as tales which begin with (A). On examining this phenomenon, we can observe that these tales proceed from a certain situation of insufficiency or lack, and it is this that leads to quests analogous to those in the case of villainy. We conclude from this that **lack can be considered as the morphological equivalent of seizure.**

A tale, while omitting villainy, very often begins directly with a lack. For example, a princess steals the hero's talisman, creating a lack. **Insufficiency,** just as seizure, determines the next point of the complication: the hero sets out on a quest. The same may be said about the abduction of a bride as about the simple lack of a bride. In the first instance a certain act is given, the result of which creates an insufficiency and provokes a quest; in the second instance a ready-made insufficiency is presented, which also provokes a quest. In the first instance, a lack is created from without; in the second, it is realized from within.

VIIIa. ONE MEMBER OF A FAMILY EITHER LACKS SOMETHING OR DESIRES TO HAVE SOMETHING. (Definition: *lack*. Designation: a.)

It is possible to register the following forms of lack: (1) Lack of a bride (or a friend, or a human being generally). This lack is sometimes depicted quite vividly (the hero intends to search for a bride), and sometimes it is not even mentioned verbally. The hero is unmarried and sets out to find a bride—with this a beginning is given to the course of the action (a^1). (2) A magical agent is needed: apples, water, horses (a^2). (3) Wondrous objects are lacking (without magical power), such as the firebird, ducks with golden feathers (a^3). (4) A specific form (the magic egg containing the love of a princess) is lacking (a^4). (5) Rationalized forms: (money, the means of existence) are lacking (a^5).

Just as the object of seizure does not determine the structure of the tale, neither does the object which is lacking. In consequence, there is **no need to systematize all instances** for the sake of the general goals of morphology. One can limit oneself to the most important ones and generalize the rest.

IX. MISFORTUNE OR LACK IS MADE KNOWN; THE HERO IS APPROACHED WITH A REQUEST OR COMMAND; HE IS ALLOWED TO GO OR HE IS DISPATCHED. (Definition: *mediation, the* **connective** *incident*. Designation: B.)

This function brings the hero into the tale. He may be one of **two types:** (1) if a young girl is kidnapped, and disappears from the horizon of her father (and that of the listener) and if a young man goes off in search of her, then the hero of the tale is the young man and not the kidnapped girl. Heroes of this type may be termed *seekers*. (2) If a young girl or boy is seized or driven out and the thread of the narrative is linked to his or her fate and not to those who remain behind, then the hero of the tale is the seized or banished boy or girl. There are no seekers in such tales. Heroes of this variety may be called *victimized heroes*. A moment of mediation is present in both cases. The significance of this moment lies in the fact that the hero's departure from home is caused by it.

A call for help is given, with the resultant dispatch of the hero (B^1).

The hero is dispatched directly (B^2). Dispatch is presented either in the form of a command or a request. In the former instance, it is sometimes accompanied by threats; in the latter, by promises. Sometimes both threats and promises are made.

The hero is allowed to depart from home (B^3). In this instance the initiative for departure often comes from the hero himself, and not from a dispatcher. Parents bestow their blessing. The hero sometimes does not announce his real aims for leaving: he asks

---

Examples of Villainy:

- Kidnapping
- Theft
- Bodily harm
- Sudden disappearance
- Acquiring rights to a person through a deceitful agreement
- Expulsion
- Casting a spell
- Substitution
- Murder or attempted murder
- Imprisonment
- Threats
- Torment at night
- Declaration of war

"lack can be considered as the morphological equivalent of seizure"—Lack and seizure (harm) are equivalent ways of starting a story.

"Insufficiency"—Synonym for lack.

 Lack

Examples of Lack:

- Cinderella is treated like a servant.
- In "Rumpelstiltskin," the girl must spin straw into gold.

"no need to systematize all instances"—We may be able to think of stories with elements not explicitly mentioned by Propp, but he will nonetheless consider himself successful if he has successfully characterized the kinds of structures in the fairy tale.

 Mediation

"connective incident"—To fulfill this function (B), the hero must leave home. The connective incident provides the reason to leave. It may be the result of villainy or merely of lack.

"two types"—The hero may leave voluntarily, may be commanded, driven out, or abducted. Depending on the reason for the departure, heroes may be typed as:

- Seekers
- Victimized heroes.

for permission to go out walking, etc., but in reality he is setting off for the struggle.

Misfortune is announced (B⁴). For example, a mother tells her son about the abduction of her daughter that took place before his birth. The son sets out in search of his sister, without having been asked to do so by his mother. More often, however, a story of misfortune does not come from parents, but rather from various old women or persons casually encountered.

These **four preceding forms** all refer to seeker-heroes. The forms following are directly related to the victimized hero. The structure of the tale demands that the hero leave home at any cost. If this is not accomplished by means of some form of villainy, then the tale employs the connective incident to this end.

The hero condemned to death is secretly freed (B⁶). A cook or an archer spares a young girl (or boy), frees her, and instead of killing her, slays an animal in order to obtain its heart

Walter Crane, illustration for *"Rapunzel,"* 1882. The prince, who is a seeker hero, encounters the princess by chance. Thus his dispatch in the tale is almost invisible, as her song "entered into his heart and every day he went into the wood and listened to it."

and liver as proof of the murder. Incident B was defined above as the factor causing the departure of the hero from home. Whereas dispatch presents the necessity for setting out, here the opportunity for departure is given. The first instance is characteristic of the seeker-hero, and the second applies to the victimized hero.

> X. THE SEEKER AGREES TO OR DECIDES UPON COUNTERACTION. (Definition: *beginning counteraction.* Designation: C.)

 Counteraction

This moment is characterized in such words, for instance, as the following: "Permit us to go in search of your princess," etc. Sometimes this moment is not expressed in words, but a volitional decision, of course, precedes the search. This moment is characteristic only of those tales in which the hero is a seeker. Banished, vanquished, bewitched, and substituted heroes demonstrate no volitional aspiration toward freedom, and in such cases this element is lacking.

> XI. THE HERO LEAVES HOME. (Definition: *departure.* Designation: ↑.)

 **Departure**

Departure here denotes something different from the temporary absence element, designated earlier by B. The departures of seeker-heroes and victim-heroes are also different. The departures of the former group have search as their goal, while those of the latter mark the beginning of a journey without searches, on which various adventures await the hero. It is necessary to keep the following in mind: if a young girl is abducted and a seeker goes in pursuit of her, then two characters have left home. But the route followed by the story and on which the action is developed is actually the route of the seeker. If, for example, a girl is driven out and there is no seeker, then the narrative is developed along the route of the victim hero. The sign ↑ **designates the route of the hero,** regardless of whether he is a seeker or not. In certain tales a spatial transference of the hero is absent. The entire action takes place in one location. Sometimes, on the contrary, departure is intensified, assuming the character of flight.

The elements **ABC** ↑ represent the complication. Later on, the course of action is developed.

Now a new character enters the tale: this personage might be termed the *donor,* or more precisely, the *provider.* Usually he is encountered accidentally—in the forest,

---

"four preceding forms"—refers to connective incidents B¹ to B⁴, which deal with seeker heroes.

"The hero condemned to death is secretly freed"—Snow White is secretly freed by the woodsman who has been commanded to kill her. He brings back a boar's heart to the stepmother.

B⁶—Throughout this excerpt, in the interest of space, we have omitted portions of Propp's classification, in this case the details of B5, "the banished hero is transported away from home."

"↑designates the route of the hero"—What is important here is the journey, not the reason for leaving, as in function B (p. 505).

"ABC"—A function sequence in which each component depends on the previous one, and together the components form a module of the story. See the analysis of *The Wizard of Oz,* Ch. 35, p. 514, for examples.

along the roadway, etc. It is from him that the hero (both the seeker-hero and the victim-hero) obtains some agent (usually magical) which permits the eventual liquidation of misfortune. But before receipt of the magical agent takes place, the hero is subjected to a number of quite diverse actions which, however, all lead to the result that a magical agent comes into his hands.

> XII. THE HERO IS TESTED, INTERROGATED, ATTACKED, ETC., WHICH PREPARES THE WAY FOR HIS RECEIVING EITHER A MAGICAL AGENT OR HELPER. (Definition: *the first function of the donor*. Designation: D.)

The donor tests the hero (D^1), or greets and interrogates the hero (D^2). This form may be considered as a weakened form of testing. Greeting and interrogation are also present in the forms mentioned above, but there they do not have the character of a test; rather they precede it. A dying or deceased person requests the rendering of a service (D^3). This form also sometimes takes on the character of a test.

A prisoner begs for his freedom (D^4), or the hero is approached with a request for mercy (D^5). This form might be considered as a subclass of the preceding one. It occurs either after capture or while the hero takes aim at an animal with the intention of killing it.

> XIII. THE HERO REACTS TO THE ACTIONS OF THE FUTURE DONOR. (Definition: *the hero's reaction*. Designation: E.)

In the majority of instances, the reaction is either positive or negative. The hero withstands (or does not withstand) a test (E^1), answers (or does not answer) a greeting (E^2), renders (or does not render) a service to a dead person (E^3), frees a captive (E^4), or shows mercy to a suppliant (E^5).

> XIV. THE HERO ACQUIRES THE USE OF A MAGICAL AGENT. (Definition: *provision or receipt of a magical agent*. Designation: F.)

The following things are capable of serving as magical agents: (1) animals (a horse, an eagle, etc.); (2) objects out of which magical helpers appear (a flintstone containing a steed, a ring containing young men); (3) objects possessing a magical property, such as cudgels, swords, balls; (4) qualities or capacities which are directly given, such as the power of transformation into animals. All of these objects of transmission we shall conditionally term "magical agents." The forms by which they are transmitted are the following:

The agent is directly transferred (F^1). Such acts of transference very often have the character of a reward: an old man presents a horse as a gift; forest animals offer their offspring, etc. Sometimes the hero, instead of receiving a certain animal directly for his own use, obtains the power of turning himself into it. **If a hero's reaction is negative,** then the transference may not occur (F neg.), or is replaced by cruel retribution. The hero is devoured, frozen, etc. (F contr.).

The agent is pointed out (F^2), prepared (F^3), sold and purchased (F^4), or falls into the hands of the hero by chance (is found by him) (F^5).

The agent suddenly appears of its own accord (F^6), or it is eaten and drunk (F^7). This is not, strictly speaking, a form of transference, although it may be coordinated, conditionally, with the cases cited.

The agent is seized (F^8). The application of magical agents against the person who exchanged them and the taking back of objects which had been given may also be considered a special form of seizure.

Various characters place themselves at the disposal of the hero (F^9). An animal, for example, may either present its offspring or offer its services to the hero, making, as it were, a present of itself. It often happens that various magical creatures, without any warning, suddenly appear or are met on the way and offer their services and are

---

 The Donor Cycle (Functions DEF)

Example of testing:
In "The Raven" (Ch. 36, p. 531), the man fails the first test because he accepts the old woman's insistent offer and drinks, although the Raven has warned him not to eat or drink.

Example of E^1:
In "The Raven" (Ch. 36, p. 531), the man fails the second test because he falls asleep and does not see the chariot go by.

 Magical Agents:

- Animals
- Objects that produce magical helpers
- Qualities or abilities given directly to the hero

 Ways in Which the Agent Is Transferred:

- Given directly to the hero
- Pointed out by the donor
- Sold and purchased
- Appears by chance
- Eaten or drunk
- Seized
- Characters offer themselves as agents

"If a hero's reaction is negative"— If the hero refuses the magical agent, he may be punished. In "The Raven," the hero who fails the tests of the first donor must embark on a long difficult trip to the golden castle of Stromberg.

Example of F^8—
In "The Raven" (Ch. 36, p. 531), the man steals the door-opening cudgel, the cloak of invisibility, and the magic horse from the robbers.

Types of Connections in the Transmission of Magical Agents:

1. Magical agent is seized, shared, bartered.
2. Magical agent is given, shown, purchased, or pointed out by the donor; or it appears suddenly or by chance.

accepted as helpers (F). Most often these are heroes with extraordinary attributes, or characters possessing various magical qualities.

Here, before continuing with the further registration of functions, the following question may be raised: in what combination does one encounter the types of elements D (preparation for transmission), and F (transmission itself)?

If one proceeds to determine types from the forms of transmission of a magical agent, one can isolate two types of connections:

1 The seizure of a magical agent, linked with an attempt to destroy the hero, with a request for apportionment, or with a proposal for an exchange.
2. All other forms of transmission and receipt, linked with all other preparatory forms. The request for apportionment belongs to the second type if the division is actually accomplished, but to the first if the disputants are deceived.

In connection with this, one might touch upon the question of the character of donors. The second type most often presents friendly donors (with the exception of those who surrender a magical agent unwillingly or after a fight), whereas the first type exhibits unfriendly (or, at any rate, deceived) donors. These are not donors in the true sense of the word, but **personages who unwillingly furnish the hero with something.**

Within the forms of each type, all combinations are possible and logical, whether actually present or not. Thus, for example, either an exacting or a grateful donor is capable of giving, revealing, selling, or preparing an agent, or he may let the hero find the agent, etc. On the other hand, an agent in the possession of a deceived donor can only be stolen or taken by force. Combinations outside of these types are illogical.

Thus, for example, **it is not logical** if a hero, after performing a difficult task for a witch, steals a colt from her. This does not mean that such combinations do not exist in the tale. They do exist, but in these instances the storyteller is obliged to give additional motivation for the actions of his heroes.

The employment of a magical agent follows its receipt by the hero; or, if the agent received is a living creature, its help is directly put to use on the command of the hero. With this **the hero outwardly loses all significance;** he himself does nothing, while his helper accomplishes everything. The morphological significance of the hero is nevertheless very great, since his intentions create the axis of the narrative. These intentions appear in the form of various commands which the hero gives to his helpers.

At this point a more exact definition of the hero can be given than was done before. **The hero of a fairy tale** is that character who either directly suffers from the action of the villain in the complication (the one who senses some kind of lack), or who agrees to liquidate the misfortune or lack of another person. In the course of the action the hero is the person who is supplied with a magical agent (a magical helper), and who makes use of it or is served by it.

XV.   THE HERO IS TRANSFERRED, DELIVERED, OR LED TO THE WHEREABOUTS OF AN OBJECT OF SEARCH. (Definition: *spatial transference between two kingdoms, guidance.* Designation: G.)

Generally the object of search is located in "another" or "different" kingdom.

The hero flies through the air (G^1): on a steed; on a bird; in the form of a bird; on board a flying ship; on a flying carpet; on the back of a giant or a spirit.

He travels on the ground or on water (G^2): on the back of a horse or wolf, on board a ship, etc. Or he is led (G^3) by a creature (a fox leads a prince), or an object (a ball of string). Sometimes, the route is pointed out to him (G^4).

He makes use of stationary means of communication (G^5): a stairway, an underground passageway, etc.; or he follows bloody tracks (G^6).

This exhausts the forms of transference of the hero. It should be noted that "delivery,"

Types of Donors:

1. Unfriendly, or deceived
2. Friendly (although some are at first unwilling)

"personages who unwillingly furnish the hero with something"— It may seem that a donor must always be kind or friendly, but a donor can be unwilling at first. The hero may fight the donor to obtain the needed object.

"it is not logical"—The parts of the function group DEF should fit together logically. The test should match the task and the magical agent. If not, the tale is illogical or paratactic. See Ch. 2, p. 18, on parataxis.

"the hero outwardly loses all significance"—He always uses the magic object or helper. But although he is not accomplishing the deeds himself, he is still central because his *intentions* move the actions forward.

"The hero of a fairy tale"—The definition of this hero emphasizes his or her centrality to the action in terms of the functions in the sphere of this *dramatis persona*. (See p. 500.)

 Transference

"spatial transference"—There should be some sense of travel. If the hero simply walks to the location of the quest, this function is omitted.

Examples of G:

- In "The Raven," the giant transports the man (Ch. 36, p. 533).
- In *The Wizard of Oz,* the tornado transports Dorothy and Toto (Ch. 35, p. 521).

Modes of Transference:

- Flying through the air
- Traveling on the ground or on water
- Being shown the route
- Using stairs.
- Following bloody tracks

as a function in itself, is sometimes absent: the hero simply walks to the place (i.e., function G amounts to a natural continuation of function ↑). In such a case function G is not singled out.

XVI.   THE HERO AND THE VILLAIN JOIN IN DIRECT COMBAT. (Definition: *struggle*. Designation: H.)

This form needs to be **distinguished** from the struggle (fight) with a hostile donor. These two forms can be distinguished by their results. If the hero obtains an agent, for the purpose of further searching, as the result of an unfriendly encounter, this would be element D. If, on the other hand, the hero receives through victory the very object of his quest, we have situation H.

They fight in an open field (H^1) with dragons, knights, etc.; they engage in a competition (H^2) or play cards (H^3). The hero wins with the help of cleverness: a gypsy puts a dragon to flight by squeezing a piece of cheese as though it were a stone, by pretending that a blow to the back of the head was merely a whistle, etc.

XVII.   THE HERO IS BRANDED. (Definition: *branding, marking*. Designation: J.)

A brand is applied to the body (J^1). The hero receives a wound during a skirmish, thus branding him. He may also receive a ring or a kerchief (J^2).

XVIII.   THE VILLAIN IS DEFEATED. (Definition: *victory*. Designation: I.)

The villain is beaten in open combat (I^1), or in a contest (I^2), loses at cards (I^3), on being weighed (I^4); he is killed without a preliminary fight (I^5), or is banished directly.

XIX.   THE INITIAL MISFORTUNE OR LACK IS LIQUIDATED. (Definition: _____. Designation K.)

This function, together with villainy (A), constitutes a **pair**. The narrative reaches its peak in this function.
The object of a search is seized by the use of force or cleverness (K^1). Here heroes sometimes employ the same means adopted by villains for the initial seizure.

The object of the search is obtained by several personages at once, through a rapid interchange of their actions (K^2), or with the help of enticements (K^3), or as the direct result of preceding actions (K^4). If, for example, the hero kills a dragon and later marries the princess whom he has freed, there is no obtaining as a special act; rather, there is obtaining as a function, as a stage in the development of the plot. The princess is neither seized nor abducted, but she is nevertheless "obtained." She is obtained as the result of combat. Obtaining in these cases is a logical element.

The object of the search is obtained instantly through the use of a **magical agent** (K^5). The use of a magical agent overcomes poverty (K^6), or the object of search is caught (K^7).

The receipt of an object of search is sometimes accomplished by means of the same forms as the receipt of a magical agent (i.e., it is given as a gift, its location is indicated, it is purchased, etc.). Designation of these occurrences: $\mathbf{KF^1}$, direct transmission; $\mathbf{KF^2}$, indication; etc., as above.

XX.   THE HERO RETURNS. (Definition: *return*. Designation: ↓)

A return is generally accomplished by means of the same forms as an arrival. However, there is no need of attaching a special function to follow a return, since returning already implies a surmounting of space. This is not always true in the case of a departure. Following a departure, an agent is given (a horse, eagle, etc.) and then flying or other forms of travel occur, whereas a return takes place immediately and, for the most part, in the same forms as an arrival.

 Struggle with a Villain

"distinguished"—Once again, confusion between functions is resolved by considering the results.

Modes of Combat between the Hero and Villain:

- Fighting in a field
- Competing in a contest
- Playing cards

 Branding

 Defeat of the Villain

Ways in Which the Villain is Defeated:

- Loses in combat
- Loses a contest
- Loses at cards
- Loses on being weighed
- Is killed without a fight
- Is banished

 Liquidation

"pair"—This is related to a "function sequence" in that two functions are linked in the accomplishment of a single action. But with a pair, the functions are not as closely related.

"magical agent"—In "Rumplestiltskin," the magical agent is actually the little man himself.

"KF^1 . . . KF^2"—These are examples of pairs, two functions that fit together to make a sequence.

 Return

Pursuit

Example of Pursuit:
In *The Wizard of Oz,* Dorothy and her friends are pursued by the Wicked Witch of the West (see Ch. 35, p. 522).

 Rescue

Example of Rescue:
In *The Wizard of Oz,* Dorothy and friends gain entrance to the Emerald Castle (Ch. 35, p. 522).

"this is far from always being the case"—See p. 512 for the ways in which multiple chains of action, called "moves," are woven into a single tale.

move A series of related functions. For a more detailed description, see p. 512.

"the number of tales in each text"—To chart the structure of the tale, it is important to determine how multiple tales may combine in a single story.

 Unrecognized Arrival

 Unfounded Claims

 Difficult Task

"all instances present in our material"—Tasks appear in folktales from all traditions. For example, in "Rumpelstiltskin," the king gives the princess the task of spinning straw into gold.

James Marsh, illustration for *"Rumpelstiltskin."* In this story the title character functions as a donor at first, but becomes a false hero when he lays claim to the queen's child.

XXI.   THE HERO IS PURSUED. (Definition: *pursuit, chase.* Designation: Pr.)

The pursuer flies after the hero (Pr^1), demands the guilty person (Pr^2) or pursues the hero, rapidly transforming himself into various animals, etc. (Pr^3). This form at several stages is also connected with flight.

Pursuers turn into alluring objects and place themselves in the path of the hero (Pr^4).

XXII.   RESCUE OF THE HERO FROM PURSUIT. (Definition: *rescue.* Designation: Rs.)

He is carried away through the air on an animal (sometimes he is saved by lightning-fast fleeing) (Rs^1).

The hero flees, placing obstacles in the path of his pursuer (Rs^2). He throws a brush, a comb, a towel; they turn into mountains, forests, lakes.

The hero, while in flight, changes into objects which make him unrecognizable (Rs^3). A princess turns herself and the prince into a well and dipper, a church and priest. The hero hides himself during his flight (Rs^4), or is hidden by blacksmiths (Rs^5).

The hero saves himself while in flight by means of rapid transformations into animals, stones, etc. (Rs^6). The hero flees in the form of a horse, a ring, a seed, a falcon. The actual transformation is essential to this form. Flight may sometimes be omitted; such forms may be considered as a special subclass.

A great many tales end on the note of rescue from pursuit. The hero arrives home and then, if he has obtained a girl, marries her, etc. Nevertheless, **this is far from always being the case.** A tale may have another misfortune in store for the hero: a villain may appear once again, may seize whatever the hero has obtained, may kill him, etc. In a word, an initial villainy is repeated, sometimes in the same forms as in the beginning, and sometimes in other forms which are new for a given tale. With this a new story commences.

This phenomenon attests to the fact that many tales are composed of two *series* of functions which may be labeled **"moves."** A new villainous act creates a new "move," and in this manner, sometimes a whole series of tales combine into a single tale. Nevertheless, the process of development which will be described below does constitute the continuation of a given tale, although it also creates a new move. In connection with this, one must eventually ask how to distinguish **the number of tales in each text.**

XXIII.   THE HERO, UNRECOGNIZED, ARRIVES HOME OR IN ANOTHER COUNTRY. (Definition: *unrecognized.* Designation: o.)

Here two classes are distinguishable: (1) arrival *home,* in which the hero stays with some sort of artisan, serving as an apprentice; (2) he arrives at the court of some *king,* and serves as either a cook or a groom.

XXIV.   A FALSE HERO PRESENTS UNFOUNDED CLAIMS. (Definition: *unfounded claims.* Designation: L.)

If the hero arrives home, the false claims are presented by his brothers. If he is serving in another kingdom, a general, a water-carrier, or others present them.

XXV.   A DIFFICULT TASK IS PROPOSED TO THE HERO. (Definition: *difficult task.* Designation: M.)

This is one of the tale's favorite elements. We shall enumerate **all instances present in our material,** with an approximate arrangement into groups:

Ordeal by food and drink
Ordeal by fire

Riddle guessing and similar ordeals
Ordeal of choice
Hide and seek
To kiss the princess in a window
To jump up on top of the gates
Test of strength, adroitness, fortitude
Test of endurance
Tasks of supply and manufacture
Other tasks, such as to pick berries from a certain bush or tree.

XXVI. THE TASK IS RESOLVED. (Definition: *solution*. Designation: N.)

Forms of solution correspond exactly to the forms of task. Certain tasks are completed before they are set, or before the time required by the person assigning the task.

XXVII. THE HERO IS RECOGNIZED. (Definition: *recognition*. Designation: Q.)

He is recognized by a mark, a brand, or by a thing given to him. In this case, recognition serves as a function corresponding to branding and marking. The hero is also recognized by his accomplishment of a difficult task. Finally, the hero may be recognized immediately after a long period of separation. In the latter case, parents and children, brothers and sisters, etc., may recognize one another.

XXVIII. THE FALSE HERO OR VILLAIN IS EXPOSED. (Definition: *exposure*. Designation: Ex.)

This function is, in most cases, connected with the one preceding. Sometimes it is the result of an uncompleted task. Most often, it is presented in the form of a story. Sometimes a song is sung telling of what has occurred and exposing the villain.

XXIX. THE HERO IS GIVEN A NEW APPEARANCE. (Definition: *transfiguration*. Designation: T.)

A new appearance is directly effected by means of the magical action of the helper (T^1). The hero builds a marvelous palace (T^2), or he puts on new garments (T^3). There might also be rationalized and humorous forms (T^4). Actual changes in appearance do not take place in these cases, but a new appearance is achieved by deception: false evidence of wealth and beauty is accepted as true evidence.

XXX. THE VILLAIN IS PUNISHED. (Definition: *punishment*. Designation: U.)

The villain is shot, banished, tied to the tail of a horse, commits suicide, and so forth. In parallel with this we sometimes have a magnanimous pardon (U neg).

XXXI. THE HERO IS MARRIED AND ASCENDS THE THRONE. (Definition: *wedding*. Designation: W.)

1. A bride and a kingdom are awarded at once, or the hero receives half the kingdom at first, and the whole kingdom upon the death of his parents (W^{**}).
2. Sometimes the hero simply marries without obtaining a throne, since his bride is not a princess (W^*).
3. Sometimes only accession to the throne is mentioned (W^*).
4. If a new act of villainy interrupts a tale shortly before a wedding, then the first move ends with a betrothal, or a promise of marriage (w^1).
5. The hero sometimes receives a reward or some other compensation in place of the princess' hand (w^o).

At this point the tale draws to a close. It should also be stated that there are several actions of tale heroes in individual cases which do not conform to, nor are defined by, any

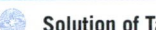
Solution of Task

Recognition

Example of Recognition:
The golden shoe fits Cinderella perfectly. The prince then looks at her face carefully and confirms that she is the bride he is seeking.

Exposure

Example of Exposure:
In "The Goose Girl," the King exposes the false bride at the wedding banquet (Ch. 36, p. 531).

Transfiguration

Example of Transfiguration:
In "The Goose Girl," when the old King learns that she is really a princess, he has her dressed in royal clothing so all will know her status (Ch. 36, p. 531).

Punishment

Example of Punishment:
In "Cinderella," pigeons pick out the eyes of the stepsisters.

Wedding

Examples of Wedding:
- Cinderella marries the prince
- In "The Raven," the man who rescues the princess marries her (Ch. 36, p. 534)
- In "The Frog Prince," the princess, who "rescues" the prince, marries him

of the functions already mentioned. They are either forms which cannot be understood without comparative material, or they are forms transferred from tales of other classes (anecdotes, legends, etc.). We define these as unclear elements and designate them with the sign X.

Just what are the conclusions that may be drawn from the foregoing observations? First of all, a few general inferences. We observe that, actually, the number of functions is quite limited. Only some 31 functions may be noted. The action of all tales included in our material develops within the limits of these functions. The same may also be said for the action of a great many other tales of the most dissimilar peoples. Further, if we read through all of the functions, one after another, we observe that one function develops out of another with logical and artistic necessity. We see that not a single function excludes another. They all belong to a single axis and not to a number of axes.

Now we shall give several individual, though highly important deductions. We observe that a large number of functions are arranged in pairs (prohibition-violation, reconnaissance-delivery, struggle-victory, pursuit-deliverance, etc.). Other functions may be arranged according to groups. Thus villainy, dispatch, decision for counteraction, and departure from home (ABC↑), constitute the complication. Elements DEF also form something of a whole. Alongside these combinations there are some individual functions (absentations, punishment, marriage, etc.).

Combining Sequences of Functions to Make a More Complex Tale

Now that the main elements of the tale have been indicated and several attendant features have been clarified, we may proceed to break down the texts into their components.

First of all, at this point the question arises as to what is meant by a tale.

Morphologically, a tale may be termed any development proceeding from villainy (A) or a lack (a), through intermediary functions to marriage (W*), or to other functions employed as a denouement. Terminal functions are at times a reward (F), a gain or in general the liquidation of misfortune (K), an escape from pursuit (Rs), etc. This type of development is termed by us a **move.**

Each new act of villainy, each new lack creates a new move. **One tale may have several moves,** and when analyzing a text, one must first of all determine the number of moves of which it consists. One move may directly follow another, but they may also interweave; a development which has begun pauses, and a new move is inserted. Singling out a move is not always an easy matter, but it is always possible with complete exactitude. Special devices of parallelism, repetitions, etc., lead to the fact that one tale may be composed of several moves.

The combination of moves may be as follows:

1. One move directly follows another. An approximate scheme of such combinations is:

    I. A ————— W*

        II. A ——— W²

2. A new move begins before the termination of the first one. Action is interrupted by an episodic move. After the completion of the episode, the completion of the first move follows as well. The scheme is:

    I. A ————— G . . . . K ———— W*

        II. a ———————— K

3. An episode may also be interrupted in its turn, and in this case fairly complicated schemes may result.

⚙ Conclusions

- Propp's functions cover actions in all of his tales, and a great many others
- Functions always develop logically from other functions
- No function excludes another
- Many functions are arranged in pairs or groups. (For more on this, see Introduction, p. 500.)

⚙ What Is Meant by a Tale?

move Any development proceeding from Villainy (A) or lack (a) through . . . to marriage (W) or other terminal function (F, K, or Rs). Each new lack creates a new move.

"One tale may have several moves"—For an illustration of this, see the Proppian analysis of *The Wizard of Oz,* Ch. 35, p. 514.

⚙ Different Combinations of Moves

Walter Crane, illustration for *"The Frog Prince,"* 1882. This story can be viewed from the point of view of the princess or the prince. However, the pictured scene is unequivocal: the initial misfortune is liquidated as the prince returns to his original form.

I._____ . . . . _____ . . . .

II. _____ . . . . _____

III. _____

4. A tale may begin with two villainies at once, of which the first one may be liquidated completely before the other is. If the hero is killed and a magical agent is stolen from him, then first of all the murder is liquidated, and then the theft is liquidated also.

A_2^{14} {I._____ K^9

{II. . . . . ._____ K^1

5. Two moves may have a common ending.

I. _____ . . . .} _____

II. _____}

6. Sometimes a tale contains two seekers. The heroes part in the middle of the first move. They usually part with omens at a road marker. This road marker serves as a disuniting element. (Parting at a road marker we shall designate by the sign <. Sometimes, however, the road marker amounts to a simple accessory.) On parting, the heroes often give one another a signaling object; we shall designate the transference of a signaling object with the sign Y. The schemes of such tales are:

II._____ . . . .}

I._____ <Y } _____

. . . . .III._____}

These are the chief methods of combining moves.

Further Reading

Propp, Vladimir. *The Morphology of the Folktale*. Ed. Louis A. Wagner, trans. Laurence Scott. Austin, TX: University of Texas Press, 1968.

35

A Proppian Analysis of *The Wizard of Oz*

WHAT TO EXPECT . . . The classic film, *The Wizard of Oz,* is based on the novel, *The Wonderful Wizard of Oz,* by L. Frank Baum. The movie differs from the book because of creative choices made by the movie's writers and directors. These innovations actually give the movie mythical dimensions that are lacking in the book, and students of mythology can find in it many of the characteristics of the traditional fairy tale. Because of this, you can apply the techniques of Proppian analysis to compare the film with the novel or with other stories. For a detailed explanation of Proppian analysis, see Chapter 34, p. 499.

In this chapter, you will see that the Proppian functions, moves, and sphere of action are present, but may not always occur in the order presented by Propp. At times a single moment in the film may contain a couple of Proppian moves, while at other times, a single move may play out over the course of several events. As you practice, compare the elements of this analysis with the explanations by Propp in Chapter 34.

Although *The Wizard of Oz* was made in 1939, its appeal has endured through several generations; it is often shown on television and is today regarded as a classic. Because many people in our culture are familiar with this movie, a discussion of it should bring back familiar images for many readers. Our discussion of the film is intended both to shed light on its structure and appeal, and give you practice with using Proppian analysis and weighing the sorts of decisions it calls for. As will be shown, subjecting *The Wizard of Oz* to Proppian analysis highlights the fairy tale nature of the movie: it has an elaborate, but quite standard structure, as defined by Propp. This fact in itself provides a clue to long-standing appeal of the film.

Although *The Wizard of Oz* is based on a children's story, it is not, in the strict sense, a folk- or fairy tale. Unlike folk- and fairy tales, the movie was not handed down through oral tradition, so we might not have been able to apply the same methods of analysis to it that work with folktales. However, it turns out that the development of the movie underwent a process of refining and honing that could be considered analogous to the kind of shaping that folktales undergo as they are passed from person to person. Before it was finished, the film used the talents of ten writers,[1] who worked in collaboration with a variety of directors, producers, and actors, reshap-

---

[1] The screen credits read, "Screenplay by Noel Langley, Florence Ryerson, and Edgar Allen Woolf. Adaptation by Noel Langley." However the writers assigned to the film (not all of whom made contributions to the script) were: Herman Mankiewitz, Ogden Nash, Noel Langley, Herbert Fields, Samuel Hoffenstein, Florence Ryerson, Edgar Allen Wolf, Jack Mintz, Sid Silvers, and John Lee Mahin. In addition, contributions were made by director Mervyn LeRoy, producer Arthur Freed, lyricist Yip Harburg, and others.

ing the script dozens of times, adding and subtracting whole scenes and characters. This process of retelling and reshaping the story both to fit the new teller's concerns and interests, and to generalize its appeal to increased numbers of listeners resembles the evolution of a folktale.

The movie is based on *The Wonderful Wizard of Oz* by L. Frank Baum. This book, however, does not have a well-developed Proppian structure. Much of the story consists of inconsequential Proppian moves. Over and over, Dorothy and her companions travel to a new part of Oz, meet an obstacle, a monster or a new group of fantastic people, and solve some problem associated with it. These travels are all in the context of Dorothy's need to get home, but the story is structured as a series of more or less independent episodes. The movie, in contrast, is about one main problem that Dorothy spends the whole movie trying to solve: how to get from Oz home to Kansas.

As the screenplay evolved, the story was pushed increasingly toward the characteristics of a traditional fairy tale. Why did this happen? As in the oral tradition, it was not the case, as far as we know, that the tellers consciously shaped the story toward a traditional structure. Rather, this was the structure they were familiar with, and as successful writers, their instincts suggested that it was this structure that would appeal to the greatest number of people. As we view the result of their efforts, we see that the instincts of the writers were correct,[2] and that *The Wizard of Oz* has endured precisely because its story was shaped toward a structure that people know and love.

At the same time, the appeal of the movie can also be ascribed to its novelty. It was not just a humble fairy tale; it was a technicolor extravaganza. With its shift from the opening black and white scenes in Kansas to the glorious full color of the scenes in Oz, the movie highlights the rich, sensuous effects we as modern audiences find delightful in the media of film and television. In addition, the movie provides just enough in the way of special effects that it feels modern despite the considerable technical progress since 1939.

Another feature contributing to the popularity of the movie is that, unlike the book, it was written for a variety of audiences, both adults and children. In a way reminiscent of modern children's shows like *Sesame Street, The Wizard of Oz* has appeal on multiple levels, incorporating as it does elements of musical comedy, vaudeville, burlesque, and slapstick with the more conventionally "uplifting" material often considered suitable for children. Baum intended his story for children and counted on the willing suspension of disbelief that children typically bring to such stories. However, the movie was designed to appeal to whole families and thus included a variety of jokes and routines that would be more comprehensible to adults. In addition, the scriptwriters developed a whole new opening segment of the movie in Kansas to rationalize the fantasy elements and make them acceptable to adults. (The initial Kansas scenes are discussed on pp. 519–20; the rationalization process that often takes place in myth is discussed on p. 20.)

THE MEANING OF *THE WIZARD OF OZ*

Over the years, there has been much study and debate devoted to the meaning of L. Frank Baum's book, *The Wonderful Wizard of Oz*. Although the focus here is on the 1939 movie *The Wizard of Oz,* considering Baum's intentions in the book may help us understand the movie better. The most prominent theories about Baum note the relationship between the green of the

---

[2]Not everyone agrees that the process was a successful one. Aljean Harmetz wrote in *The Making of the Wizard of Oz* that in adapting Baum's book, the production team "coarsened" it and damaged Baum's original concept by turning the story into a dream (36, 39). Critics were not uniformly enthusiastic either. Russel Maloney wrote in *The New Yorker* that the film was a "stinkeroo" and displayed "no trace of imagination, good taste, or ingenuity" (Harmetz, 21).

Emerald City and the color of money. Accordingly, the book has been taken as a parable about the dangers of departing from a gold standard, or an appeal to return to more simple agrarian values. However, William Leach has pointed out that L. Frank Baum was a showman and a salesman, much like the Wizard himself, and that, rather than decrying the values of Oz and the Emerald City, Baum seems to have been admiring of them. Leach points to the novel's contrast between the drabness of Kansas and the multicolored splendor of Oz. Although Dorothy does not want to remain in Oz, it continues to be the land of her dreams even when she returns home to Kansas. The addition of the Miss Gulch–Toto storyline highlights the difficulty of life in Kansas even more than the book did, and the movie emphasizes the desirability of Oz by having Dorothy sing of her imagined dreamland while in Kansas. The effect is that *The Wizard of Oz* emphasizes the wonders of modern urban life and the colorful array of goods and services it can make available to us. This aspect of the movie can be seen particularly in Dorothy's gawking at the splendors of the Emerald City and in the neat assembly line that cleans and beautifies her and her friends before they see the Wizard.

In addition to Baum's interest in showmanship and consumerism, his other writings suggest that he admired two philosophical ideas that can be found in *The Wonderful Wizard of Oz:* he valued a movement called theosophy and was a strong believer in equal rights for women. Theosophy teaches that human beings can achieve happiness if they recognize and learn to tap the goodness and the talents that they already possess. This idea can certainly be found throughout Baum's book and survives into its adaptation into the movie. Dorothy and her companions eventually achieve what they are seeking by discovering that it has always been present inside themselves. This includes the brains, heart, and courage sought by her companions, as well as Dorothy's own desire to get home, which is eventually satisfied by using the ruby slippers correctly when her desire to go home is strong enough.

Also, Baum's concern for women's rights is apparent both in the book and in the movie. Throughout the story, women are treated on a par with men. Oz is a kingdom run by both men and women, some good and some bad. Dorothy requires a lot of help in her adventures, and she also requires rescuing on occasion. However, in the end, it is she who destroys the Wicked Witch, and often it is her job to rescue her companions. Of the longings and aspirations of all the characters, it is Dorothy's goals that the story treats with the greatest reverence. Even the end of the story reflects Baum's concerns with gender equality. He wanted to avoid ending his story with a wedding, as old-fashioned fairy tales did, in part because he thought that such automatic unions were unfair to women.

To these ideas of Baum, the writers at MGM added a variety of other feelings and concepts that can still be detected in the movie. Ryerson and Woolf, the team of writers who worked most on the script after Noel Langley, believed that it was lacking in emotion. One of their contributions was to emphasize the theme of "There's no place like home" throughout the movie. The Dorothy of Baum's book also wants to return to Kansas, but her expressions of this desire do not contain any sentimentalization or generalization about the importance of home. After the departure of Ryerson and Woolf, Yip Harburg, the movie's lyricist (who is not usually included in the list of the movie's ten writers), worked to blend their contributions with those of the first writer, Noel Langley. One of Harburg's main contributions was the scene in which the Wizard gives the Scarecrow a diploma, the Tin Woodsman a testimonial, and the Lion a medal. Harburg was less of a sentimentalist than Ryerson and Woolf, and viewed these elements as expressing the "satiric and cynical idea of the Wizard handing out symbols because I was so aware of our lives being the images of things rather than the things themselves" (Harmetz, 58). It is ironic that these cynical touches blended so well with Baum's more uplifting theosophical principles. Although the film contains a variety of different points of view, it nonetheless ends up seeming like a unified, if complicated, work of art.

One of the most interesting aspects of *The Wizard of Oz* has been its significance for homosexual audiences. Although, as far as we know, this effect was not intended by the film's writers, the story of Dorothy working in close concert with her trio of male companions is likened by homosexuals to the interaction of a group of gay men with a strong female figure. Dorothy is stronger than her companions, and they are able to rely on her for help; her ability to support her companions can be taken to refer to the greater acceptability to society of a heterosexual orientation. At the same time, the story is not developed as a romance with a wedding at the end, so gay men can identify with Dorothy's companions without her intruding on their fantasies about each other. Thus, L. Frank Baum's intention of promoting gender equality has resulted in a story that is also more open to gender preference. The connection homosexuals have felt with the movie and with Dorothy has been generalized to an identification with the star who played her. Judy Garland has through the years served as an important icon for gay ritual and spectacle: dressing up as Judy is such a standard element of many a drag queen's repertoire that by now it represents a cliché in gay culture. Some people see a more serious link between the star and the gay community in the fact that the Stonewall riots, which are considered the birth of the gay liberation movement, began on June 27, 1969, the day of Judy Garland's funeral.

HOW TO PERFORM A PROPPIAN ANALYSIS

In Chapter 34 (p. 499), we explain that, according to Propp, a folktale will consist of a series of functions, from "A" or "a," an initial harm or a lack, to "W," a wedding or other ceremony suggesting the transfer of power from generation to generation; typically the wedding occurs in circumstances that suggest that the initial lack or harm was liquidated. The functions are actions or events whose designations are roughly in alphabetical order. As the story is told, however, the sequence of functions can undergo various groupings and repetitions. The story may even start over in the middle, with a new A and a new sequence of functions to resolve it, again in alphabetical order. However, each story will not have all the functions in Propp's list.

Thus, it may seem that a Proppian analysis of a folktale is simply a matter of identifying the code letters that pertain to the actions of the story. However, although Proppian analysis is rather straightforward, looking only for the elements listed in the functions can cause trouble. For example, every wedding in a story is not necessarily a W. The wedding at the beginning of "Rumpelstiltskin" must be thought of as a misfortune that comes to the miller's daughter because of her father's bragging. She is forced to marry the king, who believes she can spin straw into gold and continues to call upon her to do so. By any account, this is a misfortune, not a joyous occasion, whether we look at it as her marrying a man who does not see her true talents for what they are, or as simply the practical problem of her being asked to do something she doesn't know how to do.

Some preliminary steps are necessary to a successful Proppian analysis, and the first of these is to identify the main *dramatis personae* of the story. This Latin term means "actors" and refers to the main generic categories of characters in the story: hero, villain, donor, false hero, victim, and so forth. Each of these *dramatis personae* will have a sphere of action including some of the functions and not others. For instance, in the beginning of "Rumpelstiltskin," the miller, who brags that his daughter can spin straw into gold, is a villain, so he cannot cause a happy function like W. However, A is within his sphere of action as a villain and is appropriately assigned to the wedding that takes place there.

After identifying the *dramatis personae,* we need to look for the lack or harm in the story. Each time there is a new lack or harm, a new sequence of functions, a move, starts in the story, and should be traceable to its conclusion. As explained in Chapter 34 (p. 504), the causes of a lack or harm can be explained in great detail in the story, or they can simply pop up without much motivation at all. The story can begin, "Jack woke up one morning and set out to seek his fortune." No reason for the lack is given; it is simply how the story begins. In other stories, the lack or harm can be provided with an elaborate explanation in the form of a series of actions by a villain. As already mentioned, the harm in "Rumpelstiltskin" is the miller's daughter being married to the king, who believes she can spin straw into gold. A large part of the beginning of the story consists of nothing but background information explaining how this lack or harm came about; Propp calls this the "Preparatory Part." For a successful Proppian analysis, we need to identify the lack or harm, and identify any Preparatory Part that caused it.

One other point arises as a problem for newcomers to Proppian analysis: it is not always clear when to assign a new function. It may help to understand that functions are not evenly distributed throughout the story. It is tempting to try to assign a function to every paragraph or so, but this is not how Proppian analysis works. Rather, some functions take a long time to be completed in the story, while others can be represented by a single word, or several functions may be included in the same sentence or group of words. For example, there are four functions in the single sentence, "Jack woke up one morning and set out to seek his fortune:"

- a (lack)—Jack noticed he was poor.
- B (connective incident)—The departure is prepared for; although it is not mentioned in the story, Jack presumably considered his choices.
- C (counteraction)—Jack decided to leave home to seek his fortune. This also is not specifically mentioned in the story, but it is implied by his setting out.
- ↑ (departure)—Jack left home.

On the other hand, the fulfillment of a single function can take a long time. For example, in *The Wizard of Oz,* the Wizard gives Dorothy the task of bringing back the broom of the Wicked Witch of the West. The next twenty minutes or so are taken up with fulfilling this task. This whole section of the movie consists of only one function, N, the fulfillment of a difficult task.

Quick Greek Primer for Use with Propp's Functions

α	alpha	ϵ	epsilon
β	beta	ζ	zeta ("ZAY-ta")
γ	gamma	η	eta ("AY-ta")
δ	delta	θ	theta

Small variations in order do not affect the status of the Proppian analysis. However, if many of the functions are very far from their standard order, it may be necessary to conclude that the story is not a traditional fairy tale. For example, in the Preparatory Part of *The Wizard of Oz,* the actual order of functions is $\alpha\beta\epsilon\zeta\eta\theta\gamma\delta$, not the standard $\alpha\beta\gamma\delta\epsilon\zeta\eta\theta$. That is, we do not hear about the interdiction which Dorothy has violated ($\gamma\delta$) until after Miss Gulch appears with the sheriff's order and takes Toto ($\epsilon\zeta\eta\theta$). This variation is small enough to have no significance. In addition, the change can be explained by Miss Gulch's use of a flashback to report earlier events. You will see in the analysis, however, that we do not rearrange the functions into the proper order; the analysis should report them in the order found in the story, without rearranging the story.

To summarize, therefore, we would say that a Proppian analysis should consist of the following steps:

1. Read through the whole story before you start analyzing it. Don't try to figure it out as you read the first time; this will lead to the misidentifications we described before.
2. Identify the *dramatis personae.*
3. Look for the harm(s) or lack(s) in the story.

4. Identify the Preparatory Part(s), which are the section(s) of the story that come before the lack(s) or harm(s).

5. Fill in the appropriate functions in each part of the story, to correspond to the spheres of influence of the *dramatis personae*.

THE KANSAS OPENING SCENES: A PROBLEM FOR PROPPIAN ANALYSIS

The Kansas portion of Baum's book is brief and bleak; there are only six pages before Dorothy is whisked away by the tornado and finds herself in Oz. Martin Gardner noted that the word "gray" is used nine times in four paragraphs (*The Annotated Wizard of Oz,* 19). For the most part, the movie is easier to analyze as a fairy tale than the book. However, the opening of the movie greatly expands the Kansas section of the book by introducing a series of new scenes. At the beginning of the movie, Dorothy is in Kansas, living with her Uncle Henry and Auntie Em and her dog, Toto. Even before the difficulties about Toto come to a head and create the standard problems found in a Proppian preparatory section, Dorothy is listless and unhappy in these scenes, as reflected by her singing "Somewhere Over the Rainbow," in which she expresses an undefined yearning for a happier place.

The initial scene in Kansas represents a major contribution on the part of the scriptwriters of the movie. However, writer Noel Langley felt that the modern view of fantasy required grounding the Oz elements of the movie in a realistic portrait of the world: "You cannot put fantastic people in front of an audience unless they have seen them as human beings first." Consequently he expanded the Kansas scene and included in it real-world versions of the main characters whom Dorothy would meet in Oz, including Miss Gulch, the scarecrow, and the tin woodsman (Harmetz, 34).

However, in doing a Proppian analysis of *The Wizard of Oz,* we find that the newly added Kansas scenes introduce some complications. The movie changes the contribution of Kansas from providing merely a preparatory section to being a whole separate move of the story with its

Judy Garland as Dorothy, in the barnyard of her home in Kansas, singing "Somewhere Over the Rainbow." The movie expands this part of the story, so it represents a major deviation from the pacing of the story as written by L. Frank Baum. The segment, in black and white, emphasizes the bleakness of Dorothy's life at this point, but the song, which was an afterthought, gives the episode its particular character, and greatly contributes to the popularity of the film.

own villain, lack, and resolution. In this Kansas move of the movie, the real-world versions of the Oz characters represent different *dramatis personae* than they do in Oz. The following chart shows the shifts in the *dramatis personae* of the movie:

Kansas	Oz
Hero: Dorothy	Hero: Dorothy
Villain: Miss Gulch	Villain: Wicked Witch of the West
Donor: Professor Marvel	Donors: Scarecrow, Tin Woodsman, Cowardly Lion
	False Hero: Wizard

The shift of characters in a story to different *dramatis personae* during different moves is not unusual in Proppian analysis, but in many cases it seems to represent changes in the story caused by oral composition; that is, as the story passes from teller to teller, it acquires new features that don't quite fit with its previous elements. Here, however, the shift is caused by a deliberate attempt of the storytellers to fit the fairy tale into a more believable or logical context.

This is actually ironic because, in writing his story, L. Frank Baum intended to produce a new kind of fairy tale, one that would seem more believable to his readers. This caused him *not* to represent the scenes in Oz as a dream sequence. He wanted them to seem real to emphasize the presence of magic in our everyday lives, and not just our dreams. However, his presentation did not fit with what the screenwriters of *The Wizard of Oz* considered acceptable to their audience.

OTHER ISSUES RELATING TO A PROPPIAN ANALYSIS OF *THE WIZARD OF OZ*

Having determined the *dramatis personae* of each part of the story, it only remains to locate the harm(s) or lack(s) to figure out the number of moves in the story. As mentioned before, the opening segment in Kansas contains its own lack: Miss Gulch takes away Toto. Toto returns, but Dorothy realizes that Miss Gulch will return again to take him. At this point, Dorothy realizes she lacks the power to keep Toto while staying with her aunt and uncle. This lack is never clearly resolved by the movie. At the end, Dorothy is happy to be home, and her aunt is tender toward her. Toto's precarious situation never comes up. We may be supposed to assume that, like the Wicked Witch of the East, Miss Gulch has been killed by the tornado, so that Toto is now safe from her evil plans. Or perhaps Auntie Em, relieved that Dorothy is all right, will work harder at defending her niece's need to keep her dog. Or maybe Dorothy will work harder at keeping track of Toto and make the issue moot. The earlier situation is not resolved, but there is an implication at the end of the story that things are less bleak and that Dorothy now has the power she lacked at the beginning. This kind of incomplete settling of the problems of a story is not atypical of fairy tales, where the overall effect is more important than the logical resolution of every aspect of the tale.

Once in Oz, Dorothy experiences a second lack: she is away from home and wishes she could return. This lack is resolved at the end of the story, when Dorothy uses the ruby slippers to return to Kansas. This second lack constitutes the second and final move of the story.

The Wizard of Oz, then, consists of two moves, one set in Kansas, and a second, embedded in the first, set in Oz. The Oz move achieves complete resolution, while the Kansas move has some unresolved elements at the end. However, the disappearance from the final scene of Miss Gulch, the villain of the Kansas move, suggests that this move as well has achieved some kind of resolution, and this is confirmed by Dorothy's pronouncement at the end that "There's no place like home."

With these elements sketched out for ourselves, we are ready to embark on a full-scale Proppian analysis of *The Wizard of Oz*.

Dorothy lives in Kansas, on a farm run by her Auntie Em and Uncle Henry. She has a dog, Toto, who has a tendency to run off after rabbits.

At the beginning of the movie, Dorothy is out walking. When she comes into the yard, **she encounters Hickory,** Hunk, and Zeke, three farm hands who serve as real-world counterparts to the Tin Woodsman, Scarecrow, and the Cowardly Lion in the Oz part of the story. When she gets in the house, Dorothy discovers that Miss Gulch is there talking to her Auntie Em. This is why her Aunt has called her in.

As Dorothy listens, Miss Gulch produces an order from the sheriff to take Toto. Dorothy tries to get Toto to run away, but he comes when he hears the sound of her voice. Miss Gulch takes Toto.

From the discussion that results, we gather that Dorothy has been told to keep Toto away from Miss Gulch, but she has not always been successful at this. Apparently, Toto got away and barked and snapped at Miss Gulch, and this has caused her to seek the sheriff's order to have him destroyed.

Miss Gulch takes Toto away in a basket, but he escapes and returns to Dorothy.

Dorothy realizes that Miss Gulch will come back and take Toto again. To keep her dog safe, she must run away. She packs a suitcase and leaves.

She reaches the wagon of Professor Marvel, a traveling performer who at first seems annoyed to see her, but she persists in talking to him and he finally agrees to tell her fortune. They go into his wagon and he has her close her eyes.

Upon peeking into Dorothy's basket and finding a picture of Auntie Em, Professor Marvel describes for Dorothy a vision of her aunt putting her hand to her heart and falling to the ground in grief that Dorothy has run away. Dorothy is filled with an urgent desire to go home.

Dorothy hurries home, arriving just as a tornado is on the verge of hitting the farm. Her family has been looking for her, but has just given up and gone into the storm cellar. She can't get the door of the storm cellar open, so she rushes inside, arriving in her room carrying Toto, just as the storm hits. The tornado picks up the house and whirls it about in the air.

In the ensuing action, several things happen at more or less the same time. The house lands with a thud. When Dorothy steps out of it, she discovers that she has arrived in a magical, colorful land. She also discovers that her house has feet sticking out from under it. It has landed on and killed someone. She soon meets Glinda and the Munchkins and learns that she is in Oz, and that her house has fallen on the Wicked Witch of the East, setting the Munchkins free from their evil ruler.

The Wicked Witch of the West appears and wants to take the ruby slippers from her dead sister's feet, but at Glinda's instruction, Dorothy puts them on herself. Eventually, at the end of the story, the slippers allow Dorothy to go home. However, for most of the story, their function is to show people that she is special. Glinda tells Dorothy that she has acquired a powerful enemy in the Wicked Witch of the West.

Dorothy seems not to notice, but in arriving in Oz, she has now come to a land where she can remain and live safely without losing Toto.

Dorothy is offered the chance to remain as ruler of the Munchkins, but she wants to go home to Kansas. She questions Glinda and learns that the Wizard of Oz may be able to help her do this. So she sets off for the Emerald City, where he lives, to ask for his help. Glinda tells her that the path to take is the Yellow Brick Road. Dorothy starts off along the Yellow Brick Road.

Along the way, Dorothy finds herself involved in a conversation with a scarecrow who is fastened to a post beside the road. He is a challenge to talk to because he is easily confused; eventually the Scarecrow tells Dorothy that he wishes he had a brain. She agrees to let him come along on her journey so that he too may be able to get help from the Wizard of Oz.

Dorothy and the Scarecrow come upon a Woodsman made completely of tin. He has become paralyzed by rust; they oil him, enabling him to move again. The Tin Woodsman also

 Preparatory Part

α—Initial situation
β—Absentation

"she encounters Hickory"—No function: not every interesting part of the story necessarily corresponds to a function.

ϵ—Reconnaissance by the villain
ζ—Delivery of Dorothy to the villain
η—Trickery. The sheriff's order shows that Miss Gulch has already taken action against Toto.
θ—Villainy
γ—Interdiction
δ—Interdiction is violated

 First Move

a—Lack of a place to be where she can keep Toto
B—Connective incident
C—Counteraction
↑—Departure
D—Testing by a donor, Professor Marvel
E—Hero's reaction
F—Hero acquires a magical agent, the urgent desire to go home. She experiences this need throughout her travels.
G—Hero is transferred to a magical place, Oz
H—Combat with a villain. The encounter with each witch could be viewed as a separate combat, but we have combined them as two parts of the same incident.
I—Villain is defeated
J—Hero is branded. It may seem as if Glinda were a donor and the slippers a magical agent, but such an agent helps the hero accomplish a task, and the slippers do not do this. Rather, the slippers identify Dorothy as a special person.
K—The initial misfortune is liquidated.

Andy Warhol, *Myths (The Witch)*, 1981.

Second Move

a—Lack, of home
B—Connective incident
C—Counteraction
↑—Departure
D—Testing by a donor, the Scare-crow
E—Hero's reaction
F—Hero acquires a magical com-panion. The donor may provide help in the form of a helper who will assist the hero in his or her tasks.
D—Testing by a donor, the Woodsman
E—Hero's reaction
F—Hero acquires a magical com-panion
Pr—Pursuit
Rs—Rescue. These elements appear slightly out of order. This scene is here to remind us of the threat of the Wicked Witch while Dorothy is gathering her forces.
D—Testing by a donor, the Lion
E—Hero's reaction
F—Hero acquires a magical com-panion
Pr—Pursuit
Rs—Rescue. Some functions, like o and Q or Pr and Rs, tend to come in pairs. If the hero arrives unrecognized, sooner or later she will be recognized. If the hero is pursued, she is usually rescued.
o—Hero arrives unrecognized.
Q—Hero is recognized. Here the recognition is immediate. Often there is a greater interval, with other things occurring between these two functions.
L—Claims of the false hero, the Wizard

"he also asks to come along . . . "—We now have three donor cycles. Trebling, the tendency to form groups of three, often occurs in folk tales.

asks to come along on the journey to see the Wizard. His goal is to acquire a heart. Dorothy agrees to let him come along on her journey, and he joins her and the Scarecrow as they travel along the Yellow Brick Road.

The Wicked Witch of the West appears briefly, issuing threats at Dorothy and her compan-ions. This begins her pursuit of the group. She throws a ball of fire at the scarecrow. Dorothy and the Tin Woodsman put out the fire and the trio continue their trip.

The trio is menaced by a lion who threatens Toto. Dorothy immediately leaps to her dog's defense. The lion's attack collapses; it turns out that he is a great coward who is afraid of his own shadow. When he learns of the Wizard, **he also asks to come along** on the journey to acquire courage. Dorothy agrees to let him come along, and she and her three companions travel together toward the Emerald City.

Dorothy and her companions reach the enchanted field of sleepy poppies. The Wicked Witch, who has been tracking them in her crystal ball, knows they will be overcome by sleep, and has her winged monkeys circling overhead, ready to bring them to her when they succumb. However, the Scarecrow and the Tin Man are not affected by the poppies, and they call out for help. Glinda sends a snowstorm that awakens Dorothy and the Cowardly Lion, and they continue on their way. They reach the gate of the Emerald City but are unrecognized as no one answers their knock. When a guard finally opens the door, he doesn't want to let them in until Dorothy introduces herself and points out her ruby slippers, causing him to recognize her. After, this, they are immediately admitted and taken to a hall where they hear the voice of the Wizard. He agrees to grant them their wishes if they bring back the broomstick of the Wicked Witch of the West.

As Dorothy and her companions try to reach the witch's castle unnoticed, she and Toto are captured by the Witch. She tries to take the ruby slippers from Dorothy, but realizes they can only be removed at the girl's death. She gives Dorothy one hour to live. The Scarecrow and the Lion, trying to rescue Dorothy, disguise themselves as the Witch's guards and sneak into the castle. However, the Witch discovers them and attacks the Scarecrow with a flaming torch. When Dorothy throws a bucket of water to extinguish the flames, she misses and the water lands on the Witch, melting her and causing her death.

Returning with the Witch's broom, Dorothy asks the Wizard to keep his promise. The Wizard tries to delay doing so, and is eventually unmasked as a humbug. He is a little man behind a curtain who has been running a special effects machine, not the great and powerful Oz.

The Wizard now sets about fulfilling the wishes of Dorothy's companions. Actually, he explains that they have always had the talents they were requesting. He gives the Scarecrow a diploma, the Lion a medal, and the Tin Man a small clock in the shape of a heart. In each case, the Wizard declares that the gifts are intended as evidence of the talents they already have.

The Wizard intends to take Dorothy back to Kansas in the hot-air balloon that originally brought him to Oz. To replace his government, he leaves Dorothy's companions to rule Oz in his stead, calling upon them to use their newly discovered brains, heart, and courage. The Wizard climbs into the basket of the balloon and it sails away. Dorothy, however, is left behind as the balloon rises just as she is retrieving Toto, who has again run off.

Glinda now appears and tells a forlorn Dorothy that she has always had the ability to get home in the ruby slippers. At Glinda's instruction, she taps her heels together three times and keeps repeating "There's no place like home" until she is back in Kansas. She is in her bed and surrounded by the worried faces of the farm hands and her aunt and uncle. It seems as if she was injured or frightened in the tornado, but everything is all right now.

Thus, the complete analysis of the film *The Wizard of Oz* is as follows:

Move I. In Kansas: $\alpha\beta\epsilon\zeta\eta\theta\gamma\delta$
    aBC↑(Dorothy runs away)   DEF (Prof. Marvel)   G (to Oz)
    HIJ (Witch)   K

    or: aBC↑   DEF   G   HIJ   K

Move II. In Oz:
    aBC↑ (Dorothy decides to find the Wizard)   DEF (Scarecrow)
    DEF (Tin Man)   DEF (Lion)   PrRs (poppy field)   o (at the city gate)
    Q   L   MN (bring the Witch's broom)   ExU   W↓   K

    or: aBC↑   DEF   DEF   DEF   PrRs   oQ   L   MN   Ex   U   W↓   K

We can see that the film has the structure of a standard fairy tale; the standard structure is interrupted only by the dubious relationship of the worlds of Kansas and Oz, an element introduced into the story by writer Noel Langley's desire to overcome the skepticism of adult audiences by rationalizing the fantastic events of the plot in a realistic world, where they can take on the aspect of a delirious dream. Thus the doubt that remains at the end of the movie can be considered a deliberate antithesis to the fairy tale form, in an attempt to make the fairy tale itself as acceptable as possible to a resistant audience: it is the exception that proves the rule that the film gains its power by representing a traditional tale.

Further Reading

Harmetz, Aljean. *The Making of The Wizard of Oz.* New York, NY: Delta (Dell), 1977.

Second Move (continued)

M—Difficult task: bringing back the broom of the Witch
N—Accomplishment of the difficult task
Ex—False hero is exposed
U—False hero is punished. The Wizard loses his kingdom and is set adrift, presumably, to start over somewhere else.
W—This function often stands for a wedding, but Propp says it can also be represented by "a monetary reward or some other form of compensation." (See Ch. 34, p. 511.)
↓—Return
K—Liquidation of initial misfortune. This is not clearly spelled out; See Introduction, p. 520.

"As Dorothy and her companions try to reach the witch's castle unnoticed"—This long sequence is all the accomplishment of the difficult task. (See p. 517.)

36

Household Tales

WILHELM AND JAKOB GRIMM

WHAT TO EXPECT . . . Wilhelm and Jakob Grimm, philologists from a strong religious tradition, collected tales, edited them, and published revisions of their collections between 1812 and 1857. Their dual purposes—to preserve living artifacts from ancient times and to illustrate moral values and demonstrate the necessity for pious, moral behavior—is evident, especially in the tales in this chapter: "The Goose Girl," "The Raven," and "Faithful John." The marginal analysis of these stories includes techniques developed by Vladimir Propp (Ch. 34, p. 499), Claude Levi-Strauss (Ch. 20, p. 280), Carl Jung (Ch. 32, p. 468), Otto Rank (Introduction, Part 3, p. 155), and Victor Turner (Ch. 26, p. 373). It may be useful at this point to look back to the key elements of each analysis that figures in this chapter.

As you read, note how folktales often emphasize plot at the expense of character development, and point out the particulars of how the stories in this chapter enter the realm of myth by reflecting the inherent values of the audience. Compare the stories in this chapter to other traditional fairy tales you know, with a view to finding stories that have some of the same elements. Consider other stories you have read or seen that may have elements of a coming of age story like "The Goose Girl" or the inclusion of the hero or heroine's best friend like "Faithful John." What interpretive elements used in this chapter can you apply to these stories, to enrich your understanding of them?

Wilhelm and Jakob Grimm were the authors and editors of perhaps the most famous collection of folk and fairy tales in the modern Western tradition. They began collecting their *Children's and Household Stories* almost 200 years ago. They were born in the 1780s in Germany, and as they were growing up, their country fell under the control of France under Napoleon. Living under foreign rule caused a strong desire among their countrymen to look back to their old Germanic roots as a way of assessing their cultural worth.

Like many other learned people of their time, called Germany's Romantic period, the Grimms felt that collecting and publishing native works of literature and folk poetry was important for preserving their national spirit. This corresponded to a serious interest in the early periods of Germanic history and culture, and was intensified by translations of the old epic poems into modern German and publication of new novels and poetry imbued with the old themes. The Grimms saw fairy tales as a genre closely related to the epic poetry of the Middle Ages and earlier, and they were eager to bring to the forefront what they considered the most important reason for collecting and publishing—their firm beliefs concerning the spiritual life of their readers. However, they also viewed these stories as living artifacts from ancient times that continued to evolve according to the belief expectations of successive generations.

The process of bringing the fairy tales to light began with finding sources for the stories. Since the Grimm brothers lived in the area near Frankfurt-on-Main in Hesse, many of their tales come from that region. In recent years, our understanding of the brothers' methodology has changed quite a bit. Scholars used to believe that they operated much like anthropologists,

Jakob and Wilhelm Grimm.

traveling around and looking for peasant storytellers, and then arranging immediately to listen to them and write down the tales they recited. However, there is much evidence now that a few middle-class women, who were recognized for their storytelling talents, visited the brothers periodically and recited their stories several times, as Jakob and Wilhelm wrote them down.

There are additional reasons to think that the Grimms' tales are more literary versions than true folktales. The brothers collected all sorts of stories, including magical fairy tales, horror stories, tall tales, and comical accounts. We know from their introductions to the many editions of their collection that their intent was to "awaken the thoughts of the heart." From their first edition in 1812, they kept revising the texts and notes until the seventh and final edition was published in 1857. By late in the nineteenth century, the book took its place as a true best seller.

Education was one of the main reasons that fairy tales were collected, edited, and published: like earlier European collectors, the Grimm brothers wished to provide their readership with models of the moral values of society. However, unlike their predecessors, the Grimms were very much influenced by the ideals of Romanticism. In fact, we might say that Romanticism is the critical environment for the tales. The philosophy of this movement looked back to what people considered a less complicated life, highlighted by more basic—or natural—human qualities. These fundamental values are what the Grimms' villains repeatedly violate. As we study the tales, we see that growth in charity is an integral part of the characters' development: improving oneself means being natural, displaying the kind of caring and love that arises from one's internal spiritual well-being. Examples of this include parents sacrificing for their children, as well as characters helping those in need and striving to improve their own willingness to care about others.

However, there is a more personal aspect of the Grimms' selecting and editing, one that is consistent with their beliefs. In *The Owl, the Raven and the Dove,* G. Ronald Murphy shows that Wilhelm and Jakob incorporated elements of three major Western belief systems that were important to their audience (Classical Greek, Medieval Germanic, and Christian): he points out that many elements in the Western tradition originated in ancient times and were reworked through the years according to the expectations of the audience. This reworking is obvious in the motifs and situations in many of the Grimm stories. For example, Wilhelm, who was the primary editor, reworked earlier versions of "Little Red Riding Hood" from edition to edition, refining artistic aspects, as well as adding elements that were very important to his Christian beliefs, especially the concept of spiritual love. As you read "Faithful John," take note of the assimilation of the ancient Greek, the Germanic, and the Christian traditions that were certainly key for the Grimm brothers, and expected by the majority of their readers. (For a discussion of the power of audience expectations, see the Introduction to Anne Sexton's "Snow White," Ch. 42, p. 637.)

Household Stories has become a worldwide success and has influenced collectors in many other cultures to preserve the artistic folk heritage as part of their people's intellectual culture. The Grimms' stories are familiar to most of us from versions found in animated Disney films and illustrated books for children. We might even say that the brothers created genuine classics that continue to provide a connection with the interior life as well as to "awaken the thoughts of the heart."

FAIRY TALE AS MYTH

In some ways, fairy tales are different from the myths of ancient peoples found throughout this book.[1] The genre of the fairy tale shares elements with both the oral tradition of the folktale and the more consciously structured tradition of literary circles found throughout Europe. In seventeenth-century France in particular, small gatherings of people met to develop their language skills and to refine the art of storytelling. Such gatherings provided a popular activity for women as well as men. The groups were called *salons,* from the French word for the type of room where they met.

Salon participants wrote and reworked stories they knew from the general practice of storytelling, but they did not have a folklorist's interest in maintaining the integrity of the stories they were telling. Thus they were content to rationalize the stories as they reworked them, adding characters and events, and changing the emphasis of the stories in many cases to reflect their own values and ethics. In French circles, this code was called *civilité,* a kind of standard for morally and socially correct living. The fairy tales that had their origins in the salons were then told again and again, and were collected and dispersed widely by literary collectors like Charles Perrault. His major collection appeared just at the end of the seventeenth century and contained such stories as "Little Red Riding Hood," "Cinderella," and "Sleeping Beauty."

The tales by Perrault and many other writers became part of a general body of storytelling material and were carried over linguistic, social, and geographical borders throughout Europe. The audiences of these tales were varied in their views of the world and moral beliefs, and storytellers altered the tales to fulfill their expectations. By this process of reworking and retelling, the fairy tale enters the realm of myth: the story takes on elements that reflect the values of the audience, and retellings spread the message of those values to contemporaries as well as to future generations. However, through the process of revision in the literary setting of its time, the stories published by the Grimm brothers developed a more sophisticated writing style and a more logical structure than can be expected in a genuine folktale.

The process of reshaping fairy tales continues today, although the writing and revising of literary fairy tales for adults is no longer a popular pastime in our society. Current American versions of the Grimms' tales have been reworked primarily for children. In this process, the tales have been revised to minimize or eliminate the violence and bloodshed in their nineteenth-century versions. For example, in the Grimms' story, one of Cinderella's stepsisters cuts off her heel and the other her toes to fit into the slipper that the Prince has brought to determine his true bride. And in the same story, birds peck out the eyes of the sisters as punishment for their wickedness. These changes reflect the fact that many in our society believe that children should be shielded from the more brutal facts of grown-up life.

---

[1] For more on the distinctions between these two forms of stories, see the introduction to the work of Vladimir Propp, who studied Russian folktales, Ch. 34, p. 499.

However, some have defended the violent aspects of the tales collected by the Grimm brothers; psychologist Bruno Bettelheim argues in *The Uses of Enchantment* that this element of fairy tales provides an outlet for feelings that are an important component of a child's upbringing. Bettelheim bases his theories on Sigmund Freud and on Otto Rank's concept of the *family romance*. According to this theory, the child is dissatisfied with its parents and fantasizes getting rid of them. According to Rank, these feelings correspond to an element found in many fairy tales, where the hero is rejected by his parents: it may be that a parent dies, or goes off to war (or, as in "The Raven," the child leaves the parent). According to Bettelheim, both parents and child win by the creation and telling of these stories, because both are set free by the symbolic representation of the feelings involved in these situations. Another prominent aspect of European fairy tales is the splitting of the mother figure into a kind, caring biological mother and a wicked, destructive stepmother. According to Bettelheim, this helps the child attribute good things to its "real" mother and assign guilt for bad events to a person of lesser importance.

The process of reshaping fairy tales for new audiences continues today, so that we can, by studying it, follow the development of our own mythological traditions. For example, Chapter 42, "Mythological Themes in Poetry," includes Anne Sexton's reimagined "Snow White" (p. 637), and Chapter 44, "Mythological Themes in Modern Narrative," includes "The Tiger's Bride," Angela Carter's modern retelling of "Beauty and the Beast" (p. 670). Carter's version features a much more active heroine who chooses to align herself with the beast because she is attracted to him. This shows that a "classical" fairy tale can be reworked very satisfactorily for a contemporary audience. Carter's story is also unusual for our time in being directed primarily at adults, as were the stories of the Grimm brothers.

The introduction to each of the individual tales incorporates various possible interpretations. Each highlights a possible point of view, although it should not be surprising that most of the tales can be interpreted from several perspectives. See Chapter 38 (p. 560) for a discussion of the insights to be gained from multiple analyses of a tale.

"The Goose Girl"

This selection from *Household Stories* can be viewed as a tale about growing up and the trials involved in the process. Victor Turner has suggested that tales like this one are comparable to the initiation ceremony that marks the child's transition from a subordinate state to the full rights and powers of adulthood. In such rites of passage, the candidates for adulthood are sequestered from the community and undergo a series of trials or ritual abuse in what is called the liminal or transitional point of the ceremony, before they are admitted to their new status in society. Similarly, in this tale, the Goose Girl leaves her home and family and undergoes a period of humiliation when she becomes a servant tending geese, and her own servant takes her place as the master. Such inversion of social roles is characteristic of the rite of passage (see Turner, Ch. 26, p. 375).

The following outline shows the progress of the action in a fairy tale involving a maturation and initiation cycle. It draws on some of the characteristics of the family romance as defined by Otto Rank (see Introduction to Part 3, p. 155).

1. The child is separated from her natural mother.
2. The mother tries to provide surrogate protection.
3. A substitute mother mistreats the child.
4. The child journeys far from home.
5. The child undergoes trials of separation. (Here, she is betrayed and loses her identity.)
6. The child is subjected to trials of her fortitude and virtue. (Here, she must work as a peasant despite her noble status, and she is pursued by her companion.)

These stories come from:
Grimm Brothers, *Household Stories*.*

7. The child stands the test. (Here, she is helped by nature: the wind blows Conrad's hat away and he must chase it.)
8. The child's true identity is discovered.
9. She assumes her rightful place in society.

There lived once an old Queen, whose husband had been dead many years. She had a beautiful daughter who was promised in marriage to a King's son living a great way off. When the time appointed for the wedding drew near, and the old Queen had to send her daughter into the foreign land, she got together many costly things, furniture and cups and jewels and adornments, both of gold and silver, everything proper for the dowry of a royal Princess, for she loved her daughter dearly.

She gave her also a waiting gentlewoman to attend her and to give her into the bridegroom's hands; and they were each to have a horse for the journey, and the Princess's horse was named **Falada, and he could speak.** When the time for parting came, the old Queen took her daughter to her chamber, and with a little knife she cut her own finger so that it bled; and she held beneath it a white napkin, and on it fell **three drops of blood;** and she gave it to her daughter, bidding her take care of it, for it would be needful to her on the way. Then they took leave of each other; and the Princess put the napkin in her bosom, got on her horse, and set out to go to the bridegroom. After she had ridden an hour, she began to feel very thirsty, and she said to the waiting-woman,

"Get down, and fill my cup that you are carrying with water from the brook; I have great desire to drink."

"Get down yourself," said the waiting-woman," and if you are thirsty stoop down and drink; I will not be your slave."

And as her thirst was so great, the **Princess** had to get down and to stoop and drink of the water of the brook, and **could not have her gold cup to serve her.** "Oh dear!" said the poor Princess. And the three drops of blood heard her, and said,

"If your mother knew of this, it would break her heart."

But the Princess answered nothing, and quietly mounted her horse again. So they rode on some miles farther; the day was warm, the sun shone hot, and the Princess grew thirsty once more. And when they came to a water-course she called again to the waiting-woman and said,

"Get down, and give me to drink out of my golden cup." **For she had forgotten all that had gone before.** But the waiting-woman spoke still more scornfully and said,

"If you want a drink, you may get it yourself; I am not going to be your slave."

So, as her thirst was so great, the Princess had to get off her horse and to stoop towards the running water to drink, and as she stooped, she wept and said,

"Oh dear!" And the three drops of blood heard her and answered,

"If your mother knew of this, it would break her heart!"

And as she drank and stooped over, **the napkin** on which were the three drops of blood fell out of her bosom and **floated down the stream,** and in her distress she never noticed it; not so the waiting-woman, who rejoiced because she should have power over the bride, who, now that she had lost the three drops of blood, had become weak, and unable to defend herself. And when she was going to mount her horse again the waiting-woman cried,

"Falada belongs to me, and this jade to you." And the Princess had to give way and let it be as she said. Then the waiting-woman ordered the Princess with many hard words to take off her rich clothing and to put on her plain garments, and then **she made her swear to say nothing of the matter** when they came to the royal court;

"Falada . . . could speak"—Animals with magical powers very often turn out to be helpers in fairy tales.

"three drops of blood"—The mother will protect the daughter even if her physical presence is limited to three drops of her blood. The drops of blood on a napkin hint at the onset of menstruation, and suggest that the time of the wedding represents a rite of passage for the girl as she moves into her adult role as a wife. (See Victor Turner, Ch. 26, p. 373.) L. Hinton notes that, in the legend of the Holy Grail, Perceval notices three drops of blood in the snow; they signal "a turning point in his development."

"Princess . . . could not have her gold cup to serve her"—The princess fails at her attempt to command her servant and will soon be deprived of the symbols of her royal status. This element of the story represents the little girl's reluctance to grow up.

"For she had forgotten all that had gone before."—This seems to be a phrase inserted by the storyteller to rationalize the events in the tale. (For an explanation of rationalization, see Ch. 7, p. 79.)

"the napkin . . . floated down the stream"—The princess loses the protection of her mother.

"she made [the princess] swear to say nothing of the matter"—The waiting-woman is now in charge, since both women will be judged according to their clothing and horse.

"Falada noticed and remembered"—This is a foreshadowing that as a helper, Falada will refer to her suffering later.

"thinking she was his bride"—Hinton notes that he is as yet "unconscious of the dark side of the feminine."

Household Stories by the Brothers Grimm. Trans. Lucy Crane. (New York: Macmillan and Company, 1886), 20–31, 43–51.

threatening to take her life if she refused. And all the while **Falada noticed and remembered.**

The waiting-woman then mounting Falada, and the Princess the sorry jade, they journeyed on till they reached the royal castle. There was great joy at their coming, and the King's son hastened to meet them, and lifted the waiting-woman from her horse, **thinking she was his bride;** and then he led her up the stairs, while the real Princess had to remain below. But **the old King,** who was looking out of the window, saw her standing in the yard, and **noticed how delicate and gentle and beautiful she was,** and then he went down and asked the seeming bride who it was that she had brought with her and that was now standing in the courtyard.

"Oh," answered the bride, "I only brought her with me for company; **give the maid something to do,** that she may not be for ever standing idle."

But the old King had no work to give her; until he bethought him of a boy he had who took **care of the geese,** and that she might help him. And so the real Princess was sent to keep geese with **the goose-boy, who was called Conrad.**

Soon after the false bride said to the Prince,

"Dearest husband, I pray thee do me a pleasure."

"With all my heart," answered he.

"Then" said she, "send for the knacker, that he may carry off the horse I came here upon, and make away with him; he was very troublesome to me on the journey." For **she was afraid that the horse might tell** how she had behaved to the Princess. And when the order had been given that Falada should die, it came to the Princess's ears, and she came to the knacker's man secretly, and **promised him a piece of gold** if he would do her a service. There was in the town a great dark gateway through which she had to pass morning and evening with her geese, **and she asked the man to take Falada's head and to nail it on the gate,** that she might always see it as she passed by. And the man promised, and he took Falada's head and nailed it fast in the dark gateway.

Early next morning as she and Conrad drove their geese through the gate, she said as she went by,

O Falada, dost thou hang there?

And the head answered,

> Princess, dost thou so meanly fare?
> But if thy mother knew thy pain,
> Her heart would surely break in twain.

But she went on through the town, driving her geese to the field. And when they came into the meadows, she sat down and undid her hair, which was all of gold, and when Conrad saw how it glistened, **he wanted to pull out a few hairs for himself.** And she said,

> O wind, blow Conrad's hat away,
> Make him run after as it flies,
> While I with my gold hair will play,
> And twist it up in seemly wise.

Then there came **a wind strong enough to blow Conrad's hat far away** over the fields, and he had to run after it; and by the time he came back she had put up her hair with combs and pins, and he could not get at any to pull it out; and he was sulky and would not speak to her; so they looked after the geese until the evening came, and then they went home.

"the old King . . . noticed how delicate and gentle and beautiful she was"—Despite her lowly clothing, the Princess looks special. The idea that the hero should be beautiful, that is blessed by God, is not unusual in fairy tales.

"give the maid something to do"—The girl receives a lowly task. Such humiliation is a usual part of rites of passage. See Turner, Ch. 26, p. 375.

"care of the geese"—Geese have erotic qualities because of their "long phallic necks" (Hinton) and their association with Aphrodite, the Greek goddess of love.

"the goose-boy, who was called Conrad"—Personal names are uncommon in fairy tales. Generic descriptions are more the rule ("the king," "the serving woman").

"she was afraid that the horse might tell"—The servant woman also knows the magical powers of the horse.

"[she] promised him a piece of gold . . . and she asked the man to take Falada's head and nail it on the gate"—The princess assures the continuity of her connection with her mother by retaining Falada's head. Bettelheim notes that the head speaks "the helpless grief of her mother." However, Hinton points out that she is now choosing to hear the previously neglected sentiments of her mother.

"O Falada, dost thou hang there?" —The Goose Girl's question and the horse's lament occur three times, as will Conrad's attempt to take strands of the girl's hair. In European tales, events often happen in threes. This may be a storytelling technique, or may be related to a much older and deeper belief. (See Jung, Ch. 32, p. 468.)

"he wanted to pull out a few hairs for himself"—Freudian readings of fairy tales interpret Conrad's desire for her hair as an expression of sexual desire.

"a wind strong enough to blow Conrad's hat far away"—Nature helps the princess maintain her virginity. Nature, also in the form of animal helpers or hiding places in trees and rocks, often takes on the role of benevolent protector/mother.

The next morning, as they passed under the dark gateway, the Princess said,

> **O Falada,** dost thou hang there?

"O Falada . . . Princess . . . O wind"—One reason for the use of such repetition is that these stories were collected from the oral tradition, where repetition helps engage the audience. (See Ch. 23, p. 341.)

And Falada answered,

> **Princess,** dost thou so meanly fare?
> But if thy mother knew thy pain,
> Her heart would surely break in twain.

And when they reached the fields she sat down and began to comb out her hair; then Conrad came up and wanted to seize upon some of it, and she cried,

> **O wind**, blow Conrad's hat away,
> Make him run after as it flies,
> While I with my gold hair will play,
> And do it up in seemly wise.

Then the wind came and blew Conrad's hat very far away, so that he had to run after it, and when he came back again her hair was put up again, so that he could pull none of it out; and they tended the geese until the evening. And after they had got home, Conrad went to the old King and said," I will tend the geese no longer with that girl!"

H. J. Ford. Illustration for *"The Goose Girl,"* 1919.

"Why not?" asked the old King.

"Because she vexes me the whole day long," answered Conrad. Then the old King ordered him to tell how it was.

"Every morning," said Conrad," as we pass under the dark gateway with the geese, there is an old horse's head hanging on the wall, and she says to it,

> **O Falada,** dost thou hang there?

And the head answers,

> **Princess,** dost thou so meanly fare?
> But if thy mother knew thy pain,
> Her heart would surely break in twain.

And besides this, Conrad related all that happened in the fields, and how he was obliged to run after his hat.

"The old King . . . went behind the gate"—The king is also acting as a mother-figure here because of his concern for the Goose Girl and Conrad.

The old King told him to go to drive the geese next morning as usual, and he himself **went behind the gate** and listened how the maiden spoke to Falada; and then he followed them into the fields, and hid himself behind a bush; and he watched the goose-boy and the goose-girl tend the geese; and after a while he saw the girl make her hair all loose, and how it gleamed and shone. Soon she said,

> O wind, blow Conrad's hat away,
> And make him follow as it flies,
> While I with my gold hair will play,
> And bind it up in seemly wise.

Then there came a gust of wind and away went Conrad's hat, and he after it, while the maiden combed and bound up her hair; and the old King saw all that went on. At last he went unnoticed away, and when the goose-girl came back in the evening he sent for her, and asked the reason of her doing all this.

"That I dare not tell you," she answered, "nor can I tell any man of my woe, for when I was in danger of my life I swore an oath not to reveal it." And he pressed her sore, and left her no peace, but he could get nothing out of her.

At last he said, "If you will not tell it me, tell it to the iron oven," and went away. **Then she crept into the iron oven,** and began to weep and to lament, and at last she opened her heart and said,

"Here I sit forsaken of all the world, and I am a King's daughter, and a wicked waiting-woman forced me to give up my royal garments and my place at the bridegroom's side, and I am made a goose-girl, and have to do mean service. And if my mother knew, it would break her heart."

Now the old King was standing outside by the oven-door listening, and he heard all she said, and he called to her and told her to come out of the oven. And **he caused royal clothing to be put upon her,** and it was a marvel to see how beautiful she was.

The old King then called his son and proved to him that he had the wrong bride, for she was really only a waiting-woman, and that the true bride was here at hand, she who had been the goose-girl. The Prince was glad at heart when he saw her beauty and gentleness; and a great feast was made ready, and all the court people and good friends were bidden to it. The bridegroom sat in the midst with the Princess on one side and the waiting-woman on the other; and the false bride did not know the true one, because she was dazzled with her glittering braveries. When all the company had eaten and drunk and were merry, the old King gave the waiting-woman a question to answer, as to what such a one deserved, who had deceived her masters in such and such a manner, telling the whole story, and ending by asking,

"Now, what doom does such a one deserve?"

"No better than this," answered the false bride, "that she be put naked into a cask, studded inside with sharp nails, and be dragged along in it by two white horses from street to street, until she be dead."

"Thou hast spoken thy own doom," said the old King; "as thou hast said, so shall it be done." And when the sentence was fulfilled, the Prince married the true bride, and ever after they ruled over their kingdom in peace and blessedness.

> "Then she crept into the iron oven"—Freudian interpreters consider the oven a womb symbol, while L. Klein points out that it symbolizes transformation by cooking. Turner might see it as representing a liminal state. When the princess climbs inside, she enters another state of being, one in which she can speak freely, isolated from the world. When she comes out of the oven, she enters a new life, the life her mother originally intended for her, as the bride-to-be of the prince, but she does so when she is ready and on her own terms. Thus the rite of passage from girl to Queen is completed through the use of the oven.

> "he caused royal clothing to be put upon her"—Clothing makes her beautiful and reveals her royal status. This reverses the effects of the change to lowly clothes that the waiting-woman demanded earlier.

> "No better than this"—She names her own punishment without realizing it. This happens often in the Grimms' tales. It provides a satisfying irony for the audience that just as the villain seems to have won, he or she causes her own doom.

"The Raven"

In many fairy tales, as Vladimir Propp showed, there is an elaborate opening situation that sets the scene for the actions of the hero by explaining the origin of the harm or lack that must be resolved in the main move of the tale (see Ch. 34, p. 503). However, this tale shows that every tale does not necessarily have an elaborate opening situation. "The Raven" begins with a queen's wish that her child be transformed into a raven. There is no explanation for why her thoughtless words result in the transformation of her child. Nor is there any suggestion that she regrets the effect of her comment. The transformation of the child is presented matter-of-factly, without any attention to the human emotions that would necessarily attend such an event. Here, as in "Faithful John," it is worthwhile remembering that fairy tales emphasize plot over character development and often represent events without providing motivations for the characters who perform them.

In its present form, the story contains a lesson about self-restraint. The nameless hero of the tale is willing to help, but his weaknesses in the first move prevent him from saving the girl. His impediments are the very human longing for food, drink, and sleep. In this sense, this fairy tale is reminiscent of the *Epic of Gilgamesh,* in which the hero tries to achieve immortality but fails the test set by Utnapishtim: Gilgamesh is told to remain awake for seven days and seven nights but is unable to do so. However, the emphasis of "The Raven" is somewhat different, since fairy tales do not call for actions on the same grand scale as do myths. As the tale continues, the hero is given a different challenge and manages to save the girl, even though he was not able to overcome his human limitations. See Chapter 38 for a detailed analysis of this tale.

There was once a Queen and she had a little daughter, who was as yet a babe in arms; and once the child was so restless that the mother could get no peace, do what she would; so **she lost patience,** and seeing a flight of ravens passing over the castle, she opened the window and said to her child,

"Oh, that thou wert a raven and couldst fly away, that I might be at peace."

No sooner had she uttered the words, than the child was indeed changed into a raven, and fluttered from her arms out of the window. And **she flew into a dark wood** and stayed there a long time, and her parents knew nothing of her. Once a man was passing through the wood, and he heard the raven cry, and he followed the voice; and when he came near it said,

"I was born a King's daughter, and have been bewitched, but thou canst set me free."

"What shall I do?" asked the man.

"Go deeper into the wood," said she, "and thou shalt find a house and an old woman sitting in it: **she will offer thee meat and drink, but thou must take none;** if thou eatest or drinkest thou fallest into a deep sleep, and canst not set me free at all. In the garden behind the house is a big heap of tan, stand upon that and wait for me.

"Three days, at about the middle of the day, shall I come to thee in a car drawn by four white horses the first time, by four red ones the second time, and lastly by four black ones; and if thou art not waking but sleeping, thou failest to set me free."

The man promised to do all she said.

"But ah!" cried she, "I know quite well I shall not be set free of thee; something thou wilt surely take from the old woman."

But the man promised yet once more that certainly he would not touch the meat or the drink. But when he came to the house the old woman came up to him.

"My poor man," said she to him, "you are quite tired out, come and be refreshed, and eat and drink."

"No," said the man, "I will eat and drink nothing."

But she left him no peace, saying, "Even if you eat nothing, take a draught out of this cup once and away."

So he was over-persuaded, and he drank.

In the afternoon, about two o'clock, he went out into the garden to stand upon the tan-heap and wait for the raven. As he stood there he felt all at once so tired, that he could bear it no longer, and laid himself down for a little; but not to sleep. But no sooner was he stretched at length than his eyes closed of themselves, and he fell asleep, and slept so sound, as if nothing in the world could awaken him.

At two o'clock came the raven in the car drawn by four white horses, but she was sad, knowing already that the man would be asleep, and so, when she came into the garden, there he lay sure enough. And she got out of the car and shook him and called to him, but he did not wake.

The next day at noon the old woman came and brought him meat and drink, but he would take none. But she left him no peace, and persuaded him until he took a draught out of the cup. About two o'clock he went into the garden to stand upon the tan-heap, and to wait for the raven, but he was overcome with so great a weariness that his limbs would no longer hold him up; and whether he would or no he had to lie down, and **he fell into a deep sleep.** And when the raven came up with her four red horses, she was sad, knowing already that the man would be asleep. And she went up to him, and there he lay, and nothing would wake him.

The next day the old woman came and asked what was the matter with him, and if he wanted to die, that he would neither eat nor drink; but he answered,

"I neither can nor will eat and drink."

"she lost patience"—Fairy tales often point out that bad behavior creates problems. This can be the result of violating an interdiction. Here, the mother is violating her natural relationship to the child by making such an impatient wish. G. R. Murphy points out that her words can be "performative" or "magic" on the child's soul.

"she flew into a dark wood"—This is a case of Propp's absentation (see Ch. 34, p. 503). The mother has caused the child to become a bird, whose nature is to fly away.

"What shall I do? . . . Go deeper into the wood"—The princess' words function like an interdiction. Interdictions may be positive or negative. Three interdictions at once signal the structure of events. This is an indication that the tale is rooted in an oral tradition:

- Go deeper into the wood.
- Accept no food or drink.
- Wait on the tan heap.

"she will offer thee meat and drink, but thou must take none"—The temptation to eat is a test of whether the hero can control the most basic of instincts. It is found in the story of the Garden of Eden (Ch. 5, p. 55). Thus, the garden in this story recapitulates the scene in Genesis. Compare also the New Testament account of the temptation of Jesus Christ in the desert, Matthew 4:2–4.

"So he was over-persuaded, and he drank"—This is part of a failed donor cycle.

"he fell into a deep sleep"—His breaking the second interdiction, "thou must take none," leads to his breaking the final one, waiting on the tan heap. Like the temptation to eat, the temptation to sleep is a test of whether the hero can control a basic instinct. It is also found in the *Epic of Gilgamesh* (Ch. 15, p. 191), and in the New Testament where the disciples fall asleep while waiting for Jesus, who is praying in the garden in Matthew 14:32–41.

But she brought the dishes of food and the cup of wine, and placed them before him, and when the smell came in his nostrils he could not refrain, but took a deep draught. When the hour drew near, he went into the garden and stood on the tan-heap to wait for the king's daughter; as time went on he grew more and more weary, and at last he laid himself down and slept like a stone. At two o'clock came the raven with four black horses, and the car and all was black; and she was sad, knowing already that he was sleeping, and would not be able to set her free; and when she came up to him, there he lay and slept. She shook him and called to him, but she could not wake him. **Then she laid a loaf by his side** and some meat, and a flask of wine, for now, however much he ate and drank, it could not matter. And she took a ring of gold from her finger, and put it on his finger, and her name was engraved on it. And lastly she laid by him a letter, in which was set down what she had given him, and that all was of no use, and further also it said,

"I see that here thou canst not save me, but if thy mind is to the thing, come to the golden castle of Stromberg: I know well that if thou willst thou canst." And when all this was done, she got again into her car, and went to the golden castle of Stromberg.

When the man waked up and perceived that he had been to sleep, he was sad at heart to think that she had been, and gone, and that he had not set her free. Then, catching sight of what lay beside him, he read the letter that told him all. And **he rose up and set off at once** to go to the golden castle of Stromberg, though he knew not where it was. And when he had wandered about in the world for a long time, he came to a dark wood, and there spent a fortnight trying to find the way out, and not being able. At the end of this time, it being towards evening, he was so tired that he laid himself down under a clump of bushes and went to sleep.

The next day he went on again, and in the evening, when he was going to lie down again to rest, he heard howlings and lamentations, so that he could not sleep. And about the hour when lamps are lighted, he looked up and saw a light glimmer in the forest; and he got up and followed it, and he found that it came from a house that looked very small indeed, because **there stood a giant** before it. And the man thought to himself that if he were to try to enter and the giant were to see him, it would go hard but he should lose his life. At last he made up his mind, and walked in. And the giant saw him.

"I am glad thou art come," said he; "it is now a long time since I have had anything to eat; I shall make a good supper of thee."

"That may be," said the man, "but I shall not relish it; besides, if thou desirest to eat, **I have somewhat here that may satisfy thee.**"

"If that is true," answered the giant, "thou mayest make thy mind easy; it was only for want of something better that I wished to devour thee."

Then they went in and placed themselves at the table, and the man brought out bread, meat, and wine in plenty.

"This pleases me well," said the giant, and he ate to his heart's content. After a while the man asked him if he could tell him where the golden castle of Stromberg was.

"I will look on my land-chart," said the giant, "for on it all towns and villages and houses are marked."

So he fetched the land-chart which was in his room, and sought for **the castle,** but it **was not to be found.**

"Never mind," said he, "I have up-stairs in the cupboard much bigger maps than this; we will have a look at them." And so they did, but in vain.

And now the man wanted to pursue his journey, but the giant begged him to stay a few days longer, until his brother, who had gone to get in provisions, should return. When the brother came, they asked him about the golden castle of Stromberg.

"When I have had time to eat a meal and be satisfied, I will look at the map."

"Then she laid a loaf by his side"—The Raven leaves gifts that will help the man free her: bread and wine, a gold ring with her name, a letter.

"he . . . set off at once"—This quest might be compared with that of Gilgamesh (see Ch. 15, p. 143), although, as is typical of a myth, the hero of the epic is a much more important and well-defined figure.

"there stood a giant"—Because the man chooses to confront the giant, he acts heroically. In many tales, monsters or giants guard treasures; here, the giant becomes a helper.

"I have somewhat here that may satisfy thee"—The man gives the giant bread and wine left for him by Raven. This gift acts as a substitute for the threat of death for the man. The raven-princess has acted as a donor as well as a victim, and now her gift helps prepare for her rescue.

"the castle . . . was not to be found"—Very often in myths and tales, the most miraculous places are uncharted, and are discovered only through the hero's bravery and ingenuity. (Compare *Gilgamesh,* Ch. 15, p. 185.)

M. Drott. A Variation on *"Princess on a Glass Mountain."*

That being done, he went into his room with them, and they looked at his maps, but could find nothing: then **he fetched other old maps,** and they never left off searching until they found the golden castle of Stromberg, but it was many thousand miles away.

"How shall I ever get there?" said the man.

"I have a couple of hours to spare," said the giant, "and I will set you on your way, but I shall have to come back and look after the child that we have in the house with us."

Then the giant bore the man until within about a hundred hours' journey from the castle, and saying,

"You can manage the rest of the way by yourself," he departed; and the man went on day and night, until at last he came to the golden castle of Stromberg. It stood on a **mountain of glass,** and he could see the enchanted Princess driving round it, and then passing inside the gates. He was rejoiced when he saw her, and began at once to climb the mountain to get to her; but it was so slippery, as fast as he went he fell back again. And when he saw this he felt he should never reach her, and he was full of grief, and resolved at least to stay at the foot of the mountain and wait for her. So he built himself a hut, and sat there and waited a whole year; and every day he saw the Princess drive round and pass in, and was never able to reach her.

One day he looked out of his hut and saw **three robbers fighting,** and he called out, "Mercy on us!" Hearing a voice, they stopped for a moment, but went on again beating one another in a dreadful manner. And he cried out again, "Mercy on us!" They stopped and listened, and looked about them, and then went on again. And he cried out a third time, "Mercy on us!" and then, thinking he would go and see what was the matter, he went out and asked them what they were fighting for. One of them told him he had found a stick which would open any door only by knocking at it; the second said he had found a cloak which, if he put it on, made him invisible; the third said he was possessed of a horse that would ride over everything, even the glass mountain. Now they had fought because they could not agree whether they should enjoy these things in common or separately.

"Suppose we make a bargain," said the man; "it is true I have no money, but I have other things yet more valuable to exchange for these; I must, however, make trial of them beforehand, to see if you have spoken truth concerning them."

So they let him mount the horse, and put the cloak round him, and they gave him the stick into his hand, and as soon as he had all this he was no longer to be seen; but laying about him well, he gave them all a sound thrashing, crying out,

"Now, you good-for-nothing fellows, **you have got what you deserve;** perhaps you will be satisfied now!"

Then he rode up the glass mountain, and when he reached the castle gates he found them locked; but **he beat with his stick upon the door** and it opened at once. And he walked in, and up the stairs to the great room where sat the Princess with a golden cup and wine before her: she could not see him so long as the cloak was on him, but drawing near to her he pulled off the ring she had given him, and threw it into the cup with a clang.

"This is my ring," she cried, "and the man who is to set me free must be here, too!"

But though she sought through the whole castle she found him not; he had gone outside, seated himself on his horse, and thrown off the cloak. And when she came to look out at the door, she saw him and shrieked out for joy; and he dismounted and took her in his arms, and she kissed him,

"Now hast thou set me free from my enchantment, and **tomorrow we will be married."**

"Faithful John"

This story seems to incorporate sections of several different stories into a single tale. The parts are not well blended, however, and the overall effect is somewhat confusing. Despite these continuity problems, the story of "Faithful John" is a powerful and fascinating tale that represents the tensions involved in a variety of social relationships, including friendship and marriage. The separate parts—or moves, as Propp would call them—of the tale are:

- the prince's courting of his bride
- the threats to the king's marriage
- the recovery of John by the king.

Each of these parts of the tale seems to have the capacity to be a complete tale on its own, but in this version of the story, the three components are condensed and their elements are incompletely synthesized. Each move is launched by a new harm or lack: in the first, the prince is overwhelmed by love of the golden princess and goes to seek her as his wife. In the second move, John overhears the dire predictions of the three witches, and it is their forebodings that form the harm beginning the second move. The third move begins with John's being turned to stone.

Besides these three components, the story has an extended initial situation that seems related only to the first move, as it specifies the events that lead to the courtship of the golden princess. Perhaps because of this elaborate opening, the first move is even more foreshortened than the other aspects of the tale.

In addition to the Proppian analysis we have sketched out, the tale lends itself to other methods of interpretation, including the Levi-Straussian (or structuralist) contrast between nature and culture, and the Jungian perspective that considers the tale in terms of archetypes. The marginal notes will indicate some of the key elements of each of these methods of analysis.

For many readers, the most puzzling and difficult part of the story is the prince's killing of his children to save John in the third move. If this were a novel or a psychological study instead of a fairy tale, the listeners might be horrified at this development in the plot. However, the logic of the tale de-emphasizes the inhumane aspects of the infanticide. In fact, the story seems to regard this act as a positive step, as it serves as a solution to the problem of John's being turned to stone. It may be helpful in understanding this attitude of the tale to remember that a folk- or fairy tale emphasizes plot at the expense of character development. The children who are killed (and resurrected) are not portrayed as real babies whose loss is mourned. Rather, they are abstract representations of the king's marriage to culture, which has been shown in the first move to represent an excessive force that tears the prince away from his friend John. Thus, the death of these "children of culture" is merely a way of restoring the balance between nature and culture in the tale, and returning the newly married king to a balance of interests between his wife and his best friend. Any young man who has ever argued with a girlfriend for the right to spend the occasional night "out with the boys" will appreciate the essential nature of this solution.

The emphasis on the faithfulness of John not only in the title of this tale, but also as the crux of its plot, illustrates the moral values expressed by the tale; see the general introduction on p. 525.

There was once **an old King,** who, having fallen sick, thought to himself, "This is very likely my death-bed on which I am lying."

Then he said, "Let Faithful John be sent for."

Faithful John was his best-beloved servant, and was so called because he had served the King faithfully all his life long. When he came near the bed, the King said to him,

"Faithful John, I feel my end drawing near, and my only care is for my son; he is yet

"an old King"—Neither the King nor his son is given a personal name; the emphasis of the story is on Faithful John, whose name actually signifies his virtue.

of tender years, and does not always know how to shape his conduct; and unless you promise me to instruct him in all his actions and be a true foster-father to him, I shall not be able to close my eyes in peace."

Then answered Faithful John, "I will never forsake him, and will serve him faithfully, even though it should cost me my life."

And the old King said, "Then I die, being of good cheer and at peace." And he went on to say,

"After my death, **you must lead him through the whole castle,** into all the chambers, halls, and vaults, and show him the treasures that in them lie; but the last chamber in the long gallery, in which lies hidden the picture of the Princess of the Golden Palace, **you must not show him.** If he were to see that picture, he would directly fall into so great a love for her, that he would faint with the strength of it, and afterwards for her sake run into great dangers; so you must guard him well."

And as Faithful John gave him his hand upon it, the old King became still and silent, laid his head upon the pillow, and died.

When the old King was laid in the grave, Faithful John told the young King what he had promised to his father on his death-bed, and said,

"And I will certainly hold to my promise and be faithful to you, as I was faithful to him, even though it should cost me my life."

When the days of mourning were at an end, Faithful John said to the Prince,

"**It is now time that you should see your inheritance;** I will show you all the paternal castle."

Then he led him over all the place, upstairs and downstairs, and showed him all the treasures and the splendid chambers; **one chamber only he did not open,** that in which the perilous picture hung. Now the picture was so placed that when the door opened it was the first thing to be seen, and was so wonderfully painted that it seemed to breathe and move, and in the whole world was there nothing more lovely or more beautiful. The young King noticed how Faithful John always passed by this one door, and asked,

"Why do you not undo this door?"

"There is something inside that would terrify you," answered he. But the King answered,

"I have seen the whole castle, and I will know what is in here also." And he went forward and tried to open the door by force.

Then Faithful John called him back, and said, "I promised your father on his death-bed that you should not see what is in that room; it might bring great misfortune on you and me were I to break my promise."

But the young King answered, "I shall be undone if I do not go inside that room; I shall have no peace day or night until I have seen it with these eyes; and I will not move from this place until you have unlocked it."

Then Faithful John saw there was no help for it, and he chose out the key from the big bunch with a heavy heart and many sighs. When the door was opened he walked in first and thought that by standing in front of the King he might hide the picture from him, but that was no good, the King stood on tiptoe, and looked over his shoulder. And when he saw the image of the lady that was so wonderfully beautiful, and so glittering with gold and jewels, **he fell on the ground powerless.** Faithful John helped him up, took him to his bed, and thought with sorrow, "**Ah me! the evil has come to pass,** what will become of us?"

Then he strengthened the King with wine, until he came to himself. The first words that he said were,

"Oh, the beautiful picture! Whose portrait is it?"

"It is the portrait of the Princess of the Golden Palace," answered Faithful John. Then the King said,

"My love for her is so great that if all the leaves of the forest were tongues they could not utter it! I stake my life on the chance of obtaining her, and you, my Faithful John, must stand by me."

The faithful servant considered for a long time how the business should be begun; it seemed to him that it would be a difficult matter to come only at a sight of the Princess. At last he thought out a way, and said to the King,

"All that she has about her is of gold—tables, chairs, dishes, drinking-cups, bowls, and all the household furniture; in your treasury are five tons of gold, let the goldsmiths of your kingdom work it up into all kinds of **vessels and implements,** into all kinds of birds, and wild creatures, and wonderful beasts, such as may please her; then we will carry them off with us, and go and seek our fortune."

Walter Crane, illustration for *"Faithful John"* from the 1886 English edition of *Household Stories*. This picture shows the king on the voyage to win his bride.

The King had all the goldsmiths fetched, and they worked day and night, until at last some splendid things were got ready. When a ship had been loaded with them, Faithful John put on the garb of a merchant, and so did the King, so as the more completely to disguise themselves. Then they journeyed over the sea, and went so far that at last they came to the city where the Princess of the Golden Palace dwelt.

Faithful John told the King to stay in the ship, and to wait for him.

"Perhaps," said he, "I shall bring the Princess back with me, so take care that everything is in order; let the golden vessels be placed about, and the whole ship be adorned."

Then he gathered together in his apron some of the gold things, one of each kind, landed, and went up to the royal castle. And when he reached the courtyard of the castle there stood by the well a pretty maiden, who had two golden pails in her hand, and she was drawing water with them, and as she turned round to carry them away **she saw the strange man, and asked him who he was.** He answered,

"I am a merchant," and opened his apron, and let her look within it.

"Ah, what beautiful things!" cried she, and setting down her pails, she turned the golden toys over, and looked at them one after another; then she said,

"The Princess must see these; she takes so much pleasure in gold things that she will buy them all from you."

Then she took him by the hand and led him in, for she was the chamber-maid.

When the Princess saw the golden wares she was very pleased, and said,

"All these are so finely worked that I should like to buy them of you."

But the faithful John said,

"I am only the servant of a rich merchant, and **what I have here is nothing to what my master has in the ship**—the cunningest and costliest things that ever were made of gold."

The Princess then wanted it all to be brought to her; but he said,

"That would take up many days; so great is the number of them, and so much space would they occupy that there would not be enough room for them in your house."

But the Princess's curiosity and fancy grew so much that at last she said,

"Lead me to the ship; I will myself go and see your master's treasures."

Then Faithful John led her to the ship joyfully, and the King, when he saw that her beauty was even greater than the picture had set forth, felt his heart leap at the sight.

"The faithful servant considered for a long time"—Faithful John is a helper in the Proppian sense. He provides the young King with a plan for winning the princess, and he will also carry out the plan.

"vessels and implements"—These objects show that the King has fallen under the spell of culture, and Faithful John helps him create a wonderful, but artificial world of golden images.

"Faithful John told the King to stay in the ship"—John takes responsibility for bringing the Princess to the King. The reliance of the helpless king on the stratagems of his servant can be viewed as a commentary on the weakness of the nobility and their dependence on the bourgeoisie. Note also the reliance of the Goose Girl on her waiting-woman.

"she saw the strange man, and asked him who he was"—Faithful John was wise in dressing himself and the king as merchants. The first contact is on equal terms, servant-to-servant.

"what I have here is nothing to what my master has in the ship"—Classical tales often present incidents of groups of three. Here, Faithful John parlays three requests of the Princess into her visiting the ship.

"Faithful John . . . gave orders for the ship to push off"—In fulfilling his promise to the King, Faithful John tricks the Princess. Such an action might be considered villainous, but Faithful John's motives are noble, keeping him in the role of helper rather than villain.

"Oh that I had died rather than fallen into his power"—The princess fears that she has been abducted for dishonorable ends, but she is soon won over by the blandishments of the king. Nonetheless, the scene contains the barely hidden threat of rape. In some respects, this story is reminiscent of the scene between Vertumnus and Pomona in Ovid's *Metamorphoses* XIV, 625–771.

"No merchant am I, but a King"—Now that he is with the Princess, the King may reveal his true standing; in fact he must, in order to win her.

"she willingly consented to become his wife"—If this were a tale only of the wooing of the Princess of the Golden Palace, it might end here. But this is the tale of Faithful John, and the focus returns to him.

"he understood [the ravens] quite well"—Understanding animals is a widespread motif which usually shows how special people can receive crucial information from nature through nonhuman communication. A popular example of this is Dr. Doolittle, and a classic example is Siegfried, who could understand the birds after licking his fingers which were covered with the blood of the dragon that he'd just slain.

"What does that avail him?"—Through overhearing the conversation of the ravens, Faithful John learns of the price the helper must pay—being turned gradually into stone. The dangers discussed by the ravens serve as the prophecy of harm to be averted in the tale's second move. The damage which results to John will be the harm launching the third move.

"He who knows it and does it will be turned into stone" Faithful John learns the dangers and the antidotes—and the price he will have to pay. This increases his heroic stature.

"the young Queen . . . will die"—In the third repetition, both the consequences to the helper (turning into stone) and the danger to the Queen increase. The first two situations are actually threats to the young King, but the last is to the Queen herself.

Then she climbed up into the ship, and the King received her. **Faithful John** stayed by the steersman, and **gave orders for the ship to push off,** saying, "Spread all sail, that she may fly like a bird in the air."

So the King showed her all the golden things, each separately—the dishes, the bowls, the birds, the wild creatures, and the wonderful beasts. Many hours were passed in looking at them all, and in her pleasure the Princess never noticed that the ship was moving onwards. When she had examined the last, she thanked the merchant, and prepared to return home; but when she came to the ship's side, she saw that they were on the high seas, far from land, and speeding on under full sail. "Ah!" cried she, full of terror, "I am betrayed and carried off by this merchant. **Oh that I had died rather than have fallen into his power!**"

But the King took hold of her hand, and said,

"**No merchant am I, but a King,** and no baser of birth than thyself; it is because of my over-mastering love for thee that I have carried thee off by cunning. The first time I saw thy picture I fell fainting to the earth."

When the Princess of the Golden Palace heard this she became more trustful, and her heart inclined favorably towards him, so that **she willingly consented to become his wife.** It happened, however, as they were still journeying on the open sea, that Faithful John, as he sat in the forepart of the ship and made music, caught sight of three ravens in the air flying overhead. Then he stopped playing, and listened to what they said one to another, for **he understood them quite well.** The first one cried,

"Ay, there goes the Princess of the Golden Palace."

"Yes," answered the second; "but he has not got her safe yet."

And the third said,

"He has her, though; she sits beside him in the ship."

Then the first one spoke again,

"**What does that avail him?** When they come on land a fox-red horse will spring towards them; then will the King try to mount him; and if he does, the horse will rise with him into the air, so that he will never see his bride again." The second raven asked,

"Is there no remedy?"

"Oh yes; if another man mounts quickly, and takes the pistol out of the holster and shoots the horse dead with it, he will save the young King. But who knows that? And he that knows it and does it will become stone from toe to knee." Then said the second,

"I know further, that if the horse should be killed, the young King will not even then be sure of his bride. When they arrive at the castle there will lie a wrought bride-shirt in a dish, and it will seem all woven of gold and silver, but it is really of sulphur and pitch, and if he puts it on it will burn him to the marrow of his bones." The third raven said,

"Is there no remedy?"

"Oh yes," answered the second; "if another man with gloves on picks up the shirt, and throws it into the fire, so that it is consumed, then is the young King delivered. But what avails that? **He who knows it and does it will be turned into stone** from his heart to his knee." Then spoke the third,

"I know yet more, that even when the bride-shirt is burnt up the King is not sure of his bride; when at the wedding the dance begins, and **the young Queen** dances, she will suddenly grow pale and fall to the earth as if she were dead, and unless some one lifts her up and takes three drops of blood from her right breast, she **will die.** But he that knows this and does this will become stone from the crown of his head to the sole of his foot."

When the ravens had spoken thus among themselves they flew away. Faithful John had understood it all, and from that time he remained quiet and sad, for he thought to himself that were he to conceal what he had heard from his master, misfortune would befall; and were he to discover it **his own life would be sacrificed.** At last, however, he said within himself,

"**I will save my master,** though I myself should perish!"

So when they came on land, it happened just as the ravens had foretold, there sprang forward a splendid fox-red horse.

"Come on!" said the King, "he shall carry me to the castle," and was going to mount, when Faithful John passed before him and mounted quickly, drew the pistol out of the holster, and shot the horse dead. Then the other servants of the king cried out (for they did not wish well to Faithful John),

"How shameful to kill that beautiful animal that was to have carried the king to his castle." But the King said,

"Hold your tongues, and let him be: he is my Faithful John; he knows what is the good of it."

Then they went up to the castle, and there stood in the hall a dish, and the wrought bride-shirt that lay on it seemed as if of gold and silver. The young King went up to it and was going to put it on, but Faithful John pushed him away, picked it up with his gloved hands, threw it quickly on the fire, and there let it burn. The other servants began grumbling again, and said,

"Look, he is even burning up the king's bridal shirt!"

But the young King said,

"Who knows but that there may be a good reason for it? **Let him be,** he is my Faithful John."

Then the wedding feast was held; and the bride led the dance; Faithful John watched her carefully, and all at once she grew pale and fell down as if she were dead. Then he went quickly to her, and carried her into a chamber hard by, laid her down, and kneeling, **took three drops of blood from her right breast.**

Immediately she drew breath again and raised herself up, but the young King witnessing all, and not knowing why Faithful John had done this, grew very angry, and cried out,

"Throw him into prison!"

The next morning Faithful John was condemned to death and led to the gallows, and as he stood there ready to suffer, he said,

"He who is about to die is permitted to speak once before his end; may I claim that right?"

"Yes," answered the King, "it is granted to you." Then said Faithful John,

"I have been condemned unjustly, for I have always been faithful," and he related how he had heard on the sea voyage the talk of the ravens, and how he had done everything in order to save his master. Then cried the King,

"O my Faithful John, pardon! pardon! lead him down!"

But **Faithful John, as he spoke the last words, fell lifeless, and became stone.**

The King and Queen had great grief because of this, and the King said,

"Ah, how could I have evil-rewarded such faithfulness!" and he caused the stone image to be lifted up and put to stand in his sleeping-room by the side of his bed. And as often as he saw it he wept and said,

"**Would that I could bring thee back** to life, my Faithful John!"

After some time the Queen bore twins—two little sons—that grew and thrived, and were the joy of their parents. One day, **when the Queen was in church,** the two children were sitting and playing with their father, and he gazed at the stone image full of sadness, sighed, and cried,

"Oh that I could bring thee back to life, my Faithful John!"

Then the stone began to speak, and said,

"his own life would be sacrificed" —This is the Suffering Servant motif, which the Grimms would have known from Isaiah 52.

"I will save my master"—Faithful John decides to persevere in his loyalty to both kings. Once again, the role of the storyteller is significant (see p. 525). The story reflects the views of the Grimms' informants. We see in "Faithful John" a great admiration for the constancy of the servant class, culminating in the servant sacrificing his life for his master.

"Let him be"—The King trusts his servant, despite the apparently treacherous behavior.

"[he] took three drops of blood from her right breast"—This action, though it saves the Queen's life, appears to be a violation of the bride and a usurping of her husband's "right" to her body.

"Faithful John . . . became stone"—The magical force takes over just as the King realizes his verdict was unjust. Changing into stone is a risk Faithful John took, which illustrates his devotion.

"Would that I could bring thee back"—The King wants to become a helper, but does not know how.

"when the Queen was in church" —This could be a rationalization, providing a way to remove the Queen now, so that she, too, can be tested when she returns. (For more on rationalization, see p. 79.) It is also likely to be a device for the Grimms to incorporate elements from the New Testament Palm Sunday reading which includes a similar dialog, culminating in a promise similar to "All that I have in the world I will give up for thee!"

"Yes, thou canst bring me back to life again, if thou wilt bestow therefore thy best-beloved." Then cried the King,

"All that I have in the world will I give up for thee!" The stone went on to say,

"If thou wilt cut off the heads of thy two children with thy own hand, and besmear me with their blood, I shall receive life again."

The King was horror-struck at the thought that he must put his beloved children to death, **but he remembered all John's faithfulness, and how he had died for him,** and he drew his sword and cut off his children's heads with his own hand. And when he had besmeared the stone with their blood life returned to it, and Faithful John stood alive and well before him; and he said to the king,

"Thy faithfulness shall not be unrewarded," and, taking up the heads of the children, he set them on again, and **besmeared the wound with their blood,** upon which in a moment they were whole again, and jumped about, and went on playing as if nothing had happened to them.

Now was the King full of joy; and when he saw the Queen coming he put Faithful John and the two children in a great chest. When she came in he said to her,

"Hast thou prayed **in church?**"

"Yes," answered she, "but I was thinking all the while of Faithful John, and how he came to such great misfortune through us."

"Then," said he, "dear wife, we can give him life again, but it will cost us both our little sons, whom we must sacrifice."

The Queen grew pale and sick at heart, but said,

"**We owe it him,** because of his great faithfulness."

Then the King rejoiced because she thought as he did, and he went and unlocked the chest and took out the children and Faithful John, and said,

"God be praised, he is delivered, and our little sons are ours again"; and he related to her how it had come to pass.

After that they all lived together in happiness to their lives' end.

Further Reading

Warner, Marina. *From the Beast to the Blonde*. London: Chatto & Windus, 1994.

Zipes, Jack. *The Brothers Grimm: From Enchanted Forests to the Modern World*. New York, NY: Routledge, 1988.

Marginal notes:

"but he remembered all John's faithfulness, and how he had died for him"—This is another Christian echo. The King honors Faithful John's command in order to reward his faithful service.

"besmeared the wound with their blood"—This is an echo of Exodus and Passover, commemorating how marking one's door with blood caused the Jews to be spared. It might also be a remnant of very ancient beliefs in the life-giving power of blood. Levi-Strauss also discusses this in Ch. 20.

"in church"—This puts the material since "the Queen was in church" (p. 539) into the religious interpretive framework.

"We owe it to him"—The Queen has been tested and is proven worthy because she also puts faithful service before all else. We might note that Abraham's willingness to sacrifice Isaac is parallel.

Cupid and Psyche

APULEIUS

WHAT TO EXPECT . . . "Cupid and Psyche," which is part of a longer Latin work called the *Metamorphoses*, represents a unique combination of myth and fairy tale. It includes elements more common to myth: deities are major characters, and gods exhibit characteristics familiar from earlier mythic traditions—in particular, they are vindictive when they feel humans overstep their boundaries. However, the work also contains elements that are hallmarks of the fairy tale as described by Propp (Ch. 34, p. 499), including traditional donor figures, identifiable moves within the plot development, well-defined tasks to be accomplished by the hero, and a happy ending.

Many of the characters are deities, but they often behave in unflattering, human ways, marking the story as belonging to a society that still knew the tradition but had given up belief in it. As you read, look for instances of irony and humor that would have appealed to this Roman audience, and give reasons why, based on what you have learned about Apuleius' society. Consider the story as a member of that "dark" tradition that is harder to analyze by means of Jungian analysis. What insights does this perspective give you?

The story of Cupid and Psyche is included in a longer work called the *Metamorphoses*, a novel written in Latin during the second century C.E. (A different book with the same name as the work by Ovid 15 excerpted in Ch. 4.) The main character of this novel is Lucius, a young man who, as a result of his curiosity about magic, is turned into an ass and goes through a series of adventures before he succeeds at having the spell reversed. While focusing primarily on the story of Lucius, the novel consists of the witty interweaving of a variety of narrators and narrative levels; also, a variety of other stories are told, both by Lucius and by other characters. An old woman tells the story of Cupid and Psyche to calm a young bride kidnapped on her wedding day and held for ransom by the robbers. It is part of the complicated irony of the *Metamorphoses* that the story of Cupid and Psyche ends happily, but the story of the bride becomes a tragedy as she is murdered by the robbers and never lives to enjoy life with her bridegroom.

In our discussion of the differences between fairy tales and myths (see Introduction to Part 6, p. 495), we have noted that the characters in fairy tales tend to be generic figures with names like "Jack" or "the old woman" who resolve their problems through the use of magic and trickery. In contrast, the characters in myths tend to have unique names, personalities, and talents. For example, in a story with Heracles as its hero, we would expect a quite different resolution of any difficulties than in a story about Loki. In the *Metamorphoses,* the cook's narrative about Cupid and Psyche represents a unique blend of myth and fairy tale.

The characters in this story are gods, but they do not always behave as gods. Venus, in particular, acts a great deal like the wicked stepmother or the witch in a fairy tale who tries to prevent the heroine from growing up or makes her life difficult as she tries to become an independent adult. Yet at the same time, the story is also a myth because it deals with issues relating to religion and proper devotion to the gods. Psyche is so beautiful that people abandon the worship of Venus and instead perform rituals that treat the girl as a goddess.

In the course of the story, Venus reestablishes her authority after rebuffing the threat from Psyche, as Demeter does in the *Hymn to Demeter*, defining her worship at Eleusis (see Ch. 27, p. 389). The view of Venus in the story of Cupid and Psyche is consistent with her portrayal in the *Metamorphoses* as a whole: in the end, her cult gives way to the worship of the goddess Isis who, at the end of the novel, saves Lucius, the main character, from the enchantment that traps him in the body of a donkey. Isis was originally an Egyptian goddess whose worship was quite widespread in Hellenistic and Roman times. She was seen as a giver of life, a healer, and mistress of the universe. "The function of Isis as a metaphysical anchor is symbolized on her robe in the representation of stars ordering themselves obediently around a moon, which of course is to be identified with the goddess herself" (Shumate, 314). Through initiation into the cult of Isis, worshippers achieved a personal relationship with her, and they were promised rebirth through the goddess.

Graham Anderson has shown that the story of Cupid and Psyche is related to a series of Hittite texts from the second millennium B.C.E. In

these texts the mother of the god Telepinus commissions Kamprusepas, the goddess of healing, to soothe the anger of the god: the reasons for his anger are in a damaged portion of the tablet, but its result is that no creature on earth is able to engage in sex. Kamprusepas soothes Telepinus by giving him wheat, from which she separates the chaff, and then wool from the sheep of the sun god, and finally olive oil, a traditional equivalent for the waters of life. Then his anger is sealed in a container in the underworld. Anderson argues that Apuleius adapts these tasks to create the tasks Venus gives Psyche. The effect of these tasks is to overcome her anger and the anger of her son Cupid, so that their marriage can resume.

Venus (Aphrodite), a first or second century C.E. copy of a 2nd century B.C.E. Greek original. This statue represents the innocent beauty of the goddess of love as she is surprised while bathing. In "Cupid and Psyche," the heroine embodies this quality more successfully than the goddess herself.

Bruno Bettelheim notes that the resulting story created by Apuleius is the earliest version we have in the Western tradition of an animal groom story. Other stories of this type include "Beauty and the Beast" and "The Frog Prince." We include Angela Carter's version of "Beauty and the Beast" in Chapter 44, p. 670; see the introduction of that chapter for more discussion of the theme. The version of the story presented in this chapter seems to have been composed by Apuleius, who drew upon earlier stories about a link between the soul or Psyche and the god of love. With its unique combination of myth and fairy tale, the story seems to have been invented by Apuleius. Note though, that Apuleius does not call this story "Cupid and Psyche"; that title was added later, when people began to excerpt it from the longer novel into which it is so well integrated.

The link between Cupid and Psyche was not limited to Apuleius' imagination, however. C. Schlam points out that both Cupid and Psyche were traditionally represented as winged creatures representing Love and the Soul, respectively, and showing the pitfalls of their interaction. By the fifth and fourth centuries B.C.E., the couple were often portrayed embracing in terra cotta and bronze reliefs. By Hellenistic times, there were figures portraying the Eros bound or burned, sometimes by a winged girl or by a butterfly. There were also portraits of Psyche tortured by Eros in similar ways. However, until the story told by Apuleius, Psyche at least was seen more as an abstraction than as a character with a real personality. As a result of the familiar artistic representations, however, readers would have assumed that Psyche's mysterious husband was Cupid, and thus what was hidden from her would not have mystified Apuleius' audience. Philosophical portraits of the relationship between Love and the Soul are at least as old as Plato's *Phaedrus* (4th c. B.C.E.), and parts of Apuleius' tale can be read as symbolizing the struggles which the soul must go through to become worthy of the divine power of Love.

Erich Neumann divides the story into five parts: the Introduction, the Marriage of Death, the Act, the Four Tasks, the Happy End. We have added a section called the Wanderings, but for the rest we echo Neumann's division in our marginal notes.

Introduction

Once upon a time there lived in a certain city a king and queen, and they had three daughters remarkably beautiful. But though the two elder girls were as comely as you could wish, yet it didn't strike you dumb with despair to have a look at them—while as for the youngest girl, all man's praising words were too poor to touch (let alone becomingly adorn) a beauty so glorious, so victorious.

Citizens in crowds, and droves of pilgrims, were attracted by the loveliness. Already the word had gone abroad through the nearby cities and bordering countries that **Venus had had a Second Birth** (this time from earth, not water): a Venus endowed with the flower of virginity, and germinated from a distillation of the stars.

Every day the tale drifted farther. Soon the neighbouring islands, most of the mainland, scores of provinces, were echoing with the news. Many were the hurrying men that made long journeys by land and over the deep seas, only to gaze upon this splendid product of the age. **No one set sail for Paphos;** no one set sail **for Cnidos**—no, not even **for Cythera**—to come into the presence of Venus. Her sacred rites were forgotten; **her shrines were falling into ruin;** her cushions were trampled on; her ceremonies were neglected; her images were ungarlanded; and the old ashes lay dirtying the desolate altar.

A young girl had supplanted her, and the divinity of the mighty goddess was worshipped in the shrine of a human face. In her morning walks the virgin was propitiated by the **victims and food-offerings** due to the missing Venus. When she strolled down the street, the people rushed out and presented her with votive tablets; or they strewed her way with flowers.

This intemperate attribution of divine rights and qualities to a mortal girl deeply incensed the actual Venus. Transported with indignation, and shaking her head in a towering rage, she uttered the following soliloquy: "I **the primal Mother of all living,** I the elemental Source of energy, I the fostering Venus of the girdled earth—I am degraded to sharing my empire and honour with a mere wench. **A girl that will one day die** borrows the power of my name. It meant nothing then that shepherd Paris, whose good taste and integrity Love himself admitted, set me above the other great goddesses as the Queen of Beauty. I shall take measures that she may soon be sorry for her charlatan charms."

So anon she summoned **her son, that winged lad,** the naughty child who has been so spoilt that he despises all social restraint. Armed with flames and arrows he flits in the night from house to house. He severs the marriage-tie on all sides; and unchastised he perpetrates endless mischief, and he does everything save what he ought to do. This

---

*Apuleius. *The Golden Ass,* trans. Jack Lindsay, 105–142, 239–242. Copyright © 1932. Used by permission of University of Indiana Press.

This story comes from:
Apuleius, *The Metamorphoses, or The Golden Ass.**

"Once upon a time"—The opening is typical of the generic introduction of a fairy tale, which does not feature a specific time or place. However, the casting of characters will turn out to be quite a bit less generic than the setting.

"Venus had had a Second Birth" —In her beauty, Psyche contends, although unintentionally, with the gods. This aspect of the story is typical of myths, not fairy tales, and calls to mind the stories about Prometheus, who rivaled Zeus and was punished for his effrontery. (See Ch. 24, p. 353.)

"No one set sail for Paphos . . . for Cnidos . . . for Cythera"— These were shrines throughout the Greek world devoted to the cult of Venus.

"her shrines were falling into ruin"—These symptoms of neglect are bound to elicit the anger of the goddess.

"victims and food-offerings"— Devotion to Psyche is represented as a false religion. The story is not just a fairy tale, but also functions as a myth in representing the devotion due to the goddess of love.

"the primal Mother of all living" — Venus was the goddess of love who caused plants and animals to procreate, and thus was responsible for the creation of everything in the world.

"A girl that will one day die"—The phrase is an important one, as it distinguishes between humans, who are mortal, and the eternal gods.

"her son, that winged lad"—The Greek poets in the 7th c. first described love as a deity making humans fall in love by hitting them with a whip or an axe. In Euripides, he uses a bow and arrows. Later, he becomes the son of Venus and Mars, the god of war. Cupid is a boy with wings. He can be seen as any age, from a baby to a young man.

Psyche Greek for "soul."

"I beseech you . . . by the tie of mother-love, by the sweet wounds of your arrowhead"—Though she is herself a god, and also Cupid's mother, Venus' request is a prayer, as she recognizes that her son does not have to comply.

"Let the virgin be gripped with most passionate love for the basest of mankind"—We don't find out for a long time what happens to Psyche as a result of Venus' efforts. What follows is written as a mystery story in which we do not know the identity of her lover.

"She trod the spray-tips of the tossing waters"—Apuleius emphasizes the difference between Venus and Psyche by representing the traditional portrait of the goddess as she looked when she was born from the waves of the sea, (See Ch. 3, p. 31.)

"the Milesian God . . . composer of this Milesian Tale"—Apollo was Milesian, as he had an oracle at Didyma near Miletus. Here Apuleius emphasizes the parallel between the god and himself as the creator of this Milesian Tale. This genre consisted of lewd short stories.

"it is a raging serpent she must wed"—In Greek and Roman society, a girl's father chose her husband, so she might find herself married to a stranger she considered abhorrent. This practice is also represented in the Homeric *Hymn to Demeter,* see Ch. 27, p. 385.

"hymeneal songs"—Hymns of praise to Hymen, the god of marriage, were a traditional part of the wedding ceremony.

"death-marriage"—The ceremony is a rite of passage, representing the end or death of childhood, as the partners cease to be children (see Turner, Ch. 26, p. 375). Also at an end are the associations of the bride with her own family. In some societies like Rome, marriage marks the entry of the bride into the family of the groom. In societies like our own, the married couple is seen as constituting a new family. The convention of tears at a wedding represents the feelings of the parents at the "loss" of their child.

lad prone enough to harm on his own lewd initiative, Venus whetted on with her words. She brought him to the city of our tale and pointed out **Psyche**—for that was the name given to the girl. Moaning and incoherent with wrath, Venus related the story of her rival's beauty and insolence.

"**I beseech you,**" she said, "**by the tie of mother-love, by the sweet wounds of your arrowhead,** by the honeyed warmth of your torch, provide your parent with her revenge, her full revenge. Exact heavy retribution for these contumelious charms. And, above everything else, do your best to give her the fate that I ordain. **Let the virgin be gripped with most passionate love for the basest of mankind**—one that Fortune has stripped of his rank and estate, and almost of his skin—one so vile that his wretchedness has no parallel anywhere."

Thus she spoke. Whereupon with loose-lipped kisses she long and closely farewelled the lad, and then sought the margin of the tide-swept shore. **She trod the spray-tips of the tossing waters** with her rosy feet; and lo, the sea fell calm over all its glossy surface.

The Marriage of Death

Meanwhile Psyche, for all her manifest beauty reaped no benefit from her preeminence. She was gazed at by all, praised and mazed; but no man king or prince or even commoner, raised any pretensions to her hand in marriage.

Accordingly the sorrowing father of this ill-fated girl suspected the wrath of the gods; and dreading some visitation from heaven, he consulted the ancient oracle of **the Milesian God.** With prayers and sacrifices he besought the powerful deity to bestow a marriage-bed and a husband on this slighted maid.

Apollo, though a Grecian and Ionic yet (for love of the **composer of this Milesian Tale**) gave a Latin response which translates as follows:

> King, stand the girl upon some mountain-top
> adorned in fullest mourning for the dead.
> No mortal husband, King, shall make her crop
> **it is a raging serpent she must wed,**—
> which, flying high, works universal Doom,
> debilitating all with Flame and Sword.
> Jove quails, the Gods all dread him—the Abhorred!
> Streams quake before him, and the Stygian Gloom.

When the announcement of the holy oracle was delivered, the king, formerly so pleased with life, dragged himself sadly home and unfolded to his wife the injunctions of this melancholy response. They all lamented, wept, groaned, for several days. But at last arrived the dread hour when the shocking oracle must be consummated. The procession was formed for the fatal wedding of the unfortunate girl.

The torches burned dully, choked with ash and soot; and the tunes of the marriage-flute were replaced by plaintive Lydian melodies. The gay **hymeneal songs** quavered away into doleful howls; and the bride wiped her tears with the nuptial veil itself.

The entire city turned out to show its mourning respect for the afflicted family. A day of public lamentation was at once sympathetically ordered. The **death-marriage** was sorrowfully solemnized; and the funeral of the living bride moved on, attended by the whole populace.

Thus the weeping Psyche was present, not at her wedding, but at her funeral; and while the anguished parents, horrified unendurably, strove to delay the ghastly procession, the girl herself exhorted them to submit.

"When the tribes and the nations were hymning me with divine honours, when all their voices chimed in titling me the second Venus, that was the hour for grief and tears, that was the hour when you should have given me up for lost. Now I feel, now I realize, that **Venus is my murderess,** and none other. Lead forward, and stand me up on the rock to which the response devoted me. Why should I lag? Why should I shrink aside from the coming of Him that has been born to destroy the world?"

The virgin said no more. She took her place in the flocking procession and strode onwards resolutely. At length they arrived at the appointed crag on a precipitate mountain-top; and there they deposited the girl and left her.

But **as Psyche lay trembling** apprehensively and weeping on the top-shelf of the crag, a gentle breath of fondling Zephyrus fluttered and tweaked her dresses, and puffed them up. Gradually raised on the palm of a tranquil wind she was smoothly wafted down the steep and rocky slope and laid softly on the lap of the valley, on flower-sprinkled turf.

Psyche, pleasantly reposing in a tender verdant nook on a couch of dewy grasses, felt all her agitated limbs relax; and **she drifted into a sweet sleep,** from which she awoke fully refreshed. Her mind was now at peace. She saw a grove composed of tall and thick-boughed trees. She saw a fountain flashing with waters like glass in the middlemost of the grove.

Near to the plashing foot of the fountain there stood **a palace built not by human hands** but by divine power. You had but to give one glance into the hall to know that you stood before the gorgeous pleasure-house of a god. The lofty ceilings, delicately fretted out of citronwood and ivory, were upheld by pillars of gold. The walls were completely crusted with silver modelling, while shapes of wild beasts and of other animals flanked the entrance.

The pavement itself was a mosaic of gems splintered and fitted together so as to weld their colours and to represent various objects. All the other parts of this extensive mansion were equally splendid beyond estimation.

Invited by this delightful outlook, Psyche approached nearer and timidly affecting courage, she crossed the threshold. **The lovely vista lured her on;** and she wandered through the premises, wondering at all she saw. Farther in, she found magnificent storerooms crammed with every luxury. No wish but found its fulfillment there.

While she was gazing round in rapture, a bodiless voice addressed her. "Why, lady," it asked, "do you stand astonished at this fine show? All that you see is yours. Hie therefore to the bedroom, and rest your wearied body on the couch; and when you so desire, arise and bathe yourself. We whose voices you hear are your handmaidens."

Psyche **felt herself happy and safe** in these counsels of divine providence. She hearkened to the aerial Voices, and soothed away all her tiredness—first in sleep, and then in the bath. The moment this was done, she saw near by a half-moon dais with a raised seat and all the materials for a restorative meal. Joyously she seated herself.

Immediately cups of nectarous wine and relays of dishes garnished with every conceivable dainty were set before her by some spiritual agency; for not a servant appeared. And though she could see no human being, yet she heard people speaking around her; and these Voices were her only servants.

After she had sumptuously dined, One entered unseen and sang; and Another played on a lyre, and both lyre and lyrist were unseen. When these diversions were over, Psyche yielded to the suggestions of the dusk and **retired to bed;** and when the veils of night were drawn, an insinuating murmur floated into her ears. Then, afraid for her maidenhead in that lonely place, she quailed and was all the more shaken because she did not know what threatened.

But as she shuddered the anonymous bridegroom drew near, and climbed into bed, and made Psyche his bride, and departed hastily before sunrise. At once the waiting-voices entered the bedroom and solicitously tended the young bride with her ruptured virginity.

"Venus is my murderess"—The portrait of the goddess of creation as dealing death is quite ironic. In addition, Apuleius is a devotee of Isis, not Venus.

"as Psyche lay trembling"—Given the oracle ("a raging serpent she must wed"), Psyche expects a fate like Andromeda, who was fastened to a rock as prey for a sea monster, and rescued by Perseus.

"she drifted into a sweet sleep"—Sleep is often represented as a transition state before passage into a magical or divine realm. For instance, Odysseus, in Homer's *Odyssey,* sleeps on the magical ship that carries him back to Ithaca after a 20–year absence.

"a palace built not by human hands"—A magical dwelling place like this often indicates that the hero has "crossed the threshold" into another realm. Jung would point out that Psyche has descended into the unconscious, where she will encounter archetypes involved in her individuation (Ch. 32, p. 477.)

"The lovely vista lured her on"—While Psyche begins to enjoy herself in her new home, the careful reader remembers the prophecies and wonders what horrible things await the foolish girl.

"While she was gazing round in rapture"—The voices urge her to accept her part in the "fine show" of her new house. She is told to sleep again, although she has just awakened.

"felt herself happy and safe"—Psyche will later have to pay the price of her commitment to pleasures she does not understand. In this respect, Psyche is seen as parallel to Lucius, the main character of the *Metamorphoses'* frame story, who is initially captivated by the false pleasures offered by witchcraft and must undergo a path of suffering until he achieves true wisdom.

"retired to bed"—Psyche sleeps again, the third such interlude before she meets her new husband, whose lack of a bodily form and particular attributes is part of the illusion.

Thus her life went on, day after day; and **habit brought its trails of pleasure,** and the sound of the unknown Voices was the solace of her solitude. One day, Psyche's husband remarked—for she could feel and hear him, she could do all but see him— "Psyche, my precious, my darling wife, termagant Fortune has an ugly trick ready for you, which needs (I think) the shrewdest counterblast on our part. Your sisters, dismayed by the report of your death, are endeavouring to trace you. They will climb up yonder crag. If then you should chance to hear their outcry, **make no answer, do not even look their way.** If you act otherwise, you will bring on me a heavy misfortune and on yourself utter destruction."

Psyche promised, assuring him that she would be an obedient wife. But when he and the night drained away together, **the poor girl spent the whole next day in weeping and moaning.** A little later, her husband (appearing at her side somewhat earlier than usual) embraced her as she wept, and thus expostulated:

"O Psyche, my love, is this what you promised me? **What am I your husband to expect of you now?** What am I to hope for? Daylong and nightlong you grieve, and you lie within my embrace as on a cross of torment. So be it. Do as you desire, and follow the destructive bias of your whims. When repentance comes, you will remember my warning too late."

At this she begged and swore that she would kill herself, till she extorted from her husband the licence that she desired, to see **her sisters,** soothe their grief, and give her sisters as much gold and jewels as she wished.

But **one condition he emphasized** so repeatedly as to scare her: never to let any guile of the sisters lure her into inquiries concerning her husband's identity—or by her sacrilegious curiosity she would cast herself down from her exalted height of Fortune and never again enjoy his embraces.

She thanked her husband gratefully. "O no," she said, restored to cheerfulness, "I'd rather die a hundred times than lose your darling caresses. **I love you, desperately love you, whoever you are**. I cherish you like my own soul. I would not exchange you for Love himself. But all the same I think you ought to grant my prayer. Bid Zephyrus this coachman of yours to fetch my sisters down—as I was fetched. "

And **she kissed him persuasively, and murmured endearments, and twined him with her arms and legs,** and said in a wheedling whisper, "O my honey, O my husband, O you sweet sweet soul of your Psyche."

Unable to resist her coaxing compulsion, her husband felt his will reluctantly drown beneath her kisses. He promised that she should have all her wishes; and then at the first smudge of light he vanished from the arms of his wife.

The sisters had inquired the locality of the crag where Psyche had been left. They hurriedly climbed the slope; and standing on the rock they wept and beat their breasts till the boulders and scarps resounded with their inconsolable screams. They called on their hapless sister by name till **the piercing echoes of their grief reached all the way down the valley. Psyche in her agitation ran wildly out of the palace.**

"Hallo there!" she called back. "Why are you making yourselves so miserable, and all for nothing? Here is the person you mourn. Cease this wailing. Dry those tears that have wetted your cheeks for so long. In a moment you can hold in your arms the sister that you're lamenting."

Then she summoned Zephyrus and informed him of her husband's permission. **Obeying her commands,** in a jiffy he brought the sisters gliding unharmed down to Psyche upon the downiest blast. In a tangle of embraces, a flurry of kisses, the girls turned one to the other until the tears sealed for a space burst forth again—this time from excess of joy. What sparkling gems, what parquets of gold, she treads.

"Now come inside," said Psyche." Come into our house and learn to smile again— You must cheer up with your Psyche now."

Margin notes:

"habit brought its trails of pleasure"— Psyche's new life is represented as a delusion, as she lives in a haze of pleasure without understanding or reflection. Neumann calls this phase a "variant of the hero's engulfment by the whale-dragon monster." Campbell refers to it as "in the belly of the whale" (see Ch. 14, p. 163).

"make no answer, do not even look their way"—The first of the interdictions Psyche goes on to violate. Her disobedience results in the harm that will end this long preparatory section and lead to the first move. (See Ch. 34, p. 503.)

"the poor girl spent the whole next day in weeping and moaning"— Because she is immature, Psyche promises obedience to her new husband, but betrays him, without meaning to because she has so little control over her feelings.

"What am I your husband to expect of you now?"—The story begs the question of who this husband is. The reader and Psyche share the desire to unravel the mystery of his identity. This is part of Apuleius' cleverness.

"her sisters"—Neumann describes them as a man-hating matriarchal force, and considers them Psyche's shadow. On this element of a Jungian analysis, see Ch. 32, p. 475.

"one condition he emphasized"— This is a new interdiction, which Psyche violates in the end.

"I love you, desperately love you, whoever you are"—The immaturity of Psyche's attachment is expressed by these ironic words.

"she kissed him . . . and twined him with her arms and legs"— Psyche is no longer the innocent bride. She now knows how to use sexual charms to get her own way.

"The sisters had inquired the locality of the crag"–The storyteller leaves out a great deal here, about how Psyche contacts her sisters and invites them to visit her.

"the piercing echoes of their grief reached all the way down the valley. Psyche in her agitation ran wildly out of the palace"—Psyche appears as agitated as her sisters. Apuleius emphasizes their wild behavior to make all of them, including Psyche, appear slightly ridiculous.

With this prologue she showed them all the resources of her house of gold, and introduced them to the household of attendant Voices. She gave them a tiptop entertainment—first, all the luxuries of the bath; then, the spirit-served delicacies of her table—till, at length satiated by the inexhaustible supply of god-sent riches, **the elder sisters began to nourish a jealous hatred** in the depths of their hearts. One of them was particularly tireless in interrogating Psyche minutely as to who was the master of this divine residence, what kind of man he was, and how he shaped as a husband.

Psyche however managed to follow out her husband's instructions and let nothing slip to betray her secret. But making the best of the situation **she told them that he was a young man, extremely handsome**, with cheeks just shaded by the downiest of beardlets—and that most of his time was employed in country-sports and mountain-hunting. Then, to save herself from any contradictory phrases that would expose the truth, she loaded her sisters with gold and jewelled necklaces; and calling Zephyrus she bade him convey them back to the summit.

When these orders had been obeyed, the excellent sisters returned home, burning with rancorous jealousy that swelled at every step. Soon they were chattering with mutual indignation. One said to the other:

"So now you see how daft and cruel and unjust is Fortune! Did it overjoy you to find that we sisters, though we have the same parentage, have very different lots? Here are we, the elders by birth, delivered as bondsmaids to foreign husbands, packed far away from homeland and parents, like exiles. That's our life. And here is the youngest daughter, the end-product of our mother's decrepit womb, owning all that wealth and a god for a husband—and she doesn't even know how to make a proper use of her good fortune. You saw, sister, what a mass of necklaces lie about the house, and what value they are—what glistening stuff, what sparkling gems, what parquets of gold, she treads carelessly underfoot. If in addition to this she has the fine-looking husband that she describes, then there is no woman happier in the whole world. Perhaps when he is in the clutch of long habit and the ties of their affection are strengthened, **this god of a husband will make her a goddess too**.

"By Hercules, that's what he's done. That's the explanation of her airs and graces. Think of her. Think of her condescending pride. The woman breathes the goddess already, she with her attendant Voices and her ladyship over the very winds. But I (poor nothing) am fettered to a husband older than my father, a man who's balder than a pumpkin and as passionate as a peascod, a man who (to make matters worse) locks and bars up the whole house, the suspicious fool!"

"And I," answered the other, "**I have to lie down tamely under a husband who's tortured and twisted with gout**, and who consequently cultivates my venus-plot very sparsely. I spend most of the time in chafing his crippled chalky fingers and scalding my daintly white hands with stinking fomentations, filthy napkins, and horrid poultices. My role is not wife but nurse-of-all-works. You, sister, seem to tolerate your position with quite a deal of patience—I might say, low-spiritedness—for I believe in saying what I think. For my part I won't endure for another moment the good fortune that has dropped into the lap of one who doesn't deserve it. **Recollect also how overbearingly, how sneeringly she behaved toward us**; and how her puffed-up attitude peeped out of every boast that she couldn't control as she showed us around; and how she bundled on us against her will a few oddments of her huge wealth; and how then, bored with our company, she gave orders for us to be swept-up and blurted and whizzed away. I'm not a woman, I can't squeeze out another breath, unless I bring down this fine erection of fortunes; and if these insults rankle in you too, as they certainly ought, then let us concert some workable plan. First of all, let us agree not to show these things we're carrying to anyone—not even our parents. In short, we must not admit that we know she's alive and well. It is quite enough to have had the vexation of seeing

Psyche, Roman, from the Early empire. This statue shows the beauty of Psyche in the everyday task of pouring water. The emphasis is on the girl's humanity rather than on the divine status she achieves by the end.

"let's return equipped to lessen her pride"—The sisters' plans and their deployment are compared to a military assault.

"sworn in conspiracy"—The sisters cannot admit Psyche has a good marriage. Thus, they emerge as perfect villains for the preparatory section of the fairy tale.

"He reluctantly received them"—Even the servants shun Psyche's sisters; their malice is transparent to everyone, except, to Psyche.

reticule Purse.

"the hidden snare"—More military language to characterize the sisters' plan against Psyche.

"Psyche · . . . produced a fresh fiction"—Like a character in a comedy, Psyche is careless and is trapped by her own lies.

"if she has never seen his face, it must be a god that she has married"—The sister's logic is correct. The irony is that they are much shrewder than Psyche, and thus able to manipulate her successfully. From this point they are not trying to find out the identity of her husband. Rather, they want to confirm their hypothesis and ruin her marriage.

what we have seen, without scattering abroad the news of her glory among the family and the whole city. For there's no glory when nobody knows how rich she is. We'll teach her that we're not her slaves but her elder sisters. So for the present let's return to our husbands and our poor mediocre houses; and then after thoroughly digesting the situation **let's return equipped to lessen her pride.**"

[Omitted section: Psyche's husband warns her again about her sisters.]

But the brace of sisters, **sworn in conspiracy**, went straight from shipboard to the crag, made with haste. They did not even dawdle for the arrival of the carrier-wind, but leaped into the valleydepth with uncontrollable foolhardiness. Zephyrus however was mindful of the royal command. **He reluctantly received them** on the bosom of his soughing blast and bore them to the ground. With quickening steps the pair restlessly dashed into the house; and hiding behind the name of sisters they embraced their quarry. Then, strewing a smile upon the pit of their hoarded guile, they flattered her.

"Psyche, you're not as slim as you used to be. Soon you'll be a mother. Oh, you can't think what a joy for us all you're carrying in your **reticule**. The whole house will simply be wild with delight. Oh, how happy we will be to amuse your golden baby. For if he only matches his parents in beauty—and so he must— then he'll be a pure love."

Thus with a prattle that sounded like affection they won Psyche over. She at once made them seat themselves to recover from the fatigues of travel. She had them laved in warm flowing baths and entertained them at a choice repast where most-tasty dishes and concoctions marvellously came and went. She ordered the harp to twang, and it rippled sweetly—the flute to play, and its notes issued forth—the choir to sing, and they sang. The music ravished the souls of the hearers with its delicious cadences; but not a performer was to be seen.

But not all the honeyed song with its tempering sweetness mitigated one whit the wickedness of the scheming women. They guided the conversation towards **the hidden snare** and made deftly oblique inquiries as to the husband, what kind of a man he was, and where he was born, and what was his family.

Psyche in extreme artfulness forgot her former account and produced a fresh fiction. She said that her husband was a merchant from the adjoining province, a man of tremendous wealth, now middle-aged with a sprinkle of grey in his hair. Then again she abruptly changed the subject, loaded her sisters with presents, and sent them back on their wind-carriage. But while they were returning home, borne aloft on the tranquil breath of Zephyrus, they conferred as follows:

"What are we to say, sister, of the lurid lies of that idiot? One moment her husband is a young fellow that trims a beard of the softest down. The next moment he's a middle-aged man with hair showing silvery. Who can this be that in so brief a space suddenly becomes changed into an old man? There's only one explanation, my sister; and that is that this worthless woman is telling us a string of lies, or that she doesn't know herself what her husband looks like. But whichever supposition is true, she must as soon as possible have all these riches whipped away from her. And yet **if she has never seen his**

face, it must be a god that she has married and a god that she is bearing us under her belt. If that's so, and if she does become the mother of a divine babe (which heaven forbid), I'll string myself up on the spot in a noose.

Thus inflamed, the sisters tossed feverishly awake all night. Then, desperate in the morning, they rushed back to the crag, and by the usual vehicle of wind descended in frenzy. **They squeezed out some tears from under their lids, and guilefully said to Psyche**:

"Here you sit smiling when it's only blissful ignorance that stops you from seeing the terrible danger you're in. But we, who watch over your affairs so vigorously, are nailed on a cross of painful apprehension. We have discovered for an absolute fact something that in true sympathy with all sorrow and misfortune we cannot keep to ourselves any longer. We've discovered that it's a monstrous, twining, twisted, coiling, venomous, swollen-throated, ravenously gaping-jawed Serpent that reposes with you secretly in the night. Don't you recall the Pythian Responses that announced you the destined bride of a bloodthirsty beast? Besides, many of the country-folk who go hunting in these regions, and scores of the neighbours, saw him gliding home in the evening from his pasturage and swimming across the shoals of the river hard by.

"Everybody is saying that he won't long keep on pampering you with enticing complaisances in the way of food. But as soon as your womb is fully rounded with pregnancy he will gobble you up as an appetizing morsel in a prime state. So it's up to you to decide whether you want to listen to us, your sisters, who are thinking only of your best advantages—whether you want to escape death and to come to live with us, safe from all attacks; or whether you want to be engulfed in the bowels of a cruel beast.

"But if you're so keen on your rural solitude full of nothing but Voices—so attached to the filthy and dangerous embraces of clandestine lust, and the caresses of a poisonous serpent—at least we have discharged our duty like loving sisters."

Psyche (poor girl), so sincere herself and so tender-hearted, was stiff with horror at this dreadful disclosure. **Whirled out of all her senses**, she took no heed of her husband's admonitions and of her own promises. She felt herself swept before an avalanche of anguish. Trembling, with all the blood shocked out of her face, she managed at last in a strangled voice to falter out a few words:

"O my dearest sisters, you're still as loving as ever. You've acted as you ought, as your sisterly duty dictated. I'm sure that all you've been told seems to me genuine. For **I've never seen my husband's face, and I don't know where he comes from**. I only hear him whispering at night. I have to accept a husband of unknown standing, a shape that flees the light. So I agree that you must have hit the truth. He is some monster. He spends his time in frightening me from looking at him, and in threatening me with some great evil for being curious about his face. So if you can bring a ray of hope to your poor misguided sister, don't lose a moment. For if you neglect that, you'll undo all the good which your care has done me so far."

The wicked women, having thus **won the approaches to their sister's defenceless heart**, emerged from their ambushes and frankly assaulted the simple girl's panic-stricken meditations with the drawn sword of craft.

Accordingly the first answered. "Since the bond of blood obliges us to consider no personal danger when your life is at stake, we will show you the only road which leads to safety. **This plan is the result of our long, long thought**. On the side of the bed where you usually lie, hide a very sharp razor, whetted on the palm of your hand to the finest edge. And hide a lamp, trimmed and full of oil, a lamp that burns with a steady flame, behind some of the bedroom-hangings. Make all these arrangements with the utmost precaution. When the Thing has slid into the chamber and climbed up on the bed, wait until he's stretched out and begun to breathe heavily inside the coils of sleep. Then slip out of the sheets and tiptoe on bare feet slowly along the floor. Rescue the lamp from its shroud, and by the light's direction find the moment for this glorious deed. Boldly lift up your right-hand. Slash the blade down with all your strength, and sever the head of the baneful Serpent at the nape of the neck. And don't think we'll be far. We shall be anxiously standing by for the signal that your safety is secured. Then together we'll remove all this property; and and we'll soon see you married to a human being like yourself."

With all these arguments they poured flame into the vitals of their sister; and when they saw that she was fully kindled, they at once abandoned her. Afraid to be caught within the area of the approaching crisis, they were carried to the crag by the usual sudden blast; and hastening with brisk terror to the quay, they sailed away.

But Psyche, left alone (if a girl tormented by wild Furies can be considered alone), flooded and ebbed with sorrows like a stormy sea. She began to prepare for the ugly deed with assured intention and obdurate heart; but almost immediately she hesitated irresolute, distracted with wavering impulses and decisions. She hurried, then lagged. She was bold, then timid. She was doubtful, then furious. And (strangest of all) in the same person she hated the beast but loved the bridegroom. Yet as evening drew on the night, she made a last demented effort and prepared the scene for her wicked deed.

Night came; and her husband came; and after some amorous skirmishes he fell into a heavy sleep. Then drooping in body and mind, yet fed with unusual strength by the cruelty of fate, she brought forth the lamp and seized the knife, boldly shedding her sex.

The Act

But as soon as she raised the lamp and unbared the mystery of her bed, **she saw the sweetest and gentlest of all wild creatures:** Cupid himself, a beautiful god beautifully lying on the couch. At sight of him the flame burned cheerfully higher, and the razor dulled its sacrilegious edge.

But as for Psyche, she was terrified at the sight. She lost all self-control; and swooning, pallid, trembling, she dropped on her knees and sought to hide the knife—deep in her own bosom. And so she would have done, had it not been that the blade, shrinking from such an atrocity, fell to the floor out of her heedless hands. And then, for all her faintness and fear, she felt her flagging spirits revive as she gazed at the beauty of the god's face.

On the shoulders of the flying god there bloomed dewy plumes of gleaming whiteness; and though the wings themselves were laid at rest, yet the tender down that fringed the feathers frisked in a continuous running flutter. The rest of his body was so smoothly warmly rounded that Venus could look on it and feel no pang at having borne such a

Eros. Alabastron from Apulia, undated.

child. At the foot of the couch lay his bow, his quiver, and his arrows: the gracious weapons of the mighty god.

While **Psyche stood spellbound** with insatiable delight and worship, impelled by wonder she began to handle her husband's weapons. She drew one of the arrows out of the quiver and tested its sharpness, on the tip of her thumb. But pressing unduly hard (for her hand still trembled) she pricked the skin and evoked some tiny drops of rose-red blood. Then, burning more and more with desire for Cupid, she laid herself broadly upon him; and opening her mouth with forward kisses she applied herself eagerly to the embrace, fearing only that he would wake too soon.

But while she stirred above him in the extremity of agonized joy, the lamp (actuated either **by treachery, or by base envy,** or by a desire to touch so lovely a body—to kiss it in a lamp's way) spewed a drop of glowing oil from the point of its flame upon the god's right shoulder.

O bold and reckless lamp! base officer of love! to burn the very god of Flame—you that some lover, inspired by the need to possess the beloved even at night, first devised.

The god, thus burnt, leaped out of bed; and spying the scattered evidences of Psyche's forfeited truth, he rose into the air. He alighted upon a nearby cypress and gravely admonished her from its swaying top:

"O simple-hearted Psyche! Putting aside the commands of **my mother Venus who had bidden me infatuate you with some base wretch and degrade you to his bed,** I chose rather to fly to you myself as a lover. I acted rashly, well I know. I the world-famous archer stabbed myself with my own arrowhead. I took you for my wife—only to have you think me a wild bear and raise the blade to sever my head . . . which bears those very eyes that loved you so fondly.

"This it was I bade you always to beware. This it was against which my loving-heart forewarned you. But as for those fine advisers of yours, they shall pay heavily for their pernicious interference. My flight is penalty enough for you."

The Wanderings

As he ended, he spread his wings and soared out of sight. But Psyche lay prostrate on the ground and strained her eyes after her winging, vanishing husband, harassing her mind with most piteous outcries; and **when his wings with sweeping strokes had rapt him out of her life** into the vast distance, she crawled to a nearby river and threw herself from the bank into the waters. But the gentle stream, in horror and in reverent fear of the god who can heat even the dank water-deeps, took Psyche on the soft curl of a wave and laid her safe on the thick green turf of the bank.

It chanced that at this moment Pan the country-god was seated on the river-lip, embracing Echo, goddess of the mountainside. He was teaching her to sing all kinds of tunes. Near by, she-goats gamboled along the winding pasture of the banks, cropping the weedy tresses of the river. The goatfoot god, aware of Psyche's sad fate, compassionately called the sick and stricken girl to his side, and comforted her with friendly words:

"Pretty maiden, I am a country-fellow, a shepherd, but my mind is stored with much odd knowledge as the result of long experience. **If I may hazard a guess (which among wise men goes by the title of a divination)** I judge by these halting and stumbling steps, and by the extreme paleness of your face, and by the incessant sighs you heave, and by the sad look in your eyes, that you are madly in love.

"Hearken then to me. Seek no longer to lose your life by dashing yourself to pieces or by any other such recourse of despair. Lay grief aside. Cease your sorrow. Woo Cupid with adoring prayers. For he is the mightiest of the gods, a wanton lad and spoilt. **Press him with grateful offers of compliance.**"

"Psyche stood spellbound"—This parallels the scene near the beginning where Cupid pricks himself with his own arrow: Neumann says, the "original unity of the embrace in the darkness is transcended, and with Psyche's heroic act suffering, guilt and loneliness have come into the world."

"by treachery, or by base envy"—The joke provides a level of ironic distance which keeps the reader from being overly involved in the fate of the characters.

"O bold and reckless lamp!"—The speaker here is Apuleius, himself, who interrupts his own story, breaking through both the layer of Lucius' storytelling and that of the old woman to sing a brief hymn to the lamp held by Psyche.

"my mother Venus . . . had bidden me infatuate you with some base wretch and degrade you to his bed"—We were witness to this scene, but have not been told what Cupid did afterwards. Here Cupid tells Psyche, "I chose . . . to fly to you myself as a lover" and "I . . . stabbed myself with my own arrowhead." He describes his actions as rash; presumably they represented defiance of his overbearing mother.

"when his wings . . . had rapt him out of her life"—The elaborate preparatory section of the tale is over, and the lack which drives the first move has taken place. On the theories of Propp about fairy tales, see Ch. 34, p. 499.

"If I may hazard a guess (which among wise men goes by the title of a divination)"—The story that Apuleius tells has both mythical or religious elements and comic or ironic ones. This statement belongs in both categories, functioning to show the sophisticated nature of the author's religiosity, as he both accepts and questions the value of his beliefs.

"Press him with grateful offers of compliance."—Neumann suggests the god's advice to Psyche is "be feminine and win his love."

Praxiteles, *Capitoline Venus,* Roman copy (early Imperial age) of Greek 5th-c. B.C.E. original made for the sanctuary of Aphrodite at Knidos. The original of this statue was much-copied in antiquity. It shows that, despite her shrewish portrayal by Apuleius, the Romans thought of Aphrodite as beautiful and in some instances modest about her beauty.

"Cupid . . . lay moaning in his mother's bedroom"—Jung suggests that if a man's mother has a negative influence on him, his behavior is characterized by "irritable, depressed moods, uncertainty, insecurity, and touchiness." This description certainly fits Cupid's behavior to Psyche earlier, as well as his helplessness and dependency here. For more on the Jungian concept of the *anima,* which is heavily affected by a man's relationship with his mother, see Ch. 32, p. 479.

Thus spoke the shepherd-god; and Psyche, making no reply beyond an obeisance to his divinity, wandered on.

She traveled through many peoples, resolute in quest of Cupid; and **Cupid, wounded by the lampspilth, lay moaning in his mother's bedroom.** Then a white seagull, the bird that skims across the waves of the sea with its wings, dived down into the bosom of the waters. There, accosting Venus as she washed and swam, the bird informed her that her son was confined to bed, complaining of a severe burn; that his cure was doubted; and that gossip and insult of all kinds were being bandied about among mankind, involving the reputation of the whole Venus family. "The lad has been whoring in the mountains." "What is the name of the wench that seduced my ingenuous-hearted son who's not yet in man's clothes? Is she one of the tribe of Nymphs, or of the company of the Hours, or of the choir of the Muses, or of my own train of Graces?"

The garrulous bird said, "Let me see . . . if my memory doesn't deceive me, her name's Psyche."

"Psyche!" Venus cried in a fury of indignation. "Surely he hasn't picked out Psyche, the pretender to my throne of beauty, the rival of my renown! And, insult added to injury, he has taken me as a bawd, for it was my finger that pointed the way to the trollop."

With this complaint she rose up out of the sea, and hurried to her Golden Chamber, where she found her sick son, just as she had been told. Before she was through the door, she began yelling at him. "Fine goings-on! so perfectly in accord with our position in the scheme of things and your good name! First of all, **you trample on the express orders of your mother**—your queen I should say. Next, you refuse to stretch my enemy on the cross of dirty embraces. More, at your age you, a mere boy, entangle yourself in a low lewd schoolboy affair—just to annoy me with a woman I hate for daughter-in-law.

"However, I'll see that you're sorry for your games. You'll learn what a sour and bitter thing marriage is. But **now that you've made a laughing-stock of me,** what am I to do? Whither shall I wander? What snare will hold this slippery young scoundrel?

"I shall believe that I have atonement for my injury when I have shorn those golden locks which my hands have so often dressed—when I have clipped those wings which I have dyed in my bosom's fount of nectar."

Meanwhile, no longer able to continue the search for her flyaway husband, Psyche abandoned all hope of safety. Thus she communed with her own thoughts:

"What support can I expect to find, what remedy for my anguish, when even goddesses, no matter how sympathetic, must deny me their good word? Whither shall I turn, when there are snares on every side? **What roof may shelter me, what darkness hide me, from the inescapable eyes of mighty Venus?**

"There is nothing for it then, Psyche, but to bid your heart be manly, renounce boldly all shiverings of hope, deliver yourself a hostage to your mistress's wrath, and humbly (if not too late) wear down her cruelty. Who knows, moreover, whether you may not find in his mother's house one whom you have sought so long?"

Thus she prepared herself for a doubtful submission, which seemed to mean certain destruction; and she sought in her mind for the words with which to preface her surrender. **Venus, dropping all earthly methods of inquiry,** returned to heaven. She ordered out the chariot presented to her on the threshold of their marriage. The golden chariot adorned with exquisite carvings. The coach of the goddess was followed by irrepressibly chirruping sparrows, who wantoned as they went, while other **sweet-voiced birds announced the approach of the goddess with cheering honey-trills of song.**

She drove direct to the lordly citadel of Jove, and with a haughty air expressed herself as in urgent need of the services of the crier-god Mercury; nor did the sky-blue brow of Jove refuse its nod. Exultant Venus, companioned by Mercury, precipitately descended from heaven, and thus earnestly addressed him:

"Brother of Arcady, you know well that your sister Venus never did anything without the presence of Mercury; and you must have heard how long I have been vainly searching for my absconded slave-girl. **The only resource left is to have you make public proclamation after her, with due offerings of reward.** Then get to work at once. Do as I bid. **Broadcast a full description** with all details, so that no one can plead ignorance as an excuse for the crime of naughtily sheltering her."

"you trample on the express orders of your mother"—Neumann notes that Venus is behaving like a wicked stepmother here. In what follows, Psyche will be saving him from her, causing him to grow up.

"now that you've made a laughing-stock of me"—This story is not the first to represent the goddess of Love in a humorous way. In Homer's *Odyssey,* a work dating to the 8th c. C.E., the poet Demodocus tells a story in which Aphrodite (Venus) is caught by Hephaistos (Vulcan) with her adulterous lover Ares, to the amusement of the other gods (*Odyssey* VIII.266–366).

"What roof may shelter me, what darkness hide me, from . . . Venus?"—The goddess' power was well-known. The most famous account is by Sappho, "My tongue breaks off and I am left here bereft of speech, struck dumb. My skin takes fire . . . and there is emptiness before my eyes, and in my ears such thunder that sweat pours over me."

"Venus, dropping all earthly methods of inquiry"—This draws upon the standard Roman procedure for reclaiming a runaway slave.

"sweet-voiced birds announced the approach of the goddess with cheering honey-trills of song"—Two-part nouns ("honey-trills") and adjectives ("sweet-voiced") make this sound like the poet Homer. The solemnity of the elevated language will be deflated by Venus' comic behavior when she finds Psyche.

"'The only resource left is to have you make public proclamation. . . . Broadcast a full description.—These details show the way storytellers incorporate laws and customs from their own societies in the mythical stories they tell.

"by way of reward seven times a Kiss of Bliss and once a Kiss honeyed-beyond-measure"—The humorous reward is reminiscent of ancient Greek comedy, in which the gods behave to some extent normally, while parodying their own powers. For example, in *The Frogs* of Aristophanes, Dionysos, often portrayed as wearing feminine robes (normal attribute), goes down to Hades, and behaves like a total coward (parody).

So saying, she handed him a booklet containing Psyche's name and other particulars and thereupon departed home. Mercury obediently set to work. He travelled across the face of the earth, dutifully performing the required offices of crier. He announced:

"Ho, if anyone can produce in person, or give information as to the place of concealment of a certain runagate princess, a slave-girl of Venus, Psyche by name, let him hie to Mercury the crier at the rear of the Murtian Sanctuary, and receive **by way of reward seven times a Kiss of Bliss and once a Kiss honeyed-beyond-measure** by the interjection of her alluring tongue."

The Realm of Venus

After this specifying proclamation, all mankind were converted into rivals zealously competing for the coveted prize. Psyche consequently banished all remaining hesitations; and she was nearing the gates of her lady's dominion, when she was met by one of Venus's best servants, Mistress Habit by name. At once Habit bawled out at the top of her voice:

"wicked wench . . . harlotries"—Venus' servant lords it over Psyche without much concern for logic. Here she speaks of Psyche's immoral behavior, while Venus later refers to herself as the girl's mother-in-law, implying a wedded union.

"prisoner"—Psyche will perform tasks set by Venus. Her deeds will resemble those of Heracles, whose labors to satisfy a malicious Hera (see Ch. 31, p. 453). Psyche will even visit the underworld, as did Heracles. Yet her way of accomplishing the tasks contrasts her abilities with those of Heracles.

"So here you are, you **wicked wench!** You know who's mistress now, eh? Or do you pretend, to add to the rest of all your **harlotries,** that you don't know what a world of trouble we've been taking to sniff you out? I'm glad you've fallen in my hands and not another's; for you've strayed into the very jaws of hell, and you'll find that what's coming to you (you rebel) has a very nasty edge to it."

With that she grabbed Psyche by the hair and dragged the unresisting girl along to Venus. As soon as the mistress recognized the maltreated **prisoner,** she burst into a loud laugh—the laugh of a person in a rage—and tossed her head and scratched behind her right ear.

"At last," she said, "you've condescended to call on your mother-in-law. Or perhaps you meant to visit your husband, who lies at death's door because of your doings? Make yourself at ease. I'll receive you as a good mother should. Where," she called, "are those servants of mine, Care and Sorrowing?"

The pair entered, and Psyche was handed over to their ministrations. They followed out their mistress's instructions, scourging and tormenting the poor girl; and when she had been racked on the cross of pain, they brought her back for Venus to gloat upon.

"whore-fruit . . . the glorious scion that is to make me a doting grandmother"—Now it is Venus who combines incompatible descriptions. She justifies her view later by speaking in negative legal terms of the union of Cupid and Psyche ("unequal marriages . . . cannot possibly be considered binding"). There is some irony in seeing the goddess of love, who is supposed to be desirable and young, as a grandmother.

Again Venus laughed harshly. "Look at her," she said. "The **whore-fruit** that swells her belly quite stirs my pity, since there lodges **the glorious scion that is to make me a doting grandmother.** Of course I shall be happy to be made a grandmother in the very flower of my age; and the son of a cheap slave-girl will be the grandson of Venus. And yet I'm talking nonsense in calling him my grandchild; for unequal marriages, consummated in a country-hole without witnesses or the father's consent, cannot possibly be considered binding in law. The child therefore will be born a bastard—that is, if I allow you to bring the brat to birth at all."

The Four Tasks

"taking wheat, barley, mullet, poppyseed, pease, lentils, and beans"—Here Psyche receives her first task from Venus. Sorting tasks are often found in fairy tales. Psyche, as the representative of the human soul, is the perfect character to perform such a task, which psychologists say symbolizes the unconscious' attempt to organize and characterize its experiences. She is assisted by ants, creatures from the earth, which represent her deeply seated instincts.

After this denunciation she leaped upon Psyche, tore her clothes into shreds, tugged out her hair, shook her by the head, and beat her black and blue. Then **taking wheat, barley, mullet, poppyseed, pease, lentils, and beans,** and mixing them into a single confused hillock, she said:

"To my eyes you're such an ugly slut that the only way you're ever likely to get a lover is by working your fingers off for him. Separate this promiscuous mass of seeds. Sort out each grain; and collect them all in their original heaps. See to it that you obtain my approval by having the task finished when I return at dusk."

Committing the huge heap of seeds to Psyche's care, she departed for a marriage-banquet. But Psyche did not lift a hand towards the hopelessly confused mound. She sat staring in silent stupefaction at the impossible task. Just then **an ant** (tiny toiler of the fields), **realizing what a monstrous labour had been set the girl,** felt himself revolted with pity for the mighty godling's mate and with anger at the mother-in-law's cruelty. Dashing busily about, he summoned the whole tribe of ants that were at work in the nearby meadows, invoking them thus:

"Have pity, O ye nimble-footed swarms born from Great Mother Earth. Have pity and come promptly on all feet to the succour of the wife of Love, a sweet-faced girl in danger of her life."

Then quickly more and more of the six-footed people flurried and scurried in waves of haste, sorting the mass, carting it grain by grain away—until at last when every grain was separated into its right heap they hurriedly vanished. When night came, Venus returned from the nuptial feast, warm with wine and redolent of balsam, her whole body twined with glowing rose-wreaths. As soon as she saw the incredible task duly done, "Slut," she said, "this is no work of your hands. He did it all, the lad you seduced to the hurt of both of you." Then casting her a crust of brown bread, she retired to sleep.

Meanwhile Cupid was shut in his bedroom, in solitary confinement, partly to prevent him from chafing his wound by some act of wanton self-indulgence, partly to keep him apart from his beloved. The lovers, thus divided though beneath the same roof, passed a long and bitter night. But the moment that **Aurora came riding up,** Venus called Psyche and spoke as follows:

"Do you see that strip of woodland growing along the banks of the river where the greenery bends down over the spring hard by? Shining sheep wander there, with thick fleeces the colours of gold, pasturing without a shepherd. I bid you to **go thither and bring me** speedily back, by whatever means you like, **some of the wool of their fleeces.**"

Psyche went out willingly, not to perform the set task but to find release from her miseries by jumping off a rock into the river. But when she came to the river, **a green-growing reed** (foster nurse of flowing music), divinely inspired by a soft breath of articulate sweetness, thus **murmured a prophecy:**

"Poor Psyche, so tired, so sorrowful, pollute not my holy waters with your lamentable death; nor seek yet to approach the **dangerous wild-sheep** that fill these banks with terror. While burning in the rays of the sun, they borrow his heat; they range in formidable frenzy; and with buttings of their sharpened horns and rocklike heads, or (as oft happens) with their poisonous bites, they worry men to death. Then wait till the sun of noon has slackened the reins of his heat—till the spirit of the river breathes out a lulling influence, and beasts sleep. Lie hidden meanwhile under the shade of that lofty plane-tree which drinks from the same breast of waters as myself. As soon as the sheep have ceased from wandering in madness and lie down to rest, then shake the branches of the neighbouring trees and you will find the woolly gold is sticking richly to the lower twigs."

Thus the single-hearted reed humanely showed the wretched Psyche how to save her life. Psyche carefully went ahead with the instructions, and found that they paid her well. **The theft was easy** and she returned to Venus with a bosomful of the downy burning gold. But even then, after the success of this perilous second task, she was unable to earn her mistress's regard. Smiling bitterly with knitted brows, Venus said to her:

"I am not deceived. **This deed is also bastardly mothered.** Next time I shall test you properly, to see if you are really imbued with such resolution, my stout-heart, and with such singular providence. Do you see the top of yonder high and precipitous mountain? From that crest there gush the dusky waters of a black springhead, which

"an ant . . . realizing what a monstrous labour had been set the girl"—In many tales, the hero acquires the help of the ants or other small animals by championing them in some fashion, say by turning his horse aside so it does not walk on the ants in the road. Here the appearance of the ant is motivated only by generosity.

"Aurora came riding up"—Aurora is the goddess of the dawn. Instead of saying, "the sun rose," Apuleius comically presents her casual appearance as a character.

"go thither and bring me . . . some of the wool of their fleeces" —The second task is more difficult than the first: the danger it poses is hidden by Venus.

"a green-growing reed . . . murmured a prophecy"—Again, a donor appears without prior effort by Psyche. Lena Ross suggests that here Apuleius refers to the story of Syrinx, a nymph Pan tried to rape; she begged to be turned into a reed to escape.

"dangerous wild-sheep"—The animals of the sun are traditionally viewed as dangerous. In the *Odyssey,* Zeus punishes Odysseus' crewmen who kill and eat the cattle of Helios, the sun; the hides of the animals crawl and their meat lows as they cook it (XII.127–419). With this task, Apuleius begins a series of links between Psyche and Heracles. In his eighth labor, Heracles must contend with the man-eating mares of Diomedes (see Ch. 31, p. 456).

"The theft was easy"—Heracles defeats the man-eating animals with his strength. Neumann suggests that, following Pan's suggestion at the start of her wanderings, Psyche prevails through her feminine qualities.

"This deed is also bastardly mothered"—Venus would like to see Psyche "sweat a little," but the girl's pains and difficulties in the previous quest have not been revealed to her. She switches tactics, and this time states the task while revealing its dangers and difficulties.

Raphael (1483–1520), *Psyche and Venus.*

are dammed-up in the valley below; and thence they seep through to the Stygian Marshes, and feed the hoarse torrent of Cocytus. Out of the depths of that loftily bubbling spring fetch me this phial full of icy water."

With these words she gave her a bottle of cut crystal, adding even more savage threats than previously. Psyche began the climb towards the summit of the mountain with anxious care; for she thought that there at last she would find the conclusion of her miseries. But as soon as she reached the skirts of the described ridge, she saw the deadly difficulty of the enterprise. For a tall boulder, huge in bulk rugged and affording no foothold, **vomited** from the midst of its stone-jaws the **ugly jets of spring water** which, falling straight out of a cavernous hole that sloped downward, ran into a deep, narrow, covered water-course and were thus carried underground into the valley below. **On both sides** along the cracked crags **there crawled** with long outstretched necks a brood of **fierce dragons,** keeping unflagging watch **with indefatigable eyes**—the relentless glare beating on lidless sockets.

Psyche stood chilled to stone before the improbability of the task. But **the royal bird of high Jove** (swooping eagle) suddenly appeared, coming with wide-spread wings **mindful of his ancient obligations to Cupid**—by whose agency he had rapt-up **the Phyrgian lad** to be Jove's cupbearer.

Therefore, bringing timely aid, the eagle transferred his allegiance to the perplexed wife of the god, and left the trails of Jove high in the heavens. Flapping about the girl's face, he thus addressed her:

"Ah, simple one, unlearned in the world's ways, how can you hope ever to dip a finger or snatch one drop of this holy and no-less murdering stream? Have you never heard that these **Stygian waters** are dreaded by all the gods, including Jove himself; and that as you mortals swear by the Power of the Gods, so the gods swear by the Majesty of Styx? But give me that phial."

Without another word he tore the bottle from her and gripped it in his claws. He steered his veering course to left and right until he reached the crest and filled the phial from the quarrelling waters that told him to be gone or it would be the worse for him. But he pretended that Venus herself had dispatched him for the draught; and by this stratagem he managed to approach near enough for success. Psyche joyously received the full bottle, and returned quickly to Venus; but even now she could not appease the wrath of the offended goddess. For, menacing her with heavier and more vicious shames, the latter finally said with an implacable smile:

"You seem to me a witch as subtly witted as you are blackhearted, or how did you dispose so nimbly of my commands? But there is one task more, my puppet. **Take this box,**" she went on, handing it over, "**and go instantly to the depths of hell** and the ghastly home of death. Then present the box to Proserpine and say: Venus's compliments, and would you please send back a scrap of your beauty, at least enough to eke out a winter's day; for Venus regrets that through her devotion to her son's sick-bed, she has wasted and fretted all her own. But don't linger on the way, for I must prink myself with this borrowed beauty before I go to the Theatre of the Gods."

Now Psyche saw that she was trembling on the brink and that she was frankly designated for immediate destruction; for Venus had dropped her mask and bidden the girl take herself off on a message to Tartarus and the Shades. So she thought that the quickest way to obey would be to go to the top of a high tower and jump; for this seemed to her the straight road down, the easiest road by far, to hell.

But when she got there, **the tower suddenly spoke to her.** "Why, poor girl," it said, "do you seek death by dashing yourself to pieces? Why do you thoughtlessly collapse under the final danger that you are called on to face? Once your spirit is driven out of your body, you'll be packed off to the depth of Tartarus quick enough; but you won't be able to return on any pretext. Hearken to me. Lacedaemon, a noble city of Achaia, is not far hence. Seek out Taenarus, which is hidden deviously near by. There you will find the ventilation-hole of hell; and through the yawning door leads down an untrodden track. Cross that threshold, and hold on straight along that passage, and you will come to the kingdom of death. But beware of pressing forward unprovisioned into those caverns of darkness. You must take in each hand a sop of **barley-bread soaked in honey-wine, and in your mouth two bits of money.** When you have travelled a fair part of your hellish journey, you will encounter a lame ass laden with wood, and an ass-driver lame as well. The man will ask you to pick up some of the chips that have dropped out of the load. Do not stop; do not answer; pass quickly. Then go directly on till you come to the Dead River, where Charon, after extorting his due price, ferries the incoming traffic across to the Farther Shore in his patched skiff. Greed, you see, flourishes among the dead. Neither Charon nor the great god Dis, his father, does anything unfee'd. The poor man on his deathbed must not forget his viaticum; and if he should have no money in his fist, men refuse to let him breathe his last. Therefore, to this foul old man give one of the coins you carry for your fare; but make him take it with his own fingers from your mouth.

A colossal dog, sprouting three large fiercely ravening heads, snaps and barks thunderously at the dead, whom he may scare but cannot injure. Unwearyingly before the threshold and dark Palace of Proserpine he stands, guard of the Plutonian Void. Appease this dog with one of your sops, and pass safely on. Then you will find yourself in the very presence of Proserpine, who will receive you with all kindly courtesy. She will bid you seat yourself on cushions and eat of a luxurious meal. But you must sit on the ground and ask for a scrap of brown bread. Then explain your message; and after taking what she gives you, return, diverting the fanged dog with the remaining sop. Give the greedy ferryman the coin that you have reserved. He will row you back, and you can retrace your steps till you come to the Choir of the Stars of Heaven. But I give you one especially strong warning. **Do not open or peep into the box you carry, and repress all curiosity** as to the Imprisoned Treasure of Divine Beauty."

Thus that discerning Tower offered Psyche its vaticinatory services. Psyche went straightway to Taenarus, correctly equipped herself with coins and sops, and ran down the infernal passage. She passed the stumbling ass without a word, paid the river-fare to the ferryman, bribed the raging dog with the sop of bread, and entered the mansion of Proserpine. She refused the seat of ease and the morsel of luxury. Sitting humbly at the queen's feet and gnawing only a slice of wholemeal bread, she performed the embassy of Venus. The box was at once secretly filled, closed, and handed to her. **She** then cheated with the second sop the howling dog, paid the sculler with the other coin, and **emerged from hell, brimming over with new life.**

She gazed once more upon the sun and worshipped the tide of Light. Then, despite her anxiety to complete her errand, she felt a rash curiosity mount to her head. "Here now," she murmured, "what a foolish carrier of divine beauty am I, who do not cull the tiniest little smudge for myself, so that I may please my beautiful lover."

"the tower suddenly spoke to her"—Once again, Apuleius provides no motivation for the help Psyche receives from the tower. He seems less interested in the human aspects of this part of his story, and here devotes his efforts to providing his heroine with a crash course in the proper way to undertake this trip.

"barley-bread soaked in honey-wine . . . two bits of money"—These were the standard items needed to enter Hades successfully and were used by Heracles. The lame ass and ass driver, the entreaties of the old man, and the invitation of Proserpine were perhaps invented by Apuleius.

"A colossal dog, sprouting three large fiercely ravening heads"—Cerberus is the traditional guardian of the entrance of Hades.

"Do not open or peep into the box you carry, and repress all curiosity"—Curiosity is a great temptation in Greek myth. Pandora, the first woman, is given a box or a cask that she opened, and released trouble and care for human beings. In this story, Psyche has already gotten into trouble through curiosity about her husband's identity. In Apuleius' frame story, Lucius' curiosity about witchcraft results in his being turned into an ass.

"She . . . emerged from hell, brimming over with new life"—A trip to Hades or hell signals the death of the traveler, and thus the return represents a rebirth. Psyche, who has been passive for most of the story, is reborn into taking some initiative. Unfortunately, she moves immediately in a direction which was warned against by her helper, the tower.

Antonio Canova, (1757–1822), *Psyche brought back to life by the kiss of Amor.*

With this intention she opened the box. But it held no Recipe of Beauty. In it lurked Sleep of the Innermost Darkness, the night of Styx, which freed from its cell rushed upon her and penetrated her whole body with a heavy cloud of unconsciousness and enfolded her where she lay. For she collapsed doubled-up on the ground; and there she lay without the slightest stir, a corpse asleep.

The Happy End

"he roused Psyche"—Psyche's failure at last rouses Cupid from his passivity and he intervenes to save her. This represents his liberation from the bonds of his mother, and her incestuous hold on him suddenly evaporates.

But Cupid's wound had now healed into a scar; and he himself could not bear his long separation from Psyche. So he slipped out through the high window of his chamber, where he was enclosed. His wings, strengthened by their rest, bore him even swiftlier than before, as he hastened to find his Psyche. Delicately purging her of the Sleep, which he put back in its original lair the box, **he roused Psyche** with a charming prick of his Arrow.

"Look now," he said. "Again you have ruined yourself, unhappy one, by your uncontrollable curiosity. Now go ahead and complete the business with which my mother entrusted you. I shall see to the rest."

"Cupid . . . had recourse again to tricks"—Here his tricks seem to consist of in pleading his case while looking like a pathetic and loveable young man who was bound to be attractive to the bisexual father of the gods.

With these words her lover rose airily on his wings, while Psyche lost no time in carrying Proserpine's present to Venus. But **Cupid,** wasted and lean-jawed with excess of love, **had recourse again to his tricks.** On wings of haste he climbed the peak of heaven; and kneeling before great Jove, he pleaded his cause.

Jove stroked the cheeks of Cupid, and taking the lad's hand kissed it. "Although, my son and master," he said, "you never pay me the respect which the Parliament of Gods voted me—although, on the contrary, you assault with swarming blows this breast of mine, in which repose the laws of the Elements and the motions of the Stars—although you defile my life with continual episodes of earthly lust, to the subversion of the Laws, the **Julian Edict against Adultery,** and the Social Order—though you injure my name and fame with the blots of fornication, transforming my serene majesty into snakes, flames, wild beasts, birds, and cattle—yet, remembering by reputation for moderate action, remembering that you have been nursed in these very hands, I shall grant your prayer. At the same time you are aware that you had been strengthening your position. . . .

So, if there is any young girl on earth at the moment showing a particular aptitude in charms, you ought to make her mine in recompense for my present services."

Having thus spoken, he bade Mercury summon forthwith an Assembly of the Gods and announce that if any member of the Heavenly Host stayed away he (or she) should be **fined ten thousand pieces of money.** This threat soon packed the Celestial Theatre; and taking his seat on the exalted throne lofty Jupiter made the following speech:

"**Conscript Gods,** enrolled in the scroll of the Muses, this youth whom I have reared with my own hands is thoroughly well known to you all. I have deemed it advisable to restrain the heated impulses of his young blood by some means or other. No further reasons need be adduced beyond the daily scandal that he creates with adulteries and all manner of profligacy. All occasion for this must be removed, and his youthful sportiveness must be hampered with nuptial fetters. He has chosen a girl and seduced her. Let him take her and possess her. Let him hold her in his arms and never depart from the delight of that embrace."

Then turning to Venus he continued: "And you, my daughter, dry your tears; and do not fear that the family-tree and your rank will suffer from this wedding with a mortal. **For I shall legislate that the marriage is not a misalliance** but perfectly in accord with usage and the civil code.

He then instructed Mercury to snatch Psyche up and bring her to heaven; and on her arrival he handed her a cup of ambrosia. "Drink this, Psyche," he said, "and become immortal. Cupid will never swerve from your embrace and you will live in an eternally celebrated wedlock."

So it was done; and a glorious marriage-banquet was served. The bridegroom reclined in the seat of honour, holding Psyche to his breast; and Jupiter was seated similarly with Juno; and so on with all the other gods in their right precedence.

Then Jupiter was presented with a bowl of nectar (the wine of the gods) by **his special cupbearer the country-lad,** while Liber filled for the rest. Vulcan cooked the dinner; the Hours emblazoned everything with roses and other flowers; the Graces scattered balsam; the Muses sang in harmony; Apollo chanted to his lyre; and beautiful Venus danced, her gestures chiming with the music. The arrangement of the concert was as follows: the Choir, Muses; Flautist, Satyrus; piper, Paniscus. Thus at last Psyche was properly married to Cupid; and in due time she bore him a daughter, whom we call Joy.

Julian Edict against Adultery In 18 c.e., the Roman Emperor Augustus passed a series of moral reform laws, promoting marriage and childbirth and discouraging adultery.

"fined ten thousand pieces of money"—A humorous reference to the Roman practice of fining those who did not do their duty by appearing at assemblies.

"Conscript Gods"—An ironic echo of the title used to address the Roman Senate, who were called "conscript fathers," in reference to the fact that they had been called upon (or conscripted) to serve by the votes of their fellow citizens.

"For I shall legislate that the marriage is not a misalliance"—Throughout this section, Jupiter is humorously portrayed as an emperor who maintains the outward form of republican government, but uses it to provide a stamp of approval for his own wishes. Such behavior was typical of Roman emperors.

"his special cupbearer the country-lad"—Ganymede, the young man Jupiter's eagle refers to in helping Psyche earlier.

Further Reading

Apuleius, *The Golden Ass.* Trans. Jack Lindsay. Bloomington, IN: University of Indiana Press, 1932.

38

Using Multiple Analyses to Highlight Different Aspects of the Same Tale

WHAT TO EXPECT . . . Because the various methods of analyzing myths are based on achieving different, specific ends, using more than one method can provide a deeper understanding of the myth and the society that "owns" it. This chapter puts into practice methods of analysis described in detail in earlier chapters: looking for the various aspects of myth (Ch. 1, p. 3), Campbell's Hero's Quest (Ch. 14, p. 159), Levi-Strauss' anthropological structuralist analysis (Ch. 20, p. 280), Jung's psychological analysis (Ch. 32, p. 468, and Ch. 33, p. 485), and Propp's morphological analysis (Ch. 34, p. 499, and Ch. 35, p. 514).

In this chapter there is a historical discussion centering on the significance of Mother Goose and her relationship to fairy tales. In considering the Grimms' "The Goose Girl" and "The Raven" from several perspectives, including psychological, historical, and sociological, you will see that the synergy among methods provides a more comprehensive understanding of the stories and their audience.

As you read, compare the Proppian and Jungian analyses of "The Raven" and the Levi-Straussian and Jungian analyses of "Who Framed Roger Rabbit" with ideas in the earlier chapters defining the methods of analysis used. Look for stories and films in your own repertoire that can be interpreted in similar ways.

Students who are learning different theories about myth will sometimes wonder which analysis is the best one or the right one to use. The answer is often very simple: try different analyses and find the one that shows you most about how a story works. A successful analysis will highlight patterns of various sorts occurring in the story. You will be able, from these patterns, to learn more about what the message or the meaning of the story might be to different people at different times. At times, the use of several analyses of the same story will give you even more information about the impact of the story. The purpose of this chapter is to illustrate the use of multiple analyses, both to make the use of such a methodology clearer and to provide added insight into what may constitute the meaning of a myth or fairy tale.

This chapter is meant to complement the discussion in Chapter 33 (p. 485), which shows that performing several Jungian analyses on the same story may be a way of learning more about the story's significance. The main difference here is that instead of performing multiple Jungian analyses, we are recommending different kinds of analyses whose significance can be brought into harmony with each other.

In this chapter, we assume familiarity with a variety of different ways of looking at a fairy tale. You can go right ahead and read this chapter without backtracking, but if some of the discussion leaves you confused, you may want to go back to the original chapters that explain the method of analysis being used. We provide references throughout to earlier chapters. The methods of analysis referred to in this chapter include the following: functional analysis, which considers the different kinds of insights a story may provide about its culture (Ch. 1, p. 13); analysis according to the Hero's journey pattern found in Campbell's *Hero with a Thousand Faces* (Ch. 14, p. 159); Levi-Straussian or structuralist analysis (Ch. 20, p. 280); Jungian analysis (Ch. 32, p. 468 and Ch. 33, p. 485); and Proppian analysis, which is also called structuralist in a very different sense from the analysis of Levi-Strauss (Ch. 34, p. 499 and Ch. 35, p. 514).

Introduction: Meanings of a Myth or Fairy Tale

In discussing the **meaning of myths** or fairy tales, it is a good idea to remember the perspectives that Victor Turner identifies as relevant to the study of rituals, as they also apply to the study of fairy tales. Perhaps the most important distinction we will want to make is that between being "inside" a culture and being "outside" of it. Turner points out that there are **three different points of view** from which to view any ritual: exegetical, operational, and positional. The exegetical perspective refers to how a person participating in a ritual would explain it; the operational perspective explains how a person from the outside, like an anthropologist or other scholar, would describe what happened at the ritual; and the positional perspective refers to the role of the ritual in the whole complex of symbols and meanings found in the culture, and thus can represent an insider's point of view, but is usually associated with an outsider's perspective. Turner's ideas on perspective apply as well to the meaning of myths as they do to the study of ritual. For the most part, as students, we are looking at the meaning of the myth from outside the culture, and considering its meaning in relationship to the other symbols and stories found in the culture (positional perspective). But we also need to consider its meaning to the people within the culture (exegetical perspective).

For example, we can say that the myth of Demeter explained the seasons to the Greeks (see Ch. 27, p. 399f.), but what do we mean when we say this? Are we saying that an ancient Greek did not understand the fact that the seasons were caused by the changes in the sun's relationship to earth? It is important to remember Turner's positional dimension and to consider how the belief in the myth of Demeter fit with other beliefs of the Greeks. Greek science was actually rather far advanced for its time: it was well known that the sun moved north to south and back again. Either Thales or his pupil Anaximander, who lived in the sixth century B.C.E., discovered the oblique angle of the zodiac, which is how we explain the seasons today. All the same, all ancient Greeks weren't identical, any more than are people in our own time. Some had a better understanding of science than others. Surveys of our students in turn-of-the-century America suggest that many can't explain what causes the seasons, so it would not be surprising if this were true of some ancient Greeks as well. Thus, we have to assume that for some ancient Greeks the story was literally true, while for others it was just a story that had some meaning, but didn't substitute for science any more than such a story would for many in our day.

Multiple Perspectives on a Story

Even though the Greeks did not, for the most part, view it as a substitute for a scientific explanation of the seasons, the story's importance was great, as it was associated with the rituals of Demeter at Eleusis, a major institution in Greece for centuries. In that sense it is in some ways similar to the stories about extraterrestrials' appearance at Roswell, New Mexico, in 1957. **Attitudes toward this story run the gamut** from literal belief to debunking a false story (the common sense of the word "myth," and not the one we have been using in this book). At the same time, for many people in our culture, these stories about extraterrestrials are symbolic or playful. As we can see in the discussion of the television show *The X-Files* in Ch. 40, p. 590, the stories about Roswell can have a meaning for people, even if they don't consider them completely true. And they certainly can, in the positional sense, tell us something about our society, for which

---

"meaning of myths"—Myths are often related to rituals. At least provisionally, the same concepts can be applied to studying them as to studying rituals. Their meaning can be formulated "inside" (within the rules of the culture) or "outside" a story.

"three different points of view"—Victor Turner's ideas on ritual are discussed more fully in Ch. 26, p. 373. They include the following perspectives:

- Exegetical: explanation from inside the culture
- Operational: explanation by a figure from outside the culture
- Positional: relationship of a ritual or myth to all the other beliefs in the culture (can be inside, mostly outside)

Example: The story of Demeter.

inside the culture—The story explained the seasons to the Greeks.

outside the culture—The story explains the science of the Greeks to us in relation to our own beliefs in science, as long as we are careful to put it in perspective with what historians and other scholars have shown about Greek science.

"Attitudes toward this story run the gamut"—It is important to remember that any society includes a range of opinions and beliefs about any phenomenon, including the meaning of the stories told by its members.

Frontispiece, *Tales of My Mother Goose*, by Charles Perrault, 1697. Note that Mother Goose, seated at the left, is a woman, not an animal.

Example:
"The Goose Girl"—meanings of a myth as seen from outside the culture.

 **The Association Between "The Goose Girl" and Mother Goose**

 **Historical Bases for Mother Goose**

These ideas come from: Marina Warner, *From the Beast to the Blonde: on Fairy Tales and their Tellers.*

 **Links between the Queen of Sheba and Mother Goose**

"Warner argues that the goose foot marks a storyteller whose stories portray a . . . subversive world"— Fairy tales are subversive because they gave more freedom to women and to women's wisdom than did society at large. A similar trend can be seen in the worship of Dionysus, the Greek god of wine, which involved stories about women who were freed from their household tasks to celebrate the worship of the god. In fact, such stories do not overturn societal rules, but they do make them more tolerable by providing a break from their strict enforcement. (See Ch. 31, p. 459f.)

 **Links between Bertha, Mother Goose, and "The Goose Girl"**

"Trust No One" (the motto of the television show) has definite meaning. Thus, we can suggest that, even within our society, there is more than one way of looking at or thinking about a story. Thus, multiple analyses of a story can highlight aspects of its meaning that occur inside the culture or outside of it, depending on how we have framed our inquiry and how much information we have at our disposal about the people who told the stories and the intellectual and political history of their culture.

For example, let us consider "The Goose Girl," a fairy tale collected by the Brothers Grimm. (See Ch. 36, p. 527 for the text of the story.) In this story, the main character, the princess, is put in charge of a flock of geese and possesses a horse whose head continues to tell tales even after the animal is killed and its head is hung up on a fence.

The association of the princess with geese and with magical stories is of special interest to some scholars because in our culture, we associate fairy tales with Mother Goose, an old woman who was supposed to have been their originator.

We can learn something about "The Goose Girl" from the real women who are associated with it. Various women have been identified as the real Mother Goose, including Marie-Jeanne L'Héritier de Villandon, who wrote fairy tales in her own right and may have influenced the famous writer of fairy tales Charles Perrault, who subtitled his 1697 book, *Tales of My Mother Goose.* Another figure connected with Mother Goose is Dorothea Viehmann, from whom the Grimm Brothers got many of their stories, including "The Goose Girl." The brothers included Viehmann's portrait as the frontispiece of their collection; in the English translation of the tales, it is identified as Gammer (meaning "old wife") Grethel and the stories are called *Gammer Grethel's Fairy Tales.* However, Marina Warner, in her study of fairy tales, says, "A figure like Mother Goose turns out to have a recorded, empirical history, [and] to be compacted of many beliefs." So it is worthwhile to consider the various stories that are linked with Mother Goose and that may be connected to "The Goose Girl" as well.

Among the components of our image of Mother Goose, Warner includes the Queen of Sheba, who visited Solomon in the Bible and, impressed by his wisdom, was converted to the worship of Yahweh (1 Kings 10:1–13, 2 Chr. 9:1–12). In medieval stories and portraits, the Queen of Sheba is represented as having the foot of a goose, and refusing to step with it on a bridge made of the wood that will become the cross on which Christ is crucified. In Warner's view, the goose foot symbolizes the heathen or demonic aspects of the Queen and has the same meaning in representations of Mother Goose, whose stories constituted instruction in the female realm of the nursery. **Warner argues that the goose foot marks a storyteller whose stories portray a bawdy, vulgar, and subversive world** in which the differences between human beings are defined according to morality and not gender or social status. In this world, society's limits on women's sphere of action and its criticism of women's wisdom are routinely violated and challenged.

Warner traces a connection between the Grimm Brothers' Goose Girl and the historical Bertha, the mother of the great French leader Charlemagne. She was reputed to have "a foot much larger than any other woman of her day," and she was portrayed with a single webbed foot like that of a goose. In a mid-thirteenth-century poem called **"Big-Footed Bertha,"** the minstrel Adenet describes how Aliste, Bertha's maid, **takes the queen's rightful place as Pepin's bride** and queen and makes up horrendous charges against her, but eventually the queen is reinstated and the maid is punished. Warner concludes that the meaning of this story is that the association with geese is a charge that "proper" society makes against women who refuse to be limited by the roles set out for them. However, the ability to tell stories is what frees women from the shameful charge of deformity, which is an "attempt to contain and subdue the heterodox." Through storytelling, women are able to take their place in society on their own terms, because their fascinating stories can't be passed up, even by those who disapprove of them.

The Value Added Component of Multiple Analyses

What, then do we learn when we consider "The Goose Girl" in light of the historical information associated with it? Originally, we interpreted the story psychologically and found in it the reluctance of the heroine to assume the role that society had set out for her (see Ch. 36, p. 527). We saw the time she spent as a goose girl as a liminal period in which she was halfway between being a child and becoming a wife, the status she assumed at the end of her journey. At the same time, we interpreted the story sociologically, and saw that the girl moved from the end of the scale Levi-Strauss designated as incest (staying home) to the one called exogamy (going to a foreign land to marry), and thus, with some reluctance, she satisfied her society's requirements for marriage. If Warner's view of this story is correct, the historical perspective it provides does not cancel out our earlier interpretations, but enhances them. It allows us to see the girl's resistance to her social role in a historical context and to suggest that such resistance itself contributed to the formation of society. In other words, the individuality of the heroine can make a contribution to society, not just her compliance. This is most easily seen in the links between the Goose Girl and Bertha, the mother of Charlemagne, and by the suggestion that an entire genre of stories arose to communicate the woman's point of view represented by the Mother Goose stories.

In most cases, the performance of multiple analyses of the same myth or fairy tale offers additional insights into the story: the overlap or synergy between different analytical methods permits us to understand aspects of the story, or of the story's meaning, that would not have been clear from any one of the analyses performed by itself. Thus, taking "The Goose Girl" as an example, we saw in Chapter 36 (p. 527) that psychological analysis gave us insight into the personal growth of the heroine. Sociological analysis allowed us to view the marriage customs of the time as an external barrier with which the heroine had to contend to make space for her internal development. This perspective highlighted the heroine's lack of resistance to the servant girl who usurped her place. This allowed us to observe that, because the princess was not ready to assume the place of a grown-up bride, she unwittingly made it easy for the servant girl to overpower and replace her. One of the meanings of the story thus becomes the description of an ongoing struggle between the needs of the individual and the customs of the society.

If we add the historical perspective of Marina Warner's analysis to the previously mentioned two levels, we are able to see another group of meanings of the fairy tale. We are now reminded of the trickster aspect of the Goose Girl, who, in undergoing a **rite of passage** from young girl to young woman, exhibits a kind of resistance to her society's values and uses her "goose-footed" ways, which the society typically thinks are shameful, to circumvent those demands that she is not ready to meet. In this perspective, the Goose Girl is no longer alone in her resistance to the marriage customs of her society. She joins an ongoing tradition of women who get their own way and who stealthily undermine the structures of society to express their individuality and make space for their own concerns and values. In this light, the outrage of Conrad at the Goose Girl's behavior is seen as the reluctance of society to the subversion of its male-oriented values. At the same time, the assistance of the old king can be seen as the flexibility and resilience of society itself, which grows stronger from incorporating the stories and tricks of individuals and thus on some level makes space for the autonomy of women, as long as it does not go too far.

A Taxonomy of Meanings for Myths

The taxonomy in Table I represents an attempt to classify the different kinds of meanings to which we can aspire by applying the theories detailed in this book. It is not surprising that different analyses of the same story can be complementary, as the different theories we apply to myth operate in different domains or aspects. We can show this by bringing up, from the first

---

"Big-Footed Bertha"—This European figure has something in common with the heroine of the comical American song "My Darling Clementine," whose feet were so big that she wore herring boxes for shoes (Warner, 126).

"takes the queen's rightful place as Pepin's bride"—This incident seems to have found its way into several Grimm's fairy tales. In addition to "The Goose Girl," it is also found in "The Brother and Sister."

 Multiple Analyses of "The Goose Girl"

Psychological insights The story is about a girl who is growing up.

Sociological insights In the story, the heroine struggles with her society's marriage customs.

Historical insights The Goose Girl takes her place in a long line of heroines who get their own way through trickery and storytelling. Thus we can compare her to Scheherazade, the princess in "A Thousand and One Nights" who saves her life each day by telling another story. Although Scheherazade is resourceful and shrewd and the Goose Girl is much more passive, the historical view highlights their resemblance.

 The Goose Girl as a Reluctant Wife

 The Goose Girl as a Trickster Figure

"rite of passage"—Turner focuses extensively on this kind of ritual, which marks the transition of a member of society from one level of status to another. Such rituals have a liminal period when the initiates are actually between the two states and thus have a freedom from the rules of both. In this liminal period, there is a freedom to joke, to play, and to disrupt the traditional restrictions of society. While she is in disguise, the Goose Girl is clearly in a liminal state, and her behavior toward Conrad marks her freedom. For more on the liminal state, see Ch. 26, p. 375.

Table I. Kinds of Insights Produced by Different Analyses of Myths and Fairy Tales

Kinds of insights into myth:	Jung	Rank	Theories Campbell Hero	Levi-Strauss	Propp
Psychological "individuals"	X	X	X		X
Anthropological "cultures"	X	X	X	X	X
Social or sociological "groups"				X	X
Metaphysical "god and death"	X	X	X		X
Aetiological "reasons"				X	X
Cosmological "science"				X	X
Historical "past events"				X	X

 Comments on the Table

society A group of human beings who regularly work together toward a goal or series of goals, and are bound by a series of rules for behavior. These rules are enforced in formal and informal ways by the society, whether they are written, unwritten, or even unspoken.

culture All the components used by a group or society for transmitting and perpetuating its goals and values. It includes the stories, customs, laws, and art of the group, as well as the body of intellectual and emotional insights that guide the shaping of group life.

 Proppian Analysis of "The Raven"

Preparatory Section:

α—Initial situation
γ—Interdiction
δ—Violation (child cries)
θ—Complicity

First Move:

A—Harm (child becomes raven)
B—Connective incident
C—(Hero's) counteraction
$\uparrow$—(Hero's) departure

Old woman as donor:
D—Testing by donor
D—Testing by donor
D—Testing by donor

chapter of this book, the kinds of insights that mythology can provide us and by considering how they are related with respect to the forms of analysis we have been discussing.

Table I describes the most likely range of possibilities available within each form of analysis. For example, the column labeled "Levi-Strauss" includes check marks under "anthropological" and "sociological" insights because this method of analysis typically leads us to conclusions about the storyteller's society and how it works, or about the culture and what it expects of people living within it. There are no check marks under "psychological," not because this method of analysis never provides insight into the psychology of individuals living within the society or the culture, but because that is not the primary focus of this method of analysis. In addition, it should not be assumed that every analysis incorporates all the areas checked off in the chart. For example, in the Levi-Strauss column, the "aetiological," "cosmological," and "historical" insights are checked because structuralist analysis often illuminates these domains, not because every structuralist analysis must deal with them.

We have seen that multiple analyses of the same story can enrich our understanding of a myth or fairy tale. In some instances, the use of different methods of analysis for the same tale can also serve as a way of completing our understanding of the nature or "logic" of the tale. We have put the word "logic" inside quotation marks because fairy tales and myths are often, in the strict sense, paratactic or illogical. As explained in Chapter 2 (p. 18), this often results from oral transmission. As people are telling a story, they may not notice inconsistencies in their account because they (and their audience) know the point they intended to make, and any aspects of the story that do not fit together can be ignored. In modern times, we often observe logical flaws and inconsistencies the second time we see a movie; these problems did not strike us the first time. Or we might see a movie with someone who is very attuned to small details, or "nit-picking" as it is often called, and he or she will point out that some details were inconsistent or inaccurate. If the story is good enough, such inconsistencies often don't matter to a large proportion of the audience. However, performing multiple analyses on a story can sometimes show that, despite inconsistencies or gaps in one way of looking at the story, it is logical or sensible from another, different perspective.

"The Raven": Attempts to Fill in the Gaps through Multiple Analyses

In the fairy tales collected by the Grimm Brothers, there are often elements that don't make sense but have nonetheless become a part of the story. "The Raven" is the story of a little girl who is turned into a raven by her mother and is eventually rescued from this transformation by the hero. A Proppian analysis of this story can show us its underlying structure. (For more on Proppian analysis, see Ch. 34, p. 499, and Ch. 35, p. 514.)

According to **Proppian** terminology, the story's first action or move is launched in the preparatory section, when a baby violates what seems to be an unspoken command (or interdiction) not to cry, and as a result, the mother, who is portrayed as a villain, turns her into a raven. This harm begins the first move. The Raven flies off into the woods and stays there a long time. Eventually, a hero appears who wants to counteract the harm and rescue her. At the Raven's suggestion, he goes to the house of an old woman and is tested by her. The old woman seems to be in the category that Propp calls a donor: a person who gives the hero something magical to use later in completing a task. However, the donor cycle here is not completed. The hero tries to resist the old woman's offers of food and drink, but three times gives in to the temptation, and a new harm results.

In the new move, which describes the actions occurring after the new harm, the Raven is sent to a distant castle, but she first communicates briefly with the hero and tells him that if he wants to help, he must find her there. He doesn't even know where this castle is. He then finds a giant with a map and manages to obtain his help in getting to the castle. There the hero obtains three magical objects by tricking some robbers, uses these to storm the citadel where the girl is being held, and finally sets her free.

As sometimes happens with fairy tales, the parts of "The Raven" are not well integrated. The section of the story dealing with the old woman donor seems to represent a separate segment that seems incompletely related to the other events in the story. The fairy tale provides no personality for the queen: her reaction to the transformation is not included. We are not told why the old woman has power over the Raven. It would be easy enough to link the old woman with the queen, or with the Raven's wandering in the woods after her transformation, but the story does not provide any such connection. Nor is there any explanation of why the hero's failure with the old woman results in the removal of the Raven to the distant castle. Because of these missing connections, the events of the story seem arbitrary and illogical.

However, a Jungian analysis of "The Raven" can in part compensate for the story's gaps in logic. If we consider the hero as the main character whose perspective we will use for a Jungian analysis, we can then interpret the story as his process of individuation. We see that the hero first encounters the Raven, who is an **anima** figure for him, and as such is intended to bring him to his true Self. However, the Raven cannot stay with the hero, as she has been enchanted. Thus, the hero is left first to deal with the old woman, who is also an anima figure. When the hero is unsuccessful at the tests given him by the old woman, the Raven is taken farther away from him and he must again seek her. It is then that he encounters the giant and the robbers, who help him and enable him to perform the task of freeing the Raven from her enchantment.

In the context of Jungian analysis, it is not surprising that the hero is unsuccessful with dealing with the old woman, but does much better with the giant and the robbers. Jung argued that each person had first to deal with a same-sex figure who embodied aspects of his personality that he had not yet accepted, his **shadow.** In "The Raven," the giant can be interpreted as such a shadow figure, particularly because the hero shows, in his encounter with the old woman, that he does not as yet know how to restrain his desire to eat and drink. The giant seems to be the same way: when he first meets the hero, he declares that he wants to eat him and is dissuaded from this plan only when the hero, who has been provided with magical food and drink, offers this to the giant. It is when the hero figures out ways of dealing with his shadow figures that he is at last ready to be united with his anima. First he must negotiate with the greedy giant, and then he has to trick the quarrelsome robbers, also shadow figures, who when he meets them are arguing about how to share their magical possessions.

Second Move:

A—Harm (Raven sent away)
B—Connective incident
C—Counteraction
↑—Departure

← Giant as donor:
D—Testing by a donor
E—Hero's reaction
F—Hero acquires a magical agent (the help of the giant)
G—Hero is transferred to a magical place (the giant carries him)

Robbers as donors:
D—Testing by a donor
E—Hero's reaction
F—Hero acquires magical agents (stick cloak, horse)

o—Hero arrives unrecognized (invisible)
M—Difficult task (glass mountain)
N—Accomplishment of the difficult task
Q—Hero is recognized (drops ring into glass)
T—Transformation (of the Raven back into a girl)
W—Wedding

 Jungian Analysis of "The Raven"

anima A female figure that appears in dreams and stories and helps to guide the hero to his true self. The same hero can have different anima figures, according to his personality and level of maturity. The mother of the dreamer or storyteller is influential on the nature of the anima figures produced by that person. (See Ch. 32, p. 479.)

shadow This figure need not necessarily be evil, but it often appears in a threatening form. In this story, the giant first tries to eat the hero. In some cases it is necessary to defeat or destroy the shadow, but when the hero successfully obtains its help, as occurs in this story, it can greatly enhance the hero's accomplishments.

A Jungian psychological interpretation of "The Raven" seems to suggest that the hero fails with the first donor, the old woman, because he is not yet ready to deal with his anima. Before he can successfully meet her, in any form, he must come to terms with various shadow figures who represent his shortcomings. Once he has incorporated these figures into his sense of himself, he can reap the benefits of relating to them, and move on to be united with the Raven, who represents his anima.

Roger Rabbit: Multiple Analyses and Modern Storytelling

Modern authors who write in the style of classic stories are attuned to the different kinds of meanings that a fairy tale or myth can have. For example, the Disney movie, **Who Framed Roger Rabbit?** can be analyzed in the same way as a fairy tale. It is based on the book by Gary Wolf called *Who Censored Roger Rabbit?* In the movie, the detective Eddie Valiant is duped into framing a cartoon character named Roger Rabbit.

Eddie has agreed to help Roger only because his detective agency is down on its luck, but his help backfires, resulting in a murder charge for Roger. Eddie vowed not to have anything to do with Toons years ago, when an unidentified Toon got away with killing his brother. Before this incident, Eddie and his brother used to have a reputation for helping Toons.

The movie was considered a technological breakthough, as it incorporates cartoon figures intermingled with film footage of real people. Toons are represented as a minority that suffers discrimination and whose members are forced into jobs with inferior working conditions and consigned to the community of Toontown. As Eddie Valiant tries to help Roger Rabbit, he comes up against Judge Doom, a sinister figure who wants to destroy all of Toontown.

Like a classic fairy tale, this film can be analyzed in a variety of ways. Jungian analysis shows that **Doom is Eddie's first shadow figure.** When we first meet Eddie, he is full of self-loathing and is drinking himself into an early grave. In many respects he is like Doom himself, who we learn at the end of the movie is actually a Toon in disguise who is bent on destroying his own kind. To defeat Judge Doom, Eddie eventually has to let go of his own angry and morose attitude and adopt the silly and slap-happy style of his other shadow figure, Roger Rabbit. When Eddie dances and cavorts like a Toon, Judge Doom and his boys are destroyed and Toontown is set free.

This story provides, in fable form, sociological insight into American race relations and racial prejudice. The Toons can be compared to any oppressed minority: because they are "different," Toons must accept inferior jobs and inferior working conditions, and they are forced to live in a ghetto. Levi-Straussian analysis would note that the communities of Los Angeles represent extremes of a scale with nature at one end and culture at the other. Los Angeles is seen as the height of culture, while Toontown represents nature, as its residents are simple and for the most part, good-hearted and good-natured. Ironically, Judge Doom, who wants to be accepted as a real person and not a Toon, embodies the **most extreme vision of technological LA.** His dream is to destroy Toontown to build the entrance to a freeway. The contrast between nature and culture is made clear when Eddie Valiant leaves LA and crosses the threshold to Toontown: he is immediately surrounded by cartoon birds and trees like those in early Disney cartoons, and the music changes to a bucolic theme. By the end of the movie, a balance is achieved between the two worlds. Toontown saves LA from Judge Doom's freeway, while Eddie Valiant saves Toontown from destruction and sets it free by finding the deed to the community and giving it to the Toons themselves.

Near the end of the movie, the writers have included themes that allow the story to have aetiological significance. Judge Doom's plans for another freeway are defeated, but this climax

---

Who Framed Roger Rabbit?—A more detailed analysis of this film is available on the Internet at: http://www.coas.drexel.edu/humanities/faculty/thury/Final_Paper_Sample2.html.

 Jungian Analysis of Who Framed Roger Rabbit?

"Doom is Eddie's first shadow figure"—Said author Gary Wolf in an interview, "Roger Rabbit is actually autobiographical. Roger is the essence of fun and good humor. Eddie is the soul of logic and by-the-book methodology. Together they make up one good person."

 Levi-Straussian Analysis of Who Framed Roger Rabbit?

"most extreme vision of technological LA"—Doom says of his planned freeway, "You lack vision. I see a place where people get on and off the freeway. On and off. Off and on. All day, all night. Soon where Toontown once stood will be a string of gas stations, inexpensive motels, restaurants that serve rapidly prepared food, tire salons, automobile dealerships, and wonderful, wonderful billboards reaching as far as the eye can see. My God, it'll be beautiful."

From *Who Framed Roger Rabbit?* Eddie Valiant, with his shadow, the title character.

occurs after he has already destroyed what Tim Dirks calls the **"vast system of electric trolleys which once criss-crossed the LA Basin."**

Thus the movie provides an explanation for why a major city like Los Angeles does not have a viable system of public transportation. As real myths can provide an aetiology for particular geographic or cultural characteristics, so the fictitious tale of Roger Rabbit provides an explanation for the rise of the car culture that LA is famous for. What is the point of such a false aetiology? In the first place, it makes the story seem more myth-like by giving it a characteristic which myths and fairy tales often have. In addition, it points out a real historical fact that many people probably do not know, namely that Los Angeles once actually had a public transportation system. And it focuses our attention on a real issue, namely the advantage of public transportation over the use of cars and freeways, both in terms of ecology and given the congestion of freeways, in terms of saving time.

It is not hard to see that the three kinds of analyses we have applied to *Who Framed Roger Rabbit?* complement each other. The psychological analysis shows Eddie Valiant coming to terms with Roger Rabbit as a shadow figure. In exactly the same way, according to Levi-Straussian analysis, Los Angeles comes to terms with Toontown. The private detective, like his hometown, achieves a kind of equilibrium by accepting his natural instincts and using them to temper his hard-headed or scientific nature. The contribution of the aetiological analysis to our understanding of the movie is, however, an ironic one. In the real world, as we know, Los Angeles was not saved from freeways, so our enjoyment of the triumph of Roger Rabbit is tempered by our understanding that, despite Eddie's efforts, LA has not been saved from pollution and congestion.

Who Framed Roger Rabbit? is what Disney calls a family film, one designed to be viewed at the same time by audiences of different ages. Our aetiological analysis of this movie shows that, along with the fantasy-level triumph of the hero that can appeal to both adults and children, the movie's meaning also includes an aspect of wistfulness over what has been lost. It suggests that, unfortunately, Eddie Valiant is just a fictional character, no more real as a human than Roger Rabbit is as a Toon. Thus, Eddie's triumphs are not real and serve only to point up that for us, Judge Doom's twisted vision of the future of Los Angeles represents reality.

 Aetiological Analysis of Who Framed Roger Rabbit?

"vast system of electric trolleys which once criss-crossed the LA Basin"—At one point Eddie says, "Who needs a car in LA? We got the best public transportation system in the world."

These ideas come from: Tim Dirks, Review of *Who Framed Roger Rabbit?*

 Value Added in Multiple Analyses of *Who Framed Roger Rabbit?*

Further Reading

Dirks, Tim. Review of *Who Framed Roger Rabbit?*, http://www.filmsite.org/whof.html (accessed 8 February 2003).

Warner, Marina. *From the Beast to the Blonde: On Fairy Tales and Their Tellers*. London: Chatto and Windus, 1994.

Wolf, Gary. *Who Censored Roger Rabbit?* New York, NY: Ballantine, 1981.

Wolf, Gary. "Q & A with Gary Wolf," *Interesting Roger Rabbit Facts*. http://www.cc.gatech.edu/~jimmyd/roger-rabbit/roger_rabbit_facts.html (accessed 28 June 2004).

Part 7

Myth in a Contemporary Context

A survey of today's publications, popular and academic, would yield a wide variety of claims that particular stories, alone or in combination, represent the essence of what it means to be human and a participant in contemporary society. The range of stories some consider relevant to our self-definition includes traditional tales like those in the Bible, historical accounts of the heroic survivors of oppression, and even mass-media extravaganzas like *Star Wars* or *Spiderman*. Some might even include the memoirs of contestants in so-called reality TV shows like *Survivor* or *American Idol*. Among the more interesting suggestions in this line is the idea that we should see ourselves in the portraits of the Romans drawn in the Asterix and Obelix books and movies. This French series depicts a town of ornery Gauls (the ancestors of the modern-day French) who will not succumb to domination by the monolithic but inept Roman Empire under Julius Caesar. These Romans have been interpreted as the Nazis, or today's French government, or as representing American mass culture. Whether we see ourselves as superheroes, villains, or just plain ordinary folks struggling to get along may well depend on where we turn and whose stories we listen to.

However, it is well nigh impossible to assess the merits of these disparate portraits from the point of view of mythology. Since myths are stories honed by the passage of time, it is very difficult to pinpoint what a contemporary myth is. By the time a story

Asterix sizes up a large Roman opponent who is not much of a threat, as a potion brewed by the village sage gives the diminutive French hero superpowers. The significance of the enemy seems to have changed since the debut of the comic in 1959. Since its origin, it depicts a wide range of French and European concerns. These days, Asterix films are seen throughout Europe, and their meaning has acquired an additional international perspective, so that the grandiose, inept Roman adversary easily becomes assimilated to Europeans' view of the United States.

has become a myth, it is usually no longer contemporary. And to complicate matters even further, our "modern times" are inspired by a wide range of traditional myths that hark back to principles and values held by generations of women and men. These include the stories told by the many religions, as well as a variety of stories about the foundation and history of individual cultures and nations that are constantly adjusted and interwoven to satisfy the needs of the group by reflecting their values.

Some of the issues to consider in the pursuit of contemporary myths are delineated in the work of Victor Turner. Two of his ideas about ritual apply also to myths and thus are relevant to any effort to look for modern myths:

1. A ritual looks different to those inside a culture and to those outside it: Turner distinguishes between the exegetical, operational, and positional views of a ritual. These concepts highlight our unique perspective in describing what happens in our culture (exegetical view), but remind us that we may leave out important aspects of a ritual or myth because we are as blind to them as a fish is to water (operational view), and that, as members of a culture, we may be unaware of the place a particular story holds in our value system (positional). (See Ch. 26, p. 374.)

2. The role of ritual is different in a homogeneous traditional society than it is in a heterogeneous industrial society. In such a modern society, rituals and myths are associated with voluntary, and even leisure, activities and are not woven into the work-life and the unified society of the culture. Thus, even when we speak of serious stories that convey strong values, the take-it-or-leave-it attitude of our culture implies that the myths do not define us in the same way that the story of Hercules embodied the values of fifth-century-B.C.E. Greeks or even first-century-C.E. Romans. (See Ch. 26, p. 382f.)

Some people would suggest that contemporary storytelling is for entertainment only and represents no meaning at all. This viewpoint is dubbed the "bubble gum fallacy" by Jewett and Lawrence in their classic analysis of the significance of the *Star Trek* original series. They counter that, although we may be unaware of it, the stories we enjoy in the movies and on television are satisfying because they interweave timeless mythic patterns with conflicts that signify in a veiled form the political and ethical dilemmas that confront us in real life. They argue that the shows that achieve widespread popularity are those with heroes that reflect the values we hold.

Despite the many warnings and reservations that attend the quest for contemporary myths, we regularly find ourselves in contact with stories that seem to have a character or function similar to those of some of the classic stories of mythology. As a result, throughout this book we have mentioned a wide variety of stories found in our popular culture, not because those stories are identical with mythological tales, but because they transmit some of the thrill that has come from traditional tales in other societies.

In the spirit of the multiplicity of choices characteristic of our time as delineated by Victor Turner (see Ch. 26, p. 384), we suggest that students of mythology may want to study any and all stories they find stirring, whether the emotions they

Pandals are temporary structures erected at the Durga Pujo in Calcutta, a festival in honor of the Durga. They are made of wood, cloth and bamboo and contain altars to the goddess. The structure above represents Hogwarts, the school attended by Harry Potter.

evoke are fascination or anger. Perhaps the genius of contemporary mythmaking in postindustrial societies is to make us aware of our ongoing and evolving self-definition through the choices we make to enjoy and appreciate a variety of different stories.

In the face of a great multitude of competing stories, we have chosen only three for this section. The saga of Daniel Boone is included because his story shares some characteristics with the stories of "nation-founding" heroes collected by Otto Rank. At the same time, the details of Daniel Boone's story, though firmly based in history, incorporate some "spin" from an eighteenth-century commercial venture and as such are relevant to our modern-day sense of ourselves that often has to be disentangled from, or reconciled with, the goals of commercial enterprises. The comparison of the recent television show *Firefly* with the classic film *Stagecoach* showcases the stories arising through the globalization of the American Western and its reshaping in the context of contemporary technology through the genre of science fiction. This series also illustrates how popular entertainment—like myths from ancient times—reflects the audiences' most basic hopes and fears. The third chapter in this section relates the Harry Potter series of books and films to Otto Rank's classic work on the characteristics of a hero. This series has become a global phenomenon, as shown by the representation of Hogwarts, Harry Potter's school, at the Durga Pujo, a festival in Calcutta, India.

The diverse mythology-based studies in this section reflect the way that mythological meaning emerges from the stories told through mass media, both long ago and in global contemporary society. Many other stories can, and should, be brought into consideration as representing contemporary myths. In this book, these include the stories of John Updike (Ch. 44, p. 664), and Leslie Silko (Ch. 43, p. 644). Also of interest may be the discussion of the films *The Wizard of Oz* (Ch. 35, p. 514) and *Who Framed Roger Rabbit?* (Ch. 38, p. 566).

Futher Reading

Bjørklid, Finn, tr. and ed. by Nicolai Langfeldt. "A Celtic Gaul named Asterix," http://heim.ifi.uio.no/~janl/ts/asterix-article.html posted 9/29/1996, accessed 11/01/2008 (Norwegian original: *Tegn*, 4/94).

Jewett, Robert and John Shelton Lawrence. *The American Monomyth*. Garden City, NY: Anchor Press, 1977.

A Study of the Construction of the Daniel Boone Myth

WHAT TO EXPECT . . . The story of Daniel Boone, the American frontiersman, was shaped into patterns that had, and continue to have, meanings for storytellers and their audiences. This chapter's reading comes from Richard Slotkin's comprehensive work on the American frontier from 1600 to 1860. Slotkin focuses on the life of Daniel Boone written by John Filson in 1784. Slotkin's analysis provides an opportunity to study a myth in the making. Some of Filson's process involves ignoring historical and sociological facts about Boone's actual accomplishments and the role of Native Americans in the colonists' lives, while adding elements that enhance his status as hero and his wife's role as the ideal pioneer woman. Your first impulse may be to consider Filson a dishonest narrator, but it is worthwhile looking for ways in which he tried to be truthful. This discussion takes us back to our attempts to define myth in Chapter 1 (p. 3) and our statement that "mythological stories reveal true things about the culture that originated them." Consider Filson's story in this light and see if you can support this statement.

In this chapter, we look at stories about Daniel Boone, the North American pioneer. Boone, who was born in 1734, played a significant role in the exploration and settlement of Kentucky in particular and the U.S. western frontier in general. As suggested in the introduction to this part, it is a complicated task to turn the lens of mythology on our own heroes, and especially on a historical figure like Boone. Since we are inside the culture, it is hard if not impossible for us to study it without introducing our own biases into the analysis. It is not clear whether modern-day citizens of the United States would acknowledge that we considered Boone a hero or admired his accomplishments. To some extent, people's response to Boone will depend on their political views: what they think represent the United States' accomplishments, and what directions they think their country's future actions should take. Nonetheless, by many accounts of the development of Americans' sense of themselves, the story of Daniel Boone has had a significant effect on how the citizens of the United States explain their actions and how they define themselves in relation to their country.

Another difficulty with Daniel Boone is that he is a historical figure. As a result, some may believe that the story of his life consists of a determinate set of facts, and therefore is not mythology. In fact, such views represent the attitude toward mythology that we have argued against in this book. In Chapter 1, we pointed out that, according to the most common definition of the word used today, *myth* means a false story. In this book, however, we have suggested that regardless of their fidelity to historical detail, myths are actually true stories because they embody the principles and values of individuals and societies. When we are looking at a story in the remote past, like the adventures of Gilgamesh or the capture of Troy, it is difficult to determine which aspects of the story rely on historical facts and which represent cultural truths that have transformed idiosyncratic historical details into more universally applicable stories.

Let us consider Gilgamesh, who with his companion Enkidu, conquered Humbaba, the king of the cedar forest (see Ch. 15, p. 179). Certainly, the story of this act must have stirred the citizens of Uruk in somewhat the same way as American settlers were once inspired by tales of Daniel Boone's settlement of Kentucky. Although the adventures of Gilgamesh are shrouded in antiquity, they too are based on historical fact. Ancient documents tell us that Gilgamesh was the king of Uruk in Mesopotamia at around 2700 B.C.E. However, as Boone's story is so much closer in time to our own, we have many more details about the circumstances of his life. We know that the conquest of the Native Americans who lived in Kentucky before its colonization by Boone and his companions took place over many years and consisted of a series of encounters, some honorable and some treacherous, on each side. In contrast, the conquest of Humbaba is presented as a single expedition in which heroic action belonged exclusively to Gilgamesh and Enkidu. The manifold details of the ancient story have disappeared from our sight, leaving behind an account of the universal forces of nature and culture that clashed in the cedar forest. (See a Levi-Straussian view of Gilgamesh for an analysis of the myth in this light, Ch. 16, p. 193.)

Here is another example. It may well be the case that a historical figure named Odysseus never existed, although Homer's portrait of him is quite successful at representing him as an actual person (see Ch. 1, p. 10). Scholars who study the *Odyssey* point out that its hero is an individual with particular features, starting from the old hunting scar on his leg acquired while he was proving himself on his first boar hunt. Odysseus displays a host of characteristics we usually associate with individuals: he cries and laughs, he experiences fear and undergoes spiritual and psychological growth. Nonetheless, Homer's portrait of this hero is probably a composite that embodies aspects of many Greek leaders in the Bronze Age. However, the individual historical details that underlie Odysseus' struggles are too remote from us to compete with his life story as a hero.

In contrast, we have abundant historical evidence that Daniel Boone did exist, as well as volumes of testimony to his characteristics as a particular individual. His life consisted of many activities each day, and we have records that attest to hundreds of things he did and said. From this material we know that Boone was a poor reader, that in his youth he went on some wild forays in pursuit of women and drink, and that he encountered a host of legal difficulties in business ventures. There are accounts of Boone's courtship of his wife, as well as details of his marriage and stories about how he brought up the nine of his children who lived beyond infancy. In addition, Daniel Boone grew up surrounded by Native Americans, and there are records of a wide range of his encounters with them, from his childhood onward, including his adoption into the Shawnee tribe as a grown man. In a sense we are too close to Boone. We can see many aspects of him as a man. Our own perspectives will of course shape what we notice and what we make of it; that is, it remains for us to determine which, if any, of these characteristics are relevant to his status as hero.

In examining and evaluating the myth of Daniel Boone, we are confronted with a vast supply of material on his life. Lyman Copeland Draper, a nineteenth-century historian, roamed the west in a wide-ranging search for historical sources documenting the trans-Appalachian migration, including stories, letters, account books, and family records. Draper amassed 486 volumes, which include the most important sources for information relating to the life of Daniel Boone. The Draper Manuscript Collection at the State Historical Society of Wisconsin includes a five-volume life of Boone, as well as extensive interviews with Boone's relatives, and documents and interviews relating to Boone and to Kentucky.

However, investigation of Boone's life does not stop with the extensive Draper collection. John Bakeless, a notable twentieth-century biographer of Boone, provides a four-page list of acknowledgements that catalogues the materials he consulted in his effort to represent Boone's life accurately. Bakeless reports working at the Library of Congress, the library of the New York

Bar Association, and the libraries of many local historical societies. At Bakeless' request, libraries and records offices across the country tracked down previously unknown newspaper stories, maps, and legal records, including Boone's marriage certificate. To represent the Native American aspect of Boone's story, Bakeless studied the records of the Smithsonian Institution's Bureau of American Ethnology and consulted an expert on the Shawnee language.

In fact, over time, different accounts of Boone's life have emphasized some of the information in these sources and neglected some of it. But the information chosen was not randomly selected; the facts of Boone's life were shaped into patterns that had meaning for the storytellers and their audiences. Based on these patterns, there arose the stories we as a society know best about Daniel Boone. These stories survive because they once seemed to define the nature of the American West. As a result, the story of Boone gives us a chance to consider myths in the making. We can examine the historical detail of the life of the hero as well as the stories that were told about him. Of course, looking at all the stories relating to Boone is much too big a task for us here. We will limit ourselves to the discussion of one account of his life that was influential in the development of the United States as we know it, John Filson's *The Discovery, Settlement And present State of Kentucke: . . . To which is added . . . I. The Adventures of Col. Daniel Boon.* Filson's narrative, written in 1784, purported to be an autobiography of Boone. This account by Filson, which is widely available on the Internet, has been the focus of extensive analysis by Richard Slotkin in *Regeneration through Violence: The Mythology of the American Frontier, 1600–1860,* from which we provide excerpts in this chapter.

The relationship of the authors whose works are discussed in this chapter.

Slotkin's book is a study of the stories European-Americans told about themselves as they settled in the New World. He analyzes a variety of different materials, including sermons and tracts written by religious groups, accounts of the war with the Indians, and personal narratives describing captivity by the Indians. He finds the Filson account of Boone's life a highly significant component of the myth that shaped the American frontier and thus determined the character of the United States of America as a nation. In this sense, the Boone of Filson's narrative can be compared with Sargon, Cyrus, and Romulus—heroes, described by Otto Rank, who undertook heroic quests to establish a nation. For a discussion of these heroes who have an important role in the nation's identity and sense of mission, see Introduction to Part 3, p. 156f.

To demonstrate the strength of Slotkin's argument, we have annotated his analysis with excerpts from the Little Golden Book version of Boone's life, written by Irwin Shapiro in 1956. It will be apparent from these annotations that a modern version of the Daniel Boone story, written for very young children more than 150 years after Filson's account, reproduces the fundamental elements of his narrative of Daniel Boone's life, as outlined by Slotkin.

As noted in the opening paragraph of this introduction, the meaning of the myth of Daniel Boone for Americans will depend in part on their beliefs about the history and the destiny of the United States. For those whose values emphasize sensitivity to the culture and claims of Native Americans, the expansion of the frontier will represent the story of imperialistic self-aggrandizement at the expense of a native people. For those who emphasize the role of the United States as a great nation that exerts a positive force throughout the world, the life of Daniel Boone will represent just one chapter in a story that embodies human striving and progress. In all probability, many readers will see aspects of both perspectives in the story of Daniel Boone.

Before we examine Filson's narrative in more detail, it will be helpful to consider two broader aspects of the myth of Daniel Boone: the relationship of the hero to Native Americans and the role of women in the conquest of the frontier.

LEARNING FROM THE INDIANS, DEFEATING THE INDIANS

Daniel Boone's legend represents him as blazing a trail in the uncharted wilderness. However, the territory that Boone explored was far from empty or uncharted. North America had been settled for centuries by native populations, although as European colonization continued, it did become emptied of much of its native population. Scholars today estimate that in 1492, the Indian population had been somewhere between 5,000,000 and 10,000,000. By 1800, it had fallen to around 600,000. In *New Worlds for All: Indians, Europeans and the Remaking of Early America,* Colin Calloway notes that Europeans who came to America often built their towns on the sites of previous Indian settlements. For example, when the Pilgrims settled at Plymouth, they found fields that had been cultivated by the Indians, but abandoned after an epidemic in 1617. By the time of Daniel Boone, much of eastern North America had become emptied of its original inhabitants. Indians died of European diseases, or they were pushed back as the new settlers' hunting, farming, and lumbering practices cleared the land and depleted its animal population. The settlers saw the animals in the new world as salable commodities, while the Indians regarded them as sacred spirits to be hunted only for survival. As they became active in the fur trade that met the extensive needs of European markets, rather than supplying only their own villages and families, these values necessarily changed.

Calloway notes that each of these two cultures was changed extensively by contact with the other. Every schoolchild in the United States learns that the settlers were able to achieve their independence and to defeat the armies of King George III by fighting "Indian style." The interaction between the Europeans and natives was not so limited or one-directional, however. Changes were evident in the agricultural practices, diet, clothing, dwelling design, as well as social structure and values of each side. Through imports from the colonies, Europeans' health improved as their diet was enriched by a variety of previously unknown foods from America. The introduction of the potato, with its shorter growing season, shifted the balance of power to northern countries like Russia and England, at the expense of Mediterranean countries like Spain and France. At the same time, Native American culture was extensively modified by the introduction of steel implements and weapons, and by reliance on the previously unknown horse.

George Caleb Bingham, *Daniel Boone Escorting Settlers through the Cumberland Gap,* 1851–52. Oil on canvas, 36½ x 50¼. Mildred Lane Kemper Art Museum, Washington University in St. Louis. Gift of Nathaniel Phillips, 1890. Boone is remembered for blazing the trail through the Cumberland Gap, though he was not the first European-American settler to do so. Of course, Indians, the native Americans, had known about the Cumberland Gap before the European settlers came. Their understanding of the wilderness and how to survive in it formed the basis of the wisdom of the backwoods community with which Boone associated himself.

However, many of the stories the American settlers told about themselves did not reflect this reciprocity of cultural exchange in the New World. The myth of Daniel Boone portrays its hero as a self-made man, a hunter and explorer who relied only on his instincts for blazing a trail in the wilderness. The Little Golden Book account of his life explains that when Daniel was twelve, his father gave him a rifle, and he "took to hunting right off. He brought home many a deer that weighed as much as he did." However, John Faragher explains in *Daniel Boone: The Life and Legend of an American Pioneer* that when Daniel went out into the woods near his home, he encountered other backwoods hunters of both European and Native American descent who roamed the woods and taught him the skills associated with their way of life. Although men from both cultures lived in the backwoods, hunting as a way of life was more characteristic of the Indians than the settlers. As a rule, in European countries, hunting was practiced primarily as a sport, not a means of livelihood. The settlers learned woods lore and hunting techniques from the natives, while both groups favored the use of European firearms and ammunition. Faragher notes that, by the eighteenth century, "these two groups were fully acculturated to each other" and shared fundamental moral values as well as styles of housing and dress (22).

When Daniel Boone was growing up, Indian visitors were not unusual, and it is clear from the stories we have about the explorer as a boy that he learned a great deal by questioning and observing them. Contemporary historical accounts preserved in the Draper Manuscript Collection document these encounters, reporting that he even basted a turkey like an Indian, and his hunting and tracking skills were on a par with those of the natives. However, the legend of Daniel Boone elevates him above the give-and-take associated with this blended culture and represents him as accomplishing great deeds by means of his raw talent as a woodsman. For example, according to legend, Daniel Boone blazed a trail through the mountains to Kentucky by way of the Cumberland Gap. In fact, Boone learned of the Cumberland Gap in 1768 from John Findley, who knew it as a path used by Cherokee warriors to attack the Shawnee. Boone, his brother Squire, and their friend William Hall had tried without success to reach Kentucky the previous year by a more easterly path (Lofaro, 25). It should be clear that seeing Boone's accomplishment in the light of his exchange with Findley does not necessarily diminish his greatness as an explorer. It does present us with a different vision of the exploration of Kentucky: westward expansion depended on cooperation as much as on solitary daring, and it called for learning from Native Americans as much as defeating them.

The settlement of the western lands was itself problematic and raises the question of the motive behind Daniel Boone's explorations. Did Boone explore Kentucky simply because he loved roaming the wilderness? Would we consider him less of a hero if we thought that he acted to develop land for real estate speculation? Some historians have suggested that Daniel Boone had been hired as a scout by Richard Henderson, who had formed a company to explore the western territory. Such efforts would have had to be clandestine, as the Royal Proclamation of 1763 declared that the western lands belonged to the Indians (Elliott, 58–59; Lofaro, 23–24). However, the legal status of westward expansion was far from clear: many of the colonies had charters that entitled them to the land west of the Allegheny Mountains. As a result, merchants and speculators did not take the proclamation seriously. George Washington pronounced it "an expedient to quiet the minds of the Indians" (Elliott, 44).

Although European law may well have supported the claims of colonists traveling westward, the Shawnee, who were squeezed between the Cherokee in the south and west, and the Iroquois on the north and east, fiercely defended Kentucky as their own territory. The legend of Daniel Boone reflects the American colonists' attempt to wrest territory from the Native Americans. Western colonization involved bloody battles, uneasy truces with accommodation being made by both sides, as well as periods of cooperation and assimilation, often followed by new treaties and fresh betrayals. The European powers (France and England) encouraged and supported attacks by their Native American allies to further their own territorial ambitions.

Boone's exploration of Kentucky culminated in the founding of Boonesborough in 1775. The town was attacked regularly by Indians; in 1778, Boone was captured, adopted by the Shawnee, and lived with the tribe for four months, until he saw that they were massing for an extensive attack on the colonists. He escaped and rescued Boonesborough from Indian attack, and went on to found and defend other settlements in Indian country.

Adoption by the Shawnee and eventual escape from their midst play a prominent role in the second half of Filson's Boone narrative. (The Slotkin excerpt discusses the early part of Filson's story.) Although Filson does not explicitly say so, Boone's treatment by the Shawnee suggests that, once again, he was able to use the skills he had gained from contact with the Indians to advance the position of American settlers. He fit well into Shawnee society. To quote Filson's narrative, "I became a son, and had a great share in the affection of my new parents, brothers, sisters, and friends. I was exceedingly familiar and friendly with them, always appearing as cheerful and satisfied as possible, and they put great confidence in me. I often went a hunting with them, and frequently gained their applause for my activity at our shooting-matches." Once again, an examination of the complex interactions between European-American colonists and Native American peoples suggests that the reality of the historical Boone is only partially represented in the legend Filson contributed to American culture.

In *Regeneration through Violence,* Slotkin discusses other figures in American legend whose understanding can be enhanced by a closer examination of the culture of colonial America. For example, starting in 1823, James Fenimore Cooper wrote a series of novels about life on the American frontier. Like Filson's account of the adventures of Daniel Boone, Cooper's *Leatherstocking Tales* have helped to shape the way that Americans tell the story of the founding of their nation. In fact, it is generally agreed that Natty Bumppo, the hunter whose story runs throughout Cooper's many-volumed narrative, is significantly influenced by and, to some extent, based on Filson's Boone. Natty is a white man who has learned the ways of Native Americans as he hunts with them in the wilderness. Slotkin explains that, for this kind of hero, "Moral truth emerges only when [he] totally immerses himself in his wilderness environment and . . . discovers truths about himself and his world that were . . . hidden to him. In solitude and isolation his acts of war and hunting awaken him to his kinship with creation, to a sense of reality, and of religious and social duty" (507). There is little room in this story of the American hero for the interaction of disparate cultures that learn from each other.

REBECCA BOONE AS A PIONEER WOMAN

When Daniel Boone was 21, he married 17-year-old Rebecca Bryan, a tall, strong woman who was to be the mother of his ten children. According to a variety of historical sources, Rebecca Boone's experiences were fairly typical of the lives of frontier women. Backwoods hunters and explorers like her husband did not devote much of their time and energy to the tending or protection of their households. Since Daniel was often away or roaming the woods, Rebecca was in effect the head and sole support of a household that included her own children and, at various points, an assortment of nieces, nephews, and grandchildren. Her work included cooking and cleaning, fetching water, and providing for the family's clothes by spinning, weaving, and sewing. In addition, it fell to her to cultivate the fields and hunt small game. When Indians or brigands attacked, as they did from time to time, it was up to Rebecca to protect her family and move them to safety. Through her years as Daniel's wife, Rebecca Boone buried two sons who had been killed by Indians and endured the kidnapping and eventual rescue of her daughter Jemima.

Rebecca was equal to the hard work and danger of frontier life; in addition, she had the emotional strength to endure its loneliness. Although Daniel Boone was by no means a womanizer or a philanderer, stories about him suggest that he was not always faithful to his wife while away from her. During one of his adventures, Daniel was absent for such a long time that

Rebecca moved her family back east. At another time, Rebecca believed he was dead and sought consolation in the arms of his brother. When Daniel returned, he found his wife tending a child that looked like him but could not have been his. This experience was not uncommon on the frontier. In such circumstances some men sent away the wife and child, but Boone alluded to his own sexual misadventures and accepted the addition to the family.

In the context of mythical heroes and their adventures, we can easily see Rebecca Boone as a figure of great stature. She can be compared to Penelope, who endures loneliness and distress during her husband Odysseus' absence, or to Dejaneira, who must adjust her own goals and ambitions to her husband Heracles' sense of mission. Like Hecuba, Andromache, or Clytemnestra, Rebecca Boone is in charge of her household when she endures the tragic loss of family members to warfare, treachery, and misadventure. However, despite the abundance of historical records representing Rebecca Boone's strength in her own right, Filson's life of Daniel Boone largely ignores her, mentioning only that she was the "first white woman" to cross into Kentucky. His account was aimed at an audience accustomed to minimizing the experiences and accomplishments of women. Filson wrote to fire the imagination of this audience, spurring them to acquire land in Kentucky—land to be bought and owned by men. According to the social and religious values of the time, men saw themselves as the masters of their wives and families. Thus, to highlight her husband's exploits, Filson represents Rebecca as a generalized amiable spouse, eliminating the historical details of her life and ignoring the Boone family legends that emphasized her activities.

In some sense, the legends surrounding Rebecca Boone reflect the tensions between men and women in eighteenth-century society. Faragher refers to one kinsman of Boone's who said women were proud and "needed kind subduing" and to another family acquaintance who, in his toast to the groom of one of Boone's sisters, said she would make a fine wife "if you will take her down at the first loaf" (46). Contemporary sources report several stories about Daniel Boone that seem intended to make clear his dominance over his spouse. According to one that Boone himself liked to tell, when he was courting Rebecca, he took the opportunity to test her character. As he sat with her at a local picnic, he flipped his knife casually in the grass, in the process cutting a large hole in her new muslin apron. Such fine cloth was not easy to come by on the frontier. When she did not raise a fuss, he was assured that she would make a suitable wife. According to another family story, Daniel took some ribbing from Rebecca and her sisters when he came in to dinner wearing a blood-spattered hunting shirt after dressing a deer. He responded with a jibe about the cleanliness of the cup he was drinking from, saying to the cup, "You, like my hunting shirt, have missed many a good washing." Filson's narrative does not include either story; in his account, the dominance of Boone as husband is undisputed.

In telling about Daniel and Rebecca Boone's courtship and marriage, Slotkin notes that Filson omits a story about Rebecca Boone that was widely known in her lifetime. According to the "fire-hunt" legend, Boone was hunting one night, using a torch to attract a deer to his stand. Slotkin notes that when Boone saw a glimmer of light in the dark, he prepared to fire, but "some intuition stayed him. He moved toward the gleams, pushed aside the brush, and discovered Rebecca, who turned and fled home." Thus Rebecca narrowly escaped being shot by Daniel, who mistook her for a deer, recognizing her just in time. He began to court her soon afterwards. Faragher points out that this legend suggests men must curtail their free-ranging activities to interact with women: "Rebecca is placed in deadly peril by Boone's pursuit of his occupation" (44). However, Slotkin argues that the story also represents some themes commonly found in Native American myths. Both the existence and the suppression of the fire-hunt legend provide a fine example of the interplay of European and Native-American cultures that was characteristic of life in America in the late eighteenth century.

This legend featured one of several hunting techniques routinely practiced by Native Americans that involved fire. Fire was used to attract prey, as well as to drive them from their dens.

Plots of land were burned to produce new growth, superior fodder to draw grazers; traps were baited with fired grass. Smoke repelled mosquitoes and flies and thus served to lure deer. Native Americans routinely used fire to burn off large areas of woods and grassland to log timber for building, to produce rich grazing land for their animals, and to prepare fields for agriculture. Native ceremonies and rituals involved the use of fire for purification and entertainment. Perhaps the association of fire with so many native practices explains the Boone family's rejection of the fire-hunt legend. Boone himself claimed that he did not engage in fire-hunting, but the practice was widely used in the backwoods culture from which he learned to interact with the wilderness.

The fire-hunt legend about Daniel and Rebecca Boone has other Native American associations as well. Slotkin compares it to native creation stories in which the earth is seen as a mother goddess, a representative of the creative forces of nature, who brings forth crops from her body. In a version of the story told by the Delaware Indians, humans live underground until a hunter tracking a deer follows it to the surface. The story attached to Rebecca Boone seems to owe its origins to influence by the Indian myth. At the same time, this would explain the logic of its suppression by Filson, whose choice would have been in accordance with the attitudes and expectations of his audience. The story emphasizes the role of Rebecca Boone, who is seen as a divine creature responsible for leading the people to a new and rich land. As a result, it better fits the values of Indian societies, which often accorded women and children higher status than they enjoyed among the European settlers. These settlers "sought to subordinate women in their program of restructuring Indian societies along European lines: men, not clan mothers, must dominate society" (Calloway, 191).

Miriam Story Hurford, *The Boone family,* as pictured in Irwin Shapiro's *Daniel Boone* for Little Golden Books (1956). This children's story reflected the Filson version of Daniel Boone's achievements. Here Rebecca sits quietly in the background, doing household tasks with a daughter, while Daniel, drawn larger in the foreground, seems to be teaching a son about the use and care of a rifle. In real life, Rebecca was often alone during her husband's trips and had charge of the defense of the family as well as of household tasks.

According to the fire-hunt legend, Rebecca is the wild spirit of nature that Daniel pursues and with which he eventually achieves closeness. Thus, the story represents the alien beliefs and values that people would encounter during life on the frontier. By omitting it, Filson glosses over two topics that might disquiet his audience and cause them to lose interest in acquiring land in Kentucky: the social tensions typical of eighteenth-century society and the blending of cultures that occurred in frontier America.

As is clear from the brief survey, we know a fair amount about Rebecca Boone; the minimal role she plays in the legend of Daniel Boone does not result from lack of information. It is also clear that her subsidiary role does not correspond to the historical facts about her life and activities. However, representing her as a heroic figure would not have served the ends Filson was trying to advance in his life of her husband. Because Filson's account proved to be very influential in shaping the myth of Daniel Boone, Americans who were inspired or motivated by this myth had little reason to include in their national vision the importance of a strong woman as a leader or role model.

Filson's Motivation for Writing about Boone

In 1784 John Filson, a schoolmaster turned surveyor and land speculator, returned from two years in Kentucky. In Wilmington, the metropolis of his home state of Delaware, he published the *Discovery, Settlement and Present State of Kentucke,* an elaborate real-estate promotion brochure designed to sell farm lands in the Dark and Bloody Ground to easterners and Europeans. Sales resistance was likely to be high. The Revolution had just ended, and the **bloody Indian wars** which had decimated the Kentucky settlements were still sputtering out in petty raids and secret murders. Thus Filson faced the classic problem of writers about the frontier: how to portray the promise of the frontier without destroying his own credibility by glossing over the obviously perilous realities of the pioneer's situation.

Filson attempted to persuade his audience by composing, as an appendix to that book, a literary dramatization of a hero's immersion in the elemental violence of the wilderness and his consequent emergence as the founder of a nascent imperial republic. In "The Adventures of Col. Daniel Boon" Filson created a character who was to become the **archetypal hero of the American frontier,** copied by imitators and plagiarists and appearing innumerable times under other names and in other guises—in literature, the popular arts, and folklore—as the man who made the wilderness safe for democracy. The Boone narrative, in fact, constituted the first nationally viable statement of a myth of the frontier.

Myth, as I would define it, **is a narrative formulation of a culture's world view and self-concept,** which draws both on the historical experience of that culture and on sources of feeling, fear, and aspiration (individual and universal/archetypal) deep in the human subconscious and which can be shown to function in that culture as a prescription for historical action and for value judgment.

A myth is a narrative which concentrates in a single, dramatized experience the whole history of a people in their land. **The myth-hero embodies or defends the values of his culture** in a struggle against the forces which threaten to destroy the people and lay waste the land. Myth grows out of the timeless desire of men to know and be reconciled to their true relationship to the gods or elemental powers that set in motion the forces of history and rule the world of nature. In the case of the American colonies, whose people were not native to the soil, this desire took the form of a yearning to

This excerpt comes from:
Richard Slotkin, *Regeneration through Violence: The Mythology of the American Frontier, 1600–1860.**

"bloody Indian wars"—A major part of the experience of European settlers in America was fighting with the Native American people already living there. Any account the settlers gave of their actions had to portray this struggle as a meaningful one.

"archetypal hero of the American frontier"—In Carl Jung's theory, the word "archetype" refers to mythic concepts or images that are universal to all human beings, no matter what their culture, Here Slotkin provides detailed analysis of Filson's narrative (see p. 583f). Then Slotkin provides an overview of what he takes to be the archetypal aspects of his story (see p. 587). On Jung, see Ch. 32, p. 468.

"Myth . . . is a narrative formulation of a culture's world view and self-concept"—Myth provides a representation of both historical experiences and the subconscious forces underlying them.

"The myth-hero embodies or defends the values of his culture"—The stories the European settlers told about themselves demonstrated that they had done the right thing in coming to America.

*Richard Slotkin, *Regeneration Through Violence: The Mythology of the American Frontier, 1600–1860,* 268–311 (excerpts). Harper Perennial. Copyright © 1996. Reprinted by permission of Brandt & Hochman Literary Agents, Inc.

"fulfillment of their own destiny as children of Jehovah"—Initially, the colonists saw coming to America as enhancing their religious faith. Slotkin notes their destiny was establishing "an exemplary community of saints" from which they would train leaders to return and govern a "redeemed England" (41). Later, they came to view their destiny as remaining in the New World.

"to qualify as myth"—In Slotkin's view, the requirements for a successful myth are that it

- allows the audience to identify with the hero
- can grow as the culture changes
- "dramatize . . . the interdependence"—Slotkin argues that a successful myth about Boone would
- recount the events of Boone's life ("Boone's destiny")
- validate the past actions of the community ("historical mission")
- fulfill the values expressed by the religious community ("destiny appointed . . . by . . . divine Providence")

"interaction between themselves . . . and the dark races belonging to their land"—To justify their actions, the American colonists had to fashion an ideology that attached a positive moral value to defeating the Indians.

"hunter and husbandman"—Slotkin argues Filson portrayed Boone as both. Many of Boone's exploits are the violent activities of a hunter, but his motive is to open new territory to peaceful settlement by farmers. Filson's view proved long-lived and influential.

Crèvecoeur Michel de, 18th-c. diplomat and farmer who wrote about what it meant to be American in colonial times.

"immortality of Filson's vision"—This section provides excerpts of Slotkin's extensive analysis of Filson's narrative. The Little Golden Book version of Boone's life, written in 1956, says, "The days of Daniel Boone are long since gone, [but] there are folks who say that from the woods [there still] comes a voice calling, 'Come along, come along, Daniel Boone.' And the same folks say that if you listen hard enough, you will hear your name called too."

prove that they truly belonged to their place, that their bringing of Christian civilization to the wilderness represented the **fulfillment of their own destiny as children of Jehovah** (rather than a perversion of that destiny) and of the land's destiny as the creation of God. (This yearning, common to all the colonies, was most clearly and intensely articulated by the Puritans.)

Filson's narrative, then, **to qualify as myth,** would have to draw together all the significant strands of thought and belief about the frontier that had been developed in the historical experience of the colonies, concentrate those experiences in the tale of a single hero, and present that hero's career in such a way that his audience could believe in and identify with him. Moreover, the tale would have to be constructed in such a way that it could grow along with the culture whose values it espoused, changing and adjusting to match changes in the evolution of that culture. Otherwise the tale would lose that essential quality of seeming to be drawn from the original sources of cultural experience. Ultimately, Filson's tale would have to **dramatize convincingly the interdependence** of **Boone's destiny**, the **historical mission** of the American people, and the **destiny appointed for the wilderness by natural law and divine Providence**. The evidence suggests that the Boone legend first put before the public by Filson did, in fact, fulfill these requirements.

The adoption by the national reading public of the myth of Daniel Boone implied their acceptance of a certain myth-scenario of **interaction between themselves, their land, and the dark races belonging to their land.** In Filson's legend and in the myth that grew out of it, the roles and characters of **hunter and husbandman** are ambiguously equated through the association of the hero's career of seminomadic wandering, violence, and opportunity-seeking with the agrarian imagery and morality expounded by Jefferson and **Crèvecoeur.** Implicit in this ambiguity is a scenario of national progress in which the land and its resources are to be "cultivated" through their quick exploitation and given their "improved" value by speculation and in which the Indian is to be redeemed through the expropriation of his land, physical removal to desert and inhospitable regions, or (if necessary) extermination.

Filson's Boone Narrative

"The Adventures of Col. Daniel Boon" is the key to the **immortality of Filson's vision of** the West and of the fame of his hero, Daniel Boone. This chapter of *Kentucke* proved far more popular than the rest of the book. It was lifted out of its context and reprinted as a separate pamphlet in anthologies of Indian war narratives and captivity narratives, and in popular literary periodicals in both Europe and the United States. It became the vehicle by which Filson's version of the frontier myth was transmitted to the literary giants of the American Renaissance and to the European Romantics.

The Boone narrative, though ostensibly Boone's own narration of his adventures, is actually Filson's careful reworking of Boone's statements and of the legends that Filson had heard about Boone from his fellow frontiersmen. The narrative is a **literary myth,** artfully contrived to appeal to men concerned with literature; it is not folk legend. Filson selects incidents for portrayal and breaks into the strict chronology of events in order to establish in his reader's mind a sense of the rhythm of Boone's experience and to emphasize certain key images and symbols that define the meaning of Boone's experience.

Boone's "Adventures" consist of a series of initiations, a series of progressive immersions that take him deeper into the wilderness. These initiations awaken Boone's sense of his own identity, provide him with a natural moral philosophy, and give him progressively deeper insights into the nature of the wilderness. Each immersion is followed by a return to civilization, where Boone can apply his growing wisdom to the ordering of his community, and by a momentary interlude of meditation and contemplation, in which Boone can review his experience, interpret it, and formulate the **wisdom gained from it.** As a result of these rhythmic cycles of immersion and emergence, he grows to become the commanding genius of his people, their hero-chief, and the man fit to realize Kentucky's destiny.

Filson casts Boone's adventures as a personal narrative, a form developed by the Puritans as a literary form of witness to an experience of God's grace. But **Filson revolutionizes the Puritan forms by substituting nature or the wilderness for Jehovah as his symbol of deity.** The impression conveyed by the Puritan personal narrative is that of a tightly closed, systematic, intimate universe, God and man—a universe manageable in size but containing all important things. The wilderness is the realm of chaos, impinging on the ordered cosmos but somehow outside the world protected by God. Filson, however, substitutes all of the wilderness landscape, its ambiguous and even hellish elements as well as its pure and paradisiacal qualities (its wigwams as well as its settlements), for the Word of God in the symbolic universe of Boone's personal narrative. He thus expands the boundaries of that universe to include the wild continent as an integral and vital part of the divine plan for the regeneration of man. At the same time, by retaining the individual experience as the central focus and source of perspective in his narrative, he preserves the sense of organic unity and order that the Puritan form possessed.

The Boone narrative begins with an account of and an apology for the hero's motivation for leaving his family and moving to Kentucky. The account is carefully calculated to overcome the objections made by opponents of emigration from Increase Mather to Buffon. **If a man is civilized, why would he leave society for the savage solitude of the forest?** And if he is not civilized, how can he be set up as a hero for civilized men to emulate? Boone's justification is largely pragmatic: the final results of his act are good, whatever his motives. He creates a new society through his emigration, and he does not destroy the existing society by leaving it. He returns in the end to his family. Thus the trinity of values on which Anglo-American society is based—social progress, piety, and the family—is invoked at the outset as the basic standard for judging Boone's actions. But Filson reinforces this defense by having Boone present himself as a man nurtured in the values of the eighteenth century, so that he can further justify his emigration by appealing to the "divinities" of natural religion—natural law, human reason (and the desire for knowledge), and divine Providence:

> Curiosity is natural to the soul of man, and interesting objects have a powerful influence on our affections. Let these influencing powers actuate, by the permission or disposal of Providence, from selfish or social views, yet in time **the mysterious will of heaven** is unfolded, and we behold our own conduct, from whatever motives excited, operating to answer the important designs of heaven. Thus we behold Kentucke, lately an howling wilderness, . . . rising from obscurity to shine with splendor, equal to any other of the stars of the American hemisphere.

This passage provides a major insight into the pattern of experience that is rhythmically repeated throughout the Boone narrative and the whole of *Kentucke.* **Boone enters the wilderness in a state of innocence and naiveté,** unsure of his own motivations and of the ultimate outcome of his adventures, but trusting in the strength of his own character and **the goodness of nature** to create ultimate good out of present confusion. This trusting immersion in the wilderness ultimately results in the attainment of self-knowledge and an understanding of the design of God—a state of awareness which Boone attains when he is able to stand above his experience, view it from outside, and exercise his reason upon it in order to reduce it to its essential order.

This pattern of experience is followed in the first crucial section of the narrative, in which Boone is initiated into a knowledge of the wilderness of Kentucky. With four friends, he enters Kentucky in 1769, after a fatiguing journey and "uncomfortable

"literary myth"—For the characteristics of a literary or written myth, see Ch. 2, p. 19. For the difference between the literary version of a myth and other versions, see Ch. 25, p. 361.

"Boone's 'Adventures' consist of a series of . . . progressive immersions that take him deeper into the wilderness"—In the Little Golden Book, Boone keeps guiding settlers, but each time he says, "Too many people! Too crowded! I need more elbowroom!" and travels successively farther West.

"wisdom gained from it"—Boone must have learned many of his skills from the Native Americans who lived around him. Filson represents nature as his teacher, as does the Little Golden Book: "Daniel listened to the wind in the trees . . . . [He] took to hunting right off."

"Filson revolutionizes the Puritan forms by substituting nature or the wilderness for Jehovah as his symbol of deity"—Filson draws upon and revises previous types of storytelling. In earlier accounts, the colonists were described as achieving a new level of meaning through their struggles in the wilderness, gaining salvation through their increased reliance on God. In the Puritan world view, humans are depraved creatures requiring "rigid chastisement by God and government." As a result, in Puritan narratives, humans never stand out; Jehovah is the only hero. According to Filson, Boone also achieves greater meaning in life through communing with nature in the wilderness.

Here Slotkin is quoting from:
John Filson, *Kentucke,* 49–50.

"If a man is civilized, why would he leave society for the savage solitude of the forest?"—Levi-Strauss has shown that myths usually embody a tension or a conflict between nature and culture. (See Ch. 20, p. 292.)

"the mysterious will of heaven"—the force that Slotkin identifies with natural law. It is this force that will provide Boone with newfound wisdom in the course of his journey into Kentucky.

Miriam Story Hurford, *Daniel Boone* listening to nature, illustration from The Little Golden Book.

"Boone enters the wilderness in the state of innocence and naiveté"— In a sense, Boone is undergoing -an initiation. After the trials he will experience in the wilderness, he will achieve a different status in society, that of the hunter-husbandman. See Victor Turner's discussion of initiation rituals, and their relationship to myth, Ch. 26, p. 375f.

"the goodness of nature"—Slotkin finds that Boone represented natural law, an important concept in colonial America. In the 17th c., philosophers Thomas Hobbes and John Locke distinguished between the laws that humans created in civilized societies and what they called "natural law." They identified the content of natural law by studying human beings apart from their societies. Locke's idea that nature gives humans "inalienable rights," can be found in the U.S. Declaration of Independence.

"So much does friendship triumph over misfortune . . ."—Turner notes that neophytes who are undergoing initiation together "tend to develop an intense comradeship," see Ch. 26, p. 376f.

"it requires but a little philosophy to make a man happy"—The wilderness teaches Boone lessons that will make him a better citizen when he reenters society. In Campbell's terms, he becomes "master of both worlds" (Ch. 14, p. 165).

Here Slotkin is quoting from John Filson, *Kentucke*, 53–54.

"He must be stripped to the barest essentials for survival"—Like all initiations, Boone's adventures require him to shed all the indications of his previous status in society. Turner describes the initiation of a new chief among the Ndembu, as follows: "a chief is just like a slave on the night before he succeeds." In the course of this initiation, the chief-to-be is dressed in rags. He must sit patiently on a mat while those with a grudge against him berate him. Turner compares this phase of initiation to death or to being in the womb. (See Ch. 26, p. 376.)

weather as a prelibation of our future suffering." The naive hero is exposed to a series of experiences that give him direct knowledge of both the terror and the beauty of Kentucky.

As they proceed into the wilderness, Boone and one companion are captured, their other friends driven off, their camp and furs plundered. The two men manage to escape their captors and return to camp, where they find Boone's brother Squire arrived before them. This coincidence provides Boone with an opportunity for one of those philosophical asides in which he finds the essential meaning of his experience and derives from that meaning a practical wisdom. In this case he discovers that friendship and human society are balm for the hurts inflicted by human enmity and evil: "[Our] meeting so fortunately in the wilderness made us reciprocally sensible of the utmost satisfaction. **So much does friendship triumph over misfortune** . . . and substitute . . . happiness in [its] room" (Filson, 53). Soon his companion is killed by Indians, and Boone and Squire are left alone in the wilderness. Yet he can still maintain his cheerfulness and confidence, indulge in civilized conversation, and articulate a stoic philosophy of asceticism and self-control:

> Thus situated, many hundred of miles from our families in the howling wilderness, I believe few would have enjoyed the happiness we experienced. I often observed to my brother. You see now how little nature requires to be satisfied. Felicity . . . is rather found in our own breasts than in the enjoyment of external things . . . **it requires but a little philosophy to make a man happy**. . . . This consists in a full resignation to the Will of Providence, and a resigned soul finds pleasure in a path strewed with briars and thorns.

Boone's initiation into knowledge of the wilderness cannot be accomplished, however, while even one civilized amenity remains to him. **He must be stripped to the barest essentials for survival,** in order to meet nature directly and without encumbrances. Thus, when their supplies run low, Squire returns to the settlement, leaving Boone with no trace of civilized life except his rifle—"without bread, salt or sugar, without company of my fellow creatures or even a horse or dog." The dark elements in the wilderness have all but subdued the light. Death has nearly triumphed over life, loneliness has succeeded companionship, and melancholy passions have all but toppled the controlling power of "philosophy and fortitude" (Filson, 54). But at this point the narrative takes a sudden turn, and Boone's melancholy is converted into a vision of the beauty and order of nature, which strengthens his spirit and gives him the determination to settle permanently in Kentucky.

> One day I undertook a tour through the country, and the diversity and beauty of nature . . . expelled every gloomy and vexatious thought. . . . I surveyed the famous river Ohio that rolled in silent dignity, marking the western boundary of Kentucke with ***inconceivable grandeur.*** At a vast distance I beheld the mountains lift their venerable brows, and penetrate the clouds. All things were stilled. I kindled a fire near a fountain of sweet water, and feasted on the loin of a buck which a few hours before I had killed.
>
> The sullen shades of night soon overspread the whole atmosphere, and the earth seemed to gasp for the hovering moisture. I laid me down to sleep, and I awoke not until the sun had chased away the night.

This scene is the crisis of the book, for from this first initiation into the knowledge of nature Boone derives the "philosophy and fortitude" and the vision of future paradise in Kentucky which enable him to emerge from the later ordeals he must face. The scene is crucial to the operation of the narrative as myth, since it is here that the human hero achieves communion with the gods of nature.

The Boone Narrative as Myth

Part of Filson's success can be attributed to his conscious artistry in altering and ordering his raw materials for literary presentation. He departed in a number of ways from the facts of Boone's career in order to fit him into the necessary mold of hunter-husbandman-philosopher. Boone was fifty years old when Filson met him, the patriarch of a large and still-expanding family and the possessor of a great reputation among his fellow frontiersmen. To characterize him as a novice receiving his initiation into the ways of the wilderness, **Filson had to suppress the facts** that Boone was in his late thirties when his "Adventures" began, that he had long been familiar with the conditions of life in the wilderness, and that he had already developed the mental attitude and physical prowess needed for survival.

But Filson was also fortunate in that the real Boone's character and activities contributed to the legend's credibility—over the next forty years of Boone's (and the legend's) life—in large and even small ways. By an uncanny coincidence, Boone's personal history embodied the symbolic patterns of **Voltaire's and Rousseau's** imagery: Boone was born of good Quaker parents in Pennsylvania and was formally adopted by the good savages of the Shawnee nation. His personal philosophy of life apparently combined the Indian love of hunting, personal freedom, and combat with the Quaker's scrupulous morality, disapproval of cruelty and waste and gentleness toward the helpless. It was part of the legend that developed early in his life that he killed neither Indian nor animal, except when compelled by necessity, and that he took no scalps.

Filson's portrayal of Boone as a hunter-husbandman is accurate as far as it goes, but it falls short of depicting Boone's real attitude toward farming. Although Boone did stake out and work a subsistence farm in the manner of the physiocratic yeoman, **he never did fit into the yeoman's mold.** He was primarily a hunter and trapper, who cleared only as much of his land as was needed for kitchen crops and a little salable tobacco to keep his family fed during his long absences.

2. Rebecca Boone as a Character in the Myth

"Boone's courtship of his wife"—Rebecca Bryan Boone was a strong and capable woman who cared for a large family during her husband's frequent absences. See "Rebecca Boone as a Pioneer Woman," p. 578.

"omitted by Filson"—Slotkin suggests that fire-hunting did not fit Filson's version of the legend of Daniel Boone because it represented him as a solitary, animal-like hunter. Contemporary accounts record Boone's distaste for the custom, but the basis of his feelings is not reported. He may have felt it called for an unnecessary display of sharpshooting, or it may have violated his sense of fair play in hunting.

"Rebecca underwent the most considerable change"—On the accomplishments of Boone's wife, see "Rebecca Boone as a Pioneer Woman," p. 579.

"eliminates"—In minimizing Rebecca Boone's accomplishments, Filson was tailoring his story to his audience. In Boone's time, people felt that a man should dominate his spouse. This attitude was based on the religious beliefs of the time, and resulted in tension between men and women, who operated in different realms and often had different priorities and concerns. See "Rebecca Boone as a Pioneer Woman," p. 579.

"Boone's wife"—The Little Golden Book version of Boone's marriage reflects Filson's emphasis. It reads, in entirety: "'All a man needs to be happy is a good gun, a good horse, and a good wife,' Daniel said. He had a good gun and a good horse, and in time he married a good wife. He raised a family of boys and girls, and they were good too."

The most significant of the legends that had gathered around Boone before Filson met him centers on his love of the wilderness and his sense of identification with the land. This legend constitutes an eighteenth-century Kentucky equivalent of the primitive divine king and sacred marriage myths, in which a tribal hero meets and cohabits or weds with an avatar of the feminine nature spirit, thus insuring renewed life to both tribe and land.

The legend concerns **Boone's courtship of his wife,** Rebecca Bryan. He was fire-hunting one dark night, stalking the forest with a blazing torch whose light was supposed to attract a deer to his stand. The deer would have to be killed by a shot aimed between the two points of reflected firelight that would mark its eyes, because the animal would be otherwise invisible. After a long wait Boone saw the double gleam and prepared to fire, but some intuition stayed him. He moved toward the gleams, pushed aside the brush, and discovered Rebecca, who turned and fled home. According to the legend, she told her family she had been scared by "a painter," or panther, and soon afterward Daniel came courting.

The fire-hunt legend was well known to the Boones themselves, and they often repeated it to their children (who refused to believe it). Yet this legend and others which show Boone as the wild, lonely hunter were neglected or **omitted by Filson.** (Later, western writers like Timothy Flint and Romantics like Fenimore Cooper rediscovered them and worked them into the literary versions of the Boone myth.) Filson wished to retain the idea that Boone's hunting trips initiated him into a deep intimacy with the powers of nature and that the health of his spirit was essential to the realization of nature's plan for the Kentucky land. Being committed to the philosophy and pastoral imagery of physiocracy, he would have wished to deny that the wild, man-shy spirit of the deer symbolized nature in Kentucky or that the symbolic hero of the American frontier had the lonely, restless spirit of the hunting panther, rather than the virtuous placidity of the yeoman.

Filson made other important alterations of the facts in his new images of Boone, Rebecca, and the wilderness. **Rebecca underwent the most considerable change.** In life a strong and intelligent woman, she stood almost as tall as Daniel Boone, who himself was over the average in height. It was she who held their large family together while he vanished on long hunts, which might last a season or a couple of years. When he was taken by the Shawnee and presumed dead, she packed up her family and moved east to Carolina by herself through Indian country at the height of the Indian wars. When he grew old and was attacked by rheumatism, she accompanied him on hunts, helped him kill game, and was accounted a fair shot.

Filson all but **eliminates** Rebecca Boone from his account. She appears only as "my wife," never by name, and no attention is paid to her considerable accomplishments as provider and protector. She first appears in Boone's meditation on his loneliness during the first exploration of Kentucky; in this passage the thought of his family far away in the settlement inclines him to melancholy, and he has to put aside the sentiment. Next, she appears as the "first white woman" to stand beside the Kentucky river, a symbol of the establishment of civilization on the river and of the settlement's weakness and exposure to the savagery of the wilderness. She does not appear again until after Boone has returned from his Shawnee captivity and beaten off the Indian attack on Boonesborough. Then the reader learns that she returned to Carolina, heartbroken over the thought of his death. For Filson, Rebecca is simply a generalized "amiable Spouse," subject to the conventional weaknesses of the sentimental heroine, suffering deprivations and heartbreak without acquiring (in the narrative) a personality of her own.

Even in Filson's account, **Boone's wife** remains a symbol of the spirit of nature. But where the folk myth emphasizes her wildness and freedom and shyness of man, Filson's myth emphasizes her civilized qualities, her conformity to the conventional idea of

Thomas Moran, a member of the Hudson River School, painted *The Chasm* of the Colorado, 1873–74.

woman in Anglo-American society—a morally strong but physically weak creature in need of a hero's protection, a victim suffering dutifully under physical discomfort and the pangs of womanly sentiment, so completely identified with her role as wife and mother that she has no identity independent of her social role.

The **archetypal hero** begins in a state of innocence or unawareness of the powers that are latent in himself and in his environment. Filson's Boone narrative fits the archetype rather closely. In the first cycle of adventures, Boone begins by dwelling on a peaceful farm. Curiosity and the spirit of adventure lure him willingly to the threshold of Kentucky.

After preliminary struggles with the Indians and his own melancholy fears, he descends into **the western wilderness,** which (as we have seen) **is archetypal of the unconscious hidden mind,** the kingdom of dreams, death's Valhalla. He submits to the ordeal of captivity and battle with the Indian presence and is initiated in the wilderness life by means of hunting the deer. He tastes the land's sweetness and returns with his vision to the world of his past, there to quicken the frontiersmen's ambition and aspiration.

Next, in the captivity cycle of his adventures, he leaves the peaceful island of Boonesborough to hunt deer and salt, is carried over the threshold of the Indians' world in defeat and captivity, is initiated and adopted into the tribe, resists a series of temptations that test his character, and returns with the new wisdom to become the war chief of his people. His return is at once a resurrection (his wife has thought him dead) and a transformation (he has become a hero and chief).

In a final test, he goes forth to battle, is plunged into misery and despair by his son's death, but returns to the land of death to retrieve and appropriately inter his son's body. **He emerges with renewed strength**—a superhuman strength from which his land and people will draw sustenance and which they will employ to achieve peace and to establish their settlements in the land (apotheosis).

The Complex Influences on Filson's Boone Tale

Although Filson's Boone has the Romantics' emotional rapport with nature, trust in intuitive wisdom, and ability to feel strong passions, his greatest need is for order. Thus he modulates his passions to the controllable level of sentiments by the exercise of reason. Although moved by the "ruins . . . of a world" which greet him in his first

 3. Daniel Boone as the Archetypal Hero

"archetypal hero"—Slotkin's use of the word "archetypal" can be taken in two senses here: (1) it means "typical" or "standard"; (2) it refers to Jung's explanation "archetype," an image or concept that is found in all human beings. See Ch. 32, p. 470f.

"the western wilderness . . . is archetypal of the unconscious hidden mind"—In Jung's view, the adventures of the hero in the real world represent each person's internal search for meaning.

"He emerges with renewed strength"—Joseph Campbell describes the journey of the hero in an account that includes the ideas of Jung. Campbell points out that the hero typically returns from his journey bearing a treasure or boon that makes life better for himself and others. (See Ch. 14, p. 165.)

"Hudson River school"—These 19th-c. Romantics painted landscapes representing the natural beauty of the untouched American wilderness.

"means to a social end"—In his opening, Slotkin notes that a myth can be successful only insofar as it reflects and expresses the values of the society from which it comes. Here he is summing up the ways in which the myth of Daniel Boone satisfies this criterion.

"maintenance of civilization against the powers of the wilderness"—In Slotkin's view, Filson's version of the Daniel Boone myth represents the tension between two conflicting forces, nature and culture.

"Cooper's Leatherstocking Tales" —James Fenimore Cooper wrote a series of stories involving a character named Natty Bumppo who was thought to be based on Daniel Boone. (See p. 578.)

Crèvecoeur—In *Letters from an American Farmer* (1782) and *Sketches of Eighteenth Century America* (1925), he shed light on the nature of the American colonists. (See note on p. 582.)

"Filson ceased to control his version of the myth not long after he had written it"—The essence of Filson's story survives in versions that modify many of the "factual" details in his story; that is, future versions of the story, while contradicting details of Filson's narrative, nonetheless maintained his emphasis on Daniel Boone as someone who found philosophical meaning in nature.

attempt to cross the mountains, Boone, like the **Hudson River school** painter, is more moved by the sunlit vistas from his sweet spring on the mountaintop. Great passions are necessary to his realization of his full potential for human feeling; but in order for him to attain heroic stature, he must restrain his passion, forget private grief, and attend to the public good.

For Filson, Boone's solitary hunting trips are, not ends in themselves, but **means to a social end.** Solitude has value in the Boone narrative only insofar as it contributes to the ultimate creation of a better society; hunting is noble only insofar as it clears the way for husbandry. Sentiments are of use only because they lead to self-knowledge and consequently to a higher quality of self-restraint.

The lesson of the frontier experience was that the **maintenance of civilization against the powers of the wilderness** was possible only through complete knowledge of one's own capacity for good and evil and of the wilderness's inherent threats and promises. Too much preoccupation with darkness would have weakened Boone's ability to resist the terrors of his environment and construct a viable social order. He had to retain a positive vision of a perfected civilization as his final goal.

In this concern Filson's Boone prefigures that peculiar sense of social place, mission, and obligation that informs the characters of **Cooper's Leatherstocking Tales** and the works of Emerson, Whitman, and their generation. Even in the darker writers of the American Renaissance, like Hawthorne and Melville, who did not put forward positive visions of an ideal America, the sense of obligation to society or civilization appears as a feeling of spiritual malaise or guilt for having pursued art into an antisocial wilderness of darkness, chaos, and blood.

Like **Crèvecoeur**'s study of American character, Filson's Boone narrative offers a kind of composite portrait, containing many possible hero types—some themselves expressing antithetical values—within a single figure. Filson's Boone, however, is more hunter, warrior, and wanderer than he is farmer, while Crèvecoeur's farmer enters Boone's world only by compulsion.

Boone's personal myth continued to grow, as the old hunter continued to pursue his seasonal hunting and exploring expeditions until he was well into his eighties. **Filson ceased to control his version of the myth not long after he had written it,** and the literary version of the myth embarked on a long career of modification by European rationalists and Romantics and by American spokesmen for the northeastern, southern, and western sections of the new nation. Several distinct but related variations resulted, the peculiar emphasis and direction of each determined by the cultural needs and prejudices of the different sections and intellectual periods. Through them all, two major themes persisted: the Filsonian vision of the frontier hero as an untutored republican-gentleman-philosopher and the folk vision of Boone as the mighty hunter, child of the wilderness, and exemplar of values derived from sources outside Anglo-American civilization.

Futher Reading

Calloway, Colin G. *New Worlds for All: Indians, Europeans and the Remaking of Early America.* Baltimore, MD: The Johns Hopkins University Press, 1997.

Slotkin, Richard. *Regeneration Through Violence: The Mythology of the American Frontier, 1600–1860.* New York, NY: HarperCollins, 1996.

Stagecoach and *Firefly*

Science Fiction and the Journey into the Unknown

WHAT TO EXPECT . . . Because entertainment media are targeted to specific audiences, and they reflect the values and beliefs of those viewers, they can exhibit important lessons for students of mythology. One popular genre that especially lends itself to mythological discussion is science fiction.

This chapter, through its analysis of Joss Whedon's television series *Firefly* and his film *Serenity*, considers how such entertainment reflects the concerns of its audience by examining the underlying assumptions of these works about the place of human beings in the cosmos.

The methodology used in this chapter is comparative, looking at the science fiction stories in *Firefly* and *Serenity* in relation to the classic Western film *Stagecoach*. As you read, consider the relationship of the world represented in this film to the frontier world portrayed by Filson in his account of Daniel Boone in Chapter 39, p. 573.

In addition, consider the journeys described in this chapter in relation to what Joseph Campbell says about the hero's journey in Chapter 14, p. 159. Also, compare what you learn about the audiences of Whedon's works with your understanding of ancient Romans with respect to Ovid's representation of science in Chapter 4, p. 42. Relate Turner's discussion of the liminoid (relating to an individual's ability to join a range of social groups) in Chapter 26, p. 373, to the events in the series and the film. Consider which of the insights provided by myth, as described in Chapter 1, relate to the material in this chapter: anthropological, metaphysical, cosmological, aetiological, sociological, psychological, historical.

In the discussion below, we are not assuming that you have seen *Firefly* or *Serenity*. We will describe the elements of the show and movie that are necessary for our discussion. However, the series and movie are widely available on DVD, so if you are intrigued by the account in this chapter, you will be able to find them.

Science fiction writers create a universe informed by science, and they craft narratives set in worlds whose science, history, and culture are very different from our own. However, at the core of such writing, we find powerful stories charged with meaning related to the beliefs, tensions, and conflicts of our own time—the domain of mythology. Because of its flexibility and widespread appeal, science fiction can provide useful insights into the ways mythology permeates contemporary culture.

Before we delve further into the mythological aspects of this genre, let us pause for a brief note about terminology. It is possible to make a distinction between science fiction and fantasy, and between "hard" science fiction (stories with meticulous attention to the laws of physics, cosmology, mathematics, and biology), "soft" science fiction (stories focused on the social sciences and on character), "space opera" (starships battling to win galaxies), and fantasy (stories with elves, dragons, and other magical creatures). We will not dwell on these distinctions here.

Rather, we will point out the wide range of media that can be considered science fiction, including the story lines of many Japanese *manga* and the narrative elements of video games, television shows, and of course, movies. These various narratives are used to represent all the different kinds of issues we are concerned with in contemporary society. They are of particular interest to us in our study of contemporary approaches to mythology because we can see in many of them the complexity of science and the ambivalence we feel toward it.

Science does not represent a belief system in the way that religion does, but nonetheless it can play an important role in how we define ourselves and how we view our lives and our place in society. And this is especially true in America—more Americans believe that science will be important to our future than the citizens of any other industrialized country (Campbell and Curtis, 262).

THE IDEOLOGY AND SCIENCE OF *STAR TREK*

To understand the role of science in recent popular culture, it is helpful to look back at the middle of the last century. In the late sixties, the belief in the wide-ranging positive effect of science on our society was far greater than it is now. In popular culture, this attitude was expressed by the television show *Star Trek*. The original series was about the crew of the starship *Enterprise* who are on a mission to explore the galaxy; as often as not, the captain and crew wind up trying to convince the inhabitants of the planets they travel to that they should be more like us, because our culture and values are superior to theirs. The emphasis is on the values of the group, and often individuals on the ship and on the planets have to subordinate their personal happiness to the good of the group.

Star Trek takes place in a future in which science has solved all the main problems we experience today, like poverty, hunger, and disease. Jewett and Lawrence suggest that the meaning of the series is connected to the beliefs and values of the society from which it draws its audience. In particular the show celebrated "the freeing of the human spirit from superstition and narrow-mindedness" and wore "the cloak of empirical science" (9). The original *Star Trek* spawned several new series as well as a number of feature films that were broadcast through the 2004–2005 season. Both the series and the films are still widely available.

Although a variety of scientific disciplines play incidental or occasional roles in the series, the one most essential to the story line of *Star Trek* is physics. Space travel across great distances is accomplished through manipulating the properties of matter and antimatter in a device called a warp drive. This involves a variety of imaginary inventions based on real physical principles, in some cases reinforced by robotic or mechanical components. The advanced physics represented on the *Enterprise* is matched by advances in other scientific areas as well, but most problems are solved by traveling across amazing areas of space in a short time and beaming to the site, as well as other feats achieved through advances in physics.

THE X-FILES: NEW SCIENCE FICTION FOR A NEW ERA

Like *Star Trek, The X-Files* appeared at a critical juncture in our views of science in society. This science fiction series ran from 1993 to 2003 and featured a very different world view. The show detailed the adventures of two FBI special agents, Fox Mulder and Dana Scully, who are assigned to investigate cases involving unexplainable phenomena. Their investigations are wide ranging. *The X-Files,* at first sight, seems to explore the relationship, or if you prefer, the battle, of human beings and extraterrestrials. However, the battleground in this series is definitely on the home front, not the outer reaches of the galaxy. Lavery, Hague, and Cartwright suggest that *The X-Files* reflects the ongoing questioning of authority in the political sphere (2). The show in fact reflects a growing isolationist conservatism in American society. In line with this perspective, the

In an episode of *The X-Files* titled "The Erlenmeyer Flask" (123), FBI agent Fox Mulder discovers a lab in a seemingly deserted shed. On this show science often consists of secret biology experiments performed by lone individuals.

show represents "dystopian images of decrepit and corrupted technology" (Novotny, 107). In this world, the plot emphasizes the eclectic choices individuals make in building their own value systems, operating independently of the realm of organized religion. On every level, the show encourages the adoption of one of its maxims, "Trust No One." That is, the stories emphasize the inherent untrustworthiness of any social organization.

The model of science represented in *The X-Files* reinforces our vision of ourselves as separate entities, individuals first and members of social units later, if at all. The entity to be protected from invasion is the body, not the country. It is to this realm of anxiety that *The X-Files* speaks. In the context of the show's concerns, the only reliable scientific discoveries are those by the X-Files investigators themselves, who are seen as making connections between remote phenomena widely separated by geographic distances and as bridging the boundaries of a range of disciplines. The scientific theories applied by the agents are drawn from a variety of scientific domains, but biology of different kinds is most prominent. In particular, many episodes of the series turn on the agents' understanding of the behavior of DNA and vaccines, in the light of aliens' desire to produce a human–alien hybrid and to wage war through the use of cancer, making the biology of that disease prominent in the series.

THE FILM *STAGECOACH*

In the present chapter, Fred Erisman explains the connections between the science fiction television series *Firefly* and the Western genre, notably John Ford's *Stagecoach*. This film was made in 1939 and is viewed as one of the great achievements of its director. The great filmmaker Orson Welles described himself as viewing *Stagecoach* over and over as an important element of his preparation for making his masterpiece *Citizen Kane* (Lowrie, 27). Famed Japanese director Akira Kurosawa is said to have drawn on Ford's film for elements of his own films *The Seven Samurai* and *Yojimbo* (Goodwin, 166–67).

It has never been a secret that *Firefly* creator Joss Whedon intended to make a Western set in space. Erisman's article shows us *how* Whedon developed the themes and concepts he wove into the television series. For us as students of mythology, this analysis shows the way the archetypical hero's journey plays out in new stories that reflect the perspectives of our ever-changing world.

INTRODUCTION TO *FIREFLY*

Firefly was the brainchild of Joss Whedon, creator of the incredibly popular *Buffy the Vampire Slayer* series. There were 14 episodes of the show, which ran in the 2002–2003 season and was hailed as one of the best science fiction television series ever made (Burrow).

The story is set in 2507, when most earthdwellers have moved to another solar system centered on a star with many planets and even more moons. "Through giant atmosphere processing plants, terraforming technologies, gravity regulation, and the introduction of every known form of Earthlife," each planet has become its own earth-like homeworld (Whedon, 12).

The Central Planets are home to the descendents of America and China, former rivals who have achieved peace through forming a heavy-handed governing structure, the Alliance. The episodes of *Firefly* take place just after the Alliance has won the War for Unification, defeating the Independents and forcing its government on the more frontier-like outer planets. Though the Alliance won, it was a "Pyrrhic victory" (Lackey, 66) that severely depleted the resources of the governing structure, limiting its ability to supply and patrol its extensive holdings. Mal Reynolds, the captain of the run-down freighter called *Firefly*, and his second in command, Zoe Washburne, fought on the side of the Independents or Browncoats in the war. They operate on the edges of the Alliance's influence in the various illegal or semilegal missions they undertake. The ship's other passengers represent a cross-section of twenty-sixth century society and include a highly respectable courtesan, a preacher with a mysterious past, and a doctor and his sister on the lam from a forced bio-engineering program of the Alliance.

The film *Serenity* continues the storyline beyond the series, while explaining some of the backstory, notably the origin of the cannibalistic Reavers, savage humans who raid ships and rape, cannibalize, skin, and kill the passengers. The plot pits captain Mal Reynolds against the nameless Operator, who believes fanatically in the nobility of the Alliance until he learns, at the end of the movie, that it is responsible for the creation of the Reavers.

FIREFLY AND BIOLOGY

Like *The X-Files, Firefly* is science fiction that relies extensively on biology for shaping its universe and creating the complications of its plot. Especially prominent in the backstory of *Firefly* is the process of terraforming, through which lifeless planets and moons are made habitable for human beings. The solar system to which human civilization has been moved is created through the use of a variety of techniques coming from biology. In effect, terraforming involves recreating the process of evolution in a short time span to provide a world like our own. This requires a range of experimentation with the geological, biological, chemical, and psychological processes necessary to human life. Terraforming particularly informs the premise of the show, since its outcome is the creation of a world with resources inadequate for the humans on the outer planets. As a result, Darwinian natural selection manifests itself, and the brutal forces of human history operate again in a new setting, despite the advances of science.

In addition, the process of experimentation rooted in biology results in interfering with the nature of humanity itself, like the failed project described in the film *Serenity*. This experiment took place on the planet Miranda and resulted in the creation of the Reavers. The original plan was to alter human nature by rendering it more serene through the introduction of a chemical into the air system, but the result is to produce two extremes: the majority of the populace becomes so placid that it dies out, while a small proportion of the inhabitants become the cannibalistic, brutal creatures who are feared throughout the series.

In the film *Serenity*, we see another aspect of River's experience with the gifted program she is fleeing. She has been taught a wide range of martial arts skills and when these are triggered, she has, in effect, been turned into a killer. Above we see her after she has single-handedly defeated a band of the fierce Reavers.

The biological tinkering that resulted in the creation of the Reavers is, apparently, only one manifestation of a range of programs manipulating human biology without the consent of the subjects. Another such program affects the plot of *Firefly* even more directly. Doctor Simon Tam and his sister River, two of the passengers on the ship, are fleeing a program designed to turn bright young people into human weapons by modifying their cognitive processes. At a young age, River was sent to a special school for gifted students that turned out to be a cover for this program. Her brother Simon, a brilliant surgeon, abandoned his promising career to rescue his sister and now lives a fugitive's life with her on *Firefly*, helping her deal with the nightmares and the bizarre, at times dangerous, behavior resulting from the experiments performed on her while she was forced to participate in this government program.

FIREFLY AND CONSERVATISM

Like the early *Star Trek*, *Firefly* represents the world of organized religion with reservation if not suspicion. In the episode "Our Mrs. Reynolds," Mal finds himself married to a con artist in a backwater community after unwittingly participating in a wedding ceremony he believes is a victory celebration over bandits. In "Safe," passenger River is kidnapped and nearly burned as a witch by superstitious folk on Jiangyin. At the same time, the moral choices of the crew of *Serenity* represent the eclectic individualistic philosophy prevalent in *The X-Files*. In *Serenity*, the passenger Shepherd Book, a man of the cloth, challenges Captain Mal Reynolds, telling him that he'll need "belief" to get him through. Mal is displeased: "I ain't looking for help from on high. That's a long wait for a train that don't come." However, Book responds, "When I talk about belief, why do you always assume I'm talking about God?" Later in the film, Mal does make a decision to express his moral beliefs by fighting against the unquestioning stance of the Operative who wants to bring about "a world without sin," an affront to the Captain's belief in personal liberty.

The series also reflects a constant tension between the good of the individual and the good of the ship or the "family," as explained by Fred Erisman below. *Star Trek Voyager* was a television show produced from 1995 to 2001 and set in the original series' universe, but with a different cast and crew. In *Voyager*, a human is recaptured after a lengthy indoctrination by the collective called the Borg and takes a position on the ship. This crewmember, known as Seven of Nine, is the focus of many episodes about how to balance the relationship between the individual and the collective, as represented by the crew. The issue is very reminiscent of the one that arises in *Firefly*, but the emphasis in Whedon's show is very different. In *Firefly*, the engineer Kaylee is seen as the focus of the collective efforts of the show, while the captain Mal more often than not represents the values of the individual. The result is that the call for the collective has much less prominence, represented as it is by a character who is charming but quixotic and does not have the authority to defend herself.

Mal and his first mate Zoe are seen as rebels trying to escape the grasp of the great collective, the Alliance, making them much like Mulder and Scully fighting the military-industrial complex in *The X-Files*. Joss Whedon has said that Mal is "somewhat of a reactionary . . . a conservative kind of Libertarian guy." As such, Mal represents "rugged individualism," a philosophy associated with extremely conservative political values suggesting the importance of restricting the role of government. Indeed, liberal Joss Whedon has said, "if Mal and I sat down to dinner, we'd have a terrible time" (11).

Media scholar Henry Jenkins has pointed out that it is important for those who study popular culture to be attentive to the reactions of the fans who actually watch the shows, and not merely to spin their theories in the isolation of the ivory tower (86). A brief investigation of online reactions to the show reveals that fans are as likely to identify with the libertarian aspects of Mal's politics as they are to see the show as a call for sacrifice to the good of the collective. For example, one fan notes, "I found that there's a good number of libertarian Firefly fans on the official FOX board. Many libertarians are attracted to the strong anti-authoritarian themes, as well Firefly's portrayal of the importance of 'the right to bear arms,' so to speak"(CANTTAKESKY). Another online discussant says, "Firefly drips with good old fashioned Heinleinesque libertarianism" (Hinson, comment by Brandybuck Aug. 8, 2005). In this respect, *Firefly* successfully represents the conservative ideology that has emerged as a significant aspect of the modern-day political scene. However, despite his libertarian associations, in episode after episode Mal is shown to have a soft spot for his crew, and winds up jeopardizing individual gain and profit to protect the crew from harm and bring its members back together as a community.

Firefly as a Western

This story comes from: *"Stagecoach* in Space: The Legacy of *Firefly*,"

When Joss Whedon's science fiction television series, *Firefly*, premiered in September, 2002, there was no denying it was a Western. In succeeding frames of the opening

*Fred Erisman. "*Stagecoach* in Space: The Legacy of *Firefly*," *Extrapolation* 47.2 (2006) 249–58. Printed with permission.

credits a pistol cocked with a threatening click; the protagonist faced the camera stalwartly alone, a pistol strapped low on his thigh; accompanied by a trusted sidekick, he stood off a cluster of mounted, duster-clad ne'er-do-wells; and horses stampeded into the foreground, spooked by the low-flying spaceship above them. All the while, an off-screen voice wailed the lyrics of the series' theme:

> Take me out to the black,
> Tell them I ain't comin' back.
> Burn the land and boil the sea;
> **You can't take the sky from me** ("Serenity").

The series' roots in the tradition of the Western story and the Western film were apparent for all to see.

Far less apparent, however, is the degree to which the series draws upon a single Western classic, John Ford's *Stagecoach* (1939), to shape its structure and its nature. Ford's film, which made John Wayne a star and netted Academy Awards for supporting actor Thomas Mitchell and score composer Richard Hageman, establishes the model from which *Firefly* builds. In the fourteen segments filmed (only eleven of which were aired before the series was untimely cancelled), Whedon and his cast make clear their debt to the earlier film. Whedon, in fact, remarks that, in planning his ensemble cast, he mused: "**Millennium Falcon,** yes. *Stagecoach,* better . . . , so I decided to go from five [characters] to nine," making his cast match Ford's in number ("Here's How It Was"). From that beginning, he, the writers, and the cast go on to demonstrate how, had circumstances permitted, the film's structure, context, and motifs might be translated into a future world far from the Western frontier.

The Journey in *Stagecoach*

The basic structure of *Stagecoach* is the familiar one of **the journey**. Six passengers, a lawman, and the driver set out from Tonto to travel to Lordsburg, picking up a ninth person along the way. They are a disparate group: Buck, the driver (Andy Devine), has a job to do; Curly, the marshal (George Bancroft), rides shotgun to search for the Ringo Kid, who has broken jail; pregnant Lucy Mallory (Louise Platt) is on her way to join her cavalry officer husband; Peacock (Donald Meek), a whiskey salesman called "Reverend" by the group, wants only "to return to the bosoms of his family"; Hatfield (John Carradine), a gambler and disgraced Southern aristocrat, goes along to protect Lucy Mallory; Gatewood (Berton Churchill), a banker, is absconding with his bank's cash; while drunken Doc Boone (Thomas Mitchell) and the prostitute Dallas (Claire Trevor) have been driven out of town by the self-righteous women of the Law and Order League. The final passenger, the Ringo Kid (John Wayne), has escaped prison to avenge the murder of his brother by the Plummer brothers. En route to Lordsburg, Doc Boone delivers Lucy's baby, the group fends off an Indian attack, Hatfield is killed and Peacock wounded, Ringo and Dallas fall in love, and Curly, turning a blind eye to the letter of the law, sends the two off to start life anew on Ringo's ranch.

The journey in and of itself, however, in Ford's hands becomes the "**journey into hell**"—a device by which "the hero (in this case the group) must undertake a journey that brings him face to face with mirror images of his own weaknesses and flaws, but in the form of powerful obstacles for him to overcome before he can . . . emerge, cleansed and reborn, into the light" (Place, 32). Thus, each of the principal characters, and especially Dallas and Ringo, must examine his or her beliefs and principles before the film can end. Doc Boone overcomes drunkenness to deliver a baby; Hatfield shows a glimmer of vestigial honor in his efforts to protect Lucy; Peacock, a Milquetoast character, finds courage and determination within himself; and Curly, a dedicated law

---

"You can't take the sky from me"—This sentiment attests to the rugged individualism of the Independents and the ideology of *Firefly* captain Mal Reynolds. At the same time, it finds a responsive chord in the libertarian political views prominent in our own time. See Introduction, p. 593.

Millennium Falcon—The space ship operated by smuggler Han Solo in Star Wars IV and figuring in the second and third film as well. Like *Firefly*, she is a ship that has seen better days. Solo says of her, "she may not look like much, but she's got it where it counts, kid."

"the journey"—Mythological tales are often structured by this plot device. For Joseph Campbell's extensive analysis of the hero's journey and the ways it is used to express mythological content and structure the ritual elements of a culture, see Ch. 14, p. 159.

🔵 The Characters of *Stagecoach*

Hero	The Ringo Kid
Driver/pilot	Buck
Doctor	Doc Boone
Woman needing protection	Lucy Mallory
Priest	"Reverend" Peacock (whiskey salesman)
Whore	Dallas
Other	Hatfield the gambler
Characters	Gatewood the dishonest banker
	Curly the marshal

"journey into hell"—The literary term for this is *katabasis*. Many mythological heroes undergo a *katabasis*, including Heracles (see Ch. 31, page 458.) and Orpheus, the poet who travels to the underworld to bring back his wife Eurydice who has died by stepping on a snake. Persephone (Ch. 27, p. 391) is also taken to the underworld when she is snatched by Aidoneus, and Psyche is sent there by her mother-in-law Venus (Ch. 37, page 556). The self-knowledge that attends a *katabasis* can be seen as corresponding to the interior process described by Carl Jung as the "process of individuation" (see Ch. 32, page 475).

officer, comes to understand that personal law can transcend statutory law. The evolution of the principal characters catalyzed by the circumstances of the journey gives the film much of its distinctiveness.

The Journey in *Firefly*

That same distinctiveness resonates in *Firefly*, where nine diverse characters set out on an **endless voyage** from one planetary settlement to another. The time is 500 years in the future, five years after a global war has left only two superpowers, the United States and China, and galactic government has been centralized into the authoritarian Alliance. The similarities between casts are noteworthy; the differences are even more so. The vehicle, spaceship rather than stage, is named *Serenity*. Buck, the serio-comic driver, becomes Wash, the pilot (Alan Tudyk); drunken Doc Boone becomes the uptight surgeon Simon Tam (Sean Maher), who, with his tormented sister, River (Summer Glau), is on the run from Alliance officials; "Reverend" Peacock is replaced by an actual cleric, the enigmatic Shepherd Book (Ron Glass), whose peaceful calling masks an intriguing familiarity with crime and weapons; and, in an especially telling reversal, the prostitute Dallas becomes Inara Serra (Morena Baccarin), a licensed and respected Companion whose clients include women as well as men and whose presence aboard the ship gives it "a certain respectability" ("Out of Gas").

Three characters have no direct counterparts in the film: the ship's engineer, Kaylee Frye (Jewel Staite), unschooled but a genius with machines; the first officer, Zoe (Gina Torres), an army buddy of *Serenity*'s captain and the "resident hard-ass chick," who carries as a sidearm a sawed-off Winchester 94 rifle; and **muscleman Jayne Cobb** (Adam Baldwin), a humorously mercenary thug with a rudimentary sense of honor ("Here's How It Was"). The fourth character, however, could have stepped from the film—Malcolm Reynolds (Nathan Fillion), owner and captain, and a spiritual kinsman to the Ringo Kid. A former sergeant in the Independent forces opposing the Alliance, a "**man of faith**, a man of action . . . before he had everything taken away from him," he is the person who, among them all, is most on the "journey into hell." Betrayed by his own leaders, he has taken up a semi-legitimate life on the **fringes of civilization**, seeking the freedom denied him at home and surrounding himself with a crew that represents "bits of himself that he had lost" ("Commentary to 'Serenity'"). In episode after episode, he encounters obstacles that test his mettle and that of his associates; when Inara says to Simon, "You're lost in the woods. We all are. Even the captain. Only he likes it that way," Mal interjects: "No, the only difference is the woods are the only place I can see a clear path" ("Serenity"). As he walks that path, he strives to recover himself and his sense of life.

The Challenge of the Wilderness

The journey undertaken by **both sets of characters** takes place within a distinctive context—a hostile environment offering little by way of support, and forcing them to turn inward for the resources they need to overcome its perils. For *Stagecoach*, the environment is Monument Valley, in northern Arizona, a desert region whose monotony is broken by towering stone monoliths. It is a dramatic setting in its own right, but, in Ford's hands, becomes more. It is, one critic has observed, symbolic of the forces of nature, which offer man neither aid nor obstacle but are only a **stage upon which he can work out his dreams**. . . . Within it an enclosed worldview is not only possible but necessary. Within it life (and the living of it) must be created through the efforts of man—the environment does not do it for them (Place, 36–37).

"endless voyage"—The goal of the original *Star Trek* series was the exploration of space, a similarly indeterminate goal.

🛰 The Characters of *Firefly*

Hero	Mal Reynolds, the Captain
Driver/ pilot	Wash
Doctor	Simon Tam
Woman needing protection	River Tam
Priest	Shepherd Book
Whore	Inara Serra
Other Characters	Kaylee, the engineer
	Zoe, the second in command
	Jayne, the mercenary

"muscleman Jayne Cobb"—Jayne can be compared to Heracles in being more a man of brawn than intellect. (See Ch. 31, p. 450.)

"man of faith"—See the Introduction, p. 594, on *Firefly*'s stance on religion. For Mal Reynolds, religion represents a moral stance rather than a relationship with a reality beyond his own. His attitude is a natural outgrowth of his individualistic, libertarian principles.

"fringes of civilization"—The world of *Firefly* melds the Western frontier and the Interzone. The latter term is from cyberpunk, a form of science fiction about "marginalized, alienated loners" living "on the edge of society in a generally dystopic future" brought about by "rapid technological change, an ubiquitous datasphere of computerized information, and invasive modification of the human body" (Person). An Interzone is "a liminal space where industrial artifact becomes street art" (Sobystil).

"both sets of characters"—*Stagecoach* and *Firefly* have characters who face comparable challenges in similar situations.

"stage upon which he can work out his dreams"—In American legend, Daniel Boone finds similar inspiration in the wilderness; see Ch. 39, p. 583.

This context is one that Ford found especially provocative, and he used it, in one form or another, in many subsequent films.

Even in *Stagecoach*, however, the essential elements already exist. Like the omnipresent Nature of Stephen Crane's "The Open Boat" or Frank Norris's *McTeague*, **the Valley is neither malevolent nor benevolent**; it simply is, and its aridity and overwhelming expanses reduce human concerns almost to nothingness. The external context, in short, provides "a **wilderness of insecurity**. The townspeople gather in their town, an artificial world, for protection from a menacing and chaotic outer space, from which they isolate themselves"(Gallagher, 391). Part of the contextual menace, however, comes from human as well as natural perils. The Valley is populated by Apaches, **indigenous savages of immeasurable ruthlessness**, and their attack upon the stage brings the action to a climax. Indians and horses die; Peacock takes an arrow through the chest and Hatfield is killed as he **prepares to shoot Lucy to protect her from mutilation and rape**; the stage's defenders are down to their last rounds of ammunition, and only the timely intervention of the United States Cavalry saves the day. In their savagery, the Apache offer a secondary threat that the travelers must constantly keep in mind, a threat they can overcome only with the aid of the military.

The crew of *Serenity* face a comparable situation, albeit in an environment infinitely more lethal than that of Arizona, and populated by hostiles who make the Apache seem innocuous. The environment is, of course, interplanetary space—an airless realm where the slightest failure of human effort can bring lingering (and often instant) death—and its perils play an important part in two segments of the show. In "Out of Gas," the eighth installment of the series, *Serenity* is disabled by an engine room explosion, and its life support systems fail. As the show proceeds, the shipboard temperature drops and the atmosphere thickens with CO_2. Every person aboard recognizes the imminence of death, either from suffocation or freezing; their only alternative seems to be to surrender themselves to the vacuum of space, and their spirits are not helped by the doctor's off-hand description of the effects of suffocation.

It is, however, **the airlessness of space** that poses the greatest danger. Shipboard life is dependent upon an intricate network of interdependent systems to shut in air and refresh its oxygen; excursions outside *Serenity*, when they become necessary, require the elaborate protection of a spacesuit, which carries its own kind of menace. When Jayne twits Simon for quailing at the thought of going outside the ship in flight, the doctor remarks: "I suppose it's just the thought of a little Mylar and glass being the only thing separating a person from . . . nothing." And Jayne, ever the unfeeling realist, replies: "It's impressive what 'nothing' can do to a man" ("Bushwhacked"). Jayne himself comes in for his own taste of airlessness when Malcolm, angered by his betrayal of Simon and River, shuts him in an airlock and cracks the door as the ship climbs out of the atmosphere. Malcolm, grilling him, points out that "You'll be a lot thinner once you get sucked out that hole," and Jayne, in uncharacteristic terror, cries: "That ain't no way for a man to die!" ("Ariel"). So inexorable, and so final, is the threat of space that even the hard-shelled Jayne succumbs to its menace.

For all its dangers, space is a known constant. The crew knows of its dangers long before they embark on their journey and they prepare themselves, mentally and materially, to deal with it. Less predictable and in some ways even more menacing is the human threat. As participants in illegal trade, the crew expects and takes in stride the hazards of their work: a swindle, a double-cross, or a set-up. These elements go with the territory, and they are as proficient in their execution as the folk with whom they deal. The greater human threat is two-fold: on the one hand, the Alliance, with its enforced adherence to arbitrary laws, and, on the other, the Reavers, feral humans unrivaled in their anarchy and bestiality.

"the Valley is neither malevolent nor benevolent"—The aridity of the Western land is in sharp contrast with the lush wilderness experienced by Daniel Boone (see Ch. 39, page 585). However, the significance of the wilderness is the same: it is the "promised land."

"wilderness of insecurity"—Budd notes that "*Stagecoach* marks the journey from Tonto to Lordsburg with images of gates and fences which spatially separate the relative safety of the towns and way stations from the open desert where the stagecoach is vulnerable to Indian attack" (63).

"indigenous savages of immeasurable ruthlessness"—Slotkin (Ch. 39, p. 582) points out that the European colonists in America were forming a new identity as Americans. Edward Said has noted that, in a process like this, the distinctions that are generated, like the designation of other groups as barbarians, can be arbitrary (54).

"prepares to shoot Lucy to protect her from mutilation and rape"—In *Firefly*, it is considered a kindness to accord similar treatment to victims captured by the Reavers.

"the airlessness of space"—The arid desert can be as deadly as space, and require similarly elaborate preparation from travelers. Both groups are constantly threatened by hostile environments.

In *Stagecoach*, the "wilderness of insecurity" harbors Indians who are portrayed as savage and relentless; they emerge from it to attack the passengers in their vehicle.

"Whereas the military in *Stagecoach* is a source of rescue, in *Firefly* it becomes a threat."—Like the FBI in *The X-Files*, the Alliance and its military forces represent the peril of the establishment and its "big science." In comparison, the crew of *Firefly* operate with very limited technological resources.

"the Reavers are a constant peril"—These creatures can be compared to the Apache threat in *Stagecoach,* but in science fiction terms, humans' misuse of science represents the greatest danger—the enemy is not the other, but ourselves. The contrast between the Reavers and "civilized" humans is similar to the one in the *Epic of Gilgamesh*, where Gilgamesh and Enkidu battle Humbaba, the king of the cedar forest, and Enkidu is reminded of his kinship with the wild Humbaba. (See Ch. 15, p. 178.)

"reduced themselves to the lowest of beasts"—This explanation is given in the series. In *Serenity*, the origin of the Reavers is explained as being caused by a government program.

"a quiet questioning of conventional morality"—The western frontier represents the edge of civilization, and as such, is a suitable location for unconventional behavior. It represents what Victor Turner would call a liminal space, an inherently unstable area on the threshold between two dominant forces (see Ch. 26, p. 375). The recent television series *Deadwood* represented the South Dakota frontier town around the time of its annexation to the Union. The town is populated by shady characters, including Al Swearingen, a brothel owner and saloon-keeper whose morals are in some ways superior to those of some of the more "civilized" people in town.

Whereas the military in *Stagecoach* is a source of rescue, in *Firefly* it becomes at best an annoyance, at worst a threat. Its minions turn up at awkward times, flexing their authority and running rough-shod over the concerns of civilians. The Alliance does nothing to retrieve a shipment of vital medical goods hijacked in "The Train Job"; they arbitrarily board and search *Firefly* in "Bushwhacked" and confiscate the ship's cargo; a military goon squad bullies an innocuous, Jewish postal clerk in "The Message"; and a running concern throughout the series is the program of psychological mutilation that Alliance authorities have carried out on River. Though he's undeniably a biased source, Malcolm handily sums up a prevailing attitude toward the Alliance when he says that it's typical of them to "Unite all the planets under one rule so that everybody can be interfered with or ignored equally" ("The Train Job"). The Alliance is not the cavalry that will turn up in times of need, and its unpredictability only adds to the uncertainty that Malcolm and his crew face.

If the Alliance is an uncertain nuisance, **the Reavers are a constant peril**, lurking always on the fringes of consciousness and so terrible in their actions as to require constant readiness should they appear. For the sheltered Simon, they are the stuff of "campfire stories . . . men gone savage on the edge of space," but for the space-savvy crew members, they are very real, indeed. Should *Serenity* be captured, Zoe tells Simon, the Reavers will "rape us to death, eat our flesh, and sew our skins into their clothing. And if we're very, very lucky, they'll do it in that order" ("Serenity"). Even the normally tolerant Malcolm minces no words when talking of them: "Reavers ain't men. Or they forgot how to be. Come to just nothin'. They got out to the edge of the galaxy, to that place of nothin', and that's what they became" ("Bushwhacked"). Compared with the Indians of *Stagecoach*, the Reavers are infinitely more terrifying; whereas the Apache (by the standards of 1939) were naturally savage, carrying out depredations because such was their inherent nature, the Reavers, once upon a time men, have abdicated all that it means to be human, and have **reduced themselves to the lowest of beasts**. Hazards abound in the world of *Firefly* even more extensively than in that of *Stagecoach*, and the crew must accept their reality if life is to continue.

While the structure and context of *Stagecoach* have their analogues in *Firefly*, it is in the similarity of themes that the two works come closest. Among these themes, three in particular stand out. First of all, *Stagecoach* offers **a quiet questioning of conventional morality**. The most outwardly "respectable" character, the banker, Gatewood, is an embezzler. The gambler, Hatfield, for all his aristocratic pretensions, has been rumored to shoot men in the back. The most compassionate and humane of the passengers is the whiskey salesman, Peacock, untouched by the ravages of his trade, while Doc Boone and Dallas even take pride in their outcast status. As Doc says to her, "These dear ladies of the Law and Order League are scouring out the dregs of the town. . . . Come on—be a proud, glorified dreg like me." Just who, the film asks, are the upright citizens, who are the dregs, and who decides the criteria to be applied?

A similar questioning of the conventional appears in *Firefly*. Inara is the most obvious agent; **she is a prostitute**, yet her trade is openly accepted while that of the rest of the crew is scorned, and she becomes the "nurturer" aboard the ship ("Here's How It Was"). One show, "Shindig," affirms the point explicitly. At a formal ball, where she is the invited guest of a local aristocrat while Mal has crashed it in search of work, she confronts him: "You have no call trying to make me ashamed of my job. What I do is legal. And how's that smuggling coming?" Mal replies: "My work's illegal, but at least it's honest," and, to Inara's puzzled "What?" he points to the ornately dressed and posturing guests and adds, "Well this—the lie of it" ("Shindig"). For Mal, a life of openly acknowledged shadiness is preferable to a socially acceptable one that requires hypocrisy and pretense, and the viewer is left to ruminate upon the question.

A second shared theme is *Stagecoach*'s questioning of conventional "civilization."

The film opens and closes in two established, "civilized" settlements, Tonto and Lords-burg, presumably **bastions of all that is right** and proper in the midst of an untamed wilderness. Yet, as the action proceeds, we discover that the towns' "civilization" also incorporates prejudice, coercion, narrow-mindedness, and injustice. Doc Boone speaks for another kind of civilization, one determined by individualistic and humane values, as he opens and closes the film. At the outset, being run out of town with Dal-las, he wryly remarks: "We're the victims of a foul disease called social prejudice, my child." And, in the penultimate line of the film, as Ringo and Dallas ride out of the story and off to Ringo's isolated ranch, he turns to Curly and says, "Well, they're saved from the blessings of civilization." For Doc, and for much of *Stagecoach*, the ideal of "civilization" is a two-faced one, carrying persecution as well as benefits, and, for a cer-tain type of person, one that is profitably challenged, even ignored.

Firefly shares the film's skepticism toward civilization. The tension between civiliza-tion and freedom is, to be sure, a long-standing element in both the Western and sci-ence-fiction (Mogen, 98–107). In *Firefly*, however, it comes to the foreground, explicitly examined in the contrast between the authoritarianism of the Alliance and the inner world of *Serenity*. The opening segment sets the scene: after *Serenity* unexpectedly encounters an Alliance cruiser, Jayne wonders: "What the hell are they doin' out this far, anyhow?" To this, Kaylee replies, simply: "Shinin' the light of civilization" ("Serenity"). "Bushwhacked" extends the contrast. The **iconoclastic Mal** permits Shepherd Book to conduct a funeral service for victims of the Reavers, then, when an Alliance ship appears, remarks: "Looks like civilization has finally caught up with us." At segment's end, after the Alliance commander has confiscated their cargo but let the ship go, Mal comments: "Couldn't let us profit. Wouldn't be civilized" ("Bushwhacked").

The Travelers as Family

Yet, as other segments make explicit, the world in which Mal and the crew operate is a kind of civilization, with rules, standards, and values peculiarly its own, yet no less

"she is a prostitute"—Science fic-tion as a genre allows us to ques-tion society by reshaping the roles in it. In the society of *Firefly*, a companion represents a high rank within society. Ford's assignment of virtue to Ringo the outlaw and Dallas the prostitute in *Stagecoach* provides societal critique. The con-trast resembles the one discussed by Victor Turner. In his view, in modern postindustrial society, the *liminoid* challenge the very founda-tions on which the culture is built. In traditional society, a *liminal* cri-tique would normally occur without disrupting the structure of the cul-ture. (See Ch. 26, page 380.)

"bastions of all that is right'"—It is hard to say where the questioning of a specific instance becomes the rejection of all government. In this contrast between Tonto and Lords-burg, Erisman is describing the for-mer, but in *Firefly*, Mal Reynolds' rejection of governmental attempts at civilization can definitely be seen as libertarianism. This is a political philosophy based on strong sup-port for individual liberty. Its propo-nents generally view most restric-tions imposed by the government as a violation of liberty. See Intro-duction, p. 593.

"iconoclastic Mal'"—The captain can be seen as a Trickster figure who rebels against authority and undermines it, while maintaining the values at the heart of civiliza-tion. In this respect, he resembles Prometheus, who rebels against Zeus in Greek mythology while providing human beings with the elements they need to build civi-lization. See Ch. 24, p. 353.

In *Serenity*, Reavers drag away a young trading post resident, already preparing to tear him limb from limb. The captain will shoot him to prevent a horrible death at their hands.

The stagecoach passengers form a "Fordian community" as they share a peaceful moment while waiting for the birth of Lucy Mallory's child. Clockwise from left to right, they are: Mr. Peacock, Curly, Buck, Hatfield, and the Ringo Kid

"What defines a man?"—For ancient society, this question was likely to be asked in a religious, theological, or ritual context. In Sophocles' *Oedipus the King*, the debate is about whether human beings should be obedient to the gods, or should see themselves as "self-made" or "children of chance." See Ch. 25, p. 362.

valid than those of conventional society. "Jaynestown," the seventh installment of the series, brings the debate into the foreground. The entire episode is a rumination upon social order, exploring the issues of both social and individual needs by considering society's need for heroes and the question of "**What defines a man?**" For the strait-laced Simon, this boils down to an understanding of what, precisely, are the things a person holds crucial. Kaylee twits him for his (to her) excessive propriety, saying, "What's so damn important about bein' proper? It don't mean nothin' out here in the black." And Simon calmly disagrees, affirming his growing sense of self-determination: "It means more out here. It's all I have" ("Jaynestown"). Civilization is all that separates humanity from the animals, yet it is not something to be accepted unthinkingly. There are many forms of civilization, and each person, and each community, must decide which is the most appropriate.

The final shared theme arises in the very notion of community, for both *Stagecoach* and *Firefly* pose, as an alternative to conventional civilization, what one critic has called the "Fordian community." As seen throughout Ford's films, this is "the family, almost always depicted as an isolated pocket of existential security, as a refuge from loneliness (but, like 'home,' it is an ideal rarely attained, and generally imperfect, fragmented, lacking one parent.)" The leader of this community most often is a solitary man who "seldom reaps life's humble pleasures. He is often a combination of soldier, judge, and priest, symbolizing his intervention, authority, and self-sacrifice. . . . He is purer than the average man in service of such accepted values as tolerance, justice, medical duty, preservation of family, and love" (Gallagher, 479–80). The pattern resonates throughout both stories.

The surviving passengers of *Stagecoach* form just such a group, albeit one not homogeneous or trouble-free. The birth of Lucy Mallory's child breaks down one set of socially-determined barriers, bringing drunk and lawman, prostitute and prig together in a moment of cherished domesticity. The passengers come to see new strengths and merit in the drunken doctor and the wimpish whiskey salesman, and share in their disdain for the thieving banker, who has violated his depositors' trust. If they go their separate ways at film's end, they go with a new understanding of human kinship, individual integrity, and social interdependence. Marshal Curly, the nominal leader, grows in his tolerance for Ringo's offenses and his appreciation of Ringo and Dallas's love, while Ringo himself, in many ways the spiritual leader, reflects the stoic calm and inherent honor of the Fordian hero. The community has reshaped and redefined itself, and all are stronger for their participation.

Stagecoach may have served to establish the Fordian community, but it is *Firefly* that brings it to its fullest expression. Within the isolated confines of the ship, the crew and the captain coalesce into a distinctive family group—one not without its strains, to be sure, but one that strengthens all its members in its functioning. Family groupings appear in the show from the outset. Zoe and Wash are married and talk of having a child; Simon and River are siblings; Kaylee, according to actress Jewel Staite, "**makes sure that everybody remembers that we are one big family**, and all we have is each other" ("Here's How It Was"). However, Mal has had this goal in mind (albeit inarticulately) all along, as he visualizes what his crew will be like: "They must feel the need to be free. Take jobs as they come. They never have to be under the heel of nobody ever again" ("Out of Gas"). He expands this later, telling the unscrupulous Saffron that he has chosen to surround himself with "People who trust each other, who do for each other and ain't always lookin' for the advantage" ("Our Mrs. Reynolds"). He threatens to toss Jayne from the airlock for betraying Simon and River, saying "You turn on any of my crew, you turn on me!," and he answers Simon's question as to why he has risked the ship and crew to rescue the doctor and River from kidnapers by saying "You're on my crew. Why are we still talking about this?" ("Ariel," "Safe").

"makes sure that everybody remembers that we are one big family"—Kaylee was described above as "unschooled but a genius with machines." Her role shows the downplaying of physics in the series, as much of the drama of running the ship is resolved on a personal level of her battle with what seem to be the gears of mechanical devices. In addition, she spends much of it mooning over the doctor, whose role is much more tied to biology. See the Introduction, p. 592, for a discussion of biology as the dominant science of our time. In this respect, *Firefly* resembles *The X-Files*; see p. 591.

The crew of *Serenity* sitting like a family around the long dining table of the ship, listening to their captain while making a difficult decision about how to defeat their adversary. From left to right: companion Inara Serra, mercenary Jayne Cobb, pilot Hoban Washburne, and second-in-command Zoe Washburne.

This simple lesson, that families look out for one another, is not lost on Simon; his upbringing in his own privileged but dysfunctional family has contributed to his becoming a fugitive, and *Serenity* is the closest thing to a real home that he and River have enjoyed for several years. And he, in turn, is **willing to see the others in family terms**. Patching up the wounded Jayne, knowing that Jayne betrayed him and his sister to the Alliance, he says:

> You're on this table, you're safe. 'Cause I'm your medic, and however little we may like or trust each other, we're on the same crew. Got the same troubles, same enemies, and more than enough of both. Now, we could circle each other and growl, sleep with one eye open, but that thought wearies me. I don't care what you've done. I don't know what you're planning on doing, but I'm trusting you. I think you should do the same. 'Cause I don't see this working any other way. ("Trash")

Professional obligations come second to family obligations; Simon and Jayne are on the same crew—of **the same "family"**—and they will, must trust each other.

Binding them all together is, not surprisingly, Mal—the Fordian hero writ large. He can be ruthless (as when he shoots down the Alliance agent holding the wounded Kaylee at gunpoint), and he can be compassionate (as when he gives Shepherd Book the go-ahead for a funeral service despite an urgent need for *Serenity* to leave the vicinity). He can be shifty (as when he double-crosses Saffron, who has double-crossed him), and he can be upright (as when he returns the medications he has hijacked to the community where "others need this more"). Throughout the series, though, he is driven by a single urge: his need to do what he believes is right, proper, and appropriate. He responds to Book's call "to do the right thing" in checking out a derelict ship, and, in turn, tells Book he has taken Simon and River on board, despite their fugitive status and his dislike for Simon, "Because it's the right thing to do" ("Serenity," "Bushwhacked," "Trash," "The Train Job"). Long ago betrayed by his military superiors and condemned to life in a society that disdains his beliefs, he lives by his inherent, ingrained sense of personal honor. He values his freedom above all other traits, and he readily endorses and supports the like-thinking folk about him. He is the heart of the

"willing to see the others in family terms"—The closeness of the crew is represented as an ongoing series of individually negotiated relationships and not the outcome of automatic social values like those on *Star Trek*. Each moment must be negotiated, and there is never any guarantee that a crew member will survive an episode.

"the same 'family'—Victor Turner has noted that in the "'high culture' context of complex societies," individuals make idiosyncratic choices about the groups they will belong to, out of a wide range of competing choices available (see Ch. 24, pp. 382–83). Here we see the crew of *Serenity* choosing to forge a family unit out of strangers with a similar cast of mind.

crew, the central father-figure who draws them into the unified, trusting, and even loving group that they become.

Throughout its fourteen episodes, *Firefly* plays out its stories in an extended homage to John Ford and *Stagecoach*. Like its forbearer, it builds upon character as much as action, human responses as much as setting. We come away from the program's sadly truncated history with a renewed sense of human integrity and human endeavor, just as we do from *Stagecoach*, *High Noon*, *Shane*, and a host of other memorable films that confirm our belief in principle, compassion, and the imperative to do what is right and necessary whatever the larger society might say. It incorporates **allusions to many attributes of the Western** as it develops its motifs, but it always comes back to the foundation of *Stagecoach*, the model that gives it its shape and its direction.

Firefly is a testament to the continuing vitality of the Western, and, even more, to the vitality and versatility of science fiction. The Western grows from circumstances and events of the last third of the nineteenth century; science fiction grows from circumstances still to come, in a future both near and distant. The Western, perhaps, is being left behind by history, but science fiction stands ready to take up its cause. Both genres attest to the resilience and strength of the human spirit; both give us occasion to reflect upon what we have done, and may yet do, with technology and human society; and both compel us to consider again and again the essential question of what it means to be human. We would do well to pay them heed.

"allusions to many attributes of the Western"—Erisman notes that in the *Firefly* episode "Trash," for example, a priceless historic artifact, the prototype of a hand-held laser pistol, is called "The Lassiter" after the name of the pistol-packing hero of Zane Grey's classic Western *Riders of the Purple Sage*.

Further Reading

Jenkins, Henry. *Textual Poachers: Television Fans and Participatory Culture.* New York, NY: Rutledge, 1992.

Jewett, Robert, and John Shelton Lawrence. *The American Monomyth.* Garden City, NY: Anchor Press, 1977.

Noyes, Mimi. *The Firefly Episode Guide: An Unofficial, Independent Guide to Joss Whedon's Firefly with Complete Facts and Critiques*, 2nd. ed. Port Orchard, WA: Lightning Rod Publishers, 2007.

Harry Potter

A Rankian Take on the Hero of Hogwarts

What to Expect . . . Harry Potter is both a figure in popular culture and an extremely well-known contemporary literary character; as a result, he can provide us with a range of insights into how heroes operate in our society and what they show us about ourselves. This chapter investigates the young wizard and the series of books in which he appears from the perspective of psychologist Otto Rank. As you read, look for a greater understanding of trends in psychology and how they apply to mythology. The question Rank wanted to answer in his studies was "Where does mythology come from?" His investigations showed that it was part of human nature to tell mythological stories, and that this aspect of our humanity emerges from the way we interact with the members of our families. Thus, the fundamental concept you will encounter here is Rank's family romance, which explains how hero myths result from basic family conflicts that transcend culture and history.

In this chapter, M. Katherine Grimes applies Rank's theories to the Harry Potter series and updates them to reflect the social conditions of our time. As a result, she presents new perspectives on the books and films about Harry Potter and the mission of Hogwarts School of Witchcraft and Wizardry. Her discussion leads us to reexamine the role of female characters as heroes, and to think about the importance of the mother figure in mythological stories, as well as to ponder the significance of the themes of birth and rebirth.

Before you read this chapter, you might review the discussion of heroes in the Introduction to Part 3, page 25 and the examination of C. G. Jung's archetypal hero in Chapter 32, page 468. As you read this chapter, compare Harry Potter with other heroes like Gilgamesh (Ch. 15, page 166), Mwindo (Ch. 22, page 305), and Rama (Ch. 17, page 203).

The psychological theories of Sigmund Freud and Otto Rank have used the images found in myth to explain conflicts in the human unconscious. (For more about these ideas, see the Introduction to Part 3, p. 155.) By the same token, the theories of these psychologists can enrich our understanding of the meaning of myth. We began this book by suggesting that myths are not just false stories. Rather, they express important truths about the experiences of human beings. Interestingly, the psychological view is yet another perspective from which the traditions preserved as mythology represent such truths.

Rank identified a process called the family romance and argued that it has produced a wide range of stories about the birth and adventures of heroes. Rank himself collected stories from all over the world to show how the family romance worked, but his theories apply as well to other stories as yet unknown and even untold. In this chapter, M. Katherine Grimes shows the relevance of Rank's ideas to the beloved and popular series of Harry Potter books by J. K. Rowling. When Grimes wrote this article, only the first four books had been published: *Harry Potter and the Sorcerer's Stone* (1997; hereafter *Stone*), *Harry Potter and the Chamber of*

Secrets (1998; hereafter *Chamber*), *Harry Potter and the Prisoner of Azkaban* (1999; hereafter *Prisoner*), and *Harry Potter and the Goblet of Fire* (2000; hereafter *Goblet*). As you will see below, however, she was able to forecast the outcome of the series on the basis of her analysis. We have supplemented her views in the marginalia below with additional detail from the last three books: which are *Harry Potter and the Order of the Phoenix* (2003; hereafter *Phoenix*), *Harry Potter and the Half-Blood Prince* (2005; hereafter *Prince*), and *Harry Potter and the Deathly Hallows* (2007; hereafter *Hallows*).

If Freud and Rank are correct, then myths come from the human unconscious, and the forces that create them are innate in every human being. "Innate" means "born in" and refers to the complex of features that makes human beings what they are. For example, language learning ability is innate: every normal human child is born with the ability to develop language. The child is not born speaking Japanese or Hindi or English, but rather has the structures in her brain that allow her to develop language through interaction with her environment. It is not a particular language that is innate in the child, but the ability to develop language.

Grimes' analysis shows that the Harry Potter stories are a wonderful illustration of the way stories with mythological meaning continue to enthrall people in contemporary society, providing them with images expressing their fears, hopes, and dreams.

OTTO RANK AND THE FAMILY ROMANCE

Like Freud, Rank was a clinical practitioner. As part of this profession, he studied the behavior of his patients who were neurotic. However, Freud used the behavior of neurotic patients to

Otto Rank

explain human nature in general, while Rank preferred to consider the behavior of normal subjects and derive from it an understanding of neurotics. His theories about family relationships developed from actual clinical experiences with both parents and children.

Rank generally agreed with Freud that a complex kind of possessive anger underlies the dynamic of the family. However, he insisted that daughters as well as sons exhibit such behavior. This complex of feelings, he maintained, motivates the creation of the hero myth. Therefore, we might say that Rank sees myth as arising out of basic human conflicts. He understands the child's wanting the mother for itself as one of the most basic conflicts in life: first the (male) child idealizes its parents, but ultimately he is disenchanted with them. He sees that his parents are not perfect and comes to believe they are not of the high social stature he would like. The child substitutes more exalted figures for his parents in his imaginings, because he wants to return to what he sees as the "vanished happy time" of early childhood.

In the child's view, the parents are first seen as ideals. As he meets other grown-ups and compares his parents' actions and abilities with them, the child becomes dissatisfied and often feels rejected. Sexual rivalry is often involved in these feelings of rejection. As the child notices the existence of sexual relationships, he begins to imagine his role as part of the sexual relationship of his parents. The child then resents the role his father enjoys and wishes such a relationship with his mother.

Because his parents do not live up to his expectations, the child fantasizes about getting rid of them. This feeling arises as the child is trying to establish his independence. However, despite any negative feelings, the child still harbors his original affection for his parents. Rank emphasizes that the child does not really want to do away with his parents, but that he enjoys imaginary scenarios in which things work out to his advantage. These fantasies and daydreams express important emotions that children may not be aware of. The child's complex of feelings of longing and rejection, love, and anger together make up the phenomenon that Rank calls the family romance.

THE MYTH OF THE BIRTH OF THE HERO

For the child, one of the mechanisms for coping with the feelings he experiences in the family romance is to transform them into a myth. In this story, the child sees himself as an exceptional person who is unjustly treated by tyrannical older relative (usually a father), but who accomplishes great deeds and is recognized far and wide for these actions. The way that these ideas of the child are reflected in the Oedipus myth is outlined in this book in Chapter 25, "Looking Back at Heroes" (p. 360).

In his book *The Myth of the Birth of the Hero*, Rank showed the same common pattern in stories about heroes from many parts of the world dating from the twenty-fourth century B.C.E., as shown in the table. He believed that people create these heroes as a way of expressing the sense of powerlessness a child feels in the family. If, like the hero, the child can fulfill the unlikely task of defeating the powerful oppressor, then he can succeed in satisfying his individual psychic needs. For the child, who resents the power wielded by his parents, the hero's task is always to overpower them. This process is called projection, the reversal of relationship roles. In the myth, the son's real-life rebellion against the father is reversed, so that it is the father who is hostile to the son, not vice versa. And Rank points out that the great myths through the ages emphasize such defeats of oppressive power by the hero. Note,

A Selection of Heroes Whose Stories Are Studied by Otto Rank in *The Myth of the Birth of the Hero*

Sargon	24th c. B.C.E.	Mesopotamia	Founded Babylon and destroyed the walls of Uruk, whose construction is celebrated in the *Epic of Gilgamesh*
Moses	1500 (1200) B.C.E.	Israel	Led the Hebrew people out of Egypt to the Promised Land
Paris	nonhistorical: 8th c. B.C.E.	Troy	Son of the king; brought about the Trojan War, which caused the downfall of the city
Romulus	nonhistorical: 8th c. B.C.E.	Rome	Founder of Rome, first a city, then an empire
Cyrus	6th c. B.C.E.	Persia	Founded the Persian Empire
Hercules	nonhistorical: throughout classical antiquity	Greece and Rome	Hero who performed 12 labors, extending across and beyond the Greek world; was later made a god
Oedipus	nonhistorical: 5th c. B.C.E.	Greece	King of Thebes who killed his father and married his mother. This brought about the downfall of his regime, though he was considered a hero in Athens
Jesus	1st c. C.E.	Christian	Founder of Christianity
Tristan	nonhistorical: 12th c. C.E.	Celtic, European	Folklore figure in courtly romances who became a knight of King Arthur's Round Table

though, that a great number of the heroes Rank describes are in the final analysis the builders of nations, cultures, and religions. Though their stories express the rebellion of the son against the father, these heroes at the same time channel the creative energies of the son into the creation of a new way of life.

Although children themselves do not create great myths, as adults they contribute to the existing lore of their culture, adding to or modifying stories in ways that reflect their own experience and feelings. In this way, the myths of a group become the illustrations of psychological situations and the embodiment of human fears and anxieties.

Rank's theory includes us all, for he says that all humans share the psychological experiences he has described. He says that human beings, by their basic nature, tell stories about heroes. We create hero myths because we unconsciously represent our infantile struggles in the adventures of the hero. We idealize ourselves through our conception of the hero, the ego. In the excerpt below, through applying Rank's observations, Grimes gives us a new perspective on the books and films about Harry Potter.

UPDATING RANK TO INVESTIGATE *HARRY POTTER*

The influence is not all in one direction, however. In one respect in particular, Grimes updates Rank's observations to the social conditions of our time. When Freud and Rank wrote, the family was dominated by the father, but in our day we have a rather different idea of how its dynamics should work. Today the influence of women and mothers is more important to our understanding of the family, and limits to the role of women are much less well accepted.

The traditional Freudian update of the story of the hero would be to describe a woman hero whose identity is defined by her competition with her mother for the affections of the opposite-sex parent, her father. This is the dynamic of Freud's Electra complex. However, modern feminist Freudians like Nancy Chodorow (*The Reproduction of Mothering: Psychoanalysis and the Sociology of Gender*) are more inclined to consider the roles of both parents in the development of the child, and thus the hero. And in fact, the change in the status of women in our society has not occurred in such a way as to make credible stories that plug women into the same roles as men. There are of course exceptions to this limitation, but the norm has been to craft stories reflecting the continued importance of men in our society, but with an increased role for women.

In this scene from *Stone*, the villain, Lord Voldemort (left), separates Harry Potter (background right) from his parents (foreground right). The scene shows the hero and his family forming Rank's ideal "family romance," which is shattered by the evil father substitute who inhabits the body of a teacher at Hogwarts.

Some scholars have, in fact, criticized the Harry Potter stories as not featuring powerful enough women. Noted folklorist Jack Zipes says, "girls are always left to gawk and gaze at Harry's stunning prowess." He cites scholar Christine Schoefer as saying, "'Harry's fictional realm of magic and wizardry perfectly mirrors the conventional assumption that men do and should run the world'" (179). We might note the activities and influence of Hermione Granger and other Hogwarts women as evidence in the other direction.

Whatever view we have of this issue, we can agree that women play much more vital roles in the Harry Potter stories than they do in the myths collected by Otto Rank. Thus, to make sense of these stories, Grimes considers first the role of the father, as a traditional Rankian analyst would, and then develops the role of the mother in the formation of the young wizard, expanding the traditional analysis to represent more closely the view of our society. (See the section following, on mother figures, p. 611.)

Since humans have existed, adults have attempted to make sense of our world through myth. Otto Rank applied his teacher Sigmund Freud's theories of dreams and mythology to many of the world's mythical and legendary heroes, both well and little known. According to Robert A. Segal in his introduction to *In Quest of the Hero*, both Freud and Rank believed that myths are "the disguised, symbolic fulfillment of repressed, overwhelmingly **Oedipal wishes** lingering in the adult mythmaker or reader." In *The Myth of the Birth of the Hero*, originally published in 1909, Rank wrote what Segal calls "the classic Freudian analysis of hero myths."

According to Rank, hero myths, such as the stories of Oedipus, Moses, and Jesus, contain ten basic elements, eight of which have been fulfilled by Harry Potter:

1. The boy is the son of royal or even immortal parents—Harry Potter's parents are a wizard and a witch.
2. Difficulties precede the conception, and in some cases the mother is a virgin—As of book four, we do not yet know the details of Harry's conception.
3. The child's life is threatened when **dream or oracle** warns the father or another royal personage that the boy will be a danger—Voldemort, a sort of prince of evil, has reason to fear Harry and tries to kill him.
4. The boy is separated from his parents—Harry's parents are dead.
5. The boy is exposed, often in a **basket or other receptacle**—Harry is laid on the doorstep of his aunt and uncle in a bundle of blankets.
6. The boy is put into water, either to kill him or to save him—Harry and the other first-years are ferried to Hogwarts across a lake, and before Harry can be free from the Dursleys, Hagrid must fetch him from across a large body of water.
7. The child is rescued by animals or underlings, often shepherds—Harry is rescued by **Hagrid, a gamekeeper**, and is later aided by his godfather in the form of a dog and his father in the form of a stag.
8. The baby is suckled or reared by animals or lowly persons—Harry's aunt and uncle, the Dursleys, are lowly persons, as is Hagrid, but in a very different way.
9. The hero is eventually recognized as such, often because of a mark or a wound—Harry's attack by Voldemort has left him with a scar on his forehead, a sign that other wizards recognize.
10. The hero is reconciled with his father (or his representative), OR he exacts revenge upon his father—Like the condition about conception, this characteristic has not yet been met in Rowling's novels.

The universality of these characteristics in the world's myths and legends has caused much speculation as to both why they are ubiquitous and why they are popular.

Father Figures

In the upcoming section, Grimes discusses the father figure, the most important personage of a traditional Rankian analysis. An examination of the elements of the family romance listed above will show that it is the father who receives the warning not to bear a son (item 3), and that reconciliation or revenge for his banishment from his original family involves the father (item 10).

Almost all Rankian heroes are threatened by their fathers or by some other man, often a royal figure, who has power over them. Oedipus's father, Laius, ordered the boy

"Oedipal wishes"—Rank believed that the characteristics of the family romance were a result of the child's anger at his father for interfering with the child's desire for exclusive access to the mother. Interestingly, the child projected his anger on the father figure, so in the stories it is the father who is angry with the son. Rank explained that children store away these feelings and later express them by telling and appreciating stories that exhibit them. See the Introduction (p. 605) for more detail on this process.

The ideas underlying Grimes' analysis come from: Otto Rank, *The Myth of the Birth of the Hero.*

"dream or oracle"—In *Phoenix*, we learn that the basis of Voldemort's fear is a prophecy (839).

"basket or other receptacle"—Moses is rescued from the Pharaoh by being placed in a basket. Jesus is born in a stable and placed into a manger, a receptacle for feeding animals.

"Hagrid, a gamekeeper"—In Harry's third year, Hagrid becomes Hogwarts teacher of the "Care of Magical Creatures," and throughout the series he delights in breeding, raising, and taming all sorts of animals.

Snape in *Harry Potter and the Sorcerer's Stone.*

Origin of Threats to the Hero (Rankian View)

Oedipus	father
Paris	father
Telephus	grandfather
Perseus	grandfather
Gilgamesh	grandfather
Moses	father figure
Jesus	father figure
Romulus and Remus	father figure

"threatened not by his father but by the evil Voldemort"—In much of the series, the main father figure is the ambiguous Professor Snape, the Potions Master at Hogwarts. Though Harry's mentor Professor Dumbledore urges the boy to believe he is on the right side, Snape ridicules and punishes him throughout the series. He is also responsible for the death of Dumbledore in *Prince*, but the event is revealed in the next book as more of a collaboration than a murder. Snape's actual allegiance is not revealed until the last book, *Hallows*, where he is shown to have had a complex relationship with both Voldemort and Dumbledore. Despite his menacing behavior toward Harry, Snape is seen finally as his protector, and in the Epilogue, which occurs nineteen years after *Hallows*, Harry has a son named Albus Severus, and refers to Snape as "probably the bravest man I ever knew" (758). In *Hallows*, Harry defeats and kills Voldemort.

exposed Leaving a child in the wilderness is referred to by this term. It was a common form of population control in societies that did not consider a child fully human until later in life.

boggart In British folklore, these are hairy, malevolent household spirits that dress in ragged clothes and bring bad luck: they make milk go sour and candles blow out. In Harry Potter's world, this is a spirit that likes to live in a cupboard and takes on the shape of whatever a person fears most.

exposed, as did Paris's father, Priam. Telephus, son of Hercules; Perseus, son of Zeus; and Gilgamesh are all victims of their maternal grandfathers, and Moses is threatened by the Pharaoh, the father of his adoptive mother. Jesus is threatened by Herod, the Roman ruler of Judea; Romulus and Remus were also condemned to death by a king.

Harry Potter is **threatened not by his father but by the evil Voldemort**, the dark lord, who has numerous ties with the boy. First, he and Voldemort have wands with feathers from the same bird, the Phoenix named Fawkes that belongs to headmaster Albus Dumbledore. Second, Voldemort has tried to kill Harry, and when he fails, he disappears for a decade. In fact, that defeat almost kills Voldemort. Third, by the end of *Harry Potter and the Goblet of Fire*, Voldemort has been revived by the boy's blood (642–43).

Because it is the father or father figure who has attempted to destroy the child, there must come a time of reckoning between the hero and his attacker. Otto Rank points out that the hero has two choices: to try to reconcile with the father, or to avenge himself against his enemy. Sometimes the tale ends with a combination of these climaxes; the son's assumption of his father's throne is a kind of reconciliation, in the sense that the boy has become the man his father was, but the usurpation is also a sort of revenge or overthrow.

Moses overcomes the man who tried to destroy him, the Pharaoh of Egypt, who ordered all male Hebrew children put to death during Moses' infancy and later sentenced the grown Moses to death for killing an Egyptian. Because the Pharaoh is Moses' adoptive grandfather, as the child had been found and adopted by the ruler's daughter, when Moses' God sends him to save the Hebrews from their captors, Moses settles a personal score as well as a national one.

Oedipus avenges his father's attempt to have him killed, as well, but he does so unawares; he does not know that the traveler he kills in anger is his father, King Laius of Thebes. Paris of Troy is reconciled with his father, Priam, even though the king had sent a slave to leave the infant Paris to be **exposed**. The story of Romulus and Remus combines the themes of vengeance and reconciliation. Romulus kills his great-uncle, the king who had tried to kill him and his brother, and is reconciled with his grandfather, from whom he had been long separated.

J. K. Rowling's first four books about Harry Potter give the boy six fathers or father surrogates, each of whom is suggested by a father or father figure in myth and legend, but none of whom is completely satisfactory. Among them, they represent adults' needs to see fathers as both earthly and immortal.

First, of course, is Harry's real father, James Potter, whom Voldemort kills when Harry is only a year old. The boy has great longing to know his father, as we see very clearly in four episodes. The first occurs in *Harry Potter and the Sorcerer's Stone,* in chapter 12, "The Mirror of Erised." The mirror shows those who look into it their greatest desire; for Harry, this desire is to see his parents. In fact, as he looks into the mirror, Harry sees himself, his parents, and his other ancestors. He sees himself in his father, for they both are tall and thin with messy dark hair and glasses. Seeing his family for the first time in his memory, Harry is mesmerized. Rowling writes, "The Potters smiled and waved at Harry and he stared hungrily back at them" (*Sorcerer's Stone,* 208–9). It is also in the first book that Harry is given something of his father's: an invisibility cloak, which allows him to move through Hogwarts [and beyond] without being seen.

Again in *Harry Potter and the Prisoner of Azkaban*, Harry encounters his father. With his Defense against the Dark Arts teacher, he is learning to fight his fears by summoning a Patronus, the word, of course, derived from the Latin word for "father." The **boggart** whom he must learn to defeat takes the shape of an evil dementor, a deathlike creature who can suck the soul from a person; when it appears, it causes Harry to hear his parents' voices as he relives the attack on his family by Voldemort. Consequently, the boy is torn between wanting to defeat the boggart/dementor and wanting to hear his parents again.

He learns in chapter 18, "Moony, Wormtail, Padfoot, and Prongs," about **his father's experiences as a schoolboy.** Young James Potter and three of his friends broke the rules of the magical world by becoming Animagi, wizards who turned themselves into animals, without permission. James Potter's alternate self was a stag. Later, in *Harry Potter and the Prisoner of Azkaban*, Harry's father's manifestation as a stag becomes directly relevant. Real dementors are chasing the boy and his godfather, Sirius Black, and Harry summons a patronus. It appears in the form of a stag, and across the lake Harry thinks he sees his own father. As he views the scene from the present looking back on the past, he waits for his father to appear. But he later learns that he and his friend Hermione Granger have turned back time using a **Time-Turner**, and "[h]e hadn't seen his father—he had seen himself." Subsequently he shouts the spell "EXPECTO PATRONUM" and sees his Patronus, the stag, Prongs, the animal incarnation of his father (*Prisoner of Azkaban*, 411–12).

Although James Potter's death separates him from his son, Harry's feelings about his father are not ambivalent. He identifies with his father and sees him as his protector. Later he tells his headmaster, Albus Dumbledore, of what he thought he saw and says that he realizes his thinking he saw his father was foolish because James Potter is dead. Dumbledore reassures him, telling him how much he looks like his father. He tells the boy, "Your father is alive in you, Harry. . . . [I]n a way, you did see your father last night. . . . You found him inside yourself" (*Prisoner of Azkaban*, 427–28).

Thus, Harry's father has three manifestations: the animal Prongs, the spirit, and Harry's identification with him. He represents the animal part of our nature, the spirit or soul, and immortality through future generations. He is both **the father who deserts the child** and the one who protects him, the god who puts us in this dangerous world filled with death, including the knowledge of our own at an unknown time, and the god who sustains us and gives us renewed life. Finally, he is the creator who lives on in us.

Vernon Dursley is the first father figure Harry remembers. The **epitome of the bad father**, Dursley shows strong favoritism to his own son, Dudley, and treats Harry as a pariah, failing to acknowledge his nephew's birthdays, making him sleep in a cupboard under the stairs, forcing him to stay out of sight when guests visit, and forbidding him to speak of his magical gifts. He tries to keep Harry from learning his parents' true identities and hides him when he begins receiving letters telling him to report to Hogwarts. He shouts at Harry during one of the boy's miserable summers on Privet Drive, "I WILL NOT TOLERATE MENTION OF YOUR ABNORMALITY UNDER THIS ROOF!" (*Chamber of Secrets*, 2). In short, Uncle Vernon tries to stifle Harry and keep him from being his true self. Harry's only consolation is that his uncle fears his magical powers. Rowling writes that Dursley treats Harry "like a bomb that might go off at any moment, because Harry Potter *wasn't* a normal boy" (*Chamber of Secrets*, 3). Vernon Dursley represents one aspect of the lowly figure in the archetypal heroic myth. His ordinariness stands in stark contrast to the wizards in Harry's new world at Hogwarts.

Rubeus Hagrid represents the other aspect of this figure. Associated with animals, both as a hunter and a keeper of magical creatures, Hagrid reminds one of the shepherds and cattleherds who take in abandoned children throughout mythology—the shepherds who save Oedipus, find Paris, and visit Jesus at the time of his birth; the cattle herder who saves Cyrus the Great; the swineherd who rears Romulus and Remus; the ox-herders who rear Hercules; and the overseer who rears Gilgamesh. Hagrid is also Keeper of the Keys, a status symbolizing Dumbledore's trust. A wild-looking half-giant, Hagrid is not a brilliant man but a kind one who delivers the infant Harry to his

"His father's experiences as a schoolboy"—According to Rank, the hero is a king's son whose father has been warned by a prophecy to avoid bearing a child. Harry's father is no king, but he is an outstanding wizard, who develops additional abilities as an Animagus to protect his childhood friend Remus Lupin (*Prisoner*, 259). In *Phoenix*, James becomes the kind of complex figure typical of Rowling's characterization. Harry learns that when a student at Hogwarts, his father tormented his fellow student Severus Snape (*Phoenix*, 640–50). "For nearly five years the thought of his father had been a source of comfort, of inspiration. Whenever someone had told him he was like James he had glowed with pride inside. And now . . . now he felt cold and miserable at the thought of him" (*Phoenix*, 653–54). In *Hallows*, however, James stands beside Harry in his final struggle with death, and Harry's attitude toward his father seems to be healed (700).

Time-Turner Mythology often alludes to a time outside of time, as noted by historian of religion Mircea Eliade (35–36). In *Youth Without Youth*, Francis Ford Coppola films a novel by Eliade to capture this concept. Manohla Dargis notes Coppola "blurs dreams and everyday life and suggests that through visual and narrative experimentation he has begun the search for new ways of making meaning, new holy places" (*New York Times*, December 16, 2007).

"the father who deserts the child"—James' desertion is involuntary. He is actually betrayed to Voldemort by someone he trusts as a friend, Peter Pettigrew, who, like him, is an Animagus. And, like Oedipus' father Laius, James is killed by his son. He dies because of a prophecy involving his son, a prophecy that the one who can destroy Voldemort will be born at the end of July, in the year of Harry's birth (*Phoenix*, 841). As a result, Voldemort attacks the family, but does not succeed at killing Harry, only his parents.

"epitome of the bad father"—The Dursleys represent the lowly parents who receive the child after he is abandoned by his royal parents. They are not wizards like Harry's parents. In addition, they represent the parody of parenting. Folklorist Jack Zipes criticizes the Harry Potter stories, saying that Harry behaves like a Boy Scout (180). However, despite his hero status, Harry misbehaves regularly. At Hogwarts Harry's "misbehavior" is in some ways principled, as when he defies Headmistress Dolores Umbridge (*Phoenix*). However, the scenes with the Dursleys verge on slapstick and provide a range of lighthearted misbehavior in *Stone*, *Chamber*, *Prisoner*, and *Phoenix*.

Rank notes that the hero may need to "play the fool" as a way of expressing his rebellion against the father (p. 605). Trickster tales explain this motif differently: the hero may appear as the buffoon, not because of weakness, but as a way of performing actions that blur the boundaries between the several worlds he inhabits. See p. 376 for a discussion of liminality.

"Voldemort is neither the boy's father nor his grandfather"— According to Rank, the son's real-life rebellion against the father (see Introduction, p. 605) is reversed in the myth through a process called projection, so that it is the father who is hostile to the son, not vice versa. As the child realizes his hostility toward the father, he works to justify it and projects his hostile attitude onto the father. The child/hero eventually attempts to reduce his hostility toward his father. Rank calls this attenuation. The result of attenuation is that in many of the stories Rank describes, it is not the father who is out to harm the son, but a grandfather or even an unrelated figure in authority. In some stories, like that of Harry Potter, both the hero and his parents are persecuted by the tyrant, which brings the hero closer to his mother.

aunt and uncle and the boy Harry to Hogwarts. He continues to befriend Harry and his friends as well.

Sirius Black is Harry's godfather, his father's best friend. Sirius is in hiding because he has been framed for murder, so he befriends Harry primarily through correspondence. However, when Harry is in real trouble, Sirius appears, often in the shape of a dog. Thus, Sirius represents the animals throughout mythology who appear to protect abandoned children: the bear who nurses Paris, the wolf who nurses Romulus and Remus and the woodpecker who guards them, the eagle who saves Gilgamesh, the doe who nurses Siegfried, and the swan who feeds Lohengrin. While it is true that most of the animals who save children are female, the animal who comes to Harry's rescue is male, a father figure. Many children in Rankian hero myths have earthly fathers who serve as surrogates for immortal patriarchs. Joseph, the father of Jesus, epitomizes this father archetype. It is Joseph who saves Jesus by taking him to Egypt when Herod orders male children of the Hebrews killed. Sirius serves in a similar fashion as the earthly protector of Harry Potter, whose father's death deprives the boy of his rightful protector.

Voldemort represents the evil king in the Rankian heroic tale. Like the Pharaoh, Herod, and Romulus and Remus's uncle King Amulius, **Voldemort is neither the boy's father nor his grandfather**, but an evil person with power who fears losing that power to another and thus attempts to kill the usurper in childhood. However, as noted earlier, Voldemort and Harry share a number of bonds: their similar wands and their shared blood are the strongest. Voldemort's failed attempt to kill the boy also binds them. The symbolic connection of their wands in *Harry Potter and the Goblet of Fire is* particularly fascinating, if the two are not related. Voldemort plans to kill Harry, but wants to play with him first, so he commands him to duel. Reminding Harry of the death of his father, he says, "And now you face me, like a man . . . the way your father died" (*Goblet of Fire*, 660). Then Voldemort attacks Harry with the Cruciatus Curse. When Voldemort halts the curse long enough to taunt Harry, the boy crouches behind Voldemort's father's gravestone, then matches Voldemort curse for curse. As the two foes point their wands at each other, jets of light emerge from each wand and connect, forming one light. This beam lifts both Voldemort and Harry into the air. Harry and Voldemort struggle, and Harry hears the song of a phoenix, noteworthy because his and Voldemort's wands both contain feathers from Albus Dumbledore's phoenix, Fawkes. After a time, ghostly figures are emitted from Voldemort's wand: Harry's friend Cedric Diggory, whom Voldemort has just killed; a man; a woman; and, as noted above, Harry's father and mother. The three Potters, with the help of Voldemort's other victims, are able to overcome Voldemort, and Harry escapes back to Hogwarts (*Goblet of Fire*, 663–68).

At least two points are relevant here. First, those who have been attacked by Voldemort join with his latest victim to foil his attempt. Second, **the phallic imagery of the two wands** is inescapable. Harry is emasculated when his wand is taken from him, and Voldemort can draw blood. But once Harry's wand is returned, he can block the power of Voldemort. The two beams from the wands of Voldemort and Harry Potter combine to both repel each other and bind the enemies in a golden web that can transport them and even raise the dead, if only temporarily. Good and evil both attract and repulse one another, and good wins, again if only temporarily. Voldemort's wand is rendered useless; he is symbolically castrated, rendered impotent, during this encounter.

Albus Dumbledore is the antithesis of Voldemort. He uses power purely for good, and he, too, assumes a paternal role in the orphaned Harry's life. It is significant that the most admirable and respected character in the Harry Potter series is not a government official but the head of a school, as Rowling clearly suggests that the one who can help shape the minds and character of the next generation of leaders is the most important person in a society. Dumbledore serves that role, mentoring Harry and his friends, serving as a role model, and, most important of all, taking on the task of rallying all good to fight all evil. We see this at the end of *Harry Potter and the Goblet of Fire,* when Dumbledore sends emissaries to the giants and to the other schools to form alliances to fight Voldemort. **Dumbledore is the idealized father**, the dream of every child—the father who is godlike: omnipotent, omniscient, and benevolent, always on the side of good. Dumbledore is to Harry what God is to Jesus, what Zeus is to Hercules, what Mars is to Romulus and Remus, perhaps not literally, but figuratively.

In the fairy tale, the Seven Dwarves become *Snow White's* "lowly parents."

Harry, the fatherless boy, has a plethora of father-figures, both positive and negative. He looks to some for comfort and rescue, fears the attack of others, and tries to please most of them.

Mother Figures

The focus on mother figures is not part of Otto Rank's analysis in *The Myth of the Birth of the Hero,* but it is clearly needed to provide a convincing explanation of the Harry Potter stories. In this sense, the next section represents A. Katherine Grimes' updating of Rank, or even a critique of his views. Rank based his analysis on the dynamics of the family as it appeared to him in 1909. He suggested that the family romance by itself was adequate to explain the stories he collected. In fact, those stories themselves were a product of their age, arising in societies with a more limited view of women than our own. Although the stories Rank described have not changed, our view of them has, and certainly stories written more recently place more importance on the role, as well as on the importance, of women. Joseph Campbell is another scholar who developed views that would correct the views of Freud and Rank by placing more emphasis on the role of women: see Chapter 14, page 163.

Sometimes it is the biological mother who saves her child, as Sargon's mother bore him in hiding and floated him down the river in a vessel that protected him; Moses' mother hid him for three months, then floated him on the river in a basket; and Siegfried's mother put him in a glass vessel to protect him. Often a surrogate mother saves the child, as the Pharaoh's daughter saved Moses, Polybus's wife Periboa saved Oedipus, and the wife of the swineherd saved Romulus and Remus.

Harry Potter has three mothers or mother figures. The first is his biological mother, Lily Potter, who like many Rankian mothers of heroes is born of relatively ordinary parents: Lily, though herself a witch, is the daughter of Muggles, the sister of the very ordinary Petunia Dursley. Her child, however, is not ordinary at all, for he is a wizard like his father. This pattern is found in the births of Jesus, Hercules, Paris, and other heroes who have mortal mothers but immortal fathers. The mothers, too, are extraordinary, resulting in their being chosen to have these special children.

Lily is her son's savior. When Voldemort attacks the Potter family, Lily says to him, as Harry hears years later when dementors attack him, "Not Harry, please no, . . . kill me instead" (*Prisoner of Azkaban,* 179). Her love for Harry, combined with his own innate greatness, is enough to save the boy from death, just as **a few drops of Hera's milk** are enough to render Hercules immortal. As Albus Dumbledore tells Harry in the first book, "Your mother died to save you. If there is one thing Voldemort cannot understand, it is love. . . . [T]o have been loved so deeply, even though the person who loved us is gone, will give us some protection forever" (*Sorcerer's Stone,* 299).

"the phallic imagery of the two wands"—Like his teacher Freud, Rank believed that the physical differences between men and women represented their roles in society. Thus, the phallus symbolized the power of a man. Later psychologists have adapted these theories to the different sexual roles found in our own society. Zipes describes Harry as the "ultimate detective" with "a phallic wand" (179–80).

"Dumbledore is the idealized father"—The headmaster's high status serves as a reminder of Harry's "divine" parentage. All the same, in the earlier stories, Harry operates at some distance from Dumbledore, and thus their relationship echoes the Rankian hero's rejection by his father. Dumbledore does not seem to protect Harry in his battles with Voldemort or rescue him from the escaped Death Eater who seems determined to destroy him. The Headmaster is unable to prevent the entry of a terrified Harry into the Triwizard tournament, and his absence from Hogwarts leaves Harry victim to the terrifying reign of Dolores Umbridge. Dumbledore at last undertakes to guide Harry in *Phoenix* and *Prince,* but even there, he does not share with Harry the secrets that lead to his death and to Harry's final struggle with Voldemort in *Hallows.* The Headmaster of Hogwarts emerges as a complex figure, as evidenced by Rowling's recent revelation that she conceives of him as a gay man who suffered a great tragedy the one time he was in love (Finn): this "tragedy" may well have influenced his response to Harry.

The spirit of *Harry's mother* at the end of the film version of *Goblet,* appearing to him in his struggle with Voldemort.

"Harry Potter has three mothers"—The material Grimes presents here shows the influence of the mother on the hero, an aspect of mythology not investigated by Rank but vital to modern understanding of the hero. The psychologist who does consider the importance of the mother is Carl Jung. In Jung's view, these mother figures represent different forms of the hero's anima (see Ch. 32, p. 479). Joseph Campbell integrates the views of Rank and Jung (see Ch. 14, p. 159).

"a few drops of Hera's milk . . ." —There are various explanations for the immortality of Hercules: this one comes from Rank, *The Myth of the Birth of the Hero* (38). See also Chapter 31, p. 459, for the idea that the hero becomes a god after his death on Mount Oeta.

Persephone—This story is included in Ch. 27, p. 385. See also the discussion of the influence of this ancient Greek myth (p. 390) in allowing us to see the importance of the mother-daughter bond and the significance of relationships between women.

"appears to have very little interest in her nephew"—All the same, it is Petunia Dursley whose blood-tie to her sister Lily keeps Harry safe from Voldemort as he is growing up, as explained in *Phoenix* (836).

"evil stepmother"—See other analyses of this important element of the fairy tale, Ch. 34, p. 503, and Ch. 36, p. 527.

"this does not mean we want our hero to have an easy time of it"— In the Mwindo Epic (Ch. 22, p. 305), Mwindo's father tries to prevent his birth. In Oedipus the King, Oedipus' father tries to have him killed right after his birth (Ch. 19, p. 256).

Nicolas Poussin, (1594–1665), *Moses Set Adrift on the Waters.*

Lily Potter returns to Harry when he is threatened by dementors; he hears her voice from the past. He also sees her when he looks into the Mirror of Erised. And when Voldemort tries to kill him again at the end of *Harry Potter and the Goblet of Fire*, the spirit of his mother comes from her killer's wand. It is she who gives him the instructions that save his life. Harry follows her directions, and Voldemort's victims, including Lily Potter, shield the boy as he runs from the evil wizard (*Goblet of Fire*, 667–68). The hero's mother has helped save him again. It is significant that J. K. Rowling's own answer to the question "What would you see in the Mirror of Erised?" was, "I would probably see my mother, who died in 1990. So, the same as Harry." Lily Potter has a parallel in Demeter, for whom the world stopped when she lost her daughter, **Perse-phone**, to the god of the underworld and began again only when her daughter was returned to her, though for only part of each year. Like Achilles' mother, who tried to protect her son by dipping him in the Styx, these are women whose lives center around motherhood and who love and try to protect their offspring.

Petunia Dursley, Lily Potter's sister, is Harry's first surrogate mother. Like her husband, she favors her own child over Harry and **appears to have very little interest in her nephew**. Mrs. Dursley is more reminiscent of the **evil stepmother** in folk and fairy tales—Cinderella's stepmother is probably the greatest example—than she is of mythical surrogates; however, her type is common in such literature as Charlotte Bronte's *Jane Eyre,* the title character of which has a monstrous aunt who far prefers her own children and locks Jane in a room. In mythology, there are women who conspire with their husbands against children, often in variations on the Oedipus myth, or even themselves send the children to be exposed.

Molly Weasley finds love and room for Harry even with all seven of her own brood to care for. In fact, at the end *of Harry Potter and the Goblet of Fire,* when Harry has won the Triwizard Tournament and survived the attack by Voldemort, Mrs. Weasley is at Hogwarts in lieu of his own family. She is the poor woman whose husband serves the leader, in this case the Minister of Magic, who takes in the foundling, the generous woman who is a foil to the insufferable Petunia Dursley and shows Harry what a mother's love should be. She is like the cattle-herder's wife who saves Cyrus the Great, and the swineherd's wife who rears Romulus and Remus.

Themes of Birth and Rebirth

In the next section, A. Katherine Grimes discusses a theme that is very important to the thinking of Otto Rank: birth. In addition to *The Myth of the Birth of the Hero*, Rank wrote a book titled *The Trauma of Birth*, in which he argued that the hero's adventures are part of an effort to overcome the difficult experience of having to leave his mother's womb, and his search for glory is the seeking for an effort to recover his unconsciously remembered earlier blissful state.

While parents and their surrogates figure greatly in myths, it is the hero or heroine who matters most to us, the person with whom we identify, whose happiness and well-being are our concern. Everyone else in the story matters to us primarily as he or she matters to our hero. We want our hero to live happily ever after, even to be resurrected after death. We care about this person to the extent that the destruction of others, even children, has little effect on us. Consider the ease with which Greek playwrights get us past the killing of Hercules' family, focusing instead on his suffering. Biblical writers move right past all the dead Hebrew children, all the dead Egyptian children, and all the dead people of the world in the story of Noah and his ark. Our hero represents us, and as long as we survive, we can get past the deaths of hundreds of innocents.

However, **this does not mean that we want our hero to have an easy time of it**. First, ease is not exciting. Second, ease does not aid maturity. One must be tested and withstand the test. We do not want even our gods to be perfect, but we do want them to be triumphant. Our myths and legends make that clear. Hera tries to kill Hercules. Laius tries to have Oedipus left to die. The Pharaoh and Herod try to exterminate all little Hebrew boys in their attempts to prevent Moses and Jesus from taking their thrones. But our little heroes are survivors, and we rejoice in their triumph.

Harry Potter, too, experiences the trials of the world's mythological heroes. Attacked as a child by the evil Voldemort, he loses his parents and barely escapes with his life. He endures years of persecution and loneliness in the household of his aunt, uncle, and cousin. Like Hercules, he has his own labors: he must fight a troll, a basilisk, and Voldemort again and again, sometimes in one form and sometimes in another. Like other Rankian heroes, he sometimes asks to be relieved of his tasks, often denying the warning of his aching scar, hoping, like Oedipus, that if he ignores the warning, he can avoid the risk.

But **the risk always comes**, and Harry faces it directly. He defeats Voldemort time after time and wins battles against Tom Riddle, the basilisk, the dragon who guards her egg, and Peter Pettigrew. He wins Quidditch matches and the Triwizard Tournament. Like children reading fairy tales and adolescents reading more realistic books, adults, too, identify with mythological heroes and believe that we can stand up against life's slings and arrows.

Rank points out what should be obvious but what might get lost in this discussion: "The myths are certainly not constructed by the hero, least of all by the child hero"; instead, they are "created by adults, by means of retrograde childhood fantasies." Rank explains, "The ego of the child behaves," then, "like the hero of the myth, and . . . the hero should always be interpreted merely as a collective ego" (70–71, 62).

In short, Rank's theories explain myths **the way Bettelheim explains fairy tales**: they provide us with allegories to understand our own worst and best impulses, to help us understand birth, death, sex, identity, and good and evil.

Mythology almost always explains birth as a mystical, magical event, one ordained by the gods. Thus, despite Laius's fear inculcated in him by the oracle at Delphi that his son would kill him, he gets drunk and impregnates Jocasta, resulting in the birth of Oedipus.

The idea of rebirth, too, appears in myth. When Moses delivers the Israelites from Egypt, he parts the Red Sea and walks his newly freed people through it in a remarkable birth image—the rebirth of a people into their Promised Land.

Otto Rank cites as one of the characteristics of the hero that he is often put into water, either to send him to his death or to save him (57). The story of Moses' mother's placing him in a basket and placing him in the Nile, from which he is drawn by the Pharaoh's daughter, has numerous parallels, including Romulus and Remus's being placed in a tub on the Tiber, then washing ashore, and the Hindu hero Karna's being placed in a basket and floated down a river into the Ganges, from which a charioteer and his wife save him (Rank, 16).

The themes of birth and rebirth are part of understanding ourselves and our identities, as well as the concept of sex. They also make us believe, both as adults and as children, that we have second chances, that we do not have to remain the way we were born. Oddly, these themes combine the ideas of destiny and freedom. If we are destined to greatness, a lowly birth will not prevent us from achieving distinction. On the other hand, even if we are born as though destined for nothing, we can be reborn as persons of eminence and great deeds. In short, we are not doomed by our birth, as Dumbledore tells Cornelius Fudge, the Minister of Magic: "[I]t matters not what someone is born, but what they grow to be!" (*Goblet of Fire*, 708).

After four books, the circumstances surrounding Harry Potter's conception and birth are still unknown to us. However, birth imagery is quite common in the works.

"the risk always comes"—In *Hallows*, Harry leaves the comparative safety of Hogwarts and roams the countryside like Rama or Gilgamesh in the wilderness (see Ch. 17, p. 203, and Ch. 15, p. 166, respectively). He is aided by Prongs, the Patronus derived from his appreciation of his father.

"the way Bettelheim explains fairy tales"—In *The Uses of Enchantment*, Bruno Bettelheim suggests that fairy tales are useful to children because, at different stages of their lives, they identify with different characters in them, using this identification to achieve a symbolic resolution of crises in their real lives. For more detail, see Ch. 34, pp. 507–508.

"rescuing his friend Ron Weasley" —The role of Harry's companions is not a major part of Grimes' analysis, though it is an important part of the books. Psychological analysis like that of Rank and Jung tends to focus on the individual, but part of the delight of the Harry Potter stories is to see Harry's interactions with his classmates. Much of what Grimes says about Harry could be applied to Ron as well, and in some respects, as here, Ron is a projection of Harry, who, despite his different background, expresses Harry's fears and hopes. Here rescuing Ron is, for Harry, identical to saving himself. The differences between Harry and his companions are clearer when we consider Hermione, however. She demonstrates some kinds of competence that come harder to Harry, like the sensitivity to the plight of the oppressed house elves. This theme is much more prominent in the books than the films.

While baby Harry is not placed in a basket in the water, his delivery to Hogwarts contains strong elements of rebirth symbolism, and he later has life-changing experiences with water. When he receives letters announcing that he is to begin school at Hogwarts, his aunt and uncle take him to an island to hide him from whoever is sending the mail. He is carried from the island across the water by Hagrid, just as numerous other heroes are delivered from the water by shepherds, gamekeepers, and other folk who work with animals (*Sorcerer's Stone*, 44–65). In fact, all first-year students—and, significantly, only the first-years—are ferried across water to Hogwarts, a sort of rebirth completed when the Sorting Hat puts them into their new houses. Again in *Goblet of Fire*, Harry has a significant experience with water, this time the lake around Hogwarts School. As part of the Triwizard Tournament, he has the task of **rescuing his friend Ron Weasley** from the merpeople at the bottom of the lake. He learns of his task by opening a dragon egg under water in a bath (*Goblet of Fire*, 458–66). Then by eating a substance called gillyweed, he becomes capable of breathing through gills, like a fish. He finds his friend, as well as three other captives, and then, after other contestants rescue two of the captives, carries Ron and a child back to the surface, just as he loses the ability to breathe under water (*Goblet of Fire*, 493–504). Again, the birth imagery is unmistakable: like a fetus, he does not need oxygen, but as he is reborn as a hero, a savior of his friends, he must again breathe air.

Birth and rebirth imagery function in two ways for readers. First, they help us establish identity, for it is upon our births that most cultures mark us as individuals distinct from our parents, as unique persons. Second, they reflect our attitude of wonderment toward the idea of sex, especially sex between our parents, a taboo subject for most children and many adults.

Lord Raglan: The Pattern of Hero Stories ("Hero," pp. 212–13)

1. His mother is a royal virgin.
2. His father is a king, and
3. Often a near relative of the mother, but
4. The circumstances of his conception are unusual, and
5. He is also reputed to be the son of a god.
6. At birth an attempt is made, usually by his father or maternal grandfather, to kill him, but
7. He is spirited away, and
8. Reared by foster-parents in a far country.
9. We are told nothing of his childhood, but
10. On reaching manhood he returns or goes to his future kingdom.
11. After a victory over the king and/or a giant, dragon, or wild beast,
12. He marries a princess, often the daughter of his predecessor and
13. Becomes king.
14. For a time he reigns uneventfully and
15. Prescribes laws but
16. Later loses favor with the gods and or his people and
17. Is driven from the throne and the city, after which
18. He meets with a mysterious death
19. Often at the top of a hill.
20. His children, if any, do not succeed him.
21. His body is not buried, but nevertheless
22. He has one or more holy sepulchres.

Death, the obverse of birth, is even more of a mystery. We have both a fear of death and an obsession with it, partly because no one can really explain it. The **threat of death** appears at the very beginning of almost every hero myth: Oedipus's father tries to have him killed; the Pharaoh tries to have Moses killed—in fact, the Hebrew God slaughters the first-born sons of the Egyptians, making Exodus full of infanticide; and Herod tries to have Jesus killed. Harry Potter, too, is almost the victim of Voldemort's plots to kill him.

To our delight, our hero archetypes always escape the attempted murder. Of course this is comforting: we believe that we, too, can escape early death. However, in *The Hero: A Study in Tradition, Myth, and Drama*, myth ritualist **Lord Raglan** lists twenty-two similarities among heroic tales, five of which relate to the hero's death. Otto Rank brings us to the hero's triumph, not to his demise. However, most myths and legends do take us to the end of the lives of the heroes.

Mythology is our earliest form of literature. Fairy tales are probably our second. More realistic narratives came much later, just as more representational painting followed long after the symbolic paintings found in caves. We have much reason to believe that fairy tales grew from mythology and that more realistic literature grew from these tales. Perhaps the early development of mythology stems from adults' desire to explain the world to ourselves. Only later did we feel it necessary to explain it to children. Finally, when we had made our way through the greatest mysteries, such as where the sun goes at night, we turned toward those more mundane ones of everyday reality, such as prejudice.

Harry Potter is **Everyboy and Everyman**, the Everyman or Everywoman we all know is inside us, whether we are six, sixteen, or sixty, the Everyman who knows he is special, that great things lie in store for him which others do not yet recognize. We are that boy in the cupboard under the stairs just waiting for our letter from Hogwarts, just waiting for Hagrid to come and take us from the humdrum and unjust Dursleys to an exciting, magical world in which our unique heroism allows us to catch the Golden Snitch, look evil full in the face, and win.

> "threat of death"—In *Hallows*, Harry views Snape's memories and he "understood at last that he was not supposed to survive. His job was to walk calmly into Death's welcoming arms" (691). And he does so in his final confrontation with Voldemort. Afterward, Harry finds himself face to face with Dumbledore, who explains, "You had accepted, even embraced, the possibility of death, something Voldemort has never been able to do. Your courage won . . ." (711).

> Lord Raglan—See the table for the pattern described by this twentieth-century folklorist who believed that mythological stories were based on ritual dramas. The basis for the pattern was Sophocles' Oedipus the King (see Ch. 19, p. 231). Grimes' analogy here is an appropriate one for Harry Potter, however, as this hero must undergo his own death in order to triumph over his adversary.

> "Everyboy and Everyman"—This phrasing is a play on the title of the medieval play named *Everyman* after its main character, who symbolizes all human beings. When Death calls Everyman, none of his friends, the allegorically named Beauty, Kindred, and Worldly Goods, are willing to go with him, but Good Deeds is.

Further Reading

Bettelheim, Bruno. *The Uses of Enchantment: The Meaning and Importance of Fairy Tales.* New York, NY: Alfred A. Knopf, 1976.

Eliade, Mircea. *The Myth of the Eternal Return: Or Cosmos and History.* Trans. Willard R. Trask. Bollingen Series XLVI. Princeton, NJ: Princeton University Press, 1989.

Finn, Natalie. "J.K. Rowling Outs Dumbledore." *E! Online*, October 19, 2007. http://www.eonline.com/news/article/index.jsp?uuid=c2b40da2-2406-4e8f-bc89-6fc11d1b0e41&entry=index&sid=rss_topstories&utm_source=eonline&utm_medium=rssfeeds&utm_campaign=rss_topstories (accessed 8 January 2008).

Grimes, M. Katherine. "Harry Potter: Fairy Tale Prince, Real Boy, and Archetypal Hero." in *The Ivory Tower and Harry Potter: Perspectives on a Literary Phenomenon*, ed. Lana A. Whited. Columbia, MO: University of Missouri Press, 2002.

Raglan, Lord. "The Hero of Tradition," *Folklore* 45.3 (1934): 212–231.

Rank, Otto. *The Myth of the Birth of the Hero.* New York, NY: Alfred A. Knopf, 1959.

Zipes, Jack. "The Phenomenon of Harry Potter, or Why All the Talk?" In *Sticks and Stones: The Troublesome Success of Children's Literature from Slovenly Peter to Harry Potter*. New York: Routledge, 2002.

Part 8

Myth and Literature

We usually make a distinction between mythological stories in themselves and mythology as an element of a literary work. In a sense, this classification is incomplete because we also have works like Sophocles' *Oedipus at Thebes,* which are mythological stories in the form of literary pieces. To some extent, the distinction is one of currency: Sophocles wrote his play at the time when the story he used was still "alive" in his culture, with an altar to the hero cult of Oedipus at Athens. Even so, there is distinction between the story of Oedipus as told by Sophocles and the story of the hero as told in different ways by different storytellers (see Ch. 25, p. 361ff.). In this section, however, we move away from "living" mythology and ritual to literary works by artists who incorporate the stories, places, and characters from the mythological tradition in their own efforts.

As we read these literary works—or listen to song lyrics or view films containing elements of the mythological tradition—we can gain much more information and enjoyment if we are aware of the mythological connections they include. For example, the stories of Zeus' unfaithfulness to his wife Hera and of her frightful jealousy (e.g., see her treatment of Heracles, Ch. 31, p. 453) add another dimension to the appreciation of W. B. Yeats' "Leda and the Swan" (see Ch. 42, p. 634). Or knowing that Medusa was able to frighten men to death through her dreadful appearance makes clear a reference such as "[such a character] was a real Medusa." Likewise, the story of Helen of Troy's beauty causing the Trojan War can lead readers to think of a 3000-year-old tradition when a modern writer refers to a woman as a "Helen of Troy."

In some cases, understanding mythological stories can provide access to what almost amounts to a secret language of unspoken references. For example, by naming a character Penelope, an author can refer to the extraordinary faithfulness of the wife of Odysseus to her husband while he was away from home for twenty years because of the Trojan War. A character named Loki can be used to evoke the stories associated with the Icelandic trickster god, who was as mischievous as he was undependable. Mythological place names can enrich our reading in the same way: the mention of Valhalla always conjures up visions of a kind of heavenly home, and the Augean stables (see Heracles, Ch. 31, p. 446) live in our imagination as a metaphor for unbelievable mess and filth.

Changing Views on Using Myth in Literature

People's interest in classical mythology varies throughout history. In the late-sixteenth- and mid-seventeenth centuries in Europe, and in the past forty years in America, mythological themes have been popular in art and in literature. Today we find numerous references to classical and Western mythologies in what we read, hear, and see, but this has not always been the case.

In the early days of Christianity in Europe, manuscripts about the ancient Greek and Roman gods were frowned on, as they represented stories about a rival religion, one which, in the minds of most people, had been replaced by Christianity. Today, almost no one would bother to object to a story about Heracles or Apollo, but in those days a story like that was viewed as a threat to people's religious values. As a result, they got rid of texts with ancient stories in them, or stored them in remote places where they were often lost or destroyed. In the period known as the Dark Ages (late fifth through eleventh centuries), many manuscripts from Rome and ancient Greece were destroyed, either by the people who owned them or by various marauding groups. Such invaders also destroyed a great deal of written material from Christian times. In addition, very little new creative literature was produced during this time, since the greatest intellectual effort was spent on preserving and copying Biblical texts.

By the Middle Ages, literary production grew at a constant pace, but the fear of non-Western, non-Christian influence led to an emphasis in art and literature on Biblical, religious, and ethnically heroic themes. There was not much knowledge of classical literature at this time in the West, except for Latin works by the poet Ovid. And when writers alluded to Ovid in their works, they tended to "Christianize" the material, using it as allegory for Christian beliefs. The most common manifestation of mythology we might find during this period is the writing down of native European stories, such as Snorri Sturluson's eddas. (See Ch. 7, p. 78; Ch. 13, p. 147; and Ch. 18, p. 218)

However, when the wars called the Crusades (lasting 200 years from the end of the eleventh century) took many Europeans to Jerusalem and other parts of the Middle East, things began to change. In the great libraries maintained by Islamic empires, these Christians rediscovered the works of ancient Greek and Roman writers that often incorporated mythological stories. Some of these works were brought back from the Holy Land for study, while the rekindling of interest in Classical times caused others to be brought out of storage areas in Europe. This surge of interest in ancient Greek and Roman culture, called the Renaissance ("rebirth"), moved geographically from Italy northward and westward. It was also spurred on by the Greek and Arabic learning that Islamic scholars brought to Europe in the twelfth and thirteenth centuries.

Appreciation of all kinds of ancient and non-Western texts continued to grow, and the invention of the printing press in the mid-fifteenth century made classical literature more accessible to the reading public. What had been taboo because it was pagan became a valued source of information for science and art. In turn, the lively interest in ancient Greece and Rome helped lead to a general shift from the religious and theological perspective to a more secular focus on all aspects of human nature (thus, the name "Humanism"). By the early sixteenth century, classical literature was taught regularly, and before the century ended, European writers borrowed freely from ancient works.

This trend continued throughout the seventeenth century in England, where George Chapman's translations of the *Iliad* and the *Odyssey* made Homer's epics even more widely accessible. An example of their popularity is the use of mythological figures and themes in court entertainments such as *masques*. These were theatrical performances in which members of educated society acted out scenes inspired by mythological and pastoral themes. In these performances, a succession of rapidly changing scenes featured elaborately costumed, masked figures of gods, monsters, heroes, satyrs, and fairies dancing to fanciful music. One of the most famous of these masques is John Milton's *Comus,* whose main character is the Roman god of revelry. Because most literate people were so familiar with traditional myths and their characters, poets often alluded to mythological figures in their works, even if the ancient story was not the main theme. William Shakespeare does this in some of his plays, even incorporating a masque featuring Ceres (Roman goddess of agriculture) and Juno (Roman queen of the gods) into *The Tempest*.

In the late eighteenth century, classical mythology again came into favor in Europe. The influence of ancient Greece and Rome is still apparent in the architecture of that period, and much of English poetry shows a love for what was viewed as the serene, balanced life of ancient times. A good example of this trend is the popularity of a type of poem called the pastoral. In it, Greek shepherds and shepherdesses inhabit an idealized and tranquil landscape, which in its simplicity seemed an antidote to the increasingly industrialized and urban world of the readers.

Among the English Romantic poets of the nineteenth century, John Keats and Percy Bysshe Shelley offer us examples of continuing interest in classical mythology. Shelley's *Prometheus Unbound* (1820) was based on *Prometheus Bound* by the Greek dramatist Aeschylus. Shelley kept the underlying structure of the original story, in which Prometheus, who is an advocate for human beings, defies Zeus, who wants to keep all good things, including fire, from them. However, in Shelley's version, Jupiter (the Roman counterpart of Zeus) represents evil in the abstract, and Prometheus uses knowledge as a weapon to banish the taint of evil from human nature. This symbolic drama, fashioned from Aeschylus' version of the Prometheus myth, shows Shelley's belief that social reform, which is the moral responsibility of human beings, can bring about the elimination of evil. This is a good example of how a poet may effectively avoid being boring and didactic by dramatizing contemporary ideas in the guise of an ancient story.

Later, the interest in ancient cultures and their mythologies was fueled from a different source of energy. From the mid-eighteenth and throughout the nineteenth centuries, the English, Germans, and other Europeans were getting to see actual remnants of the cultures of classical mythology without traveling to the Middle East. Archeologists were returning to Europe with statuary and huge pieces of ancient monuments. The personages and events depicted on these again excited the interest of the public as well as the academic communities. We can get a glimpse of this by reading Keats' "Ode on a Grecian Urn," in which he describes the scene on a Greek cup called a *kylix,* praising its timelessness and its beauty.

Even in contemporary American literature we find references to mythology that enrich our enjoyment. For example, John Updike's novel, *The Centaur,* contains a treasure trove of metaphors from ancient Greek mythology. The more of them we can recognize as we read, the more we can participate in the events of the book. Although *The Centaur* is set in a small Pennsylvania town in the mid-twentieth century, all of the major characters are modern versions of major Greek deities. The actions of these re-embodiments take place in the world we know, although their underlying motivations are rooted in their mythological identities.

We would also point out the growing body of literature in the United States that reveals the richness of Native American mythology. Those by American Indian authors use integral parts of Native American culture to enrich their writing. As we read more of the work, we learn more of this culture; and as we learn more, our enjoyment expands. The piece in this section, Leslie Marmon Silko's "Yellow Woman," is a modern presentation of a traditional Indian story about a young woman's abduction by spirits and her eventual return to society. Silko's version of the story blurs the lines between native beliefs and modern, nontraditional motivations and social practices. The reader is drawn into the woman's dilemma as she grapples with her situation: is this man her abductor and she Yellow Woman, as he insists; or is he a predator and she one of his naively willing partners?

Fairy Tales in Literature

In Part 6, we showed the relationship between folk- and fairy tales and mythology. We see many instances of such stories in modern literature. In the first place, we find many versions of classical fairy tales aimed at particular audiences. These stories, or "duplications," maintain the ideas and belief system of the original but alter them to suit a new audience (Zipes, 8–9). For example, many popular American Cinderella stories omit the sisters' cutting off parts of their feet or the birds' pecking out their eyes.

However, there are also more creative incorporations of old tales into other perspectives and styles of writing. Jack Zipes dubbed these "revisions," as they are different from duplications, most obviously because they draw upon a well-honored tradition without remaining bound to its aims or style of writing. In reflecting the new creator's ideas and the expected new audience's tastes, these revisions can also change readers' views of the old, traditional patterns, images, and codes (Zipes, 9–10).

A good example of a revised fairy tale is the version of "Beauty and the Beast," called "The Tiger's Bride," in Chapter 44 (p. 670ff.). Interesting revisions of other Grimms tales include a pessimistic "Sleeping Beauty" story meant for adults in Anne Sexton's collection of poems, *Transformations,* and Jane Yolen's "Sleeping

Ugly," a humorous parody of the same tale for children. In this, the heroine is "Plain Jane" and the prince is "Jojo"; thus the story turns what the child expects into the opposite, making it a comic reference.

In these modern takes on the fairy tale, the basic premise and traditional conclusion are overturned. These stories appeal to more sophisticated audiences who are familiar with the original, but are more interested in the beliefs of their own times. Once again, the same principles apply to these modern fairy tales as were mentioned in relation to literary works with allusions to the gods and heroes of classical myths: the more familiar the reader is with the earlier work, the richer is her experience with the later one.

Further Reading

Zipes, Jack. *Fairy Tale As Myth, Myth As Fairy Tale.* Lexington: The University Press of Kentucky, 1994.

Mythological Themes in Poetry

42

WHAT TO EXPECT . . . Because poets use figurative language to express personal and universal concepts and feelings, they often rely on allusions to characters and events from mythology. This chapter discusses how a selection of poets from the seventeenth through twentieth centuries— John Milton, John Keats, Alfred Lord Tennyson, William Butler Yeats, Hilda Doolittle, and Anne Sexton—enrich their creations and thus increase the depth of their readers' experiences by including mythological references in them.

As you read, note how the various poetic genres, such as pastoral and sonnet, affect the tone of the poem. Consider the way references to mythical and fairy tale figures affect your understanding of the poem's meaning, and examine whether the twentieth-century poems speak more directly to you and your peers. What does the varying treatment of myth tell you about how the tastes and expectations of readers have changed over the centuries?

Poetry is a kind of literature that especially lends itself to the inclusion of mythological material. Because it relies on expressing ideas and feelings in a kind of figurative shorthand, poetry can be greatly enriched through use of images from the storehouse of mythology. For example, when the reader is familiar with Greek mythology, William Butler Yeats' poem "Leda and the Swan" immediately evokes the images and emotions related to the classical story of Zeus' conquest of a human woman, giving Yeats a rich palette of images and associations with which to convey his thoughts—which were actually about Ireland in his own time.

Through the centuries, material from myth has been incorporated into poetry, enhancing not only its depth of expression, but also its impact on the audience. Readers who can draw on the broader experience expressed in the myth can relate more immediately to the images in the poem. Many authors combine classical Greek and Roman myth with stories from the Christian and Hebrew traditions. The inclusion of material from Bible stories is neither aimed at promoting belief nor at supporting skepticism. Rather, our culture imbues all of these stories with feelings and associations that the poet can evoke with a single name or phrase. Such material lends itself to incorporation in a variety of poetic expressions. For example, the pastoral is a poetic form that can readily express the disparate views of nature popular in different eras. This stylized genre dates back to ancient times and includes rural scenes and the charming flirtations conducted by stereotypical rural figures.

In the English Renaissance when nature was viewed as an ideal, John Milton (1608–1674) drew on mythological scenes and characters to embody the glorious goal of fame that he felt was denied a young poet who had died before his prime. Using these disparate elements, he constructed a great poem, "Lycidas," that incorporated the classical themes typical of the pastoral, but at the same time represented his personal attitudes and perspectives. For readers familiar with the ancient stories Milton drew on, the events in the poem take on a resonance and grandeur directly related to their understanding of the mythological material. Milton's approach was quite different from the pastoral as conceived later by John Keats (1795–1821). Keats wrote at the start of the industrial age, at a time when poetry was used to draw an elaborate idealized portrait of people's relationship with nature as this tie was being threatened. Keats also included mythological figures in his version of the pastoral.

In his turn, William Butler Yeats (1865–1939) was also able to incorporate mythological elements in representing the grand sweep of individualism in a more modern style of poetry. To achieve the effect he wanted, Yeats reformulated the characteristics of the mythological figures he incorporated. Thus, mythological themes set the scene for the disturbance of cosmic proportions, which is the rape of Leda in "Leda and the Swan," and the presentation of his personal philosophy in "The Second Coming."

In general, the imaginative language typical of poetry provides an opportunity for shaping literary works through the use of mythological figures and allusions. Thus, if readers are familiar with the characters and situations that constitute various mythological traditions, they can get a much richer picture from a literary work. In this sense, mythology not only forms a kind of shorthand, but it also allows readers to compare the ways in which beliefs and moral values have changed throughout human history.

This section contains poetic selections by six poets from the mid-seventeenth to the late-twentieth centuries, including a variety of recognized poetic forms, from epic through pastoral and sonnet to blank verse and experimental form.

John Milton (1608–1674)

John Milton was a statesman, scholar, and poet. He served with Oliver Cromwell, who governed England when Charles I was deposed. After the restoration of the monarchy in 1660, Milton returned to private life and devoted himself to his poetry. As a young man, he had written sonnets in Italian and traveled to Italy, where he held discussions with Galileo and other learned figures.

Mihály Munkácsy, *Blind Milton dictating* Paradise Lost *to his daughters,* 1877.

Milton lived during the English Renaissance, a period named from the French word for "rebirth." At this time (in England, sixteenth and seventeenth centuries), Europeans were rediscovering literary works from ancient Greek and Roman authors that had been put aside during the Middle Ages because they were considered in conflict with Christianity. In Renaissance writing, it was customary to bring in a variety of names and events from a wide range of poetical conventions, historical events, and stories, including those from mythology. As a writer, Milton carried in his head a vivid vision of the world, which linked classical Greek and Roman learning, as well as the Hebrew Bible and the New Testament, in a continuous line of human endeavor leading directly to the ideas of his own time.

When Milton wrote about any idea, he wanted to express it clearly in all its ramifications; thus, he drew from the author and time period that provided him with the most powerful concepts or the most memorable imagery for making his point. Because he was a man of extensive learning, Milton had at his command a vast repertoire of authors and works from which he could weave together ideas in his own writing. He could read Greek, Latin, and Hebrew fluently, and even after he became totally blind in 1651, he continued his learned studies and his writing. He had Hebrew scripture and other great works read to him daily and dictated his own compositions.

Today, Milton is best known for his epic poem *Paradise Lost* (1667), which deals with what in the opening line is called "man's first disobedience." Milton portrays the weaknesses of Adam and Eve and the ebullient attractiveness of Satan, often enriched by references from classical Greek and Latin mythology. The command of a wide range of literary styles and allusions is apparent in Milton's earlier works, as well.

Before he was 30 years old, Milton composed the pastoral poem "Lycidas," which mourns the death of Edward King, a Cambridge University classmate, who was drowned in a boating accident in the Irish Sea. This poem represents Milton's own personal grief, but expresses it in a traditional poetic form derived from classical Greek and Roman writers going as far back as the third century B.C.E. The poem is a lament, one of the three types of pastoral. (The other two are the singing match between two poets and the monologue.)

"Lycidas" is a good example of the English pastoral form, which was most popular in that country between 1550 and 1750. The name of the genre is derived from *pastor,* Latin for "shepherd." This kind of poetry represents the ideas and feelings of its author by projecting them into stories about shepherds and rural life. The writers of pastoral poetry were not interested in the realistic details of country life; they saw the countryside as an idealized place to which a busy city person could withdraw to recover a sense of himself after the efforts of everyday life.

In this poem, Milton does not refer to his former classmate by his real name, but calls him "Lycidas," a name often used for a shepherd in pastoral poetry. In Renaissance writing, it was customary to bring in a variety of names and events from poetical conventions, historical events, and stories in mythology.

Lycidas

Yet once more, **O ye laurels,** and once more,
Ye myrtles brown, with ivy never sear,
I come to pluck your berries harsh and crude,
And with forced fingers rude
Shatter your leaves before the mellowing year.   5
Bitter constraint and sad occasion dear
Compels me to disturb your season due:
For Lycidas is dead, dead ere his prime,
Young Lycidas, and hath not left his peer.

"O ye laurels . . . Ye myrtles"— Milton sets the scene for a pastoral, starting with idealized vegetation. The plants he mentions are also traditional materials for garlands.

Who would not sing for Lycidas? **He knew**   10
Himself to sing, and build the lofty rime.
He must not float upon this watery bier
Unwept, and welter to the parching wind,
Without the meed of some melodious tear.
Begin, then, **Sisters of the sacred well,**   15
That from beneath the seat of **Jove** doth spring,
Begin, and somewhat loudly sweep the string.
Hence with denial vain and some coy excuse;
So may some gentle muse
With lucky words favor my destined urn,   20
And as he passes turn
And bid fair peace be to my sable shroud!
For we were nursed upon the selfsame hill,
Fed the same flock, by fountain, shade, and rill.
Together both, **ere the high lawns appeared**   25
Under the opening eyelids of the morn,
We drove afield, and both together heard
What time the gray-fly winds her sultry horn,
Battening our flocks with the fresh dews of night,
Oft till the star that rose at evening, bright,   30
Toward heaven's descent had sloped his westering wheel.
Meanwhile the rural ditties were not mute,
Tempered to **the oaten flute;**
Rough Satyrs danced, and Fauns with cloven heel
From the glad sound would not be absent long,   35
And old Damoetas loved to hear our song.

But, oh! the heavy change, now thou art gone,
Now thou art gone, and never must return!
Thee, Shepherd, thee the woods and desert caves,
With wild thyme and **the gadding vine o'ergrown,**   40
And all their echoes mourn.
The willows, and the hazel copses green,
Shall now no more be seen,
Fanning their joyous leaves to thy soft lays.
As killing as the canker to the rose,   45
Or taint-worm to the weanling herds that graze,
Or frost to flowers, that their gay wardrobe wear,
When first the white-thorn blows—
Such, Lycidas, thy loss to shepherd's ear.

Where were ye, **Nymphs,** when the remorseless deep   50
Closed o'er the head of your loved Lycidas?
For neither were ye playing on the steep
Where **your old bards, the famous Druids,** lie,
Nor on the shaggy top of **Mona** high,
Nor yet **where Deva spreads her wizard stream:**   55
Aye me! I fondly dream
"Had ye been there"—for what could that have done?

"He knew himself to sing"—
Edward King was a poet, the
most noble of ancient callings.

"Sisters of the sacred well"—The
Muses were daughters of Zeus
who guarded a spring (or "well") of
inspiration at his temple. Poets called
on them for inspiration in the creative
arts.

Jove Jupiter, the supreme
Roman god, counterpart of Zeus.

"Fed the same flock"—According
to the imagery Milton uses, a poet
is a shepherd, so the closeness
Milton feels for the dead young
man is expressed in terms of their
shared activities as shepherds.

"ere the high lawns appeared"—
Before civilization altered nature.

"the oaten flute"—Even the musical instrument is rustic, made
from the hollowed-out reed of an
oat stalk.

"the gadding vine o'ergrown"—It
is beyond the order that civilization
imposes.

"Fanning their joyous leaves to thy
soft lays"—Lycidas pleased nature
with his poetry.

Nymphs From a Greek word for
"girl," these minor deities were
not associated with excessive sexual appetite, as suggested by our
word "nymphomaniac."

"your old bards, the famous
Druids"—Ancient celtic priests.

Mona Angelsea, in the Irish Sea,
was said to be the home of the
Druids.

"where Deva spreads her wizard
stream"—Shifts in the course of
the River Dee, between Wales and
England, were thought to predict
changes in luck between the two
countries.

What could the Muse herself that **Orpheus** bore,
The Muse herself, for her enchanting son,
Whom universal nature did lament,   60
When, by the rout that made the hideous roar,
His gory visage down the stream was sent,
Down the swift **Hebrus** to the Lesbian shore?

   Alas! what boots it with uncessant care
To tend the homely, slighted shepherd's trade,   65
And strictly mediate the thankless Muse?
Were it not better done as others use,
To sport with Amaryllis in the shade,
Or with the tangles of Neaera's hair?
Fame is the spur that the clear spirit doth raise   70
(That last infirmity of noble mind)
To scorn delights, and live laborious days;
But the fair guerdon when we hope to find,
And think to burst out into sudden blaze,
Comes the **blind Fury with th' abhorred shears,**   75
And slits the thin-spun life. "But not the praise,"
Phoebus replied, and touched my trembling ears;
"Fame is no plant that grows on mortal soil,
Nor in the glistering foil
Set off to the world, nor in broad rumor lies,   80
But lives and spreads aloft by those pure eyes
And perfect witness of all-judging Jove;
As he pronounces lastly on each deed,
Of so much fame in heaven expect thy meed."

   O fountain **Arethuse,** and thou honored flood,   85
Smooth-sliding **Mincius,** crowned with vocal reeds,
That strain I heard was of a higher mood.
But now my oat proceeds,
And listens to the Herald of the Sea
That came in Neptune's plea.   90
He asked the waves and asked the felon winds, What hard
mishaps hath doomed this gentle swain?
And questioned every gust of rugged wings
That blows from off each beaked promontory.
They knew not of his story;   95
And sage **Hippotades** their answer brings,
That not a blast was from his dungeon strayed;
The air was calm, and on the level brine
Sleek **Panope** with all her sisters played. It was that fatal   100
and perfidious bark,
Built in the eclipse, and rigged with curses dark,
That sunk so low that sacred head of thine.

   Next, **Camus,** reverend sire, went footing slow,
His mantle hairy, and his bonnet sedge,

Orpheus Son of Apollo and the muse, Calliope, tried and failed to save his wife Euridice from the underworld.

Hebrus—Maddened by what they saw as Orpheus' excessive lamenting for Eurydice, Thracian women tore him to pieces and threw his head and lyre into this river.

"blind Fury with th' abhorred shears, And slits the thin-spun life"—The Fates, Clotho, Lachesis, and Atropos, had control over human life. Clotho spun the thread of life, Lachesis offered an element of chance, and Atropos cut it, causing death. The Furies were avenging goddesses.

Phoebus Phoebus (Apollo), god of poetry.

Arethuse A fountain in Sicily named for the sea nymph who tried to escape the hunter Alpheus and was changed into a spring. He then changed into a river and eventually mingled with the waters of her spring.

Mincius River in Italy near Virgil's birthplace.

"He asked the waves"—Neptune was not responsible for Lycidas' death.

Hippotades Aeolus, the Greek god of the winds.

Panope One of the Nereids, nymphs of the sea.

Camus The spirit of the River Cam, which runs through Cambridge, England. King (Lycidas) and Milton were classmates at Cambridge University.

"that sanguine flower"—The hyacinth was created from the blood of the youth Hyacinthus by Apollo as a symbol of his grief.

"Pilot of the Galilean Lake"—St. Peter, a fisherman in Galilee, was promised the keys to the kingdom of heaven (Matt. 16:19). He wears a miter as a sign of being bishop.

"sheep-hook"—As bishop, Peter also carries a crozier, a stylized shepherd's staff with a hook-like end. The Christian "shepherd" adds an element from Milton's culture to the classical shepherds with which the genre of this poem is identified.

Alpheus The hunter who became a river god after pursuing Arethuse, the water nymph who was changed into a spring to escape him.

Sicilian Muse Said to be the muse who inspired Theocritus, who was Sicilian.

"the swart star sparely looks"— When Sirius, the dog star, was at its zenith, people believed it would blacken vegetation.

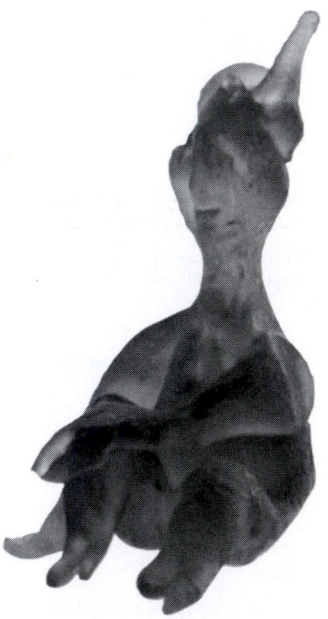

Egidio Costantini, after a sketch by Pablo Picasso, *Satyr,* 1964. This glass sculpture catches a satyr in an unguarded moment, one horn standing up and one back.

Inwrought with figures dim, and on the edge   105
Like to **that sanguine flower** inscribed with woe.
"Ah! who hath reft," quoth he, "my dearest pledge?"
Last came, and last did go,
The **Pilot of the Galilean Lake;**
Two massy keys he bore of metals twain   110
(The golden opes, the iron shuts amain).
He shook his mitered locks, and stern bespake:
"How well could I have spared for thee, young swain,
Enow of such as, for their bellies' sake,
Creep, and intrude, and climb into the fold!   115
Of other care they little reckoning make
Than how to scramble at the shearers' feast,
And shove away the worthy bidden guest.
Blind mouths! that scarce themselves know how to hold
A **sheep-hook,** or have learned aught else the least   120
That to the faithful herdsman's art belongs!
What recks it them? What need they? They are sped;
And when they list, their lean and flashy songs
Grate on their scrannel pipes of wretched straw;
The hungry sheep look up, and are not fed,   125
But swoln with wind and the rank mist they draw,
Rot inwardly, and foul contagion spread;
Besides what the grim wolf with privy paw
Daily devours apace, and nothing said.
But that two-handed engine at the door   130
Stands ready to smite once, and smite no more."

Return, **Alpheus,** the dread voice is past
That shrunk thy streams; return, **Sicilian Muse,**
And call the vales, and bid them hither cast
Their bells and flowerets of a thousand hues.   135
Ye valleys low, where the mild whispers use
Of shades, and wanton winds, and gushing brooks,
On whose fresh lap **the swart star sparely looks,**
Throw hither all your quaint enameled eyes,
That on the green turf suck the honeyed showers,   140
And purple all the ground with vernal flowers.
Bring the rathe primrose that forsaken dies,
The tufted crow-toe, and pale jessamine,
The white pink, and the pansy freaked with jet,
The glowing violet,   145
The musk-rose, and the well-attired woodbine,
With cowslips wan that hang the pensive head,
And every flower that sad embroidery wears;
Bid amaranthus all his beauty shed,
And daffodillies fill their cups with tears,   150
To strew the laureate hearse where Lycid lies.
For so, to interpose a little ease,
Let our frail thoughts daily with false surmise.

Aye me! Whilst thee the shores and sounding seas
Wash far away, where'er thy bones are hurled,   155
Whether beyond the stormy Hebrides,
Where thou **perhaps under the whelming tide**
Visit'st the bottom of the monstrous world;
Or whether thou, to our moist vows denied,
Sleep'st by the fable of **Bellerus** old,   160
Where the great Vision of the guarded mount
Looks toward Namancos and Bayona's hold.
Look Homeward, Angel, now, and melt with ruth;
And, O ye dolphins, waft the hapless youth.

Weep no more, woeful shepherds, weep no more,   165
For Lycidas, your sorrow, is not dead,
Sunk though he may be beneath the watery floor;
So sinks the day-star in the ocean bed,
And yet anon repairs his drooping head,
And tricks his beams, and with new-spangled ore   170
Flames in the forehead of the morning sky.
So Lycidas sunk low, but mounted high,
Through **the dear might of Him that walked the waves,**
Where, other groves and other streams along,
With nectar pure his oozy locks he laves,   175
And hears the unexpressive nuptial song,
In the blest kingdoms meek of joy and love.
In solemn troops, and sweet societies,
That sing, and singing in their glory move,
And wipe the tears forever from his eyes.   180
There entertain him all the saints above,
Now, Lycidas, the shepherds weep no more;
Henceforth thou art the Genius of the shore,
In thy large recompense, and shalt be good
To all that wander in that perilous flood.   185

Thus sang **the uncouth swain** to th' oaks gray;
He touched the tender stops of various quills,
With eager thought warbling his Doric lay.
And now the sun had stretched out all the hills,
And now was **dropped into the western bay.**   190
At last he rose, and twitched his mantle blue;
Tomorrow to fresh woods and pastures new.

> "perhaps under the whelming tide"—The poet wonders if his friend lies under the Irish Sea.

> **Bellerus** Legendary giant said to be buried in Cornwall, England, at Lands' End.

> "the dear might of Him that walked the waves"—Although most of the allusions here come from classical mythology, this refers to the redemptive power of Christ, whose walking on the water of the Sea of Galilee is reported in Matthew.

> "the uncouth swain"—The poet. "Uncouth" here has the older connotation of "not sophisticated," like the shepherds of the pastoral genre.

> "dropped into the western bay"—This echoes the ancient idea that the sun was drawn by a chariot across the sky, lifted up from the eastern horizon and dropped in the west into the water that surrounded the earth.

John Keats (1795–1821)

John Keats, who rose from middle-class surroundings to be acclaimed as one of the finest poets in the English language, reflects both the ideas of his times and the concerns of fellow poets. The literary period that coincides with his life almost exactly has been called Romantic by later students of literature. And although we may now link the word "romantic" with "love," the term—when it refers to the writing of Keats and his contemporaries—is much more closely related to "feeling." More specifically, poetry of the Romantic movement was concerned with demonstrating as directly as possible how the poet *feels* about the subject of the poem or narrative. Before this, he or she was expected to provide a reasoned description of the subject in other words, and in so doing, to present a picture of the world to the reader. With the Romantics, the focus was on the poet's emotional response—that is, the poet, not the subject, is central.

In this period, people read the works of the great poets of the past in an effort to learn from them something of the innermost being of the creator. These efforts included not only the great works of the Middle Ages, but also the ancient Greek and Latin masterpieces. Virgil was the Latin poet who described the mythical background of the founding of Rome. His work had become accessible to English speakers in translations by Henry Howard in the mid-sixteenth century. Homer was a blind Greek poet considered by many as the founder of the epic genre. He recounted the story of the Trojan War in the *Iliad* and the homecoming of its hero, Odysseus, in the *Odyssey*. The great translation of Homer's work by George Chapman, published in 1611 and 1616, opened up truly new worlds for Keats and his contemporaries. Keats' poem, "On First Looking into Chapman's Homer," gives us some indication of the importance of such reading to people of this time. This is an immediate response, a most direct outpouring of his feelings. He is said to have written the poem early in the morning after an all-night reading of Chapman with his teacher. He was 21 years old and had decided to set aside a medical career for poetry. He published his first book of poetry in 1817, and at the end of that year, he completed "Endymion."

Considering his enthusiastic allusions to people, places, and events from classical mythology, it is interesting that Keats makes no distinction between the particulars of the Greek and Roman traditions. For example, in the poem "To Homer," he refers to Jove rather than Zeus and Neptune rather than Poseidon while addressing the greatest of classical Greek poets.

Both "Chapman" and "To Homer" are sonnets, poems consisting of fourteen lines with a specific meter and rhyme scheme. Like traditional sonnets, they present or describe the situation in the first eight lines and comment on it in the next six. In "Chapman," Keats describes his own experience of the "one wide expanse" that was ruled by "deep-browed Homer." He says he felt like "some watcher of the skies / When a new planet swims into his ken." Later in life, Keats' poetry still showed great enthusiasm for the legacy of Greek mythology as he had experienced it while reading Homer. In his poetic imagination, the ancient gods themselves made the universe (the heavens, the seas, and the earth) accessible to Homer, in spite of his blindness. As we read the poem we might notice that in the final lines Keats moves Homer inside the realm of the mythological system itself, equating him with "Dian, Queen of Earth, and Heaven, and Hell."

Keats also enriched his more mature works, including "Lamia" (1819), with the imagery of ancient classical mythology. Because of this, it is not surprising that Percy Bysshe Shelley chose Greek mythology as the vehicle for lamenting the early death of his good friend in "Adonais, An Elegy on the Death of John Keats."

"giant ignorance"—Keats regrets that he does not know the Greek language.

Cyclades Greek islands in the Aegean Sea.

To Homer*

> Standing aloof in **giant ignorance,**
> Of thee I hear and of the **Cyclades,**
> As one who sits ashore and longs perchance
> To visit dolphin-coral in deep seas.
> So thou wast blind!—but then the veil was rent;   5

*"To Homer." Reprinted by permission of the publisher from *John Keats' Complete Poems*. Edited by Jack Stillinger. Cambridge, MA: The Belknap Press of Harvard University Press, p. 199. Copyright © 1978, 1982 by the President and Fellows of Harvard College.

For **Jove** uncurtained Heaven to let thee live,
And **Neptune** made for thee a spumy tent,
And **Pan** made sing for thee his forest-hive;

Aye, on the shores of darkness there is light,
And precipices show untrodden green;   10
There is a budding morrow in midnight,
There is **a triple sight** in blindness keen;
Such seeing hadst thou, as it once befell
to Dian, Queen of Earth, and Heaven, and Hell.
(1848)

Jove Roman head god, also known as Jupiter, counterpart to Greek Zeus.

Neptune Roman god of the sea, counterpart to Poseidon.

Pan Greek god of woods, fields, and flocks.

"A triple sight"—This is a double allusion, to two different methods of classifying the world: Diana was worshipped by some cults as a three-figured goddess ruling nature on earth, the moon, and in hell. Traditionally, these regions are commanded by Jove (heaven), Neptune (sea), and Pan (forest).

Alfred Lord Tennyson (1809–1892)

Alfred Lord Tennyson, the son of a rural minister, studied at Cambridge University and became England's poet laureate in 1850.

Although his style is different from that of Keats, Tennyson also took much of his subject matter from history and classical myth. In addition, many of his poems concerned events of his own day, such as "The Charge of the Light Brigade" on the famous battle of the Crimean War, and events of the future in "Locksley Hall." Tennyson loved the engineering and technical inventions of his Victorian age because they gave him a satisfaction of human progress. He was also keenly interested in history, especially the classical past.

"The Lotus-Eaters" (1830), an epic poem, is based on an episode in the *Odyssey*. In it, on their long return voyage from Troy, Odysseus and his men land in a place where they are given lotus to eat. This causes forgetfulness and thus a loss of their desire to return home. Tennyson updates and expands this theme for his own readers by presenting a picture of great weariness and a desire for rest and even death:

Surely, surely, slumber is more sweet than toil . . .
O rest, brother mariners, we will not wander more.

"Tithonus" (1860) is also based on Greek mythology. It is the story of a Trojan prince loved by Eos, the goddess of dawn, who convinced the gods to grant him eternal life but neglected to ask for eternal youth. And so, in this poem, the aged Tithonus tells Eos:

Can thy love, thy beauty make amends . . .
Let me go; take back thy gift.

He regrets living outside human boundaries:

Why should a man desire in any way
To vary from the kindly race of man.

In "Ulysses," Tennyson also uses a basic story from Greek mythology to illustrate a theme common to the human condition—aging. Some who are familiar with this poem have raised the question: is Ulysses (Greek Odysseus) a great hero, or is he irresponsible for trying to regain the thrill of his youth? As for his personal view, Tennyson explained that the poem expressed his own need to go on in life after the death of Arthur Hallam, his best friend from their student days.

Comparing this poem to others, students of mythology might conclude that Tennyson's Ulysses is closer to Dante's in the *Inferno* (XXVI) than to the Homeric hero. Homer's Odysseus did not seek out travel or exploration; his lengthy travels arose only because Poseidon, the god of the sea, was angry with him and diverted him as he was trying to get home from the Trojan War. In line with the attitude of his own times toward exploration, Tennyson re-envisions Ulysses as an explorer who traveled for the joy of it. He portrays Ulysses as becoming restless after returning to Ithaca and wanting to set out on another voyage. After only a brief time at home, Tennyson's Ulysses persuades some of his followers to join him on a trip seeking to go beyond the limits of the known universe.

Ulysses

"an idle king . . . with an aged wife"—Ulysses has returned safely to the ever-faithful Penelope, but the routines of the court bore him.

It little profits that **an idle king,**
By this still hearth, among these barren crags,
Matched **with an aged wife,** I mete and dole
Unequal laws unto a savage race,
That hoard, and sleep, and feed, and **know not me.**   5

"know not me"—Ulysses' experiences have isolated him, so he feels estranged from the people he rules.

I cannot rest from travel; I will drink
Life to the lees. All times I have enjoyed
Greatly, have suffered greatly, both with those
That loved me, and alone; on shore, and when
Through scudding drifts **the rainy Hyades**   10
Vexed the dim sea. I am become a name;

"the rainy Hyades"—A group of stars in the constellation Taurus. When they rose, people expected rain.

For always roaming with a hungry heart
Much have I seen and known—cities of men
And manners, climates, councils, governments,
Myself not least, but honored of them all—   15
And drunk delight of battle with my peers,
Far on the ringing plains of windy Troy.
I am a part of all that I have met;
Yet all experience is an arch wherethrough
Gleams that untraveled world, whose margin fades   20
For ever and ever when I move.
How dull it is to pause, to make an end,
To rust unburnished, not to shine in use!
As though to breathe were life. Life piled on life
Were all too little, and of one to me   25
Little remains; but every hour is saved
From that eternal silence, something more,
A bringer of new things; and vile it were
For some three suns to store and hoard myself,
And this gray spirit yearning in desire   30
To follow knowledge like a sinking star,
Beyond the utmost bound of human thought.

Romare Bearden, *The Return of Ulysses,* 20th c. Art © Romare Bearden Foundation/Licensed by VAGA, New York, NY. While her husband was away, Penelope was besieged by suitors who wanted her to go on to another marriage. She delayed them, saying she could not marry until she completed a shroud for her aged father-in-law. She wove the garment during the day, and unraveled it at night to delay her suitors. The loom in the lower left is a tribute to her struggle.

    This is my son, mine own Telemachus,
To whom I leave the scepter and the isle—
Well-loved of me, discerning to fulfill   35
This labor by slow prudence **to make mild
A rugged people,** and through soft degrees
Subdue them to the useful and the good.
Most blameless is he, centered in the sphere

". . . to make mild a rugged people"—Whereas Ulysses urges his men to continue their adventures, Telemachus represents the opposite type of person, the wise and patient administrator.

Of common duties, decent not to fail 40
In offices of tenderness, and **pay**
Meet adoration to my household gods,
When I am gone. He works his work, I mine.

There lies the port; the vessel puffs her sail:
There gloom the dark, broad seas. My mariners, 45
Souls that have toiled, and wrought, and thought with me—
That ever with a frolic welcome took
The thunder and the sunshine, and opposed
Free hearts, free foreheads you and I are old;
Old age hath yet his honor and his toil. 50
Death closes all; all but something ere the end,
Some work of noble note, may yet be done,
Not unbecoming men that strove with Gods.
The lights begin to twinkle from the rocks;
The long day wanes; the slow moon climbs; the deep 55
Moans round with many voices. Come, my friends.
'Tis not too late to seek a newer world.
Push off, and sitting well in order smite
The sounding furrows; for my purpose holds
To sail beyond the sunset, and the baths 60
Of all the western stars, until I die.
It may be that the gulfs will wash us down;
It may be we shall touch the **Happy Isles,**
And see the great Achilles, whom we knew.
Though much is taken, much abides; and though 65
We are not now that strength which in old days
Moved earth and heaven, that which we are, we are:
One equal temper of heroic hearts,
Made weak by time and fate, but strong in will
To strive, to seek, to find, and not to yield. 70
(1842)

> "pay meet adoration to my household gods, when I am gone"—This is a concern that would have been very important for the ancient warrior.

> "To sail beyond the sunset"—In ancient Greek cosmology, the stars set into the water that surrounded the flat earth. Thus, Ulysses knows he is taking a tremendous risk in this expedition.

> **Happy Isles** Elysium, or the Isles of the Dead, were thought to be in the far western ocean. This was the place where heroes like Achilles were believed to live after death. Compare this idea to that of Valhalla in the *Prose Edda*, Ch. 18, p. 225.

William Butler Yeats (1865–1939)

William Butler Yeats was born in Dublin, but his family's heritage connected him to both Ireland and England. His ancestors had come from England to settle in Ireland. Yeats lived in London for most of his teenage years, and in adulthood he lived alternately in Dublin and London, as well as going out to the Irish countryside in Sligo, the home of his mother's family.

His connection to these three different places influenced Yeats' development as a poet. In London he worked with the important poets of the day, who emphasized an elevated, literary language. From the unsophisticated, natural people of Sligo he learned a strong attachment to local folklore and a sense of language influenced by Gaelic, the native language of the area. In Dublin he interacted with people who vigorously supported the revival of traditional Irish culture and encouraged the political nationalism that such movements engender. Yeats was at the forefront of this work, founding the Irish National Theatre in Dublin in 1899. However, Yeats' contributions as a poet were recognized well beyond his native lands; in 1923, he was the recipient of the Nobel Prize for Literature.

The two poems by Yeats, "Leda and the Swan" and "The Second Coming," illustrate his views on the political and cultural situation in Ireland and include his ideas about the dissolution of his contemporary civilization. By alluding to classical mythology and the Bible, he strengthens the effect of his work on the reader. For example, in "Leda and the Swan," he draws on a story about Zeus, the head of the Greek gods. According to this story, Zeus often visited earth in animal form, and his union with Leda produced two daughters, Helen and Clytemnestra. Helen's elopement with the Trojan Paris caused the destruction of Troy, and Clytemnestra murdered her husband, Agamemnon. Only a small part of this mythology actually appears in the poem, which is about Zeus' affair with Leda. However, knowing the full background can enrich our interpretation of the sonnet, because Yeats draws upon the atmosphere created by this mythological background.

In his writings about his poetry, Yeats notes his changing view of this poem. At one time he explained that he had originally been approached by a political journal for a poem, and envisioned "Leda and the Swan" as a metaphor for the domination of Ireland by England. However, as he worked on the poem, he felt it lose the political connotation and take on a much more universal significance. The poem reflected his views on the development of civilization, according to which Zeus' visit to Leda corresponded to the annunciation by the angel to the Virgin Mary that she was to bear Jesus, the Son of God. Yeats considered this union of Zeus and Leda the beginning of Greek civilization, as he viewed the birth of Christ as the beginning of the next great civilization.

In "The Second Coming," Yeats also represents a world view combining Judaeo-Christian mythology with his own personal religious discoveries. He was a follower of a group called the anthroposophists, who tried to develop a new and more personal religion. Much of anthroposophy is based on the religious experiences of individuals. From his own experiences and those of others, Yeats developed a personal philosophy that included the view that we (and society) experience life in a circular pattern, (a "gyre"), like a spiral that gets wider as it gets higher. From this vantage point, as we experience new events, we have built upon—and can see—our old experiences. In "The Second Coming," he speaks of "the widening gyre." As the gyre expands out of control, "the center cannot hold": civilization is falling apart. Yeats saw his society as standing on the edge of a defunct civilization, awaiting the start of a new one. He believed that civilization and culture as we know it would soon come to an end and be replaced by new ones.

Leda and the Swan*

"the great wings"—Except for the title, we might not guess that the great wings belong to a swan; and when we know that Zeus often came to women in the shape of an animal, we can make the connection with the classical Greek myth concerning the tragic fate of the children engendered by this coupling.

A sudden blow: **the great wings** beating still
Above the staggering girl, her thighs caressed
By the dark webs, her nape caught in his bill,
He holds her helpless breast upon his breast.

How can those terrified vague fingers push   5
The feathered glory from her loosening thighs?
And how can body, laid in that white rush,
But feel the strange heart beating where it lies?

---

*"Leda and the Swan." Reprinted with the permission of Scribner, an imprint of Simon and Schuster Adult Publishing Group. From *The Collected Works of W.B. Yeats, Volume I: The Poems, Revised,* edited by Richard J. Finnegan, 214–215. Copyright 1928 by The Macmillan Company; copyright renewed 1956 by Georgie Yeats.

A shudder in the loins engenders there
The broken wall, the burning roof and tower   10
And Agamemnon dead.

                             Being so caught up,
So mastered by the brute blood of the air,
Did she put on his knowledge with his power
Before the indifferent beak could let her drop?
(1924)

The Second Coming*

 Turning and turning in the widening gyre
The falcon cannot hear the falconer;
Things fall apart; the center cannot hold;
Mere anarchy is loosed upon the world,
The blood-dimmed tide is loosed, and everywhere   5
The ceremony of innocence is drowned;

The best lack all conviction, while the worst
Are full of passionate intensity.
Surely some revelation is at hand;
Surely the Second Coming is at hand.   10
The Second Coming! Hardly are those words out
When a vast image out of **Spiritus Mundi**
Troubles my sight: somewhere in sands of the desert
A shape with **lion body and the head of a man,**
A gaze blank and pitiless as the sun,   15
Is moving its slow thighs, while all about it
Reel shadows of the indignant desert birds.
The darkness drops again; but now I know
That twenty centuries of stony sleep
Were vexed to nightmare by a rocking cradle,   20
And what rough beast, its hour come round at last,
Slouches towards Bethlehem to be born?
(1920)

"The broken wall"—In the sonnet form, the final six lines comment on the situation presented in the first eight. Here, the "broken wall" can refer to the loss of Leda's virginity. But it can also be tied to the destruction of the house—both the structure and the inhabitants—of Agamemnon. He was murdered by his wife, Clytemnestra, for having had their daughter, Iphigenia, put to death. In turn, Clytemnestra and her complicitous lover, Aegisthus, were put to death by her son, Orestes.

"The Second Coming"—This title is ironic. The usual connotation is for the coming of Christ at the end of the world to judge all human beings. The purpose of his first coming was to redeem mankind from its sins. Yeats' "second coming" is based on his spiral theory of civilization, rather than on traditional religious belief.

"Mere anarchy is loosed upon the world"—Some scholars interpret this as a reference to the Russian Revolution in 1917.

Spritus Mundi Literally, "Spirit of the World." According to the concept, all individual souls are connected through the "Great Memory." Yeats considered this to be a universal subconscious where the past of the human race was preserved. Compare this idea with Jung's collective unconscious, Ch. 32, p. 469.

"lion body and the head of a man"—This describes the sphinx, which is more often portrayed as having a woman's head. See the story of Oedipus, Ch. 19, p. 231.

Hilda Doolittle (1886–1961)

Hilda Doolittle, a student of classical languages and literature at Bryn Mawr College in the late nineteenth century, has become more keenly appreciated in the later twentieth century. She had collaborated for many years with Ezra Pound and was active in literary circles in England, her adopted home.

   Her published poems include lyrics such as "Helen" and "Leda," both of which illustrate her affinity for updating themes from Greek mythology.

*"The Second Coming." Reprinted with the permission of Scribner, an imprint of Simon and Schuster Adult Publishing Group. From *The Collected Works of W.B. Yeats, Volume I: The Poems, Revised,* edited by Richard J. Finnegan, 187. Copyright 1924 by The Macmillan Company; copyright renewed 1952 by Bertha Georgie Yeats.

Leda and the Swan, Roman 1st c. C.E.

Most interesting in "Leda" is the physical absence of the female figure, except in the title. Compared with Yeats' sonnet, "Leda and the Swan," this work seems at first to describe a quiet sunset scene on a marsh. Only when we reach the last verse, and only if we know the story of the chief Greek god Zeus coming to women in the guise of animals, do we connect the Leda of the title with the red swan of the verse.

Leda*

Where **the slow river**
meets the tide,
a red swan lifts red wings
and darker beak,
and underneath **the purple down**   5
of his soft breast
uncurls his coral feet.

Through the **deep purple**
of the dying heat
of sun and mist,   10
the level ray of sun-beam
has caressed
the lily with **dark breast,**
and flecked with richer gold
its golden crest.   15

Where the slow lifting
of the tide,
floats into the river
and slowly drifts
among the reeds,   20
and lifts the yellow flags,
he floats
where tide and river meet.

Ah kingly kiss—
no more regret   25
nor old deep memories
to mar the bliss;
where the low sedge is thick,
the gold day-lily
outspreads and rests   30
beneath soft fluttering
of red swan wings
and the warm quivering
of the red swan's breast.
(1919)

"the slow river . . . the purple down of his soft breast"—The image here is serene and soft, especially compared with the opening of Yeats' Leda poem: "A sudden blow."

"deep purple of the dying heat . . . dark breast and flecked with richer gold"—Purple and gold are regal colors, suggesting the status of this stately bird.

"he floats where tide and river meet"—Again, the vocabulary suggests passivity and calm on the part of the swan.

"Ah kingly kiss"—This first indication of another being's presence continues the allusion to a regal figure.

"beneath soft fluttering"—Compared with the tumult and violence of Yeats' counterpart poem, the description here belies the nature of the action.

Anne Sexton (1928–1974)

Anne Sexton, the noted American poet and recipient of numerous awards, lived a psychologically troubled life and began writing poetry in 1952 on the advice of her psychiatrist. She raised three daughters and taught creative writing in prestigious programs while battling mental illness. Even the title of her first volume of poetry, *To Bedlam and Part-Way Back* (1960), reflects her intense confrontation of the situation in her work.

Her final two collections also reveal the very personal nature of her work: *The Death Notebooks,* on mourning the deaths of her loved ones, and *The Awful Rowing Towards God,* which expresses a hope of abandoning doubt and finding God. This last work was written during her final hospital stay before her suicide in 1974.

For students of mythology and the fairy tale, Sexton's 1971 collection, *Transformations,* provides an opportunity to enjoy the poems as "insiders" of sorts. Each of the poems in the collection "transforms" a Grimm Brothers' tale into a late-twentieth-century commentary on the traditional tale. Like Angela Carter's "Beauty and the Beast" reworking (see "The Tiger's Bride," Ch. 44, p. 670), these poems preserve the essential moves of the classical tale. (For more on moves as defined by Propp, see Ch. 34, p. 512.) However, the emphasis on the old moral code has been replaced by a spirited, almost impertinent, commentary on the characters and their activities. For example, in "Snow White and the Seven Dwarfs," Snow White is a "dumb bunny" for disobeying the dwarfs and opening the door to her stepmother.

The many comparisons—the similes and metaphors—used to describe people and events move the feeling of the work to a slangy, even cartoon-like, level. For example, the dwarfs are "those little hot dogs," and when they revive Snow White after the poisoned comb incident, "She opened her eyes as wide as Orphan Annie." However, there is a serious reason for this wit and humor: whereas in the traditional tale, the teller is distanced and the emphasis is exclusively on the events of the story, in *Transformations* the first-person narrator is sympathetic but irreverent. Using the surprising, contemporary metaphors allows Sexton to portray the main characters as flawed individuals rather than as paradigms of virtue.

Some of our enjoyment comes from having our expectations suddenly undercut. For example, if we know the Grimms' tales and are familiar with the classical fairy tale format and moral codes, we are surprised when the queen is presented with the heart she believes is Snow White's and she "chewed it up like cube steak."

In fact, Sexton surprises us in other ways. For example, where most revisions focus on updating the morals and overturning the codes of conduct implicit in the originals, Sexton updates by satirizing and shifting the point of view—but ultimately shocks by returning to the old values. For an example of this, read the closing lines of the following poem, which seems to say that Snow White turns out to be like all women of the old stereotype. The final four lines, which are certainly not characteristic of the Grimm Brothers in tone or style, are what we might expect of a vibrant, irreverent poet like Anne Sexton.

Snow White and the Seven Dwarfs*

> **No matter what life you lead**
> **the virgin is a lovely number:**
> cheeks as fragile as cigarette paper,
> arms and legs made of Limoges,
> lips like Vin De Rhone,   5

"No matter what life you lead"—Like the other poems in *Transformations*, this begins with a preface that introduces Sexton's intended emphasis.

"the virgin is a lovely number"—Slangy language is the first clue to Sexton's irreverent treatment of the classic tale. It also depersonalizes the virgin, taking away her individuality, and focusing on her more universal message.

---

* "Snow White and the Seven Dwarfs." From *Transformations* by Anne Sexton 3–9. Copyright © 1971 by Anne Sexton. Reprinted by permission of Houghton Mifflin Company. All rights reserved.

rolling her china-blue doll eyes
open and shut.
Open to say,
Good Day, Mama,
and shut for the thrust   10
of the unicorn.
She is unsoiled.
She is as white as a bonefish.

Once there was a lovely virgin
called Snow White,   15
Say she was thirteen,
Her stepmother,
a beauty in her own right,
though eaten, of course, by age,
would hear of no beauty surpassing her own.   20
Beauty is a simple passion,
but, oh, my friends, in the end
you will dance the fire dance in iron shoes.
The stepmother had a mirror to which she referred—
something like the weather forecast—   25
a mirror that proclaimed
the one beauty of the land.
She would ask,
Looking glass upon the wall,
who is fairest of us all.   30
Pride pumped in her like poison.

Suddenly one day the mirror replied,
Queen, you are full fair, 'tis true,
but Snow White is fairer than you.

Until that moment Snow White   35
had been **no more important**
than a dust mouse under the bed.
But now the queen saw brown spots on her hand
and four whiskers over her lip
so she condemned Snow White   40
to be hacked to death.
Bring me her heart, she said to the hunter,
and I will salt it and eat it.
The hunter, however, let his prisoner go
and brought a boar's heart back to the castle   45
The queen chewed it up like a cube steak.
Now I am fairest, she said,
lapping her slim white fingers.

Snow White walked in the wildwood
for weeks and weeks.   50

"Once there was"—The tale begins with a traditional fairy-tale opening.

"but, oh, my friends"—Sexton addresses the reader directly. In classical tales, there is no room for the reader, since the storyteller concentrates on the action, not the audience.

"something like the weather forecast"—The mirror is not magic, although it does produce mysterious information, which Sexton jokingly equates with the weather forecast.

"no more important than a dust mouse under the bed. But now"—Nothing has actually changed except the queen's perception. In a classic tale, this psychological shift would not be expressed so graphically.

"lapping her slim white fingers"—This sign of physical satisfaction also represents the more grotesque moral satisfaction.

At each turn there were twenty doorways
and at each stood a hungry wolf,
his tongue lolling out like a worm.
The birds called out lewdly,
talking like pink parrots,   55
and the snakes hung down in loops,
each a noose for her sweet white neck.
On the seventh week
she came to the seventh mountain
and there she found the dwarf house.   60
It was as droll as a honeymoon cottage
and completely equipped with
seven beds, seven chairs, seven forks
and seven chamber pots.
Snow White ate seven chicken livers   65
and lay down, at last, to sleep.

The dwarfs, those little hot dogs,
walked three times around Snow White,
the sleeping virgin. They were wise
and wattled like small czars.   70
Yes. It's a good omen,
they said, and will bring us luck.
They stood on tiptoes to watch
Snow White wake up. She told them
about the mirror and the killer-queen   75
and they asked her to stay and keep house.
Beware of your stepmother,
they said.
Soon she will know you are here.
While we are away in the mines   80
during the day, you must not
open the door.

Looking glass upon the wall . . .
The mirror told
and so the queen dressed herself in rags   85
and went out like a peddler to trap Snow White.
She went across seven mountains.
She came to the dwarf house
and Snow White opened the door
and bought a bit of lacing.   90
The queen fastened it tightly
around her bodice,
as tight as an Ace bandage,
so tight that Snow White swooned.
She lay on the floor, a plucked daisy.   95
When the dwarfs came home they undid the lace
and she revived miraculously.

"The birds called out lewdly, talking like pink parrots, and the snakes hung down in loops"—Although the forest is threatening, the cartoon-like character of the description lightens the effect.

"It was as droll as a honeymoon cottage"—The irony is that the virgin and "those little hot dogs" are not at all suited to make use of a "honeymoon cottage."

"Looking glass upon the wall"—Sexton expects the reader to be familiar enough with the tale that the incantation does not need to be repeated.

"She was as full of life as soda pop."—This line is actually unnecessary after "she revived miraculously," but it adds to the tone of the work by focusing on the light and ephemeral image of soda pop.

She was as full of life as soda pop.
Beware of your stepmother,
they said. She will try once more.   100

Looking glass upon the wall . . .
Once more the mirror told
and once more the queen dressed in rags
and once more Snow White opened the door.
This time she bought a poison comb,   105
a curved eight-inch scorpion,
and put it in her hair and swooned again.
The dwarfs returned and took out the comb
and she revived miraculously.
She opened her eyes as wide as Orphan Annie.   110
Beware, beware, they said,
but the mirror told,
the queen came,
Snow White, the dumb bunny,
opened the door   115
and she bit into a poison apple
and fell down for the final time.
When the dwarfs returned
they undid her bodice,
they looked for a comb,   120
but it did no good.
Though they washed her with wine
and rubbed her with butter
it was to no avail.
She lay as still as a gold piece.   125
The seven dwarfs could not bring themselves
to bury her in the black ground
so they made a glass coffin
and set it upon the seventh mountain
so that all who passed by   130
could peek in upon her beauty.
A prince came one June day
and would not budge.
He stayed so long his hair turned green
and still he would not leave.   135
The dwarfs took pity upon him
and gave him **the glass Snow White—**
its doll's eyes shut forever—
to keep in his far-off castle.
As the prince's men carried the coffin   140
they stumbled and dropped it
and the chunk of apple flew out
of her throat and she woke up miraculously.

And thus Snow White became the prince's bride.
The wicked queen was invited to the wedding feast   145

"She opened her eyes . . . beware . . . the mirror told, the queen came"—In four short lines, the essentials of the plot are covered. The value of the poem lies not in recounting a story that the reader already knows, but in giving it renewed significance through contemporary narrative style and wry commentary.

Hans Makart, *Snow White receives the poisoned comb*, 1872.

"the glass Snow White—its doll's eyes shut forever"—Referring to Snow White as a doll and "it" removes her from the human realm and makes it unnecessary for her to exhibit genuine emotion. She is an invention, not a person; the reader is free to enjoy the joke.

and when she arrived there were
red-hot iron shoes,
in the manner of red-hot roller skates,
clamped upon her feet.
First your toes will smoke   150
and then your heels will turn black
and you will fry upward like a frog,
she was told.
And so she danced until she was dead,
a subterranean figure,   155
her tongue flicking in and out
like a gas jet.
Meanwhile Snow White held court,
rolling her china-blue doll eyes open and shut
and **sometimes referring to her mirror**   160
as women do.

"red-hot iron shoes"—The original Grimm Brothers version says she would have to dance in iron shoes over red-hot coals until she died. This description is therefore accurate, even if much more disturbingly graphic.

"her tongue flicking in and out like a gas jet"—Again, the cartoon image intrudes, causing the reader to shift emotional gears.

"Meanwhile . . . as women do."—A change from the "happily ever after" ending, these lines show that Snow White is no different from others and that she might just follow in the stepmother's footsteps.

Further Reading

Middlebrook, Diane Wood. *Anne Sexton, a Biography.* Boston, MA: Houghton Mifflin, 1991.

Sexton, Anne, *Transformations.* Boston, MA: Houghton Mifflin, 1971.

43

Mythological Themes in Native American Literature

WHAT TO EXPECT . . . Although Native American sacred rites and narratives have almost always been passed down in the particular tribe's own language, there is a long history of Native American writers in English, often to protest injustice by the English-speaking world.

Myth is an integral part of Native American fiction, since the stories are anchored in the ancient beliefs of the storyteller. Leslie Marmon Silko's "Yellow Woman" illustrates the nature of storytelling by incorporating her mythic heritage into contemporary life and bringing her characters together with mythic figures across cultures and time. Using traditional storytelling techniques, Silko shows how the ancient Yellow Woman myth is an integral part of her culture's psyche. She accomplishes this through interweaving the traditional story with a modern version and by emphasizing the duality of the main characters: they live in both the real and the mythical worlds, that is, they are part of the contemporary society and the timeless age represented by the mythology of their culture. The resulting story is polyvalent: there is no one right way to interpret it. As you read through this story, list for yourself all the valid interpretations you think of as you read, noting both the contradictory ones and the ones that can be rationalized (see Ch. 25, p. 363) into a noncontradictory narrative.

As you read, consider how the man in the story can also be considered a trickster (see Ch. 24, p. 353) or, more particularly, a *ka'tsina* figure (p. 646). Note also Yellow Woman's activities as representative of the steps in Joseph Campbell's delineation of the journey of the hero (Ch. 14, p. 161). Consider a Jungian analysis of the story: what archetypes can you identify?

Until the 1990s, Native American creative literature was not likely to be part of the curriculum in United States schools and colleges. Despite a lively public interest in the creative arts of Native Americans, especially jewelry, pottery, weaving, and ancient artifacts, American Indian poets are only slowly entering the literary canon dealt with in English and Comparative Literature classes.

FROM THE BEGINNING

Like other ancient peoples, the first Americans already had an oral tradition when they crossed the Bering Straits from Asia to present-day Alaska during the Ice Age. This tradition has continued through their history to the present.

As contact with European colonists increased in what is now the continental United States and Canada, the native peoples found that their lives, their cultures, and their languages were at risk. Many learned Eastern Native Americans wrote practical works to make their culture known to white society. Some learned English at missionary schools as early as the late seventeenth century, but only in 1772 was the first work by a Native American published: Mohegan

Samson Occom's "Sermon Preached at the Execution of Moses Paul." As a Protestant minister, Occom was interested in influencing his own people. However, most early American Indian writing in English was intended to protest injustice in a form that the colonizers could understand. They continued their own sacred rites and narratives in their own languages.

In the 1870s the U.S. government decided that Native American children could best be "civilized" by educating them in English-only boarding schools, like the Carlisle School in Pennsylvania. One of the earliest students, Lakota Sioux Luther Standing Bear, published "My People the Sioux" as an adult in 1928 to explain the conditions of his forced reculturation and his personal views to a broad audience—a tactic that others such as Yankton Sioux Zitkala-Su and Santee Sioux Charles Alexander Eastman also used successfully.

D'Arcy McNickle, who by family ties is Cree, Salish, and Kootenai, was born on the Flathead Reservation in Montana. He was of the generation that, for the most part, grew up on reservations—that is, land "reserved" for Native Americans who had actually been moved off their own ancestral lands by the government. An outstanding figure in modern Native American literature, McNickle published *The Surrounded* in 1936, the same year he joined the U.S. Bureau of Indian Affairs. While he worked for the Bureau, he was instrumental in getting bills passed that were crucial to self-governance on reservations. He is remembered especially for his successes in achieving a better life for Native Americans, though he also published novels and many scholarly nonfiction works.

However, until N. Scott Momaday's *House Made of Dawn* won a Pulitzer Prize for fiction in 1968, Native American literature had little impact on the broader American reading public. Since then, there has been a steadily growing interest accompanied by the publication of novels, short stories, and poetry by writers from a wide variety of tribal backgrounds. Most have a university education; many are professors and teachers of writing.

SOME GENERAL CHARACTERISTICS OF CONTEMPORARY NATIVE AMERICAN FICTION

Like their colonial era works in English, much contemporary fiction by Native Americans represents Indian life and culture in relation to continuing problems with the federal government. Examples of this include Vizenor's *Darkness in St. Louis Bearheart,* which presents satirical views of federal Indian agents and tribal officials, as well as others on the reservation who do not fully embrace native beliefs. Welch's *Winter in the Blood* and *Fool's Crow* similarly address issues concerning life on the reservation and the centrality of nature in Native American culture. Modoc tribe member Michael Dorris' *The Broken Cord: A Family's Struggle with Fetal Alcohol Syndrome,* is a nonfiction account describing the tragic life of an adopted son.

A newly emerging characteristic of more recent Native American literary works is the prevalence of poetic style and mythical themes. In the acclaimed short story "Yellow Woman" (p. 644), Leslie Silko interweaves stories from Native American oral tradition with contemporary characters and settings to fashion a haunting tale set in the present. In *Ceremony,* Silko's extensive use of oral tradition enriches not only by informing the reader about Indian culture, but also by proposing that dealing with the world via native ways can restore individuals as well as civilizations. In fact, some scholars maintain that by bringing together situations from Western thought and experiences within the Native American tradition, contemporary Indian writers are helping to build bridges between cultures that have not understood one another very often or very well. Thus we see a new style of achieving some of the same goals intended by the practical literature of Native Americans in the colonial era.

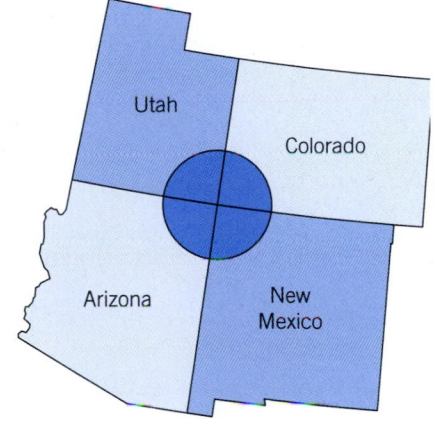

■ Four Corners

The term "Four Corners" refers to the intersecting corners of four states: Colorado, Utah, New Mexico, and Arizona. This region is home to some 300,000 Native Americans, including the Navajo and Hopi Indian Reservations. Because Native Americans from different tribes were relegated to this area, which was "reserved" for them, the cultures of different Indian tribes sometimes intersect and interact there. The story in this chapter is set here.

MYTH AS AN INTEGRAL PART OF NATIVE AMERICAN FICTION

The storytelling that underlies Native American fiction is actually the glue in these stories—the force attracting readers from the different cultures, across time and space. In these stories, the linear time that Western culture relies on is often absent, and dreams may well be as real and as dynamic as any waking, physical experience. These ambiguities allow for a seamless interaction between the past and present, between ancestors and offspring. Thus, characters are able to move freely among the old stories retold or reenacted; the mythic tradition is alive in the present.

These stories are anchored in the ancient belief system of the storyteller, who is bringing the reader inside the narrative. As this happens, reality is brought into question, and understanding and meaning come from the narrative itself. For this process to be successful, the storyteller must evoke the art of traditional storytelling, even if the work is intended from the outset to be printed. Paul Zolbrod, in *Reading the Voice: Native American Oral Poetry on the Page,* stresses the impact of the oral tradition in contemporary works. Although his work focuses heavily on poetry, the principles also apply to prose. In explaining his "wish to examine the traditional Native American material from within, according to its own manner of composition, its medium of transmission, and its original purpose" (8), he notes that the world view of a culture as expressed in Native American stories with a mythological basis is rooted in "a shared sacred vision of the universe" (2). As we showed in Chapter 27, when a society is guided by an oral tradition, its ceremonies are an important part of the community life cycle, and the link to the sacred is experienced in daily life.

Not all of the mythological references in these stories will necessarily be understood immediately by the reader whose belief system is firmly rooted in the Western mainstream. William Bevis emphasizes the obstacles: "In the handling of plot and nature the novels of McNickle, Momaday, Silko, and Welch are Native American. . . . [T]hese works are drenched in a tribalism most whites neither understand nor expect in the works of contemporary Indians, much less when they are professors" (15); all four have taught at universities. However, as noted earlier, Native American fiction offers opportunities for greater reciprocal understanding. Besides, these are very good stories!

Further Reading

Zolbrod, Paul. *Reading the Voice: Native American Oral Poetry on the Page.* Salt Lake City, UT: University of Utah Press, 1995.

Yellow Woman

LESLIE MARMON SILKO

Leslie Marmon Silko's grandfather was a white man from the Midwest, and her mother was from the Laguna Pueblo people. Silko, whose ancestry also includes a Mexican line, was born in 1948 and grew up in the Laguna Pueblo in New Mexico, the home of her maternal family. As a child, she spoke Keresan, a Native American language, and learned stories told by her mother, her aunts, and numerous others in the pueblo. As an adult, Silko finished her formal education at the University of New Mexico and has achieved recognition as a major writer and storyteller. Her many awards include a MacArthur Fellowship and citation by the State of New Mexico as a living cultural treasure.

In her collection titled *Storyteller,* Silko explains that the story "Yellow Woman" illustrates the nature of storytelling, a concept central to her own thinking and one she has described in various essays and interviews. "Storytelling brings us together, despite great distances between cultures, despite great distances in time" (*Yellow Woman and a Beauty of the Spirit,* 72). That is, as members of a group tell stories, they pass along vital information about their heritage, while incorporating the significance of that heritage into contemporary life. In *Storyteller,* Silko speaks specifically about the influence her great aunt, Susie, had on her as a child. Silko describes her with admiration as a "brilliant woman, a scholar of her own making," who was even more important because:

> She was of a generation, the last here at Laguna,
> that passed down an entire culture
> by word of mouth
> an entire history
> an entire vision of the world
> which depended upon memory
> and retelling by subsequent generations.

Jar (olla). Acoma people, U.S.A. Early 20th c. This pot shows a traditional design of the Pueblo people.

   In Silko's view, storytelling is a primary vehicle for the transmission of cultural information. This corresponds to Levi-Strauss' explanation of the role of mythology (see Ch. 20, p. 281): traditional stories represent events passed down through generations. As the stories are told and retold, the events may be altered or even replaced by other elements, depending on variations or developments in the society's experiences. However, as the story travels through time, it carries information about earlier generations to their descendents, who in turn modify the story according to their experiences and pass it on. Levi-Strauss would note that this accumulation of stories comprises the culture of the society. As we mentioned in the introduction to this part (p. 617), the study of mythology encourages us to be open to other cultures and literatures, and the more we understand about the stories underlying a literary work, the deeper will be our satisfaction in reading it.

   Silko has noted that many variations of the Yellow Woman story exist—it is called "Kochininako" in the Keres tradition—and she herself has also written others. In a sense, because the story is about a woman lured away by a mysterious figure, it could be classified under the Aarne–Thompson motif of abduction (See Introduction to Part 6, "Folktale and Myth," p. 495). However, a literary work allows or even elicits multiple levels of interpretation, so we can ascribe different kinds of motivations to the characters and find multiple layers of meaning in the story. In the version included here, as in many others, the protagonist is an independent thinker, attached to her culture but not averse to going against conventions, and intrigued by the excitement of the taboo. The woman is not looking for trouble, but does go out alone, beyond the security of the pueblo. For more on this idea of striking out into the unknown, see Joseph Campbell's discussion of the quest of the hero (Ch. 14, p. 159). The hero's journey includes leaving home, traveling to a distant and unfamiliar destination, going through an initiation, and ultimately returning home to the recognition of one's own family.

   The power of Silko's story is enhanced by its first-person narrator, a contemporary woman who accepts her connection to two worlds: contemporary society and the timeless age represented by the mythology of her people. Through her narration, the reader is given a vivid sense of her perception that she is turning into the mythical Yellow Woman. At the same time, she maintains a hold on her everyday reality: the pueblo is just on the other side of the mesa, her family will talk about her disappearance, and so forth. The woman in this story is not alone in her duality: the story also represents its other character, the man Silva, as both human and mythological, a figure viewed by some as a *ka'tsina*. Helen Jaskoski explains that *ka'tsinas* are supernatural beings closely identified with natural elements and animals (34). The *ka'tsina* is often seen as a trickster, a figure functioning at the edge of society and representing the forces that work to question or challenge established authority in that society (see Ch. 21, p. 297). In fact, the story highlights the trickster elements in Silva's progressively stronger seduction techniques. Another characteristic of the trickster is often his alienation from society, his "otherness."

Kachina spirit. These figures are used in communal dances to evoke spirits repesenting societal values. The tradition is not Navajo, but Hopi.

This story comes from: Leslie Marmon Silko, *Storyteller.**

"I looked at him beside me"—The story is told as a reflection in which the Yellow Woman looks back on her experiences. We are not told until much later in the story what her temporal perspective is.

"the same river"—Nature provides a tangible reckoning point in time and space.

"I remembered him asleep"— Memory and imagination prompt her to go back to him.

"I knelt down to touch him"—In waking him, she undoes all of her preparations to leave. Thus, she cooperates with the tradition that Yellow Woman stays with the man for a longer time. Her action also brings to mind the Proppian function called complicity, in which the victim cooperates with the machinations of the villain (see Ch. 34, p. 504).

He may have alienated himself from his own culture, or may be an intruder from another. In this Yellow Woman version, it is not clear where Silva comes from, but the woman assumes he is Navajo, a nearby but "other" tribe. This transference moves the cause of the danger from her own people to a suspicious stranger.

In other Yellow Woman stories, the seducer is Arrow-Boy, also a Pueblo hero figure. Arrow-Boy is a variant of the figure Dirty Boy, who often appears in other North American Indian tales. Generally, the figure is portrayed as lazy, dirty, or physically disabled, but actually turns out to be a handsome hero. In the typical story, this Dirty Boy responds to the kindness of an acquaintance—usually someone viewed negatively by his own group. For the reader familiar with Navajo tradition, Silko's story may raise, and frustrate, the expectation that woman will serve as the kindly figure who will transform Silva. Anthropologist Ruth Benedict notes that, like many Native American mythical figures, Yellow Woman also can appear as a variety of characters, including a bride, a witch, a chief's daughter, bear woman or even an ogress or female *ka'tsina*. (For more on Benedict, see Ch. 8, p. 90.)

The more familiar we are with these aspects of storytelling in Native American culture, the more fully we can enjoy stories like the following one. As she tries to interpret her place in her world and figure out what is happening to her, Silko's Yellow Woman both grows closer to her own traditions and comes to share in broader human psychological challenges. As Silko herself has said, "Pueblo expression resembles something like a spider's web—with many little threads radiating from the center, crisscrossing one another. . . . My task [as storyteller] is a formidable one: I ask you to set aside a number of basic approaches you have been using and will probably continue to use, and instead, to approach language from the Pueblo perspective, one that embraces the whole of creation and the whole of history and time" (*Yellow Woman and a Beauty of the Spirit,* 48–49).

My thigh clung to his with dampness, and I watched the sun rising up through the tamaracks and willows. The small brown water birds came to the river and hopped across the mud, leaving brown scratches in the alkali-white crust. They bathed in the river silently. I could hear the water, almost at our feet where the narrow fast channel bubbled and washed green ragged moss and fern leaves.

I looked at him beside me, rolled in the red blanket on the white river sand. I cleaned the sand out of the cracks between my toes, squinting because the sun was above the willow trees. I looked at him for the last time, sleeping on the white river sand.

I felt hungry and followed the river south the way we had come the afternoon before, following our footprints that were already blurred by lizard tracks and bug trails. The horses were still lying down, and the black one whinnied when he saw me but he did not get up—maybe it was because the corral was made out of thick cedar branches and the horses had not yet felt the sun like I had. I tried to look beyond the pale red mesas to the pueblo. I knew it was there, even if I could not see it, on the sand-rock hill above the river, **the same river** that moved past me now and had reflected the moon last night.

The horse felt warm underneath me. He shook his head and pawed the sand. The bay whinnied and leaned against the gate trying to follow, and **I remembered him asleep** in the red blanket beside the river. I slid off the horse and tied him close to the other horse, I walked north with the river again, and the white sand broke loose in footprints over footprints.

"Wake up."

He moved in the blanket and turned his face to me with his eyes still closed. **I knelt down to touch** him.

"I'm leaving."

He smiled now, eyes still closed. "You are coming with me, remember?" He sat up now with his bare dark chest and belly in the sun.

"Where?"

"To my place."

"And will I come back?"

He pulled his pants on. I walked away from him, feeling him behind me and smelling the willows.

"Yellow Woman," he said.

I turned to face him. "Who are you?" I asked.

He laughed and knelt on the low, sandy bank, washing his face in the river. "**Last night you guessed my name,** and you knew why I had come."

I stared past him at the shallow moving water and tried to remember the night, but could only see the moon in the water and remember his warmth around me.

"But I only said that you were him and that I was the Yellow Woman—**I'm not really her**—I have my own name and I come from the pueblo on the other side of the mesa. Your name is Silva and you are a stranger I met by the river yesterday afternoon."

He laughed softly. "What happened yesterday has nothing to do with what you will do today, Yellow Woman."

"I know—that's what I'm saying—**the old stories** about the *ka'tsina* spirit and the Yellow Woman **can't mean us.**"

My old grandpa liked to tell those stories best. There is one about Badger and Coyote who went hunting and were gone all day, and when the sun was going down they found a house. There was a girl living there alone, and she had light hair and eyes and she told them that they could sleep with her. Coyote wanted to be with her all night so he sent Badger into a prairie-dog hole, telling him he thought he saw something in it. As soon as Badger crawled in, **Coyote blocked up the entrance** with rocks and hurried back to Yellow Woman.

"Come here," he said gently.

He touched my neck and I moved close to him to feel his breathing and to hear his heart. **I was wondering** if Yellow Woman had known who she was—if she knew she would become a part of the stories. Maybe she'd had another name that her husband and relatives called her so that only the *ka'tsina* from the north and the storytellers would know her as Yellow Woman. But I didn't go on; I felt him all around me, pushing me down into the white river sand.

Yellow Woman went away with the spirit from the north and lived with him and his relatives. She was gone for a long time, but then one day she came back and brought twin boys.

"Do you know the story?"

"What story?" He smiled and pulled me close to him as he said this. I was afraid lying there on the red blanket. All I could know was the way he felt, warm, damp, his body beside me. **This is the way it happens in the stories.** I was thinking, with no thoughts beyond the moment she meets the *ka'tsina* spirit and they go.

"I don't have to go. **What they tell in stories was real only then,** back in time immemorial, like they say."

He stood up and pointed at my clothes tangled in the blanket. "Let's go," he said.

I walked beside him, breathing hard because he walked fast, his hand around my wrist. I had stopped trying to pull away from him, because his hand felt cool and the sun was high, drying the riverbed into alkali. I will see someone, eventually I will see someone, and then I will be certain that he is only a man—**some man from nearby**—and I will be sure that I am not Yellow Woman. Because she is from out of time past and I live now and I've been to school and there are highways and pickup trucks that Yellow Woman never saw.

"Yellow Woman"—He identifies her as the mythical personage.

"Last night you guessed my name"—Because of her familiarity with the Yellow Woman stories, the narrator had seen herself as the abducted woman, and thus placed him in the role of the magical *ka'tsina* that carries her off.

"I'm not really her"—The woman tries to maintain her contemporary identity. Campbell would note that the story here represents the psychological aspect of myth (see Ch. 1, p. 6).

"the old stories . . . can't mean us"—She tries again to deny her connection with the myth.

"Coyote blocked up the entrance"—For more on Coyote as a trickster, see Ch. 20, p. 287.

"I was wondering"—The narrator interprets what is happening to her. She differentiates between the Yellow Woman of the old stories and herself, but the ambiguity she finds in each event prevents her from escaping the mythical role.

"This is the way it happens in the stories . . . 'What they tell . . . was real only then'"—He tries to bring her into the story, but she continues to argue that she cannot actually be the mythical Yellow Woman.

"some man from nearby"—She expects that his "reality" will become evident when compared with a current, tangible figure. This is much the same as someone having an unpleasant experience who hopes that something will prove that the experience is "just a dream."

It was an easy ride north on horseback. I watched the change from the cottonwood trees along the river to the junipers that brushed past us in the foothills, and finally there were only pinons, and when I looked up at the rim of the mountain plateau I could see pine trees growing on the edge. Once I stopped to look down, but the pale sandstone had disappeared and the river was gone and the dark lava hills were all around. He touched my hand, not speaking, but **always singing softly** a mountain song and looking into my eyes.

I felt hungry and wondered what they were doing at home now—my mother, my grandmother, **my husband, and the baby.** Cooking breakfast, saying, "Where did she go?—maybe kidnapped." And Al going to the tribal police with the details: "She went walking along the river."

The house was made with black lava rock and red mud. It was high above the spreading miles of arroyos and long mesas. I stood there beside the black horse, looking down on the small, dim country we had passed, and I shivered.

"Yellow Woman, come inside where it's warm."

He lit a fire in the stove. It was an old stove with a round belly and an enamel coffeepot on top. There was only the stove, some faded Navajo blankets, and a bedroll and cardboard box. The floor was made of smooth adobe plaster, and there was one small window facing east. He pointed at the box.

"There's some potatoes and the frying pan." He sat on the floor with his arms around his knees pulling them close to his chest and he watched me fry the potatoes. I didn't mind him watching me because he was always watching me—he had been watching me **since I came upon him** sitting on the riverbank trimming leaves from a willow twig with his knife. We ate from the pan and he wiped the grease from his fingers on his Levi's.

"Have you brought women here before?" He smiled and kept chewing, so I said, "Do you always use the same tricks?"

"What tricks?" He looked at me like he didn't understand.

"The story about being a *ka'tsina* from the mountains. The story about Yellow Woman."

Silva was silent; his face was calm.

"I don't believe it. **Those stories couldn't happen now,**" I said.

He shook his head and said softly, "**But someday they will talk about us,** and they will say, 'Those two lived long ago when things like that happened.'"

He stood up and went out. I ate the rest of the potatoes and thought about things—about the noise the stove was making and the sound of the mountain wind outside. I remembered yesterday and the day before, and then I went outside.

I walked past the corral to the edge where the narrow trail cut through the black rim rock. I was standing in the sky with nothing around me but the wind that came down from the blue mountain peak behind me. I could see faint mountain images in the distance miles across the vast spread of mesas and valleys and plains. I wondered who was over there to feel the mountain wind on those sheer blue edges—who walks on the pine needles in those blue mountains.

"Can you see the pueblo?" Silva was standing behind me.

I shook my head. "We're too far away."

"From here I can see the world." He stepped out on the edge. "The Navajo reservation begins over there." He pointed to the east. "The Pueblo boundaries are over here." He looked below us to the south, where the narrow trail seemed to come from. "The Texans have their ranches over there, starting with that valley, the Concho Valley. The Mexicans run some cattle over there too."

"Do you ever work for them?"

"I steal from them," Silva answered. The sun was dropping behind us and the shadows were filling the land below. I turned away from the edge that dropped forever into the valleys below.

"always singing softly"—This prompts us to question whether he is simply singing or working a magic spell.

"my husband, and the baby"—This is not simply the romantic lark of a young girl, but a serious event for a woman with responsibilities.

"since I came upon him"—We finally learn how she met him. That he seemed so nonthreatening conflicts with the idea that she was abducted. Both interpretations are, however, possible.

"Those stories couldn't happen now. . . . But someday they will talk about us"—Again, she tries to convince herself, and he points out that stories form a continuum: today's events are tomorrow's stories.

"From here I can see the world.—Far above the everyday world, they are like mythical deities. Silko's descriptions show that they are standing on the Continental Divide, the ridge from which waters flow to the Pacific and the Gulf of California, the Gulf of Mexico, the Hudson Bay, and the Arctic Ocean. The action of the story takes place in the area we call "Four Corners." For more about this region, see the Introduction, p. 643.

"I steal from them"—Silva reveals himself as a trickster figure. For more on tricksters, see Ch. 23, p. 339.

"I'm cold," I said, "I'm going inside." I started wondering about this man who could speak the Pueblo language so well but who lived on a mountain and rustled cattle. I decided that this man Silva must be Navajo, because Pueblo men don't do things like that.

"You must be a Navajo."

Silva shook his head gently. "Little Yellow Woman," he said, "you never give up, do you? I have told you who I am. The Navajo people know me, too."

He knelt down and unrolled the bedroll and spread the extra blankets out on a piece of canvas. The sun was down, and the only light in the house came from out-side—the dim orange light from sundown.

I stood there and waited for him to crawl under the blankets.

"What are you waiting for?" he said, and I lay down beside him. He undressed me slowly like the night before beside the river—kissing my face gently and running his hands up and down my belly and legs. He took off my pants and then he laughed.

"Why are you laughing?"

"You are breathing so hard."

I pulled away from him and turned my back to him.

He pulled me around and pinned me down with his arms and chest. "You don't understand, do you, little Yellow Woman? **You will do what I want.**"

And again he was all around me with his skin slippery against mine, and I was afraid because I understood that his strength could hurt me. I lay underneath him and I knew that he could destroy me. But later, while he slept beside me, I touched his face and I had a feeling—the kind of feeling for him that overcame me that morning along the river. I kissed him on the forehead and he reached out for me.

When I woke up in the morning, he was gone. It gave me a strange feeling because for a long time I sat there on the blankets and looked around the little house for some object of his—**some proof that he had been there** or maybe that he was coming back. Only the blankets and the cardboard box remained. The .30-30 that had been leaning in the corner was gone, and so was the knife I had used the night before. He was gone, and I had my chance to go now. But first I had to eat, because I knew it would be a long walk home.

I found some dried apricots in the cardboard box, and I sat down on a rock at the edge of the plateau rim. There was no wind and the sun warmed me. I was surrounded by silence. I drowsed with apricots in my mouth, and I didn't believe that there were highways or railroads or cattle to steal.

When I woke up, I stared down at my feet in the black mountain dirt. Little black ants were swarming over the pine needles around my foot. They must have smelled the apricots. I thought about my family far below me. They would be wondering about me, because this had never happened to me before. The tribal police would file a report. But if old **Grandpa** weren't dead, he **would tell them what happened**—he would laugh and say, "Stolen by a *ka'tsina*, a mountain spirit. She'll come home—they usually do." There are enough of them to handle things. My mother and grandmother will raise the baby like they raised me. Al will find someone else, and they will go on like before, except that **there will be a story** about the day I disappeared while I was walking along the river. Silva had come for me; he said he had. I did not decide to go. I just went. Moonflowers blossom in the sand hills before dawn, just as I followed him.

That's what I was thinking as I wandered along the trail through the pine trees.

It was noon when I got back. When I saw the stone house I remembered that **I had meant to go home.** But that didn't seem important any more, maybe because there were little blue flowers growing in the meadow behind the stone house and the gray squirrels were playing in the pines next to the house. The horses were standing in the corral, and there was a beef carcass hanging on the shady side of a big pine in front of the house. Flies buzzed around the clotted blood that hung from the carcass. Silva was washing his hands in a bucket full of water. He must have heard me coming because he spoke to me without turning to face me.

"You must be Navajo"—With this remark, the narrator tries once again to distance herself from Silva. Once again, he deflects her attempt.

"You will do what I want"—This threatening remark is a reference to the stories about *ka'tsinas* and their power over humans.

"some proof that he had been there"—She is still searching for clues that will tell her if the situation is real.

"Grandpa . . . would tell them what happened"—The elders are true keepers of the stories. He would base his response to a current situation on the mythical tradition.

"there will be a story"—The Yellow Woman tradition will continue and she will become a part of it.

"I had meant to go home"—She did not decide, and he did not force her physically. This helps to link her disappearing to a fate required by the myth.

"I've been waiting for you."

"I went walking in the big pine trees."

I looked into the bucket full of bloody water with brown-and-white animal hairs floating in it. Silva stood there letting his hand drip, examining me intently.

"Are you coming with me?"

"Where?" I asked him. "To sell the meat in Marquez."

"If you're sure it's ok."

"I wouldn't ask you if it wasn't," he answered.

He sloshed the water around in the bucket before he dumped it out and set the bucket upside down near the door. I followed him to the corral and watched him saddle the horses. Even beside the horses he looked tall, and **I asked him again if he wasn't Navajo.** He didn't say anything; he just shook his head and kept cinching up the saddle.

"But Navajos are tall."

"Get on the horse," he said, "and let's go."

The last thing he did before we started down the steep trail was to grab the .30-30 from the corner. He slid the rifle into the scabbard that hung from his saddle.

"Do they ever try to catch you?" I asked.

"They don't know who I am."

"Then why did you bring the rifle?"

"Because we are going to Marquez where the Mexicans live."

The trail leveled out on a narrow ridge that was steep on both sides like an animal spine. On one side I could see where the trail went around the rocky gray hills and disappeared into the southeast where the pale sand rock mesas stood in the distance near my home. On the other side was a trail that went west, and as I looked far into the distance I thought I saw the little town. But Silva said no, that I was looking in the wrong place, that I just thought I saw houses. After that I quit looking off into the distance; it was hot and the wildflowers were closing up their deep-yellow petals. Only the waxy cactus flowers bloomed in the bright sun, and I saw every color that a cactus bloom can be; the white ones and the red ones were still buds, but the purple and the yellow were blossoms, open full and the most beautiful of all.

Silva saw him before I did. **The white man** was riding a big gray horse, coming up the trail towards us. He was traveling fast and the gray horse's feet sent rocks rolling off the trail into the dry tumbleweeds. Silva motioned for me to stop and we watched the white man. He didn't see us right away, but finally his horse whinnied at our horses and he stopped. He looked at us briefly before he lapped the gray horse across the three hundred yards that separated us. He stopped his horse in front of Silva, and his young fat face was shadowed by the brim of his hat. He didn't look mad, but his small, pale eyes moved from the blood-soaked gunny sacks hanging from my saddle to Silva's face and then back to my face.

"Where did you get the fresh meat?" the white man asked.

"I've been hunting," Silva said, and when he shifted his weight in the saddle the leather creaked.

"The hell you have, Indian. You've been rustling cattle. We've been looking for the thief for a long time."

The rancher was fat, and sweat began to soak through his white cowboy shirt and the wet cloth stuck to the thick rolls of belly fat. He almost seemed to be panting from the exertion of talking, and he smelled rancid, maybe because Silva scared him.

Silva turned to me and smiled, "**Go back up the mountain,** Yellow Woman."

The white man got angry when he heard Silva **speak in a language he couldn't understand.** "Don't try anything, Indian. Just keep riding to Marquez. We'll call the state police from there."

Andy Warhol, *Kachina Dolls,* 1986. This modern rendition of *ka'tsina* spirits indicates the ways in which artists in modern society choose from material from a variety of cultures. For a traditional figure of this type, see p. 646.

"I asked him again if he wasn't Navajo"—She is trying to make him "real" by placing him in her everyday realm of experience.

"The white man"—She had wished another man would come by so she could dispel the idea that Silva was a mythical being. However, this man is an intruder, foreign to her world, and serves to threaten rather than ameliorate the situation.

"Go back up the mountain"—Silva tells the woman to leave, thus removing the evidence from the scene that might reveal his sinister, trickster character.

"speak in a language he couldn't understand"—Their common language unites the woman to Silva, separating her from the modern world of the white man.

The rancher must have been unarmed because he was very frightened and if he had a gun he would have pulled it out then. I turned my horse around and the rancher yelled, "Stop!" I looked at Silva for an instant and there was **something ancient and dark—something I could feel in my stomach—in his eyes,** and when I glanced at his hand I saw his finger on the trigger of the .30-30 that was still in the saddle scabbard. I slapped my horse across the flank and the sacks of raw meat swung against my knees as the horse leaped up the trail. It was hard to keep my balance, and once I thought I felt the saddle slipping backward; it was because of this that I could not look back.

I didn't stop until I reached the ridge where the trail forked. The horse was breathing deep gasps and there was a dark film of sweat on its neck. I looked down in the direction I had come from, but I couldn't see the place. I waited. The wind came up and pushed warm air past me. I looked up at the sky, pale blue and full of thin clouds and **fading vapor trails left by jets.**

I think four shots were fired—I remember hearing four hollow explosions that reminded me of deer hunting. There could have been more shots after that, but I couldn't have heard them because my horse was running again and the loose rocks were making too much noise as they scattered around his feet.

Horses have a hard time running downhill, but I went that way instead of uphill to the mountain because I thought it was safer. I felt better with the horse running southeast past the round gray hills that were covered with cedar trees and black lava rock. When I got to the plain in the distance I could see the dark green patches of tamaracks that grew along the river; and beyond the river I could see the beginning of the pale sandrock mesas. I stopped the horse and looked back to see if anyone was coming; then I got off the horse and turned the horse around, wondering if it would go back to its corral under the pines on the mountain. It looked back at me for a moment and then plucked a mouthful of green tumbleweeds before it trotted back up the trail with its ears pointed forward, carrying its head daintily to one side to avoid stepping on the dragging reins. When the horse disappeared over the last hill, the gunny sacks full of meat were still swinging and bouncing.

I walked toward the river on a wood-hauler's road that I knew would eventually lead to a paved road. I was thinking about waiting beside the road for someone to drive by, but by the time I got to the pavement I had decided it wasn't very far to walk if **I followed the river back** the way Silva and I had come.

The river water tasted good, and I sat in the shade under a cluster of silvery willows. I thought about Silva, and I felt sad at leaving him; still, there was something strange about him, and I tried to figure it out all the way back home.

I came back to the place on the river bank where he had been sitting the first time I saw him. **The green willow leaves that he had trimmed from the branch were still lying there,** wilted in the sand. I saw the leaves and I wanted to go back to him—to kiss him and to touch him—but the mountains were too far away now.

And I told myself, because I believe it, he will come back sometime and be waiting again by the river.

I followed the path up from the river into the village. The sun was getting low, and I could smell supper cooking when I got to the screen door of my house. I could hear the voices inside—my mother was telling my grandmother how to fix Jell-O and my husband, Al, was playing with the baby. **I decided to tell them that some Navajo had kidnapped me,** but I was sorry that old Grandpa wasn't alive to hear my story because it was the Yellow Woman stories he liked to tell best.

Further Reading

Silko, Leslie Marmon. *Storyteller*. New York, NY: Seaver Books, 1981, 54-62.

"something ancient and dark . . . in his eyes"—Silva reveals himself as a sinister figure with a connection to primordial evil.

"fading vapor trails left by jets"—This anchors the woman in the modern world, although she does not reflect on its significance because of the ominous situation.

Canyon de Chelly National Monument, Arizona, U.S.A. The view that Yellow Woman was looking out on would have looked like this.

"I followed the river back"—This brings the telling full circle and also demonstrates the helpfulness of nature, an important element in many stories we've read, such as the Grimms' tales (see Ch. 36, p. 529).

"The green willow leaves . . . were still lying there"—This is a clue that she had not been gone long, which is a variant of most Yellow Woman stories. Usually, the woman returns only after many months, during which she has borne a child or twins. In this story, the Yellow Woman figure returns to her previous situation and is free to present her own version of what happened.

"I decided to tell them that some Navajo had kidnapped me"—Even at its end, the story still doesn't resolve the narrator's attitude to her experience with Silva: was it just an escapade, or a piece of her people's tradition? The story admits of both interpretations.

44

Mythological Themes in Modern Narrative

WHAT TO EXPECT . . . As societies become more and more diverse, creative literature exhibits an increasing variety of themes, styles, and viewpoints, These, in turn, help readers to understand the diverse cultural contexts of their own worlds, although the conclusions may be more ambiguous than in older societies with monolithic value structures. The three selections in this chapter illustrate the dual role of fiction in the twentieth century, as it relates to the study of mythology.

James Joyce's *Ulysses* intertwines the author's Dublin experiences and Greek mythology, particularly Homer's story of Odysseus. John Updike's *The Centaur* focuses on the relationship of a father and son in Olinger, Pennsylvania. However, the characters simultaneously operate in the spheres of Greek mythology, exhibiting the characteristics of the gods in settings that are momentarily transformed from everyday Olinger to ancient, mythical Greece: myth and reality coexist. Look for elements of the hero's experience as described by Joseph Campbell (Ch. 14, p. 159) in these stories: you won't find the whole structure without reading the whole of each novel, but you can ask yourself which parts of the hero's journey appear in the excerpts in this chapter. Jungian analysis (Ch. 32, p. 468) is also likely to be incomplete here, but aspects of it might be interesting to identify, as well.

Angela Carter's "The Tiger's Bride" reutilizes the Beauty and the Beast theme; that is, it retains the basic components of the old story, but revises it to fit another audience—your own. In doing so, it represents contemporary sensibilities: Carter's Beauty is initially dissatisfied but never afraid, and in the end, the ultimate irony is that she decides to renounce her humanness and join The Beast. As you read, consider how the fact that this is an "Animal Bridegroom" story (see also Ch. 37, p. 541) affects your reaction to Beauty's emotional, psychological, and physical transformation. Think about whether this story lends itself to Proppian analysis (Ch. 34, p. 499), and if so, what adjustments would you make in such an analysis?

To some extent, our view of the role and value of mythology in relation to modern fiction will be inseparable from our view of the status and significance of modern fiction and, even more broadly, of modern literature in itself. For the literature of the past, the place of mythology seems much more straightforward: mythology represented a kind of symbolic language that could be used, to the degree desired, to focus the effects that the author wanted to have. Mythology represented something: its actual meaning varied from age to age and from genre to genre, but whatever it was, the author could bring it to bear and, suddenly, the significance of mythology had been deployed. This process continues to this day. As John Vickery notes, myths in a sense resemble scenarios or scripts, and each work of literature "assigns specific values to the mythic variables" (190).

However, several factors have interfered with this straightforward enactment of the creative process, and this interference has produced results that can be very interesting for those inspired by the modern study of mythological traditions.

STUDY OF MYTHOLOGY BROADENS CULTURAL UNDERSTANDING

In the first place, as a result of familiarity with the contents of some of the studies presented in this book, we as a society are much more aware of the cultural context of the mythological stories we read, so we hesitate to pull them up like flowers from their environment and to incorporate them into a new arrangement that has little or nothing to do with their natural cultural habitat. We wonder, "Who was Helen of Troy?" and we seek to explain her behavior in Homer by considering that her world was a so-called "shame culture" and not, like ours, motivated by the internal mechanism of guilt. From the vantage of such sociological insights, it is harder to see the beautiful Helen simply as "the face that launched a thousand ships and toppled the topless towers of Ilium" (Christopher Marlowe, *Dr. Faustus*).

However, at the same time, as Victor Turner (see Ch. 26, p. 373) has shown, we are increasingly a diverse society whose members operate without undertaking a lifelong commitment to a single cultural role. Rather, we are much more likely to take our pleasure by constructing a shifting mosaic of choices from the diverse range of alternatives available in our society. As a result, as a society, we understand diverse cultural contexts better, perhaps, than we used to. Paradoxically, however, authors are ever more comfortable with jumping from one cultural context to another and putting the resulting contrasting perspectives to good artistic use. A good example of this can be found in the previous chapter, in "Yellow Woman," by Leslie Marmon Silko (see Ch. 43, p. 644). The main character of this story shifts back and forth between her own modern family life and the traditional, mythic world of her ancestors, and the reader comes to appreciate the dissonant perspectives.

MODERN WRITERS USE MYTHS TO COMMENT ON HUMAN CONCERNS

Thanks to Levi-Strauss and those who have studied him (see Ch. 20, p. 280, and Ch. 16, p. 193), we are much more aware that myths consist of a variety of different and likely contradictory stories, all highlighting a series of ultimately coherent values at the heart of a society. However, myth represents a way of solving problems not for individuals, but for societies, and therein lies another problem in bringing mythic material into modern fiction. While mythic ideation strives for the general, the idealized, the circular, modern writing emphasizes the particular and the individualistic. A corollary of the multiplicity of roles we undertake in modern society is the importance of the locus of these choices, the individual who undertakes them.

Modern writers have found ways of shaping mythical material into eloquent commentary on the difficulties encountered by the individual in modern society, as shown in the excerpt from *The Centaur* presented in this chapter. In it John Updike provides a melding of the world of ancient Greek gods and heroes and that of ordinary middle-class individuals in a small town in America. The effect is to create a work of fiction which focuses in mythic terms on the choices made by the individual.

MODERN WRITERS USE MYTHOLOGICAL ALLUSIONS TO ENRICH THEIR WORK

Modern fiction itself has increasingly moved away from a concern with the straightforward telling of a story. In a sense, modernist and postmodernist claims in this direction are, of course, overstated, and fiction writing has, at least since Boccaccio, thrived on the interplay of multiple layers of ambiguity. Nonetheless, the irresolvable disintegration of character and plot, which can be said to characterize modern fiction, may at first seem to be at odds with the meaning- and message-laden nature of mythological stories. We have spent 43 chapters showing many of the different kinds of insights that myths and the forms of storytelling related to them can provide. How then can an artistic form whose predominant stance, as Northrup Frye has observed, is irony and thematic detachment make use of such material?

Frye notes that irony and allegory represent opposite ends of a scale. Our literature does not tend toward large-scale allegory: we do not use mythological characters to represent abstract concepts. In particular, we do not use the gods and heroes of mythology to represent our own gods and heroes, because we tend more toward skepticism than religious piety and hero worship. As a result, it is difficult for us to recognize or acknowledge abstract principles and values; we find them limiting and see them as separating members of our diverse society from each other, rather than uniting them to toil in the same vineyard for the good of all humankind. And yet, perhaps even more than before, there is room in the fiction of such a splintered, cynical age for allusions to myths and fairy tales. In the collection *Burn Your Boats,* Angela Carter takes a variety of fairy tale motifs and reimagines them in a way that will not seem hokey or alien even to modern adult readers. Carter's "The Tiger's Bride" (included in this chapter) satisfies the need of the modern reader for ironic detachment by focusing in a humorous way not on uplifting morals we should learn, but on our flaws and limitations as human beings. The point of Carter's story is not philosophical but grimly, playfully, evocative of our modern values: "The tiger will never lie down with the lamb; he acknowledges no pact that is not reciprocal. The lamb must learn to run with the tigers" (p. 680).

MYTHOLOGICAL ELEMENTS PROVIDE THE READER WITH INTERPRETIVE CHOICES

Finally, the playfulness of modern fiction exacerbates a tendency that has been present in fiction since its inception. The role of fiction as such has remained the same, despite the changing concerns of our day. As E. Gould notes, "All fiction however much it looks like reality, is a refusal to accept that the real world is quite enough" (138). In the past, fiction compensated for its unreality by providing connections to philosophical, social scientific, or political theories, that is, to real world referents whose conceptual framework informs the fictional world evoked in the novel. However, modern fiction with its "lack of mimetic faithfulness" begs the question of conceptual meaning or value in favor of what Gould calls an "epiphanic moment," the sudden emergence of a moment of truth in the reader, who becomes the builder of the story from the discontinuous clusters of imagistic material that form the novel's core. In this process, the individual reader constructs a new meaning from the mythological elements provided by the author, in an atmosphere where mythology has become permanently separated from the culture that originated it and the belief system that sustained it. Thus, Gould would argue that modern fiction capitalizes on the ability of modern readers to choose and gives them a kind of story that of itself has mythological significance, whether its writer incorporates mythological themes or not. In this chapter, we present an excerpt from James Joyce's *Ulysses* to show that such fiction is even more powerful insofar as it also incorporates, in its own way, the figures and themes of traditional mythology.

Thus, the twentieth-century fictional works in this chapter show us how creative writers continue the ancient storyteller tradition by treating mythological themes according to their own belief systems. Though James Joyce and John Updike use the stories of the ancient Greeks as the basis of their own creative efforts, not surprisingly, they no longer share those beliefs. Angela Carter has crafted her modern Beauty and the Beast story without any kind of dedication to the social values implied by the fairy tale. On the contrary, her version adds ironic twists that undermine the values of the original tale and shape it in a direction the contemporary reader of fantasy enjoys. All three of these writers show great respect for the old themes, but they use the modern literary devices their audiences expect. In essence, this is what storytellers have always done— create narratives from their own belief systems and alter them as aspects of that system change.

MYTHOLOGICAL CONNECTIONS HELP US WITH OUR OWN NARRATIVES

For us, too, life is an ever-changing narrative. We are surrounded by a panoply of myths and tales. We accept those that have meaning for us and usually ignore the others. American students are in some ways barraged by mythological references in all sorts of narrative, especially in popular culture. Our personal spiritual beliefs, as well as our ethnic and local traditions, are also vital representations of the fact that our life experiences are attended by countless possible narratives, some of which we eventually recognize, while others recede unfulfilled or unrecognized as our experiences unfurl themselves. All of these real and potential narratives are interwoven with our broader contemporary context and with the stories in our past.

What we have learned from this book will help us read our own narratives. Students of mythology can find great enrichment in discerning the interplay of the mythological and the everyday. They can also find satisfaction in realizing that mythological stories and figures represent a broad range of human nature, like the factual and psychological aspects of our own situations.

Thus, we might say that reading the modern fictional narratives presented in this chapter can be the first step in our harnessing of the traditions we have studied to craft stories about our life experiences, using our understanding of mythology to spark our creativity and enrich our own narratives.

Further Reading

Carter, Angela. *Burning Your Boats: Stories.* London: Chatto and Windus, 1995.

Gould, Eric. *Mythical Intentions in Modern Literature.* Princeton, NJ: Princeton University Press, 1981.

Ulysses

JAMES JOYCE

James Joyce (1882–1941), one of the most important writers shaping modern fiction, is recognized for his innovative use of language, plot construction, and character portrayal. His writing style represented a revolution in the use of the English language as well as a landmark in the development of twentieth-century modernism, a movement that challenged what it viewed as traditional style and content of literary works. Joyce was a complex character, but one of the most important aspects of his artistry is his Irishness. However, he left his native land just after the turn of the century, living in self-imposed exile on the continent. Except for short visits to Ireland in 1909 and 1912, he spent the rest of his life in Trieste, Paris, and Zürich. Yet the setting of his works was almost always his native Dublin, and the characters were based on family, friends, and acquaintances.

Joyce's most powerful writing portrays his own time and place in works such as *Dubliners,* a collection of stories, and the novels *A Portrait of the Artist as a Young Man* and *Finnegan's Wake.* His masterpiece, *Ulysses,* ties together Dublin themes and Greek mythology, specifically the story of Odysseus' wanderings in Homer's *Odyssey.* In naming this novel, Joyce used the Roman form of the hero's name.

HOMER'S *ODYSSEY*

Although many readers never wonder who Homer was, scholars debate whether the works attributed to him—the *Iliad,* the *Odyssey,* and the Homeric hymns—were all written by the same person, or if a poet named Homer actually existed at all. It is assumed that both of the epic poems, the *Iliad* and the *Odyssey,* were originally recited or sung to an audience by a professional performer who might also have played the lyre as accompaniment. Some scholars believe that Homer, or the poet who wrote down these epics, merely collected stories from the

James Joyce at 22, photographed in Dublin in 1904 by friend and fellow University College student Constantine P. Curran. When Joyce was later asked what he was thinking about while being photographed, he replied, "I was wondering would he lend me five shillings."

long oral tradition, perhaps contributing original material and a scheme of organization. Others attribute to a single poet, Homer, the talent and creativity to produce a refined poetic work based on traditional tales.

Homer's compositions are great literary works in their own right. In addition, they are valuable to the student of mythology because of the stories they tell about the hero Odysseus, as well as their rich narrative background: the references to gods and heroes whose stories are told in other myths, including Calypso, Circe, Poseidon, Cyclops, Scylla, Helios, and Hades. (For examples, see Ch. 1, p. 9, for the Trojan War.) Since Homer's epics were written down rather early (in the sixth century B.C.E.), we have in them descriptions of these mythological figures that date back to the times when the religion that incorporated them was still alive. We can compare Homer's stories to those of classical Greece in the fifth century and thus track the development of the mythic figures he describes through the course of Greek culture.

JOYCE'S *ULYSSES*

Joyce published *Ulysses* in 1922, and although the novel was controversial because of its widespread innovation in language, its sexual candor, and its irreverence toward religion, it has become a staple of literary studies in the English-speaking world for its innovative use of language and its intertwining of themes. The action takes place on a single day, June 16, 1904 (now widely referred to as *Bloomsday*), in Dublin. The main character, Leopold Bloom, performs the routine actions of a typical day. However, this day is punctuated as well by singular events, such as attending a fellow Dubliner's funeral. The novel does not indicate any explicit mention of the characters and events of Homer's *Odyssey* beyond that found in his title, but the main characters and episodes are based on those in Homer's epic. Bloom corresponds to Odysseus, and his travels ultimately bring him together with a figurative son in Stephen Dedalus (Telemachus). In the course of his day, Bloom navigates the Ormond Bar in the face of alluring barmaids (Sirens), and he must vanquish other suitors when returning to his wife Molly (Penelope). Also identifiable in the course of the story are Circe, the Cyclops, Scylla, and Hades. Therefore, the more familiar readers are with the classic Greek story, the more fully they can enjoy the modern English one.

The interplay of the traditions is straightforward in some places and quite subtle in others. The excerpts from the Hades episode contain several references to Greek mythology. Most obvious is the fact that in some sense the episode corresponds to Odysseus' visit to Hades: Leopold Bloom is attending a funeral and meditating on death and dying. It becomes obvious that the carriage of the mourners and the hearse carrying the deceased correspond to the vessel used to convey the dead across the River Styx. In addition, the Homeric underworld has four rivers, and the funeral entourage in Dublin crosses four rivers or canals.

Another analogy to Homer is the frequent mention of the monuments the funeral entourage passes on the way to the cemetery. During his stay in the underworld, Odysseus speaks to the shades of great men and praises their deeds. This motif is transferred to Joyce's work, but most of the monuments described are statues of great Irish political heroes such as Charles Parnell and Daniel O'Connell. And in a humorous twist not present in Homer, Bloom remarks about Sir Philip Crampton's memorial fountain bust: "Who was he?" This fits Bloom's view of the world, since he philosophizes often about the futility of living well, concluding that one is always forgotten sooner or later and that one's good works diminish and disappear. However, he speaks of the dead with the same kind of regret and longing for the past that Odysseus does.

As we can see, not all of the references to Homer and the myths of the Greeks are straightforward and obvious. Some are perverted for the sake of irony, such as Bloom's wife, Molly. Homer's Penelope is a model of fidelity because she vigorously wards off many suitors while Odysseus is away. If Bloom is an Odysseus figure, we might expect his wife to be a Penelope counterpart. Leopold's wife, Molly, also has suitors, men that Leopold knows, but she is known for entertaining them, not defusing their ardor. Even as he is attending Paddy Dignam's funeral, Bloom fears that Molly is with her lover Blazes Boylan, a concert promoter who is arranging Molly's next performance.

In the end, however, Bloom represents the universal human tendency to make do with the present, and even look forward to the future. This mirrors Odysseus' optimism when he is released from Hades to continue his journey home. In fact, Bloom's final remark of the chapter after the funeral is, "How grand we are this morning."

THE HADES EPISODE

In the course of his day, Leopold Bloom, who corresponds to Homer's Odysseus, attends the funeral of Paddy Dignam. The episode gives Joyce a chance to express his misgivings about

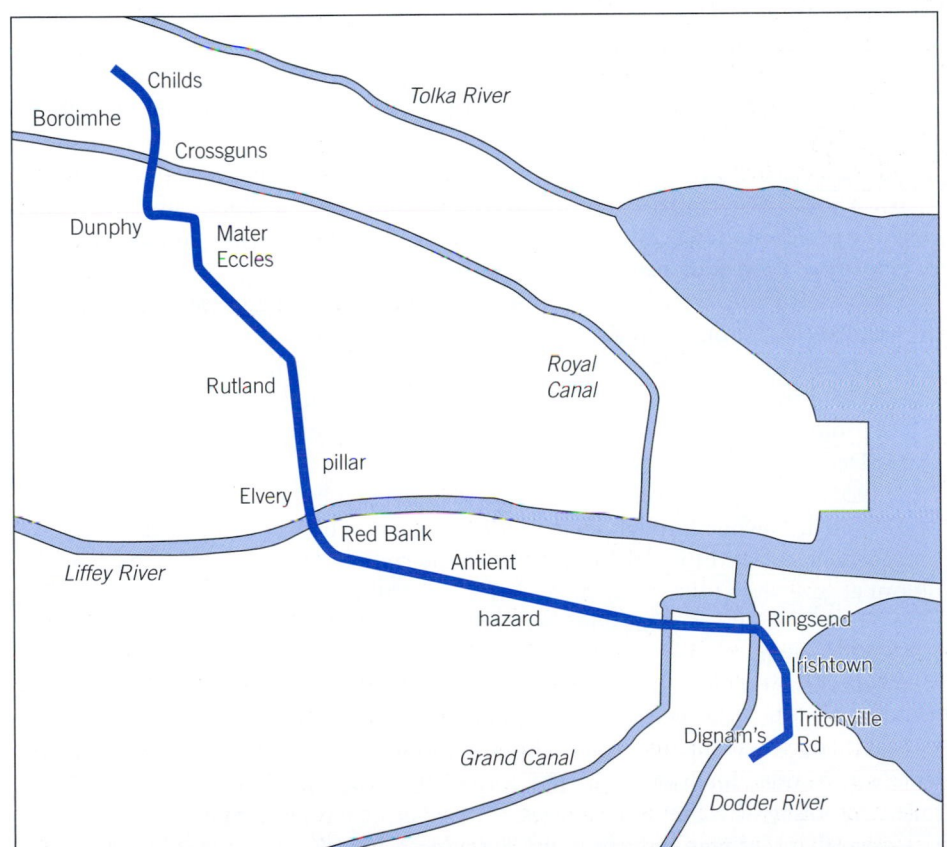

Dublin (detail): Map showing the path of the funeral procession in James Joyce's *Ulysses*.

religion, and his musings about the futility of life, a theme characteristic of the modern movement, as well as to ponder the history of the Irish people. These issues contrast ironically with Homer's Odysseus, who enters the underworld out of the need to satisfy the demands of the gods and to fulfill what he views as the destiny of his country and his family.

At the funeral, Bloom is seated in a carriage with Martin Cunningham, Jack Power, and Simon Dedalus, the father of his friend Stephen. The path of the funeral procession is through the streets of Dublin from Dignam's to the cemetery in Glasnevin, as shown in the map.

Martin Cunningham, first, poked his silkhatted head into the creaking carriage and, entering deftly, seated himself. Mr Power stepped in after him, curving his height with care.

—Come on, Simon.

—After you, Mr Bloom said.

Mr Dedalus covered himself quickly and got in, saying:

—Yes, yes.

—After you, Mr Bloom said.

—Are we all here now? Martin Cunningham asked. **Come along Bloom.**

Mr Bloom entered and sat in the vacant place. He pulled the door to after him and slammed it tight till it shut tight. He passed an arm through the armstrap and looked seriously from the open carriage window at the lowered blinds of the **avenue.** One dragged aside: an old woman peeping. Nose whiteflattened against the pane. Thanking her stars she was passed over. Extraordinary the interest they take in a corpse. Glad to see us go we give them such trouble coming. Job seems to suit them. **Huggermugger** in corners. Slop about in **slipperslappers** for fear he'd wake. Then getting it ready. Laying it out. **Molly** and Mrs Fleming making the bed. Pull it more to your side. Our winding-sheet. Never know who will touch you dead. Wash and shampoo. I believe they clip the nails and the hair. Keep a bit in an envelope. Grow all the same after. Unclean job.

All waited. Nothing was said. Stowing in the wreaths probably. I am sitting on something hard. Ah, that **soap** in my hip pocket. Better shift it out of that. Wait for an opportunity.

All waited. Then wheels were heard from in front, turning: then nearer: then horses' hoofs. A jolt. Their carriage began to move, creaking and swaying. Other hoofs and creaking wheels started behind. The blinds of the avenue passed and **number ten** with its craped knocker, door ajar. **At walking pace.**

They waited still, their knees jogging till they had turned and were passing along the tramtracks. Tritonville road. Quicker. The wheels rattled rolling over the cobbled causeway and the **crazy glasses** shook rattling in the doorframes.

—What way is he taking us? Mr Power asked through both windows.

—Irishtown, Martin Cunningham said. Ringsend. Brunswick street.

Mr **Dedalus** nodded, looking out.

—That's a fine old custom, he said. I am glad to see it has not died out.

All watched awhile through their windows caps and hats lifted by passers. Respect. The carriage swerved from the tramtrack to the smoother road past Watery lane. Mr Bloom at gaze saw a lithe young man, clad in mourning, a wide hat.

—There's a friend of yours gone by, Dedalus, he said.

—Who is that?

—Your son and heir.

—Where is he? Mr Dedalus said, stretching over across.

The carriage, passing the open drains and mounds of rippedup roadway before the tenement houses, lurched round the corner and, swerving back to the tramtrack, rolled on noisily with chattering wheels. Mr Dedalus fell back, saying:

—Was that **Mulligan** cad with him? His *fidus Achates!*

These excerpts come from: Joyce, *Ulysses,* Paris, 1922 (84–110).

Most notes come from: Gifford, *Ulysses Annotated,* Episode Six.

"Come along Bloom"—This implies a certain distance between Cunningham and Bloom. In fact, Bloom is the only Jew in the carriage, and his religion places a distance between him and the funeral rites.

"avenue"—Newbridge Avenue.

"Huggermugger"—secretly.

"slipperslapper"—Old Mother Slipper Slapper is a poor old woman in a folk song, and here represents how Joyce sees Ireland.

Molly Bloom's wife. He remembers the death of his infant son Rudy, his wife and the maid laying him out eleven years ago. He has not had sex with Molly since.

"soap"—Bought for a visit to the public baths, just before this episode.

"number ten"—Dignam's is 10 Newbridge Avenue.

"At walking pace"—This was the custom for a funeral entourage.

"crazy glasses"—Crazed glass, with small cracks in it.

Dedalus Stephen Dedalus, Simon's son and Bloom's friend.

Mulligan Simon disapproves of his son's friend Buck Mulligan.

"*fidus Achates*"—In Virgil's *Aeneid,* the hero's faithful friend is called Achates, and Virgil often refers to him with this phrase; *fidus* means "faithful." Aeneas also takes a trip to the underworld, and Achates helps him in his preparations.

—No, Mr Bloom said. He was alone.

—Down with his aunt Sally, I suppose, Mr Dedalus said, the Goulding faction, the drunken little **costdrawer** and Crissie, papa's little lump of dung, the wise child that knows her own father.

Mr Bloom smiled joylessly on Ringsend road. Wallace Bros: the bottleworks: **Dodder** bridge.

Richie Goulding and the legal bag. Goulding, Collis and Ward he calls the firm. His jokes are getting a bit damp. Great card he was. Waltzing in Stamer street with Ignatius Gallaher on a Sunday morning, the landlady's two hats pinned on his head. Out on the rampage all night. Beginning to tell on him now: that backache of his, I fear. Wife **ironing** his back. Thinks he'll cure it with pills. All breadcrumbs they are. About six hundred per cent profit.

Ulysses and Teiresias, detail of Greek red-figure vase, 5th c. B.C.E. In Homer, Odysseus' purpose in visiting Hades was to speak to Teiresias, the prophet-priest, who would give him guidance on how to appease Poseidon, the god of the sea, who was preventing his homecoming.

—He's in with a lowdown crowd, Mr Dedalus snarled. That Mulligan is a contaminated bloody doubledyed ruffian by all accounts. His name stinks all over Dublin. But with the help of God and His blessed mother I'll make it my business to write a letter one of those days to his mother or his aunt or whatever she is that will open her eye as wide as a gate. **I'll tickle his catastrophe,** believe you me.

He cried above the clatter of the wheels.

—I won't have her bastard of a nephew ruin my son. A **counterjumper**'s son. Selling tapes in my cousin, Peter Paul M'Swiney's. Not likely.

He ceased. Mr Bloom glanced from his angry moustache to Mr Power's mild face and Martin Cunningham's eyes and beard, gravely shaking. Noisy selfwilled man. Full of his son. He is right. Something to hand on. If little Rudy had lived. See him grow up. Hear his voice in the house. Walking beside Molly in an Eton suit. My son. Me in his eyes. Strange feeling it would be. From me. Just a chance. Must have been that morning in **Raymond terrace** she was at the window watching the two dogs at it by the wall of the **cease to do evil.** And the sergeant grinning up. She had that cream gown on with the rip she never stitched. Give us a touch, Poldy. God, I'm dying for it. How life begins.

Got big then. Had to refuse the **Greystones concert.** My son inside her. I could have helped him on in life. I could. Make him independent. Learn German too.

—Are we late? Mr Power asked.

—Ten minutes, Martin Cunningham said, looking at his watch.

Molly. **Milly.** Same thing watered down. Her tomboy oaths. O jumping Jupiter! Ye gods and little fishes! Still, she's a dear girl. Soon be a woman. Mullingar. Dearest Papli. Young student. Yes, yes: a woman too. Life, life. . . .

He closed his left eye. Martin Cunningham began to brush away crustcrumbs from under his thighs.

—What is this, he said, in the name of God? **Crumbs?**

—Someone seems to have been making a picnic party here lately, Mr Power said.

All raised their thighs, eyed with disfavour the mildewed buttonless leather of the seats. . . .

"costdrawer"—Cost accountant.

Dodder The first of the four rivers the procession will cross.

Richie Goulding Stephen's mother's brother.

"ironing"—Massaging.

"I'll tickle his catastrophe"—Page with a drawn sword says in defense of Falstaff, in Shakespeare, *Henry IV, Part II,* lines 65–66: "I'll tickle your catastrophe (backside)."

"counterjumper"—Shop clerk.

"Raymond terrace"—Rudy was conceived there, before the Blooms moved to their present address.

"cease to do evil"—Motto over the gate of the jail in South Circular Road.

"Greystones concert"—A stylish summer resort. Molly Bloom is a singer whose concert had to be canceled because of her pregnancy.

Milly Bloom's daughter.

"Crumbs?"—The men discover that previous occupants have left food and that the carriage is also in a state of decay. Ancient gravesites in the Middle East reveal that the custom in many cultures was to supply the corpse with food for the journey to the afterlife.

The carriage halted short.

—What's wrong?

—We're stopped.

—Where are we?

Mr Bloom put his head out of the window.

—**The grand canal,** he said.

Gasworks. Whooping cough they say it cures. Good job Milly never got it. Poor children! Doubles them up black and blue in convulsions. Shame really. Got off lightly with illnesses compared. Only measles. Flaxseed tea. Scarlatina, influenza epidemics. Canvassing for death. Don't miss this chance. Dogs' home over there. Poor old **Athos!** Be good to Athos, Leopold, is my last wish. Thy will be done. We obey them in the grave. A dying scrawl. He took it to heart, pined away. Quiet brute. Old men's dogs usually are. . . .

They went past the bleak pulpit of Saint Mark's, under the railway bridge, past the Queen's theatre: in silence. Hoardings: Eugene Stratton, Mrs Bandmann Palmer. Could I go to see *Leah* tonight, I wonder. I said I. Or *The Lily of Killarney?* Elster Grimes Opera Company. Big powerful change. Wet bright bills for next week. *Fun on the Bristol.* Martin Cunningham could work a pass for the Gaiety. Have to stand a drink or two. As broad as it's long.

He's coming in the afternoon. Her songs.

Plasto's. Sir Philip Crampton's memorial fountain bust. Who was he?

—How do you do? Martin Cunningham said, raising his palm to his brow in salute.

—He doesn't see us, Mr Power said. Yes, he does. How do you do?

—Who? Mr Dedalus asked.

—**Blazes Boylan,** Mr Power said. There he is airing his **quiff.** Just that moment I was thinking.

Mr Dedalus bent across to salute. From the door of the Red Bank the white disc of a straw hat flashed reply: passed.

Mr Bloom reviewed the nails of his left hand, then those of his right hand. The nails, yes. Is there anything more in him that she sees? Fascination. Worst man in Dublin. That keeps him alive. They sometimes feel what a person is. Instinct. But a type like that. My nails. I am just looking at them: well pared. And after: thinking alone. Body getting a bit softy. I would notice that: from remembering. What causes that? I suppose the skin can't contract quickly enough when the flesh falls off. But the shape is there. The shape is there still. Shoulders. Hips. Plump. Night of the dance dressing. Shift stuck between the cheeks behind.

He clasped his hands between his knees and, satisfied, sent his vacant glance over their faces. . . .

They passed under the hugecloaked **Liberator**'s form.

Martin Cunningham nudged Mr Power.

—Of the **tribe of Reuben,** he said.

A tall blackbearded figure, bent on a stick, stumping round the corner of Elvery's elephant house showed them a curved hand open on his spine.

—In all his pristine beauty, Mr Power said.

Mr Dedalus looked after the stumping figure and said mildly:

—The devil break the hasp of your back!

—Mr Power, collapsing in laughter, shaded his face from the window as the carriage passed **Gray's** statue.

—**We have all been there,** Martin Cunningham said broadly. His eyes met Mr Bloom's eyes. He caressed his beard, adding:

—Well, nearly all of us.

"The grand canal"—The second of the four rivers crossed by the procession.

"Gasworks"—This odoriferous plant processed coal into gas for lighting and heating. This is the beginning of one of Leopold Bloom's frequent interior monologues that give the reader a chance to see how he thinks as well as to fill out the background of events. Note that in this episode, almost all of the meditations deal with death.

Athos One of Alexandre Dumas' Three Musketeers. The dog of Bloom's father, who committed suicide, is here conflated with Argos, Odysseus' old dog who recognizes his master on his return.

Plasto's Hat shop near Bloom's house.

Sir Philip Crampton (1777–1858) Surgeon from Dublin who served as surgeon general of Her Majesty's Forces.

Blazes Boylan A concert promoter who is arranging Molly's next concert. He is also her lover, and is on his way to meet her while Bloom is out.

"quiff"—Lock of hair fixed by hair oil to the forehead. This implies that Boylan was a bit of a dandy.

"Liberator"—Statue of Daniel O'Connell 12 feet tall and on a high pedestal. He was a political leader who led a successful campaign for the repeal of laws limiting the rights of Catholics.

"tribe of Reuben"—Jewish. Reuben saved his younger brother Joseph, but entered into adultery with his father's concubine.

Gray Sir John Gray (1816–75), Protestant Irish newspaperman and politician.

"We have all been there"—In the grasp of hostile Jewish moneylenders.

Mr Bloom began to speak with sudden eagerness to his companions' faces.

—That's an awfully good one that's going the rounds about **Reuben J and the son.**

—About **the boatman?** Mr Power asked.

—Yes. Isn't it awfully good?

—What is that? Mr Dedalus asked. I didn't hear it.

—There was a girl in the case, Mr. Bloom began, and he determined to send him to the isle of Man out of harm's way but when they were both. . . .

—What? Mr Dedalus asked. That confirmed bloody hobble-dehoy is it?

—Yes, Mr Bloom said. They were both on the way to the boat and he tried to drown . . .

—Drown **Barabbas!** Mr Dedalus cried. I wish to Christ he did!

—No, Mr Bloom said, the son himself . . .

Martin Cunningham thwarted his speech rudely.

—Reuben J and the son were piking down the quay next the river on their way to the isle of Man boat and the young chiseller suddenly got loose and over the wall with him into the **Liffy.**

—For God's sake! Mr Dedalus exclaimed in fright. Is he dead?

—Dead! Martin Cunningham cried. Not he! A boatman got a pole and **fished him out** by the slack of the breeches and he was landed up to the father on the quay. More dead than alive. Half the town was there.

—Yes, Mr Bloom said. But the funny part is . . .

—And Reuben J, Martin Cunningham said, **gave the boatman a florin** for saving his son's life.

A stifled sigh came from under Mr. Power's hand.

—O, he did, Martin Cunningham affirmed. Like a hero. A silver florin.

—Isn't it awfully good? Mr Bloom said eagerly.

—**One and eightpence too much,** Mr Dedalus said drily.

Mr Power's choked laugh burst quietly in the carriage. **Nelson's pillar.**

—Eight plums for a penny! Eight for a penny!

—We had better look a little serious, Martin Cunningham said.

Mr Dedalus sighed.

—Ah then, indeed, he said, poor little Paddy wouldn't grudge us a laugh. Many a good one he told himself.

—The lord forgive me! Mr Power said wiping his wet eyes with his fingers. Poor Paddy! I little thought a week ago when I saw him last and he was in his usual health that I'd be driving after him like this. He's gone from us.

—As decent a little man as ever wore a hat, Mr Dedalus said. . . .

The carriage climbed more slowly the hill of Rutland square. Rattle his bones. Over the stones. Only a pauper. Nobody owns.

—In the midst of life, Martin Cunningham said.

—But the worst of all, Mr Power said, is **the man who takes his own life.**

Martin Cunningham drew out his watch briskly, coughed and put it back.

—The greatest disgrace to have in the family, Mr Power added.

Charon in a boat, ferrying souls across the Styx. Roman marble relief from a sarcophagus, 3rd c. C.E.

"Reuben J and the son"—Refers to an actual newspaper story about a dock worker who saved the life of a solicitor's son. Joyce fictionalizes it, making the worker Jewish and a boatman. The son, Reuben J. Dodd Jr., was at school with Joyce.

"the boatman"—In Greek mythology, the boatman, Charon, ferries the deceased over the River Styx to Hades.

Barabbas The criminal released instead of Jesus, at the request of the mob. See Matthew 27:20, Mark 15, Luke 23, and John 18.

Liffy—The third river crossed by the funeral procession.

"fished him out"—The irony here is that the boatman *saves* the man from death, and figuratively moves him further away from the afterlife.

"gave the boatman a florin"— In Greek tradition, the deceased were buried with coins to be paid the boatman Charon for ferrying them to Hades. In the story, "Cupid and Psyche," Psyche takes coins with her for this purpose when she visits Hades (Ch. 37, p. 556.)

"One and eightpence too much" —A florin was 24 pence, or two shillings. Simon Dedalus suggests that Dodd's son is worth only 6 pence, half a shilling.

"Nelson's pillar"—Monument with 13-foot statue of British Admiral Lord Nelson (1758–1805). It is one of the few monuments in this chapter that is no longer standing, as it was bombed by the Irish Republican Army in 1966.

"the man who takes his own life"—This conversation evokes Bloom's memory of the death of his father. Odysseus encounters his mother in the underworld, learning of her death from the sight of her shade. By the sudden turn of the conversation, Joyce achieves a similar effect of surprise in his hero.

—Temporary insanity, of course, Martin Cunningham said decisively. We must take a charitable view of it.

—They say a man who does it is a coward, Mr Dedalus said.

—**It is not for us to judge,** Martin Cunningham said.

Mr Bloom, about to speak, closed his lips again. Martin Cunningham's large eyes. Looking away now. Sympathetic human man he is. Intelligent. Like Shakespeare's face. Always a good word to say. They have no mercy on that here or infanticide. Refuse christian burial. They used to drive a stake of wood through his heart in the grave. As if it wasn't broken already. Yet sometimes they repent too late. Found in the riverbed clutching rushes. He looked at me. And that awful drunkard of a wife of his. Setting up house for her time after time and then pawning the furniture on him every Saturday almost. Leading him the life of the damned. Wear the heart out of a stone, that. Monday morning start afresh. **Shoulder to the wheel.** Lord, she must have looked a sight that night Dedalus told me he was in there. Drunk about the place and capering with Martin's umbrella:

—*And they call me the jewel of Asia,*
Of Asia,
The geisha.

He looked away from me. He knows. Rattle his bones. . . .

As they turned into Berkeley street a streetorgan near the **Basin** sent over and after them a rollicking song of the halls. **Has anybody here seen Kelly?** Kay ee double ell wy. Dead march from *Saul.* He's as bad as old **Antonio.** He left me on my ownio. Pirouette! The *Mater Misericordiae.* **Eccles street.** My house down there. Big place. Ward for incurables there. Very encouraging. Our Lady's Hospice for the dying. Deadhouse handy underneath. Where old Mrs Riordan died. . . .

—Dunphy's, Mr Power announced as the carriage turned right.

Dunphy's corner. Mourning coaches drawn up drowning their grief. A pause by the wayside. Tiptop position for a pub. Expect we'll pull up here on the way back to drink his health. Pass round the consolation. **Elixir of life**. . . .

In silence they drove along Phibsborough road. An empty hearse trotted by, coming from the cemetery: looks relieved.

Crossguns bridge: the **royal canal**. . . .

The stonecutter's yard on the right. Last lap. Crowded on the spit of land **silent shapes** appeared, white, sorrowful, holding out calm hands, knelt in grief, pointing. Fragments of shapes, hewn. In white silence: appealing. The best obtainable. Thos. H. Dennany, monumental builder and sculptor. . . .

Paltry funeral: coach and three carriages. It's all the same. Pallbearers, gold reins, requiem mass, firing a volley. Pomp of death. Behind the hind carriage a hawker stood by his barrow of cakes and fruit. Simnel cakes those are, stuck together: **cakes for the dead. Dogbiscuits.** Who ate them? Mourners coming out. . . .

Titian (Tiziano Vecelli) (ca. 1488–1576), *Sisyphus.*

"It is not for us to judge"—Of the party in the carriage, only Martin Cunningham is aware of the circumstances of the elder Bloom's death.

"Shoulder to the wheel"—Cunningham is described as Sisyphus, the mythical king punished by having to roll a boulder uphill for eternity.

Basin A rectangular reservoir called the City Basin.

"Has anybody here seen Kelly?"—The refrain from the American version of a song about a man who abandons his sweetheart.

Saul Handel's Dead March from the oratorio *Saul* is traditionally played at British military funerals. It accompanies the defeated Israelites recovering their dead from the battle of Gilboa.

Antonio Ice cream seller who betrays his benefactors in a song.

Mater Misericordiae Largest hospital in Dublin at the time.

Eccles street Where Bloom's own house is located.

"Elixir of life"—rough translation of the Irish *uisce beatha* (water of life), the origin of the word "whiskey."

Royal Canal Last of the four rivers crossed by the funeral procession.

"silent shapes"—The statues in the stonecutter's yard resemble the shades of the dead who inhabit Hades.

"cakes for the dead"—Like many other ancient cultures, the Greeks supplied the dead with food for the journey. Joyce's irony here is that these are for "mourners coming out."

"Dogbiscuits"—Cerberus the three-headed dog guarded the entrance to the Greek underworld.

The priest took a stick with a knob at the end of it out of the boy's bucket and shook it over the coffin. Then he walked to the other end and shook it again. Then he came back and put it back in the bucket. As you were before you rested. It's all written down: **he has to do it.**

—*Et ne nos inducas in tentationem*. . . .

Holy water that was, I expect. Shaking sleep out of it. He must be fed up with that job, shaking that thing over all the corpses they trot up. What harm if he could see what he was shaking it over. Every mortal day a fresh batch: middleaged men, old women, children, women dead in childbirth, men with beards, baldheaded business men, consumptive girls with little sparrows' breasts. All the year round he prayed the same thing over them all and shook water on top of them: sleep. On Dignam now.

—*In paradisum.*

Said he was going to paradise or is in paradise. Says that over everybody. Tiresome kind of a job. But he has to say something. . . .

The coffin dived out of sight, eased down by the men straddled on the gravetrestles. They struggled up and out: and all uncovered. Twenty.

Pause.

If we were all suddenly somebody else.

Far away **a donkey brayed.** Rain. No such ass. Never see a dead one, they say. Shame of death. They hide. Also **poor papa went away.**

Gentle sweet air blew round the bared heads in a whisper. Whisper. **The boy by the gravehead** held his wreath with both hands staring quietly in the black open space. Mr Bloom moved behind the portly kindly caretaker. Well cut frockcoat. Weighing them up perhaps to see which will go next. Well it is a long rest. Feel no more. It's the moment you feel. Must be damned unpleasant. Can't believe it at first. Mistake must be: someone else. Try the house opposite. Wait, I wanted to. I haven't yet. Then darkened death chamber. Light they want. Whispering around you. Would you like to see a priest? Then rambling and wandering. Delerium all you hid all your life. The death struggle. His sleep is not natural. Press his lower eyelid. Watching is his nose pointed is his jaw sinking are the soles of his feet yellow. Pull the pillow away and finish it off on the floor since he's doomed. Devil in that picture of sinner's death showing him a woman. Dying to embrace her in his shirt. Last act of *Lucia*. *Shall I nevermore behold thee?* Bam! expires. Gone at last. People talk about you a bit: forget you. Don't forget to pray for him. **Remember him** in your prayers. Even Parnell. **Ivy day dying out.** Then they follow: dropping into a hole one after the other.

We are praying now for the repose of his soul. Hoping you're well and not in hell. Nice change of air. Out of the fryingpan of life into the fire of purgatory. . . .

An **obese grey rat** toddled along the side of the crypt, moving the pebbles. An old stager: great grandfather; he knows the ropes. The grey alive crushed itself in under the plinth, wriggled itself in under it. Good hidingplace for treasure.

Who lives there? Are laid the remains of Robert Emery. **Robert Emmet** was buried there by torchlight, wasn't he? Making his rounds.

Tail gone now.

One of those chaps could make short work of a fellow. Pick the bones clean no matter who it was. Ordinary meat for them. A corpse is meat gone bad. Well and what's cheese? Corpse of milk. I read in that *Voyages in China* that the Chinese say a white man smells like a corpse. Cremation better. Priests dead against. it. Devilling for the other firm. Wholesale burners and Dutch oven dealers. Time of the plague. Quicklime fever pits to eat them. Lethal chamber. Ashes to ashes. Or bury at sea. Where is

---

"he has to do it"—As with all ritual, the priest follows prescribed rites, blessing the coffin and the mourners with holy water. Bloom meditates on how little meaning he would find in such a repetitious job. In contrast, in Homer it is Odysseus who performs a ritual to attract the spirits of the dead.

"*Et ne nos inducas in tentationem*"—"Lead us not into temptation," the next-to-concluding words of the Lord's prayer.

"*In paradisum*"—Opening words of the anthem sung when the coffin is carried to the grave: "Into paradise may the angels lead you."

"a donkey brayed"—When this occurs at noon, it is supposed to indicate the coming of rain. Gifford suggests that Bloom may be confused about the saying.

"poor papa went away"—Bloom mourns his own family several times in this episode, forming a parallel to Odysseus' conversation with his dead mother in Hades.

"The boy by the gravehead"— Bloom is reminded of the death of his own son, Rudy.

Lucia The opera *Lucia di Lammermoor* features the heroine in a mad scene sung in her nightgown.

"Remember him"—As Bloom expresses one of modern mankind's major concerns, he notes the inevitability of being forgotten. A primary aim of epics such as the Odyssey is to remember heroes. Joyce intimates here that this is futile.

"Ivy day dying out"—Parnell was an Irish nationalist whose efforts failed when he came into conflict with the Catholic Church. His followers wore a leaf of ivy on the anniversary of his death.

"obese gray rat"—Odysseus talks to the spirit of the prophet Teiresias, who tells him the ceremony he needs to perform to ward off the wrath of Poseidon, god of the sea. Bloom, in contrast receives a concrete indication of his own mortality from this creature.

Robert Emmet Odysseus comes upon the shade of his boatman Elpenor, who has died while he has been away. Here Bloom is reminded of Robert Emmet (whose name is similar to the one on the tomb before him), an Irish patriot whose burial place is unknown.

"Parsee tower of silence"—The ancient custom of the followers of the Persian religion of Zoroaster was to dispose of their dead by installing them in a tower, where their bodies become food for vultures and other birds.

"Back to the world"—Leaving the Dublin cemetery through the iron gates is like leaving the ancient underworld. The difference is that leaving the underworld demanded the consent of Hades (see Ch. 27, p. 385).

"Mrs Sinico's funeral"—This is one of several cross-references to characters in other Joyce works, such as *Dubliners* and *A Portrait of the Artist as a Young Man*.

"They are not going to get me"—Bloom's optimism and relief mirrors that of Odysseus as he resumes his journey.

that **Parsee tower of silence?** Eaten by birds. Earth, fire, water. Drowning they say is the pleasantest. See your whole life in a flash. But being brought back to life no. Can't bury in the air however. Out of a flying machine. Wonder does the news go about whenever a fresh one is let down. Underground communication. We learned that from them. Wouldn't be surprised. Regular square feed for them. Flies come before he's well dead. Got wind of Dignam. They wouldn't care about the smell of it. Saltwhite crumbling mush of corpse: smell, taste like raw white turnips.

The gates glimmered in front: still open. **Back to the world** again. Enough of this place. Brings you a bit nearer every time. Last time I was here was **Mrs Sinico's funeral.** Poor papa too. The love that kills. And even scraping up the earth at night with a lantern like that case I read of to get at fresh buried females or even putrefied with running gravesores. Give you the creeps after a bit. I will appear to you after death. You will see my ghost after death. My ghost will haunt you after death. There is another world after death named hell. I do not like that other world she wrote. No more do I. Plenty to see and hear and feel yet. Feel live warm beings near you. Let them sleep in their maggoty beds. **They are not going to get me** this innings. Warm beds: warm fullblooded life.

Further Reading

Blamires, Harry. *The Bloomsday Book: A Guide through Joyce's Ulysses.* London: Methuen & Co. Ltd., 1966.

Joyce, James. *Ulysses.* Paris: Shakespeare and Company, 1922.

The Centaur

JOHN UPDIKE

John Updike, who was born in 1932, is one of America's most celebrated writers. His novels and short stories often portray the relationships of what might be called ordinary people, and in the process, these characters reveal themselves as complex individuals grappling with modern life.

Updike's characteristic theme of characters trying to find a meaningful role in life is given extra dimensions in *The Centaur,* his National Book Award–winning novel. Written in 1962, this novel takes place over three days in the winter of 1947, and focuses on the relationship of a father and teenage son, George and Peter Caldwell, in south-central Pennsylvania. Like many adolescents, Peter is often embarrassed by his father's actions—even if it is a matter of the man's being kind or charitable—and he is trying to find his own place in society, while wondering what he will do as an adult.

Peter is the narrator of the novel, writing eleven years after its major events. Therefore, some of the chapters take place in the narrator's present, in New York City, where he is an undistinguished expressionist painter. Seeing the adolescent narrator's future career gives the reader the chance to see that he has succeeded, to an extent, in his artistic aspirations and that he has achieved a respect and admiration for his father.

In fact, Peter begins to understand his father only as he tells the story. He realizes his legacy as son and artist. During the action of the novel, we see that George has explained to him what he considered the eternal progression of human endeavor and achievement: the movement from priest to teacher to artist. And Peter now accepts his responsibility as the son of a science teacher and grandson of a minister, George's father, Wesley Caldwell. This maturation fits into the mythological scheme of the novel, especially Joseph Campbell's psychological aspect of myth that shows the struggles of individuals to become mature human beings and useful members of society (see Ch. 1, p. 9).

THE STORY

George Caldwell, a high school science teacher and father of Peter, a teenage son, is experiencing a midlife crisis. The bulk of the novel consists of Peter's recollection of events involving the Caldwell family over three days in 1947. The reader discovers early that the narrative's characters inhabit not only Olinger, their hometown in rural Pennsylvania, but also simultaneously operate in the sphere of Greek mythology.

As the book opens, George Caldwell is teaching the history of the evolution of the world, and one of the disruptive students throws a missile at him. Caldwell is also Chiron, the centaur teacher of Greek gods. Wounded by the poisoned arrow, he staggers to the nearby Hummel's Garage where the proprietor removes the arrow. Hummel's garage is the forge of the Greek god Hephaestus.

In the second chapter, Peter begins to recount his experiences with his father during the three days, noting Caldwell's hypochondriacal fear that he has stomach cancer and his obsequious behavior with a revolting hitchhiker.

Interestingly, this chapter, full of realistic detail, is followed by a pastoral interlude focusing on Chiron the centaur teaching his ideal and idealistic students in an ancient Greek setting. (For more on the "pastoral," see Ch. 42, p. 625.) Here, Caldwell and Olinger are totally absent.

In a subsequent chapter, Peter recounts a dream in which, as Prometheus, he laments George's death. During this dream, he meets his "dead" father and tries to convince him to go on living.

The next chapter consists of Peter's recalling further events of the three days, and then the novel ends with Caldwell as Chiron. After spending two nights away from home because of a snowstorm and their old Buick's engine problems, Caldwell and Peter return to Olinger, only to stall again just before reaching their house. Next morning, Peter remains home with a fever while his father goes out, presumably to dig out and start the car and go to his teaching job, which he hates. The reader might guess that it is Caldwell who is going to dig out the car, but as the narration continues, it becomes clear that we are dealing with the centaur. In the excerpt the family's big, black 1936 Buick can be seen as the chariot of Zeus as well as the gateway to the afterlife. Whether Caldwell actually dies at this point is not clear. Doc Appleton had recently reported to him that the diagnostic tests for cancer proved negative. However, this ambiguity might be expected in a story with a strong emphasis on dual characters who simultaneously inhabit two worlds, yet operate discretely in each.

DUAL EXISTENCE: CONTEMPORARY HUMANS AND MYTHOLOGICAL FIGURES

We selected the final chapter from *The Centaur* as our excerpt because it illustrates well how the novel operates. In some poetic works, the use of mythological material would involve symbolism or allegory; in such a symbolic presentation, the figurative representation of the character is substituted for a literal one, creating a kind of artistic overlay. However, in Olinger, Pennsylvania, *The Centaur's* world, myth and realism coexist: the novel is not an allegory, and the dual nature of the characters is not symbolic. The characters simultaneously inhabit both the everyday, real world, and the eternally present mythological sphere. Even when the narrative shifts in midsentence between the worlds, the action is continuous and the characters operate smoothly with no marked transition.

For example, within the first two pages, when Caldwell/Chiron has been wounded, he walks down the hall on his way to Hummel's garage, where the owner has metalworking tools to remove the arrow. During this walk, phrases and descriptions reveal the unexpected equine characteristics of a character who was assumed to be a human being. In other words, it becomes clear that George Caldwell is Chiron: "Each time the feathers brushed the floor, the shaft worked in his wound. He tried to keep that leg from touching the floor, but the jagged clatter of the three remaining hooves sounded so loud he was afraid one of the doors would snap open and another teacher emerge to bar his way. In this crisis his fellow-teachers seemed herdsmen of terror, threatening to squeeze him back into the room with the students" (4–5).

Chiron was conceived when Cronos, the son of Uranus (or Ouranus, "sky") sought his infant son Zeus who had been hidden by his mother Rhea in Crete. As a result of his parentage Chiron was immortal, and because of his talents he was entrusted with educating the Olympian youth. It was he who taught healing to Apollo's son Asclepius, who became the god of medicine. However, a poisoned arrow mistakenly shot by one of his students, Heracles, wounded the centaur; the pain was everlasting and so severe that he wanted to die. He begged Zeus to let him go to Hades in place of Prometheus, who was suffering for his rebellion against the head god. Zeus finally granted his wish. (For more on Heracles, see Ch. 31, p. 446, and on Prometheus see Ch. 24, p. 353.)

It is not only George Caldwell and his son Peter who inhabit both worlds; all of the major Olinger characters are also mythological figures. The correspondences require readers to call on their knowledge of Greek mythology, because they are often subtle and much more complex than merely identifying attributes or characteristic behavior. As an introduction, the chart (p. 667) provides an outline of some of the important characters in the novel.

Pamphaios, Centaur Chiron carrying the young Achilles. Attic red-figure amphora, 525 B.C.E. In Greek mythology, centaurs are creatures that are human to the waist, but have the lower body of a horse. They are half-civilized creatures who are often unable to control their instincts and their emotions. However, Chiron is an unusual centaur who, unlike his fellows, is cultivated and learned.

WHAT HAPPENED? WHAT HAPPENS?

Some readers of *The Centaur* presume that Caldwell commits suicide. But considering his dual existence as father and centaur, it is more logical that his "death" is metaphorical: the giving up of his spirit to the pain and disillusionment of teaching and everyday life. He will return to the demands at Olinger High for the sake of his son. Test results have just confirmed that he does not have cancer as he had suspected, and especially during the past three days as they tried to get home, George realizes a special closeness and responsibility to his son.

This respect and responsibility is also evident in the fact that, more than a decade later, Peter brings together his creative powers and his mythological responsibility to tell the story (see "nostalgia," Ch. 1, p. 10), thus remembering and celebrating his father's legacy. In fact, by telling the story "warts and all," he actually elevates his father's life, making it easier for the reader to understand that he simultaneously inhabits the mundane and mythological realms.

In *The Centaur,* Updike illustrates the importance of mythological thought in the development of contemporary individuals, as described by Campbell's psychological aspect of myth. The novel's significance can be viewed in a broader, societal perspective as well. The twentieth-century British poet W. H. Auden explained the value of literature by saying that history tells us what happened, while literature tells us what happens. Mythology, like literature, tells us what happens and thus helps us find our place in the world. Speaking specifically of *The Centaur,* Donald J. Greiner spells out the relationship between these realms: "The mythic frame of the novel reflects the divisions between soul and body, heaven and earth, immortality and the ordinary, and Olympus and Olinger. Unable to be sure of one, humanity creates the other in order to consider both. That is, *man makes metaphors to explain his predicament, and the hero straddles the extremes*" (109).

In this view of the novel, George Caldwell straddles the extremes, but finds that he cannot unify his split nature as the immortal centaur and the mortal George Caldwell. In the end, as Chiron accepts death to atone for the mythical Prometheus, Caldwell sacrifices figuratively for the sake of his son Peter—he returns to his appalling teaching job. And by continuing his mundane life in a

Character	Greek Deity	Example of Correspondence
Vera Hummel	Venus	A shapely, provocative physical education teacher whom Chiron meets as she emerges from the Olinger High locker room shower, the Arcadian woodland pond.
Mr. Hummel	Hephaestus	Owner of Hummel's garage, where Caldwell/Chiron goes to have the arrow removed from his leg. The Olinger garage is also the primeval metal workshop of the god Hephaestus. Like Hephaestus, Hummel walks with a limp.
Mr. Zimmerman	Zeus	Principal of Olinger High. Mr. Zimmerman holds as much power over Caldwell as Zeus does over Chiron and the Greek deities. Like Zeus, Zimmerman is duplicitous and promiscuous. When he visits Caldwell/ Chiron's class, he moves about the room fondling the young girls.
Mrs. Herzog	Hera	Although Hera is the wife of Zeus, Mrs. Herzog is not Mr. Zimmerman's spouse. She takes on the role in fact by carrying on a sexual affair with him, and by sharing administration of the school as head of the parent-teacher association.
Minor Kretz	Minos	Mr. Kretz's luncheonette, the main hangout for the Olinger High students, is a maze of counters and booths filled with exuberant young people trying to make their way through the crowd to meet with friends. The maze on Crete surrounded the beastly Minotaur and prevented young people from escaping him and his voracious appetite.
Cassie Caldwell	Demeter (called Ceres in the novel, after the Roman version of the goddess)	Peter's mother and George's wife. Mrs. Caldwell is a Ceres counterpart who has moved the family from the town to the country so they can live closer to nature. (For the story of Demeter, see Ch. 27, p. 385.)
Pop Kramer	Cronos (See Kronos in Ch. 3, p. 32.)	Cassie Caldwell's father, who lives with the Caldwell family, is the respected elder, the keeper of the family history, and follower of world events through daily newspaper reading. He is typically found in the family kitchen as Cassie tries to get George and Peter out on time. Appropriately to his identity as Cronos, Pop Kramer refers repeatedly to the one of two clocks that is accurate, while George is adamant in pacing himself according to the other timepiece, a cheap and inaccurate model.

small town in Pennsylvania, he sets up the circumstances for his son to finish his education and take his place in the continuum of human existence. Thus, the mythological dimension of the novel provides Updike with a power image showing the inevitable fragmentation of human beings in modern society.

Alone **he walked through the white width.** His hooves clattered, the fourth scraping (bone against bone), on the limestone plateau, sunstruck from above. Was the dome bronze or iron? From Sky to Earth, they said, an anvil would fall nine days and nights; and from Earth again it would fall nine days and nights and on the tenth day strike Tartaros. In the first days, **when Uranus nightly coupled with Gaia,** the distance must have been less. Perhaps now it was more, perhaps—the thought deepened his sickness—**an anvil could fall forever from Sky** and never strike Earth. For indeed, was it not **Mother Ge,** who from her damp clefts had once freely brought forth the **Hundred-handed,** the metal-wielding One-eyed, deep-swirling Oceanus, Caeus and Crius and Hyperion and Iapetus, Theia and Rhea, Themis and Mnemosyne and gold-crowned Phoebe and lovely Tethys the mother of Philyra; Ge who when watered by the blood-drops of **her consort**'s mutilation brought forth the avenging Erinnyes and the gentler Meliai, the shadows of ash-trees and the nurses of Zeus; Ge who brought forth Pegasos

This excerpt is from: John Updike, *The Centaur,* Chapter IX.*

"he walked through the white width"—Caldwell/Chiron walks across the snow to the Buick in the yard.

"when Uranus nightly coupled, with Gaia"—Hesiod describes their union in the *Theogony.* Throughout this chapter, Updike bases the Centaur's reveries on this literary work (see Ch. 3, pp. 29–35).

"an anvil could fall forever from Sky"—Knowing the ancient story but caught in modern doubt, he fears uncertainty.

Mother Ge Another name for Gaia.

"Hundred-handed"—The Hecatoncheires, monsters who helped Zeus defeat the Titans. (See Ch. 3, p. 33.)

"her consort"—Cronos.

* This excerpt is Chapter IX of *The Centaur,* by John Updike. Copyright © 1962, 1963 by John Updike. Used by permission of Alfred A. Knopf, a division of Random House, Inc.

Ceres Goddess of the harvest, Roman counterpart of Demeter. (See Ch. 27, p. 386.)

"the twelve"—The main Greek gods were twelve in number.

"The pain in his tissues"—Chiron accepted death to escape the pain of his wound.

Hekate **A member of the older** generation of the gods, associated with Gaia, the earth, and with the underworld. She fought with the Giants against the Olympian gods, but a victorious Zeus did not punish her because of her great power. She plays a role in the story of the kidnapping of Persephone (see Ch. 27, p. 392).

"The scene he had left behind"— This paragraph melds aspects of Caldwell as father of Peter and Chiron as benefactor of Prometheus. (See Introduction, p. 665.)

Ocyrhoe Daughter of Charon, who functions in the mythological component of the novel as the equivalent of Peter.

"a king is born"—A reference to the birth of Christ at Christmas, and to the king who is sacrificed in James Frazer's *Golden Bough.* Frazer, an anthropologist at the turn of the 20th c., was influential in his day but is not much accepted today. He believed that ancient Greek religion had a basis of human sacrifice, involving a king who marries a priestess of the mother goddess and after a time is sacrificed for the good of his people.

"the sky of his father's God"—In this scene, George is walking with Wesley Caldwell, his father. This phrase briefly anchors the story in the mythological component by mention of the Centaur's father Cronos, and his father Ouranus (Sky).

"but the boy took it to heart"—As Caldwell reflects on his father's words, he is consoled and becomes optimistic. This passing down of wisdom is cited earlier, when George tells Peter from priest to teacher to artist.

from the drops of the Gorgon's blood and who mating with Tartaros brought forth her youngest and most terrible son Typhoeus, whose lower body was two wrestling serpents and whose arms stretched from sunrise to sunset and who flung whole mountains daubed with his blood and for a time hid the sinews of Zeus himself in a bear's pelt—was it not Mother Ge who had summoned easily from her brown belly such prodigies now entranced by a strange quietude? White, she was white, death's own color, sum of the spectrum, wherever the centaur's eye searched. He wondered, Had not the castration of Sky worked a terrible sterility upon Gaia, though she herself had cried aloud for rescue?

The plants by the side of the road he walked were bare of leaves and sparse in variety. Orchard grass the signature of **Ceres,** sumac the dermal poison, dogwood whose bark was a mild purge, mulberry and pin oak and choke cherry, staple of hedgerows. Sticks. In this season they were barren of virtue and the ground of blank snow made them calligraphic. He searched their scribble for a word and found none. There was no help. There was not one of **the twelve** he had not consulted and not one had given him the answer. Must he wander forever beneath the blank gaze of the gods? 👁 👁 **The pain in his tissues** barked and tore like a penned pack of dogs. Set them free. *My Lord, set them free.* As if in fury at his prayer there poured through his mind like the foul congested breath of **Hekate** the monstrous tumble of aborted forms and raging giants that composed the sequence of creation: a ferment sucked from the lipless yawn of Chaos, the grisly All-father. *Brug.* His wise mind gaped helplessly ajar under this onrush of horror and he prayed now for only the blessing of ignorance, of forgetting. Politic, he had long ago made it his policy to ask the gods only what he believed they could not help giving. The gates narrowed; he mercifully forgot a little of what he knew.

The scene he had left behind him came to trouble his mind. His child lying fevered. His heart moved in pity for **Ocyrhoe,** his one seedling with her wealth of hair. Needed a haircut. Poor kid, needed everything. Poverty. His inheritance, deskful of debts and a Bible, he was passing it on. Poverty the last child of Ge. Sky, emasculate, had flung himself far off raging in pain and left his progeny to parch upon a white waste that stretched its arms from sunrise to sunset.

Yet even in the dead of winter the sere twigs prepare for their small dull buds. In the pit of the year **a king is born.** Not a leaf falls but leaves an amber root, a dainty hoof, a fleck of baggage to be unpacked in future time. Such flecks gave the black thatch of twigs a ruddy underglow. Dully the centaur's litmus eye absorbed this; slowly the chemistry of his thought altered. The intervals between the hedgerow trunks passed him like ragged doorways and he remembered walking on some church errand with his father down a dangerous street in Passaic; it was Saturday and the men from the sulphur works were getting drunk. From within the double doors of a saloon there welled poisonous laughter that seemed to distill all the cruelty and blasphemy in the world, and he wondered how such a noise could have a place under **the sky of his father's God.** In those days he customarily kept silent about what troubled him, but his worry must have made itself felt, for he remembered his father turning and listening in his backwards collar to the laughter from the saloon and then smiling down to his son, "All joy belongs to the Lord."

It was half a joke **but the boy took it to heart.** All joy belongs to the Lord. Wherever in the filth and confusion and misery, a soul felt joy, there the Lord came and claimed it as his own; into barrooms and brothels and classrooms and alleys slippery with spittle, no matter how dark and scabbed and remote, in China or Africa or Brazil, wherever a moment of joy was felt, there the Lord stole and added to his enduring domain. And all the rest, all that was not joy, fell away, precipitated, dross that had never been. He thought of his wife's joy in the land and Pop Kramer's joy in the newspaper and his son's joy in the future and was glad, grateful, that he was able to sustain these for yet a space more. The X-rays were clear. **A white width of days stretched ahead.** The time left him possessed a skyey breadth in which he swam like a true grandchild of Oceanus; he discovered that in giving his life to others he entered a total freedom. Mt. Ide and Mt. Dikte from opposite blue distances rushed toward him like clapping waves and in the upright of his body **Sky and Gaia mated again.** Only goodness lives. But it does live.

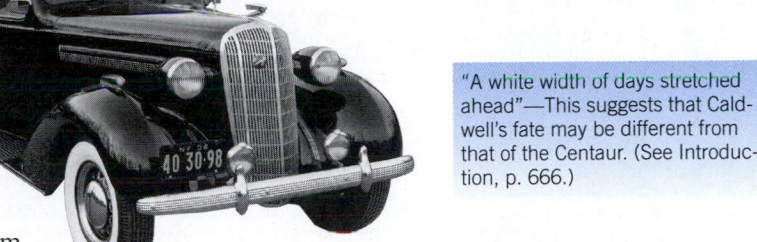

A '36 Buick.

"A white width of days stretched ahead"—This suggests that Caldwell's fate may be different from that of the Centaur. (See Introduction, p. 666.)

Now he came to the turn in the road. A hundred strides ahead of him he saw **the Buick** like a black mouth he must enter. It had been an undertaker's car. It made a black spot against the heaped snow, fifty-fifty he could get it out. Above the brow of the field on his left **the Amishman's silo** poked with its conical hat of corrugated iron; an abandoned windmill stood stark; a few grackles wheeled above the buried stubble.

Brutish landscape.

The invisible expanse **the centaur** had in an instant grasped retreated from him with a pang; he focused forward at the car and his heart felt squeezed. An ache spread through his abdomen, where the hominoid and equine elements interlocked. Monsters are most vulnerable in their transitions.

Black.

They really put the shellac on those old pre-war Buicks. As Chiron drew nearer, the shattered grille looked astonished. He saw now that this was the mouth of a tunnel he must crawl through; the children he was committed to teach seemed in his brain's glare-struck eye the jiggling teeth of a grinder, a multi-colored chopper. He had been spoiled. In these last days he had been saying goodbye to everything, tidying up the books, readying himself for a change, a journey. **There would be none; Atropos** had opened her shears, thought twice, smiled, and permitted the thread to continue spinning.

Chiron bit back a belch and tried to muster his thoughts. A steep weariness mounted before him. The prospect of having again to maneuver among Zimmerman and Mrs. Herzog and all that overbearing unfathomable Olinger gang made him giddy, sick; how could his father's seed, exploding into an infinitude of possibilities, have been funneled into this, this paralyzed patch of thankless alien land, these few cryptic faces, those certain four walls of **Room 204?**

Drawing closer to the car, close enough to see an elongated distortion of himself in the fender, he understood. This was a chariot **Zimmerman** had sent for him. His lessons. He must order his mind and prepare his lessons.

Why do we worship Zeus? Because there is none other.

Name the five rivers of the dead. Styx, Acheron, Phlegethon, Kokytos, and Lethe.

Who were the daughters of Nereus? Agaue, Aktaia, Amphitrite, Autonoe, Doris, Doto, Dynamene, Eione, Erato, Euagore, Euarne, Eudora, Eukrante, Eulimene, Eunike, Eupompe, Galateia, Galene, Glauke, Glaukonome, Halia, Halimede, Hipponoe, Hippothoe, Kymo, Kymodoke, Kymothoe, Laomedeia, Leiagora, Lysianassa, Melite, Menippe, Nemertes, Nesaie, Neso, Panopeia, Pasithea, Pherousa, Ploto, Polynoe, Pontoporeia, Pronoe, Proto, Protomedeia, Psamathe, Sao, Speio, Themisto, Thetis, and Thoe.

What is a hero? A hero is a king sacrificed to Hera.

Chiron came to the edge of limestone; **his hoof scratched.** A bit of pale pebble rattled into the abyss. He cast his eyes upward to the dome of blue and perceived that it

"Sky and Gaia mated again"—Renewal of the mythic process of creation offers hope and optimism to the modern human.

"the Buick"—The car that has kept George and Peter away from home, but has also given rise to their adventures, which have helped reveal the true nature of the father to the son.

"the Amishman's silo"—Many farms in southeastern Pennsylvania are worked by Amish families, members of a Pietist religious denomination.

"the centaur"—From the house, Peter sees his father trudge to the car, but George is operating dually as Chiron/George.

"There would be none"—George will continue his journey as father, teacher, man.

Atropos One of the three Fates. It is she who cuts off the thread of a human life, bringing about its end.

"Room 204"—Caldwell's classroom at Olinger High.

Zimmerman The principal of Olinger High, a Zeus figure.

"Why do we worship Zeus?"—This is the material the Centaur teaches his Olympian students, rather than what Caldwell teaches in Olinger.

"his hoof scratched"—The figure here is the Centaur, with no reference to Caldwell.

Translation of the Greek: "And having received an incurable wound, he went off to the cave. And he willingly went there to die; and although he was immortal and thus not able to die, when Prometheus exchanged fates with him, in order that Chiron might die in his stead, then the Centaur died" (Taylor, 125). The classical Greek explanation (from Apollodorus, *Library* 2.5.4) provides a necessary link between the original myth and the current story. In doing so, Updike emphasizes the relationship between myth and reality as well as the heroism of apparently mundane lives.

was indeed a great step. Yes, in seriousness, a very great step, for which all the walking in his life had not prepared him. Not an easy step nor an easy journey, it would take an eternity to get there, an eternity as the anvil ever fell. His strained bowels sagged; his hurt leg cursed; his head felt light. The whiteness of limestone pierced his eyes. A little breeze met his face at the cliff-edge. His will, a perfect diamond under the pressure of absolute fear, uttered the final word. *Now.* ἀνί ατον δὲ ἔχων τὸ ἕλκος εἰς τὸ σπήλαιον ἀπαλλάσσεται κἀκεῖ τελευτῆσαι βουλόμενος καὶ μὴ δυνάμενος ἐπείπερ ἀθάνατος ἦν, ἀντιδόντος Διὶ Προμηθέως αὐτὸν ἀντ᾽ αὐτοῦ γενησόμενον ἀθάνατου οὕτως ἀπέθανεν. Chiron accepted death.

EPILOGUE

Zeus had loved his old friend, and lifted him up, and set him among the stars as the constellation Sagittarius. Here, in the Zodiac, now above, now below the horizon, he assists in the regulation of our destinies, though in this latter time few living mortals cast their eyes respectfully toward Heaven, and fewer still sit as students to the stars.

Further Reading

Updike, John. *The Centaur.* New York, NY: Alfred A. Knopf, 1962.

The Tiger's Bride

ANGELA CARTER

Angela Carter (1940–1992) was a writer of fairy tales and fantastic stories who lived in England and the United States; she was also a teacher of writing and an award-winning novelist. Among Carter's best known works are *Nights at the Circus, Several Perceptions, The Bloody Chamber,* and *The Magic Toyshop.* Besides adapting this last work for film, she wrote the film script for *The Company of Wolves.*

"The Tiger's Bride" is among several of Carter's stories using the Beauty and the Beast theme. It is readily recognizable as a close, but modern relative of the classic versions of the story we have known from childhood. This story is a good example of a reutilized fairy tale, one which retains its basic components according to the Aarne–Thompson classification (see Part 6 Introduction, p. 497), but revises the action to suit it to another audience (Zipes, 9–10). In a reutilized fairy tale like this one, the other audience is usually the author's contemporary society or a poet's representation of a particular philosophy. In a sense, reutilization is actually what also happens in the oral tradition: each teller stresses those events and characteristics that are most meaningful for her and her audience, and she glosses over or leaves out what is not valued or not understood by her audience. However, in the hands of a literary artist, these choices might be much more deliberate and the alterations more encompassing. Thus, reutilization is a more decisive and more conscious process than reworking.

However, Marina Warner, who has studied literary fairy tales, notes that they still have embedded in them remnants of ancient beliefs and traditions. Therefore, tracing the evolution of these tales can give us historical and cultural information that otherwise might not be immediately evident. (For more of Warner's analyses, see Ch. 38, p. 562.) In Angela Carter's version, Beauty is lost to The Beast by her father in a card game; Warner explains that this is a modern variation of the tradition described in older stories of fathers giving daughters in marriage without consulting them. The moral teaching in these stories was that girls are virtuous and good when they are obedient and receptive to authority. And traditionally, the accepting brides are rewarded for their obedience when The Beast ultimately turns into the expected handsome prince and offers marriage.

In contrast, in Carter's version, the father is not a responsible patriarch providing for his daughter according to the rules of his society, but an irresponsible gambler who can't control his addiction. Virtue resides in Beauty, who accepts the sentence brought upon her by her father's gambling mania. The irony of Beauty's situation is compounded by The Beast's regression into an increasingly bestial state (instead of any revelation of his noble human qualities). Finally, Beauty decides to renounce her humanness and join The Beast: there is no prince, no return to human society, and most impressively—no regret. The events in Carter's version of the story recall the stereotypical features of the original, only to critique the values they are based on and to pay homage to the value of individual choice, as expressed through an ironic and irreverent portrayal of idiosyncratic sexuality.

THE ANIMAL BRIDEGROOM MOTIF

Marina Warner explains that the motif of the animal bridegroom is very ancient and widespread, with some very old versions in India and China. The Roman tale by Apuleius called "Cupid and Psyche" (see Ch. 37, p. 541) is the earliest story we have of the Beauty and the Beast type in Western literature. In western Europe, the earliest written version of the tale, "Beauty and the Beast," was written in 1740 by Madame de Villaneuve. It was a production of the French literary salons, which are discussed in the Introduction to the Grimms' tales (Ch. 36, p. 526). This classic tale is characterized by its intricate plot and sophisticated narrative structure. Here, the bridegroom is actually a prince who has met his fate as beast because he refused his guardian's propositions. But Belle recognizes him as the true noble he is, and her caring becomes his salvation. Like Carter's version of the story, this one also provides a view of contemporary problems, revealing the corruption at the French court, which allows the prince to be transformed into a beast through the arbitrary behavior of his guardian.

In many tales involving animal bridegrooms, the female figure is somehow at fault; she must atone for her limited appreciation of The Beast's virtues and learn that it is wrong to fear him, because his repulsiveness is in the eye of the beholder. Warner argues that such tales seem designed to teach girls to accept the husband chosen for them according to the social situation of the times. While sons went off joyfully to find a bride, daughters often didn't know what kind of family they were marrying into and going to spend the rest of their life with. Thus, tales like "Beauty and the Beast" warned girls of their responsibility to make the best of marriages arranged perhaps without their consent or even knowledge. When the method of selecting a marriage partner changed and women had more choice in the process, animal bridegroom tales changed, too.

The underlying assumptions in classic Beauty and the Beast tales also illustrate the maternal role of women storytellers, who used these stories in teaching young girls how to live in society. For example, you can look at The Beast as someone "other" who does not belong to Beauty's usual world. Telling the story in this way would have been quite consoling for girls who were worried about having husbands chosen for them, because the originally threatening Beast is eventually recognized as a prince and a potentially loving bridegroom.

In fact, Madame Leprince de Beaumont, who was by profession a governess in England, wrote a version of the tale that inspired the classic 1946 film by the French Surrealist dramatist Jean Cocteau. In *La Belle et le Bête*, the Beast does not have to change because Beauty grows to recognize the real hero in him. Marina Warner puts it this way: female love and sympathy redeem the brute in man (297).

Angela Carter's story "The Tiger's Bride" gives us yet another type of Beauty, one who is different from the classic characters and might be seen as representing our contemporary sensibilities. Here there is none of the moralizing of the eighteenth-century tales and the nineteenth-century Grimms' stories. Although Carter's Beauty is initially dissatisfied with the uncertain and mysterious situation, she is never afraid, and it becomes obvious that she is impressed and excited by The Beast's animal nature. Most significantly, this story ends not with the Beast's transformation into a prince, but Beauty's transformation into a creature like him. The contemporary reader might not be surprised at all at this reversal; in fact we might even have come to expect that heroes, monsters, and Beauties cross previously forbidden boundaries.

This story comes from: Angela Carter, *The Bloody Chamber.**

"My father lost me"—Carter's opening is designed to shock us, and to make it clear that this story is set in a more real world than the magical "time out of time" represented by a fairy tale's conventional opening, "Once upon a time."

"the Devil's picture books"—This name for cards introduces the theme of the Devil's role in the fairy tale, making it akin to such trickster tales as "The Devil's Daughter." However, Carter's use of this theme, as of the other precursors of her story, is to turn it toward the playful and ironic.

"my father . . . rids himself of the last scraps of my inheritance"—Losing is described ironically here. "Rid" and "donate" are words with a positive connotation, especially since they represent a conscious action by the father.

"grand seigneur . . . Milord"—These are titles of respect for a person who has been granted primary authority. As the story unfolds, we will sense the irony of the title.

"the still mask . . . the yellow eyes"—These are the first physical signs that there is a mystery.

"his huge crest of a tiger . . . was it to do with the heraldic signature"—Such questioning and ambiguity do not usually appear in fairy tales because the characters are standard types whose behavior is expected by the audience.

My father lost me to The Beast at cards.

There's a special madness strikes travelers from the North when they reach the lovely land where lemon trees grow. We come from countries of cold weather; at home, we are at war with nature but here, ah! you think you've come to the blessed plot where the lion lies down with the lamb.

Everything flowers; no harsh wind stirs the voluptuous air. The sun spills fruit for you. And the deathly, sensual lethargy of the sweet South infects the starved brain; it gasps: "Luxury! more luxury!" But then the snow comes, you cannot escape it, it followed us from Russia as if it ran behind our carriage, and in this dark, bitter city has caught up with us at last, flocking against the windowpanes to mock my father's expectations of perpetual pleasure as the veins in his forehead stand out and throb, his hands shake as he deals **the Devil's picture books.** The candles dropped hot, acrid gouts of wax on my bare shoulders. I watched the furious cynicism peculiar to women whom circumstances force mutely to witness folly, while **my father,** fired in his desperation by more and yet more draughts of the firewater they call "grappa", **rids himself of the last scraps of my inheritance.** When we left Russia, we owned black earth, blue forest with bear and wild boar, serfs, cornfields, farmyards, my beloved horses, white nights of cool summer, the fireworks of the northern lights. What a burden all those possessions must have been to him, because he laughs as if with glee as he beggars himself; he is in such a passion to donate all to The Beast.

Everyone who comes to this city must play a hand with the *grande seigneur;* few come. They did not warn us at Milan, or, if they did, we did not understand them—my limping Italian, the bewildering dialect of the region. Indeed, I myself spoke up in favor of this remote, provincial place, out of fashion two hundred years, because, oh irony, it boasted no casino. I did not know that the price of a stay in its Decembral solitude was a game with **Milord.**

The hour was late. The chill damp of this place creeps into the stones, into your bones, into the spongy pith of the lungs; it insinuated itself with a shiver into our parlor, where Milord came to play in the privacy essential to him. Who could refuse the invitation his valet brought to our lodging? Not my profligate father, certainly; the mirror above the table gave me back his frenzy, my impassivity, the withering candles, the emptying bottles, the colored tide of the cards as they rose and fell, **the still mask** that concealed all the features of The Beast but for **the yellow eyes** that strayed, now and then, from his unfurled hand towards myself.

"*La Bestia!*" said our landlady, gingerly fingering an envelope with **his huge crest of a tiger** rampant on it, something of fear, something of wonder in her face. And I could not ask her why they called the master of the place, *La Bestia*—**was it to do with the heraldic signature**—because her tongue was so thickened by the phlegmy, bronchitic

---

*"The Tiger's Bride," from *The Bloody Chamber.* Copyright © The Estate of Angela Carter, 1979. Reproduced by permission of the Estate of Angela Carter c/o Rogers, Coleridge & White Ltd., 20 Powis Mews, London W11 1JN.

speech of the region I scarcely managed to make out a thing she said except, when she saw me: *"Che bella!"*

Since I could toddle, always the pretty one, with my glossy, nut-brown curls, my rosy cheeks. And born on Christmas Day—her "Christmas rose," my English nurse called me. The peasants said: "The living image of her mother," crossing themselves out of respect for the dead. My mother did not blossom long; bartered for her dowry to such a feckless sprig of the Russian nobility that she soon died of his gaming, his whoring, his agonising repentances. And The Beast gave me the rose from his own impeccable if outmoded buttonhole when he arrived, the valet brushing the snow off his black cloak. **This white rose, unnatural, out of season, that now my nervous fingers ripped, petal by petal, apart** as my father magnificently concluded the career he had made of catastrophe.

This is a **melancholy, introspective region; a sunless, featureless landscape, the sullen river** sweating fog, the shorn, hunkering willows. And a **cruel city;** the sombre piazza, a place uniquely suited to public executions, under the beetling shadow of that malign barn of a church. They used to hang condemned men in cages from the city walls; unkindness comes naturally to them, their eyes are set so close together, they have thin lips. Poor food, pasta soaked in oil, boiled beef with sauce of bitter herbs. A funeral hush about the place, the inhabitants huddled up against the **cold** so you can hardly see their faces. And they lie to you and cheat you, innkeepers, coachmen, everybody. God, how they fleeced us.

The treacherous South, where you think there is no winter but forget to take it with you.

My senses were increasingly troubled by the fuddling perfume of Milord, far too potent a reek of purplish civet at such close quarters in so small a room. He must bathe himself in scent, soak his shirts and underlinen in it; **what can he smell of, that needs so much camouflage?**

I never saw a man so big look so two-dimensional, in spite of the quaint elegance of The Beast, in the old-fashioned tailcoat that might, from its looks, have been bought in those distant years before he imposed seclusion on himself; he does not feel he need keep up with the times. There is a crude clumsiness about his outlines, that are on the ungainly, giant side; and he had an odd air of self-imposed restraint, as if fighting a

"This white rose . . . my nervous fingers ripped . . . apart"—The flower represents Beauty, who had been a Christmas rose, but who now metaphorically destroys the symbol of herself that the Beast has provided.

"melancholy . . . featureless . . . sullen . . . cruel"—These characteristics of the landscape and the city segué into a similar characterization of the inhabitants: "unkindness comes naturally . . . they lie . . . and cheat . . . they fleeced us."

"cold"—Beauty, who comes from Russia, does not expect Italy to be cold, but the temperature seems part of the uncaring atmosphere of the palace.

"what can he smell of, that needs so much camouflage?"—Beauty raises questions that also disturb the reader. Carter draws us deeply into the story by anticipating our concerns.

In the Walt Disney animated film, *Beauty and the Beast,* Belle, the beauty, loves and educates a benevolent animal.

battle with himself to remain upright when he would far rather drop down on all fours. He throws our human aspirations to the godlike sadly awry, poor fellow; only from a distance would you think The Beast not much different from any other man, although he wears **a mask with a man's face painted most beautifully upon it.** Oh, yes, a beautiful face; **but one with too much formal symmetry** of feature to be entirely human: one profile of his mask is the mirror image of the other, too perfect, uncanny. He wears a wig, too, false hair tied at the nape with a bow, a wig of the kind you see in old-fashioned portraits. A chaste silk stock stuck with a pearl hides his throat. And gloves of blond kid that are yet so huge and clumsy they do not seem to cover hands.

He is a carnival figure made of paper-mache and crepe hair; and yet **he has the Devil's knack at cards.**

His masked voice echoes as from a great distance as he stoops over his hand and he has such a growling impediment in his speech that only his valet, who understands him, can interpret for him, as if his master were the clumsy doll and he the ventriloquist.

The wick slumped in the eroded wax, the candles guttered. By the time my rose had lost all its petals, my father, too, was left with nothing.

"Except the girl."

Gambling is a sickness. My father said he loved me yet he staked his daughter on a hand of cards. He fanned them out; in the mirror, I saw wild hope light up his eyes. His collar was unfastened, his rumpled hair stood up on end, he had the anguish of a man in the last stages of debauchery. The draughts came out of the old walls and bit me, I was colder than I'd ever been in Russia, when nights are coldest there.

A queen, a king, an ace. I saw them in the mirror. Oh, I know he thought he could not lose me; besides, back with me would come all he had lost, the unravelled fortunes of our family at one blow restored. And would he not win, as well, The Beast's hereditary palazzo outside the city; his immense revenues; his lands around the river; his rents, his treasure chest, his Mantegnas, his Guilio Romanos, his Cellini salt-cellars, his titles . . . the very city itself.

You must not think my father valued me at less than a king's ransom; but at **_no more_ than a king's ransom.**

It was cold as hell in the parlor. And it seemed to me, child of the severe North, that it was not my flesh but, truly, my father's soul that was in peril.

My father, of course, believed in miracles; what gambler does not? In pursuit of just such a miracle as this, had we not traveled from the land of bears and shooting stars?

So we teetered on the brink.

The Beast bayed; laid down all three remaining aces.

The indifferent servants now glided smoothly forward as on wheels to douse the candles one by one. To look at them you would think that nothing of any moment had occurred. They yawned a little resentfully; it was almost morning. We had kept them out of bed. The Beast's man brought his cloak. My father sat amongst these preparations for departure, staring on at the betrayal of his cards upon the table.

The Beast's man informed me crisply that he, the valet, would call for me and my bags tomorrow, at ten, and conduct me forthwith to The Beast's palazzo. *Capisco?* So shocked was I that I scarcely did *capisco;* he repeated my orders patiently, he was a strange, thin, quick little man who walked with an irregular jolting rhythm upon splayed feet in curious, wedge-shaped shoes.

Where my father had been as red as fire, now he was white as the snow that caked the windowpane. His eyes swam; soon he would cry.

"'Like the base Indian,'" he said; **he loved rhetoric.** "'One whose hand/Like the base Indian, threw a pearl away/Richer than all his tribe . . .' I have lost my pearl, my pearl beyond price."

"a mask with a man's face painted most beautifully upon it . . . but one with too much formal symmetry"—The face painted on the mask is too perfect and therefore makes him seem nonhuman.

"he has the Devil's knack at cards"—This is an indication that he has sinister intentions. In folktales, it is a common motif that the Devil challenges an unsuspecting victim to cards or a game of chance and then wins an inordinate prize because of his supernatural powers.

"Except the girl"—This is most likely the suggestion of the Beast, but it might as well be the father's. His "sickness" has caused him to treat his daughter as a possession that he may wager. However, in several of the Grimms' tales, the father allows harm to come to daughter because he is absent or inattentive.

"no more than a king's ransom"—This is the kind of unexpected twist Carter uses that shows us that this is not a reverent retelling of a tale, but rather a playful, critical commentary on it.

"The indifferent servants"—There is a total lack of emotion on the part of the other participants in the scene. Their mechanical movements and precise directions lead the reader to suspect they are not human.

"he loved rhetoric"—The father responds not with his own words, but with those from another's poem.

Feast scene from the film *The Company of Wolves.* As they reveal their basic animal natures, London guests are transformed into beasts at a dinner party.

At that, **The Beast made a sudden, dreadful noise,** halfway between a growl and a roar; the candles flared. The quick valet, the prim hypocrite, interpreted unblinkingly: "My master says: If you are so careless of your treasures, you should expect them to be taken from you."

He gave us the bow and smile his master could not offer us and they departed.

I watched the snow until, just before dawn, it stopped falling; a hard frost settled, next morning there was a light like iron.

The Beast's carriage, of an elegant if antique design, was black as a hearse and it was drawn by a dashing black gelding who blew smoke from his nostrils and stamped upon the packed snow with enough sprightly appearance of life to give me some hope that not all the world was locked in ice, that horses are better than we are, and, that day, **I would have been glad to depart with him to the kingdom of horses,** if I'd been given the chance.

The valet sat up on the box in a natty black and gold livery, clasping, of all things, **a bunch of his master's damned white roses** as if a gift of flowers would reconcile a woman to any humiliation. He sprang down with preternatural agility to place them ceremoniously in my reluctant hand. My tear-beslobbered father wants a rose to show that I forgive him. When I break off a stem, I prick my finger so he gets his rose all smeared with blood.

The valet crouched at my feet to tuck the rugs about me with a strange kind of unflattering obsequiousness yet he forgot his station sufficiently to scratch busily beneath his white periwig with an over-supple index finger as he offered me what my old nurse would have called an "old-fashioned look," ironic, sly, a smidgeon of disdain in it. And pity? No pity. His eyes were moist and brown, his face seamed with the innocent cunning of an ancient baby. He had an irritating habit of chattering to himself under his breath all the time as he packed up his master's winnings. I drew the curtains to conceal the sight of my father's farewell; my spite was sharp as broken glass.

Lost to The Beast! **And what, I wondered, might be the exact nature of his "beast-liness"?** My English nurse once told me about a tiger-man she saw in London, when she was a little girl, to scare me into good behavior, for I was a wild wee thing and she could not tame me into submission with a frown or the bribe of a spoonful of jam. If you don't stop plaguing the nursemaids, my beauty, the tiger-man will come and take you away. They'd brought him from Sumatra, in the Indies, she said; his hinder parts were all hairy and only from the head downwards did he resemble a man.

And yet The Beast goes always masked; it cannot be his face that looks like mine.

But the tiger-man, in spite of his hairiness, could take a glass of ale in his hand like a good Christian and drink it down. Had she not seen him do so, at the sign of The George, by the steps of Upper Moor Fields when she was just as high as me and lisped and toddled, too? Then she would sigh for London, across the North Sea of the lapse of years. But, if this young lady was not a good little girl and did not eat her boiled beetroot, then the tiger-man would put his big black traveling cloak lined with fur, just like your daddy's, and hire **the Erl-King's** galloper of wind and ride through the night straight to the nursery and—

Yes, my beauty! GOBBLE YOU UP!

How I'd squeal in delighted terror, **half believing her, half knowing** that she teased me. And there were things I knew that I must not tell her. In our lost farmyard, where the giggling nursemaids initiated me into the mysteries of what the bull did to the cows, I heard about the waggoner's daughter. Hush, hush, don't let on to your nursie we said so: the waggoner's lass, hare-lipped, squint-eyed, ugly as sin, who would have taken her? Yet, to her shame, her belly swelled amid the cruel mockery of the ostlers and her son was born of a bear, they whispered. Born with a full pelt and teeth; that proved it. But, when he grew up, he was a good shepherd, although he never married, lived in a hut outside the village and could make the wind blow any way he wanted to besides being able to tell which eggs would become cocks, which hens.

The wondering peasants once brought my father a skull with horns four inches long on either side of it and would not go back to the field where their poor plough disturbed it until the priest went with them; for this skull had the jaw-bone of a *man*, had it not?

Old wives' tales, nursery fears! I knew well enough the reason for the trepidation I cosily titillated with superstitious marvels of my childhood on **the day my childhood ended.** For now my own skin was my sole capital in the world and today I'd make my first investment.

We had left the city far behind us and were now traversing a wide, flat dish of snow where the mutilated stumps of the willows flourished their ciliate heads athwart frozen ditches; mist diminished the horizon, brought down the sky until it seemed no more than a few inches above us. As far as eye could see, not one thing living. How starveling, how bereft **the dead season of this spurious Eden** in which all the fruit was blighted by cold! And my frail roses, already faded. I opened the carriage door and tossed the defunct bouquet into the rucked, frost-stiff mud of the road. Suddenly a sharp, freezing wind arose and pelted my face with a dry rice of powdered snow. The mist lifted sufficiently to reveal before me an acreage of half-derelict facades of sheer red brick, the vast man-trap, the megalomaniac citadel of his palazzo.

It was a world in itself but a dead one, a burned-out planet. I saw The Beast bought solitude, not luxury, with his money.

The little black horse trotted smartly through the figured bronze doors that stood open to the weather like those of a barn and the valet handed me out of the carriage on to the scarred tiles of the great hall itself, into the odorous warmth of a stable, sweet with hay, acrid with horse dung. An equine chorus of neighings and soft drummings of hooves broke out beneath the tall roof, where the beams were scabbed with last summer's swallows' nests; a dozen gracile muzzles lifted from their mangers and turned towards us, ears erect. **The Beast had given his horses the use of the dining room.** The walls were painted, aptly enough, with a fresco of horses, dogs and men in a wood where fruit and blossom grew on the bough together.

"the Erl-King"—In an early 19th-c. German poem, Johann Wolfgang von Goethe told the legend of the Erl-King, a spirit who entices children to come with him to the land of the dead.

"half believing . . . half knowing"—Beauty tries to sort out the present situation by recalling old tales that were only partly based on fact. With this reference, Carter reminds us that we are in the midst of a fairy tale, while at the same time bringing into question the value of such tales. The effect is comic.

"the day my childhood ended"—Beauty recognizes that the present, despite its fairy-tale quality, is real and that she is going to have to be responsible for herself. The difficulties she faces remind us that this is another story about a young girl who is betrayed by a father who forces her into a bad marriage. In a sense, this becomes just another tale of a young girl's passage through exogamy into adulthood. See also the stories of Persephone (Ch. 27, p. 385) and the Grimms' fairy tale, "The Goose Girl" (Ch. 36, p. 527).

"the dead season of this spurious Eden"—The setting of the tale mocks its fairy-tale nature.

"The Beast had given his horses the use of the dining room."—A sign that the house belongs to animals, rather than to people.

The valet tweaked politely at my sleeve. Milord is waiting.

Gaping doors and broken windows let the wind in everywhere. We mounted one staircase after another, our feet clopping on the marble. Through archways and open doors, I glimpsed suites of vaulted chambers opening one out of another like systems of Chinese boxes into the infinite complexity of the innards of the place. He and I and the wind were the only things stirring; and all the furniture was under dust sheets, the chandeliers bundled up in cloth, pictures taken from their hooks and propped with their faces to the walls as if their master could not bear to look at them. The palace was dismantled, as if its owner were about to move house or had never properly moved in; The Beast had chosen to live in an uninhabited place.

The valet darted me a reassuring glance from his brown, eloquent eyes, yet a glance with so much queer superciliousness in it that it did not comfort me, and went bounding ahead of me on his bandy legs, softly chattering to himself. I held my head high and followed him; but for all my pride, my heart was heavy.

Milord has his eyrie high above the house, a small, stifling, darkened room; he keeps his shutters locked at noon. I was out of breath by the time we reached it and returned to him the silence with which he greeted me. I will not smile. He cannot smile.

In his rarely disturbed privacy, The Beast wears a garment of Ottoman design, a loose, dull purple gown with gold embroidery round the neck that falls from his shoulders to conceal his feet. The feet of the chair he sits in are handsomely clawed. He hides his hands in his ample sleeves. The artificial masterpiece of his face appalls me. A small fire in a small grate. A rushing wind rattles the shutters.

The valet coughed. To him fell the delicate task of transmitting to me his master's wishes.

"My master—"

A stick fell in the grate. It made a mighty clatter in that dreadful silence, the valet started, lost his place in his speech, began again.

"My master has but one desire."

The thick, rich, wild scent with which Milord had soaked himself the previous evening hangs all about us, ascends in cursive blue from the smoke hole of a precious Chinese pot.

"He wishes only—"

Now, in the face of my impassivity, the valet twittered, his ironic composure gone, for the desire of a master, however trivial, may yet sound unbearably insolent in the mouth of a servant and his role of go-between clearly caused him **a good deal of embarrassment.** He gulped; he swallowed, at last contrived to unleash an unpunctuated flood.

"My master's sole desire is to see the pretty young lady unclothed nude without her dress and that only for one time after which she will be returned to her father undamaged with bankers' orders for the sum which he lost to my master at cards and also a number of fine presents such as furs, jewels and horses—"

I remained standing. During this interview, my eyes were level with those inside the mask that now evaded mine as if, to his credit, he was ashamed of his own request even as his mouthpiece made it for him. *Agitato, molto agitato,* the valet wrung his white-gloved hands.

"Desnuda—"

I could scarcely believe my ears. I let out **a raucous guffaw;** no young lady laughs like that! my old nurse used to remonstrate. But I did. And do. At the clamor of my heartless mirth, the valet danced backwards with perturbation, palpitating his fingers as if attempting to wrench them off, expostulating, wordlessly pleading. I felt that I owed it to him to make my reply in as exquisite Tuscan as I could muster.

"Gaping doors and broken windows"—By using a series of clichés, Carter is leading the reader to associate this place with numerous scenes in modern horror stories.

"Milord has his eyrie . . ."—Beauty's account of past events ends here. She has now brought us up to date, and Carter emphasizes this by switching to present tense. The change may seem a lapse in Beauty's storytelling style, but it may also indicate that the situation continues into the present moment of telling the tale.

"The valet coughed"—Unexpectedly, Carter returns to the use of the narrative past: we have returned to the events of the story.

"a good deal of embarrassment"—This contradicts our earlier perception that the servant is cold and uncaring. It is a signal that the Beast and his valet, when at home, reveal a complexity of character that they mask in their dealings with the outside world.

"My master's sole desire"—Ironically, the Beast reveals that his terms are much more humane than those of Beauty's father.

"a raucous guffaw"—With this response, Beauty shows that expressing genuine emotion is more important to her than observing the restraints of polite society. Also, this is our first indication that there is something about Beauty that will fit with the Beast.

"**You may put me in a windowless room,** sir, and I promise you I will pull my skirt up to my waist, ready for you. But there must be a sheet over my face, to hide it; though the sheet must be laid over me so lightly that it will not choke me. So I shall be covered completely from the waist upwards, and no lights. There you can visit me once, sir, and only the once. After that I must be driven directly to the city and deposited in the public square, in front of the church. If you wish to give me money, then I should be pleased to receive it. But I must stress that you should give me only the same amount of money that you would give to any other woman in such circumstances. However, if you choose not to give me a present, then that is your right."

How pleased I was to see I struck The Beast to the heart! For, after a baker's dozen heart-beats, one single tear swelled, glittering, at the corner of the masked eye. A tear! A tear, I hoped, of shame. **The tear trembled for a moment on an edge of painted bone,** then tumbled down the painted cheek to fall, with an abrupt tinkle, on the tiled floor.

The valet, ticking and clucking to himself, hastily ushered me out of the room. A mauve cloud of his master's perfume billowed out into the chill corridor with us and dissipated itself on the spinning winds.

A cell had been prepared for me, a veritable cell, windowless, airless, lightless, in the viscera of the palace. The valet lit a lamp for me; a narrow bed, a dark cupboard with fruit and flowers carved on it bulked out of the gloom.

"I shall twist a noose out of my bed linen and hang myself with it," I said.

"Oh, no," said the valet, fixing upon me wide and suddenly melancholy eyes. "Oh, no, you will not. You are a woman of honor."

And what was *he* doing in my bedroom, this jigging caricature of a man? Was he to be my warder until I submitted to The Beast's whim or he to mine? Am I in such reduced circumstances that I may not have a lady's maid? As if in reply to my unspoken demand, the valet clapped his hands.

"To assuage your loneliness, madame . . ."

A knocking and clattering behind the door of the cupboard; the door swings open and out glides a soubrette from an operetta, with glossy, nut-brown curls, rosy cheeks, blue, rolling eyes; it takes me a moment to recognize her, in her little cap, her white stockings, her frilled petticoats. She carries a looking glass in one hand and a powder puff in the other and there is a musical box where her heart should be; she tinkles as she rolls towards me on her tiny wheels.

"**Nothing human lives here,**" said the valet.

My maid halted, bowed; from a split seam at the side of her bodice protrudes the handle of a key. She is a marvelous machine, the most delicately balanced system of cords and pulleys in the world.

"We have dispensed with servants," the valet said. "We surround ourselves instead, for utility and pleasure, with simulacra and find it no less convenient than most gentlemen."

This clockwork twin of mine halted before me, her bowels churning out a settecento minuet, and offered me the bold carnation of her smile. Click, click—she raises her arm and busily dusts my cheeks with pink, powdered chalk that makes me cough, then thrusts towards me her little mirror.

I saw within it not my own face but that of my father, **as if I had put on his face** when I arrived at The Beast's palace as the discharge of his debt. What, you self-deluding fool, are you crying still? And drunk, too. He tossed back his grappa and hurled the tumbler away.

Seeing my astonished fright, the valet took the mirror away from me, breathed on it, polished it with the ham of his gloved fist, handed it back to me. Now all I saw was

---

"You may put me in a windowless room"—Beauty's proposal: she moves to what she considers a much more impersonal encounter, and she also moves the idea of payment to a less central position.

"The tear trembled . . . on an edge of painted bone"—It is ironic that the tear, the expression of human emotion, lingers on the mask, which hides the Beast's own face.

"And what was *he* doing in my bedroom"—Traditional tales typically lack this kind of introspection. Only in rare circumstances do we get even a very rudimentary view into the hero's thoughts, and even this is formulaic. For example, a character may ask herself, "What am I to do now?" Such a question is more a device to encourage audience participation; in contrast, Carter here gives us a question arising from the character's internal speculations.

"Nothing human lives here"—The valet reveals to the reader as well as to Beauty what we might have suspected. The Beast's household is a peculiar blend of the nonhuman, ranging from mechanical beings to those with animal natures. But if this is so, what about the valet himself, and The Beast? Carter invites the reader to consider mysterious aspects of the story she is telling.

"as if I had put on his face"—Like the Beast's mask, Beauty's mirror is something that reveals as well as hides.

myself, haggard from a sleepless night, pale enough to need my maid's supply of rouge.

I heard the key turn in the heavy door and the valet's footsteps patter down the stone passage. Meanwhile, my double continued to powder the air, emitting her jangling tune but, as it turned out, she was not inexhaustible; soon she was powdering more and yet more languorously, her metal heart slowed in imitation of fatigue, her musical box ran down until the notes separated themselves out of the tune and plopped like single raindrops and, as if sleep had overtaken her, at last she moved no longer. **As she succumbed to sleep, I had no option but to do so too.** I dropped on the narrow bed as if felled.

Time passed but I do not know how much; the valet woke me with rolls and honey, I gestured the tray away, but he set it down firmly beside the lamp and took from it a little shagreen box, which he offered to me.

I turned away my head.

"Oh, my lady!" Such hurt cracked his high-pitched voice! He dextrously unfastened the gold clasp; on a bed of crimson velvet lay a single diamond earring, perfect as a tear.

I snapped the box shut and tossed it into a corner. This sudden, sharp movement must have disturbed the mechanism of the doll; **she jerked her arm** almost as if to reprimand me, letting out a rippling fart of gavotte. Then she was still again.

"Very well," said the valet, put out. And indicated it was time for me to visit my host again. **He did not let me wash or comb my hair.** There was so little natural light in the interior of the palace that I could not tell whether it was day or night.

You would not think the Beast had budged an inch since I last saw him; he sat in his huge chair, with his hands in his sleeves, and the heavy air never moved. I might have slept an hour, a night, or a month, but his sculptured calm, the stifling air remained just as it had been. The incense rose from the pot, still traced the same signature on the air. The same fire burned.

Take my clothes off for you, like a ballet girl? Is that all you want of me?

"The sight of a young lady's skin **that no man has seen before**—" stammered the valet.

I wished I'd rolled in the hay with every lad on my father's farm, to disqualify myself from this humiliating bargain. That he should want so little was the reason why I could not give it; I did not need to speak for The Beast to understand me.

A tear came from his other eye. And then he moved; he buried his cardboard carnival head with its ribboned weight of false hair in, I would say, his arms; he withdrew his, I might say, hands from his sleeves and **I saw his furred pads, his excoriating claws.**

The dropped tear caught upon his fur and shone. And in my room for hours I heard those paws pad back and forth outside my door.

When the valet arrived again with his silver salver, I had a pair of diamond earrings of the finest water in the world; I threw the other into the corner where the first one lay. The valet twittered with aggrieved regret but did not offer to lead me to The Beast again. Instead, he smiled ingratiatingly and confided: "My master, he say: invite the young lady to go riding."

"What's this?"

He briskly mimicked the action of a gallop and, to my amazement, tunelessly croaked: "Tantivy! tantivy! a-hunting we will go!"

"I'll run away. I'll ride to the city."

"Oh, no," he said. "Are you not a woman of honor?"

He clapped his hands and my maidservant clicked and jangled into the imitation of life. She rolled towards the cupboard where she had come from and reached inside it

---

Sidebar notes:

"As she succumbed to sleep, I had no option but to do so too."—Beauty behaves as her clockwork twin does. Of course, the difference is that her sleep is genuine, while that action of her robot-double is a nonhuman response.

"she jerked her arm"—The robot responds to Beauty's violent reaction.

"He did not let me wash or comb my hair."—The Beast is not interested in the hygiene of Beauty's culture, although it is obvious that she wants to present herself properly as a guest.

"that no man has seen before"—The irony of this statement becomes clear as the reader becomes more and more convinced that the potential viewer is not a man.

"I saw his furred pads, his excoriating claws"—In expressing human sorrow, The Beast reveals his animal nature. However, what is remarkable here is Beauty's sober, dispassionate reportage of a discovery that should have been shocking and frightening.

"My very own riding habit"—Such events that cannot be explained in ordinary life often occur in fairy tales. See for example, the restoration of Faithful John and the king's sons, Ch. 36, p. 539.

"if you have enough money, anything is possible"—Carter again twists the suspension of disbelief required by a fairy tale and deflates it into a cynical explanation.

Paolo Veronese (1528–1588), *Landscape with Ruins,* in a trompe l'oeil style.

trompe l'oeil   A type of painting that depicts things so realistically that our eye is tricked into thinking they are real. Here, even the pony is fooled and tries to eat the painted grass. This is another example of how Carter mixes fantasy and reality.

"A profound sense of strangeness"—The reason for the strangeness is her realization that she no longer lives in the rational world of her childhood. Although she has grown older and wiser, she now understands that she shares the same reputation as the horses and The Beast and his valet: they do not count as substantial beings. She sees herself as no more substantial than the mechanical doll.

to fetch out over her synthetic arm my riding habit. Of all things. **My very own riding habit,** that I'd left behind me in a trunk in the loft in the country house outside Petersburg that we'd lost long ago, before, even, we set out on this wild pilgrimage to the cruel South. Either the very riding habit my old nurse had sewn for me or else a copy of it perfect to the lost button on the right sleeve, the ripped hem held up with a pin. I turned the worn cloth about in my hands, looking for a clue. The wind that sprinted through the palace made the door tremble in its frame; had the north wind blown my garments across Europe to me? At home, the bear's son directed the winds at his pleasure; what democracy of magic held this palace and the fir forest in common? Or, should I be prepared to accept it as proof of the axiom my father had drummed into me: that, **if you have enough money, anything is possible?**

"Tantivy," suggested the now twinkling valet, evidently charmed at the pleasure mixed with bewilderment. The clockwork maid held my jacket out to me and I allowed myself to shrug into it as if reluctantly, although I was half mad to get out into the open air, away from this deathly palace, even in such company.

The doors of the hall let the bright day in; I saw that it was morning. Our horses, saddled and bridled, beasts in bondage, were waiting for us, striking sparks from the tiles with their impatient hooves while their stablemates lolled at ease among the straw, conversing with one another in the mute speech of horses. A pigeon or two, feathers puffed to keep out the cold, strutted about, pecking at ears of corn. The little black gelding who had brought me here greeted me with a ringing neigh that resonated inside the mist roof as in a sounding box and I knew he was meant for me to ride.

I always adored horses, noblest of creatures, such wounded sensitivity in their wise eyes, such rational restraint of energy at their high-strung hindquarters. I lirruped and hurrumphed to my shining black companion and he acknowledged my greeting with a kiss on the forehead from his soft lips. There was a little shaggy pony nuzzling away at the *trompe l'oeil* foliage beneath the hooves of the painted horses on the wall, into whose saddle the valet sprang with a flourish as of the circus. Then The Beast wrapped in a black fur-lined cloak, came to heave himself aloft a grave grey mare. No natural horseman he; he clung to her mane like a shipwrecked sailor to a spar.

Cold, that morning, yet dazzling with the sharp winter sunlight that wounds the retina. There was a scurrying wind about that seemed to go with us, as if the masked, immense one who did not speak carried it inside his cloak and let it out at his pleasure, for it stirred the horses' manes but did not lift the lowland mists.

A bereft landscape in the sad browns and sepias of winter lay all about us, the marshland drearily protracting itself towards the wide river. Those decapitated willows. Now and then, the swoop of a bird, its irreconcilable cry.

A profound sense of strangeness slowly began to possess me. I knew my two companions were not, in any way, as other men, the simian retainer and the master for whom he spoke, the one with clawed forepaws who was in a plot with the witches who let the winds out of their knotted handkerchiefs up towards the Finnish border. I knew they lived according to a different logic than I had done until my father abandoned me to the wild beasts with his human carelessness. This knowledge gave me a certain fearfulness still; but, I would say, not much . . . I was a young girl, a virgin, and therefore men denied me rationality just as they denied it to all those who were not exactly like themselves, in all their unreason. If I could see not one single soul in that wilderness of desolation all around me, then the six of us—mounts and riders, both—could boast amongst us not one soul, either, since all the best religions in the world state categorically that not beasts nor women were equipped with the flimsy, insubstantial things when the good Lord opened the gates of Eden and let Eve and her familiars tumble out. Understand, then, that though I would not say I privately engaged in metaphysical speculation as we rode through the reedy approaches to the river, I certainly meditated on the nature of my own state, how I had been bought and sold, passed from hand to hand. That clockwork girl who powdered my cheeks for me; had I not been allotted the same kind of imitative life amongst men that the doll-maker had given her?

Yet, as to the true nature of the being of this clawed magus who rode his pale horse in a style that made me recall how **Kublai Khan's** leopards went out hunting on horseback, of that I had no notion.

> **Kublai Khan** Grandson of Genghis Khan, founder of the Mongol Dynasty in China in the 13th c. Khan figured in stories brought back by explorers who traveled to the Far East in the European age of exploration. Here Carter draws upon the magical character of this period of China's history.

We came to the bank of the river that was so wide we could not see across it, so still with winter that it scarcely seemed to flow. The horses lowered their heads to drink. The valet cleared his throat, about to speak; we were in a place of perfect privacy, beyond a brake of winter-bare rushes, a hedge of reeds.

"**If you will not let him see you without your clothes—**"

I involuntarily shook my head—

"—you must, **then,** prepare yourself for the sight of my master, naked."

> "**If . . . then**"—This is an unexpected consequence. The irony lies in the fact that Beauty's "punishment" for not submitting to The Beast's requirement is not physical and not directly related to her personal well-being. It seems to be related to William Blake's poem "The Tyger" in which the human observer is in complete awe of the overwhelming power of the animal.

The river broke on the pebbles with a diminishing sigh. My composure deserted me; all at once I was on the brink of panic. I did not think that I could bear the sight of him, whatever he was. The mare raised her dripping muzzle and looked at me keenly, as if urging me. The river broke again at my feet. I was far from home.

"You," said the valet, "must."

When I saw how scared he was I might refuse, I nodded.

The reed bowed down in a sudden snarl of wind that brought with it a gust of the heavy odor of his disguise. The valet held out his master's cloak to screen him from me as he removed his mask. The horses stirred.

The tiger will never lie down with the lamb; he acknowledges no pact that is not reciprocal. **The lamb must learn to run with the tigers.**

> "**The lamb must learn to run with the tigers**"—This is a fateful statement for Beauty and surprising to those familiar with the Bible. In Isaiah 11:6, we read of the wolf lying down with the lamb. Here, again, Carter reverses what is expected.

A great, feline, tawny shape whose pelt was barred with **a savage geometry** of bars the color of burned wood. His domed, heavy head, so terrible he must hide it. How subtle the muscles, how profound the tread. The annihilating vehemence of his eyes, like twin suns.

> "**a savage geometry**"—This expression evokes Blake's "Tyger": "What immortal hand or eye Dare frame thy fearful symmetry." This is an example of how familiarity with one literary work can enrich the reader's enjoyment of others. As the introduction to this part (p. 620) notes, familiarity with myths can also greatly enrich a reader's enjoyment.

I felt my breast ripped apart as if I suffered a marvelous wound.

The valet moved forward as if to cover up his master **now the girl had acknowledged him but I said: "No."** The tiger sat still as a heraldic beast, in the pact he had made with his own ferocity to do me no harm. He was far larger than I could have imagined. From the poor, shabby things I'd seen once, in the Czar's menagerie at Petersburg, the golden fruit of their eyes dimming, withering in the far North of captivity. Nothing about him reminded me of humanity.

I therefore, shivering, now unfastened my jacket, to show him I would do him no harm. Yet I was clumsy and blushed a little, for no man had seen me naked and I was a proud girl. Pride it was, not shame, that thwarted my fingers so; and a certain trepidation lest this frail little article of human upholstery before him might not be, in itself, grand enough to satisfy his expectations of us, since those, for all I knew, might have grown infinite during the endless time he had been waiting. The wind clattered in the rushes, purled and eddied in the river.

> "**now the girl had acknowledged him but I said: 'No'**"—This change from speaking impersonally about "the girl" to "I" suggests that the Beast's original plan, to be acknowledged by a human virgin, now has a more personal consequence. "The girl" not only acknowledges him, but accepts him because "Nothing about him reminded me of humanity."

I showed his grave silence my white skin, my red nipples, and the horses turned their heads to watch me, also, as if they, too, were courteously curious as to the fleshy nature of women. Then The Beast lowered his massive head; Enough! said the valet with a gesture. The wind died down. All was still again.

Then they went off together, the valet on his pony, **the tiger running before him like a hound,** and I walked along the river bank for a while. I felt I was at liberty for the first time in my life. Then the winter sun began to tarnish, a few flakes of snow drifted from the darkening sky and, when I returned to the horses, I found The Beast mounted again on his grey mare, cloaked and masked and once more, to all appearances, a man,

> "**the tiger running before him like a hound**"—The tiger briefly abandons all pretense of being human before returning, again disguised as a man. Compare this with the nature–culture opposition described by Levi-Strauss (Ch. 20, p. 281f.)

Horace Pippin, *Holy Mountain III,* August 9, 1945.

while the valet had a fine catch of waterfowl dangling from his hand and the corpse of a young roebuck slung behind his saddle. I climbed up on the black gelding in silence and so we returned to the palace as the snow fell more heavily, **obscuring the tracks** that we had left behind us.

The valet did not return me to my cell, but, instead, to an elegant, if old-fashioned boudoir with sofas of faded pink brocade, a jinn's treasury of Oriental carpets, tintinnabulation of cut-glass chandeliers. Candles in antlered holders struck rainbows from the prismatic hearts of my diamond earrings that lay on my new dressing table at which my attentive maid stood ready with her powder puff and mirror. Intending to fix the ornaments in my ears, I took the looking glass from her hand, but it was in the midst of one of its magic fits again and I did not see my own face in it but that of my father; at first I thought he smiled at me. Then I saw he was smiling with pure gratification.

He sat, I saw, in the parlor of our lodgings, at the very table where he had lost me, but now he was busily engaged in counting out a tremendous pile of banknotes. **My father's circumstances had changed already;** well-shaven, neatly barbered, smart new clothes. A frosted glass of sparkling wine sat convenient to his hand beside an ice bucket. The Beast had clearly paid cash on the nail for his glimpse of my bosom and paid up promptly, as if it had not been a sight I might have died of showing. Then I saw my father's trunks were packed, ready for departure. Could he so easily leave me here?

There was a note on the table with the money, in a fine hand. I could read it quite clearly. "The young lady will arrive immediately." Some harlot with whom he'd briskly negotiated a liaison on the strength of his spoils? Not at all. For at that moment, the valet knocked at my door to announce that I might leave the palace at any time hereafter, and he bore over his arm a handsome sable cloak, my very own little gratuity, The Beast's morning gift, in which he proposed to pack me up and send me off.

When I looked at the mirror again, my father had disappeared and all I saw was a pale, hollow-eyed girl whom I scarcely recognized. The valet asked politely when he should prepare the carriage, as if he did not doubt that I would leave with my booty at the first opportunity while my maid, whose face was no longer the spit of my own, continued bonnily to beam. **I will dress her in my own clothes, wind her up, send her back to perform the part of my father's daughter.**

"Leave me alone," I said to the valet.

He did not need to lock the door, now. I fixed the earrings in my ears. They were very heavy. Then I took off my riding habit, left it where it lay on the floor. But, when I got down to my shift, my arms dropped to my sides. I was unaccustomed to nakedness. I was so unused to my own skin that to take off all my clothes involved a kind of flaying. I thought The Beast had wanted a little thing compared with what I was prepared to give him; but it is not natural for humankind to go naked, not since first we hid our loins with fig leaves. He had demanded the abominable. I felt as much atrocious pain as if I was stripping off my own underpelt and the smiling girl stood poised in the oblivion of her balked simulation of life, watching me peel down to the cold, white meat of contract and, if she did not see me, then so much more like the marketplace, where the eyes that watch you take no account of your existence.

And it seemed my entire life, since I had left the North, had passed under the indifferent gaze of eyes like hers.

Then I was flinching stark, except for his irreproachable tears.

I huddled in the furs I must return to him, to keep me from the lacerating winds that raced along the corridors. I knew the way to his den without the valet to guide me.

No response to my tentative rap on his door.

Then the wind blew the valet whirling along the passage. He must have decided that, if one should go naked, then all should go naked; without his livery, he revealed himself, as I had suspected, a delicate creature, covered with silken moth-grey fur, brown fingers supple as leather, chocolate muzzle, the gentlest creature in the world. He gibbered a little to see my fine furs and jewels as if I were dressed up for the opera and, **with a great deal of tender ceremony,** removed the sables from my shoulders. The sables thereupon resolved themselves into a pack of black squeaking rats that rattled immediately down the stairs on their hard little feet and were lost to sight.

The valet bowed me inside The Beast's room.

> "with a great deal of tender ceremony"—The valet reverently welcomes Beauty to The Beast's world. In a traditional story, the fur cape's becoming rats might be a repulsive event, but here it is a positive view of animals being released to their natural state.

The purple dressing gown, the mask, the wig, were laid out on his chair, a glove was planted on each arm. The empty house of his appearance was ready for him but he had abandoned it. There was a reek of fur and piss; the incense pot lay broken in pieces on the floor. Half-burned sticks were scattered from the extinguished fire. A candle stuck by its own grease to the mantle piece lit two narrow flames in the pupils of the tiger's eyes.

He was pacing backwards and forwards, backwards and forwards, the tip of his heavy tail twitching as he paced out the length and breadth of his imprisonment between the gnawed and bloody bones.

He will gobble you up.

Nursery fears made flesh and sinew; earliest and most archaic of fears, fear of devourment. The beast and his carnivorous bed of bone and I, white, shaking, raw, approaching him as if offering, in myself, the key to **a peaceable kingdom** in which his appetite need not be my extinction.

> "a peaceable kingdom"—This is a general name for paintings representing paradise by showing a lion and a lamb lying side-by-side in a lush, well-ordered forest. Famous examples include a 19th-c. painting by Edward Hicks, as well as one facing by Horace Pippin.

He went still as stone. He was far more frightened of me than I was of him.

I squatted on the wet straw and stretched out my hand. I was now within the field of force of his golden eyes. He growled at the back of his throat, lowered his head, sank onto his forepaws, snarled, showed me his red gullet, his yellow teeth. I never moved. He snuffled the air, as if to smell my fear; he could not.

Slowly, slowly he began to drag his heavy, gleaming weight across the floor towards me.

A tremendous throbbing, as of the engine that makes the earth turn, filled the little room; he had begun to purr.

The sweet thunder of his purr shook the old walls, made the shutters batter the windows until they burst apart and let in the white light of the snowy moon. Tiles came crashing down from the roof; I heard them fall into the courtyard far below. The reverberations of his purring rocked the foundations of the house; the walls began to dance. I thought: "It will all fall, everything will disintegrate."

> "The sweet thunder of his purr"—The animal's expression of contentment, his purring, causes the last traces of culture to disappear.
>
> "He will lick the skin off me!"—In another situation, this would be equal to "He will gobble you up." But Beauty ignores the feeling she has referred to as the "earliest and most archaic fear." In fact, the licking itself transforms her into a creature of nature.

He dragged himself closer and closer to me, until I felt the harsh velvet of his head against my hand, then a tongue, abrasive as sandpaper. **"He will lick the skin off me!"**

And each stroke of his tongue ripped skin after successive skin, all the skins of a life in the world, and left behind a nascent patina of shiny hairs. My earrings turned back to water and trickled down my shoulders; I shrugged the drops off my beautiful fur.

Further Reading

Warner, Marina. *From the Beast to the Blonde: On Fairy Tales and Their Tellers*. London: Chatto and Windus. 1994.

Zipes, Jack. *Fairy Tale As Myth, Myth As Fairy Tale*. Lexington, KY: The University Press of Kentucky, 1994.

GLOSSARY OF GODS, HEROES, AND ANTIHEROES

As a rule, there are many different versions of almost any mythological tale. The compact format of this glossary does not permit us to provide an exhaustive list of versions and sources. Doubtless, assiduous students of mythology will find much to add to our brief descriptions, but we hope these will nonetheless provide a useful reference.

Achilles—Greek. Son of Peleus and Thetis. Noblest Greek warrior at Troy.

Actaeon—Greek. A hunter who comes upon Diana while she is bathing, and is then turned into stag and torn apart by hounds.

Adad—Babylonian god of storms and winds.

Adonis—Greek god of vegetation, who is loved by Aphrodite. Can be compared to Egyptian Osiris and Mesopotamian Tammuz.

Aegisthus, Aegisthos—Greek. Lover of Clytemnestra and killed by Orestes, her son.

Aeneas—Greek. Son of Aphrodite and Anchises. Warrior in the Trojan War and supposed ancestor of the Romans. Hero of Virgil's *Aeneid*.

Aeolus—Greek god of the winds, also known as Hippotades.

Æsir—Race of Norse gods led by Odin and Thor, living at Asgard.

Agadzagadza—Uganda. Lizard who pretends to be the sky god Mugulu, but actually brings about death on earth.

Agamemnon—Greek. King of Mycenae; husband of Clytemnestra, father of Iphigenia. Murdered by Clytemnestra for having Iphigenia put to death.

Agni—Hindu. Vedic god of fire.

Aidoneus—Greek. Another name for Hades, usually in poetry.

Air-Spirit People—Native American. Insects; earliest creatures in the Navajo Creation Story. Because of their evil ways, they are forced to wander until they finally escape to higher worlds by flying through a hole in the sky.

Alcmene—Greek mortal. Wife of Amphitryon, mother of Heracles by Zeus, granddaughter of Perseus and Andromeda.

All-Father—Norse. Another name for Odin.

Alpheus—Greek. Hunter who became a river god after pursuing Arethusa, the water nymph who was changed into a spring to escape him.

Amazons—Greek. Tribe of warrior women thought to live near the Black Sea.

Amma—Egg-shaped creation goddess of Mali. Gives birth to two sets of twins; makes earth from a fragment of the placenta of Ogo, one of her creations.

Amphitrite—Greek sea goddess, daughter of Nereus, wife of Poseidon.

Amphitryon—Greek. Husband of Alcmene, who was the mother of Heracles.

Amun—Egyptian god worshiped in Thebes and Hermopolis. He caused the ram-headed Khnum to create humans from clay.

Anansi, Nancy—West African. A trickster figure who can use magic for both good and evil purposes. Many African-American tales about Anansi come from the Ashanti people of Ghana.

Andromache—Greek. Wife of Hector, mother of Astyanax, daughter of Eëtion.

Andromeda—Greek. Daughter of Cassiopeia and King Cephus of Ethiopia.

Anshar—Akkadian sky god. Descendant of Apsu and Tiamat, husband of his sister Kishar, father of Anu, great-grandfather of Marduk.

Antigone—Greek. Daughter of Oedipus and Jocasta; walled up in a tomb as punishment for burying her dead brother, Polyneices. Also sister of Ismene and Eteocles.

Anu—Akkadian. Father of the gods; god of the heavens. Counterpart of Sumerian An.

Anubis—Egyptian god of the dead who weighs the hearts of the deceased. Portrayed with the head of a jackal. Son of Nephthys and Osiris. Presided over funerals and conducted souls to the underworld.

Anunnaki—Sumerian grouping of gods of fertility and gods of the underworld under An and Enlil. They serve as judges, for example, of when men are to die.

Aphrodite—Greek goddess of love, born from the sea. Mother of Eros. Counterpart of Roman Venus.

Apollo—Greek god of the sun, poetry, music, and medicine. Son of Zeus and Leto, twin of Artemis, father of Asclepius. Worshipped at the oracle at Delphi. Also known as Phoebus.

Apsu—Akkadian. With Tiamat, progenitor of Mesopotamian pantheon.

Ares—Greek god of war. Son of Zeus and Hera. Counterpart of Roman Mars.

Arges—Greek. One of the Cyclopes. According to Hesiod, a son of Uranus and Gaia.

Ariadne—Greek. Daughter of King Minos of Crete and Pasiphae, who gave Theseus the thread that allowed him to escape from the Labyrinth. She was deserted by Theseus on Naxos and later married Dionysus.

Artemis—Greek goddess of the hunt. Daughter of Leto and Zeus, sister of Apollo. Associated also with the moon and virginity.

Aruru—Akkadian earth goddess who assisted Marduk in creating humans. Counterpart of Sumerian Ki.

Asa-Thor—Norse. Son of Thor and his wife, Earth.

Asclepios—Greek god of medicine and healing. Son of Apollo; pupil of Chiron, the centaur. Counterpart of Roman Aesculapius.

Ask—Norse. First man. Created from an ash tree.

Astarte—Phoenician goddess of love and fertility who was associated with Egyptian Hathor.

Astraea—Greek goddess of justice. Daughter of Zeus and Themis. In Ovid's *Metamorphoses,* the last of the immortals.

Athena—Greek goddess of wisdom and war. Daughter of Zeus, born from his head. Counterpart of Roman Minerva.

Atlas—Greek Titan. Son of Iapetus and Clymene. Father of the Hesperides, the Hyades, and the Pleiades. Prometheus' brother, who fought against Zeus and the Olympian gods. He was punished by having to hold the earth and heavens on his back.

Atropos—Greek Fate who cuts the thread of human life, bringing about its end.

Atum—Egyptian sun god who conducts the final judgment before Osiris. By himself, father of Shu and Tefnut.

Aurora—Roman goddess of the dawn. Counterpart of Greek Eos.

Aya—Mesopotamian. Dawn, bride of the sun gods.

Bacchae—Greek. Female attendants of Dionysus, usually women who participated in orgiastic rites and wild dancing through the mountains called the Bacchanalia.

Bacchus—Roman god of wine and revelry. Counterpart of Greek Dionysus.

Baldr, Balder—Norse god of light and peace. Son of Odin and Frigg, husband of Nanna; Hodr unwittingly killed him.

Bastet—Egyptian goddess who often had the features of a cat. Later identified with Isis.

Bel—Akkadian. Alternate name for Enlil. Replaced by Akkadian god Marduk.

Bellerophon—Greek. Grandson of Sisyphus. Corinthian hero who accomplishes a series of tasks with the help of Pegasus, the winged horse, including killing the Chimera.

Berserks—Norse. Warriors who battled with extraordinary fury and energy.

Bharata—Hindu. In Valmiki's *Ramayana,* Rama's half-brother, by Kaikeyi.

Bor—Norse, Æsir. Father of Odin.

Boreas—Greek north wind, one of the four winds ruled by Zephyrus. Counterpart of Roman Aquilo.

Bow-Priests—Southwestern Native American spiritual leaders. As the two brothers in the Zuni Emergence Myth, they use long prayersticks to help their people ascend to the next world.

Bragi—Norse god of poetry and elegance. Son of Odin and husband of Idun.

Briareus—Greek. Monstrous child of Gaia and Uranus, one of the Hecatoncheires.

Brontes—Greek. One of the Cyclopes. Child of Gaia and Uranus.

Buri—Norse. First of the gods, ancestor of the Æsir created when the cow Audhumla licked the block of ice in the *Prose Edda.* Father of Bor, who is the father of Odin.

Cadmus, Cadmos—Greek, Brother of Europa. Legendary founder of the Greek city of Thebes.

Centaurs—Greek. Creatures with the upper body of a man and the lower body of a horse, who lived mainly in Thessaly.

Cerberus, Cerberos—Greek. Three-headed dog which guards the entrance to Hades.

Ceres—Roman goddess of agriculture. Counterpart of the Greek Demeter.

Ch'ang-O—Chinese. Moon goddess who stole the elixir of immortality that had been given to her husband Yi, the archer.

Chaos—Greek. The infinite void or the shapeless universe before creation. Also, the deity ruling it.

Charon—Greek. Boatman who ferries the dead across the River Styx into Hades.

Ch'ih Yu—Chinese. God of war and culture hero who invented metallurgy and metal weapons.

Chiron, Cheiron—Greek, Centaur who taught many Greek heroes, including Achilles, Asclepius, and Jason.

Circe—Greek. Enchantress on the island of Aeaea who turns men into swine. Daughter of Helios.

Clotho—Greek Fate who spins the thread of life.

Clytemnestra—Greek. Daughter of Leda and Zeus, wife of Agamemnon, mother of Orestes.

Cottos, Kottos—Greek. Monstrous child of Gaia and Uranus. One of the Hecatoncheires.

Council of the Gods—Roman. In Ovid's *Metamorphoses,* it decides to destroy humankind by a flood.

Coyote—Native American. Trickster figure and culture hero; sometimes a malevolent shapechanger. Often travels with a companion such as a fox or bear; credited with introducing work, pain, and death to the world.

Cretan Bull—Greek. Savage bull transported by Heracles and allowed to roam near Marathon until captured by Theseus.

Cronos, Kronos—Greek. Head of the Titans. Son of Uranus and Gaia, father of Zeus. Counterpart of Roman Saturn.

Cupid—Roman god of love. Son of Venus and Mercury or Mars. Counterpart of Greek Eros. Also called Amor.

Cybele—Asia Minor. Mother goddess.

Cyclopes—Greek. One-eyed giants Brontes, Arges, and Steropes. According to Hesiod, sons of Uranus and Gaia.

Cythera—Greek. An epithet of Aphrodite because of her birth from the sea near Cythera. Also the name of a shrine devoted to Aphrodite off the coast of the Peloponneses, where she was said to have been born.

Daedalus, Daedalos—Greek. Athenian architect who built the Labyrinth on Crete for King Minos. He made wings for himself and his son Icarus for their escape from Crete.

Damkina—Mesopotamian. Wife of Ea, mother of Marduk.

Daphne—Greek nymph. Daughter of the river god Peneus. She was changed into a tree to escape the advances of Apollo, who loved her.

Dasaratha—Hindu. Rama's father. King of Ayodhya.

Deianeira—Greek. Wife of Heracles, who poisoned him unwittingly by giving him a shirt dipped in the poisoned blood of Nessus. Daughter of Achelous.

Demeter—Greek goddess of agriculture, especially grain. Daughter of Cronus and Rhea, mother of Persephone by Zeus. Counterpart of Roman Ceres.

Demophöon—Greek. Son of King Celeus of Eleusis and Metaneira; nursed by Demeter.

Deucalion—Greek. Son of Prometheus. He and his wife, Pyrrha, were the sole survivors of the Flood.

Diana—Ancient Greek goddess of woods and fertility. Later, by identification with the Greek goddess Artemis, she also became goddess of the moon and healing.

Dionysus, Dionysos—Greek god of fertility, dreams, and wine. Son of Zeus and Semele, whose father was Cadmus. Counterpart of Roman Bacchus.

Donar—Germanic god of thunder, corresponding to the Norse god Thor. Associated with Roman Hercules.

Ea—Akkadian god of wisdom and fresh waters; one of the creators of mankind. Son of Apsu and Marduk. Counterpart of Sumerian Enki.

Einherjar—Norse. Spirits of dead warriors who follow Odin to fight on Vigrid at Ragnarok.

Embla—Norse. First woman; created by the gods from a tree.

Enki—Sumerian god of fresh water and wisdom. Helper of humans. Counterpart of Akkadian Ea.

Enkidu—Sumerian. In the *Epic of Gilgamesh,* human created by Ninsun as a companion for her son, Gilgamesh.

Enlil, Ellil—Sumerian king of the gods; god of earth and wind. Father of Ninurta.

Ennugi—Mesopotamian. Guardian god of canals.

Eos—Greek goddess of dawn. Counterpart of Roman Aurora.

Epimetheus—Greek. Son of Iapetus and Clymene, brother of Prometheus and Atlas, husband of Pandora.

Erebos, Erebus—Greek. Son of Chaos, brother and husband of Nyx (night). Personification of darkness and the unknown. Also, region of darkness in the underworld where the dead reside.

Ereshkigal—Sumerian and Akkadian goddess of death. Queen of the underworld, sister of Ishtar, spouse of Nergal, mother of Ninazu. Another name for Irkalla.

Eros—Greek god of love. According to Hesiod, one of the first gods. Counterpart of Roman Cupid.

Esu-Elegbara—West African. Trickster who interprets the wishes of the gods to humans and guards the barrier which separates the worlds of the humans and the gods.

Eteocles—Greek mortal. Son of Oedipus and Jocasta, who killed his brother Polyneices in a civil war and then died of his wounds.

Europa—Greek. Daughter of the king of Phoenicia and Telephassa, sister of Cadmus. Abducted to Crete by Zeus in the form of a bull; Minos was one of her children with Zeus.

Eurydice—Greek. Bride of Orpheus confined eternally to Hades after Orpheus failed in his attempt to rescue her. Also called Agriope.

Eurystheus—Greek. King of Mycenae who imposed Heracles' labors.

Faro—Bambara. Creator of seven heavens.

Fates—Greek goddesses of destiny: Clotho, Atropos, and Lachesis. The Greeks called them Moirai, and the Romans called them Parcae.

Fenrir—Norse. Monstrous wolf who tries to eat the sun. Son of Loki and Angerboda. At Ragnarok, he swallows Odin and is killed by Vidar.

Freyja, Freya—Norse. Vanir fertility goddess who claims half of the fallen warriors in battle. (Odin claims the other half.) Wife of Od, mother of Hnoss, sister of Freyr, daughter of Njord. A shapechanger.

Freyr, Frey—Norse. Son of the wind and sea god Njord and brother of Freyja, who controls the sun, rain, and harvest. Originally associated with the Vanir, later with the Æsir. Fertility god of the Swedes in eleventh century.

Frigg, Frigga—Norse. Goddess of the heavens and queen of Asgard. Wife of Odin, mother of Baldr. Associated with childbirth.

Fu Hsi—Chinese. Culture hero who invented writing, music, and the domestication of animals.

Furies, Furiae—Roman goddesses of vengeance. Counterparts of the Greek Erinyes or Eumenides.

Gaia, Gaea, Ge—Greek goddess. Mother Earth. Mother and wife of Uranus; by Uranus, mother of the Titans, Cyclopes, and Hecatonchieres.

Ganymede—Greek. Cupbearer of the gods on Mt. Olympus. Son of Tros and Callirhoe. He was taken to Olympus by Zeus and later made immortal.

Ge—Another name for the Greek earth goddess Gaia.

Geb—Egyptian earth god. Father of Isis and Osiris.

Gefjon—Norse. Æsir giantess.

Giants, Gigantes—Ancient Greek. Monster children of Gaia who fought the Olympians and were defeated.

Gilgamesh—Sumerian. Legendary king, hero of Sumerian and Babylonian epics.

Graces—Greek goddesses of grace and beauty: Aglaia, Euphrosyne, and Thalia. Daughters of Eurynome and Zeus. Counterparts of the Roman Gratiae.

Gyges—Greek. Monstrous child of Uranus and Gaia.

Hades, Aidoneus—Greek god of the underworld. Son of Cronus and Rhea, husband of Persephone. Known as Pluto to the Romans. Counterpart of the Roman Dis. Also, a name for the underworld itself.

Hanuman—Hindu. In the *Ramayana,* a noble monkey who leads the monkey army to fight for Rama.

Harmonia—Greek. Daughter of Ares and Aphrodite, wife of Cadmus.

Hathor—Egyptian goddess of fertility, love, and joy, often represented with the head, horns, or ears of a cow. In some stories, she is the mother of Horus; in others, his consort.

Hebe—Greek goddess of youth and spring. Daughter of Zeus and Hera, later wife of Heracles.

Hecate, Hekate—Greek. Goddess of the moon, often seen carrying a torch. Also associated with Gaia, the earth, and with the underworld.

Hecatoncheires—Greek. Monster sons of Uranus and Gaia who helped Zeus defeat the Titans.

Hector—Greek hero in the *Iliad*. Son of Priam of Troy and Hecuba; husband of Andromache.

Hecuba—Greek. Wife of King Priam of Troy; mother of Hector, Paris, and Polydorus.

Heimdall—Norse god of dawn and light who guards Asgard. At Ragnarok, he blows his horn Gjoll to awaken the gods.

Hel—Norse goddess. Daughter of Loki and Angerboda. Rules over Niflheim, the kingdom of death. Also another name for Niflheim, the underworld for the wicked.

Helen of Troy—Greek mortal. Daughter of Zeus and Leda, wife of Menelaus of Sparta, sister of Castor, Pollux, and Clytemnestra.

Helios—Ancient Greek god of the sun. Son of the Titan Hyperion and Theia, father of Circe and Pasiphae. Represented as driving a chariot across the sky. Counterpart of the Roman Sol.

Hephaistos—Greek god of fire, forges, metalwork, and handicrafts. Son of Zeus and Hera, husband of Aphrodite. Counterpart of the Roman Vulcan.

Hera—Greek. Queen of the Olympian goddesses. Daughter of Cronus and Rhea, wife of Zeus, mother of Hephaistos, Ares, and Hebe. Counterpart of the Roman Juno.

Heracles—Greek. Son of Zeus and Alcmene who gained immortality by completing twelve labors. Counterpart of the Roman Hercules.

Hermes—Greek god of travelers, commerce, flocks, and cunning. Son of Zeus and Maia; he conducts souls to the underworld. As a messenger god, he is the counterpart of Roman Mercury.

Hermod—Norse. Son of Odin. Rode to Hel to negotiate the return of Baldr to Asgard.

Hesperides—Greek nymphs. Daughters of Erebos and Nyx, or of Atlas and Hesperus, or of Phorcys and Ceto. According to Hesiod, guardians of the Golden Apples.

Hippolyte—Greek. Daughter of Ares and Queen of the Amazons.

Hodr—Norse god who was blind. He was tricked by Loki into throwing a mistletoe branch which killed Baldr.

Horus—Egyptian sun god usually portrayed as a falcon or as a man with the head of a falcon. He represented the living king of Egypt. In one of his forms, he was also known as Harpocrates, a child nursing at the breast of Isis. Associated with the Greek Apollo.

Hou Chi—Chinese. Culture hero and god who taught humans to sow grain.

Hsi Wang Mu—Chinese. Representative of the element "yin." She cultivates the peach tree of immortality and brews a tea from its fruit.

Humbaba, Huwawa—Sumerian. In the *Epic of Gilgamesh,* giant guardian of the cedar forest, slain by Enkidu.

Hyacinthus—Greek youth loved by, and accidentally killed by, Apollo. The hyacinth flower sprang from his blood.

Hyades—Greek nymphs. Sisters of the Pleiades who nurtured the baby Dionysus and as a reward were placed among the stars. Seven stars that make up the face of the bull in the constellation Taurus.

Hyperion—Greek Titan. Son of Uranus and Gaia; father of Helios, Eos, and Selene by his sister Theia. Sometimes identified with Helios and Apollo.

Hyperionides—Greek. Another name for Helios, the sun; the name means he was the son of Hyperion.

Iangura—Nyanga Democratic Republic of the Congo. Sister of Mwindo and wife of Mukiti, the water serpent.

Iapetos—Greek Titan. Son of Uranus and Gaia; father of Prometheus, Epimetheus, and Atlas by Clymene.

Indra—Hindu. Vedic chief god, god of thunder and rain. Leads warriors in battle, sitting in a chariot pulled through the air by green horses.

Iolaos—Greek. Heracles' half-brother and son of Iphicles, who accompanied him on some of his adventures.

Iphicles—Greek. Son of Alcmene and Amphitryon. Heracles' twin brother, whose birth was hastened by Hera because Zeus had declared that the child about to be born would be the next king of Mycenae.

Iphigeneia—Greek. Daughter of Agamemnon and Clytemnestra, sister of Orestes and Electra. Agamemnon sacrificed her to Artemis to ensure good winds to take the Greek ships to Troy; Artemis rescued her and she became one of the goddess' priestesses.

Iris—Roman goddess of the rainbow. Juno's messenger.

Irkalla—Mesopotamian. Another name for Ereshkigal, Queen of the underworld.

Ishtar—Assyrian and Babylonian. Goddess of love, fertility, and war. Daughter of Anu. Identified with the Phoenician goddess Astarte and the Sumerian Inanna.

Isis—Egyptian goddess of fertility and the moon. Daughter of Geb (earth) and Nut (sky). Mother of Horus, sister and wife of Osiris. Usually represented as a woman with a cow's horns and a solar disk between them. Associated with Greek Artemis.

Ismene—Greek. Daughter of Oedipus and Jocasta; sister of Antigone, Eteocles, and Polyneices. She did not join Antigone in the forbidden burial of their slain brother, Polyneices.

Jatayu—Hindu. The celestial eagle who guards Sita for Rama; later killed by Ravana.

Jocasta, Jokasta—Greek. Wife of King Laius of Thebes, mother and wife of Oedipus. Mother, by Oedipus, of Antigone, Ismene, Eteocles, and Polyneices.

Jove—Roman supreme deity. Counterpart of the Greek Zeus. Also known as Jupiter.

Juno—Roman queen of the gods, protector of women and marriage. Daughter of Saturn, sister and wife of Jupiter. Counterpart of Greek goddess Hera.

Jupiter—Roman. Son of Saturn and Ops. Counterpart of Greek Zeus. Also known as Jove.

Kaikeyi—Hindu. In the *Ramayana,* one of King Dasaratha's three wives. Stepmother of Rama, who forced him into exile so her own son, Bharata, could rule.

Kaikuzi—Uganda. Son of Mugulu. In the Creation Story, he helps Kintu in trying to overcome Warumbe, but fails.

Kali—Hindu goddess of destruction. Wife of Shiva in his aspect as destroyer. She represents the all-devouring aspect of Devi, the Hindu mother goddess, but also represents positive creativity. Also known as Chandi Durga, Parvati, Sakti, Uma, and Mata.

Kasiyembe—Nyanga. Democratic Republic of the Congo. In the Mwindo epic, Mukiti's head man, who is charged with guarding Iangura.

Kausalya—Hindu. In Valmiki's *Ramayana,* one of King Dasaratha's three wives. Mother of Rama.

Kintu—Uganda. Semilegendary first king, and also a legendary immortal figure involved in the creation of the world.

Kishar—Mesopotamian. Descendant of Apsu and Tiamat, sister and wife of Anshar, with him mother of Anu, great-grandmother of Marduk.

Kore, Core—Greek. Persephone, especially as a symbol of virginity. "Kore" means "maiden."

Kronides—Greek. Another name for Zeus, meaning "son of Cronus."

Kuan Yin—Chinese goddess of compassion. After Buddhism arrived in China, she was considered the incarnation of a male bodhisattva.

Labdacus—Greek. Father of Laius, grandson of Cadmus. Legendary king of Thebes.

Lachesis—Greek Fate who determines the length of the thread of life. A personification of destiny.

Lahamu—Mesopotamian. Daughter of Apsu and Tiamat, sister and wife of Lahmu, with him mother of Anshar and Kishar, grandmother of Ea.

Laius—Greek. King of Thebes. Great-grandson of Cadmus, husband of Jocasta, father of Oedipus, by whom he was killed.

Lakshmana—Hindu. Rama's half-brother by Sumitra. Made immortal because he took his own life to spare Rama from death.

Laomedon—Greek. King of Troy. Father of Priam and Hesione.

Leda—Greek. Mother of Castor, Pollux, Helen, and Clytemnestra by Zeus, who came to her in the form of a swan. Wife of King Tyndareus of Sparta.

Leto—Greek. Mother of Apollo and Artemis by Zeus. Counterpart of the Roman Latona.

Leucothea—Greek sea goddess who protected sailors. In the *Odyssey,* she saved Odysseus after Poseidon capsized his vessel.

Leviathan—Judaeo-Christian. Biblical sea monster that embodies all evil.

Lisa—Benin. Fon (Dahomey) people. Son of Nana Boluku, who completes the task of creating the universe with his sister Mawu.

Loki—Norse trickster god of discord and mischief who lives in Asgard. Son of Laufey and the giant Farbauti, brother of Byleist and Helbindi, husband of Sigyn, and father of Nari. Also the father of Fenrir, Jormungand (the Midgard Serpent), and Hel by the giantess Angrboda. He tricked Hodr into killing Baldr.

Loricus—Icelandic. Nobleman of Thrace. Foster father of Thor. In the *Prose Edda,* Thor kills Loricus and his wife and takes over Thrace.

Lugulbanda—Mesopotamian. A king of Uruk, god and shepherd, father and protector of Gilgamesh.

Maenads—Greek. Female worshippers of Dionysus. Also called Bacchantes.

Maia—Greek. Eldest of the Pleiades. Daughter of Atlas and Pleione, mother of Hermes by Zeus.

Marduk—Babylonian head god, son of Ea. Originally a god of thunderstorms; later, a chief Sumerian deity. Creator of the universe from the body of Tiamat.

Maricha—Hindu. In the *Ramayana,* Rakshasa demon, Ravana's adviser.

Mars—Roman god of war and agriculture. Counterpart of the Greek Ares.

Mawu—Benin. Fon (Dahomey) people. Daughter of Nana Boluku, who completes the task of creating the universe with her brother Lisa.

Medea—Greek Enchantress. Daughter of Aeëtes, wife of Jason and then King Aegeus of Athens, niece of Circe. Helped Jason get the Golden Fleece and killed their children when he deserted her.

Medusa—Greek. Monster daughter of Phorcys and Ceto who could turn people to stone by looking at them. The only one of the three Gorgons to be mortal, she was killed by Perseus.

Megara—Greek. Daughter of Creon, wife of Heracles. Heracles killed their children in a fit of madness.

Menelaus—Greek. Husband of Helen, brother of Agamemnon. King of Sparta at the time of the Trojan War.

Mercury—Roman god of commerce, travelers, science, and thievery. Son of Jupiter and Maia. Counterpart of Greek Hermes. Also known as Hermanubis in Rome, a combination of Hermes and Anubis.

Metaneira—Greek. Wife of King Celeus of Eleusis who took Demeter in to nurse her child.

Metis—Greek Titan. First wife of Zeus, daughter of Oceanus and Tethys, mother of Athena. Athena was born from Zeus' head after he had swallowed Metis. Her name means "wisdom" or "thought."

Midgard Serpent—Norse serpent curled around the edge of the earth (Midgard). Son of Loki and the giantess Angrboda. Killed by Thor at Ragnarok. Poison from the Serpent then kills Thor.

Mimir—Norse being who lives in the roots of Yggdrasil and guards a spring. Odin receives great wisdom through his advice.

Minos—Greek. Son of Zeus by a human mother, Europa. King of Crete who ordered Daedalus to build the Labyrinth. Husband of Pasiphae, father of Ariadne and Androgeus. After his death, he became a judge in the lower world.

Minotaur—Greek monster offspring of Pasiphae and King Minos. He lived in the Cretan Labyrinth, feeding on human flesh, until Theseus, helped by Ariadne, killed him.

Mnemosyne—Greek Titan. Goddess of memory. Daughter of Uranus and Gaia, mother of the Muses by Zeus.

Mugulu, Gulu—Uganda. An important sky deity. Father of Warumbe, the god of death.

Muisa—Nyanga. Democratic Republic of the Congo. A god of the underworld. Father of Kahindo, spirit of good fortune.

Mukiti—Nyanga. Democratic Republic of the Congo. Water serpent who marries Iangura, sister of Mwindo.

Muses—Greek. Nine sister goddesses of arts, sciences, poetry, and song: Calliope, Clio, Euterpe, Thalia, Melpomene, Terpsichore, Erato, Polyhymnia, and Urania. Daughters of Zeus and Mnemosyne. Counterparts of the Roman Camenae.

Musoka—Nyanga. Democratic Republic of the Congo. Female water spirit for whom the Nyanga have a special cult.

Mwindo—Nyanga. Democratic Republic of the Congo. Hero who exhibits miraculous traits even at birth and performs extraordinary deeds with the help of the gods.

Nambi—Uganda. Daughter of Mugulu (Gulu), an important sky god.

Namtar—Sumerian and Akkadian demon of the underworld; the negative aspect of fate. Personification of death.

Nana Boluku—Benin. Androgynous creator of the universe for the Fon (Dahomey) people. Daughter Mawu and son Lisa complete the creation.

Narcissus—Greek. Beloved of Echo. Son of the river god Cephisus and the nymph Liriope. Fell in love with his own reflection in a pool and wasted away from unfulfilled desire.

Nephilim—Judaeo-Christian. Biblical reference to a bygone race of mighty creatures or giants.

Nephthys—Egyptian. Sister of Isis and Osiris; sister and wife of Seth.

Neptune—Roman god of the sea. Counterpart of Greek Poseidon.

Nereids—Greek. Group of 50 sea nymphs who were the daughters of Nereus and the Oceanid Doris.

Nergel—Akkadian. Ruled the world of the dead with Ereshkigal. He helped cause the Flood by pulling out the great dams.

Nerthus—Germanic goddess of fertility, joy, and devotion. Visited her people in a wagon. Later, her characteristics are associated with Frey and the Vanir.

Nessus—Greek. Centaur killed by Heracles as he attempted to seduce his wife, Deianeira. Before he died, Nessus gave her the poisoned shirt that caused Heracles' death.

Nidhogg—Norse. Serpent in Niflheim who gnaws at the root of Yggdrasil, the World Tree.

Ninsun—Sumerian goddess noted for wisdom. Wife of Lugulbanda, mother of Gilgamesh.

Ninurta—Sumerian and Babylonian god of war, wells, and irrigation; the south wind. Son of Enlil.

Njord—Norse. Vanir god of ships and the sea. Father of Freyr and Freyja. Husband of Skadi.

Nkuba—Nyanga. Democratic Republic of the Congo. Husband of Chinawezi, the mother of all things; father of Gihanga, a cultural hero who brought prosperity and founded the mythical kingdom of Rwanda. He and Chinawezi divided the world, and he moved to the sky to become the god of lightning, bringing life-giving rain.

Noah—Judaeo-Christian. Father of the only family spared by the Flood in Genesis.

Norns—Norse equivalents of the Greek Fates, goddesses who control the destinies of humans. Counterparts of the Anglo-Saxon Wyrd and similar to the Greek Moirai and the Roman Parcae.

Nudimmud—Akkadian. Alternate name for Ea.

Nü-Kwa—Chinese. Creator goddess of humans; saves humankind from cosmic catastrophe when one of the pillars holding the sky collapses.

Nut—Egyptian goddess of the sky. Mother of Osiris.

Nyamwindo—Nyanga. Democratic Republic of the Congo. Mother of Mwindo.

Nymphs—Greek. Protective lesser deities dwelling in rivers, streams, fountains, mountains, and woods.

Oceanus—Greek Titan. Son of Uranus and Gaia. With Tethys, his wife, father of the river gods, and nymphs of the rivers and seas.

Ocyrhoe, Okyrhoe—Greek. Daughter of Charon.

Odin—Norse. Æsir god of war, wisdom, and poetry. Husband of Friyg, son of Bor and Bestla. Counterpart of the Germanic Wotan and Anglo-Saxon Wodan.

Odysseus—Greek. King of Ithaca. Husband of Penelope, father of Telemachus. Leader in the Trojan War and hero of the *Odyssey*. His Latin name is Ulysses.

Oedipus—Greek. Son of Laius of Thebes and Jocasta. Murders Laius and unwittingly marries his mother. With her, he fathers Antigone, Ismene, Eteocles, and Polyneices.

Ongo, Yurugu—Mali. Consort of Amma in creating humans.

Orpheus—Greek god of music and poetry. Son of Calliope, and husband of Eurydice, whom he followed into the underworld after her death. Hades gave permission for him to lead her back to earth, but he violated the interdiction not to look back.

Osiris—Egyptian chief deity, judge of the dead. Killed and dismembered by his brother Seth, and reassembled by his sister and wife Isis. Usually represented as a man with a beard wearing an *atef* crown and partly wrapped as a mummy.

Pan—Greek god of the woods, fields, and flocks. Represented with the upper body of a man and the legs (and sometimes horns and ears) of a goat.

Pandora—Greek. The first woman, created by Hephaistos at the command of Zeus. Wife of Epimetheus. She opened the box (or jar) that had been given her, unwittingly releasing all evils that could affect humans.

Paris—Greek. Son of Priam of Troy and Hecuba, brother of Cassandra. Helped by Aphrodite, to whom he had awarded the apple of discord in a beauty contest. Abducted Helen, causing the Trojan War.

Pasiphae—Greek. Wife of King Minos of Crete, mother of Ariadne, and of the Minotaur by the Cretan Bull.

Patroclus—Greek. Hero in the Trojan War. Son of Menoetius, friend of Achilles. He was slain by Hector.

Pemba—Bambara. Mali. Creator of earth with Faro, who descended from the sky. Twin of sister Musokoroni.

Penelope—Greek. Wife of Odysseus who rejected suitors while he was gone, fighting at Troy.

Pentheus—Greek. Son of Agave and Echion, King of Thebes. In Euripides' play, *The Bacchae*, he is forced to accept the worship of Dionysus.

Persephone—Greek. Daughter of Demeter by Zeus. Abducted to Hades, but allowed to return to earth for part of the year. Counterpart of the Roman Proserpina.

Perseus—Greek. Son of Zeus by the human Danae. Founder-king of Mycenae. Slayer of the Gorgon Medusa with the help of Hermes and Athena. He later saved Andromeda from a sea monster.

Phaethon—Greek. Son of Helios and Clymene. Borrowed the chariot of the sun and was struck down by Zeus when he came dangerously close to earth.

Phoebe—Greek Titan. Daughter of Uranus and Gaia, mother of Leto. Later identified with the moon, Artemis, and the Roman goddess Diana.

Phoebus—Greek. Epithet of Apollo as the sun god. The name means "radiant" or "bright."

Pholus—Greek. Centaur killed accidentally by Odysseus' poisoned arrow.

Pi-hia yüan-kün—Chinese. Goddess who protects women in childbirth and with her helpers assists with childhood diseases.

Pluto—Greek name for Hades, meaning "wealthy one" or "wealth giver."

Polyneices—Greek. Son of Oedipus and Jocasta, brother of Antigone, Ismene, and Eteocles. He killed his brother Eteocles in a civil war, and died of his wounds.

Poseidon—Greek god of the sea and earthquakes. Son of Cronus and Rhea, brother of Zeus, husband of Amphitrite, father of Pegasus by Medusa. Counterpart of the Roman Neptune.

Powakas—Southwest Native American. Evil creatures that cause others to become evil. In the Hopi Creation Story, almost all are shut out of society.

Priam—Trojan. King at the time of the Trojan War. Husband of Hecuba, father of Hector, Paris, Polydorus, and Cassandra. Killed during the capture of Troy.

Prometheus—Greek Titan. Son of Iapetus and Clymene, brother of Epimetheus and Atlas, father of Deucalion or Pyrrha. Stole fire from Olympus for humans and was punished by Zeus by being chained to a rock where an eagle ate his liver daily. Rescued by Heracles. The name means "forethought."

Proserpina—Roman counterpart of the Greek Persephone.

Proteus—Greek god of the sea. Served Poseidon; a shapechanger.

Psyche—Greek. A personification of the soul who, in the form of a beautiful girl, was loved by Eros (Cupid) and became his wife.

Ptah—Egyptian god who created the universe. Menes, the King of the first dynasty, established his temple at Memphis.

Pyrrha—Greek. Daughter of Epimetheus. With her husband, Deucalion, sole survivor of the Flood.

Rakshasas—Hindu. Demons who are hostile to humans. They are shapechangers who sometimes eat human flesh. In the *Ramayana*, Ravana belongs to this group.

Rama—Hindu. Hero of the *Ramayana*. Any of the three avatars of Vishnu: Balarama, Parashurama, or Ramachandra.

Ravana—Hindu. In the *Ramayana*, a rakshasa, a monster with 10 heads and 20 arms. King of Ceylon who abducts Sita and is later defeated by her husband, Rama.

Raven—Native American. One of the animal deities of many peoples in the northwest area of North America who bring fire, rain, natural features, and order to society. They are tricksters and sometimes also shapechangers.

Re, Ra—Egyptian. A sun god whose cult was centered in Heliopolis; worshipped throughout ancient Egypt as the creator of the universe. Usually represented as a falcon-headed man with the solar disk and *uraeus* (a rearing cobra with a swollen neck) on his head.

Rhea—Greek Titan, mother goddess. Daughter of Uranus and Gaia; sister and wife of Cronus; mother of Zeus, Demeter, Hades, Hera, Poseidon, and Hestia.

Romulus—Roman. Founder of Rome in 753 B.C.E. and first king. Son of Mars and Rhea Silvia. With his twin brother Remus, he was abandoned, nursed by a she-wolf, and raised by a shepherd. Later made into a god by the Romans.

Satrughna—Hindu. Rama's half-brother by Sumitra; twin of Lakshmana.

Saturn—Italo-Roman god. "Hellenized" in the third century B.C.E. Counterpart of the Greek Cronus; father of Jupiter and ruler during the Golden Age.

Satyrs—Greek. Wild woodland deities who are part human, part horse, and sometimes part goat. As attendants of Dionysus (Bacchus), they are preoccupied with drinking and lovemaking. Counterparts of the Roman Fauns.

Semele—Greek. Daughter of Cadmus of Thebes and Harmonia, mother of Dionysus by Zeus.

Seth—Egyptian. Osiris' brother and murderer. Represented as a donkey or other mammal and considered a personification of the wind. According to Plutarch, counterpart of Greek Typhon.

Shamash—Mesopotamian sun god. In the *Epic of Gilgamesh*, he provides fierce winds to help Gilgamesh and Enkidu defeat Humbaba.

Sheburungu—Nyanga. Democratic Republic of the Congo. Name given to Ongo, the creator god.

Shemwindo—Nyanga. Democratic Republic of the Congo. Banyanga chief, father of Mwindo, brother of Iyngura.

Shen Nüng—Chinese. Culture hero who introduced agriculture, commerce, and pharmacopoeia to humankind.

Shiva, Siva—Vedic, and later Hindu, god of destruction, sensuality, and aestheticism. His name means "the Destroyer." Third member of the Trimurti, with Brahma, the Creator, and Vishnu, the Preserver. Sometimes a helper of humans.

Shu—Egyptian god of the air. Created by Atum. Father of Nut.

Siddhartha—Vedic. Epithet of Buddha meaning "he who has attained his goal."

Siduri—Mesopotamian goddess of brewing and wisdom. Advises Gilgamesh about mortality, as well as revealing how he might find Utnapishtim.

Sif—Norse goddess. Wife of Thor.

Sisyphus—Greek. Son of Aeolus. Mythical king of Corinth punished by having to roll a boulder uphill for eternity in Hades.

Sita—Hindu. In the *Ramayana*, wife of Rama, daughter of Mother Earth and King Janaka; incarnation of Lakshmi, Vishnu's wife. Abducted by Ravana and later rescued.

Skadi—Norse. Wife of Njord.

Sphinx—Greek. Monster usually represented with the head and breast of a woman, the body of a lion, and wings of an eagle. Lurked outside Thebes, killing all who could not solve her riddle. When Oedipus solved it, she killed herself.

Spider Grandmother—Native American. One of several spider figures who help humans, often by using magic.

Steropes—Greek. According to Hesiod, one of the Cyclopes.

Strife—Greek. Another name for Eris. Counterpart of the Roman Discordia.

Sugreeva—Hindu. In the *Ramayana*, Monkey King who helps Rama find Sita.

Sumitra—Hindu. In the *Ramayana*, one of Dasaratha's three wives and mother of Lakshmana and Satrughna, the half-brothers of Rama.

Surt—Norse. Muspell giant and ruler who is to defeat Freyr and destroy the world by fire at Ragnarok.

Syrdon—Legendary figure in Ossetic myth who shares many of Loki's characteristics.

Tammuz—Sumerian and Babylonian shepherd god who took the place of his wife Inanna or Ishtar in the underworld. The name means "faithful son."

Tawa—Native American. Hopi Sun Spirit, creator of the first world.

Tefnut, Tefenet—Egyptian. Moisture, created by Atum, along with Shu, Air, in the first stage of creation.

Telemachus—Greek. Son of Odysseus and Penelope. Helped his father kill Penelope's suitors.

Teliko—Bambara. Mali. Begotten by Yo, the creative spirit. Spirit of the air who gives birth to aquatic twins from whom come all humans.

Tethys—Greek. Titan daughter of Gaia and Uranus. Mother, by Oceanus, of Metis and Proteus.

Themis—Greek. Daughter of Gaia. Goddess of order, justice, and the seasons. Mother of the Fates.

Theseus—Greek. Son of Poseidon. Kills the Minotaur and marries the Amazon queen Hippolyte.

Thetis—Greek sea goddess. Achilles' mother.

Thökk—Norse. Giantess who refused to weep for the dead Baldr, thus preventing him from escaping from Hel.

Thor—Germanic. Æsir god of thunder, lightning, rain, and fertility, who lived in Asgard. Son of Odin. Known for his strength, size, and appetite.

Thoth—Egyptian god of writing and knowledge, represented as an ibis.

Tiamat—Bablyonian goddess identified with water. Killed by Marduk, who created the universe from her body.

Ti K'u—Chinese. Culture hero who invented music.

Titans—Greek. Monster children of Uranus and Gaia. Ruled the universe until they waged war with the Olympian gods and lost to Zeus.

Tiwaz—Ancient Germanic god of the sky and war. Associated with the Norse Tyr and Anglo-Saxon Tiu.

Triton—Greek sea god. Son of Poseidon and Amphritite. Represented with human head and upper body, and the lower body of a fish, blowing on a conch shell.

Ture—African tradition. Zande people. Spider trickster.

Tyche—Greek goddess of chance, therefore of luck. Associated with the Roman Fortuna.

Typhon, Typhoon—Greek monster. Opponent of Zeus, according to Hesiod.

Tyr—Norse god of war and strife. Son of Odin who lost his hand to Fenrir the wolf. Counterpart of the Anglo-Saxon Tiw.

Uranus, Ouranos—Greek. Original god of the sky. Husband and son of Gaia; with her, father of the Titans and Cyclopes.

Urshanabi—Mesopotamian. Ferryman of Gilgamesh to Utnapishtim in the land of Dilmun.

Utgard-Loki—Norse. In the *Prose Edda*, when Thor and Loki visit Giantland, Utgard-Loki uses trickery to defeat them in contests.

Utnapishtim—Mesopotamian. In the *Epic of Gilgamesh*, the sole survivor of the flood with his wife. Made immortal by the gods. Gilgamesh seeks him out in order to gain immortality.

Vali—Hindu. In the *Ramayana*, elder brother of Sugreeva, who has banished him.

Vali—Norse, Æsir. Son of Odin who avenges Baldr.

Valkyries—Norse. Warrior goddesses, attendants of Odin who choose who will die in battle, and wait on the dead warriors in Valhalla.

Vanir—Norse family of gods, including Frey and Freyja, who granted peace and plenty.

Venus—Italo-Roman fertility goddess. Adopted by the Romans who identified her with the Greek Aphrodite, goddess of love and beauty.

Vidar—Norse. Son of Odin who avenges his father by killing Fenrir at Ragnarok.

Vishnu—Hindu. Most important and supreme god, who was worshipped also in the earlier Vedic tradition.

Vishwamritra—Hindu. In the *Ramayana*, a sage who travels with Rama and counsels him.

Vulcan—Early Roman god of fires and metalworking. Son of Jupiter. Counterpart of the Greek Hephaistos.

Water Spider—Native American. One of several spider figures helpful to humans. In the Zuni Emergence Myth, the creature who helps the people locate the middle of the world.

Wodan—Anglo-Saxon chief god. Counterpart of the Norse Odin and Germanic Wotan. The Romans equated him with Mercury.

Wotan—Germanic chief god. Counterpart of Norse Odin and the Anglo-Saxon Wodan.

Yellow Emperor, the—Chinese. Culture hero and god who taught pottery and shipbuilding, the use of armor and wheeled carts.

Ymir—Norse. Primeval giant killed by Odin and his brothers, who used parts of his body to create the world. Also called Aurgelymir.

Yo—Bambara. Creative spirit. Gives birth to Faro, Pemba, and Teliko.

Yü the Great—Chinese. God who was born miraculously from a rock. Saved humanity by digging channels to alleviate a deadly flood.

Zeus—Greek. Chief sky god. Defeated the Titans to become ruler of the universe from Mt. Olympus. Counterpart of the Roman Jupiter.

Additional Works Cited

ABOUT THE COVER

Calte, Beverley. "Biography for the catalogue of the exposition, 'Francis Picabia, Japon, Août 1999–Février 2000.'" Paris, 1999. Friends of Picabia. http://www.picabia.com/biograph/bio_ev_p1.htm to http://www.picabia.com/biograph/bio_ev_p6.htm. Accessed on November 8, 2008.

PART 1 INTRODUCTION TO STUDYING MYTH

1. What Is Myth?

Dodds, E. R. *The Greeks and the Irrational.* Berkeley: University of California Press, 1951.

Doniger, Wendy. "Minimyths and Maximyths and Political Points of View." In *Myth and Method,* eds. Laurie L. Patton and Wendy Doniger, 109–27. Charlottesville: University Press of Virginia, 1996.

Eliade, Mircea. "Towards a Definition of Myth." In *Mythologies,* Vol. I, ed. Yves Bonnefoy, 3–5. Chicago: University of Chicago Press, 1991.

Frye, Northrop. *The Great Code: The Bible and Literature.* New York: Harcourt, 1982, 31–52.

Korfmann, Manfred. "Troia, an Ancient Anatolian Palatial and Trading Center." *Classical World* 91.5 (1998): 369–85.

Raaflaub, Kurt A. "Homer, the Trojan War, and History." *Classical World* 91.5 (1998): 386–403.

Rose, C. B. "Troy and the Historical Imagination." *Classical World* 91.5 (1998): 405–13.

2. Ways of Understanding Myth

Myers, K. Sara. *Ovid's Causes: Cosmogony and Aetiology in the Metamorphoses.* Ann Arbor: University of Michigan Press, 1994.

Ong, Walter. *Orality and Literacy: The Technologizing of the Word.* London and New York: Methuen, 1982.

Segal, Charles. *Landscape in Ovid's "Metamorphoses": A Study in the Transformations of a Literary Symbol.* (Hermes Einzelschrift 23.) Wiesbaden: Franz Steiner Verlag, 1969.

PART 2 MYTHS OF CREATION AND DESTRUCTION
PART 2A MYTHS OF CREATION

3. Greek Creation Stories

Clay, Jenny Strauss. *The Politics of Olympus: Form and Meaning in the Major Homeric Hymns.* Princeton, NJ: Princeton University Press, 1989.

Doherty, Lillian. "Women in the Hesiodic *Catalogue of Women.*" In *Laughing with Medusa: Classical Myth and Feminist Thought,* eds. Vanda Zajko and Miriam Leonard, 297–325. Oxford: Oxford University Press, 2006.

Eliade, Mircea. *The Myth of the Eternal Return: Or Cosmos and History.* Trans. Willard R. Trask. Bollingen Series XLVI. Princeton, NJ: Princeton University Press, 1974.

Hesiod. *Theogony, Works and Days: Theognis, Elegies.* Trans. Dorothea Wender. London: Penguin Books, Ltd., 1976.

Kirk, G. S. "The Structure and Aim of the *Theogony.*" In *Hésiode et son influence, Entretiens Hardt 7,* 61–107. Geneva: Fondation Hardt, 1962.

Kirk, G. S., and J. E. Raven. *The Presocratic Philosophers.* Cambridge: Cambridge University Press, 1957.

Merkelbach, R., and M. L. West. *Hesiodi Fragmenta Selecta.* In *Hesiodi Theogonia, Opera et Dies, Scutum,* 3rd ed., ed. F. Solmsen. Oxford: Oxford University Press, 1990.

Mondi, Robert. "ΧΑΟΣ and the Hesiodic Cosmogony." *Harvard Studies in Classical Philology* 92 (1989): 1–41.

Nagy, Gregory. *Greek Mythology and Poetics.* Cornell, NY: Cornell University Press, 1990.

Ovid. *The Metamorphoses.* Trans. Allen Mandelbaum. New York: Harcourt, 1993.

Peabody, Berkley. *The Winged Word: A Study in the Technique of Ancient Greek Oral Composition as Seen Principally through Hesiod's "Works and Days."* Albany: SUNY Press, 1975.

Tyrrell, William Blake, and Frieda S. Brown. *Athenian Myths and Institutions.* Oxford: Oxford University Press, 1991.

Verdenius, W. J. *A Commentary on Hesiod: "Works and Days," vv. 1–382.* Leiden: E. J. Brill, 1985.

Vernant, Jean–Pierre. "Hesiod's Myth of the Races: an Essay in Structural Analysis." In *Structuralism in Myth*, ed. Robert A. Segal, 247–76. New York: Garland, 1996.

Walcot, P. *Hesiod and the Near East*. Cardiff: University of Wales Press, 1966.

West, M. L. *Hesiod, Theogony, Edited with Prolegomena and Commentary*. Oxford: Clarendon Press, 1966.

4. Ovid's Creation Story

Galinsky, G. Karl. *Ovid's "Metamorphoses": An Introduction to the Basic Aspects*. Berkeley: University of California Press, 1975.

Segal, Charles. *Landscape in Ovid's "Metamorphoses": A Study in the Transformations of a Literary Symbol*. (Hermes Einzelschrift 23.) Wiesbaden: Franz Steiner Verlag, 1969.

5. Biblical Creation Stories

Anderson, Bernhard W. *Understanding the Old Testament*, 3rd ed. Englewood Cliffs, NJ: Prentice-Hall, 1975.

Rad, Gerhard von. *Genesis: A Commentary*. Trans. John H. Marks. Philadelphia: Westminster Press, 1961.

6. *Enuma Elish*: A Mesopotamian Creation Story

Bottero, Jean. *Religion in Ancient Mesopotamia*. Trans. Teresa Lavender Fagan. Chicago: The University of Chicago Press, 2001.

Harris, Rikvah. "The Conflict of Generations in Ancient Mesopotamian Myths." *Comparative Study in Society and History*. 34. 4 (October 1992): 621–35.

Heidel, Alexander. *The Babylonian Genesis: The Story of Creation*, 2nd ed. Chicago: The University of Chicago Press, 1951.

Jacobsen, Thorkild. "The Battle between Marduk and Tiamat." *Journal of the American Oriental Society* 88.1 (1968): 104–108.

King, L. W., ed. *Enuma Elish: The Seven Tablets of Creation*. Vol. 1: *English Translations*. London: Luzac and Co., 1902. (New York: AMS Press Inc., 1976).

Machinist, Peter. "Rest and Violence in the Poem of Erra." *Journal of the American Oriental Society* 103.1 (1983): 221–26.

7. The *Prose Edda*'s Creation Stories

Crossley-Holland, Kevin. *Norse Myths*. New York: Pantheon, 1980.

Orchard, Andy. *Dictionary of Norse Myth and Legend*. London: Cassell, 1997.

8. Native American Creation Stories from the Southwestern United States

Barnes, Nellie. *American Indian Verse: Characteristics of Style*. Lawrence: University Press of Kansas, 1922.

Brotherston, Gordon. *The Book of the Fourth World: Reading the Native Americans Through Their Literature*. Cambridge: Cambridge University Press, 1993.

Frisbie, Charlotte. *Southwestern Indian Ritual Drama*. Albuquerque: University of New Mexico Press, 1980.

Ortiz, Alfonso, and William C. Sturtevant, eds. *Handbook of North American Indians: Southwest*. Washington, DC: U.S. Government Printing Office, 1983.

Witherspoon, Gary. *Language and Art in the Navajo Universe*. Ann Arbor: University of Michigan Press, 1977.

Wyman, Leland. *Blessingway*. Tucson: University of Arizona Press, 1970.

9. African Creation Stories

Abrahamsson, Hans. *The Origin of Death: Studies in African Mythology*. Upsala: Studia Ethnographica Upsaliensia III, 1951.

Bascom, William. *African Folktales in the New World*. Bloomington: Indiana University Press, 1992.

Helser, Albert D. *African Stories*. New York: Fleming H. Revell Co., 1930.

Johnston, Sir Harry. *The Uganda Protectorate*, Vol. II. London: Hutchinson & Co., 1902.

Mair, Lucy P. *An African People in the Twentieth Century*. New York: Russell and Russell, 1965.

Oliver, Roland. *The African Experience: Major Themes in African History from Earliest Times to the Present*. New York: HarperCollins, 1991.

10. Nü Kwa: A Chinese Creator Goddess

"The Chinese Language." Columbia University, East Asian Curriculum Project, April 11, 2007. http://afe.easia.columbia.edu/china/language/teach.htm (accessed 21 December 2007).

Birrell, Anne M. *Chinese Mythology: An Introduction*. Baltimore, MD: Johns Hopkins University Press, 1993.

Bodde, Derk. *Essays on Chinese Civilization*, eds Charles Le Blanc and Dorothy Borei. Princeton, NJ: Princeton University Press, 1981.

http://www.virtualtourist.com/travel/Asia/China/Zhejiang_Sheng/Putuoshan-1032139/Things_To_Do-Putuoshan-BR-1.html#0, 24 November, 2003 (accessed 29 December 2007).

Chau, Adam Yuet. *Miraculous Response: Doing Popular Religion in Contemporary China*. Palo Alto, CA: Stanford University Press, 2005.

Davies, Philip. "The Goddess Myth." *New Directions*, April 2001. http://trushare.com/71APR01/AP01GODD.htm (accessed 29 December 2007).

Gunde, Richard. *Culture and Customs of China*. Westport, CN: Greenwood Press, 2002.

Kerényi, Karl. *Prometheus: Archetypal Image of Human Existence*, trans. Ralph Manheim. London: Thames and Hudson, 1963.

King, R. Todd. "Nanshan Temple" http://rtoddking.com/chinawin2005_synt.htm Winter 2005, accessed 29 December, 2007.

Knapp, Bettina. "China's Fragmented Goddess Images," in *Women in Myth*. Albany, NY: State University of New York Press, 1996.

Law, Pui-lam. "The revival of folk religion and gender relationships in rural China: A preliminary observation." *Asian Folklore Studies* 64.1 (2005): 89–109.

Maspero, Henri. *Taoism and Chinese Religion*. Tr. Frank A. Kierman, Jr. Amherst, MA: University of Massachusetts Press, 1981.

Paul, Diana Y. *Women in Buddhism*. Berkeley, CA: University of California Press, 1985.

Stone, Merlin. *Ancient Mirrors of Womanhood*. Boston, MA: Beacon Press, 1990.

Tan, Billy. "Nanshan Guan Yin: In The Spirit of Compassion." http://streetwisdom.spaces.live.com/cns!1DA7FABBA126F4C!2917.entry 1 November 2007, accessed 29 December 2007.

Thompson, Laurence G. *Chinese Religion: An Introduction*, 2nd ed. Encino, CA: Dickenson Publishing, 1975.

World Desk Reference, 4th ed. London: Dorlink Kindersley, 2002.

PART 2B: MYTHS OF DESTRUCTION

11. Ovid's Flood Story

Anderson, William S. *Ovid's Metamorphoses Books 1–5, Edited, with Introduction and Commentary*. Norman: University of Oklahoma Press, 1997.

Galinsky, G. Karl. *Ovid's Metamorphoses: An Introduction to the Basic Aspects*. Berkeley: University of California Press, 1975.

Myers, K. Sara. *Ovid's Causes: Cosmogony and Aetiology in the Metamorphoses*. Ann Arbor: University of Michigan Press, 1994.

Segal, Charles. *Landscape in Ovid's Metamorphoses: A Study in the Transformations of a Literary Symbol*. (Hermes Einzelschrift 23.) Wiesbaden: Franz Steiner Verlag, 1969.

12. Biblical Flood Stories

Anderson, Bernhard W. *Understanding the Old Testament*, 3rd ed. Englewood Cliffs, NJ: Prentice-Hall, 1975.

Rad, Gerhard von. *Genesis: A Commentary*. Trans. John H. Marks. Philadelphia, PA: Westminster Press, 1961.

13. Ragnarok

Crossley-Holland, Kevin. *Norse Myths*. New York: Pantheon, 1980.

Murphy, G. Ronald, S.J. *The Owl, the Raven, and the Dove*. New York: Oxford University Press, 2000.

Orchard, Andy. *Dictionary of Norse Myth and Legend*. London: Cassell, 1997.

PART 3: HEROES AND TRICKSTERS

15. The *Epic of Gilgamesh*

Dalley, Stephanie, ed. and trans. "The Epic of Gilgamesh." In *Myths from Mesopotamia*, 38–135. Oxford: Oxford University Press, 1989.

Foster, Benjamin R., ed. and trans. *The Epic of Gilgamesh*. New York, NY: Norton, 2001.

Gardner, John, and John Maier. *Gilgamesh: Translated from the Sîn-leqi-unninni Version*. New York, NY: Alfred A. Knopf, 1984.

George, Andrew W., ed. and trans. *The Epic of Gilgamesh*. New York, NY: Penguin, 1999.

Heidel, Alexander. *The Epic of Gilgamesh and Old Testament Parallels*. Chicago, IL: The University of Chicago Press, 1963.

Jacobsen, Thorkild. *The Treasures of Darkness: A History of Mesopotamian Religion*. New Haven, CN: Yale University Press, 1976.

O'Brien, Joan V. *In the Beginning: Creation Myths from Ancient Mesopotamia, Israel, and Greece*. Chico, CA: Scholars Press, 1982.

Tigay, Jeffrey H. *The Evolution of the Gilgamesh Epic*. Philadelphia, PA: University of Pennsylvania Press, 1982.

17. The *Ramayana*

Das, Nobin Chandra. *A Note on the Ancient Geography of Asia*. Varanasi: Bharat–Bharati, 1896, reprinted 1971.

O'Flaherty, Wendy Doniger. "Sita and Helen, Ahayal and Alcmena: A Comparative Study." *History of Religions* 37 (1997): 21–29.

Sharma, Ramashraya. *A Socio–Political Study of the Valmiki Ramayana*. Delhi: Motilal Banarsidass, 1971.

18. Heroes in the *Prose Edda*—Snorri Sturluson

Crossley-Holland, Kevin. *Norse Myths*. New York, NY: Pantheon, 1980.

Dumézil, Georges. *Gods of the Ancient Northmen*. Berkeley, CA: University of California Press, 1973.

———. *Loki*. Berkeley: University of California Press, 1959.

Orchard, Andy. *Dictionary of Norse Myth and Legend*. London: Cassell, 1997.

19. *Oedipus the King*—Sophocles

Ahl, Frederick, *Sophocles' Oedipus: Evidence and Self-Conviction*. Ithaca, NY: Cornell University Press, 1991.

Arnott, Peter D. *Greek Scenic Conventions in the Fifth Century B.C.* Oxford: Clarendon Press, 1962.

Jones, John. *On Aristotle and Greek Tragedy*. Stanford, CA: Stanford University Press, 1962.

Segal, Charles, *Oedipus Tyrannus: Tragic Heroism and the Limits of Knowledge*, 2nd ed. New York, NY: Oxford University Press, 2001.

20. The Structural Study of Myth—Claude Levi-Strauss

Huizinga, Johan. *Homo Ludens: A Study of the Play-Element in Culture*. Boston: Beacon Press, 1967.

Levi–Strauss, Claude. *Structural Anthropology*. New York: Basic Books, 1963.

21. Raven: A Native American Trickster

Fienup-Riordan, Anne. *Eskimo Essays: Yupik Lives and How We See Them*. New Brunswick, NJ: Rutgers University Press, 1994.

Erdoes, Richard, and Alfonso Otriz, eds. *American Indian Trickster Tales*. New York, NY: Penguin, 1998.

Goodchild, Peter. *Raven Tales: Traditional Stories of Native Peoples*. Chicago, IL: Chicago Review Press, 1991.

Hyde, Lewis. *Trickster Makes This World: Mischief, Myth, and Art*. New York, NY: Farrar, Straus and Giroux, 1998.

Leeming, David Adams. *The World of Myth: An Anthology*. New York, NY: Oxford University Press, 1990.

———, and Jake Page. *God: Myths of the Male Divine*. New York, NY: Oxford University Press, 1996.

Pelton, Mary Helen, and Jacqueline DiGenaro. *Images of a People: Tlingit Myths and Legends*. Englewood, CO: Libraries Unlimited, Inc., 1992.

22. The Mwindo Epic

Biebuyck, Daniel. "Nyanga Circumcision Masks and Costumes." *African Arts* 6.2 (1973): 20–25, 86–92.

———. *Hero and Chief: Epic Literature from the Banyanga, Zaire Republic*. Berkeley, CA: University of California Press, 1978.

23. African and African-American Trickster Stories

Abrahams, Roger D. *African Folktales: Traditional Stories of the Black World*. New York, NY: Pantheon Books, 1983.

———. *The Man-of-Words in the West Indies: Performance and the Emergence of Creole Culture*. Baltimore, MD: The Johns Hopkins University Press, 1983.

———. *Afro-American Folktales: Stories from Black Traditions in the New World*. New York, NY: Pantheon Books, 1985.

Bascom, William. *African Folktales in the New World*. Bloomington, IN: Indiana University Press, 1992.

Bennett, Louise. *Anancy Stories and Dialect Verse* (new series). Nendeln, Liechtenstein: Kraus Reprint, 1973; Kingston, Jamaica: Pioneer Press, 1950.

Edwards, Jay. "Structural Analysis of the Afro-American Trickster Tale." In *Black Literature & Literary Theory*, ed. Henry Louis Gates Jr. New York, NY: Routledge, 1990, 81–103.

Evans-Pritchard, E. E. *The Zande Trickster*. Oxford: Clarendon Press, 1967.

Fenik, Bernard. *Studies in the Odyssey*. (Hermes Einzelschrift 30.) Wiesbaden: Franz Steiner Verlag, 1974.

Harris, Joel Chandler. *Uncle Remus: His Songs and Sayings.* New York, NY: D. Appleton and Company, 1917.

Hurston, Zora Neale. *Mules and Men.* New York, NY: Harper-Perennial, 1990 (1935).

Lester, Julius. *Black Folktales.* New York: Grove Weidenfield, 1970.

Parsons, Elsie Clews. "Folklore of the Antilles, French and English." *Memoirs of the American Folklore Society* 26.3 (1943): 97–100.

Pelton, Robert D. *The Trickster in West Africa: A Study of Mythic Irony and Sacred Delight.* Berkeley and Los Angeles, CA: University of California Press, 1980.

24. Prometheus: The Greek Trickster

Aeschylus. *The Oresteia Trilogy.* ed. Robert W. Corrigan, trans. George Thomson. New York, NY: Dell Publishing Company, 1965.

Hesiod. *Theogony, Works and Days: Theogonis, Elegies.* Trans. Dorothea Wender. New York, NY: Penguin Books Inc., 1973 and 1976.

Roberts, John W. *From Trickster to Badman: The Black Folk Hero in Slavery and Freedom.* Philadelphia, PA: University of Pennsylvania Press, 1989.

25. Looking Back at Heroes: The Different Versions of a Myth

Ahl, Frederick. *Sophocles' Oedipus: Evidence and Self-Conviction.* Ithaca, NY: Cornell University Press, 1991.

Deubner, Ludwig. *Attische Feste.* Berlin: Akademie-Verlag, 1956.

Freud, Sigmund. *The General Introduction to Psychoanalysis.* Trans. Joan Riviere. New York, NY: Washington Square Press, 1960.

Kirk, G. S., and J. E. Raven. *The Presocratic Philosophers.* Cambridge: Cambridge University Press, 1957.

Lord, Albert. *The Singer of Tales.* Cambridge, MA: Harvard University Press, 1960.

McCormick, Kathleen, and Gary Waller, with Linda Flower. *Reading Texts: Reading, Responding, Writing.* Lexington, MA: Heath, 1987.

Segal, Charles. *"Oedipus Tyrannus": Tragic Heroism and the Limits of Knowledge.* New York, NY: Twayne, 1993.

26. Ritual— Victor Turner

Turner, Victor. *The Ritual Process: Structure and Anti-Structure.* New York: NY, Aldine de Gruyter, 1969.

———. "Symbols in African Ritual." *Science* 79 (March 16, 1972): 1100–1105.

———. "Liminal to liminoid in play, flow, and ritual: An essay in comparative symbology." *The Anthropological Study of Human Play* 60.3 (Summer 1974): 53–92. (Ed. E. Norbeck. Houston, TX: Rice University Studies.)

———. *On the Edge of the Bush: Anthropology as Experience.* Tucson: University of Arizona Press, 1985.

27. Demeter and Persephone: The Homeric *Hymn to Demeter*

Bachofen, Johann. *Myth, Religion, and Mother Right, Selected Writings of J. J. Bachofen.* Trans. Ralph Manheim. Princeton, NJ: Princeton University Press, 1967.

Bianchi, Ugo. *Selected Essays on Gnosticism, Dualism, and Mysteriosophy.* Leiden: Brill, 1978, 196–216.

Campbell, Joseph. "Mythological Themes in Creative Literature and Art." In *Myths, Dreams and Religion,* ed. Joseph Campbell, 138–75. New York: E. P. Dutton, 1970.

Clay, Jenny Strauss. *The Politics of Olympus: Form and Meaning in the Major Homeric Hymns.* Princeton, NJ: Princeton University Press, 1989.

Downing, Christine, ed. *The Long Journey Home.* Boston, MA: Shambhala, 1994.

Frazer, Sir James G. *The Golden Bough: A Study in Magic and Religion,* abridged and ed. Robert Fraser. London and New York: Oxford University Press, 1994.

Jonas, Hans. *The Gnostic Religion,* 2nd ed. Boston: Beacon Press, 1958.

Martin, Luther H. *Hellenistic Religions: An Introduction.* Oxford: Oxford University Press, 1987.

Mylonas, George E. *Eleusis and the Eleusinian Mysteries.* Princeton, NJ: Princeton University Press, 1961.

Segal, Robert A. *Joseph Campbell: An Introduction.* New York: Mentor, 1990.

Slater, Philip. *The Glory of Hera: Greek Mythology and the Greek Family.* Boston, MA: Beacon Press, 1971.

Sowa, C. A. *Traditional Themes and the Homeric Hymns.* Chicago, IL: Bolchazy-Carducci, 1984.

28. Isis and Osiris

The Ancient Egyptian Coffin Texts, Spells 74 and 76. Trans. R. O. Faulkner. Warminster, UK: Aris & Phillips, 1973.

The Ancient Egyptian Pyramid Texts. Translated into English. Trans. R. O. Faulkner. Oxford: Oxford University Press, 1998.

Cott, Jonathan. "Isis and Osiris: A Conversation with James P. Allen." In *Isis and Osiris: Exploring the Goddess Myth,* 27–33. New York, NY: Doubleday, 1994.

———. "A Conversation with Robert S. Bianchi." In *Isis and Osiris: Exploring the Goddess Myth,* 87–95. New York, NY: Doubleday, 1994.

Cumont, Franz. *Oriental Religions in Roman Paganism.* New York, NY: Dover, 1956 (reprint of 1911 edition).

Griffiths, John Gwyn, ed. and trans. *Plutarch's "De Iside et Osiride,"* with commentary. Cardiff: University of Wales Press, 1970.

Lesko, Leonard H. "Ancient Egyptian Cosmogonies and Cosmology." In *Religion in Ancient Egypt: Gods, Myths and Personal Sacrifice,* ed. Byron E. Shafer, 88–122. Ithaca, NY: Cornell University Press, 1991.

Richter, Daniel S. "Plutarch on Isis and Osiris: Text, Cult, and Cultural Appropriation." *Transactions of the American Philological Association* 131 (2001): 191–216.

Russmann, Edna R. *Eternal Egypt: Masterworks of Ancient Art from the British Museum.* Exhibition catalog. Berkeley, CA: University of California Press, 2001.

Shaw, Ian, ed. *The Oxford History of Ancient Egypt.* Oxford: Oxford University Press, 2000.

Silverman, David P. "Divinity and Deities in Ancient Egypt." In *Religion in Ancient Egypt: Gods, Myths and Personal Sacrifice,* ed. Byron E. Shafer, 7–87. Ithaca, NY: Cornell University Press, 1991.

Tarn, W. W. *Hellenistic Civilization,* 3rd ed. rev. with G. T. Griffith. Cleveland, OH: Meridian, 1952 (1927).

29. "Deciphering a Meal"—Mary Douglas

Bulmer, Ralph. "Why Is the Cassowary Not a Bird? A Problem of Zoological Taxonomy Among the Karam of the New Guinea Highlands," *Man,* new ser. 2 (1967): 5–25.

Fuller, Roy. *Owls and Artificers: Oxford Lectures on Poetry*. New York, NY: Library Press, 1971.

30. The Rituals of Northern Europe—H. R. Ellis Davidson

Dumézil, Georges. *Gods of the Ancient Northmen*. Berkeley, CA: University of California Press, 1973.

Murphy, G. Ronald, S.J. *The Saxon Savior: The Germanic Transformation of the Gospel in the Ninth-Century Heliand*. New York, NY: Oxford University Press, 1995.

Orchard, Andy. *Dictionary of Norse Myth and Legend*. London: Cassell, 1997.

31. Heracles and Dionysus

Dodds, E. R., ed. *Euripides Bacchae*, with introduction and commentary. Oxford, UK: Clarendon Press, 1960.

Farnell, L. R. *Greek Hero Cults and Ideas of Immortality*. Oxford, UK: Clarendon Press, 1921.

Hard, Robin, trans. and ed. *Apollodorus: The Library of Greek Mythology*. Oxford, UK: Oxford University Press, 1997.

Kirk, G. S. *The Nature of Greek Myths*. Middlesex, UK, and New York, NY: Penguin, 1974.

Seaford, Richard. *Dionysos*. London: Routledge, 2006.

Sowa, Cora Angier. *Traditional Themes and the Homeric Hymns*. Chicago: Bolchazy-Carducci Publishers, 1984.

PART 5 MYTHS AND DREAMS

32. *Man and His Symbols*—C. G. Jung

Bennett, E. A. *What Jung Really Said*. London: Macdonald, 1966.

Jung, C. G. "A Psychological Approach to the Dogma of the Trinity." In C. Jung, *The Collected Works of C. G. Jung*, Vol. II, 2nd ed. Princeton, NJ: Princeton University Press, 1969.

———. *Psyche and Symbol. A Selection from the Writings of C.G. Jung*. Ed. Violet S. Laszlo. Garden City, NY: Doubleday Anchor Books, 1958.

33. How to Perform a Jungian Analysis of a Myth or Fairy Tale

Barthelme, Donald. *Snow White*. New York, NY: Bantam, 1968.

Frantz, Marie-Louise von. *Shadow and Evil in Fairy Tales*, Rev. ed. Boston, MA: Shambala, 1995.

———. *The Interpretation of Fairy Tales*, Rev. ed. Boston, MA: Shambala, 1996.

Hillman, James. *The Dream and the Underworld*. New York, NY: Harper & Row, 1979.

Jacoby, Mario, Verena Kast, and Ingrid Riedel. *Witches, Ogres and the Devil's Daughter: Encounters with Evil in Fairy Tales*. Boston, MA: Shambala, 1992.

Jung, Carl. *Man and His Symbols*. Trans. M. L. von Frantz, Joseph L. Henderson, Jolande Jacobi, and Aniela Jaffé. New York, NY: Laurel, 1968.

Stevens, Anthony. *Private Myths: Dreams and Dreaming*. Cambridge, MA: Harvard University Press, 1995.

PART 6 FOLKTALE AND MYTH

34. *The Morphology of the Folktale*—Vladimir Propp

Bettelheim, Bruno. *The Uses of Enchantment: The Meaning and Importance of Fairy Tales*. New York, NY: Vintage Books, 1989.

Douglas, Mary. "Children Consumed and Child Cannibals: Robertson Smith's Attack on the Science of Mythology." In *Myth and Method*, eds. Laurie L. Patton and Wendy Doniger, 29–51. Charlottesville, VA: University Press of Virginia, 1996.

35. A Proppian Analysis of *The Wizard of Oz*

Baum, L. Frank. *The Wonderful Wizard of Oz*. Ed. with analytical articles, William R. Leach. Belmont, CA: Wadsworth, 1991.

Baum, L. Frank, ed. Michael Patrick Hearn. *The Annotated Wizard of Oz*, Centennial Edition. New York, NY: Norton, 2000.

36. *Household Tales*—Wilhelm and Jakob Grimm

Bettelheim, Bruno. *The Uses of Enchantment: The Meaning and Importance of Fairy Tales*. New York, NY: Vintage Books, 1989.

Grimm, Brothers. *Household Stories by the Brothers Grimm*. Trans. Lucy Crane. New York, NY: Dover Publications, Inc., 1963.

Hinton, Ladson. "'*The Goose Girl*': Puella and Transformation." In *Psyche's Stories: Modern Jungian Interpretations of Fairy Tales*, Vol. I. Eds. Murray Stein and Lionel Corbett, 141–53. Wilmette, IL: Chiron Publications, 1991.

Klein, Lucille. "'*The Goose Girl*': Images of Individuation." In *Psyche's Stories: Modern Jungian Interpretations of Fairy Tales*, Vol. I. Eds. Murray Stein and Lionel Corbett, 155–66. Wilmette, IL: Chiron Publications, 1991.

Murphy, G. Ronald, S.J. *The Owl, the Raven, and the Dove*. New York, NY: Oxford University Press, 2000.

Tatar, Maria. *The Hard Facts of the Grimms' Fairy Tales*. Princeton, NJ: Princeton University Press, 1987.

———. *Off With Their Heads: Fairy Tales and the Culture of Childhood*. Princeton, NJ: Princeton University Press, 1992.

———. *No Go the Bogeyman*. New York, NY: Farrar, Straus and Giroux, 1998.

Zipes, Jack. *Fairy Tale as Myth*. Lexington, KY: The University Press of Kentucky, 1994.

———. ed. *The Oxford Companion to Fairy Tales*. New York, NY: Oxford University Press, 2000.

37. Cupid and Psyche—Apuleius

Anderson, Graham. *Fairytale in the Ancient World*. London: Routledge, 2000.

Bettelheim, Bruno. *The Uses of Enchantment: The Meaning and Importance of Fairy Tales*. New York, NY: Vintage Books, 1989.

Neumann, Erich. *Amor and Psyche: The Psychological Development of the Feminine: A Commentary on the Tale by Apuleius*. Trans. Ralph Manheim. New York, NY: Pantheon Books for the Bollingen Foundation, 1956.

Ross, Lena B. "'*Cupid and Psyche*': Birth of a New Consciousness." In *Psyche's Stories: Modern Jungian Interpretations of Fairy Tales*, Vol. I. Eds. Murray Stein and Lionel Corbett, 65–90. Wilmette, IL: Chiron Publications, 1991.

Sappho. "My Tongue Is Broken –31." Trans. Ken Hope. http://www.northshore.net/homepages/hope/Sapphotongue.html (accessed 19 June 1999).

Schlam, Carl C. *The Metamorphoses of Apuleius: On Making an Ass of Oneself*. Chapel Hill, NC: University of North Carolina Press, 1992.

Shumate, Nancy. *Crisis and Conversion in Apuleius' Metamorphoses*. Ann Arbor, MI: University of Michigan Press, 1996.

Winkler, John J. *Auctor & Actor: A Narratological Reading of Apuleius's Golden Ass.* Berkeley, CA: University of California Press, 1985.

PART 7 MYTH IN A CONTEMPORARY CONTEXT

39. A Study of the Construction of the Daniel Boone Myth

Bakeless, John. *Daniel Boone: Master of the Wilderness.* Harrisburg, PA: Stackpole Company, 1939, reprinted 1965.

Cavan, Seamus. *Daniel Boone and the Opening of the Ohio Country.* New York, NY: Chelsea House Publishers, 1991.

Elliott, Lawrence. *The Long Hunter: A New Life of Daniel Boone.* New York, NY: Reader's Digest Press, 1976. Distributed by Crowell Company.

Faragher, John Mack, *Daniel Boone: The Life and Legend of an American Pioneer.* New York, NY: Holt, 1992.

Lofaro, Michael A. *The Life and Adventures of Daniel Boone.* Lexington, KY: The University Press of Kentucky, 1978.

Pyne, Stephen J. *Fire in America: A Cultural History of Wildland and Rural Fire.* Princeton, NJ: Princeton University Press, 1982.

Shapiro, Irwin. *Daniel Boone.* New York, NY: Simon and Schuster, Little Golden Books, 1956.

40. *Stagecoach* and *Firefly*: Science Fiction and the Journey into the Unknown

Firefly: The Complete Series. DVD, Twentieth Century Fox, 2003. Included is the interview "How It Was: the Making of Firefly" and commentary by cast and creators.

Budd, Michael. "A Home in the Wilderness: Visual Imagery in John Ford's Westerns." *Cinema Journal* 16.1 (1976): 62–75.

Burrow, Robert. "*Firefly*: the Complete Series." *The Times* (London), April 17, 2004.

Campbell, Robert A., and James E. Curtis. "The Public's Views on the Future of Religion and Science: Cross–National Survey Results." *Review of Religious Research* 37.3 (1996): 260–67.

CANTTAKESKY. June 24, 2003 "Wondering What Sort of Fans *Firefly* Attracts." Fireflyfans.net Forum, http://www.fireflyfans.net/thread.asp?b=2&t=2179 (accessed 20 November 2007).

Erisman, Fred. "Stagecoach in space: the legacy of Firefly." *Extrapolation* 47.2 (2006): 249–58.

Gallagher, Tag. *John Ford: The Man and His Films.* Berkeley, CA: University of California Press, 1986.

Goodwin, James. *Akira Kurosawa and Intertextual Cinema.* Baltimore, MD: Johns Hopkins University Press, 1991.

Hinson, Sara T. "Freedom and Firefly" *Brainwash: Aff's Weekly Online Magazine,* 7 August 2005, http://www.affbrainwash.com/archives/020132.php.

Lackey, Mercedes. "*Serenity* and Bobby McGee." In *Finding Serenity,* ed. Jane Espenson. Dallas, TX: Benbella Books, 2005.

Lavery, David, Angela Hague, and Marla Cartwright. "Generation X—The X-Files and the Cultural Moment," "Deny All Knowledge." In *Reading The X Files,* eds. David Lavery, Angela Hague, and Marla Cartwright, 1–221. Syracuse, NY: Syracuse University Press, 1996.

Lowrie, Peter. *The Cinema of Orson Welles.* New York, NY: A. S. Barnes, 1965.

Mogen, David. *Wilderness Visions: The Western Theme in Science Fiction Literature,* 2nd ed. San Bernardino, CA: Borgo Press, 1993.

Novotny, Patrick. "No Future! Cyberpunk, Industrial Music, and the Aesthetics of Postmodern Disintegration." In *Political Science Fiction,* eds. Donald M. Hassler and Clyde Wilcox. Columbia, SC: University of South Carolina Press, 1997, 99—123.

Place, J. A. *The Western Films of John Ford.* Secaucus, NJ: Citadel Press, 1974.

Person, Lawrence. "Notes Toward a Postcyberpunk Manifesto." *Slashdot,* http://features.slashdot.org/article.pl?sid=99/10/08/2123255.

Said, Edward, *Orientalism.* New York, NY: Vintage, 1979.

Sobstyl, Edrie. "Cyberpunk: Liminal Space Cadets." *Enculturation,* 3.1 (Spring 2000). http://enculturation.gmu.edu/3_1/sobstyl.html.

Whedon, Joss. *Serenity: the Official Visual Companion.* London: Titan Books, 2005.

41. Harry Potter: A Rankian Take on the Hero of Hogwarts

Rowling, J. K. "Barnes and Noble Chat with J. K Rowling." 20 October, 2000 *Accio Quote!* http://accio–quote.org/articles/2000/1000–livechat–barnesnoble.html.

PART 8 MYTH AND LITERATURE

43. Mythological Themes in Native American Literature

Aarne, Antti. *The Types of the Folk-Tale; a Classification and Bibliography.* Trans. and enl. by Stith Thompson. Helsinki: Suomalainen Tiedeakatemia, Academia Scientarum Fennica, 1928.

Bevis, William. "Native American Novels: Homing In." In *Critical Perspectives on Native American Fiction,* ed. Richard F. Fleck, 15–23. Washington, DC: Three Continents Press, 1993.

Fleck, Richard F., ed. *Critical Perspectives on Native American Fiction.* Washington, DC: Three Continents Press, 1993.

Horne, Dee. *Contemporary Indian Writing: Unsettling Literature.* New York, NY: Peter Lang, 1999.

Jaskoski, Helen. *Leslie Marmon Silko: A Study of Her Short Fiction.* New York, NY: Twayne Publishers, 1998.

Larson, Charles R. *American Indian Fiction.* Albuquerque, NM: University of New Mexico Press, 1978.

Ramirez, Susan Berry Brill de. *Contemporary American Indian Literatures and the Oral Tradition.* Tucson, AZ: The University of Arizona Press, 1999.

Silko, Leslie Marmon. *Yellow Woman and a Beauty of the Spirit: Essays on Native American Life Today.* New York, NY: Simon and Schuster, 1996.

Smith, Patricia Clark, and Paula Gunn Allen, "Earthy Relations, Carnal Knowledge: Southwestern American Indian Women Writers and Landscape." In *The Desert is No Lady: Southwestern Landscapes in Women's Writing and Art,* eds. Vera Norwood and Janice Monk, 174–96. New Haven, CN: Yale University Press, 1987.

Stein, Rachel. *Shifting the Ground: American Women Writers' Revisions of Nature, Gender, and Race.* Charlottesville, VA: University Press of Virginia, 1997.

Trout, Lawana. *Native American Literature: An Anthology.* Lincolnwood, IL: NTC Publishing Group, 1998.

Witalic, Jane, ed. *Native North American Literature: Biographical and Critical Information on Native Writers and Orators from the United States and Canada from Historical Times to the Present.* New York, NY: Gale Research Inc., 1994.

44. Mythological Themes in Modern Narrative

Apollodorus, *The Library of Greek Mythology*, Robin Hard, trans. and ed. Oxford, UK: Oxford University Press, 1997.

Barger, Jorn. "Advanced notes for Ulysses ch6 (Hades). February 2000 (updated February 2001). http://www.robotwisdom.com/jaj/ulysses/notes06.html#54 (accessed February 21, 2003).

Burgess, Anthony. *Joysprick: An Introduction to the Language of James Joyce.* New York, NY: Harcourt Brace Jovanovich, 1973.

Detweiler, Robert. *John Updike.* Boston, MA: Twayne Publishers, 1984.

Frye, Northrup. "The Road of Excess." In *Myth and Symbol: Critical Approaches and Applications*, 3–20. Lincoln, NE: University of Nebraska Press, 1963.

Gifford, Don, with Robert J Seidman. *"Ulysses" Annotated: Notes for James Joyce's "Ulysses."* Berkeley, CA: University of California Press, 1983.

Greiner, Donald J. *John Updike's Novels.* Athens, OH: Ohio University Press, 1984.

Pritchard, William H. *Updike: America's Man of Letters.* South Royalton, VT: Steerforth Press, 2000.

Taylor, Larry E. *Pastoral and Anti–Pastoral Patterns in John Updike's Fiction.* Carbondale, IL: Southern Illinois University Press, 1971.

Vickery, John B. "Literary Criticism and Myth: Anglo-American Critics." In *Literary Criticism and a Myth*, ed. Joseph P. Strelka, 210–37. University Park, PA: Pennsylvania State University Press, 1980.

———. "Orpheus and Persephone: Uses and Meanings." In *Classical Mythology in 20th Century Thought and Literature*, eds. Wendell M. Aycock and Theodore M. Klein, 187–212. Lubbock, TX: Texas Tech Press, 1980.

Art Credits

Index

The letters *c*, *f*, *m*, and *t* following a page number denote chart, figure, map, and table, respectively.

Aarne-Thompson motifs, 497, 645, 670
Abrahams, Roger D., 340, 341, 345–46, 350
absentation, Proppian, 503, 532
Abydos, 406*m*, 413
Achates, 658
Acheron, 459
Achilles, 10, 12, 136, 184, 393, 396, 452, 611, 666*f*
Actaeon, 163
Adam, 483
Adam and Eve, 55, 56, 56*f*, 124
Adam of Bremen, 439
Adonis, 440
Aeolus, 12, 133, 627
Aeschylus, 9, 12, 136, 250, 356, 390, 619
Aesir, 82, 83, 84, 87, 147, 151, 219, 222, 223, 228, 229, 431, 437
aetiological insights, 7, 8, 13, 74, 102, 113, 138, 230, 345, 356, 402*c*, 436, 449, 564, 564*c*, 566–67
Agadzagadza, 109
Agamemnon, 10, 293, 634
Agave, 286, 462, 464
Ages of Man, 18, 29, 36, 39–41, 130,
Agni, 207
Ahl, Frederick, 232, 252, 361
Aidoneus. *See* Hades
Air-Spirit People, 95–96
Akkadia, 58, 59*c*, 166
Alaska, 295–304, 296*m*
Alcmene, 35, 447, 453
Alexandria, 9, 406*m*
All-father, 84, 221, 223, 442
alligators in the sewers, 5, 5*f*, 6
Alphaeus (Alphaios), 627, 628
Amazons, 456
Amphion, 286
Amphitrite, 35, 45
Amphitryon, 450, 453
Amun, 405

Anansi (Nancy), 296–97, 340, 345, 348
Anasazi, 91, 95
Anaxagoras, 43, 45
Anaximander, 561
Andromache, 579
Angrboda, 148
anima, 390, 469, 475, 479–80, 487–88, 491, 493, 552, 566, 613
animal bridegroom, 350–52, 542, 670–83
animus, 469, 475, 481–82, 487–89
animals, 418, 424–27. *See also* Coyote, Joel Chandler Harris, Petrel, Raven, "The Tiger's Bride"
Annunaki / Anukki, 66, 75, 184, 188
Anshar, 58*c*, 62, 63*c*, 67–73
"Ant's Burden, The," 345–47
anthropological insights, 6, 11, 13*c*, 18, 280–93 passim, 402*c*, 561, 564*c*
anthropomorphism, 51, 55, 140, 168, 298, 406, 634
Antigone, 277*f*, 285, 293
Antiope, 286
Anu, 57, 58*c*, 63*c*, 70, 74, 172, 184
Anubis, 406, 407, 413
Aphrodite, 9, 11, 29, 32*f*, 33, 35, 38, 412, 496, 529, 552. *See also* Venus
Apollo, 34, 162, 237, 238*f*, 241, 242, 247, 249, 250, 252, 257*f*, 260, 410, 412, 456, 457, 627, 666
Apollodorus, 3, 156, 453–59, 460, 463–64, 669
Apotheosis, 169
Apsu, 57, 58*c*, 61, 62, 65–66, 72, 75
Apuleius, 413, 414–16, 480, 541–59 passim, 671
Arcadia, 132, 456
archeology, 11*f*, 121, 167, 212, 220, 229, 429–30
archetypes, 117, 162, 163, 177, 468–70, 472, 486–91, 535, 544, 581, 587. *See also* individual archetypes
Ares, 27, 35, 240, 456, 553

Arethuse (Arethusa), 627, 628
Argeiphontes, 398
Arges, 30, 31*c*
Ariadne, 35
Aristophanes, 450, 453
Aristotle, 43, 233–34, 459
Arnott, Peter, 232
Arp, Jean, 398
Artemis, 34, 239, 241, 241*f*, 455
Artha, 206
Arthur, 156, 605*c*
Aruru, 172
Aryans, 204, 207
Ascalaphos, 458, 459
asceticism, 212, 388
Asclepius (Aesclepias), 410, 450, 666
Asgard, 88, 222, 435, 437, 438, 439–44
Ash-Boy, 289, 646
Assurbanipal, 58, 167
Assyria/Assyrians, 57, 58*m*, 59*c*
Astana Tombs, 111*m*, 122*f*, 124
Astarte, 410, 413, 414
Asterix, 569, 569*f*
Astraea, 49
Athapaskans, 95
Athena (Athene), 9, 34, 35, 38, 47, 239, 453
Athens, 232, 239
Atlas, 35, 357, 449
atonement of the father, 164
Atropos, 34, 627, 669
attenuation, 611
Atum, 102, 102, 404–09 passim, 408*c*
Auden, W. H., 666
audience, 299, 341–44, 350, 362
Augean stables, 448, 455, 457, 618
Augustus Caesar, 21, 44
Aurora, 555
Auster, 46
autochthony, 284, 464
Auyodhaya (Ayodhya), 203, 209
Aya, 177

702